Library and Book Trade Almanac™

formerly **The Bowker Annual**

2016 | 61st Edition

Library and Book Trade Almanac™

formerly **The Bowker Annual**

2016 | 61st Edition

Editor Catherine Barr
Consultant Karen Adams

 Information Today, Inc.

Published by Information Today, Inc.
Copyright © 2016 Information Today, Inc.
All rights reserved

International Standard Book Number 978-1-57387-520-2
International Standard Serial Number 2150-5446
Library of Congress Catalog Card Number 55-12434

Information Today, Inc.
143 Old Marlton Pike
Medford, NJ 08055-8750
Phone: 800-300-9868 (customer service)
          800-409-4929 (editorial queries)
Fax: 609-654-4309
E-mail (orders): custserv@infotoday.com
Web Site: http://www.infotoday.com

Printed and bound in the United States of America

US $289.50

ISBN 13: 978-1-57387-520-2

28950>

9 781573 875202

Dedication

The 2016 edition of the *Library and Book Trade Almanac* is dedicated with great fondness to the late Dave Bogart.

For more than twenty years, Dave's diligence and editorial vision made the publication an essential resource for librarians, publishing industry leaders, and information professionals everywhere. From the earliest inroads of computers and automation systems into the library and research world to our current state where it sometimes seems that all human knowledge is available electronically, Dave chronicled the changing times and technologies that affected a profession he regarded so highly.

Dave was the perfect editor to track down just the right source or to make sure that the data presented was accurate and verified, having honed those skills in his years as a newspaper reporter. But even under the pressure of pulling together multiple pieces of information from disparate sources under tight deadlines, Dave always kept his sense of humor and the priorities of life in perspective.

Information Today, Inc. also expresses its gratitude to Catherine Barr for continuing the work necessary to produce this edition of the *Library and Book Trade Almanac*.

Contents

Part 1
Reports from the Field

Part 2
Funding and Grants

Part 3
Library/Information Science Education, Placement, and Salaries

Part 4
Research and Statistics

Part 5
Reference Information

Part 6
Directory of Organizations

Preface

Welcome to the 61st edition of the *Library and Book Trade Almanac*. This book has evolved over the years but continues to provide a mix of analysis and practical information that will keep you abreast of developments in the publishing and library worlds.

Our Special Reports this year cover varied topics:

- Jamie Campbell Naidoo writes about the effective use of digital media in children's libraries
- A group of experts discuss how "embedded" librarians can offer very useful services, particularly in specialized arenas such as hospitals
- Heather Morrison looks at access to government information, with close attention to the current situation in Canada

Part 1 continues with the usual reports from federal agencies and national associations as well as accounts of the activities of the International Federation of Library Associations and Institutions and Library and Archives Canada.

Part 2 provides details of key funding for libraries, and Part 3 contains professional information—tips on employment opportunities, salary and placement studies, a list of accredited master's degree programs, and scholarship sources and award recipients.

Part 4 gathers together statistics that will be helpful in predicting library expenditures and justifying budgets: average acquisition expenditures, price indexes, library construction, and so forth.

Parts 5 and 6 supply basic reference information: ISBN, ISSN, and SAN details; lists of recommended books and other materials; literary prizes; and a directory of library and book trade organizations in the United States and abroad.

Finally, you'll find a list of National Information Standards Organization (NISO) standards, a calendar of events, a list of acronyms, and indexes by organization and subject.

Compiling this book is a complex task and we are grateful to all who have made contributions. Special thank yous are owed to Karen Adams for her help as consultant editor and to Christine Weisel McNaull, who makes the whole thing possible.

Catherine Barr
Editor

Part 1
Reports from the Field

Special Reports

Digital Media in the Children's Library

Jamie Campbell Naidoo

Foster-EBSCO Endowed Associate Professor
University of Alabama School of Library and Information Studies

A salient theme in the current field of children's librarianship is that of digital media[1] usage of young children and the role that children's librarians can play in facilitating purposeful interactions among their young patrons with this evolving format. In 2010 the iPad revolutionized the way in which children interact with technology, offering touch-screen opportunities for active learning and engagement. Over time, an unexpected effect of the iPad was to offer creative, innovative children's librarians a chance to reach digital natives as never before in library programming. By way of e-books and digital apps, librarians could create individualized, active, and unique media-rich experiences that, when wed with printed books and traditional skills such as storytelling and puppetry, fostered literacy development.

This report provides a snapshot of how digital media, particularly digital apps and digital picture books, have been received by public children's librarians and describes some of the key concerns and opportunities for using these materials with young children.

Brief Historical Overview

Since 2011 there has been considerable interest within the children's librarian community to better understand the ways in which digital apps and digital picture books and other digital media can be evaluated, curated, and used appropriately in library storytime programs. Beginning that year, children's librarian Cen Campbell started Little eLit (http://littleelit.com) as a way to document her experiences incorporating digital media (specifically digital apps) in children's storytimes to promote early literacy development. Two years later the website became "a crowd-sourced, grass-roots professional learning network to develop promising practices for the incorporation of new media into library collections, services and programs for families with young children" (Little eLit, 2016). Many of the librarians associated with Little eLit became staunch advocates for using digital media in the children's library, sharing anecdotes, advice, and program plans to support developmentally appropriate practice. These librarians offered webinars, wrote articles, and rallied other children's librarians to become curators of digital apps and early adoptees of digital media usage in children's library programming.

As their enthusiasm and ranks grew, so did the strong voices from the other side of the profession advocating for tech-free children's library spaces filled with wholesome, sacrosanct books, puppets, hands-on manipulatives, and flannel boards. Kathy Kleckner (2013), a children's librarian in the Dakota Country Library System (Minnesota), demonstrated strong opposition to the use of digital tablets in library storytimes in her post "The Screen Free Story Time Is the Best Story Time" on the Association for Library Service to Children (ALSC) Blog. Kleckner emphasized the role of the library in promoting early literacy development, stressing that screens have no place in helping young children learn in the library. She offered a list of six reasons why traditional storytime practices are preferable to digital tablets. Other librarians throughout the year also proffered their concerns on the ALSC listserv, particularly during discussions about substituting a specific app for a book or traditional literacy activity during storytime.

That same year, the Institute of Museum and Library Services (IMLS) published the *Growing Young Minds: How Museums and Libraries Create Lifelong Learners* report that emphasized the role of libraries in promoting multiple literacies (reading, informational, cultural, and digital) and closing the achievement gap between low- and high-income children. The report described ten major ways museums and libraries can support early literacy skills, STEM learning, Common Core Standards, and digital literacy to assist children in their educational attainment and growth. The seventh suggestion on their list was the ability of libraries and museums to link new digital technology to learning. According to the report, "With their free public access to the Internet, libraries are important community digital hubs, with expertise in promoting digital, media, and information literacy. Museums and school and public libraries are rich sources of accessible digital media, educational apps, videos, and audio- and e-books, with staff trained to help parents and youth select age-appropriate, content-based, curriculum-linked materials. They help close the digital divide for children, families, and caregivers who lack alternate sources of access" (IMLS 2013, p. 22). Almost all librarians understood their role in promoting traditional reading and information literacy, but some were not so certain they should be promoting digital or media literacy. Their questions tackled tough issues such as: Does promoting digital or media literacy take away from the library's goal to promote the love of reading and books? Do digital picture books, digital apps, and other forms of digital media surpass the printed word in the lives of children? Will using digital media in library programming for children and their families interfere with the healthy development of young children? Should librarians only promote the use of print materials since children have enough exposure to the screen in their daily life by way of everything from educational videos to video games? Will the use of digital media actually create a larger digital divide rather than bringing disparate cultural groups together?

In 2014 several children's librarians along with ALSC conducted an official survey of children's librarians to answer the research question: "What is the landscape in public libraries around the country with respect to new media use in programming for young children ages zero to five?" (Mills, Romeijn-Stout, Campbell, and Koester, 2015, p. 28). In doing so, the librarians hoped to address some of the concerns that the children's librarian community had about digital media usage in the children's library and gain a better understanding of how librarians are using digital media with young patrons. Results of the survey indicated that of the 415 respondents, 71 percent use digital media in library services and programs for young children and their families. Specifically, 40 percent include digital media in storytimes, 31 percent use digital media in other types of children's programming, 26 percent make tablets available for checkout within the library, 20 percent offer tablets for checkout outside the library, and 41 percent have mounted tablets with digital apps loaded on them (Mills et al., 2015). Hardly any librarians mentioned that they serve as media mentors, recommending or curating lists of high-quality digital media. The researchers noted that this finding "sets the stage for a larger discussion around the concept of media mentorship: how library staff can be positive models and guides in implementing research-based best practices to help families manage their media use (Mills et al., 2015, p. 31). Although many children's librarians offered their patrons access to tablets and digital apps either by way of specific programs or services, other librarians still had concerns about digital media usage with young children, indicating that more research is needed to determine the potential harmful influences of digital media on children younger than the age of six. These librarians also suggested that as a profession, children's librarians should adapt slowly and only add a device to programs if there is a direct benefit for the children. This last point is one that almost all librarians—whether for or against digital media usage with young children—agreed that digital media usage should be purposeful and not merely adopted just because it is available. Although the number of librarians responding to the survey was representative of only a portion of the practicing children's librarians in the nation, the majority indicated that they intend to increase their digital media usage in the future, highlighting the saliency of this topic in the profession.

Just a year later, ALSC published the white paper *Media Mentorship in Libraries Serving Youth* that attempted to answer some of the continued questions that librarians had about digital media usage with young children and the specific role of librarians as media mentors. It emphasized the importance of digital media to foster digital literacy development in young children and called for children's librarians to become media mentors who not only recommend high-quality, educational, interactive digital apps and e-books to children and families but also use them in library programming. When used purposefully, appropriately, and in moderation, digital apps, digital picture books, and other forms of digital media can play an integral role in supporting the development of all children. This report highlighted some of the additional concerns and opportunities relating to using digital media in the children's library and described how librarians can reach underserved and underrepresented populations who may not ordinarily use the library and its resources. The white paper also asserted the position of ALSC that:

- "Every library have librarians and other staff serving youth who embrace their role as media mentors for their community.
- Media mentors support children and families in their media use and decisions.
- Library schools provide resources and training to support future librarians and youth services practitioners in serving as media mentors.

- Professional development for current librarians and youth services practitioners include formal training and informal support for serving as media mentors" (Campbell, Haines, Koester, and Stoltz, 2015, p. 7).

To demonstrate the importance of librarians serving as media mentors, ALSC updated its *Competencies for Librarians Serving Children in Public Libraries* (http://www.ala.org/alsc/edcareeers/alsccorecomps) in 2015 to include a stronger focus on the inclusion of serving diverse and underserved populations as well as incorporating language that calls for children's librarians to be knowledgeable not only of quality print materials but digital media as well. Competency II.4 states that librarians serving children should be able to "[identify] the digital media needs of children and their caregivers through formal and informal customer-service interactions and [apply] strategies to support those needs." Competency IV.1 suggests that a children's librarian "[demonstrate] knowledge, management, use and appreciation of children's literature, multimodal materials, digital media, and other materials that contribute to a diverse, current, and relevant children's collection." Collectively, these two statements reinforce ALSC's growing commitment to serving diverse, digital natives in public libraries.

Presently, ALSC is discussing the prospect of creating an award to either honor high-quality digital apps or acknowledge a particularly innovative, dynamic children's librarian who has successfully and purposefully integrated digital media in library programs and exemplifies the qualities of a media mentor. The establishment of the award would further cement ALSC's position on digital media in the children's library and champion librarians for putting the ALSC Competencies into action.

Children's Digital Media Usage

Contemporary children are digital natives. They have never known a time when some sort of digital device, such as a computer, smartphone, or digital tablet, was not present. Although they may not have had access to these devices, they are nonetheless aware of them in larger society. By the age of two years, almost all children have interacted with a mobile device, and many have used it or the Internet for some sort of media-related activity: playing a game, reading an e-book, interacting with a digital app, and so on. Below is a sampling of the statistics relating to children's media usage:

- 67 percent of children ages 2 to 13 years with Internet access have read an e-book, and almost all (92 percent) consumed e-books at least once a week (Bryant, 2014).
- More than a fourth (28 percent) of children ages 0 to 8 years have read an e-book or had one read to them (Common Sense Media, 2013).
- 72 percent of children ages 0 to 8 years have used a mobile device for media activity, up from 38 percent in 2011. Similarly, 38 percent of children ages 0 to 2 years have used a mobile device for media activity, up from 10 percent in 2011 (Common Sense Media, 2013).

- 65 percent of 6- to 8-year-old children and 56 percent of 9- to 11-year-old children have read an e-book, up from 28 percent and 22 percent, respectively, in 2010. However, more than three quarters (77 percent) still prefer print books to their digital counterparts (Scholastic, 2015).

These findings, which do not include TV viewing, suggest that children's digital media usage is increasing over time and at younger ages; indeed, they live in a digital world. Yet reports from researchers, child psychologists, and pediatricians have suggested for decades that screen time and media usage should be significantly limited or entirely eliminated from the lives of young children. The American Academy of Pediatrics (AAP) 1999 report, updated in 2011 and 2013, is an example of the earliest and continually strictest of these warnings about screen time, suggesting that children younger than two years of age should not have access to screens (AAP, 1999; Brown and AAP, 2011; AAP, 2013). These reports indicate that screen time in all its forms—TV viewing, computer and mobile device usage, and so on—can be detrimental to a child's cognitive and emotional development, particularly if the screen time includes passive viewing and involves children younger than two years. However, in fall 2015 AAP released a report that provided guidelines to parents on media usage with young children and suggested that its forthcoming 2016 statement on children's media usage would take into account that digital media can be another environment for young children to learn, hinting that AAP may relax its guidelines to include purposeful, limited, joint, and interactive media engagement that involves both the parent and young child (Brown, Shifrin, and Hill, 2015).

In 1996 the National Association for the Education of Young Children (NAEYC, 1996) published its initial statement about the use of technology with children ages three to eight, officially supporting technology integration in learning programs for young children. More recently, NAEYC partnered with the Fred Rogers Center for Early Learning and Children's Media to revise the 1996 statement to include new digital media and to address concerns about technology and digital media usage with infants and young children (NAEYC and the Fred Rogers Center for Early Learning and Children's Media, 2012). This statement indicates that *developmentally appropriate* technology and digital media can be *purposefully* integrated into learning environments. The keywords here are *developmentally appropriate* and *purposeful*. Many types of print and digital media are available for children; however, just as particular books or films are created for a specific age range, new digital media are also developed for assigned age ranges based on physical and psychological developmental stages. Digital apps that are appropriate for an eight-year-old child will not be suitable for a four-year-old. Similarly, digital media and technology should serve a purpose when used with children. In an educational setting such as a library or classroom, librarians should select digital media that teach a particular skill or enhance their print materials. When sharing digital media with young children, librarians should encourage caregivers to actively engage with their children as they explore a particular digital app, digital picture book, and so on.

Lisa Guernsey, an expert on the use of digital media with children to support multiple literacy, suggests it is okay and even encouraged for young children to interact with digital media as long as librarians and caregivers remember the "three Cs": content, context, and child (Guernsey, 2012; Guernsey and Levine, 2015). Each of these is explained in detail below.

Content

Similar to the NAEYC and the Fred Rogers Center for Early Learning and Children's Media 2012 statement, this guideline asks librarians to consider the purpose of the digital content. Are children using digital media to read a story, learn a skill, or engage in creative play? Are these activities developmentally appropriate? What social messages about particular cultural groups do children glean from a particular digital app, digital picture book, or e-book? Are stereotypes being created or reinforced? Is advertising or in-app purchases prominent throughout an app?

High-quality digital media can offer librarians considerable flexibility in meeting the individualized learning and literacy needs of all children and can provide unique opportunities to extend concepts presented in a storytime. Creative digital apps can be used by English language learners to record digital stories, songs, puppet skits, and more that are culturally relevant and in their first language. This is particularly meaningful if a library does not have print materials that reflect the language and culture of a particular child.

Context

The context of how a librarian uses a particular piece of digital media with children is extremely important. Digital media should never be used as a substitute for bonding time between children and caregivers nor should it replace opportunities to interact with high-quality children's literature. On the contrary, digital apps, digital picture books, and other forms of digital media can be used to augment learning through interactive, hands-on creative explorations. Digital apps can be used to supplement whole-group learning in storytimes with modeling performed by the librarian using a digital tablet and projection system.

Similarly, a digital app can also serve as a medium for individual learning activities performed between caregivers and children after a storytime program. Digital media interaction should not be a solo activity. Children need to be involved in joint media engagement with their peers, caregivers, family members, and librarians. Collaboratively, they should be exploring, learning, modeling, and creating. In his book *Technology and Digital Media in the Early Years*, Donohue (2015) and other authors provide numerous examples of how educators can incorporate digital media into learning activities to meet various learning standards and competencies suggested by professional associations. The book also emphasizes the role of children's librarians in working with educators to facilitate active and purposeful digital media usage.

Child

Every child is unique in his or her literacy development. Although we can identify patterns of growth and development, the rate at which a child acquires various literacy skills depends on his or her natural abilities and home environment. What may work for one child or a group of children may not be successful or relevant for other children. Whereas one child may flourish with a diet of equal parts social interaction with peers, screen time, and engagement with print, another child may need greater doses of one or the other depending on his or her individual physical and cognitive development. Children in supportive homes that have had previous shared learning experiences with a caregiver or older family member while reading a book or interacting with a digital storybook app will respond differently than children who have been left alone to use digital media. Each child has unique interests that influence his or her engagement with various forms of digital media. A creative app that involves creating a puppet and performing a virtual puppet show might appeal more to a child with an interest in dramatic play than a child with a keen interest in science and discovery.

Socioeconomic status also plays a role in a child's media engagement. If caregivers do not have access to digital media, then their level of digital literacy will be lower than that of caregivers who have ready access to digital media. As such, the digital divide between those with access to technology and digital media and those without creates an environment where low-income caregivers may not have the same opportunity to actively participate in joint media engagement as their higher income peers. In their study of public libraries in Philadelphia, Neuman and Celano (2012) observe that caregivers from more economically disadvantaged areas do not actively engage with their children during their interactions with digital media, but high-income caregivers are often co-viewing and actively participating. Similarly, the higher income caregivers provide opportunities for children to experience higher order critical thinking skills while the lower income caregivers do not.

So what does this mean for children's librarians? Today's children have been exposed to digital media at a young age. Some digital media can be good for a child if it is developmentally appropriate and purposeful. Children's librarians have an opportunity to engage nontraditional library users through the use of digital media to augment their current collections and programs. In essence, children's librarians can become well-respected media mentors.

Librarians as Media Mentors

Although many parents seemingly understand that digital media such as storybook, creative, or gaming apps hold benefits for their young children in fostering literacy skills and preparing them to be digital citizens, parents are mindful of the amount of time their children spend with the apps and generally prefer the use of print books over storybook apps and real-world experiential learning opportunities in lieu of virtual ones (Howard and Wallace, 2016; Rideout, 2014). Unfortunately, other parents allow their children to use digital media with little or no guidance, giving them virtually unlimited time and opportunity to explore apps on their phones or tablets (Rideout, 2014). A children's librarian, serving as a media mentor, can prove essential in helping these parents find the best digital media to meet their children's literacy needs while also modeling the necessary engagement that parents should have with their children when they use digital media.

According to Campbell and Kluver (2015), librarians working with children are especially suited to be media mentors for educators, parents, and children for the following reasons. Children's librarians:

- Know how to evaluate, select, and recommend all types of print and digital media
- Can develop dynamic early literacy programs that promote the love of reading and lifelong learning
- Understand the importance of equity of access for all children to print and digital materials
- Are well-suited for collaborative projects with community-based organizations that involve learning with technology

Campbell, Haines, Koester, and Stoltz (2015) also note that "media mentors support children and their families in their decisions and practice around media use. This role encompasses a variety of strategies for support, with each child or family requiring individual mentoring to ensure that support is respectful, appropriate, and relevant" (p. 7). Essentially, there are three types of media mentorship: digital media advisory, programming with digital media, and providing access to curated digital media (Campbell, Haines, and ALSC, 2016). Digital media advisory involves librarians helping parents understand the current research and professional statements relating to digital media usage and young children. Programming with digital media includes librarians modeling how to use a particular digital app or other digital media to promote literacy and creating cohesive programs using both books and digital to foster learning. Librarians can also be media mentors when they provide parents with recommended lists of digital media as well as information on the various resources available.

It is essential that children's librarians get training as media mentors in their library education or through continued professional development. Unfortunately, most library programs do not address this topic in the youth services curriculum. The exceptions are ALA-accredited programs such as the University of Alabama School of Library and Information Studies, the University of Illinois at Urbana-Champaign Graduate School of Library and Information Science, the University of Washington Information School, and Kent State University School of Library and Information Science. This leaves many children's librarians to find professional resources, workshops, and webinars to help them understand how to effectively become media mentors. Highly useful sources to fill this void are the robust Little eLit website (http://littleelit.com); ALSC's Media Mentorship webpage (http://www.ala.org/alsc/mediamentorship); the free e-book *Young Children, New Media, and Libraries: A Guide for Incorporating New Media into Library Collections, Services, and Programs for Families and Children Ages 0–5* (Koester, 2015); and the book *Becoming a Media Mentor: A Guide for Working with Children and Families* (Campbell, Haines, and ALSC, 2016). The publication *Family Time with Apps: A Guide to Using Apps with Your Kids* (The Joan Ganz Cooney Center at Sesame Workshop, 2014), available in English and Spanish, is also perfect for children's librarians to share with caregivers when explaining the educational uses of digital apps and assisting in the selection of high-quality digital apps to use at home.

Types of Digital Media

The idea of using digital media in library programming causes great consternation for many children's librarians. Ostensibly, reluctant librarians are concerned that digital media will replace cherished books and traditional literacy activities, such as puppetry and storytelling with the flannel board, and make way for a completely digital library. Without a doubt, children need physical books, but there is also considerable opportunity and increasing support for the use of digital media in storytimes as well. When thinking about how to use new digital media in library programs, it is essential to understand the differences and learning potential that various types of digital media offer children and their families. A non-interactive digital picture book or e-book for children is quite different than an interactive digital storybook or creative app that encourages children to tap, swipe, and explore a particular topic or story.

For the most part, e-books are created for specialized e-readers (such as Nooks or Kindles) and have limited interactivity options beyond resizing text, highlighting particular passages, searching content for specific words or phrases, and audio narration. Some e-books for children are predominantly text based, such as a digital version of a children's novel, and other e-books include photographs and illustrations that would be found in the print version of a children's picture book. Because their interactivity is quite limited, the potential for using e-books in children's library programming is primarily limited to displaying the books on the overhead to read as a group during storytime or making them available on computers and other digital devices in the children's area for independent exploration.

Interactive digital picture books are becoming more popular, particularly in our ever-increasing digital society. These often include animations, sounds, music, and expressive readings of the text. Usually these books run directly from an online website; librarians make them available to patrons via the children's department webpage, and librarians may use them in storytimes to supplement print stories or extend learning on a particular topic.

Apps are standalone software applications—generally created for the Android or Apple operating systems—that run on a mobile digital device such as a smartphone or digital tablet. Some apps offer passive entertainment in which the children have very little interaction, and others are more interactive, allowing children to drive the action via various cause-and-effect motions (e.g., tapping, swiping). Children's apps are generally divided into three major types: book apps, gaming apps, and creative apps. Book apps include storybook and picture book apps. The interactivity within the app varies greatly from product to product, but the best and recommended type of book app for children's libraries are interactive storybook apps designed to engage children and extend literacy concepts via developmentally appropriate screen interactions and shared activity between the child and caregiver. Interactive storybook apps usually have sound (e.g., narration, music), multiple language modes, imbedded games, and hotspots where a child points to something on the screen to cause an action, narration, and sometimes animation. Some book apps are specifically created for the app platform, and others are adapted from other digital formats. Yokota and Teale (2014) describe the downsides of this latter format and provide useful criteria for thinking critically about the book app format.

Gaming apps consist of challenges to be achieved via some type of digital strategy game. Some gaming apps, called educational apps, are created for the specific purpose of teaching a particular skill or concept. Other gaming apps mirror typical video and computer games and are created solely for entertainment purposes. Activities might unintentionally teach a skill or concept, and there may be violence such as kicking, punching, or killing. The best type of gaming apps for libraries are those that are developmentally appropriate for children, scaffold their learning, and are enjoyable with opportunities for collaborative and interactive play.

Creative apps generally provide specific tools to develop or design an end product such as a recorded story, puppet show, comic book, musical score, or feltboard scene. The best creative apps are nonprescriptive, allow for free play, and promote educational exploration and engagement. Sometimes the most successful use of creative apps is to highlight their use during a storytime and then allow children free play (with their caregivers or other children) via individual tablets or tablet kiosks. Because of their often open-ended nature, creative apps hold great potential for librarians interested in meeting the needs of English language learners.

Evaluating Digital Media

Just as a good children's librarian would not dream of reading a book during storytime without first reading it aloud to herself, the same librarian would not want to feature an app or other type of digital media in a storytime without first learning about its functionality, evaluating its ease of use, and analyzing its depiction of genders and cultural groups. Established in 1997 by the ALSC Children and Technology Committee and updated in 2013 by the ALSC Great Websites Committee, *ALSC Great Websites for Kids Selection Criteria* is one of the most helpful tools for evaluating digital media such as websites, digital picture books, and apps. These criteria establish basic guidelines for ensuring the content of digital media is developmentally appropriate, accurate, and easy to navigate. Specifically, they allow children's librarians to examine the following:

- **Authorship or sponsorship.** Identify who created a particular type of digital media and their authority in the subject matter.
- **Purpose.** Discern why a particular example of digital media was created and what it intends to teach children.
- **Design and stability.** Evaluate how children can access and use the content in the digital media and ensure that it is easy to navigate, accessible, updated regularly, clutter free, and loads easily.
- **Content.** Analyze the information in the digital media to ensure accuracy, developmental appropriateness, correct grammar and spelling, bias-free images and text, advertisement-free material, and privacy protection (Association for Library Service to Children, 2013).

Multiple resources are available to help children's librarians select the best digital media. These range from top lists of recommended apps to professional review sources of all types of digital media. Some of the more common ones are listed below:

- *AASL Best Apps for Teaching and Learning* (http://www.ala.org/aasl/standards/best/apps). Initiated in 2013 by the American Association of School Librarians (AASL), this annual list of the best children's and youth apps selects software because of its high potential for curricular connections that support the association's standards for school librarianship and cultivate children's learning in libraries through creativity, active participation, innovation, and collaboration.
- *Children's Technology Review* (http://childrenstech.com). This longstanding, trusted subscription-based resource includes reviews for a wide range of children's digital media.
- *Common Sense Media* (https://www.commonsensemedia.org/app-reviews). A free comprehensive resource, this website categorizes and reviews various types of children's digital media, commenting on their suitability for children. Librarians should use their best judgment when using this resource because the reviewers are quite conservative in their views of topics appropriate for children.
- *Digital Storytime* (http://digital-storytime.com). This highly useful online resource categorizes and reviews apps by a variety of topics and themes. It also allows librarians to search for specific language options to locate media for their English language learners and provides interviews as well as new stories relating to digital media usage with children on the companion blog Digital Media Diet (http://digitalmediadiet.com).
- *Little eLit* (http://littleelit.com/app-lists-reviews). Part of the robust Little eLit website, this webpage includes a list of app review websites, specialized lists of apps, and links to blog posts about app reviewing.

Although all of these resources provide useful information for reviewing apps, librarians may discover that a particular app they want to use in library programming has not been reviewed. Luckily, the blog Learning in Hand with Tony Vincent (http://learninginhand.com/blog/ways-to-evaluate-educational-apps.html) provides several helpful checklists and toolkits to assist librarians, parents, and educators in evaluating digital apps. These checklists can be modified for a variety of different purposes relating to the roles of a media mentor.

Diversity in Digital Media

Children need access to diverse digital media, as well as diverse books, to provide opportunities for them to see reflections (mirrors) of their cultural experiences and glimpses (windows) into the cultures of children who are different. A piece of digital media is embedded with the cultural beliefs of the app developers and content creators such as authors, artists, and designers. When children engage with a digital picture book, e-book, or digital app, they are introduced to various social and cultural messages. These messages can influence how children perceive their culture, the culture of their peers, and other cultures around the world. Both print and digital media play important roles in helping children formulate their self-concept and identity, and learn social cues that dictate how to respond in particular situations (Vygotsky, 1986; Cortés, 2002). Stereotypes in digital media can foster a child's misunderstanding about a particular culture.

Unfortunately, the predilection of cartoon animators to caricature and over-simplify non-white cultures is equally practiced by app developers and other de-signers of digital media, resulting in stereotyping of cultural groups. This is partic-ularly evident in digital apps. For example, in the digital storybook app *The Dream* by Swipea Kids (http://www.swipea.com/the-dream-an-arabic-tale-for-ios.html), the developers introduce children to a clichéd view of Arab culture, imbued with factually incorrect information. The idea of people from other cultures wearing costumes versus typical dress is reinforced in one of the imbedded games in which children are encouraged to help the female character select a *costume* to wear. A hijab and abayah are then presented for children to choose from. Using the loaded word *costume* suggests that children are helping the character try on a cultural identity rather than experiencing it.

Recent conversations about diversity in children's literature have identified this same propensity to stereotype, particularly when depicting cultural groups such as African Americans. In late 2015 and early 2016 librarians, educators, re-searchers, children's book creators, and publishers all weighed in on discussions about recent children's picture books depicting happy, smiling slaves eager to please their white masters. Sadly, because of the sheer number of apps available on a daily basis and the lack of quality control measures that are more rigid in traditional children's publishing, similar stereotypes depicting cultural groups can go virtually unnoticed in digital apps for children. Rarely do stereotyped digital media for children receive the same attention as their printed counterparts. Naidoo (2014) observes:

> Because issues of racism, stereotyping, whitewashing, and other social concerns are still hot topics in children's and young adult literature, we must be similarly cautious about the presence of these issues in digital media. Conversations regarding these "hot button" top-ics have been ongoing since before Nancy Larrick's (1965) article "The All-White World of Children's Books,"[2] and we have no reason to believe that the digital media industry is any more socially conscious than the children's book industry. . . . A glance through the iTunes store reveals that most apps are created with a monocultural child in mind—the white, middle-class child. Essentially the "All-White World of Children's Books" with the aid of digital enhancements has now morphed into the "All-White World of Children's Book Apps." While some culturally sensitive apps and other digital media are available to help them explore global cultures, children are predominantly exposed to apps with an embed-ded, socially constructed script perpetuating the notion of a singular culturally generic ex-perience. As in the children's literature world, this generic experience generally represents White, middle class culture (pp. 125–26).

Many forms of digital media only feature generic animals or nonhuman cartoon characters as protagonists, offering children little opportunities for any type of cultural connection. In a study of digital apps for children, Vaala, Ly, and Levine (2015) note that fewer than half featured human characters, and those that did feature human characters presented a relatively generic ethnicity based on skin tone, leaving the researchers to question which specific cultural group was being represented. Culturally generic digital media rob children of opportunities to make social connections and learn social scripts to help them interact with others and succeed in our pluralistic society.

When choosing culturally diverse digital media to use in storytimes or other library programs, children's librarians should consider how the topic of diversity is introduced to children. The best media present culture and diversity naturally to children. The adage "show, don't tell" is equally as applicable to digital media as it is to children's books. Digital media that place heavy emphasis on convincing children that it is okay to be different may not be as successful in fostering cultural pride and understanding as media that highlight the accomplishments and contributions of various cultures to our global society. Below are additional guidelines to consider when selecting culturally diverse digital media. Diverse apps, e-books, and other digital media should:

- Feature characters who represent the broad spectrum of diversity (e.g., racial, ethnic, gender, family composition, ability, religion) in a community.
- Allow kids to see cross-cultural characters interacting with each other to understand the ways that we are all the same, same but different.
- Offer unique ideas, stories, and information celebrating specific cultures.
- Provide children with new ways to make cross-cultural connections within our larger global culture.
- Scaffold children's literacy development in their home or first language.
- Avoid "token" characters to fill a diversity quota (Naidoo, 2014; Nankani, 2015).

Some app developers and children's program researchers understand the importance of providing opportunities for all children to interact with diverse cultures via digital media. They have consciously attempted to infuse diversity into discussions and reports on children's digital media. The Joan Ganz Cooney Center at Sesame Workshop recently published the report *Diverse Families and Media: Using Research to Inspire Design*. One of the authors of this report emphasizes that diversity in children's media matters and describes Sesame Workshop's commitment to providing this diversity in the digital media it creates (Pressey, 2016). At the same time, two app developers have created the Diversity in Apps movement (http://diversityinapps.com), which is similar to the widely publicized We Need Diverse Books (http://diversebooks.org) campaign in children's publishing. Diversity in Apps is intended to mobilize educators, researchers, and app designers to proactively focus on highlighting the need for diversity in digital media and creating high-quality digital apps featuring diverse cultures.

Sandhya Nankani (2015), the founder of the Indie publisher and content development company Literary Safari, observes that often apps representing cultural diversity get lost in the landslide of other digital apps available for children. She notes that app stores such as iTunes and Google Play use algorithms to suggest apps to potential buyers that are based on buyers' previous purchases and perceived needs. This often keeps multicultural apps buried in the search results. It is incumbent upon vigilant children's librarians and media mentors to sift through the available sources and find those diamonds in the rough to augment print materials in library storytimes and programs for children.

Concluding Remarks

Public libraries have always served as welcoming spaces to promote the love of traditional reading literacy and scaffold lifelong learning. As society and technology have changed, the role of the public library has expanded to also promote technology and media in their multiple formats and foster other types of literacies such as information literacy, digital literacy, and cultural literacy. Successful public libraries are the heart of their communities, creating a third space or informal public gathering place where children and their families can come together to learn about the world around them through both print and digital materials and culturally rich library programs that incorporate all media formats.

Although this report has attempted to capture some of the current topics in the field of children's librarianship relating to digital media usage with children in the public library, the landscape is in a constant state of motion. New research studies, statements by child development and media associations, and trade reports are published regularly in an attempt to best understand the influence of digital media on young children as well as the media consumption habits of these diverse users. Now is an exciting time for children's librarians to explore the potential for using digital media in the library and embracing their role as media mentors. Koester (2015) observes, "The topic of new media, young children, and libraries is still in its infancy; it is continually developing and ever-evolving as new technology emerges and libraries determine new and productive ways to wield these tools in support of their mission to serve children and families" (p. 112). Many children's librarians are welcoming this evolving role, and others are taking time to better understand the changing digital world and their role as storytellers and early literacy educators in it. This reluctance is understandable, particularly if librarians believe that using digital media in the children's library is a binary choice: either you use digital media and let it take precedence over children's books during storytime or you ban the use of new media in children's programs. However, this is not the case. Simon and Nemeth (2012) remind librarians that they have a myriad of choices when planning storytime programs: "It's about the choices you make: your curriculum, your practice, and how you use whatever materials you plan for children to explore and learn from—not whether or not the material is digital. Rejecting technology for your program because it can be used inappropriately or because some applications are inappropriate is like throwing the baby out with the bathwater!" (p. 19). The baby and the bathwater are here to stay as the statistics of children's digital media usage suggest. It's time for children's librarians as media mentors to provide the bubbles!

References

American Academy of Pediatrics (AAP), Committee on Public Education. "Media Education." Part 1. *Pediatrics* 104, no. 2 (1999): 341–43.

American Academy of Pediatrics (AAP), Council on Communications and Media. (2013). "Children, Adolescents, and the Media." *Pediatrics-Springfield* 132 (5): 958–61.

Association for Library Service to Children (ALSC). "Great Websites for Kids Selection Criteria." ALSC, 2013. Accessed April 7, 2016. http://gws.ala.org/about/selection-criteria.

Brown, Ari, and American Academy of Pediatrics (AAP), Council on Communications and Media. "Media Use by Children Younger than 2 Years." *Pediatrics* 128, no. 5 (2011): 1,040–45.

Brown, Ari, Donald L. Shifrin, and David L. Hill. "Beyond 'Turn It Off': How to Advise Families on Media Use." *American Academy of Pediatrics News* 36, no. 10 (2015). Accessed April 6, 2016. http://www.aappublications.org/content/36/10/54.

Bryant, Alison. *What a Difference a Year Makes: Kids and E-Reading Trends 2012–13*. PlayCollective LLC and Digital Book World. January 2014. Accessed April 6, 2016. http://store.digitalbookworld.com/what-difference-a-year-makes-childrens-report-t3592.

Campbell, Cen, Claudia Haines, Amy Koester, and Dorothy Stoltz. *Media Mentorship in Libraries Serving Youth*. White Paper. Association for Library Service to Children (ALSC), 2015. Accessed April 6, 2016. http://www.ala.org/alsc/sites/ala.org.alsc/files/content/2015%20ALSC%20White%20Paper_FINAL.pdf.

Campbell, Cen, Claudia Haines, and the Association for Library Service to Children (ALSC). *Becoming a Media Mentor: A Guide for Working with Children and Families*. American Library Association, 2016.

Campbell, Cen, and Carisa Kluver. "Access, Content, and Engagement: How Children's Librarians Support Early Learning in the Digital Age." In Chip Donohue (ed.). *Technology and Digital Media in the Early Years: Tools for Teaching and Learning* (pp. 235–249). Routledge, 2015.

Common Sense Media. *Zero to Eight: Children's Media Use in America 2013*. Fall 2013. Accessed April 7, 2016. http://www.commonsensemedia.org/research/zero-to-eight-childrens-media-use-in-america-2013.

Cortés, Carlos. *The Making, and Remaking, of a Multiculturalist*. Teachers College Press, 2002.

Donohue, Chip (ed.). *Technology and Digital Media in the Early Years: Tools for Teaching and Learning*. The All-White World of Children's Literature.

Guernsey, Lisa. *Screen Time: How Electronic Media—From Baby Videos to Educational Software—Affects Your Young Child*. Basic Books, 2012.

Guernsey, Lisa, and Michael H. Levine. *Tap, Click, Read: Growing Readers in a World of Screens*. Jossey-Bass, 2015.

Howard, Vivian, and Maureen Wallace. "Today's Tech Literacy Tools: Parental Perceptions of Apps for Preschoolers." *Children and Libraries* 14, no. 1 (2016): 3–9.

Institute of Museum and Library Services (IMLS). *Growing Young Minds: How Museums and Libraries Create Lifelong Learners*. June 2013. Accessed April

6, 2016. http://www.imls.gov/assets/1/AssetManager/GrowingYoungMinds. pdf.

The Joan Ganz Cooney Center at Sesame Workshop. *Family Time with Apps: A Guide to Using Apps with Your Kids*. December 2014. Accessed April 6, 2016. http://www.joanganzcooneycenter.org/publication/family-time-with-apps.

Kleckner, Kathy. "The Screen Free Story Time Is the Best Story Time." ALSC Blog. June 14, 2013. Accessed April 6, 2016. http://www.alsc.ala.org/ blog/2013/06/the-screen-free-story-time-is-the-best-story-time.

Koester, Amy (ed.). *Young Children, New Media, and Libraries: A Guide for Incorporating New Media into Library Collections, Services, and Programs for Families and Children Ages 0–5*. Little eLit: 2015. Accessed April 6, 2016. http://littleelit.com/book.

Little eLit. "About Little eLit." 2016. Accessed April 6, 2016. http://littleelit.com.

Mills, J. Elizabeth, Emily Romeijn-Stout, Cen Campbell, and Amy Koester. "Results from the Young Children, New Media, and Libraries Survey: What Did We Learn?" *Children and Libraries* 13, no. 2 (2015): 26–32, 35.

Naidoo, Jamie Campbell. *Diversity Programming for Digital Youth: Promoting Cultural Competence in the Children's Library*. Libraries Unlimited, 2014.

Nankani, Sandhya. "Mind the (Diversity) Gap in Kids' Digital Media." The Joan Ganz Cooney Center Blog. January 27, 2015. Accessed April 6, 2016. http:// www.joanganzcooneycenter.org/2015/01/27/mind-the-diversity-gap-in-kids-digital-media.

National Association for the Education of Young Children (NAEYC). *Technology and Young Children—Ages 3 Through 8*. Position Statement. Washington, DC: NAEYC, 1996.

National Association for the Education of Young Children (NAEYC) and the Fred Rogers Center for Early Learning and Children's Media. (2012). *Technology and Interactive Media as Tools in Early Childhood Programs Serving Children from Birth Through Age 8*. Joint position statement. Washington, DC: NAEYC; Latrobe, PA: Fred Rogers Center for Early Learning and Children's Media. Accessed April 6, 2016. http://www.naeyc.org/content/technology-and-young-children.

Neuman, Susan B., and Donna C. Celano. *Giving Our Children a Fighting Chance: Poverty, Literacy and the Development of Information Capital*. Teachers College Press, 2012.

Pressey, Briana. "Diversity in Children's Media Matters." The Joan Ganz Cooney Center Blog. Accessed April 6, 2016. http://www.joanganzcooneycenter. org/2016/04/06/diversity-in-childrens-media-matters.

Rideout, Victoria J. *Learning at Home: Families' Educational Media Use in America*. The Joan Ganz Cooney Center at Sesame Workshop. January 2014. Accessed April 6, 2016. http://www.joanganzcooneycenter.org/publication/ learning-at-home.

Scholastic. *Kids and Family Reading Report*. 5th ed. Scholastic. January 2015. Accessed April 7, 2016. http://www.scholastic.com/readingreport/downloads. htm.

Simon, Fran, and Karen Nemeth. *Digital Decisions: Choosing the Right Technology Tools for Early Childhood Education*. Gryphon House, 2012.

Vaala, Sarah, Anna Ly, and Michael H. Levine. *Getting a Read on the App Stores: A Market Scan and Analysis of Children's Literacy Apps*. The Joan Ganz Cooney Center at Sesame Workshop. December 2015. Accessed April 6, 2016. http://www.joanganzcooneycenter.org/wp-content/uploads/2015/12/jgcc_gettingaread.pdf.

Vygotsky, Lev. *Thought and Language*. MIT Press, 1986.

Yokota, Junko, and William H. Teale. "Picture Books and the Digital World." *The Reading Teacher* 67, no. 8 (2014): 557–85.

Endnotes

1. Note that the use of the term *digital media* is used fluidly to include digital apps, online games, e-books, digital picture books, and dynamic Web resources. At times a differentiation between digital apps and other types of digital media is made to make a pertinent point.

2. Larrick, Nancy. "The All-White World of Children's Books." *Saturday Review* (September 11, 1965): 63–65. Larrick's article is often cited as one of the influential articles in the children's literature world that provided a "wake-up call" to the paucity and scarcity of children's books about non-white cultural groups.

Embedded Librarianship: Experiences of Early Adopters Offering Informationist Services

Jaime Friel Blanck, Blair Anton, Terrie R. Wheeler,
Claire Twose, Rob Wright, Jennifer Darragh

This chapter will introduce the concept of the embedded librarian and will in-corporate examples of embedded library services at Johns Hopkins University. An *embedded librarian* is also commonly referred to as an *informationist*, and we will be using these terms interchangeably throughout this chapter. Embedded librarianship refers to a model of information service wherein librarians partici-pate in academic and research arenas alongside their users. This service delivery model provides a dedicated librarian as a contact person for the faculty, staff, and students in specific departments. It involves being located, at least part of the time, outside the library in physical proximity to specific departments where the librarian partners with users on an ongoing basis. This can be in the form of the librarian having working space within the department or librarian participation in departmental meetings and activities. Librarians can also be embedded in vir-tual environments such as course management software systems used in distance education. This close proximity allows for more frequent contact and for deeper, longer-lasting collaborations between librarians and researchers. By focusing on a limited number of small groups, embedded librarians can immerse themselves in the content of the discipline and create customized information services that most effectively meet user needs.

Embedded librarians form partnerships with the user community rather than acting simply as service providers. Through these partnerships, librarians become fully integrated members of project and research teams. This requires proactively reaching out to stakeholders and persuasively presenting the skills and services li-brarians can bring to these teams. This can be one of the most challenging aspects of becoming embedded and is very different from traditional modes of librarian-ship, where the user is the party to initiate contact. Promoting information services is an ongoing activity and should be based on a needs assessment (discussed in greater detail later in the chapter). When talking with clients about the value a librarian can bring to a project or department, be prepared with examples. Users often have a fixed idea of what a library is and what services a librarian provides. It is the responsibility of the librarian to analyze the results of needs assessments and offer suggestions to stakeholders about how the library can enhance the qual-ity or productivity of their work.

Embedded librarians/informationists still provide many traditional services associated with libraries, such as training on information resources, performing literature searches, supporting current awareness, and maintaining a collection of

Jaime Friel Blanck is Clinical Informationist at the William H. Welch Medical Library, Johns Hopkins University. Blair Anton is Associate Director of Informationist Services at the William H. Welch Medical Library, Johns Hopkins University. Terrie R. Wheeler is Director of the Samuel J. Wood Library and C. V. Starr Biomedical Information Center, Weill Cornell Medicine. Claire Twose is Associate Director of Research Services at William H. Welch Medical Library, Johns Hopkins University. Rob Wright is Basic Sciences Informationist at William H. Welch Medical Library, Johns Hopkins University. Jennifer Darragh is Data Services and Sociology Librarian, Milton S. Eisenhower Library, GIS and Data Services, Johns Hopkins University.

online resources. Embedded librarians may also support data management, participate in the systematic review process (beyond the literature search), and participate in curriculum design. In a 2008 systematic review of the role of informationists, Rankin et al. identified a tri-partite model of competencies of successful informationists in the medical domain (Rankin, Grefsheim, & Canto, 2008):

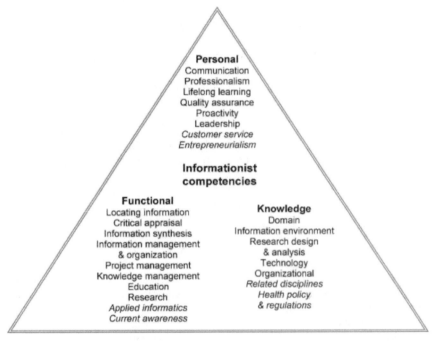

Informationists must also possess strong interpersonal skills in order to build relationships and establish trust among collaborators. Adaptability to the cultural specifics of disciplines other than information science is necessary, as is an ongoing interest in deepening one's personal knowledge of discipline-specific topics. Perhaps the most important quality of successful embedded librarians is the motivation to continually acquire new skills and seek out new collaborations.

Identifying High-Value Informationist Practices

One key to the successful planning of embedded library services is to identify activities of high value to project and research teams. Identifying the value of a knowledge worker has traditionally been challenging, because it is very difficult to measure knowledge conveyed or transformed into new knowledge or practice. In health care, knowledge becomes valuable when it facilitates excellent patient care with the least amount of resources. This may be through saving time, preventing needless tests or procedures, avoiding adverse drug reactions, or shortening length of stay. Value in other domains may include increasing the quality of faculty publications, increasing the number of funded grants, or improving the ability of students to locate and critically appraise the research literature. This section will focus on best practices for identifying areas of high value for embedded library services in an organization.

From the outset of any partnership, there must be clear communication to establish the roles and responsibilities of the team and the informationist. Clear communication between the team served and the information center providing the informationist allows the information center to customize its services to the research team. These customized services may be documented in a memorandum of understanding or through more informal channels of communication. The information center may request that the informationist be included in all of the clinical or research activities of the team. It may also specify that the informationist be assigned a mentor on the team who can provide advice regarding the continuing education that would best equip the informationist to work with the team. Generally such conversations also outline periodic requests for feedback on the service, which can include focus groups, survey responses, or other means for gathering the end-user's perspective. In practice, groups receiving informationist services at minimal or no charge are eager to provide the mentoring, inclusion in team activities, and evaluation of the efficacy of the informationist program in return for having such a highly skilled and valuable team member made available to them.

Interviewing the team leader to identify areas through which the informationist could have the greatest potential impact on the mission or science of the team is a highly valuable exercise. The team leader sees the mission of the team in the larger context of the organization as well as within the larger discipline. Hence the team leader may be able to best articulate the value of proposed services that the informationist might bring to the research team.

Embedding an informationist in a clinical or research team allows the informationist, with appropriate domain or subject expertise, to function as another team member. In this manner the library goes to the researcher, rather than vice versa, and the informationist can provide information as needed to advance the research effort of the team. Physically embedding an informationist into a clinical or research team is not always required to achieve these results. An informationist may be assigned to work with several different groups, and rotate among them on a weekly or semi-weekly basis. This still achieves the goal of having the informationist become a full team member, but allows them to work with several teams, rather than just one or two. Another method, termed an "in-context" informationist, takes informationists with specific subject expertise and enables them to interface with many different groups through their domain or subject expertise. In-context informationists generally work out of the library, with researchers coming to them from a wide variety of groups across an organization for specialized consulting services. However, like the embedded informationist, the in-context informationist seeks to understand workflows and introduce information solutions to advance the organization's mission. An example of an in-context informationist service is a health science library's bioinformatics support service.

Another potential high-value service is integrating information into the workflow of the team when and where it is needed, while not disrupting the workflow of the investigator. This can be done either electronically through alerting services products such as LibGuides, or by inserting the informationist into the workflow to provide real-time literature searches. Increasingly the value of the informationist is in outlining the workflows of a research process and identifying how master data can be captured once and reused many times for reporting purposes. This concept of developing systems that capture data once, with APIs that export structured data downstream into other systems, is becoming increasingly valued in scientific organizations. Data reporting activities are ever increasing in these organizations, while time, staff, and funding are not.

The informationist may support the educational mission of the team in impactful ways by facilitating journal clubs, providing instruction in how to use bioinformatics or statistical tools, or becoming experts who train team members in particular software workflows employed by the team, such as lab notebooks or data management tools such as REDCap.

An informationist can cultivate the team's scholarly output by training the research team on how to comply with the National Institutes of Health's Public Access Policy, creating publication strategies, or creating portals where PDFs of relevant articles are placed for convenient citation while writing a research paper. A step further in this direction would be for the informationist to take on the role of the managing editor of a special issue of a journal to which the scientific team contributes. Efforts like this can get new scientific knowledge into publication as much as six months earlier, indicating the value of the informationist to the scientific team. Another way a clinical informationist can champion the team's scholarly output is by locating evidence-based papers that support a particularly challenging clinical diagnosis or therapy. These papers can be placed in an environment like Faculty of 1000 Prime's new "project" and annotated by team members. Informationists can also provide advice on crafting data management and sharing plans that can promote the dissemination of the data produced during research.

While we have discussed some methods for gathering data on the impact of the informationist program, such as interviewing the team leader or a focus group, another standard tool for quantitative and qualitative data capture is the survey. Done well, this tool can be used to capture how information provided by the informationist supported decision making, changed treatment decisions, avoided unnecessary tests, or shortened or avoided an in-patient admission. Over time, this kind of quantitative information will illustrate the value that the informationist brings to the team in terms that leadership understands, and can better illustrate the value proposition that the informationist provides to the team. Formal assessment strategies for embedded library services will be discussed in greater detail later in this chapter.

Promotion Strategies for the Informationist Program

Informationist programs that follow the above best practices and consistently demonstrate their value to their organizations will likely not need any promotion, because their value will spread among investigators by word of mouth. However, there are some simple strategies that can ensure that the informationist program, and as a result the library or information center, becomes integral to the success of the organization. Try to avoid traditional advertising, and focus on marketing to specific user groups based on identified needs. Develop suites of services that target demand areas, and begin introducing these services as soon as a new investigator joins the organization. If at an academic organization, begin by cultivating the students in their first year. The sooner students or new investigators become dependent upon the services of the information center, the more likely they will return for more complex services later. The informationist may also need to create buy-in among new members of a team. Setting up a system where the team leader or a senior investigator introduces the informationist to each new investigator with an example of how the informationist has supported the science of the senior investigator will go a long way in building trust. In this manner the junior team members will learn to accept and seek out the services offered by the informationist.

Researchers may not immediately perceive how they can incorporate evolving embedded library services into their workflows. Developing a document that describes these services, with examples of their impacts, can help investigators envision where embedded library services can benefit them. Developing tiers of services, from basic to more complex, allows faculty to select the level of support they need. As an investigator's initial information needs are satisfied, move them along to more advanced services that may exceed their expectations. As expectations are exceeded, and services remain reliable and consistent, the informationist cultivates the trust of the investigators, earning their loyalty over time. This manner of introducing information services is simple, strategic, and highly successful. Periodic assessments of the use of services can help ensure that client expectations are met or exceeded.

Informationists in the Biomedical Sciences

Patterns of embedded librarianship can be traced back to earlier models of librarianship, including branch librarians working with specific subject collections and departments or clinical librarians acting as part of a larger health professional team in addition to working in a medical library. Gertrude Lamb is credited with creating the clinical medical librarian role in the early 1970s at the University of Missouri-Kansas City School of Medicine (Lamb, 1982). This model of librarianship recognized that physicians' information needs most often occur when physicians are actively engaged in patient care, when they do not have access to the physical library or the services of a librarian. Clinical librarians began embedding themselves into the medical team during patient rounds and providing information from the medical literature to answer clinicians' questions and support patient care. Davidoff and Florance proposed the profession of informationists as an evolved information profession expanded from the clinical medical model (Davidoff & Florance, 2000). They specified that informationists must have experience or education in both information science and a medical/scientific discipline. Education in non-information fields does not need to be through formal coursework, but can be gained through continuing education, self-study, or on-the-job experience. Amid the rapid proliferation of biotechnology research in the late 1980s, Cunningham et al. surveyed researchers and librarians at nine major medical centers across the United States to learn more about the amount of biotechnology research being conducted and how libraries were supporting this research (Cunningham, Grefsheim, Simon, & Lansing, 1991). The survey results demonstrated that biotechnology researchers were using library resources, but that there were gaps in the library collections and in librarians' understanding of the information needs of these researchers. By 1990, in response to a call by the National Library of Medicine to prioritize the information needs of biotechnology researchers, reports of liaison programs targeting this group began to appear in the literature (Pratt, 1990). The informationist role has also expanded into public health, including the specialized role of "disaster information specialist" as an embedded model for more effectively supporting the public health response to disasters (Featherstone, 2012)

In addition to the above discipline-specific roles for informationists, the role of the data services informationist has evolved to meet user needs. Due to recent funding mandates, these services have grown to include research data management or RDM (Akers, 2014). Research data services have been offered by research institutes, specialty archives, and university academic departments for more than 50 years (Martinez-Uribe, 2014). Historically, the numeric data that these services revolved around were predominantly from national and international government producers, as well as from disciplines in the social sciences where empirical data sharing practices were encouraged (Feinberg et al., 1985; Sieber, 1991). In addition, the desire to share data from empirical research in the social sciences spurred the development of archives such as the Inter-University Consortium for Political and Social Research (ICPSR) ("ICPSR: The Founding and Early Years"). The development of research data services within libraries on academic research university campuses grew over the latter half of the 20th century as natural extensions of government documents programs (providing access to the U.S. Census) and the centralization of magnetic tape reading services (Treadwell, 1994).

Research Support

Literature searching to support original research is a core service requiring a considerable investment of time and effort. It involves working with researchers to develop search strategies that include controlled vocabularies, keywords, appropriate syntax, relevant field tags, and validated search filters. Examples of databases commonly searched include PubMed, Embase, Web of Science, Scopus, TOXLINE, and BIOSIS. Informationists must also be experts at searching for grey literature, which is information not published in the journal literature. Examples of grey literature include clinical trials registries, data sets, statistics produced by government agencies, white papers, and conference proceedings. Search strategies vary in their level of complexity and comprehensiveness depending upon the intended uses for the searches. Intended uses include self-education on a new area of research, decision-support for ongoing research, literature reviews, scoping reviews, and systematic reviews. In the case of systematic reviews, research teams are usually created to undertake these time-consuming projects via departmental research committees. Informationist skills and expertise are highlighted in these collaborations. Informationists often educate users interested in undertaking systematic reviews about the nature of the project they are embarking on, and alternative, valid review strategies that may better meet their needs. When a systematic review is undertaken the informationist role often begins with the formulation of a specific, answerable research question and can include developing and conducting expert searches, managing citations, and serving on review teams. Literature searches can also support other areas of research such as preparing grant applications, presentations, lectures, and identifying journal options for authors seeking to publish an article.

Biological data searching is literature searching's counterpart, finding information that addresses a researcher's question through well-structured queries of databases. Biological data searching involves a different set of databases and the information retrieved takes a different form, including the features of molecules and descriptions of processes within living things. Examples of such information include DNA sequences, protein structures, gene expression data, and biological pathways. Databases searched through the informationist program at the Welch Medical Library at Johns Hopkins University include those from the National Center for Biotechnology Information (NCBI), the European Molecular Biology Laboratory–European Bioinformatics Institute (EMBL–EBI), and a variety of other sources. NCBI databases searched include Gene, Genome, Protein, the Conserved Domain Database, and the Gene Expression Omnibus. EMBL–EBI databases searched include ArrayExpress, Expression Atlas, and InterPro. Tools used from other sources include FlyMine, FlyBase, and PaxDb. Specific examples of projects in which biological data searching support was provided include GEO/ArrayExpress datasets for gene expression, InterPro searches for conserved protein domains, and searches for orthologs of Drosophila genes.

Librarians embedded to support research data access and management use a growing range of RDM services. An environmental scan of academic research libraries revealed that common RDM services included training in best practices and assistance with metadata creation and with deposit of data into institutional or disciplinary repositories (*SPEC Kit 334: Research Data Management Services*, 2013).

Educational Support

Informationists participate in academic planning activities that go above and beyond typical library instruction sessions that regularly occur as part of the educational curriculum. At Johns Hopkins University, the informationists at the Welch Medical Library have been invited to participate in the curricula of the Schools of Medicine and Public Health. An informationist serves as a member of the Education Policy and Curriculum Committee (EPCC) for the School of Medicine (SOM). Established by the dean of the medical faculty, the EPCC is a standing SOM committee and the institutional body responsible for the overall design, management, and evaluation of a coherent and coordinated medical school curriculum associated with the MD degree and other related educational priorities. Another informationist is an instructor in the Transition to the Wards course. This is a three-week course that covers basic clinical skills that rising third-year students will need to master before they begin their clinical rotations. Informationists work with SOM faculty to schedule and plan education activities. Information skills are woven into clinical practice in realistic scenarios of how they will interact with clinical information systems while caring for patients. Mastery of clinical information seeking is measured as part of the Objective Structure Clinical Examination (OSCE) at the end of the course. For almost 10 years, informationists have co-taught alongside a faculty member in the 6-credit course called "Systematic Reviews and Meta-Analysis" offered through the Bloomberg School of Public

Health. In this course, informationists lead several classes to provide instruction on how to create a high-quality systematic review search strategy and work with small groups of students to identify viable research topics and provide guidance on their final projects. An informationist partners with the education librarian from the Eisenhower Library at Johns Hopkins to embed support for the students of the Masters of Education for the Health Professions (MEHP) program. All of the students are physicians and nurses pursuing further coursework to strengthen their skills as clinical educators. The librarians worked closely with the head of the program to research similar programs when the degree was initially created.

Support for Information Discovery

Empowering researchers to successfully discover information independently is an important goal for libraries. The Welch Medical Library provides instruction to patrons about the use of tools for literature and biological data searching. These tools include PubMed, Embase, Scopus, Web of Science, and BIOSIS for literature searching. Workshops have also been conducted on a variety of NCBI-associated databases used for finding biological data, including BioSystems, dbSNP, Epigenomics, Gene, HomoloGene, International HapMap, and OMIM. In addition to these sessions, which have been informationist-created and typically given to a small audience, the library has hosted special-event presentations from outside groups, including NCBI and HINARI, that have been held in larger venues on campus.

The library has also created a suite of Web pages on a variety of topics to help users quickly get to specialized information. These web pages include LibGuides, which cover specific topics of interest for a broad audience of users. These guides provide support for finding grant funding, writing and publishing, and complying with the NIH Public Access Policy. The Emergency Medicine and Public Health LibGuide was developed through a partnership between an Emergency Medicine faculty member and two informationists. This guide was designed as a reference for researchers whose work spans public health and emergency medicine. It contains information pertinent to this population of users, including funding opportunities and links to current articles on disaster medicine and selected infectious diseases. There are also guides called specialty portals that were created in-house using Drupal-based templates. The Basic Sciences Portal has pages with protocols, key databases, model organism resources, Hopkins core facilities, and database tutorials. The Bioinformatics Portal is organized according to major "-omics" fields and was developed using input from faculty, a core bioinformatics textbook, bioinformatics directories, resources linked from Hopkins lab web pages, and portals created by other libraries. The resulting portal organizes core resources in logical categories, offers detailed descriptions, includes tutorials, and highlights Hopkins centers, facilities, and tools.

A key priority for the data informationist at Johns Hopkins is connecting researchers to data sets, either to support their contribution to these sets or to help facilitate access to support their knowledge discovery. Keeping abreast of the availability of new and existing data repositories across disciplines and agencies is beneficial, as is understanding the requirements for submitting data into these repositories (*SPEC Kit 334: Research Data Management Services*, 2013)

When instructions for deposit aren't clear, data librarians typically understand the various components needed for data discoverability and data usability, such as proper metadata assignment, data dictionaries, and codebooks. Assisting researchers as an embedded team member could be at varying levels. For example, a more surface-level involvement (meaning less likely to need to be included on the project's Institutional Review Board application/approval) could be to create tailored "best practices" workshops based on the discipline area of the project. Many academic libraries already offer some best practices training, but in more of a broad-brush approach ("NIH Data Sharing Repositories," 2013). A deeper-level option involves a hands-on approach working with the project team and the actual data (which would require Institutional Review Board clearance and inclusion on the Institutional Review Board application/approval). In the hands-on approach, the data librarian would attend project team meetings; review study protocols, reports and other associated documentation; and work with the data files themselves. With this level of inclusion, the data librarian would be able to assist with the development of a proper metadata schema, data documentation (dictionaries and user's manuals), and file formatting for sharing as well as long-term preservation.

Clinical Practice Support

Physicians, nurses, and other health care providers have unique information needs. Ideally, their information requests are satisfied by concise, highly relevant answers that are delivered quickly in usable formats at the point of care. Establishing department office hours in close proximity to medical units increases visibility for an embedded information service and helps build relationships between clinical informationists and these users. Information services provided include, but are not limited to, the following:

- Utilizing point-of-care resources, demonstrating the array of general and specialty-specific tools for these needs
- Searching for and retrieving literature—completing a literature search and summarizing findings in response to clinical questions
- Providing domain expertise for information re This chapter will present many examples This chapter will present many examples sources—going beyond the literature databases to knowledgably guide clinicians and researchers to websites, potential collaborators, databanks, outreach partners, training opportunities, etc.
- Instruction on library resources and workflow software in a variety of formats, including online synchronous and in-person at departmental events such as seminars and journal clubs
- Consultation services relating to research, publication, and scholarship

Clinical librarians provide embedded services in a variety of venues where they engage with clinicians. Clinical informationists have found themselves invited to participate in a variety of activities that integrate their skills into the clinical workflow to assist in finding answers to questions about patient care. Welch Medical Library informationists participate in regularly scheduled departmental activities, such as case conferences for the Pediatric Intensive Care Unit, Pediatrics Department morning report, and the Anesthesiology and Critical Care Medicine morbidity and mortality meetings. In these contexts, they are able to provide point-of-care, evidence-based information that contributes to patient care and decision-making. Informationists participate in the General Internal Medicine Evidence-Based Medicine rounds where each resident presents a clinical question from a current patient case and a library and faculty member work with them to locate and analyze the evidence to put into practice. Another informationist is integrated into the Emergency Medicine Evidence-Based Medicine rounds where she is the co-instructor on strategies for conducting high-quality literature and systematic reviews. Yet another informationist works with the Johns Hopkins Hospital Nursing Residency Program supporting new nurses who must complete an evidence-based practice project.

Clinical librarians also assist in answering questions relating to health care administration and policy, practice standards, and guidelines. Informationists serve on hospital-wide, multidisciplinary committees, to find current policies relating to care standards, or to find literature that is used to create policies. Examples of these committees include the Johns Hopkins Hospital Ethics Committee, the JHH Nursing Evidence-based Practice aCommittees, and the Pediatric Nursing Standards of Care Committee.

Critical Partnerships

Forming critical partnerships is essential to expanding and sustaining embedded librarian services. Leadership at the Welch Medical Library recognized the potential for embedded RDM assistance and successfully received funding through an NLM Administrative Supplement grant[10] for informationist services to assist an NIH-funded project with their data management needs. Specifically, two Welch informationists worked with the research team to reformat, reorganize, and better annotate data from a colorectal cancer project. This effort involved meetings with the project team to discuss the overall study measurement methods, data formatting needs, and end goals. The informationists devoted a few hours of restructuring work one day per week over a period of two years. This proved to be a positive learning experience in which librarians were able to work more deeply within a particular discipline and garner a deeper understanding of how medical research teams work. While this particular effort was grant-funded, funding isn't absolutely necessary in order to pursue opportunities to provide some level of hands-on data management assistance as an embedded librarian/informationist within a project team.

Relationships with researchers form the foundation of the basic science program. The basic science informationist has been a member of multiple, faculty-led systematic review teams, playing roles including search strategy development, citation management, title–abstract review, and manuscript preparation. Less-formal collaborations have been critical to the success of a variety of initiatives, particularly those involving bioinformatics support. Faculty and staff from the Center for Computational Genomics, the Center for Resources in Integrative Biology, and the Transgenic Mouse Core Laboratory offered valuable advice about the design and content of the Bioinformatics Portal. Other groups, such has the Graduate Student

Association and the Postdoctoral Association, played an important role in advertising special events such as the NCBI and UCSC Genome Browser workshops. A faculty member with the McKusick–Nathans Institute of Genetic Medicine was instrumental in bringing the UCSC Genome Browser speaker to campus.

Informationist Program Assessment and Evaluation

Program assessment should be part of any plan for new embedded library services programs. Assessment and evaluation are often used interchangeably (Hodges, 2011; Issel, 2014). For the purposes of this discussion, consider assessment as an understanding of the state or condition of something, and evaluation as the passing of judgment of some kind. In program evaluation, that judgment is often how valuable the program is to the organization. Program assessment is the process of objectively understanding the state or condition of a program, usually obtained by observation and measurement. A program assessment may be used to evaluate the program's value. This evaluation or "judgment" is accomplished by comparing it with similar programs, with a standard, or by identifying outcomes that the institution deems valuable to its overall mission. To develop a construct for objectively assessing a program, a logic model is often used (Foundation, 2004). Below is a sample logic model for an informationist program supporting a scientific research and clinical care organization, developed by one of the authors (TW).

This logic model provides an informationist program mission, activities, outputs, and outcomes, along with resources that go into the program to ensure its success. The outcomes determine the value of the program to the organization, or its success.

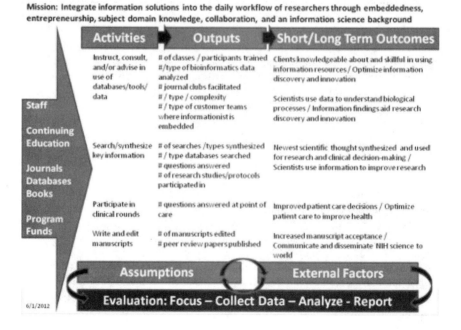

Needs assessments of users may occur in a multitude of ways, including electronic surveys used judiciously, focus groups, and in-person individual interviews. Interviews with users may range from informal to semi-structured, to critical incident, highly structured interviews. Any interaction with a user is an opportunity to discuss information use, management, dissemination and storage as well as pain points and barriers to information access. Librarians should investigate departments they work with to learn more about culture and structure, faculty information-seeking behaviors, what library services are valued, access issues, information dissemination, and sharing practices.

Considerations When Starting an Embedded Librarianship Service

Ideally, planning embedded library services begins with a sound understanding of the mission and goals of the parent institution. A philosophy statement should clearly define the type and extent of services, the scope of services and to whom they will be provided, goals for the success of services, and how new services will improve or be different from existing traditional services. Transparency about ongoing assessment and evaluation measures is needed, as well as goals directed at how the program will improve services to users in the community. It should be understood that assessment is ongoing and iterative.

Externally, consider who to approach to get buy-in from high-level stakeholders of the library. Look for library users who support new service delivery as an avenue to participate in research, clinical practice, and education. Library champions are individuals who fit these roles well and can typically be found in teaching, clinical care, or research roles themselves. Characteristically, those who favor more proactive service provision are more innovative, multidisciplinary thinkers. Identify potentially receptive user groups and attend their open department activities such as grand rounds and seminars. Contact key department members and ask to speak at a department meeting to start a dialogue about information needs and the services an informationist could provide to meet them. Emphasize visibility and presence with office hours and other regularly scheduled department activities. Relationship building is critical and good communication methods are necessary for ongoing awareness of where an informationist can add value.

Factors for Success

One of the most important qualities needed for starting an embedded library service is the personal motivation of the library staff involved. Since the training required to stay current in both information skills and discipline-specific knowledge is continual, the library staff must be driven to acquire these new skills and specialized knowledge. The cooperation of all library staff is essential, as professional librarians will spend more time outside of the library. Support staff are encouraged to take on duties that allow this to happen. Strong interpersonal skills are also important because librarians must be able to sell themselves and their skills, be professional, and be approachable. Embedded librarians often have to convince research team members of the value of their services. They must have good communication skills, the ability to work with many different personality types, and the ability to recognize the different needs of different types of professionals. The support of champions within departments is vital to helping to build support for the service. A champion can be an influential faculty member who will promote the service to his/her students or sponsor librarian partnerships with key departmental activities.

There are several characteristics that apply to the parent institution that affect the success of embedded library services. These types of services flourish in a collaborative, multidisciplinary team environment. A health care environment that currently embraces multidisciplinary teams is more likely to see a librarian as another member of a professional team. A culture that supports lifelong learning will be more likely to embrace embedded information services. These types of institutions tend to welcome librarians and understand how they contribute to a team's knowledge base.

Successful programs must be based on needs assessments and targeted to specific populations. Librarians will also have to be effective marketers to raise awareness of the availability of these new services. Having a strong sense of service orientation is essential. Embedded librarians support researchers' workflows and must be flexible in working with them to find the best solutions.

Embedded librarian programs can be successful and sustainable if the factors discussed above are all present. These types of programs can add value to researcher productivity, enhance the dissemination of new knowledge, and speed the rate of new discoveries.

References

Akers, K. G. (2014). "Going Beyond Data Managment Planning: Comprehensive Research Data Services." *College & Research Libraries News, 75*(8), 435.

Cunningham, D., Grefsheim, S., Simon, M., and Lansing, P. S. (1991). "Biotechnology Awareness Study, Part 2: Meeting the Information Needs of Biotechnologists." *Bull. Med. Libr. Assoc., 79*(1), 45–52.

Davidoff, F., and Florance, V. (2000). "The Informationist: A New Health Profession?" *Ann. Intern. Med., 132*(12), 996–998.

Featherstone, R. M. (2012). "The Disaster Information Specialist: An Emerging Role for Health Librarians." *Journal of Library Administration, 52*(8), 731–753. doi:10.1080/01930826.2012.746875.

Feinberg, S. E., Martin, Margaret E., Straf, Miron L. (1985). *Sharing Research Data*. Washington, D.C.: National Academy Press.

Foundation, W. K. K. (2004). *W. K. Kellogg Foundation Logic Model Development Guide: Using Logic Models to Bring Together Planning, Evaluation, and Action*. Battle Creek, Michigan: W. K. Kellogg Foundation.

Hodges, B. C. V., Donna M. (2011). *Assessment and Planning in Health Programs* (2nd ed.). Sudbury, MA: Jones and Bartlett Learning.

ICPSR: The Founding and Early Years. Retrieved from http://www.icpsr.umich.edu/icpsrweb/content/membership/history/early-years.html.

Issel, L. M. (2014). *Health Program Planning and Evaluation* (3rd ed.). Burlington, MA: Jones and Bartlett Learning.

Lamb, G. (1982). "A Decade of Clinical Librarianship." *Clinical Librarian Quarterly, 1*(1), 2–4.

Martinez-Uribe, L. (2014). Chronology of Data Library and Data Centers. Retrieved from http://iassistdata.org/blog/chronology-data-library-and-data-centres.

NIH Data Sharing Repositories. (2013, December 9 2015).

Pratt, G. F. (1990). "A Health Sciences Library Liaison Project to Support Biotechnology Research." *Bull. Med. Libr. Assoc., 78*(3), 302–303.

Rankin, J. A., Grefsheim, S. F., and Canto, C. C. (2008). "The Emerging Informationist Specialty: A Systematic Review of the Literature." *J. Med. Libr. Assoc., 96*(3), 194–206. doi:10.3163/1536-5050.96.3.005.

Sieber, J. E. (1991). *Sharing Social Science Data: Advantages and Challenges* (Vol. 128). Newbury Park, California: SAGE Publications.

SPEC Kit 334: Research Data Management Services. (2013). Retrieved from http://publications.arl.org/Research-Data-Management-Services-SPEC-Kit-334/.

Treadwell, W. C., and Cogswell, J. A. (1994). "The Machine Readable Data Center: A Model Approach to Data Services in Academic Libraries." *Library Hi Tech, 12*(1), 87–92.

Access to Government Information:
An Overview of a Growing Area for Libraries

Heather Morrison

Assistant Professor
École des sciences de l'information / School of Information Studies
University of Ottawa

This article covers the long-term trend toward increasing access to government information in the Canadian and global contexts. The story begins in the 1980s with the federal Access to Information Act (ATI), granting Canadians broad-based rights to access government information, including personal information about them gathered by the government, and the establishment of the Office of the Information Commissioner. Canadian provinces have enacted similar legislation often referred to as FOIP (Freedom of Information and Protection of Privacy). Publicly funded libraries, including academic libraries, are subject to ATI/FOIP legislation and in some cases are responsible for responding to ATI/FOIP requests. In 2008 Canada, along with a number of governments, made a commitment to the Open Government Partnership. The basic idea is to set the default to "open" for government information, to bring forward a new era of accountability and transparency, to open access to government data to spur innovation, and to use social media as the basis for greater citizen engagement. To fulfill the potential of open government, information will need to be gathered, curated, described, and made accessible, and people will need to learn how to make use of the information. It will likely be fully evident to every librarian that the skills needed for this kind of work are the basics of librarianship. There is potential for growth in roles for the profession, whether recognized as the tradition of librarianship or under the new terminology of the information professional. It is important to recognize that open government is a complement to, but not a replacement for, ATI.

Access to Information and Freedom of Information Legislation at the National Level

Bazillion (1984) provides some historical context on the then recent Access to Information and Privacy Acts bundled together and passed in 1983 under Bill C-43. At the time, Canada was seen as far behind the United States in terms of open access to government information. In Canada, advocacy for access to information predates the 1983 acts by decades. For scholars in the areas of social sciences and history, access to information about government actions and decisions is essential to scholarship, and lengthy embargoes on access are a key reason why our knowledge in this area is of necessity more historical than relevant to the current social situation. Although the aim of the 1983 Access to Information Act was to give individuals the right to examine official records of personal or scholarly use, even before enactment of the legislation this was seen as a mixed blessing by advocates of open government. For example, in 1981, the Canadian Historical Association complained that access was closed off to sources previously available in the Public

Archives of Canada, including correspondence and records relating to the Royal Canadian Mounted Police, in anticipation of this legislation.

Canada's implementation of access to information, as explained by Bazillion, reflects a combination of the British (Westminster) influence and the approach of the Liberal governments that, at that time, had held power in Canada almost continuously for two decades. The Liberals' perspective on accountability included adherence to a principle of ministerial responsibility. One advantage of this in the long term was an emphasis on preservation of records. A disadvantage from the point of view of access to information is that this is likely a factor in Canada's tendency to emphasize government confidentiality and ministerial discretion in both legislation and judicial review, one of the primary critiques of Canada's ATI legislation. Bazillion notes the influence of the Official Secrets Act, based on a British precedent and virtually unchanged since 1939, intended to restrict access to classified information, but which in theory forbids all access to government information. Along with a tradition of oaths of secrecy taken by civil servants and cabinet ministers, this has led to a Canadian approach to ATI that leans more toward secrecy than U.S. legislation has. Bazillion's discussion of the issues surrounding overclassification and excessive delays in declassification reads like a preview of the more recent discussion of these issues brought to the forefront by Wikileaks.

Further research into the historical context of ATI would be beneficial. Current legislation and policies may reflect an obsolete historical context. There was a need for secrecy in the Second World War, reflected in the Official Secrets Act, that is no longer relevant today. On the other hand, we cannot predict with any certainty the potential for future wars. Analysis of the advisability and usefulness of a secretive approach to government information in previous wartimes could be helpful to shape current and future legislation in this area.

In 1985 the government of Canada enacted the current Access to Information Act, which can be found in consolidated form including all amendments (most recently July 2015) on the Justice Canada website. Highlights follow.

> The Access to Information Act (ATIA) provides the right to access records under the control of a federal government institution in accordance with the principles that government information should be available to the public, that necessary exceptions to the right of access should be limited and specific, and that decisions on the disclosure of government information should be reviewed independently of government.

> "As Canada's Federal Court ruled in a decision on ATIA, 'Parliament considers access to information in Canada and document retention as essential components of citizens' right to government information' (*Bronskill v. Minister of Canadian Heritage,* 2011 FC 983 at para. 17). Access to information, according to the court, is integral to our democracy." (Clément, n.d.)

> "FOI laws do not simply assert a right of access. They also codify restrictions on access to information. The law, for instance, protects the Prime Minister's Office from having to disclose information. As Ann Rees explains, 'the ATIA is as much about the codification of secrecy and executive branch control of government information as it is about granting the public, including parliamentarians, access to government records. In defining what the pub-

lic may know, the ATIA also defines what the public may not know, with the scales heavily weighed in favour of the latter.'" (As cited in Clément, 2015).

Mandatory and discretionary exemptions

"Mandatory exemptions are introduced with the wording ' . . . the head of a government institution shall refuse to disclose . . . ' which indicates that there is no option but to refuse access to the information. There are some "shall" provisions, however, which contain certain conditions under which the information can be nevertheless be disclosed.

For example, subsection 13(1) of the ATIA says that federal government institutions 'shall refuse to disclose' any record obtained in confidence from a provincial government. However, subsection 13(2) says that federal government institutions 'may disclose' that record if the provincial government either consented to the disclosure or made the information public.

Discretionary exemptions are introduced with the wording ' . . . the head of a government institution may refuse to disclose . . .'. In these instances, government institutions have the option to disclose or to protect the information" (Office of the Privacy Commissioner of Canada, 2008).

Sections 13 to 24 establish the exemptions to access under the act. Sections 68 and 69 of the act define the types of information that are not applicable under the act.

Exemptions include:

RESPONSIBILITIES OF GOVERNMENT: Information obtained in confidence; Where disclosure authorized; Federal-provincial affairs; International affairs and defence; Law enforcement and investigations; Security; Policing services for provinces or municipalities; Records relating to investigations, examinations and audits (Auditor General of Canada, Commissioner of Official Languages for Canada, Information Commissioner, and Privacy Commissioner); Records relating to investigations (Commissioner of Lobbying); Investigations, examinations and reviews under the Canada Elections Act; Director of Public Prosecutions; Public Sector Integrity Commissioner; Public Servants Disclosure Protection Act; Safety of individuals; Economic interests of Canada; Economic interests of certain government institutions.

PERSONAL INFORMATION: Personal information; Where disclosure authorized.

THIRD PARTY INFORMATION: Third party information; Product or environmental testing; Methods used in testing; Preliminary testing; Disclosure if a supplier consents; Disclosure authorized if in public interest; Public Sector Pension Investment Board; Canada Pension Plan Investment Board; National Arts Centre Corporation.

OPERATIONS OF GOVERNMENT: Advice, etc.; Exercise of a discretionary power or an adjudicative function; Testing procedures, tests and audits; Internal audits; Solicitor-client privilege.

STATUTORY PROHIBITIONS: Statutory prohibitions against disclosure; Review of statutory prohibitions by Parliamentary committee; Severability.

The act does not apply to the following material:
(a) published material or material available for purchase by the public;
(b) library or museum material preserved solely for public reference or exhibition purposes; or
(c) material placed in the Library and Archives of Canada, the National Gallery of Canada, the Canadian Museum of History, the Canadian Museum of Nature, the National Museum of Science and Technology, the Canadian Museum for Human Rights or the Canadian Museum of Immigration at Pier 21 by or on behalf of persons or organizations other than government institutions." (*Access to Information Act*, RSC 1985, c A-1, p. 10)

Furthermore, the act does not apply to: the Canadian Broadcasting Corporation; Atomic Energy of Canada, Confidences of the Queen's Privy Council for Canada; and, a Certificate under the Canada Evidence Act.

Office of the Information Commissioner

"The Office of the Information Commissioner was established in 1983 under the *Access to Information Act*—Canada's freedom of information legislation—to assist individuals and organizations who believe that federal institutions have not respected their rights under the *Act*" (Office of the Information Commissioner of Canada, 2014, Who We Are).

The role of the information commissioner as described on the departmental website is:

> The Information Commissioner provides arms-length oversight of the federal government's access to information practices. [The Commissioner] encourages and assists federal institutions to adopt approaches to information-sharing that meet the objectives of the ATIA, and advocates for greater access to information in Canada.
>
> The Commissioner relies on persuasion to solve disputes, asking for a Federal Court review only if an individual has been improperly denied access and a negotiated solution has proved impossible. (Information Commissioner of Canada, n.d.)

The [Commissioner's] annual report for 2015–2016 had not been published at the time of this report. Ongoing work includes some of the following topics:

• Call on governments to create a duty to document
• Call on governments to respect rights in information sharing agreements
• Encouraging Access to Information Act reform

- Conducting national and international benchmarking (documenting global best practices; partnering with national and international experts)
- Documenting the health of the access system.

Open Government Partnership

"The Open Government Partnership is a multilateral initiative that aims to secure concrete commitments from governments to promote transparency, empower citizens, fight corruption, and harness new technologies to strengthen governance. In the spirit of multi-stakeholder collaboration, OGP is overseen by a Steering Committee of governments and civil society organizations.

To become a member of OGP, participating countries must:

- endorse a high-level Open Government Declaration (http://www.opengov partnership.org/about/open-government-declaration)
- deliver a concrete action plan, developed with public consultation
- commit to independent reporting on their progress going forward." (Open Government Partnership, 2015)

"The Open Government Partnership formally launched on September 20, 2011, when the 8 founding governments (Brazil, Indonesia, Mexico, Norway, Philippines, South Africa, United Kingdom, United States) endorsed the Open Government Declaration, announced their country action plans, and welcomed the commitment of 38 governments to join the Partnership.

OGP held its first annual high-level meeting on April 17–18, 2012, in Brasilia, Brazil. Since its launch, OGP has grown to become a global community of government reformers, civil society leaders, and business innovators, who together are advancing a new standard of good governance in the 21st century. Through concrete commitments announced via OGP action plans, over fifty-five governments are taking important steps towards greater transparency, accountability and participation that will ultimately improve the lives of people around the world." (U.S. Department of State, n.d., The Open Government Partnership).

"Canada joined the Open Government Partnership (OGP) in April 2012, and remains committed to the principles of the OGP's Open Government Declaration. Canada's membership in the OGP provides key opportunities to advance our open government agenda, share and learn from international best practices, and collaborate with our OGP colleagues on solutions that benefit citizens globally. As co-chair of the OGP's Open Data Working Group, Canada works with governments and civil society organizations on defining shared principles for open data, including the use of common standards that will help align open data services offered around the world." (Government of Canada, 2016, Canada's Action Plan on Open Government).

Open Government and Open Data in Canada

"Open Government is about greater openness and accountability, strengthening democracy and driving innovation and economic opportunities for all Canadians." (Government of Canada, 2016, Open Government). The Government of Canada is committed to an Action Plan on Open Government Action Plan which is reviewed on a regular basis. The current Action Plan is for 2014–2016.

Access to Information and Libraries

International Federation of Library Associations and Institutions (IFLA)

In 2008 the IFLA Governing Board adopted the IFLA Manifesto on Transparency, Good Governance and Freedom from Corruption. This document clarifies for libraries globally the connection between access to information style legislation and the library value and role of helping to safeguard democratic rights through providing access to information. This IFLA Manifesto prescribes proactive involvement in advocacy for access to information legislation in countries where this has not yet been enacted, and provides guidance to libraries on providing services to help citizens make use of these rights.

Specifically, the manifesto calls for:

1 Where a country has information access or freedom of information laws, librarians should seek to make the library a centre where citizens can be assisted in drawing up and submitting information requests.

2 Where a country does not have information access or freedom of information laws, or such laws are not effective, librarians should support initiatives to draft, amend, promote and protect such laws from neglect.

3 Training should be organised for librarians and users in the use of the type of information that will improve citizens' understanding of the laws and assist them in the pursuit of their rights and entitlements.

4 Libraries should collect information materials issued by official bodies, particularly those that deal with citizens' rights and entitlements. They should seek to make information that is issued by official bodies more comprehensible and accessible (through indexes, abstracts, search support, etc.). They should also organise digitisation and other preservation programmes for official information relating to laws, rights and entitlements, and facilitate access to existing databases of these types of information.

5 Libraries should be made available as venues for the promotion of information rights (through posters and other publicity methods) and librarians should seek to raise awareness of the right to information.

A search of Library and Information Science Abstracts for the subject "access to information" illustrates the international scope of interest and activity in this area. Following are a few recent examples of articles in this area: Ward (2014) talks about building free access to law in Africa; Zhang (2014) covers public access to legal information in China; Baxter (2014) discusses the use of freedom of information legislation in a specific case in northeast Scotland; Oswald (2012) talks about freedom of information in cyberspace; Gimenez-Chornet (2012) addresses the impact of public access on transparency in Spain; Silva and Silva (2012) talk about the use of comic books to explain access to legal information in Brazil; and Relly (2012) reports on a cross-national study on the influence of information access on the control of corruption.

Library and Archives Canada (2015) provides the kind of service described by IFLA: information about how to place an access to information request, monthly reports on ATI requests, and an online database of completed ATIP requests—a step that is designed for efficiency, so that once a request is filled, others with the same request can access the information directly.

Larsen (2013) discusses the use of access to information legislation and procedures as an emerging and growing area in academic research. Traditionally librarians have served an important role in helping people to obtain the information that they need. Now that access to information legislation is almost ubiquitous in Canada, it may be a good idea for librarians to learn how to help people make use of ATI legislation and processes. For example, often a major stumbling block to ATI requesting is simply that the requester does not know exactly what to request. As a result, a requester may submit a very general question that would take an enormous amount of time to answer, where a reference interview to assist the requester in developing a more precise question would be much more effective for the requester and time efficient for the government.

A LISA search for "open government" yields more than 1,000 results, most very recent and focused on the practical uses of open data and open government, whether documents that are now freely available or new tools. A few examples from 2015 and 2016: Dreher, McCallum, and Waller (2016) speak to the potential of new media for participation by Australia's indigenous peoples in policy making; Gordon-Murnane (2015) discusses "Do It Yourself Data and Tools Courtesy of the Government" in *Online Searcher;* Tristao (2015) talks about public access to newly declassified federal government materials; and Wijnhoven, Ehrenhard, and Kuhn (2015) discuss "open government objectives and participation motivations" per se in *Government Information Quarterly.*

Wikileaks and the International Library Community

Recent controversy surrounding Wikileaks and perspectives of civil groups including the international library community is summarized by Karhula (2012) on behalf of IFLA. In brief, Wikileaks defends its release of documents through referral to article 19 of the Universal Declaration of Human Rights. The U.S. government, an early leader in establishing the Open Government Partnership, reacted in what some would describe as an ironic manner, not only denouncing the leaks but also invoking the espionage act for what a number of journalists have described as activity that fits well within the tradition of investigative journalism. In the United States, the Library of Congress blocked access to Wikileaks while the American Library Association (and library associations from other countries) moved towards a resolution in support of Wikileaks on the grounds of academic freedom. Morrison (2011) discusses the history and controversy behind the Wikileaks resolution and the related resolution in support of whistleblower Bradley (now Chelsea) Manning and why libraries should be involved. In brief, the American Library Association, while in support of whistleblowing in principle, was reluctant to commit to earlier forms of resolutions calling for specific support for the individuals behind the actions.

Conclusion

Access to information legislation embodies the traditional library value of access to information and is an early (but still essential) implementation of the emerging area of open government. In Canada, access to information legislation, usually paired with privacy legislation, is almost ubiquitous at federal, provincial, and territorial levels. This is a global phenomenon, and Canada is perhaps more typical of developed countries than a leader in this area. This is an area of growing interest in librarianship, as an area of policy advocacy, sometimes a service area for library and/or information professionals, with the potential for growth in providing reference and information literacy support for ATI requesting in libraries of all types.

References

Access to Information Act, RSC 1985, c A-1. Retrieved February 28, 2016, from http://laws-lois.justice.gc.ca/eng/acts/A-1/.

Baxter, G. (2014). "Open for Business? An Historical, Comparative Study of Public Access to Information About Two Controversial Coastal Developments in North-East Scotland." *Information Research,* 19(1).

Bazillion, R. J. (1984). "The Effect of Access and Privacy Legislation on the Conduct of Scholarly Research in Canada. *Social Science Information Studies,* 4(1), 5–14. doi:10.1016/0143-6236(84)90045-0.

Clément, D. (n.d.). Freedom of Information. Retrieved from http://historyofrights. ca/encyclopaedia/main-events/freedom-information/.

Clément, D. (2014). "Brokering Access: Power, Politics and Freedom of Information Process in Canada." *Surveillance and Society,* 12(4), 600–601.

Clément, D. (2015). "'Freedom' of Information in Canada: Implications for Historical Research." *Labour/Le Travail,* 75. Retrieved from http://historyofrights.ca/about/recent-publications-on-human-rights/.

Dreher, T., McCallum, K., and Waller, L. (2016). "Indigenous Voices and Mediatized Policy-Making in the Digital Age." *Information, Communication & Society,* 19(1), 23.

Gimenez-Chornet, V. (2012). "Public Access to Documents Supports Transparency in Public Administration." *Profesional de la Informacion,* 21(5), 504–508.

Gordon-Murnane, L. (2015). "Do It Yourself Data and Tools Courtesy of the Government." *Online Searcher,* 39 (5), 16–22.

Government of Canada. (2016). Open Government. Retrieved March 5, 2016, from https://www.canada.ca/en/transparency/open.html.

Information Commissioner of Canada. (n.d.). In *Wikipedia*. Retrieved March 5, 2016, from https://en.wikipedia.org/wiki/Information Commissioner_of_Canada.

International Federation of Library Associations (IFLA) (2008). *IFLA Manifesto on Transparency, Good Governance and Freedom from Corruption*. Retrieved February 28, 2016, from http://www.ifla.org/publications/ifla-manifesto-on-transparency--good-governance-and-freedom-from-corruption?og=30.

Janning, N. (2012). "A Delicate Balance: National Security, Government Transparency, and Free Speech."
DttP: Documents to the People, 40(4), 10–14. Retrieved from http://search.proquest.com/docview/1347769228?accountid=14701

Karhula, P. (2012). "What Is the Effect of Wikileaks for Freedom of Information?" Retrieved March 5, 2016, from http://www.ifla.org/publications/what-is-the-effect-of-wikileaks-for-freedom-of-information.

Kniffel, L. (2011). "Federal Ban of WikiLeaks Website Embroil Library of Congress." *American Libraries,* 42(1–2), 26–27. Retrieved from http://search.proquest.com/docview/869787039?accountid=14701.

Larsen, M. (2013). *Access in the Academy: Bringing ATI and FOI to Academic Research.* Vancouver, British Columbia: The British Columbia Freedom of Information and Privacy Association. Retrieved February 28, 2016, from https://fipa.bc.ca/access-in-the-academy-bringing-foi-and-ati-to-academic-research/.

Library and Archives Canada (2015). Access to Information and Privacy (website). Retrieved February 28, 2016, from http://www.bac-lac.gc.ca/eng/transparency/atip/Pages/atip.aspx

Morrison, H. (2011). "Wikileaks: A Library Issue?" Information Policy Committee Virtual Salon. *BCLA Reporter* 3:3. Retrieved February 28, 2016, from bclabrowser.ca/index.php/browser/article/download/279/391.

Office of the Information Commissioner of Canada. (2014). Retrieved March 5, 2016, from http://www.oic-ci.gc.ca/eng/abu-ans_who-we-are_qui-sommes-nous.aspx.

Office of the Privacy Commissioner of Canada. (2008). Chapter 5: Exemptions and Exclusions. Retrieved from https://www.priv.gc.ca/au-ans/atip-aiprp/manual_chap5_e.asp.

Open Government Partnership. (2015). Retrieved March 5, 2016, from http://www.opengovpartnership.org/about.

Oswald, M. (2012). "Freedom of Information in Cyberspace: What Now for Copyright?" *International Review of Law, Computers and Technology,* 26(2–3), 245–255. doi:http://dx.doi.org/10.1080/13600869.2012.698452.

Relly, J. E. (2012). "Examining a Model of Vertical Accountability: A Cross-National Study of the Influence of Information Access on the Control of Corruption." *Government Information Quarterly,* 29(3), 335–345. doi:http://dx.doi.org/10.1016/j.giq.2012.02.011.

Schallier, W. (2012). What WikiLeaks Teaches Us About Libraries. *META: Tijdschrift Voor Bibliotheek & Archief, 88*(3), 32–34. Retrieved from http://search.proquest.com/docview/1622284399?accountid=14701

Schuman, D., & Feltren, E. (2012). "The State of Open Government": A Panel Discussion Depository Library Council Meeting and Federal Depository Library Program Conference, October 19, 2011, Arlington, Virginia. *Government Information Quarterly, 29*(4), 608–609. doi:http://dx.doi.org/10.1016/j.giq.2012.06.006

Silva, A. G., and Silva, L. G. (2012). "Legal Information Access Through Comic Books and Booklets." *Informacao & Informacao,* 17(1), 166–183. doi:http://dx.doi.org/10.5433/1981-8920.2012v17n1p166.

Tristao, M. S. (2015). "Declassified: Public Access to Previously Classified Federal Government Materials." *DttP.Documents to the People,* 43(4), 15.

U.S. Department of State. (n.d.). The Open Government Partnership. Retrieved March 5, 2016, from http://www.state.gov/j/ogp/index.htm.

Ward, R. (2014). "Building Free Access to Law in Africa: Some Examples of Successful Projects." *Legal Information Management,* 14(4), 290–300. doi:http://dx.doi.org/10.1017/S1472669614000590.

Wijnhoven, F., Ehrenhard, M., and Kuhn, J. (2015). "Open Government Objectives and Participation Motivations." *Government Information Quarterly,* 32(1), 30–42. doi:http://dx.doi.org/10.1016/j.giq.2014.10.002.

Zhang, X. (2014). "Public Access to Primary Legal Information in China: Challenges and Opportunities." *Legal Information Management,* 14(2), 132–142. doi:http://dx.doi.org/10.1017/S1472669614000322.

Acknowledgment

Thank you very much to Lisa Desautels, M.I.S., for preparation of research notes/background material.

Appendix

ATI and Privacy Legislation in the Canadian Provinces/Territories: Overview

Alberta

"The Commissioner oversees and enforces the administration of Alberta's three access and privacy laws to ensure their purposes are achieved."The Freedom of Information and Protection of Privacy Act (FOIP Act) came into force on October 1, 1995. The FOIP Act was the first access and privacy law in Alberta and provided the foundations on which the OIPC was created. The FOIP Act provides individuals with the right to request access to information in the custody or control of public bodies while providing public bodies with a framework for conducting the collection, use and disclosure of personal information." More information is available on the website of the Office of the Information and Privacy Commissioner of Alberta (https://www.oipc.ab.ca/).

The Personal Information Protection Act (PIPA), which came into force on January 1, 2004, "provides individuals with the right to request access to their own personal information while providing private sector organizations with a framework for conducting the collection, use and disclosure of personal information." PIPA applies to provincially-regulated private sector organizations and to "certain defined non-profit organizations and only to the extent that those organizations are involved in commercial activities." More information is available on the website of the Office of the Information and Privacy Commissioner of Alberta (https://www.oipc.ab.ca/).

The Health Information Act (HIA), which came into force on April 25, 2001, "provides individuals with the right to request access to their own health information in the custody or under the control of health custodians while providing custodians with a framework for conducting the collection, use and disclosure of health information.

The act also gives individuals the right to request corrections and to have custodians consider their wishes regarding how much of their health information is disclosed or made accessible through Alberta Netcare, the province's electronic health record system." Additional information is available on the website of the Office of the Information and Privacy Commissioner of Alberta (https://www.oipc.ab.ca/).

British Columbia

"Established in 1993, the Office of the Information and Privacy Commissioner provides independent oversight and enforcement of B.C.'s access and privacy laws, including:

The Freedom of Information and Protection of Privacy Act ("FIPPA"), which applies to over 2,900 "public bodies including ministries, local governments, schools, crown corporations, hospitals, municipal police forces, and more;

The Personal Information Protection Act ("PIPA"), which applies to over 380,000 private sector "organizations including businesses, charities, associations, trade unions and trusts."

The Information and Privacy Commissioner enforces both FIPPA and PIPA. The Privacy Act covers disputes between private citizens and is outside of the commissioner's jurisdiction."

The Freedom of Information and Protection of Privacy Act sets out the access and privacy rights of individuals as they relate to the public sector. FIPPA establishes an individual's right to access records—this includes access to a person's own "personal information" as well as records in the custody or control of a "public body"."

There are certain exceptions to accessing records—for example, a public body cannot disclose information that is deemed to be harmful to law enforcement, personal privacy or public safety. Policy advice and legal advice are also excluded. These exceptions are spelled out in sections 12 to 22.

FIPPA also sets out the terms under which a public body can collect, use and disclose the "personal information" of individuals. Public bodies are held accountable for their information practices—FIPPA requires that they take reasonable steps to protect the privacy of personal information they hold.

The Personal Information Protection Act came into effect in January 2004, and sets out how private sector "organizations" can collect, use and disclose personal information. There are more than 300,000 organizations in B.C. covered by PIPA, including businesses and corporations, unions, political parties, and not-for-profits doing business in B.C.

Under PIPA, individuals have the right to access their own personal information. The law also sets out the rules by which organizations can collect, use and disclose personal information from customers, clients and/or employees. PIPA requires organizations to protect and secure personal information against unauthorized use or disclosure.

Additional information is available on the website of the Office of the Information and Privacy Commissioner for British Columbia (https://www.oipc.bc.ca/about/about-us/).

Manitoba

The Manitoba Ombudsman—Access and Privacy division "is responsible for upholding access to information and privacy rights by investigating complaints and reviewing compliance with The Freedom of Information and Protection of Privacy Act (FIPPA) and The Personal Health Information Act (PHIA)." Additional information is available on the website of the Manitoba Ombudsman—Access and Privacy Division (https://www.ombudsman.mb.ca/).

New Brunswick

The commissioner oversees "the application of rules governing access to information and the protection of privacy in the public and health care sectors. These rules have been codified in two statutes that came into effect on September 1, 2010: the Right to Information and Protection of Privacy Act and the Personal Health Information Privacy and Access Act."

"The Right to Information and Protection of Privacy Act grants members of the public a general right to access information, including your own personal information, held by provincial public bodies. This legislation also establishes rules for provincial public bodies about the collection, use, disclosure and protection of personal information.

"The Personal Health Information Privacy and Access Act regulates the handling of personal health information in New Brunswick's health care sector. This statute sets out rules for all aspects of the handling of personal health information, from collection, use and disclosure to secure storage and destruction by all health care providers. This legislation also gives individuals the right to request and receive a copy of their own personal health information from their health care providers."

Additional information is available on the website of the Office of the Access to Information and Privacy Commissioner for New Brunswick (http://info-priv-nb.ca/default.asp).

Newfoundland and Labrador

Newfoundland and Labrador's Information and Privacy Commissioner has a "broad range of responsibilities and powers under both the Access to Information and Protection of Privacy Act, 2015 (ATIPPA, 2015) and the Personal Health Information Act (PHIA).

"Oversight of these Acts includes conducting reviews of decisions and investigating and attempting to resolve complaints about access to information and protection of privacy involving public bodies under the ATIPPA, 2015 and custodians of personal health information under the PHIA. The Commissioner may also make recommendations in order to uphold the Acts and encourage better compliance".

Additional information is available on the website of the Office of the Information and Privacy Commissioner for Newfoundland and Labrador (http://www. oipc.nl.ca/).

Northwest Territories

The Access to Information and Protection of Privacy Act gives individuals a legal right to request access to information held by Northwest Territories public bodies. Businesses, individuals and organizations can request access to information help by public bodies via the Government of the NWT's Access and Privacy Office. Additional information is available on the website of Government of the Northwest Territories (http://services.exec.gov.nt.ca/service).

Nova Scotia

"The Office of the Information and Privacy Commissioner for Nova Scotia (NS OIPC) support the Commissioner to resolve freedom of information matters through research, investigation, analysis and mediation. If a matter cannot be settled through mediation, it is referred to the Review Officer for consideration.

The Privacy Review Officer Act ['PRO Act'] was proclaimed into law in September 2009. Citizens who feel that provincial public bodies have breached their privacy can now complain by making a Request for Review to the Privacy Review Officer as the designated oversight body. The Privacy Review Officer Act does not apply to municipal public bodies and there is no similar legislation at this time.

The Personal Health Information Act ['PHIA'] came into force on June 1, 2013. PHIA governs the collection, use, disclosure, retention, disposal and destruction of personal health information. It gives citizens a right to file a Request for Review of decisions made by health custodians to the NS OIPC."

Additional information is available on the website of the Office of the Information and Privacy Commissioner for Nova Scotia (http://foipop.ns.ca/).

Nunavut

"The Access to Information and Protection of Privacy Act has two objectives. Firstly, to allow the public a means to obtain information which the government or a government body holds. The second is to ensure that private, personal information which is held by a government agency is used only for the purpose it was intended and is not improperly disclosed to anyone either inside or outside of government.

Access to information requests are handled by coordinators within each department of the Government of Nunavut. Issues of personal privacy are dealt with directly by the Information and Privacy Commissioner."

Additional information is available on the website of the Information and Privacy Commissioner of Nunavut (http://www.info-privacy.nu.ca/).

Ontario

Under the Freedom of Information and Protection of Privacy Act (FIPPA) and the Municipal Freedom of Information and Protection of Privacy Act (MFIPPA), citizens have a right to ask certain public sector organizations in Ontario for the recorded information they hold.

For information on the right to request access to general information held by government organizations, or to request access to personal information, see the brochure *Access to Information under Ontario's Information and Privacy Acts* (https://www.ipc.on.ca/English/Resources/Educational-Material/Education-al-Material-Summary/?id=278). For additional information on requesting access to personal information, or correction of that information, see the brochure, *Your Privacy and Ontario's Information and Privacy Commissioner* (https://www.ipc.on.ca/english/Resources/Educational-Material/Educational-Material-Summary/?id=285).

"The *Personal Health Information Protection Act* gives individuals the right to request access to records of their personal health information." The Information and Privacy Commissioner must ensure the right to access is protected.

Additional information is available on the website of the Information and Privacy Commissioner of Ontario (https://www.ipc.on.ca/english/Home-Page/).

Prince Edward Island

The Freedom of Information and Protection of Privacy Act came into effect in Prince Edward Island on November 1, 2002.

"Pursuant to the Act, all public bodies are obliged to adopt a policy of accountability, openness and transparency, and to provide a right of access to information, with limited exceptions. They are also obliged to ensure the protection of an individual's personal privacy."

Additional information is available on the website of the Legislative Assembly of Prince Edward Island, Information and Privacy Commissioner (http://www.assembly.pe.ca/index.php3).

Québec

La Commission d'accès à l'information du Québec « exerce les fonctions et pouvoirs édictés dans sa loi constitutive de 1982, la Loi sur l'accès aux documents des organismes publics et sur la protection des renseignements personnels (Loi sur l'accès). Elle est principalement chargée de l'application de cette loi et de la Loi sur la protection des renseignements personnels dans le secteur privé (Loi sur la protection dans le secteur privé). Pour la mise en œuvre des mandats qui lui sont confiés, la Loi sur l'accès crée deux sections à la Commission : une section de surveillance et une section juridictionnelle. »

Additional information is available on the website of the Commission d'accès à l'information du Québec (http://www.cai.gouv.qc.ca/).

Saskatchewan

The commissioner "ensures that public bodies respect the privacy and access rights of the citizens of Saskatchewan by:

1 Informing members of the public of their information rights
2 Resolving access and privacy disputes between individuals and public bodies
3 Making recommendations on appeals from access to information decisions by public bodies
4 Investigating and resolving privacy complaints
5 Issuing recommendations on public bodies' policies and practices
6 Commenting on proposed laws and policies

The IPC of Saskatchewan has oversight over three statutes and regulations:

- The Freedom of Information and Protection of Privacy Act (FOIP; http://www.qp.gov.sk.ca/documents/English/Statutes/Statutes/F22-01.pdf; FOIP Regulations http://www.qp.gov.sk.ca/documents/English/Regulations/Regulations/F22-01R1.pdf)
- The Local Authority Freedom of Information and Protection of Privacy Act (LA FOIP; http://www.qp.gov.sk.ca/documents/English/Statutes/Statutes/L27-1.pdf; LA FOIP Regulations http://www.qp.gov.sk.ca/documents/English/Regulations/Regulations/L27-1R1.pdf)
- The Health Information Protection Act (HIPA; http://www.qp.gov.sk.ca/documents/english/Statutes/Statutes/H0-021.pdf; HIPA Regulations http://www.qp.gov.sk.ca/documents/English/Regulations/Regulations/H0-021r1.pdf)

Additional information is available on the website of the Office of the Saskatchewan Information and Privacy Commissioner (http://www.oipc.sk.ca/default.htm).

Yukon

"The ATIPP Act gives the public a right of access to information held by the Yukon government. Much of this information is available by way of routine disclosure. Other information can be requested through a Request for Access to Records, also known as an Access Request, under the ATIPP Act.

The act guarantees certain fundamental rights for individuals including:

- access to records in the custody and control of Yukon government departments and designated public bodies with certain exceptions;
- access to individuals' own personal information and the right to request correction of wrong information;
- privacy of personal information in the custody or under the control of public bodies;

- protection against unauthorized collection, use, disclosure of personal information; and
- independent review of decisions made by public bodies about access and privacy."

Additional information is available on the website of the Yukon Information and Privacy Commissioner (http://www.ombudsman.yk.ca/yukon-information-and-privacy-commissioner/for-the-public).

Federal Agency and Federal Library Reports

Library of Congress

10 First Street S.E., Washington, DC 20540
202-707-5000
http://www.loc.gov

David S. Mao

Acting Librarian of Congress

Founded in 1800, the Library of Congress is the largest library in the world, with more than 162 million items in various languages, disciplines, and formats. As the world's largest repository of knowledge and creativity, the library's mission is to support the U.S. Congress in fulfilling its constitutional duties and to further the progress of knowledge and creativity for the benefit of the American people.

The library's collections are housed in its three buildings on Capitol Hill and in climate-controlled facilities for books at Fort Meade, Maryland. Its audiovisual materials are held at the Packard Campus for Audio-Visual Conservation in Culpeper, Virginia. The library also provides global access to its resources through its popular website, http://www.loc.gov.

Legislative Support to Congress

Serving Congress is the library's highest priority, particularly in the area of legislative support. The library provides such support to Congress through the Congressional Research Service (CRS), the Law Library, and the U.S. Copyright Office. In 2015 the library circulated approximately 20,540 volumes from its collections to members of Congress.

During the year, the library responded to more than 597,000 congressional reference requests. CRS supported Congress with policy analyses as it considered such key domestic issues as Medicare, Medicaid, and the Children's Health Insurance Program; reauthorization of the Elementary and Secondary Education Act; and analysis of the Ebola outbreak abroad and control of the disease at home. Experts provided support as lawmakers addressed the U.S. budget, federal debt, the deficit and tax reform, and gave legal advice on executive discretion regarding immigration reform. In the area of foreign affairs, CRS supported congressional review of developments in Iraq, Syria, and activities in the Islamic State.

Report compiled by Audrey Fischer, Public Affairs Specialist, Library of Congress

These posed major challenges to U.S. global interests, as did the situations in Iran, Libya, Yemen, Egypt, and other sub-Saharan African countries. CRS experts advised Congress on trade-related issues such as the U.S. Trade Promotion Authority, the Trans-Pacific Partnership, the U.S.–EU Transatlantic Trade and Investment Partnership and the reauthorization of the U.S. Export–Import Bank, as well as U.S.–China relations.

The Law Library—the world's largest law library, comprising more than 5 million items, including 2.92 million volumes—provided Congress with comprehensive international, comparative, and foreign law research based on the most current information available. During the year, the Law Library staff answered 4,590 congressional inquiries and prepared 869 legal research reports, special studies, and memoranda in response to congressional inquiries. Foreign law specialists provided Members of Congress with reports relating to many pressing U.S. legislative issues, including regulations concerning defense procurements, assisted suicide, taxation of citizens living abroad, child labor in family agriculture, family and medical leave, the impact of the United Nations General Assembly and Security Council resolutions on domestic legislation, decentralization of power in Ukraine, and late-term abortion laws. Many of these reports are available to the public on the Law Library's website.

The U.S. Copyright Office provided policy advice and technical assistance to Congress on important copyright laws and related issues. Throughout the year, the Copyright Office continued to assist the comprehensive review of the nation's copyright laws initiated in 2013 by Rep. Bob Goodlatte (R-Va.), chair of the House Judiciary Committee. The committee held two law-review hearings in 2015. One addressed copyright issues in education and for the visually impaired. The other, "The Register's Perspective on Copyright Review," featured Register of Copyrights Maria A. Pallante as the sole witness. The House Judiciary Committee also held a hearing about Copyright Office operations and funding in which it considered limits on the ability of the office to meet the needs of digital-age stakeholders.

Legislative Transparency

To support transparency in government, the Library of Congress, in collaboration with the U.S. Congress and the Government Printing Office, provides online access to the nation's legislative information on the mobile-friendly website Congress.gov. Congress.gov provides members of Congress, legislative agencies, and the public with accurate, timely, and complete legislative information. The site is presented by the Library of Congress using data from the U.S. House of Representatives, the Senate, the Government Publishing Office, the Congressional Budget Office, and the Congressional Research Service.

As a result of a series of system updates in 2015, more than 1 million items pertaining to the legislative process are accessible on stationary computers or mobile devices. The site contains metadata for legislation starting with 1973 (the 93rd Congress), full text of the legislation beginning in 1993 (the 103rd Congress), and both the *Congressional Record* and committee reports dating back to 1995 (the 104th Congress). New content includes treaty documents, nominations, executive communications, and the Federalist Papers.

Along with the growth in the volume of data on the site, additional features have been added. Users can now sign up to receive e-mail alerts any time a member of Congress introduces a bill, there is an action on a particular bill, or a new issue of the *Congressional Record* is available on the site.

To make Congress.gov more accessible to people with disabilities, a new feature, "Listen to This Page" reads the legislative summaries aloud. A new video series, "Two-Minute Tips," provides tutorials such as "Creating and Using Congress. gov Email Alerts," "Search Terms and Facets," and "Navigating a Bill." These short videos join a nine-part series on the legislative process, written by CRS experts.

Security

During 2015 the library's Office of Security and Emergency Preparedness focused on strengthening protective services, personnel security, and emergency preparedness programs. Collections security was also enhanced through expansion of the Site Assistance Visit Program, which partnered physical security with preservation elements. The office also implemented additional access controls and electronic security measures for the library's highest-level collections and financial assets. Lastly, the office continued to upgrade its emergency communications systems, including mass alert notifications, mobile radio equipment, and the emergency public address system.

In collaboration with the Office of Security and Emergency Preparedness, the Information Technology Services Office (ITS) worked to ensure the continuity of operation at an Alternate Computing Facility in the event of a pandemic or other emergency. During the year, the ITS Security Group was involved in assessing a governance, risk, and compliance system to better manage the library's continuous monitoring activities. ITS ensured that the library's mission-critical systems are reliable and secure and that the technology infrastructure that supports these systems was uncompromised. ITS also ensured that the library's information technology infrastructure and the services it provides continued to adapt to new technology and respond to other changes and requirements. The library's current IT infrastructure includes five data centers in four building locations.

Library Realignment and Strategic Planning

On May 18, 2015, Librarian of Congress James H. Billington announced a plan for realignment of certain programs and operations to better support the institutional vision described in the 2016–2020 Strategic Plan. Both plans became effective on October 1, 2015.

The realignment was initiated to strengthen the information technology and other support functions, elevate the outreach function, consolidate digital and analog collection management, provide a better support structure for staff, improve overall management, and ultimately result in even better service to the library's customers.

The plan involves three main elements: the reassignment of Office of Strategic Initiatives functions to the newly created Office of the Chief Information Officer; the establishment of a new National and International Outreach service unit to encompass many of the offices and functions previously performed by Library Services; and the alignment of support services in a new Office of the Chief Operating Officer.

The organizational realignment provided an updated foundation for moving the library forward during a time of transition following the September 30 retirement of Librarian of Congress James H. Billington and the appointment of David S. Mao as Acting Librarian of Congress.

Budget

The Consolidated and Further Continuing Appropriations Act (P.L. 113-235), signed by the president on December 16, 2014, provided a fiscal 2015 appropriation for the library of $630.853 million, including authority to spend up to $39.9 million in offsetting receipts. The president signed a continuing resolution on September 30, 2015, to provide legislative branch funding from October 1 through December 18, 2015. The 2016 Consolidated Appropriations Act 2016 (Public Law 114-113), signed by the president on December 18, 2015, provided an appropriation of $642 million, including authority to spend up to $42.1 million in offsetting collections.

Development

The library's development efforts in 2015 raised a total of $7.52 million, representing 866 gifts from 579 donors. These gifts, including $3.1 million in cash gifts, $3.03 million in new pledges, $999,580 in in-kind gifts, and $398,336 received through planned gifts, were made to 63 library initiatives. The library forged partnerships with 229 first-time donors, who gave a total of $1,443,535.

Private gifts supported new and continuing initiatives throughout the library, including exhibitions, acquisitions, and other scholarly programs. The James Madison Council—the library's private-sector advisory group—continued to provide substantial support for library initiatives, including literacy programs, fellowships, symposia, and the World Digital Library. Gifts from members totaled $2.75 million. James Madison Council Chairman and National Book Festival Co-Chairman David M. Rubenstein, AARP, Wells Fargo, the *Washington Post*, the Institute of Museum and Library Services, and a number of additional supporters donated more than $2.6 million in cash and in-kind gifts to support the library's 2015 National Book Festival.

Educational Outreach

The library's outreach to teachers focuses on the use of primary sources in the classroom. Over the past two decades, digital technology has allowed the Library of Congress to make many of its collections accessible in K–12 classrooms in the United States and around the world. Access to these resources assists educators in meeting curriculum goals and creating lifelong learners. The Teachers Page, the library's Web-based resource for teachers, includes lesson plans that meet curriculum standards. In 2015 the site recorded nearly 5 million visits.

The Educational Outreach Team expanded the Interactive Student Discovery Series for Apple iPads, which can be downloaded free of charge on iBooks. Six new Library of Congress Student Discovery Sets were added to the Teachers Page during the year, bringing the total to 12. The series brings together historical artifacts and one-of-a-kind documents on a wide range of topics, from history to science to literature.

Through its Teaching with Primary Sources Program (TPS) the library is providing educators with methods and materials that build student literacy skills, content knowledge, and critical-thinking abilities. Through workshops, conferences, and webinars, the TPS program served more than 22,000 teachers in 392 congressional districts in 2015. Many of these received instruction through the TPS Consortium, composed of the library's 28 partner institutions across the country.

From print journals to social media, the library sought to connect with educators around the nation. The Educational Outreach Team hosted 28 webinars for educators and reached more than 10,000 followers on its @TeachingLC, a Twitter feed for K–12 educators offering primary sources, inspiration, and ideas. The team also published 124 posts on its "Teaching with the Library of Congress" blog, to showcase the library's collections and strategies for using them in the classroom, and to encourage readers to share their teaching strategies.

Literacy Promotion

The Library of Congress promotes reading and literacy through the Center for the Book, the National Book Festival, the appointment of a National Ambassador for Young People's Literature, and through its popular literacy-promotion website, http://www.Read.gov.

Center for the Book

The Center for the Book was established by Congress in 1977 to "stimulate public interest in books and reading." A public–private partnership, the center sponsors educational programs that reach readers of all ages through a network of 50 affiliated state centers, collaborations with more than 80 nonprofit reading promotion partners and through the Young Readers Center and Poetry and Literature Center at the Library of Congress. The center also maintains and updates the library's http://www.Read.gov.

In collaboration with the Children's Book Council (CBC) and the CBC Foundation, and with support from publishers, the center sponsors the National Ambassador for Young People's Literature. In 2015 two-time Newbery Medal-winner Kate DiCamillo served the second year of her two-year term as National Ambassador for Young People's Literature. She continued to focus on her platform, "Stories Connect Us."

Working with the Poetry and Literature Center, Charles Wright, the library's Poet Laureate Consultant in Poetry for 2014–2015, presided over the literary season, which featured many distinguished poets and writers reading from their works.

The Center for the Book played a major role in presentation of the 2015 Library of Congress National Book Festival, participating in planning the festival, inviting and scheduling authors and illustrators, and organizing the Pavilion of the States.

The Young Readers Center in the Thomas Jefferson Building continued to grow in popularity, with new programs and activities for children that attracted nearly 30,000 visitors during the year.

More than 50,000 young readers from across the country participated in the center's 2014–2015 Letters About Literature competition. Open to students in grades 4 through 12, the competition challenged young people to write letters to their favorite authors explaining how their works changed their lives. The top letters in each competition level for each state were chosen. Then national winners and runners-up were chosen in each of three competition levels.

For the third year, the Center for the Book administered the Library of Congress Literacy Awards, an initiative supported and originated by philanthropist David M. Rubenstein.

The awards recognize and support organizations and institutions in the United States and abroad that have made significant contributions to combating illiteracy.

Collections

In 2015 the library added 1.7 million items to its collection through purchase, gift, exchange, or transfer from other government agencies, bringing the total to more than 162 million items in various formats. This figure included more than 38 million cataloged books and other print materials, 70 million manuscripts, 17 million microforms, 15 million visual materials (photographs, posters, prints, and drawings), 7.1 million pieces of sheet music, 5.6 million maps, 3.6 million audio materials, 1.7 million moving images, and more than 3.3 million items in miscellaneous formats. An increasing amount of incoming material is in digital format.

Important New Acquisitions

The library receives millions of items each year from copyright deposits, federal agencies, and purchases, exchanges, and gifts.

The U.S. Copyright Office forwarded more than 615,000 copies of works with a net value of $29.3 million to the library's collections in 2015; more than 347,000 of these copies were received from publishers under the mandatory deposit provisions of the law. Contributions from the James Madison Council helped the library acquire a number of items, including letters from two iconic American composers, Leonard Bernstein and George Gershwin; two original design drawings for murals in the library's Thomas Jefferson Building by distinguished American artist Elihu Vedder; and a unique 1864 illustrated map of Andersonville Prison.

The library also acquired many significant items and collections by gift or purchase, including the following:

- The American Folklife Center acquired a significant collection of oral histories provided by responders to the September 11, 2001, terrorist attack on the New York World Trade Center.

- The Geography and Map Division received the donated Archive of the Association of American Geographers (1904–present), the oldest professional geographers' organization in the United States.
- The Law Library acquired *Year Books of Edward V to Henry VIII*, a group of separately printed yearbooks covering the years 1483 through 1535. This completes the Law Library's preeminent collection of the earliest printed records of the decisions of medieval English judges.
- The Motion Picture, Broadcasting, and Recorded Sound Division acquired recordings from the pioneering folk music label Stinson Records, featuring Woody Guthrie, Pete Seeger, Josh White, Lead Belly, Mary Lou Williams, the band Sonora Matancera, and many others.
- The Music Division received through donation the papers of composer, pianist, and conductor Marvin Hamlisch.
- The Prints and Photographs division received 540 Civil War stereographs from the Robin G. Stanford Collection, including rare images of President Lincoln's funeral procession through several cities.
- The Rare Book and Special Collections Division received, as a gift made possible by the GHR Foundation to mark the historic address of Pope Francis to Congress, one of only 12 copies of the Apostles Edition of the Saint John's Bible, a contemporary illuminated manuscript produced by the monks of Saint John's Abbey and University.

Cataloging

The library provided cataloging records to the nation's 122,000 public, school, academic, and research libraries and other institutions that rely on the library's bibliographic data. In 2015 the library cataloged in its Voyager system 268,250 new works on 271,977 separate bibliographic records. Production of full- and standard-level original cataloging totaled 183,979 bibliographic records. The library and other member institutions of the international Program for Cooperative Cataloging created 296,466 name and series authority records, and 4,934 subject authorities. The library served as secretariat for the program and created 84,659 of the name and series authority records and 3,474 of the subject authorities. Dewey Decimal Classification numbers were assigned to 103,346 titles as a service to other libraries throughout the world that use that system to organize their collections.

Bibliographic Framework Initiative

Since 2011 the Library of Congress has been leading a bibliographic framework initiative (BIBFRAME) to plan for the evolution from the present framework to the future, not only for the Library of Congress but also for the institutions that depend on bibliographic data shared by the library and its partners. In 2015 the library continued development of BIBFRAME to replace MARC 21 as a cataloging metadata standard in order to reap the benefits of newer technology, particularly data linking. The library continued to build on the work and tools developed in

2014: a stable version of the vocabulary and data-entry editing and transformation tools that convert MARC records to BIBFRAME descriptions. These tools were updated and combined with other new components to support a BIBFRAME pilot to allow input of native BIBFRAME descriptions. Approximately 35 library catalogers created bibliographic descriptions, in both BIBFRAME and in MARC—the latter for distribution through the library's Cataloging Distribution Service. The results of the pilot will be evaluated and plans will be made for a second pilot in 2016. BIBFRAME, coupled with the already implemented RDA: Resource Description and Access, is paving the way for a seismic transformation in bibliographic control. With these two standards, the Library of Congress, along with other libraries, will be able to share and use metadata in ways never-before possible, with great savings of time, energy, and resources.

Reference Services

More than 897,000 items were circulated for use by patrons working at the library in 2015. The library's staff responded to more than 457,000 reference requests. Of these, more than 155,000 were received online, including queries that were handled through the Ask a Librarian service.

Patrons continued to register in person for the library-issued user card. Those patrons submit hundreds of requests for materials using the Integrated Library System's (ILS) automated Call Slip function in the LC Online Catalog. The ILS contains 9 million authority records that provide references from variant forms of names and from narrower to broader subject headings within the Library of Congress subject headings.

The library added 87 new encoded archival description finding aids online, bringing the total to 2,225 Web-accessible finding aids covering more than 60.2 million archival items in the library's collections.

Online Resources

The library continued to add high-quality digital content to its website. During the year, 8.6 million new digital files were added, bringing the total to 60.9 million, including files from the National Digital Newspaper Program.

The library's website at http://www.loc.gov gives users access to the institution's vast resources, such as its online catalogs; selected collections in various formats; copyright, legal, and legislative information; library exhibitions; and videos and podcasts of library events. Consistently recognized as one of the top federal sites, the website recorded more than 90.2 million visits and 481.7 million page views during the year.

The library successfully managed a fourth year of the overall Web Strategy implementation effort. The project focused on functional, content, and process work across the library's Web presence. Highlights include usability improvements to the core search and browse toolset for loc.gov that allows access to 21 million items, including new gallery, grid, and slideshow tools for visualizing library content; the addition of newly digitized primary-source collections including the James Monroe Papers, the Andrew Jackson Papers, the Archive of Recorded Poetry and Literature, and the Archive of Hispanic Literature on Tape.

The library continued development of Congress.gov, a premier destination for legislative information. Progress made in 2015 includes search and browse improvements, enhancements to appropriations data, improved data exchange with legislative partners, and the addition of new content.

Social Media

The library continued to participate in media-sharing and social networking sites to promote its collections, programs, and events. Library of Congress events, booktalks, and concerts reached extensive audiences through the library's YouTube and iTunesU channels.

The YouTube channel continued to grow with the addition of nearly 400 new videos. Since the site's debut in 2009, the YouTube channel has garnered nearly 11 million video views by users around the world. Content on the iTunesU channel has been viewed or heard via downloads and streams more than 3.8 million times since its launch in June 2009. New content added in 2015 included interviews from the Civil Rights History Project, professional development content for teachers, public domain videos from the library's collections, scholarly symposia, poetry readings, concerts, and each presentation from the 2015 Library of Congress National Book Festival.

Thousands of photo enthusiasts continued to not only access but also help identify library photos from the early 1900s through the photo-sharing project on Flickr. During the year, the library added over 2,400 photos to its Flickr account, bringing the total to more than 22,000. The images have received 216 million views since 2008.

In addition to its main Facebook site—with more than 364,019 "friends"—the library offers Facebook pages for the Law Library, the American Folklife Center, Performing Arts, the National Digital Information Infrastructure and Preservation Program, and the National Library Service for the Blind and Physically Handicapped.

The library's Twitter presence includes feeds for the World Digital Library, the digital preservation program, the Congressional Research Service, teacher resources, the Law Library, legislative resources, map collections, the John W. Kluge Center, library events, and the Register of Copyrights. The library's ten Twitter accounts had more than 926,000 followers at the end of the year.

The library's Pinterest account has more than 5,600 followers and includes content on 46 boards featuring the library's collections, exhibitions, publications, and events such as the National Book Festival.

The library's main blog—among the first federal blogs at the time of its launch on April 24, 2007—has since been joined by 14 other blogs generated by the Copyright Office; the Law Library; the National Digital Preservation and Information Infrastructure Program; the Music, Prints and Photographs, and Science, Technology and Business Divisions; the Poetry and Literature Center; the Educational Outreach Office; the American Folklife Center; the National Library Service for the Blind and Physically Handicapped; the Packard Campus for Audio-Visual Conservation; and the John W. Kluge Center. In 2015 the library's blogs received nearly 5.7 million visits, and a new blog focusing on the National Book Festival was added.

In August the library launched its presence on Instagram and began sharing images from current events, concerts, and exhibitions. The Instagram channel ended the year with more than 2,300 followers.

Global Access

The Library of Congress acquires global resources through cooperative agreements and exchanges with other nations, through its overseas offices, and the World Digital Library initiative. The overseas offices collect and catalog materials from 86 countries in some 150 languages and 25 scripts, from Africa, Asia, Latin America, and the Middle East. These items are accessible in the library's area studies reading rooms. Selected items have been digitized—many through cooperative digitizing projects—and are accessible on the library's website.

Overseas Offices

The library's six overseas offices (located in Cairo, Islamabad, Jakarta, Nairobi, New Delhi, and Rio de Janeiro) acquired, cataloged, and preserved materials from parts of the world where the book and information industries are not well developed. Those offices acquired 213,363 items for the Library of Congress and, on a cost-recovery basis, provided 320,109 items to other U.S. libraries through their Cooperative Acquisitions Programs. In 2015 the library continued the West Africa Acquisitions Pilot Project in collaboration with the Council of American Overseas Research Centers to select, purchase, and provide bibliographic services for materials from 11 West African countries. In fiscal 2015 the project acquired 5,835 collection items. These acquisitions strengthen the library's holdings in the areas of literature, social sciences, and current events in West Africa.

World Digital Library

The World Digital Library (WDL) is a website, accessible from anywhere in the world, which presents in digital form, free of charge, documents of historical significance about numerous countries and cultures. Participation has grown to 190 partners in 81 countries. At year's end the WDL website contained 12,268 items, containing more than 610,522 images, in 128 languages. A highlight of the year was the public release of the new user interface—the first full redesign of the website since its initial launch in 2009. The new interface better accommodates use on mobile devices. In 2015 the WDL website recorded more than 6.8 million visits—nearly double the total of the previous year. Page views amounted to 30.8 million, up from 24.1 million the previous year.

Noteworthy content added to the site from partner institutions included the only known copy of the journal believed to have been written on board the ship during Vasco da Gama's first voyage to India, 1497–1499, from the Municipal Library of Porto, Portugal; the oldest surviving document written in Catalan, 1080, from the National Library of Catalonia, Barcelona; all 39 of the first editions produced between 1584 and 1619 at the press in Lima (the oldest press in South America and the second-oldest in the New World), in Spanish, Latin, Quechua, and Aymara, from the National Library of Peru; two of three existing parts of the *Book of Hours of Simon de Varie*, 1455, from the National Library of the Netherlands; seven Mesoamerican codices, including the *Codex Vergara, Codex Azcatitlan*, the *Aubin Tonalamatl*, and the *Codex Mexicanus*, from the National Library of France; five manuscripts associated with Fray Bernardino de Sahagún, compiler of the *Florentine Codex*, circa 1540–1574, from the Newberry Library and the complete run of the *Cherokee Phoenix*, the first Native American newspaper in the United States, 1828–1834, from the Library of Congress.

The WDL team worked in cooperation with the library's custodial divisions to select hundreds of items from the library's collections to digitize for inclusion in the WDL on a new scanner dedicated specifically for this purpose.

A key objective of the WDL project is to build digital library capabilities in the developing world. To that end, the WDL continued to maintain and process content from digital conversion centers at the Egyptian National Library and Archives in Cairo, the National Library of Uganda in Kampala, and the Iraq National Library and Archive in Baghdad.

Preservation

Preserving its unparalleled collections—from cuneiform tablets to born-digital items—is one of the library's major activities in support of its vision to further human understanding and wisdom. During the year, more than 9 million items from the library's collections were bound, treated, mass-deacidified, microfilmed, or otherwise reformatted. The Preservation Directorate surveyed the preservation needs of 1.4 million items from the library's general and special collections, including books, photographs, maps, audiovisual materials, and other formats. More than 155,000 items were bound, 62,000 were housed in protective containers and 66,000 were treated or repaired. Nearly 206,000 files were digitally copied and archived. An additional 1.3 million units (volumes/sheets) were deacidified and more than 6 million pages were microfilmed, with an additional 2.3 million pages microfilmed by the library's Overseas Office in New Delhi.

The library's preservation research program conducted analyses and assessments of factors that endanger the library's collections, investigated ways to reduce inherent risks and the effects of the use of collection items, and helped reduce environmental risks to the collections.

The congressionally mandated National Digital Information Infrastructure and Preservation Project (NDIIPP), administered by the library's Office of Strategic Initiatives, continued to collect and preserve at-risk digital content of cultural and historical importance.

Books

During 2015 the library transferred 67,450 volumes to its climate-controlled off-site storage facility at Fort Meade, Maryland, and its storage facility in Landover, Maryland, bringing the total to 5.2 million items housed offsite. In most cases, items can be retrieved and sent to Capitol Hill within 24 hours. Under the Additional Service Copy Program, 93,806 duplicate volumes were withdrawn. To address overcrowding in the bookstacks of the Thomas Jefferson and John Adams Buildings on Capitol Hill, a temporary collection storage facility was leased in Cabin Branch, Maryland, to house 3.1 million books in Fort Meade-compatible containers. Library staff began planning for the construction and transfer of collections to Fort Meade Module 5.

Newspapers

In partnership with the National Endowment for the Humanities, the library sponsors the National Digital Newspaper Program, a project to digitize and provide free and public access to American newspapers that are in the public domain. During 2015 more than 1.84 million newspaper pages were scanned, bringing the total to 10 million pages since the project's inception. The scanned newspapers are accessible on the library's Chronicling America website, a free national searchable database of nearly 1,900 historic American newspapers published in 38 states, Puerto Rico, and the District of Columbia between 1836 and 1922. In 2015 the site logged more than 42 million page views and 3.9 million visits.

Audiovisual Collections

The Packard Campus for Audio-Visual Conservation in Culpeper, Virginia, houses the library's recorded sound and moving image collections—the world's largest and most comprehensive. In 2015 the Packard Campus digitally preserved nearly 54,000 moving image and recorded sound collection items. Highlights include the digitization of 3,000 hours of content from the Studs Terkel Collection (in collaboration with the Chicago History Museum) and the processing of 2,000 lacquer discs from the Les Paul Collection.

At year's end the Packard Campus Data Center held 6.2 petabytes of collection content comprising nearly 1.5 million digital files. This includes more than 205,000 files from 18,200 public broadcasting programs recently acquired from the American Archive of Public Broadcasting and ingested into the Digital Archive.

Films

It is estimated that half the films produced before 1950 and 80 percent to 90 percent of those made before 1920 are gone forever. The library is working with many organizations to prevent further losses. Under the terms of the National Film Preservation Act of 1988, the Librarian of Congress—with advice from the National Film Preservation Board—began selecting 25 films annually for the National Film Registry to be preserved for all time. The films are chosen on the basis of whether they are "culturally, historically, or aesthetically significant."

On December 16, 2015, the library announced the following additions to the National Film Registry, which brought the total of films on the list to 675.

Being There (1979)

Black and Tan (1929)

Dracula (Spanish-language version) (1931)

Dream of a Rarebit Fiend (1906)

Eadweard Muybridge, Zoopraxographer (1975)

Edison Kinetoscopic Record of a Sneeze (1894)

A Fool There Was (1915)

Ghostbusters (1984)

Hail the Conquering Hero (1944)

Humoresque (1920)

Imitation of Life (1959)

The Inner World of Aphasia (1968)

John Henry and the Inky-Poo (1946)

L.A. Confidential (1997)

The Mark of Zorro (1920)

The Old Mill (1937)

Our Daily Bread (1934)

Portrait of Jason (1967)

Seconds (1966)

The Shawshank Redemption (1994)

Sink or Swim (1990)

The Story of Menstruation (1946)

Symbiopsychotaxiplasm: Take One (1968)

Top Gun (1986)

Winchester '73 (1950)

The legislation also directs the library to support archival research projects that would investigate the survival rates of American movies produced in all major categories during the 19th and 20th centuries. With funding from the National Film Preservation Board, the library initiated the Silent Film Project, the goal of which is to borrow, catalog, digitally preserve, and ensure the availability of silent films for public viewing and research. Private collectors may engage in the project by lending their small-gauge silent films that do not otherwise survive or only survive in a less complete form. All borrowed films are scanned for preservation and access purposes.

Sound Recordings

The National Recording Preservation Act of 2000 mandates the preservation of the nation's historic sound recordings, many of which are at risk of deterioration. It directs the Librarian of Congress to name sound recordings of aesthetic, historical, or cultural value to the National Recording Registry, to establish an advisory National Recording Preservation Board, and to create and implement a national plan to assure the long-term preservation and accessibility of the nation's audio heritage.

On March 25, 2015, the Librarian of Congress announced the addition of the following 25 sound recordings to the National Recording Registry, bringing the total to 425.

Vernacular Wax Cylinder Recordings at University of California, Santa Barbara Library (c.1890–1910)

The Benjamin Ives Gilman Collection, recorded at the 1893 World's Columbian Exposition at Chicago (1893)

"The Boys of the Lough"/"The Humours of Ennistymon," Michael Coleman (1922)

"Black Snake Moan"/"Match Box Blues," Blind Lemon Jefferson (1927)

"Sorry, Wrong Number," episode of *Suspense* radio series (1943)

"Ac-Cent-Tchu-Ate the Positive," Johnny Mercer (1944)

Radio Coverage of President Franklin D. Roosevelt's Funeral, Arthur Godfrey et al. (April 14, 1945)

Kiss Me, Kate, original cast album, (1949)

John Brown's Body, film soundtrack (1953)

"My Funny Valentine," the Gerry Mulligan Quartet featuring Chet Baker (1953)

"Sixteen Tons," Tennessee Ernie Ford (1955)

"Mary Don't You Weep," the Swan Silvertones (1959)

Joan Baez, Joan Baez (1960)

"Stand by Me," Ben E. King (1961)

New Orleans' Sweet Emma Barrett and Her Preservation Hall Jazz Band, Sweet Emma and Her Preservation Hall Jazz Band (1964)

"You've Lost That Lovin' Feelin'," The Righteous Brothers (1964)

The Doors, The Doors (1967)

Stand! Sly and the Family Stone (1969)

Lincoln Mayorga and Distinguished Colleagues, Lincoln Mayorga (1968)

A Wild and Crazy Guy, Steve Martin (1978)

Sesame Street: All-Time Platinum Favorites (1995)

OK Computer, Radiohead (1997)

Old Regular Baptists: Lined-Out Hymnody from Southeastern Kentucky, Indian Bottom Association (1997)

The Miseducation of Lauryn Hill, Lauryn Hill (1998)

Fanfares for the Uncommon Woman, Colorado Symphony Orchestra (1999)

Oral History

The Library of Congress has been collecting and preserving the nation's oral history since the 1930s, when the Works Progress Administration's (WPA) Federal Writers' Project documented the experiences of former slaves and of Americans living through the Great Depression. The American Folklife Center became the repository for these oral histories and others, such as the man-on-the-street interviews after the attack on Pearl Harbor on December 7, 1941, and similar interviews following the terrorist attacks of September 11, 2001.

Launched in 2000 at the behest of Congress, the Veterans History Project in the American Folklife Center is preserving and making available the recollections of those in the armed services dating to World War I. The Veterans History Project marked its 15th anniversary with the launch of a new Web presentation featuring 15 collections from the project's permanent archive. In recognition of the 70th anniversary of VJ-Day in 2015, the project launched a major campaign to preserve the stories of World War II veterans residing in and around the nation's capital. During the year more than 5,000 personal recollections were deposited in the library, bringing the total to more than 100,000 since the project's inception. Many of these stories are accessible on the project's website.

In 2003 documentary producer Dave Isay was inspired by the library's WPA collections to launch StoryCorps, an innovative oral history project in which ordinary Americans record one another's stories. The more than 51,400 audio interviews that comprise the StoryCorps project reside in the Library of Congress, where they can be accessed onsite. In addition to weekly broadcasts on National Public Radio's *Morning Edition*, selected interviews are available as downloadable podcasts from NPR and as animated shorts on the StoryCorps website. In November the project introduced technology that makes it possible for anyone to participate via a new app or through the StoryCorps.me site. The ability to conduct and share interviews independent of a StoryCorps recording booth provides a global platform whereby anyone in the world can record and upload an oral history. The library will regularly gather copies of these uploaded interviews from the StoryCorps.me site for long-term preservation.

Under the Civil Rights History Project Act of 2009, Congress directed the Library of Congress and the Smithsonian Institution's National Museum of African American History and Culture to conduct a survey of existing oral history collections with relevance to the civil rights movement, and to record new interviews with people who participated in the movement, over a five-year period beginning in 2010. The library has since completed the survey and launched the Civil Rights History Project website, which provides information about civil rights collections housed in more than 1,500 archives, libraries, museums, and other repositories around the country, including the Library of Congress. In 2015 the American Folklife Center, which manages the project at the library, made these interviews and other related materials available on the project website in conjunction with the opening of the library's exhibition *Civil Rights Act of 1964: A Long Struggle for Freedom*. The American Folklife Center cataloged 7,292 civil rights-related items, digitized 17,101 items in various formats, and expanded the project website.

Digital Preservation and Management

The National Digital Information Infrastructure and Preservation Program (NDIIPP) was mandated by Congress in 2000 to develop a nationwide strategy to collect and preserve high-risk digital materials of high value to the American people and the nation's lawmakers. The library continued to add high-quality digital content to the its website through internal scanning operations, contracted services, and collaborations with outside partners. In 2015, 8.6 million new digital files were added, bringing the total to 60.9 million, including 6.6 million files from the National Digital Newspaper Program. Using repository software, OSI staff added 608 terabytes of content to the library's digital collection, for a total of more than 2.6 petabytes of digital collections under library management.

Web Archiving

In 2015 the library's Web Archiving Team continued to provide project management and technical support for 39 active Web archive collections. During the year the team archived 179 terabytes of Web content (1.6 million documents), bringing the total to 763 terabytes (10.8 billion documents) in the library's Web archive collections.

U.S. Copyright Office

Congress enacted the first copyright law in May 1790; in 1870 it centralized the national copyright function in the Library of Congress. The U.S. Copyright Office in the Library of Congress administers certain major provisions of the U.S. copyright law and provides expert and impartial advice about copyright law and policy to Congress, federal agencies, the courts, and the public. The collections of the Library of Congress have been created largely through the copyright deposit system.

During 2015 the Copyright Office registered more than 443,000 copyright claims, of which 94 percent were filed online, and recorded thousands of copyright transfer documents. Additionally, the office processed hundreds of notices terminating transfers of copyrights made in the 1970s, most of which pertained to musical works.

The Copyright Office invited three rounds of public comments and held public hearings in Washington, D.C., and Los Angeles in relation to the sixth triennial rulemaking proceeding under section 1201 of the copyright law. Section 1201 provides that, upon the recommendation of the Register of Copyrights, the Librarian of Congress may designate certain classes of works as exempt from the prohibition against circumventing technological measures that control access to copyrighted works.

Copyright Royalty Judges

The Copyright Royalty Judges administer the provisions of Chapter 8 of Title 17 of the Copyright Act, which is related to setting royalty rates and terms as well as determining the distribution of royalties for certain copyright statutory licenses. In 2015 licensees remitted approximately $314 million in television retransmission and other royalties. The judges approved distributions of approximately $378 million from 22 different royalty funds. The judges finalized five matters, three of which were proceedings by stipulation or adjudication and published five agreed partial-distribution notices for comment. The judges also published final rates and terms for two statutory licenses, proposed rates and terms for one statutory license, cost-of-living adjustments for three established rates, and five notices of intent to audit.

National Library Service for the Blind and Physically Handicapped

The National Library Service for the Blind and Physically Handicapped (NLS) was established in 1931 when President Herbert Hoover signed the Pratt-Smoot Act into law. In 2015 NLS circulated nearly 22 million copies of braille and recorded books and magazines to more than 862,000 reader accounts through a network of more than 100 cooperating libraries. Through its digital talking-book program, NLS continued to distribute digital players and audiobooks on flash-memory cartridges in specially designed mailing containers to libraries nationwide.

During the year NLS contracted for the production of 3,564 audio books and also selected 20 audio recordings of books from recordings provided free of charge by the commercial publishers Audible, Inc.; Hachette; Penguin; Random House; and Scholastic. NLS also added materials to its Braille Audio Reading Download (BARD) offerings with those produced by network libraries, thus expanding the scope and quantity of available titles. The 2015 additions to BARD comprised 1,393 talking books, 227 braille books, and 10 audio magazines, bringing the total to nearly 65,000 items. In June the free BARD mobile app became available through Google Play for devices running Android OS 4.1 or later.

The John W. Kluge Center

The John W. Kluge Center was established in 2000 with a gift of $60 million from the late John W. Kluge, Metromedia president and founding chair of the James Madison Council (the library's private-sector advisory group). The center's goal is to bring the world's scholars to the Library of Congress to use the institution's vast resources and interact with policymakers in Washington.

During 2015 the Kluge Center brought scholars and interns in the humanities and social sciences to Washington. Senior scholars, pre- and post-doctoral fellows, and interns researched topics of historical and contemporary significance in the fields of humanities, social sciences, foreign policy, and law. The center hosted its first-ever Kluge Fellows in Digital Studies. A highlight of the year was ScholarFest, the Kluge Center's celebration of its 15-year history, which welcomed more than 70 current and former Kluge scholars for two days of scholarly conversations.

Publications

Each year the library publishes books, calendars, and other printed products featuring its vast content. All told, more than 200 library publications are in print and can be purchased in bookstores nationwide and from the library shop.

Among the titles published in 2015 were the following four volumes featuring items drawn from the library's collections.

To Know Wisdom and Instruction by Levon Avdoyan (published in association with the Armenian eBook Initiative) is the companion publication to the library's 2012 exhibition marking the quincentenary of Armenian printing. Drawing from the Armenian collections of the Library of Congress, the e-book contains 75 color images highlighting the varieties of the Armenian literary tradition from manuscripts through contemporary publishing.

Mapping the West with Lewis and Clark by Ralph E. Ehrenberg and Herman J. Viola (published in association with Levenger Press) sheds new light on the cartographic discoveries of these explorers. Drawing from period maps in the library's Geography and Map Division and other repositories, the book examines the critical role that maps played in Thomas Jefferson's vision of a formidable republic that would no longer be eclipsed by European empires.

Jacob Riis: Revealing New York's Other Half by Bonnie Yochelson (published in association with Yale University Press) is the first comprehensive study and complete catalogue of Riis's world-famous images, which he used to support his views on social reform. The book is the companion volume to new Riis exhibitions at four venues in the United States and Denmark, including the Library of Congress.

Facing Change: Documenting America by Leah Bendavid-Val (published in association with the nonprofit Facing Change: Documenting America) is a national portrait of America today, featuring the work of ten of the country's most celebrated contemporary photojournalists. The volume also includes historic documentary photographs from the library's collections.

Exhibitions

From pre-Columbian artifacts to rare 15th-century Bibles, from Thomas Jefferson's personal library to the art and architecture of the building named for him, continuing exhibitions offer something for everyone. The library's exhibitions can be viewed online at http://www.loc.gov/exhibits/.

In 2015 new library exhibitions celebrated the 200th anniversary of the library's acquisition of Thomas Jefferson's library (*Out of the Ashes: A New Library for Congress and the Nation*, May 8, 2015–May 2016); marked the 1640 publication of the first book printed in America (*First Among Many: The Bay Psalm Book and Early Moments in American Printing*, June 4, 2015–January 2, 2016); and honored the work of 20th-century political cartoonists (*Pointing Their Pens: Herblock and Fellow Cartoonists Confront the Issues*, March 21, 2015–March 19, 2016) and the art of theatrical design *Grand Illusion: The Art of Theatrical Design,* February 12, 2015–July 25, 2015. The library also honored the life and legacy of its music patron, Elizabeth Sprague Coolidge (1864–1953) with a display in the Performing Arts Reading Room (August 13, 2015–January 23, 2016).

To commemorate the 150th anniversary of its delivery, the library placed on display the original manuscript of President Abraham Lincoln's Second Inaugural Address for four days in March in the Great Hall of the Thomas Jefferson Building. President Barack Obama viewed the document at the library on March 8.

The library also displayed its copy of *The Apostles Edition of The Saint John's Bible* (September 26, 2015–January 2, 2016), which was given to the library on the occasion of the Pope's visit to Washington, D.C., on September 24.

Special Events

During the year the library presented hundreds of public events such as poetry and literary programs, concerts, film screenings, lectures, and symposia, many of which were broadcast live or archived on the library's website at http://www.loc.gov/webcasts/. For a list of upcoming events, visit http://www.loc.gov/loc/events/. For concert information, go to www.loc.gov/concerts/.

Literary Events

The 15th annual Library of Congress National Book Festival, held September 5, 2015, drew a capacity crowd of book-lovers to the free, public event in the Walter E. Washington Convention Center in Washington, D.C. This year the festival celebrated its 15th anniversary and the 200th anniversary of Thomas Jefferson's personal library coming to the Library of Congress. The 12-hour festival featured presentations and book-signings by more than 170 bestselling authors on 19 stages and program areas.

The Center for the Book sponsored more than 20 public programs during the year. Many of these were part of the popular Books & Beyond literary series, which highlights new books by authors who drew on the library's vast resources to produce their works. In February the center hosted a two-day conference on romance fiction.

The Poetry and Literature Center offered numerous poetry readings and literary events during the year. Charles Wright concluded his tenure as Poet Laureate Consultant in Poetry with a conversation with former Poet Laureate Charles Simic held on April 30. Juan Felipe Herrera gave his inaugural reading as the 21st Poet Laureate Consultant in Poetry on September 15.

Concerts

Since 1925 the library's Coolidge Auditorium has provided a venue for world-class performers and world premieres of commissioned works. Sponsored by the Music Division with support from private donors, the 2014–2015 season featured 95 individual events, including 27 major concerts, 40 lectures and talks, and 5 world premieres of musical compositions commissioned by the library. The Music Division's public programming also included a series of lectures delivered by curators and other experts, as well as symposia and displays of collection items. The concerts were complemented by guest speakers, curators, panels, film screenings, and displays of rarely seen manuscripts, letters, and memorabilia from the library's holdings. All concerts were presented free of charge in the library's historic, 500-seat Coolidge Auditorium.

The library's 89th concert season celebrated American performers and music through performances by some of the nation's most legendary musicians. They included popular Broadway composers Steven Lutvak (*A Gentleman's Guide to Love and Murder*), Jeanine Tesori (*Thoroughly Modern Millie*), and David Yazbek (*The Full Monty* and *Dirty Rotten Scoundrels*); and performers Etienne Charles (Creole Soul) and Nels Cline of Wilco, whose music embraces diversity in the national community.

The noontime folklife concert series known as "Homegrown: The Music of America" brought the multicultural richness of American folk arts from around the country to the nation's capital. Presented by the American Folklife Center in cooperation with the Kennedy Center Millennium Stage, the series ran from June through September.

Symposia and Lectures

During the year, various library divisions sponsored programs and lectures on a wide range of topics. These programs provided an opportunity to share ideas, celebrate diversity, and showcase the library's collections. The following are examples of these programs:

The African and Middle Eastern Division's programs included an Armenian Vardanants Day event, which featured a presentation by Carnegie Fellow Susan Harper on "American Humanitarianism in the Armenian Crucible, 1915–1923." The division's Hebraic Section continued its "Treasures from the Hebraic Section" series, and the African Section's "Conversations with African Poets and Writers" series entered its fourth year.

The American Folklife Center presented ten programs in its Benjamin Botkin lecture series. To launch the annual International Conference of Indigenous Archives, Libraries and Museums, the American Folklife Center and the Association of Tribal Archives, Libraries and Museums presented a symposium titled "Civil Rights, Identity, and Sovereignty: Native American Perspectives on History, Law, and the Path Ahead."

The John W. Kluge Center sponsored more than 30 public programs during the year on topics that included foreign policy, religion, American history and government, the earth and the environment, and arts and culture. A highlight of the year was ScholarFest, the Kluge Center's celebration of its 15-year history, which welcomed more than 70 current and former Kluge scholars for two days of scholarly conversations. Other public programs included the inaugural Daniel K. Inouye Distinguished Lecture featuring former Secretaries of State Madeleine Albright and Colin Powell; a conference on the legacy of Vaclav Havel featuring Secretary of State Madeleine Albright and Sen. John McCain; and a three-part seminar series on astrobiology and the humanities. Called the Blumberg Dialogues, the series features 23 scholars and scientists and was part of the NASA/ Library of Congress Astrobiology Program.

The Law Library continued its lecture series to celebrate the 800th anniversary of Magna Carta and the display of the Great Charter at the Library of Congress. In conjunction with the library's exhibition on the Civil Rights Act of 1964, photojournalist Bob Adelman and retired executive director of the American Civil Liberties Union (ACLU) Ira Glasser discussed their work and experiences during the civil rights movement. In recognition of Human Rights Day in December, the Law Library of Congress and the library's African and Middle Eastern Division hosted a panel discussion on Islamic law reform.

The Science, Technology and Business Division's lecture series included talks by NASA scientist Douglas Morton on climate and wildfires in the 21st century, by Dr. Daniel R. Lucey on Ebola in West Africa, and by Gabriel Weimann of the University of Haifa on terrorism in cyberspace. Big data, underground water supplies in space, community gardens, and the Fukushima explosion were some of the other topics covered by this series.

Film Screenings

The library's Packard Campus Theater continued its popular film screenings that showcase the film, television, radio, and recorded sound collections of the Library of Congress. The Art Deco-style theater is one of only five venues in the country equipped to show original classic film prints on nitrate film stock as they would have been screened in theaters before 1950. The theater also features a custom-made organ that provides live musical accompaniment for silent movies to enhance the cinematic experience. During 2015 the Packard Campus offered 145 public events in its 205-seat theater, including the screening of more than 190 films held by the library. Nearly 11,000 people attended these screenings. Among the live events held at the theater was a production featuring the Metropolitan Washington Old-Time Radio Club, which re-created episodes of two 1949 radio shows.

Honors and Awards

Gershwin Prize for Popular Song

The Library of Congress celebrated Willie Nelson's career and his selection as the 2015 recipient of the Library of Congress Gershwin Prize for Popular Song in Washington, D.C., with a series of events, culminating in a star-studded concert at DAR Constitution Hall on November 18. Named for George and Ira Gershwin, the prize honors a living music artist's lifetime achievement in promoting song to enhance cultural understanding; entertaining and informing audiences; and inspiring new generations. The two-day celebration began with a presentation and special display in the library's historic Thomas Jefferson Building with a group of the nation's lawmakers, who recognized Nelson for his contributions to popular music.

With a career that spans six decades, Nelson's music pushes genre boundaries and his lyrics give voice to America's heartland. He put his imprint forever on country music and introduced it to new audiences by expanding music's avenues in the 1970s to create "outlaw country." He has continually broadened his musical language, crossing into jazz, blues, folk, rock, and Latin styles. A guitar virtuoso with a unique voice, Nelson is an artist whose work continues to inspire new musicians of diverse genres. The November concert was taped for public broadcast on PBS stations nationwide in January 2016.

John W. Kluge Prize

Jürgen Habermas and Charles Taylor, two of the world's most important philosophers, received the library's John W. Kluge Prize for Achievement in the Study of Humanity at a ceremony held September 29 in the Great Hall of the Thomas Jefferson Building. Habermas and Taylor, the 9th and 10th recipients of the award, will share $1.5 million. Ordinarily the prize carries a $1 million award, but in 2015 the Kluge Prize was increased to $1.5 million in recognition of the Kluge Center's 15th anniversary.

Library of Congress Prize for American Fiction

Louise Erdrich received the Library of Congress Prize for American Fiction during the 2015 Library of Congress National Book Festival on September 5. The prize honors an American literary writer whose body of work is distinguished not only for its mastery of the art but for its originality of thought and imagination. Erdrich is the author of such critically acclaimed novels as *Love Medicine, The Last Report on the Miracles at Little No Horse, The Plague of Doves,* and *The Round House.*

Literacy Awards

Created and sponsored by philanthropist David M. Rubenstein, the Library of Congress Literacy Awards seek to reward those organizations that have been doing exemplary, innovative and easily replicable work over a sustained period of time and to encourage new groups, organizations, and individuals to become involved. Recipients of the 2015 annual awards were announced on October 28.

The winners were Room to Read, San Francisco, California (David M. Rubenstein Prize, $150,000, for groundbreaking or sustained record of advancement of literacy by an individual or entity); SMART, Oregon (American Prize, $50,000, for a project developed and implemented successfully during the past decade for combating illiteracy and/or aliteracy); and Mother Child Education Foundation, Turkey (International Prize, $50,000, for the work of an individual or nation or nongovernmental organization working in a specific country or region).

Living Legend Award

The Library of Congress Living Legend Award honors those who have made significant contributions to America's diverse cultural, scientific, and social heritage. First presented in 2000, during the library's bicentennial celebration, the award has been given to artists, writers, filmmakers, physicians, entertainers, sports figures, public servants, and musicians who have enriched the nation through their professional accomplishments and personal excellence. In 2015 the award was presented to Glenn Jones, a pioneer in cable television and in dissemination of knowledge through digital networks, and to musician Marta Casals Istomin.

Rebekah Johnson Bobbitt Prize

The Rebekah Johnson Bobbitt National Prize for Poetry was awarded to Patricia Smith on April 6 for her book *Shoulda Been Jimi Savannah*. The prize is awarded for an American poet's lifetime achievements, or the most distinguished book of poetry published in the preceding two years. Awarded at the Library of Congress, the Bobbitt Prize is a biennial $10,000 award donated by the family of Rebekah Johnson Bobbitt of Austin, Texas, in her memory.

Additional Sources of Information

Library of Congress website	www.loc.gov
Main phone number	202-707-5000
Reading room hours and locations	www.loc.gov/rr/
	202-707-6400
General reference	www.loc.gov/rr/askalib/
	202-707-3399
	TTY 202-707-4210
Visitor information	www.loc.gov/visit/
	202-707-8000
	TTY 202-707-6200

Exhibitions	ww.loc.gov/exhibits/
	202-707-4604
Copyright information	www.copyright.gov
	202-707-3000
Copyright hotline (to order forms)	202-707-9100
Library catalogs	www.catalog.loc.gov/
Cataloging Information	www.loc.gov/aba/
Services for the Blind and Physically Handicapped	www.loc.gov/nls/
	202-707-5100
	TDD 202-707-0744
Literacy promotion	www.read.gov
Teachers Page	www.loc.gov/teachers/
Legislative information	www.Congress.gov
Library of Congress Shop (credit card orders)	888-682-3557
	www.loc.gov/shop

Federal Library and Information Network (FEDLINK)

Blane K. Dessy

Interim Executive Director

Summary

During fiscal year (FY) 2015 the Federal Library Information Network (FED-LINK) continued its mission to achieve better utilization of federal library and information resources; provide the most cost-effective and efficient administrative mechanism for providing necessary services and materials to federal libraries and information centers; and serve as a forum for discussion of federal library and information policies, programs, and procedures, to help inform Congress, federal agencies, and others concerned with libraries and information centers.

FEDLINK's Advisory Board (FAB) focused its bimonthly meetings on a variety of broad federal information issues including FEDLINK's status as the commodity manager of Information Retrieval for the Federal Strategic Sourcing Initiative (FSSI), the Library of the United States Project (LOTUS), interlibrary loan groups among federal libraries, new technologies for federal librarians, FED-LINK's research agenda, and the Federal Library Census.

The governing body structure of FEDLINK includes a number of committees, working groups, and ad hoc committees that all completed an ambitious agenda in fiscal 2015. Notably, the American Indian Library Initiative participated in the ATALM (Association of Tribal Archives, Libraries and Museums) annual conference, the Education Working Group featured agency options for internship programs and began work on a federal library mentoring project, and the FEDGrey Working Group hosted GreyNet 16, GreyNet International's annual conference.

The Awards Committee announced the following awards:

- 2014 Federal Library/Information Center of the Year in the Large Library/Information Center Category (with a staff of 11 or more employees): Barr Memorial Library, Fort Knox U.S. Army Garrison, Kentucky
- 2014 award in the Small Library/Information Center Category (with a staff of 10 or fewer employees): Darnall Medical Library, Walter Reed National Military Medical Center
- 2014 Federal Librarian of the Year: Richard James King, Branch Chief and Information Architect, National Institutes of Health Library, Bethesda, Maryland
- 2014 Federal Library Technician of the Year: Maria Walls, Library Technician, U.S. Department of Justice

The Human Resources Working Group (HRWG) completed revising the 1410 series and sent out the revision to the FEDLINK Federal Advisory Board and to more than 40 federal librarians who volunteered to review the draft revision from a variety of federal agencies. Following the review, the HRWG addressed and adjudicated the comments and completed additional revisions.

In FY 2014 FEDLINK continued its publication program as a digital communication provider and used the FEDLIB listserv to communicate critical advocacy and program information to more than 2,000 electronic subscribers. New resources for FY 2015 include revisions to the member handbook, adding award-winning exemplars to the website, and a number of research documents on federal information purchasing and strategic sourcing.

FEDLINK continued to enhance its fiscal operations while providing its members with $75.7 million in transfer-pay services, $5.9 million in direct-pay services, and an estimated $106.5 million in the Direct Express service. In total, approximately $188 million of information resource purchasing was done on FEDLINK contracts. This saved federal agencies more than $36.7 million in vendor volume discounts and approximately $49.9 million in cost avoidance.

FEDLINK staff highlighted services at national conferences such as the American Library Association (ALA), Computers in Libraries, National Contracts Management Association World Congress, and the Government Contracts Management Symposium. Staff also represented FEDLINK at regional events such as the House of Representatives Subscription Fair. They also assisted the ALA Federal and Armed Forces Librarians Round Table (FAFLRT) track activities affecting federal libraries and host programs at the annual conference on working in a federal library and best practices for library internships. Staff members also participated in additional national conferences, workshops, and meetings, including CENDI and Computers in Libraries.

FEDLINK continued to provide federal agencies cost-effective access to an array of automated information resources for online research and support for federal library functions. FEDLINK members procured an array of publications in various formats: print and electronic journals, print and electronic books, sound recordings, audiovisual materials, items via document delivery and interlibrary loan, and access to databases of full text, indexes, abstracts, and a variety of other data. Federal libraries obtained support for many functions such as acquisitions, cataloging and related technical processing services, staffing support, information management, resource sharing, information industry market research and library services benchmarking, integrated library systems, digitization, digital archiving, and preservation and conservation services via Library of Congress/FEDLINK contracts with more than 125 vendors.

FEDLINK issued many Requests for Proposals (RFPs) and Requests for Quotes (RFQs). An RFP "open season" established new agreements for preservation and conservation services with six companies, bringing the total to 27 vendors, and expanding the range of services available. Two other "open season" RFPs added a serials subscription agent and several information retrieval vendors. FEDLINK awarded a contract for Interlibrary Loan Fee Management and renewed option years for staffing support and bibliographic resources. In total, FEDLINK issued 40 RFQs for agencies' requirements for these services.

FEDLINK Executive Report

The Advisory Board focused its bimonthly meetings on a variety of broad federal information issues including FEDLINK's status as the commodity manager of Information Retrieval for the Federal Strategic Sourcing Initiative (FSSI), the Library of the United States Project (LOTUS), interlibrary loan groups among federal libraries, new technologies for federal librarians, FEDLINK's research agenda, and the Federal Library Census.

The American Indian Libraries Working Group's first year was filled with outreach and educational initiatives. After building an infrastructure for the group itself and identifying program objectives, the group heard from an archivist with the state of New Mexico (Department of Cultural Affairs) who is developing an online access project with the Museum of Indian Arts and Culture. The group then presented a workshop at the annual Association of Tribal Libraries and Museums (ATALM) and developed programming for a later event on connecting American Indian and federal libraries.

FEDLINK held two expositions in FY 2015. The 2014 Fall Expo featured "The Global Synergy of Federal Information" with discussions of international collections, acquisitions, parallel universes of information, and the latest on programs engaging and participating in the worldwide-networked community. In the spring of 2015 the FEDLINK Expo "Innovation in Federal Libraries" explored the methods and the tools that make federal libraries the center of innovation for both the missions of their agencies and for the benefit of all their users.

The Strategic Sourcing Initiative continued throughout the fiscal year with research reports on federal spending on information and efforts to develop further strategic sourcing of information resources for federal agencies.

FEDLINK Fees

The final budget for FY 2015 held membership fees steady for transfer-pay customers to 6 percent on amounts exceeding $100,000; 6.75 percent below $100,000 and 4 percent on amounts equal to or exceeding $1,000,000. Direct-pay fees remained at FY 2009 levels, as did Direct Express fees of 0.75 percent for all participating commercial online information services vendors.

Accounts Receivable and Member Services

FEDLINK processed registrations from federal libraries, information centers, and other federal offices for a total of 327 signed Interagency agreements (IAAs) and more than 844 IAA amendments for agencies that added, adjusted, or ended service funding. FEDLINK executed service requests by generating 3,132 delivery orders that LC/Contracts and Grants issued to vendors.

Transfer-Pay Accounts Payable Services

Staff members efficiently processed vendor invoices and earned approximately $13,000 in discounts for prompt payment of FEDLINK customer invoices. FEDLINK continued to maintain open accounts for five prior years to pay invoices for members. FEDLINK completed the closing of FY 2010. Statements are issued to members for the current year and prior years.

Direct Express Services

The FEDLINK Direct Express Program now includes 94 vendors offering database retrieval services. The program is set up to provide customers procurement and payment options similar to GSA in which the vendors pay a quarterly service fee to FEDLINK based on customer billings for usage.

Budget, Revenue, and Risks Reserves

In FY 2015, FEDLINK Fee Revenue from signed IAAs was approximately $285,000 lower than FY 2014. The expenditures for FY 2015 were approximately $133,000 lower than FY 2014 due to not filling positions, delayed projects, and a reduced research program. FEDLINK's Reserve requirement for FY 2015 continues to be solvent. The program holds reserves for: 1) mandatory requirements for shutdown and bankruptcy risks; 2) continuity of operations requirements for mission essential systems; and 3) compliance risk mitigation initiatives.

National Agricultural Library

U.S. Department of Agriculture, Abraham Lincoln Bldg.,
10301 Baltimore Ave., Beltsville, MD 20705-2351
E-mail agref@nal.usda.gov
World Wide Web http://www.nal.usda.gov

Jennifer Gilbert
Special Assistant to the Director

The U.S. Department of Agriculture's National Agricultural Library (NAL) is one of the world's largest and most accessible agricultural research libraries, offering service directly to the public via its website, http://www.nal.usda.gov.

The library was instituted in 1862 at the same time as the U.S. Department of Agriculture (USDA). It became a national library in 1962 when Congress established it as the primary agricultural information resource of the United States (7 USCS § 3125a). Congress assigned to the library the responsibilities to

- Acquire, preserve, and manage information resources relating to agriculture and allied sciences
- Organize agricultural information products and services and provide them within the United States and internationally
- Plan, coordinate, and evaluate information and library needs relating to agricultural research and education
- Cooperate with and coordinate efforts toward development of a comprehensive agricultural library and information network
- Coordinate the development of specialized subject information services among the agricultural and library information communities

NAL is located in Beltsville, Maryland, near Washington, D.C., on the grounds of USDA's Henry A. Wallace Beltsville Agricultural Research Center. Its 15-story Abraham Lincoln Building is named in honor of the president who created the Department of Agriculture and signed several of the major U.S. laws affecting agriculture.

The library employs about 100 librarians, information specialists, computer specialists, administrators, and clerical personnel, supplemented by about 50 volunteers, contract staff, and cooperators from NAL partnering organizations.

NAL's reputation as one of the world's foremost agricultural libraries is supported and burnished by its expert staff, ongoing leadership in delivering information services, expanding collaborations with other U.S. and international agricultural research and information organizations, and its extensive collection of agricultural information, searchable through AGRICOLA (AGRICultural On-Line Access), the library's bibliographic database.

In 2012 NAL reorganized to better align its functions with its overall strategic plan, which includes simplified access to all NAL content, expansion of digital content, and the integration of scientific data sets and discovery tools.

The Collection

The NAL collection dates to the congressionally approved 1839 purchase of books for the Agricultural Division of the Patent Office, predating the 1862 establishment of USDA itself. Today NAL provides access to billions of pages of agricultural information—an immense collection of scientific books, journals, audiovisuals, reports, theses, artifacts, and images—and to a widening array of digital media, as well as databases and other information resources germane to the broad reach of agriculture-related sciences.

The library's collection contains more than 8 million items, dating from the 16th century to the present, including the most complete repository of USDA publications and the world's most extensive set of materials on the history of U.S. agriculture.

Building the Collection

NAL has primary responsibility for collecting and retaining publications of USDA and its agencies, and it is the only U.S. national library with a legislated mandate to collect in the following disciplines: plant and animal health, welfare, and production; agricultural economics, products, and education; aquaculture; forestry; rural sociology and rural life; family and consumer science; and food science, safety, and nutrition. In addition to collecting as comprehensively as possible in these core subject areas, NAL collects extensively in many related subjects, such as biology, bioinformatics, biochemistry, chemistry, entomology, environmental science, genetics, invasive species, meteorology, natural resources, physics, soil science, sustainability, water quality, and zoology.

Rare and Special Collections

The NAL Rare and Special Collections program emphasizes access to and preservation of rare and unique materials documenting the history of agriculture and related sciences. Items in the library's special collections include rare books, manuscripts, nursery and seed trade catalogs, posters, objects, photographs, and other rare materials documenting agricultural subjects. Materials date from the 1500s to the present and include many international sources. Detailed information about these special collections is available on the NAL website at https://special collections.nal.usda.gov.

Special collections of note include the following:

- The U.S. Department of Agriculture History Collection (https://special collections.nal.usda.gov/usda-history-collection-introductionindex), assembled over 80 years by USDA historians, includes letters, memoranda, reports, and papers of USDA officials, as well as photographs, oral histories, and clippings covering the activities of the department from its founding through the early 1990s.

- The U.S. Department of Agriculture Pomological Watercolor Collection (http://usdawatercolors.nal.usda.gov) includes more than 7,000 detailed, botanically accurate watercolor illustrations of fruit and nut varieties developed by growers or introduced by USDA plant explorers. Created between 1886 and the 1940s, the watercolors served as official documentation of the work of the Office of the Pomologist and were used to create chromolithographs in publications distributed widely by the department. Although created for scientific accuracy, the works are artistic treasures in their own right. The full collection has been digitized and is now available online.
- The Henry G. Gilbert Nursery and Seed Trade Catalog Collection (https:// specialcollections.nal.usda.gov/guide-collections/henry-g-gilbert-nursery-and-seed-trade-catalog-collection), begun in 1904 by USDA economic botanist Percy L. Ricker, has grown to comprise more than 200,000 U.S. and foreign catalogs. The earliest items date from the late 1700s, but the collection is strongest from the 1890s to the present. Researchers commonly use the collection to document the introduction of plants to the United States, study economic trends, and illustrate early developments in American landscape design.
- The Rare Book Collection (https://specialcollections.nal.usda.gov/guide-collections/rare-book-collection) highlights agriculture's printed historical record. It covers a wide variety of subjects but is particularly strong in botany, natural history, zoology, and entomology. International in scope, the collection documents early agricultural practices in Britain and Europe, as well as the Americas. Of particular note are the more than 300 books by or about Carl Linnaeus, the "father of taxonomy," including a rare first edition of his 1735 work *Systema Naturae*.
- Manuscript collections (https://specialcollections.nal.usda.gov/guide-collections/index-manuscript-collections), now numbering more than 400, document the story of American agriculture and its influence on the world.

NAL continues to digitize these and other unique materials to share them broadly via its website and has published detailed indexes to the content of many manuscript collections to improve discovery. AGRICOLA, NAL's catalog, includes bibliographic entries for special collection items, manuscripts, and rare books. The library provides in-house research and reference services for its special collections and offers fee-based duplication services.

Preservation/Digitization

NAL is committed to the preservation of its print and non-print collections. It continues to monitor and improve the environmental quality of its stacks to extend the longevity of all materials in the collection. The library has instituted a long-term strategy to ensure the growing body of agricultural information is systematically identified, preserved, and archived.

NAL's digital conversion program has resulted in a growing digital collection of USDA publications and many non-USDA historical materials not restricted by copyright. NAL is in the midst of a large-scale project to digitize agricultural literature and provide online access to the general public. Important and distinctive items were selected from the NAL collection, with an initial focus on USDA-issued publications and nursery and seed trade catalogs. In 2014 NAL digitized and created citation information for 38,698 items. Publications are accessible at https://archive.org/details/usdanationalagriculturallibrary.

NAL Digital Collections

NAL has undertaken several projects to digitize, store, and provide online access to more than 1.5 million pages of historic print documents and images, primarily from USDA. In an effort to unify all digital content, the library launched an interface for the NAL Digital Collections (http://naldc.nal.usda.gov) accompanied by policies for collecting, storing, and making publicly available federally funded research outcomes published by USDA scientists and researchers. Long-range plans include collecting, maintaining, and providing access to a broad range of agricultural information in a wide variety of digital formats. The result will be a perpetual, reliable, publicly accessible collection of digital documents, data sets, images, and other items relating to agriculture. As of the end of 2014 NAL's digital repository of full-text content comprised nine collections, including nearly 50,000 peer-reviewed journal articles authored by USDA researchers, and more than 30,000 historical documents and reports. The public downloads approximately 3 million full-text items each year.

AGRICOLA

AGRICOLA comprises an online catalog and citation database of NAL collections and delivers worldwide access to agricultural information through its searchable Web interface (http://agricola.nal.usda.gov). Alternatively, users can access AGRICOLA on a fee basis through several commercial vendors, or they can subscribe to the complete AGRICOLA file, also on a fee basis, from the National Technical Information Service within the U.S. Department of Commerce.

The AGRICOLA database covers materials in all formats, including printed works from the 16th century onward. The records describe publications and resources encompassing all aspects of agriculture and allied disciplines. AGRICOLA, updated daily, includes the following two components:

- NAL Public Access Catalog, containing more than 1 million citations to books, audiovisual materials, serial titles, and other materials in the NAL collection. (The catalog also contains some bibliographic records for items cataloged by other libraries but not held in the NAL collection.)
- NAL Article Citation Database, consisting of more than 3 million citations to serial articles, book chapters, reports, and reprints. NAL has chosen and is implementing automated indexing/text analytics software to produce its Article Citation Database. This application combines semantic analysis, machine learning, and human rules to automatically assign subject terms to journal articles.

LCA Digital Commons

NAL launched the LCA Digital Commons, a life cycle inventory database, to address the lack of information resources regarding the life cycle of agricultural products. The LCA Digital Commons provides, through a fully searchable Web interface (http://www.lcacommons.gov), peer-reviewed crop production data sets for commodity crops measuring the material and energy flows to and from the environment.

Information Management and Information Technology

Over the past quarter century, NAL has applied increasingly sophisticated information technology to support the ever more complex and demanding information needs of researchers, practitioners, policymakers, and the general public. Technological developments spearheaded by the library date back to the 1940s and 1950s, when NAL Director Ralph Shaw invented "electronic machines" such as the photo charger, rapid selector, and photo clerk. Over the years NAL has made numerous technological improvements, from automating collections information to delivering full-text and image collections digitally on the Internet.

NAL has fully implemented the Voyager integrated library management system from Ex Libris, Ltd. The system supports ordering, receiving, and invoice processing for purchases; creating and maintaining indexing and cataloging records for AGRICOLA; circulating print holdings; and providing a Web-based online catalog for public searching and browsing of the collection. In addition, the system is fully integrated with an automated interlibrary loan and document delivery system by Relais International that streamlines services and provides desktop delivery of needed materials.

English-Spanish Agricultural Thesaurus and Glossary

NAL is known for its expertise in developing and using a thesaurus, or controlled vocabulary, a critical component of effective digital information systems. The NAL Agricultural Thesaurus (NALT) (http://agclass.nal.usda.gov/agt.shtml) is a hierarchical vocabulary of agricultural and biological terms, organized according to 17 subject categories. It comprises primarily biological nomenclature, with additional terminology supporting the physical and social sciences.

The 15th edition of NALT, issued in 2016, contains more than 120,600 terms and nearly 4,950 definitions. Taxonomic terms from every biological kingdom were expanded in this edition, along with common names of species. Plant species were added following taxonomic verification by the Germplasm Resources Information Network (GRIN). Terminology for genetic soil types was modified according to *USDA Keys to Soil Taxonomy, Twelfth Edition,* 2014. Fish taxonomy was expanded following taxonomic verification from Fishbase. Other subject areas expanded include terms in chromatography, receptors, bacteria, fungi, breeds of animals, endangered species, insects, chemicals, enzymes, economics, food, wood, and forestry.

NALT continues to be available as Linked Open Data. NAL can now connect its vocabulary to other linked data vocabularies, which, in turn, will connect NALT to the larger semantic Web. Such interconnections will help programmers create meaningful relationships that will make it easier to locate related content.

Associated with NALT, the NAL Glossary provides definitions of agricultural terms. The 2015 edition contains 4,488 definitions, ranging across agriculture and its many ancillary subjects, an increase of 667 definitions from last year. Most definitions are composed by NALT staff. (Suggestions for new terms or definitions can be sent by e-mail to agref@ars.usda.gov.)

NAL publishes Spanish-language versions of the thesaurus and glossary, which carry the names *Tesauro Agrícola* and *Glosario,* respectively. Both are updated concurrently with the annual release of the English-language version. The 2016 edition of the Spanish-language version of NALT contains more than 96,700 terms and 4,880 definitions.

The thesaurus and glossary are primarily used for indexing and for improving the retrieval of agricultural information, but they can also be used by students (from fifth grade up), teachers, writers, translators, and others who are seeking precise definitions of words from the agricultural sciences. Users can download all four publications—English and Spanish thesaurus and glossary—in both machine-readable (MARC 21, RDF-SKOS, and XML) and human-readable (doc, pdf) formats at http://agclass.nal.usda.gov/download.shtml.

Library Services

NAL serves the agricultural information needs of customers through a combination of Web-based and traditional library services, including reference, document delivery, and information center services. The NAL website offers access to a wide variety of full-text resources, as well as online access to reference and document delivery services. In 2014 the library provided nearly 8,000 reference transactions, fulfilled more than 1.2 million full-text article requests, and satisfied more than 5,000 requests for interlibrary loans.

The main reading room in the library's Beltsville facility features a walk-up service desk, access to an array of digital information resources (including full-text scientific journals), current periodicals, and an on-site request service for materials from NAL's collection. Services are available 8:30 to 4:30 Monday through Friday, except federal holidays.

NAL's reference services are accessible online using the Ask a Question form on the NAL Web pages; by use of e-mail addressed to agref@ars.usda.gov; by telephone at 301-504-5755; or by mail to Research Services, National Agricultural Library ARS/USDA, 10301 Baltimore Avenue, Beltsville, MD 20705. Requesters receive assistance from Research Services staff in all areas and aspects of agriculture, but staff particularly answer questions, provide research guidance, and make presentations on topics not addressed by the seven subject-focused information centers of the library.

NAL's seven information centers are reliable sources of comprehensive, science-based information on key aspects of U.S. agriculture, providing timely, accurate, and in-depth coverage of their specialized subject areas. Their expert staff offer extensive Web-based information resources and advanced reference services. Each NAL information center has its own website and is a partner in AgNIC.

- The Alternative Farming Systems Information Center (AFSIC) (http://afsic.nal.usda.gov) specializes in identifying and accessing information relating to farming methods that maintain the health and productivity of the entire farming enterprise, including the world's natural resources. This focus includes sustainable and alternative agricultural systems, crops, and livestock.

- The Animal Welfare Information Center (AWIC) (http://awic.nal.usda.gov) provides scientific information and referrals to help ensure the proper care and treatment of animals used in biomedical research, testing, teaching, and exhibitions, and by animal dealers. Among its varied outreach activities, the center conducts workshops for researchers on meeting the information requirements of the Animal Welfare Act.

- The Food and Nutrition Information Center (FNIC) (http://fnic.nal.usda.gov) provides credible, accurate, and practical resources for nutrition and health professionals, educators, government personnel, and consumers. FNIC maintains a staff of registered dietitians who can answer questions on food and human nutrition.

- The Food Safety Research Information Office (FSRIO) (http://fsrio.nal.usda.gov) delivers information on publicly funded—and, to the extent possible, privately funded—food safety research initiatives. Its Research Projects Database, with more than 8,500 projects cited, provides ready access to the largest searchable collection of food safety research being conducted within U.S. and international governmental agencies.

- The National Invasive Species Information Center (NISIC) (http://www.invasivespeciesinfo.gov) delivers accessible, accurate, referenced, up-to-date, and comprehensive information on invasive species drawn from federal, state, local, and international sources.

- The Rural Information Center (RIC) (http://ric.nal.usda.gov) assists local officials, organizations, businesses, and rural residents working to maintain the vitality of rural areas. It collects and disseminates information on such diverse topics as community economic development, small business development, health care, finance, housing, environment, quality of life, community leadership, and education.

- The Water Quality Information Center (WQIC) (http://wqic.nal.usda.gov) collects, organizes, and communicates scientific findings, educational methodologies, and public policy issues relating to water quality and agriculture.

In addition to these information centers, NAL manages the popular Nutrition.gov website (http://www.nutrition.gov) in collaboration with other USDA agencies and the Department of Health and Human Services. This site provides vetted, science-based nutrition information for the general consumer and highlights the latest in nutrition news and tools from across federal government agencies. The site is an important tool for disseminating the work of multiple federal agencies in a national obesity prevention effort. A team of registered dietitians at NAL's Food and Nutrition Information Center maintains Nutrition.gov and answers questions on food and nutrition issues.

Web-Based Products and Services

The NAL websites, which encompass nearly all the content and services described here, collectively receive millions of pageviews per month from people seeking agricultural information.

DigiTop

DigiTop, USDA's Digital Desktop Library, delivers the full text of thousands of journals and hundreds of newspapers worldwide, provides 17 agriculturally significant citation databases, supplies a range of digital reference resources, and offers focused, personalized services. Navigator is a component of DigiTop that allows cross-searching of multiple bibliographic databases. This system includes AGRICOLA; AGRIS; BIOSIS; CAB Abstracts; Fish, Fisheries, and Aquatic Biodiversity Worldwide; Food Science and Technology Abstracts; GEOBASE; GeoRef; MEDLINE; Wildlife and Ecology Studies Worldwide; Scopus; and Zoological Record. The Navigator service allows researchers to access nearly 79 million records at once and is updated weekly. DigiTop is available to the entire USDA workforce worldwide—more than 100,000 people—around the clock. NAL staff provide help desk and reference services, continuous user education, and training for DigiTop users.

Document Delivery Services

NAL's document delivery operation responds to thousands of requests each year from USDA employees and from libraries and organizations around the world. NAL uses the Relais Enterprise document request and delivery system to support document delivery. With Relais fully integrated with the Voyager library system, with DigiTop, and with other Open-URL and ISO ILL compliant systems, NAL customers can request materials or check on the status of their requests via the Web, and the needed materials can easily be delivered electronically. Document requests can also be submitted via OCLC (NAL's symbol is AGL) and DOCLINE (NAL's libid is MDUNAL). Visit http://www.nal.usda.gov/services/request.shtml for details.

Networks of Cooperation

The NAL collection and information resources are supplemented by networks of cooperation with other institutions, including arrangements with agricultural libraries at U.S. land-grant universities, other U.S. national libraries, agricultural libraries in other countries, and libraries of the United Nations and other international organizations.

AgNIC

The library serves as secretariat for the Agriculture Network Information Center (AgNIC) Alliance, a voluntary, collaborative partnership that hosts a distributed network of discipline-specific agricultural information websites at http://www.agnic.org. AgNIC provides access to high-quality agricultural information selected by its 53 partner members, which include land-grant universities, NAL, and other institutions globally. Together they offer more than 80 information and subject specialists, more than 60 topics covered comprehensively, and links to more than 5 million full-text and bibliographic items.

AGLINET

Through the Agricultural Libraries Network (AGLINET), NAL serves as the U.S. node of an international agricultural information system that brings together agricultural libraries with strong regional or country coverage and other specialized collections. NAL functions as a gateway to U.S. agricultural libraries and resources, fulfilling requests for information via reciprocal agreements with several other libraries, information centers, and consortia. As an AGLINET member, NAL agrees to provide low-cost interlibrary loan and photocopy service to other AGLINET libraries. Most materials requested through AGLINET are delivered digitally, although reproductions via fiche or photocopy are used when appropriate. AGLINET is administered by the Food and Agriculture Organization of the United Nations.

National Library of Medicine

8600 Rockville Pike, Bethesda, MD 20894
301-496-6308, 888-346-3656, fax 301-496-4450
E-mail publicinfo@nlm.nih.gov
World Wide Web http://www.nlm.nih.gov

Kathleen Cravedi
Director, Office of Communications and Public Liaison

Melanie Modlin
Deputy Director, Office of Communications and Public Liaison

The National Library of Medicine (NLM) is one of the 27 Institutes and Centers of the National Institutes of Health (NIH). Founded in 1836 as the Library of the Surgeon General of the Army, NLM has evolved into the world's largest biomedical library.

In today's increasingly digital world, NLM carries out its mission of enabling biomedical research, supporting health care and public health, and promoting healthy behavior by

- Building and providing electronic information resources used billions of times each year by millions of scientists, health professionals, and members of the public
- Creating and maintaining information systems that provide free public access to results of biomedical research supported by NIH and by other government and private funders
- Supporting and conducting research, development, and training in biomedical informatics, computational biology, data science, and health information technology
- Coordinating a 6,000-member National Network of Libraries of Medicine that promotes and provides access to health information in communities across the United States

Through its information systems, a cutting-edge informatics research portfolio, and extensive partnerships, NLM plays an essential role in catalyzing and supporting the translation of basic science into new treatments, new products, improved practice, useful decision support for health professionals and patients, and effective disaster and emergency preparedness and response.

The range of information that NLM organizes and disseminates is enormous, including genetic, genomic, biochemical, and toxicological data; images; published and unpublished research results; decision support resources; scientific and health data standards; informatics tools for system developers; and health information for the public. Scientists, health professionals, and the public can search or download information directly from an NLM website, find it via an Internet search engine, or use an app that provides value-added access to NLM data. Thousands of commercial and nonprofit system developers regularly use the applications programming interfaces (APIs) that NLM provides to fuel private sector innovation.

Delivering High-Quality Information Services

Central to NLM services is the world's largest, continually expanding collection of biomedical literature in all media and a broad array of authoritative digital databases encompassing information for scientists, health professionals, the public, and the librarians and information specialists who serve them. NLM develops and uses sophisticated information systems to support the complex operations necessary to acquire, describe, index, archive, and provide rapid access to physical and digital materials. Special attention is given to developing systems to build and refine electronic databases and services and to responding to changes in user needs and behaviors.

In 2014 NLM greatly expanded the quantity and range of high-quality information readily available to scientists, health professionals, and the general public. Advances included:

- The indexing of more than 765,000 new journal articles for PubMed/MEDLINE, NLM's most heavily used database, which contains more than 24 million references to articles in the biomedical and life sciences journals and delivers information to about 2 million users a day
- Growth in the PubMed Central (PMC) digital archive, which now provides public access to the full-text versions of more than 3.3 million research articles, including those produced by NIH-funded researchers
- Expansion of ClinicalTrials.gov, which now includes more than 181,000 registered studies and summary results for more than 15,700 trials, including many not available elsewhere
- A doubling of the number of tests in the Genetic Testing Registry, where users can find detailed information on more than 33,000 genetic tests
- More than 20 percent growth in the database of Genotypes and Phenotypes (dbGaP), which connects individual-level genomic data with individual-level clinical information and now contains nearly 600 studies involving more than 840,000 people
- Improved dissemination methods and new tools to aid the use of the U.S. clinical terminology standards required for interoperability of electronic health records

NLM also continued to expand access to its rare and unique historical collections by digitizing rare books, manuscripts, pictures, and historical films. In 2014 a total of 2,460 printed historic books, 4,319 historic images, and 895 manuscripts were digitized and added to NLM's Digital Collections, a free online archive of biomedical books and videos. These collections are heavily used by scholars, the media, and the general public.

As the percentage of users accessing NLM databases with mobile phones and tablets continues to rise, NLM is redesigning many of its Web interfaces so that the information display adjusts automatically to the size of the device. In 2014 the library released new "responsive design" versions of AIDS*info,* the Department of Health and Human Services (HHS) authoritative source of HIV/AIDS treatment and prevention information, and of DailyMed, which includes Food and

Drug Administration (FDA)-approved structured label information for medications marketed in the United States. NLM continued to be a leading player in social media among HHS agencies with active Facebook, Twitter, Flickr, Pinterest, and YouTube accounts (including the very popular @medlineplus Twitter feed and a Spanish-language counterpart), several online newsletters, and its National Network of Libraries of Medicine, which covers the United States and hosts 8 Facebook pages, 10 Twitter feeds, and 12 blogs. NLM is consistently ranked among the most liked, most followed, and most mentioned organizations among small government agencies with social media accounts.

Promoting Public Access to Information

NLM has extensive outreach programs to enhance awareness of its diverse information services among biomedical researchers, health professionals, librarians, patients, and the public. To improve access to high-quality health information, NLM works with the National Network of Libraries of Medicine and has formal partnerships such as Partners in Information Access for the Public Health Workforce and the Environmental Health Information Outreach Partnership with Historically Black Colleges and Universities, tribal colleges, and other minority serving institutions.

The member institutions of the National Network of Libraries of Medicine are valued partners in ensuring that health information, including NLM's many services, is available to scientists, health professionals, and the public. The network is coordinated by eight regional medical libraries and is composed of academic health sciences libraries, hospital libraries, public libraries, and community-based organizations.

In 2014 dozens of community-based projects were funded nationwide to enhance awareness of and access to health information, including in disaster and emergency situations, and to address health literacy issues. As part of its outreach efforts, NLM continually solicits feedback from users on how existing resources can be improved.

NLM also fosters more informal community partnerships and uses exhibitions, the media, and new technologies in its efforts to reach underserved populations and to promote interest among young people in careers in science, medicine, and technology. The library continues to expand its successful traveling exhibitions program as another means to enhance access to its services and promote interest in careers in science and medicine. Examples of these exhibitions include "Every Necessary Care and Attention: George Washington and Medicine" and "Surviving and Thriving: AIDS, Politics, and Culture."

With assistance from other NIH components and outside partners, NLM continues to increase the distribution of *NIH MedlinePlus* magazine, and its Spanish-language counterpart, *NIH Salud.* The magazine, which is also available online in Spanish and English, is distributed to doctors' offices, health science libraries, Congress, the media, federally supported community health centers, select hospital emergency and waiting rooms, and other locations where the public receives health services.

Information Systems, Standards, Research Tools

NLM's advanced information services have long benefitted from its intramural research and development (R&D) programs. The library has two organizations that conduct advanced R&D on different aspects of biomedical informatics: the Lister Hill National Center for Biomedical Communications (LHC) and the National Center for Biotechnology Information (NCBI). Both apply their research results to the development of new information services and tools for scientists, informatics researchers, and software developers.

LHC, established in 1968, conducts and supports research in such areas as the development and dissemination of health information technology standards; the capture, processing, dissemination, and use of high-quality imaging data; medical language processing; high-speed access to biomedical information; and advanced technology for emergency and disaster management.

NCBI, created in 1988, conducts R&D on the representation, integration, and retrieval of molecular biology data and biomedical literature, in addition to providing an integrated, genomic information resource consisting of more than 40 databases for biomedical researchers at NIH and around the world. NCBI's development of large-scale data integration techniques with advanced information systems is key to its expanding ability to support the accelerated pace of research made possible by new technologies such as next-generation DNA sequencing, microarrays, and small molecule screening. GenBank at NCBI, in collaboration with partners in Britain and Japan, is the world's largest annotated collection of publicly available DNA sequences. GenBank contains 175 million sequences from more than 310,000 different species. NCBI's Web services for access to these data provide the information and analytic tools for researchers to accelerate the rate of genomic discovery and facilitate the translation of basic science advances into new diagnostics and treatments.

NLM was also a pioneer in developing and sharing novel medical language resources and innovative algorithms and tools, including the UMLS (Unified Medical Language System), MetaMap, Medical Text Indexer (MTI), and SemRep, to advance research in natural language understanding and biomedical text mining. This research has been applied to indexing, information retrieval, question answering, and literature-based discovery to assist NLM's high-volume data creation and service operations, to help other NIH components to identify and summarize new knowledge useful in updating clinical guidelines, and to add standard terminology and codes to clinical and clinical research data to enhance their research value. NLM has many joint research activities with other NIH components and other federal agencies, including collaborations with FDA to use natural language processing and NLM terminology resources to extract adverse event data from publications indexed for PubMed/MEDLINE and drug-drug interactions from product labels submitted by manufacturers.

NLM has also made advances that will facilitate health information exchange and meaningful use of electronic health records (EHRs). NLM researchers have developed advanced and heavily used APIs for medication data, nomenclature, and high-quality pill images, including information submitted to FDA; produced novel algorithms for validating vocabulary components of electronic clinical quality measure specifications in cooperation with the Centers for Medicare and

Medicaid Services; and analyzed frequency data from multiple private healthcare organizations and the Veterans Health Administration to produce manageable subsets of large standard clinical vocabularies. They have also developed effective techniques for mapping clinical vocabularies to administrative code sets and have established partnerships to test the use and impact of personal health records.

NLM's Personal Health Record (PHR) project has developed open source software components that can be used by PHR and EHR developers to provide capabilities that help individuals to manage health and health care for themselves and their families. The strong use of vocabulary standards in the NLM PHR software components enables many computer-generated features such as personalized reminders, automatic calculation of health measures, and direct links to such information sources as MedlinePlus. The use of standards in these components will also enable the direct importing of the consumer's own data from clinical sources.

Administration

The director of the Library, Donald A. B. Lindberg, M.D., is guided in matters of policy by a board of regents consisting of 10 appointed and 11 ex officio members.

Table 1 / Selected NLM Statistics*

Library Operations	Volume
Collection (book and non-book)	26,648,261
Items cataloged	18,755
Serial titles received	17,439
Articles indexed for MEDLINE	765,850
Circulation requests processed	259,285
For interlibrary loan	188,912
For on-site users	70,373
MEDLINE/PubMed Searches	2,650,894,898
Budget Authority	$328,000,000
Staff	830

*For fiscal year ending September 30, 2014

National Technical Information Service

U.S. Department of Commerce, Alexandria, VA 22312
800-553-NTIS (6847) or 703-605-6000
World Wide Web http://www.ntis.gov

The National Technical Information Service (NTIS) is the nation's largest and most comprehensive source of government-funded scientific, technical, engineering, and business information produced or sponsored by U.S. and international government sources. NTIS is a federal agency within the U.S. Department of Commerce.

Since 1945 the NTIS mission has been to operate a central U.S. government access point for scientific and technical information useful to American industry and government. NTIS maintains a permanent archive of this declassified information for researchers, businesses, and the public to access quickly and easily. Release of the information is intended to promote U.S. economic growth and development and to increase U.S. competitiveness in the world market.

The NTIS collection of approximately 3 million titles covers more than 350 subject areas and contains products available in various formats. Such information includes reports describing research conducted or sponsored by federal agencies and their contractors; statistical and business information; multimedia training programs; databases developed by federal agencies; and technical reports prepared by research organizations worldwide. NTIS maintains a permanent repository of its information products.

More than 200 U.S. government agencies contribute to the NTIS collection, including the National Aeronautics and Space Administration; the Environmental Protection Agency; the departments of Agriculture, Commerce, Defense, Energy, Health and Human Services, Homeland Security, Interior, Labor, Treasury, Veterans Affairs, Housing and Urban Development, Education, and Transportation; and numerous other agencies. International contributors include Canada, Japan, Britain, and several European countries.

NTIS on the Web

NTIS offers Web-based access to information on government scientific and technical research products. Visitors to http://www.ntis.gov can search the entire collection dating back to 1964 free of charge. NTIS provides many of the technical reports for purchase on CD, paper copies, or downloaded pdf files. RSS feeds of recently catalogued materials are available in major subject categories.

NTIS Database

The NTIS Database offers unparalleled bibliographic coverage of U.S. government and worldwide government-sponsored research information products acquired by NTIS since 1964. Its contents represent hundreds of billions of research dollars and cover a range of important topics including agriculture, biotechnology, business, communication, energy, engineering, the environment, health and safety, medicine, research and development, science, space, technology, and transportation.

The NTIS Database can be leased directly from NTIS and can also be accessed through several commercial services. To lease the NTIS Database directly from NTIS, contact the NTIS Office of Product Management at 703-605-6515.

NTIS National Technical Reports Library

The National Technical Reports Library (NTRL) enhances accessibility to the NTIS technical reports collection. Subscription rates are based on institutional FTE levels. NTRL operates on a system interface that allows users to do queries on the large NTIS bibliographic database. The intent is to broadly expand and improve access to more than 2.5 million bibliographic records (pre-1960 to the present) and more than 700,000 full-text documents in pdf format that are directly linked to that bibliographic database.

NTIS offers several valuable research-oriented database products. To find out more about accessing the databases, visit http://www.ntis.gov/products/ntrl.

AGRICOLA

As one of the most comprehensive sources of U.S. agricultural and life sciences information, the AGRICOLA (Agricultural Online Access) Database contains bibliographic records for documents acquired by the U.S. Department of Agriculture's National Agricultural Library. It is available at http://www.ntis.gov/products/databases/agricola.

Energy Science and Technology

The Energy Science and Technology Database (EDB) is a multidisciplinary file containing worldwide references to basic and applied scientific and technical research literature. The information is collected for use by government managers, researchers at the national laboratories, and other research efforts sponsored by the U.S. Department of Energy, and the results of this research are transferred to the public. The database is available at http://www.ntis.gov/products/databases/energy-science-technology.

FEDRIP

The Federal Research in Progress Database (FEDRIP) provides access to information about ongoing federally funded projects in such fields as the physical sciences, engineering, and life sciences. To access FEDRIP, go to http://www.ntis.gov/products/databases/federal-research-in-progress.

Online Subscriptions

NTIS offers quick, convenient online access, on a subscription basis, to the following resources:

U.S. Export Administration Regulations

U.S. Export Administration Regulations (EAR) provides the latest rules controlling the export of U.S. dual-use commodities, technology, and software. Step by step, EAR explains when an export license is necessary and when it is not, how to obtain an export license, policy changes as they are issued, new restrictions on exports to certain countries and of certain types of items, and where to obtain further help.

This information is available through NTIS in loose-leaf form, on CD-ROM, and online. An e-mail update notification service is also available.

World News Connection

World News Connection (WNC) was an NTIS online news service accessible via the World Wide Web. It made available English-language translations of time-sensitive news and information culled from non-U.S. media in more than 100 countries. WNC was provided by the Open Source Center (OSC), operated by the Central Intelligence Agency (CIA), and its content was updated throughout every government business day. It was made available by NTIS through the Dialog Corporation. The service ceased operation at the end of 2013.

Special Subscription Services

NTIS eAlerts

More than 1,000 new titles are added to the NTIS collection every week. NTIS prepares a list of search criteria that is run against all new studies and research and development reports in 16 subject areas. An NTIS eAlert provides a twice-monthly information briefing service, by e-mail, covering a wide range of technology topics. For more information, call the NTIS Subscriptions Department at 703-605-6060.

NTIS Selected Research Service

NTIS Selected Research Service (SRS) is a tailored information service that delivers complete electronic copies of government publications based on customers' needs, automatically, within a few weeks of announcement by NTIS. SRS includes the full bibliographic information in XML and HTML formats. Users choose between Standard SRS (selecting one or more of the 320 existing subject areas) or Custom SRS, which creates a new subject area to meet their particular needs. Custom SRS requires a one-time fee to cover the cost of strategy development and computer programming to set up a profile. Except for this fee, the cost of Custom SRS is the same as the Standard SRS. Through this ongoing subscription service, customers download copies of new reports pertaining to their field(s) of interest as NTIS obtains the reports. To place an order, call 800-363-2068 or 703-605-6060.

This service is also available in CD-ROM format as Science and Technology on CD, which delivers the documents digitized and stored in pdf format.

Federal Science Repository Service

Collections of scientific and technical documents, images, videos, and other content represent the mission and work of an agency or other institution. To help preserve these collections, NTIS formed a joint venture with Information International Associates, Inc. of Oak Ridge, Tennessee, to develop for federal agencies a searchable, digital Federal Science Repository Service (FSRS). FSRS provides a supporting infrastructure, long-term storage, security, interface design, and content management and operational expertise. An agency can utilize this entire service or select components, resulting in the design of an agency-specific repository that serves as a distinct gateway to its content. For more information, visit http://www.ntis.gov/products/fsrs.

NTIS Customer Service

NTIS's automated systems make shopping online at NTIS safe and secure. Electronic document storage is fully integrated with NTIS's order-taking process, allowing it to provide rapid reproduction for the most recent additions to the NTIS document collection. Most orders for shipment are filled and delivered anywhere in the United States in five to seven business days. Rush service is available for an additional fee.

Key NTIS Contacts for Ordering

Order by Phone

Sales Desk 800-553-6847 or 703-605-6000
8:00 A.M.–6:00 P.M. Eastern time, Monday–Friday

Subscriptions 800-363-2068 or 703-605-6060
8:30 A.M.–5:00 P.M. Eastern time, Monday–Friday
TDD (hearing impaired only) 703-487-4639
8:30 A.M.–5:00 P.M. Eastern time, Monday–Friday

Order by Fax

24 hours a day, seven days a week 703-605-6900

Order by Mail

National Technical Information Service
5301 Shawnee Rd.
Alexandria, VA 22312

RUSH Service (available for an additional fee) 800-553-6847 or 703-605-6000
Note: If requesting RUSH Service, please do not mail your order

Order Online

Direct and secure online ordering http://www.ntis.gov

United States Government Publishing Office

732 North Capitol St. N.W., Washington, DC 20401
World Wide Web http://www.gpo.gov

Gary Somerset

Media and Public Relations Manager
202-512-1957, e-mail gsomerset@gpo.gov

The U.S. Government Printing Office (GPO) was created when President James Buchanan signed Joint Resolution 25 on June 23, 1860. GPO opened its doors for business nine months later on March 4, 1861, the same day Abraham Lincoln took the oath of office to become the 16th president of the United States. On that day GPO began operation in buildings purchased by Congress, at the same address it occupies today.

A historic moment occurred for GPO in December 2014 when President Barack Obama signed into law a bill changing the agency's name to the U.S. Government *Publishing* Office. The new name reflects the increasingly prominent role that GPO plays in providing access to government information in digital formats through GPO's Federal Digital System (FDsys), apps, e-books, and related technologies. The information needs of Congress, federal agencies, and the public have evolved beyond only print, and GPO has transformed itself to meet its customers' needs.

Under Title 44 of the United States Code, GPO is responsible for the production and distribution of information products for all three branches of the federal government. These include the official publications of Congress, federal agencies, and the courts. Today GPO provides products in print and a variety of digital forms, all of which are born digital. In addition GPO produces passports for the Department of State and secure credentials for many government agencies.

As the federal government's official, digital, secure resource for gathering, producing, cataloging, providing access to, and preserving published information in all forms, GPO has disseminated millions of publications to the public.

GPO's Superintendent of Documents and its Library Services and Content Management (LSCM) organizations administer and manage the four programs required by Title 44:

- The Federal Depository Library Program (FDLP)
- Cataloging and indexing (C&I)
- Distributing government publications to the International Exchange Service
- The By-Law Program, under which certain government publications are distributed to members of Congress and to other government agencies as mandated by law

FDLP dates back to 1813 when Congress first authorized legislation to ensure the provision of certain congressional documents to selected universities, historical societies, and state libraries. At that time, the secretary of state was responsible for distributing publications. In 1857 the secretary of the interior assumed oversight of printing and the designation of depositories. In the Printing Act of 1895 the governance of the depository program was transferred to the Office of the Superintendent of Documents at GPO. Duties remained largely unchanged until 1993, when Public Law 103-40, the Government Printing Office Electronic Information Access Enhancement Act, amended GPO's duties to not only provide public access to printed publications but to Internet-accessible publications as well. Two centuries after the start of FDLP, the program continues to serve a vital need of the public through the partnership with federal depository libraries located in nearly every congressional district.

GPO is obviously a much different agency in the digital age than it was years ago. While its name has changed, its mission—"Keeping America Informed" is as important and relevant as ever. FDLP and GPO's information dissemination programs are examples of the agency's longstanding commitment to permanent public access to U.S. government information.

Collaboration

Digital Partnerships with Federal Depository Libraries

Since 1997 GPO has developed strategic partnerships with federal depository libraries and other federal agencies to increase access to electronic federal information. All branches of federal government are transitioning away from print, and federal materials are coming to GPO for publishing. This is due to budgetary pressures, open government initiatives, and increasing access to electronic solutions.

One avenue to address this has been to develop strategic partnerships to ensure permanent public access to electronic content, assist depositories in providing access to electronic material, and help libraries better manage their depository collections. Partnerships also allow GPO to take advantage of the expertise and services of federal depository librarians and federal agencies.

Partnership Updates

GPO currently maintains partnerships with sixteen depository libraries, eight federal agencies, and two institutions. During fiscal year (FY) 2014 LSCM signed three new partnership agreements:

- University of North Texas (UNT)—This partnership ensures permanent public access to the university's large current and future digital collections of U.S. government content that are within scope of FDLP. These collections now contain approximately 50,000 federal government information products on a wide range of interesting topics. Notable examples are World War II newsmaps; documents on early aircraft, engines, and more from the National Advisory Committee for Aeronautics; and annual reports from the U.S. Department of Agriculture's experiment stations from 1901 to 1954. Under the agreement, GPO guarantees public access to these materials in perpetuity.
- University of Colorado, Boulder—This is a cooperative cataloging partnership. The university is creating bibliographic records for historic publications from the U.S. Geological Survey Bulletins series and the Bureau of

Mines Reports of Investigations series. GPO will enhance the records by verifying the Superintendent of Documents Classification System (SuDoc) number and performing needed authority work to the subject headings and corporate names. The records will then be available through GPO's Catalog of U.S. Government Publications (CGP) and OCLC.

- Boston Public Library (BPL)—In commemoration of the 50th anniversary of the release of the Warren Commission report on the assassination of President John F. Kennedy, GPO made the complete report and the 26 volumes of hearings testimony available on FDsys through a partnership with BPL. The hearing transcripts were digitized by BPL. This partnership ensures permanent public access to Warren Commission resources.

During FY 2014 LSCM renewed one partnership:

- University of Illinois at Chicago—This partnership ensures permanent public access to the content in DOSFAN, a digital library of electronically archived information produced by the U.S. Department of State from 1990 to 1997 that includes the archived websites of the U.S. Arms Control and Disarmament Agency and the U.S. Information Agency.

Work continued on several cooperative cataloging partnerships:

- University of Florida—LSCM's partnership with the University of Florida combines cooperative cataloging and permanent public access to digitized content. As material is digitized, the university will share bibliographic records with GPO. Records will be added to CGP, and records for the digitized versions will be created with persistent URLs (PURLs). During FY 2014 work was completed on more than 1,600 bibliographic records for titles from the National Recovery Administration.
- University of Iowa—LSCM completed work to convert the University of Iowa's Dublin Core records for their digitized poster collection to 1,454 MARC records. Each poster was also assigned a PURL, and these records are available through CGP.
- University of Montana—LSCM began working with the university's Mansfield Library in 2011 to add bibliographic records to CGP for historic U.S. Forest Service publications. Mansfield Library staff members create bibliographic records for Forest Service publications and submit them to LSCM. Cataloging and classification staff at LSCM verify the SuDoc class and item number and add subject and corporate name headings to the records. As a result of this partnership, more than 1,900 Forest Service records have been added to CGP.
- University of North Texas—LSCM's partnership with the university combines cooperative cataloging and permanent public access to digitized content. During FY 2014 LSCM staff created or updated bibliographic records for titles in the following university digital collections: Federal Register, Congressional Record, World War I, Government Documents General, World War II Newsmaps, and U.S. Experiment Station Reports.

GPO and DPLA

GPO also developed a new partnership with the Digital Public Library of America (DPLA), a repository of digitized content from U.S. libraries, archives, and museums, all available to the public free of charge. In September 2014 GPO and DPLA partnered to increase public access to government information made available through CGP. More than 150,000 records from CGP are available to the public via the DPLA website (http://dp.la). Examples of records include the federal budget; federal laws, such as the Patient Protection and Affordable Care Act; federal regulations; transcripts of congressional hearings; and reports and other documents. GPO continuously adds records to CGP, which will also be available through DPLA, increasing public discoverability of and access to federal government information. GPO adds approximately 1,000 new records to DPLA each month.

During the year LSCM staff participated in and collaborated with a number of outside groups in support of FDLP and the Cataloging and Indexing Program, including CENDI and the CENDI Policy Working Group (CENDI is an interagency working group of senior scientific and technical information managers representing 14 U.S. federal agencies): the CENDI Digitization Specifications Working Group, Ex Libris Users of North America, the Federal Agencies Digitization Guidelines Initiative (FADGI) Preservation Working Group, the FADGI Audio-Visual Working Group, the FADGI Still Image Digitization Working Group, the FADGI Still Image File Format Working Group, the Federal Library and Information Network (FEDLINK), the American Indian Libraries Initiative, the Federal Web Archiving Coordination Group (National Archives and Records Administration, Library of Congress, and GPO), the International Internet Preservation Consortium, the National Digital Strategy Advisory Board, OCLC, the Program for Cooperative Cataloging (Library of Congress), the Science.gov Alliance, the Society of American Archivists, and the Society for Imaging Science and Technology.

Key GPO Tools

Federal Digital System (FDsys)

GPO's Federal Digital System (FDsys) (http://www.fdsys.gov) provides free online access to official publications from the three branches of the federal government. The content in FDsys is available in multiple formats including pdf, XML, audio, and photographs. FDsys provides access to digitized historical content and serial publications that are updated daily.

GPO adds content to FDsys regularly and continuously implements enhancements to system functionality. FDsys offers the public access to approximately 50 collections of government information, and more than 10 million documents are indexed by the FDsys search engine. As of September 2014 FDsys provided access to more than 856,000 searchable online titles and received an average of 34 million retrievals a month.

Catalog of U.S. Government Publications (CGP)

Under the requirements of sections 1710 and 1711 of Title 44, GPO is charged with cataloging a comprehensive index of public documents issued or published by the federal government that are not confidential in character. The goals of the Cataloging and Indexing Program are to:

- Develop a comprehensive and authoritative national bibliography of U.S. government publications
- Increase the visibility and use of government information products
- Create a premier destination for information searchers

This undertaking serves libraries and the public nationwide and enables people to locate desired government publications in all formats. The main public interface for the access of cataloging records is CGP.

The identification and creation of online bibliographic catalog records for new U.S. federal government publications, in all published formats, is accomplished through daily operations. A separate retrospective effort is necessary to build online bibliographic records for historical and fugitive (uncataloged but relevant) materials. This effort is known as the National Bibliographic Records Inventory Initiative (NBRII).

NBRII endeavors to provide an online bibliographic record or serial holding record for historical records not currently captured in CGP. These records include:

- Fugitive materials, with a focus on publications issued prior to 1976
- Older publications where bibliographic records exist only in a non-electronically available resource, such as a catalog card or other paper bibliographic record.
- Materials that were previously cataloged with such minimal information that they require critical record enhancement to reach a full-level bibliographic record

Enhancement/Progression/Innovation

Notable additions to FDsys during FY 2014 included the following:

Warren Commission Report and Hearings

GPO made available the official, digital version of the Warren Commission hearings on FDsys in FY 2014. Georgetown University's Lauinger Library provided a copy of the report to GPO for digitizing, and the Boston Public Library digitized the 26 hearing volumes. The commission was created by President Lyndon Johnson and chaired by Chief Justice Earl Warren and presented its findings on September 24, 1964. The commission also released 26 volumes of hearing transcripts, produced by GPO, composed of testimony from 550 witnesses and other evidence.

U.S. Courts Opinions Collection

GPO enhanced the U.S. Courts Opinions Collection by providing public access to the opinions of the U.S. Court of International Trade, along with the opinions of 31 additional courts (appellate courts, bankruptcy courts, and district courts). The number of courts available on FDsys was expanded from the initial 29 courts in FY 2012 to 95 by the end of FY 2014. The collection saw almost 51 million content retrievals on FDsys for FY 2014.

U.S. House of Representatives Bill Summaries

In February 2014 GPO partnered with the Library of Congress to make House of Representatives bill summaries available in XML format for bulk data download from FDsys. Bill summaries are prepared by the Library of Congress's Congressional Research Service and describe the most significant provisions of a piece of legislation. They also detail the effects the legislative text may have on current law and federal programs. The bill summaries are part of the FDsys bulk data repository starting with the 113th Congress. Making House bill summaries available in XML permits data to be reused and repurposed for mobile Web applications, data mashups, and other analytical tools by third party providers, which contributes to openness and transparency in government. This project commenced at the direction of the House Appropriations Committee and is in support of the task force on bulk data established by the House.

CIA Audiobook

GPO made an audiobook available for the first time on FDsys in FY 2014. Published by the Central Intelligence Agency (CIA), the audiobook, "Getting to Know the President: Intelligence Briefings of Presidential Candidates, 1952–2004," is a historical account of the information-sharing process between the intelligence community and presidential candidates and presidents-elect during campaigns and administration transitions. The audiobook is available in an MP3 format on FDsys.

Historic Bound Congressional Record

GPO has been collaborating with the Library of Congress to digitize volumes of the Bound Congressional Record dating from 1873 to 1998 and to provide access through FDsys. The entire Digitized Bound Congressional Record (DBCR) project, covering the period 1873 to 1998, contains approximately 2,085 parts and a total of 2.6 million pages. The digitized content must be reviewed and descriptive content metadata must be identified and recorded prior to providing access on FDsys. As of the end of FY 2014 nearly all volumes of the Bound Congressional Record had been digitized.

Cataloging and CGP Accomplishments

GPO Among Top Ten Original Catalogers

GPO was again named one of the world's top ten original catalogers in OCLC's annual report for FY 2013 (released in FY 2014). During FY 2013 GPO added 13,793 new records for U.S. government information products to WorldCat, a database of bibliographic information built by libraries around the world and OCLC.

GPO was a founding member of the OCLC network in 1976, and has reached several important milestones as an active contributor to WorldCat. In 1992 a GPO cataloger contributed the 100,000th record to the OCLC Bibliographic Database, and in 1999 another GPO cataloger contributed the 43,000,000th record.

National Bibliographic Records Inventory

Projects associated with the National Bibliographic Records Inventory in FY 2014 included the following:

- Historic Shelflist Transcription—LSCM continued transcribing all non-OCLC cards in its historic shelflist. Contract staff transcribe the shelflist cards, check in serial issues, and add Library of Congress subject headings and corporate name authority to records. By the end of FY 2014 there were 157,623 shelflist records available through CGP.
- Monthly Catalog Transcription—Beginning in January 2013 LSCM initiated an effort to transcribe entries from volumes of the *Monthly Catalog of U.S. Government Publications.* In FY 2014 transcription of entries from the 1895 and 1898 volumes was completed. More than 9,600 Monthly Catalog records are available through CGP.
- Serials Management Plan—In FY 2014 more than 54,770 serial issues were checked into CGP, and 559 publication patterns were created for serial titles. In addition, 785 previously uncataloged serial titles were identified, and new bibliographic records for those titles were created and added to CGP.
- LSCM Internal Manual Records Conversion—Beginning in June 2013 GPO staff have been adding information for historic and current serial issues of government publications from internal GPO sources of CGP. In FY 2014 information for 41,500 historic serial issues of U.S. government publications from internal GPO sources were added to CGP.

E-Books Added to FDLP

In February 2014 GPO introduced more than 100 titles in new e-book formats to FDLP. The new formats, MOBI and EPUB, are available to the public free of charge using CGP. All e-book titles available through CGP are federal publications of public interest or educational value within the scope of Title 44, sections 1902–1903. The titles made available through this program were previously self-distributed on federal websites and available to the public at no cost; they join the growing number of online resources that have been a vital part of FDLP for more than 20 years.

By the end of FY 2014 more than 150 e-book titles were available through CGP through this program. More information is available at FDLP.gov's e-books page.

Resource Description and Access

After the successful implementation of Resource Description and Access (RDA) in early 2013 Library Technical Services librarians engaged in training and outreach to the FDLP community in 2014 to assist in RDA application. GPO librarians presented three webinars in GPO's Library Technical Services Webinar and

Webcast Series, all of which cover the interpretation of RDA for government documents—Congressional Publications: An Overview; Name Authority Records in RDA; and Archiving and Cataloging Federal Agency Websites.

Cataloging Record Distribution Program

The Cataloging Record Distribution Program (CRDP) continued in FY 2014 through a contract with MARCIVE, Inc. Through this program, 82 libraries receive free bibliographic records that correspond to their item number selection profile. The annual survey of participants validated the success of the program, with nearly all of the libraries indicating that the CRDP meets expectations and increases access to government information or has made it easier for the libraries to provide it.

FDLP Academy

FDLP Academy was launched by LSCM in FY 2014 as a new resource for educational tools on government information. This educational program was created to support the FDLP community and to advance federal government information literacy. The mission of FDLP Academy is to create and deliver enhanced educational opportunities to the FDLP community by fostering collaboration, by facilitating knowledge sharing, and through the application of new methods and use of multiple media.

FDLP Academy enhances federal government information knowledge through events and conferences coordinated by GPO and webinars and webcasts on a wide variety of government information topics. Many sessions are presented by GPO staff, while others are presented by staff from other federal agencies and from members of the FDLP community, as recruited and hosted by GPO.

Through this program, 51 live webinars were presented to 3,803 attendees, eight recorded webcasts had more than 900 views, and four live classroom sessions attracted 41 attendees during the fiscal year. Collaborators with GPO through this program have included representatives of the U.S. Department of Energy, the U.S. Census Bureau, the National Institutes of Health, the U.S. Department of Health and Human Services, the National Oceanic and Atmospheric Administration, and many more.

FDLP Academy resources include

- An FDLP Events Calendar with information on upcoming events and related registration information
- A Webinars and Webcasts Archive with links to recordings and handouts of all past webinars and webcasts, categorized by learning track (FDsys, GPO, Agency, or FDLP Community)
- An Events and Conferences page with information about GPO's annual FDLP events
- An Events and Conferences Archive with links to recordings and handouts of all past FDLP events and conferences that have been broadcast virtually
- A collection of FDsys training videos

- A form to request specialized training or to volunteer to share expertise through a webinar hosted by GPO

Web Archiving Initiative

GPO continues to be an Archive-It partner for website-level harvesting and has made a number of advances in collection development. LSCM staff members have completed archiving the websites of the Y3 SuDoc classification scheme, which encompasses the committees, commissions, and independent agencies, and have begun to develop a concept for special collections of online content. The first effort began as a request from the Superintendent of Documents to archive federal Web resources that would be beneficial to the Native American community. LSCM envisions similar special collections in the future.

Since the beginning of this program, LSCM staff have focused on increasing the number and types of agencies being archived. LSCM also wants to focus on maintenance of existing collections by completing regular crawls. A workflow has been developed for improving the frequency of crawls on existing collections, and implementation began in FY 2014.

LSCM continues to welcome nominations for Web archiving. The FDLP community can nominate websites through a number of avenues, including Document Discovery, askGPO, or through a direct e-mail to LSCM's Web Archiving team.

The current size of GPO's collection in Archive-It is 3.5 terabytes with more than 24 million documents crawled. There are 57 agencies represented on GPO's Archive-It site and 65 records in CGP.

To avoid duplication of effort, GPO has worked with other federal agencies that are Web archiving in order to foster better communication and cooperation relating to long-term preservation and access initiatives.

In fall 2014 GPO joined with the Library of Congress and the National Archives and Records Administration in forming a Federal Web Archiving Working Group. The group meets monthly to discuss Web archiving strategies and coordinated efforts. Members plan to expand outreach and communication efforts in 2015.

There is an extensive project page on FDLP.gov that provides more information and FAQs on the Web archiving program.

Recognizing Depository Libraries

On April 30, 2014, during the Depository Library Council Meeting and Federal Depository Library Conference, GPO recognized four libraries for their achievements and initiatives in 2013 and 2014. These "libraries of the year" were selected for their leadership, educational outreach, and commitment to providing free public access to federal government information.

These were the honorees:

The University of Iowa Libraries, the state's regional depository library, was honored for its successful blending of partnerships and projects within the institution, the local community, GPO, and the nation. The libraries were found to be exemplary in their cataloging and preservation initiatives. One project included the identification, cataloging, and digitization of nearly 1,500 large-format posters issued by the federal government.

The Ottenheimer Library at the University of Arkansas, Little Rock, was honored for its leadership in scholarship activities that promote government information and depository libraries nationwide. The library is a leader in coordinating federal documents activities at the state level. It was instrumental in acquiring support and financing for the online U.S. Congressional Serial Set while continuing to preserve and maintain the tangible volumes on campus under a cooperative agreement with other institutions in the area.

The State Library of Arizona was honored for its active participation in the electronic distribution of online cataloging records project, creation of the state master plan for depository libraries, and collaboration in the development of a biennial multi-state virtual depository library conference.

Brooklyn College Library was honored for its leadership and mentoring activities for library staff in the greater New York City area. The library provides access and staff with expertise for a wide range of tangible and electronic resources for the public, providing a basis for transitioning from a traditional to a modern library.

Depository Library Spotlight

GPO Depository Library Spotlight highlights a federal depository library and describes the unique services it offers. This feature appears on the GPO website, gpo. gov, and in the *FDLP Connection* newsletter.

The following depositories were highlighted in FY 2014: Hesburgh Libraries, University of Notre Dame; San Diego Public Library; Las Vegas Library of the Las Vegas-Clark County Library District; and Arizona State University Libraries.

LSCM Metrics

Notable LSCM Metrics for FY 2014:

- New titles acquired (online and tangible): 13,384
- Number of serial issues checked in: 64,779
- Searches of CGP: 25,605,364
- Total titles cataloged: 13,697
- Total PURLs created: 11,345
- Total titles distributed: 6,193
- Total copies distributed: 1,363,635
- Number of federal depository libraries: 1,174
- Total titles available through GPO: 1,286,466

Public Access Assessment

Regular communication and consultation between individual depository libraries and GPO staff strengthen and benefit FDLP. A Public Access Assessment (PAA) is a review by a GPO librarian of an individual federal depository library's operation and services; it is one of the significant ways in which GPO communicates and shares information with individual libraries in FDLP. PAAs are intended to support each library through sharing of best practices, recognition of notable achievements, and recommendations so the library can continue enhancing its operation and services. The assessment involves a review of library documentation and a conference call with depository library personnel.

GPO also performs PAAs, pursuant to 44 U.S.C. §19, to ensure that resources distributed to federal depository libraries are readily accessible to all library users, including the general public, and that libraries are complying with requirements and regulations outlined in "Legal Requirements and Program Regulations of the Federal Depository Library Program." If necessary, GPO advises libraries on how to reach greater compliance and requests related follow-up action. Information about PAAs is available to depository library personnel in featured newsletter articles, a webcast, and an FDLP.gov guidance article. In FY 2014 GPO completed 107 PAAs in Colorado, Indiana, Louisiana, Montana, Nevada, New York, Oklahoma, Pennsylvania, Tennessee, and Wisconsin.

National Archives and Records Administration

700 Pennsylvania Ave. N.W., Washington, DC 20408
202-357-5000
World Wide Web http://www.archives.gov

The National Archives and Records Administration (NARA), an independent federal agency, is the nation's record keeper. NARA safeguards and preserves the important records of all three branches of the federal government so that the people can discover, use, and learn from this documentary heritage. NARA ensures continuing access to records that document the rights of American citizens, the actions of government officials, and the history of the nation.

NARA carries out its mission through a national network of archives and records centers stretching from Boston to San Francisco and Atlanta to Seattle, in addition to 13 presidential libraries that document administrations back to that of Herbert Hoover—a total of 46 facilities nationwide.

The agency includes the National Historical Publications and Records Commission (NHPRC), the grant-making arm of NARA; the Office of the Federal Register, which publishes the official records of the actions of the government; the Information Security Oversight Office (ISOO), which oversees the government's classification programs; the National Declassification Center (NDC), which is streamlining the declassification process; and the Office of Government Information Services (OGIS), which reviews agencies' Freedom of Information Act (FOIA) administration and practices.

NARA also assists federal agencies, the courts, and Congress in documenting their activities by providing records storage, offering reference service, administering records management programs, scheduling records, and retiring non-current records to federal records centers. NARA also provides training, advice, and guidance on many issues relating to records management.

NARA's constituents and stakeholders include educators and their students at all levels, a history-minded public, family historians, the media, the archival community, and a broad spectrum of professional associations and researchers in such fields as history, political science, law, library and information services, and genealogy.

The size and breadth of NARA's holdings are staggering. NARA's electronic records holdings amount to nearly 700 terabytes of data, which includes the 2010 census. This consists of records that were "born digital" and managed in a digital form throughout their life cycle.

In addition, NARA maintains traditional holdings that will be converted to digital form for preservation purposes and to ensure access to them far into the future. This, along with the ever-growing quantity of "born digital" records, creates a big data challenge for NARA and the federal government.

NARA's current traditional holdings include more than 11 billion pages, 18 million maps, 50 million photographs, 600,000 artifacts, and 360,000 motion picture films. In addition, 18 Federal Records Centers (FRCs), located around the country, provide storage for about 69 billion pages of non-current records for 400 federal agencies.

NARA is currently operating under a Strategic Plan for fiscal years 2014 to 2018, which sets its long-term objectives. It has four strategic goals: Make Access

Happen, Connect with Customers, Maximize NARA's Value to the Nation, and Build Our Future Through Our People. Specific initiatives are under way at NARA to reach each goal.

Records and Access

Information Security Oversight Office

The Information Security Oversight Office (ISOO) is responsible to the president for policy and oversight of the government-wide security classification system, the National Industrial Security Program, and the emerging federal policy on "controlled unclassified" information. ISOO receives policy and program guidance from the assistant to the president for national security affairs and National Security Council staff in the Executive Office of the President.

ISOO oversees the security classification programs (classification, safeguarding, and declassification) in both government and industry. It is also responsible for exercising NARA's authorities and responsibilities as the executive agent for controlled unclassified information. ISOO contributes materially to the effective implementation of the government-wide security classification program and has a direct impact on the performance of thousands of government employees and contract personnel who work with classified national security information. For more information on ISOO, visit http://www.archives.gov/isoo.

National Declassification Center

In December 2009 President Barack Obama directed an overhaul of how documents created by the federal government are classified and declassified. This initiative aims at promoting transparency and accountability of government. The president also directed the creation of the National Declassification Center (NDC), located within NARA.

NDC is leading the streamlining of the declassification process throughout the federal government. In particular, it is accelerating the processing of historically valuable classified records in which more than one federal agency has an interest. NDC met the president's initial December 31, 2013, goal for the center by successfully addressing referrals and quality assurance problems within the backlog of 352 million pages of accessioned federal records at NARA that were previously subject to automatic declassification. NDC maintained that momentum by meeting its 2014 and 2015 quality assurance goals as well.

NDC also oversees the development of common declassification processes among agencies, and it is prioritizing declassification based on public interest and the likelihood of declassification. For more information about NDC, go to http://www.archives.gov/declassification.

Office of Government Information Services

OGIS's role as the FOIA Ombudsman encompasses a full range of activities, including daily interaction with customers, strategic outreach, and communications and training programs. OGIS also provides dispute resolution training for the

FOIA staff of federal agencies, and it works closely with key FOIA stakeholders, including the requester community and open-government advocates.

The Open Government Act of 2007 created OGIS with three statutorily defined functions. OGIS offers mediation services to help resolve FOIA disputes. It reviews agency FOIA policies, procedures, and compliance. And it makes recommendations to Congress and the president to improve the administration of FOIA as necessary.

As part of the second Open Government National Action Plan, the OGIS director chairs the FOIA Federal Advisory Committee. There are ten members from within government and ten nongovernmental members who have considerable FOIA expertise. The FOIA Advisory Committee works to improve focus on three key issues: oversight and accountability of agency FOIA programs, FOIA fees, and proactive disclosures.

For more information about OGIS, visit http://ogis.archives.gov or follow OGIS on Twitter @FOIA_Ombuds.

Electronic Records Archives

The Electronic Records Archives (ERA) system captures electronic records and information, regardless of format, saves them permanently, and provides access to them. ERA development was completed at the end of fiscal year (FY) 2011, and ERA moved to an operations and maintenance phase at the beginning of FY 2012.

The focus then shifted to increasing the use of ERA by federal departments and agencies in anticipation of ERA becoming mandatory by the end of 2012 for federal agency use in scheduling and transferring permanent electronic records to NARA. The adoption of ERA by federal agencies has led to the transfer of increasing volumes of electronic records to NARA for preservation and eventual access through its public access portal, the National Archives Catalog (NAC).

From 2013 through 2015 NARA made several improvements to better meet the needs of all stakeholders that rely on the ERA system to schedule, transfer, preserve, and provide access to the permanently valuable digital heritage of the federal government.

In early 2016 ERA held 670 terabytes of information in electronic form. For 2016 NARA will continue to evolve the ERA system to improve its capabilities and performance to meet the growing challenges in preserving and providing access to electronic records. For more information about ERA, see http://www.archives.gov/era.

Applied Research Division

NARA's Applied Research Division serves as the agency's center for advanced and applied research capabilities in the fields of computer science, engineering, and archival science. The division's staff conducts research on new technologies, both to be aware of new types of electronic record formats that will need to be preserved and to evaluate new technologies that might be incorporated into electronic records management and preservation systems at NARA to increase their effectiveness. The staff also helps NARA managers and employees acquire the knowledge and skills they need to function effectively in e-government through presentations on new technologies. For more information, visit http://www.archives.gov/applied-research.

National Archives Catalog

Today anyone with a computer connected to the Internet can search descriptions of more than 86 percent of NARA's nationwide holdings and view digital copies of some of its most popular documents through NARA's updated National Archives Catalog. By the end of 2016 NARA will have 95 percent of its vast holdings described in the catalog. Currently the catalog contains more than 8 million descriptions of archival holdings. Included are more than 2,186,000 digital copies of high-interest documents, representing many of the holdings highlighted on NARA's numerous social media platforms and in the Public Vaults, NARA's permanent interactive exhibition. The catalog is available on the Internet at http://www.archives.gov/research/catalog.

NARA's Website

The online entrance to the National Archives is its award-winning website, http://www.archives.gov, which provides the most widely available means of electronic access to information about and services available from NARA. Links to various sections provide help to the particular needs of researchers, including veterans and their families, educators and students, and the general public—as well as records managers, journalists, historians, information security specialists, members of Congress, and federal employees.

The NARA website provides

- Directions on how to contact NARA and do research at its facilities around the country
- Direct access to certain archived electronic records at http://www.archives.gov/aad
- Digital copies of selected archived documents
- An Internet Web form, at http://www.archives.gov/contact/inquire-form.html, for customer questions, reference requests, comments, and complaints
- Electronic versions of *Federal Register* publications
- Online exhibits
- Selected articles about U.S. history from *Prologue* (http://www.archives.gov/publications/prologue), the agency's quarterly magazine
- Classroom resources for students and teachers
- Online tools such as eVetRecs (http://www.archives.gov/veterans/military-service-records), which allows veterans and their next-of-kin to complete and print, for mail-in submission, requests for their military service records

Copies of military pension records from the American Revolution through World War I, census pages, land files, court records, and microfilm publications can be ordered online at http://www.archives.gov/shop. Researchers can also submit reference questions about various research topics online. In FY 2015 NARA welcomed 24 million Web visitors and received more than 80 million page views on its websites.

Digitization Projects

Within its Office of Innovation, NARA is working to digitize its traditional (paper) holdings to preserve them and provide greater access to them. The Office of Innovation will accelerate NARA's innovation activities and culture, support innovation in public access delivery, and demonstrate leadership in the archival and information access field.

As a result of these efforts, the National Archives digitized and added more than 5 million digital objects to the National Archives Catalog (https://catalog. archives.gov/) in FY 2015.

While the National Archives Catalog gives users the ability to view digitized records, the amount of material digitized and fully made available online is limited compared with the total holdings of the National Archives.

To better facilitate access of records, the online catalog has also recently been upgraded and now features more participatory elements, including new tagging and transcription tools to further engage citizen archivists and help make holdings more discoverable to researchers. At the end of FY 2015 citizen archivists had contributed more than 91,000 tags and 35,000 transcriptions to the catalog, with the latter growing at 5 percent each week.

Most of NARA's holdings currently are available only from the archival facility in which they are stored. Through a series of digitization projects, NARA is working to vastly increase online public access to more of its holdings. In 2014 the agency updated the digitization strategy (http://www.archives.gov/digitization/ strategy.html) to deal with digitization efforts, which include working with partners in the private sector. In 2016 NARA will be adding millions of images to the catalog. These images were created by its private industry digitization partners. More information about the digitization partnerships is available at http://www. archives.gov/digitization/index.html.

Social Media

NARA uses multiple social media platforms to increase access to the records in its holdings, which is at the heart of its mission. The main goals of social media at NARA are to increase awareness about archival holdings and programs and to enrich the agency's relationship with the public through conversations about its services and holdings. In addition to expanding access, use of social media creates a more collaborative work environment and increases communication and knowledge sharing both within NARA and externally with other federal agencies.

The National Archives has more than a dozen blogs, including one by the Archivist of the United States. NARA also offers historical videos from its holdings and videos of recent public events on the agency's YouTube channel. The agency shares photographs and documents from its collections through Flickr Commons. Across the country, more than 200 NARA staff contribute actively to the agency's 130 social media (http://www.archives.gov/social-media/) accounts (including Facebook, Twitter, Tumblr, Instagram, and others). In FY 2015 almost 250 million people viewed content posted to those social media platforms, up significantly over the previous fiscal year's total of 141 million.

Followers can also use Really Simple Syndication (RSS) feeds of the "Document for Today" feature, NARA news, and press releases. Several mobile apps and e-books have been developed and are available free of charge in the iTunes store and Android Market for Today's Document, DocsTeach, and recent exhibits.

Social media also allow NARA's researchers, friends, and the public to become "citizen archivists" by tagging, sharing, and transcribing documents. For more information, go to http://www.archives.gov/citizen-archivist.

Additional information about NARA's social media projects is available at http://www.archives.gov/social-media.

National Archives Museum

The National Archives Museum, a set of interconnected resources made possible by a public-private partnership between NARA and the National Archives Foundation, provides a variety of ways to explore the power and importance of the nation's records.

The Rotunda for the Charters of Freedom at the National Archives Building in Washington, D.C., is the centerpiece of the National Archives Museum. On display are the Declaration of Independence, the Constitution, and the Bill of Rights—known collectively as the Charters of Freedom. The Public Vaults is a 9,000-square-foot permanent exhibition that conveys the feeling of going beyond the walls of the Rotunda and into the stacks and vaults of the working archives. Dozens of individual exhibits, many of them interactive, reveal the breadth and variety of NARA's holdings.

Complementing the Public Vaults, the Lawrence F. O'Brien Gallery hosts a changing array of topical exhibits based on National Archives records. The 290-seat William G. McGowan Theater is a showplace for NARA's extensive audiovisual holdings and serves as a forum for lectures and discussions. It also is home to the Charles Guggenheim Center for the Documentary Film at the National Archives.

An expanded museum shop opened in 2012, and a new exhibition gallery and visitor orientation plaza opened in 2013. The David M. Rubenstein Gallery houses a permanent interactive exhibit, "Records of Rights," which documents the struggles and debates over civil rights and liberties throughout American history. The Rubenstein Gallery is also the new home for a 1297 copy of the Magna Carta, owned by Rubenstein.

Inside the Boeing Learning Center, the ReSource Room is an access point for teachers and parents to explore documents found in the exhibits and to use NARA records as teaching tools. The center's Constitution-in-Action Learning Lab is designed to provide an intense field trip adventure for middle and high school students that links to curriculum in the classroom.

DocsTeach (http://www.docsteach.org) is an education website designed to provide instruction to teachers in the best practices of teaching with primary sources. Using documents in NARA's holdings as teachable resources, DocsTeach strongly supports civic literacy. This tool gives all teachers access to primary sources, instruction in best practices, and opportunities to interact with their counterparts across the nation.

When developing the DocsTeach site, the agency established an online community that served as a virtual meeting place for NARA's education team and colleagues from schools, institutions, and organizations nationwide to collaborate and share innovative ideas and best practices for this online resource.

The National Archives Museum has expanded to the National Archives in New York City, which is located in the Alexander Hamilton U.S. Custom House at the southern tip of Manhattan. There NARA has not only a new research area but also a learning center for education and public programs and a welcome center with exhibit space. The new Learning Center incorporates many of the resources and activities found in the Washington, D.C., building.

At its Kansas City, Missouri, field office at 400 West Pershing Road, NARA also has a welcome center, changing exhibitions, workshops, and other public programs.

A set of Web pages now makes the National Archives Museum available anywhere. An illustrated history of the Charters of Freedom can be found there, as well as information on educational programs, special events, and current exhibits at the National Archives.

Those traveling to Washington can bypass the public line during peak tourist season by making online reservations at http://www.recreation.gov. For more information, see "The National Archives Museum" at http://www.archives.gov/nae. An online version of the "Records of Rights" exhibition is available at http://recordsofrights.org.

NARA facilities hosted about 4.5 million physical visitors in FY 2015, of which about 3.5 million were headed to exhibits, 887,000 to public programs, and 85,000 to research rooms. More than a million visited the National Archives Museum in Washington, and exhibits in the 13 presidential library museums were visited by about 2.2 million.

Research Services

Few records repositories serve as many customers as NARA. In FY 2015 there were nearly 85,000 researcher visits to NARA facilities nationwide, including archives, presidential libraries, and federal records centers. More than a million people requested information in writing.

National Archives Research Centers

At the Robert M. Warner Research Center in the National Archives Building in Washington, D.C., and the Steny Hoyer Research Center at the National Archives at College Park, Maryland, researchers can consult with staff experts on federal records held in each building and submit requests to examine original documents.

The Warner Research Center holds approximately 275,000 rolls of microfilmed records, documenting military service prior to World War I, immigration into the United States, the federal census, the U.S. Congress, federal courts in the District of Columbia, the Bureau of Indian Affairs, and the Freedmen's Bureau. The center also contains an extensive, ever-expanding system of reference reports, helping researchers conduct research in federal documents.

Executive branch records housed in the National Archives Building include those of the Bureau of Indian Affairs and of civilian agencies responsible for maritime affairs. Military records in this building include records of the Army before World War I and the Navy and Marine Corps before World War II. In addition, the National Archives Building holds many records relating to the federal government's interaction with individuals; these are often consulted for genealogical research.

The Hoyer Research Center in College Park holds textual records of civilian agencies from 1789, investigative records and military holdings that include records from the Army and Army Air Forces dating from World War I and Navy, Marine Corps, intelligence, defense-related, and seized enemy records dating from World War II. In addition to textual records, special media records include motion pictures, still photographs and posters, sound recordings, maps, architectural drawings, aerial photographs, and electronic records. A research room for accessioned microfilm holds records of the Department of State's Berlin Document Center and other World War II-era captured documents.

Regional Archives

NARA has 12 regional archives where the public can do research. They are located in or near Boston, New York, Philadelphia, Atlanta, Chicago, St. Louis, Kansas City, Fort Worth, Denver, Riverside (California), San Francisco, and Seattle. Archived records of regional significance, as well as, in some locations, immigration records, are available for use by the public in these regional archives.

Presidential Libraries

NARA operates the libraries and museums of the 13 most recent U.S. presidents, beginning with Herbert Hoover, whose library is in West Branch, Iowa. The others are Franklin D. Roosevelt, Hyde Park, New York; Harry S. Truman, Independence, Missouri; Dwight D. Eisenhower, Abilene, Kansas; John F. Kennedy, Boston; Lyndon Baines Johnson, Austin; Richard Nixon, Yorba Linda, California; Gerald R. Ford, Ann Arbor (library) and Grand Rapids (museum), Michigan; Jimmy Carter, Atlanta; Ronald Reagan, Simi Valley, California; George Bush, College Station, Texas; William J. Clinton, Little Rock; and George W. Bush, Dallas.

In FY 2015 more than 2.1 million people visited exhibits in the presidential library museums; the libraries had more than 10,000 researcher visits. At http://www.archives.gov/presidential-libraries, visitors can learn about the presidential library system as a whole and link to individual library websites to learn about the lives of the presidents and the times in which they served.

Federal Records Centers

NARA also serves federal agencies, the courts, and Congress by providing records storage, reference service, training, advice, and guidance on many issues relating to records management.

A network of 18 Federal Records Centers (FRCs) stores 30 million cubic feet (about 75 billion pages) of non-current records for 400 agencies. In FY 2015 these records centers replied to more than 9 million requests for information and records, including more than 1 million requests for information regarding military and civilian service records provided by the National Personnel Records Center in St. Louis.

In addition, NARA has records centers in or near Atlanta; Boston; Chicago; Dayton; Denver; Fort Worth; Kansas City; Kingsridge (near Dayton), Ohio; Lee's Summit, Missouri; Lenexa, Kansas; Philadelphia; Pittsfield, Massachusetts; Riverside, California; San Francisco; Seattle; and Suitland, Maryland.

Genealogy Research

Genealogy research brings hundreds of thousands of people to NARA facilities every year. In its holdings NARA has census records dating back to 1790, records dealing with immigration, land and pension records, and passenger lists from ships arriving from all over the world.

NARA is often considered the first stop in searching for one's ancestry, at its facilities in the Washington, D.C., area or one of its 12 regional archives around the country. At these locations, NARA staff offers genealogy workshops to show the public how to look through documents dating back to the Revolutionary period.

NARA also offers an annual Genealogy Fair, which is now a "virtual" event at which NARA staff provides tips and techniques for researching genealogy records at the National Archives. Lectures are designed for experienced genealogy professionals and novices alike.

NARA also maintains close relationships with genealogical associations as well as organizations such as Ancestry.com, which can be accessed without charge at any NARA location.

The National Archives has the census schedules on microfilm available from 1790 to 1940. (Most of the 1890 Census was destroyed in a Department of Commerce fire, although partial records are available for some states.)

Archives Library Information Center

The Archives Library Information Center (ALIC) provides access to information on American history and government, archival administration, information management, and government documents. ALIC is located in the National Archives at College Park. Customers also can visit ALIC on the Internet at http://www.archives.gov/research/alic, where they will find "Reference at Your Desk" Internet links, staff-compiled bibliographies and publications, and an online library catalog. ALIC can be reached by telephone at 301-837-3415.

Government Documents

Government publications are generally available to researchers at many of the 1,250 congressionally designated federal depository libraries throughout the nation. A record set of these publications also is part of NARA's archival holdings. Publications of the U.S. Government (Record Group 287) is a collection of selected publications of government agencies, arranged by the SuDoc classification system devised by the Office of the Superintendent of Documents, U.S. Government Publishing Office (GPO).

The core of the collection is a library established in 1895 by GPO's Public Documents Division. By 1972, when NARA acquired the library, it included of-

ficial publications dating from the early years of the federal government and selected publications produced for and by federal government agencies. Since 1972
the 25,000-cubic-foot collection has been augmented periodically with accessions
of government publications selected by the Office of the Superintendent of Documents as a byproduct of its cataloging activity. As with the federal depository
library collections, the holdings in NARA's Record Group 287 comprise only a
portion of all U.S. government publications.

NARA Publications

Historically NARA has published guides and indexes to various portions of its
archival holdings. Many of these are still in print, though the most up-to-date
information about NARA holdings now is available almost exclusively through
online searches at http://www.archives.gov. The agency also publishes informational leaflets and brochures and NARA's flagship publication, *Prologue,* a scholarly magazine published quarterly.

Some publications appear on NARA's website, at http://www.archives.gov/
publications/online.html, and many are available from NARA's Customer Service
Center in College Park, by calling 800-234-8861 or 866-272-6272 (in the Washington, D.C., area, 301-837-2000) or faxing 301-837-0483. The NARA website's
publications homepage, http://www.archives.gov/publications, provides more detailed information about available publications and ordering.

General-interest books about NARA and its holdings that will appeal to anyone with an interest in U.S. history, exhibition catalogs, and facsimiles of certain
documents are published by the National Archives Foundation. They are for sale
at the foundation's myArchives Store in NARA's downtown Washington building
and via the NARA website's eStore page at http://www.myarchivesstore.org.

Federal Register

The *Federal Register* is the daily gazette of the U.S. government, containing presidential documents, proposed and final federal regulations, and public notices of
federal agencies. It is published by the Office of the Federal Register and printed
and distributed by GPO. The two agencies collaborate in the same way to produce the annual revisions of the *Code of Federal Regulations (CFR).* Free access
to the full text of the electronic version of the *Federal Register* and *CFR,* and to
an unofficial, daily-updated electronic *CFR* (the *e-CFR*), is available via http://
www.fdsys.gov. Federal Register documents scheduled for future publication are
available for public inspection at the Office of the Federal Register (800 North
Capitol St. N.W., Washington, DC 20002) or online at the electronic Public Inspection Desk (http://www.federalregister.gov/public-inspection). Federalregister.
gov provides access to proposed rules and rules published in the *Federal Register*
and open for public comment (the website https://www.federalregister.gov and the
multiagency website http://www.regulations.gov also provide means to comment
on these documents).

The full catalog of other Federal Register publications is posted at http://
www.ofr.gov and includes the *Compilation of Presidential Documents, Public Papers of the Presidents,* slip laws, *United States Statutes at Large,* and the *United*

States Government Manual. Printed or microfiche editions of Federal Register publications also are maintained at federal depository libraries (http://www.gpo.gov/libraries).

The Public Law Electronic Notification Service (PENS) is a free subscription e-mail service for notification of recently enacted public laws. Varied subscriptions to the daily *Federal Register* are available from http://www.federalregister.gov. Additional information about Federal Register programs appears on Facebook (http://www.facebook.com/federalregister) and Twitter (@FedRegister).

The Office of the Federal Register also publishes information about its ministerial responsibilities associated with the operation of the Electoral College and ratification of constitutional amendments and provides access to related records. Publication information concerning laws, regulations, and presidential documents and services is available from the Office of the Federal Register (telephone 202-741-6070). Information on Federal Register finding aids, the Electoral College, and constitutional amendments is available through http://www.archives.gov/federal-register.

Publications can be ordered by contacting GPO at http://bookstore.gpo.gov, or by toll-free telephone at 866-512-1800. To submit orders by fax or by mail, see http://bookstore.gpo.gov/help/index.jsp.

Grants

The National Historical Publications and Records Commission (NHPRC) is the national grants program of the National Archives. The Archivist of the United States chairs the commission and makes grants on its recommendation. NHPRC's 14 other members represent the president (two appointees), the Supreme Court, the Senate and House of Representatives, the departments of State and Defense, the Librarian of Congress, the American Association for State and Local History, the American Historical Association, the Association for Documentary Editing, the National Association of Government Archives and Records Administrators, the Organization of American Historians, and the Society of American Archivists.

The commission's mission is to provide opportunities for the American people to discover and use records that increase understanding of the nation's democracy, history, and culture. Through leadership initiatives, grants, and fostering the creation of new tools and methods, the commission connects the work of the National Archives to the work of the nation's archives. NHPRC grants help archives, universities, historical societies, professional organizations, and other nonprofit organizations to establish or strengthen archival programs, improve training and techniques, preserve and process records collections, and provide access to them through finding aids, digitization of collections, and documentary editions of the papers of significant historical figures and movements in American history. The commission works in partnership with a national network of state archives and state historical records advisory boards to develop a national archival infrastructure. For more information about the Commission, visit http://www.archives.gov/nhprc. For more information about the projects it supports, go to http://www.facebook.com/nhprc.

Customer Service

Few records repositories serve as many customers as NARA. In FY 2015 there were about 85,000 researcher visits to NARA facilities nationwide, including archives, presidential libraries, and federal records centers. At the same time, more than a million customers submitted written requests for information.

NARA also maintains an Internet form (http://www.archives.gov/contact/inquire-form.html) to facilitate continuous feedback from customers about what is most important to them and what NARA might do better to meet their needs.

Administration

The head of NARA is David S. Ferriero, who was appointed Archivist of the United States in 2009 by President Obama. As of March 1, 2016, the agency employed 2,928 people, of whom 2,855 were full-time permanent staff members working at NARA locations around the country.

National Center for Education Statistics

U.S. Department of Education, Institute of Education Sciences
Potomac Center Plaza, 550 12th St. S.W., 4th fl., Washington, DC 20202

Christopher A. Cody
Academic Libraries, Integrated Postsecondary Education Data System

Chelsea Owens
School Library Media Centers, Schools and Staffing Survey

In an effort to collect and disseminate more complete statistical information about libraries, the National Center for Education Statistics (NCES) initiated a formal library statistics program in 1989 that included surveys on academic libraries, school library media centers, public libraries, and state libraries.* At the end of December 2006, the Public Libraries Survey and the State Library Agencies Survey were officially transferred to the Institute of Museum and Library Services (IMLS). The Academic Libraries Survey and the School Library Media Centers Survey continued to be administered and funded by NCES. However, the School Library Media Centers Survey was incorporated into the School and Staffing Survey (SASS), and the Academic Libraries Survey was incorporated into the Integrated Postsecondary Education Data System (IPEDS). [For detailed information on the surveys now being handled by IMLS, see "Institute of Museum and Library Services Library Programs" in Part 2 and "Highlights of IMLS and NCES Surveys" in Part 4—Ed.]

The library surveys conducted by NCES are designed to provide comprehensive nationwide data on the status of libraries. Federal, state, and local officials, professional associations, and local practitioners use these surveys for planning, evaluating, and making policy. These data are also available to researchers and educators.

Past information about elementary and secondary public school library media centers is available on the School and Staffing Survey website, http://nces.ed.gov/surveys/sass/. The Library Statistics Program's website, http://nces.ed.gov/surveys/libraries, provides links to data search tools, data files, survey definitions, and survey designs for the Academic Libraries Survey from 1996 to 2012. The IPEDS Academic Libraries Information Center, http://nces.ed.gov/ipeds/Section/Alscenter, contains current survey definitions and designs, and the IPEDS Data Center at http://nces.ed.gov/ipeds/datacenter/ contains data files for the Academic Libraries component beginning in 2014. The two library surveys conducted by NCES are described below.

Academic Libraries

The IPEDS Academic Libraries (AL) component provides descriptive statistics from academic libraries in the 50 states, the District of Columbia, and, if appli-

---

*The authorization for the National Center for Education Statistics (NCES) to collect library statistics is included in the Education Sciences Reform Act of 2002 (PL 107-279), under Title I, Part C.

cable, the outlying areas of the United States (Guam, the Commonwealth of the Northern Mariana Islands, Puerto Rico, and the U.S. Virgin Islands).

NCES surveyed academic libraries on a three-year cycle between 1966 and 1988. From 1988 to 1998, AL was a component of IPEDS collected on a two-year cycle. From 2000 to 2012, the Academic Libraries Survey separated from IPEDS but remained on a two-year cycle as part of the Library Statistics Program. IPEDS and ALS data were still linked by the identification codes of the postsecondary education institutions. In aggregate, these data provide an overview of the status of academic libraries nationally and by state. Beginning with the 2014–2015 collection cycle, AL was reintegrated back into IPEDS.

AL collects data on libraries in the entire universe of degree-granting postsecondary institutions using a Web-based data collection system. The survey component collects counts of library books, e-books, media, and databases, both in the physical and electronic formats. Academic libraries are also asked to report salaries, wages, and fringe benefits, if paid from the library budget; materials and services expenditures; operations and maintenance expenditures; and total expenditures. Libraries with reported total expenditures over zero but less than $100,000 were required to report collections data, while those with expenditures equal to or greater than $100,000 were required to report collections and detailed expenditures data.

A First Look report, "Academic Libraries: 2012" (NCES 2014-038), was released on the NCES website in February 2014, as were the final data file and documentation for the 2012 ALS (NCES 2014-039). NCES has developed a Web-based peer analysis tool for AL called "Compare Academic Libraries" (https://nces.ed.gov/surveys/libraries/compare/). This tool currently uses AL 2012 data. A First Look report, "Enrollment and Employees in Postsecondary Institutions, Fall 2014; and Financial Statistics and Academic Libraries, Fiscal Year 2014" (NCES 2016-005), was released in November 2015. AL 2014 data and all future library data collected will be available via the IPEDS Data Center tool. Academic library statistics information can be obtained from Christopher A. Cody, Integrated Postsecondary Education Data System, e-mail IPEDS@ed.gov.

School Library Media Centers

National surveys of school library media centers in elementary and secondary schools in the United States were conducted in 1958, 1962, 1974, 1978, and 1986, 1993–1994, 1999–2000, 2003–2004, 2007–2008, and 2011–2012.

NCES, with the assistance of the U.S. Bureau of the Census, conducted the School Library Media Center Survey as part of the Schools and Staffing Survey (SASS). SASS is the nation's largest sample survey of teachers, schools, and principals in K–12 public and private schools. Data from the school library media center questionnaire provide a national picture of public school library staffing, collections, expenditures, technology, and services. Results from the 2011–2012 survey can be found in "Characteristics of Public Elementary and Secondary School Library Media Centers in the United States: Results from the 2011–12 Schools and Staffing Survey" (NCES 2013–315).

NCES also published a historical report about school libraries titled *Fifty Years of Supporting Children's Learning: A History of Public School Libraries and Federal Legislation from 1953–2000* (NCES 2005-311). Drawn from more than 50 sources, this report gives descriptive data about public school libraries since 1953. Along with key characteristics of school libraries, the report also presents national and regional standards, and federal legislation affecting school library media centers. Data from sample surveys are provided at the national, regional, and school levels, and by state.

NCES has recently redesigned the Schools and Staffing Survey into the National Teacher and Principal Survey (NTPS). NTPS will focus on teachers, principals, and the schools in which they work. The redesigned study collects counts of the number of school library media centers. The first NTPS (2015–2016) is currently in the field for data collection. Results will be available in summer of 2017.

Additional information on school library media center statistics can be obtained from Chelsea Owens, e-mail chelsea.owens@ed.gov.

NCES has included some library-oriented questions relevant to the library usage and skills of the parent and the teacher instruments of the new Early Childhood Longitudinal Study (ECLS). For additional information, visit http://nces.ed.gov/ecls. Library items also appear in National Household Education Survey (NHES) instruments. For more information about that survey, visit http://nces.ed.gov/nhes.

NCES included a questionnaire about high school library media centers in the Education Longitudinal Study of 2002 (ELS: 2002). This survey collected data from tenth graders about their schools, their school library media centers, their communities, and their home life. The report, "School Library Media Centers: Selected Results from the Education Longitudinal Study of 2002" (ELS: 2002) (NCES 2005-302), is available on the NCES website. For more information about this survey, visit http://nces.ed.gov/surveys/els2002.

How to Obtain Printed and Electronic Products

Reports are currently published in the First Look format. First Look reports consist of a short collection of tables presenting state and national totals, a survey description, and data highlights. NCES also publishes separate, more in-depth studies analyzing these data.

Internet Access

Many NCES publications (including out-of-print publications) and edited raw data files from the library surveys are available for viewing or downloading at no charge through the Electronic Catalog on the NCES website at http://nces.ed.gov/pubsearch.

Ordering Printed Products

Many NCES publications are also available in printed format. To order one free copy of recent NCES reports, contact the Education Publications Center (ED Pubs) at http://www.edpubs.org, by e-mail at edpubs@edpubs.ed.gov, by toll-free telephone at 877-4-ED-PUBS (1-877-433-7827) or TTY/TDD 877-576-7734, by fax at 703-605-6794, or by mail at ED Pubs, P.O. Box 22207, Alexandria, VA 22304.

Many publications are available through the Education Resources Information Clearinghouse (ERIC) system. For more information on services and products, visit the EDRS website at http://www.eric.ed.gov.

Out-of-print publications and data files may be available through the NCES Electronic Catalog on the NCES website at http://nces.ed.gov/pubsearch or through one of the 1,250 federal depository libraries throughout the United States (see http://catalog.gpo.gov/fdlpdir/FDLPdir.jsp). Use the NCES publication number included in the citations for publications and data files to quickly locate items in the NCES Electronic Catalog. Use the GPO number to locate items in a federal depository library.

Defense Technical Information Center

Fort Belvoir, VA 22060
World Wide Web http://www.dtic.mil

Michele Finley
Public Affairs Officer

The Defense Technical Information Center (DTIC) is responsible for developing, coordinating, and enabling a strong scientific and technical information (STINFO) program for the Assistant Secretary of Defense for Research and Engineering, and the Department of Defense (DoD) scientific and technical (S&T) enterprise. In this role, DTIC sets policy for scientific and technical information exchanges for the research and engineering community. DTIC's aim is to maximize the availability, use, and collaboration of technical information resulting from DoD-funded technical activities while ensuring restrictions to safeguard national security, export control, and intellectual property rights.

Since its inception in 1945 DTIC has served as a vital link in the transfer of defense-related information. The center offers access to more than 4 million research records to engineers, researchers, scientists, and information professionals in laboratories, universities, and the acquisition field. DTIC's mission is to collect and deliver rapid, accurate, and reliable technical research, development, test, and evaluation information to DoD customers. As a DoD field activity, DTIC is under the office of the Under Secretary of Defense for Acquisition, Technology, and Logistics and reports to the Assistant Secretary of Defense, Research and Engineering (ASD[R&E]).

In 2013 DTIC marked nine years as a DoD field activity and saw the renewal of its field activity charter. Signed by Deputy Secretary of Defense Ashton B. Carter, the charter, in force until 2018, reaffirmed DTIC's position as DoD's central scientific, research, and engineering information support activity for ASD(R&E). In 2013 DTIC also saw the approval of DoD Instruction 3200.12, "DoD Scientific and Technical Information Program (STIP)." Now an instruction, this issuance establishes policy and responsibilities and proposes procedures for DTIC to carry out STIP. The instruction outlines the vital role played by DTIC in collecting, indexing, cataloging, and providing storage for scientific and technical information obtained from DoD components and their contractors, non-DoD organizations, and foreign sources.

The instruction reiterates that DoD should sustain a coordinated program to manage scientific and technical information, which will maximize resources while eliminating duplication of efforts by the reuse of DoD research, development, test, and evaluation investments and assets. DoDI 3200.12 can be found on the DoD Issuances website, http://www.dtic.mil/whs/directives/corres/pdf/320012p.pdf.

In 2014 DoD Manual 3200.14, Volume 2, "Principles and Operational Parameters of the DoD Scientific and Technical Information Program (STIP): Information Analysis Centers (IACs)," was updated. The DoD establishes IACs to acquire, digest, analyze, evaluate, synthesize, store, publish, and distribute STI and engineering data in a clearly defined specialized field or subject area of significant DoD

DTIC is a registered service mark of the Defense Technical Information Center interest or concern. Additionally IACs provide advisory and other user services to their authorized user community. This volume describes the DoD IAC Program and implements its policy, principles, and concepts for procedural functions and is available at http://www.dtic.mil/whs/directives/corres/pdf/320014vol2.pdf.

Early in 2015 the Defense Acquisition Regulation Supplement clause on Electronic Submission of Technical Reports was updated to require electronic submissions instead of paper copies of approved final scientific or technical reports of research funded by DoD. This reaffirms the requirement for all final scientific and technical reports on DoD-funded research to be submitted to DTIC.

Reaching Customers

DTIC offers its suite of services to a diverse population of the defense community. Because of the nature of the information it handles, some of DTIC's products are only accessible to the federal government and its contractors. While DTIC also has a public website and search, there are advantages to accessing the secured sites. These value-added services include having research assistance from trained information professionals and having access to limited (not publicly available) information. More information about who is eligible to access DTIC's suite of products can be found at http://www.dtic.mil/dtic/registration.

Who uses DTIC information? Some of its more than 25,000 users are:

- Acquisition community
- Active duty military personnel
- Congressional staff
- DoD and federal contractors
- Engineers
- Faculty and students at military schools
- Historians
- Information professionals/librarians
- Intelligence community
- Logistics management specialists
- Researchers
- Scientists
- Security managers
- Software engineers and developers

Resources

DTIC's holdings include technical reports on completed research; research summaries of planned, ongoing, and completed work; independent research and development summaries; defense technology transfer agreements; DoD planning documents; budget data; DoD directives and instructions; international agreements; conference proceedings; security classification guides; command histories; and special research collections that date back to World War II. DoD-funded research-ers are required to search DTIC's collections to ensure that they do not under-take unnecessary or redundant research. The general public can access "unclassi-fied, unlimited" information, including many full-text downloadable documents, through the public DTIC website at http://www.dtic.mil. The information on the site is free of charge, and no registration is required.

Information Sources

DTIC information is derived from many sources, including DoD organizations (ci-vilian and military) and DoD contractors; the Information Analysis Centers, U.S. government organizations and their contractors; nonprofit organizations working on DoD scientific, research, and engineering activities; academia; and foreign governments. DTIC accepts information in print, nonprint (CDs and DVDs), and electronically over the Web. DTIC gets information from the defense community, for the defense community, on defense topics and more. Having a full range of sci-ence and technology and research and development information within the DTIC collection ensures that technological innovations are linked to defense develop-ment and acquisition efforts. New research projects can begin with the highest level of information available. This avoids duplication of effort, maximizing the use of DoD project dollars and saving taxpayer dollars.

Creating Tools for DoD

DTIC continues to play a key role in DoD by producing collaboration tools (often not available to the public) to help the defense research and engineering com-munity work in a secure environment. In order to utilize many of these websites, individuals must be eligible to access DTIC's products.

In a more networked world, the defense workforce needs the tools to cre-ate, share, and reuse knowledge developed both within DoD and by its external partners (industry and academia, for example). DTIC has made strides in creating and hosting sites aimed at enhancing the ability of DoD to connect internally and externally. In addition, DTIC is working to map relationships to enable users to access the life cycle of research projects from planning to final results. DTIC em-ploys technology to verify and validate information submitted and improve user confidence in DoD research documentation.

The Research and Engineering (R&E) Gateway provides the means to con-nect the acquisition enterprise (DoD Labs); Federally Funded Research and De-velopment Centers (FFRDCs); Program Executive Offices; Acquisition, Technol-ogy, and Logistics (AT&L) commands; and Combatant commands (CCMDs). In an access-controlled environment, all of DTIC's unclassified assets, tools, and community interaction capabilities foster innovation, competition, and identifica-tion of solutions. DoD conducts research at its 60-plus labs, in the FFRDCs, in DTIC's IACs, through contracts and grants, and across 17 distinct priority area communities of interest. This work is available through the R&E Gateway. In ad-dition, the R&E Gateway offers access to official defense scientific and technical information, collaborative tools, and subject matter experts. The gateway helps the defense S&T community build on past work, collaborate on current projects, and avoid duplication of effort. With better connections within DoD, the development and delivery of technologies to the armed forces can be accelerated.

The R&E Gateway is the entry point to DTIC's suite of tools. Some of the tools within the gateway are:

- DTIC Collection Search—This tool aids in the quick discovery of public and access-controlled DoD research projects and documents, as well as people (subject matter experts), places (organizations), and content (past and current research) from DoDTechSpace. DTIC continually works to enable additional features within its search capabilities and from commercial partners to improve information discovery and relevance.

- DoDTechipedia—Designed by DTIC in 2008, DoDTechipedia was one of the first DoD scientific and technical wikis. A secure online system, it facilitates transparency and communication among DoD scientists, engineers, program managers, and the armed forces. It helps members of the DoD S&T community collaborate and identify solutions for technology challenges. Among its numerous features are interest area pages for DoD personnel and DoD contractors to work together on challenges and solutions.

- DoDTechSpace—A social business tool, DoDTechSpace is a place for DTIC's customers to collaborate, share, find, and post information. It connects the defense research and engineering community, DoD laboratories, and other DoD agencies, while providing current and next-generation researchers with advanced Web 2.0 tools. Offering real-time discussions on capability needs and solutions, events, and people, this collaborative environment can support community activities, social networking, lessons learned, and discussions.

- DoD Budget Tools—DTIC publishes searchable congressional budget data shortly after its release and offers both public and access-controlled sites to review and analyze DoD research and engineering funding data. The center posts reports from the House and Senate committees that oversee the DoD budget information, all of which can be found on the public site http:// www.dtic.mil/congressional_budget. DTIC posts this reformatted budget data within days of its release on the Congress.gov legislative information website operated by the Library of Congress. The budget data is thoroughly checked prior to posting, ensuring its accuracy and reliability.

- Defense Innovation Marketplace—The Defense Innovation Marketplace was launched in late 2011 and continues to be used as an online resource (both public and access-controlled) for the purpose of "connecting industry with government customers." Creation of this site was a direct result of the "Better Buying Power" initiative within DoD, which called for the department to deliver better value by improving the way it was doing business. In short, industry submits information about DoD-related ideas and projects, which helps DoD to see what industry is developing. The site helps the department plan acquisitions and identify potential research gaps.

These tools are available through the R&E Gateway at https://www.dtic.mil. Links to these sites are also available through DTIC's public website at http://www.dtic.mil.

DoD Information Analysis Centers (IACs)

DoD Information Analysis Centers (IACs), established under DoD Manual 3200.14, Vol. 2, serve as a vital resource in providing timely, relevant information directly to users when and where it is needed. IACs serve as a bridge between the armed forces and the acquisition/research community, providing essential technical analysis and data support to a diverse customer base, to include the Combatant Commands (CCMDs), Program Executive Offices, the Office of the Secretary of Defense, Defense Agencies, and the military services. IACs actively partner and collaborate with Defense R&E focus groups and communities of interest in specialized fields or specific technologies. IACs create and maintain comprehensive knowledge analysis centers that include historical, technical, scientific, and other data and information collected worldwide. They are staffed with scientists, engineers, and information specialists to provide research and analysis to customers with diverse, complex, and challenging requirements. IAC operations directly support the fighting forces, and play an ongoing and critical role in solving key CCMD operational issues such as cybersecurity, unmanned aerial vehicles, human–machine teaming, and improvements to the ballistic resistance of body armor. More information on IACs is available at http://iac.dtic.mil.

Expanding Free Training Opportunities

Webinars have been mainstays of the opportunities offered to DTIC registered users to learn about DTIC's products and services. Three webinars, on DoDTechSpace, DoDTechipedia, and DTIC Search, are offered on a monthly basis.

"DTIC Boot Camp: S&T Resources for the DoD Community" offers hands-on training (at DTIC headquarters), including sessions about the center's numerous resources as well as instruction about submitting documents. This interactive one-day workshop is held monthly for users. DTIC users can request additional training sessions at DTIC headquarters or at their own locations.

DoD Scientific and Technical Information (STINFO) training is offered in one- and three-day classes that review the management and conduct of an organizational STINFO program. It can be held at DTIC or requested off-site.

Public Access to Federally Funded Research

DTIC is in a leading role for the department's efforts to implement public access to published journal articles and digital data from research funded by taxpayers. In this role, DTIC is actively working with partners across the services, other federal agencies, and publishers.

Summary

DTIC protects and preserves DoD's multibillion-dollar investment in research, which empowers the acquisition enterprise through innovative tools, information systems, and decision support capabilities. DTIC is uniquely positioned to support and unleash the value of DoD's R&D portfolio.

Education Resources

National Library of Education

Knowledge Utilization Division
National Center for Education Evaluation and Regional Assistance
Institute of Education Sciences, U.S. Department of Education
400 Maryland Ave. S.W., Washington, DC 20202
World Wide Web http://ies.ed.gov/ncee/projects/nle

Pamela Tripp-Melby

Director
202-453-6536, e-mail pamela.tripp-melby@ed.gov

The U.S. Department of Education's National Library of Education (NLE), created in 1994, is the primary resource center for education information in the federal government, serving the research needs of the Department of Education, the education community, and the public. NLE resides in the National Center for Education Evaluation and Regional Assistance, Institute of Education Sciences.

NLE was created by Public Law 103-227, the Educational Research, Development, Dissemination, and Improvement Act of 1994, and reauthorized under Public Law 107-279, the Education Sciences Reform Act of 2002. The act outlines four primary functions of NLE:

- Collect and archive information, including products and publications developed through, or supported by, the Institute of Education Sciences; and other relevant and useful education-related research, statistics, and evaluation materials and other information, projects, and publications that are consistent with scientifically valid research or the priorities and mission of the institute, and developed by the department, other federal agencies, or entities
- Provide a central location within the federal government for information about education
- Provide comprehensive reference services on matters relating to education to employees of the Department of Education and its contractors and grantees, other federal employees, and the public
- Promote greater cooperation and resource sharing among providers and repositories of education information in the United States

NLE works closely with the Education Resources Information Center (ERIC). ERIC collects and archives information and provides a central location within the federal government for information about education. Because ERIC serves as the major public program, it is covered separately. [See "Education Resources Information Center" below.—Ed.]

The primary responsibility of NLE is to provide information services to agency staff and contractors, the general public, other government agencies, and other libraries. Located in the agency's headquarters building in Washington, D.C., the library houses current and historical collections and archives of information on education issues, research, statistics, and policy; there is a special emphasis on agency publications and contractor reports, as well as current and historical federal education legislation.

NLE has a staff of 12 as of 2015, four full-time federal staff and eight contract librarians. Staffing and organizational structure are kept flexible to support changing needs and to allow for fast, competent response to customer requests, institutional initiatives, and advances in technology. NLE's primary customer base includes about 5,000 department staff nationwide; department contractors performing research; education organizations and media; and academic, special, and government libraries. All services are supported by NLE's budget, which in fiscal year 2015 is approximately $2 million.

Collections

The focus of NLE's collection is on education issues, with an emphasis on research and policy, with some materials on related topics including law, public policy, economics, urban affairs, sociology, history, philosophy, psychology, and cognitive development. In addition to current materials, the collection has books dating from the early 19th century, including approximately 800 books on education research in the United States and more than 25,000 historical textbooks. Some of these books were donated to the library by Henry Barnard, the first U.S. Commissioner of Education.

NLE maintains collections of historical documents associated with its parent agency, the U.S. Department of Education, having a complete collection of ERIC microfiche; research reports reviewed by the What Works Clearinghouse and special panels; and publications of or relating to the department's predecessor agencies, including the National Institute of Education and the U.S. Office of Education in the Department of Health, Education, and Welfare. These collections include reports, studies, manuals, statistical publications, speeches, and policy papers. NLE also serves as a selective federal depository library under the U.S. Government Publishing Office program.

Services

NLE provides reference and other information services, including legislative reference and statistical information services, to department staff, to the education community at large, and to the general public, as well as offering document delivery services to department staff and interlibrary loan services to other libraries and government agencies.

Contact Information

The U.S. Department of Education Research Library can be contacted by e-mail at askalibrarian@ed.gov. The library's reference desk is available by telephone from 9 A.M. to 5 P.M. weekdays, except federal holidays, at 800-424-1616 (toll free) or 202-205-5015, and by fax at 202-401-0547. For the hearing-impaired, the toll-free number for the Federal Relay Service is 800-877-8339.

Located in the department's headquarters building at 400 Maryland Ave. S.W., the library is open to researchers by appointment from 9 A.M. to 5 P.M. weekdays, except federal holidays.

Education Resources Information Center

Knowledge Utilization Division
National Center for Education Evaluation and Regional Assistance
Institute of Education Sciences, U.S. Department of Education
555 New Jersey Ave. N.W., Washington, DC 20208
World Wide Web http://eric.ed.gov

Erin Pollard
Program Officer, ERIC
202-219-3400, e-mail erin.pollard@ed.gov

The Education Resources Information Center (ERIC) is the world's largest and most frequently used digital library of education resources. It is composed of more than 1.5 million bibliographic records and more than 340,000 full-text materials indexed from 1966 to the present. Each ERIC bibliographic record contains an abstract of a journal article or non-journal document (for example, a technical report or conference paper), along with such indexed information as author, title, and publication date.

Background

ERIC has served the information needs of schools, institutions of higher education, educators, parents, administrators, policymakers, researchers, and public and private entities for decades, through a variety of library services and formats—first in paper copy, then in microfiche, and today exclusively in electronic format. ERIC provides service directly to the public via its website, http://eric.ed.gov.

With more than 50 years of service to the public, ERIC is one of the oldest programs in the U.S. Department of Education. As the world's largest education resource, it is distinguished by two hallmarks: free dissemination of bibliographic records and the collection of gray literature such as research conference papers and government contractor reports.

The authorizing legislation for ERIC is part of the Education Sciences Reform Act of 2002, Public Law 107-279. This legislation envisioned ERIC subject areas or topics (previously covered by the ERIC Clearinghouses) as part of the totality of enhanced information dissemination to be conducted by the Institute of Education Sciences. In addition, information dissemination includes material on closing the achievement gap and on educational practices that improve academic achievement and promote learning.

ERIC Mission

ERIC's mission is to provide a comprehensive, easy-to-use, searchable, Internet-based bibliographic and full-text database of education research and information for educators, researchers, and the general public. Terms defining the ERIC mission are as follows:

- *Comprehensive:* The ERIC digital library consists of journal articles and non-journal materials, including materials not published by commercial publishers that are directly related to education and education research.
- *Easy-to-use and searchable:* ERIC users will be able to find the education information they need quickly and efficiently.
- *Electronic:* ERIC is an entirely electronic system comprising the ERIC website and the digital library. It links to libraries, publishers, and commercial sources of journal articles, and is made available to commercial database vendors through authorization agreements.
- *Bibliographic and full-text:* Bibliographic records convey the information that users need in a simple and straightforward manner, and, whenever possible, full-text journal articles and non-journal materials are included free of charge in the digital library. Other full-text articles and materials, whenever possible, will be immediately available for purchase through an online link to the publisher's website.

Selection Standards

The selection policy provides that all materials added to the ERIC database are rigorous and relevant sources of research directly related to the field of education. The majority of the journals indexed in ERIC are peer-reviewed, and peer-reviewed status is indicated for all journals indexed since 2004 when this data began to be documented by the ERIC system. The collection scope includes early childhood education through higher education, vocational education, and special education; it includes teacher education, education administration, assessment and evaluation, counseling, information technology, and the academic areas of reading, mathematics, science, environmental education, languages, and social studies.

To be considered for selection, all submissions must be in digital format and accompanied by author permission for dissemination. For individual document submissions, authors (copyright holders) can upload materials through a link on the ERIC website. Journal publishers, associations, and other entities with multiple documents also submit electronic content following guidance and instructions consistent with provider agreements from ERIC.

ERIC Collection

In addition to being the largest education library, ERIC is one of the few collections to index non-journal materials as well as journal literature. The largest share of the collection consists of citations to journal articles (more than 825,000 records), and a smaller portion consists of non-journal materials (more than 725,000 records). The non-journal materials are frequently called gray literature, materials that are not easy to find and are not produced by commercial publishers. In ERIC, the gray literature consists of research syntheses, dissertations, conference proceedings, and such selected papers as keynote speeches, technical reports, policy papers, literature reviews, bibliographies, congressional hearings and reports, reports on federal and state standards, testing and regulations, U.S. Department of Education reports (such as those produced by the department's What Works Clearinghouse and the National Center for Education Statistics), and working papers for established research and policy organizations.

The ERIC selection policy was recently revised and can be found at http://eric.ed.gov/?selection. The list of journals approved for indexing can be found at http://eric.ed.gov/?journals, and the list of non-journals approved for indexing can be found at http://eric.ed.gov/?nonjournals.

To facilitate electronic access to more archived materials, ERIC launched a microfiche digitization project in 2006; this project was concluded in 2009. The project scope was to digitize and archive microfiche full-text documents containing an estimated 43 million pages and to provide copyright due diligence by seeking permission from the copyright holders to make the electronic version available to users.

Approximately 340,000 full-text documents, indexed 1966–1992, were converted from microfiche to digital image files, and more than 65 percent of these documents were added to the ERIC digital library.

In 2010 ERIC established a partnership with ProQuest to begin indexing education-related doctoral dissertations from 700 academic institutions worldwide. More than 17,900 recent records from the ProQuest Dissertations and Thesis Database have been added to the ERIC collection.

ERIC Website

In August 2013 ERIC released a new website to provide an improved level of service to the community at a reduced cost to taxpayers. The new home page has a light visual design that emphasizes ERIC's most crucial features—Search and Thesaurus. The search feature is fast, robust, and fully comparable to widely used commercial search products. Additionally, the ERIC Thesaurus is integrated with ERIC Search, increasing its ease of use. Easy-to-find limiters allow searchers to retrieve only records with full text in ERIC and/or only peer-reviewed materials. The goal of the website is to make its use easier and more productive for novice users and skilled searchers alike. New functionality is being added on an ongoing basis, and there are plans for new support tools designed especially for practitioners and new ERIC users.

Automated systems for acquisition and processing help to reduce the total time required to produce a database record, and most records are processed in fewer than 30 days. New content is added to the ERIC database every day, and ERIC publishes approximately 4,000 new records to the ERIC digital library each month. New updates to the database will be available to download at eric.ed.gov/download.

The website also provides links to find ERIC on Facebook and Twitter. This feature provides frequent news updates, links, and downloadable materials, with the goal of broadening ERIC outreach.

ERIC Access

Use of ERIC continues to grow. In addition to the government-sponsored website at http://www.eric.ed.gov, ERIC is carried by search engines including Google and Google Scholar, MSN, and Yahoo!, as well as by commercial database providers including EBSCO, OCLC, OVID, ProQuest, SilverPlatter, and Dialog. ERIC is also available through statewide networks in Ohio, Texas, Kentucky, and North Carolina.

The ERIC digital library can be reached toll-free by telephone in the United States, Canada, and Puerto Rico at 800-LET-ERIC (800-538-3742), Monday through Friday, 9 A.M. to 7 P.M. eastern time. Questions can also be transmitted via the message box on the "Contact Us" page on the ERIC website.

National Association and Organization Reports

American Library Association

50 E. Huron St., Chicago, IL 60611
800-545-2433
World Wide Web http://www.ala.org

Sari Feldman
President

The American Library Association (ALA)—the oldest, largest, and most influential library association in the world—was founded in 1876 in Philadelphia and later chartered in the Commonwealth of Massachusetts. ALA has approximately 58,000 members, including librarians, library trustees, and other interested people from every state and many nations. The association serves public, state, school, and academic libraries, as well as special libraries for people working in government, commerce and industry, the arts, and the armed services or in hospitals, prisons, and other institutions.

ALA's mission is "to provide leadership for the development, promotion, and improvement of library and information services and the profession of librarianship in order to enhance learning and ensure access to information for all."

ALA is governed by an elected council, which is its policy making body, and an executive board, which acts for the council in the administration of established policies and programs. In this context, the executive board is the body that manages the affairs of the association, delegating management of its day-to-day operation to the executive director. ALA also has 37 standing committees, designated as committees of the association or of the council. ALA operations are directed by the executive director and implemented by staff through a structure of programmatic offices and support units.

ALA is home to 11 membership divisions, each focused on a type of library or library function. They are the American Association of School Librarians (AASL), the Association for Library Collections and Technical Services (ALCTS), the Association for Library Service to Children (ALSC), the Association of College and Research Libraries (ACRL), the Association of Specialized and Cooperative Library Agencies (ASCLA), the Library and Information Technology Association (LITA), the Library Leadership and Management Association (LLAMA), the Public Library Association (PLA), the Reference and User Services Association (RUSA), United for Libraries, and the Young Adult Library Services Association (YALSA).

ALA also hosts 20 round tables for members who share interests that lie outside the scope of any of the divisions. A network of affiliates, chapters, and other organizations enables ALA to reach a broad audience.

Key action areas include diversity, equitable access to information and library services, education and lifelong learning, intellectual freedom, advocacy for libraries and the profession, literacy, transforming libraries, and organizational excellence.

ALA offices address the broad interests and issues of concern to ALA members; they track issues and provide information, services, and products for members and the general public. Current ALA offices are the Chapter Relations Office (CRO), the Development Office, the Governance Office, the International Relations Office (IRO), the Office for Accreditation, the Office of Government Relations (OGR), the Office for Human Resource Development and Recruitment (HRDR), the Office for Information Technology Policy (OITP), the Office for Intellectual Freedom (OIF), the Office for Library Advocacy (OLA), the Office for Diversity, Literacy and Outreach Services (ODLOS), the Office for Research and Statistics (ORS), the Public Awareness Office (PAO), the Public Programs Office (PPO), and the Washington Office.

ALA's headquarters is in Chicago. OGR and OITP are located at ALA's Washington Office, and United for Libraries is located in Philadelphia. ALA also has an editorial office for *Choice*, a review journal for academic libraries, in Middletown, Connecticut.

ALA is a 501(c)(3) charitable and educational organization.

Leadership and Strategic Planning

Sari Feldman, executive director of the Cuyahoga County Public Library, Parma, Ohio, was inaugurated as ALA president at the 2015 Annual Conference in San Francisco.

Feldman's presidency focused on the Libraries Transform™ Campaign, an effort to increase public awareness of the value, impact, and services provided by libraries and library professionals. The campaign showcases the transformative nature of today's libraries and elevates the critical role libraries play in the digital age. The purpose of the campaign is to amplify the message that libraries today are less about what they have for people, and more about what they do for and with people. The goal of the campaign is to increase funding support for libraries and advance information policy issues in alignment with ALA's advocacy priorities.

Julie Todaro, dean of library services at Austin (Tex.) Community College, will be inaugurated as ALA president at the 2016 Annual Conference in Orlando.

Three new ALA Executive Board members were elected by the ALA Council in a vote taken at the 2015 ALA Midwinter Meeting. Loida Garcia-Febo, Julius C. Jefferson, Jr., and Mike L. Marlin are each serving three-year terms that will conclude in June 2018.

In a planning retreat at the 2014 Midwinter Meeting, the ALA Executive Board identified three areas of strategic direction to guide the association into the future: Advocacy, Information Policy, and Professional and Leadership Development. Throughout 2014 and 2015, in-person and virtual forums provided the broadest possible opportunity for member groups to contribute to the vision, assumptions, goals, strategies, and objectives in each of the three areas. ALA Council approved the new ALA strategic plan at the 2015 Annual Conference in San Francisco.

Highlights of the Year

New Public Awareness Campaign

In October 2015 ALA President Sari Feldman officially launched Libraries Transform™, a national public awareness campaign designed to increase awareness of and support for the transforming library and to shift perception of the library from "obsolete" or "nice to have" to essential. The campaign seeks to energize library professionals and build external advocates to influence local, state, and national decision makers. As part of the national launch, Feldman toured a variety of institutions in Washington, D.C., including the Smithsonian Library, Thomson Elementary School Library, George Washington University Gelman Library, and Martin Luther King Jr. Memorial Library to see firsthand how libraries are transforming to ensure individual opportunity and community progress. Simultaneously, banners and posters of provocative "Because" statements were hung around public, school, academic, and special libraries across the country to spread the word about the transforming library. In D.C., street teams were interacting directly with the public by handing out flyers and asking people to participate in entertaining quizzes about the transformed library. Since the launch, thousands of people have interacted with the campaign through social media and the libraries transform.org website.

Washington, D.C., Advocacy

ALA awarded Senator John Cornyn (R-Tex.) the 2015 James Madison Award during the 17th Annual Freedom of Information Day in Washington, D.C., in March 2015. Senator Cornyn spearheaded efforts to support open access to taxpayer-funded research and to improve the public's right to know government information.

In April the White House announced the launch of "ConnectED: Library Challenge," a new initiative to ensure that all students receive public library cards through their schools. ALA President Courtney Young met with President Barack Obama about the new program and called on school and public library leaders to work collaboratively with school administrators and civic leaders to ensure that every student has a public library card.

More than 400 library advocates met in Washington, D.C., in May to speak with their legislators about the importance of libraries as part of the 41st annual National Library Legislative Day. The Honorable Former Senator Byron Dorgan (D-N.Dak.) started the briefing by speaking about the importance of constituent advocacy. Additional speakers included ALA President Courtney Young, Patrice McDermott, director of Openthegovernment.org, and several congressional staff experts.

The ALA Washington Office welcomed more than 75 luminaries to a reception in October to celebrate 70 years of advocacy to the nation's legislators and policy makers on behalf of libraries and librarians.

Legislation to limit the Librarian of Congress's tenure to a renewable term of ten years was passed by Congress in early November. ALA urged the president to nominate a professional librarian for the office following the retirement of Dr. James Billington.

After a decade of ALA advocacy, the Senate and House agreed on a new education bill that the president signed into law in December. The Every Student Succeeds Act (ESSA) includes many school library provisions that were not present in the previous legislation and were included in ESSA in large part due to ALA's grassroots efforts.

Technology and Information Policy

The 2015 Digital Inclusion Survey found that nearly all (97.5%) public libraries offer free wireless Internet access. Technology training is offered in nearly all (98.0%) public libraries, and nearly all offer education and learning programs (99.5%) and summer reading programs (98.4%). Almost 80% of libraries offer programs that aid patrons with job applications, interview skills, and résumé development. Three-fourths of libraries offer community, civic engagement, or e-government programs. Nearly all libraries offer patrons assistance in completing online government forms.

Broadband speeds in U.S. public libraries have improved significantly in recent years yet continue to lag behind national broadband connectivity standards, according to "Broadband Quality in Public Libraries," a supplementary report released jointly in April by ALA and the Information Policy and Access Center at the University of Maryland College Park as part of the Digital Inclusion Survey.

In late April ALA joined other founding member trade and civil society organizations to launch "Re:Create: Innovators, Creators and Consumers United for Balanced Copyright." The group is a new coalition formed in anticipation of congressional efforts to revise copyright law. Detailed information about Re:Create, its mission, objectives, and positions on a broad range of issues is online at recreatecoalition.org.

In June ALA released a National Policy Agenda for Libraries, developed in coordination with other major library organizations, as the latest activity from the "Policy Revolution!" initiative. The agenda articulates two broad themes—building library capacity to advance national priorities and advancing the public interest. Among the areas for capacity building are education and learning, entrepreneurship, and health and wellness. Public interest topics include balanced copyright and licensing, systems for digital content, and privacy and transparency.

In late October the Librarian of Congress approved a request filed jointly nearly a year before by the Library Copyright Alliance, educators, and academic institutions to expand the permissible use of "clips" from copyrighted motion pictures in several ways within the higher education community and, notably, to extend this "Section 1201 exemption" to include K–12 settings.

With the Georgia Public Library Service and the Chief Officers of State Library Agencies (COSLA), OITP launched the E-Rate Clearinghouse in November. The clearinghouse is designed to help libraries take advantage of E-rate program changes to support network infrastructure upgrades.

President Sari Feldman and other ALA leaders held a series of meetings in December with senior corporate executives and library marketing executives of

Simon & Schuster, HarperCollins, and Penguin Random House. ALA's most specific request was to expand the options for library e-book lending business models to give libraries, and subsequently readers, more choice. This visit represents ALA's ninth such delegation effort over the last several years.

OITP issued "Toward a More Printed Union: Library 3D Printing Democratizes Creation" in December. The paper highlights the multifaceted 3D printing leadership of libraries and urges public and private sector leaders to leverage this leadership to unlock the full potential of 3D printing technology for all Americans.

After months of planning and coordinating, the U.S. Department of Housing and Urban Development (HUD) and the White House launched "ConnectHome," with ALA as a named national partner. The initiative seeks to extend broadband access to public housing through 28 pilot cities.

Professional and Leadership Development

A presidential initiative of ALA President Courtney Young included a partnership with ALA chapters to provide career development facilitation training. Twenty ALA chapters selected representatives from their states to participate in the training; sessions at the ALA 2015 Midwinter Meeting were followed by 14 weeks of virtual contacts and assignments.

The Library Support Staff Online Resource Center website was completely updated in 2015. The site is designed to provide resources of interest for library support staff, paraprofessionals and those interested in library work, and provides information on education, training, certification, and financial assistance.

The Emerging Leaders program enables newer librarians from across the country to participate in problem-solving workgroups, network with peers, gain insight into ALA structure, and have an opportunity to serve the overall profession in a leadership capacity. There were 50 participants in 2015, and nearly 750 have participated in the program since it began in 1997 as a one-year program under ALA President Mary R. Somerville and was revived in 2006 under ALA President Leslie Burger.

Standards for Accreditation

The ALA Council approved the revised Standards for Accreditation of Master's Programs in Library and Information Science at the 2015 Midwinter Meeting. The new standards place an emphasis on planning, assessment, and evaluation to sustain quality. The standards require programs to demonstrate how the results of evaluation are applied.

National Celebrations and Observances

The theme of National Library Week 2015 was "Unlimited Possibilities @ your library" and author David Baldacci served as honorary chair.

ALSC celebrated the 19th anniversary of "Día, El día de los niños/El día de los libros" on April 30. Día helps children and families from all cultural and linguistic backgrounds become critical thinkers, lifelong learners, and active global citizens.

Author and television host Brad Meltzer served as honorary chair of Preservation Week, April 26–May 2. Sponsored by ALCTS, the "Pass It On" theme allowed for a week of celebrating the importance of preserving personal and community cultural heritage, and brought workshops, webinars, information resources, and more to libraries across the nation.

The May 1–7 Choose Privacy Week's theme, "Who Reads the Reader?," focused on how the rapid development of online and digital technologies has given governments and corporations alike the ability to track, record, and monitor our communications and reading habits—a very real threat to the reader's right to privacy.

Snoopy served as honorary chair of Library Card Sign-up Month in September and more than 2,000 libraries received permission to use free Peanuts artwork on their library cards.

Banned Books Week, September 27–October 3, focused on the themes of "Diverse Books Need Us" and young adult literature, both frequent targets of contemporary challenges. More than half of banned books on record are by authors of color or about topics affecting people of color.

Center for the Future of Libraries

The Center for the Future of Libraries continued to promote its growing trends collection, with new write-ups of Haptic Technology, Badging, Fandom, and more. An association-wide group of experts, broadly representative of the many constituencies within the library community, has been appointed to advise and shape the center's work.

Equity, Diversity, and Inclusion

In 2015 the ALA Task Force on Equity, Diversity, and Inclusion launched a series of short surveys to provide information for the development of a plan to build more equity, diversity, and inclusion among our members, the field of librarianship, and our communities.

Library Services for Children

In March 2015 the ALSC Board of Directors voted to adopt a white paper titled "Media Mentorship in Libraries Serving Youth." The paper was written for ALSC by Cen Campbell, Claudia Haines, Amy Koester, and Dorothy Stoltz. The paper explores the role of children's librarians as mentors of new media and responsibility to support families in their intentional, appropriate, and positive use of media.

ALSC launched "Babies Need Words Every Day: Talk, Read, Sing, Play" with shareable resources designed to bridge the 30 Million Word Gap by providing parents with proven ways to build their children's literacy skills. "Babies Need Words Every Day" resources include eight visually appealing posters that deliver simple, effective rhymes, games, and other suggestions for immediate, enriching ways to communicate with babies.

Serving Teens

With support from Best Buy, YALSA awarded 20 Teen Tech Week grants to libraries to support activities aimed at helping teens build digital literacy skills. The theme of the March 8–14, 2015, Teen Tech Week was "Libraries Are for Making."

Libraries across the country joined with YALSA to celebrate Teen Read Week (TRW) on October 18–24 with the theme "Get Away @ your library." TRW is an opportunity for libraries to showcase all the great literacies, resources, and services they provide for and with teens and their families.

YALSA's "Badges for Learning" program helps learners earn seven micro-credentials that align with YALSA's Competencies for Librarians Serving Youth. In the program, library workers earn a micro-credential by completing lessons that enable individuals to develop skills they need to successfully work for and with teens. The badges can be used on résumés and in online spaces to demonstrate expertise to colleagues, administrators, and current and potential employers.

School Libraries and Librarians

More than 2,600 educators, authors, and exhibitors gathered in Columbus, Ohio, November 5–8, 2015, for AASL's 17th National Conference and Exhibition, "Experience Education Evolution." New at the 2015 conference was the fact that more than 10 percent of attendees were school administrators who received complimentary registration in order to learn side-by-side with their school librarians.

In 2015 AASL joined the national movement for Future Ready Schools as a coalition partner. The Alliance for Excellent Education and U.S. Department of Education are leading the Future Ready Schools effort with the support of the Leading Education by Advancing Digital Commission and a coalition of national experts.

AASL released a new member-created resource to help school librarians promote the ways their programs transform teaching and learning. Available on the AASL website, the tool offers strategies, practical tips, and key messages school librarians can implement immediately.

A new public service announcement (PSA) featuring Academy Award-winning actress and bestselling author Julianne Moore was available from AASL as part of the 30th anniversary of School Library Month in April 2015. In the PSA, Moore spoke about how school librarians empower students to succeed in school and beyond.

AASL launched a companion website for its professional journal, *Knowledge Quest*. A new vehicle to empower school librarians as they transform learning for their students, the site offers breaking news and blogs, and encourages conversations to inspire insightful professionals and stronger communities.

Academic Libraries

ACRL released a new report—"Academic Library Contributions to Student Success: Documented Practices from the Field"—which synthesized results from more than 70 higher education institutions from across North America that recently completed team-based assessment projects. These projects, from the first year of "Assessment in Action: Academic Libraries and Student Success (AiA)," resulted in promising and effective approaches to demonstrating the library's value to students' academic success.

As part of its 75th anniversary celebration in 2015, ACRL released "New Roles for the Road Ahead: Essays Commissioned for ACRL's 75th Anniversary" authored by Steven J. Bell, Lorcan Dempsey, and Barbara Fister.

In February ACRL released the "Framework for Information Literacy." The Framework is organized into six frames, each consisting of a concept central to information literacy, a set of knowledge practices, and a set of dispositions. The six concepts are: authority is constructed and contextual, information creation as a process, information has value, research as inquiry, scholarship as conversation, and searching as strategic exploration.

Keeping Up With . . . is an online current awareness publication from ACRL featuring concise briefs on trends in academic librarianship and higher education. Entries for 2015 included affordable course content, beacons, library value, and critical librarianship.

Intellectual Freedom

ALA Editions released the ninth edition of OIF's *Intellectual Freedom Manual* in April 2015. The new edition was completely revised and includes new features in addition to ALA policy statements and documents on intellectual freedom. The second volume of the manual was released in July and features essays and articles on the development of ALA's intellectual freedom policies.

The Newsletter on Intellectual Freedom ceased publication in December 2015. The newsletter will be recast in Spring 2016 as *In Libris Libertas: A Journal of Intellectual Freedom and Privacy*. The new journal will include peer-reviewed articles, reports on challenges to reading and privacy, court cases addressing First Amendment and privacy, and bibliographies.

Membership

More than 3,500 friends and trustee groups become ALA members in September 2015 at the conclusion of a successful pilot project between United for Libraries and ALA. Under the arrangement, friends and trustee groups within a state can become statewide group members and have access to United for Libraries and ALA training and support programs under a blanket agreement with the state library agency.

Programs and Partners

Public Library Initiatives

PLA's advocacy training curriculum "Turning the Page: Supporting Libraries, Strengthening Communities" became available for free download in 2015. The package includes an Advocacy Training Implementation Guide and a set of 15 training sessions that each include a trainer script, PowerPoint presentation, and handouts. An Advocacy Action Plan Workbook accompanies the training so that participants can develop an advocacy plan for their libraries in real-time.

Since launching in June PLA's "Project Outcome" has quickly met public library demand and desire for standardized performance measures. "Project Outcome" is dedicated to helping public libraries understand and share the true impact of essential library services and programs with simple survey instruments and an easy-to-use process for measuring and analyzing outcomes. The surveys were designed and developed by the Performance Measurement Task Force comprising library leaders, researchers, and data analysts.

Libraries Transforming Communities

ALA and the Harwood Institute for Public Innovation partnered on "Libraries Transforming Communities (LTC)," an ALA initiative that sought to strengthen libraries' roles as core community leaders and change-agents. In 2015 ALA released a free, six-part online course designed to help libraries strengthen their role as core community leaders and work with residents to bring about positive change. The LTC initiative was funded by the Bill and Melinda Gates Foundation, and the ten public libraries participating in the initiative concluded their 18-month projects in December.

Building STEAM with Día Toolkit

ALSC launched a free downloadable "Building STEAM with Día Toolkit." The toolkit provides a research-based overview of the importance of intentionally planning for the inclusion of diverse content and community partners in programming centered on science, technology, engineering, arts, and math. The toolkit was made possible by the Dollar General Literacy Foundation.

Beyond Words Disaster Relief Grants

Old Dock Elementary School in Whiteville, North Carolina, and James Monroe Elementary in Edison, New Jersey, were the recipients of the 2015 catastrophic disaster relief grants offered as a part of the AASL Beyond Words Grant funded by the Dollar General Literacy Foundation. Since 2012 two catastrophic grants are awarded yearly to schools that suffered a 90 percent or greater loss to the school library program due to a natural disaster, fire, or an act recognized by the federal government as terrorism.

Conferences and Workshops

ACRL 2015 National Conference

More than 5,000 library staff, exhibitors, speakers, and guests from all 50 states and 24 countries attended the ACRL 2015 Conference, held March 25–28 in Portland, Oregon. Themed "Creating Sustainable Community," the conference offered more than 500 programs that explored a host of pressing issues affecting higher education. Key topics included the changing nature and role of academic and research librarians, libraries as partners in higher education, scholarly communication, libraries and social justice, assessment, and trends in information literacy instruction, along with a variety of technology-related subjects such as e-textbooks, mobile services, and social media.

2015 Annual Conference

The 2015 ALA Annual Conference & Exhibition, June 25–30 in San Francisco, brought 22,696 attendees and exhibitors from all over the world.

The Opening General Session kicked off with cheers for that morning's announcement of the historic Supreme Court decision on marriage equality. As the litigator responsible for invalidating a key section of the Defense of Marriage Act (DOMA) two years to the day earlier, Roberta A. Kaplan was an especially timely and inspiring speaker, and surprise guest Nancy Pelosi, minority leader of the House of Representatives, added to the celebration. Pelosi attended to honor managers who kept the Enoch Pratt Free Library and its branches open and engaged with the Baltimore community during the civil unrest in April 2015.

"Show Your Pride" was a consistent conference theme, with special events and programs, and the wrap-up of ALA's first time sponsoring the nationwide GLBT Book Month. Around 100 conference attendees marched with staff from the San Francisco Public Library in Sunday's exuberant Pride Parade that passed just blocks from the conference site, while others cheered them on. Many other areas of equality, diversity, and inclusion provided a focus at the conference. Dozens of attendees suggested possible actions relating to diversity and inclusion by completing the sentence on the Networking Uncommons wall: "In order to improve the climate of diversity and inclusion within ALA, I plan to_____."

Some content was organized around ALA's three strategic directions: advocacy, information policy, and professional and leadership development. Rooms were packed for sessions on digital content, community engagement, the impact and potential of the newest technologies, digital literacy, the state of the school library, privacy and surveillance, services for makers, accessible gaming, innovative services for English Language Learners and immigrants, services for veterans, financial education, intellectual property and 3D printing, sustainable libraries, and many more.

Standing-room-only Auditorium Speaker sessions included writers, activists, thought-leaders, actors, and artists Gloria Steinem, Haifaa al-Mansour, Sarah Vowell, Nick Offerman, Joshua Davis with Rick Jacobs and David Thomson, Edwidge Danticat, and Sonia Manzano. At the President's Program, Courtney Young presented Sarah Lewis, whose "Embrace the Near Win" was selected as one of TED Talks' 2014 Collection of the Most Powerful Talks.

ALA at IFLA Congress in Cape Town

More than 3,000 delegates from 120 countries attended the IFLA Congress held in Cape Town, South Africa, August 15–21. ALA President Sari Feldman and Past-President Courtney Young led a delegation of 275 U.S. library professionals. President Feldman represented ALA at numerous high-level meetings and discussed ALA accreditation as a panelist at the "Quality Assurance of Library and Information Science" program. ALA member Donna Scheeder was inaugurated as the new IFLA President on August 21, and will serve a two-year term. ALA Executive Board Member Loida Garcia-Febo was re-elected to another two-year term on the IFLA Governing Board.

ALSC National Institute

The ALSC National Institute with the theme of "Believe. Build. Become" was held September 15–17, 2015, in Charlotte, North Carolina. The institute featured educational programming and inspirational speakers. A number of award-winning authors and illustrators were present and a special reception, held at ImaginOn, was a highlight event.

Sharjah International Book Fair/ALA Library Conference

Approximately 300 librarians gathered at the Sharjah International Book Fair (SIBF) in the United Arab Emirates, November 10–12, for the second SIBF/ALA Library Conference, ALA's most ambitious international professional development event. Librarians participated in the three days of programs, training, and networking, in both Arabic and English, with translation provided. ALA President Sari Feldman's opening keynote on Libraries Transform was followed by 17 concurrent sessions and poster sessions on a wide range of topics for all types of libraries.

LITA Forum

More than 270 attendees participated in the 2015 LITA Forum, November 12–15 in Minneapolis. Attendees participated in more than 55 sessions and heard three keynote speakers. LITA partnered with LLAMA to provide content specifically for administrators and managers at the forum.

2016 Midwinter Meeting

More than 11,700 attendees and exhibitors shared the latest library-related trends, updates, innovations, products, titles, and services at the 2016 ALA Midwinter Meeting and Exhibits in Boston, January 8–12, 2016.

With an emphasis on ALA's new national public awareness campaign, Libraries Transform, dozens of updates, discussion groups, workshops, and several high-profile speakers addressed in different ways how libraries are less about what they *have* and more about what they do *for* and *with* people. The "Because of You" branding at Midwinter honored library workers for their role in transforming libraries.

Several future-forward sessions were sponsored by ALA's Center for the Future of Libraries, the Office for Diversity, Literacy, and Outreach Services, and the Task Force on Equity, Diversity and Inclusion. They included the well-attended "Libraries Transform: Understanding Change," a three-hour interactive exploration with trainers from Kotter International, experts in the process and leadership of change, around libraries' current context and the question, "What do I need to be doing now to move my library into the future?" "Libraries Transform: Civic and Social Innovation" offered drop-in sessions with Boston-based civic and social innovators for two outward-looking forums exploring the changes happening in our communities, leading to engaged discussion about how those changes relate to libraries.

In "Creativity, Innovation and Change: Libraries Transform in the Digital Age," Harvard Law School's Jonathan Zittrain, ALA President Sari Feldman, ALA President-Elect Julie Todaro, and Director of ALA Office for Information Technology Policy Alan Inouye examined innovative library environments and how we can leverage them to illustrate our value to decision-makers and influencers at both national and local levels.

An interactive workshop, "If I Hadn't Believed It, I Wouldn't Have Seen It: Exploring Systemic Racism and Its Implications for Our Lives and Work," sponsored by the Office for Diversity, Literacy, and Outreach Services with the Task Force on Equity, Diversity, and Inclusion, engaged attendees at two sessions in an exploration of how race, systemic racism, and racial privilege have implications for our personal and professional lives.

Senator Cory Booker, featured speaker on the President's Program, addressed a standing-room-only crowd. In his impassioned talk, he focused on seeing opportunity and hope rather than just challenges. The senator talked about libraries as "treasures for all," and great equalizers in advancing digital inclusion.

ALA kicked off its 140th Anniversary at Midwinter with a "Because of You: Libraries Transform" cake celebration in front of the timeline in the ALA Lounge that offered a glimpse of how ALA has been engaged in supporting library transformation since 1876, and invited people to add their own highlights to the record.

Grants and Contributions

Research on Student Achievement

AASL was awarded a grant from the Institute of Museum and Library Services to discover what works at that intersection of formal and informal learning in the school library learning space, in order to provide reliable information to assess the impact of specific actions in library programs and by certified school library staffing.

Curiosity Grants

ALSC awarded 79 Curiosity Create grants of up to $7,500 each, made possible through a $800,000 donation from Disney. The grants spanned a broad range of geographic regions and service populations to support libraries in promoting exploration and discovery programming for children ages 6 to 14.

Google Grants to Boost Federal Advocacy

OGR received $25,000 through Google's Washington-based policy office to underwrite two initiatives: a series of advocacy videos to be jointly written and produced with the Harry Potter Alliance; and a series of events to be held at libraries around the country.

Public Programming

Grants from PPO enable libraries of all types, sizes, and budgets to boost their offerings and infuse their communities with new ideas. In 2015 the National Endowment for the Humanities (NEH) provided funding for the following programs: "Latino Americans: 500 Years of History" was awarded to 203 libraries to facilitate informed discussion in their communities about the long and fascinating history of Latinos in the United States; 50 sites received grants for the Great Stories Club, a reading and discussion program that gives at-risk youth the chance to read, reflect, and share ideas on topics that resonate with them; 50 sites were selected for a nationwide tour of Shakespeare's First Folio.

The U.S. National Library of Medicine provided funding for 104 libraries to host the traveling exhibition "Native Voices: Native Peoples' Concepts of Health and Illness."

The Institute of Museum and Library Services provided funding for ten libraries to offer "StoryCorps @ your library," allowing them to collect oral histories at their libraries.

The AARP Foundation provided funding to develop the AARP Integrated Services for Older Adults model for public libraries. Four public libraries were chosen as pilot sites for the new program, becoming a one-stop location for vulnerable older adults to receive assistance in their communities in AARP's four priority areas: hunger, income, housing, and isolation.

In collaboration with the Smithsonian's National Museum of Natural History Human Origins Program, PPO selected 19 public libraries to host the traveling exhibition "Exploring Human Origins: What Does It Mean to Be Human?"

Twenty-four public libraries from across the country will host interactive science- and technology-focused traveling exhibitions, bringing learning about the stars and planets, earth science and climate change, and technology to audiences of all ages. The exhibitions are offered by PPO in collaboration with the Space Science Institute National Center for Interactive Learning, the Lunar and Planetary Institute, and the Afterschool Alliance.

The Financial Industry Regulatory Authority (FINRA) Investor Education Foundation gave ALA more than $1.6 million to support financial literacy education in U.S. public libraries. The funding will support the development of a traveling exhibition on personal finance topics, which will tour public libraries nationwide over a two-year period. The FINRA Foundation support will also fund a research study of financial literacy resources and services available in U.S. public libraries.

Publishing

ALA Editions/ALA Neal-Schuman

The ALA Editions publishing strategy focuses on professional development titles whereas the Neal-Schuman publishing strategy focuses on library education. Together the two imprints published 50 titles in fiscal year (FY) 2015. Lead titles on the professional development side included Rebecca Vnuk's *The Weeding Handbook*, Ben Bizzle's *Start a Revolution: Stop Acting Like a Library*, and Paige Andrews's *RDA and Cartographic Resources*. Lead titles on the library education side included *Preserving Our Heritage* by Michelle Valerie Cloonan and *Introduction to Reference Sources in the Health Sciences, 6th edition,* by Jeffrey Huber and Susan Swogger. ALA Editions authors have played a substantial role in online continuing education for the profession and Neal-Schuman's rich content and author-experts allow ALA to expand the range and number of its growing list of e-books.

ALA TechSource

ALA TechSource, which continues to be the source for two enduring periodicals, *Library Technology Reports* and *Smart Libraries Newsletter*, also develops and presents online content for professional development through webinars and e-courses. It produces both original and re-purposed content (from ALA Editions and Neal-Schuman authors) for its growing list of programs. It also produces the ground-breaking AL Live series for *American Libraries* magazine. AL Live streams live interviews and panel discussions that are underwritten by industry sponsors and are free to participants. They can be viewed in real time from home, library, or a favorite wifi spot, and allow viewers to interact with hosts and expert panelists via active live chat. Notable webinars included "Building Great Programs for Patrons in the 20s and 30s" by Katie LaMantia and Emily Vinci, "How to Respond to a Security Incident in Your Library" by Steve Albrecht, and "Copyright, Licensing and the Law of eBooks" by Mary Minow. Notable e-courses included "Music Cataloging with RDA" by Sonia Archer-Capuzzo and "Basic Reference Skills for Non-Reference Librarians" by Francisca Goldsmith.

RDA: Resource Description and Access

Total users now number 8,500, a 10 percent increase over FY 2014, and the renewal rate is increasing. International sales are strong and growing. The RDA Toolkit now includes German, Spanish, and Finnish translation with Italian scheduled for release in the spring of 2016. Germany has adopted RDA as its national cataloging standard. Development is moving strongly into linked data. Training in RDA and RDA-related issues is offered from a number of sources, including regular, well-attended, free "RDA Toolkit Essentials" webinars and a number of "Janeathons" that offer live hackathon-like seminars to practice applying RDA principles to cataloging exercises.

ALA Graphics

Celebrities, beloved book characters, tie-ins with movies adapted from books, and event-related themes all continued to inspire ALA Graphics products and customers. Collaborating with units across ALA to create new posters, bookmarks, and other products for library-related celebrations is a hallmark of ALA Graphics' success every year: National Library Week (April) and Library Card Sign-up Month (September) with PAO; Banned Books Week (September) and Choose Privacy Week (May) with OIF; Teen Read Week (October) and Teen Tech Week (March) with YALSA; School Library Month (April) with AASL; Día (April) with ALSC; and National Friends of Libraries Week (October) with United for Libraries. Four catalogs mailed and distributed during the fiscal year introduce a host of new products, and FY 2015 included a range of posters featuring popular book characters, READ celebrities, TV series, and book-to-movie-inspired images, many with accompanying bookmarks, included the following: character posters featuring Olaf from the Disney movie *Frozen*, Pizzoli's Pals, another version of Bad Kitty to coincide with the publication of a new book in the popular series, Kate DiCamillo's Flora and Ulysses, Cece Bell's El Deafo, and the adoption of Snoopy as the Honorary Chair of Library Card Sign-up month. A Super Heroes series featured Wonder Woman, Bat Girl, Superman, and The Flash. Celebrity posters included Jane Lynch, Tim Howard, and Octavia Spencer.

Booklist Publications

The multi-platform suite of 13 products includes a new digital version of the magazine, The Booklist Reader, which aggregates all its e-newsletters, *Booklist* webinars (sponsor-supported online programs, free to registrants); Booklist Delivers (an e-blast service delivering sponsors' HTML promotions to the *Booklist* audience), *Booklist Online* (now serving more than 1.75 million pages per month), 22 print issues of *Booklist* and four issues of *Book Links*. *Booklist* webinars have continued to be a high-profile success, with well over 60,000 registrants (averaging 400 for each program) for the 40 to 50 programs moderated by *Booklist* editors and special guests. Registrants who are unable to attend can access archived recordings. In post-webinar surveys, 91.2 percent of attendees said the programs are useful. All past webinars can be accessed through the *Booklist* webinar archive. In conjunction with RUSA, *Booklist* co-sponsors the Andrew Carnegie Medal for Excellence in Fiction and Nonfiction. Awards in 2015 went to Anthony Doerr for *All the Light We Cannot See* and *Just Mercy: A Story of Justice and Redemption* by Bryan Stevenson. Both authors spoke in acceptance of the awards at the standing-room-only presentation at Annual Conference. *Booklist* programs at Annual Conference and Midwinter include the ERT/Booklist Author Forum and a popular new program called "Read and Rave," which brings together a panel of young adult and middle grade collection development librarians who roam the exhibit aisles in search of galleys to rave about.

American Libraries

American Libraries' new website, americanlibrariesmagazine.org, now includes responsive design and generated a 45 percent increase in sessions. On the homepage, *AL* introduced a Twitter-like feed called Latest Library Links, which provides up-to-date content about the industry and ALA. An increase in online-only content also boosted views, thanks in part to the hiring of a senior editor dedicated to generating and posting digital content. The magazine published many high-profile interviews featuring big names such as musician Pharrell Williams, bestselling author James Patterson, and National Book Award winners Jacqueline Woodson and Ursula K. Le Guin. Social media engagement includes more than 46,000 Twitter followers, nearly 9,000 Facebook fans, and 32 Pinterest boards with almost 5,000 pins. *AL*'s Twitter post about speaker Sonia Manzano's (a.k.a. "Maria") retirement from *Sesame Street* went viral, getting picked up by major news outlets such as *The New York Times*, the Associated Press, NPR, and *The Washington Post*. The publishing calendar included six print issues, one digital issue, and several digital supplements that covered ALA Online Learning, the State of America's Libraries Report, E-Content, American Dream Starts @ your library (with ALA's Office for Diversity, Literacy, and Outreach Services), and the IFLA edition—a print issue of which was distributed at the IFLA conference in Cape Town, South Africa. A final wrap-up piece appeared in a digital version of the supplement, accessible to all ALA members. AL Live, a live, interactive, sponsored streaming webinar produced in conjunction with ALA TechSource, continued to garner nearly 2,000 viewers per episode. AL Direct, the twice-a-week digital newsletter, will be approaching its 10th anniversary in 2016.

American Booksellers Association

333 Westchester Ave., Suite 202, White Plains, NY 10604
914-406-7500
World Wide Web http://www.bookweb.org

Founded in 1900, the American Booksellers Association (ABA) is a national not-for-profit trade organization that works to help independently owned bookstores grow and succeed.

ABA's core members are key participants in their communities' local economies and culture, and to assist them ABA creates relevant programs; provides education, information, business products, and services; and engages in public policy and industry advocacy. The association actively supports and defends free speech and the First Amendment rights of all Americans. A volunteer board of booksellers governs the association.

At the end of 2015 independent bookstore members of ABA reported another year of growth both in numbers and overall business, as well as strong holiday sales. The national resurgence in independent stores continued, with new stores opening, established stores finding new owners, and a new generation coming into the business as owner/managers and frontline booksellers.

In 2015 ABA welcomed 60 independent bookstores that opened in 31 states and the District of Columbia. In another sign of the health of independent bookstores, 16 established ABA member businesses were bought by new owners.

Following the final rush of holiday shoppers, booksellers reported healthy sales in 2015 and an equally encouraging start to 2016. A strong kickoff on Small Business Saturday, November 28, launched a successful holiday season for independent bookstores, boosted by "buy local" campaigns and widespread media coverage that trumpeted local booksellers and the unique draw of neighborhood stores.

Nationally, ABA reported that, based on the more than 500 stores reporting to the weekly Indie Bestsellers List, unit sales of books maintained the growth seen over the past few years, with an increase over 2014 of a little more than 10 percent.

ABA member bookstores and other independent businesses experienced strong sales growth in 2015, buoyed by their strong community ties and growing public awareness of the benefits of locally owned businesses, according to the results of the 2016 Independent Business Survey. Released in February 2016, the ninth annual survey conducted by the Institute for Local Self-Reliance in partnership with Advocates for Independent Business gathered data from more than 3,200 locally owned businesses, including members of ABA.

Survey respondents reported brisk sales in 2015, with revenue growing 6.6 percent on average in 2015, up from 5.3 percent the previous year. Independent retailers, who made up just under half the sample, saw revenue increase 4.7 percent in 2015. Holiday sales at local stores also grew by an average of 3.1 percent, beating the performance of many national chains and coming in ahead of the 1.6 percent rise in December retail sales reported by the U.S. Department of Commerce.

The survey results suggest that the strength of the independent sector is owed partly to an improving economy and partly to the spread of the "buy local" movement. Two-thirds of respondents in cities with an active Local First, or "buy local," campaign said that the initiative is having a noticeable positive impact on their business, including attracting new customers and fostering increased loyalty among existing customers. Survey respondents cited a wide range of direct benefits from "buy local" campaigns, with about one-third of businesses in Local First cities reporting that the initiative had led them to become more engaged in advocating on public policy issues and 45 percent saying they had resulted in more awareness and support among city officials.

However, the survey found that independent businesses are facing a number of challenges, including a lack of credit for businesses seeking to grow. One in three independent businesses applying for a bank loan in the last two years reported being unable to secure one. That figure was 54 percent among minority-owned businesses, and 41 percent among young firms, whose expansion has historically been a key source of net job growth.

Other challenges included public policy issues, competition from large Internet companies and large competitors that can use their market power to secure better pricing and terms from suppliers, the rising cost of commercial rent, and steep swipe fees set by credit card companies.

For the third year in a row, Indies First, a national campaign of activities and events in support of independent bookstores, marked another successful kickoff to the holiday shopping season on Small Business Saturday. Nearly 500 independent bookstores participated, inviting hundreds of authors into their stores to serve as honorary booksellers for the day.

Unit sales of books were up slightly over 2014 for the week including Indies First on Small Business Saturday. According to the Small Business Saturday Consumer Insights Survey, released on November 30, 2015, by American Express and the National Federation of Independent Business, total spending among U.S. consumers who were aware of Small Business Saturday increased by 14 percent in 2015, reaching $16.2 billion spent at independent retailers and restaurants on the day, up from $14.3 billion in 2014.

In December 2015 author James Patterson awarded $250,000 in holiday bonuses to independent bookstore employees to thank them for their dedication to spreading the joy of reading. Anyone was allowed to nominate a bookseller by answering the question, "Why does this bookseller deserve a holiday bonus?" Bonuses of $2,500 and $5,000 were awarded to 87 independent booksellers out of 2,848 nominations received.

"These grants and bonuses are my humble acknowledgment of some of the terrific work taking place in libraries and bookstores," Patterson said. ABA CEO Oren Teicher said "Once again, we are enormously grateful for James Patterson's wonderful generosity. Nobody puts their money where their mouth is more than Jim. Providing extra financial support to individuals who spend their entire day putting books into the hands of customers and spreading the joy of reading is an extraordinary gesture."

Also in 2015 booksellers celebrated the inaugural Independent Bookstore Day on May 2 with author events, discounts and giveaways, tasty treats, and special literary-themed merchandise available exclusively at 400 bookstores across the country. Results from a survey of the participating stores showed solid sales gains, with 80 percent of the responding stores reporting a sales increase over the first Saturday of May 2014. ABA created an interactive Independent Bookstore

Day map on its IndieBound.org website that allowed users to find bookstores that would be hosting events and selling the special literary-themed merchandise.

In July 2015 independent bookstores and other locally owned businesses across the nation took part in the fourth annual Find Waldo Local community-building event. Co-sponsored by the American Booksellers Association and Where's Waldo? publisher Candlewick Press, the campaign invited shoppers to pick up passports at any of 250 participating bookstores throughout July and to visit nearby businesses to hunt for the famous children's book character, earning stamps to be redeemed for prizes along the way.

In October ABA launched the Revisit and Rediscover program, a new feature on the Indie Next Lists that provides the independent bookstore channel opportunities to showcase and support favorite backlist titles. The initiative was developed in response to requests from booksellers and publishers to find new ways of highlighting the strong backlist works that provide a foundation for both bookstores and publishing houses. Two panels of booksellers compiled lists of enduring backlist titles they consider critical for bookstores to have on their shelves at all times. The first round of featured titles debuted on the December Indie Next List and the Winter Kids' Indie Next List fliers.

Also in October ABA launched a test designed to increase traffic to member stores—and to their e-commerce websites—by improving the online shopping experience for an initial purchase on IndieBound.org. ABA will evaluate the test results and report back to members in 2016.

Association and Governance

The results of balloting by the bookstore members of ABA to elect three directors to serve three-year terms on the ABA Board (2015–2018) were announced in May 2015.

In keeping with the 2011 amendment to ABA's Bylaws, which established two-year terms for board officers, Betsy Burton of The King's English Bookshop in Salt Lake City, Utah, was elected to a two-year term (2015–2017) as ABA president, and Robert Sindelar of Third Place Books in Lake Forest Park, Washington, was elected to serve a two-year term as vice president/secretary.

Elected to three-year terms (2015–2018) as directors were Valerie Koehler of Blue Willow Bookshop in Houston, Texas; Pete Mulvihill of Green Apple Books in San Francisco, California; and Jonathon Welch of Talking Leaves . . . Books in Buffalo, New York. This marked the second three-year term for Koehler and Welch, and the first for Mulvihill.

Continuing on the 10-member board were Sarah Bagby of Watermark Books and Café in Wichita, Kansas; John Evans of DIESEL, A Bookstore in Oakland, Larkspur, and Brentwood, California; Jamie Fiocco of Flyleaf Books in Chapel Hill, North Carolina; Matthew Norcross of McLean & Eakin Booksellers in Petoskey, Michigan; and Annie Philbrick of Bank Square Books in Mystic, Connecticut.

Leaving the board was Steve Bercu of BookPeople in Austin, Texas, who finished his second year as ABA president at the end of May.

At its July meeting, the ABA board unanimously approved a proposal to amend the association's bylaws in order to increase the number of booksellers serving on the board from 10 to 11. In explaining the reasoning behind this decision, ABA President Betsy Burton said that, "one more place at the board table will encourage the opportunity for diversity," and that the proposed change would also improve the association's governance by avoiding tie votes.

The change was approved by the membership in a vote that concluded on October 26. With more than 10 percent of ABA membership participating in the balloting—which the association's bylaws require for the voting process to be valid—the amendment passed with 299 in favor and 1 opposed.

Book Awards

The winners of the 2015 Indies Choice Book Awards and the E. B. White Read-Aloud Awards, as voted by independent booksellers nationwide, were announced in April 2015.

The **2015 Indies Choice Book Award winners** "reflecting the spirit of independent bookstores nationwide" were:

- Adult Fiction: *All the Light We Cannot See: A Novel* by Anthony Doerr (Scribner)
- Adult Nonfiction: *Being Mortal: Medicine and What Matters in the End* by Atul Gawande (Metropolitan Books)
- Adult Debut Book: *The Martian: A Novel* by Andy Weir (Crown)
- Young Adult: *The Darkest Part of the Forest* by Holly Black (Little, Brown)

E. B. White Read-Aloud Awards "reflecting the playful, well-paced language, the engaging themes, and the universal appeal embodied by E. B. White's collection of beloved books":

- Middle Reader: *Brown Girl Dreaming* by Jacqueline Woodson (Nancy Paulsen Books)
- Picture Book: *Sam and Dave Dig a Hole* by Mac Barnett, illus. by Jon Klassen (Candlewick)

Indie Champion Award "presented to the author or illustrator who booksellers feel has the best sense of the importance of independent bookstores to their communities at large and the strongest personal commitment to foster and support the mission and passion of independent booksellers":

- Neil Gaiman and Amanda Palmer (HarperCollins/Hachette)

Indie booksellers choose three classic picture books each year for induction into the **Picture Book Hall of Fame**. The 2015 inductees were:

- *Blueberries for Sal* by Robert McCloskey (Viking)
- *Frog and Toad* by Arnold Lobel (HarperCollins)
- *If You Give a Mouse a Cookie* by Laura Numeroff, illus. by Felicia Bond (HarperCollins)

The **2015 Honor Award** recipients were:

- Adult Fiction: *The Bone Clocks: A Novel* by David Mitchell (Random House); *The Magician's Land: A Novel* by Lev Grossman (Viking); *The Museum of Extraordinary Things: A Novel* by Alice Hoffman (Scribner); *Natchez Burning: A Novel* by Greg Iles (William Morrow); *Station Eleven: A Novel* by Emily St. John Mandel (Knopf).
- Adult Nonfiction: *Can't We Talk About Something More Pleasant? A Memoir* by Roz Chast (Bloomsbury); *The Empathy Exams: Essays* by Leslie Jamison (Graywolf); *In the Kingdom of Ice: The Grand and Terrible Polar Voyage of the USS Jeannette* by Hampton Sides (Doubleday); *Just Mercy: A Story of Justice and Redemption* by Bryan Stevenson (Spiegel & Grau); *On Immunity: An Inoculation* by Eula Biss (Graywolf).
- Adult Debut: *Fourth of July Creek: A Novel* by Smith Henderson (Ecco); *I Am Pilgrim: A Thriller* by Terry Hayes (Emily Bestler Books/Atria); *Painted Horses: A Novel* by Malcolm Brooks (Grove Press); *The Queen of the Tearling: A Novel* by Erika Johansen (Harper); *Shotgun Lovesongs: A Novel* by Nickolas Butler (Thomas Dunne).
- Young Adult: *Glory O'Brien's History of the Future* by A. S. King (Little, Brown); *Noggin* by John Corey Whaley (Atheneum); *The Shadow Hero* by Gene Luen Yang, illus. by Sonny Liew (First Second); *Tell Me Again How a Crush Should Feel: A Novel* by Sara Farizan (Algonquin); *This One Summer* by Jillian Tamaki and Mariko Tamaki (First Second).

E. B. White Read-Aloud:

- Middle Reader: *The Boundless*, by Kenneth Oppel, illus. by Jim Tierney (Simon & Schuster); *The Fourteenth Goldfish* by Jennifer L. Holm (Random House); *A Snicker of Magic* by Natalie Lloyd (Scholastic); *The Terrible Two* by Mac Barnett and Jory John, illus. by Kevin Cornell (Amulet); *The War That Saved My Life* by Kimberly Brubaker Bradley (Dial).
- Picture Book: *Goodnight Already!* by Jory John, illus. by Benji Davies (HarperCollins); *Kid Sheriff and the Terrible Toads* by Bob Shea, illus. by Lane Smith (Roaring Brook); *Last Stop on Market Street* by Matt de la Peña, illus. by Christian Robinson (Putnam); *The Smallest Girl in the Smallest Grade* by Justin Roberts, illus. by Christian Robinson (Putnam); *This Is a Moose* by Richard T. Morris, illus. by Tom Lichtenheld (Little, Brown).

Indie Champion:

- Authors United, represented by Douglas Preston (Hachette); Jeff Kinney (Abrams); Dav Pilkey (Scholastic); Richard Russo (Knopf/Vintage); Garth Stein (Simon & Schuster, HarperCollins).

Personnel

ABA experienced personnel changes during 2015. In March Robyn DesHotel was appointed chief financial officer to replace long-time ABA CFO Eleanor Chang. A graduate of Rice University and the Stanford Graduate School of Business with more than 20 years of finance-related experience, DesHotel came to ABA from PEN American Center, Inc., where she had served as the organization's director of finance and administration since 2010.

At the end of June Neil Strandberg left his position as ABA's director of technology to join the staff of Shelf Awareness as director of technology and operations. Following the restructuring of the organization's technology department, ABA CEO Oren Teicher announced the promotion of Marketing and Content Technology Manager Greg Galloway to ABA technology director; with this promotion, Galloway joined ABA's senior staff. Geetha Nathan, lead developer for IndieCommerce, was promoted to manager of IndieCommerce. After further reorganization, Phil Davies joined ABA's IndieCommerce Department in January 2016, stepping into the newly minted position of IndieCommerce director.

On June 27 former CEO Avin Mark Domnitz, who served from 1997 to 2009, died of cancer at the age of 71. Domnitz was the owner of Dickens Books and then co-owner of the Harry W. Schwartz Bookshops in Milwaukee, Wisconsin, when his many years of service to independent booksellers began. He served on the ABA board for two terms and was president of the association from 1994 to 1996. Domnitz was honored by his ABA colleagues at BookExpo America 2015.

Member Education

The 11th Winter Institute (Wi11), held in Denver, Colorado, January 23–26, 2016, brought close to 600 ABA member booksellers, 100-plus authors, and 40 international guests from Australia, New Zealand, the Netherlands, and France to the Sheraton Downtown Denver Hotel.

Wi11 featured three days of keynote addresses and featured speakers, education sessions, rep picks presentations, publisher/bookseller focus groups, and breakout sessions. The event was made possible by the generous support of lead sponsor Ingram Content Group and 72 publisher sponsors. Booksellers and international guests had the opportunity to take tours of bookstores in the Denver area.

In celebration of ABA's new Revisit and Rediscover backlist initiative, the opening reception was followed by the first annual Backlist Book Swap, where hundreds of booksellers and publishers shared their favorite backlist books. Those who participated were encouraged to bring a copy of their favorite "under-read" book, a title at least five years old and still in print.

ABA CEO Oren Teicher welcomed booksellers on January 25 and shared new evidence that the resurgence of independent bookstores is continuing apace: Overall sales across the network of independent bookstores were up 10 percent in 2015, almost 8 percent on a per store basis, Teicher said, and total book sales at indie bookstores exceeded $500 million last year, which does not count non-book or other store revenues.

"In a year that saw bricks-and-mortar retailers pressured by lots of things, independent bookstores once again fulfilled their mission of putting the right books in the hands of readers and book buyers while growing their businesses in what obviously remains a challenging environment," said Teicher. "At ABA, we appreciate these challenges and we know that not every store in every community is seeing this growth, but the important fact is that nationally you are succeeding, and we will continue to work hard to see that growth across the country."

On the same day representatives from the economics consulting group Civic Economics released "Amazon and Empty Storefronts: The Fiscal and Land Use Impact of Online Retail," a groundbreaking new study commissioned by ABA that details the overall negative impact that Amazon has had on Main Street retailers and jobs. The study revealed that the real costs and ramifications of Amazon's expansion have been even more pronounced than many people had thought.

The study found that in 2014 Amazon sold $44.1 billion worth of retail goods nationwide, and that this growth and retail displacement resulted in a total of more than $1 billion in revenue lost to state and local governments. In addition, the study estimates that the shift to online sales has resulted in a national reduction in demand for retail space totaling over 100 million square feet, the equivalent of more than 30,000 traditional storefronts employing 136,000 workers

ABA awarded 67 scholarships to the Winter Institute, including several aimed at fostering diversity. Fifty-eight scholarships were supported by the event's publisher sponsors; five were sponsored by the Book Industry Charitable Foundation (Binc), a nonprofit dedicated to providing financial assistance to booksellers; and three were awarded in honor of former ABA CEO Avin Mark Domnitz, including one awarded by ABA to a bookseller at a store participating in this year's ABACUS survey, and two supported by memorial contributions to ABA following his death. Candlewick Press again awarded a scholarship to a bookseller active in the Candlewick Handselling Indie Recognition Program (CHIRP).

In 2015 ABA staff traveled around the country during the regional spring forums, meeting with approximately 350 member booksellers during the months of March and April. Held in conjunction with the regional bookseller associations, the annual forums are designed to provide an opportunity to share ideas, discuss industry issues, and receive updates on various association projects. At this year's forums, ABA presented a new education session, "Exploring New Markets," which examined opportunities provided by customer demographics and proven sales and marketing initiatives, as well as the practical steps necessary for booksellers to implement appropriate programs in their bookstores.

In May 2015 the annual BookExpo America conference and trade show was held at the Javits Convention Center in New York City. ABA hosted two networking events for editors and publicists—"Meet the Editor" and "Publicists Speed Dating"—open exclusively to ABA bookseller members. "Publicists Speed Dating" provided stores with the opportunity to meet one-on-one with publicists for approximately 12 minutes each to learn what publicists look for when planning an author tour, while "Meet the Editor" allowed booksellers to meet in a small group with book editors at a publisher's New York City offices for a behind-the-scenes peek at the editing process.

In fall 2015 ABA presented the all-new education session "The Economics of Publishing and How They Impact Booksellers" at each of the eight fall regional trade shows. Leading publishing executives provided booksellers with important insights into the financial realities they face every day.

A special bookseller workshop focused on human resources in conjunction with the Pacific Northwest Booksellers Association and New England Independent Booksellers Association trade shows. The new, in-depth education event, presented by Dr. John Sherlock, director of the Master of Science in Human Resources Program at Western Carolina University, covered essential aspects of HR for small businesses.

ABA's programming regarding children's bookselling also continued to grow in 2015.

The ABC Children's Group at ABA welcomed 190 booksellers to Pasadena, California, in April 2015 for an upbeat and energetic ABC Children's Institute, ABA's third standalone event for children's booksellers.

ABA published its annual financial survey of participating independent bookstores, the ABACUS report, once again in 2015. Stores participating in the ABACUS project receive a customized report that analyzes their financial results, including comparisons with other businesses based on multiple criteria (such as sales level, store size, and community type) in addition to year-to-year trending information.

ABACUS helps participating stores benchmark key economic indicators and create a roadmap for growth and profitability. In addition, ABACUS is used in aggregate by ABA to create timely education for all members.

The IndieCommerce team completed its execution of the migration of several hundred stores' e-commerce websites to the Drupal 7 platform. Throughout the process, IndieCommerce staff communicated and worked with bookstores in a number of ways, including through dedicated e-mail updates, conference calls, a series of webinars, and sessions and one-on-one meetings at BookExpo America.

Advocacy

ABA's vigorous advocacy efforts on behalf of member bookstores continued during 2015.

Among other activities, ABA focused much of its advocacy resources on the growing minimum wage issue, in addition to the ongoing sales tax fairness campaign and health care reform.

As a growing number of cities tackle the question of raising the minimum wage, ABA called on mayors across the country to include indie retailers, such as booksellers, in any discussions on increasing the minimum wage in their cities.

To assist booksellers in advocating for minimum wage policies that take into account the economic realities of independent retailing, ABA also created the Minimum Wage Legislative Tool Kit, which provides a number of items to help booksellers work with lawmakers, town officials, and the media to develop good minimum wage policy. Included is an interactive spreadsheet and a "Minimum Wage Impact Calculator," a powerful visual tool that booksellers can use when meeting with key decision-makers.

ABA continued to work with the Marketplace Fairness Coalition, which includes a diverse array of trade associations and businesses of all sizes, in order to more effectively advocate for its members in the nation's capital.

In addition, Advocates for independent Business (AIB), a coalition of independent trade associations and businesses that ABA co-founded in late 2013, continued to advocate on behalf of independent business. In response to the subsidies and tax incentives that Amazon has been receiving from a growing number of municipalities to entice the online giant to open distribution centers, AIB and the Institute for Local Self-Reliance (ILSR) created and released a one-page fact sheet, "5 Things Local Officials Need to Know Before Welcoming an Amazon Warehouse," which provides data that reveal how these deals actually do more harm than good to local economies. Between 2012 and 2014, Amazon received $431 million in local tax incentives and other subsidies from local and state governments to finance its warehouse expansion. But Amazon has a long history of shirking its obligation to collect and remit sales tax, and still does not collect in 19 of the 45 states that collect and remit sales tax.

In addition, ABA, as part of a broad coalition of booksellers and authors, asked the U.S. Supreme Court to review a decision by the Second Circuit Court of Appeals in the case *U.S. v. Apple*, which found that Apple violated antitrust law by coordinating with major U.S. book publishers to influence the price of e-books.

The friend-of-the-court brief created by the Authors Guild, Authors United, the American Booksellers Association, and Barnes & Noble was filed in December in the interest of competitive e-book pricing, and was a continuation of the efforts of authors and booksellers to ensure that the nation's book markets aren't controlled by a single dominant player.

The brief highlights the benefits of a competitive e-book economy and argues that Apple's entry into the e-book market enhanced competition by decreasing the average price of e-books and increasing the number of e-book titles and of e-book distributors. This, the brief notes, has led to technological improvements in the e-book market and enhanced freedom of expression and access to e-books.

On the health reform front, ABA continued to provide its members with key information about the Affordable Care Act, such as how to claim health care tax credits and how to purchase insurance through exchanges.

After merging in late 2014 with the American Booksellers Association, the American Booksellers for Free Expression, or ABFE (formerly known as the American Booksellers Foundation for Free Expression, or ABFFE), dove right into its free speech advocacy efforts as the year started. Joining with the National Coalition Against Censorship (NCAC), ABA and ABFE condemned the January 7, 2015, terrorist attack on French satirical magazine *Charlie Hebdo*, in which ten staffers were killed by gunmen who stormed the publication's Parisian headquarters.

Later in the year ABFE served as a sponsor of Banned Books Week along with such organizations as the American Library Association, the Association of American Publishers, and PEN American Center. Nationwide, bookstores put their own unique spins on Banned Books Week with creative events, social media posts, and eye-catching displays that celebrate the freedom to read. The 2015 event focused on YA books that have been challenged or banned.

Association of Research Libraries

21 Dupont Circle N.W., Washington, DC 20036
202-296-2296, e-mail arlhq@arl.org
World Wide Web http://www.arl.org

Kaylyn Groves
Senior Writer and Editor

The Association of Research Libraries (ARL) is a nonprofit organization of 124 research libraries in the United States and Canada. ARL's mission is to influence the changing environment of scholarly communication and the public policies that affect research libraries and the diverse communities they serve. ARL pursues this mission by advancing the goals of its member research libraries, providing leadership in public and information policy to the scholarly and higher education communities, fostering the exchange of ideas and expertise, facilitating the emergence of new roles for research libraries, and shaping a future environment that leverages its interests with those of allied organizations.

The year 2015 saw transformation for the association. ARL and its member libraries began implementing the Strategic Framework and System of Action that were developed in 2014. The System of Action fosters efforts in five areas: the ARL Academy, Collective Collections, Innovation Lab, Libraries That Learn, and Scholarly Dissemination Engine. Four enabling capacities address advocacy and public policy, assessment, diversity and inclusion, and member engagement and outreach across all initiatives within the System of Action.

Below are highlights of the association's achievements in 2015, many of which were undertaken in partnership with member libraries or other organizations. For links to additional information about these accomplishments and an infographic of ARL's 2015 transformations and impact in higher education and society, visit http://www.arl.org/about/arl-key-accomplishments-in-2015.

Advocacy and Public Policy

ARL's Advocacy and Public Policy capacity includes analysis of legal and legislative public policy issues and encompasses advocacy for issues of timely importance to the research library and higher education community.

In February the association published *Research Library Issues* (*RLI*) no. 285, a special issue focusing on recent developments in U.S. copyright law as well as international copyright agreements. Many of these developments have significant implications for research libraries and higher education, such as affirming the right to provide access to digitized text for people with print disabilities.

In late February 64 organizations and institutions participated in Fair Use Week, an annual celebration of the doctrines of fair use and fair dealing, which allow the use of copyrighted materials without permission from the copyright holder under certain circumstances. Fair Use Week 2015 was organized by ARL, and participants included universities, libraries, library associations, and a number of other organizations. Over the course of the week, more than 90 blog posts, 13 videos, 2 podcasts, a comic book, ARL's "Fair Use Fundamentals" infographic, and several other resources were released. See "Fair Use Week 2015 Highlights" on the ARL website for an overview and links to many of the week's resources.

Also in February the U.S. Federal Communications Commission (FCC) voted in favor of adopting rules to protect and promote the open Internet, also known as net neutrality. The Open Internet Order ensures that Internet providers do not create "fast lanes" for those willing and able to pay a premium and "slow lanes" for everyone else—and that the Internet remains open and available to all. ARL participated actively with partner organizations in FCC's Open Internet proceeding that led to the adoption of the Open Internet Order, which incorporated many of the joint principles filed by library and higher education organizations in 2014. In September ARL joined the American Library Association, Association of College and Research Libraries, and Chief Officers of State Library Agencies in submitting an amicus brief in the DC Court of Appeals case *United States Telecom Association, et al.,* v. *Federal Communications Commission (FCC) and the United States of America.* The brief expresses these organizations' support of FCC's Open Internet Order establishing rules protecting net neutrality.

In March and October ARL presented two free webinars about the accessibility of electronic resources. The March webinar, "Working Together: Research Libraries and Publishers on the Value of Inclusive Learning Resources," raised awareness about the value of producing or procuring accessible born-digital resources to support library users of all abilities. The October webinar, "Library and Publisher Roles in Making E-Resources Accessible to Users of All Abilities," looked at recent successes and challenges to spur an active dialogue about the future of the digital book and the roles of research libraries and publishers in facilitating improved access to information.

In June the U.S. Senate voted in favor of the USA Freedom Act—legislation that bans the bulk collection of phone records that has been practiced by the National Security Agency since 2006—and President Obama signed the bill into law. ARL supported this bill as the first step forward in meaningful surveillance reform.

Also in June ARL's Accessibility and Universal Design Working Group launched a new blog devoted to facilitating web accessibility in research libraries, as an enhancement of ARL's Web Accessibility Toolkit. The working group hopes the blog will stimulate discussion of accessibility issues in the research library community, and encourages individuals to share their ideas and knowledge by contributing posts to the blog.

In October the U.S. Court of Appeals for the Second Circuit unanimously ruled in *Authors Guild* v. *Google*—also known as the "Google Books" case—that Google's mass scanning and digital indexing of books for use in creating a searchable online library constituted a legal "fair use" of copyrighted material rather than an infringement. ARL supported Google in this ten-year case. For an in-depth analysis of the Second Circuit's decision, see the ARL issue brief on the Google Books case. The Library Copyright Alliance—consisting of the American Library Association, Association of Research Libraries, and Association of College and Research Libraries—updated its one-page "Google Books Litigation Family Tree," summarizing the case's chronology in a graphical format.

Also in October the Library of Congress released its final rules for the current three-year cycle of the Digital Millennium Copyright Act's (DMCA) Section

1201 rulemaking. The updated rules continue to support access for people who are print disabled by allowing them to circumvent technological protection measures on literary works distributed electronically. The rules also expand a copyright exemption for motion picture excerpts for educational purposes. ARL, as part of the Library Copyright Alliance, submitted five filings in the rulemaking process in February.

The 12 negotiating parties for the Trans-Pacific Partnership Agreement (TPP)—a large regional trade agreement that had been under negotiation since 2010—announced the conclusion of the agreement in October. ARL had been actively involved over the course of the negotiations, and the release of the final text revealed mixed results. While there are some areas of text that are disappointing, overall the final language of the copyright provisions improved significantly from the initial proposals made by the United States. The final text includes more flexibility for the TPP parties and also includes language supporting limitations and exceptions, including for those with print disabilities. ARL published an issue brief on the final TPP text regarding intellectual property.

Over the course of the year, ARL worked closely with the Obama administration and members of Congress to support ratification of the World Intellectual Property Organization (WIPO) Marrakesh Treaty to Facilitate Access to Published Works for Persons Who Are Blind, Visually Impaired, or Otherwise Print Disabled. The Marrakesh Treaty is a significant achievement as the first WIPO treaty dedicated to limitations and exceptions, focusing on the rights of users rather than increasing the rights of rightholders. The United States has signed but not yet ratified the treaty; it was expected that the treaty would be sent to the Senate in early 2016 for ratification. ARL published an issue brief on the Marrakesh Treaty background and ratification status in December.

ARL Academy

With the ARL Academy initiative, the association is fostering the development of an agile, diverse workforce and the inspiring leadership necessary to meet present and future challenges. (See the "Diversity and Inclusion" section below for accomplishments specific to that area.)

In 2015 ARL published three *Workforce Transformation Stories* in which library leaders describe new workplace developments and promote organizational change: "Communities of Practice to Deepen Leadership Practice" and "Creating an Aboriginal Internship" by Jill Mierke, director of human resources for the University of Saskatchewan Library, and "Changes in Hiring Accelerate and Enhance Culture Change" by Joyce E. B. Backus, associate director for library operations, and Kathel Dunn, program coordinator of the Associate Fellowship Program, at the U.S. National Library of Medicine.

ARL, Columbia University Libraries, Cornell University Libraries, and the University of Toronto Libraries held a pilot Library Liaison Institute in June. Nearly 50 liaison librarians from the three institutions convened at Cornell for two days to examine—through a mix of presentations and active learning experiences—future models for structuring liaison work, and to discuss ways to measure the impact of liaison work on fulfilling the mission of the university. In December ARL published the final report of the event, which summarizes the institute and provides critical reflections and recommendations for reorganizing liaison work as well as guidance for offering future Library Liaison Institutes.

Also in June the association created the Julia C. Blixrud Memorial Fund to honor the memory and extend the legacy of long-time ARL staff member Julia Blixrud. The fund supports a scholarship for one master of library and information science (MLIS) student or recent graduate to attend the ARL Fall Forum each year. The forum is a one-day conference on a topic of interest to the research library community, held immediately after ARL's Fall Meeting in Washington, D.C., each October. Generous contributions from the community have established the memorial fund for the scholarship, to which organizations and individuals are welcome to contribute. In addition to the scholarship, ARL founded an annual keynote lecture at the Fall Forum in memory of Julia.

In November ARL selected 28 individuals to participate in the 2016–2017 Leadership Fellows program. This executive leadership program facilitates the development of future senior-level leaders in large research libraries and archives. Three sponsor libraries—University of Alberta, Colorado State University, and Duke University—and the Leadership Fellows Advisory Group are helping to design and support the 2016–2017 offering of this program.

ARL in November released *Evolution of Library Liaisons*, SPEC Kit 349, an exploration of the changing role of library liaison, the shifting goals and strategies of liaison programs at ARL member libraries, and the factors that influence these changes on an institutional level. A December webcast presented the SPEC survey findings and enabled webcast participants to discuss trends with the survey authors.

Assessment

ARL's Assessment capacity collects data that offer information and support decision making. This capacity also creates processes for collecting and disseminating analytics and metrics.

A series of four webinars in March and April focused on data visualization for library stories. Using Tableau software, libraries can better harness, analyze, and report their data to internal and external stakeholders. Video recordings of the series are freely available on ARL's YouTube channel.

In June the association published the *ARL Annual Salary Survey 2014–2015*, which analyzes salary data for all professional staff working in the 125 ARL member libraries in fiscal 2014–2015. The data show that Canadian ARL librarians' salaries kept pace with inflation, but U.S. ARL librarians' salaries did not.

In August Quinn Galbraith was appointed a visiting program officer (VPO) for 2015–2016 to research salary trends using the ARL Annual Salary Survey data. Galbraith, a social science librarian and former human resources manager for the Harold B. Lee Library at Brigham Young University (BYU), is examining whether minority- and gender-based differences in salaries can be explained by such factors as family size, family-related leaves, attitudes toward promotion, and years of experience, among other variables. The ARL Assessment Committee is serving in an advisory capacity on the project. In an effort to examine these additional variables, Galbraith distributed a survey to 44 ARL libraries; more than 1,250 librarians responded. He will use this data in conjunction with 35 years of ARL

Annual Salary Survey data to conduct his analysis. Galbraith recently published the results of a separate survey of 719 librarians at ARL institutions, examining academic librarians' job satisfaction and work/life balance: "The Impact of Faculty Status and Gender on Employee Well-being in Academic Libraries" by Quinn Galbraith, Leanna Fry, and Melissa Garrison, in *College & Research Libraries* 77, no. 1 (January 2016): 71–86.

In October ARL published *ARL Statistics 2013–2014*, *ARL Academic Health Sciences Library Statistics 2013–2014*, and *ARL Academic Law Library Statistics 2013–2014*. These are the latest in a series of annual publications that describe the collections, staffing, expenditures, and service activities of member libraries.

Also in October the Integrated Postsecondary Education Data System (IPEDS) Academic Libraries Component adopted revised definitions for fiscal year (FY) 2015 as a result of recommendations made by a joint ARL, ACRL, and ALA task force. The task force offered a free webinar to inform academic libraries of the changes and help the community prepare to complete the FY 2015 IPEDS Academic Libraries Component survey.

Collective Collections

With the Collective Collections initiative ARL is motivating the creation of deep and wide platforms for ensuring that knowledge resources are accessible and sustained through federated networks of print, digital, data, and artifactual repositories, created and managed by collectives of institutions in North America and beyond. SHARE is a key part of this strategy, operating at the network level and unifying distributed resources.

ARL—in partnership with the Association of American Universities, Association of Public and Land-grant Universities, and Center for Open Science—in 2015 further developed the SHARE initiative, higher education's venture to promote accessibility of research:

In April the project launched the public beta of SHARE Notify, which generates a feed of research release events—such as posting a preprint to a disciplinary repository, depositing a data set into a data repository, publishing a peer-reviewed article—from diverse sources. By the end of the year the SHARE Notify database included more than 3 million research releases contributed by 77 data providers.

In June 60 individuals from universities, corporations, nonprofit organizations, and government agencies gathered in Washington, D.C., for the second SHARE Community Meeting. Participants included SHARE Working Group members, SHARE Notify beta participants, technical partners, and other stakeholders. Most of the meeting was devoted to a small number of breakout task groups to explore specific issues, helping to define SHARE's opportunities, scope out limitations and boundaries, and identify what successful execution will look like and who it will benefit.

In September ARL appointed two visiting program officers to work on SHARE from September 2015 to March 2017. Cynthia Hudson-Vitale, digital data librarian in research data and GIS services at Washington University in St.

Louis Libraries, is providing outreach and engagement support for SHARE. Rick Johnson, program co-director for the Digital Initiatives and Scholarship Program and head of data curation and digital library solutions at University of Notre Dame's Hesburgh Libraries, is fostering SHARE metadata enhancements and strengthening partnerships between SHARE and other research data stewards and providers.

In October the Institute of Museum and Library Services (IMLS) and the Alfred P. Sloan Foundation awarded ARL a joint $1.2 million grant to expand and enhance SHARE's open data set of research and scholarly activities across their life cycle. The grant will help support SHARE's investigations with several research universities about the value and challenges of tracking and reporting their research activities. The grant will also help the team increase the quantity of sources coming into the SHARE data set, and add or impute missing elements to improve the quality of the data set.

In July ARL released *Community-Based Collections*, SPEC Kit 347, an exploration of collections that have been amassed not by one individual but by a collective, which may take the form of a museum, ethnic or cultural organization, or other diaspora group active in the documentation of its past. In August the association offered a webcast that presented the SPEC survey findings and enabled webcast participants to discuss trends with the survey authors.

Diversity and Inclusion

ARL's diversity programs recruit people from underrepresented racial and ethnic groups into careers in research libraries, into the field of music and performing arts librarianship, and into the archives and special collections professional workforce.

At ALA Midwinter in January ARL hosted the 11th Annual Leadership Symposium for MLIS students participating in ARL diversity recruitment programs. The symposium focuses on topics relating to major strategic areas, as well as transitioning into, and building career networks in, research libraries and archives. Thirty-six students participated in the three-day event.

Research Library Issues (*RLI*) no. 286 was published in April, a special issue focusing on fostering diversity and inclusion in research library operations and culture. The three articles in this issue cover recruitment and retention of staff from traditionally underrepresented groups, organizational climate and health, and library services to people with disabilities.

In May ARL and the Society of American Archivists (SAA) selected six MLIS students specializing in archival studies to participate in the 2015–2017 ARL/SAA Mosaic Program. Funded by IMLS, this program strives to promote much-needed diversification of the archives and special collections professional workforce.

Seven ARL partner institutions hosted internships for the 2015 ARL Career Enhancement Program fellows. Fourteen MLIS students from underrepresented racial and ethnic minority groups participated in a six- to twelve-week practical field experience as a major component of this diversity recruitment fellowship. The Career Enhancement Program is funded by IMLS and ARL member libraries.

In July a selection committee chose four recipients for the 2015 ARL/Digital Library Federation (DLF) Forum Fellowships for Underrepresented Groups. Each fellow received financial support to attend the DLF Forum in Vancouver in October. The fellows wrote blog posts reflecting on their experiences at the forum.

The July 2015 issue of *Synergy: News from ARL Diversity Programs* features three essays by former ARL diversity and leadership program participants on advancement for library and information professionals at various stages in their careers, from library school students to mid-career librarians.

In August ARL chose 18 MLIS students to participate in the 2015–2017 Initiative to Recruit a Diverse Workforce (IRDW) as ARL Diversity Scholars. Underwritten by ARL member libraries, the IRDW offers financial benefits and leadership development to participants.

Also in August, ARL and the Music Library Association (MLA) selected four MLIS students to participate in the 2015–2017 ARL/MLA Diversity and Inclusion Initiative. This initiative—funded by IMLS, ARL, and MLA—seeks to address the growing need for professional staff in music and performing arts libraries to better reflect the changing demographics of students and faculty in those fields.

In December ARL and five partner institutions recruited a 2016 cohort of six Career Enhancement Program fellows. The new fellows participated in the 12th ARL Annual Leadership Symposium in Boston in early January 2016 and will complete internships in ARL member libraries throughout the winter/spring term. The ARL Career Enhancement Program is funded by IMLS and the partner institutions.

Scholarly Dissemination Engine

With the Scholarly Dissemination Engine initiative ARL is promoting wide-reaching and sustainable publication of research and scholarship to ensure that such publications retain and enhance rigor and quality, embed a culture of rights sympathetic to the scholarly enterprise, and use financial models that are sustainable.

In March the ARL/ACRL Institute on Scholarly Communication held its first unconference, ScholCommCamp, in Portland, Oregon. During this community-driven experience, participants shared skills, learned what has worked at other campuses, and built plans to improve their libraries' scholarly communication programs.

In May ARL released *Scholarly Output Assessment Activities*, SPEC Kit 346, which explores current ARL member library activities that help scholars manage and measure their output and impact. A June webcast presented the SPEC survey findings and enabled webcast participants to discuss trends with the survey authors.

Published in September, *Research Library Issues* (*RLI*) no. 287 offers an overview of the history of scholarly communication from its beginnings in the 17th century to recent innovations in digital and hybrid publishing.

Also in September, ARL released *Rapid Fabrication/Makerspace Services*, SPEC Kit 348, an exploration of current ARL member library engagement with 3D printing, rapid fabrication and digitization technologies, and makerspaces. An October webcast presented the SPEC survey findings and enabled webcast participants to discuss trends with the survey authors.

The Fall Forum 2015, "Research Partnerships in Digital Scholarship for the Humanities and Social Sciences," took place in Washington, D.C., in October. This year's forum launched the Julia C. Blixrud Memorial Lecture along with the Julia C. Blixrud Scholarship, which supports the attendance of one master of library and information science (MLIS) student or recent graduate at the Fall Forum each year. The 2015 lecturer was Tara McPherson of the University of Southern California, and the scholarship recipient was Liz Hamilton of Northwestern University Press.

In December representatives from Asia, Europe, and North America—including ARL's Elliott Shore and Kathleen Shearer, Rick Luce (Oklahoma), and Leslie Weir (Ottawa)—gathered at the invitation-only Berlin 12 Open Access Conference to discuss a proposal to flip subscription-based journals to open access models. For a summary of the key points of the proposal and a description of the discussions and concerns raised at the conference, read the Association of Research Libraries report on the Berlin 12 Open Access Conference, available on the ARL website.

Spring and Fall Association Meetings

ARL holds two meetings of all member representatives each year. The Spring Meeting is hosted by a member library or libraries; the Fall Meeting is hosted by ARL in Washington, D.C.

President Deborah Jakubs (Duke University) convened the Spring 2015 Meeting in Berkeley, California. The theme was "Global Connections of Research Libraries" and program sessions explored international copyright issues, shared print repositories, and tools and services for open science. Member representatives, ARL Leadership Fellows, and ARL staff discussed the transition to ARL's new Strategic Framework and System of Action. This meeting also marked the completion of the 2013–2015 ARL Leadership Fellows program with recognition of the fellows for their achievements. All available presentation slides are linked from the speakers' names or session titles in the summary of the program sessions on the ARL website.

Jakubs convened the Fall 2015 Meeting on October 6–7. The Strategic Thinking and Design Transition Team presented its final report, and System of Action groups presented their interim reports. The meeting schedule on the ARL website provides an annotated outline of the program sessions.

During the October 7 Business Meeting, the ARL membership ratified the board's election of Mary Case (Illinois at Chicago) as ARL vice president/president-elect. Three new board members were elected by the membership to serve three-year terms: Lorraine Haricombe (Texas at Austin), Steven Smith (Tennessee, Knoxville), and Ann Thornton (Columbia). At the end of the meeting, Jakubs transferred the president's gavel to Larry Alford (Toronto), who then started his one-year term as ARL president. View a photo roster of the ARL Board of Directors on the association's website.

Strategic Thinking and Design

ARL embarked upon an intensive and extensive Strategic Thinking and Design process in the fall of 2013 to reimagine the future of the research library and reshape ARL to help bring that future into being.

In February 2015 the association released the final report on the Strategic Thinking and Design work that ARL conducted from the fall of 2013 through the spring of 2014. The report includes a detailed description of the innovative process as well as the Strategic Framework and the System of Action that emerged from the process.

In early 2015 a Strategic Thinking and Design Transition Team worked with the ARL board, committees, and senior staff to develop recommendations for implementing the new framework. The Transition Team reported its recommendations at the Spring Meeting. Five design teams composed of ARL library directors and ARL staff/visiting program officer liaisons were appointed to further develop the scope and contextual framework of each System of Action initiative in order to define the breadth, focus, and type of projects that could be undertaken. The five initiatives are the ARL Academy, Collective Collections, Innovation Lab, Libraries That Learn, and Scholarly Dissemination Engine. Four enabling capacity committees composed of ARL library directors and ARL staff liaisons were appointed to address their respective issues—advocacy and policy, assessment, diversity and inclusion, and member engagement and outreach—across all initiatives and projects within the System of Action.

To support the new design teams and the Coordinating Committee, two visiting program officers were appointed to serve from June 2015 to May 2016; a part-time program director was hired in October. Melissa Just, associate university librarian for research and instructional services at Rutgers University, is a visiting program officer for the Libraries That Learn Design Team. Mark Robertson, associate university librarian for information services at York University, is a visiting program officer for the Innovation Lab Design Team. As program director for research and strategic initiatives, Elizabeth Waraksa is working closely with the Coordinating Committee to foster the development of project activities brought forward by member directors, staff, or partners in response to the System of Action.

The Scholarly Publishing and Academic Resources Coalition

Heather Joseph

Executive Director

21 Dupont Circle N.W., Suite 800, Washington, DC 20036
202-296-2296, e-mail sparc@sparcopen.org
World Wide Web http://www.sparcopen.org

Background and Mission

SPARC (the Scholarly Publishing and Academic Resources Coalition) works to enable the open sharing of research outputs and educational materials in order to democratize access to knowledge, accelerate discovery, and increase the return on our investment in research and education. As a catalyst for action, SPARC focuses on collaborating with other stakeholders—including authors, publishers, libraries, students, funders, policymakers, and the public—to build on the opportunities created by the Internet, promoting changes to both infrastructure and culture needed to make "open" the default for research and education.

SPARC counts more than 600 members globally, including 210 members in North America—representing seven Canadian provinces, 45 states, and the District of Columbia. The membership includes several institutions from outside North America and affiliate memberships of four major library associations. In addition to SPARC's three global affiliates (SPARC Europe, SPARC Japan, and SPARC Africa), this broad and comprehensive representation helps reinforce the coalition's international focus.

Its members are primarily academic and research libraries that use the resources and support provided by SPARC to actively promote open access to scholarly articles, the open sharing of research data, and the creation and adoption of open educational resources (OER) on their campuses.

Strategy

SPARC works internationally to make the open agenda the default mode for research and education through the adoption of open access, open data, and open education policies and practices. SPARC's strategy focuses on four strategic pillars critical to ensuring the open sharing and broad use of knowledge:

- Advocacy—raising the public policy profile of the open agenda
- Education—increasing the understanding of the benefits of the open agenda
- Collaboration—working with stakeholders to encourage the emergence of new norms that support the open agenda
- Incubation—advancing new demonstrations of scalable business models that sustainably support open sharing of these materials

Priorities

SPARC's strategy focuses on reducing barriers to the access, sharing, and use of knowledge. The highest priority is advancing the understanding and implementation of policies and practices that make openness the default for research outputs and educational materials—including journal articles, digital data, and educational resources.

The following were among key priorities in 2015:

Advocacy/Policy Strategy. The top priority for SPARC was to raise the public policy profile of open access to the outputs of research—including journal articles, data, and educational resources. SPARC advanced this priority by:

- Leading efforts to advocate for policies that open up access to journal articles, data, and educational resources on the institutional, state, national, and international levels
- Identifying and capitalizing on opportunities to open new advocacy fronts
- Supporting research on social/economic benefits of open access to research outputs
- Leading the U.S. National Open Access Working Group, and establishing a new Working Group on Open Data
- Working with media outlets to promote public awareness of open access
- Working with public and private research funders to create and implement open access policies
- Expanding communications and outreach efforts to maximize reach of campaigns
- Actively participating in coalitions working on target "open" issue areas
- Participating in and promoting productive collective efforts to build scalable capacity to support effective implementations of open access policies
- Hosting (or co-hosting) annual meeting on issues relating to open access to journal articles, data, and educational resources

Communications Reset. A key priority for SPARC was to retool communications efforts to better reflect the breadth of its expanded program portfolio by:

- Conducting a comprehensive review of current communications assets and priorities
- Analyzing recommended changes to the communications portfolio and creating a new strategic communications plan that emphasizes SPARC's role in the wider "open" movement
- Creating a new communications plan in concert with technical/IT platform changes required by SPARC's recent move to the New Venture Fund

Member Outreach. SPARC worked to articulate how SPARC's programs specifically support its members' campus education and advocacy activities by:

- Creating and refining members-only services (i.e., a monthly digest of key developments along with suggested campus-based responses; a new web area containing "talking points" documents, slide decks, and other communications tools for campus use, etc.)
- Expanding a successful OA/OER education "roadshow" for member campuses
- Creating OA and OER toolkits and other resources for campus use
- Building out resources for promoting/supporting the adoption of campus-based, faculty-driven open access policies and funds
- Sponsoring Open Access Week and its growing related activities
- Updating the "Author Rights" educational campaign
- Continuing the production and promotion of targeted educational materials

Continuing Priorities in 2015

Globalization. SPARC continued to expand its presence and programs to reflect and support the global nature of scholarly communications by:

- Actively promoting the updated SPARC brand as a reflection of global presence and activity
- Co-sponsoring biennial meetings outside the United States with partner organizations
- Developing SPARC brand-based MOU templates for use by prospective international partners
- Establishing SPARC-branded activities in South Africa
- Identifying new opportunities and establishing partnerships with key stakeholders in other global regions

Student Campaign. SPARC promoted the inclusion of students and student organizations in all areas of open access by:

- Providing financial and managerial resources to support the operations of this rapidly growing program;
- Co-funding an additional staff person for the Right to Research Coalition (R2RC)
- Strengthening joint advocacy efforts with R2RC and member organizations to leverage community presence on open access, open data, OER, and related issues
- Developing and presenting regular joint SPARC/student educational programs
- Supporting R2RC in organizing OpenCon for Students and Early Stage Researchers
- Seeking additional support/partnerships to help strengthen ongoing R2RC activities

Open Access Infrastructure Support. SPARC continued its leadership role in promoting digital repositories and open access publishing outlets by:

- Supporting academy-based publishing initiatives
- Actively partnering with OA publishers to promote awareness and adoption of open access journal publishing options
- Collaborating with university presses, scholarly societies, and other non-profit publishing initiatives to develop educational materials highlighting successful alternative publishing models for journals, monographs, and other scholarly communication genres
- Providing expert consulting services exploring and supporting transition strategies for subscription-based publishers to move to open-access models;
- Contributing to evaluations of potential business models supporting community-wide open access infrastructure
- Partnering with key digital repository organizations to promote educational programs of interest to the community
- Participating in workshops and symposia on access issues

Ensuring Organizational Stability and Strength. SPARC continued to place a premium on ensuring that its organizational structure is designed to achieve its mission by:

- Expanding representation on the SPARC Steering Committee to include experts in key issues areas and constituencies (i.e. data, OER, students)
- Deploying flexible employment arrangements to ensure high-level talent can be strategically deployed to meet changing resource needs
- Identifying and capitalizing on opportunities to build internal capacity, via ongoing monitoring of dues structure, grant funding for program support, expanded partnership arrangements, etc.
- Promoting and expanding member retention and recruitment efforts

Program Activities and Outcomes in 2015
Advocacy and Policy

- SPARC continued to achieve significant success with its high-profile policy advocacy program. As a direct result of its work in securing the 2013 White House Directive on Public Access, 13 U.S. federal agencies released plans in 2015 for policies ensuring that articles and data resulting from their funded research be made freely available.

- SPARC and its member organizations actively contributed to the ongoing consultations that resulted in the three major Canadian Research Councils issuing a new, harmonized Tri-Agency Open Access Policy in early 2015.
- The SPARC-supported "Fair Access to Science and Technology Research (FASTR) Act," a bill that would codify the White House Directive into law, successfully advanced through the U.S. Senate Homeland Security and Governmental Affairs Committee.
- SPARC introduced a new campaign to educate declared 2016 U.S. presidential candidates on the importance of open access, open data, and OER, and to advocate for the inclusion of these issues in campaign events and platforms.
- SPARC staff worked with the White House and U.S. federal agencies to raise the profile of OER as a policy issue, co-organizing a government-wide workshop on open licenses and OER, and leading coalition efforts to advocate for Executive Branch actions in support of OER.
- SPARC also worked to generate support for "open" practices within the foundation community. With support from the Robert Wood Johnson Foundation, SPARC convened leading research foundations (including the Gates Foundation, the Arnold Foundation, and the Soros Foundation) to explore the adoption of open access funder policies, and the establishment of an ongoing open access "community of practice" of research foundations in North America.
- To generate direct input on its programming from its members, SPARC established three new members-only advisory groups to help develop new programs and services, and to refine efforts to best serve members.
- To keep members ahead of the curve in understanding the latest developments in the scholarly communication environment, SPARC hosted regular webcasts (free to members) on important topics ranging from the Elsevier article "sharing" policy, to complying with new public access mandates, to developing campus rights-retention-based open access policies.
- SPARC continued to provide a full suite of educational tools and opportunities, ranging from "directors only" calls connecting SPARC members to thought leaders in scholarly communication to regular webcasts.

Communication and Media

SPARC was regularly consulted and quoted as an expert source on topics relating to scholarly communication. SPARC and SPARC-sponsored programs were featured in both the national and trade press, in outlets including the *New York Times, Times Higher Education, Science, Inside Higher Ed, Chronicle of Higher Education, Boston Herald, Library Journal,* NBC News, and Salon. SPARC staff also authored articles for various publications.

Through its website, SPARC highlighted the work of open access champions. SPARC honored the Bill and Melinda Gates Foundation and the Open Access Button developers David Carroll and Joseph McArthur with its 2015 Innovator Awards.

Campus Education

SPARC actively supported members' local, campus efforts by providing SPARC-sponsored speakers for campus events, practical guides, talking points, templates, and expert counsel on campus open access and OER issues.

With continued support from the Hewlett Foundation, SPARC expanded its OER program to provide regular campus-based opportunities for education and advocacy in support of the creation and adoption of OER. In partnership with ACRL, SPARC co-hosted the first Scholarly Communications Institute devoted to OER.

SPARC supported campus-based policy action in conjunction with a panel of experts to promote resources that support data-driven, community-engaging, and successful open access policy development. SPARC provides Web and administrative support for the Coalition of Open Access Policy Institutions (COAPI), a group of U.S. and Canadian institutions that have implemented or are in the process of implementing campus-based open access policies. SPARC also serves as a platform for the work of COAPI.

In keeping with its commitment to partner with the next generation of leaders, SPARC and the Right to Research Coalition (R2RC) co-hosted OpenCon 2015 on November 14–16 in Brussels, Belgium. In its second year, OpenCon brought together more than 100 students and early career academic professionals from approximately 40 countries to advance open access, OER, and open data. Since the inaugural event in 2014, more than 5,000 individuals from 150 countries have applied to attend OpenCon.

Through the R2RC, SPARC partnered with Texas A&M University to secure a grant to develop programming for the first ever "SECU Academic Collaboration Award" Workshop. The program brought teams of library directors and leaders together with student government leaders with the aim of identifying and developing ongoing campus open access and OER collaborations.

SPARC provided incubation support for the student-led "Open Access Button" project, a browser-based app that lets readers register when they've hit an article behind a paywall, maps those instances, and ultimately, will provide access to an open version of the article where possible.

SPARC's annual International Open Access Week continues. The 2015 kick-off event reflected the theme of "Open for Collaboration," with SPARC and the Wikimedia Library co-sponsoring a global, virtual edit-a-thon for open access-related content on Wikipedia.

SPARC-ACRL Forums

A major component of SPARC's community outreach occurs at meetings of the American Library Association (ALA) when SPARC works with the Association of College and Research Libraries (ACRL) and its scholarly communication committee to bring current issues to the attention of the community.

In January 2015 the SPARC-ACRL Midwinter forum, "The Integration of Open Education Resources into Your Library," was held in Chicago. In June a second forum, "Advancing 'Open' Through Library Partnerships with Students and Early Career Researchers," was held in San Francisco at ALA's Annual Meeting.

Governance

SPARC is guided by a steering committee. The 2015 committee members were Jun Adachi (Japanese National Institute of Informatics; for SPARC Japan), Prudence Adler (Association of Research Libraries), Juan Pablo Alperin (Simon Fraser University), Theresa Byrd (University of San Diego), Ada Emmett (University of Kansas), Lorraine Haricombe (University of Texas Austin), Loubna Ghaouti (Universite Laval), Vivian Lewis (McMaster University), Virginia Steel (UCLA), John Ulmschneider (Virginia Commonwealth University), Mary Marlino (University Corporation for Atmospheric Research), Barbara Dewey (Pennsylvania State University), Deborah Jakubs (Duke University), Mary Case (University of Illinois Chicago).

4r

Council on Library and Information Resources

1707 L St. N.W., Suite 650, Washington, DC 20036
202-939-4754
World Wide Web http://www.clir.org
Twitter @CLIRNews

Kathlin Smith
Director of Communications

The Council on Library and Information Resources (CLIR) is an independent, nonprofit organization that forges strategies to enhance research, teaching, and learning environments in collaboration with libraries, cultural institutions, and communities of higher learning. CLIR President Charles Henry leads the 13-member staff.

CLIR is supported by fees from sponsoring institutions, grants from public and private foundations, contracts with federal agencies, and donations from individuals. A list of current sponsors, members, and funders is available at http://www.clir.org/about/current-sponsors-and-funders.

CLIR's board establishes policy, oversees the investment of funds, sets goals, and approves strategies for their achievement. A full listing of CLIR board members is available at http://www.clir.org/about/governance.

In 2015 CLIR had five Distinguished Presidential Fellows: Michael Edson, of the Smithsonian Institution; Stephen G. Nichols, of Johns Hopkins University; Elliott Shore, of the Association for Research Libraries; Michael F. Suarez, of the University of Virginia; and John Unsworth, of Brandeis University.

CLIR's activities in 2015 are described in the following sections.

Digital Libraries

Digital Library Federation

Strategy meets practice at the Digital Library Federation (DLF). DLF is a robust and diverse community of practitioners who advance research, learning, and the public good through the creative design and wise application of digital library technologies. Through its programs, working groups, and initiatives, DLF connects CLIR's vision and research agenda to a network of practitioners working in digital libraries, archives, labs, and museums. The organization promotes work on standards and best practices; research and data management across disciplines; aggregation and preservation services for digital collections; digital library assessment; and services that expand access to resources for research, teaching, and learning.

In April 2015 Bethany Nowviskie became director of DLF, succeeding Rachel Frick, who left the organization in September 2014. Nowviskie had been a distinguished presidential fellow at CLIR, president of the Association for Computers and the Humanities, and director of the internationally known Scholars' Lab at the University of Virginia Library.

In 2015 DLF partnered with the Samuel H. Kress Foundation to initiate a museums cohort within DLF. The initial group of new-member museums and museum libraries includes the Dallas Museum of Art, the Philadelphia Museum of Art, and the New York Art Resources Consortium (NYARC), which represents the libraries and archives of the Brooklyn Museum, the Frick Collection, and MoMA, the Museum of Modern Art. Representatives of these organizations will join the Smithsonian Institution Libraries, a longtime DLF member, in engaging in a series of continuing conversations over the coming year on how DLF and the broader digital library community might better engage and support museums and museum libraries.

DLF members post regular updates on their work in the blog series DLF Contribute, available at https://www.diglib.org/topics/contribute/.

The following paragraphs describe current initiatives at DLF. Additional information can be found on DLF's website, https://www.diglib.org.

DLF Forum. The DLF Forum is convened annually and is open to digital library practitioners from member institutions and the broader community. The forum serves as a meeting place, marketplace, and congress. As a meeting place it provides an opportunity for DLF working groups, affiliated organizations, and community members to conduct business and present their work. As a marketplace of ideas, the forum provides an opportunity to disseminate experiences and develop best practices, and to support a broader level of information sharing among digital library professionals. As a congress, the forum provides an opportunity for DLF to continually review and assess its programs with input from the community at large.

The 2015 DLF Forum, in Vancouver, British Columbia, was the first to take place outside the United States. The largest to date, it drew some 600 attendees, including those attending DLF's affiliated events. A Liberal Arts Preconference was held in conjunction with the forum. The one-day meeting was designed to foster conversation and build community among those who work with digital libraries or digital scholarships at liberal arts colleges. A fuller report on the forum, and links to live-streamed sessions, is available at http://www.clir.org/pubs/issues/issues108/issues108#forum.

Digital Library Assessment. The DLF Digital Library Assessment group, formed in 2014, met during the 2015 Forum to share problems, ideas, and solutions. The group continues its work year-round through a dedicated e-mail list and a DLF-supported wiki. Membership is open to anyone interested in learning about or collaborating on the improvement of digital library assessment measures. Current subcommittees are focusing on tools and best-practices documents to support cost assessment, to measure digital library analytics, to standardize digital library content citations, and to assess user needs and usability. Links to the group's recent draft and finalized white papers are available at https://www.diglib.org/groups/assessment/.

Digitizing Special Formats Wiki. DLF is curating a list of resources for professionals planning projects involving the digitization of rare and unique materials. The list, available at https://wiki.diglib.org/Digitizing_Special_Formats, includes introductory and reference materials relevant to digitizing cultural heritage.

National Digital Stewardship Alliance. In October 2015 the National Digital Stewardship Alliance (NDSA) announced that it had selected DLF to serve as NDSA's home starting in January 2016. Launched in 2010 by the Library of Congress as a part of the National Digital Information Infrastructure and Preservation Program, NDSA works to establish, maintain, and advance the capacity to preserve the nation's digital resources for the benefit of present and future generations. For an inaugural four-year term, the Library of Congress provided secretariat and membership management support to NDSA, contributing working group leadership, expertise, and administrative support. Today, NDSA has 165 members, including universities, government and nonprofit organizations, commercial businesses, and professional associations. The mission and structure of NDSA will remain largely unchanged. It is a distinct organization within CLIR and DLF, with all organizations benefiting from the pursuit of common goals while leveraging shared resources. More information on NDSA is available at https://ndsa.diglib.org.

DLF eResearch Network. The DLF eResearch Network (eRN) is a cohort-based learning and networking experience designed to help academic and research libraries devise collaborative strategies for data management support. eResearch Network members develop plans appropriate for their institutions through collaboration, resource sharing, webinars, and custom consultations by eRN faculty. Network members come from colleges and universities of varying size. To date, 13 institutions from across the United States and Canada have participated in the eRN, and the 2016 cohort will be the largest yet.

The 2015 DLF eRN cohort kicked off with an in-person meeting in April, co-located with the Research Data Access and Preservation (RDAP) summit in Minneapolis. Work concluded with a meeting at the 2015 DLF Forum in Vancouver. Over the course of the program, participants from five institutions learned more about data management surveys; some identified and filled needs for repository software, conducted outreach with local scholars and administrators, and piloted educational workshops.

Openlab Workshop. In December 2015 CLIR co-hosted a series of meetings to assess the feasibility of a new venture, Openlab, to accelerate change in the GLAM (gallery, library, archive, and museum) sector. Openlab is envisioned as a solutions lab, convener, and consultancy. The idea for Openlab, spearheaded by CLIR Distinguished Presidential Fellow Michael Edson, grew from an observation that GLAMs are not leveraging their use of technology to address the grand challenges of our time, and are not at the forefront of debates that affect the public good.

A workshop held on December 2 at the offices of the American Alliance of Museums was preceded by a day of ignite talks and an unconference that generated ideas and participation from a larger community than could be accommodated in a workshop setting. More than 100 professionals from 80 institutions attended the unconference and ignite talks, and 36 individuals participated. The meetings were supported with funding from the National Endowment for the Humanities Office of Digital Humanities and Division of Public Programs. Information and materials from Openlab events are available at the project's wiki, at http://openlabworkshop.wikispaces.com/. The site includes videos of the ignite talks, unconference session notes, and workshop information.

Assessment of National Digital Stewardship Residency Programs

With funding from the Institute of Museum and Library Services (IMLS), CLIR is assessing the impact of five National Digital Stewardship Residency (NDSR) initiatives. Between 2012 and 2015 the IMLS Laura Bush 21st Century Librarian Program funded a series of five projects designed to build capacity in the information services and cultural heritage professions for the collection, management, preservation, and distribution of digital assets to the American public. By the summer of 2016, 35 recent graduates of master's programs in library and information science and related fields will have completed working residencies at leading U.S. institutions in the field of digital stewardship.

In fall 2015 a research team led by former CLIR Postdoctoral Fellow Meridith Beck Sayre began gathering data through interviews, site visits, and a survey in order to evaluate the significance of the residency experience for the residents and their host institutions, to identify the differences among the five projects and the perceived effects of those differences on the residents, and to articulate the factors common to successful and productive residencies. In late 2016 the team will produce a report with recommendations for future initiatives that build on the work of the residents and their mentors. CLIR will publish the report at the conclusion of the project.

International Image Interoperability Framework Consortium

In fall 2015 CLIR became administrative host to the International Image Interoperability Framework Consortium (IIIF-C). Formed in June 2015, the consortium aims to standardize and improve sharing and display of image-based scholarly resources on the Web.

Founding members of the consortium are the British Library, Oxford University, Stanford University, Bayerisches Staatsbibliothek (Bavarian State Library), Bibliothèque nationale de France (National Library of France), Cornell University, Nasjonalbibliotek (National Library of Norway), Princeton University, Wellcome Trust, and Yale University.

IIIF-C aims to reduce the inefficiency and redundancy that result from incompatibility in how images are delivered, and to collaboratively produce an interoperable technology and community framework for image delivery. The framework includes two application programming interfaces (APIs). The Image API provides access to the image content and technical descriptions. The Preservation API gives structural and descriptive information about the image's context so that it can be appropriately rendered for a Web-based viewing environment.

Study on Needs in Continuing Education for Managing Cultural Heritage Data

In September 2013 IMLS awarded CLIR a grant to examine federally mandated plans for open access and their implications for continuing education needs for libraries, museums, and other cultural heritage institutions. Under this grant, CLIR is conducting research in three areas. Part 1 is a highly structured content analysis of select federal agency plans for supporting open access to data and publications, identifying the commonalities and differences among the plans with emphasis on access to data. Part 2 takes the results of the content analysis and traces its implications for IMLS program areas and the cultural heritage institutions they serve. Part 3 identifies gaps in continuing education opportunities for cultural heritage professionals, assessing the readiness of the current professional workforce and identifying how best to address the needs and close the gaps in the immediate and longer term. Final results will be released by summer 2016.

Committee on Coherence at Scale

CLIR established the Committee on Coherence at Scale for Higher Education in October 2012, in partnership with Vanderbilt University. The committee's charge is to examine emerging national-scale digital projects and their potential to help transform higher education in terms of scholarly productivity, teaching, cost-efficiency, and sustainability. The committee currently comprises 24 members, representing university and college presidents and provosts, heads of national education associations and other organizations, and library and information science deans. The committee meets twice yearly.

In spring 2015 the University of Pittsburgh's iSchool announced the first two iFellows under the new doctoral fellowship program for information science students that support research for the Committee on Coherence at Scale. Timothy Schultz, Ph.D. student at Drexel University's iSchool, and Wei Jeng, Ph.D. student at the University of Pittsburgh's iSchool, were selected from a competitive pool of applicants. Timothy Schultz's research will dive into the world of "big data" as it pertains to collaborating, visualizing, and sharing information in the medical industry. Wei Jeng's research will focus on her interest in information sharing, with an emphasis on investigating how scholars communicate and share research data with one another. The program, funded by an award from the Andrew W. Mellon Foundation, will ultimately support ten iFellows in total.

Scholarship and Research

Postdoctoral Fellowship Program

CLIR's Postdoctoral Fellowship Program offers recent Ph.D. graduates an opportunity to work on projects that forge and strengthen connections among library collections, educational technologies, and current research. Launched in 2004, the program has supported 130 fellows at 60 host institutions across the United States and Canada. Since 2012, in response to a growing recognition within the professional community that research data management poses particular challenges to libraries and other departments serving today's researchers, CLIR expanded the program's focus to data curation. With grant support from the Alfred P. Sloan and Andrew W. Mellon foundations, CLIR seeks to help host institutions establish staffing models, policies, resources, and services relating to research data curation through matching those institutions with Ph.D.'s with expertise relevant to their needs.

In May 2015 CLIR announced the award of 14 postdoctoral fellowships: five Postdoctoral Fellowships in Academic Libraries, five CLIR/DLF Postdoctoral Fellowships in Data Curation for Visual Studies, and four CLIR/DLF Postdoctoral Fellowships in Data Curation for the Sciences and Social Sciences. The Fellowships in Data Curation for Visual Studies were launched with funding from the Andrew W. Mellon Foundation. In June CLIR received additional funding from the Mellon Foundation to support five two-year Fellowships in Data Curation for Medieval Studies, starting in July 2016. An animated overview of the data curation program, produced in fall 2015, is available at http://www.clir.org/fellowships/postdoc/info. A list of current and previous fellows is available at http://www.clir.org/fellowships/postdoc/fellowsupdate.

All new fellows attended a summer seminar, hosted at Bryn Mawr College, addressing issues faced by 21st-century libraries, including data curation and management. The seminar provided an opportunity for fellows to participate in cohort-building activities. Fellows' supervisors joined the seminar for one day to discuss expectations and establish effective communication strategies.

In September 2015 CLIR published a volume of essays written by 20 previous and present CLIR postdoctoral fellows, in which they reflect on their experiences and, more broadly, on the direction of academia. The essays focus on working conditions associated with creating a new profession of expertise and responsibilities in light of emerging forms of scholarly communication and pedagogy. The volume, titled *The Process of Discovery: The CLIR Postdoctoral Fellowship Program and the Future of the Academy*, is available at http://www.clir.org/pubs/reports/pub167.

Cataloging Hidden Special Collections and Archives

Launched in 2008 with the support of the Andrew W. Mellon Foundation, CLIR's Cataloging Hidden Special Collections and Archives Program announced its final round of 19 grants in December 2014. The program, which had supported efforts to expose unknown or underused cultural materials, has been succeeded by a new program to digitize hidden collections, described below.

A capstone event for the Cataloging Hidden Special Collections and Archives program was held in March 2015 at the Kislak Center for Special Collections, Rare Books and Manuscripts at the University of Pennsylvania Libraries. The symposium, titled "Innovation, Collaboration, and Models," and the unconference that preceded the symposium drew 172 participants, including representatives from 62 Hidden Collections projects. More than 75 presenters and discussion leaders contributed to the program, vividly illustrating the impact that the Hidden Collections initiative has had over its seven-year history. Grant recipients addressed problems that today's library and cultural heritage professionals face as they organize collections and make them accessible to scholars and other users. In October CLIR published the symposium proceedings, which are available at http://www.clir.org/pubs/ reports/pub169.

Since its inception, the program has awarded 129 grants amounting to $27.5 million. Grants have gone to academic libraries, museums, public libraries, archives, and historical societies, among other types of cultural institutions.

Through the grant program, one quarter of the funded projects were collaborative partnerships. By June 2015 grant recipients reported the archival processing of at least 2,952 collections, comprising a reported 53,608 linear feet, an additional 4,229 cubic feet, plus 960 boxes of mixed materials. Recipients have created item-level descriptions for a reported 273,728 items, including 50,551 books and manuscripts; 46,702 audio and audiovisual recordings; 29,393 items of ephemera; 27,125 pamphlets; 15,600 pamphlet plays; 8,560 maps and map series; 6,956 artifacts; 5,537 artworks; and 2,978 architectural drawings.

Digitizing Hidden Special Collections and Archives

In January 2015 CLIR announced a major new program to fund the digitization of rare and unique content in cultural memory institutions, thanks to a grant from the Andrew W. Mellon Foundation. The national competition is built on the model of CLIR's Cataloging Hidden Special Collections and Archives program. Developed through consultation with digital library practitioners and funders, and with input from the broader community, the program is designed to:

- encourage approaches to digitization that make possible new kinds of scholarship in the digital research environment
- support the digitization of entire collections, rather than selected items
- promote strategic partnerships, as few institutions have the capacity to handle and scan the wide array of objects in their collections
- promote best practices for ensuring the long-term availability and discoverability of digital files
- ensure that digitized content is made available to the public as easily and completely as possible

The two-stage application process was completed by late July 2015, and the first round of 18 awards, totaling $4 million, was announced January 4, 2016. A list and description of the projects is available at http://www.clir.org/hiddencollections/awards/for-2015.

Mellon Dissertation Fellowships

In 2015, 15 graduate students were selected to receive Mellon Dissertation Fellowships. The fellowship program, initiated in 2002, is intended to help graduate students in the humanities and related social science fields pursue doctoral research using original sources and gain skill and creativity in using original source materials in libraries, archives, museums, and related repositories. To date, the program has supported 194 graduate students who have carried out their dissertation research in public and private libraries and archives worldwide. A list of current and past fellowship recipients is available at http://www.clir.org/fellowships/mellon/fellrecipients.html. A brief video, in which Mellon Dissertation Fellows talk about the impact of the fellowship on their work, is available at https://vimeo.com/138078078. An assessment of the program's reach and impact will be available in 2016.

Leadership Education and Cultivation

Leading Change Institute

CLIR and EDUCAUSE hosted the second Leading Change Institute (LCI) May 31–June 5, 2015. Thirty-six participants joined deans Elliott Shore, executive director of the Association of Research Libraries, and Joanne Kossuth, vice president for operations and CIO at the Olin College of Engineering. In the months since LCI, participants have joined deans Shore and Kossuth for regular, hour-long online chats, allowing them to continue exchanges beyond the institute and to provide ongoing support and advice for one another.

LCI aims to prepare and develop the next generation of leaders in libraries, information services, and higher education by engaging those who seek to further develop their skills for the benefit of higher education. A list of participants from 2015 and previous years is available at http://www.clir.org/initiatives-partnerships/leading-change-institute.

Chief Information Officers Group

CLIR's Chief Information Officers Group is composed of 30 directors of organizations that have merged their library and technology units on liberal arts college and university campuses. A list of members is available at http://www.clir.org/initiatives-partnerships/cios. At their meetings and via a listserv, members discuss library and computing issues as an integrated whole. They have explored such topics as recent changes in merged organizations, strategic and tactical issues concerning cloud computing, trends in the uses of technology in teaching, and effective ways to provide faculty support.

Rovelstad Scholarship in International Librarianship

Kelly Grogg, a library and information sciences student at the University of Iowa, was selected to receive the 2015 Rovelstad Scholarship in International Librarianship. Grogg spent two years teaching at a rural high school in Cambodia through the U.S. Peace Corps. Grogg has a B.A. in English Literature from the University of Iowa and works as a graduate research assistant in Special Collections and University Archives. The Rovelstad Scholarship provides travel funds for a student of library and information science to attend the annual meeting of the World Library and Information Congress, which took place in Cape Town, South Africa, in August 2015.

National Institute for Technology in Liberal Education (NITLE)

In April 2015 it was announced that the National Institute for Technology in Liberal Education (NITLE) would migrate from its home at Southwestern University to CLIR on July 1, 2015. The decision to move NITLE to CLIR stemmed from a recognition that the two organizations' programmatic interests are closely aligned and that CLIR could help expand NITLE's audience and potential collaborators. In addition, the environment for liberal arts colleges has changed fundamentally in

15 years, and the transition provides an opportunity to re-evaluate NITLE's focus and activities.

Shortly after the migration, W. Joseph King was appointed NITLE interim director to oversee planning, member relations, and outreach. Since the migration, CLIR has been managing a rigorous analysis and assessment of the organization. The assessment, based on surveys and interviews, will identify the opportunities and challenges facing NITLE and will be completed in spring 2016.

Publications

The Center of Excellence Model for Information Services, by Joy Kirchner, José Diaz, Geneva Henry, Susan Fliss, John Culshaw, Heather Gendron, and Jon E. Cawthorne. February 2015. Available at http://www.clir.org/pubs/reports/pub163. Used in a variety of industries, the center of excellence (CoE) model is designed to attract the most talented researchers in a particular field, enhance collaboration, and improve access to the resources needed for their research. This report examines the feasibility of using the CoE model to provide the new services required for the effective use of digital information.

ARSC Guide to Audio Preservation, Sam Brylawski, Maya Lerman, Robin Pike, Kathlin Smith, eds. May 2015. Available at http://www.clir.org/pubs/reports/pub164. A practical introduction to caring for and preserving audio collections, the guide is aimed at individuals and institutions that have recorded sound collections but lack the expertise in one or more areas to preserve them. Nine chapters, contributed by a range of experts, cover audio conservation and preservation, recorded sound formats and their associated risks, appraisal, related copyright issues, and disaster preparedness. The guide offers advice on making informed decisions about digitization, as well as strategies for managing digital content. An appendix to the guide focuses on fair use and sound recordings.

Getting Found: SEO Cookbook, by Patrick O'Brien and Kenning Arlitsch. May 2015. Available at http://www.clir.org/pubs/reports/pub165. *Getting Found* provides a step-by-step video guide to help libraries measure and monitor the search engine optimization (SEO) performance of their digital repositories. It includes everything necessary to implement a preconfigured Google Analytics dashboard that continuously monitors SEO performance metrics relevant to digital repositories.

The Once and Future Publishing Library, by Anne Okerson and Alex Holzman. July 2015. Available at http://www.clir.org/pubs/reports/pub166. This report explores the revitalization of library publishing and its possible future, and examines elements that influence the success and sustainability of library publishing initiatives. Authors include results of a survey they conducted to better understand how current library publishing initiatives are supported financially.

The Process of Discovery: The CLIR Postdoctoral Fellowship Program and the Future of the Academy, by John C. Maclachlan, Elizabeth A. Waraksa, and Christa Williford, eds. September 2015. Available at http://www.clir.org/pubs/reports/pub167. This volume celebrates the first decade of CLIR's Postdoctoral Fellowship Program by bringing together 20 previous and current CLIR postdoctoral fellows to reflect on their experiences and, more broadly, on the direction of academia. Each essay is a look into the working conditions associated with creating a new profession of expertise and responsibilities in response to emerging forms of scholarly communication and pedagogy.

Building Expertise to Support Digital Scholarship: A Global Perspective, by Vivian Lewis, Lisa Spiro, Xuemao Wang, and Jon E. Cawthorne. October 2015. Available at http://www.clir.org/pubs/reports/pub168. This report explores the expertise required to support a robust and sustainable digital scholarship program. It focuses first on defining and describing the key domain knowledge, skills, competencies, and mindsets at prominent digital scholarship programs. It then identifies the main strategies used to build this expertise, both formally and informally. The work examines leading digital scholarship organizations in China, India, Taiwan, the United Kingdom, Germany, Mexico, Canada, and the United States, and provides recommendations to help those currently involved in or considering embarking on a digital scholarship program.

Innovation, Collaboration and Models: Proceedings of the CLIR Cataloging Hidden Special Collections and Archives Symposium, March 2015, Cheryl Oestreicher, ed. November 2015. Available at http://www.clir.org/pubs/reports/pub169. This volume documents the capstone event to the seven-year Cataloging Hidden Special Collections and Archives program, funded by the Andrew W. Mellon Foundation. In the proceedings, more than 20 symposium presenters examine inter-institutional collaboration, student and faculty involvement, cataloging, arrangement and description, audiovisual collections, science collections, and outreach.

CLIR Annual Report, 2014–2015. December 2015.

CLIR Issues 103–108.

Re:Thinking blog series, http://connect.clir.org/blogs/allrethinkingblogs.

Association for Library and Information Science Education

ALISE Headquarters, 2150 N. 107th St., Suite 205, Seattle, WA 98133
206-209-5267, fax 206-367-8777, e-mail office@alise.org
World Wide Web http://www.alise.org

Samantha Hastings
President 2015–2016

The Association for Library and Information Science Education (ALISE) is an independent, nonprofit professional association, founded in 1915 as the Association of American Library Schools (AALS). It changed to its current name in 1983 to reflect more accurately the mission, goals, and membership of the association. Its mission is to promote innovation and excellence in research, teaching, and service for educators and scholars in library and information science and cognate disciplines internationally through leadership, collaboration, advocacy, and knowledge creation.

Membership

Membership is open to individuals and institutions. Personal members can include anyone interested in the objectives of the association, with categories including full-time (faculty member, administrator, librarian, researcher, or other interested individual); new professional (doctoral students as they transition to faculty member status, maximum of three years); part-time/retired (part-time or adjunct faculty, or retired professionals); and student (doctoral or other students, maximum of six years). Institutional members include schools with programs accredited by the American Library Association (ALA) and other U.S. and Canadian schools that offer a graduate degree in library and information science or a cognate field. International affiliate institutional membership is open to any school outside the United States or Canada that offers an educational program in library and information science at the professional level as defined or accepted by the country in which the school is located. Associate institutional membership status is accorded to libraries and organizations other than schools of library and information science.

Structure and Governance

ALISE is constituted of operational groups including the board of directors; committees; the council of deans, directors, and program chairs; school representatives; and special interest groups (SIGs). The association was managed from 2006 to July 2014 by the Medical Library Association, with Kathleen Combs as executive director. After a national search, SBI Association Management in Seattle was selected to manage ALISE starting in August 2014, with Andrew Estep as executive director. The board of directors is composed of seven elected officers serving three-year terms. Officers for 2015–2016 were Samantha K. Hastings (University of South Carolina), president; Louise Spiteri (Dalhousie University), vice-president/president-elect; Clara M. Chu (University of Illinois at Urbana-Champaign), past president; Denice Adkins (University of Alabama), secretary/treasurer; Laurie Bonnici (University of Alabama), director for membership services; Carol Tilley (University of Illinois at Urbana-Champaign), director for external relations; and Leanne Bowler (University of Pittsburgh), director for special interest groups. At the end of the January 2016 Annual Conference, Bonnici and Chu concluded their terms of service and two newly elected officers joined the board: Dietmar Wolfram (University of Wisconsin–Milwaukee), vice-president/president-elect, and Cecilia Salvatore (Dominican University), director for membership services.

The board establishes policy, sets goals and strategic directions, and provides oversight for the management of the association. Face-to-face meetings are held in January in conjunction with the Annual Conference and in spring and fall to focus on policy, planning, programmatic, and other matters. For the remainder of the year, business is conducted through teleconferences and e-mail.

Committees play a vital role in carrying out the work of the association. Since fall 2008 an open call for volunteers to serve on committees has been used to ensure broader participation in committee service, with members for the coming year appointed by the vice-president/president-elect for most committees. Principal areas of activity include awards, budget and finance, conference program planning, governance, nominations, research competitions, and tellers. (See http://www.alise.org/mc/page.do?sitePageId=86452 for a full list.) Each committee is given an ongoing term of reference to guide its work as well as the specific charges for the year. Task forces can be charged to carry out tasks outside the scope of the existing standing committees. For example, the board established the ALISE Committee on Accreditation Reform in Education (CARE), chaired by Tula Giannini, to address concerns regarding the quality and process of accreditation of LIS professional education. It is working with the American Library Association (ALA) Subcommittee on Accreditation to enhance the quality of LIS education and the accreditation process. The board is also working with ALA in providing statistics in searchable formats.

The ALISE Council of Deans, Directors, and Program Chairs consists of the chief executive officers of each ALISE institutional member school. The group convenes at the Annual Conference and discusses issues via e-mail in the interim. Tula Giannini (Pratt University) and Seamus Ross (University of Toronto) serve as 2014–2016 co-chairs.

Within each institutional member school, a school representative is named to serve as a direct link between the membership and the ALISE board. These individuals communicate to the faculty of their school about ALISE and the association's events and initiatives and provide input on membership issues to the ALISE board.

Special interest groups (SIGs) enable members with shared interests to communicate and collaborate, with a particular emphasis on programs at the Annual Conference. New SIGs are established as areas of interest emerge. Ongoing SIGs, grouped by thematic clusters, are:

- *Roles and Responsibilities*: Assistant/Associate Deans and Directors, Doctoral Students, New Faculty, Part-time and Adjunct Faculty, Student Services
- *Teaching and Learning*: Curriculum, Distance Education, Innovative Pedagogies
- *Topics and Courses*: Archival/Preservation Education; Development and Fundraising; Gender Issues; Historical Perspectives; Information Ethics; Information Policy; International Library Education; Multicultural, Ethnic, and Humanistic Concerns; Research; School Library Media; Technical Services Education, Youth Services

Communication

ALISE communication channels are mainly electronic. The organization's presence on social media including Facebook, LinkedIn, and Twitter has grown. LinkedIn continues to be ALISE's most popular social media tool with 1,786 members in January 2016.

Publications

The ALISE publications program has four components:

- The *Journal of Education for Library and Information Science* (*JELIS*) is a peer-reviewed quarterly journal edited by Peta Wellstead. The journal is a scholarly forum for discussion and presentation of research and issues within the field of library and information science (LIS) education. Dr. Wellstead transitioned *JELIS* to an online journal, with its first electronic issue published in January 2015. The journal is open access at a green level.
- The *ALISE Directory of LIS Programs and Faculty in the United States and Canada* is published annually in electronic format and is freely available to members. Listings of faculty for each school include teaching and research areas, using codes from the LIS Research Areas Classification Scheme that ALISE maintains. The classification is currently under revision.
- The *ALISE Library and Information Science Education Statistical Report* publishes data collected annually from its institutional members on their curriculum, faculty, students, income and expenditures, and continuing professional education. In 2015 the report moved to an Excel format, which allows users to further analyze the data. Members can gain free access to existing reports by logging in on the members-only area of the website.
- The ALISE website is the public face of the association and provides information about the association and news of activities and opportunities of interest to members. It provides login access to the MemberClicks system,

where members can access members-only benefits (reports, member directory, etc.), renew membership, register for the conference and webinars, and access other services.

Annual Conference

The ALISE Annual Conference is held immediately before the ALA Midwinter Meeting. The 2016 conference, also the centennial conference, drew almost 400 attendees to Boston, January 5th–8th, to explore the theme "Radical Change: Inclusion and Innovation," celebrating the far-reaching impact of Eliza T. Dresang's work. Program Co-Chairs Kathleen McDowell (University of Illinois) and Lisa Hussey (Simmons College), with President Hastings, planned ALISE traditional conference offerings (presentations, poster sessions, and networking and placement opportunities); and continued some new programs: the ALISE President's Program, an unConference, and the unCommons—a gathering place to share, debate, brainstorm, and network. The Pre-Conference Workshop on innovative education for the future and the ALISE Academy on radical change led off the conference.

Professional Development

Starting in Spring 2014 ALISE launched the ALISE Xchange Forums, a webinar series offered free to members to facilitate virtual engagement with research and other membership interests during the year between conferences. The webinars have been successful, and ALISE plans to continue to offer them, creating a Professional Development Committee to review opportunities.

ALISE is also contributing to the future direction of professional development nationally. It is a founding member of the Coalition to Advance Learning in Archives, Libraries and Museums (coalitiontoadvancelearning.org). The coalition is supported by grants from the Institute of Museum and Library Services, and the Bill and Melinda Gates Foundation, with administration provided by OCLC. The goal of the group is to work in deliberate coordination across organizational boundaries to devise and strengthen sustainable continuing education and professional development programs that will transform the library, archives, and museum workforce in ways that lead to measurable impact on the nation's communities.

Grants and Awards

ALISE supports research and recognizes accomplishments through its grants and awards programs. Research competitions include the ALISE Research Grant Competition, the ALISE/Bohdan S. Wynar Research Paper Competition, the ALISE/Dialog Methodology Paper Competition, the ALISE/Eugene Garfield Doctoral Dissertation Competition, the ALISE/Linworth Youth Services Paper Award, and the OCLC/ALISE Library and Information Science Research Grant Competition. Support for conference participation is provided by the University of Washington

Information School Youth Services Graduate Student Travel Award, the Doctoral Student to ALISE Award, and the ALISE Diversity Travel Award to the ALISE Annual Conference. This last award was created in collaboration with the ALA Office for Diversity Spectrum Scholarship Program, which created a parallel award, the ALA/ALISE Spectrum Travel Award to ALISE, partially funded by ALISE.

Awards recognizing outstanding accomplishments include the ALISE/Norman Horrocks Leadership Award (for early-career leadership), the ALISE/Pratt-Severn Faculty Innovation Award, the ALISE Service Award, the ALISE Award for Professional Contribution, the ALISE/Connie Van Fleet Award for Research Excellence in Public Library Services to Adults, and the LJ/ALISE Excellence in Teaching Award, sponsored by Rowman & Littlefield, a collaboration with *Library Journal*, which also had its own teaching award. Winners are recognized at an awards luncheon at the Annual Conference. [For a list of award winners, see http://www.alise.org/awards-grants.]

Collaboration with Other Organizations

ALISE seeks to collaborate with other organizations on activities of mutual interest. A critical collaboration with ALA is joint work on revising accreditation of professional LIS education. ALISE members are serving as representatives to national organizations, including the FEDLINK Network, the 2016 IFLA Conference National Committee, the ALA Committee on Education, the ALA Library Services and Technology Act Committee, the ACRL Committee on Education, and the Coalition to Advance Learning in Archives, Libraries and Museums.

ALISE continues to build its international connections, with members serving on IFLA Standing Committees that address education and research, and support of initiatives to address access to information, including the Lyon Declaration that calls on the United Nations to incorporate information in advancing equity and sustainability in the development of the UN post-2015 millennium goals, which will shape policies worldwide.

Conclusion

ALISE is guided by its strategic plan, "Setting in Motion a New Century of Leadership Strategic Directions, 2014–2017," and looks forward to new developments led by President Sam Hastings.

International Reports

International Federation of Library Associations and Institutions

Mailing Address: P.O. Box 95312, 2509 CH The Hague, Netherlands
Physical Address: Prins Willem-Alexanderhof 5, 2595 BE The Hague, Netherlands
Tel. 31-70-3140884, fax 31-70-3834827, e-mail ifla@ifla.org
World Wide Web www.ifla.org

Beacher Wiggins
Director for Acquisitions and Bibliographic Access, Library of Congress
Corresponding Member, IFLA Standing Committee on Government Libraries, 2015–2017

The International Federation of Library Associations and Institutions (IFLA) is the preeminent international organization representing librarians, other information professionals, and library users. Despite budgetary pressures, throughout 2015 IFLA promoted its four core values: freedom of access to information and expression, as stated in Article 19 of the Universal Declaration of Human Rights; the belief that such access must be universal and equitable to support human well-being; delivery of high-quality library and information services in support of that access; and the commitment to enabling all members of IFLA to participate without regard to citizenship, disability, ethnic origin, gender, geographical location, political philosophy, race, or religion.

Throughout the year, IFLA promoted an understanding of libraries as cultural heritage resources that are the patrimony of every nation.

World Library and Information Congress

The World Library and Information Congress (WLIC)/81st IFLA General Conference and Council attracted 3,188 registered, paying attendees from 112 countries to Cape Town, South Africa, August 15–21, 2015. The number of attendees was nearly identical to the 3,222 from 132 countries who attended the 2014 WLIC in Lyon, France, and far exceeded the number of registrations at the 2013 WLIC in Singapore (2,704) and the 2012 WLIC in Helsinki, Finland (2,486). Ms. Ujala Satgoor, president of the Library and Information Association of South Africa (LIASA) for 2012–2015, chaired the National Committee that planned the Cape Town conference, with incoming LIASA president Ms. Segametsi Molawa as co-chair.

The conference theme, "Dynamic Libraries: Access, Development, and Transformation," was highlighted by the keynote address by Dr. Rob Adam, director-designate of the Square Kilometer Array South Africa Project and a political prisoner during South Africa's apartheid era. The Square Kilometer Array is the largest radio telescope system on Earth, with components in nine African countries and in Australia. The keynote address by this distinguished theoretical nuclear physicist indicates libraries' growing emphasis on supporting research in the sciences and on compiling, preserving, and accessing "big data" resources. The Cape Town conference offered delegates opportunities for service, including "Gift a Book, Change a Life" with the American Library Association International Relations Committee, which collected approximately 430 new books and 41 DVDs for Cape Town schoolchildren, and the Knitting Librarians project that created 67 blankets for Nelson Mandela Day to aid Cape Town's neediest citizens.

Seventeen satellite meetings, organized by IFLA sections, afforded more-detailed discussions on specific topics such as the role of libraries in the United Nations Sustainable Development Goals; personal career management; digital preservation; and online newspapers. The satellite meetings were held in Botswana, Namibia, and in South Africa's major centers in Cape Town, Durban, Pretoria, and Stellenbosch.

The next World Library and Information Congress will take place in Columbus, Ohio, United States, in August 2016. The 2017 meeting will be held in Wrocław, Poland (formerly called Breslau). Under the current IFLA WLIC conference planning guidelines, the conference cities are selected three years in advance, and at each WLIC the IFLA Governing Board announces the specific location of the conference that will take place two years later. The 2017 conference in Poland will be followed by conferences in Latin America or the Caribbean region (2018), and again in Europe (2019). The IFLA Governing Board is committed to continuously improving both the conference experience for participants and the financial security of the organization. Although the exhibitor fees and registration are higher than for most conferences in the library community, WLIC historically has not made money for IFLA, and the custom of convening all registered participants in opening and closing ceremonies limits the number of cities that can host the conference to those with conference halls seating at least 3,000 people. Furthermore, member organizations have commented that it is difficult to send representatives to both the general conference and the numerous specialized satellite meetings that occur at a distance from the general conference site. The current seven-year planning cycle and conference model were adopted after a consultation in early 2010 that Pleiade Management and Consultancy of Amsterdam conducted for IFLA. Through its Governing Board, IFLA retains overall ownership of each conference, and the Governing Board, IFLA Headquarters, and the conference National Committee (the local organizing committee) are responsible for each conference overall. Program content is guided by the IFLA Professional Committee. Actual conference planning and services are contracted to a "congress secretariat" or event management company. The Helsinki, Singapore, Lyon, and Cape Town conferences were managed by the K.I.T. Group of Berlin, Germany. A more extensive review of conference governance, the host city selection process, the planning cycle, and financial management is planned after the site of the 2018 conference is announced and all of IFLA's regions have hosted at least one recent conference.

Five Key Initiatives

In 2010 IFLA's Governing Board adopted a new Strategic Plan for the years 2010–2015. The plan, grounded in the four core values, set forth four strategic directions: empowering libraries to enable their user communities to have equitable access to information; building the strategic capacity of IFLA and that of its members; transforming the profile and standing of the library profession; and representing the interests of IFLA's members and their users throughout the world. The five key initiatives for 2010–2015 were the digital content program, international leadership development for librarianship, outreach for advocacy and advancement of the profession, cultural heritage disaster reconstruction, and the multilingualism program. The Governing Board determined priority activities every two years under the strategic plan. The Governing Board developed a new Strategic Plan in 2015 to take effect in 2016.

Digital Content Program

In its digital content program, IFLA advocates vigorously for open access to digital content and for the right of libraries to benefit from fair use and exemptions from copyright restrictions. The federation's position is that the current framework of copyright exceptions is not adequate for the digital era. Through participation in the World Intellectual Property Organization's Standing Committee on Copyright and Related Rights (SCCR), IFLA has worked toward a binding international instrument on copyright limitations and exceptions that will enable the world's libraries to continue their historic mission of providing universal access to knowledge and information. With the International Council on Archives (ICA), Electronic Information for Libraries (EIFL), and Corporación Innovarte, IFLA's Committee on Copyright and Other Legal Matters drafted the Treaty Proposal on Copyright Limitations and Exceptions for Libraries and Archives (TLIB). It would protect libraries in the areas of preservation, right of reproduction and supply of copies, legal deposit, library lending, parallel importation, cross-border uses, orphan works, retracted and withdrawn works, liability of libraries and archives, technological measures of protection, contracts, and the right to translate works. Following intensive efforts by IFLA and its partners throughout 2013 and 2014 to gain the support of WIPO member states for the proposed TLIB, the SSCR in 2015 reviewed a study by American copyright lawyer Kenneth Crews of existing copyright exceptions for libraries and museums in 188 countries.

IFLA continues to be an active participant in follow-up to the World Summit of the Information Society (WSIS), which held two summits in Geneva, Switzerland (2003) and Tunis, Tunisia (2005). IFLA sends representatives to the Internet Governance Forum, a series of annual follow-up meetings to the WSIS; in 2015 the Governance Forum took place in João Pessoa, Brazil. IFLA is responsible for reporting to UNESCO on two of the eleven WSIS action lines, Action Line C3: Access to Information and Action Line C8: Cultural Diversity and Identity, Linguistic Diversity, and Local Content. The follow-up activities have become part of the "WSIS+10" review that commenced in 2013, ten years after the Geneva summit. In January 2013 the IFLA Governing Board issued a revised Position on Internet Governance that states clearly the issues IFLA believes should be addressed in any post-WSIS framework, especially the right of equitable public access to the

Internet, and advocates a multi-stakeholder model of Internet governance. IFLA's membership and officers worked tirelessly in 2014 and 2015 to ensure that the review would acknowledge the place of libraries in the WSIS vision of a people-centered, inclusive and development-oriented information society. The WSIS+10 review was presented at the United Nations General Assembly High-Level Meeting, December 15–16, 2015, and the General Assembly adopted the review's outcome document that calls for bridging the digital divide and welcoming participation by all stakeholders.

In January 2015 IFLA released its Sustainable Development Toolkit, to assist libraries in promoting the role of information in sustainable development from 2015 through 2030. At the Lyon WLIC in August 2014 IFLA had promulgated the Lyon Declaration on Access to Information and Development and publicly invited other stakeholders in the information society to co-sign. The declaration states that access to information has a central role in sustainable development for all of the world's people, and it calls on member states of the United Nations to acknowledge the necessity of access to information and the skills to use information effectively, and to ensure that this necessity is recognized in the United Nations' post-2015 development agenda. The declaration attracted more than 500 co-signers. Most are libraries, library associations, or institutions of higher education, but the co-signers also include the Wellcome Foundation, Wikipedia Foundation, and Engineers for Social Responsibility.

The officers of IFLA, particularly incoming president Donna Scheeder, achieved a milestone when the United Nations included, as Target 16.10 of its 2030 Agenda for Sustainable Development, the aim to "ensure public access to information and protect fundamental freedoms, in accordance with national legislation and international agreements."

International Leadership and Advocacy Program

Planning for this key initiative essentially began at the 2012 WLIC in Helsinki, Finland, and is being carried out through IFLA's existing Action for Development Through Libraries (ALP) program. The Building Strong Library Associations initiative provides training materials and mentoring to help library associations build capacity. The ALP International Leaders program sponsors in-person sessions for emerging library leaders at each WLIC. The ALP program also contributed to the federation's goals for sustainable development.

Cultural Heritage Disaster Reconstruction Program

Since 1996 IFLA has been a founding member of the International Committee of the Blue Shield (ICBS) to protect cultural property in the event of natural and human disasters. Its current partners in ICBS are the International Council on Archives, the International Council on Monuments and Sites, the International Council of Museums, and the Coordinating Council of Audiovisual Archives Associations. In 2015 the IFLA North American regional center for preservation and conservation, hosted at the Library of Congress, continued to develop a network of colleague institutions to provide a safety net for library collections during emergencies. An additional focus in 2015 was IFLA's work to help libraries recover from the earthquake that struck Nepal on April 25. Also in 2015 IFLA began building a Risk Register for Documentary Cultural Heritage, to be launched the following year.

Multilingualism Program

Recognizing that the Internet is now a prevalent means of communication and resource sharing, IFLA continues efforts to make its website at http://www.ifla.org multilingual. The website is available now in English, French, and Spanish versions. To assist libraries in China, francophone Africa, the Arab world, and Russia, IFLA maintains four language centers at the National Library of China in Beijing; the Central Library of Cheikh Anta Diop University in Dakar, Senegal; the Bibliotheca Alexandrina in Alexandria, Egypt; and the Russian State Library in Moscow.

Grants and Awards

IFLA continues to work with corporate partners and national libraries to maintain programs and opportunities that would otherwise not be possible, especially for librarians and libraries in developing countries. The Jay Jordan IFLA/OCLC Early Career Development Fellowships provide four weeks of intensive experience, based in OCLC headquarters in Dublin, Ohio, for library and information science professionals from countries with developing economies who are in the early stages of their careers. The fellows for 2015 were from Pakistan, the Philippines, Serbia, Swaziland, and Zimbabwe. At the Cape Town WLIC in August 2015 OCLC and IFLA announced the fellows for 2016, from Bangladesh, Kenya, Nigeria, the Philippines, and Serbia. (The American Theological Library Association ended its co-sponsor role in 2013.) Since its inception in 2001, the program has supported 75 librarians from 38 countries with developing economies.

The Frederic Thorpe Awards, established in 2003, are administered by the IFLA Libraries Serving Persons with Print Disabilities Section and the Ulverscroft Foundation of Leicester, England, which Thorpe founded to support visually impaired people. The Ulverscroft Foundation renewed the program as the Ulverscroft/IFLA Best Practice Awards (Frederic Thorpe Awards) in 2006, 2007, 2008, 2010, and 2011, with no award in 2009 or 2012. In 2013 the Ulverscroft Foundation again began funding the award. The 2013 award supported a Serbian librarian to visit the Royal National Institute of Blind People (RNIB) National Library for the Blind in the United Kingdom. In 2014 and 2015 the Frederic Thorpe Award program was revamped in order to resume the awards in 2016 in the form of travel grants for three librarians from countries with developing economies to attend the two-day satellite meeting of the IFLA Libraries Serving Persons with Print Disabilities Section planned in conjunction with the 2016 WLIC in Columbus, Ohio.

The Bill and Melinda Gates Foundation Access to Learning Award was presented annually from 2000 to 2014 to a library, library agency, or comparable organization outside the United States that was innovative in providing free public access to information. To IFLA's regret, the Gates Foundation announced in 2014 that it would conclude its Global Libraries program within the next three to five years. The final Access to Learning Award was presented at the 2014 WLIC in Lyon, France, to Sri Lanka's e-Library Nenasala Program.

Numerous awards and grants encourage travel to the annual IFLA conferences. The IFLA International Marketing Award includes a stipend and travel to the conference for representatives of the winning libraries. The Emerald Group sponsored the award from 2008 through 2014. After a hiatus in 2015, it became the IFLA/BibLibre International Marketing Award in 2016. BibLibre, a library systems and services vendor in Marseille, France, made a commitment to award three stipends in 2016 and to continue its sponsorship through 2018.

The Council on Library and Information Resources (CLIR) sponsors the Rovelstad Scholarship in International Librarianship that brings one international library science student to the WLIC each year. In 2015 the awardee was Kelly Grogg, Olson Graduate Research Assistant in Special Collections and University Archives, University of Iowa Libraries. The Dr. Shawky Salem Conference Grant, the Kwarim Ltd. Conference Grant, and the Naseej (Arabian Advanced Systems Co.) Conference Grant support conference attendance from Arab countries. Many national library professional associations subsidize travel to the IFLA conference for their members; the Comité Français IFLA supports travelers from any francophone country. The Aspire Award supports travel to conferences of IFLA and of CILIP, the Chartered Institute of Library and Information Professionals (United Kingdom), in memory of Dr. Bob McKee (1950–2010), chief executive of CILIP.

The IFLA Academic and Research Libraries Section sponsors an annual competition awarding conference registration and travel support for three contestants from Africa, Latin America, and the Asia/Pacific region. Formerly the De Gruyter/Saur Research Paper Award, this competition was co-sponsored by Ex Libris and Sage in 2015. The Section on Education and Training sponsors a Student Paper Award, funded by the library services vendor ekz (ekz.bibliotheksservice GmbH), for library science students.

With IFLA, the large commercial publisher Brill sponsors the Open Access Award for initiatives in the area of open access monograph publishing. The first award, in 2013, recognized Open Book Publishers, Cambridge (United Kingdom). In 2014 the award was presented to Knowledge Unlatched, a United Kingdom project to ensure that scholarly publications are open accessible once the costs of publication have been met. The 2015 recipient was the Directory of Open Access Books (DOAB), a discovery service for open-access books that is operated by the OAPEN Foundation, headquartered at the Koninklijke Bibliotheek, The Hague. The award includes funding to attend the WLIC and a cash award of 1,000 euros.

The IFLA Honorary Fellowships, the IFLA Medal, and the IFLA Scroll of Appreciation recognize service to IFLA by individuals. The IFLA Scroll of Appreciation was presented to the National Committee for the Cape Town WLIC in 2015, in keeping with the customary award to each National Committee for the WLIC. In addition, Susan Schnuer, associate director of the Mortenson Center for International Library Programs, University of Illinois, received the Scroll of Appreciation in Cape Town in recognition of her distinguished service to the international library community. An IFLA Medal was not awarded in 2015. Ingrid Parent, university librarian of the University of British Columbia and a former president of IFLA (2011–2013), was named an IFLA Honorary Fellow in 2015.

Membership and Finances

IFLA has more than 1,500 members in 150 countries. Initially established at a conference in Edinburgh, Scotland, in 1927, it has been registered in the Netherlands since 1971 and has headquarters facilities at the Koninklijke Bibliotheek (Royal Library) in The Hague. Although IFLA did not hold a General Conference outside Europe and North America until 1980, there has since been steadily increasing participation from Asia, Africa, South America, and Australia. The federation now maintains regional offices for Africa (in Pretoria, South Africa); Asia and Oceania (in Singapore); and Latin America and the Caribbean (in Mexico City since 2011; formerly in Rio de Janeiro, Brazil). The organization has seven official working languages: Arabic, Chinese, English, French, German, Russian, and Spanish. It maintains four language centers: for Arabic, in Alexandria, Egypt; for Chinese, in Beijing, China; for the French-speaking communities of Africa, in Dakar, Senegal; and for Russian, in Moscow, Russia. The language centers contribute to more effective communication with their respective language communities by providing translations of IFLA publications and becoming involved in local or regional professional events.

IFLA offers a range of membership categories: international library associations, national library associations, other associations (generally regional or special library associations), institutions, institutional sub-units, one-person libraries, school libraries, association affiliates (limited to three consecutive years and open only to national associations with operating budgets of 10,000 euros or less, to encourage membership in countries with developing economies), personal affiliates, student affiliates, new graduate members, and non-salaried personal members. Association and institution members have voting rights in the IFLA General Council and IFLA elections and may nominate candidates for IFLA offices. Institutional sub-units, one-person libraries, and school libraries have limited voting rights for section elections; association affiliates and personal members do not have voting rights but may submit nominations for any IFLA office, and individuals may run for office themselves. Except for affiliates, membership fees are keyed to the UNESCO Scale of Assessment and the United Nations List of Least Developed Countries, to encourage participation regardless of economic circumstances.

UNESCO has given IFLA formal associate relations status, the highest level of relationship accorded to nongovernmental organizations by UNESCO. In addition, IFLA has observer status with the United Nations, WIPO, the International Organization for Standardization, and the World Trade Organization, and associate status with the International Council of Scientific Unions.

IFLA has extended consultative status to many organizations in the information field, including the Arab League Educational, Cultural and Scientific Organization; Conference of Directors of National Libraries; European Dyslexia Association; International Council on Archives; International Standard Serial Number (ISSN) International Centre; International Board on Books for Young People; International Organization for Standardization (ISO); International Publishers Association; World Blind Union; and World Federation of the Deaf.

More than a dozen corporations in the information industry have formed working relationships with IFLA as corporate partners. The corporate partners provide financial and in-kind support and in turn gain the opportunity to convey information about their products and services to IFLA members and others who pay attention to IFLA's publications and activities. Several levels of corporate partnership are available. Most prominently, in 2014 OCLC became IFLA's first and sole Platinum Partner, providing support at an extraordinary level. Most corporate partners choose to support IFLA at one of three levels: gold (annual support equaling 3,500 euros), silver (annual support equaling 2,000 euros), or bronze (annual support equaling 1,000 euros). Gold Corporate Partners in 2015 were Emerald and Sage Publications. De Gruyter Saur was a Silver Partner, and Bronze Partners were Brill, Elsevier, Gale Cengage Learning, Innovative Interfaces Inc., Rockefeller University Press, and Sabinet. IFLA's Associate Partners were Annual Reviews, Axiell, Harrassowitz, and nbd/biblion. A review of the current corporate partnership program began in 2012 and is ongoing, in recognition that corporate sponsors need the benefits of IFLA institutional membership as well as opportunities to expose their products and services to the IFLA community.

In addition, a number of national libraries provide financial support to IFLA either directly or in-kind. In 2014 the Bill and Melinda Gates Foundation announced that it would donate approximately $4.9 million to IFLA over the next five years.

The IFLA Foundation (Stichting IFLA) was established in 2007. The foundation accepts private donations and bequests and also is funded by other IFLA income. It gives funding priority to proposals and projects that promise to have a long-term impact in developing and strengthening IFLA; are clearly related to at least one of IFLA's strategic priorities; and are not likely to be funded by other bodies. The foundation also occasionally makes grants for attendance at the World Library and Information Conference; the grants are administered by the IFLA headquarters and governance structure rather than directly by the foundation. The foundation's board of trustees consists of IFLA's president, president-elect, treasurer, secretary general, and an appointed expert in foundation law and management.

Personnel, Structure, and Governance

The secretary general of IFLA is Jennefer Nicholson, former executive director of the Australian Library and Information Association. Ms. Nicholson planned to retire on May 31, 2016, and the IFLA Governing Board has announced that her successor will be Gerald Leitner, currently secretary general of the Austrian Library Association.

At IFLA Headquarters, Fiona Bradley manages development programs; Joanne Yeomans is professional support officer; Julia Brungs and Asha Uche-Roosberg are both policy and projects officers. Stuart Hamilton was named deputy secretary general in 2014 and also continues as director for policy and advocacy, with Christina de Castell as manager for policy and advocacy. The editor of the quarterly *IFLA Journal* is Stephen W. Witt, succeeding J. Stephen Parker. Esther Doria is the voucher program administrator. Louis Takács is content editor for the IFLA website. The IFLA manager for conference and business relations is Josche Ouwerkerk. Christine Zuidwijk is IFLA's financial officer, and Ina Dijkstra is the human resources adviser while the federation seeks to hire a human resources officer. Tatjana Hoeink is the membership officer and Helen Mandl is the manager for member services.

New officers and board members took office at the close of the 2015 conference in Cape Town. Donna Scheeder, retired from the Congressional Research Service, Library of Congress, and currently president of Library Strategies International, is the new president of IFLA, succeeding Sinikka Sipilä, secretary-general of the Finnish Library Association. The new president-elect is Glòria Pérez-Salmerón of FESABID (Federación Española de Sociedades de Archivística, Biblioteconomía, Documentación y Museística). The treasurer is Christine Mackenzie, chief executive officer of Yarra Plenty Regional Libraries, Victoria, Australia.

Under the revised 2008 IFLA Statutes, the 19 members of IFLA's Governing Board (plus the secretary general, ex officio) are responsible for the federation's general policies, management and finance. Additionally, the board represents the federation in legal and other formal proceedings. The board is composed of the president, president-elect, secretary general (ex officio), ten directly elected members, the chair of the Professional Committee, the chairs of each IFLA division, and the chair of the Standing Committee of the Management of Library Associations Section, currently Barbara Schleihagen, executive director, Deutsche Bibliotheksverband. Current members, in addition to Scheeder, Pérez-Salmerón, Nicholson, and Schleihagen, are Margaret Allen (Australia), Kirsten Boelt (Denmark), Loida Garcia-Febo (United States), Ágnes Hajdu Barát (Hungary), Ngian Lek Choh (Singapore), Andrew McDonald (United Kingdom), Ellen Ndeshi Namhila (Namibia), Victoria Owen (Canada), and Christine Wellems (Germany), plus the chairs of the Professional Committee and divisions, named below.

The Governing Board delegates responsibility for overseeing the direction of IFLA between board meetings, within the policies established by the board, to the IFLA Executive Committee, which includes the president, president-elect, treasurer, chair of the Professional Committee, two members of the Governing Board (elected every two years by members of the board from among its elected members), and IFLA's secretary general, ex officio. The current elected Governing Board members of the Executive Committee are Ngian and McDonald.

The IFLA Professional Committee monitors the planning and programming of professional activities carried out by IFLA's two types of bodies: professional groups—five divisions, forty-four sections, and special interest groups—and strategic programs (formerly called core programs or core activities). The Professional Committee is composed of one elected officer from each division, plus a chair elected by the outgoing committee; the president, the president-elect, and the professional support officer, who serves as secretary; the chairs of the CLM and FAIFE committees, and two elected members of the Governing Board, currently Boelt and Wellems. Maria Carme Torras i Calvo, library director, Universitetsbiblioteket i Bergen, Norway, chairs the Professional Committee.

The five divisions of IFLA and their representatives on the Professional Committee are I: Library Types (Raissa Teodori, Italy); II: Library Collections (Frederick Zarndt, United States); III: Library Services (Viviana Quiñones, France); IV: Support of the Profession (Perry Moree, Netherlands); and V: Regions (Victoria Okojie, Nigeria). The chair of the Copyright and Legal Matters Committee is Evelyn Woodberry (Australia). The chair of the Freedom of Access to Information and Freedom of Expression Committee is Martyn Wade, national librarian of

Scotland. A total of forty-four sections focus on topical interests, such as statistics and evaluation, library theory and research, and management and marketing, or on particular types of libraries or parts of the world.

The six strategic programs, which replace the former five core activities, are Action for Development Through Libraries (ALP, originally Advancement of Librarianship); Preservation and Conservation (PAC); IFLA UNIMARC Strategic Programme, which maintains and develops the Universal MARC Format, UNIMARC; Committee on Standards; Free Access to Information and Freedom of Expression (FAIFE); and Copyright and Other Legal Matters (CLM). The UNIMARC Strategic Programme has a separate office headed by Maria-Inês Cordeiro at the National Library of Portugal in Lisbon. Two other longstanding IFLA projects are the IFLA website and the IFLA Voucher Scheme, which replaced the IFLA Office for International Lending. The voucher scheme enables libraries to pay for international interlibrary loan requests using vouchers purchased from IFLA rather than actual currency or credit accounts. By eliminating bank charges and invoices for each transaction, the voucher scheme reduces the administrative costs of international library loans and allows libraries to plan budgets with less regard to short-term fluctuations in the value of different national currencies. The voucher scheme has also encouraged participating libraries to voluntarily standardize their charges for loans.

To ensure an arena within IFLA for discussion of new social, professional, or cultural issues, the Professional Committee approves the formation of special interest groups for a limited time period. There currently are discussion groups for Access to Information Network/Africa (ATINA); Agricultural Libraries; Big Data; E-Metrics; Environmental Sustainability and Libraries; LGBTQ (Lesbian, Gay, Bisexual, Transgender, Queer/Questioning) Users; Library and Information Science Education in Developing Countries; Library History; National Information and Library Policy; National Organizations and International Relations; New Professionals; Radio Frequency Identification (RFID); Religious Libraries in Dialogue; Semantic Web; and Women, Information, and Libraries. Special interest groups operate for a maximum period of three years. If there is sufficient interest, a special interest group may then become a permanent IFLA section. The Indigenous Matters Section was established from a special interest group in 2015.

Library and Archives Canada: 2015—The Year of Possibilities

Guy Berthiaume
Librarian and Archivist of Canada

The year 2015 opened up many possibilities for Library and Archives Canada (LAC), and allowed the organization to translate a broad vision of access into a working reality. There were four main priorities identified at the beginning of the year: increasing access to Canada's documentary heritage, developing a coherent approach to stakeholders, establishing LAC as a client-driven organization and making sure that LAC has the necessary infrastructure to fulfill its mandate.

One of the key factors in achieving these priorities was giving LAC staff the chance to contribute their ideas and their expertise, leveraging their individual and collective strengths to put LAC at the leading edge of archival and library science and new technologies. Harnessing the views of staff is part of LAC's overall commitment to consultation.

From June to December 2015 LAC gathered the views of its users, its main stakeholders, and its employees. It conducted four focus groups, five employee consultation sessions, a public opinion survey, a town hall, and a formal discussion with its Stakeholder's Forum, the twelve Canadian professional associations with which staff deal frequently. The ideas generated by these consultations helped to develop a road map, a three-year plan for 2016 to 2019, so that the work of LAC will meet the needs of its clients. LAC also get to know its clients better, allowing it to stay relevant, optimize its content and services, and demonstrate its value to Canadians as a whole.

LAC is one of many organizations that represent the interests of Canada's archival and library communities abroad. As a combined library and archives, and as a departmental agency within Canada's federal government, LAC has a unique opportunity, at home and abroad, to connect communities, facilitate discussions, compare standards, and share professional perspectives. LAC is committed to engaging with international networks in an open and inclusive way, and in this spirit it completed an International Engagement Strategy in 2015. The goal of this strategy is to promote coherence among LAC's various international activities, and to better position LAC to play an active role internationally—with other national memory institutions and alongside other Canadian experts.

Increasing Access

A digital strategy for LAC was an important focus of 2015, one that will ensure a long-term, secure system for preserving digital content and making it available. The work of creating this strategy has been undertaken in consultation with the government of Canada, and the provincial and territorial governments. LAC is now looking into commercially available solutions for a secure digital platform, which other archives could then benefit from.

Report prepared by Sandra Nicholls, Senior Writer, Library and Archives Canada

The digital strategy will mean that LAC can:

- Build the right technology platform to achieve its goals
- Ensure its collections include new forms of born-digital content
- Digitize those portions of its analog collections in greatest demand
- Ensure high-quality metadata is provided
- Facilitate the use of its holdings by anyone, anywhere, anytime
- Promote its holdings and engage with clients
- Play a leadership role among the network of memory institutions
- Be aware of client needs
- Inform decisions with the best use of data
- Build a digital culture

Documentary heritage is a cornerstone of all democratic societies, and, throughout the world, memory institutions such as LAC are creating targeted approaches to digitizing their national heritage. Canada's National Heritage Digitization Strategy (NHDS) has been developed in collaboration with the Stakeholder's Forum, and draws from international best practices, such as the Digital Public Library of America and the Swedish Digisam initiative. The official launch of the strategy is scheduled for June 2016.

LAC has already been actively digitizing materials together with some of its partners. For example, with Canadiana.org, LAC digitized 35 million pages of archival material on microfilm, and with Ancestry.ca, LAC digitized and indexed 11 archival collections representing 3 million pages online. New partnerships with these two partners are underway, for newspaper reels and certificates of military instruction.

LAC in the Community

Canada's national library and archives has always been involved at the community, grassroots level. It's part of LAC's mandate. But in 2015 LAC took this commitment even further through new kinds of partnerships and collaborative arrangements.

The Documentary Heritage Communities Program (DHCP) was introduced in June 2015. It provides financial help directly to community organizations across Canada so they can preserve, promote, and provide access to their collections. Archives, library associations, historical societies, and other heritage groups can all apply for this funding, which totals $1.5 million per year over five years.

The program funded 65 projects in its first year. Recipients included the Inuit Broadcasting Corporation, the Dr. James Naismith Basketball Foundation, Les Amis des Jardins de Métis, the Canadian Association of Research Libraries, the Prairie Tractor and Engine Museum Society, the Vancouver Holocaust Education Centre, and the Fédérations des associations de familles du Québec.

LAC is also bringing researchers and specialists from across Canada together to discuss how LAC works, and as a way to find solutions to common problems. For example, the Acquisitions Advisory Committee invites art experts and historians to look at the best ways of adding to its collections. The Services Consultation Committee looks at the kinds of services it offers, and how they can be improved.

The TD Summer Reading Club is a national program that gets children to read—in 2015 participants enjoyed some 1.2 million books. The program is offered by LAC in partnership with TD Bank, the Toronto Public Library, and libraries across the country. During the summer of 2015 more than 2,000 libraries hosted the program, and more than 650,000 children discovered the fun of reading.

Since 1965 LAC has collected theses and dissertations working together with Canadian universities; in 2015 LAC consulted more than 75 universities to design a new approach. As a result, universities can now manage licenses for this intellectual property directly with their students. The theses portal continues to grow in popularity, with more than 43,000 new titles submitted in 2014–2015, and more than 600,000 downloads.

LAC and Bibliothèque et Archives nationales du Québec (BAnQ) signed a partnership in 2015 that will allow BAnQ to provide digital publications directly to LAC, with the publisher's permission. This means that up to 10,000 digital publications from Quebec publishing houses could be added to LAC's collection over the next two years.

The Continuing Record of Government

There is a new trend in government: making it more open. More than 68 countries have joined the Open Government Partnership, including Canada. LAC has a key role to play by opening up government information and making it more available to the public.

LAC has all kinds of government records, including documents about Canada's military history, trade relations, residential schools, and even how Canada celebrates its birthdays. Taking one "block" of records at a time, and seeing if it can remove any restrictions, LAC has opened 18 million pages of records since 2010. From April 1, 2015, to December 31, 2015 alone, LAC made 5,802,398 pages of government records openly available to the public.

LAC also continues to create historical data sets, everything from census data to records of land grants, and then puts them on Canada's open data portal. In 2015 LAC created new data sets, covering topics ranging from environmental observations to Canadian airmen of the First World War, studies of immigrants, and the results of Canadian elections.

LAC's Public Identity

LAC is an active player in Canada's cultural life. Through public programs and special events, exhibitions and joint displays, an active loans program, and the creative use of its public spaces, LAC engages clients with the cultural heritage of an entire nation.

Visitors from around the world toured LAC's Preservation Centre in 2015, from Serbia's ambassador to architectural students from Carleton University to representatives of the National Archives of the United Arab Emirates. LAC's flagship building at 395 Wellington Street, in the heart of Canada's capital city, Ottawa, was extensively renovated in 2015, offering a much-needed focal point for the public programming. With its marbled stairways and engraved glass windows, 395 Wellington speaks to the noble and enduring purpose of a national archives and library.

A major exhibition was held in its sunken floor lobby in 2015. "Hockey Marching as to War" explored the impact of the First World War on hockey players, and the way it transformed organized hockey during and after the war. Items featured included reproductions of photographs, posters and documents from the collections of LAC and the Hockey Hall of Fame (HHOF), and digital copies of Canadian Expeditionary Force files and the attestation papers of more than 25 HHOF inductees.

The second floor reading room is now the go-to site for public events and cultural activities, as well as a place of quiet beauty for people to read. The room is flanked by two murals created by famous Quebec artist Alfred Pellan. Among the public program highlights in 2015:

- David Fricker, the director general of the National Archives of Australia, gave a public talk on e-Government and Policy Responses from the National Archives of Australia.
- Dr. Robert Darnton, university librarian emeritus at Harvard, gave a talk on the digital public library of America and where he sees the future of books, libraries, and information.
- Sherry Simon from the French Department at Concordia University brought literary Montreal in the 1940s to life with her talk on Yiddish Language Modernism in "Montreal: A Tale of Three Cities."
- Pierre Anctil, professor of history at the University of Ottawa, gave a talk on the modernist Yiddish poetry of Jacob-Isaac Segal.

Whether a national treasure or a hidden gem, LAC is also proud to contribute items for public display at museums, archives, libraries, and other memory institutions large and small. Here are a few that LAC helped put on display in 2015.

- The 1982 Proclamation of the Constitution Act was loaned to the Canadian Museum for Human Rights for its grand opening in Winnipeg.
- The earliest known oil portrait of former Prime Minister Sir John A. Macdonald was displayed at Macdonald's former residence, historic Bellevue House in Kingston, Ontario.
- The *Red River Expedition at Kakabeka Falls*, Ontario, an 1877 painting by Frances Anne Hopkins, traveled to the Art Gallery of Ontario in Toronto, the Crystal Bridges Museum of American Art in Arizona, and the Pinacoteca do Estado de São Paulo in Brazil.

LAC also contributed to exhibitions at the Canadian Museum of Immigration at Pier 21, the Library of Parliament, the Museum of Canadian History, Canada's Hockey Hall of Fame, the National Gallery of Canada, the Musée des beaux-arts de Montréal, the Canadian Centre for Architecture in Montreal, and the Galt Museum and Archives in Lethbridge, Alberta, among others.

Also in 2015, the groundwork was set for an innovative new series known as *Signatures*. *Signatures* is both a magazine and a public program featuring lively and informal discussions between the Librarian and Archivist of Canada and individual donors to LAC. Both the journal and the conversations interpret the living cultural, civic, historical, and literary record of Canada as reflected in its documentary heritage.

LAC in the World

As Librarian and Archivist of Canada, Guy Berthiaume was elected in 2015 as the chair of the Standing Committee on National Libraries at the International Federation of Libraries and Library Associations (IFLA). This global organization represents the voice of the library and information community around the world. The National Libraries section supports national libraries as guardians of the world's intellectual heritage.

Organizations from more than 45 countries make up the International Internet Preservation Consortium, which is dedicated to collecting and preserving the knowledge found on the global web, and then making it available. LAC's chief information officer was voted in as the chair of its steering committee for 2015.

Conclusion

In 2015 LAC continued its journey to self-definition by opening up numerous possibilities for growth and change, and re-imagining the future for an organization which is, at once, a government agency, an archives, and a library. By consistently demonstrating its value to Canadians, providing an accessible link between the past, present, and future, and staying open to new kinds of collaborations and partnerships, LAC has ensured that it will be around for the future, whatever that future holds.

Part 2
Funding and Grants

Funding Programs and Grant-Making Agencies

National Endowment for the Humanities

400 7th St. S.W., Washington, DC 20506
202-606-8400, 800-634-1121
TDD (hearing impaired) 202-606-8282 or 866-372-2930 (toll free)
E-mail info@neh.gov, World Wide Web http://neh.gov

The National Endowment for the Humanities (NEH) is an independent federal agency created in 1965. It is one of the largest funders of humanities programs in the United States.

Because democracy demands wisdom, NEH promotes excellence in the humanities and conveys the lessons of history to all Americans, seeking to develop educated and thoughtful citizens. It accomplishes this mission by providing grants for high-quality humanities projects in six funding areas: education, preservation and access, public programs, research, challenge grants, and digital humanities.

Grants from NEH enrich classroom learning, create and preserve knowledge, and bring ideas to life through public television, radio, new technologies, museum exhibitions, and programs in libraries and other community places. Recipients typically are cultural institutions, such as museums, archives, libraries, colleges and universities, and public television and radio stations, as well as individual scholars. The grants

- Strengthen teaching and learning in the humanities in schools and colleges
- Preserve and provide access to cultural and educational resources
- Provide opportunities for lifelong learning
- Facilitate research and original scholarship
- Strengthen the institutional base of the humanities

Over nearly half a century, NEH has reached millions of people with projects and programs that preserve and study the nation's culture and history while providing a foundation for the future.

The endowment's mission is to enrich cultural life by promoting the study of the humanities. According to the National Foundation on the Arts and the Humanities Act, "The term 'humanities' includes, but is not limited to, the study of the following: language, both modern and classical; linguistics; literature; history; jurisprudence; philosophy; archaeology; comparative religion; ethics; the history, criticism, and theory of the arts; those aspects of social sciences which have humanistic content and employ humanistic methods; and the study and application of the humanities to the human environment with particular attention to reflecting our diverse heritage, traditions, and history and to the relevance of the humanities to the current conditions of national life."

The act, adopted by Congress in 1965, provided for the establishment of the National Foundation on the Arts and the Humanities in order to promote progress and scholarship in the humanities and the arts in the United States. The act included the following findings:

- The arts and the humanities belong to all the people of the United States.
- The encouragement and support of national progress and scholarship in the humanities and the arts, while primarily matters for private and local initiative, are also appropriate matters of concern to the federal government.
- An advanced civilization must not limit its efforts to science and technology alone, but must give full value and support to the other great branches of scholarly and cultural activity in order to achieve a better understanding of the past, a better analysis of the present, and a better view of the future.
- Democracy demands wisdom and vision in its citizens. It must therefore foster and support a form of education, and access to the arts and the humanities, designed to make people of all backgrounds and locations masters of technology and not its unthinking servants.
- It is necessary and appropriate for the federal government to complement, assist, and add to programs for the advancement of the humanities and the arts by local, state, regional, and private agencies and their organizations. In doing so, the government must be sensitive to the nature of public sponsorship. Public funding of the arts and humanities is subject to the conditions that traditionally govern the use of public money. Such funding should contribute to public support and confidence in the use of taxpayer funds. Public funds provided by the federal government ultimately must serve public purposes the Congress defines.
- The arts and the humanities reflect the high place accorded by the American people to the nation's rich culture and history and to the fostering of mutual respect for the diverse beliefs and values of all persons and groups.

What NEH Grants Accomplish

Since its founding, NEH has awarded more than 69,300 competitive grants.

Interpretive Exhibitions

Interpretive exhibitions provide opportunities for lifelong learning in the humanities for millions of Americans. Since 1967 NEH has awarded approximately $300 million in grants for interpretive exhibitions, catalogs, and public programs, which are among the most highly visible activities supported by the endowment. NEH support finances exhibitions; reading, viewing, and discussion programs; Web-based programs; and other public education programs at venues across the country.

Renewing Teaching

Over NEH's history, more than 100,000 high school and college teachers have deepened their knowledge of the humanities through intensive summer study supported by the endowment; tens of thousands of students benefit from these better-educated teachers every year.

Reading and Discussion Programs

Since 1982 NEH has supported reading and discussion programs in the nation's libraries, bringing people together to discuss works of literature and history. Scholars in the humanities provide thematic direction for the discussion programs. Using selected texts and such themes as "Work," "Family," "Diversity," and "Not for Children Only," these programs have attracted more than 2 million Americans to read and talk about what they've read.

Chronicling America

NEH's National Digital Newspaper Program is supporting projects to convert microfilm of historically important U.S. newspapers into fully searchable digital files. Developed in partnership with the Library of Congress, this long-term project ultimately will make more than 30 million pages of newspapers accessible online. For more on this project, visit http://chroniclingamerica.loc.gov.

Stimulating Private Support

About $2 billion in humanities support has been generated by NEH's Challenge Grants program, which requires most grant recipients to raise $3 in nonfederal funds for every dollar they receive.

Presidential Papers

Ten presidential papers projects, from Washington to Eisenhower, have received support from NEH. Matching grants for the ten projects have leveraged millions of dollars in nonfederal contributions.

New Scholarship

NEH grants enable scholars to do in-depth study. Jack Rakove explored the making of the Constitution in his *Original Meanings* and James McPherson chronicled the Civil War in his *Battle Cry of Freedom*. Projects supported by NEH grants have earned nearly 20 Pulitzer Prizes.

History on Screen

Since 1967 NEH has awarded approximately $300 million to support the production of films for broad public distribution, including the Emmy Award-winning series *The Civil War*, the Oscar-nominated films *Brooklyn Bridge, The Restless*

Conscience, and *Freedom on My Mind,* and film biographies of John and Abigail Adams, Eugene O'Neill, and Ernest Hemingway. More than 20 million people have watched Ken Burns's critically acclaimed *The War* (2007), which chronicles the United States in World War II. More than 8 million saw the April 2010 debut of *The Buddha,* a documentary made for PBS by filmmaker David Grubin, and it has been streamed into hundreds of classrooms nationwide.

American Voices

NEH support for scholarly editions makes the writings of prominent and influential Americans accessible. Ten presidents are included, along with such key figures as Martin Luther King, Jr., George C. Marshall, and Eleanor Roosevelt. Papers of prominent writers—among them Emily Dickinson, Walt Whitman, Mark Twain, and Robert Frost—are also available.

Library of America

Millions of books have been sold as part of the Library of America series, a collection of the riches of the nation's literature. Begun with NEH seed money, the nearly 200 published volumes include the works of such figures as Henry Adams, Edith Wharton, William James, Eudora Welty, and W. E. B. Du Bois.

The Library of America also received a $150,000 grant for the publication of *American Poetry: The Seventeenth and Eighteenth Centuries* (two volumes) and an expanded volume of selected works by Captain John Smith—a key figure in the establishment of the first permanent English settlement in North America, at Jamestown, Virginia—and other early exploration narratives.

Technical Innovation

NEH support for the digital humanities is fueling innovation and new tools for research in the humanities. Modern 3D technology allows students to visit things ranging from ancient Egypt to the 1964–1965 New York World's Fair. Spectral imaging was used to create an online critical edition of explorer David Livingstone's previously unreadable field diary of 1871.

Science and the Humanities

The scientific past is being preserved with NEH-supported editions of the letters of Charles Darwin, the works of Albert Einstein, and the 14-volume papers of Thomas Edison. Additionally, NEH and the National Science Foundation have joined forces in Documenting Endangered Languages (DEL), a multiyear effort to preserve records of key languages that are in danger of becoming extinct.

EDSITEment

EDSITEment (http://edsitement.neh.gov) assembles the best humanities resources on the Web, drawing more than 400,000 visitors each month. Incorporating these Internet resources, particularly primary documents, from more than 350 peer-reviewed websites, EDSITEment features more than 500 online lesson plans in all areas of the humanities. Teachers use EDSITEment's resources to enhance lessons and to engage students through interactive technology tools that hone critical-thinking skills.

Federal-State Partnership

The Office of Federal-State Partnership links NEH with the nationwide network of 56 humanities councils, which are located in each state, the District of Columbia, Puerto Rico, the U.S. Virgin Islands, the Northern Mariana Islands, American Samoa, and Guam. Each council funds humanities programs in its own jurisdiction.

Directory of State Humanities Councils

Alabama

Alabama Humanities Foundation
1100 Ireland Way, Suite 202
Birmingham, AL 35205-7001
205-558-3980, fax 205-558-3981
http://www.alabamahumanities.org

Alaska

Alaska Humanities Forum
161 E. First Ave., Door 15
Anchorage, AK 99501
907-272-5341, fax 907-272-3979
http://www.akhf.org

Arizona

Arizona Humanities Council
Ellis-Shackelford House
1242 N. Central Ave.
Phoenix, AZ 85004-1887
602-257-0335, fax 602-257-0392
http://www.azhumanities.org

Arkansas

Arkansas Humanities Council
407 President Clinton Ave., Suite 201
Little Rock, AR 72201
501-320-5761, fax 501-537-4550
http://www.arkhums.org

California

Cal Humanities
312 Sutter St., Suite 601
San Francisco, CA 94108
415-391-1474, fax 415-391-1312
http://www.calhum.org

Colorado

Colorado Humanities
7935 E. Prentice Ave., Suite 450
Greenwood Village, CO 80111
303-894-7951, fax 303-864-9361
http://www.coloradohumanities.org

Connecticut

Connecticut Humanities Council
37 Broad St.
Middletown, CT 06457
860-685-2260, fax 860-685-7597
http://cthumanities.org

Delaware

Delaware Humanities Forum
100 W. Tenth St., Suite 1009
Wilmington, DE 19801
302-657-0650, fax 302-657-0655
http://dehumanities.org

District of Columbia

Humanities Council of Washington, D.C.
925 U St. N.W.
Washington, DC 20001
202-387-8393, fax 202-387-8149
http://wdchumanities.org

Florida

Florida Humanities Council
599 Second St. S.
St. Petersburg, FL 33701-5005
727-873-2000, fax 727-873-2014
http://www.flahum.org

Georgia

Georgia Humanities Council
50 Hurt Plaza S.E., Suite 595
Atlanta, GA 30303-2915
404-523-6220, fax 404-523-5702
http://www.georgiahumanities.org

Hawaii

Hawai'i Council for the Humanities
First Hawaiian Bank Bldg.
3599 Waialae Ave., Room 25
Honolulu, HI 96816
808-732-5402, fax 808-732-5432
http://www.hihumanities.org

Idaho

Idaho Humanities Council
217 W. State St.
Boise, ID 83702
208-345-5346, fax 208-345-5347
http://www.idahohumanities.org

Illinois

Illinois Humanities Council
17 N. State St., No. 1400
Chicago, IL 60602-3296
312-422-5580, fax 312-422-5588
http://www.prairie.org

Indiana

Indiana Humanities
1500 N. Delaware St.
Indianapolis, IN 46202
317-638-1500, fax 317-634-9503
http://www.indianahumanities.org

Iowa

Humanities Iowa
100 Library, Room 4039
Iowa City, IA 52242-4038
319-335-4153, fax 319-335-4154
http://humanitiesiowa.org

Kansas

Kansas Humanities Council
112 S.W. Sixth Ave., Suite 210
Topeka, KS 66603

785-357-0359, fax 785-357-1723
http://www.kansashumanities.org

Kentucky

Kentucky Humanities Council
206 E. Maxwell St.
Lexington, KY 40508
859-257-5932, fax 859-257-5933
http://www.kyhumanities.org

Louisiana

Louisiana Endowment for the Humanities
938 Lafayette St., Suite 300
New Orleans, LA 70113-1782
504-523-4352, fax 504-529-2358
http://www.leh.org

Maine

Maine Humanities Council
674 Brighton Ave.
Portland, ME 04102-1012
207-773-5051, fax 207-773-2416
http://www.mainehumanities.org

Maryland

Maryland Humanities Council
108 W. Centre St.
Baltimore, MD 21201-4565
410-685-0095, fax 410-685-0795
http://www.mdhc.org

Massachusetts

Mass Humanities
66 Bridge St.
Northampton, MA 01060
413-584-8440, fax 413-584-8454
http://www.masshumanities.org

Michigan

Michigan Humanities Council
119 Pere Marquette Drive, Suite 3B
Lansing, MI 48912-1270
517-372-7770, fax 517-372-0027
http://michiganhumanities.org

Minnesota

Minnesota Humanities Center
987 E. Ivy Ave.
St. Paul, MN 55106-2046
651-774-0105, fax 651-774-0205
http://www.minnesotahumanities.org

Mississippi

Mississippi Humanities Council
3825 Ridgewood Rd., Room 311
Jackson, MS 39211
601-432-6752, fax 601-432-6750
http://www.mshumanities.org

Missouri

Missouri Humanities Council
543 Hanley Industrial Court, Suite 201
St. Louis, MO 63144-1905
314-781-9660, fax 314-781-9681
http://www.mohumanities.org

Montana

Humanities Montana
311 Brantly
Missoula, MT 59812-7848
406-243-6022, fax 406-243-4836
http://www.humanitiesmontana.org

Nebraska

Nebraska Humanities Council
215 Centennial Mall South, Suite 330
Lincoln, NE 68508
402-474-2131, fax 402-474-4852
http://www.humanitiesnebraska.org

Nevada

Nevada Humanities
1670-200 N. Virginia St.
P.O. Box 8029
Reno, NV 89507
775-784-6587, fax 775-784-6527
http://www.nevadahumanities.org

New Hampshire

New Hampshire Humanities Council
117 Pleasant St.
Concord, NH 03301-3852

603-224-4071, fax 603-224-4072
http://www.nhhc.org

New Jersey

New Jersey Council for the Humanities
28 W. State St., 6th floor
Trenton, NJ 08608
609-695-4838, fax 609-695-4929
http://www.njch.org

New Mexico

New Mexico Humanities Council
4115 Silver Ave. S.E.
Albuquerque, NM 87108
505-633-7370, fax 505-633-7377
http://www.nmhum.org

New York

New York Council for the Humanities
150 Broadway, Suite 1700
New York, NY 10038
212-233-1131, fax 212-233-4607
http://www.nyhumanities.org

North Carolina

North Carolina Humanities Council
320 East 9th St., Suite 414
Charlotte, NC 28202
704-687-1520, fax 704-687-1525
http://www.nchumanities.org

North Dakota

North Dakota Humanities Council
418 E. Broadway, Suite 8
P.O. Box 2191
Bismarck, ND 58502
701-255-3360, fax 701-223-8724
http://www.ndhumanities.org

Ohio

Ohio Humanities Council
471 E. Broad St., Suite 1620
Columbus, OH 43215-3857
614-461-7802, fax 614-461-4651
http://www.ohiohumanities.org

Oklahoma

Oklahoma Humanities Council
Festival Plaza
428 W. California, Suite 270
Oklahoma City, OK 73102
405-235-0280, fax 405-235-0289
http://www.okhumanities.org

Oregon

Oregon Council for the Humanities
921 S.W. Washington St., #150
Portland, OR 97205
503-241-0543, fax 503-241-0024
http://www.oregonhumanities.org

Pennsylvania

Pennsylvania Humanities Council
325 Chestnut St., Suite 715
Philadelphia, PA 19106-2607
215-925-1005, fax 215-925-3054
http://www.pahumanities.org

Rhode Island

Rhode Island Council for the Humanities
131 Washington St., Suite 210
Providence, RI 02903
401-273-2250, fax 401-454-4872
http://www.rihumanities.org

South Carolina

Humanities Council of South Carolina
2711 Middleburg Drive, Suite 203
P.O. Box 5287
Columbia, SC 29254
803-771-2477, fax 803-771-2487
http://www.schumanities.org

South Dakota

South Dakota Humanities Council
1215 Trail Ridge Rd., Suite A
Brookings, SD 57006
605-688-6113, fax 605-688-4531
http://sdhumanities.org

Tennessee

Humanities Tennessee
306 Gay St., Suite 306
Nashville, TN 37201
615-770-0006, fax 615-770-0007
http://www.humanitiestennessee.org

Texas

Humanities Texas
1410 Rio Grande St.
Austin, TX 78701
512-440-1991, fax 512-440-0115
http://www.humanitiestexas.org

Utah

Utah Humanities Council
202 W. 300 North
Salt Lake City, UT 84103
801-359-9670, fax 801-531-7869
http://www.utahhumanities.org

Vermont

Vermont Humanities Council
11 Loomis St.
Montpelier, VT 05602
802-262-2626, fax 802-262-2620
http://www.vermonthumanities.org

Virginia

Virginia Foundation for the Humanities and
  Public Policy
145 Ednam Drive
Charlottesville, VA 22903-4629
434-924-3296, fax 434-296-4714
http://www.virginiafoundation.org

Washington

Humanities Washington
1015 Eighth Ave. North, Suite B
Seattle, WA 98109
206-682-1770, fax 206-682-4158
http://www.humanities.org

West Virginia

West Virginia Humanities Council
1310 Kanawha Blvd. East
Charleston, WV 25301
304-346-8500, fax 304-346-8504
http://www.wvhumanities.org

Wisconsin

Wisconsin Humanities Council
222 S. Bedford St., Suite F
Madison, WI 53703-3688
608-262-0706, fax 608-263-7970
http://www.wisconsinhumanities.org

Wyoming

Wyoming Humanities Council
1315 E. Lewis St.
Laramie, WY 82072-3459
307-721-9243, fax 307-742-4914
http://www.thinkwy.org

American Samoa

Amerika Samoa Humanities Council
P.O. Box 5800
Pago Pago, AS 96799
684-633-4870, fax 684-633-4873
http://ashcouncil.org

Guam

Guam Humanities Council
222 Chalan Santo Papa
Reflection Center, Suite 106

Hagatna, Guam 96910
671-472-4460, fax 671-472-4465
http://www.guamhumanitiescouncil.org

Northern Marianas Islands

Northern Marianas Humanities Council
P.O. Box 506437
Saipan, MP 96950
670-235-4785, fax 670-235-4786
http://northernmarianashumanities.org

Puerto Rico

Fundación Puertorriqueña de las Humanidades
109 San José St., 3rd floor
Box 9023920
San Juan, PR 00902-3920
787-721-2087, fax 787-721-2684
http://www.fphpr.org

Virgin Islands

Virgin Islands Humanities Council
1829 Kongens Gade
St. Thomas, VI 00802-6746
340-776-4044, fax 340-774-3972
http://www.vihumanities.org

NEH Overview

Common Good: Humanities in the Public Square

The Common Good is a new initiative of the National Endowment for the Humanities designed to demonstrate the critical role humanities scholarship can play in our public life.

The launch of this initiative coincided with NEH's celebration of its 50th anniversary beginning in 2015. NEH's enabling legislation speaks eloquently of the need to attend to "the relevance of the humanities to the current conditions of national life." Today, as our country grapples with both remarkable opportunities and extraordinary challenges, the "conditions of national life" suggest that this need is greater than ever.

Through NEH's traditional grant-making programs and several special initiatives, The Common Good will encourage humanities scholars to turn their attention to topics that have widespread resonance with the American people and that lend themselves to the methods and concerns of the humanities. For more information, visit www.neh.gov/commongood/about.

Contact: 202-606-8446, e-mail commongood@neh.gov.

Division of Education Programs

Through grants to educational institutions and professional development programs for scholars and teachers, this division is designed to support study of the humanities at all levels of education.

Grants support the development of curriculum and materials, faculty study programs among educational institutions, and conferences and networks of institutions.

Contact: 202-606-8500, e-mail education@neh.gov.

Seminars and Institutes

Grants support summer seminars and institutes in the humanities for college and school teachers. These faculty-development activities are conducted at colleges and universities in the United States and abroad. Those wishing to participate in seminars should submit their seminar applications to the seminar director.

Contact: 202-606-8471, e-mail sem-inst@neh.gov.

Landmarks of American History and Culture

Grants for Landmarks workshops provide support to school teachers and community college faculty. These professional development workshops are conducted at or near sites important to American history and culture (such as presidential residences or libraries, colonial era settlements, major battlefields, historic districts, and sites associated with major writers or artists) to address central themes and issues in American history, government, literature, art history, and related subjects in the humanities.

Contact: 202-606-8463, e-mail landmarks@neh.gov.

Division of Preservation and Access

Grants are made for projects that will create, preserve, and increase the availability of resources important for research, education, and public programming in the humanities.

Support may be sought to preserve the intellectual content and aid bibliographic control of collections; to compile bibliographies, descriptive catalogs, and guides to cultural holdings; and to create dictionaries, encyclopedias, databases, and electronic archives. Applications also may be submitted for education and training projects dealing with issues of preservation or access; for research and development leading to improved preservation and access standards, practices, and tools; and for projects to digitize historic U.S. newspapers and to document endangered languages. Grants are also made to help smaller cultural repositories preserve and care for their humanities collections. Proposals may combine preservation and access activities within a single project.

Contact: 202-606-8570, e-mail preservation@neh.gov.

Division of Public Programs

Public humanities programs promote lifelong learning in American and world history, literature, comparative religion, philosophy, and other fields of the humanities. They offer new insights into familiar subjects and invite conversation about important humanities ideas and questions.

The Division of Public Programs supports a wide range of public humanities programs that reach large and diverse public audiences through a variety of program formats, including interpretive exhibitions, radio and television broadcasts, lectures, symposia, interpretive multimedia projects, printed materials, and reading and discussion programs.

Grants support the development and production of television, radio, and digital media programs; the planning and implementation of museum exhibitions, the interpretation of historic sites, the production of related publications, multimedia components, and educational programs; and the planning and implementation of reading and discussion programs, lectures, symposia, and interpretive exhibitions of books, manuscripts, and other library resources.

Contact: 202-606-8269, e-mail publicpgms@neh.gov.

Division of Research Programs

Through fellowships to individual scholars and grants to support complex, frequently collaborative research, the Division of Research Programs contributes to the creation of knowledge in the humanities.

Fellowships and Stipends

Grants provide support for scholars to undertake full-time independent research and writing in the humanities. Grants are available for a maximum of one year and a minimum of two months of summer study.

Contact: 202-606-8200, e-mail (fellowships) fellowships@neh.gov, (summer stipends) stipends@neh.gov.

Research

Grants provide up to three years of support for collaborative research in the preparation for publication of editions, translations, and other important works in the humanities, and in the conduct of large or complex interpretive studies, including archaeology projects and humanities studies of science and technology. Grants also support research opportunities offered through independent research centers and international research organizations.

Contact: 202-606-8200, e-mail research@neh.gov.

Office of Challenge Grants

Nonprofit institutions interested in developing new sources of long-term support for educational, scholarly, preservation, and public programs in the humanities can be assisted in these efforts by an NEH Challenge Grant. Grantees are required to raise $3 in nonfederal donations for every federal dollar offered. Both federal and nonfederal funds may be used to establish or increase institutional endowments and therefore guarantee long-term support for a variety of humanities needs. Funds also can be used for limited direct capital expenditures where such needs are compelling and clearly related to improvements in the humanities.

Contact: 202-606-8309, e-mail challenge@neh.gov.

Office of Digital Humanities

The Office of Digital Humanities encourages and supports projects that utilize or study the impact of digital technology on research, education, preservation, and public programming in the humanities. Launched as an initiative in 2006, Digital Humanities was made permanent as an office within NEH in 2008.

NEH is interested in fostering the growth of digital humanities and lending support to a wide variety of projects, including those that deploy digital technologies and methods to enhance understanding of a topic or issue; those that study the impact of digital technology on the humanities; and those that digitize important materials, thereby increasing the public's ability to search and access humanities information.

The office coordinates the endowment's efforts in the area of digital scholarship. Currently NEH has numerous programs throughout the agency that are actively funding digital scholarship, including Humanities Collections and Resources, Institutes for Advanced Topics in the Digital Humanities, Digital Humanities Challenge Grants, Digital Humanities Start-Up Grants, and many others. NEH is also actively working with other funding partners in the United States and abroad in order to better coordinate spending on digital infrastructure for the humanities.

Contact: 202-606-8401, e-mail odh@neh.gov.

A full list of NEH grants programs and deadlines is available on the endowment's website at http://www.neh.gov/grants.

Institute of Museum and Library Services Office of Library Services

955 L'Enfant Plaza North, S.W., Suite 4000, Washington, DC 20024-2135
202-653-4657, fax 202-653-4600
World Wide Web http://www.imls.gov

Kathryn K. Matthew
Director

Maura Marx
Deputy Director for Library Services

Vision and Mission

The vision of the Institute of Museum and Library Services (IMLS) is a democratic society where communities and individuals thrive with broad public access to knowledge, cultural heritage, and lifelong learning.

Its mission is to inspire libraries and museums to advance innovation, lifelong learning, and cultural and civic engagement. It provides leadership through research, policy development, and grant making.

Strategic Goals

- IMLS places the learner at the center and supports engaging experiences in libraries and museums that prepare people to be full participants in their local communities and our global society.
- IMLS promotes museums and libraries as strong community anchors that enhance civic engagement, cultural opportunities, and economic vitality.
- IMLS supports exemplary stewardship of museum and library collections and promotes the use of technology to facilitate discovery of knowledge and cultural heritage.
- IMLS advises the president and Congress on plans, policies, and activities to sustain and increase public access to information and ideas.
- IMLS achieves excellence in public management and performs as a model organization through strategic alignment of resources and prioritization of programmatic activities, maximizing value for the American public.

There are 123,000 libraries and 35,000 museums in the United States. IMLS supports the full range of libraries, including public, academic, research, special, and tribal, and the full range of museums including art, history, science and technology, children's museums, historical societies, tribal museums, planetariums, botanic gardens, and zoos. Nearly 170 million people in the United States over the age of 14 (69 percent of the population) are library users, and every year 148 million over the age of 18 visit a museum.

Overview

U.S. museums and libraries are at the forefront of the movement to create a nation of learners. As stewards of cultural heritage with rich, authentic content, they provide learning experiences for everyone. With built infrastructure in nearly every community in the nation, robust online networks, and dedicated and knowledgeable staff, they connect people to one another and to the full spectrum of human experience.

The role of IMLS is to provide leadership and funding for the nation's museums and libraries—resources these institutions need to fulfill their mission of becoming centers of learning for life, crucial to achieving personal fulfillment, a productive workforce, and an engaged citizenry.

The Museum and Library Services Act, which includes the Library Services and Technology Act (LSTA) and the Museum Services Act (MSA), authorizes IMLS to support the following activities:

LSTA

- Enhance coordination among federal programs that relate to library and information services
- Promote continuous improvement in library services in all types of libraries in order to better serve the people of the United States
- Facilitate access to resources in all types of libraries for the purpose of cultivating an educated and informed citizenry
- Encourage resource sharing among all types of libraries for the purpose of achieving economical and efficient delivery of library services to the public
- Promote literacy, education, and lifelong learning and enhance and expand the services and resources provided by libraries, including those services and resources relating to workforce development, 21st century skills, and digital literacy skills
- Enhance the skills of the current library workforce and recruit future professionals to the field of library and information services
- Ensure the preservation of knowledge and library collections in all formats and enable libraries to serve their communities during disasters
- Enhance the role of libraries within the information infrastructure of the United States in order to support research, education, and innovation
- Promote library services that provide users with access to information through national, state, local, regional, and international collaborations and networks

MSA

- Encourage and support museums in carrying out their public service role of connecting the whole of society to the cultural, artistic, historical, natural, and scientific understandings that constitute our heritage

- Encourage and support museums in carrying out their educational role as core providers of learning and in conjunction with schools, families, and communities
- Encourage leadership, innovation, and applications of the most current technologies and practices to enhance museum services through international, national, regional, state, and local networks and partnerships
- Assist, encourage, and support museums in carrying out their stewardship responsibilities to achieve the highest standards in conservation and care of the cultural, historic, natural, and scientific heritage of the United States to benefit future generations
- Assist, encourage, and support museums in achieving the highest standards of management and service to the public, and ease the financial burden borne by museums as a result of their increasing use by the public
- Support resource sharing and partnerships among museums, libraries, schools, and other community organizations
- Encourage and support museums as a part of economic development and revitalization in communities
- Ensure museums of various types and sizes in diverse geographic regions of the United States are afforded attention and support
- Support efforts at the state level to leverage museum resources and maximize museum services

A general provision of the Museum and Library Services Act calls for IMLS to develop and implement policy to ensure the availability of museum, library, and information services throughout the U.S. Specific duties include the following: advising the president, Congress, and other federal agencies and offices on museum, library, and information services in order to ensure the creation, preservation, organization, and dissemination of knowledge; engaging federal, state, and local governmental agencies and private entities in assessing the needs of museum, library, and information services, and coordinating the development of plans, policies, and activities to meet such needs effectively; carrying out programs of research and development, data collection, and financial assistance to extend and improve the nation's museum, library, and information services; ensuring that museum, library, and information services are fully integrated into the information and education infrastructures.

Funding

In fiscal year (FY) 2015, Congress appropriated $180,909,000 for the programs authorized by LSTA. The Office of Library Services within IMLS, under the policy direction of the IMLS director and deputy director, administers LSTA programs. The office comprises the Division of State Programs—which administers the Grants to States program—and the Division of Discretionary Programs, which administers the National Leadership Grants for Libraries program, the Laura Bush 21st Century Librarian Program, the Native American Library Services program, and the Native Hawaiian Library Services program. IMLS presents annual awards to libraries through the National Medal for Museum and Library Service program. Additionally, IMLS supports two award programs administered by the President's Committee on the Arts and the Humanities: the National Arts and Humanities Youth Program Awards and the National Student Poets Program.

Library Statistics

The president's budget request for FY 2015 included funds for IMLS to continue administering the Public Libraries Survey (PLS) and the State Library Administrative Agencies Survey. In addition to reporting on the survey data, IMLS provides shorter research products to highlight report findings. These brief reports leverage the survey data to address a wide range of public policy priorities, including education, employment, community and economic development, and telecommunications policy.

In the Data Collection section of the IMLS website (www.imls.gov/research-tools/data-collection), visitors can link to data search tools, the latest available data for each survey, other publications, and survey definitions.

Public Libraries Survey

Descriptive statistics for more than 9,000 public libraries are collected and disseminated annually through a voluntary census, the Public Libraries Survey (PLS). The survey is conducted through the Public Library Statistics Cooperative (PLSC, formerly the Federal-State Cooperative System [FSCS]). In FY 2015 IMLS completed the 27th collection of this data. In 2015, final imputed data files for the FY 2013 Public Libraries Survey (PLS) were made available in the PLS Data Files section of the IMLS website. The PLS is designed as a universal survey whose FY 2013 frame consisted of 9,290 public libraries as identified by state library agencies (9,228 public libraries in the 50 states and the District of Columbia and 62 public libraries in the outlying areas of American Samoa, Guam, the Northern Mariana Islands, Puerto Rico, and the U.S. Virgin Islands). The Compare Public Libraries Tool and the Public Library Locator Tool on the IMLS website were updated with FY 2013 data, along with the new IMLS Data Catalog (data.imls.gov), which allows users to access and analyze IMLS data and create charts, graphs and maps without the need of technical statistical or GIS mapping software.

The survey collects identifying information about public libraries and each of their service outlets, including street address, city, county, zip code, and telephone number. The survey collects data on staffing; type of legal basis; type of geographic boundary; type of administrative structure; type of interlibrary relationship; type and number of public service outlets; operating revenue and expenditures; capital revenue and expenditures; size of collection (including number of electronic books, audio and video resources, and databases); and such service measures as number of reference transactions, interlibrary loans, circulation, public service hours, library visits, circulation of children's materials, number of programs (including programs for children and for young adults), program attendance, number of Internet terminals used by the general public, and number of users of electronic resources. This survey also collects several data items about outlets, including geo-location information (such as latitude and longitude), number of books-by-mail-only outlets, number of bookmobiles by bookmobile outlet, and square footage of the outlet.

The 50 states and the District of Columbia have participated in data collection from the survey's inception in 1989. In 1993 Guam, the Commonwealth of the Northern Mariana Islands, Puerto Rico, and the U.S. Virgin Islands joined in the survey, and American Samoa provided data for FY 2013 for the first time. The first release of Public Libraries Survey data occurred with the launch of the updated Compare Public Libraries Tool on the IMLS website. The data used in this Web tool are final but do not include imputations for missing data. (Imputation is a statistical means for providing an estimate for each missing data item.)

An important feature of the public library data tools is the availability of locale codes for all administrative entities and outlets. These locale codes allow users to quickly identify which library outlets and administrative entities are located in cities, suburbs, towns, or rural areas. The locale codes are based on an address's proximity to an urbanized area (a densely settled core with densely settled surrounding areas). The locale code system classifies territory into four major types: city, suburban, town, and rural. Each type has three subcategories. For city and suburb, these gradations are based on population size: large, midsize, and small. Towns and rural areas are further distinguished by their distance from an urbanized area. They can be characterized as fringe, distant, or remote. The coding methodology was developed by the U.S. Census Bureau as a way to identify the location of public schools in the National Center for Education Statistics' (NCES's) Common Core of Data. Each library outlet and administrative entity survey has one of the twelve locale codes assigned to it.

Locale codes provide a new way to analyze library services in the U.S. By incorporating objective measures of rurality and urbanicity into the data files, researchers and practitioners can benchmark services in a fundamentally different way by basing comparisons on community attributes as well as the attributes of the libraries themselves. In other words, library services in rural remote areas can now be compared with library services in other rural remote areas of the state or country using a standardized urbanicity/rurality metric that is applied consistently to each library. Once communities of interest have been selected, comparisons can be made to any data that are available in the survey whether financial, operational, or service output related.

State Library Administrative Agencies Survey

The State Library Administrative Agencies Survey collects and disseminates information about the state library administrative agencies in the 50 states and the District of Columbia. A State Library Administrative Agency (SLAA) is the official unit of state government charged with statewide library development and the administration of federal funds under the IMLS Grants to States program. SLAAs' administrative and developmental responsibilities affect the operation of thousands of public, academic, school, and special libraries. SLAAs provide important reference and information services to state governments and sometimes also provide service to the general public. SLAAs often administer state library and special operations such as state archives and libraries for the blind and physically handicapped and the state Center for the Book.

The SLAA Survey began in 1994 and was administered by NCES until 2007. Beginning with FY 1999 data, the survey used a Web-based data collection system and included imputations for missing data. IMLS has shifted to a biannual data collection of the survey. In FY 2015 the FY 2014 data file was released.

National Medal for Museum and Library Service

The National Medal for Museum and Library Service honors outstanding institutions that make significant and exceptional contributions to their communities. Selected institutions demonstrate extraordinary and innovative approaches to public service, exceeding the expected levels of community outreach and core programs generally associated with its services. The medal includes a prize of $5,000 to each recipient, an awards ceremony held in Washington, D.C., and a visit from StoryCorps to interview community members about how the library or museum affected their lives. The 2015 ceremony was held at the White House on May 18.

Winners of the medal in 2015 were Amazement Square, Lynchburg, Virginia; Cecil County Public Library, Elkton, Maryland; Craig Public Library, Craig, Alaska; Embudo Valley Library and Community Center, Dixon, New Mexico; Los Angeles Public Library, Los Angeles, California; Louisiana Children's Museum, New Orleans, Louisiana; Museum of Northern Arizona, Flagstaff, Arizona; New York Hall of Science, Queens, New York; the Schomburg Center for Research in Black Culture, New York, New York; and the Tech Museum of Innovation, San Jose, California.

State-Administered Programs

In FY 2015 approximately 85 percent ($154,848,000) of the annual federal appropriation under LSTA was distributed through the Grants to States program to SLAAs according to a formula set by the law. The formula consists of a base amount for each SLAA—the 50 states, Puerto Rico, and the District of Columbia receive $680,000 each; other U.S. territories receive $60,000 each—plus a supplemental amount based on population (Table 1).

SLAAs may use the appropriation for statewide initiatives and services. They may also distribute the funds through competitive subawards to, or cooperative agreements with, public, academic, research, school, or special libraries. For-profit and federal libraries are not eligible applicants. Grants to States funds have been used to meet the special needs of children, parents, teenagers, the unemployed, senior citizens, and the business community, as well as adult learners. Many libraries have partnered with community organizations to provide a variety of services and programs, including access to electronic databases, computer instruction, homework centers, summer reading programs, digitization of special collections, access to e-books and adaptive technology, bookmobile service, and development of outreach programs to the underserved. States are required by law to match the IMLS

**Table 1 / Library Services and Technology Act, State Allotments
FY 2015 (H.J. Res 83; Public Law 113-235)**
Total Distributed to States: $154,848,000

State	Federal Funds from IMLS (66%)[1,2]	State Matching Funds (34%)	Total Federal and State Funds
Alabama	$2,476,238	$1,275,638	$3,751,876
Alaska	952,890	490,883	1,443,773
Arizona	3,173,382	1,634,773	4,808,155
Arkansas	1,778,761	916,331	2,695,092
California	15,052,678	7,754,410	22,807,088
Colorado	2,663,845	1,372,284	4,036,129
Connecticut	2,012,231	1,036,604	3,048,835
Delaware	1,026,557	528,832	1,555,389
Florida	8,048,596	4,146,246	12,194,842
Georgia	4,420,116	2,277,029	6,697,145
Hawaii	1,205,813	621,176	1,826,989
Idaho	1,285,415	662,183	1,947,598
Illinois	5,451,043	2,808,113	8,259,156
Indiana	3,123,514	1,609,083	4,732,597
Iowa	1,830,898	943,190	2,774,088
Kansas	1,755,667	904,435	2,660,102
Kentucky	2,314,771	1,192,458	3,507,229
Louisiana	2,117,896	1,091,037	3,208,933
Maine	1,172,672	604,104	1,776,776
Maryland	2,893,697	1,490,692	4,384,389
Massachusetts	3,178,539	1,637,429	4,815,968
Michigan	4,350,678	2,241,258	6,591,936
Minnesota	2,701,369	1,391,614	4,092,983
Mississippi	1,789,025	921,619	2,710,644
Missouri	2,925,990	1,507,328	4,433,318
Montana	1,059,140	545,618	1,604,758
Nebraska	1,376,920	709,322	2,086,242
Nevada	1,731,619	892,046	2,623,665
New Hampshire	1,171,459	603,479	1,774,938
New Jersey	3,990,753	2,055,842	6,046,595
New Mexico	1,452,508	748,262	2,200,770
New York	7,929,546	4,084,918	12,014,464
North Carolina	4,363,304	2,247,763	6,611,067
North Dakota	953,909	491,408	1,445,317
Ohio	4,974,547	2,562,645	7,537,192
Oklahoma	2,116,453	1,090,294	3,206,747
Oregon	2,150,600	1,107,885	3,258,485
Pennsylvania	5,416,459	2,790,297	8,206,756
Rhode Island	1,070,842	551,646	1,622,488
South Carolina	2,469,980	1,272,414	3,742,394
South Dakota	996,021	513,102	1,509,123
Tennessee	3,105,919	1,600,019	4,705,938
Texas	10,665,018	5,494,100	16,159,118
Utah	1,770,068	911,853	2,681,921
Vermont	912,082	469,860	1,381,942
Virginia	3,764,107	1,939,085	5,703,192

Table 1 / **Library Services and Technology Act, State Allotments
FY 2015 (H.J. Res 83; Public Law 113-235)**
Total Distributed to States: $154,848,000

State	Federal Funds from IMLS (66%)[1,2]	State Matching Funds (34%)	Total Federal and State Funds
Washington	3,295,633	1,697,750	4,993,383
West Virginia	1,365,372	703,373	2,068,745
Wisconsin	2,663,262	1,371,983	4,035,245
Wyoming	896,374	461,768	1,358,142
District of Columbia	924,058	476,030	1,400,088
Puerto Rico	1,928,368	993,402	2,921,770
American Samoa[4]	80,129	0	80,129
Northern Marianas[4]	79,389	0	79,389
Guam[4]	119,926	0	119,926
Virgin Islands[4]	98,364	0	98,364
Pacific Territories[3,5]	253,590	130,637	384,227
Total	$154,848,000	$79,575,553	$234,423,553

1 The IMLS Federal funds (allotments) are calculated using the current minimum base set into law (P.L. 108-81) and population figures from the Bureau of the Census (BOC) published in December 2014.
Population data is pulled from the BOC. Data used in the state allotment table are calculated based on the most recent Census data available at the time of the grant award notification. Therefore, the population data used in the FY2015 table is what was available on the BOC website http://www.census.gov/popest/ as of December, 2014.
Population data for American Samoa, Northern Marianas, Guam, Virgin Islands, Marshall Islands, Federated States of Micronesia, and Palau is used from the Census International Programs International Database. http://www.census.gov/population/international/data/idb/informationGateway.php This table reflects what was available as of December, 2014.
2 The agency is required to reduce the FY2015 allotment of any State that did not meet their FY2012 Maintenance of Effort (MOE) requirement and did not apply for, or receive, a waiver of the requirement. Those funds deducted from states not meeting the MOE requirement have been distributed across the remaining states in accordance with (1).
3 Aggregate allotments (including administrative costs) for Palau, Marshall Islands, and Federated States of Micronesia are awarded on a competitive basis to eligible applicants after taking into consideration recommendations from the Regional Educational Laboratory—Pacific (REL-P).
4 Waived pursuant to 48 U.S.C. § 1469a(d).
5 Subject to the provisions of U.S.C. § 1469a(d).

grant with non-federal funds at a 1-to-2 (non-federal to federal) ratio. No more than 4 percent of a state's program funds may be used for administrative costs.

A Special Rule, 20 USCA 9131(b)(3)(C), authorizes a small competitive grants program for four U.S. territories (American Samoa, the Commonwealth of Northern Mariana Islands, Guam, and the U.S. Virgin Islands) and three Freely Associated States (the Federated States of Micronesia, the Republic of the Marshall Islands, and the Republic of Palau). The funds for this grant program are taken from the total allotment for the Freely Associated States. In FY 2015 a total of $253,590 was available for the seven entities. This amount included a set-aside of 5 percent for the contractor for the Regional Educational Laboratory—Pacific, Mid-continent Research for Education and Learning (McREL) to facilitate the grants review process, in accordance with IMLS legislation. The total amount awarded in FY 2015, therefore, was $240,000.

The IMLS-funded programs and services delivered by each SLAA support the purposes and priorities set forth in LSTA. The SLAAs determine goals and objectives for the Grants to States funds through a planning process that includes statewide needs assessments. These goals and objectives are included in each state's statutorily required five-year plan on file with IMLS.

On a rotating basis, IMLS Grants to States program staff members conduct site visits to SLAAs to provide technical support and to monitor the states' success in administering the program. In 2015 program officers visited eight SLAAs in Alabama, Delaware, Florida, Iowa, Massachusetts, South Carolina, South Dakota, and Vermont. Each site visit includes a critical review of the administration of the LSTA program at the SLAA as well as trips into the field to visit libraries that are recipients of subawards or beneficiaries of statewide IMLS-funded projects. For more information about state priorities and projects, see www.imls.gov/programs.

Discretionary Grants Programs

In FY 2015 IMLS's four library discretionary programs awarded the following total amounts: National Leadership Grants: $12,039,953; Laura Bush 21st Century Librarian Program: $9,609,274; Native American Library Services: $ 3,311,000; and Native Hawaiian Library Services: $550,000.

National Leadership Grants for Libraries

The National Leadership Grants for Libraries program provides funding for research and innovative model programs to enhance the quality of library services nationwide. National Leadership Grants are competitive and intended to produce results useful for the broader library community.

For FY 2015 there were four categories of National Leadership Grants for Libraries:

Project Grants ($10,000 to $2,000,000)

This category supports fully developed projects for which needs assessments, partnership development, feasibility analyses, prototyping, and other planning activities have been completed.

Research Grants ($10,000 to $2,000,000)

These grants support the investigation of key questions important to library or archival practice. The term "research" includes systematic study directed toward fuller scientific knowledge or understanding of the subject studied. It also includes activities involving the training of individuals in research techniques where such activities utilize the same facilities as other research and development activities and where such activities are not included in the instruction function.

Planning Grants (up to $50,000)

This category allows project teams to perform preliminary planning activities, such as analyzing needs and feasibility, solidifying partnerships, developing project work plans, or developing prototypes or proofs of concept. These activities should have the potential to lead to a full project, such as those described in Project Grants above.

National Forum Grants (up to $100,000)

These grants provide the opportunity to convene qualified groups of experts and key stakeholders to consider issues or challenges that are important to libraries or archives across the nation. Grant-supported meetings are expected to produce reports for wide dissemination with expert recommendations for action or research that address a key challenge identified in the proposal. The expert recommendations resulting from these meetings are intended to guide future applications to the NLG-Libraries program. National Forum Grant recipients are required at the end of the project to submit to us a brief white paper for public distribution summarizing those expert recommendations, which we will post online.

The program received 267 complete and eligible proposals in FY 2015. Collectively, these proposals requested over $98 million. In March 2015 the program announced 6 awards to libraries and archives, totaling $4.1 million, and in August 2015 the program announced 17 awards to libraries and archives, totaling $6.4 million (for details, see www.imls.gov/grants/awarded-grants).

In addition to these awards to libraries and archives, remaining program funds were used to sponsor special initiatives, out-of-cycle special opportunities, and other projects, including 21 Sparks! Ignition Grants and multiple other small awards in support of efforts such as the National Medal for Museum and Library Service and the interagency Performance Partnership Pilots for Disconnected Youth (P3).

Laura Bush 21st Century Librarian Program

The Laura Bush 21st Century Librarian Program provides competitive grants to support projects to recruit and educate the next generation of librarians and library leaders; build institutional capacity in graduate schools of library and information science and develop faculty who will help in this endeavor; and support programs of continuing education and training in library and information science for librarians and library staff. In FY 2015 the program offered three funding categories for Project Grants up to $500,000, Planning Grants up to $50,000 and National Forum Grants up to $100,000 in the following project categories:

Doctoral Programs

- Develop faculty to educate the next generation of library and archives professionals. In particular, increase the number of students enrolled in doctoral programs that will prepare faculty to teach master's students who will work in school, public, academic, research, and special libraries and archives.
- Develop the next generation of library and archives leaders to assume positions as managers and administrators.

Master's Programs

- Educate the next generation of librarians and archivists in nationally accredited graduate library programs to meet the evolving needs of the profession and society.

Early Career Development

- Support the early career development of new faculty members in library and information science by supporting innovative research by untenured, tenure-track faculty.

Research

- Investigate issues and trends affecting library and archival practices.
- For all research projects, except Early Career Development Projects, all eligible library entities may apply, either individually or collaboratively.

Programs to Build Institutional Capacity

- Develop or enhance curricula within graduate schools of library and information science to better meet the needs of cultural heritage and information professionals.
- Broaden the library and information science curriculum by incorporating perspectives from other disciplines and fields of scholarship.
- Develop projects or programs of study to increase the abilities of future library and archives professionals in developing the 21st century skills of their users, including information and digital literacy skills.

Continuing Education

- Improve the knowledge, skills, and abilities of library and archives staff through programs of continuing education, both formal and informal, including post-master's programs such as certificates of advanced study, residencies, enhanced work experiences, and other training programs for professional staff.

IMLS received a total of 121 applications in the Laura Bush 21st Century Librarian Program in FY 2015. In March 2015 the program announced 16 awards to libraries and archives, totaling $5.15 million, and in August 2015 the program announced 11 awards to libraries and archives, totaling $3.4 million (for details, see www.imls.gov/grants/awarded-grants).

Native American/Native Hawaiian Library Services Grants

The Native American and Native Hawaiian Library Services program provides opportunities for improved library services to an important part of the nation's community of library users. The program offers three types of support:

1 Basic library services grants in the amount of $6,000, which support core library operations on a noncompetitive basis for all eligible Indian tribes and Alaska Native villages and corporations that apply for such support
2 Basic library services grants with a supplemental education/assessment option of $1,000 to provide funding for library staff to attend continuing education courses and/or training workshops on- or off-site, for library

staff to attend or give presentations at conferences related to library services, or to hire a consultant for an on-site professional library assessment

3 Enhancement grants, which support new levels of library service for activities specifically identified under the LSTA

Collectively, these programs received 256 applications in FY 2015. IMLS funded 227 of these proposals, totaling $3,313,000. This included basic grants and basic grants with the education/assessment option to 214 tribes, and 13 enhancement grants (for details, see www.imls.gov/grants/awarded-grants).

The Native Hawaiian Library Services program provides opportunities for improved library services through grants to nonprofit organizations that primarily serve and represent Native Hawaiians, as the term "Native Hawaiian" is defined in section 7207 of the Native Hawaiian Education Act (20 U.S.C. 7517). In FY 2015 IMLS awarded four grants in this program, totaling $550,000 (for details, see www.imls.gov/grants/awarded-grants).

Museum and Library Cooperative and Interagency Agreements

IMLS has numerous cooperative and interagency agreements to support and enhance agency priorities and services to the library and museum community:

Sundance Film Forward
Sundance Institute—Park City, Utah

• Film Forward is an international touring program designed to enhance greater cultural understanding and dialogue in both the U.S. and abroad by engaging underserved audiences, particularly 18–24 year olds, through the exhibition of films, workshops, and conversations with filmmakers. It is an initiative of the President's Committee on the Arts and Humanities and the Sundance Institute, supported by IMLS, the National Endowment for the Arts (NEA), and the National Endowment for the Humanities (NEH).

Integrating Early Learning Activities with State Systems
The BUILD Initiative—Boston, Massachusetts

• The BUILD Initiative was launched in May 2002 by a consortium of private foundations. Its aim is to stimulate public investments in early learning and help coordinate programs, policies, and services for young children. BUILD and IMLS have a year-long effort to integrate museums and libraries into statewide early childhood systems.

Learning Labs Community of Practice
National Writing Project—Berkeley, California

• The National Writing Project (NWP) is a professional development network that reaches more than 100,000 teachers across the country. With IMLS support, NWP has partnered with the Association of Science-Technology Centers (ASTC) to build an open online Community of Practice (CoP) to expand access to peer-driven professional learning for educators both in and beyond the current network of Learning Labs, originally funded by IMLS and the MacArthur Foundation. Launched in January 2015, the YOUmedia Network CoP connects educators in libraries, museums, community organizations, and schools, and is free and open to share, learn, engage in discussions, and contribute resources and materials. More than 170 members have engaged in ongoing webinars, resource development activities, and cross-site support discussions. The NWP plans to expand the community in the next year and offer targeted resources and learning opportunities that support the creation and development of learning labs sites.

Clinic Networks and Early Learning
Reach Out and Read, Inc.—Boston, Massachusetts

- IMLS funded Reach Out and Read to develop Prescription for Success, a year-long project aimed at helping more families benefit from museum and library services that foster literacy development in young children. As a national nonprofit organization comprised of doctors and nurses who encourage family reading habits, Reach Out and Read will explore new ways doctors and their staff can collaborate with museums and libraries. It will also survey and document current partnerships between its network and libraries and museums, create an online toolkit of best literacy practices, and further develop statewide library and museum collaborations in Colorado, Connecticut, and South Carolina.

Open Source eBook Platform
New York Public Library—New York, New York

- The New York Public Library (NYPL), in close collaboration with the Digital Public Library of America (DPLA), and 19 partner libraries and library consortia from across the country will use IMLS funds to expand and provide outreach for the Library Simplified open source eBook platform. Through this work, the partners aim to unify and improve the eBook borrowing and reading experience for library users across the country. The project directly supports technology development and implementation of the Open eBooks initiative, an effort to make eBooks available to children and youth from low-income families. The project also supports a broader strategy to enhance open source software tools for public library systems across the country to provide access to eBooks.

One Card Convening
Urban Libraries Council—Washington, D.C.

- The Urban Libraries Council (ULC) will identify strategies and define models for barrier-free access to learning for kids, from Universal Library Card adoption to fully integrated municipal One Card systems. On April 30, 2015, President Obama issued the ConnectED Library Challenge calling upon library leaders to work with their mayors, school leaders and librarians to create or strengthen partnerships so that every child enrolled in school can receive a library card. In response, ULC successfully rallied over 30 public libraries and their communities to answer the challenge. To ensure success, the cooperative agreement will identify and share leading practices for adoption of universal or one card systems. ULC will also describe and document successful programs and models so that other cities and counties across the United States can successfully implement a program that ensures a library card in every student's hand.

Sustaining and Advancing Indigenous Cultures
Association of Tribal Archives, Libraries, and Museums—Oklahoma City, Oklahoma

- The Association of Tribal Archives, Libraries, and Museums (ATALM) will provide two annual conferences with continuing education programs targeted to the needs of tribal archivists, librarians, and museum staff; and will conduct a survey of tribal archives, libraries, and museums, followed by a report documenting activities, challenges, and needs. Funded activities will contribute to improving the informational, educational, and cultural programs and services available to the nation's 4.5 million indigenous peoples, and $150,000 of award funds will be used to support conference scholarships.

Digital Skills for Digital Librarians
Mozilla Foundation—Mountain View, California

- The Mozilla Foundation, in collaboration with the Technology and Social Change Group (TASCHA) at the University of Washington Information School, will refine and launch an open source curriculum, training, tools, and credentials for a library audience to learn web literacy skills and develop digital competencies. The project intends to empower library staff to provide patrons with opportunities to develop the digital skills they need for better success in such areas as education, workforce development, and civic engagement. The project will first identify core digital literacy badges for library professionals that include technical and 21st century skills aligned with Mozilla's Web Literacy Map. The team will pilot the resources in five public library systems representing geographic, demographic, and experiential diversity. Emphasis will be placed on underserved communities, and populations will be selected for testing. In addition, one school of library information studies will also be selected to test curriculum, training, and credentials.

Performance Partnership Pilots for Disconnected Youth
U.S. Department of Education—Washington, D.C.

- IMLS is one of six federal agencies contributing to Performance Partnership Pilots for Disconnected Youth (P3), a newly authorized federal program. Other participating agencies include the U.S. Departments of Education, Labor, Health and Human Services, and Justice, as well as the Corporation for National and Community Service. From the first year's applicant pool, agencies announced nine pilots from states, localities, tribal governments, and their partners to test strategies for reaching "disconnected youth." The initiative allows awarded pilots to blend funds that they already receive from participating agencies, request waivers around those federal funds, and receive supplemental start-up grants of up to $700,000. The P3 program is intended to break down silos and improve educational and workforce outcomes for disconnected youth, and it has been authorized for an additional two years of pilots.

Museum Assessment Program
American Alliance of Museums—Washington, D.C.

• The Museum Assessment Program (MAP) helps museums assess their strengths and weaknesses, and plan for the future. A MAP assessment requires the museum staff and governing authority to complete a self-study. Following the study, a site visit is conducted by one or more museum professionals, who tour the museum and meet with staff, governing officials, and volunteers and produce a report evaluating the museum's operations, making recommendations, and suggesting resources. Three types of MAP assessments are offered: Organizational; Collections Stewardship; and Community Engagement. In FY 2015 the Museum Assessment Program received 123 applications and funded 111 museums in 40 states.

Museums for All
Association of Children's Museums—Arlington, Virginia

• The Association of Children's Museums is working with IMLS to establish a nationwide museum access program that encourages visitation at all types of museums. Piloted with children's museums and, if successful, eventually expanding to include all types of museums, Museums for All will invite low-income families to visit participating museums for a nominal fee. By promoting affordable museum experiences, ACM and IMLS can encourage families of all backgrounds to visit museums regularly, building lifelong museum habits that bolster museums' role as community anchors.

National Arts and Humanities Youth Program Awards
President's Committee on the Arts and the Humanities—Washington, D.C.

• The National Arts and Humanities Youth Program Award is the Nation's highest honor for out-of-school arts and humanities programs in museums, libraries and other youth-serving organizations. The awards recognize and support excellence in programs that open new pathways to learning, self-discovery, and achievement for young people.

National Book Festival
The Library of Congress—Washington, D.C.

• This effort supports the Library of Congress National Book Festival's "Pavilion of the States," which highlights the work of state library agencies and regional library services. Representatives from state libraries and Centers for the Book across the country interact with festival attendees (adults and children) and provide information on their state's literary heritage and its local libraries, book festivals, activities dedicated to promoting local authors and reading, and careers and opportunities in library and information science. The "Pavilion of the States" is one of the most highly attended activities at the National Book Festival with a diverse audience of families, teachers and students.

Chief Officers of State Library Agencies (COSLA)—Lexington, Kentucky

- IMLS funding supports the participation of representatives from throughout the U.S. and the territories in the National Book Festival. Representatives use this opportunity to talk about the enormous variety of reading programs around the country and the critical role of libraries in the community.

National Digital Stewardship Residency Program
The Library of Congress—Washington, D.C.

- The program, administered by the Library of Congress and supported by IMLS, allows ten recent master's program graduates in relevant fields to complete a nine-month residency at various institutions in the Washington, D.C. area. Accepted residents attend an intensive two-week digital stewardship workshop at the Library of Congress. Thereafter, residents move to a host institution to work on significant digital stewardship projects. All ten members of the first NDSR cohort received jobs in the field by the end of the residency. IMLS and the Library of Congress renewed the project in 2014 for two more cohorts. IMLS also funded similar NDSR programs in Boston and New York. These efforts will increase the capacity of the library and archives professions to manage, preserve and provide access to the nation's cultural heritage in digital formats.

National Medal for Museum and Library Service: StoryCorps Recordings
StoryCorps—Brooklyn, New York

- This Cooperative Agreement highlights the contributions that IMLS National Medal for Museum and Library Service award winners have made to their communities. A team from StoryCorps visits each award winner and conducts interviews with community members about how the library or museum affected their lives.

National Student Poets Program
Alliance for Young Artists and Writers—New York, New York

- Along with the NEA on behalf of the President's Committee on the Arts and Humanities, this agreement supports the National Student Poets Program, a national initiative that highlights the work of young poets for a national audience. The program also tries to inspire other young people to excellence in their creative endeavors and showcase the role of writing and the arts in academic and personal success.

Maker/STEM Education Support for 21st Century Community Learning Centers
Exploratorium—San Francisco, California

- The Exploratorium worked with IMLS and the Department of Education to develop and deliver STEM-rich making and tinkering programs for elementary school-aged children in a select set of 21st Century Community Learning Centers (CCLC). Professional development, activities, tools, and other resources were provided to support programming in 25 sites in five states.

STEM Video Game Challenge
Joan Ganz Cooney Center at Sesame Workshop—New York, New York

- This award helps museums and libraries in the STEM Video Game Challenge, sponsored by the Joan Ganz Cooney Center and other funders, by holding workshops at 20 institutions for youth to develop students' ability to participate in the Challenge.

Supporting Making in Museums and Libraries
Children's Museum of Pittsburgh—Pittsburgh, Pennsylvania

- Supporting Making in Museums and Libraries is designed to build the capacity of libraries and museums to develop effective maker spaces and related programs for learning. Working with the Exploratorium, Maker Education Initiative, Chicago Public Library and North Carolina State University Library, the Children's Museum is developing a framework to guide the development of effective maker spaces, supported by a website, downloadable publication, and additional tools and resources.

Federal Partnerships

Americans depend upon libraries and museums to deliver a wide range of public services. As more and more government services are only available online, museums and libraries have an increased role in the delivery of federal information and services. In the past three years, federal agencies are increasingly seeking partnerships with IMLS, as they recognize the power that libraries and museums have in reaching the American public.

IMLS was one of three federal agencies in 2015 (along with NASA and the National Park Service) that collaborated with the U.S. Department of Education around its 21st Century Community Learning Center (CCLC) program, the largest out-of-school program in the nation. The initiative will expand programs and benefit more underserved students in sites nationwide. Specifically, IMLS partnered with the Exploratorium, the San Francisco-based science museum with a history of innovation in maker education, to increase Science, Technology, Engineering, and Mathematics (STEM) programming for underserved students in sites nationwide. Beginning in spring 2015, the Exploratorium introduced students at 25 21st CCLC sites in communities in California, Florida, New York, Pennsylvania, and Texas to STEM-rich making and tinkering activities, building on the growing maker movement. It also supported local networks of science museums and youth serving programs so they can work directly with the 21st CCLC sites.

IMLS is one of six federal agencies contributing to Performance Partnership Pilots (P3), a newly authorized federal program. Other participating agencies include the U.S. Departments of Education, Labor, Health and Human Services, and Justice, as well as the Corporation for National and Community Service. The P3 program is intended to break down silos and improve educational and workforce outcomes for disconnected youth through programs offered by states, localities, tribal governments, and their partners.

In 2013 the U.S. Citizenship and Immigration Services (USCIS) signed a memorandum of understanding with IMLS pledging to support local libraries' services to new immigrants. More than 55 percent of people who immigrated to the U.S. within the last 15 years use the public library at least once a week and more mock naturalization interviews take place at public libraries than at any other community institution. In FY 2014 and FY 2015 IMLS worked with USCIS to conduct a webinar series to help librarians meet the needs of new immigrants and to provide libraries with resources on citizenship and immigration. By the end of FY 2015 ten webinars had been held with over 900 total attendees, covering a range of USCIS products and services of interest to libraries.

IMLS is working with the Consumer Financial Protection Bureau (CFPB) to help libraries access and use financial education tools. In 2015 CFPB continued its financial literacy webinars for libraries, established partnerships at the individual library and statewide level, and worked with IMLS on plans for future dissemination of financial education information to libraries.

In 2015 IMLS continued working with the Office of Career, Technical, and Adult Education (OCTAE) at the U.S. Department of Education to encourage effective collaborations between libraries and federally funded adult education programs. The goal of this joint effort is to enhance the skills, employability, and quality of life of youths and adults with low skills. In 2015 IMLS and OCTAE conducted a series of webinars. IMLS also works with the Employment and Training Administration (ETA) of the U.S. Department of Labor, to address workforce development challenges. In October 2014, IMLS, ETA, and OCTAE presented a webinar to libraries around the new Workforce Innovation and Opportunity Act (WIOA) and discussed ways that public and community college libraries could receive funding for employment skills training and job search.

In June 2015 representatives from USCIS, CFPB, OCTAE, and ETA participated in an IMLS Focus convening for library leaders and professionals entitled, "Engaging Communities." One purpose of the meeting was to highlight federal partners, and a white paper summarizing the meeting and its takeaways was published in September.

IMLS worked with the Federal Communications Commission (FCC) in 2015 to disseminate new information about its programs to libraries. Following the FCC's First E-rate Modernization Order in July 2014, which began the reform of this critical program for broadband access, the FCC adopted a Second Order in December 2014, which ensures that all libraries and schools have access to high-speed broadband connectivity. In addition to raising funding levels, the order revises language defining what constitutes "rural," a very positive change for the many libraries and schools whose discount rates had been in question.

IMLS participates in the International Visitor Leadership Program (IVLP) run by the U.S. Department of State, Bureau of Educational and Cultural Affairs, which brings international visitors to the U.S. to learn about cultural organizations. As part of the program, IMLS met with visitors from a number of countries in 2015, including Uzbekistan and Brazil.

As part of an ongoing partnership with NEA, IMLS participated in the May 2015 Summit on Creative Aging in America: A Pre-Conference to the 2015 White House Conference on Aging. This preconference addressed needs related to life-long learning and the arts and viable federal government solutions.

IMLS works with federal agencies through the Partners in Tourism initiative—advancing the nation's National Tourism Strategy and spotlighting the role of cultural heritage organizations in supporting economic development through tourism.

IMLS participates in the multi-agency Informal Science Education Forum, which brings together Federal agency representatives to share information and resources on STEM-focused programming.

IMLS administers a sub-initiative of the Let's Move! program called Let's Move! Museums and Gardens to help millions of museum and garden visitors learn about healthy food choices and promote physical activity through interactive exhibits and programs. Over 650 museums participate in the Let's Move! Museums and Gardens program.

IMLS has an ongoing partnership with the President's Committee on the Arts and the Humanities, and the Alliance for Young Artists & Writers to present the National Student Poets Program, the nation's highest honor for young poets (grades 9–11) presenting original work.

In 2015 IMLS partnered with the Congressional Maker Caucus to organize the first Capitol Hill Maker Faire on June 11, 2015, a celebration of making in the nation's capital, which was held in conjunction with the National Week of Making. It was an entertaining and interactive event for attendees, including members of Congress and their staff. Preceding the faire, there was a series of panel discussions with leaders of the Maker movement discussing its impact on the economy, education, and community development. Additionally, IMLS program staff actively participate in an interagency working group focused on advancing making that is organized by the White House Office of Science and Technology Policy.

IMLS worked with the White House on several new initiatives in 2015, including the Open eBooks initiative and ConnectED Library Challenge, which strengthen student learning by improving access to public libraries and reading materials, particularly for children from low-income families. IMLS was represented in the president's new interagency Broadband Opportunity Council (BOC) charged with developing a framework of recommendations to support broadband deployment and adoption.

Evaluation of IMLS Programs

IMLS's evaluation strategy during FY 2015 continued to address the diverse needs of the Grants to States formula grant program and its discretionary grant programs. The work balanced capacity-building efforts to improve program and performance data with summative evaluations of completed grant projects. The following section highlights achievements during the year.

Measuring Success

The Measuring Success initiative is a long-term strategic planning effort begun in FY 2011 to improve performance reporting for the Grants to States program. The aim of the initiative is to increase the comparability of program data within and across the participating states. Standardization of program data will also increase the utility of the data for monitoring project accomplishments over time and comparing library service initiatives with other educational and social programming at the local level.

In FY 2015 IMLS worked collaboratively with 16 state partners to test the new State Program Reporting tool and roll it out to 37 additional states. Continued build-out of the new reporting tool in FY 2015 was enabled through a contract with the private firm Information International Associates.

IMLS Conferences and Activities

IMLS Focus Convenings

In FY 2015 IMLS hosted a series of three strategic priority meetings, each focused on a different priority. The sessions were designed to help inform future strategies, particularly for the agency's National Leadership Grant program and Laura Bush 21st Century Librarian Program. The first convening, held at the District of Columbia Public Library on April 28, examined national digital initiatives. The second, held at the Kansas City (MO) Public Library on May 14, addressed learning in libraries, and the third, held at the Los Angeles Public Library on June 2, focused on engaging communities. More information, including convening videos and white papers, is available at www.imls.gov/news-events/events-archive.

Measuring Success

In April 2015 the Grants to States program held a two-day conference in Herndon, Virginia, for representatives from the State Library Administrative Agencies (SLAAs). Following a series of lead-up webinars, the conference officially rolled out the new State Program Report framework to all the states, along with a sandbox system for testing it. Representatives from 16 pilot states were paired with other states at the conference to serve as mentors throughout the year.

In July 2015 IMLS staff also held a special half day training session for SLAA attendees of the Research Institute for Public Libraries in Colorado to address the next phase of the Measuring Success initiative.

Library Statistics State Data Coordinators Conference

The seventh IMLS-sponsored Library Statistics State Data Coordinators Conference was held in Louisville in December 2014. The conference included training for the state representatives on data collection and input, a review of existing data elements included in the Public Libraries Survey, workshops on data presentation and analysis, and a comprehensive review of survey data elements for the FY 2015 survey and beyond.

Data Catalog

In February 2015 IMLS hosted an Open Data Open House for a small group of stakeholders to discuss ideas for the agency's new online data catalog (data.imls. gov). The site allows users to access and analyze IMLS data and create charts, graphs and maps without the need of technical statistical or GIS mapping software.

Continuing Education

To develop a consensus around continuing education and professional development (CE/PD) priorities, IMLS continued to support the work of the Coalition to Advance Learning in Archives, Libraries and Museums, a collaboration of associations from all three professions. As part of this work, IMLS staff led two webinars in February 2015 focused on the key elements of a project plan. The coalition held its third in-person convening in March 2015, where planning for the deployment of other cross-cutting topics continued.

Crowdsourcing

Funding from IMLS and NEH supported a May 2015 convening to explore the potential for crowdsourcing to broaden the reach of a diverse array of institutions. Lead organizers included Dartmouth College and the University of Maryland–College Park, with additional support from the Alfred P. Sloan Foundation. The meeting, "Engaging the Public: Best Practices in Crowdsourcing Across the Disciplines," brought together more than 60 stakeholders from the humanities, sciences, and cultural heritage domains to share their experiences managing digital projects that invite contributions from virtual volunteers.

IMLS Website and Publications

The IMLS website (www.imls.gov) provides information on the various grant programs, including funded projects and application forms, as well as special agency initiatives and staff contacts. The website highlights model projects developed by libraries and museums throughout the country and provides information about IMLS-sponsored conferences, webinars, and publications. A grant search tool, detailing awarded IMLS grants is at www.imls.gov/grants/awarded-grants.

In September 2015 IMLS launched a website redesign to address the agency's growing number of audiences and expanding role. The new website enhanced the agency's mission, increased accessibility, and simplified content management.

In early 2015 IMLS released an annual report for FY 2014, which highlighted how the agency furthered learning, community, and content goals through its grant making and other activities. The report is available online at www.imls.gov/publications/2014-annual-report.

Through an electronic newsletter, *Primary Source*, and the *UpNext* blog, IMLS provides information on grant deadlines, success stories, and opportunities. Information on subscribing to the IMLS newsletter is also located on the website, along with guidelines for each of the grant programs and other publications.

IMLS is on twitter @US_IMLS and Facebook (www.facebook.com/USIMLS).

Part 3
Library/Information Science Education, Placement, and Salaries

Library Employment Sources on the Internet

Catherine Barr

Library school graduates of 2014 found jobs more easily than their counterparts in 2013, according to *Library Journal's* article "Placements and Salaries 2015: The Expanding Info Sphere" [see pp. 254–267 for the full report.—*Ed.*]. The average starting salary again increased, but many job titles did not directly reflect librarianship skills.

Librarians and information professionals have many options to consider when seeking employment both within and outside the library field. The following is not a comprehensive list of the hundreds of relevant job-related sites on the Internet. These are, however, some of the best starting places for a general job search in this ever-widening field. Many offer additional information that will be helpful to those considering a career in librarianship or a change in position, including advice on conducting a successful search, writing résumés, preparing for interviews, and negotiating salaries.

Before spending a lot of time on any website, users should check that the site has been updated recently and that out-of-date job listings no longer appear.

The Directory of Organizations in Part 6 of this volume may also prove useful, and many large libraries and library associations maintain Facebook pages that may give details of vacancies.

Background Information

The Bureau of Labor Statistics of the Department of Labor provides an overview of the work librarians do and average salaries in various sectors (schools, academia, government, and "other information services") at this page: http://www.bls.gov/oes/current/oes254021.htm. Maps show where the most jobs are located and where the salaries are highest. A useful companion page (http://www.bls.gov/ooh/Education-Training-and-Library/Librarians.htm#tab-1) looks at work environments, necessary qualifications, and similar occupations (with information on archivists, curators, museum technicians, and conservators; library technicians and assistants; and teachers).

The American Library Association (ALA) has a user-friendly introduction to librarianship at all levels—from pages and library assistants to managers and directors—at LibraryCareers.org (http://www.ala.org/educationcareers/careers/librarycareerssite/home). There are also links to discussions of career paths, education choices, and core competencies. This site will be particularly useful for young people considering a possible career in librarianship. A companion page is "ALA Overview of Library Support Staff" (http://www.ala.org/offices/hrdr/librarysupportstaff/library_support_staff_resource_center).

San José State University's School of Library and Information Science has created a "Career Development" page (http://slisweb.sjsu.edu/resources/career_development/index.htm) that aims to "help our students, alumni, and prospective students navigate a myriad of career opportunities, learn about emerging trends in the field, and develop an effective job search strategy." "Emerging Career Trends for Information Professionals: A Snapshot of Job Titles in Summer 2014" provides an interesting analysis of job listings and their requirements. A lively career blog at http://slisapps.sjsu.edu/blogs/career/ and links to career webinars are also useful.

The focus on alternatives to traditional librarianship is echoed in the many print and online publications about the profession, among them:

- *The Atlas of New Librarianship* by R. David Lankes (MIT, 2011)
- *Career Q&A: A Librarian's Real-Life, Practical Guide to Managing a Successful Career* by Susanne Markgren and Tiffany Eatman Allen (Information Today, 2013)
- "Getting the Library Job You Want" by Joseph Thompson, *Reference and User Services Quarterly* (Winter 2014)
- *The Librarian's Skillbook: 51 Essential Career Skills for Information Professionals* by Deborah Hunt and David Grossman (Information Edge, 2013)
- *LIS Career Sourcebook: Managing and Maximizing Every Stop of Your Career* by G. Kim Dority (Libraries Unlimited, 2012)
- *Making the Most of Your Library Career* ed. by Lois Stickell and Bridgette Sanders (ALA Editions, 2014)
- *The New Information Professional: Your Guide to Careers in the Digital Age* by Judy Lawson and Joanna Kroll (Neal-Schuman, 2010)
- *What Do Employers Want? A Guide for Library Science Students* by Priscilla K. Shontz and Richard A. Murray (Libraries Unlimited, 2012)

There are also many resources that address the challenges facing jobseekers and suggest strategies for success. A number of chats and webinars can be found on the ALA JobLIST site at http://www.ala.org/educationcareers/employment/career-resources. The April 2010 issue of *College and Research Library News* includes an article—"Making the Best of the Worst of Times: Global Turmoil and Landing Your First Library Job"—that looks at job listings and how to prepare for an interview. And https://opencoverletters.com/ provides actual examples of cover letters with details of names and institutions redacted.

Those who have succeeded in getting an interview will find these resources helpful:

- "Congratulations! You've Landed an Interview: What Do Hiring Committees Really Want?" by Megan Hodge and Nicole Spoor. *New Library World* Vol. 113 Iss: 3/4, pp. 139–161 (2012). This article gives the results of a survey of members of library hiring committees, offering insight for jobseekers in the public and academic library fields.

- The Library Interview Question "Database," a spreadsheet on Google Drive available at http://tinyurl.com/InterviewQuestionsRepository, gives fascinating insight into the kinds of questions job applicants may encounter. Participants describe the level of interview, the kind of position involved, the questions they were asked, and the questions they themselves asked in return.
- Finally, should you be agonizing over what to wear to an interview, visit http://librarianhirefashion.tumblr.com/ for photographs of suitable and unsuitable attire, with comments by librarians who hire.

General Sites/Portals

How to Apply for a Library Job

http://liswiki.org/wiki/HOWTO:Apply_for_a_library_job

A general guide with advice on phone, video, and in-person interviews.

ALA JobLIST

http://joblist.ala.org

Sponsored by the American Library Association and the Association of College and Research Libraries, this site is free for jobseekers, who can post their résumés and browse recent job postings or search jobs by library type, date, state, institution name, salary range, and other parameters offered in the advanced search function. Employers can choose from a menu of print and electronic posting combinations.

ALA JobLIST: Career Development Resources

http://www.ala.org/educationcareers/employment/career-resources

This ALA site lists job placement opportunities at forthcoming conferences, along with details of workshops and tips on various aspects of the job search. At the top of the page, you can do a quick search for job openings by state. Also available on this page are links to career assessment resources, advice on creating effective resumes and cover letters, general career information, and tips on job hunting, interviews, negotiating salaries, and so forth. A multimedia section includes webinars and podcasts on various aspects of job searches.

San José State University Job Listing Sites and Resources

http://slisweb.sjsu.edu/career-development/job-search/job-listing-sites-and-resources

This page provides an extensive list of library employment sites as well as tips on conducting an effective job search, with webcasts and advice on creating an e-portfolio. A related page, Professional Associations (http://slisweb.sjsu.edu/resources/orgs.htm), is a comprehensive listing of organizations in the United States and abroad that will be helpful to jobseekers with specific interests.

INALJ

http://inalj.com/

This community of information professionals working to help find and share jobs and job hunting advice is also present on Facebook, Twitter, and LinkedIn. Along with regularly updated, well-organized job listings (domestic and international), this site offers interesting articles and interviews, inspiring success stories, plus an extensive list of keywords for job searches that reveals the breadth of opportunities in the field. Check individual states for openings; the "last updated" date on splash pages may not apply.

Metropolitan New York Library Council

http://metro.org/career-resources/

A job board for library and related organizations in the NYC area, plus a calendar of events.

The Riley Guide

http://www.rileyguide.com

In addition to job listings (try http://www.rileyguide.com/info.html#lib to access positions suitable for librarians), the Riley Guide allows users to explore all aspects of job hunting, from proper preparation to résumés and cover letters, researching and targeting employers, and networking, interviewing, and negotiating salaries and job conditions.

Sites by Sector

Public Libraries

Public library openings can be found at all the general sites/portals listed above.

Careers in Public Librarianship

http://www.ala.org/pla/tools/careers

The Public Library Association offers information on public librarianship, with a webcast on finding and keeping public library jobs

Competencies for Librarians Serving Children in Public Libraries

http://www.ala.org/ala/mgrps/divs/alsc/edcareeers/alsccorecomps/

A detailed listing of skills and knowledge required to be a children's librarian in a public library.

School Libraries

School library openings can be found at many of the sites listed above and general education sites, and comprehensive employment sites such as Monster.com often include school library openings.

AASL: Recruitment to School Librarianship

http://www.ala.org/ala/mgrps/divs/aasl/aasleducation/recruitmentlib/aaslrecruitment.cfm

The American Association of School Librarians hosts this site, which describes the role of school librarians, salary and job outlooks, and mentoring programs; provides testimonials from working library media specialists; and offers state-by-state information on licensure, scholarships, library education, job hunting, mentoring, and recruitment efforts.

Special and Academic Libraries

AALL Career Center

http://www.aallnet.org/main-menu/Careers/career-center

Maintained by the American Association of Law Libraries, this site has an online job board and useful tips for job seekers (in academic libraries, court libraries, and law firms).

Careers in Law Librarianship

http://www.lawlibrarycareers.org/

This excellent site answers the question "Is a career as a law librarian right for you?" and provides broad information on the profession, educational requirements, and available financial assistance.

Association of College and Research Libraries

http://www.ala.org/acrl/

Under the heading Professional Tools, there are useful descriptions of various positions and information on recruitment and retention. Job listings are found at ALA JobLIST (see above).

ASIS&T: Careers

https://www.asist.org/about/careers/

The Careers page maintained by the Association for Information Science and Technology offers access to a Jobline, profiles of selected members, and continuing education information.

Association of Research Libraries: Leadership & Recruitment

http://www.arl.org/leadership-recruitment

In addition to user-friendly listings of openings at ARL member institutions and at other organizations, there is information on ARL's diversity programs plus a database of research library residency and internship programs.

Chronicle of Higher Education: Vitae

https://chroniclevitae.com/

Listings can be browsed, with geographical options, using keywords. Articles and advice on job searching are also available.

EDUCAUSE Job Posting Service

http://www.educause.edu/Jobs

EDUCAUSE member organizations post positions "in the broad field of information technology in higher education."

HigherEdJobs.com

http://www.higheredjobs.com

The category "Libraries" is found under Administrative Positions.

Medical Library Association: Career Center

http://www.mlanet.org/p/cm/ld/fid=352

The Medical Library Association offers much more than job listings here, with brochures on medical librarianship, a video, career tips, and a mentor program.

Music Library Association Job Openings

http://www.musiclibraryassoc.org/?page=JobsAndCareers

Along with job postings and a résumé review service, this site features useful career resources.

SLA: Career Center

http://www.sla.org/career-center/

The Career Center is the place to apply for jobs, post résumés, and find information on career enhancement.

Government
Library of Congress

http://www.loc.gov/hr/employment

An extensive survey of what it's like to work at the library, the kinds of employees the library is seeking, the organizational structure, benefits, current job openings, internships, fellowships, and volunteering.

National Archives and Records Administration

http://www.archives.gov/careers/

In addition to information on employment opportunities, internships, and volunteering, NARA provides profiles of employees and interns, describing the kinds of work they do.

Serials
NASIG Jobs

http://nasigjobs.wordpress.com/

Managed by the North American Serials Interest Group. Accepts serials-related job postings.

Library Periodicals
American Libraries

See ALA JobLIST above.

Library Journal

http://www.libraryjournal.com

Job listings are found under the Job Zone tab found under the Careers heading, which also leads to archived articles relating to employment.

School Library Journal

http://www.schoollibraryjournal.com

Click on the Job Zone tab for access to a general list of job openings (jointly maintained with *Library Journal*).

Employment Agencies/Commercial Services

A number of employment agencies and commercial services in the United States and abroad specialize in library-related jobs. Among those that keep up-to-date listings on their Web sites are:

Advanced Information Management

http://www.aimusa.com

Specializes in librarians and support staff in a variety of types of libraries across the country.

LAC Group

http://careers.lac-group.com/

An easy-to-use list of openings that can be sorted by function, location, and keyword. The LibGig site (http://www.libgig.com/) was created by the LAC Group and offers news, career profiles, and résumé consultation.

Listservs and Networking Sites

Many listservs allow members to post job openings on a casual basis.

ALA Think Tank

https://www.facebook.com/groups/ALAthinkTANK/

A lively Facebook group with nearly 12,000 members who post and comment on all aspects of librarianship.

LIBJOBS

http://www.ifla.org/en/mailing-lists

LIBJOBS is a mailing list for librarians and information professionals seeking employment. It is managed by the International Federation of Library Associations and Institutions (IFLA). Subscribers to this list receive posted job opportunities by e-mail.

LIS New Prof Network

https://twitter.com/lisnpn

A Twitter forum with news, blogs, and postings of general and specific (job openings, grants, etc.) interest.

PUBLIB

http://www.webjunction.org/documents/webjunction/PubLib_Overview.html

Public library job openings often appear on this list.

Blogs

hls: How Would You Hack Library School?

http://hacklibschool.wordpress.com/

A blog that looks at various aspects of librarianship and its evolution.

Library Career People

http://librarycareerpeople.com/

This attractive and user-friendly blog is maintained by librarians Tiffany Allen, Susanne Markgren, and Carrie Netzer Wajda and is intended to "create an enlightening discussion forum, and career development archive, of professional guidance and advice for librarians, library staff, and those thinking of entering the profession."

Placements and Salaries 2015:
The Expanding Info Sphere

Suzie Allard

Library and information science (LIS) graduates are finding their place in a market that demands creativity, flexibility, and a solid set of LIS skills that represent the profession's foundations and future. This year's list of job titles reflects ones we know well from the bedrock of our field (children's librarian, reference librarian) and those that are less familiar from the frontiers ahead (content strategy consultant, data steward). However, familiarity can be an illusion. In many cases, jobs with the same title list very different sets of job responsibilities. Answering this challenge requires job seekers to identify desired skill sets very carefully and to consider jobs with unfamiliar titles. Future job seekers may want to consider this competency-based approach when conducting their job search.

This year 37 of the 52 LIS schools in the United States reported there were 4,331 graduates in 2014, with 31.8 percent (1,379 graduates) of these graduates participating in the *LJ* survey. Overall, 2014 graduates successfully found jobs, with 83 percent of those responding to the employment status question saying they have full-time employment (though not necessarily in a library). This is a marked increase over the 69.6 percent reported last year for the 2013 graduates. The average starting salary also has improved, to $46,987, up 2.9 percent over 2013.

Although success in finding a job was high, the search process demanded perseverance and preparation. Applicants faced significant challenges including concerns over qualifying for "entry level" jobs that require previous experience; well-saturated local markets, particularly in areas with LIS schools; and the need to have strong in-person social networking skills. Successful completion of a search required being well prepared for the process, stamina to stay engaged over the longer term, and willingness to adjust expectations. One troubling indicator is that unemployment has increased over last year, to 5.9 percent.

LIS schools reported that the hiring market for LIS students was healthy, which is supported by the high number of graduates reporting full-time employment and rising salary levels. More than a quarter of the schools reported an increase in available positions, and only 18 percent recorded a decrease in positions. Some schools (11 percent) also reported that salary levels were higher than last year, while only 3 percent of schools reported that the salary level had dropped. This was supported by the results of the graduate survey.

Salary Levels

The salary picture for 2014 graduates is generally good news. Among the 1,156 graduates who shared their salary information, the average salary level is $46,987, an increase of 2.9 percent over last year. Salary levels for both women and men

Suzie Allard is a Professor of Information Sciences and Associate Dean of Research, University of Tennessee College of Communication and Information, Knoxville.

Adapted from *Library Journal*, October 23, 2015.

Table 1 / Status of 2014 Graduates

School Region	Number of Schools Reporting	Number of Graduates Responding	Employed in LIS Field	Employed Outside United States	Currently Unemployed or Continuing Education	Total Answering	Percentage Employed Full-Time
Northeast	10	347	278	51	18	347	80
Southeast	7	221	148	30	24	202	82
Midwest	10	398	216	25	6	247	85
South Central	9	270	156	26	11	193	88
Pacific	4	143	9	0	0	9	79
Total	40	1,379	907	132	59	998	83

*Table based on survey responses from schools and individual graduates. Figures will not necessarily be fully consistent with some of the other data reported. Tables do not always add up, individually or collectively, since both schools and individuals omitted data in some cases.

Table 2 / Placements and Full-Time Salaries of 2014 Graduates/Summary By Region*

Region	Number of Placements	Number Responding			Low Salary		High Salary		Average Salary			Median Salary		
		Women	Men	All**	Women	Men	Women	Men	Women	Men	All**	Women	Men	All**
Northeast	283	150	40	195	$14,000	$14,000	$110,000	$75,000	$47,055	$45,703	$46,464	$45,000	$43,000	$45,000
Southeast	165	84	33	120	14,560	24,999	77,000	88,000	39,198	45,761	41,073	39,500	45,000	40,000
Midwest	270	129	31	163	14,000	29,400	90,000	170,000	44,097	61,126	47,401	42,000	45,000	43,000
South Central	195	132	30	162	17,000	22,500	75,000	75,000	42,826	41,313	42,546	41,000	42,000	41,040
Mountain	60	33	12	45	20,000	14,000	65,000	90,000	40,726	48,190	42,716	40,000	44,500	41,000
Pacific	165	60	25	88	25,000	23,800	120,000	118,000	58,981	79,080	63,987	52,000	80,000	55,200
Canada/Intl.	18	11	2	13	16,000	95,000	82,000	96,000	57,818	95,500	63,615	64,000	95,500	70,000
Combined	1,156	606	173	793	14,000	14,000	120,000	170,000	45,353	53,288	46,987	42,500	45,000	43,000

*This table represents only salaries reported as full-time. Some data were reported as aggregate without breakdown by gender or region. Comparison with other tables will show different numbers of placements.

**All includes transgender, other, and no answer.

show increases, with women's salaries displaying a slightly stronger increase (up 2.6 percent to $45,353) than men's salaries (up 2.3 percent to $53,288). Interestingly, this year men have greater representation in the results than they did last year. For 2014, the ratio is 77.8 percent women to 22.2 percent men, versus last year's ratio of 81.4 percent women to 18.6 percent men.

Salary by Region

Regionally there is considerable variation in salary levels. (This year's regional designations were not directly comparable to last year's, so changes from last year will not be reported.) Graduates holding jobs in the Pacific states report the highest average salary, $63,987, which is 36.2 percent higher than the overall average salary. Those graduates with jobs in the Southeast reported the lowest average salary, $41,073, which is 12.6 percent below this year's overall average. The distance between these salary levels likely reflects more than just a regional cost of living (COL) standard since it is nearly double the COL differential computed for two well-known cities in these regions (22 percent difference between Portland, OR, and Charleston, SC). Those graduates employed outside the United States also commanded salaries near the top of the scale, at $63,615. Salary levels for jobs in the Midwest, $47,401, and the Northeast, $46,464, are close to the overall average. Workers in the Mountain states have an average salary of $42,716.

Salary by Job Title

Job titles provided marked differences between salary level. The top five highest average salaries are for jobs that have less traditional titles. These include software engineer/developer ($85,450), usability designer/researcher ($78,075), data analyst/scientist ($72,571), digital asset manager ($62,167), and business analyst ($55,083). Outreach librarian ($51,558) and systems librarian ($50,400) are also at salary levels more than 7 percent above the overall average salary.

School library media specialist has a salary ($50,362) that is also 7 percent above the overall average salary, however, those graduates employed with the title school librarian are about 2 percent below the average salary.

Other job titles that have salaries at or above the overall average are collection development librarian ($50,200), research librarian ($49,992), head librarian ($48,825), and metadata librarian ($47,500).

The five job titles at the lowest salary levels are library technical assistant ($29,560), library associate ($31,090), library specialist ($34,083), assistant director ($34,400), and library technician ($34,975). Many of these titles suggest that they may be jobs that do not require professional training. This highlights a theme that emerged from the survey participants' comments about the job search: frustration for those graduates who found themselves employed in a job that did not require their degree.

(text continues on page 260)

Table 3 / 2014 Total Graduates and Placements by School*

Schools	Graduates			Employed			Response Rate	
	Women	Men	Total	Women	Men	Total	No. Rec'd.	Rate
Alabama	81	19	100	11	2	13	16	16.0%
Albany	56	24	80	7	4	12	14	17.5
Buffalo*	—	—	—	11	3	17	22	—
Catholic	40	18	58	5	—	5	5	8.6
Clarion	122	30	152	19	9	28	31	20.4
Dominican	115	29	144	32	4	37	54	37.5
Drexel	110	40	150	18	3	21	30	20.0
Florida State	101	29	130	13	5	20	26	20.0
Hawaii	20	4	24	5	1	7	8	33.3
Illinois*	195	68	263	—	—	101	136	51.7
Indiana–Bloomington	104	44	148	15	3	19	25	16.9
Indiana–Purdue	—	—	—	10	2	12	13	—
Iowa	16	6	22	11	1	13	17	77.3
Kentucky	68	20	88	21	4	25	32	36.4
Long Island	—	—	—	2	—	2	6	—
Louisiana State	46	10	56	4	—	4	4	7.1
Michigan*	102	73	175	78	60	138	149	85.1
Missouri–Columbia	42	13	55	3	—	3	7	12.7
NC Chapel Hill*	81	26	107	—	—	—	107	100.0
NC Greensboro	57	15	72	10	3	13	25	34.7
North Texas	237	54	291	34	11	47	57	19.6
Oklahoma	36	10	46	8	5	13	19	41.3
Pratt	84	19	103	15	2	17	23	22.3
Queens	89	29	118	5	1	7	10	8.5
Rhode Island	35	6	41	—	—	—	—	—
Rutgers	94	28	122	37	13	51	61	50.0
San Jose*	429	113	542	86	12	100	129	23.8
Simmons*	220	34	254	73	15	90	130	51.2
South Carolina	77	21	98	11	2	13	16	16.3
South Florida	80	12	92	8	4	12	17	18.5
Southern Mississippi	37	10	47	15	3	18	18	38.3
St. Catherine	47	8	55	22	1	23	33	60.0
St. John's	18	6	24	—	—	—	—	—
Syracuse	59	14	73	16	1	17	20	27.4
Tennessee	58	26	84	12	3	15	16	19.0
Texas (Austin)*	81	30	111	49	17	66	82	73.9
Texas Woman's	127	12	139	20	2	22	26	18.7
UCLA	—	—	—	—	1	1	1	—
Valdosta State	—	—	—	14	6	20	25	—
Washington*	105	22	127	—	—	4	5	3.9
Wayne State	—	—	—	9	2	11	18	—
Wisconsin–Madison*	—	—	—	28	2	31	40	—
Wisconsin–Milwaukee	106	34	140	28	8	36	42	30.0
Total	3,375	956	4,331	765	215	1,104	1,515	35.0

Tables do not always add up, individually or collectively, owing to omitted data from schools and/or individuals.

* Some schools conducted their own survey and provided reports. This table represents placements of any kind. Comparison with other tables will show different numbers of placements.

Table 4 / Placements by Average Full-Time Salary of Reporting 2014 Graduates*

	Average Salary			Median Salary		Low Salary		High Salary		Placements		Total Placements
	Women	Men	All	Women	Men	Women	Men	Women	Men	Women	Men	
UCLA	—	$110,000	$110,000	—	$110,000	$110,000	$110,000	—	$110,000	—	1	1
Michigan	$61,704	78,572	68,848	54,000	77,500	$30,000	30,000	$120,000	170,000	49	36	85
Catholic	53,000	—	53,000	50,000	—	40,000	—	74,000	—	5	—	5
San Jose	50,821	63,890	52,418	48,500	41,000	25,000	33,500	115,000	118,000	60	9	70
Texas (Austin)	50,898	50,735	50,856	47,500	47,500	17,000	22,500	110,000	97,500	49	17	66
Pratt	51,152	45,000	50,127	46,260	45,000	28,000	40,000	110,000	50,000	10	2	12
St. Catherine's	47,531	57,000	48,057	41,000	57,000	34,000	57,000	90,000	57,000	17	1	18
Long Island	47,500	—	47,500	47,500	—	45,000	—	50,000	—	2	—	2
Rutgers	47,956	46,588	47,288	48,000	42,500	14,560	28,000	87,500	75,000	31	12	44
Indiana–Bloomington	41,964	63,333	47,149	43,465	50,000	28,000	50,000	69,500	90,000	13	3	17
Dominican	45,548	40,125	44,773	44,750	44,250	25,000	27,000	76,000	45,000	24	4	28
Florida State	42,733	49,000	44,559	44,000	42,000	24,000	40,000	58,000	68,000	11	5	18
Hawaii	45,100	42,000	44,480	52,500	42,000	20,000	42,000	55,400	42,000	4	1	5
Albany	41,664	50,526	44,322	42,000	52,000	18,000	42,000	62,275	57,577	7	3	10
Missouri–Columbia	43,991	—	43,991	41,974	—	40,000	—	50,000	—	3	—	3
Simmons	43,845	44,786	43,772	42,500	44,000	27,300	30,000	81,431	62,000	61	14	76
Wisconsin–Madison	43,908	39,500	43,696	42,000	39,500	28,912	36,000	62,000	43,000	24	2	27
North Texas	43,403	43,400	43,287	40,281	43,500	20,000	27,000	92,000	54,000	27	10	38
Iowa	44,458	—	43,143	42,500	—	30,025	—	70,000	—	10	—	11

Clarion	42,821	43,313	43,000	42,250	45,000	14,000	14,000	76,000	57,500	14	8	22
Tennessee	36,208	76,500	41,964	33,500	76,500	16,000	65,000	62,000	88,000	12	2	14
Valdosta	41,883	42,000	41,922	39,500	42,000	25,000	26,000	67,000	65,000	12	6	18
NC Greensboro	39,629	49,000	41,711	41,000	49,000	28,000	36,000	48,500	62,000	7	2	9
Texas Woman's	41,485	41,000	41,431	41,000	41,000	18,865	34,000	59,300	48,000	16	2	18
Buffalo	46,493	31,333	40,808	46,000	35,000	34,000	14,000	56,000	45,000	5	3	8
Wisconsin–Milwaukee	39,814	40,733	40,019	40,000	41,500	14,000	29,400	68,000	51,000	21	6	27
Syracuse	39,537	45,000	39,878	40,162	45,000	21,000	45,000	55,500	45,000	15	1	16
Oklahoma	38,540	39,000	38,732	40,000	41,000	30,000	27,000	45,700	44,000	7	5	12
Wayne	34,750	49,500	38,438	36,750	49,500	25,000	49,000	40,000	50,000	6	2	8
Drexel	37,629	44,388	38,424	40,000	44,388	21,000	40,000	50,000	48,775	15	2	17
Queens	40,500	37,500	38,125	40,500	37,500	31,000	37,500	50,000	37,500	2	1	4
Louisiana State	38,006	—	38,006	38,000	—	33,524	—	42,500	—	4	—	4
Washington	—	—	37,500	—	—	—	—	—	—	—	—	4
South Florida	35,400	39,025	37,011	37,000	39,050	18,000	24,999	45,000	53,000	5	4	9
Indiana–Purdue	33,880	47,500	36,356	36,700	47,500	17,000	40,000	47,000	55,000	9	2	11
Kentucky	37,401	26,500	36,254	38,000	26,500	24,000	25,000	52,000	28,000	17	2	19
Alabama	36,515	34,400	36,092	30,060	34,400	27,000	23,800	72,000	45,000	8	2	10
Southern Mississippi	34,761	36,750	35,046	35,820	36,750	19,798	31,000	43,500	42,500	12	2	14
South Carolina	35,211	26,000	34,373	34,619	26,000	20,000	26,000	45,000	26,000	10	1	11

* This table represents only placements and salaries reported as full-time. Some individuals or schools omitted information, rendering information unusable.
* Some schools conducted their own survey and provided reports. This table represents placements of any kind. Comparison with other tables will show different numbers of placements.

Table 5 / Average Salary for Starting Library Positions, 2010–2014

Year	Library Schools Represented	Average Starting Salary	Difference in Average Salary	Percentage Change
2010	38	$42,556	$341	0.8
2011	41	44,565	2,009	4.7
2012	41	44,503	-$62	-0.1
2013	40	45,650	1,147	2.6
2014	39	46,987	1,337	2.9

(continued from page 256)

Salary by Library Type

Salary levels differ by library type. This year the top three library types in terms of number of placements are the public library, college/university library, and private industry. Of these three institutional types, only private industry offered salaries that exceeded the overall average at $68,424. This suggests that while graduates are finding jobs in libraries, these positions are often in libraries that cannot offer higher salaries. These top three placement situations also provide another insight: the large number of placements in private industry is an indicator of the expanding market for the LIS skill set.

Private industry is the only library type to offer an average salary markedly higher (+45.6 percent) than the overall average. Private industry salaries are particularly strong in the Pacific. While the Mountain region also has a high average salary level, this number only represents two placements, so it is difficult to compare.

The library type with the lowest salary levels is the public library ($40,635), although the average salary did increase 2.7 percent over last year. The range of salaries, from $14,000 to $118,000, suggests that the jobs filled in these organizations have substantially different responsibilities.

School and Special Libraries

School libraries, special libraries, and other kinds of organizations ($48,588, $48,536, and $48,424, respectively) reported salaries slightly above the overall average (+3.1 percent).

Jobs in school libraries show a 1.7 percent increase in average salary over last year. However, the average salary level for school libraries was increased by the strong salary numbers for placements outside the United States, which are far more noticeable this year than last year. School librarians in the Mountain states, Northeast, and Midwest reported salary levels above the overall average.

Salaries in special libraries increased over last year by 8.6 percent. Special librarians in the Mountain and Pacific regions reported the highest salaries (more than $60,000 in each area). Special librarian salaries reported in the other regions were about average.

Salaries for librarians working in other organizations, such as government agencies, vendors, or academic institutions other than libraries, averaged $48,424.

Nonprofit organizations ($44,463) is a library type that was added this year. It is difficult to draw conclusions about this category since most regions had very

Table 6 / Salaries of Reporting Professionals by Area of Job Title*

Assignment	No. Rec'd.	Percent of Total	Low Salary	High Salary	Average Salary	Median Salary
Access Services Librarian	10	2.1	$25,000	$68,000	$42,329	$39,396
Adult/Public Services Librarian	14	2.9	14,000	70,000	42,510	43,000
Archivist	32	6.7	17,000	65,000	44,763	42,750
Assistant Director	5	1.0	29,000	45,000	34,400	32,000
Branch Manager/Library Manager	9	1.9	28,000	50,000	36,444	31,000
Business Analyst	6	1.3	38,000	67,500	55,083	56,250
Cataloger/Catalog Librarian	13	2.7	25,000	56,000	37,897	40,000
Children's/Youth Services Librarian	21	4.4	26,325	56,000	43,818	44,000
Collection Development Librarian	5	1.0	32,000	69,000	50,200	45,000
Data Analyst/Scientist	7	1.5	41,000	95,000	72,571	75,000
Digital Asset Management	6	1.3	37,500	115,000	62,167	50,250
Digital Services Librarian	9	1.9	32,000	62,000	45,778	47,500
Electronic Resources Librarian	5	1.0	34,000	53,000	43,300	44,500
Head Librarian	4	0.8	40,000	59,300	48,825	48,000
Information Services Librarian	4	0.8	30,025	47,000	38,781	39,050
Librarian	56	11.7	19,798	80,000	44,892	42,000
Library Associate/ Library Assistant	21	4.4	14,560	44,000	31,090	33,000
Library Director	25	5.2	24,000	118,000	46,164	40,000
Library Specialist	6	1.3	27,000	42,500	34,083	33,750
Library Technical Assistant	5	1.0	20,000	45,000	29,560	26,000
Library Technician	8	1.7	21,000	52,000	34,975	35,000
Medical Librarian	3	0.6	25,000	44,000	36,333	40,000
Metadata Librarian	5	1.0	38,000	67,500	47,500	46,000
Outreach Librarian	8	1.7	37,500	64,000	51,558	52,500
Reference & Instruction Librarian	37	7.7	17,000	74,000	43,221	42,000
Research Assistant	4	0.8	38,000	52,500	43,375	41,500
Research Librarian	12	2.5	38,000	68,000	49,992	48,250
School Librarian	16	3.3	30,000	96,000	46,094	44,250
School Library Media Specialist	25	5.2	35,000	87,500	50,362	47,900
Software Engineer/Developer	10	2.1	36,000	170,000	85,450	78,500
Special Collections Librarian	4	0.8	26,000	42,500	35,250	36,250
Systems Librarian	5	1.0	40,000	57,000	50,400	53,000
Technical Services Librarian	6	1.3	34,237	48,775	43,169	44,000
Teen/YA Librarian	35	7.3	28,912	54,000	38,596	37,000
UX Designer/Researcher	37	7.7	37,000	120,000	78,075	77,500
Total Answering	478	100.0	14,000	170,000	46,987	43,000

* This table represents placements of any type reported by job title but only salaries reported as full-time. Some individuals omitted placement information, rendering some information unusable. Comparison with other tables may show different numbers of placements and average and median salaries.

few placements. There is only one region with a reasonable number of placements (18) to be analyzed and much like the other regions there is a substantial range between the low and high salary. It will be worthwhile to keep an eye on this category next year.

Salaries in government libraries were reported to decrease from last year, dropping 2.5 percent to $42,719. This is also a category with relatively few placements (26), so it is difficult to make regional comparisons.

Academics and Archives

Archive salaries show a 3 percent increase over last year, to $43,431. Salaries range from a low of $14,000 to a high of $110,000, which suggests that this category includes archives that have very different levels of available resources.

(text continues on page 264)

Table 7 / Comparison of Full-Time Salaries by Type of Organization and Region

	Total Placements	Low Salary	High Salary	Average Salary	Median Salary
Public Libraries					
Southeast	36	$14,560	$54,000	$35,314	$35,000
Midwest	52	14,000	87,000	40,401	40,000
South Central	49	18,865	56,000	36,291	37,000
Mountain	19	14,000	65,000	38,961	41,000
Pacific	18	35,000	118,000	56,278	50,500
Northeast	50	14,000	70,000	40,804	41,500
Canada/Intl.	5	45,000	82,000	68,200	70,000
All Public	232	14,000	118,000	40,635	40,000
School Libraries					
Southeast	9	18,000	67,000	45,056	45,000
Midwest	11	30,000	68,009	47,637	45,000
South Central	24	28,000	60,000	44,003	43,000
Mountain	3	50,000	65,000	55,000	50,000
Pacific	8	23,800	73,000	47,413	48,750
Northeast	22	30,000	87,500	52,996	50,500
Canada/Intl.	4	35,000	96,000	68,250	71,000
All School	83	18,000	96,000	48,588	47,000
College/University Libraries					
Southeast	42	20,000	88,000	41,239	40,500
Midwest	34	20,000	66,000	42,075	42,750
South Central	39	17,000	63,000	39,696	40,000
Mountain	14	24,190	58,000	40,069	40,000
Pacific	14	25,000	67,500	46,908	45,009
Northeast	49	16,000	72,000	46,265	45,000
Canada/Intl.	1	70,000	70,000	70,000	70,000
All Academic	193	16,000	88,000	42,826	42,500
Special Libraries					
Southeast	4	29,120	45,600	39,930	42,500
Midwest	10	25,000	76,000	42,850	36,750
South Central	5	27,500	50,000	42,300	44,000

Mountain	1	65,000	65,000	65,000	65,000
Pacific	6	43,000	110,000	65,167	61,250
Northeast	8	35,360	75,000	49,315	44,580
Canada/Intl.	0	—	—	—	—
All Special	34	25,000	110,000	48,536	44,580
Government Libraries					
Southeast	5	30,000	62,500	47,332	52,000
Midwest	7	28,000	62,275	46,579	48,000
South Central	8	19,798	59,300	40,950	41,750
Mountain	1	44,000	44,000	44,000	44,000
Pacific	0	—	—	—	—
Northeast	4	17,000	52,000	38,843	43,185
Canada/Intl.	0	—	—	—	—
All Government	26	17,000	62,500	42,719	44,185
Archives					
Southeast	7	24,000	60,000	42,857	42,000
Midwest	6	20,000	42,000	32,075	32,505
South Central	4	38,000	45,000	42,563	43,625
Mountain	1	36,000	36,000	36,000	36,000
Pacific	6	36,000	110,000	58,553	49,159
Northeast	12	14,000	62,000	42,792	45,500
Canada/Intl.	0	—	—	—	—
All Archives	36	14,000	110,000	43,431	42,000
Private Industry					
Southeast	7	36,000	85,000	53,643	45,000
Midwest	28	35,000	170,000	70,907	60,500
South Central	24	22,500	75,000	57,375	57,500
Mountain	2	65,000	75,000	70,000	70,000
Pacific	27	37,500	120,000	86,222	95,000
Northeast	17	34,000	110,000	58,941	50,000
Canada/Intl.	0	—	—	—	—
All Private Industry	106	22,500	170,000	68,424	66,250
Nonprofit Organizations					
Southeast	4	30,000	54,000	38,500	35,000
Midwest	8	35,500	62,000	41,688	38,000
South Central	0	—	—	—	—
Mountain	2	36,000	90,000	63,000	63,000
Pacific	1	65,000	65,000	65,000	65,000
Northeast	18	27,736	82,500	43,791	40,000
Canada/Intl.	1	45,000	45,000	45,000	45,000
All Nonprofit	34	27,736	90,000	44,463	39,500
Other Organizations					
Southeast	9	25,000	65,000	44,667	42,000
Midwest	13	22,000	69,500	47,731	50,000
South Central	12	29,000	67,500	45,950	41,000
Mountain	3	34,000	40,000	36,667	36,000
Pacific	10	34,000	110,000	60,154	50,000
Northeast	20	18,000	81,431	47,890	49,000
Canada/Intl.	2	16,000	82,000	49,000	49,000
All Other	69	16,000	110,000	48,424	45,000

This table represents only full-time salaries and all placements reported by type. Some individuals omitted placement information, rendering some information unusable.

(continued from page 262)

College and university library salaries averaged $42,826, which is comparable to last year. The Pacific and Northeast had the highest salaries. The South Central region was the lowest paying at $39,696. Similar to the archives, there is a wide range of salary levels, from a low of $16,000 to a high of $88,000, which suggests that this category, too, includes institutions that have very different missions and financial profiles.

Titles and Tasks from Core to Cutting Edge

In the Field

The last several years of results identified emerging employment areas that are working with LIS skill sets in new ways, in both libraries and other organizations. This year we focused on whether graduates are employed in or outside of the LIS field, since there are ambiguities about defining what constitutes a professional position. It means that some direct comparisons to prior years cannot be made, but it accurately captures the idea that professional positions can require LIS skills regardless of the type of situation. Some examples of job areas that are using LIS skills include: social media, data curation, data analytics, e-learning, organizational development (fundraising), user experience, and competitive intelligence.

Providing the Foundations

Reflecting the foundations of our field, more than three-quarters of the job titles reported by survey participants include the term librarian in the title. These titles represent the diverse skills and services of the LIS profession. Naturally, the responsibilities for the myriad positions vary greatly.

Nearly 12 percent of the respondents hold the title of "librarian," which represents a wide array of responsibilities and pay levels, ranging from $19,798 to $80,000, with an average salary level of about $44,892. Highlighting the need to employ a competency-based approach to identifying the job responsibilities for these positions is the list of responsibilities noted by librarians, including programming, collection development, curriculum development, supervision, and administration.

School media specialists/school librarians account for 8.5 percent of the jobs attained among these 2014 graduates with an average salary of roughly $48,000. Responsibilities that graduates noted for this position include those that were listed by many (i.e., instruction, collection development, circulation) and some that were less commonly noted (i.e., technology integration, website design, digital citizenship).

The next two most common "foundation" job titles are reference/instructional librarian (7.7 percent) and teen/young adult librarian (7.3 percent). The average salary for these positions is $43,221 and $38,596, respectively. Instructional librarian responsibilities include such activities as technology training; course design, both for their own courses and assisting faculty; and tutorial instruction. The teen and young adult librarian manages the collection and the space, helping teen patrons and conducting outreach to this group

Table 8 / Full-Time Salaries by Type of Organization and Gender

	Total Placements			Low Salary		High Salary		Average Salary			Median Salary		
	Women	Men	All	Women	Men	Women	Men	Women	Men	All	Women	Men	All
Public Libraries	188	39	232	$14,000	$14,000	$92,000	$118,000	$40,232	$43,427	$40,635	$40,000	$42,000	$40,000
School Libraries	72	9	83	18,000	23,800	87,500	96,000	47,938	55,478	48,588	47,000	51,000	47,000
College/University Libraries	149	44	193	16,000	22,500	74,000	88,000	42,304	44,097	42,826	42,000	43,500	42,500
Special Libraries	31	3	34	25,000	36,000	110,000	40,000	49,492	38,667	48,536	45,000	40,000	44,580
Government Libraries	22	4	26	17,000	30,000	62,500	52,000	42,667	43,000	42,719	44,185	45,000	44,185
Archives	28	8	36	20,000	14,000	110,000	60,000	44,732	38,876	43,431	42,250	37,805	42,000
Private Industry	59	45	106	22,500	22,500	120,000	170,000	65,288	74,020	68,424	62,500	75,000	66,250
Nonprofit Organizations	27	7	34	27,736	35,000	82,500	90,000	43,490	48,214	44,463	40,000	37,500	39,500
Other Organizations	50	18	69	16,000	30,000	82,000	110,000	45,861	55,733	48,424	44,000	51,000	45,000

This table represents only full-time salaries and all placements reported by type. Some individuals omitted placement information, rendering some information unusable.

Serving Up the Future

Archivist accounts for 6.7 percent of all jobs in the first year after graduation and has an average salary of $44,763. Several of these positions were specifically designated as dealing with digital objects; one was focused on data. Responsibilities include applying metadata skills and managing the archives, whether analog or digital.

Last year it was noted that user experience (UX) specialist, including user interface designers, was an area of growth. This year, UX specialist is tied for being the third most common of job titles, at 7.7 percent. The average starting salary rose significantly over last year to $78,075 (+11.5 percent).

Other jobs that are emerging include research librarian (average salary $49,992), digital services librarian ($45,778), and outreach librarian ($51,558). For those job seekers with the right skills, some emerging areas offer higher salary levels. These include software engineer/web developer ($85,450) and data scientist ($72,571).

Skills for the Search

As noted earlier, respondents commented on the challenges of the search, with many noting that it was essential to develop the skills needed for the search and to be prepared to devote significant energy to the process. These are different from the professional LIS skills that were part of their degree program. New for this year, we are looking beyond the outcome of the search and focusing on the search process itself in hopes of providing future graduates with some insight for developing their own successful strategies. The search process begins while seekers are still students. Schools offer support to students in a variety of ways. Most schools (92 percent) post job opportunities and openings on Listservs. About half the schools post announcements on bulletin boards (both physical and electronic). Only about a third of the schools offer formal placement centers within the school, although some noted support at the university level. Half the schools noted they created job awareness through a variety of other channels, including Facebook, LinkedIn, Twitter, and blogs; supporting student chapters of professional associations; engaging alumni; and participating in information sessions or career fairs. Some schools noted that they offer individual career advisement or rely on personal outreach to employers.

Only 29 percent of the schools offer a formal mentoring program, and the design of these varied greatly ranging from student peer mentoring to alumni mentoring. About 14 percent noted that they encourage informal mentoring through professional association student chapter activities and personal relationships.

Survey participants were asked to identify resources they used during the search. In addition to school resources, other items mentioned include networking with practicing professionals; using the American Library Association job placement website; working the personal/professional network; using job websites such as indeed.com, glassdoor.com, and monster.com; exploiting regional job listing sites (i.e., usajob.gov, RAILS, KDLA); and taking advantage of professional society resources.

Survey Methods

LJ contacted all 49 of the 52 LIS schools in the United States and offered each the opportunity to participate in the survey. Forty-three of these schools responded. Of these, 38 schools completed an institutional survey reporting on the demographics of their 2014 graduates. Thirty-four schools contacted their 2014 graduates and elected either to send their graduates a link to the *LJ* Web survey or to collect paper surveys that were mailed to *LJ*. Nine schools instead decided to provide *LJ* with data the school collected from its graduates and submitted in a report to *LJ*: University of Buffalo, University of Illinois Urbana–Champaign, University of Michigan, UNC–Chapel Hill, San Jose State University, Simmons College, University of Texas–Austin, University of Washington, and University of Wisconsin–Madison. These reports did not always supply complete data.

The data analyzed for this article represents responses from 35 percent of the 4,331 graduates reported by the 43 participating schools. Among the surveys conducted by *LJ*, the response rate for 2014 graduates from each school ranged from a high of 77 percent to a low of 8.5 percent. Graduate response rates from data and reports supplied by schools ranged from 100 percent to 3.9 percent. Respondents could decline to answer any question on the survey and choose to leave the survey without completing it.

Four schools that were not able to participate last year, were able to do so this year: Queens College, University of Rhode Island, St. John's University, and University of Wisconsin–Milwaukee.

The following schools declined to participate, did not respond to calls for participation, or had no graduate participation: University of Arizona, University of Denver, Emporia State University, Kent State University, University of Maryland, North Carolina Central, and University of Pittsburgh.

Canadian LIS programs conduct their own survey and do not participate in the *LJ* annual survey. This includes programs at Alberta, British Columbia, Dalhousie, McGill, Montreal, Toronto, and Western Ontario. The University of Puerto Rico does not participate.

While this data provides a valuable overview of the graduates and their placements, there are research limitations that should be noted. Some graduates and some schools reported incomplete information, rendering some data unusable. For schools that did not complete the institutional survey, data was taken from graduate surveys and thus not full representation of all graduating classes. Additionally, not all participants answered all questions.

Strategies that students used successfully for the search began during their education by gaining experience through practicums and internships, beginning to develop professional social networks, volunteering in professional situations, and starting the search well before graduation. Several graduates mentioned using university resources to help them develop strong résumés and interview skills. After graduation, successful search strategies included casting a wide net by applying for many jobs that fit the skill set, having the ability to relocate away from saturated markets, and keeping a positive attitude.

Accredited Master's Programs in Library and Information Studies

This list of graduate programs accredited by the American Library Association is issued by the ALA Office for Accreditation. Regular updates and additional details appear on the Office for Accreditation's website at http://www.ala.org/CFApps/lisdir/index.cfm. A total of 145 U.S. and Canadian institutions offering both accredited and nonaccredited programs in librarianship are included in the 68th edition (2015–2016) of *American Library Directory* (Information Today, Inc.)

Northeast: D.C., Md., Mass., N.J., N.Y., Pa., R.I.

Catholic University of America, School of Arts and Sciences, Dept. of Lib. and Info. Science, 620 Michigan Ave. N.E., Washington, DC 20064. Bill Kules, chair. Tel. 202-319-5085, fax 319-5574, e-mail cua-slis@cua.edu, World Wide Web http://slis.cua.edu. Admissions contact: Louise Gray. Tel. 202-319-5085, fax 319-5574, e-mail grayl@cua.edu.

Clarion University of Pennsylvania, College of Business Admin. and Info. Sciences, Dept. of Lib. Science, 210 Carlson Lib. Bldg., Clarion, PA 16214. Linda L. Lillard, chair. Tel. 866-272-5612, fax 814-393-2150, World Wide Web http://www.clarion.edu/libsci. Admissions contact: Lois Dulavitch. Tel. 866-272-5612, e-mail ldulavitch@clarion.edu.

Drexel University, College of Computing and Informatics, 3141 Chestnut St., Philadelphia, PA 19104-2875. David E. Fenske, dean. Tel. 215-895-2474, fax 215-895-2494, e-mail istinfo@drexel.edu, World Wide Web http://www.cci.drexel.edu. Admissions contact: Matthew Lechtenburg. Tel. 215-895-1951, e-mail ml333@ischool.drexel.edu.

Long Island University, Palmer School of Lib. and Info. Science, C. W. Post Campus, 720 Northern Blvd., Brookville, NY 11548-1300. Valeda Dent, interim dir. Tel. 516-299-4109, fax 516-299-4168, e-mail palmer@cwpost.liu.edu, World Wide Web http://www.liu.edu/palmer. Admissions contact: Christine Prete. Tel. 516-299-2857, e-mail christine.prete@liu.edu.

Pratt Institute, School of Info. and Lib. Science, 144 W. 14 St., New York, NY 10011. Tula Giannini, dean. Tel. 212-647-7682, fax 202-367-2492, e-mail infosils@pratt.edu, World Wide Web http://www.pratt.edu/academics/information_and_library_sciences. Admissions contact: Quinn Lai. Tel. 212-647-7682, e-mail infosils@pratt.edu.

Queens College, City Univ. of New York, Grad. School of Lib. and Info. Studies, Rm. 254, Rosenthal Lib., 65-30 Kissena Blvd., Flushing, NY 11367-1597. Colleen Cool, chair. Tel. 718-997-3790, fax 718-997-3797, e-mail gc_gslis@qc.cuny.edu, World Wide Web http://www.qc.cuny.edu/academics/degrees/dss/gslis/Pages/default.aspx. Admissions contact: Roberta Brody. Tel. 718-997-3790, e-mail roberta_brody@qc.cuny.edu.

Rutgers University, School of Communication and Info., Dept. of Lib. and Info. Science, New Brunswick, NJ 08901-1071. Marie L. Radford, chair. Tel. 848-932-8797, fax 732-932-6916, e-mail mlis@comminfo.rutgers.edu, World Wide Web http://comminfo.rutgers.edu. Admissions contact: Kay Cassell. Tel. 732-932-7500 ext. 8264.

Saint John's University, College of Liberal Arts and Sciences, Div. of Lib. and Info. Science, 8000 Utopia Pkwy., Queens, NY 11439. Jeffery E. Olson, dir. Tel. 718-990-6200, fax 718-990-2071, e-mail dlis@stjohns.edu, World Wide Web http://www.stjohns.edu/dlis. Admissions contact: Deborah Martinez. Tel. 718-990-6200, e-mail dlis@stjohns.edu.

Simmons College, Grad. School of Lib. and Info. Science, 300 The Fenway, Boston, MA 02115. Eileen Abels, dean. Tel. 617-521-2800, fax 617-521-3192, e-mail gslis@simmons.edu, World Wide Web http://www.simmons.edu/gslis. Admissions contact:

Sarah Petrakos. Tel. 617-521-2868, e-mail gslisadm@simmons.edu.

Syracuse University, School of Info. Studies, 343 Hinds Hall, Syracuse, NY 13244. Elizabeth D. Liddy, dean. Tel. 315-443-2911, fax 315-443-6886, e-mail ischool@syr.edu, World Wide Web http://www.ischool.syr.edu. Admissions contact: Jill Hurst-Wahl. Tel. 315-443-2911, e-mail mslis@syr.edu.

University at Albany, State Univ. of New York, College of Computing and Info., Dept. of Info. Studies, Draper 113, 135 Western Ave., Albany, NY 12222. Philip B. Eppard, chair. Tel. 518-442-5110, fax 518-442-5367, e-mail infostudies@albany.edu, World Wide Web http://www.albany.edu/information studies/index.php. Admissions contact: Daphne Jorgensen. Tel. 518-442-5110, e-mail djorgensen@albany.edu.

University at Buffalo, State Univ. of New York, Graduate School of Educ., Lib. and Info. Studies, 534 Baldy Hall, Buffalo, NY 14260-1020. Heidi Julien, chair. Tel. 716-645-2412, fax 716-645-3775, e-mail ublis@buffalo.edu, World Wide Web http://gse.buffalo.edu/lis. Admissions contact: Radhika Suresh. Tel. 716-645-2110, e-mail gse-info@buffalo.edu.

University of Maryland, College of Info. Studies, 4105 Hornbake Bldg., College Park, MD 20742. John Carlo Bertot, MLIS Program Dir. Tel. 301-405-2033, fax 301-314-9145, e-mail ischooladmission@umd.edu, World Wide Web http://ischool.umd.edu. Admissions contact: Joanne Briscoe. Tel. 301-405-2038, e-mail ischooladmission@umd.edu.

University of Pittsburgh, School of Info. Sciences, 135 N. Bellefield Ave., Pittsburgh, PA 15260. Sheila Corrall, chair. Tel. 412-624-9420, fax 412-648-7001, e-mail lisinq@mail.sis.pitt.edu, World Wide Web http://www.ischool.pitt.edu. Admissions contact: Debbie Day. Tel. 412-624-9420, e-mail dday@sis.pitt.edu.

University of Rhode Island, Grad. School of Lib. and Info. Studies, Rodman Hall, 94 W. Alumni Ave., Kingston, RI 02881. Valerie Karno, interim dir. Tel. 401-874-2878, fax 401-874-4964, e-mail gslis@etal.uri.edu, World Wide Web http://www.uri.edu/artsci/lsc.

Southeast: Ala., Fla., Ga., Ky., La., Miss., N.C., S.C., Tenn., P.R.

East Carolina University, College of Educ., Lib. Science Degree Program, Mailstop 172, ECU, Greenville, NC 27858. John B. Harer, program coord. Tel. 252-328-4389, fax 252-328-4368, e-mail harerj@ecu.edu, World Wide Web http://www.ecu.edu/cs-educ/idp/lsed/index.cfm. Admissions contact: Camilla King. Tel. 252-328-6012, e-mail grad school@ecu.edu.

Florida State University, College of Communication and Info., School of Lib. and Info. Studies, 142 Collegiate Loop, P.O. Box 3062100, Tallahassee, FL 32306-2100. Kathleen Burnett, dir. Tel. 850-644-5775, fax 850-644-9763, World Wide Web http://slis.fsu.edu. Admissions e-mail slisgrad admissions@admin.fsu.edu, tel. 850-644-8121.

Louisiana State University, School of Lib. and Info. Science, 267 Coates Hall, Baton Rouge, LA 70803. Ed Holton, interim dir. Tel. 225-578-3158, fax 225-578-4581, e-mail slis@lsu.edu, World Wide Web http://slis.lsu.edu. Admissions contact: LaToya Coleman Joseph. E-mail lcjoseph@lsu.edu.

North Carolina Central University, School of Lib. and Info. Sciences, P.O. Box 19586, Durham, NC 27707. Irene Owens, dean. Tel. 919-530-6485, fax 919-530-6402, e-mail slisadmissions@nccu.edu, World Wide Web http://www.nccuslis.org. Admissions contact: Sofia Harrison.

University of Alabama, College of Communication and Info. Sciences, School of Lib. and Info. Studies, Box 870252, Tuscaloosa, AL 35487-0252. Ann E. Prentice, interim dir. Tel. 205-348-4610, fax 205-348-3746, e-mail info@slis.ua.edu, World Wide Web http://www.slis.ua.edu. Admissions contact: Beth Riggs. Tel. 205-348-1527, e-mail briggs@slis.ua.edu.

University of Kentucky, School of Lib. and Info. Science, 320 Little Lib., Lexington, KY 40506-0224. Jeffrey T. Huber, dir. Tel. 859-257-8876, fax 859-257-4205, e-mail ukslis@uky.edu, World Wide Web http://www.uky.edu/cis/slis. Admissions contact: Will Buntin. Tel. 859-257-3317, e-mail wjbunt0@uky.edu.

University of North Carolina at Chapel Hill, School of Info. and Lib. Science, CB 3360, 100 Manning Hall, Chapel Hill, NC 27599-3360. Gary Marchionini, dean. Tel. 919-962-8366, fax 919-962-8071, e-mail info@ils.unc.edu, World Wide Web http://www.sils.unc.edu. Admissions contact: Lara Bailey.

University of North Carolina at Greensboro, School of Educ., Dept. of Lib. and Info. Studies, 446 School of Educ. Bldg., Greensboro, NC 27402-6170. O. Lee Shiflett, interim chair. Tel. 336-334-3477, fax 336-334-4120, World Wide Web http://lis.uncg.edu. Admissions contact: Touger Vang. E-mail t_vang@uncg.edu.

University of Puerto Rico, Info. Sciences and Technologies, P.O. Box 21906, San Juan, PR 00931-1906. Mariano A. Maura, acting dir. Tel. 787-763-6199, fax 787-764-2311, e-mail egcti@uprrp.edu, World Wide Web http://egcti.upr.edu. Admissions contact: Migdalia Dávila-Perez. Tel. 787-764-0000 ext. 3530, e-mail migdalia.davila@upr.edu.

University of South Carolina, College of Mass Communications and Info. Studies, School of Lib. and Info. Science, 1501 Greene St., Columbia, SC 29208. Samantha K. Hastings, dir. Tel. 803-777-3858, fax 803-777-7938, e-mail hastings@sc.edu, World Wide Web http://www.libsci.sc.edu. Admissions contact: Tilda Reeder. Tel. 800-304-3153, e-mail tildareeder@sc.edu.

University of South Florida, College of Arts and Sciences, School of Lib. and Info. Science, 4202 E. Fowler Ave., CIS 1040, Tampa, FL 33620. James Andrews, dir. Tel. 813-974-3520, fax 813-974-6840, e-mail lisinfo@usf.edu, World Wide Web http://si.usf.edu. Admissions contact: Daniel Kahl. Tel. 813-974-8022, e-mail djkahl@usf.edu.

University of Southern Mississippi, College of Educ. and Psychology, School of Lib. and Info. Science, 118 College Drive, No. 5146, Hattiesburg, MS 39406-0001. Dorothy Elizabeth Haynes, dir. Tel. 601-266-4228, fax 601-266-5774, e-mail slis@usm.edu, World Wide Web http://www.usm.edu/slis. Admissions tel. 601-266-5137, e-mail graduatestudies@usm.edu.

University of Tennessee, College of Communication and Info., School of Info. Sciences, 451 Communication Bldg., Knoxville, TN 37996. Edwin M. Cortez, dir. Tel. 865-974-2148, fax 865-974-4967, World Wide Web http://www.sis.utk.edu. Admissions contact: Tanya Arnold. Tel. 865-974-2858, e-mail tnarnold@utk.edu.

Valdosta State Univ., Dept. of Info. Studies, 1500 N. Patterson St., Valdosta, GA 31698-0133. Linda R. Most, interim dept. head. Tel. 229-333-5966, fax 229-259-5055, e-mail mlis@valdosta.edu, World Wide Web http://www.valdosta.edu/mlis. Admissions contact: Sheila Peacock.

Midwest: Ill., Ind., Iowa, Kan., Mich., Minn., Mo., Ohio, Wis.

Dominican Univ., Grad. School of Lib. and Info. Science, 7900 W. Division St., River Forest, IL 60305. Kate Marek, dean. Tel. 708-524-6845, fax 708-524-6657, e-mail gslis@dom.edu, World Wide Web http://www.dom.edu/gslis. Admissions contact: Meagan Sather Tel. 708-524-6983, e-mail msather@dom.edu.

Emporia State University, School of Lib. and Info. Management, Campus Box 4025, 1 Kellogg Circle, Emporia, KS 66801-5415. Gwen Alexander, dean. Tel. 620-341-5203, fax 620-341-5233, e-mail sliminfo@emporia.edu, World Wide Web http://slim.emporia.edu. Admissions contact: Kathie Buckman. Tel. 620-341-5065, e-mail sliminfo@emporia.edu.

Indiana University, School of Informatics and Computing, Lib. and Info. Science, 1320 E. 10 St., LI 011, Bloomington, IN 47405-3907. Robert Schnabel, dean. Tel. 812-855-2018, fax 812-855-6166, e-mail ilsmain@indiana.edu, World Wide Web http://soic.iu.edu. Admissions contact: Rhonda Spencer.

Kent State University, School of Lib. and Info. Science, P.O. Box 5190, Kent, OH 44242-0001. Jeffrey Fruit, interim dir. Tel. 330-672-2782, fax 330-672-7965, e-mail slisinform@kent.edu, World Wide Web http://www.kent.edu/slis. Admissions contact: Cheryl Tennant.

Saint Catherine University, School of Business and Leadership, Educ. and LIS, MLIS Program/Information Management Department, 2004 Randolph Ave. No. 4125, St.

Paul, MN 55105. Deborah S. Grealy, assoc. dean/dir. Tel. 651-690-6802, fax 651-690-8724, e-mail imdept@stkate.edu, World Wide Web https:// www2.stkate.edu/mlis. Admissions contact: Kristina Sande. Tel. 651-690-6507, e-mail kmsande@stkate.edu.

University of Illinois at Urbana-Champaign, Grad. School of Lib. and Info. Science, 501 E. Daniel St., Champaign, IL 61820-6211. Allen Renear, interim dean. Tel. 217-333-3280, fax 217-244-3302, e-mail gslis@illinois.edu, World Wide Web http://www.lis.illinois.edu. Admissions contact: Penny Ames. Tel. 217-333-7197, e-mail pames@illinois.edu.

University of Iowa, Graduate College, School of Lib. and Info. Science, 3087 Main Lib., Iowa City, IA 52242-1420. David Eichmann, dir. Tel. 319-335-5707, fax 319-335-5374, e-mail slis@uiowa.edu, World Wide Web http://slis.grad.uiowa.edu. Admissions contact: Carol Ives. Tel. 319-335-5709, e-mail carol-ives@uiowa.edu.

University of Michigan, School of Info., 4322 North Quad, 105 S. State St., Ann Arbor, MI 48109-1285. Jeffrey Makie-Mason, dean. Tel. 734-763-2285, fax 734-764-2475, e-mail umsi.admissions@umich.edu, World Wide Web http://www.si.umich.edu. Admissions contact: Laura Elgas.

University of Missouri, College of Educ., School of Info. Science and Learning Technologies, 303 Townsend Hall, Columbia, MO 65211. Joi Moore, dir. Tel. 877-747-5868, fax 573-884-0122, e-mail sislt@missouri.edu, World Wide Web http://lis.missouri.edu. Admissions tel. 573-882-4546.

University of Wisconsin–Madison, College of Letters and Sciences, School of Lib. and Info. Studies, 600 N. Park St., Madison, WI 53706. Kristin Eschenfelder, dir. Tel. 608-263-2900, fax 608-263-4849, e-mail uw-slis@slis.wisc.edu, World Wide Web http://www.slis.wisc.edu. Admissions contact: Tanya Cobb. Tel. 608-263-2909, e-mail student-services@slis.wisc.edu.

University of Wisconsin–Milwaukee, School of Info. Studies, P.O. Box 413, Milwaukee, WI 53211. Char Zahrt, assistant dean. Tel. 414-229-4707, fax 414-229-6699, e-mail soisinfo@uwm.edu, World Wide Web http://www4.uwm.edu/sois.

Wayne State University, School of Lib. and Info. Science, 106 Kresge Lib., Detroit, MI 48202. Stephen T. Bajjaly, assoc. dean. Tel. 313-577-1825, fax 313-577-7563, e-mail asklis@wayne.edu, World Wide Web http://www.slis.wayne.edu. Admissions contact: Matthew Fredericks. Tel. 313-577-2446, e-mail mfredericks@wayne.edu.

Southwest: Ariz., Okla., Texas

Texas Woman's University, School of Lib. and Info. Studies, P.O. Box 425438, Denton, TX 76204-5438. Ling Hwey Jeng, dir. Tel. 940-898-2602, fax 940-898-2611, e-mail slis@twu.edu, World Wide Web http://www.twu.edu/slis. Admissions contact: Brenda Mallory. E-mail bmallory@mail.twu.edu.

University of Arizona, College of Social and Behavioral Sciences, School of Info. Resources and Lib. Science, 1515 E. 1 St., Tucson, AZ 85719. P. Bryan Heidorn, dir. Tel. 520-621-3565, fax 520-621-3279, e-mail sirls@email.arizona.edu, World Wide Web http://www.sirls.arizona.edu. Admissions contact: Geraldine Fragoso. Tel. 520-621-5230, e-mail gfragoso@u.arizona.edu.

University of North Texas, College of Info., Dept. of Lib. and Info. Sciences, 1155 Union Circle, No. 311068, Denton, TX 76203-5017. Suliman Hawamdeh, chair. Tel. 940-565-2445, fax 940-369-7600, e-mail lis-chair@unt.edu, World Wide Web http://lis.unt.edu. Admissions contact: Toby Faber. Tel. 940-565-2445, e-mail ci-advising@unt.edu.

University of Oklahoma, School of Lib. and Info. Studies, College of Arts and Sciences, 401 W. Brooks, Norman, OK 73019-6032. Cecelia Brown, dir. Tel. 405-325-3921, fax 405-325-7648, e-mail slisinfo@ou.edu, World Wide Web http://www.ou.edu/cas/slis. Admissions contact: Sarah Connelly.

University of Texas at Austin, School of Info., Suite 5.202, 1616 Guadalupe St., Austin, TX 78701-1213. Andrew Dillon, dean. Tel. 512-471-3821, fax 512-471-3971, e-mail info@ischool.utexas.edu, World Wide Web http://www.ischool.utexas.edu. Admissions contact: Carla Criner. Tel. 512-471-5654, e-mail criner@ischool.utexas.edu.

West: Calif., Colo., Hawaii, Wash.

San José State University, School of Lib. and Info. Science, 1 Washington Sq., San José, CA 95192-0029. Sandy Hirsh, dir. Tel. 408-924-2490, fax 408-924-2476, e-mail sjsu ischool@gmail.com, World Wide Web http://ischool.sjsu.edu. Admissions contact: Linda Main. Tel. 408-924-2494, e-mail lindxain@sjsu.edu.

University of California, Los Angeles, Graduate School of Educ. and Info. Studies, Dept. of Info. Studies, Box 951520, Los Angeles, CA 90095-1520. Jonathan Furner, chair. Tel. 310-825-8799, fax 310-206-3076, e-mail info@gseis.ucla.edu, World Wide Web http://is.gseis.ucla.edu. Admissions contact: Susan Abler. Tel. 310-825-5269, e-mail abler@gseis.ucla.edu.

University of Denver, Morgridge College of Educ., Lib. and Info. Science Program, 1999 E. Evans Ave., Denver, CO 80208-1700. Mary Stansbury, chair. Tel. 303-871-3587, fax 303-871-4456, e-mail mary.stansbury@du.edu, World Wide Web http://www.du.edu/education. Admissions contact: Kristina Coccia. E-mail kristina.coccia@du.edu.

University of Hawaii, College of Natural Sciences, Lib. and Info. Science Program, 2550 McCarthy Mall, Honolulu, HI 96822. Andrew Wertheimer, chair. Tel. 808-956-7321, fax 808-956-5835, e-mail slis@hawaii.edu, World Wide Web http://www.hawaii.edu/lis.

University of Washington, The Information School, 370 Mary Gates Hall, Seattle, WA 98195-2840. Harry Bruce, dean. Tel. 206-685-9937, fax 206-616-3152, e-mail ischool@uw.edu, World Wide Web http://ischool.uw.edu. Admissions contact: Tel. 206-543-1794, e-mail mlis@uw.edu.

Canada

Dalhousie University, School of Info. Management, Kenneth C. Rowe Management Bldg., Halifax, NS B3H 3J5. Louise Spiteri, dir. Tel. 902-494-3656, fax 902-494-2451, e-mail sim@dal.ca, World Wide Web http://www.sim.management.dal.ca. Admissions contact: JoAnn Watson. Tel. 902-494-2471, e-mail joann.watson@dal.ca.

McGill University, School of Info. Studies, 3661 Peel St., Montreal, QC H3A 1X1. France Bouthillier, dir. Tel. 514-398-4204, fax 514-398-7193, e-mail sis@mcgill.ca, World Wide Web http://www.mcgill.ca/sis. Admissions contact: Kathryn Hubbard. Tel. 514-398-4204 ext. 0742, e-mail sis@mcgill.ca.

University of Alberta, School of Lib. and Info. Studies, 3-20 Rutherford S., Edmonton, AB T6G 2J4. Anna Altmann, interim dir. Tel. 780-492-4578, fax 780-492-2430, e-mail slis@ualberta.ca, World Wide Web http://www.slis.ualberta.ca. Admissions contact: Lauren Romaniuk. Tel. 780-492-4140, e-mail slisadmissions@ualberta.ca.

University of British Columbia, School of Lib., Archival, and Info. Studies, Irving K. Barber Learning Centre, Suite 470, 1961 East Mall, Vancouver, BC V6T 1Z1. Caroline Haythornthwaite, dir. Tel. 604-822-2404, fax 604-822-6006, e-mail ischool.info@ubc.ca, World Wide Web http://www.slais.ubc.ca. Admissions contact: Dan Slessor. Tel. 604-822-2461, e-mail slais.ssc@ubc.ca.

Université de Montréal, École de Bibliothéconomie et des Sciences de l'Information, C.P. 6128, Succursale Centre-Ville, Montreal, QC H3C 3J7. Clément Arsenault, dir. Tel. 514-343-6044, fax 514-343-5753, e-mail ebsiinfo@ebsi.umontreal.ca, World Wide Web http://www.ebsi.umontreal.ca. Admissions contact: Alain Tremblay. Tel. 514-343-6044, e-mail alain.tremblay.1@umontreal.ca.

University of Ottawa, School of Info. Studies, Desmarais Bldg., Ottawa, ON K1N 6N5. Tel. 613-562-5130, fax 613-562-5854, e-mail esis@uOttawa.ca, World Wide Web http://www.sis.uottawa.ca. Daniel Paré, interim dir. Admissions contact: Marisa Simard Swangha. Tel. 613-562-5800 ext. 3392, e-mail gradsi@uottawa.ca.

University of Toronto, Faculty of Info., 140 George St., Toronto, ON M5S 3G6. Seamus Ross, dean. Tel. 416-978-3202, fax 416-978-5762, e-mail inquire.ischool@utoronto.ca, World Wide Web http://www.ischool.

utoronto.ca. Admissions contact: Adriana Rossini. Tel. 416-978-8589, e-mail adriana. rossini@utoronto.ca.

University of Western Ontario, Grad. Programs in Lib. and Info. Science, Faculty of Info. and Media Studies, Room 240, North Campus Bldg., London, ON N6A 5B7. Nick Dyer-Whitheford, acting dean; Pam McKenzie, assoc. dean. Tel. 519-661-4017, fax 519-661-3506, e-mail mlisinfo@uwo.ca, World Wide Web http://www.fims.uwo.ca. Admissions contact: Shelley Long.

Library Scholarship Sources

For a more complete list of scholarships, fellowships, and assistantships offered for library study, see *Financial Assistance for Library and Information Studies,* published annually by the American Library Association (ALA). The document is also available on the ALA website at http://www.ala.org/educationcareers/sites/ala.org.educationcareers/files/content/scholarships/right_nav_pods/2014-2015%20FALIS%20Directory.pdf.

American Association of Law Libraries. (1) A varying number of scholarships of varying amounts for graduates of an accredited law school who are degree candidates in an ALA-accredited library school; (2) a varying number of scholarships of varying amounts for library school graduates working on a law degree and non-law graduates enrolled in an ALA-accredited library school; (3) the George A. Strait Minority Stipend for varying numbers of minority librarians working toward a library or law degree; and (4) a varying number of $200 scholarships for law librarians taking courses relating to law librarianship. For information, write to: AALL Scholarship Committee, 105 W. Adams, Suite 3300, Chicago, IL 60603.

American Library Association. (1) The David H. Clift Scholarship of $3,000 for a student who has been admitted to an ALA-accredited library school; (2) the Tom and Roberta Drewes Scholarship of $3,000 for library support staff; (3) the Mary V. Gaver Scholarship of $3,000 for an individual specializing in youth services; (4) the Miriam L. Hornback Scholarship of $3,000 for an ALA or library support staff member; (5) the Christopher J. Hoy/ERT Scholarship of $5,000 for a student who has been admitted to an ALA-accredited library school; (6) the Tony B. Leisner Scholarship of $3,000 for a library support staff member; (7) the Peter Lyman Memorial/Sage Scholarship in New Media of $2,500 for a student admitted to an ALA-accredited library school who will specialize in new media; (8) the Cicely Phippen Marks Scholarship of $1,500 for a student admitted to an ALA-accredited program who will specialize in federal librarianship; and (9) Spectrum Initiative Scholarships of $6,500 for a varying number of minority students admitted to a master's degree program at an ALA-accredited library school. For information, write to: ALA Scholarship Clearinghouse, 50 E. Huron St., Chicago, IL 60611, or see http://www.ala.org/scholarships.

ALA/Association for Library Service to Children. (1) The Bound to Stay Bound Books Scholarship of $7,500 each for four U.S. or Canadian citizens who have been admitted to an ALA-accredited master's or doctoral program, and who will work with children in a library for one year after graduation; and (2) the Frederic G. Melcher Scholarship of $6,000 each for two U.S. or Canadian citizens admitted to an ALA-accredited library school who will work with children in school or public libraries for one year after graduation. For information, write to: ALA Scholarship Clearinghouse, 50 E. Huron St., Chicago, IL 60611, or see http://www.ala.org/scholarships.

ALA/Association of College and Research Libraries Thomson Reuters. The WESS-SEES De Gruyter European Librarianship Study Grant of €2,500 for up to 30 consecutive days of study in Europe. Application is electronic only. For information, e-mail Chase Ollis at collis@ala.org.

ALA/Association of Specialized and Cooperative Library Agencies. Century Scholarship of up to $2,500 for a varying number of disabled U.S. or Canadian citizens admitted to an ALA-accredited library school. For information, write to: ALA Scholarship Clearinghouse, 50 E. Huron St., Chicago, IL 60611, or see http://www.ala.org/scholarships.

ALA/International Relations Committee. The Bogle Pratt International Library Travel Fund grant of $1,000 for a varying number of ALA members to attend a first international conference. For information, write to:

Michael Dowling, ALA/IRC, 50 E. Huron St., Chicago, IL 60611.

ALA/Library and Information Technology Association. (1) The LITA/Christian Larew Memorial Scholarship of $3,000 for a U.S. or Canadian citizen admitted to an ALA-accredited library school; (2) the LITA/OCLC Minority Scholarship in Library and Information Technology of $3,000 and (3) the LITA/LSSI Minority Scholarship of $2,500, each for a minority student admitted to an ALA-accredited program. For information, write to: ALA Scholarship Clearinghouse, 50 E. Huron St., Chicago, IL 60611, or see http://www.ala.org/scholarships.

ALA/Public Library Association. The Demco New Leaders Travel Grant Study Award of up to $1,500 for a varying number of PLA members with MLS degrees and five years or less experience. For information, write to: PLA Awards Program, ALA/PLA, 50 E. Huron St., Chicago, IL 60611.

American-Scandinavian Foundation. Fellowships and grants for 25 to 30 students, in amounts from $5,000 to $23,000, for advanced study in Denmark, Finland, Iceland, Norway, or Sweden. For information, write to: Fellowships and Grants, American-Scandinavian Foundation, 58 Park Ave., New York, NY 10026, or see http://www.amscan. org/fellowships_grants.html.

Association for Library and Information Science Education (ALISE). A varying number of research grants of up to $2,500 each for members of ALISE. For information, write to: ALISE, 2150 N.W. 107th St., Suite 205, Seattle, WA 98133.

Association of Bookmobile and Outreach Services (ABOS). (1) The Bernard Vavrek Scholarship of $1,000 for a student with a grade-point average of 3.0 or better admitted to an ALA-accredited program and interested in becoming an outreach/bookmobile librarian; (2) the John Philip Award of $300 to recognize outstanding contributions and leadership by an individual in bookmobile and outreach services; (3) the Carol Hole Conference Attendance Travel Grant of $500 for a public librarian working in outreach or bookmobile services. For information, write to President, ABOS, c/o AMIGOS Library Services, 3610 Barrett Office Drive, Suite 216, Ballwin, MO 63021.

Association of Jewish Libraries. The AJL Scholarship Fund offers up to two scholarships of $1,000 for MLS students who plan to work as Judaica librarians. For information, write to: Tina Weiss, AJL Scholarship Committee, Hebrew Union College, 1 W. 4th St., New York, NY 10012.

Association of Seventh-Day Adventist Librarians. The D. Glenn Hilts Scholarship of $1,200 for a member of the Seventh-Day Adventist Church in a graduate library program. For information, write to: Lori Curtis, Association of Seventh-Day Adventist Librarians, Loma Linda University, 11072 Anderson St., Loma Linda, CA 92350.

Beta Phi Mu. (1) The Sarah Rebecca Reed Scholarship of $2,000 for a person accepted in an ALA-accredited library program; (2) the Frank B. Sessa Scholarship of $1,500 for a Beta Phi Mu member for continuing education; (3) the Harold Lancour Scholarship of $1,750 for study in a foreign country relating to the applicant's work or schooling; (4) the Blanche E. Woolls Scholarship for School Library Media Service of $2,250 for a person accepted in an ALA-accredited library program; and (5) the Eugene Garfield Doctoral Dissertation Scholarship of $3,000 for a person who has approval of a dissertation topic. For information, write to Isabel Gray, Program Director, Beta Phi Mu, c/o Drexel University College of Computing and Informatics (CCI), 3141 Chestnut St., Philadelphia, PA 19104.

Canadian Association of Law Libraries. The Diana M. Priestly Scholarship of $2,500 for a student enrolled in an approved Canadian law school or accredited Canadian library school. For information, write to: Ann Marie Melvie, Librarian, Saskatchewan Court of Appeal, 2425 Victoria Ave., Regina, SK S4P 4W6.

Canadian Federation of University Women. (1) The Alice E. Wilson Award of $6,000 for five mature students returning to graduate studies in any field, with special consideration given to those returning to study after at least three years; (2) the Margaret McWilliams Pre-Doctoral Fellowship of $13,000 for a female student who has completed at least one full year as a full-time student in doctoral-level studies; (3) the Marion Elder Grant Fellowship of $11,000 for a full-time student at any level of a doctoral program; (4) the CFUW Memorial Fellowship of $10,000 for a student who is currently enrolled in a master's program in science, mathematics, or engineering in Canada or abroad; (5) the Beverly Jackson Fellowship of $2,000 for a student over the age of 35 at the time of application who is enrolled in graduate studies at an Ontario university; (6) the 1989 Ecole Polytechnique Commemorative Award of $7,000 for graduate studies in any field; (7) the Bourse Georgette LeMoyne award of $7,000 for graduate study in any field at a Canadian university (the candidate must be studying in French); (8) the Margaret Dale Philp Biennial Award of $3,000 for studies in the humanities or social sciences; and (9) the Canadian Home Economics Association Fellowship of $6,000 for a student enrolled in a postgraduate program in Canada. For information, write to: Fellowships Program Manager, Canadian Federation of University Women, 251 Bank St., Suite 305, Ottawa, ON K2P 1X3, Canada, or visit http://www. cfuw.org/en-ca/fellowships/fellowships andawards.aspx.

Canadian Library Association. (1) The CLA Dafoe Scholarship of $5,000 and (2) the H. W. Wilson Scholarship of $2,000, each given to a Canadian citizen or landed immigrant to attend an accredited Canadian library school; and (3) the Library Research and Development Grant of $1,000 for a member of the Canadian Library Association, in support of theoretical and applied research in library and information science. For information, write to: CLA Membership Services Department, Scholarship Committee, 1150 Morrison Drive, Suite 400, Ottawa, ON K2H 8S9, Canada.

Chinese American Librarians Association. (1) The Sheila Suen Lai Scholarship and the CALA Scholarship of Library and Information Science, each $500, to a Chinese descendant who has been accepted in an ALA-accredited program. For information, write to: MengXiong Liu, Clark Library, San José State University, 1 Washington Sq., San José, CA 95192-0028.

Church and Synagogue Library Association. The Muriel Fuller Memorial Scholarship of $200 (including texts) for a correspondence course offered by the association. For infor-

mation, write to: CSLA, 10157 S.W. Barbur Blvd., No. 102C, Portland, OR 97219-5957.

Council on Library and Information Resources. The Rovelstad Scholarship in International Librarianship, to enable a student enrolled in an accredited LIS program to attend the IFLA Annual Conference. For more information, write to: Rovelstad Scholarship, Council on Library and Information Resources, 1707 L St. N.W., Suite 650, Washington, DC 20036.

Massachusetts Black Librarians' Network. Two scholarships of at least $500 and $1,000 for minority students entering an ALA-accredited master's program in library science with no more than 12 semester hours completed toward a degree. For information, write to: Pearl Mosley, Chair, Massachusetts Black Librarians' Network, 17 Beech Glen St., Roxbury, MA 02119.

Medical Library Association. (1) The Cunningham Memorial International Fellowship of $3,500 for each of two health sciences librarians from countries other than the United States and Canada; (2) a scholarship of $5,000 for a person entering an ALA-accredited library program, with no more than one-half of the program yet to be completed; (3) a scholarship of $5,000 for a minority student studying health sciences librarianship; (4) a varying number of Research, Development, and Demonstration Project Grants of $100 to $1,000 for U.S. or Canadian citizens, preferably MLA members; (5) the Thomson Reuters/MLA Doctoral Fellowship of $2,000 for doctoral work in medical librarianship or information science; (6) the Rittenhouse Award of $500 for a student enrolled in an ALA-accredited library program or a recent graduate working as a trainee in a library internship program; and (7) the Librarians without Borders Ursula Poland International Scholarship of $5,000 for a librarian working in a U.S. or Canadian health sciences library. For information, write to: MLA Grants and Scholarships, Medical Library Association, 65 E. Wacker Place, Suite 1900, Chicago, IL 60601-7298.

Mountain Plains Library Association. A varying number of grants of up to $600 for applicants who are members of the association and have been for the preceding two years.

For information, write to: Judy Zelenski, Interim Executive Secretary, MPLA, 14293 W. Center Drive, Lakewood, SD 80228.

Society of American Archivists. (1) The F. Gerald Ham Scholarship of $7,500 for up to two graduate students in archival education at a U.S. university that meets the society's criteria for graduate education; (2) the Mosaic Scholarship of $5,000 for up to two U.S. or Canadian minority students enrolled in a graduate program in archival administration; (3) the Josephine Foreman Scholarship of $10,000 for a U.S. citizen or permanent resident who is a minority graduate student enrolled in a program in archival administration; (4) the Oliver Wendell Holmes Travel Award to enable foreign students involved in archival training in the United States or Canada to attend the SAA Annual Meeting; (5) the Donald Peterson Student Travel Award of up to $1,000 to enable graduate students or recent graduates to attend the meeting; and (6) the Harold T. Pinkett Minority Student Awards to enable minority students or graduate students to attend the meeting. For details, write to: Teresa Brinati, Society of American Archivists, 17 N. State St., Suite 1425, Chicago, IL 60607, or see http://www2.archivists.org/governance/handbook/section12.

Special Libraries Association. (1) Three $6,000 scholarships for students interested in special-library work; (2) the Plenum Scholarship of $1,000 and (3) the ISI Scholarship of $1,000, each also for students interested in special-library work; (4) the Affirmative Action Scholarship of $6,000 for a minority student interested in special-library work; and (5) the Pharmaceutical Division Stipend Award of $1,200 for a student with an undergraduate degree in chemistry, life sciences, or pharmacy entering or enrolled in an ALA-accredited program. For information on the first four scholarships, write to: Scholarship Committee, Special Libraries Association, 331 S. Patrick St., Alexandria, VA 22314-3501. For information on the Pharmaceutical Division Stipend, write to: Susan E. Katz, Awards Chair, Knoll Pharmaceuticals Science Information Center, 30 N. Jefferson St., Whippany, NJ 07981.

Library Scholarship and Award Recipients, 2015

Compiled by the staff of the *Library and Book Trade Almanac*

Scholarships and awards are listed by organization.

American Association of Law Libraries (AALL)

AALL and Thomson Reuters/George A. Strait Minority Scholarship. *Winners:* Danyahel Norris, Sarah Reis, Mahum Saulat Shere, Judith Simms.

AALL Distinguished Lectureship. *Winner:* To be announced.

AALL Grants. To enable law librarians to participate in professional educational opportunities at the AALL Annual Meeting or to engage in original research on topics important to law librarianship. *Winners:* Susan Azyndar, Jennifer Baker, Erik Beck, Samantha Cabo, Susan Catterall, Diane D'Angelo, Alice Davidson, Alison Downey, Lusiella Fazzino, Shawn Friend, Dustin Green, Carolyn Hasselmann, David Isom, Amelia Landenberger, Joseph Lawson, Tameca Levermore, Kimberly Mattioli, William Mills, Dianne Oster, Rena Stoeber, Fang Wang.

AALL Marcia J. Koslov Scholarship. To an AALL member to finance conference or seminar attendance. *Winner:* Not awarded in 2015.

AALL Public Access to Government Information Award. *Winner:* Mary Alice Baish, Government Publishing Office.

AALL Spectrum Article of the Year Award. *Sponsor:* Wolters Kluwer; *Winners:* Christine Bowersox and Kristen M. Hallows for "Dialectic of Transformation: The Shaping of a Name" (April 2014).

AALL/Wolters Kluwer Law and Business Research Grant. *Winners:* To be announced.

Joseph L. Andrews Legal Literature Award. *Winners:* Mary Sarah Bilder, Charles Donahue, Jr., Ann Jordan Laeuchli, Sharon Hamby O'Connor.

Emerging Leader Award. To recognize newer members who have made significant contributions to AALL and/or to the profession and have demonstrated the potential for leadership and continuing service. *Winners:*

Nicole P. Dyszlewski, Emily R. Florio, Jane M. Larrington.

Marian Gould Gallagher Distinguished Service Award. To recognize extended and sustained service to law librarianship. *Winners:* Timothy L. Coggins, Penny A. Hazelton, Sarah (Sally) G. Holterhoff, Sarah (Sally) K. Wiant, Timothy L. Coggins, Penny A. Hazelton, Sarah (Sally) G. Holterhoff, Sarah (Sally) K. Wiant.

Innovations in Technology Award. To recognize an AALL member, special interest section, chapter, or library for innovative use of technology in the development and creation of an application or resource for law librarians or legal professionals. *Winner:* Maine State Law and Legislative Reference Library.

Law Library Advocate Award. To a law library supporter in recognition of his or her substantial contribution toward the advancement and improvement of a state, court, or county law library's service or visibility. *Winner:* To be announced.

Law Library Journal Article of the Year. *Winner:* Joseph D. Lawson, "What About the Majority? Considering the Legal Research Practices of Solo and Small Firm Attorneys."

Law Library Publications Award. *Winners:* (nonprint division) Avery Le for "The University of Florida Lawton Chiles Legal Information Center Annual Report Timeline 2013/2014"; (print) Laurel Davis and Lily Olson for "The Law in Postcards."

LexisNexis/John R. Johnson Memorial Scholarships. *Winners:* (library degree for law school graduates) Yael Bronner, Christine Mathias, Felicity Murphy, Jessica Lauren Pierucci; (library degree for those without a law degree) Lewis Giles, Janet Kearney, Elliot Kuecker, Laura Michelle Summers; (law degree for those with a library degree) Carolyn Child; (non-law degree for those with a library degree) Thomas Sneed.

LexisNexis Research Fund Grants. *Winners:* Amy Taylor for "Internet Sources in U.S. Supreme Court Records and Briefs: A Citation Analysis"; Kristina J. Alayan and Jane Bahnson for "An Empirical Study Comparing LLM Comprehension Following Live and Recorded Lectures"; Stacy Etheredge for "The Impact of the Lewis v. Casey 'Actual Injury' Requirement on Litigation Involving Prison and Jail Law Libraries"; Susan David deMaine and Benjamin J. Keele for "Access to the Justices? An Analysis on Restrictions to the Papers of the Supreme Court Justices."

Minority Leadership Development Award. *Winner:* Daniella Mia Lee-Garcia, Ninth Circuit Library, United States Court of Appeals.

Robert L. Oakley Advocacy Award. To recognize an AALL member who has been an outstanding advocate and has contributed significantly to the AALL policy agenda at the federal, state, local, or international level. *Winner:* 2012 California UELMA Advocacy Team: Michele M. Finerty, Retired, Pacific McGeorge School of Law, Sacramento, CA, Judy C. Janes, Director and Lecturer in Law, UC Davis Mabie Law Library, Davis, CA, David L. McFadden, Senior Reference Librarian, Leigh H. Taylor Law Library, Southwestern Law School, Los Angeles, CA, and Lawrence R. (Larry) Meyer, Executive Director, Law Library for San Bernardino County, San Bernardino, CA.

American Library Association (ALA)

ABC-CLIO/Greenwood Award for Best Book in Library Literature ($5,000). See "Literary Prizes, 2015" in Part 5.

ALA Excellence in Library Programming Award ($5,000). For a cultural/thematic library program or program series that engages the community in planning, sponsorship, and/or active participation, addresses an identified community need, and has a measurable impact. *Donor:* ALA Cultural Communities Fund. *Winners:* Oklahoma State University Library and its community partners for their "Science Café at OSU: Po-

tential Impacts of Oil and Gas Exploration" programs.

ALA Honorary Membership. To recognize outstanding contributions of lasting importance to libraries and librarianship. *Honoree (2014):* Patricia Glass Schuman.

ALA/Information Today, Inc. Library of the Future Award ($1,500). For a library, consortium, group of librarians, or support organization for innovative planning for, applications of, or development of patron training programs about information technology in a library setting. *Donors:* Information Today, Inc., and IIDA. *Winner:* Landis Intermediate School, Vineland, New Jersey for Sally Goode's, Landis media specialist, successful implementation of a model that taught teachers how to incorporate new technologies into the classroom.

Hugh C. Atkinson Memorial Award. For outstanding achievement (including risk taking) by academic librarians that has contributed significantly to improvements in library automation, management, and/or development or research. *Offered by:* ACRL, ALCTS, LITA, and LLAMA. *Winner:* Brian Schottlaender, Librarian at the University of California–San Diego, Audrey Geisel University.

Carroll Preston Baber Research Grant (up to $3,000). For innovative research that could lead to an improvement in library services to any specified group(s) of people. *Donor:* Eric R. Baber. *Winners:* Sharon Q. Yang, Ma Lei Hsieh, and Susan McManimon for "Experimenting with I-Learn Model and Its Impact on Students' Learning."

Beta Phi Mu Award ($1,000). For distinguished service in library education. *Donor:* Beta Phi Mu International Library and Information Science Honorary Society. *Winner:* Beverly P. Lynch, Professor, Department of Information Studies, University of California, Los Angeles (UCLA).

Bogle-Pratt International Library Travel Fund Award ($1,000). To ALA members to attend their first international conference. *Donors:* Bogle Memorial Fund and Pratt Institute School of Information and Library Science. *Winner:* To be announced.

W. Y. Boyd Literary Award. See "Literary Prizes, 2015" in Part 5.

David H. Clift Scholarship ($3,000). To worthy U.S. or Canadian citizens enrolled in an ALA-accredited program toward an MLS degree. *Winner:* Jade M. Finlinson.

Melvil Dewey Medal. To an individual or group for recent creative professional achievement in library management, training, cataloging and classification, and the tools and techniques of librarianship. *Donor:* OCLC. *Winner:* Hwa-Wei Lee, former chief of the Asian Division of the Library of Congress.

Tom and Roberta Drewes Scholarship ($3,000). To a library support staff member pursuing a master's degree in an ALA-accredited program. *Donor:* Quality Books. *Winner:* Timothy Ryan Dewysockie.

EBSCO/ALA Conference Sponsorship Award ($1,000). To enable librarians to attend the ALA Annual Conference. *Donor:* EBSCO. *Winners:* Catherine Damiani, Jennifer Evans, Lisa Horton, Alison King, Breanne Kirsch, Casey A. McCoy, Tiffany Reitz.

Equality Award ($1,000). To an individual or group for an outstanding contribution that promotes equality in the library profession. *Donor:* Rowman & Littlefield. *Winner:* Camila Alire.

Elizabeth Futas Catalyst for Change Award ($1,000). A biennial award to recognize a librarian who invests time and talent to make positive change in the profession of librarianship. *Donor:* Elizabeth Futas Memorial Fund. *Winner:* To be announced.

Loleta D. Fyan Public Library Research Grant (up to $5,000). For projects in public library development. *Donor:* Fyan Estate. *Winner:* To be announced.

Gale Cengage Learning Financial Development Award ($2,500). To a library organization for a financial development project to secure new funding resources for a public or academic library. *Donor:* Gale Cengage Learning. *Winner:* James V. Brown Library (Pennsylvania) for Own a Day, an annual fundraising campaign.

Mary V. Gaver Scholarship ($3,000). To a student pursuing an MLS degree and specializing in youth services. *Winner:* Reid Craig.

Ken Haycock Award for Promoting Librarianship ($1,000). For significant contribution to public recognition and appreciation of librarianship through professional performance, teaching, or writing. *Winner:* Nancy Kranich, Special Projects Librarian and Lecturer, Rutgers University.

Miriam L. Hornback Scholarship ($3,000). To an ALA or library support staff person pursuing a master's degree in library science. *Winner:* Marla Jo Black.

Paul Howard Award for Courage ($1,000). To a librarian, library board, library group, or an individual for exhibiting unusual courage for the benefit of library programs or services. *Donor:* Paul Howard Memorial Fund. *Winner:* Not awarded in 2015.

John Ames Humphry/OCLC/Forest Press Award ($1,000). To one or more individuals for significant contributions to international librarianship. *Donor:* OCLC/Forest Press. *Winner:* Jane Kinney Meyers.

Tony B. Leisner Scholarship ($3,000). To a library support staff member pursuing a master's degree. *Donor:* Tony B. Leisner. *Winner:* Rachel Eaton.

Joseph W. Lippincott Award ($1,000). For distinguished service to the library profession. *Donor:* Joseph W. Lippincott III. *Winner:* James G. (Jim) Neal.

Peter Lyman Memorial/Sage Scholarship in New Media. To support a student seeking an MLS degree in an ALA-accredited program and pursing a specialty in new media. *Donor:* Sage Publications. *Winner:* Justin Matthew Resti.

James Madison Award. To recognize efforts to promote government openness. *Winner:* Senator James Cornyn (Texas).

Marshall Cavendish Scholarship ($3,000). To a worthy U.S. or Canadian citizen to begin an MLS degree in an ALA-accredited program. *Winner:* Award discontinued.

Schneider Family Book Awards. See "Literary Prizes, 2015" in Part 5.

Scholastic Library Publishing Award ($1,000). To a librarian whose "unusual contributions to the stimulation and guidance of reading by children and young people exemplifies achievement in the profession." *Sponsor:* Scholastic Library Publishing. *Winner:* Judith Wines, director at the Ravena-Coeymans-Selkirk (RCS) Community Library, Ravena, New York.

Scholastic Library Publishing National Library Week Grant ($3,000). For the best public awareness campaign in support of National

Library Week. *Donor:* Scholastic Library Publishing. *Winner:* To be announced.

Lemony Snicket Prize for Noble Librarians Faced with Adversity ($3,000 plus a $1,000 travel stipend to enable attendance at the ALA Annual Conference). To honor a librarian who has faced adversity with integrity and dignity intact. *Sponsor:* Lemony Snicket (author Daniel Handler). *Winner:* Scott Bonner, Director of the Ferguson Public Library, Ferguson, Missouri.

Spectrum Doctoral Fellowships. To provide full tuition support and stipends to minority U.S. and Canadian LIS doctoral students. *Donor:* Institute of Museum and Library Services. *Winners:* Not awarded in 2015.

Spectrum Initiative Scholarships ($5,000). To minority students admitted to ALA-accredited library schools. *Donors:* ALA and Institute of Museum and Library Services. *Winners:* To be announced.

Sullivan Award for Public Library Administrators Supporting Services to Children. To a library supervisor/administrator who has shown exceptional understanding and support of public library services to children. *Donor:* Peggy Sullivan. *Winner:* Ann Burlingame, Deputy Director of Wake County Public Libraries, Raleigh, North Carolina.

H. W. Wilson Library Staff Development Grant ($3,500). To a library organization for a program to further its staff development goals and objectives. *Donor:* H. W. Wilson Company. *Winner:* Ohio Library Support Staff Institute (OLSSI).

Women's National Book Association/Ann Heidbreder Eastman Grant ($500). To support library association professional development in a state in which WNBA has a chapter. *Winner:* Award suspended.

World Book/ALA Information Literacy Goal Awards ($5,000). To promote exemplary information literacy programs in public and school libraries. *Donor:* World Book. *Winners:* Award suspended.

American Association of School Librarians (AASL)

AASL/ABC-CLIO Leadership Grant (up to $1,750). To AASL affiliates for planning and implementing leadership programs at state, regional, or local levels. *Donor:* ABC-CLIO. *Winner:* Advocacy for School Libraries Special Interest Group in New Mexico.

AASL/Baker & Taylor Distinguished Service Award ($3,000). For outstanding contributions to librarianship and school library development. *Donor:* Baker & Taylor. *Winner:* Ann M. Martin.

AASL Collaborative School Library Award ($2,500). For expanding the role of the library in elementary and/or secondary school education. *Donor:* Upstart. *Winners:* Brenda Boyer, Alison Kocis-Westgate, and Josh Chambers, Kutztown (Pennsylvania) Area High School.Stephanie Meurer, Jennifer Milstead, and Erin Kelley, Sierra Middle School (Colorado).

AASL Crystal Apple Award. To an individual, individuals, or group for a significant impact on school libraries and students. *Winner:* Terri Grief.

AASL Distinguished School Administrators Award ($2,000). For expanding the role of the library in elementary and/or secondary school education. *Donor:* ProQuest. *Winner:* Lenny Santamaria, Principal, Myra S. Barnes Intermediate School 24 (New York).

AASL/Frances Henne Award ($1,250). To a school library media specialist with five or fewer years in the profession to attend an AASL regional conference or ALA Annual Conference for the first time. *Donor:* ABC-CLIO. *Winner:* Diana Rendina, Stewart Middle Magnet School, Tampa, Florida.

AASL Innovative Reading Grant ($2,500). To support the planning and implementation of an innovative program for children that motivates and encourages reading, especially with struggling readers. *Sponsor:* Capstone. *Winner:* Clarice Marchena, Dos Puentes Elementary School, Manhattan, New York.

AASL Research Grants (up to $2,500). *Sponsor:* Capstone. *Winners:* Award suspended.

Information Technology Pathfinder Award. To library media specialists for innovative approaches to microcomputer applications in the school library media center ($1,000 to the specialist, $500 to the library). *Donor:* Follett Software Company. *Winner:* Carolyn Kirio, Kapolei Middle School, Kapolei, Hawaii.

Intellectual Freedom Award ($2,000 plus $1,000 to the media center of the recipient's choice). To a school library media specialist and AASL member who has upheld the principles of intellectual freedom. *Donor:* ProQuest. *Winner:* Not awarded in 2015.

National School Library Media Program of the Year Award ($10,000). For excellence and innovation in outstanding library media programs. *Donor:* Follett Library Resources. *Winners:* To be announced.

Association for Library Collections and Technical Services (ALCTS)

ALCTS/LBI George Cunha and Susan Swartzburg Preservation Award ($1,250). To recognize cooperative preservation projects and/or individuals or groups that foster collaboration for preservation goals. *Sponsor:* Library Binding Institute. *Winner:* Laura Word.

ALCTS Presidential Citations for Outstanding Service. *Winners:* Lenore England, Vicki Sipe, Susan Wynne.

Hugh C. Atkinson Memorial Award. *See under* American Library Association.

Ross Atkinson Lifetime Achievement Award ($3,000). To recognize the contribution of an ALCTS member and library leader who has demonstrated exceptional service to ALCTS and its areas of interest. *Donor:* EBSCO. *Winner:* Carlen Ruschoff.

Paul Banks and Carolyn Harris Preservation Award ($1,500). To recognize the contribution of a professional preservation specialist who has been active in the field of preservation and/or conservation for library and/or archival materials. *Donor:* Preservation Technologies. *Winner:* Jeanne Drewes.

Blackwell's Scholarship Award. See Outstanding Publication Award.

Ingram Coutts Award for Innovation in Electronic Resources Management ($2,000). To recognize significant and innovative contributions to electronic collections management and development practice. *Donor:* Coutts Information Services. *Winners:* Jill Emery and Graham Stone.

First Step Award (Wiley Professional Development Grant) ($1,500). To enable librarians new to the serials field to attend the ALA Annual Conference. *Donor:* John Wiley & Sons. *Winner:* Emily Cable.

Harrassowitz Award for Leadership in Library Acquisitions ($1,500). For significant contributions by an outstanding leader in the field of library acquisitions. *Donor:* Harrassowitz. *Winner:* Michale Levine-Clark.

Margaret Mann Citation (includes $2,000 scholarship award to the U.S. or Canadian library school of the winner's choice). To a cataloger or classifier for achievement in the areas of cataloging or classification. *Donor:* Online Computer Library Center (OCLC). *Winner:* Magda El-Sherbini.

Outstanding Collaboration Citation. For outstanding collaborative problem-solving efforts in the areas of acquisition, access, management, preservation, or archiving of library materials. *Winner:* Library of Congress U.S. ISSN Center and ProQuest Metadata Integration & Cataloging Section.

Outstanding Publication Award (formerly the Blackwell's Scholarship Award) ($250). To honor the year's outstanding monograph, article, or original paper in the field of acquisitions, collection development, and related areas of resource development in libraries. *Winner:* Robert Maxwell for his monograph "Maxwell's Handbook for RDA: Explaining and Illustrating RDA: Resource Description and Access using MARC 21" (Chicago: ALA Editions, 2014).

Esther J. Piercy Award ($1,500). To a librarian with no more than ten years' experience for contributions and leadership in the field of library collections and technical services. *Donor:* YBP Library Services. *Winner:* Myung-Ja (MJ) Han.

Edward Swanson Memorial Best of *LRTS* Award. To the author(s) of the year's best paper published in the division's official journal. *Winner:* Christine N. Turner for "E-Resource Acquisitions in Academic Library Consortia."

Ulrich's Serials Librarianship Award ($1,500). For distinguished contributions to serials librarianship. *Sponsor:* ProQuest. *Winner:* Maria Collins Rebecca Culbertson.

Association for Library Service to Children (ALSC)

ALSC/Baker & Taylor Summer Reading Program Grant ($3,000). For implementation of an outstanding public library summer reading program for children. *Donor:* Baker &

Taylor. *Winner:* Madison County Public Libraries (MCPL), Marshall, North Carolina.

ALSC/Booklist/YALSA Odyssey Award. To the producer of the best audiobook for children and/or young adults available in English in the United States. See Odyssey Award in "Literary Prizes, 2015" in Part 5.

ALSC/Candlewick Press "Light the Way: Library Outreach to the Underserved" Grant ($3,000). To a library conducting exemplary outreach to underserved populations. *Donor:* Candlewick Press. *Winner:* To be announced in January 2016.

May Hill Arbuthnot Honor Lectureship. To an author, critic, librarian, historian, or teacher of children's literature who prepares a paper considered to be a significant contribution to the field of children's literature. *Winner:* Author and illustrator Brian Selznick.

Mildred L. Batchelder Award. See "Literary Prizes, 2015" in Part 5.

Louise Seaman Bechtel Fellowship ($4,000). For librarians with 12 or more years of professional-level work in children's library collections, to read and study at Baldwin Library, University of Florida, Gainesville. *Donor:* Bechtel Fund. *Winners:* Bridgid Mangan, Wendy Stephens.

Pura Belpré Award. See "Literary Prizes, 2015" in Part 5.

Bookapalooza Program Awards. To provide three libraries with a collection of materials that will help transform their collection. *Winners:* To be announced in March 2016.

Bound to Stay Bound Books Scholarships ($7,000). For men and women who intend to pursue an MLS or other advanced degree and who plan to work in the area of library service to children. *Donor:* Bound to Stay Bound Books. *Winners:* Marta Denise Brandes-Meisener, Blanca Rosales Ginsberg, Lauren Gray, Jennifer Matsu.

Randolph Caldecott Medal. See "Literary Prizes, 2015" in Part 5.

Andrew Carnegie Medal for Excellence in Children's Video. To the U.S. producer of the most distinguished video for children in the previous year. *Sponsor:* Carnegie Corporation of New York. *Winners:* Paul R. Gagne and Melissa Reilly Ellard, for "Me . . . Jane" (Weston Woods).

Carnegie-Whitney Awards (up to $5,000). For the preparation of print or electronic reading lists, indexes, or other guides to library resources that promote reading or the use of library resources at any type of library. *Donors:* James Lyman Whitney and Andrew Carnegie Funds. *Winners:* Suzan Alteri and George Smathers for "Women Authored Science Books for Children 1790–1890: An Annotated Bibliography"; Dawn Amsberry and Binky Lush for "Web Accessibility Resources for Libraries"; Stacy Creel for "The Importance of Play: A Selected Bibliography of Resources Related to Learning Through Play"; Monica Dombrowski for "Gail's Toolkit"; Mary Grace Flaherty for "Read & Reach: A Resource for Promoting Physical Activity in Storytime Programs"; Lauren Hays for "An Annotated Bibliography of Analog Games and Learning"; Ladsilava Khailova for "The Stories We Share: Annotated Bibliography of K–12 Book Titles on the Experience of Immigrant Children in the United States"; Rebecca Marrall for "Women of Color in Speculative Fiction: An Annotated Bibliography of Authors"; Fatima Perkins for "Passport to Aging: Celebrate Global Perspectives"; Edward Schneider for "The DeSSCat: The First Integrated Bibliotherapy Database for Mental Health Professionals, Librarians, and the Public"; Judit Ward for "R4R: Reading for Recovery."

Century Scholarship ($2,500). For a library school student or students with disabilities admitted to an ALA-accredited library school. *Winner:* Not awarded in 2015.

Distinguished Service Award ($1,000). To recognize significant contributions to, and an impact on, library services to children and/or ALSC. *Winner:* To be announced in March 2016To be announced in March 2016.

Theodor Seuss Geisel Award. See "Literary Prizes, 2015" in Part 5.

Maureen Hayes Author/Illustrator Visit Award (up to $4,000). For an honorarium and travel expenses to make possible a library talk to children by a nationally known author/illustrator. *Sponsor:* Simon & Schuster Children's Publishing. *Winner:* Keene (New Hampshire) Public Library. *Winner:* Thibodaux (LA) Public Library

Frederic G. Melcher Scholarships ($6,000). To two students entering the field of library service to children for graduate work in an

ALA-accredited program. *Winners:* Elizabeth Pearce, Melody Tsz-way Leung.

Estela and Raúl Mora Award ($1,000 and plaque). For exemplary programs celebrating Día de los Niños/Día de los Libros. *Winner:* To be announced.

John Newbery Medal. See "Literary Prizes, 2015" in Part 5.

Penguin Young Readers Group Awards ($600). To children's librarians in school or public libraries with ten or fewer years of experience to attend the ALA Annual Conference. *Donor:* Penguin Young Readers Group. *Winners:* Elizabeth Esposito, Kristel Sexton, Kelly Shea, Caryn Wilson.

Robert F. Sibert Medal. See "Literary Prizes, 2015" in Part 5.

Laura Ingalls Wilder Medal. See "Literary Prizes, 2015" in Part 5.

Association of College and Research Libraries (ACRL)

ACRL Academic or Research Librarian of the Year Award ($5,000). For outstanding contribution to academic and research librarianship and library development. *Donor:* YBP Library Services. *Winner:* Robert A. Seal, University Libraries at Loyola University, Chicago, IL.

ACRL/CLS ProQuest Innovation in College Librarianship Award ($3,000). To academic librarians who show a capacity for innovation in the areas of programs, services, and operations; or creating innovations for library colleagues that facilitate their ability to better serve the library's community. *Winners:* Melinda Beland, Angie Cox, Melissa Gevaert, Anna Hollingsworth, Linda McLaury, University of Northern Iowa Rod Library.

ACRL/DLS Routledge Distance Learning Librarian Conference Sponsorship Award ($1,200). To an ACRL member working in distance-learning librarianship in higher education. *Sponsor:* Routledge/Taylor & Francis. *Winner:* Christina Sibley, Arizona Western College.

ACRL/CJCLS Library Resources Leadership Award. *Winner:* Mary Ann Sheble, Oakland Community College Libraries.

ACRL/EBSS Distinguished Education and Behavioral Sciences Librarian Award ($2,500).

To an academic librarian who has made an outstanding contribution as an education and/or behavioral sciences librarian through accomplishments and service to the profession. *Donor:* John Wiley & Sons. *Winner:* Not awarded in 2015.

ACRL/STS Innovation in Science and Technology Librarianship Award ($3,000). To recognize creative, innovative approaches to solving problems or improving products and services in science and technology librarianship. *Sponsor:* IEEE. *Winner:* To be announced.

ACRL/STS Oberly Award for Bibliography in the Agricultural or Natural Sciences. Awarded biennially for the best English-language bibliography in the field of agriculture or a related science in the preceding two-year period. *Donor:* Eunice Rockwood Oberly. *Winner:* James B. Beard, Harriet J. Beard, James C. Beard for "Turfgrass History and Literature: Lawns, Sports, and Golf."

ACRL/WGSS Award for Career Achievement in Women and Gender Studies Librarianship. *Winner:* Connie Phelps, Services Department, University of New Orleans.

ACRL/WGSS Award for Significant Achievement in Women and Gender Studies Librarianship. *Winner:* Nancy Goebel, Augustana Campus Library, University of Alberta.

Hugh C. Atkinson Memorial Award. *See under* American Library Association.

Coutts Nijhoff International West European Specialist Study Grant. See WESS-SEES De Gruyter European Librarianship Study Grant.

Miriam Dudley Instruction Librarian Award. For a contribution to the advancement of bibliographic instruction in a college or research institution. *Winner:* Lisa Janicke Hinchliffe, University of Illinois, Urbana-Champaign.

Excellence in Academic Libraries Awards ($3,000). To recognize outstanding college and university libraries. *Donor:* YBP Library Services. *Winners:* (university) Purdue University; (college) Amherst College; (community college) Santa Fe College.

Instruction Section Innovation Award ($3,000). To librarians or project teams in recognition of a project that demonstrates creative, innovative, or unique approaches to information literacy instruction or programming. *Donor:*

ProQuest. *Winners:* Michelle Keba, Michael Schofield, Jamie Segno, Nova Southeastern University.

Marta Lange/Sage-CQ Press Award. To recognize an academic or law librarian for contributions to bibliography and information service in law or political science. *Donor:* Sage-CQ Press. *Winner:* Not awarded in 2015.

Katharine Kyes Leab and Daniel J. Leab American Book Prices Current Exhibition Catalog Awards (citations). For the best catalogs published by American or Canadian institutions in conjunction with exhibitions of books and/or manuscripts. *Sponsor:* Leab Endowment. *Winners:* (electronic exhibitions) Eda Kuhn Loeb Music Library, Harvard University; (expensive) The Grolier Club;(moderately expensive) Thomas Fisher Rare Book Library, the University of Toronto; (inexpensive) Saint Louis University Libraries, Archives and Records Management; (brochures) Bruce Peel Special Collections Library, University of Alberta.

Ilene F. Rockman Instruction Publication of the Year Award ($3,000). To recognize an outstanding publication relating to instruction in a library environment. *Sponsor:* Emerald Group. *Winner:* Emily Drabinski, Long Island University, Brooklyn.

WESS-SEES De Gruyter European Librarianship Study Grant (formerly the Coutts Nijhoff International West European Specialist Study Grant) (€2,500). Supports research pertaining to European studies, librarianship, or the book trade. *Sponsor:* Walter de Gruyter Foundation for Scholarship and Research. *Winner:* Katharine C. Chandler, Free Library of Philadelphia Rare Book Department.

Association of Library Trustees, Advocates, Friends, and Foundations (ALTAFF). See United for Libraries.

Association of Specialized and Cooperative Library Agencies (ASCLA)

ASCLA Cathleen Bourdon Service Award. To recognize an ASCLA personal member for outstanding service and leadership to the division. *Winner:* Carol Ann Desch, Statewide Library Service, New York State Library.

ASCLA Exceptional Service Award. To recognize exceptional service to patients, the homebound, inmates, and to medical, nursing, and other professional staff in hospitals. *Winner:* Mary Morgan, Kentucky Department of Corrections, Luther Luckett Correctional Facility.

ASCLA Leadership and Professional Achievement Award. To recognize leadership and achievement in the areas of consulting, multitype library cooperation, statewide service and programs, and state library development. *Winner:* Cheryl O O'Conner, Statewide Library Service, New York State Library.

Francis Joseph Campbell Award. For a contribution of recognized importance to library service for the blind and physically handicapped. *Winner:* Adam Stephen Szczepaniak, Jr., Director and Associate State Librarian, New Jersey State Library Talking Book and Braille Center.

KLAS/National Organization on Disability Award for Library Service to People with Disabilities ($1,000). To a library organization to recognize an innovative project to benefit people with disabilities. *Donor:* Keystone Systems. *Winner:* New Port Richey (Florida) Public Library/Red Apple Training Center Adult Reading Program.

Black Caucus of the American Library Association (BCALA)

BCALA Book Literary Award. *Winners:* (best poetry) Kevin Young for *Book of Hours: Poems* (Knopf); (fiction) Lalita Tademy for *Citizen's Creek* (Atria Books); (nonfiction) Jeffrey B. Leak for *Visible Man: The Life of Henry Dumas* (University of Georgia Press); (novelist) Dwayne Alexander Smith for *Forty Acres* (Atria Books).

BCALA E-Book Literary Award. *Winner:* To be announced in January 2016.

BCALA Trailblazer's Award. Presented once every five years in recognition of outstanding and unique contributions to librarianship. *Winners:* Thomas Alford, Mary Biblo.

DEMCO/BCALA Excellence in Librarianship Award. To a librarian who has made significant contributions to promoting the status of

African Americans in the library profession. *Winner:* Wanda Brown.

E.J. Josey Scholarship Award. *Winners:* Neketta Borden, Texas Women's University; Kim McNeil-Capers, Queens College.

Ethnic and Multicultural Information and Exchange Round Table (EMIERT)

David Cohen Multicultural Award ($300). To recognize articles of significant research and publication that increase understanding and promote multiculturalism in North American libraries. *Donor:* Routledge. *Winner:* Not awarded in 2015.

EMIERT Distinguished Librarian Award. Given biennially to recognize significant accomplishments in library services that are national or international in scope and that include improving, spreading, and promoting multicultural librarianship. *Winner:* Mark Puente.

Gale Multicultural Award ($1,000). For outstanding achievement and leadership in serving the multicultural/multiethnic community. *Donor:* Gale Research. *Winner:* Award suspended.

Exhibits Round Table (ERT)

Christopher J. Hoy/ERT Scholarship ($5,000). To an individual or individuals who will work toward an MLS degree in an ALA-accredited program. *Donor:* Family of Christopher Hoy. *Winner:* Eliza Bettinger.

Federal and Armed Forces Librarians Round Table (FAFLRT)

FAFLRT Achievement Award. For achievement in the promotion of library and information service and the information profession in the federal government community. *Winner:* To be announced.

FAFLRT Adelaide del Frate Conference Sponsorship Award ($1,000). To encourage library school students to become familiar with federal librarianship and ultimately seek work in federal libraries; for attendance at the ALA Annual Conference and activities of FAFLRT. *Winner:* Not awarded in 2015.

Distinguished Service Award (citation). To honor a FAFLRT member for outstanding and sustained contributions to the association and to federal librarianship. *Winner:* To be announced.

Cicely Phippen Marks Scholarship ($1,500). To a library school student with an interest in working in a federal library. *Winner:* Not awarded in 2015.

Rising Star Award. To a FAFLRT member new to the profession in a federal or armed forces library or government information management setting. *Winner:* To be announced.

Gay, Lesbian, Bisexual, and Transgender Round Table (GLBTRT)

Stonewall Book Awards. See "Literary Prizes, 2015" in Part 5.

Government Documents Round Table (GODORT)

James Bennett Childs Award. To a librarian or other individual for distinguished lifetime contributions to documents librarianship. *Winner:* John A. Stevenson.

Bernadine Abbott Hoduski Founders Award. To recognize documents librarians who may not be known at the national level but who have made significant contributions to the field of local, state, federal, or international documents. *Winner:* Steve Beleu, Oklahoma State University.

Margaret T. Lane/Virginia F. Saunders Memorial Research Award. *Winners:* Walter Clark Wilson, William Curtis Ellis for "Surrogates Beyond Borders: Black Members of the United States Congress and the Representation of African Interests on the Congressional Foreign-Policy Agenda."

NewsBank/Readex Catharine J. Reynolds Award. To documents librarians for travel and/or study in the field of documents librarianship or an area of study benefiting their performance. *Donor:* NewsBank and Readex Corporation. *Winner:* Lynda Kellam, North Carolina Library Association's Government Resources Section (GRS).

ProQuest/GODORT/ALA Documents to the People Award. To an individual, library, organization, or noncommercial group that most effectively encourages or enhances the use of government documents in library services. *Winner:* Free Government Information.

W. David Rozkuszka Scholarship ($3,000). To provide financial assistance to individuals currently working with government documents in a library while completing a master's program in library science. *Winners:* Kelsey Cheshire, Shelly Gilliam.

Intellectual Freedom Round Table (IFRT)

John Phillip Immroth Memorial Award for Intellectual Freedom ($500). For notable contribution to intellectual freedom fueled by personal courage. *Winner:* Pam Klipsch.
Eli M. Oboler Memorial Award. See "Literary Prizes, 2015" in Part 5.
Gerald Hodges Intellectual Freedom Chapter Relations Award. *Winner:* Margery Cyr.

Library and Information Technology Association (LITA)

Hugh C. Atkinson Memorial Award. *See under* American Library Association.
Ex Libris Student Writing Award ($1,000 and publication in *Information Technology and Libraries*). For the best unpublished manuscript on a topic in the area of libraries and information technology written by a student or students enrolled in an ALA-accredited library and information studies graduate program. *Donor:* Ex Libris. *Winner:* Heather Terrell for "Reference is Dead, Long Live Reference: Electronic Collections in the Digital Age."
LITA/Christian Larew Memorial Scholarship ($3,000). To encourage the entry of qualified persons into the library and information technology field. *Sponsor:* Informata.com. *Winner:* Andrew Meyer.
LITA/Library Hi Tech Award. To an individual or institution for outstanding communication in library and information technology. *Donor:* Emerald Group. *Winner:* David Walker for the development of the open source library portal application, Xerxes.
LITA/LSSI Minority Scholarship in Library and Information Technology ($2,500). To encourage a qualified member of a principal minority group to work toward an MLS degree in an ALA-accredited program with emphasis on library automation. *Donor:* Library Systems and Services. *Winner:* Jesus Espinoza.

LITA/OCLC Frederick G. Kilgour Award for Research in Library and Information Technology ($2,000 and expense-paid attendance at the ALA Annual Conference). To bring attention to research relevant to the development of information technologies. *Donor:* OCLC. *Winner:* Ed Summers, Maryland Institute for Technology in the Humanities (MITH), University of Maryland.
LITA/OCLC Minority Scholarship in Library and Information Technology ($3,000). To encourage a qualified member of a principal minority group to work toward an MLS degree in an ALA-accredited program with emphasis on library automation. *Donor:* OCLC. *Winner:* Young-In Kim.
LITA/OITP Award for Cutting-Edge Technology in Library Services. To honor libraries that are serving their communities with novel and innovative methods. *Winners:* Not awarded in 2015.

Library History Round Table (LHRT)

Phyllis Dain Library History Dissertation Award. Given biennially to the author of a dissertation treating the history of books, libraries, librarianship, or information science. *Winner:* Miriam Intrator for "Books Across Borders and Between Libraries: UNESCO and the Politics of Postwar Cultural Reconstruction, 1945–1951."

Donald G. Davis Article Award (certificate). Awarded biennially for the best article written in English in the field of U.S. and Canadian library history. *Winner:* Not awarded in 2015.

Eliza Atkins Gleason Book Award. Presented every third year to the author of a book in English in the field of library history. *Winner:* To be awarded next in 2016.

Justin Winsor Library History Essay Award ($500). To the author of an outstanding essay embodying original historical research on a significant subject of library history. *Winner:* Sharon McQueen for "The Feminization of Ferdinand: Perceptions of Gender Nonconformity in a Classic Children's Picture Book."

Library Leadership and Management Association (LLAMA)

Hugh C. Atkinson Memorial Award. *See under* American Library Association.

John Cotton Dana Library Public Relations Awards. To libraries or library organizations of all types for public relations programs or special projects ended during the preceding year. *Donors:* H. W. Wilson Foundation and EBSCO. *Winners:* To be announced.

Library Research Round Table (LRRT)

Jesse H. Shera Award for Distinguished Published Research. For a research article on library and information studies published in English during the calendar year. *Winner:* To be announced.

Jesse H. Shera Award for Support of Dissertation Research. To recognize and support dissertation research employing exemplary research design and methods. *Winner:* Not awarded in 2015.

Map and Geospatial Information Round Table (MAGIRT)

MAGIRT Honors Award. To recognize outstanding achievement and major contributions to map and geospatial librarianship. *Winner:* Kathy Rankin.

New Members Round Table (NMRT)

NMRT Annual Conference Professional Development Attendance Award (formerly the Marshall Cavendish Award) (tickets to the ALA Annual Conference event of the winners' choice). *Winners:* April Grey, Adelphi University; Michael Mungin, James Madison University, Harrisonburg, Virginia.

NMRT Professional Development Grant (formerly the 3M/NMRT Professional Development Grant). To new NMRT members to encourage professional development and participation in national ALA and NMRT activities. *Winners:* Veronica Leigh Milliner, Nora Ohnishi.

Shirley Olofson Memorial Award ($1,000). To an individual to help defray costs of attending the ALA Annual Conference. *Win-

ner: Kai Alexis Smith, University of Notre Dame, Notre Dame, Indiana.

Student Chapter of the Year Award. To an ALA student chapter for outstanding contributions to the association. *Winner:* Student Chapter at University of South Carolina.

Office for Diversity

Achievement in Library Diversity Research Honor. To an ALA member who has made significant contributions to diversity research in the profession. *Winner:* Not awarded in 2015.

Diversity Research Grants ($2,500). To the authors of research proposals that address critical gaps in the knowledge of diversity issues within library and information science. *Winners:* Aditi Gupta for Exploring library perceptions, reading habits and library usage of the South Asian Population in BC; Win Shih for Facilitating the Learning and Academic Performance of Student Veterans; Gregory Bond for "'We Don't Employ Colored People in the Public Libraries:' The Baltimore Civil Rights Movement & the Color Line Behind the Desk at the Enoch Pratt Free Library, 1926–1946."

Office for Information Technology Policy

L. Ray Patterson Copyright Award. To recognize an individual who supports the constitutional purpose of U.S. copyright law, fair use, and the public domain. *Sponsor:* Freedom to Read Foundation. *Winner:* To be announced.

Office for Intellectual Freedom

Freedom to Read Foundation Gordon M. Conable Conference Scholarship. To enable a library school student or new professional to attend the ALA Annual Conference. *Winners:* Gretchen LeCheminant, Amy Steinbauer.

Freedom to Read Foundation Roll of Honor (citation): To recognize individuals who have contributed substantially to the foundation. *Winner:* To be announced.

Office for Literacy and Outreach Services (OLOS)

Jean E. Coleman Library Outreach Lecture. *Sponsor:* OLOS Advisory Committee. *Lecturer:* Carla D. Hayden.

Public Library Association (PLA)

Baker & Taylor Entertainment Audio Music/ Video Product Grant ($2,500 worth of audio music or video products). To help a public library to build or expand a collection of either or both formats. *Donor:* Baker & Taylor. *Winner:* Edna Zybell Memorial Library, Clarence, Iowa.

Gordon M. Conable Award ($1,500). To a public library staff member, library trustee, or public library for demonstrating a commitment to intellectual freedom and the Library Bill of Rights. *Sponsor:* LSSI. *Winner:* To be announced.

Demco New Leaders Travel Grants (up to $1,500). To PLA members who have not attended a major PLA continuing education event in the past five years. *Winners:* To be announced.

EBSCO Excellence in Small and/or Rural Public Service Award ($1,000). Honors a library serving a population of 10,000 or fewer that demonstrates excellence of service to its community as exemplified by an overall service program or a special program of significant accomplishment. *Donor:* EBSCO. *Winner:* San Juan Island Library, Friday Harbor, Washington.

Allie Beth Martin Award ($3,000). To honor a public librarian who has demonstrated extraordinary range and depth of knowledge about books or other library materials and has distinguished ability to share that knowledge. *Donor:* Baker & Taylor. *Winner:* Mary Olson, Medina County (Ohio) District Library.

Polaris Innovation in Technology John Iliff Award. To a library worker, librarian, or library for the use of technology and innovative thinking as a tool to improve services to public library users. *Sponsor:* Polaris. *Winner:* Oli Sanidas, Arapahoe (Colorado) Library District.

Charlie Robinson Award. To honor a public library director who, over a period of seven years, has been a risk taker, an innovator, and/or a change agent in a public library. *Donor:* Baker & Taylor. *Winner:* Maxine Bleiweis, Westport (Connecticut) Library.

Romance Writers of America Library Grant ($4,500). To a library to build or expand a fiction collection and/or host romance fiction programming. *Donor:* Romance Writers of America. *Winner:* Auburn (Georgia) Public Library.

Upstart Innovation Award ($2,000). To recognize a public library's innovative achievement in planning and implementing a creative community service program. *Donor:* Upstart/Demco. *Winner:* Grand Rapids (Michigan) Public Library.

Public Programs Office

Sara Jaffarian School Library Program Award for Exemplary Humanities Programming ($4,000). To honor a K–8 school library that has conducted an outstanding humanities program or series. *Donors:* Sara Jaffarian and ALA Cultural Communities Fund. *Winner:* Not awarded in 2015.

Reference and User Services Association (RUSA)

ABC-CLIO Online History Award ($3,000). A biennial award to recognize a noteworthy online historical collection, an online tool tailored for the purpose of finding historical materials, or an online teaching aid stimulating creative historical scholarship. *Donor:* ABC-CLIO. *Winner:* Joanne Murray, for "Doctor or Doctress? Explore American History Through the Eyes of Women Physicians."

ALA/RUSA Zora Neale Hurston Award. To recognize the efforts of RUSA members in promoting African American literature. *Sponsored by:* Harper Perennial Publishing. *Winner:* Carolyn Garnes, Founder and CEO of Aunt Lil's Reading Room.

Virginia Boucher–OCLC Distinguished ILL Librarian Maxine Bleiweis, Westport (Connecticut) Library.Maxine Bleiweis, Westport (Connecticut) Library. ($2,000). To a librarian for outstanding professional achievement, leadership, and contributions to interlibrary loan and document delivery. *Winner:* Lars Leon, University of Kansas.

BRASS Academic Business Librarianship Travel Award ($1,250). To recognize a librarian new to the field of academic business librarianship and support his or her attendance at the ALA Annual Conference. *Sponsor:* Business Expert Press. *Winner:* Grace Liu, University of Maine.

BRASS Award for Outstanding Service to Minority Business Communities ($2,000). To a librarian or library to recognize creation of an innovative service to a minority business community or achievement of recognition from that community for providing outstanding service. *Winner:* Award discontinued.

BRASS Emerald Research Grant Awards ($2,500). To an ALA member seeking support to conduct research in business librarianship. *Donor:* Emerald Group. *Winners:* Jason Dewland, Cindy Elliott, University of Arizona.

BRASS Gale Cengage Learning Student Travel Award ($1,250). To enable a student enrolled in an ALA-accredited master's program to attend the ALA Annual Conference. *Donor:* Gale Cengage Learning. *Winner:* Sara F. Hess, School of Information, University of Michigan.

Sophie Brody Medal. See "Literary Prizes, 2015" in Part 5.

BRASS Gale Cengage Learning Award for Excellence in Business Librarianship ($3,000). For distinguished activities in the field of business librarianship *Donor:* Gale Cengage Learning. *Winner:* Peter Z. McKay, Business Librarian, University of Florida.

BRASS Morningstar Public Librarian Support Award ($1,250). To support attendance at the ALA Annual Conference of a public librarian who has performed outstanding business reference service. *Donor:* Morningstar. *Winner:* Barbara Alvarez, Barrington Area Library (Illinois).

Gale Cengage Learning Award for Excellence in Reference and Adult Library Services ($3,000). To recognize a library or library system for developing an imaginative and unique library resource to meet patrons' reference needs. *Donor:* Gale Cengage

Learning. *Winner:* Queens Library, for the development of the "Where in Queens?" database.

Genealogical Publishing Company/History Section Award ($1,500). To encourage and commend professional achievement in historical reference and research librarianship. *Donor:* Genealogical Publishing Company. *Winner:* Michael D. Kirley, Los Angeles Public Library.

MARS Achievement Recognition Certificate ("My Favorite Martian Award"). To recognize excellence in service to the RUSA section MARS—Emerging Technologies in Reference. *Winner:* Debbie Bezanson, George Washington University.

Isadore Gilbert Mudge Award ($5,000). For distinguished contributions to reference librarianship. *Donor:* Gale Cengage Learning. *Winner:* Denise Beaubien Bennett, Engineering Librarian, University of Florida.

NoveList's Margaret E. Monroe Library Adult Services Award (citation). To a librarian for his or her impact on library service to adults. *Winner:* Neil Hollands, Adult Services Librarian, Williamsburg Regional Library.

Reference Service Press Award ($2,500). To the author or authors of the most outstanding article published in *RUSQ* during the preceding two volume years. *Donor:* Reference Service Press. *Winners:* Pauline Dewan for "Reading Matters in the Academic Library: Taking the Lead from Public Librarians."

John Sessions Memorial Award (plaque). To a library or library system in recognition of work with the labor community. *Donor:* Department for Professional Employees, AFL/CIO. *Winner:* Calcasieu Parish Library System for Southwest Louisiana (SWLA) Workforce Resource Guide.

Louis Shores Award. To an individual, team, or organization to recognize excellence in reviewing of books and other materials for libraries. *Winner:* Brad Hooper, Editor, *Booklist.*

STARS—Atlas Systems Mentoring Award ($1,250). To a library practitioner new to the field of interlibrary loan, resource sharing, or electronic reserves, to attend the ALA Annual Conference. *Donor:* Atlas Systems. *Winner:* Karen Thomas, Delaware Valley College.

Social Responsibilities Round Table (SRRT)

Jackie Eubanks Memorial Award ($500). To honor outstanding achievement in promoting the acquisition and use of alternative media in libraries. *Donor:* SRRT Alternatives in Publication Task Force. *Winner:* Not awarded in 2015.

Coretta Scott King Awards. See "Literary Prizes, 2015" in Part 5.

United for Libraries (formerly ALTAFF, Association of Library Trustees, Advocates, Friends, and Foundations)

Neal-Schuman Citizens-Save-Libraries Grants. To support library advocacy at the local level for libraries in financial difficulty. *Sponsor:* Neal-Schuman Foundation. *Winners:* To be announced

Trustee Citation. To recognize public library trustees for individual service to library development on the local, state, regional, or national level. *Winner:* Roy B. Martin, IV

United for Libraries/Baker & Taylor Awards. To recognize library friends groups for outstanding efforts to support their libraries. *Donor:* Baker & Taylor. *Winners:* To be announced.

United for Libraries/Gale Outstanding Trustee Conference Grant Award ($850). *Donor:* Gale Cengage Learning. *Winner:* Not awarded in 2015.

United for Libraries Major Benefactors Citation. To individuals, families, or corporate bodies that have made major benefactions to public libraries. *Winners:* To be announced.

United for Libraries Public Service Award. To a legislator who has been especially supportive of libraries. *Winners:* To be announced.

Young Adult Library Services Association (YALSA)

Baker & Taylor/YALSA Scholarship Grants ($1,000). To young adult librarians in public or school libraries to attend the ALA Annual Conference for the first time. *Donor:* Baker & Taylor. *Winners:* Lisa Castellano, Alicia Tate.

Dorothy Broderick Student Scholarship ($1,000). To enable a graduate student to attend the ALA AnnTo be announcedual Conference for the first time. *Sponsor:* YALSA Leadership Endowment. *Winner:* Lauren Lancaster.

BWI/YALSA Collection Development Grants ($1,000). To YALSA members who represent a public library and work directly with young adults, for collection development materials for young adults. *Donor:* Book Wholesalers, Inc. *Winners:* Chelsea Couillard-Smith, Robyn Vittek.

Margaret A. Edwards Award. See "Literary Prizes, 2015" in Part 5.

Great Books Giveaway (books, videos, CDs, and audiocassettes valued at a total of $25,000). *Winners:* (first place) Lorain City High School, Ohio; (second place) Civic Center Court Secondary School, San Francisco; (third place) Northwoods Middle School, North Charleston, South Carolina.

Frances Henne/YALSA/VOYA Research Grant ($1,000). To provide seed money to an individual, institution, or group for a project to encourage research on library service to young adults. *Donor:* Greenwood Publishing Group. *Winner:* Ligaya Scaff.

William C. Morris YA Debut Award. See "Literary Prizes, 2015" in Part 5.

Michael L. Printz Award. See "Literary Prizes, 2015" in Part 5.

YALSA/ABC-CLIO/Greenwood Publishing Group Service to Young Adults Achievement Award ($2,000). To a YALSA member who has demonstrated unique and sustained devotion to young adult services. *Donor:* Greenwood Publishing Group. *Winner:* Not awarded in 2015.

YALSA/MAE Award ($500 for the recipient plus $500 for his or her library). For an exemplary young adult reading or literature program. *Sponsor:* Margaret A. Edwards Trust. *Winner:* Peggy Hendershot.

YALSA/Sagebrush Award. See YALSA/MAE Award.

American Society for Information Science and Technology (ASIS&T)

ASIS&T Award of Merit. For an outstanding contribution to the field of information science. *Winner:* Michael E.D. Koenig.

ASIS&T Best Information Science Books. *Winners:* Ronald E. Day for "Indexing It All: The Subject in the Age of Documentation, Information, and Data (History and Foundations of Information Science)."

ASIS&T New Leaders Award. To recruit, engage, and retain new ASIS&T members and to identify potential for new leadership in the society. *Winners:* Emily Agunod, Deborah Charbonneau, Nina Collins, Suzanne Gruber, Sarah Hartmann, Hassan Zamir.

ASIS&T ProQuest Doctoral Dissertation Award ($1,000 plus expense-paid attendance at ASIS&T Annual Meeting). *Winner:* Chris Cunningham for "Governmental Structures, Social Inclusion, and the Digital Divide: A Discourse on the Affinity Between the Effects of Freedom and Access to Online Information Resources."

ASIS&T Research in Information Science Award. For a systematic program of research in a single area at a level beyond the single study, recognizing contributions in the field of information science. *Winner:* To be announced.

James M. Cretsos Leadership Award. *Winner:* Karen A. Miller, University of South Carolina.

Watson Davis Award. For outstanding continuous contributions and dedicated service to the society. *Winner:* Michael Leach, Harvard University.

Pratt Severn Best Student Research Paper Award. To encourage student research and writing in the field of information science. *Winner:* To be announced.

Thomson Reuters Doctoral Dissertation Proposal Scholarship ($2,000). *Winner:* Matthew Willis for "Patient Sociotechnical Assemblages: The Distributed Cognition of Health Information Management."

Thomson Reuters Outstanding Teacher Award ($1,500). To recognize the unique teaching contribution of an individual as a teacher of information science. *Winner:* Denise Agosto, Drexel University.

John Wiley Best *JASIST* Paper Award. *Winners:* Egon I. van den Broek, Elisabeth M.A.G. van Dijk, Richard J. Glassey, Franciska MG de Jong, Frans van der Sluis for "When Complexity Becomes Interesting."

Art Libraries Society of North America (ARLIS/NA)

ARLIS/NA Distinguished Service Award. To honor an individual whose exemplary service in art librarianship, visual resources curatorship, or a related field, has made an outstanding national or international contribution to art information. *Winner:* To be announced.

ARLIS/NA Wolfgang M. Freitag Internship Award ($3,000). To provide financial support for students preparing for a career in art librarianship or visual resource librarianship. *Winner:* Adam Beebe.

Melva J. Dwyer Award. To the creators of exceptional reference or research tools relating to Canadian art and architecture. *Winners:* Ron Williams for *Landscape Architecture in Canada* (McGill-Queens University Press).

Gerd Muehsam Award. To one or more graduate students in library science programs to recognize excellence in a graduate paper or project. *Winner:* Eva Athanasiu for "Belonging: a Brief Study on Artists' Books and Institutional Classification."

H. W. Wilson Foundation Research Awards ($1,500). *Winner:* Craig Bunch for *Interviews with Texas Artists*.

George Wittenborn Memorial Book Awards. See "Literary Prizes, 2015" in Part 5.

Asian/Pacific Americans Libraries Association (APALA)

APALA Scholarship ($1,000). For a student of Asian or Pacific background who is enrolled in, or has been accepted into, a master's or doctoral degree program in library and/or information science at an ALA-accredited school. *Winner:* To be announced.

APALA Travel Grant ($500). To a U.S. or Canadian citizen or permanent resident enrolled in a master's or doctoral degree program in library and/or information science at an ALA-accredited school, or a professional possessing a master's degree or doctoral degree in library and/or information science, to enable attendance at the ALA Annual Conference. *Winner:* To be announced.

Emerging Leaders Sponsorship. To fund participation in the 2014 class of the American

Library Association's Emerging Leaders program (ELP). *Winner:* Cynthia Orozco.

Sheila Suen Lai Research Grant. To encourage APALA members to engage in research activities relative to library and information science in general and Asian Pacific American librarianship in particular. *Winner:* To be announced.

Association for Library and Information Science Education (ALISE)

ALISE Award for Teaching Excellence. *Winner:* Renate Chancellor, Catholic University of America. *See also: Library Journal/ALISE Excellence in Teaching Award,* below.

.ALISE/Eugene Garfield Doctoral Dissertation Award. *Winner:* Kyong Eun Oh for "The Process of Organizing Personal information," Rutgers University.

ALISE/Norman Horrocks Leadership Award. To recognize a new ALISE member who has demonstrated outstanding leadership qualities in professional ALISE activities. *Winner:* Not awarded in 2015.

ALISE/LMC Paper Award. *Sponsor:* Libraries Unlimited/Linworth. *Winner:* Dana Casciotti (National Library of Medicine), Rebecca Follman, Christie Kodama, Natalie Greene Taylor, Beth St. Jean, Mega Subramaniam, (University of Marland), for "Bit by Bit: Unpacking Health Literacy Instruction for Young People."

ALISE/Pratt-Severn Faculty Innovation Award. To recognize innovation by full-time faculty members in incorporating evolving information technologies in the curricula of accredited master's degree programs in library and information studies. *Winner:* Eric Meyers, University of British Columbia.

ALISE Professional Contribution to Library and Information Science Education Award. *Winner:* Anne Gilliland, University of California, Los Angeles.

ALISE/ProQuest Methodology Paper Competition. *Winner:* Not awarded in 2015.

ALISE Research Grant Awards (one or more grants totaling $5,000). *Winners:* Julie Marie Frye (Indiana University), Maria Hasler-Barker (Sam Houston State University) for "Understanding the Role of lenguaje and interacción in Serving Patrons in Diverse Communitites."

ALISE Service Award. *Winner:* Lynne Howarth, University of Toronto.

ALISE/Jean Tague Sutcliffe Doctoral Student Research Poster Competition. *Winners:* To be announced.

ALISE/University of Washington Information School Youth Services Graduate Student Travel Award. To support the costs associated with travel to and participation in the ALISE Annual Conference. *Winner:* Rachel Magee, Drexel University.

ALISE/Bohdan S. Wynar Research Paper Competition. *Winners:* Not awarded in 2015.

Doctoral Students to ALISE Grant. To support the attendance of one or more promising LIS doctoral students at the ALISE Annual Conference. *Sponsor:* Libraries Unlimited/Linworth. *Winner:* Liya Deng, University of South Carolina.

*Library Journal/*ALISE Excellence in Teaching Award (formerly the ALISE Award for Teaching Excellence in the Field of Library and Information Science Education). *Winner:* Paul Jaeger, University of Maryland.

OCLC/ALISE Library and Information Science Research Grant Competition. To promote independent research that helps librarians integrate new technologies into areas of traditional competence and contributes to a better understanding of the library environment. *Winners:* Matthew Griffis, for "The "Place" of the Librarian in Deskless Library: Do Roaming Reference Spatial Models Create a More User-Centered Library?" University of Southern Mississippi; Jin Ha Lee, for "Appeal Factors: Enabling Crossmedia Advisory Services," University of Washington; Eric Meyers, for "Easy as Pi: Developing Computational Thinking in the Public Library," University of British Columbia.

Association of Jewish Libraries (AJL)

AJL Scholarships ($1,000). For students enrolled in accredited library schools who plan to work as Judaica librarians. *Winners:* Marci Bayer, Ilya Slavutskiy.Jemima Jarman, Elissa Sperling.

Fanny Goldstein Merit Award. To honor loyal and ongoing contributions to the association and to the profession of Jewish librarianship. *Winner:* Joy Kingsolver.

Life Membership Award. To recognize outstanding leadership and professional contributions to the association and to the profession of Jewish librarianship. *Winner:* Not awarded in 2015.

Association of Research Libraries

ARL Diversity Scholarships (stipend of up to $10,000). To a varying number of MLS students from under-represented groups who are interested in careers in research libraries. *Sponsors:* ARL member libraries and the Institute of Museum and Library Services. *Winners* Alonso Avila, DeWayne Branch, Richard Cho, Gavin Do, Joyce Gabiola, Alia Gant, John Martin, Alda Migoni, Amanda Moreno, Rebecca Orozco, Monique Perez, Yesenia Román-López, Alvarez Tarver.

Association of Seventh-Day Adventist Librarians

D. Glenn Hilts Scholarship ($1,500) for a member or members of the Seventh-Day Adventist Church who are enrolled in a graduate library program. *Winner:* Not awarded.

Beta Phi Mu

Beta Phi Mu Award. *See under* American Library Association.

Eugene Garfield Doctoral Dissertation Fellowships ($3,000). *Winners:* Tiffany Chao, University of Illinois, Urbana-Champaign; Morgan Currie, University of California, Los Angeles; Noah Lenstra, University of Illinois, Urbana-Champaign; Teresa Prendergast, University of British Columbia; Nicholas Weber, University of Illinois, Urbana-Champaign; Ayoung Yoon, University of North Carolina, Chapel Hill.

Harold Lancour Scholarship for Foreign Study ($1,750). For graduate study in a country related to the applicant's work or schooling. *Winner:* Elizabeth Cramer, for the study of international library development in India, Appalachian State University.

Sarah Rebecca Reed Scholarship ($2,250). For study at an ALA-accredited library school. *Winners:* Rebecca Greenstein, Alena Principato, University of North Carolina, Chapel Hill.

Frank B. Sessa Scholarship for Continuing Professional Education ($1,500). For continuing education for a Beta Phi Mu member. *Winner:* DawnMarin Dell, Texas Tech University School of Law Library.

Blanche E. Woolls Scholarship ($2,250). For a beginning student in school library media services. *Winner:* Kathryn Shaw, University of Alabama.

Bibliographical Society of America (BSA)

BSA Fellowships ($1,500–$6,000). For scholars involved in bibliographical inquiry and research in the history of the book trades and in publishing history. *Winners:* (Pantzer Fellowship) Claire Bourne, "'Set Forth as It Hath Been Played': Printing the Performance in Early Modern England"; (Short-term Fellowship) Anna Gialdini, "A Material, Historical and Anthropological Analysis of Greek-style Bookbindings in Renaissance Venice"; (McCorison Fellowship) Sonia Hazard, "The American Tract Society and the Materiality of Print in Antebellum America"; (Short-term Fellowship) Katherine Hindley, "The Use of Unread Words for Protection and Healing in Medieval England"; (Short-term Fellowship) Kathryn James, "Remembering the Dissolution"; (BSA-ASECS Fellowship) Rachael King, "Richard Steele, Gazetteer"; (Short-term Fellowship) Gregory Mackie, "Authenticating Oscar Wilde"; (Tanenbaum Fellowship) Katherine Parker, "Maps, Minds and the Pacific: The Production of Geographic Knowledge in Eighteenth-century Britain"; (Folter Fellowship) David Shaw, "The Bibliography of Juvenal to 1600"; (Pantzer

Senior Fellowship) Mark Towsey, "The History of Reading in the Anglophone Atlantic between 1750 and the 1820."

William L. Mitchell Prize for Research on Early British Serials ($1,000). Awarded triennially for the best single work published in the previous three years. *Winner:* Not awarded in 2015.

New Scholars Program. To promote the work of scholars who are new to the field of bibliography. *Winners:* Huub van der Linden, Jeffrey Makala, Aaron T. Pratt.

St. Louis Mercantile Library Prize in American Bibliography ($2,000). Awarded triennially for outstanding scholarship in the bibliography of American history and literature. *Sponsor:* St. Louis Mercantile Library, University of Missouri, St. Louis. *Winner:* To be awarded next in 2017.

Justin G. Schiller Prize for Bibliographical Work on Pre-20th Century Children's Books ($2,000). A triennial award to encourage scholarship in the bibliography of historical children's books. *Winner:* To be awarded next in 2016.

Canadian Library Association (CLA)

CLA Award for the Advancement of Intellectual Freedom in Canada. *Winner:* Brian Campbell, Director of Systems and Special Projects for the Vancouver Public Library, for the Advancement of Intellectual Freedom in Canada for his tireless championship of librarianship's core values of intellectual freedom and information access.

CLA/ACB Dafoe Scholarship (C$5,000). *Winner:* Kaya Fraser.

CLA Best Poster Presentation Award. To recognize outstanding poster presentations on the basis of quality, knowledge of the presenter, relevance of content, and overall appearance of the poster. *Sponsor:* Dysart & Jones Associates. *Winners:* Mary-Beth Arima for Poster 3: "Mapping Toronto—Literature and Poetry"; Sara Hossain, Stephanie Pegg for Poster 8: "Information Incarceration – the State of Prison Libraries in Ontario."

CLA Robert H. Blackburn Distinguished Paper Award. To acknowledge notable published research. *Winners:* Marni R. Harrington, Elizabeth Marshall.

CLA Emerging Leader Award. To recognize a CLA member with less than five years' experience in the library field who demonstrates leadership or active participation in association work. *Sponsor:* Counting Opinions. *Winner:* Catherine McGoveran.

CLA/Ken Haycock Award for Promoting Librarianship (C$1,000). For significant contributions to the public recognition and appreciation of librarianship. *Winner:* Leslie Weir.

CLA Library Research and Development Grant (C$1,000). *Winner:* Not awarded in 2015.

CLA/Alan MacDonald Mentorship Award. To recognize the importance of mentorship to the library community. *Sponsor:* Canadian Electronic Library. *Winner:* John Fink.

CLA/OCLC Award for Innovative Technology. *Donor:* OCLC Canada. *Winner:* The Canadian Government Information Digital Preservation Network (CGI DPN).

CLA Outstanding Service to Librarianship Award. *Donor:* ProQuest. *Winner:* Kathy Scardellato.

CLA Student Article Award. *Winner:* Gianmarco Visconti.

CLA/H. W. Wilson Scholarship ($2,000). *Winner:* Tristan Smyth.

W. Kaye Lamb Award for Service to Seniors. Awarded biennially to recognize a library that has developed an ongoing service, program, or procedure of benefit to seniors and/or a design and organization of buildings or facilities that improve access and encourage use by seniors. *Sponsors:* Ex Libris Association and CLA. *Winner:* Ajax Public Library, Ontario.

Angela Thacker Memorial Award. To honor teacher-librarians who hCelestine Bennett, Lakeshore Avenue Baptist Church Library, Oakland, California.ave made contributions to the profession through publications, productions, or professional development activities. *Winner:* Derrick Grose.

Catholic Library Association

Regina Medal. For continued, distinguished contribution to the field of children's literature. *Winner:* Judy Blume.

Chinese American Librarians Association (CALA)

CALA Conference Travel Grant. *Winners:* Chengren (Sharon) Hu, Guoying Liu, Yingqi Tang, Hanrong Wang.

CALA Distinguished Service Award. To a librarian who has been a mentor, role model, and leader in the fields of library and information science. *Winner:* Patty Wong.

CALA President's Recognition Award. *Winners:* Maria Fung, Sharon Hu, Esther Lee.

CALA Scholarship of Library and Information Science ($1,000). *Winner:* Melody Tsz-Way Leung.

Sheila Suen Lai Scholarship ($500). *Winner:* Yuehua Zhao.

Sally C. Tseng Professional Development Grant ($1,000). *Winner:* Not awarded in 2015.

Church and Synagogue Library Association (CSLA)

CSLA Award for Outstanding Congregational Librarian. For distinguished service to the congregation and/or community through devotion to the congregational library. *Winner:* Celestine Bennett, Lakeshore Avenue Baptist Church Library, Oakland, California.

CSLA Award for Outstanding Congregational Library. For responding in creative and innovative ways to the library's mission of reaching and serving the congregation and/or the wider community. *Winner:* Tallowood Baptist Church, Houston, Texas.

CSLA Award for Outstanding Contribution to Congregational Libraries. For providing inspiration, guidance, leadership, or resources to enrich the field of church or synagogue librarianship. *Winner:* Not awarded in 2015.

Helen Keating Ott Award for Outstanding Contribution to Children's Literature. *Winner:* Not awarded in 2015.

Rodda Book Award. See "Literary Prizes, 2015" in Part 5.

Coalition for Networked Information (CNI)

Paul Evan Peters Award. Awarded biennially to recognize notable and lasting international achievements relating to high-performance networks and the creation and use of information resources and services that advance scholarship and intellectual productivity. *Sponsors:* Association of Research Libraries, CNI, EDUCAUSE. *Winner:* Donald A.B. Lindberg, Director, National Library of Medicine.

Paul Evan Peters Fellowship ($5,000 a year for two years). Awarded biennially to a student or students pursuing a graduate degree in librarianship or the information sciences. *Sponsors:* Association of Research Libraries, CNI, EDUCAUSE. *Winners:* Olivia Dorsey, Jordan Eschler.

Council on Library and Information Resources (CLIR)

CLIR Postdoctoral Fellowships in Scholarly Information Resources. *Current fellows:* Laura Aydelotte, Michael Bales, Sayan Bhattacharyya, Reid Boehm, Meaghan Brown, Scout Calvert, Jacquelyn Clements, Morgan Daniels, Rachel Deblinger, Melissa Dinsman, Anne Donlon, Annie Johnson, Carrie Johnston, Dimitros Latsis, Emily McGinn, Monica Mercado, Christen Miller, Alice Motes, Tim Norris, Jessica Otis, Philip Palmer, Kyle Parry, Alicia Peaker, Fernando Rios, Elizabeth Rodrigues, Plato Smith, Todd Suomela, Yun Tai, Edward Triplett, Martin Tsang, Ana Van Guick, Mary Lindsay Van Tine, Leila Walker, Qian Zhang.

Rick Peterson Fellowship. To an early-career information technology professional or librarian who has reached beyond traditional boundaries to resolve a significant challenge facing digital libraries. *Cosponsors:* CLIR and the National Institute for Technology in Liberal Education (NITLE). *Winner:* Award suspended.

Rovelstad Scholarship in International Librarianship. To enable a student enrolled in an accredited LIS program to attend the IFLA World Library and Information Congress. *Winner:* Kelly Grogg, University of Iowa.

A. R. Zipf Fellowship in Information Management ($10,000). To a student enrolled in graduate school who shows exceptional promise for leadership and technical achievement. *Winner:* Award discontinued.

EDUCAUSE

EDUCAUSE Community Leadership Award. *Winner:* Beth Schaefer, Director of Client Services, University of Wisconsin, Milwaukee.

EDUCAUSE Leadership Award. To acknowledge leadership in higher education information technology. *Winner:* James Hilton, Dean of Libraries and Vice Provost for Digital Education and Innovation, University of Michigan, Ann Arbor.

EDUCAUSE Rising Star Award. To recognize early-career information technology professionals who demonstrate exceptional achievement in the area of information technology in higher education. *Winner:* Brandon Bernier, Director of User Services, University of Wisconsin, Madison.

Friends of the National Library of Medicine

Michael E. DeBakey Library Services Outreach Award. To recognize outstanding service and contributions to rural and underserved communities by a practicing health sciences librarian. *Winner:* Claudia DeShay, Health Sciences Digital Library and Learning Center, University of Texas Southwestern Medical Center.

Bill and Melinda Gates Foundation

Access to Learning Award ($1 million). To public libraries or similar organizations outside the United States for innovative programs that provide free public access to information technology. *Administered by:* Gates Foundation Global Libraries initiative. *Winner:* e-Library Nenasala Program of Sri Lanka, a government-run initiative to increase digital literacy and access to technology among the nation's poorest residents living in remote rural areas. Award discontinued.

Institute of Museum and Library Services

National Medal for Museum and Library Service. For extraordinary civic, educational, economic, environmental, and social contributions ($5,000). *Winners:* Amazement Square, Lynchburg, Virginia; Cecil County Public Library, Elkton, Maryland; Craig Public Library, Craig, Alaska; Embudo Valley Library and Community Center, Dixon, New Mexico; Los Angeles Public Library, Los Angeles, California; Louisiana Children's Museum, New Orleans, Louisiana; Museum of Northern Arizona, Flagstaff, Arizona; New York Hall of Science, Queens, New York; The Schomburg Center for Research in Black Culture, New York, New York; The Tech Museum of Innovation, San Jose, California.

International Association of School Librarians (IASL)

Ken Haycock and Jean Lowrie Leadership Development Grants ($1,000). To enable applicants to attend their first IASL Annual Conference. *Winner:* Neeta Bali, Kasiga School, India.

IASL School Library Technology Innovation Award. *Winner:* Not awarded in 2015.

International Board on Books for Young People (IBBY)

IBBY-Asahi Reading Promotion Award ($10,000). Awarded biennially to projects that are making a lasting contribution to reading promotion for young people. *Offered by:* International Board on Books for Young People. *Sponsor:* Asahi Shimbun. *Winners:* The Children's Book Bank, Toronto, Canada, which supports childhood literacy by providing free books and literacy support to children in low-income neighborhoods in the Toronto area; PRAESA (the Project for the Study of Alternative Education in South Africa), in recognition of its more than 20 years' work in the field of children's multilingual literacy development. Not awarded in 2015.

International Federation of Library Associations and Institutions (IFLA)

Honorary Fellowship. For distinguished service to IFLA. *Winner:* Ingrid Parent, IFLA President, 2011–2013.

IFLA Medal. To a person or organization for a distinguished contribution either to IFLA or to international librarianship. *Winners:* Not awarded in 2015.

Jay Jordan IFLA/OCLC Early Career Development Fellowships. To library and information science professionals from countries with developing economies who are in the early stages of their careers. *Winners:* Idowu Adegbilero-Iwari, Nigeria; Željko Dimitrijević, Serbia; Penninah Musangi, Kenya; Rhea Jade Nabusan, Philippines; Shaharima Parvin, Bangladesh.

Dr. Shawky Salem Conference Grant (up to $1,900). To enable an expert in library and information science who is a national of an Arab country to attend the IFLA Conference for the first time. *Winner:* Dr Enssam Mansour, Associate Professor, College of Technological Studies of the Public Authority of Applied Education and Training (PAAET), Kuwait City, Kuwait.

Frederick Thorpe Organizational Award (up to £15,000). To a library organization for development of service delivery to the visually impaired. *Sponsor:* Ulverscroft Foundation. *Winner:* Dr Enssam Mansour, Associate Professor, College of Technological Studies of the Public Authority of Applied Educa-

tion and Training (PAAET), Kuwait City, Kuwait.

Ulverscroft Foundation/IFLA Libraries Serving Persons with Print Disabilities Section Best Practice Awards. To assist the development of library services for print-disabled people and foster cooperation between library services serving these persons. *Winner:* Not awarded in 2015.

Library Journal

DEMCO/LJ Paralibrarian of the Year Award. *Winner:* Tamara Faulkner Kraus, Hickory Public Library, North Carolina.

Gale/LJ Library of the Year. *Sponsor:* Gale Cengage Learning. *Winner:* Ferguson (Missouri) Municipal Public Library.

Library Journal/ALISE Excellence in Teaching Award (formerly the ALISE Award for Teaching Excellence in the Field of Library and Information Science Education). *See under:* Association for Library and Information Science Education (ALISE).

LJ Best Small Library in America ($20,000). To honor a public library that profoundly demonstrates outstanding service to populations of 25,000 or less. *Co-sponsors: Library Journal* and the Bill and Melinda Gates Foundation. *Winner:* Belgrade Community Library, Belgrade, Montana.

LJ Librarian of the Year. *Winner:* Siobhan A. Reardon, Free Library of Philadelphia.

Library of Congress

Library of Congress Literacy Awards. *Sponsor:* David M. Rubenstein. *Winners:* (David M. Rubenstein Prize, $150,000, for a groundbreaking or sustained record of advancement of literacy by any individual or entity) First Book, which is a nonprofit social enterprise that works to further educational equity by tackling the scarcity of books and educational resources for millions of children growing up in low-income families in the United States and Canada; (The American Prize, $50,000, for a project developed and implemented successfully during the past decade for combating illiteracy and/or aliteracy) United Through Reading, a nonprofit that unites military families facing physical separation by facilitating the bonding experience of reading aloud together; (The International Prize, $50,000, for the work of an individual, nation, or nongovernmental organization working in a specific country or region) Beanstalk, a volunteer based literacy organization that provides one-on-one support to children ages 6 to 11.

Library of Congress John W. Kluge Fellowship in Digital Studies Description. To promote examination of the impact of the digital revolution on society, culture, and international relations using the library's collections and resources. *Fellow:* Iván Chaar-López.

Library of Congress Prize for American Fiction. See "Literary Prizes, 2015" in Part 5.

Medical Library Association (MLA)

Virginia L. and William K. Beatty MLA Volunteer Service Award. To recognize a medical librarian who has demonstrated outstanding, sustained service to the Medical Library Association and the health sciences library profession. *Winner:* Dolores Judkins.

Estelle Brodman Award for the Academic Medical Librarian of the Year. To honor significant achievement, potential for leadership, and continuing excellence at midcareer in the area of academic health sciences librarianship. *Winner:* Melissa Rethlefsen.

Lois Ann Colaianni Award for Excellence and Achievement in Hospital Librarianship. To a member of MLA who has made significant contributions to the profession in the area of overall distinction or leadership in hospital librarianship. *Winner:* Geneva Bush Staggs.

Cunningham Memorial International Fellowships. For health sciences librarians from countries Karen M. Albert.outside the United States and Canada, to provide for attendance at the MLA Annual Meeting and observation and supervised work in one or more medical libraries. *Winner:* Joseph Olubunmi Olorunsaye, Nigeria.

Louise Darling Medal. For distinguished achievement in collection development in the health sciences. *Winner:* HINARI Access to Research in Health Programme, World Health Organization.

Janet Doe Lectureship. *Winner:* Barbara A. Epstein, "In Their Own Words: Oral Histories of MLA Past Presidents."

EBSCO/MLA Annual Meeting Grants (up to $1,000). To enable four health sciences librarians to attend the MLA Annual Meeting. *Winners:* Krystal Buller, Suhua Caroline Fan, Erin Menzies, Michelle P. Rachal.

Ida and George Eliot Prize. To recognize a work published in the preceding calendar year that has been judged most effective in furthering medical librarianship. *Winners:* Ellen M. Aaronson, Nancy J. Allee, Ana Patricia Ayala, Tara Brigham, Elizabeth Connor, Teodora Constantinescu, Helen-Ann Brown Epstein, Ann Farrell, Tim Kenny, David Lightfoot, Jaonne M. Muellenbach, Laure Perrier, Ardis Weiss for "Effects of Librarian-Provided Services in Healthcare Settings: A Systemic Review."

Carla J. Funk Governmental Relations Award ($500). To recognize a medical librarian who has demonstrated outstanding leadership in the area of governmental relations at the federal, state, or local level, and who has furthered the goal of providing quality information for improved health. *Sponsor:* Kent A. Smith. *Winner:* Donna Timm.

Murray Gottlieb Prize. For the best unpublished essay on the history of medicine and allied sciences written by a health sciences librarian. *Sponsor:* MLA History of the Health Sciences Section. *Winner:* Not awarded in 2014.

T. Mark Hodges International Service Award. To honor outstanding achievement in promoting, enabling, or delivering improved health information internationally. *Winner:* Elena Faria Azadbakht "The Legacy of Color Vision Testing in the Railway Industry."

David A. Kronick Traveling Fellowship ($2,000). *Sponsor:* Bowden-Massey Foundation. *Winner:* Kimberly Parker.

Joseph Leiter NLM/MLA Lectureship. *Winner:* Ann McKee, "Chronic Traumatic Encephalopathy."

Donald A. B. Lindberg Research Fellowship ($10,000). To fund research aimed at expanding the research knowledge base, linking the information services provided by librarians to improved health care and advances in biomedical research. *Winner:* Lorie Kloda for "Effectiveness of Teaching Students in Occupational and Physical Therapy PICO vs. An Alternative Framework Questions Formulation: A Randomized Controlled Trial."

Lucretia W. McClure Excellence in Education Award. To an outstanding educator in the field of health sciences librarianship and informatics. *Winner:* Not awarded in 2015.

John P. McGovern Award Lectureship. Mae Jemison.

Majors/MLA Chapter Project of the Year Award. *Sponsor:* J. A. Majors Co. *Winner:* Medical Library Group of Southern California and Arizona.

Medical Informatics Section Career Development Grant ($1,500). To support a career development activity that will contribute to advancement in the field of medical informatics. *Winner:* Jennifer Dinalo.

MLA Continuing Education Awards ($100–$500). *Winners:* Leah C. Osterhaus Trzasko, Jennifer S. Walker.

MLA Scholarship (up to $5,000). For graduate study at an ALA-accredited library school. *Winner:* Catherine Hana.

MLA Scholarship for Minority Students (up to $5,000). For graduate study at an ALA-accredited library school. *Winner:* Tyler Moses.

Marcia C. Noyes Award. For an outstanding contribution to medical librarianship. *Winner:* J. Michael Homan.

President's Award. To an MLA member for a notable or important contribution made during the past association year. *Winners:* Not awarded in 2015.

Rittenhouse Award. For the best unpublished paper on medical librarianship submitted by a student enrolled in, or having been enrolled in, a course for credit in an ALA-accredited library school or a trainee in an internship program in medical librarianship. *Donor:* Rittenhouse Book Distributors. *Winner:* Nicole Dalmer for "Social Media: Evolving Assessment of Online Not awarded in 2015.Not awarded in 2015. Information Reliability."

Thomson Reuters/Frank Bradway Rogers Information Advancement Award. To recognize outstanding contributions for the application of technology to the delivery of health science information, to the science of information, or to the facilitation of the delivery of health science information. *Sponsor:* Thomson Reuters. *Winner:* Not awarded in 2015.

Music Library Association

Carol June Bradley Award. To support studies that involve the history of music libraries or special collections. *Winners:* Award Suspended.

Vincent H. Duckles Award. For the best book-length bibliography or other Award Suspended.Award Suspended. tool in music. *Winners:* John Gray for *Baila! A Bibliographic Guide to Afro-Latin Dance Musics from Mambo to Salsa* (African Diaspora Press).

Dena Epstein Award for Archival and Library Research in American Music. To support research in archives or libraries internationally on any aspect of American music. *Winner:* Gabriel Alfieri, Boston University, for research on how four major composers—Virgil Thompson, Paul Bowles, Marc Blitzstein, and Leonard Bernstein—worked with various playwrights and directors to compose incidental music for their spoken theater productions.

Kevin Freeman Travel Grants. To colleagues who are new to the profession to enable them to attend the MLA Annual Meeting. *Winners:* oy Doan, Kyra Folk-Farber, Robin Preiss, Elizabeth Surles.

Walter Gerboth Award. To members of the association who are in the first five years of their professional library careers, to assist research-in-progress in music or music librarianship. *Winner:* Not awarded in 2015.

Richard S. Hill Award. For the best article on music librarianship or article of a music-bibliographic nature. *Winner:* Linda Fairtile for "Verdi at 200: Recent Scholarship on the Composer and His Works."

MLA Citation. Awarded in recognition of contributions to the profession over a career. *Winner:* Jane Gottlieb.

Eva Judd O'Meara Award. For the best review published in *Notes. Winner:* David Hunter for "Review of Georg Friederic Händel 'Samson: Oratorio in Three Acts, HWV 57.'"

A. Ralph Papakhian Special Achievement Award. To recognize extraordinary service to the profession of music librarianship over a relatively short period of time. *Winners:* Jean Morrow.

National Library Service for the Blind and Physically Handicapped, Library of Congress

Library of the Year Awards ($1,000). *Winners:* Michigan Braille and Talking Book Library, Lansing, Michigan.

REFORMA (National Association to Promote Library and Information Services to Latinos and the Spanish-Speaking)

Elizabeth A. Martinez Lifetime Achievement Award. To recognize those who have achieved excellence in librarianship over an extended period of service and who have made significant and lasting contributions to REFORMA and the Latino community. *Winner:* Loida García-Febo.

REFORMA scholarships (up to $1,500). To students who qualify for graduate study in library science and who are citizens or permanent residents of the United States. *Winners:* (Rose Treviño Memorial Scholarship) Araceli Acosta; (REFORMA Scholarship) Elizabeth Negrete Gaylor.

Arnulfo D. Trejo Librarian of the Year Award. To recognize a librarian who has promoted and advocated services to the Spanish-speaking and Latino communities and made outstanding contributions to REFORMA. *Winner:* Madeline Peña, REFORMA LA, Los Angeles Public Library.

Society of American Archivists (SAA)

C. F. W. Coker Award for Description. To recognize creators of tools that enable archivists to produce more effective finding aids.

Winner: The Social Networks and Archival Context (SNAC) Project.

Distinguished Service Award. To recognize an archival institution, education program, nonprofit organization, or governmental organization that has given outstanding service to its public and has made an exemplary contribution to the archives profession. *Winner:* Archives Leadership Institute.

Diversity Award. To an individual, group, or Archives Leadership Institute.institution for outstanding contributions to advancing diversity within the archives profession, SAA, or the archival record. *Winners:* The Shorefront Legacy Center for the Samuel Proctor Oral History, Program, University of Florida.

Emerging Leader Award. To recognize early-career archivists who have completed archival work of broad merit, demonstrated significant promise of leadership, performed commendable service to the archives profession, or have accomplished a combination of these requirements. *Winner:* Cheryl Oestreicher, Boise State University.

Fellows' Ernst Posner Award. For an outstanding essay dealing with a facet of archival administration, history, theory, or methodology, published in *American Archivist*. *Winner:* Kit Hughes for "Appraisal as Cartography: Cultural Studies in the Archives."

Josephine Forman Scholarship ($10,000). *Sponsor:* General Commission on Archives and History of the United Methodist Church. *Winner:* Maria E. Sanchez-Tucker, University of Wisconsin, Milwaukee.

Elsie Ham and F. Gerald Ham Scholarship ($7,500). To recognize an individual's past performance in a graduate archival studies program and his or her potential in the field. *Winner:* Noah Geraci, University of California, Los Angeles.

Philip M. Hamer and Elizabeth Hamer Kegan Award. For individuals and/or institutions that have increased public awareness of a specific body of documents. *Winner:* The Legacy Center, Drexel University College of Medicine.

Oliver Wendell Holmes Travel Award. To enable overseas archivists already in the United States or Canada for training to attend the SAA Annual Meeting. *Winner:* Mary Grace Golfo, Philippines.

J. Franklin Jameson Archival Advocacy Award. For individuals and/or organizations that promote greater public awareness of archival activities and programs. *Winner:* Adrena Ifill Blagburn.

Sister M. Claude Lane, O.P., Memorial Award. For a significant contribution to the field of religious archives. *Winner:* Diane Wells, Episcopal Diocese of Olympia in Seattle.

Waldo Gifford Leland Award. To encourage and reward writing of superior excellence and usefulness in the field of archival history, theory, or practice. *Winner:* Michelle Caswell for *Archiving the Unspeakable: Silence, Memory, and the Photographic Record in Cambodia.*

Theodore Calvin Pease Award. For the best student paper ($100 and publication in *American Archivist*). *Winner:* Paige Hohmann, University of British Columbia, for "On Impartiality and Interrelatedness: Reactions to the Jenkinsonian Appraisal in the Twentieth Century."

Donald Peterson Student Travel Award (up to $1,000). To enable a student or recent graduate to attend the SAA Annual Meeting. *Winner:* Colin Post, University of North Carolina, Chapel Hill.

Harold T. Pinkett Minority Student Award. To encourage minority students to consider careers in the archival profession, and to promote minority participation in SAA. *Winners:* Talia Guzmán-González, University of Maryland, College Park; Rachel E. Winston, University of Texas at Austin.

Preservation Publication Award. To recognize an outstanding work published in North America that advances the theory or the practice of preservation in archival institutions. *Winners:* Digital POWRR Team for *From Theory to Action: "Good Enough" Digital Preservation Solutions for Under-Resourced Cultural Heritage Institutions*; (Special Commendation) National Digital Stewardship Alliance for *2015 National Agenda for Digital Stewardship.*

SAA Fellows. To a limited number of members for their outstanding contribution to the archival profession. *Honored*: Jelain Chubb, Kathy Marquis, Kathleen Williams.*Honored*: Jelain Chubb, Kathy Marquis, Kathleen Williams.

SAA Mosaic Scholarship ($5,000). To minority students pursuing graduate education in archival science. *Winners:* Desiree Alaniz, Simmons College.

SAA Spotlight Award. To recognize the contributions of individuals who work for the good of the profession and of archival collections, and whose work would not typically receive public recognition. *Winner:* Anne Ostendarp, Multimedia Archivist for the Knights of Columbus.

Special Libraries Association (SLA)

SLA Copyright Clearance Center Rising Stars Award. To SLA members in the first five years of membership who demonstrate exceptional promise of leadership. *Winners:* Susmita Chakraborty, Christine Coughlan, Kathleen Lehman.

SLA John Cotton Dana Award. For exceptional support and encouragement of special librarianship. *Winner:* Marjorie Hlava.

SLA Dow Jones Innovate Award. To an SLA member who has consistently shown innovation, leadership, and creativity in the information profession and the association. *Winner:* Not awarded in 2015.

SLA Fellows. *Honored*: Amy Affelt, P.K. Jain, Janice Keeler, Tracy Z. Maleeff, Mohamed Mubarak.

SLA Hall of Fame Award. For outstanding performance and distinguished service to SLA. *Winners:* James Matarazzo, Ethel Salonen.

SLA Presidential Citations. To SLA members for notable or important contributions during the previous year that enhanced the association or furthered its goals and objectives. *Winners:* Dorothy McGarry, Cindy Shamel, Ulla de Stricker.

Rose L. Vormelker Award. To SLA members for exceptional service through the education and mentoring of students and working professionals. *Winners:* Tom Nielsen, Rebecca Vargha.

Theatre Library Association

Brooks McNamara Performing Arts Librarian Scholarship. *Winner:* To be announced

Louis Rachow Distinguished Service in Performing Arts Librarianship Award. For extraordinary contributions to performing arts To be announcedTo be announced. *Winner:* Karen Nickeson.

George Freedley Memorial Award. *Winner:* Arnold Aronson for *Ming Cho Lee: A Life in Design.*

Richard Wall Award. See "Literary Prizes, 2015" in Part 5.

Other Awards of Distinction

American Psychological Association Excellence in Librarianship Award ($2,500). For significant contributions to psychology and behavioral sciences librarianship. *Winner:* Helen Hough, Systems Librarian for Open Source Applications, University of Texas, Arlington.

Robert B. Downs Intellectual Freedom Award. To recognize individuals or groups who have furthered the cause of intellectual freedom, particularly as it affects libraries and information centers and the dissemination of ideas. *Offered by:* Graduate School of Library and Information Science, University of Illinois at Urbana-Champaign. *Sponsor:* Libraries Unlimited/ABC-CLIO. *Winners:* HP Kids Read for promoting academic excellence and defending the role of experts, such as teachers and librarians, to select diverse reading materials that challenge their students to think critically, teach them empathy, and prepare them for the challenges of adulthood.

I Love My Librarian Awards ($5,000, a plaque, and a $500 travel stipend to attend the awards ceremony). To recognize librarians for service to their communities, schools, and campuses. Winners are nominated by library patrons. *Sponsors:* Carnegie Corporation of New York and the *New York Times. Winners:* Diane Brown, New Haven Free Public Library, Stetson Branch, New Haven, Connecticut; Doug Campbell, Willis Library, University of North Texas, Denton, Texas; Sylvia Cieply, Otto A. Fischer School Library, Orange County Juvenile Hall, Orange, California; Dona J. Helmer, College Gate Elementary School, Anchorage, Alaska; Courtney Kincaid, Hood County Library, Granbury, Texas; Leslie D. Koch, Armstrong Elementary School, Eastover, North Carolina; April Roy, Kansas City Public Library, Lucile H. Bluford Branch, Kansas City, Missouri; Elizabeth G. Rumery, Avery Point Campus Library, University of Connecticut, Groton, Connecticut; Christopher A. Shaffer, Troy University, Troy, Alabama; Shugana Williams, Mississippi Gulf Coast Community College, Perkinston Campus, Perkinston, Mississippi.

RWA Librarian of the Year. To a librarian who demonstrates outstanding support of romance authors and the romance genre. *Offered by:* Romance Writers of America. *Winner:* Lisa Schimmer, NoveList.

USBBY Bridge to Understanding Award ($1,000). To acknowledge the work of adults who use books to promote international understanding among children. *Offered by:* United States Board on Books for Young People. *Winner:* Día Family Book Club, an extension of the El Día de los Niños/El Día de los Libros project of the Association for Library Service to Children (ALSC), American Library Association. *Winner:* To be announced.

Women's National Book Association Award. Awarded biennially to a living American woman who derives part or all of her income from books and allied arts and who has done meritorious work in the world of books. *Offered by:* Women's National Book Association (WNBA). *Winner:* Amy King, SUNY Nassau Community College.

Part 4
Research and Statistics

Library Research and Statistics

Number of Libraries in the United States and Canada

Statistics are from *American Library Directory (ALD) 2016–2017* (Information Today, Inc., 2016). Data are exclusive of elementary and secondary school libraries.

Libraries in the United States

Public Libraries	16,878*
Public libraries, excluding branches	9,669
Main public libraries that have branches	1,409
Public library branches	7,209
Academic Libraries	3,635*
Community college	1,115
Departmental	199
Medical	5
Religious	7
University and college	2,520
Departmental	1,202
Law	190
Medical	235
Religious	249
Armed Forces Libraries	242*
Air Force	67
Medical	4
Army	115
Medical	22
Marine Corps	12
Navy	48
Law	1
Medical	9
Government Libraries	900*
Law	360
Medical	132
Special Libraries (excluding public, academic, armed forces, and government)	5,475*
Law	739
Medical	1,082
Religious	435

Total Special Libraries (including public, academic, armed forces, and government)	6,689
Total law	1,290
Total medical	1,489
Total religious	892
Total Libraries Counted(*)	27,130

Libraries in Regions Administered by the United States

Public Libraries	27*
Public libraries, excluding branches	9
Main public libraries that have branches	3
Public library branches	18
Academic Libraries	38*
Community college	3
Departmental	1
University and college	35
Departmental	19
Law	3
Medical	3
Religious	1
Armed Forces Libraries	2*
Air Force	1
Army	1
Navy	0
Government Libraries	3*
Law	1
Medical	1
Special Libraries (excluding public, academic, armed forces, and government)	5*
Law	3
Religious	1
Total Special Libraries (including public, academic, armed forces, and government)	14
Total law	7
Total medical	4
Total religious	2
Total Libraries Counted(*)	75

Libraries in Canada

Public Libraries	2,106*
Public libraries, excluding branches	821
Main public libraries that have branches	143
Public library branches	1,285

Academic Libraries	322*
Community college	74
Departmental	13
Religious	1
University and college	248
Departmental	173
Law	16
Medical	18
Religious	32
Government Libraries	192*
Law	27
Medical	5
Special Libraries (excluding public, academic, armed forces, and government)	629*
Law	88
Medical	145
Religious	21
Total Special Libraries (including public, academic, armed forces, and government)	728
Total law	131
Total medical	168
Total religious	72
Total Libraries Counted(*)	3,249

Summary

Total U.S. Libraries	27,130
Total Libraries Administered by the United States	75
Total Canadian Libraries	3,249
Grand Total of Libraries Listed	30,454

Note: Numbers followed by an asterisk are added to find "Total libraries counted" for each of the three geographic areas (United States, U.S.-administered regions, and Canada). The sum of the three totals is the "Grand total of libraries listed" in *ALD*. For details on the count of libraries, see the preface to the 69th edition of *ALD—Ed.*

Highlights of IMLS and NCES Surveys

The Institute of Museum and Library Services (IMLS) and the National Center for Education Statistics (NCES) collect and disseminate statistical information about libraries in the United States and its outlying areas. Two major surveys are conducted by NCES, the Academic Libraries Survey and the School Library Media Centers Survey; two others, the Public Libraries Survey and the State Library Agencies Survey, were formerly conducted by NCES, but are now handled by IMLS.

This article presents highlights from three of the most recently conducted surveys. For more information, see "National Center for Education Statistics" in Part 1 and "Institute of Museum and Library Services, Office of Library Services" in Part 2 of this volume.

Public Libraries

The following are highlights from the IMLS report *Public Libraries in the United States, Fiscal Year 2013*.

Library Use

- In FY 2013 there were 1.5 billion in-person visits to public libraries across the United States, the equivalent of more than 4.0 million visits each day. Although this reflects an increase of 17.6 percent over 10 years, libraries have experienced a decrease in physical visitation of 8.2 percent since a peak in FY 2009.
- Public libraries circulated 2.4 billion materials in FY 2013, a 10-year increase of 25.4 percent. There has been a slowing in overall circulation in recent years, with a decrease of 3.6 percent since a peak in FY 2010. However, circulation has not declined at the same rate as in-person visitation, which may be explained by the increase in access to digital materials that can be accessed remotely.
- Circulation of children's materials has seen long-term increases that may be related to increases in library programming aimed at early childhood learning and summer reading. Libraries lent 835.6 million children's books and materials in FY 2013. This is a 10-year increase of 22.7 percent, remaining stable over recent years.

Program Attendance

- There were 96.5 million attendees at public library programs in FY 2013. In support of the role of public libraries as gathering places, attendance at public library programs has continued to increase over prior years, with an increase of 28.6 percent for all programs since FY 2006.
- Children under 18 years comprised 23.1 percent of the total U.S. population in FY 2013. To meet the needs of this segment of the population, public libraries provide programming targeted to children and young adults.

Children's programming at libraries has long been a popular community resource. In addition to story hour, children's librarians have continued to meet the needs of their communities through scientifically-based programs to foster early learning and school readiness. There were 67.4 million attendees at children's programs, a 10-year increase of 29.7 percent.

- Libraries have had programs and services developed for young adults for many years, but over the past decade there has been a reconceptualization of these programs.

Public Access Computer Use

- There were 333.9 million user sessions on public access computer terminals in public libraries in FY 2013. This is a decrease of 9.2 percent from FY 2010. Many public libraries offer broadband, which can be accessed not only through the library-provided computers, but also through patrons' personal devices that they bring to the library.
- Although the uses of public access Internet computers may be decreasing, we will be exploring how to capture the many different ways that people use and access public library wireless and broadband services in future surveys.

Public Library Investments

- Public investments allow libraries to provide access to many popular services and resources. Financial investments are made by the public at the local, state, and federal levels. Public libraries direct these revenues to be spent in ways that support their local communities through services and resources. Although services may vary from place to place, most library expenditures are used to provide public resources such as the collection of materials for loan, varied programming, digital access, and knowledgeable staff.
- The PLS collects key measures of investment in public libraries: the financial investments of revenue and operating expenditures, collection size, the number of programs, the number of public access Internet computers, and levels of staffing.

Revenue

- In FY 2013 the public invested more than $11.5 billion in revenue for public libraries. After adjusting for inflation, this reflects no change from the prior year and a 10-year increase of 7.5 percent. Over $9.9 billion of public libraries' revenues (85.7 percent) came from local governments, reflecting a 10-year increase of 16.5 percent, a continuation of the increased share of library budgets. Revenue from state governments was $805.4 million, 7.0 percent of the total revenue in FY 2013.
- Although state contributions to library revenues have been steadily declining, with a 10-year decrease of 35.9 percent, there was no change in rev-

enues from states from FY 2012. The federal government provided 0.5 percent of total public library revenues.

- The remaining 6.8 percent of public library revenues came from other sources.

Operating Expenditures

- Total operating expenditures for public libraries were $10.9 billion in FY 2013, unchanged from expenditures from FY 2012 after adjusting for inflation. This is an increase of 9.1 percent over 10 years.
- The highest operating expenditures were for staffing expenses, which accounted for $7.4 billion of the total operating expenditures (67.2 percent). Although most of the expenditures for staffing are apportioned for salaries (73.7 percent), changes in the cost of health care have had a stronger impact on expenditures. Within staffing expenditures, $1.9 billion was spent on benefits. Although flat from the prior year, this budget item has increased by 54.0 percent over 10 years.
- More than $1.2 billion was spent on collections in FY 2013, unchanged from the prior year. Overall, expenditures on collections have been decreasing by 14.5 percent over 10 years. Although most public library collections expenditures still go to print materials (60.5 percent), changes in the composition of collection expenditures illustrate the ways in which public libraries are adjusting to the new models of service delivery, particularly regarding digital materials. Expenditures on electronic materials, such as e-books, were $239.3 million in FY 2013. More importantly, expenditures on electronic materials have increased by 186.8 percent over 10 years.

Collections

- Public librarians curate their collections to meet the needs of the communities they serve. Collections comprise both physical and digital materials, which may include print books, e-books, DVDs, and downloadable audio files. The average collection size across all public libraries was 116,481.6 items (median = 46,948.0), including printed materials, e-books, audio and video in all formats.
- Collections ranged from the smallest, with 399 materials, to the largest at 24,119,329.
- Print materials still make up most of public libraries' collections. There were 774.7 million print materials available at public libraries in FY 2013. This is a decrease of 4.7 percent since FY 2008, the highest volume over the prior 10 years. Public libraries also provide access to audio and video materials, including audio books and DVDs of popular movies. These collections have continued to grow. Public libraries had 46.6 million audio materials, a 10-year increase of 30.8 percent, and 59.2 million video materials, a 10-year increase of 107.0 percent.
- In FY 2013, 6,569 public libraries reported having e-books, an increase of 14.6 percent from FY 2012. For libraries that reported having e-books, their

e-book holdings ranged from 1 to 398,013 books. The average number of e-books at U.S. public libraries in FY 2013 was 20,170.0 (median = 8,770).

- In addition to e-books, public libraries provide access to digital audio and video materials. Like e-books, these materials can be downloaded and used either on devices loaned by the library or on patrons' personal devices. Most public libraries (67.3 percent) offered downloadable audio materials in FY 2013. Those libraries that offered this service ranged from 1 to 147,925 audio downloads, an average of 7,056.5 (median = 4,229.0). There were 2,725 public libraries to offer video downloads in FY 2013. Holdings ranged from 1 to 14,676 files, with an average of 1,016.1 (median = 321.0).

Public Library Programs

- Public libraries are committed to providing opportunities for learning experiences that educate and inspire people throughout their lifetime. Programs vary from digital learning and job training for adults, makerspaces for young adults, and summer reading programs and storytime for children. Public libraries have been increasing their program offerings over the previous decade.
- Public libraries offered 4.3 million programs in FY 2013, a one-year increase of 6.6 percent.

Public Access Internet Computers

- A core function of public libraries is to facilitate open access to information and ideas. In the 21st century, public libraries accomplish this by providing public access to computers and the Internet, serving as technology access points for communities.
- There were 278,733 public access Internet computers available at public libraries across the nation. This reflects a one-year increase of 2.8 percent and 10-year increase of 98.5 percent.

Public Library Staff

- One of the most important assets found in public libraries is the knowledgeable library workforce.
- Public library services were supported by 137,183 total full-time equivalent (FTE) staff. Staffing levels had fluctuated over the 10-year period prior to FY 2013. Staffing levels at public libraries declined during the recession, decreasing by 5.4 percent from a high of 145,070 in FY 2008, but stabilizing by FY 2013. Librarians composed 34.6 percent of total staff, with 47,441 librarian FTEs. This was a 10-year increase of 6.1 percent.
- There were 3.9 librarian FTEs per 25,000 people, a 3.9 percent decrease since FY 2002.
- Two-thirds (67.1 percent) of librarians had a master's of library science from an American Library Association-accredited graduate program. Half

of public libraries (52.5 percent) had at least one librarian on staff with an ALA-MLS degree.

State Library Administrative Agencies

The following are highlights from the IMLS report *State Library Administrative Agencies Survey, Fiscal Year 2012,* released in May 2014.

Revenue and Expenditures

- State Library Administrative Agency (SLAA) revenues totaled nearly $1 billion in fiscal year (FY) 2012, which represented a 27 percent decrease from FY 2003 and a 12 percent decrease from FY 2010.
- Revenues from the federal government for all SLAAs totaled $181.6 million in FY 2012. State revenues totaled $766.2 million, which included $265.8 million received from the states to support SLAA operation, $455.6 million in state aid to libraries, and $40.9 million received from the states for any other purposes (such as interagency transfers).
- Total expenditures for FY 2012 across all SLAAs were $995.5 million, which represented a 26 percent decrease from FY 2003 and an 11 percent decrease from FY 2010. When looking across the types of expenditures, $640.6 million went toward financial assistance to libraries, $335.4 million went toward operating expenditures, $14.8 million was allocated to other services, and $2.5 million was spent on capital outlay.
- More than $89 million of LSTA (Library Services and Technology Act) funds was used to support access to technology and information resources for libraries in 2012, and $36 million went toward programs and services for lifelong learning.

Workforce and Staff Development

- In FY 2012 SLAAs employed 2,814 full-time equivalent (FTE) staff, which was a decrease of 5 percent from 2010.
- In FY 2012 a total of 360 staff (13 percent of all budgeted FTEs) was reported within the service of administration, more than 600 budgeted FTEs (22 percent) were reported within library development, and 1,354 budgeted FTEs (48 percent) were reported within library services.

Services

- A total of 40 SLAAs funded or facilitated digitization programs and services in 2012, and 15 SLAAs provided preservation and conservation services to public libraries and library cooperatives.
- During FY 2012 the number of library service transactions that served the general public and state government employees reported by SLAAs included library visits (29,051), circulation transactions (45,971), reference

transactions (15,992), and interlibrary loan services provided to another library (6,222) and received from another library (2,368).

- Fifty SLAAs funded summer reading programs and continuing education programs for public libraries in FY 2012.

Identification and Governance

- Of the 50 states and the District of Columbia, three SLAAs (Michigan, New York, and Tennessee) were located within the legislative branch in state government, and 48 were located within the executive branch.
- Thirty-seven of the 51 SLAAs reported having allied operations in addition to their SLAA functions, ten reported state archives and state records management services, and eight reported some other type of allied operation.

School Libraries

The following are highlights from the NCES publication *Characteristics of Public Elementary and Secondary School Library Media Centers in the United States: Results from the 2011–2012 Schools and Staffing Survey* (NCES 2013-315).

- During the 2011–2012 school year, 79,000 of the 85,500 traditional public schools in the United States reported having a library media center, while 2,200 of the 4,500 public charter schools reported having one.
- About two-thirds (67 percent) of library media centers in traditional public schools had full-time, paid, state-certified library media center specialists, while one-third (33 percent) of those in public charter schools had this type of staff. In traditional public schools, 20 percent of library media centers did not have any paid, state-certified library media center specialists (full or part time), and 56 percent of those in public charter schools did not have this type of staff.
- The percentage of paid, professional library media center staff with a master's degree in a library-related major field was 52 percent for all public schools, 52 percent in traditional public schools, and 27 percent in public charter schools.
- During the 2010–2011 school year, public school library media centers spent an average of $9,340 for all information resources. This included an average of $6,010 for the purchase of books and $490 for the purchase of audio/video materials.
- The number of holdings in public library media centers per 100 students was 2,188 for book titles and 81 for audio/video materials at the end of the 2010–2011 school year.
- Public school library media centers provided technological services, including automated catalog(s) for student and/or staff use (88 percent), laptops for staff use outside the library media center (54 percent), laptops for

student use outside the library media center (40 percent), and technology to assist students and/or staff with disabilities (31 percent).

- The percentage of library media centers with computer workstations for student and/or staff use was 97 percent in traditional public schools and 88 percent in public charter schools. Of the library media center computer workstations, 95 percent had Internet access. Among all public school library media centers, 86 percent provided student access to online, licensed databases.

- For classes and other activities, 61 percent of public school library media centers had both flexible scheduling (available as needed) and regular scheduling (previously specified times), while 19 percent had only flexible scheduling, and 19 percent had only regular scheduling. The percentage of public school library media centers that were available for independent student use was 89 percent during regular school hours, 57 percent before school, and 54 percent after school.

- About one-fourth (24 percent) of public school library media centers were open to community members who do not attend the school and do not have children who attend the school. Of these, 61 percent had workstations that community members could use to access the Internet.

- Public school library media centers supported programs that encourage students to read (65 percent) and family literacy activities (36 percent). Per 100 students in the school, there was an average of 100 student visits to the library media center and 110 books or other materials checked out during a full week of school.

Library Acquisition Expenditures, 2015–2016: U.S. Public, Academic, Special, and Government Libraries

The information in these tables is taken from the 2015–2016 edition of *American Library Directory* (*ALD*) (Information Today, Inc.). The tables report acquisition expenditures by public, academic, special, and government libraries.

Understanding the Tables

Number of libraries includes only those U.S. libraries in *ALD* that reported annual acquisition expenditures. Libraries that reported annual income but not expenditures are not included in the count. Academic libraries include university, college, and junior college libraries. Special academic libraries, such as law and medical libraries, that reported acquisition expenditures separately from the institution's main library are counted as independent libraries.

The amount in the *total acquisition expenditures* column for a given state is generally greater than the sum of the categories of expenditures. This is because the total acquisition expenditures amount also includes the expenditures of libraries that did not itemize by category.

Figures in *categories of expenditure* columns represent only those libraries that itemized expenditures. Libraries that reported a total acquisition expenditure amount but did not itemize are only represented in the total acquisition expenditures column.

Table 1 / Public Library Acquisition Expenditures

State	Number of Libraries	Total Acquisition Expenditures	Books	Other Print Materials	Periodicals/ Serials	Manuscripts & Archives	AV Equipment	AV Materials	Microforms	Electronic Reference	Preservation
Alabama	18	18,639,316	1,184,080	1,252	23,389	2,000	—	186,619	2,013	24,566	20,400
Alaska	12	1,929,856	896,133	17,876	86,906	43,021	—	294,930	500	228,709	6,871
Arizona	22	18,183,916	3,258,036	3,700	193,031	575	—	777,971	30,481	1,170,069	—
Arkansas	10	3,323,300	1,662,840	20,564	50,526	—	23,105	699,515	—	532,570	5,000
California	67	81,259,034	31,411,940	1,588,187	2,519,450	9,000	43,417	8,382,222	67,872	8,661,349	70,311
Colorado	28	14,641,865	4,866,870	448,462	382,112	—	15,000	2,037,936	500	1,303,414	—
Connecticut	53	19,113,107	3,180,394	5,739	762,127	1,605	8,000	739,642	6,080	879,909	39,562
Delaware	4	303,475	40,000	—	5,000	—	—	—	—	—	—
District of Columbia	0	—	—	—	—	—	—	—	—	—	—
Florida	32	31,388,006	13,289,785	395,085	899,439	—	173,059	5,105,864	13,722	3,898,517	1,540
Georgia	16	4,536,812	1,391,464	42,253	76,568	—	2,026	366,137	2,350	268,969	198
Hawaii	1	4,052,293	2,361,178	66,730	135,998	—	—	—	49,347	1,439,040	—
Idaho	8	390,410	102,175	500	—	—	—	11,901	—	14,978	—
Illinois	105	34,927,512	10,602,251	81,992	699,117	3,000	75,113	3,808,276	43,939	4,668,885	26,369
Indiana	65	28,284,496	10,946,815	12,000	1,059,435	—	141,086	4,462,617	152,653	4,520,891	75,647
Iowa	59	7,112,992	2,166,240	66,914	176,393	4,000	7,013	673,421	2,993	343,055	—
Kansas	29	6,820,784	2,857,111	123,722	883,387	—	4,600	834,679	5,554	728,907	100
Kentucky	23	10,543,180	3,375,650	108,450	190,711	—	30,224	1,116,134	13,065	1,835,676	39,276
Louisiana	7	7,676,139	2,725,998	5,000	301,552	—	109,597	792,165	54,882	1,775,593	—
Maine	34	1,207,494	544,502	1,000	90,295	2,000	5,350	120,174	800	239,100	1,000
Maryland	3	10,640,301	1,823,665	—	85,337	—	—	974,786	—	175,455	—
Massachusetts	72	18,977,360	3,346,053	91,044	412,516	—	6,014	930,337	19,066	448,999	3,700
Michigan	70	29,159,919	5,856,280	217,853	354,497	—	140,831	1,729,135	10,186	1,285,498	2,102
Minnesota	31	73,857,773	2,310,619	1,403	73,122	—	83	481,502	30	192,317	516
Mississippi	10	1,378,906	603,294	—	88,964	—	—	96,239	26,000	135,492	2,162
Missouri	34	26,434,145	5,541,770	100,000	498,589	—	25,796	2,730,796	44,651	1,894,702	150

State	Count										
Montana	16	996,289	417,383	73,040	78,392	200	5,500	120,963	1,000	99,766	2,500
Nebraska	25	1,876,210	1,074,270	273,449	21,567	—	47	48,835	40	312,636	96
Nevada	5	932,628	128,500	1,193	10,558	—	—	34,634	—	20,000	—
New Hampshire	48	1,783,734	729,397	131	89,801	—	7,428	211,310	10,455	87,500	2,650
New Jersey	60	23,843,966	11,741,127	118,114	1,064,372	500	21,500	2,396,678	101,249	1,697,155	2,850
New Mexico	12	3,343,274	1,918,388	215,399	58,510	—	6,000	377,546	10,213	489,465	—
New York	107	48,013,168	15,034,382	81,818	1,163,401	3,000	287,563	3,280,551	45,663	2,385,987	8,133
North Carolina	19	9,902,430	6,152,047	1,306,038	208,415	—	7,000	673,211	8,540	456,428	—
North Dakota	15	2,097,121	699,909	385	73,529	—	35,000	164,969	3,500	558,660	1,000
Ohio	64	67,788,638	20,924,572	336,507	3,150,219	6,921	25,856	10,498,562	305,701	10,026,426	213,293
Oklahoma	12	12,749,138	4,774,914	3,528	862,264	—	—	2,078,713	3,810	1,892,349	—
Oregon	36	8,580,197	3,296,569	15,027	355,417	—	3,500	1,133,614	23,699	303,884	1,872,003
Pennsylvania	56	19,241,909	4,200,199	895,379	812,556	156,260	2,226	2,401,999	170,236	1,332,330	245,183
Rhode Island	8	9,877,726	695,680	71,214	61,005	—	—	119,609	70	831,999	1,450
South Carolina	13	11,176,562	5,079,962	46,957	120,700	5,000	7,500	2,040,492	—	916,468	10,832
South Dakota	14	1,826,083	881,131	15,756	85,749	—	16,846	308,186	50	91,081	—
Tennessee	20	6,637,633	1,774,753	270,414	138,519	—	16,600	369,335	1,200	574,271	1,724
Texas	96	54,733,768	9,655,333	334,782	787,028	—	272,843	1,757,598	52,873	2,027,493	38,650
Utah	9	3,289,767	1,874,178	1,203	47,563	—	—	797,171	30,367	401,209	—
Vermont	42	1,280,767	530,239	311	26,044	—	—	129,375	200	29,463	500
Virginia	26	11,403,923	5,145,317	151,005	470,197	44,810	—	1,350,615	40,454	1,350,794	1,339,701
Washington	22	19,396,587	2,641,299	566,925	119,593	—	54,205	648,828	622	643,264	400
West Virginia	12	5,095,574	1,384,786	3,000	78,113	—	15,000	228,352	13,500	861,966	2,900
Wisconsin	55	7,146,743	2,856,116	76,510	208,304	—	15,952	916,207	14,638	297,343	200
Wyoming	10	3,956,118	345,751	500	38,177	—	6,000	68,701	55	18,388	—
Puerto Rico	0	—	—	—	—	—	—	—	—	—	—
Total	1,615	791,752,344	220,301,345	8,258,311	20,178,454	281,892	1,616,880	69,509,052	1,384,819	64,372,985	4,038,969
Estimated % of Acquisition Expenditures			27.82	1.04	2.55	0.04	0.20	8.78	0.17	8.13	0.51

Table 2 / Academic Library Acquisition Expenditures

State	Number of Libraries	Total Acquisition Expenditures	Books	Other Print Materials	Periodicals/ Serials	Manuscripts & Archives	AV Equipment	AV Materials	Microforms	Electronic Reference	Preservation
Alabama	12	12,363,978	1,458,689	8,031	3,267,195	—	10,000	119,098	97,741	1,777,198	71,387
Alaska	4	6,770,113	556,433	20,000	2,444,608		300	77,137	16,807	938,392	18,827
Arizona	5	3,311,815	317,749		138,445	—	6,955	35,465	15,227	190,911	—
Arkansas	7	10,047,412	1,264,417	371,223	6,261,885	34,264	1,000	28,972	122,257	1,031,746	9,187
California	50	76,121,417	4,904,897	548,107	8,598,160	4,199	48,881	302,932	66,549	11,807,185	217,922
Colorado	14	21,590,192	1,102,783	24,882	1,820,672			162,972	—	4,134,010	41,037
Connecticut	10	9,850,105	1,027,191	250	2,968,126	262	80,000	51,618	8,518	1,086,622	25,311
Delaware	3	11,439,445	40,000		8,419						—
District of Columbia	4	16,518,550	1,435,677	110,000	5,900,251			3,267	34,380	1,825,723	47,000
Florida	22	32,652,972	5,009,132	856,738	13,853,756			426,437	141,498	11,746,497	174,601
Georgia	17	15,290,702	990,746	2,000	2,183,801		3,098	99,078	67,231	2,210,849	25,946
Hawaii	0	—									
Idaho	3	8,855,854	368,331	54,040	1,886,540			11,776	—	597,018	24,910
Illinois	29	53,810,443	7,897,407	7,648	16,833,097		20,000	178,242	37,529	2,983,840	119,890
Indiana	21	34,918,710	3,210,566	39,211	12,124,551		18	103,977	9,719	3,566,865	69,837
Iowa	16	24,115,952	2,242,485	394,839	4,995,622		6,000	94,803	42,545	2,188,198	78,787
Kansas	15	8,373,591	873,504	24,000	6,120,556	3,000	5,918	53,308	27,314	803,889	40,339
Kentucky	12	20,133,016	827,446	12,495	3,504,196	132	2,864	108,777	80,345	1,921,081	20,222
Louisiana	10	5,651,400	406,698	36,361	2,898,900	2,810	3,720	6,975	36,508	1,607,247	50,718
Maine	3	10,402,740	1,264,860	177,656	7,564,612				53,849	475,000	32,730
Maryland	13	11,990,942	1,504,173	8,912	8,201,673	12,434		37,787	18,398	1,777,659	35,610
Massachusetts	22	182,116,248	2,115,576	35,056	7,928,336	36,000	19,011	223,579	4,538	7,807,991	172,495
Michigan	24	23,564,210	2,357,384	141,409	9,204,832	25,203	10,000	170,039	1,407,462	6,635,944	49,959
Minnesota	16	9,557,070	1,656,679	10,000	3,769,705	280	54,455	185,782	38,367	1,342,296	95,905
Mississippi	3	572,329	84,104		149,329			11,050	—	167,346	10,500

Missouri	16	11,865,037	516,144	12,000	1,594,113	8,767	4,000	125,822	125,045	826,690	29,860
Montana	1	84,360	32,000	—	17,000	—	—	7,000	—	15,000	—
Nebraska	8	15,433,627	456,063	86,211	2,201,832	15,000	—	82,021	66,665	1,593,600	13,926
Nevada	0	—	—	—	—	—	—	—	—	—	—
New Hampshire	4	7,920,684	1,195,724	—	4,180,222	—	—	700	21,116	1,351,794	76,271
New Jersey	13	62,346,346	1,430,450	69,154	2,745,532	1,000	—	68,764	15,866	2,386,120	7,603
New Mexico	4	3,330,114	137,311	177,121	2,685,913	11,802	—	19,878	16,450	112,334	28,574
New York	47	76,896,206	7,359,903	38,136	19,867,936	86,270	176,949	457,743	137,011	16,480,586	400,710
North Carolina	25	80,223,937	3,025,681	—	8,831,819	—	1,144,575	382,687	287,139	2,474,673	80,374
North Dakota	2	2,965,537	365,806	14,193	2,011,935	—	—	30,752	684	539,766	16,594
Ohio	29	37,591,220	3,680,697	1,866	6,800,935	3,798	17,088	189,945	126,584	4,108,126	154,358
Oklahoma	9	6,336,120	661,462	—	2,339,527	2,000	—	125,951	2,452	2,159,585	7,692
Oregon	14	27,283,901	1,337,595	50,102	4,987,783	—	32,779	95,469	—	1,134,158	55,554
Pennsylvania	26	17,420,896	2,843,756	—	6,472,563	1,702	3,000	274,097	68,176	3,721,806	106,495
Rhode Island	3	1,681,147	477,893	20,000	751,097	8,000	—	38,270	8,000	391,213	6,674
South Carolina	12	9,235,576	1,087,114	—	985,064	20,000	10,000	84,449	64,255	2,697,532	65,482
South Dakota	4	3,230,118	283,665	—	776,454	—	909	11,516	13,014	577,169	18,102
Tennessee	13	18,617,026	836,493	61,462	1,427,754	—	—	41,205	84,580	2,736,516	6,917
Texas	41	56,500,087	5,381,367	—	14,728,147	6,250	168,402	228,258	241,372	6,485,159	168,448
Utah	5	9,014,776	1,145,523	—	5,052,204	—	5,000	68,800	3,500	263,379	32,276
Vermont	4	1,526,268	261,518	615,565	860,042	1,423	5,000	31,806	2,122	327,025	7,832
Virginia	21	36,897,072	5,902,711	—	11,016,563	2,000	26,871	213,059	65,070	6,434,622	83,909
Washington	11	14,372,381	1,703,911	975	7,482,834	2,000	46,000	235,372	7,900	1,814,577	18,098
West Virginia	10	3,116,419	193,350	1,964	351,813	6,750	14,300	23,070	52,944	537,115	10,778
Wisconsin	14	11,319,225	584,499	—	1,431,436	1,879	21,000	131,131	43,945	1,715,414	17,429
Wyoming	2	7,344,506	3,458,937	5,000	2,201,321	—	—	13,200	—	863,481	—
Puerto Rico	8	6,698,035	743,468	—	4,654,245	5,000	14,490	50,440	—	902,726	9,800
Total	681	1,139,269,827	88,019,968	4,036,607	249,083,351	302,225	1,962,583	5,524,476	3,780,672	131,273,673	2,856,876
Estimated % of Acquisition Expenditures			7.73	0.35	21.86	0.03	0.17	0.48	0.33	11.52	0.25

321

Table 3 / Special Library Acquisition Expenditures

State	Number of Libraries	Total Acquisition Expenditures	Category of Expenditures (in U.S. dollars)								
			Books	Other Print Materials	Periodicals/ Serials	Manuscripts & Archives	AV Equipment	AV Materials	Microforms	Electronic Reference	Preservation
Alabama	—	—	—	—	—	—	—	—	—	—	—
Alaska	—	—	—	—	—	—	—	—	—	—	—
Arizona	5	20,824	3,500	—	324	—	—	—	—	—	1,000
Arkansas	—	—	—	—	—	—	—	—	—	—	—
California	10	333,191	47,283	1,000	168,917	—	1,000	1,100	—	20,891	3,000
Colorado	—	—	—	—	—	—	—	—	—	—	—
Connecticut	1	1,000	—	—	—	—	—	—	—	—	—
Delaware	—	—	—	—	—	—	—	—	—	—	—
District of Columbia	3	309,000	61,000	—	100,000	—	—	—	2,000	145,000	1,000
Florida	2	13,600	4,650	—	7,500	—	—	—	—	—	600
Georgia	—	—	—	—	—	—	—	—	—	—	—
Hawaii	—	—	—	—	—	—	—	—	—	—	—
Idaho	—	—	—	—	—	—	—	—	—	—	—
Illinois	9	2,999,700	91,600	30,500	150,200	200	1,500	2,000	1,500	106,500	4,700
Indiana	1	87,400	—	—	—	—	—	—	—	—	—
Iowa	3	213,058	35,362	—	12,408	—	—	—	155,288	—	—
Kansas	1	6,000	3,000	—	3,000	—	—	—	—	—	—
Kentucky	—	—	—	—	—	—	—	—	—	—	—
Louisiana	1	18,000	5,000	—	13,000	—	—	—	—	—	—
Maine	1	200	—	—	—	—	—	—	—	—	—
Maryland	3	166,950	23,150	—	130,450	50	—	—	—	12,000	100
Massachusetts	1	73,000	—	—	—	—	—	—	—	—	—
Michigan	1	12,000	3,000	500	3,600	—	—	400	—	—	—
Minnesota	1	50,000	20,000	5,000	9,000	—	—	—	—	16,000	—
Mississippi	—	—	—	—	—	—	—	—	—	—	—

Missouri	1	67,500	24,000	—	29,500	—	—	—	—	14,000	—
Montana	1	17,348	15,848	—	500	—	—	—	—	1,500	—
Nebraska	1	800	300	—	—	—	—	—	—	—	—
Nevada	—	—	—	—	—	—	—	—	—	—	—
New Hampshire	2	92,000	16,000	10,000	5,000	20,000	—	—	—	32,000	9,000
New Jersey	4	21,200	9,000	—	5,000	—	—	6,000	—	—	1,200
New Mexico	2	12,500	—	—	—	—	—	—	—	—	—
New York	15	856,656	338,118	50	70,800	—	2,500	17,182	—	45,806	153,200
North Carolina	1	—	—	—	—	—	—	—	—	—	—
North Dakota	1	8,098	2,660	—	3,975	—	—	—	—	—	1,463
Ohio	7	714,455	80,551	550	73,362	882	—	850	—	31,417	5,047
Oklahoma	3	219,700	17,000	—	47,700	12,000	20,000	1,000	3,000	12,000	—
Oregon	1	600	200	—	—	—	—	—	—	400	—
Pennsylvania	1	106,357	7,108	47,812	5,059	18,351	—	4,671	—	3,322	20,034
Rhode Island	1	75,313	44,726	—	5,000	15,387	—	—	—	—	10,200
South Carolina	—	—	—	—	—	—	—	—	—	—	—
South Dakota	—	—	—	—	—	—	—	—	—	—	—
Tennessee	—	—	—	—	—	—	—	—	—	—	—
Texas	4	1,661,492	38,256	43,992	2,393	—	670	765	—	814,000	1,556
Utah	1	75,000	5,000	5,000	10,000	—	5,000	—	—	50,000	—
Vermont	—	—	—	—	—	—	—	—	—	—	—
Virginia	4	182,959	86,602	—	47,060	4,026	—	—	—	44,000	1,271
Washington	1	1,500	—	—	—	—	—	—	—	—	—
West Virginia	—	—	—	—	—	—	—	—	—	—	—
Wisconsin	2	85,500	4,000	—	20,000	—	—	—	—	60,000	—
Wyoming	—	—	—	—	—	—	—	—	—	—	—
Puerto Rico	—	—	—	—	—	—	—	—	—	—	—
Total	95	8,502,901	986,914	144,404	923,748	70,896	30,670	33,968	161,788	1,408,836	213,371
Estimated % of Acquisition Expenditures			11.61	1.70	10.86	0.83	0.36	0.40	1.90	16.57	2.51

Table 4 / Government Library Acquisition Expenditures

State	Number of Libraries	Total Acquisition Expenditures	Books	Other Print Materials	Periodicals/ Serials	Manuscripts & Archives	AV Equipment	AV Materials	Microforms	Electronic Reference	Preservation
					Category of Expenditures (in U.S. dollars)						
Alabama	2	626,295	243,777	—	575	—	—	—	—	381,472	471
Alaska	0	—	—	—	—	—	—	—	—	—	—
Arizona	0	—	—	—	—	—	—	—	—	—	—
Arkansas	0	—	—	—	—	—	—	—	—	—	—
California	8	2,148,414	575,486	—	482,354	—	3,740	—	—	318,399	1,950
Colorado	0	—	—	—	—	—	—	—	—	—	—
Connecticut	0	—	—	—	—	—	—	—	—	—	—
Delaware	0	—	—	—	—	—	—	—	—	—	—
District of Columbia	0	—	—	—	—	—	—	—	—	—	—
Florida	1	19,545	3,750	—	14,170	—	—	1,625	—	—	—
Georgia	0	—	—	—	—	—	—	—	—	—	—
Hawaii	0	—	—	—	—	—	—	—	—	—	—
Idaho	0	—	—	—	—	—	—	—	—	—	—
Illinois	0	—	—	—	—	—	—	—	—	—	—
Indiana	0	—	—	—	—	—	—	—	—	—	—
Iowa	0	—	—	—	—	—	—	—	—	—	—
Kansas	2	789,260	296,852	—	400,491	—	—	—	—	85,690	6,227
Kentucky	0	—	—	—	—	—	—	—	—	—	—
Louisiana	2	1,050,279	91,080	—	42,318	—	—	1,000	—	41,663	—
Maine	1	380,116	—	—	—	—	—	—	—	—	—
Maryland	2	214,000	93,000	11,800	98,000	—	—	7,700	—	—	3,500
Massachusetts	0	—	—	—	—	—	—	—	—	—	—
Michigan	1	35,000	—	—	—	—	—	—	—	—	—
Minnesota	2	134,500	18,000	—	61,500	—	—	—	—	55,000	—
Mississippi	0	—	—	—	—	—	—	—	—	—	—

Missouri	0	—	—	—	—	—	—	—	—	—	—
Montana	1	425,961	328,391	—	—	—	—	—	—	97,570	—
Nebraska	0	768,769	562,656	—	—	—	—	—	—	—	—
Nevada	1	—	—	—	10,803	—	—	—	3,151	186,357	5,802
New Hampshire	0	—	—	—	—	—	—	—	—	—	—
New Jersey	0	—	—	—	—	—	—	—	—	—	—
New Mexico	0	—	—	—	—	—	—	—	—	—	—
New York	0	—	—	—	—	—	—	—	—	—	—
North Carolina	0	—	—	—	—	—	—	—	—	—	—
North Dakota	0	—	—	—	—	—	—	—	—	—	—
Ohio	0	—	—	—	—	—	—	—	—	—	—
Oklahoma	0	—	—	—	—	—	—	—	—	—	—
Oregon	0	—	—	—	—	—	—	—	—	—	—
Pennsylvania	3	493,000	—	—	—	—	—	—	—	—	—
Rhode Island	1	43,425	9,961	—	31,764	—	—	814	—	886	—
South Carolina	0	—	—	—	—	—	—	—	—	—	—
South Dakota	0	—	—	—	—	—	—	—	—	—	—
Tennessee	0	—	—	—	—	—	—	—	—	—	—
Texas	0	—	—	—	—	—	—	—	—	—	—
Utah	0	—	—	—	—	—	—	—	—	—	—
Vermont	0	—	—	—	—	—	—	—	—	—	—
Virginia	1	63,090	13,355	—	42,453	—	—	6,271	—	1,011	—
Washington	0	—	—	—	—	—	—	—	—	—	—
West Virginia	1	650,000	50,000	—	400,000	—	—	—	—	200,000	—
Wisconsin	2	91,000	45,000	—	—	—	—	—	—	36,000	—
Wyoming	0	—	—	—	—	—	—	—	—	—	—
Puerto Rico	0	—	—	—	—	—	—	—	—	—	—
Total	31	7,932,654	2,331,308	11,800	1,584,428	—	3,740	17,410	3,151	1,404,048	17,950
Estimated % of Acquisition Expenditures			29.39	0.15	19.97	0.00	0.05	0.22	0.04	17.70	0.23

Public Library State Rankings, 2013

State	Library Visits per Capita	Registered Users per Capita	Circulation Transactions per Capita	Interlibrary Loans Received per 1,000 Population	Average Public-use Computers per Outlet
Alabama	45	18	46	21	21
Alaska	25	38	29	38	45
Arizona	34	39	28	32	4
Arkansas	37	25	41	45	39
California	33	24	37	20	15
Colorado	8	5	4	18	5
Connecticut	5	45	19	15	17
Delaware	36	48	33	6	8
District of Columbia	40	42	43	50	1
Florida	35	28	36	49	2
Georgia	51	49	49	24	11
Hawaii	42	4	45	51	41
Idaho	3	17	9	22	36
Illinois	7	21	12	8	14
Indiana	14	13	5	27	13
Iowa	11	7	18	19	47
Kansas	19	8	10	14	43
Kentucky	32	19	30	42	6
Louisiana	44	34	47	36	28
Maine	15	10	23	7	48
Maryland	26	20	14	33	3
Massachusetts	6	41	15	4	34
Michigan	23	40	20	11	18
Minnesota	28	2	13	17	25
Mississippi	47	35	51	48	37
Missouri	21	15	11	23	33
Montana	29	44	35	16	42
Nebraska	20	6	21	40	40
Nevada	39	46	26	31	27
New Hampshire	1	1	7	12	50
New Jersey	24	37	32	13	20
New Mexico	31	23	39	44	31
New York	18	32	24	9	23
North Carolina	43	27	42	46	12
North Dakota	46	50	34	26	44
Ohio	2	3	2	5	24
Oklahoma	30	11	27	43	29
Oregon	16	33	1	2	30
Pennsylvania	41	51	40	10	35
Rhode Island	17	47	31	3	10
South Carolina	38	29	38	35	9
South Dakota	22	30	16	34	49
Tennessee	48	36	48	41	22
Texas	49	31	44	37	7

State	Library Visits per Capita	Registered Users per Capita	Circulation Transactions per Capita	Interlibrary Loans Received per 1,000 Population	Average Public-use Computers per Outlet
Utah	4	12	3	47	26
Vermont	9	26	25	25	51
Virginia	27	22	17	39	16
Washington	12	14	6	30	19
West Virginia	50	43	50	28	46
Wisconsin	13	16	8	1	32
Wyoming	10	9	22	29	38

State	Public-use Internet Computers per 5,000 Population	Print Materials per Capita	Current Print Serial Subscriptions per 1,000 Population	Audio Physical Units per 1,000 Population	Video Physical Units per 1,000 Population
Alabama	21	39	48	42	44
Alaska	11	14	9	24	3
Arizona	37	51	46	40	37
Arkansas	33	30	37	47	39
California	49	45	41	44	45
Colorado	18	37	31	20	15
Connecticut	15	6	18	7	8
Delaware	44	44	25	36	30
District of Columbia	4	23	35	34	23
Florida	36	48	42	41	34
Georgia	46	49	51	51	50
Hawaii	51	31	49	26	47
Idaho	12	21	29	21	21
Illinois	14	15	7	8	12
Indiana	9	9	10	5	5
Iowa	5	8	4	11	10
Kansas	7	13	17	15	6
Kentucky	24	40	14	37	36
Louisiana	20	29	22	43	26
Maine	3	2	8	16	11
Maryland	39	35	28	18	29
Massachusetts	28	3	15	9	13
Michigan	17	18	16	17	16
Minnesota	22	24	26	25	33
Mississippi	30	42	43	50	49
Missouri	34	22	1	23	27
Montana	16	27	30	39	31
Nebraska	1	11	6	27	25
Nevada	50	50	45	33	28
New Hampshire	8	1	2	3	2
New Jersey	31	20	23	4	18
New Mexico	29	28	32	35	35
New York	27	16	12	22	14

State	Public-use Internet Computers per 5,000 Population	Print Materials per Capita	Current Print Serial Subscriptions per 1,000 Population	Audio Physical Units per 1,000 Population	Video Physical Units per 1,000 Population
North Carolina	45	46	44	49	51
North Dakota	19	17	20	30	32
Ohio	25	12	3	1	1
Oklahoma	26	33	39	31	43
Oregon	38	26	27	14	17
Pennsylvania	48	36	33	19	41
Rhode Island	10	7	24	32	24
South Carolina	35	41	38	46	42
South Dakota	13	10	19	28	19
Tennessee	42	43	50	45	46
Texas	41	47	47	48	48
Utah	47	32	34	12	20
Vermont	2	4	5	10	7
Virginia	40	34	40	29	40
Washington	32	38	21	13	22
West Virginia	43	25	36	38	38
Wisconsin	23	19	13	6	4
Wyoming	6	5	11	2	9

State	Total Paid FTE Staff per 25,000 Population	Paid FTE Librarians per 25,000 Population	ALA-MLS Librarians per 25,000 Population	Other Paid FTE Staff per 25,000 Population
Alabama	38	31	42	43
Alaska	27	29	28	22
Arizona	44	47	37	37
Arkansas	39	44	47	29
California	46	48	32	41
Colorado	11	28	14	9
Connecticut	8	4	3	16
Delaware	42	38	41	36
District of Columbia	1	12	1	1
Florida	45	45	30	42
Georgia	51	51	46	45
Hawaii	34	39	13	28
Idaho	15	32	39	10
Illinois	5	8	6	5
Indiana	6	14	10	4
Iowa	18	3	27	32
Kansas	7	9	20	8
Kentucky	24	10	31	34
Louisiana	16	18	26	17
Maine	13	6	11	26
Maryland	12	17	17	13
Massachusetts	17	7	5	25
Michigan	26	26	12	23

State	Total Paid FTE Staff per 25,000 Population	Paid FTE Librarians per 25,000 Population	ALA-MLS Librarians per 25,000 Population	Other Paid FTE Staff per 25,000 Population
Minnesota	33	35	24	30
Mississippi	37	16	51	50
Missouri	14	33	49	7
Montana	40	25	40	47
Nebraska	23	15	33	24
Nevada	48	50	45	44
New Hampshire	2	1	2	15
New Jersey	19	30	9	11
New Mexico	35	27	34	38
New York	9	21	8	12
North Carolina	47	49	35	40
North Dakota	41	22	44	49
Ohio	4	13	7	2
Oklahoma	30	20	29	33
Oregon	28	36	21	18
Pennsylvania	36	34	25	31
Rhode Island	20	19	4	20
South Carolina	32	37	23	27
South Dakota	25	11	43	35
Tennessee	49	46	50	46
Texas	50	43	38	48
Utah	31	40	36	21
Vermont	10	2	16	39
Virginia	29	41	19	14
Washington	21	42	18	6
West Virginia	43	24	48	51
Wisconsin	22	23	15	19
Wyoming	3	5	22	3

State	Total Operating Revenue per Capita	State Operating Revenue per Capita	Local Operating Revenue per Capita	Other Operating Revenue per Capita
Alabama	45	26	44	29
Alaska	7	24	10	10
Arizona	41	42	35	47
Arkansas	36	14	39	34
California	32	37	27	32
Colorado	10	43	8	16
Connecticut	8	35	9	3
Delaware	40	8	42	37
District of Columbia	1	49	1	51
Florida	43	22	40	43
Georgia	49	12	48	48
Hawaii	44	2	51	30
Idaho	26	28	26	18
Illinois	2	11	2	14
Indiana	12	10	13	21

State	Total Operating Revenue per Capita	State Operating Revenue per Capita	Local Operating Revenue per Capita	Other Operating Revenue per Capita
Iowa	23	32	20	12
Kansas	15	18	14	8
Kentucky	20	21	16	27
Louisiana	14	23	12	39
Maine	25	40	33	1
Maryland	16	3	23	7
Massachusetts	19	25	17	15
Michigan	21	31	18	23
Minnesota	24	15	22	13
Mississippi	50	9	50	26
Missouri	18	33	15	19
Montana	42	41	37	33
Nebraska	27	38	24	25
Nevada	33	4	38	41
New Hampshire	5	45	5	11
New Jersey	9	34	6	22
New Mexico	35	27	34	44
New York	4	13	4	5
North Carolina	46	19	45	40
North Dakota	39	16	41	28
Ohio	3	1	32	2
Oklahoma	28	30	25	36
Oregon	13	39	11	17
Pennsylvania	38	7	46	9
Rhode Island	17	5	30	6
South Carolina	37	20	36	49
South Dakota	34	50	28	45
Tennessee	51	44	47	46
Texas	48	47	43	50
Utah	30	36	21	42
Vermont	29	51	31	4
Virginia	31	17	29	38
Washington	6	46	3	31
West Virginia	47	6	49	35
Wisconsin	22	29	19	24
Wyoming	11	48	7	20

State	Total Operating Expenditures per Capita	Total Collection Expenditures per Capita	Total Staff Expenditures per Capita	Salaries and Wages Expenditures per Capita
Alabama	45	46	45	45
Alaska	7	22	10	16
Arizona	37	30	43	44
Arkansas	39	31	41	42
California	31	43	32	33
Colorado	11	5	14	11
Connecticut	5	11	4	2

State	Total Operating Expenditures per Capita	Total Collection Expenditures per Capita	Total Staff Expenditures per Capita	Salaries and Wages Expenditures per Capita
Delaware	38	40	35	36
District of Columbia	1	8	1	1
Florida	36	39	42	43
Georgia	49	50	49	49
Hawaii	44	49	44	32
Idaho	28	33	29	29
Illinois	2	4	6	4
Indiana	12	3	15	14
Iowa	24	16	21	21
Kansas	14	10	17	15
Kentucky	33	25	34	35
Louisiana	18	21	22	24
Maine	25	36	19	19
Maryland	15	9	12	13
Massachusetts	16	13	16	10
Michigan	22	27	23	25
Minnesota	23	23	24	22
Mississippi	51	51	51	51
Missouri	20	6	25	23
Montana	43	42	38	38
Nebraska	27	17	28	27
Nevada	34	32	33	34
New Hampshire	6	7	3	3
New Jersey	10	15	8	9
New Mexico	35	28	37	39
New York	3	14	2	6
North Carolina	46	47	46	46
North Dakota	42	34	40	41
Ohio	4	1	7	7
Oklahoma	26	18	27	28
Oregon	13	20	11	17
Pennsylvania	40	41	39	40
Rhode Island	17	35	13	12
South Carolina	41	38	36	37
South Dakota	32	26	30	30
Tennessee	50	48	50	50
Texas	47	45	47	47
Utah	30	12	31	31
Vermont	21	29	20	18
Virginia	29	37	26	26
Washington	9	2	9	8
West Virginia	48	44	48	48
Wisconsin	19	24	18	20
Wyoming	8	19	5	5

Per capita and per population are based on the total unduplicated population of legal service areas.

Total includes the 50 states and the District of Columbia but excludes outlying areas and libraries that do not meet the FSCS Public Library Definition.

The District of Columbia, although not a state, is included in the state rankings. Special care should be used in comparing its data to state data.

Caution should be used in making comparisons with the state of Hawaii, as Hawaii reports only one public library for the entire state.

FTE = full-time equivalent.

An ALA-MLS is a master's degree from a program of library and information studies accredited by the American Library Association.

Total revenue includes federal, state, local, and other revenue. State rankings of federal revenue are not included in this report.

Total operating expenditures includes total staff expenditures, collection expenditures, and other operating expenditures. State rankings of other operating expenditures are not included in this report.

Total staff expenditures include expenditures for salaries and wages and employee benefits. State rankings of employee benefits expenditures are not included in this report.

Source: Compiled by Carol Collier from Institute of Museum and Library Services, Public Libraries Survey, Fiscal Year 2013. Data users who create their own estimates using data from this report should cite the Institute of Museum and Library Services as the source of the original data only. Although the data in this table come from a census of all public libraries and are not subject to sampling error, the census results may contain non-sampling error. Additional information on non-sampling error, response rates, and definitions may be found in Appendix B of the report for the Public Libraries Survey.

Year in Architecture 2015: Working in Harmony

Bette-Lee Fox

Managing Editor, *Library Journal*

The 123 triumphant academic and public library construction projects that we're highlighting are large and small, dear and frugal, cautiously attentive to historic character and wildly beyond what some consider "typical" library design. Yet all feature what is at the core of today's library, the cohesion between service and the community. Among these facilities, completed between July 1, 2014, and June 30, 2015, are eight buildings judged to be the best examples of replicable public library models, *Library Journal*'s New Landmark Libraries and Honorable Mentions. They are noted on the tables that follow.

According to Academe

The new library at the University of Chattanooga is the hub of campus partnerships, home to the Art Department, Center for Advisement and Student Success, Information Technology Division, Disability Resource Center, Center for Academic and Innovative Technology, Southern Literature Association, Walker Center for Teaching and Learning, a new Gig City Studio (or Maker space), and more. The Syracuse University College of Law Library, New York, houses a collection of open spaces that foster transparency and collaboration. Its wood-paneled Reading Room receives natural light from two sides, thanks to the building's sky-lit central atrium. The Ketchum Library, University of New England, Biddeford, Maine, is now home to art exhibits, study space, book talks, lectures, receptions, classes, meetings, and noontime yoga.

The Herman B. Wells Library, Indiana University, Bloomington, reduced the number of desktop computers by nearly two-thirds, doubling seating capacity and transforming a massive open environment into a "sophisticated space that gives students options." The Thomas D. Greenley Library at Farmingdale State College, New York, offers large group study and team learning spaces, individual touch points for plugging in, private tutoring nooks, and flexible social lounge seating.

The Ruppert Commons for Research, Technology and Collaboration (The Edge) extends Duke University Libraries' mission by providing a collaborative space for interdisciplinary, team-based, and data-driven research. At the Moraine Valley Community College, Palos Hills, Illinois, wall-mounted displays in group study rooms automatically link to students who plug their devices into tables with embedded connections. The new library and learning center at Vaughn College of Aeronautics and Technology, Flushing, New York, is the final phase of the expansion, renovation, and sound abatement project at the school's main campus, which (conveniently for the aviation students) is just 200 feet from a LaGuardia Airport runway.

Adapted from *Library Journal,* November 16, 2015

Going Public

With regard to public efforts, the Riverside Library and Cultural Center, Evans, Colorado, is situated on former school property, features items from the Evans History Museum, and cohabits with a police substation, café, and banquet space.

The outdoor lawn of the Manhattan Beach Library, California, often functions as a de facto programming site, ranging from story time sessions to "Movies in the Park." The Stevenson Ranch Library, California, is situated within the Valencia Market Place shopping center. Once patrons are inside the building, the high ceilings, warm lighting, and vibrant color scheme "create a sense of openness and possibility." As well, the Castaic Library, California, rests atop a small hill overlooking an adjacent shopping center. It has a meeting room for the community as well as a separate kitchen for cooking demos.

Waccamaw Neck Branch Library, Pawleys Island, South Carolina, is located directly adjacent to a bike path and middle school. The library has a 200-seat multipurpose room with sound and AV systems; the children's area features a fish tank at the entrance. The Southwest Regional Library, Louisville Free Public Library (LFPL), Kentucky, houses two ample-sized community meeting rooms; several smaller rooms for study, reading, and collaboration; a new teen zone; and LFPL's largest children's area.

The renovated San Francisco Public Library Main Library created two new spaces: the Bridge at Main offers adult and family literacy programs, one-on-one tutoring, learning differences resource support, and more; The Mix at SFPL is an innovative, youth-designed, 21st-century teen learning space. The Snuggle Up Center at the Library Partnership: Neighborhood Resource Center, Gainesville, Florida, is designed to stimulate and encourage kids' imagination and learning. Coordination with the Partnership for Strong Families brings in more than 30 social service organizations to address the full spectrum of the community's needs.

The Family Place Library at Orion Township Public Library, Michigan, provides a unique space for children ages zero to five and their caregivers in which to read, play, and learn together. Sayville Public Library, New York, turned an underused lawn into a 750 square foot outdoor children's program area and multifunctional plaza, amphitheater, and children's event space. The design of the Athens-Limestone Public Library, Alabama, transformed an abandoned grocery store dating from the 1960s into an impressive public facility. A joint venture between Madison School & Community Recreation (MSCR), the Madison Public Library|Meadowridge Library + Meadowood Neighborhood Center, Wisconsin, revitalized an empty storefront, with both entities making use of the commercial-grade kitchen in the joint community room.

Originally opened in 1941, the Welwood Murray Memorial Library, Palm Springs, California, serves as a research library and archive for the Palm Springs Historical Society. The Northbrook Public Library, Illinois, features a 225-person auditorium; a 100-seat meeting room; and a Civic Room that seats 40, with "possibly the world's most comfortable chairs."

The 10,000 square foot Clifton Branch, Public Library of Cincinnati and Hamilton County, opened in the historic Parkview Manor with a state-of-the-art tech lab, a children's story time solarium, meeting rooms, a bike rack with built-in tire pump, a water fountain for dogs, a covered porch with built-in chess and checker tables, and special holds lockers. The Garland Smith Public Library, Marlow, Oklahoma, in a renovated National Guard Armory, grew from 3,000 square feet to 14,357 square feet. Its children's learning center provides a place for reading programs, crafts, after-school activities, and the Saturday morning movie matinee.

Fanciful Design and Wetlands

The shape of the Glendale Branch, Salt Lake City Public Library, includes a curved form that reaches out into the community while creating an outdoor plaza. Colored concrete and landscaped designs represent the geographic area along the Jordan River. South Hadley Public Library, Massachusetts, is located along the banks of the Connecticut River and mirrors the architectural elements of historic mills while providing a modern environment. A landscaped, riverfront pergola serves as an outdoor program area. The siting of the Ferndale Library, Washington, presents a threshold to both civic life and a scenic wetland. A small public plaza and meeting room with a view of Mt. Baker take advantage of the topography, raising the library well above flood levels. The Case-Halstead Public Library, Carlyle, Illinois, created a detention pond as a landscape feature.

At the new East Roswell Library, a covered bridge entry opens up to views through the building into the natural landscape beyond. The West Feliciana Parish Library, St. Francisville, Louisiana, is established as a series of small volumes, reminiscent of the additive nature of the surrounding plantation homes. The Palmetto Library, Georgia, is imagined as a series of "rooms" or small buildings nestled within its semirural landscape.

The Library at Central & Unser, Albuquerque, New Mexico, is marked by an iconic light tower and a changing LED sign reminiscent of its location on old Route 66. The front of the Sharpsburg Community Library, Pittsburgh, is accentuated by a large, yellow "swiss cheese"-like structure and storefront windows that showcase the new community room.

Airports, armories, antiquated facilities, and all-around poor functionality have met their match in this year's construction efforts. Libraries are moving up, catching up, and standing up as models of solid design and community focus.

Library Journal 2015 New Landmark Libraries Winners (NLL)		*Library Journal* 2015 New Landmark Libraries Honorable Mentions (NLLHM)	
CALIFORNIA	Palo Alto	COLORADO	Denver
LOUISIANA	Baton Rouge	GEORGIA	Atlanta
KANSAS	Lawrence	MONTANA	Billings
		WISCONSIN	Milwaukee
		CANADA	Ottawa

Table 1 / New Academic Buildings, Additions, and Renovations, 2015

Institution	Type	Status	Project Cost	Gross Area (Sq. Ft.)	Sq. Ft. Cost	Constr. Cost	Furniture/ Equip. Cost	Book Capacity	Architect
University of Tennessee, Chattanooga, Library	N		$44,300,000	184,725	$225.74	$41,700,000	$1,800,000	600,000	Derthick, Henley, & Wilkerson; Artech Design Group
Southern New Hampshire University Library Learning Commons, Manchester	N		20,000,000	50,000	281.00	14,100,000	527,647	106,501+	Perry Dean Rogers | Partners
Douglas L. Jamerson Jr. Midtown Center, St. Petersburg College, FL	N		15,564,526	50,739	252.24	12,798,226	1,625,458	2,650	Harvard Jolly Architecture
Syracuse University College of Law Library, NY	N		12,680,000	37,500	321.33	12,050,000	630,000	318,000	Gluckman Tang Architects
Vaughn College Aeronautical Academic Library, Vaughn College of Aeronautics & Technology, Flushing, NY	A		n.a.	10,788	242.12	2,611,937	652,915	26,300	John Ciardullo Associates; Ensign Engineering
*Education Commons, Felician College, Rutherford, NJ	R		10,200,000	32,000	221.88	7,100,000	3,100,000	10,000	Arcari + Iovino
Las Positas Community College Library, Livermore, CA	R		4,765,445	32,700	77.20	2,523,643	401,361	40,000	Noll & Tam Architects
Marlene and Charles Addlestone Library, College of Charleston, SC	R		3,860,000	100,000	38.60	3,860,000	n.a.	96,500+	LS3P
Herman B. Wells Library, Indiana University, Bloomington	R		3,975,000	28,000	85.71	2,400,000	1,575,000	200	Lohr Design, Inc.
Southern Illinois University School of Medicine Library, Springfield	R		2,342,818	23,350	91.37	2,133,451	209,367	11,739	HBM Architects
Thomas D. Greenley Library Information Commons, Farmingdale State College, State University of New York	R		2,161,496	24,240	55.67	1,349,390	479,824	1,116	Beatty Harvey Coco Architects
The Edge: Ruppert Commons for Research, Technology, and Collaboration, Perkins Library, Duke University, Durham, NC	R		n.a.	16,935	124.00	2,100,000	95,000	486	Shepley Bulfinch

Library	Type								Architect
Moraine Valley Community College Library, Palos Hills, IL	R		838,795	5,867	112.36	659,194	179,601	0	Legat Architects (Michael Lundeen)
Richard J. Daley Library, University of Illinois at Chicago	R		825,480	2,500	225.40	563,500	86,882	n.a.	Architects Enterprise, Ltd.
North Carolina State University Libraries, Raleigh	R		430,000	960	338.54	325,000	105,000	n.a.	RND Architects
Link Library, Concordia University Nebraska, Seward	R		56,000	924	n.a.	n.a.	n.a.	n.a.	Office Interiors & Design
Los Angeles Southwest College Library	A&R	Total	16,390,000	49,648	306.16	15,200,000	1,190,000	80,000	Carrier Johnson + CULTURE
	A&R	New	n.a.	2,500	n.a.	n.a.	n.a.	n.a.	
	A&R	Renovated	n.a.	47,148	n.a.	n.a.	n.a.	n.a.	
Charles Evans Inness Memorial Library, Medgar Evers College, City University of New York, Brooklyn	A&R	Total	16,000,000	47,000	n.a.	n.a.	n.a.	98,250	ikon.5 architects
	A&R	New	n.a.	2,000	n.a.	n.a.	n.a.	n.a.	
	A&R	Renovated	n.a.	45,000	n.a.	n.a.	n.a.	n.a.	
Arthur A. Houghton Jr. Library, Corning Community College, NY	A&R	Total	9,700,000	34,200	229.24	7,840,000	310,000	34,785	HOLT Architects
	A&R	New	n.a.	n.a.	n.a.	n.a.	n.a.	n.a.	
	A&R	Renovated	n.a.	n.a.	n.a.	n.a.	n.a.	n.a.	
**Mary Helen Cochran Library, Sweet Briar College, VA	A&R	Total	8,800,000	55,000	125.38	6,896,000	307,750	315,000	VMDO Architects
	A&R	New	n.a.	n.a.	n.a.	n.a.	n.a.	n.a.	
	A&R	Renovated	n.a.	n.a.	n.a.	n.a.	n.a.	n.a.	
Jack S. Ketchum Library, University of New England, Biddeford, ME	A&R	Total	1,118,000	3,844	281.74	1,083,000	n.a.	n.a.	JSA Architects, Inc.
	A&R	New	1,008,000	1,874	525.61	985,000.00	n.a.	n.a.	
	A&R	Renovated	110,000	1,970	49.75	98,000.00	n.a.	n.a.	

* Includes an elevator bank to meet Americans with Disabilities Act compliance.

**Sweet Briar College was officially closed in 2015, then following a lawsuit reopened for at least one more academic year.

TYPE: N=New Building; A=Addition; R=Renovation; A&R=Addition & Renovation; n.a.=not available

Table 2 / New Public Library Buildings, 2015

Community	Pop. ('000)	Code	Project Cost	Const. Cost	Gross Area (Sq. Ft.)	Sq. Ft. Cost	Equip. Cost	Other Costs	Federal Funds	State Funds	Local Funds	Gift Funds	Architect
California													
NLL Palo Alto	32	BS	$49,700,000	$27,000,000	56,000	$482.14	$1,900,000	$20,800,000	0	0	0	$48,300,000	$1,400,000 Group 4 Architecture
Stevenson Ranch	17	B	5,800,000	4,500,000	11,555	389.44	1,000,000	300,000	0	0	10,500,000	0	CWA AIA Inc.
Colorado													
NLLHM Denver	27	B	13,600,000	7,150,000	27,000	264.81	1,460,000	3,790,000	0	0	13,600,000	21,000	studiotrope Design Collective
Denver	20	B	3,170,019	2,507,357	10,000	250.74	156,496	259,206	0	0	3,170,019	0	Humphries Poli Architects
Greeley	20	B	10,000,000	7,522,500	31,404	239.54	1,250,100	1,227,400	0	$681,500	9,214,182	104,318	Roth Sheppard Architects
Hudson	10	M	3,847,880	24,026,933	11,367	211.37	124,228	457,120	0	0	3,847,880	0	Barker Rinker Seacat
Florida													
Sarasota	68	B	7,690,000	5,223,000	25,800	202.44	1,750,000	717,000	0	0	7,690,000	534,000	Harvard Jolly; Smith Const.
Tampa	5	M	7,012,728	5,163,216	23,482	219.88	1,462,251	387,261	0	0	7,012,728	0	Harvard Jolly Architecture
Zephyrhills	14	M	2,599,850	2,232,680	8,463	263.82	169,260	197,910	0	0	2,599,850	0	Harvard Jolly Architecture
Georgia													
NLLHM Atlanta	76	B	16,877,002	8,252,912	25,000	330.12	1,186,596	7,437,494	0	0	16,877,002	0	Leo A. Daly
Palmetto	28	B	7,759,523	3,830,881	11,200	342.04	531,506	2,897,136	0	0	7,259,523	500,000	Houser Walker Architecture
Roswell	200	B	12,524,891	6,135,156	17,370	353.21	617,149	4,072,586	0	0	10,824,891	1,700,000	KHAFRA; HBM Architects
Illinois													
Carlyle	3	M	4,025,200	3,255,300	10,876	299.31	200,000	569,900	0	1,618,757	0	2,770,000	Arcturis
Farmington	7	M	2,639,759	2,299,524	9,091	252.94	140,693	199,542	0	1,722,211	775,315	142,233	Apace Design
Kentucky													
Louisville	100	B	13,425,191	10,115,826	40,000	252.90	909,365	1,121,044	0	0	9,846,235	3,500,000	MSR Design; JRA Architects
Louisiana													
Alexandria	16	B	971,955	774,112	5,000	154.82	45,137	100,406	0	0	1,081,362	0	Alliance Design Group LLC
NLL Baton Rouge*	445	MS	42,192,721	34,557,917	129,000	267.89	2,216,530	4,869,074	0	0	42,192,721	64,875	Library Design Collaborative
St. Francisville	15	M	3,948,144	2,935,036	15,028	195.30	390,608	422,500	0	0	4,096,403	200,000	Hidell & Associates Architects
Youngsville	48	B	5,434,661	4,379,861	15,207	288.02	583,857	470,843	0	0	5,421,911	12,750	Architects Beazley Moliere; Dewberry
Massachusetts													
South Hadley	18	M	10,309,285	7,367,620	24,550	311.10	561,289	1,510,376	0	4,916,312	4,559,876	833,097	Johnson Roberts Associates

Minnesota													
Ely	5	M	1,566,262	1,278,462	6,630	192.83	141,842	145,958	0	458,699	976,969	130,594	Meyer Group
Excelsior	16	M	5,359,900	3,139,785	7,600	413.13	192,249	1,050,183	0	0	5,359,900	0	292 Design; MacDonald & Mack
Montana													
NLLHM Billings	147	M	21,603,907	16,513,630	66,000	250.21	1,541,375	2,656,375	0	0	19,668,747	5,000,000	Will Bruder Architects
New Mexico													
Albuquerque	38	B	10,145,429	8,457,815	25,305	334.23	822,298	865,316	0	1,212,284	7,783,145	1,150,000	Rohde May Keller McNamara
Ohio													
Cincinnati	25	B	2,751,439	2,208,719	8,000	276.09	186,125	239,260	0	0	2,751,439	0	Champlin Architecture
Pepper Pike	14	B	6,100,008	4,973,779	15,800	314.80	212,612	913,617	0	0	6,100,008	0	HBM Architects
Reading	33	B	4,620,859	4,010,415	12,000	334.20	251,554	358,890	0	0	4,620,859	0	Champlin Architecture
Whitehall	30	B	9,212,831	5,537,743	19,500	284.00	489,308	2,632,529	0	0	8,462,831	750,000	Jonathan Barnes Architecture
Rhode Island													
Tiverton	16	M	10,470,812	6,488,956	23,797	273.68	876,134	2,478,671	$475,000	4,060,003	3,650,800	2,285,009	Union Studio; Kimberly Bolan
South Carolina													
Pawleys Island	33	B	3,073,728	2,607,228	17,500	149.00	215,000	251,500	0	0	2,908,728	165,000	Tych & Walker; MDA designgroup
Tennessee													
Antioch	75	B	7,695,000	7,300,000	25,000	292.00	395,000	0	0	0	7,695,000	0	Lose & Associates; HBM Architects
Nashville	36	B	8,821,897	8,197,052	24,580	333.48	624,845	0	0	0	9,557,000	0	Hastings Architecture Associates
Texas													
Dallas	25	B	6,371,067	5,284,257	19,500	270.99	377,608	609,202	0	0	7,062,986	0	KAI Texas
Irving	50	B	12,253,441	9,740,500	52,570	185.29	1,435,326	1,077,615	0	0	12,300,000	30,000	Hidell & Associates Architects
Utah													
Salt Lake City	25	B	7,459,890	5,028,135	19,020	264.36	972,039	844,716	0	0	7,459,890	0	Architectural Nexus
Washington													
Ferndale	30	B	6,015,000	4,336,600	15,000	289.11	306,750	335,000	0	500,000	2,387,200	3,127,800	SHKS
Wisconsin													
NLLHM Milwaukee	33	B	3,420,000	2,800,000	16,500	169.70	300,000	320,000	0	0	3,420,000	10,000	HGA Architects & Engineers
Canada													
Toronto, Ont.	29	B	10,276,000	7,768,000	14,500	535.72	900,000	1,608,000	0	0	10,276,000	0	LGA Architectural; Phillip H. Carter

Symbol Code: B=Branch Library; BS=Branch & System Headquarters; M=Main Library; MS=Main & System Headquarters; S=System Headquarters; O=combined use space; n.a.=not available

Table 3 / Public Library Buildings, Additions and Renovations, 2015

Community	Pop. ('000)	Code	Project Cost	Const. Cost	Gross Area (Sq. Ft.)	Sq. Ft. Cost	Equip. Cost	Other Costs	Federal Funds	State Funds	Local Funds	Gift Funds	Architect
Alabama													
Athens	90	M	$6,696,930	$5,129,015	37,900	$135.33	$364,241	$559,800	0	$90,000	$3,200,000	$3,496,930	CMH Architects
California													
Burlingame	37	M	3,497,000	1,900,000	30,098	63.13	220,800	1,379,200	0	0	2,500,000	1,000,000	Group 4 Architecture
Castaic	19	BS	8,000,000	2,400,000	12,250	195.92	500,000	252,000	0	0	8,000,000	0	CWA AIA, Inc.
Los Angeles	42	B	3,044,000	2,600,000	5,524	470.67	157,000	287,000	$1,500,000	0	3,191,000	0	Carde Ten Architects
Manhattan Beach	31	B	25,200,000	19,200,000	21,500	893.02	1,900,000	4,100,000	0	0	26,270,496	0	Johnson Favaro Architects
Palm Springs	45	B	1,300,000	1,200,000	4,300	279.07	63,000	37,000	0	600,000	600,000	100,000	Wm. G. Kleindienst
Palo Alto	24	B	24,800,000	18,200,000	30,000	606.67	1,100,000	5,500,000	0	0	24,100,000	700,000	Group 4 Architecture
San Francisco	825	M	6,800,000	4,105,497	17,136	239.58	713,161	1,981,342	0	0	6,320,000	480,000	San Francisco Public Works
Colorado													
Englewood	98	B	2,137,034	1,776,853	45,941	38.68	236,195	123,986	0	0	2,127,034	10,000	studiotrope Design Collective
Florida													
Gainesville	20	B	270,949	167,384	14,092	11.87	77,065	26,500	0	0	205,449	65,500	McKellips & Associates
Georgia													
Hiawassee	6	B	1,021,042	868,891	8,000	106.61	51,063	101,088	0	900,000	100,000	21,041	Gardner, Spencer, Smith, Trench, Jarbeau
Illinois													
Downers Grove	50	M	2,679,637	2,116,145	67,738	31.20	520,350	43,142	0	0	2,479,637	200,000	Product Architecture + Design
Glendale Heights	34	M	1,440,000	880,000	27,000	32.59	400,000	160,000	0	0	1,440,000	0	Product Architecture + Design
North Aurora	17	M	303,385	208,471	5,778	36.08	51,514	43,400	0	0	277,000	44,000	Kluber Architects + Engineers
Northbrook	33	M	6,500,000	5,518,635	12,720	433.85	383,542	597,823	0	0	6,412,729	87,271	Dewberry
Waukegan	88	M	1,227,500	778,100	24,500	31.76	247,500	201,900	0	175,000	1,010,000	42,500	Product Architecture + Design
Indiana													
Bloomington	143	MS	1,650,900	1,252,900	19,190	65.31	307,000	91,000	0	0	1,650,900	0	Christine Matheu Architect; Kimberly Bolan
Plainfield	28	MS	230,000	100,000	7,100	14.08	100,000	30,000	0	0	230,000	10,000	Kimberly Bolan & Associates

Symbol Code: B=Branch Library; BS=Branch & System Headquarters; M=Main Library; MS=Main & System Headquarters; S=System Headquarters; O=Combined Use Space; n.a.=not available

Location		No.	Type	Value 1	Value 2	Value 3	Value 4	Value 5	Value 6	Value 7	Value 8	Value 9	Architect
Iowa	Ames	68	M	19,500,000	13,500,000	78,700	171.53	2,650,000	3,350,000	0	0	18,000,000	MSR Design
Kansas	NLL Lawrence*	91	M	19,000,000	15,677,437	66,900	234.34	795,417	2,527,146	0	0	18,000,000	Gould Evans
Louisiana	Lafayette	122	MS	13,749,522	10,579,795	65,449	161.65	1,757,368	1,412,359	0	0	40,047	MBSB Group; Dewberry
Maryland	Beltsville	28	B	2,212,563	2,060,000	25,452	80.93	54,000	98,563	0	490,000	1,722,563	Gant Brunnett Architects
	Fairmount Heights	18	B	1,204,400	1,114,000	17,764	62.70	37,500	52,900	0	0	1,204,400	Gant Brunnett Architects
	Largo	870	BS	3,758,080	3,234,000	24,858	130.10	375,000	149,080	0	0	3,758,080	Gant Brunnett Architects
Massachusetts	Boston**	656	MS	13,886,000	9,884,000	46,695	211.67	1,977,000	2,025,000	0	0	13,886,000	William Rawn Associates
	Everett	44	B	5,180,946	4,444,552	8,590	517.41	141,996	594,398	0	2,268,481	2,802,459	Johnson Roberts Associates
Michigan	Lake Orion	35	M	379,651	97,409	8,664	11.25	270,642	11,600	0	0	379,651	Kimberly Bolan & Associates
Minnesota	Saint Paul	25	B	7,991,690	6,193,439	24,000	258.06	949,910	848,341	0	0	5,026,773	LSE Architects
	Saint Paul	21	B	4,829,447	3,632,647	15,500	234.36	544,812	651,988	0	0	2,564,436	LSE Architects
	White Bear Lake	36	B	3,998,000	2,974,200	16,500	180.25	282,500	498,900	0	0	200,000	Bentz/Thompson/Rietow
New Jersey	Haworth	4	M	988,800	773,800	2,866	269.99	130,000	85,000	0	0	988,800	Arcari + Iovino
New York	Holbrook	83	M	81,438	13,866	800	17.33	62,053	5,519	0	0	113,162	Kimberly Bolan & Associates
	Long Island City	75	B	384,927	158,620	4,000	39.66	200,239	26,068	0	344,763	40,164	ADI/Applied Design Initiative
	Sayville	19	M	142,300	130,000	750	173.33	0	12,300	0	33,000	500	BBS Architects
Ohio	Cincinnati	35	B	4,359,544	3,192,430	10,000	319.24	265,553	370,000	0	0	3,545,508	McClorey & Savage Architects, Ltd.
	Dayton	12	B	2,021,600	1,311,352	4,800	273.20	261,600	448,648	0	0	2,021,600	Levin Porter Assocs.; Group 4 Architecture
	Lebanon	41	MS	750,000	580,000	6,200	93.54	170,000	0	0	0	800,000	SHP Leading Design; Cintech Construction

Symbol Code: B=Branch Library; BS=Branch & System Headquarters; M=Main Library; MS=Main & System Headquarters; O=Combined Use Space; S=System Headquarters; n.a.=not available

Table 3 / Public Library Buildings, Additions and Renovations, 2015 (*cont.*)

	Pop. ('000)	Code	Project Cost	Const. Cost	Gross Area (Sq. Ft.)	Sq. Ft. Cost	Equip. Cost	Other Costs	Federal Funds	State Funds	Local Funds	Gift Funds	Architect
Toledo	33	B	3,600,720	3,004,000	21,515	139.62	330,000	266,720	0	0	3,600,720	0	Buehrer Group Architecture
Oklahoma													
Marlow	5	O	2,018,274	1,602,313	14,357	111.65	258,042	157,919	0	0	1,710,202	308,072	Krittenbrink Architecture LLC
Pennsylvania													
Pittsburgh	12	B	3,234,000	2,509,000	8,000	313.63	190,000	535,000	0	0	50,000	3,184,000	GBBN Architects
Pittsburgh	4	B	1,012,000	870,280	2,600	334.72	60,870	80,850	0	350,000	624,565	37,435	Front Studio Architecture, LLC
Tennessee													
Nashville	25	B	438,492	438,500	4,250	77.29	62,617	47,375	0	0	438,492	0	none
Nashville	668	M	2,320,625		68,172				0	0	2,320,625	0	Gobbell Hays Partners, Inc.
Nashville	12	B	293,100	240,000	7,500	32.00			0	0	270,000	23,100	none
Utah													
Park City	8	M	9,620,000	8,116,310	54,285	149.51	802,891	700,799	0	0	9,620,000	0	Blalock & Partners
Virginia													
Charlottesville	50	O	12,124,043	6,927,677	37,320	185.63	303,670	1,871,696	0	0	12,124,043	0	HBM Architects
Norfolk	110	M	65,000,000	42,000,000	139,830	300.36	1,700,000	14,100,000	0	0	21,000,000	44,000,000	Newman Architects, PC
South Hill	7	B	55,948	19,531	884	22.09	31,301	5,116	0	0	5,000	50,948	Kimberly Bolan & Associates
Washington													
Prosser	13	B	365,374	151,578	5,920	25.60	184,214	29,582	0	0	357,374	8,000	Meier Architecture & Engineering
Renton	20	B	8,012,390	5,623,494	20,000	281.17	1,287,744	1,001,152	0	0	8,013,237	0	Schact | Aslani Architects
Wisconsin													
Grantsburg	6	M	287,406		2,500		10,000		0	0	35,000	252,406	Craig Selander, Architect, LLC
Madison	24	B	2,390,978	1,835,978	16,407	111.90	349,000	206,000	0	0	2,360,978	30,000	Engberg Anderson Architects
Canada													
NLLHM Ottawa***	45	B	10,000,000	6,750,000	24,000	281.25	2,000,000	1,250,000	0	0	10,000,000	100,000	Moriyama & Teshima
Winnipeg	35	B		14,000			165,000		0	0	957,500	3,000	LM Architectural

* Total project cost includes a separate parking structure. ** Completion of phase 1 of the two-phase renovation of Boston's Central Library. *** Figures listed in Canadian dollars

Symbol Code: B=Branch Library; BS=Branch & System Headquarters; M=Main Library; MS=Main & System Headquarters; S=System Headquarters; O=Combined Use Space; n.a.=not available

Six-Year Cost Summary

	Fiscal 2010	Fiscal 2011	Fiscal 2012	Fiscal 2013	Fiscal 2014	Fiscal 2015
Number of new buildings	70	62	34	27	29	38
Number of ARRs[1]	55	89	73	47	55	54
Sq. ft. new buildings	1,608,324	1,555,598	898,865	470,167	717,973	896,195
Sq. ft. ARRs	1,271,709	1,672,664	1,375,307	715,380	1,164,535	1,222,795
New Buildings						
Construction cost	$453,517,944	$454,425,651	$263,313,088	$139,136,298	$212,257,074	$274,900,907
Equipment cost	49,087,060	47,836,977	30,533,085	16,184,831	34,002,671	26,895,130
Site cost	28,981,431	35,104,201	14,215,747	28,272,719	18,929,131	12,031,896
Other cost	110,238,949	113,525,121	53,113,752	29,983,512	49,676,815	68,193,630
Total—Project cost	669,591,384	650,871,920	361,175,672	212,079,360	314,866,191	360,746,279
ARRs—Project cost	234,485,743	447,583,852	241,643,154	145,668,398	260,983,928	311,990,635
New & ARR Project Cost	$904,077,127	$1,098,455,772	$602,818,826	$357,747,758	$575,850,119	$672,736,914

Symbol Code: ARR=Additions, Renovations, and Remodels

Funding Sources

	Fiscal 2010	Fiscal 2011	Fiscal 2012	Fiscal 2013	Fiscal 2014	Fiscal 2015
Federal, new buildings	$8,038,118	$5,854,589	$38,465,599	$1,000,000	$25,617,538	$475,000
Federal, ARRs	10,657,831	9,270,750	18,882,075	1,684,211	6,239,463	1,500,000
Federal, total	$18,695,949	$15,125,339	$57,347,674	$2,684,211	$31,857,001	$1,975,000
State, new buildings	$67,097,479	$43,548,440	$19,558,708	$9,570,111	$64,563,247	$15,169,766
State, ARRs	27,486,827	33,147,756	9,286,208	2,017,590	19,563,872	5,251,244
State, total	$94,584,306	$76,696,196	$28,844,916	$11,587,701	$84,127,119	$20,421,010
Local, new buildings	$558,427,058	$567,608,480	$284,164,989	$192,466,192	$215,147,978	$331,311,400
Local, ARRs	251,796,891	348,642,090	184,662,609	133,692,708	188,446,449	244,614,937
Local, total	810,223,949	916,250,570	468,827,598	326,158,900	403,594,427	575,926,337
Gift, new buildings	$45,898,678	$37,374,332	$19,573,952	$12,366,431	$13,312,404	$24,430,676
Gift, ARRs	15,599,975	58,733,738	29,367,511	8,996,727	50,361,901	63,353,240
Gift, total	$61,498,653	$96,108,070	$48,941,463	$21,363,158	$63,674,305	$87,783,916
Total—Funds Used	$985,002,857	$1,104,180,175	$603,961,651	$361,793,970	$583,252,852	$686,106,263

Symbol Code: ARR=Additions, Renovations, and Remodels

Book Trade Research and Statistics

Prices of U.S. and Foreign Published Materials

Narda Tafuri

Editor, ALA ALCTS Library Materials Price Index Editorial Board

The Library Materials Price Index (LMPI) Editorial Board of the American Library Association's Association for Library Collections and Technical Services' Publications Committee continues to monitor prices for a range of library materials from sources within North America and from other key publishing centers around the world.

The U.S. Consumer Price Index (CPI) increased by only 0.7 percent in 2015, continuing the downward trend seen in 2014. CPI data are obtained from the Bureau of Labor Statistics website at http://www.bls.gov/.

The U.S. Periodical Price Index (USPPI) (Table 1), reestablished by Stephen Bosch in 2014, continues in this year's article using data provided by EBSCO Information Services. Readers are reminded that the new USPPI is based on a mix of both print and online pricing, which is a more accurate representation of an average library's journal collection. The base year for this table is set to 2010. Percent changes in average prices from previous years are noted in the chart below under the category "Periodicals."

	Percent Change				
Index	**2011**	**2012**	**2013**	**2014**	**2015**
CPI	3.0	1.7	1.5	0.8	0.7
Periodicals	4.6	5.9	6.1	6.1	7.1
Legal serials services	11.0	6.1	10.5	11.3	13.9
*Hardcover books	0.87	5.18	-2.57	6.45	0.44
+Academic books	4.6	8.0	6.3	-5.6	n.a.
+Academic e-books	-0.3	23.0	6.5	-13.7	n.a.
+Textbooks	3.5	10.6	-1.2	-7.2	n.a.
College books	4.6	2.15	4.21	-1.41	-0.59
*Mass market paperbacks	2.34	1.00	-0.28	0.57	-0.14
*Trade paperbacks	-9.99	31.96	-12.31	5.04	-2.72
*Audiobooks	-4.39	-10.96	-4.76	0.18	-15.21
*E-books	-41.17	-6.37	22.03	-9.12	-17.19
++Serials	n.a.	n.a.	7.2	6.1	6.7
++Online Serials	n.a.	n.a.	6.0	6.4	5.7
British academic books	2.77	10.81	1.67	1.0	7.1

n.a. = not available
* = figures revised based on BISAC categories
+Beginning with 2009, new data source
++Data set changes each year

The 2014 figures for Tables 3 (hardcover books), 6 (U.S. mass market paperback books), 7 (U.S. paperback books), 7A (U.S. audiobooks), and 7B (U.S. e-books), have been restated for this year's article due to late updates to the data.

U.S. Published Materials

Tables 1 through 7B indicate average prices and price indexes for library materials published primarily in the United States. These indexes are U.S. Periodicals (Table 1), Legal Serials Services (Table 2), U.S. Hardcover Books (Table 3), North American Academic Books (Table 4), North American Academic E-Books (Table 4A), North American Academic Textbooks (Table 4B), U.S. College Books (Table 5), U.S. Mass Market Paperback Books (Table 6), U.S. Paperbacks (Excluding Mass Market) (Table 7), U.S. Audiobooks (Table 7A), and U.S. E-Books (Table 7B).

Periodical and Serials Prices

The U.S. Periodical Price Index (USPPI) (Table 1) was reestablished by Stephen Bosch in 2014 and is updated for 2016 using data supplied by EBSCO Information Services. This report includes 2011–2016 data indexed to the base year of 2010. Table 1 is derived from a selected set of titles that, as much as possible will remain as the sample base for future comparisons. The data in Table 1 are created from a print preferred data pull but about half the data in the index ends up being online pricing so that the data provides a strong mix of both print and online pricing, characteristic of a current academic library's serials collection. The subscription prices used are publishers' list prices, excluding publisher discount or vendor service charges. The pricing data for 2010–2014 was based on a single report that pulled pricing information for a static set of titles for the five-year period. The pricing data for 2015 is based on the same sampling of titles, but is not an exact match due to changes that occur with serial titles. Some titles fell off the list due to pricing not being available, while other titles on the list did have pricing available that did not have pricing available in 2014. The situation continues for 2016 as this data is again based on the same sample title list as the basis for the data pull, but there are small variations in the titles that had pricing.

The USPPI in 2016 treats a little more than 5,900 titles in comparison with the original title list, which covered only about 3,700 titles. The previous versions of the USPPI treated Russian translations as a separate category. Russian translations are no longer a focus of this index and are not tracked as a category. These were once seen as a major cost factor, but this is no longer the case and therefore their inclusion in or exclusion from the index no longer makes sense. There are Russian translation titles in the index but they are not reported separately.

The main barrier to reestablishing this index was the difficulty of maintaining the title list and obtaining standard retail pricing for titles on the list. Changes in serial titles due to ceased publication, movement to open access, mergers, combining titles in packages, moving to direct orders, and publication delays are a few of the situations that can affect compilers' ability to obtain current pricing information. The new index retained that part of the title list from the previous index that remained viable and added new titles to that list based on data from EBSCO on the most frequently ordered serials in their system. From that list of serials, titles were selected for the new index to ensure that the distribution by subject was similar to the distribution in the original index. There are more titles in the selected title set than the number of titles that produced prices over the past six years. This should allow the current index to be sustainable into the future as titles fall off of the list and pricing becomes available for titles that may have been delayed, or are no longer in memberships, etc.

The first five years of data showed fairly consistent price changes across subject areas due to the fact that the pricing data took a historical look at the prices of the same set of journals. The data for 2015 and 2016 are based on the same sample list but are not the exact same list of titles as the data for 2010–2014 due to the issues mentioned above that impact pricing availability. Across subject areas, the changes in price were more volatile this year but the overall 7 percent rise mirrors increases seen in other pricing studies that nearly all show a 6 percent increase. Also at the subject level the sample sizes are smaller so a few changes can cause a large swing in the overall price for that area.

Direct comparisons between Table 1 and Table 8 should still be avoided, especially at the subject level. Both tables show the overall rate of increase in serial prices to be between 6 percent and 7 percent; however, beyond that point there is little that can reasonably be compared. Table 8 has higher overall average prices in most areas, and this is due to the survey's largest sets of data coming from the ISI Citation Indexes and Scopus, which include higher impact—and consequently more expensive—journals. Table 1 is a broader mix of journals that attempts to reflect the journal collections in an average library and therefore contains more trade and popular titles. These journals tend to be cheaper, with lower average prices. Differences in data sets will yield different results.

The most important trend seen in Table 1 is that increases in prices have remained fairly constant since the economic recovery began in 2010, hovering around 6 percent annually. Science does not dominate the list of subjects with the largest price increases. The subject areas that displayed the largest increases were quite varied: military science, general works, recreation, music, and arts and architecture. Average prices for journals in the science and technology areas are still far higher than in other areas, and that trend continues, with the average cost of chemistry journals being $4,465 and of physics journals being $3,537.

In this price index, as in similar price indexes, the data are less accurate at describing price changes the smaller the sample becomes. For that reason, drawing conclusions about price changes in subject areas with a limited number of titles will be less accurate than for large areas or the broader price index. Price changes are far more volatile where smaller data sets are used. For example, military and naval science (about 28 titles) showed average prices of $285 (2012), $301 (2013), $289 (2014), $276 (2015), and $459 (2016). If a specific inflation figure only for military and naval science is needed, it would be better to look at an average over the period or the overall number for the price study (7.1 percent) than to use the actual numbers year-by-year, i.e.: 66 percent for 2016. The variation in pricing is too volatile in smaller sample sizes to be comparable on a year-to-year basis. In

(text continues on page 350)

Table 1 / U.S. Periodicals: Average Prices and Price Indexes 2012–2016

Index Base: 2010 = 100

Subject	LC Class	Titles	2010 Average Price	2012 Average Price	2013 Average Price	2014 Average Price	2015 Average Price	2016 Average Price	Price Increase 2015–2016	Price Index (Base = 2010)
Agriculture	S	246	$579.48	$641.43	$687.22	$726.67	$780.01	$978.61	25.5%	168.9
Anthropology	GN	50	373.64	411.00	430.83	453.36	428.52	426.99	-0.4	114.3
Arts and architecture	N	115	112.39	120.62	125.24	130.70	180.35	234.50	30.0	208.6
Astronomy	QB	28	1,793.08	1,753.73	2,049.88	2,186.19	2,083.50	2,602.51	24.9	145.1
Biology	QH	330	2,053.06	2,288.26	2,405.68	2,535.65	2,727.29	2,655.14	-2.6	129.3
Botany	QK	55	1,361.09	1,491.68	1,583.36	1,667.34	1,646.31	1,926.69	17.0	141.6
Business and economics	HA-HJ	492	351.29	389.34	410.55	434.12	480.98	546.45	13.6	155.6
Chemistry	QD	124	3,396.26	3,808.31	4,024.45	4,244.38	4,335.51	4,465.42	3.0	131.5
Education	L	229	354.92	389.92	409.63	433.05	499.55	585.29	17.2	164.9
Engineering	T	542	1,244.39	1,405.36	1,486.54	1,584.81	1,692.44	1,716.47	1.4	137.9
Food science	TX	51	356.17	394.64	416.09	439.51	617.45	520.09	-15.8	146.0
General science	Q	97	998.51	1,109.61	1,153.60	1,218.88	1,401.48	1,322.20	-5.7	132.4
General works	A	131	85.84	90.73	95.41	99.14	106.87	165.98	55.3	193.4
Geography	G-GF	84	670.60	684.72	783.49	836.61	872.34	806.55	-7.5	120.3
Geology	QE	74	1,368.79	1,514.90	1,603.07	1,699.34	1,648.20	1,707.46	3.6	124.7
Heath Sciences	R	803	1,009.55	1,147.17	1,224.65	1,309.43	1,402.65	1,557.18	11.0	154.2
History	C,D,E,F	312	202.39	221.80	231.75	245.88	277.95	330.37	18.9	163.2
Language and literature	P	277	168.12	185.63	194.56	205.49	232.29	258.50	11.3	153.8
Law	K	251	214.01	231.72	239.11	251.93	297.45	355.43	19.5	166.1

Library Science	Z	107	290.02	321.24	336.34	355.38	376.47	379.89	0.9	131.0
Math and computer science	QA	329	1,242.13	1,367.86	1,406.66	1,480.16	1,623.12	1,559.12	-3.9	125.5
Military and naval science	U,V	28	239.90	285.07	301.03	288.80	276.33	458.94	66.1	191.3
Music	M	49	82.18	89.24	92.24	95.74	151.67	212.73	40.3	258.8
Philosophy and religion	B-BD, BH-BX	212	232.37	253.08	266.63	281.45	316.77	362.03	14.3	155.8
Physics	QC	148	2,845.54	2,944.32	3,282.05	3,499.54	3,538.93	3,537.87	-0.0	124.3
Political science	J	103	312.76	340.45	362.82	382.91	562.63	563.12	0.1	180.1
Psychology	BF	111	648.21	726.61	767.19	828.57	970.19	1,049.83	8.2	162.0
Recreation	GV	86	69.79	81.14	84.44	90.20	122.06	176.76	44.8	253.3
Social sciences	H	41	351.40	388.63	410.60	435.17	645.60	753.59	16.7	214.5
Sociology	HM-HX	240	482.59	538.51	567.96	608.13	717.56	760.32	6.0	157.5
Technology	TA-TT	136	535.73	592.24	624.46	679.00	723.65	775.03	7.1	144.7
Zoology	QL	117	1,454.26	1,613.42	1,675.90	1,762.83	1,816.13	1,655.65	-8.8	113.8
Total		5,998	$843.46	$934.48	$991.39	$1,051.73	$1,114.32	$1,193.10	7.1%	141.5

Compiled by Stephen Bosch, University of Arizona, based on subscription information supplied by EBSCO Information Services.

(continued from page 347)

a small sample size the change in just one or two titles could easily have a large impact on the overall price for an area.

More extensive reports from the periodical price index have been published annually in the April 15 issue of Library Journal through 1992, in the May issue of American Libraries from 1993 to 2002, and in the October 2003 issue of Library Resources and Technical Services.

The Legal Serials Services Index (Table 2) has been compiled by Ajaye Bloomstone using data collected from a number of different legal serials vendors. The base year for this index is 2009. This index presents price data covering the years 2009 through 2016.

Vendors were again asked to provide cost data on particular titles with the assumption that the title/set has been held by a large academic research law library, and the cost recorded in the index is that for the upkeep of the title in question, not the cost incurred in purchasing a new set. A nuance of legal publishing is that for some of the larger legal publishers, hard prices for a calendar year are not set at the beginning of that year but rather halfway through, so in some cases only price estimates may be available for this article. Legal serials services can be updated as new editions, regular/irregular updates ("releases") throughout the year, or added/revised volumes. The price for a title may increase or decrease from one year to the next, depending on plans for keeping a title current. It should be noted that although legal serials in print format continue to be produced, titles seem to be migrating, albeit slowly, to an electronic-only format. Some prices were provided for several titles with the caveat "no longer available for new sales." This statement would lead one to believe that the publication is being phased out. Either the title might soon no longer be available as a print product, or it may cease publication entirely, in any format.

Table 2 / Legal Serials Services: Average Prices and Price Indexes, 2009–2016
Index Base: 2009 = 100

Year	Number of Titles	Average Price	Percent Change	Index
2009	217	$1,658.20	n.a.	100.0
2010	217	1,716.30	3.5%	103.5
2011	217	1,905.20	11.0	114.9
2012	217	2,020.83	6.1	124.1
2013	217	2,233.00	10.5	134.7
2014	217	2,486.04	11.3	149.9
2015	217	2,831.00	13.9	170.7
2016	217	3,085.34	9.0	186.1

Book Prices

Tables 3 (hardcover books), 6 (mass market paperbacks), 7 (other—trade—paperbacks), 7A (audiobooks), and table 7B (e-books), prepared by Narda Tafuri, are derived from data provided by book wholesaler Baker & Taylor. Figures for

2014 are revised to reflect late updates to the Baker & Taylor database (publishers were still adding 2014 titles in early 2015); the 2015 figures given here may be similarly revised in next year's tables and should be considered preliminary. These five tables use the Book Industry Study Group's BISAC categories; for more information on the BISAC categories, visit http://www.bisg.org. The BISAC juvenile category (fiction and nonfiction) has been divided into children's and young adult.

Average book prices declined sharply in 2015. List prices for hardcovers overall (Table 3) fell by 0.44 percent. Mass market paperback prices (Table 6) showed a decrease of 0.14 percent and trade paperbacks (Table 7) declined 2.72 percent. Audiobook prices (Table 7A) have been falling since 2009, but saw an even steeper decline of 15.71 percent in 2015. E-book prices registered the greatest decrease of all—17.19 percent.

The North American Academic Books Price Indexes (Tables 4, 4A, and 4B) are prepared by Stephen Bosch. The current version of North American Academic Books: Average Prices and Price Indexes 2012–2014 (Table 4) should not be compared with the versions published in 2009 or previous years. The North American Academic Books Price Index (NAABPI) now contains many more titles in the source data, which has affected the index considerably. This is due to the fact that Coutts, now part of ProQuest, treats far more titles in their approval programs than the former Blackwell Book Services. For indexes published prior to 2009, Blackwell was a supplier of data for the index. Blackwell was purchased in 2011 by YBP and the vendor data used to create the index changed at that time. After 2009 the data comes from Coutts and YBP, prior to 2009 the data came from Blackwell and YBP. The year-to-year comparisons from 2007 on (indexes published since 2009) are now based on this new data model, and the changes in price and number of titles are not as dramatic as when looking at comparable data in the indexes that were published prior to 2009.

The overall average price for books in the NAABPI for 2014 decreased 5.6 percent, a large swing from the 6.3 percent increase seen the previous year. The average price decreased to $101.08 from $107.02. The number of titles increased dramatically from 120,822 in 2013 to 153,289 in 2014, a 27 percent increase. The decrease in price for the most recent year was primarily due to a drop in costs for the most expensive books. In 2013 there were 475 titles that cost more than $1,000 with an average price of $3,378, while in 2014 there were only 387 titles costing more than $1,000 with an average price of $1,901. Many of the books in the "greater than $1,000" category were e-books. The drop in the average price of e-book titles costing more than $1,000 was the driver in price decreases for both print and e-books in 2014.

In both 2013 and 2014 changes in the most expensive books' costs caused both the large increase in 2013 and the large decrease in 2014. When doing budget planning, it would not be wise to assume that your book costs are going to be lower since the bulk of purchasing will occur in the middle ranges and these areas are far less volatile. Book prices in the mid-range ($50–$200) have remained relatively flat, but costs have gone up due to larger numbers of titles being published.

Since 2008 two additional indexes have been available, one for e-books only (Table 4A) and another for textbooks (Table 4B). Both of these indexes are of high

(text continues on page 360)

Table 3 / Hardcover Books: Average Prices and Price Indexes, 2012–2015

Index Base: 2005 = 100

BISAC Category	2005	2012 Final			2013 Final			2014 Final			2015 Preliminary		
	Average Prices	Volumes	Average Prices	Index	Volumes	Average Prices	Index	Volumes	Average Prices	Index	Volumes	Average Prices	Index
Antiques and collectibles	$71.07	124	$69.56	97.9	137	$70.41	99.1	146	$67.04	94.3	134	$95.68	134.6
Architecture	66.99	762	80.66	120.4	879	88.92	132.7	799	89.48	133.6	895	99.47	148.5
Art	62.33	1,821	73.02	117.2	2,042	71.34	114.5	1,896	81.03	130.0	1,949	73.53	118.0
Bibles	48.05	199	37.46	78.0	197	37.43	77.9	137	33.71	70.2	178	35.74	74.4
Biography and autobiography	46.20	1,713	49.42	107.0	1,939	44.12	95.5	1,779	48.33	104.6	1,711	47.33	102.4
Body, mind and spirit	26.76	132	37.32	139.5	237	31.99	119.5	158	46.64	174.3	150	29.37	109.7
Business and economics	120.56	4,126	139.77	115.9	4,386	150.18	124.6	4,370	145.78	120.9	4,659	146.90	121.9
Children	23.14	11,920	22.97	99.3	12,179	23.78	102.8	12,763	23.99	103.7	12,988	24.03	103.8
Comics and graphic novels	32.75	735	37.86	115.6	639	37.53	114.6	664	40.31	123.1	698	37.75	115.3
Computers	113.07	981	167.06	147.7	880	139.41	123.3	901	159.86	141.4	965	150.03	132.7
Cooking	28.68	1,135	29.05	101.3	1,215	29.54	103.0	1,244	28.93	100.9	1,225	28.20	98.3
Crafts and hobbies	28.82	210	31.13	108.0	195	29.10	101.0	204	28.76	99.8	172	28.78	99.9
Design	59.41	504	64.87	109.2	399	62.97	106.0	394	67.56	113.7	457	67.62	113.8
Drama	60.81	72	76.98	126.6	76	74.53	122.6	81	81.21	133.5	59	79.99	131.5
Education	95.10	1,616	132.56	139.4	1,747	118.72	124.8	1,930	122.49	128.8	2,155	120.43	126.6
Family and relationships	25.37	213	43.07	169.8	265	36.53	144.0	209	45.46	179.2	208	57.43	226.4
Fiction	28.37	4,421	30.23	106.6	5,155	30.29	106.8	4,625	30.05	105.9	4,345	29.84	105.2
Foreign language study	116.89	221	115.16	98.5	270	115.33	98.7	220	115.88	99.1	260	140.76	120.4
Games	32.07	122	36.01	112.3	111	40.05	124.9	95	39.54	123.3	111	40.26	125.5
Gardening	38.20	134	39.94	104.6	115	37.42	98.0	97	30.64	80.2	121	38.10	99.7
Health and fitness	54.05	321	73.38	135.8	378	64.67	119.6	353	58.45	108.1	359	68.16	126.1
History	88.17	4,950	86.46	98.1	5,030	86.61	98.2	5,489	94.66	107.4	5,784	93.46	106.0
House and home	31.51	88	44.73	142.0	108	35.83	113.7	91	33.66	106.8	109	35.60	113.0
Humor	19.00	245	19.77	104.1	246	19.94	104.9	288	23.74	125.0	292	24.72	130.1

Language arts and disciplines	120.71	1,147	131.89	109.3	117.0	141.23	1,253	1,302	147.81	122.4	1,543	143.58	118.9
Law	155.28	1,900	178.81	115.2	115.1	178.70	1,966	2,105	178.45	114.9	2,169	175.45	113.0
Literary collections	74.92	258	96.92	129.4	120.3	90.16	282	271	100.18	133.7	218	113.01	150.8
Literary criticism	123.84	2,027	123.34	99.6	97.9	121.24	1,990	2,284	126.91	102.5	2,257	121.22	97.9
Mathematics	144.88	963	151.30	104.4	91.9	133.13	910	963	141.42	97.6	979	148.93	102.8
Medical	156.54	3,546	180.38	115.2	118.3	185.17	3,443	3,488	204.11	130.4	4,116	181.47	115.9
Music	77.63	524	90.51	116.6	115.1	89.37	534	540	91.28	117.6	576	95.78	123.4
Nature	67.75	371	89.94	132.8	124.4	84.27	470	420	90.35	133.4	471	89.08	131.5
Performing arts	71.74	574	90.23	125.8	131.9	94.64	583	684	94.85	132.2	773	94.70	132.0
Pets	25.45	93	23.98	94.2	100.7	25.64	107	107	24.44	96.0	89	24.78	97.4
Philosophy	127.22	1,169	105.35	82.8	83.1	105.67	1,291	1,406	109.89	86.4	1,495	106.34	83.6
Photography	56.77	865	85.88	151.3	164.2	93.22	801	841	66.87	117.8	892	68.88	121.3
Poetry	36.58	287	41.58	113.7	92.7	33.92	420	352	34.64	94.7	282	43.38	118.6
Political science	103.39	2,654	112.81	109.1	109.5	113.25	2,608	3,036	116.68	112.9	3,145	120.65	116.7
Psychology	93.85	1,100	140.31	149.5	140.6	131.91	1,171	1,193	152.10	162.1	1,363	148.46	158.2
Reference	202.23	499	396.56	196.1	176.1	356.07	409	400	320.62	158.5	359	378.60	187.2
Religion	62.29	2,730	81.93	131.5	123.8	77.10	2,804	2,538	80.02	128.5	2,474	85.91	137.9
Science	203.44	3,331	195.83	96.3	95.8	194.94	3,325	3,536	199.58	98.1	4,143	186.49	91.7
Self-help	22.43	265	24.74	110.3	125.5	28.15	377	282	25.13	112.0	284	27.78	123.9
Social science	96.17	3,139	115.79	120.4	120.3	115.72	3,335	3,328	141.10	146.7	3,825	132.77	138.1
Sports and recreation	38.77	658	51.66	133.2	122.0	47.29	690	621	60.84	156.9	606	52.77	136.1
Study aids	105.28	14	110.60	105.1	110.3	116.17	14	19	92.75	88.1	14	101.39	96.3
Technology and engineering	187.80	2,653	175.47	93.4	92.0	172.73	2,540	2,567	189.95	101.1	3,439	167.47	89.2
Transportation	68.68	225	66.85	97.3	104.5	71.76	316	248	85.61	124.6	279	83.00	120.9
Travel	37.11	205	49.73	134.0	111.3	41.30	205	181	38.16	102.8	209	34.34	92.5
True crime	29.28	70	32.37	110.6	96.3	28.20	87	78	28.83	98.5	65	42.62	145.6
Young adult	50.17	2,256	36.87	73.5	61.8	30.98	1,965	2,169	33.93	67.6	2,044	32.23	64.2
Totals	$80.36	70,288	$95.00	118.2	115.2	$92.56	72,721	73,892	$98.53	122.6	78,093	$98.96	123.1

Compiled by Narda Tafuri, University of Scranton, from data supplied by Baker & Taylor.

Table 4 / North American Academic Books: Average Prices and Price Indexes 2012–2014

Index Base: 1989 = 100

Subject Area	LC Class	1989		2012		2013		2014			
		No. of Titles	Average Price	No. of Titles	Average Price	No. of Titles	Average Price	No. of Titles	Average Price	% Change 2013–2014	Index
Agriculture	S	897	$45.13	1,402	$106.66	1,361	$99.44	1,634	$119.50	20.2%	264.8
Anthropology	GN	406	32.81	563	105.27	581	101.62	691	95.12	-6.4	289.9
Botany	QK	251	69.02	356	161.26	307	156.65	449	155.71	-0.6	225.6
Business and economics	H	5,979	41.67	11,058	115.17	11,242	117.50	14,618	108.43	-7.7	260.2
Chemistry	QD	577	110.61	787	259.27	754	238.81	988	236.90	-0.8	214.2
Education	L	1,685	29.61	4,768	95.15	4,573	96.65	6,492	88.52	-8.4	299.0
Engineering and technology	T	4,569	64.94	8,769	147.53	8,470	157.88	10,699	155.63	-1.4	239.6
Fine and applied arts	M-N	3,040	40.72	7,098	65.76	7,174	69.08	7,916	70.39	1.9	172.9
General works	A	333	134.65	162	97.19	148	110.81	232	81.99	-26.0	60.9
Geography	G	396	47.34	1,241	131.13	1,171	120.75	1,617	119.36	-1.2	252.1
Geology	QE	303	63.49	321	138.07	320	217.42	394	144.45	-33.6	227.5
History	C-D-E-F	5,549	31.34	9,857	73.31	10,301	83.35	13,944	76.50	-8.2	244.1
Home economics	TX	535	27.10	1,043	51.81	1,059	67.40	835	65.84	-2.3	242.9
Industrial arts	TT	175	23.89	430	45.58	363	43.71	306	67.78	55.1	283.7
Law	K	1,252	51.10	6,139	136.38	5,758	161.29	6,408	136.98	-15.1	268.1

Subject	LC class	No. titles	Price	No. titles	Price	No. titles	Price	No. titles	Price	% change	Index
Library and information science	Z	857	44.51	812	106.91	878	108.53	1,097	96.89	-10.7	217.7
Literature and language	P	10,812	24.99	21,813	61.12	23,203	69.50	28,986	61.52	-11.5	246.2
Mathematics and computer science	QA	2,707	44.68	4,820	122.99	4,495	133.96	5,415	111.47	-16.8	249.5
Medicine	R	5,028	58.38	9,249	130.09	8,711	128.67	11,795	153.96	19.7	263.7
Military and naval science	U-V	715	33.57	891	83.37	928	81.76	1,225	77.13	-5.7	229.8
Philosophy and religion	B	3,518	29.06	8,314	84.73	8,392	97.28	10,565	87.22	-10.3	300.1
Physical education and recreation	GV	814	20.38	2,102	64.92	2,170	85.89	2,595	69.03	-19.6	338.7
Physics and astronomy	QB	1,219	64.59	1,811	145.95	1,761	149.09	2,235	139.86	-6.2	216.5
Political science	J	1,650	36.76	3,905	110.71	3,721	106.53	5,141	104.23	-2.2	283.5
Psychology	BF	890	31.97	1,990	99.96	1,983	115.22	2,321	104.46	-9.3	326.7
Science (general)	Q	433	56.10	717	139.25	593	128.18	920	123.54	-3.6	220.2
Sociology	HM	2,742	29.36	7,044	98.63	7,260	114.34	10,021	98.58	-13.8	335.8
Zoology	QH,L,P,R	1,967	71.28	3,375	157.49	3,147	161.11	3,750	149.68	-7.1	210.0
Average for all subjects		59,299	$41.69	120,837	$100.69	120,822	$107.02	153,289	$101.08	-5.6%	242.4

Compiled by Stephen Bosch, University of Arizona, from electronic data provided by Ingrams Content Group (Coutts Information Services), and YBP Library Services. The data represent all titles (includes hardcover, trade, and paperback books, as well as annuals) treated for all approval plan customers serviced by the vendors. This table covers titles published or distributed in the United States and Canada during the calendar years listed.

Table 4A / North American Academic E-Books: Average Prices and Price Indexes 2012–2014

Index Base: 2007 = 100

Subject Area	LC Class	2007		2012		2013		2014			
		No. of Titles	Average Price	No. of Titles	Average Price	No. of Titles	Average Price	No. of Titles	Average Price	% Change 2013–2014	Index
Agriculture	S	894	$128.59	748	$150.01	730	$137.60	844	$160.32	16.5%	124.7
Anthropology	GN	382	105.28	367	130.70	317	125.90	340	115.38	-8.4	109.6
Botany	QK	287	168.18	224	176.14	197	170.44	254	198.35	16.4	117.9
Business and economics	H	9,807	97.25	7,369	136.31	6,684	138.84	8,170	122.43	-11.8	125.9
Chemistry	QD	934	213.76	595	280.25	526	268.27	596	271.52	1.2	127.0
Education	L	2,565	107.62	2,848	126.02	2,422	125.68	3,342	105.93	-15.7	98.4
Engineering and technology	T	7,176	133.60	5,365	193.12	5,069	204.78	6,127	195.67	-4.4	146.5
Fine and applied arts	M-N	1,141	84.30	1,898	114.59	1,749	116.21	2,212	100.80	-13.3	119.6
General works	A	60	107.85	83	121.94	67	109.96	108	103.65	-5.7	96.1
Geography	G	888	132.67	752	147.60	623	164.58	875	144.33	-12.3	108.8
Geology	QE	201	136.49	209	181.01	189	314.30	203	173.25	-44.9	126.9
History	C-D-E-F	4,452	93.55	5,352	111.36	4,800	116.44	6,740	95.69	-17.8	102.3
Home economics	TX	255	104.31	384	125.74	449	112.76	367	93.97	-16.7	90.1
Industrial arts	TT	20	52.73	72	70.54	86	72.30	90	100.82	39.5	191.2
Law	K	1,743	99.61	3,034	174.94	2,461	200.43	2,699	158.25	-21.0	158.9

Subject	LC class									
Library and information science	Z	308	74.70	413	123.84	439	119.44	533	117.16	-1.9	156.8
Literature and language	P	5,517	90.59	9,027	111.29	8,953	123.27	11,405	90.21	-26.8	99.6
Mathematics and computer science	QA	4,285	102.93	2,759	149.91	2,376	181.42	2,782	130.94	-27.8	127.2
Medicine	R	7,420	123.59	5,957	170.07	5,466	170.38	6,977	200.50	17.7	162.2
Military and naval science	U-V	684	82.89	503	110.54	499	106.19	642	94.88	-10.6	114.5
Philosophy and religion	B	3,612	93.77	4,609	137.82	4,146	146.45	5,340	107.85	-26.4	115.0
Physical education and recreation	GV	610	96.00	1,059	101.69	922	102.68	1,213	88.82	-13.5	92.5
Physics and astronomy	QB	1,965	142.11	1,372	179.48	1,158	187.49	1,291	158.29	-15.6	111.4
Political science	J	2,447	102.72	2,823	130.94	2,177	135.39	2,853	118.44	-12.5	115.3
Psychology	BF	1,113	83.51	1,214	132.04	1,033	163.63	1,234	125.81	-23.1	150.6
Science (general)	Q	468	117.19	427	144.13	346	148.23	490	150.21	1.3	128.2
Sociology	HM	4,139	98.02	4,400	131.34	3,966	151.15	5,308	119.37	-21.0	121.8
Zoology	QH,L,P,R	3,394	154.01	2,190	180.24	1,967	206.60	2,052	184.05	-10.9	119.5
Average for all subjects		66,767	$110.82	66,053	$142.52	59,817	$151.77	75,087	$130.95	-13.7%	118.2

Compiled by Stephen Bosch, University of Arizona from electronic data provided by Ingrams Content Group (formerly Coutts Information Services), and YBP Library Services. The data represent all e-book titles treated for all approval plan customers serviced by the vendors. This table covers titles published or distributed in the United States and Canada during the calendar years listed. It is important to note that e-books that were released in a given year may have been published in print much earlier.

Table 4B / North American Academic Text Books: Average Prices and Price Indexes 2012–2014

Index Base: 2007 = 100

Subject Area	LC Class	2007		2012		2013		2014			
		No. of Titles	Average Price	No. of Titles	Average Price	No. of Titles	Average Price	No. of Titles	Average Price	% Change 2013–2014	Index
Agriculture	S	68	$134.75	100	$140.37	62	$131.30	71	$123.05	-6.3%	91.3
Anthropology	GN	40	89.15	75	108.16	35	114.63	35	112.17	-2.1	125.8
Botany	QK	4	98.00	14	185.04	9	207.69	13	121.02	-41.7	123.5
Business and economics	H	666	110.18	1,378	140.60	849	139.79	1,037	126.85	-9.3	115.1
Chemistry	QD	80	138.70	155	186.00	99	154.16	119	149.17	-3.2	107.5
Education	L	235	79.58	589	103.20	322	99.91	444	89.06	-10.9	111.9
Engineering and technology	T	668	106.13	1,128	133.28	835	136.07	925	124.31	-8.6	117.1
Fine and applied arts	M-N	82	73.69	179	111.44	104	107.49	112	108.03	0.5	146.6
General works	A	1	48.00	8	116.81	3	120.33	4	65.08	-45.9	135.6
Geography	G	59	100.42	150	127.39	91	134.77	115	126.88	-5.9	126.4
Geology	QE	26	118.28	46	137.67	30	138.20	43	132.58	-4.1	112.1
History	C-D-E-F	72	78.41	207	97.25	106	90.00	155	94.48	5.0	120.5
Home economics	TX	54	68.23	71	106.75	50	105.95	18	116.70	10.1	171.0
Industrial arts	TT	13	73.90	27	88.60	14	87.95	9	104.47	18.8	141.4
Law	K	163	87.67	543	116.61	316	113.67	442	103.35	-9.1	117.9

Subject	LC									%	Index
Library and information science	Z	24	65.54	42	75.03	24	75.73	56	81.40	7.5	124.2
Literature and language	P	269	71.35	787	93.32	382	91.06	522	85.79	-5.8	120.2
Mathematics and computer science	QA	732	91.42	1,072	124.39	783	108.08	895	101.64	-6.0	111.2
Medicine	R	1,210	126.37	2,046	138.27	1,596	135.40	1,824	131.76	-2.7	104.3
Military and naval science	U-V	10	104.58	29	129.40	12	75.62	20	108.76	43.8	104.0
Philosophy and religion	B	85	55.51	232	73.94	122	73.20	162	69.26	-5.4	124.8
Physical education and recreation	GV	47	72.14	110	108.93	62	121.16	60	106.17	-12.4	147.2
Physics and astronomy	QB	237	107.05	323	130.77	258	119.37	278	102.04	-14.5	95.3
Political science	J	104	74.21	265	105.94	148	102.16	173	93.56	-8.4	126.1
Psychology	BF	120	100.17	287	128.83	174	132.07	183	123.97	-6.1	123.8
Science (general)	Q	24	111.30	65	102.40	35	99.37	50	86.29	-13.2	77.5
Sociology	HM	330	84.88	815	103.14	489	104.24	575	95.75	-8.1	112.8
Zoology	QH,L,P,R	250	116.73	431	136.35	256	137.69	258	126.66	-8.0	108.5
Average for all subjects		5,673	$102.52	11,174	$123.56	7,266	$122.07	8,598	$113.25	-7.2%	110.5

Compiled by Stephen Bosch, University of Arizona from electronic data provided by YBP Library Services and Ingrams Content Group. The data represent all textbook titles treated for all approval plan customers serviced by the vendors. This table covers titles published or distributed in the United States and Canada during the calendar years listed.

This index does not include paperback editions. The inclusion of these items does impact pricing in the index.

(continued from page 351)

interest to users. Based on that input, the indexes continue to be published with the base index year set to 2007. In the academic market, it has always been assumed that e-books are more expensive than their print counterparts. Users might be surprised to find that the cheaper versions of e-books, available to consumers through such channels as Amazon and the Apple Store, are not available to libraries at similar prices, if they are available at all. The e-book index clearly points out the difference in price: the average price of an e-book in 2014 was $130.95 while the average price for all books was $101.08. The average price of a print book drops to $72.69 if the e-books are removed from the overall index. In 2013 there were close to 300 titles in the index costing more than $1,000 and their average price was $4,167. In 2014, there were around 260 titles and their average price was $2,156. The e-book index (Table 4A) showed a 13.7 percent price decrease and this decrease in the prices for e-books was the driver in the overall price decrease for 2014. E-books make up about 50 percent of the base table.

The high price for e-books is not that surprising as most pricing models for academic e-books generally add a large percentage to the list print price for the purchase of the e-books. Multi-user licenses are an even larger percentage. In most situations, even single-user academic e-book titles are more expensive than their print counterparts. Responding to customer demands, vendors offer e-books on multiple platforms with multiple pricing models; consequently, there can be multiple prices for the same title. Only the first instance of a unique ISBN is included in the data, so if the same book was treated by a vendor from one e-book aggregator and then treated again from another aggregator, only the first instance of the e-book is in the index. Also, if different pricing models are available the single user price is supplied. Where multiple prices are available for different use models, the lowest price is provided. Because electronic access is where the market is going it is appropriate to have e-books as a separate index. It is also important to note that the e-book market is rapidly changing. The availability of additional pricing models could be a factor in the upward shift in e-book prices.

The cost of textbooks has been a hot topic on many college campuses. The index for textbooks documents price changes in this area. The data show that textbooks tend to be much more expensive than other types of books, with an average price of $113.25 in 2014. There was a 7.2 percent decrease in the average price in 2014 after a 1.2 percent decrease in 2013. This is still not good news for students, who are essentially hostages of the textbook market. Textbooks are still expensive and the prices are not dropping significantly despite pressure on the textbook market from alternative sources like rental services for either print or electronic versions. This is not much consolation for cash-strapped students.

The average price of North American academic books in 2014 (Table 4) decreased by 5.6 percent as compared with the 2013 average price. This is mainly due to a large decrease in the average cost of titles treated in the highest part of the price bands ($120 and up). Nearly all price bands showed only modest growth, or no growth, in the number of titles between 2010 and 2013 and then the number of titles spiked in 2014. The price band above $120 exhibited very large increases over that period. The increase in the upper price bands was primarily due to increases in e-books; their prices average well above the $120 threshold.

Figure 1 / Comparison of Titles in Sample Grouped by Price

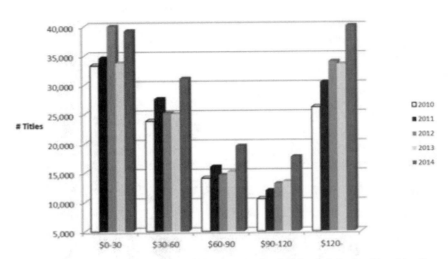

Take e-books out of the sample and the upper price bands shrink considerably. See Figure 1.

One thing that really stands out when looking at the data by price band is that the highest end of the price bands ($120 and up) has seen huge growth in the past five years, close to doubling in overall costs from $5.8 million (2010) to $9.8 million (2014). The impact on pricing from the titles in the $120-and-up price band is confirmed if you look at the actual dollar values in groups (sum of all prices for titles in the group). It is clear that the increase in the top end of the index was the main component in the overall increase as well as the decrease in the index for 2014. Until 2014 the $0–$30 price area had the largest number of titles; dollar-wise it remained the smallest portion as far as total cost (sum of all prices) goes in the index. The increase in the prices in the upper end of the index was what added to the overall level of increases. Since 2007 the cost (titles X prices) for books pricing above $120 has increased by 259 percent, while the overall costs for all books increased 120 percent. The increases in the costs of books in the upper price band represents 91 percent of the entire increase over the period covered. Again, e-books are a significant driver in that increase as within the price bands the average price remains fairly constant except for the area with prices over $120, which showed a 62 percent increase over the years 2010–2013 before a drop in 2014. See Figures 2 and 3.

The data used for this index are derived from all titles treated by the Coutts Information Services (formerly Ingram Content Group, but now Coutts is part of ProQuest) and YBP Library Services (formerly part of Baker and Taylor now part of EBSCO) in their approval plans during the calendar years listed. The index includes e-books as well as paperback editions as supplied by these vendors, and this inclusion of paperbacks and e-books as distributed as part of the approval plans has clearly influenced the prices reflected in the index figures. The index is inclusive of the broadest categories of materials as that is the marketplace in

Figure 2 / Comparison of Total Costs in Sample Grouped by Price

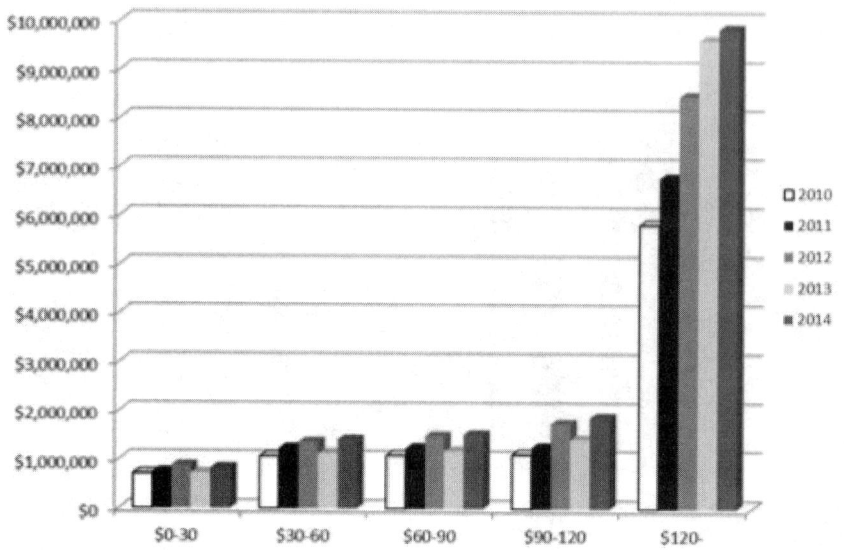

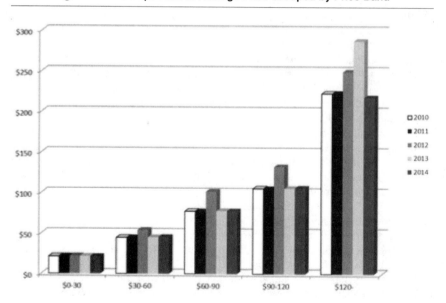

Figure 3 / Comparison of Average Price Grouped by Price Band

which academic libraries operate, and the index attempts to chart price changes that impact that market.

E-books are also now being treated in a separate index (Table 4A), so the differences in the indexes will be interesting to observe. Currently a large number of titles are not published in both print and "e" version, so the number of titles in the e-book index should remain smaller than the broader index. It is safe to say that, in the future, the number of titles in the broader index could decline and at the same time the number of e-books should rise, especially as we see more publishers move to publishing electronic versions of their books. Many e-book pricing models add extra charges of as much as 50 percent to 100 percent to the retail price. This pricing model is reflected in the higher prices for e-books. The overall price for e-books did show a decline from 2007 to 2009, but in 2011 to 2013 the prices shot up again. The year 2014 showed a decrease in average price for e-books but the overall trend is going up. The index clearly shows that, for the library market, e-books are much more expensive than print. Many publishers and e-book aggregators are still adding "e" versions of print books from backlists, and these are showing up in the index; this is also the basis for the wide swings in numbers of titles in the index from year to year.

The price index for textbooks (Table 4B) shows a 7.2 percent decrease for overall prices between 2013 and 2014. Despite the decrease, overall textbook prices are higher than regular books. These are indicators that the angst experienced by students as they purchase their texts is well justified as prices appear to be much higher than for regular academic books.

Price changes vary, as always, among subject areas. This year there were many double-digit decreases in subject areas, and a few areas showed price increases. This is a normal occurrence. What is not normal is the fact that a third of the subject areas showed double-digit price decreases. The 2014 data show that those areas with the largest decreases were very mixed, indicating that changes in publishing patterns at the subject level were not causes of the overall changes in the index. Decreases in e-book publishing in large expensive online reference works and encyclopedias caused the overall decrease.

It is good to remember that price indexes become less accurate at describing price changes the smaller the sample becomes. Geology and physical education are small samples and showed very large price changes, but to conclude that all books in those areas increased or decreased at like amounts is not correct. These areas have a small sample size (fewer than 1,000 titles) and the inclusion/exclusion of just a few large expensive items can have a major impact on prices for the category. The decreases in geology, for example, were due to a drop in the number of expensive titles. Because the sample is very small, these titles caused the overall price to drop dramatically.

The U.S. College Books Price Index (Table 5), prepared by Frederick C. Lynden, contains average price and index number data for the years 2013 through 2015 (index base year of 1989), and also the percentage change in price between 2014 and 2015.

Data for the index were compiled from 6,424 reviews of books published in *Choice* during 2015. Expensive titles ($500 or more) were omitted from the

(text continues on page 367)

Table 5 / U.S. College Books: Average Prices and Price Indexes 1989, 2013–2015

Index Base for all years: 1989 = 100

Subject	1989 No. of Titles	1989 Avg. Price per Title	2013 Avg. Price per Title	2013 Indexed to 1989	2014 No. of Titles	2014 Avg. Price per Title	2014 Indexed to 1989	2014 Indexed to 2013	2015 No. of Titles	2015 Avg. Price per Title	2015 Indexed to 1989	2015 Indexed to 2014	Percent Change 2014–2015
GENERAL *	19	$40.19	n.a.	n.a.	n.a.	n.a.	n.a.	n.a.	n.a.	n.a.	n.a.	n.a.	n.a.
HUMANITIES	21	32.33	$69.95	216.4	110	$74.73	231.1	106.8	69	$70.45	217.9	94.3	-0.1
Art and architecture	276	55.56	64.93	116.9	186	62.00	111.6	95.5	134	66.00	118.8	106.5	0.1
Fine Arts **	n.a.	n.a.	65.66	n.a.	87	60.99	n.a.	92.9	105	69.49	n.a.	113.9	0.1
Architecture **	n.a.	n.a.	72.09	n.a.	63	88.46	n.a.	122.7	44	90.81	n.a.	102.7	0.0
Photography	24	44.11	56.60	128.3	37	60.00	136.0	106.0	21	56.32	127.7	93.9	-0.1
Communication	42	$32.70	71.68	219.2	114	65.00	198.8	90.7	84	91.52	279.9	140.8	0.4
Language and literature	110	35.17	70.83	201.4	115	89.67	255.0	126.6	90	76.81	218.4	85.7	-0.1
African and Middle Eastern **	n.a.	n.a.	52.80	n.a.	18	59.32	n.a.	112.3	16	75.27	n.a.	126.9	0.3
Asian and Oceanian **	n.a.	n.a.	65.30	n.a.	21	59.37	n.a.	90.9	23	55.78	n.a.	94.0	-0.1
Classical	75	43.07	87.87	204.0	39	85.24	197.9	97.0	34	67.83	157.5	79.6	-0.2
English and American	547	30.27	72.45	239.3	365	69.18	228.5	95.5	326	67.34	222.5	97.3	-0.0
Germanic	38	32.18	73.44	228.2	30	66.44	206.5	90.5	35	72.87	226.4	109.7	0.1
Romance	97	$30.30	77.37	255.3	66	76.29	251.8	98.6	62	69.34	228.8	90.9	-0.1
Slavic	41	27.92	56.07	200.8	10	85.40	305.9	152.3	13	63.37	227.0	74.2	-0.3
Other	63	25.09	n.a.	n.a.	n.a.	n.a.	n.a.	n.a.	n.a.	n.a.	n.a.	n.a.	n.a.
Performing arts	20	29.41	59.85	203.5	37	70.72	240.5	118.2	28	57.72	196.3	81.6	-0.2
Film	82	$33.00	77.23	234.0	146	74.68	226.3	96.7	130	71.02	215.2	95.1	-0.0
Music	156	35.34	70.44	199.3	141	68.10	192.7	96.7	129	65.32	184.8	95.9	-0.0
Theater and dance	58	34.18	67.24	196.7	49	70.75	207.0	105.2	26	79.14	231.5	111.9	0.1
Philosophy	185	37.25	75.30	202.1	241	76.70	205.9	101.9	244	74.60	200.3	97.3	-0.0
Religion	174	33.49	66.32	198.0	271	68.68	205.1	103.6	290	57.51	171.7	83.7	-0.2
TOTAL HUMANITIES	2,009	$36.09	70.53	195.4	2,146	$71.35	197.7	101.2	1,903	$69.05	191.3	96.8	-0.0

SCIENCE AND TECHNOLOGY	99	$46.90	68.77	146.6	102	$59.53	126.9	86.6	67	$58.57	124.9	98.4	-0.0
History of science and technology	74	40.56	47.47	117.0	85	54.60	134.6	115.0	77	58.08	143.2	106.4	0.1
Astronautics and astronomy	22	50.56	65.56	129.7	57	57.52	113.8	87.7	66	48.00	94.9	83.4	-0.2
Biology	97	51.01	72.46	142.1	154	72.79	142.7	100.5	152	77.01	151.0	105.8	0.1
Botany	29	63.91	82.34	128.8	62	91.94	143.9	111.7	79	95.71	149.8	104.1	0.0
Zoology	53	49.21	73.03	148.4	139	58.54	119.0	80.2	115	69.55	141.3	118.8	0.2
Chemistry	21	70.76	107.12	151.4	36	86.65	122.5	80.9	30	73.21	103.5	84.5	-0.2
Earth science	34	79.44	81.36	102.4	115	84.08	105.8	103.3	119	75.86	95.5	90.2	-0.1
Engineering	87	66.74	98.47	147.5	58	91.42	137.0	92.8	57	93.02	139.4	101.8	0.0
Health sciences	94	34.91	59.12	169.3	162	66.98	191.9	113.3	151	70.27	201.3	104.9	0.0
Information and computer science	70	40.35	59.15	146.6	62	72.94	180.8	123.3	51	53.35	132.2	73.1	-0.3
Mathematics	60	48.53	65.88	135.8	85	62.64	129.1	95.1	102	67.01	138.1	107.0	0.1
Physics	22	43.94	66.47	151.3	51	58.96	134.2	88.7	44	56.54	128.7	95.9	-0.0
Sports and physical education	18	27.46	59.12	215.3	54	69.08	251.6	116.8	52	66.43	241.9	96.2	-0.0
TOTAL SCIENCE	780	$49.54	70.27	141.8	1,222	$69.20	139.7	98.5	1,162	$70.11	141.5	101.3	0.0
SOCIAL AND BEHAVIORAL SCIENCES	92	$37.09	69.48	187.3	126	$81.26	219.1	117.0	144	$81.06	218.5	99.8	-0.0
Anthropology	96	39.94	82.06	205.5	123	84.95	212.7	103.5	113	82.79	207.3	97.5	-0.0
Business management and labor	145	35.72	62.04	173.7	160	65.21	182.6	105.1	127	54.39	152.3	83.4	-0.2
Economics	332	40.75	60.24	147.8	247	60.59	148.7	100.6	238	67.44	165.5	111.3	0.1
Education	71	$34.50	65.31	189.3	138	73.24	212.3	112.1	161	77.82	225.6	106.3	0.1
History, geography and area studies	59	$42.10	76.21	181.0	117	68.10	161.8	89.4	139	70.59	167.7	103.7	0.0
Africa	44	34.85	71.76	205.9	34	71.62	205.5	99.8	34	72.54	208.1	101.3	0.0
*Ancient History ** *	n.a.	n.a.	88.88	n.a.	41	102.96	n.a.	115.8	45	95.74	n.a.	93.0	-0.1
Asia and Oceania	76	34.75	69.43	199.8	92	71.77	206.5	103.4	86	78.82	226.8	109.8	0.1
*Central and Eastern Europe ** *	n.a.	n.a.	63.73	n.a.	59	72.77	n.a.	114.2	63	68.25	n.a.	93.8	-0.1
Latin America and Caribbean	42	37.23	60.74	163.1	67	65.86	176.9	108.4	60	68.61	184.3	104.2	0.0
Middle East and North Africa	30	36.32	60.23	165.8	35	74.43	204.9	123.6	49	77.79	214.2	104.5	0.0
North America	349	30.56	63.47	207.7	441	49.60	162.3	78.1	397	50.10	163.9	101.0	0.0
*United Kingdom ** *	n.a.	n.a.	78.40	n.a.	86	72.12	n.a.	92.0	68	74.65	n.a.	103.5	0.0
Western Europe	287	42.08	74.59	177.3	122	75.99	180.6	101.9	122	69.43	165.0	91.4	-0.1

Table 5 / U.S. College Books: Average Prices and Price Indexes 1989, 2013–2015 (cont.)

Index Base for all years: 1989=100

Subject	1989 No. of Titles	1989 Avg. Price per Title	2013 Avg. Price per Title	2013 Indexed to 1989	2014 No. of Titles	2014 Avg. Price per Title	2014 Indexed to 1989	2014 Indexed to 2013	2015 No. of Titles	2015 Avg. Price per Title	2015 Indexed to 1989	2015 Indexed to 2014	Percent Change 2014–2015
Political science	28	33.56	39.98	119.1	4	124.99	372.4	312.6	3	48.98	145.9	39.2	-0.6
Comparative politics	236	37.82	70.22	185.7	202	69.93	184.9	99.6	190	79.17	209.3	113.2	0.1
International relations	207	35.74	70.52	197.3	177	73.64	206.0	104.4	187	77.80	217.7	105.6	0.1
Political theory	59	37.76	59.86	158.5	85	62.83	166.4	105.0	80	62.88	166.5	100.1	0.0
U.S. Politics	212	29.37	54.32	185.0	241	63.49	216.2	116.9	216	63.43	216.0	99.9	-0.0
Psychology	179	36.36	81.60	224.4	96	75.08	206.5	92.0	67	85.53	235.2	113.9	0.1
Sociology	178	36.36	71.22	195.9	193	78.79	216.7	110.6	169	79.70	219.2	101.2	0.0
BEHAVIORAL SCIENCES	2,722	$36.43	68.03	186.7	2,886	$68.19	187.2	100.2	2,758	$70.05	192.3	102.7	0.0
TOTAL GENERAL, HUMANITIES, SCIENCE, AND SOCIAL SCIENCE	5,511	$38.16	69.30	181.6	6,254	$69.47	182.0	100.2	5,823	$69.73	182.7	100.4	0.0
REFERENCE	636	$61.02	117.48	192.5	40	$98.18	160.9	83.6	59	$80.62	132.1	82.1	-0.2
Humanities **	n.a.	n.a.	103.51	n.a.	136	114.67	n.a.	110.8	90	106.96	n.a.	93.3	-0.1
Science and technology **	n.a.	n.a.	193.49	n.a.	43	149.99	n.a.	77.5	39	119.96	n.a.	80.0	-0.2
Social and behavioral sciences **	n.a.	n.a.	153.64	n.a.	178	134.98	n.a.	87.9	130	145.39	n.a.	107.7	0.1
TOTAL REFERENCE	636	$61.02	$143.52	235.2	397	$124.29	203.7	86.6	318	$119.38	195.6	96.0	-0.0
GRAND TOTAL	6,147	$40.52	$73.78	182.1	6,651	$72.74	179.5	98.6	6,141	72.31	178.5	99.4	-0.0

Compiled by Frederick Lynden, Brown University.

* General category no longer appears after 1999.

** Began appearing as separate sections after 1989.

n.a. = not available

analysis; thus the total number of titles reported is smaller than the actual number of books reviewed in 2015. This index includes some paperback prices; as a result, the average book price is less than if only hardcover books were included.

The average price for humanities titles in 2015 decreased by 3.22 percent from the previous year, and the average price for science and technology titles increased slightly at a rate of 1.32 percent. Finally, the average price for social and behavioral sciences increased at a rate of 2.73 percent. Nevertheless, combined, the overall subject area increase was 0.37 percent. This overall small increase is in line with the CPI increase for 2015, which has been around 0.7 percent. For all titles, which include reference, there was a small dip of 0.59 percent, caused primarily by the large decrease in reference title average prices. More and more reference titles are being published online these days.

For 2015 the overall price average for books in the four major sections of Choice—humanities, science and technology, social and behavioral sciences, and reference—was $72.31, a 0.59 percent decrease compared with the average 2014 book price of $72.74 (the overall average was corrected due to an error last year). Reference books calculated separately had an average price decrease of 3.95 percent over the previous year, with a 2015 average price of $119.38 (after items $500 or over were removed) compared with last year's average price of $124.29. However, excluding reference books, the 2015 average price was $69.73, a 0.37 percent increase over the average 2014 price of $69.47.

Questions regarding this index should be addressed to the author at his e-mail address: Flynden@stanfordalumni.org.

Foreign Prices

During 2015 the dollar continued to make significant gains against the Canadian dollar, euro, British pound sterling, and Japanese yen. The steep decline in oil prices has been a factor in the dollar's strength throughout this time period.

Dates	12/31/11*	12/31/12*	12/31/13*	12/31/14*	12/31/15*
Canada	1.0180	0.9950	1.0640	1.1580	1.3860
Euro	0.7650	0.7590	0.7260	0.8220	0.9190
U.K.	0.6370	0.6180	0.6050	0.6420	0.6750
Japan	78.0000	86.1600	105.0100	119.4500	120.4200

* Data from Bureau of Fiscal Services. U.S. Treasury Department (http://www.fiscal.treasury.gov/fsreports/rpt/treasRptRateExch/treasRptRateExch_home.htm).

Serials Prices

Average Price of Serials (Table 8) and Average Price of Online Serials (Table 8A), compiled by Stephen Bosch, provide the average prices and percent increases for serials based on titles in select serials abstracting and indexing products. The serials in this price survey are published in the United States as well as overseas and are indexed in the ISI Arts and Humanities Citation Index, ISI Science Citation Index, ISI Social Sciences Citation Index, EBSCO Academic Search Premier,

(text continues on page 382)

Table 6 / U.S. Mass Market Paperback Books: Average Prices and Price Indexes, 2012–2015

Index Base: 2005 = 100

BISAC Category	2005 Average Prices	2012 Final Volumes	2012 Final Average Prices	2012 Final Index	2013 Final Volumes	2013 Final Average Prices	2013 Final Index	2014 Final Volumes	2014 Final Average Prices	2014 Final Index	2015 Volumes	2015 Average Prices	2015 Index
Antiques and collectibles	$7.69	5	$8.99	116.9	5	$8.99	116.9	4	$8.99	116.9	n.a.	n.a.	n.a.
Architecture	n.a.	n.a.	n.a.	n.a.	n.a.	n.a.	n.a.	n.a.	n.a.	n.a.	n.a.	n.a.	n.a.
Art	n.a.	n.a.	n.a.	n.a.	n.a.	n.a.	n.a.	n.a.	n.a.	n.a.	n.a.	n.a.	n.a.
Bibles	n.a.	n.a.	n.a.	n.a.	n.a.	n.a.	n.a.	n.a.	n.a.	n.a.	n.a.	n.a.	n.a.
Biography and autobiography	7.83	4	6.73	86.0	3	9.66	123.4	6	8.98	114.7	2	$8.49	108.4
Body, mind and spirit	7.11	14	8.13	114.3	14	8.13	114.3	2	9.99	140.5	n.a.	n.a.	n.a.
Business and economics	12.47	1	7.99	64.1	n.a.	n.a.	n.a.	n.a.	n.a.	n.a.	1	8.99	72.1
Children	5.29	240	6.49	122.7	217	6.70	126.7	272	6.10	115.4	200	6.14	116.0
Comics and graphic novels	8.47	n.a.	n.a.	n.a.	n.a.	n.a.	n.a.	n.a.	n.a.	n.a.	n.a.	n.a.	n.a.
Computers	n.a.	n.a.	n.a.	n.a.	n.a.	n.a.	n.a.	n.a.	n.a.	n.a.	n.a.	n.a.	n.a.
Cooking	7.50	n.a.	n.a.	n.a.	n.a.	n.a.	n.a.	n.a.	n.a.	n.a.	1	8.99	119.9
Crafts and hobbies	n.a.	n.a.	n.a.	n.a.	n.a.	n.a.	n.a.	n.a.	n.a.	n.a.	n.a.	n.a.	n.a.
Design	n.a.	n.a.	n.a.	n.a.	n.a.	n.a.	n.a.	n.a.	n.a.	n.a.	n.a.	n.a.	n.a.
Drama	6.32	2	4.95	78.3	n.a.	n.a.	n.a.	1	9.99	158.1	n.a.	n.a.	n.a.
Education	n.a.	n.a.	n.a.	n.a.	n.a.	n.a.	n.a.	n.a.	n.a.	n.a.	n.a.	n.a.	n.a.
Family and relationships	6.98	n.a.	n.a.	n.a.	n.a.	n.a.	n.a.	n.a.	n.a.	n.a.	1	8.99	128.8
Fiction	6.34	3,894	7.05	111.2	3,524	7.00	110.4	3,603	7.09	111.9	3,235	7.10	112.0
Foreign language study	n.a.	n.a.	n.a.	n.a.	n.a.	n.a.	n.a.	1	6.99	n.a.	n.a.	n.a.	n.a.
Games	7.14	n.a.	n.a.	n.a.	1	9.99	139.9	2	9.25	129.5	1	7.99	111.9
Gardening	n.a.	n.a.	n.a.	n.a.	n.a.	n.a.	n.a.	n.a.	n.a.	n.a.	n.a.	n.a.	n.a.
Health and fitness	7.43	16	8.24	110.9	8	8.24	110.9	3	9.33	125.5	3	8.99	121.0
History	7.90	3	8.66	109.6	3	9.99	126.5	2	9.99	126.5	2	9.99	126.5
House and home	5.99	n.a.	n.a.	n.a.	n.a.	n.a.	n.a.	n.a.	n.a.	n.a.	n.a.	n.a.	n.a.
Humor	6.99	n.a.	n.a.	n.a.	2	8.00	114.4	n.a.	n.a.	n.a.	n.a.	n.a.	n.a.

Language arts and disciplines	6.99	n.a.	n.a.	n.a.	n.a.	n.a.	n.a.	1	7.99	114.3	n.a.	n.a.	n.a.
Law	n.a.	n.a.	n.a.	n.a.	n.a.	n.a.	n.a.	n.a.	n.a.	n.a.	n.a.	n.a.	n.a.
Literary collections	n.a.	2	5.95	n.a.	n.a.	n.a.	n.a.	1	4.95	n.a.	n.a.	n.a.	n.a.
Literary criticism	7.95	n.a.	n.a.	n.a.	n.a.	n.a.	n.a.	n.a.	n.a.	n.a.	n.a.	n.a.	n.a.
Mathematics	n.a.	n.a.	n.a.	n.a.	n.a.	n.a.	n.a.	n.a.	n.a.	n.a.	n.a.	n.a.	n.a.
Medical	7.83	1	8.99	114.8	n.a.	n.a.	n.a.	1	7.99	102.0	n.a.	n.a.	n.a.
Music	7.95	n.a.	n.a.	n.a.	n.a.	n.a.	n.a.	n.a.	n.a.	n.a.	n.a.	n.a.	n.a.
Nature	n.a.	1	7.99	n.a.	n.a.	n.a.	n.a.	n.a.	n.a.	n.a.	n.a.	n.a.	n.a.
Performing arts	8.23	1	9.99	121.4	1	10.99	133.5	1	10.99	133.5	1	9.99	n.a.
Pets	n.a.	n.a.	n.a.	n.a.	1	7.99	n.a.	n.a.	n.a.	n.a.	1	6.95	92.8
Philosophy	7.49	n.a.	n.a.	n.a.	n.a.	n.a.	n.a.	n.a.	n.a.	n.a.	n.a.	n.a.	n.a.
Photography	n.a.	n.a.	n.a.	n.a.	3	6.62	115.1	n.a.	n.a.	n.a.	2	6.45	112.2
Poetry	5.75	2	7.45	129.6	n.a.	n.a.	n.a.	3	9.99	n.a.	3	7.98	n.a.
Political science	n.a.	n.a.	n.a.	n.a.	n.a.	n.a.	n.a.	1	9.99	n.a.	n.a.	n.a.	n.a.
Psychology	7.97	3	8.31	121.3	3	6.49	94.7	n.a.	n.a.	n.a.	1	7.99	116.6
Reference	6.85	3	8.31	n.a.	n.a.	n.a.	n.a.	5	12.89	188.2	n.a.	n.a.	n.a.
Religion	9.96	2	7.49	75.2	n.a.	n.a.	n.a.	n.a.	n.a.	n.a.	n.a.	n.a.	n.a.
Science	n.a.	n.a.	n.a.	n.a.	n.a.	n.a.	n.a.	n.a.	n.a.	n.a.	n.a.	n.a.	n.a.
Self-help	12.45	1	7.99	64.2	n.a.	n.a.	n.a.	n.a.	n.a.	n.a.	n.a.	n.a.	n.a.
Social science	7.08	1	9.99	141.1	n.a.	n.a.	n.a.	n.a.	n.a.	n.a.	n.a.	n.a.	n.a.
Sports and recreation	7.62	1	7.99	104.9	n.a.	n.a.	n.a.	n.a.	n.a.	n.a.	n.a.	n.a.	n.a.
Study aids	n.a.	n.a.	n.a.	n.a.	n.a.	n.a.	n.a.	n.a.	n.a.	n.a.	n.a.	n.a.	n.a.
Technology and engineering	n.a.	n.a.	n.a.	n.a.	n.a.	n.a.	n.a.	n.a.	n.a.	n.a.	n.a.	n.a.	n.a.
Transportation	12.95	n.a.	n.a.	n.a.	n.a.	n.a.	n.a.	n.a.	n.a.	n.a.	1	7.99	61.7
Travel	n.a.	n.a.	n.a.	n.a.	n.a.	n.a.	n.a.	n.a.	n.a.	n.a.	n.a.	n.a.	n.a.
True crime	7.19	38	8.31	115.6	26	8.49	118.1	20	8.69	120.9	13	8.30	115.4
Young adult	6.46	44	8.94	138.4	44	9.22	142.7	44	9.42	145.9	29	8.71	134.9
Totals	$6.34	4,276	$7.06	111.4	3,855	$7.04	111.0	3,970	$7.08	111.7	3,497	$7.07	111.6

Compiled by Narda Tafuri, University of Scranton, from data supplied by Baker & Taylor.
n.a. = not available

Table 7 / U.S. Paperback Books (Excluding Mass Market): Average Prices and Price Indexes, 2012–2015

Index Base: 2005 = 100

BISAC Category	2005 Average Prices	2012 Final Volumes	2012 Final Average Prices	2012 Final Index	2013 Final Volumes	2013 Final Average Prices	2013 Final Index	2014 Final Volumes	2014 Final Average Prices	2014 Final Index	2015 Preliminary Volumes	2015 Preliminary Average Prices	2015 Preliminary Index
Antiques and collectibles	$24.80	160	$31.34	126.4	134	$34.08	137.4	139	$36.02	145.2	118	$35.51	143.2
Architecture	38.90	639	42.72	109.8	780	43.74	112.4	689	45.98	118.2	784	43.83	112.7
Art	31.28	1,718	37.93	121.3	1,697	41.70	133.3	1,679	39.58	126.5	1,800	36.73	117.4
Bibles	36.87	641	44.66	121.1	808	41.74	113.2	770	45.41	123.2	937	41.46	112.5
Biography and autobiography	19.19	2,648	20.10	104.7	3,092	19.80	103.2	2,920	20.41	106.4	2,604	20.36	106.1
Body, mind and spirit	17.48	1,061	18.35	105.0	1,013	18.31	104.7	861	18.11	103.6	664	18.21	104.2
Business and economics	71.12	9,050	86.29	121.3	7,243	88.39	124.3	7,334	92.17	129.6	8,386	102.77	144.5
Children	11.11	10,137	13.83	124.5	10,360	12.31	110.8	11,493	12.97	116.7	11,260	15.46	139.2
Comics and graphic novels	12.75	2,206	16.39	128.5	1,834	16.73	131.2	2,077	17.56	137.7	1,998	17.61	138.1
Computers	57.01	4,289	93.80	164.5	3,636	85.88	150.6	3,506	83.75	146.9	2,784	76.96	135.0
Cooking	18.30	1,297	20.48	111.9	1,190	20.06	109.6	1,279	19.65	107.4	1,103	20.44	111.7
Crafts and hobbies	18.49	1,079	19.52	105.6	1,201	18.40	99.5	1,203	18.77	101.5	1,116	19.23	104.0
Design	32.87	386	41.48	126.2	327	38.64	117.6	308	42.13	128.2	254	44.98	136.9
Drama	16.40	504	19.60	119.5	611	20.09	122.5	584	20.75	126.5	531	22.38	136.5
Education	35.10	4,189	45.94	130.9	4,195	48.89	139.3	4,380	55.91	159.3	3,698	45.65	130.1
Family and relationships	17.10	763	19.18	112.2	767	19.42	113.6	756	22.89	133.9	650	20.19	118.1
Fiction	15.74	11,063	17.07	108.4	13,231	17.00	108.0	13,114	17.28	109.8	10,341	17.15	109.0
Foreign language study	41.90	1,224	42.66	101.8	1,006	52.51	125.3	1,370	44.78	106.9	822	49.16	117.3
Games	16.53	665	15.75	95.3	619	15.64	94.6	548	17.56	106.2	450	17.70	107.1
Gardening	20.59	236	23.60	114.6	194	22.83	110.9	163	21.94	106.6	157	24.97	121.3
Health and fitness	22.81	1,181	27.90	122.3	1,095	26.30	115.3	1,108	26.78	117.4	1,034	25.76	112.9
History	33.53	6,978	42.43	126.5	6,513	37.88	113.0	7,750	40.70	121.4	6,732	38.64	115.3
House and home	19.33	148	23.49	121.5	145	20.08	103.9	949	95.61	494.6	113	20.14	104.2
Humor	12.96	395	14.18	109.4	353	14.39	111.0	344	14.97	115.5	324	14.97	115.5

Language arts and disciplines	49.14	2,282	77.38	157.5	1,875	73.94	150.5	2,151	76.56	155.8	1,715	71.89	146.3
Law	60.92	3,492	76.71	125.9	3,154	76.13	125.0	3,690	80.11	131.5	3,618	84.47	138.7
Literary collections	28.07	492	35.11	125.1	474	34.38	122.5	673	21.41	76.3	318	33.49	119.3
Literary criticism	31.99	1,597	44.22	138.2	1,587	40.32	126.0	2,554	50.49	157.8	1,760	39.66	124.0
Mathematics	75.77	2,618	97.95	129.3	1,479	86.74	114.5	1,518	90.43	119.3	984	77.42	102.2
Medical	64.27	8,268	93.79	145.9	5,120	96.56	150.2	4,605	96.33	149.9	3,618	98.39	153.1
Music	22.66	2,683	25.89	114.3	2,653	24.31	107.3	2,188	28.87	127.4	2,517	25.65	113.2
Nature	26.90	651	37.45	139.2	564	31.58	117.4	593	31.73	118.0	498	30.80	114.5
Performing arts	27.85	922	38.65	138.8	867	35.48	127.4	924	36.71	131.8	908	36.13	129.7
Pets	18.86	217	18.19	96.4	154	18.87	100.1	146	18.67	99.0	149	17.79	94.3
Philosophy	31.40	1,481	49.07	156.3	1,522	44.41	141.4	1,776	47.91	152.6	1,549	41.75	133.0
Photography	27.74	514	33.57	121.0	445	34.43	124.1	420	35.74	128.9	418	41.34	149.0
Poetry	16.09	1,959	16.55	102.9	2,399	16.62	103.3	2,279	17.64	109.6	1,901	17.81	110.7
Political science	45.65	3,522	48.73	106.7	3,555	47.80	104.7	4,114	55.48	121.5	3,534	52.09	114.1
Psychology	45.74	2,039	70.42	154.0	1,944	67.22	147.0	2,121	58.16	127.2	2,255	50.91	111.3
Reference	52.54	1,022	107.43	204.5	823	100.88	192.0	891	99.54	189.5	670	164.32	312.8
Religion	20.54	7,158	22.98	111.9	7,968	22.24	108.3	7,585	23.72	115.5	6,786	24.28	118.2
Science	71.05	7,680	93.93	132.2	4,523	90.07	126.8	4,417	88.76	124.9	2,484	90.86	127.9
Self-help	16.36	1,440	17.32	105.9	1,291	17.72	108.3	1,153	18.81	114.9	981	17.06	104.3
Social science	36.83	5,442	54.44	147.8	4,502	50.07	135.9	4,673	54.55	148.1	4,422	48.40	131.4
Sports and recreation	21.82	1,118	23.47	107.6	1,111	23.88	109.4	1,185	24.36	111.7	1,073	24.44	112.0
Study aids	30.90	590	41.74	135.1	535	47.44	153.5	1,888	44.88	145.2	797	43.40	140.4
Technology and engineering	85.80	4,519	101.91	118.8	2,805	101.16	117.9	3,688	104.67	122.0	1,809	109.54	127.7
Transportation	40.19	405	34.48	85.8	427	39.45	98.2	465	42.34	105.4	374	39.59	98.5
Travel	19.18	2,160	20.28	105.7	1,736	20.64	107.6	1,716	20.60	107.4	1,551	20.60	107.4
True crime	17.71	169	18.79	106.1	169	19.84	112.0	175	19.01	107.3	164	18.77	106.0
Young adult	14.06	3,315	17.19	122.3	2,169	16.83	119.7	2,929	18.67	132.8	2,262	20.43	145.3
Totals	$33.90	130,412	$49.96	147.4	117,895	$43.81	129.2	125,841	$46.02	135.7	107,775	$44.77	132.1

Compiled by Narda Tafuri, University of Scranton, from data supplied by Baker & Taylor.

Table 7A / U.S. Audiobooks: Average Prices and Price Indexes, 2012–2015

Index Base: 2005 = 100

BISAC Category	2005 Average Prices	2012 Final Volumes	2012 Final Average Prices	2012 Final Index	2013 Volumes	2013 Average Prices	2013 Index	2014 Volumes	2014 Average Prices	2014 Index	2015 Volumes	2015 Average Prices	2015 Index
Antiques and collectibles	n.a.	n.a.	n.a.	n.a.	n.a.	n.a.	n.a.	n.a.	n.a.	n.a.	n.a.	n.a.	n.a.
Architecture	$68.95	2	$32.45	47.1	7	$42.82	62.1	1	$59.95	86.9	2	$14.97	21.7
Art	57.51	12	37.40	65.0	3	29.95	52.1	9	39.32	68.4	9	31.65	55.0
Bibles	47.08	23	49.94	106.1	20	81.48	173.1	11	70.88	150.6	16	37.35	79.3
Biography and autobiography	37.68	1,018	47.08	124.9	1,199	41.12	109.1	982	41.60	110.4	1,231	36.65	97.3
Body, mind and spirit	26.74	126	35.99	134.6	244	26.93	100.7	181	28.51	106.6	163	23.70	88.6
Business and economics	42.11	475	38.25	90.8	452	34.51	82.0	607	29.96	71.2	703	29.48	70.0
Children	26.57	1,283	32.05	120.6	1,713	40.92	154.0	1,032	35.62	134.0	2,335	39.98	150.5
Comics and graphic novels	n.a.	4	37.48	n.a.	2	14.99	n.a.	n.a.	n.a.	n.a.	n.a.	n.a.	n.a.
Computers	41.39	4	42.73	103.2	2	52.47	126.8	18	41.26	99.7	8	30.36	73.4
Cooking	14.45	14	44.91	310.8	20	47.19	326.6	14	49.06	339.5	22	30.31	209.7
Crafts and hobbies	n.a.	1	24.95	n.a.	3	24.95	n.a.	5	24.78	n.a.	2	30.47	n.a.
Design	n.a.	3	57.30	n.a.	1	29.95	n.a.	n.a.	n.a.	n.a.	2	22.49	n.a.
Drama	23.45	111	24.09	102.7	100	32.53	138.7	59	25.91	110.5	49	29.53	125.9
Education	27.46	37	34.92	127.2	33	39.25	142.9	32	36.84	134.1	25	36.35	132.4
Family and relationships	24.58	143	43.07	175.2	119	35.16	143.0	119	32.01	130.2	162	30.86	125.6
Fiction	41.47	11,408	41.85	100.9	11,434	38.34	92.5	11,447	38.92	93.8	12,979	31.90	76.9
Foreign language study	70.04	178	65.81	94.0	114	69.35	99.0	273	64.32	91.8	118	40.66	58.1
Games	32.68	5	44.98	137.6	n.a.	n.a.	n.a.	5	47.18	144.4	1	11.99	36.7
Gardening	n.a.	5	31.99	n.a.	n.a.	n.a.	n.a.	n.a.	n.a.	n.a.	1	14.99	n.a.
Health and fitness	26.61	99	43.08	161.9	131	42.91	161.3	111	41.17	154.7	163	40.34	151.6
History	41.61	610	50.35	121.0	480	47.52	114.2	476	51.94	124.8	547	43.27	104.0
House and home	25.00	3	55.32	221.3	4	29.98	119.9	1	9.99	40.0	5	35.79	143.2
Humor	29.60	77	33.05	111.7	70	37.80	127.7	98	32.93	111.3	83	31.26	105.6

Language arts and disciplines	60.84	26	55.28	90.9	14	40.79	67.0	11	38.17	62.7	21	37.32	61.3
Law	55.32	18	51.04	92.3	16	64.24	116.1	12	62.41	112.8	10	47.59	86.0
Literary collections	24.71	35	39.87	161.3	18	37.09	150.1	41	54.10	218.9	56	40.41	163.5
Literary criticism	26.41	95	33.38	126.4	11	48.62	184.1	12	29.98	113.5	23	42.71	161.7
Mathematics	n.a.	3	51.32	n.a.	5	38.97	n.a.	5	20.59	n.a.	6	36.81	n.a.
Medical	153.72	24	49.26	32.0	24	40.98	26.7	12	37.74	24.6	27	32.31	21.0
Music	29.83	51	45.86	153.7	34	41.10	137.8	25	51.25	171.8	15	34.42	115.4
Nature	28.92	13	51.60	178.4	25	42.26	146.1	23	46.63	161.2	34	31.57	109.2
Performing arts	25.78	16	34.42	133.5	45	39.34	152.6	65	39.62	153.7	65	37.56	145.7
Pets	33.05	20	42.93	129.9	30	39.28	118.9	13	37.05	112.1	17	39.33	119.0
Philosophy	35.30	42	39.76	112.6	38	29.62	83.9	25	32.02	90.7	17	29.04	82.3
Photography	n.a.	n.a.	n.a.	n.a.	n.a.	n.a.	n.a.	n.a.	n.a.	n.a.	n.a.	n.a.	n.a.
Poetry	22.87	16	27.28	119.3	19	26.39	115.4	38	39.07	170.8	25	37.22	162.7
Political science	42.66	236	46.61	109.3	166	45.06	105.6	130	45.11	105.7	173	36.98	86.7
Psychology	35.70	85	39.45	110.5	73	43.95	123.1	96	32.57	91.2	102	35.64	99.8
Reference	21.20	11	35.44	167.2	5	49.77	234.8	8	25.99	122.6	4	15.49	73.1
Religion	26.52	577	33.05	124.6	675	29.06	109.6	698	28.74	108.4	941	26.19	98.8
Science	39.86	117	42.30	106.1	95	41.15	103.2	98	41.78	104.8	116	35.32	88.6
Self-help	23.58	386	36.91	156.5	212	31.10	131.9	231	30.43	129.0	285	30.15	127.9
Social science	35.73	116	43.50	121.7	111	38.11	106.7	103	35.46	99.2	120	31.06	86.9
Sports and recreation	28.46	37	44.06	154.8	48	39.93	140.3	52	38.52	135.4	64	34.30	120.5
Study aids	41.85	5	147.63	352.8	1	24.99	59.7	5	131.00	313.0	3	24.97	59.7
Technology and engineering	61.47	11	40.07	65.2	8	36.61	59.6	11	52.44	85.3	20	43.13	70.2
Transportation	28.00	7	46.27	165.2	10	48.68	173.9	5	52.39	187.1	9	35.98	128.5
Travel	41.91	49	35.88	85.6	37	35.89	85.6	9	47.76	114.0	26	26.37	62.9
True crime	35.97	80	45.29	125.9	136	39.89	110.9	94	34.20	95.1	105	29.05	80.8
Young adult	35.68	1,461	34.55	96.8	1,271	42.20	118.3	1,285	43.27	121.3	1,696	31.30	87.7
Totals	$40.49	19,178	$40.86	100.9	19,278	$38.92	96.1	18,588	$38.99	96.3	22,606	$33.06	81.7

Compiled by Narda Tafuri, University of Scranton from data supplied by Baker & Taylor.
n.a. = not available

Table 7B / U.S. E-Books: Average Prices and Price Indexes, 2012–2015

Index Base: 2008 = 100

BISAC Category	2008 Average Prices	2012 Final Volumes	2012 Final Average Prices	2012 Final Index	2013 Final Volumes	2013 Final Average Prices	2013 Final Index	2014 Final Volumes	2014 Final Average Prices	2014 Final Index	2015 Preliminary Volumes	2015 Preliminary Average Prices	2015 Preliminary Index
Antiques and collectibles	$55.97	168	$22.62	40.4	177	$20.96	37.4	132	$17.05	30.5	136	$9.19	16.4
Architecture	70.50	830	47.86	67.9	823	63.80	90.5	1083	144.57	205.1	501	60.77	86.2
Art	45.41	1,339	21.41	47.1	1,812	18.09	39.8	1,884	22.27	49.0	4,914	9.47	20.9
Bibles	25.79	165	13.37	51.8	495	8.76	34.0	247	9.16	35.5	191	8.69	33.7
Biography and autobiography	14.58	8,544	18.07	123.9	8,156	15.10	103.6	9,542	17.89	122.7	7,295	17.17	117.7
Body, mind and spirit	12.41	2,744	12.90	103.9	1,984	11.94	96.2	1,815	10.52	84.7	1,361	11.36	91.5
Business and economics	57.52	12,688	41.17	71.6	11,760	56.43	98.1	10,599	48.79	84.8	21,266	21.41	37.2
Children	12.01	23,942	10.63	88.5	20,257	11.53	96.0	21,565	14.62	121.8	17,454	11.84	98.6
Comics and graphic novels	25.04	628	6.68	26.7	551	7.31	29.2	1,535	6.13	24.5	3,605	8.53	34.1
Computers	66.87	4,881	70.64	105.6	4,170	54.38	81.3	4,358	66.63	99.6	4,027	62.32	93.2
Cooking	20.20	2,680	11.55	57.2	3,437	12.45	61.6	2,870	12.01	59.5	3,023	11.97	59.3
Crafts and hobbies	14.35	1,270	10.45	72.8	1,388	10.22	71.2	960	11.94	83.2	1,202	9.23	64.3
Design	36.04	221	25.27	70.1	193	26.00	72.1	144	28.03	77.8	137	26.22	72.7
Drama	29.49	2,256	7.19	24.4	1,629	7.91	26.8	1,799	9.90	33.6	1,730	7.44	25.2
Education	51.98	3,878	47.65	91.7	5,038	51.32	98.7	4,642	38.80	74.6	4,178	27.91	53.7
Family and relationships	19.88	2,208	13.81	69.5	1,927	28.32	142.5	2,200	14.11	71.0	1,756	11.39	57.3
Fiction	8.71	108,916	9.68	111.1	94,876	6.55	75.2	104,416	6.42	73.7	90,988	7.54	86.5
Foreign language study	43.01	903	23.06	53.6	1,589	16.08	37.4	1,657	16.19	37.6	1,611	19.69	45.8
Games	17.73	492	8.42	47.5	506	9.43	53.2	682	8.20	46.2	652	7.30	41.2
Gardening	20.40	408	14.41	70.6	360	13.77	67.5	311	11.59	56.8	303	11.15	54.6
Health and fitness	18.54	3,179	13.49	72.8	3,562	17.61	95.0	3,170	11.71	63.2	2,991	13.06	70.4
History	57.53	9,697	32.46	56.4	9,775	39.71	69.0	12,548	34.26	59.5	9,738	36.51	63.5
House and home	22.89	309	12.89	56.3	425	10.39	45.4	310	9.67	42.2	302	10.73	46.9
Humor	11.27	1,297	12.39	109.9	1,085	8.81	78.2	1,080	9.37	83.1	893	11.96	106.2

Language arts and disciplines	93.27	2,009	45.28	48.5	2,413	52.09	55.8	2,274	76.99	82.5	1,738	87.95	94.3
Law	81.23	2,132	72.99	89.9	1,745	94.15	115.9	1,840	99.07	122.0	1,584	101.17	124.5
Literary collections	24.50	1,823	9.95	40.6	1,468	13.90	56.7	1,615	23.78	97.1	6,311	4.97	20.3
Literary criticism	86.62	2,444	36.90	42.6	2,336	61.37	70.8	2,354	76.03	87.8	2,423	64.61	74.6
Mathematics	106.16	1,973	74.53	70.2	1,434	84.14	79.3	1,425	94.42	88.9	1,136	84.52	79.6
Medical	135.21	5,638	95.97	71.0	4,242	98.63	72.9	3,737	104.04	77.0	2,625	103.22	76.3
Music	33.83	18,723	4.85	14.3	1,942	30.36	89.7	1,431	47.07	139.1	1,602	21.06	62.3
Nature	59.76	934	38.90	65.1	1,017	33.08	55.4	952	35.52	59.4	700	41.07	68.7
Performing arts	38.06	1,231	28.74	75.5	1,599	39.69	104.3	1,421	32.68	85.9	1,262	27.99	73.5
Pets	15.91	716	14.76	92.8	750	8.41	52.9	424	10.75	67.6	298	11.29	71.0
Philosophy	79.19	2,304	37.51	47.4	2,676	56.26	71.0	2,362	61.24	77.3	1,943	55.89	70.6
Photography	30.30	471	18.89	62.3	535	22.02	72.7	556	19.79	65.3	462	17.86	59.0
Poetry	13.66	2,398	7.18	52.6	3,047	6.93	50.7	3,813	7.06	51.7	3,575	6.19	45.3
Political science	59.03	4,959	41.13	69.7	5,129	50.02	84.7	3,913	55.78	94.5	3,589	51.61	87.4
Psychology	65.30	3,023	44.76	68.5	4,119	139.89	214.2	3,273	57.59	88.2	2,091	49.56	75.9
Reference	48.33	1,392	24.74	51.2	1,543	82.84	171.4	4,062	25.72	53.2	3,407	23.87	49.4
Religion	27.29	9,644	17.76	65.1	9,800	20.59	75.4	11,208	19.21	70.4	9,217	19.66	72.1
Science	210.57	5,935	102.09	48.5	4,491	105.83	50.3	4,710	118.56	56.3	3,680	96.64	45.9
Self-help	14.15	4,978	13.50	95.4	4,299	29.36	207.5	4,825	8.57	60.6	4,005	9.83	69.5
Social science	69.42	4,446	54.35	78.3	6,941	79.66	114.8	4,888	67.16	96.7	3,865	53.11	76.5
Sports and recreation	22.44	2,607	17.82	79.4	2,727	19.47	86.8	2,344	17.87	79.6	1,815	17.48	77.9
Study aids	21.95	13,402	22.96	104.6	6,142	18.79	85.6	4,721	18.59	84.7	813	12.67	57.7
Technology and engineering	153.73	4,044	118.05	76.8	3,886	114.23	74.3	3,859	145.82	94.9	2,914	123.06	80.1
Transportation	35.47	323	24.34	68.6	327	26.12	73.6	336	19.36	54.6	331	26.62	75.0
Travel	15.61	3,686	9.74	62.4	2,546	10.96	70.2	2,320	11.28	72.3	3,163	9.19	58.9
True crime	11.60	621	15.87	136.8	616	12.03	103.7	545	12.37	106.7	458	14.78	127.4
Young adult	8.83	5,980	17.11	193.8	6,502	13.60	154.0	6,613	13.50	152.9	5,424	13.37	151.4
Totals	$57.38	301,479	$22.92	39.9	260,247	$27.97	48.7	271,370	$25.42	44.3	250,685	$21.05	36.7

Compiled by Narda Tafuri, University of Scranton, from data supplied by Baker & Taylor.

Table 8 / Average Price of Serials, Based on Titles in Select Serial Indexes, 2012–2016

Subject	LC Class	Avg. No. of Titles	2012 Avg. Price	2013 Avg. Price	2012–13 % of Price Increase	2014 Avg. Price	2013–14 % of Price Increase	2015 Avg. Price	2014–15 % of Price Increase	2016 Avg. Price	2015–16 % of Price Increase
Agriculture	S	540	$820	$876	6.9%	$940	7.3%	$987	5.0%	$1,045	5.8%
Anthropology	GN	129	426	451	5.9	493	9.4	518	5.2	545	5.0
Arts and architecture	N	207	297	345	16.2	369	6.9	392	6.3	434	10.8
Astronomy	QB	79	1,782	1,947	9.3	2,047	5.1	2,202	7.6	2,267	2.9
Biology	QH	1,259	1,846	1,951	5.7	2,076	6.4	2,199	6.0	2,320	5.5
Botany	QK	169	1,193	1,277	7.0	1,374	7.6	1,439	4.7	1,503	4.4
Business and economics	HA-HJ	1,401	982	1,040	5.9	1,115	7.2	1,189	6.6	1,268	6.6
Chemistry	QD	438	3,430	3,612	5.3	3,858	6.8	4,044	4.8	4,221	4.4
Education	L	488	582	633	8.8	686	8.3	739	7.8	791	7.0
Engineering	T	1,863	1,483	1,604	8.2	1,717	7.0	1,835	6.9	1,959	6.8
Food science	TX	95	1,076	1,150	6.8	1,239	7.8	1,327	7.1	1,384	4.3
General science	Q	262	1,054	1,109	5.2	1,173	5.8	1,256	7.1	1,321	5.2
General works	A	181	229	241	5.5	267	10.6	272	2.0	303	11.5
Geography	G-GF	296	792	876	10.5	940	7.4	992	5.4	1,054	6.3
Geology	QE	227	1,391	1,494	7.4	1,586	6.2	1,689	6.5	1,801	6.6
Health sciences	R	4,200	899	983	9.3	1,056	7.4	1,120	6.1	1,193	6.5
History	C,D,E,F	751	281	299	6.7	320	6.9	383	19.7	401	4.6

Subject	LC Class	Titles								
Language and literature	P	805	300	326	8.7	330	1.0	347	5.1	366	5.5
Law	K	433	354	377	6.5	396	5.0	423	6.9	435	2.8
Library science	Z	158	697	737	5.7	783	6.3	827	5.6	866	4.7
Math and computer science	QA	1,015	1,182	1,231	4.2	1,309	6.3	1,375	5.0	1,435	4.4
Military and naval science	U,V	91	385	424	10.0	449	5.9	493	9.8	519	5.4
Music	M	124	189	207	9.4	220	6.3	230	4.8	240	4.0
Philosophy and religion	B-BD, BH-BX	521	297	318	7.0	338	6.5	360	6.4	381	5.9
Physics	QC	493	2,868	3,072	7.1	3,234	5.3	3,349	3.6	3,468	3.5
Political science	J	252	532	571	7.2	606	6.1	636	5.0	692	8.9
Psychology	BF	319	607	652	7.5	707	8.5	757	7.0	809	6.9
Recreation	GV	113	389	423	8.9	471	11.4	500	6.2	544	8.8
Social sciences	H	129	585	630	7.7	709	12.6	744	5.0	841	12.9
Sociology	HM-HX	739	625	668	6.9	715	7.0	765	7.0	815	6.6
Technology	TA-TT	389	1,214	1,300	7.1	1,386	6.5	1,461	5.5	1,549	6.0
Zoology	QL	310	1,125	1,186	5.5	1,271	7.1	1,345	5.8	1,457	8.3
Totals		18,473	$1,035	$1,109	7.2%	$1,177	6.1%	$1,256	6.7%	$1,330	5.9%

Compiled by Stephen Bosch, University of Arizona. Data on serial pricing supplied by EBSCO and is based on titles indexed in EBSCO Academic Search Premier, EBSCO Masterfile Premier, ISI Arts and Humanities Citation Index, ISI Science Citation Index, ISI Social Sciences Citation Index, and Scopus.

Table 8A / Average Price of Online Serials, Based on Titles in Select Serial Indexes, 2012–2016

Subject	LC Class	Average No. of Titles 2012–16	2012 Avg. Price	2013 Avg. Price	2012–13 % of Price Increase	2014 Avg. Price	2013–14 % of Price Increase	2015 Avg. Price	2014–15 % of Price Increase	2016 Avg. Price	2015–16 % of Price Increase
Agriculture	S	193	$867	$916	5.8%	$962	5.0%	$999	3.8%	$1,045	4.7%
Anthropology	GN	66	569	608	6.9	647	6.4	688	6.4	725	5.3
Arts and architecture	N	72	482	515	6.9	559	8.6	592	5.9	626	5.7
Astronomy	QB	36	1,764	1,788	1.4	1,862	4.1	2,024	8.7	2,084	3.0
Biology	QH	490	1,698	1,777	4.7	1,873	5.4	1,979	5.7	2,088	5.5
Botany	QK	68	1,188	1,256	5.7	1,302	3.7	1,361	4.5	1,431	5.2
Business and economics	HA-HJ	603	1,523	1,603	5.3	1,700	6.1	1,803	6.1	1,906	5.7
Chemistry	QD	175	3,413	3,592	5.2	3,803	5.9	4,015	5.6	4,175	4.0
Education	L	289	765	811	6.0	867	6.9	926	6.8	990	7.0
Engineering	T	699	1,568	1,654	5.5	1,760	6.4	1,835	4.2	1,966	7.2
Food Science	TX	45	1,491	1,592	6.7	1,665	4.6	1,773	6.5	1,856	4.7
General science	Q	106	1,322	1,397	5.7	1,490	6.6	1,591	6.8	1,662	4.5
General works	A	26	576	637	10.4	672	5.5	700	4.2	746	6.6
Geography	G-GF	143	793	841	6.1	910	8.1	973	7.0	1,037	6.6
Geology	QE	90	1,354	1,395	3.0	1,487	6.6	1,593	7.2	1,690	6.1
Health sciences	R	1,366	1,003	1,084	8.1	1,162	7.1	1,234	6.2	1,304	5.7
History	C,D,E,F	276	428	458	7.0	482	5.3	511	5.8	541	5.9

Subject	LC Class										
Language and literature	P	304	452	495	9.6	524	5.7	546	4.4	586	7.2
Law	K	102	577	615	6.4	657	6.9	732	11.4	710	-3.0
Library science	Z	87	950	1,023	7.7	1,078	5.3	1,126	4.4	1,171	4.0
Math and computer science	QA	498	1,145	1,196	4.5	1,264	5.7	1,334	5.5	1,394	4.5
Military and naval science	U,V	42	492	541	9.9	573	6.0	633	10.3	676	6.8
Music	M	46	282	304	8.1	322	5.9	347	7.6	366	5.5
Philosophy and religion	B-BD, BH-BX	153	475	504	6.1	535	6.2	564	5.4	604	7.1
Physics	QC	229	3,018	3,198	6.0	3,378	5.6	3,502	3.7	3,655	4.4
Political science	J	138	645	688	6.7	733	6.6	775	5.8	834	7.6
Psychology	BF	147	687	710	3.4	766	7.9	816	6.5	874	7.1
Recreation	QV	52	611	648	6.2	727	12.1	775	6.5	844	9.0
Social sciences	H	57	727	782	7.6	847	8.2	874	3.3	944	7.9
Sociology	HM-HX	415	738	785	6.4	835	6.3	891	6.7	945	6.2
Technology	TA-TT	137	1,939	2,022	4.2	2,152	6.4	2,278	5.9	2,413	5.9
Zoology	QL	106	1,085	1,140	5.1	1,218	6.8	1,298	6.6	1,480	14.0
Totals		7,255	$1,181	$1,252	6.0%	$1,332	6.4%	$1,408	5.7%	$1,488	5.7%

Compiled by Stephen Bosch, University of Arizona. Data on serial pricing supplied by Ebsco and is based on online titles indexed in Ebsco Academic Search Premier, Ebsco Masterfile Premier, ISI Arts and Humanities Citation Index, ISI Science Citation Index, ISI Social Sciences Citation Index, and Scopus.

Table 9 / British Academic Books: Average Prices and Price Indexes 2012–2015

Index Base: 2009 = 100

Subject	LC Class	2009		2012		2013		2014		2015			
		No. of Titles	Average Price (£)	No. of Titles	Average Price (£)	No. of Titles	Average Price (£)	No. of Titles	Average Price (£)	No. of Titles	Average Price (£)	% Average Change 2014–2015	Index
Agriculture	S	140	53.96	183	69.29	163	68.55	134	73.28	131	73.63	0.5%	136.5
Anthropology	GN	109	53.60	145	45.73	124	55.11	109	57.63	92	59.65	3.5	111.3
Botany	QK	22	145.94	45	97.50	33	81.54	35	74.78	21	95.19	27.3	65.2
Business and economics	H-HJ	1,634	59.08	2,022	71.12	1,877	71.29	1,911	71.19	1,866	75.13	5.5	127.2
Chemistry	QD	88	101.14	144	155.82	96	149.82	91	125.67	72	127.89	1.8	126.4
Education	L	386	49.70	547	64.36	440	64.49	517	64.50	583	68.39	6.0	137.6
Engineering and technology	T-TS	796	60.97	741	76.09	758	78.35	788	76.69	732	85.51	11.5	140.2
Fine and applied arts	M, N	762	38.43	1,092	42.40	1,005	43.35	1,009	44.54	991	50.40	13.2	131.2
General works	A	15	76.73	26	78.67	17	91.58	32	72.25	21	83.47	15.5	108.8
Geography	G-GF, GR-GT	233	54.43	276	63.59	268	64.44	245	67.55	457	72.62	7.5	133.4
Geology	QE	41	53.80	51	79.33	34	77.70	33	59.80	34	60.87	1.8	113.1
History	C,D,E,F	1,572	43.41	1,880	44.74	1,690	44.63	1,725	48.11	1,835	51.22	6.5	118.0
Home economics	TX	59	39.02	47	61.06	58	67.22	38	63.79	29	85.98	34.8	220.3
Industrial arts	TT	21	24.32	42	25.47	37	35.50	27	45.43	33	46.11	1.5	189.6

Subject	LC Class	No.	Avg. price	No.	Avg. price	No.	Avg. price	No.	Avg. price	No.	Avg. price	% change	Index
Law	K	1,117	76.13	1,312	87.74	1,264	88.46	1,253	88.30	1,184	85.16	-3.6	111.9
Library and information science	Z	98	60.32	105	65.96	100	59.99	106	69.71	114	71.04	1.9	117.8
Literature and language	P	2,928	34.77	3,966	37.34	3,448	37.25	3,553	38.95	3,008	42.33	8.7	121.7
Mathematics and computer science	QA	216	49.30	266	54.93	212	61.40	180	54.91	172	57.46	4.7	116.6
Medicine	R	1,110	48.50	1,280	55.88	1,126	60.74	1,113	63.10	946	67.52	7.0	139.2
Military and naval sciences	U, V	112	48.42	163	57.71	173	48.95	201	50.67	165	53.43	5.4	110.3
Philosophy and religion	B-BD, BH-BX	1,091	45.65	1,293	54.67	1,074	53.96	1,187	52.78	1,184	56.72	7.5	124.2
Physics and astronomy	QB, QC	196	54.73	240	68.87	221	72.08	161	72.29	185	65.07	-10.0	118.9
Political Science	J	621	59.74	797	69.98	732	66.67	794	65.82	819	73.18	11.2	122.5
Psychology	BF	195	44.46	297	50.93	266	54.88	295	63.42	278	69.09	8.9	155.4
Science (general)	Q	45	41.65	72	72.50	47	54.85	54	57.89	53	62.95	8.7	151.1
Sociology	HM-HX	958	59.36	1,195	57.01	1,111	63.65	1,221	64.89	1,281	70.21	8.2	118.3
Sports & Recreation	GV	181	30.90	202	56.70	165	54.18	170	61.49	179	68.49	11.4	221.6
Zoology	QH, QL-QR	336	62.59	434	84.57	396	81.41	285	79.00	263	79.76	1.0	127.4
Total, All Books		15,082	50.42	18,863	57.51	16,935	58.47	17,267	59.05	16,728	63.22	7.1%	125.4

Compiled by George Aulisio, University of Scranton, based on information provided by YBP U.K./EBSCO.

(continued from page 367)

EBSCO Masterfile Premier, and Scopus. This is the first year where titles indexed in Scopus are included in the data. Adding Scopus expands this price survey from about 11,000 titles in 2015 to the current 18,473. The increase in the sample size makes the results more likely to accurately reflect pricing trends.

Tables 8 and 8A cover prices for periodicals and serials for a five-year period, 2012 through 2016. The 2016 pricing is the actual renewal pricing for 2016 for serials that were indexed in the selected products. These tables are derived from pricing data supplied by EBSCO Information Services and reflect broad pricing changes aggregated from titles that are indexed in the six major products mentioned above. The U.S. Periodicals: Average Prices and Price Indexes (USPPI) (Table 1) is based on price changes seen in a static set of approximately 5,900 serial titles. The Average Price of Serials (Table 8) is based on a much broader set of titles, approximately 18,400; however, the titles are not static, so this pricing study does not rise to the level of a price index. This study is still useful in showing price changes for periodicals. The indexes selected for this price survey were deemed to be fairly representative of serials that are frequently purchased in academic and public libraries. There are some foreign titles in the indexes, so the scope is broader and this may give a better picture of the overall price pressures experienced in libraries. Table 8 contains both print and online serials pricing. Table 8A is a subset of the titles treated in Table 8 and contains only online serials pricing.

The most important trend seen in the data in Table 8 is that increases in prices have remained fairly constant since the economic recovery began. Price increases have hovered around 6 percent annually since 2012. For titles with online availability (Table 8A), the rates of increase for those titles are very similar, averaging around 6 percent over the past five years. There is a difference between the average prices for print serials and online serials, so, at least for this set of data, print formats do cost less than their online counterparts. Several large publishers have made online pricing only available through custom quotes, so there is not a standard retail price and the pricing data is not available for this survey. Since these titles tend to be more expensive than titles from other publishers, this may affect the overall prices, making them lower.

Another interesting trend is that the science areas do not dominate the list of subjects with the largest price increases. The subject areas that displayed large increases were quite varied. Social sciences, general works, arts and architecture, political science, recreation, and zoology saw higher increases than most areas. Some of these same areas showed the highest increases in the online table (Table 8A) as well. Average prices of journals in the science and technology areas are by far higher than in other areas and that trend continues with the average cost of chemistry and physics journals being $4,221 and $3,468 respectively. Although these STM titles are not inflating at high rates, the impact of a 4 percent increase in a $4,000 title is much higher than a 9 percent increase on a $300 title. Online journals (Table 8A) showed similar average prices for chemistry ($4,175) and physics ($3,655).

In this price study, as in similar price surveys, the data become less accurate at describing price changes as the sample becomes smaller. For that reason, drawing conclusions about price changes in subject areas with a limited number of titles will be less accurate than for large areas or the broader price survey. Price changes are far more volatile where smaller data sets are used. For example, military and naval science (about 91 titles) showed price changes of 10.0 percent, 5.9 percent, and 9.8 and 5.5 percent between 2012 and 2016. Librarians are encouraged to look at an average price change over the period (military and naval science averaged 7.8 percent) or the overall number for the price study (5.9 percent) to calculate inflation. Year-to-year price changes in small subject areas are too unstable to be used for this purpose.

Book Prices

British Academic Books (Table 9), compiled by George Aulisio, indicates the average prices and price indexes from 2012 through 2015. The percent of change in titles and average price is calculated for 2014 to 2015, and the index price shows the percent of change between 2015 and the base year of 2009. This index is compiled using data from YBP and utilizes prices from cloth editions except when not available. YBP U.K. also profiles select titles from continental Europe and Africa. The index does not separate out more expensive reference titles. Small numbers of titles that include higher-priced reference sets may not be reliable indicators of price changes. This table does not include e-book prices.

Data on "Total, All Books" production illustrates the sum total of the LC Classes profiled in this table, not the sum total of all books profiled by YBP. In 2015 British academic books saw a 3.1 percent decrease from 17,267 titles to 16,728 titles. Historical data shows that the slight decrease in titles profiled in 2015 is not unusual.

In 2015 there was a significant overall price increase of 7.1 percent, bringing the average price for all books profiled to £63.22. The 2015 overall average price increase of 7.1 percent is well above the 3 percent to 4 percent price increase YBP U.K. predicted for 2015. Also, the 2015 increase is significantly higher than the United Kingdom's Consumer Price Index, which, according to the Office of National Statistics, was at a very modest 0.2 percent inflation in December 2015 (http://www.ons.gov.uk).

Table 9 shows how average prices have increased or decreased in comparison with the 2009 base year. For 2015 the overall index price for all LC subjects profiled in this table is at 125.4 percent. All LC Classes profiled saw a price increase with the exception of decreases in physics and astronomy (10.0 percent) and law (3.6 percent). All LC classes are currently above their 2009 base prices, except for botany, which is now at 65.2 percent of the 2009 base price. The highest increases in comparison with the 2009 base prices are sports and recreation (221.6 percent), home economics (220.3 percent), industrial arts (189.6 percent), psychology (155.4 percent), and science (general) (151.1 percent). High individual price increases from 2014 to 2015 in home economics (34.8 percent), botany (27.3 percent), and general works (15.5 percent) may be due to small samples sizes of less than 30 titles.

According to the Publishers Association, the U.K. publishing industry is in excellent financial health and saw an 8.4 percent increase in the print book market. This increase marks the first increase in five years (http://www.publishers.org.uk/policy-and-news/pa-blog/uk-publishing-2016-and-beyond/). The rise in the print book market may be attributable to Amazon.com reintroducing agency pricing and giving greater pricing control to book publishers. According to Publishing Technology, the industry introduced pricing at near-parity between e-books and print books, which seemed to encourage most consumers to purchase print editions over e-books (http://www.publishingtechnology.com/blog-article/5-predictions-for-trade-publishing-in-2016/).

The 7.1 percent price increase of 2015 is the second-highest average price increase recorded in this table, with the 10.8 percent price increase of 2012 being the highest recorded. In 2013 and 2014, the years immediately following the largest recorded price increase, there were modest average price increases of 1.7 percent and 1.0 percent, respectively. There are no reliable indicators for a 2016 industry forecast. However, given the health of the industry, the improvement in print book sales, and historical data, cautious optimism suggests the U.K. book publishing industry may return to its recent practice of modest price increases.

Using the Price Indexes

Librarians are encouraged to monitor trends in the publishing industry and changes in economic conditions when preparing budget forecasts and projections. The ALA ALCTS Library Materials Price Index Editorial Board endeavors to make information on publishing trends readily available by sponsoring the annual compilation and publication of price data contained in Tables 1 to 9. The indexes cover newly published library materials and document prices and rates of percent changes at the national and international level. They are useful benchmarks against which local costs can be compared, but because they reflect retail prices in the aggregate, they are not a substitute for cost data that reflect the collecting patterns of individual libraries, and they are not a substitute for specific cost studies.

Differences between local prices and those found in national indexes arise partially because these indexes exclude discounts, service charges, shipping and handling fees, and other costs that the library might incur. Discrepancies may also relate to a library's subject coverage; mix of titles purchased, including both current and backfiles; and the proportion of the library's budget expended on domestic or foreign materials. These variables can affect the average price paid by an individual library, although the individual library's rate of increase may not differ greatly from the national indexes.

LMPI is interested in pursuing studies that would correlate a particular library's costs with the national prices. The group welcomes interested parties to its meetings at ALA Annual and Midwinter conferences.

The Library Materials Price Index Editorial Board consists of compilers George Aulisio, Catherine Barr, Ajaye Bloomstone, Stephen Bosch, Kittie Henderson, Frederick C. Lynden, and editor Narda Tafuri.

Book Title Output and Average Prices: 2011–2015

Catherine Barr

Constance Harbison

Baker & Taylor

Overall American book title output has generally showed growing strength since the economic downturn, but this recovery has been uneven. After reaching a high of 210,772 in 2012 (up from 2009's 178,841), revised figures for 2013 show a dip to 204,402 and then a slight rebound to 205,978 in 2014. Preliminary figures for 2015 indicate a decline, but these numbers may be revised upward as late-arriving materials are added to the database.

The figures for this edition of the *Library and Book Trade Almanac* were provided by book wholesaler Baker & Taylor and are based on the Book Industry Study Group's BISAC categories. The BISAC juvenile category (fiction and nonfiction) has been divided into children's and young adult. Figures for 2013 and 2014 have been restated, reflecting late updates to the Baker & Taylor database. Figures for 2015 are preliminary.

For more information on the BISAC categories, visit http://www.bisg.org.

Output by Format and by Category

Revised results for 2014 were mixed. Output of hardcover titles was down 1.5 percent (but preliminary figures for 2015 showed a recovery); hardcovers less than $81 declined 2.93 percent after an increase of 4.90 percent; mass market paperbacks fell 1.59 percent but trade paperbacks were up 2.87 percent. The rapid increase in audiobook output stalled in 2013 (after soaring more than 43 percent in 2012) and fell a further 0.05 percent in 2014; and e-books, which had scored an impressive gain of 93.28 percent in 2012, found their momentum slowing, with a decline of 13.70 percent in 2013 and a further 3.70 percent in 2014.

Output of fiction, a key category, grew 13.07 percent in 2013 after a drop of 8.64 percent in 2012; but output fell 5.28 percent in 2014 and preliminary results for 2015 suggested another dip. Output of hardcover fiction priced at less than $81 rebounded a little more than 17 percent in 2013, but dropped just over 10 percent in 2014. In the paperback sector, mass market fiction dropped a minimal 0.47 percent in 2014 (after a 9.50 percent dip in 2013), while trade fiction fell 4.67 percent after a 19.60 percent increase in 2013. Audiobook fiction fell less than 1 percent in 2014 but figures for 2015 showed robust growth. E-book fiction output, after climbing steadily for several years, has shown uneven results, dropping in 2013 and rising in 2014. Preliminary results for 2015 are not encouraging.

The important juveniles category is broken down into children's (PreK–6) and young adult (YA; grades 7–12) titles. Overall children's books output has been rising steadily, with an increase of 6.23 percent in 2014 and the promise of another rise in 2015. Hardcover books priced at less than $81 rose less than 1 percent in 2014, while mass market lost 3.55 percent and trade paperbacks rose less than 1 percent in the same period. Children's audiobooks and e-books showed inconsistent growth, with audiobooks down 40.80 percent following an increase of 33.52 percent in 2013; e-books recovered slightly (5.14 percent) after a 15.39 percent fall in 2013, but preliminary data for 2015 indicated another decline.

Output of YA titles rose a revised 8.81 percent in 2012, but registered a decline of 25.60 percent in 2013; data for 2014 showed a rebound of 22.12 percent but preliminary 2015 figures predicted another fall. Hardcover titles priced at less than $81, which had fallen slightly in 2013, regained some ground in 2014 and appeared able to hold steady in 2015; mass market paperbacks returned to their 2012 level after a surge in 2013; and trade paperbacks recovered from their slide in 2013. YA audiobook production held steady but e-books posted a 1.97 percent hike.

Book prices overall declined or held steady in 2014, with little fluctuation from the previous year.

Table 1 / American Book Production, 2011–2015

BISAC Category	2011	2012	2013	2014	2015
Antiques and collectibles	294	289	283	289	252
Architecture	1,468	1,402	1,747	1,491	1,680
Art	3,325	3,554	4,029	3,581	3,803
Bibles	976	840	995	907	1,138
Biography and autobiography	4,496	4,365	5,122	4,699	4,316
Body, mind, and spirit	1,324	1,207	1,267	1,021	814
Business and economics	9,813	13,811	12,335	11,251	13,430
Children	21,300	22,461	23,127	24,569	24,475
Comics and graphic novels	4,212	2,941	2,495	2,742	2,694
Computers	4,391	5,379	4,693	4,539	3,765
Cooking	2,142	2,435	2,473	2,525	2,328
Crafts and hobbies	1,301	1,291	1,446	1,414	1,292
Design	856	894	732	704	711
Drama	606	578	703	671	598
Education	4,923	5,996	6,289	6,516	6,160
Family and relationships	981	977	1,046	969	862
Fiction	21,211	19,379	22,526	21,337	17,921
Foreign language study	1,463	1,483	1,501	1,626	1,145
Games	792	787	747	645	562
Gardening	368	370	315	260	278
Health and fitness	1,654	1,544	1,525	1,517	1,431
History	11,634	12,007	12,199	13,053	12,629
House and home	230	236	267	1,040	222
Humor	626	640	605	631	617
Language arts and disciplines	3,530	3,549	3,383	3,686	3,418
Law	4,979	5,476	5,530	5,885	5,891
Literary collections	870	752	797	944	537
Literary criticism	3,673	3,628	3,889	4,364	4,023
Mathematics	2,781	4,100	2,726	2,776	2,140
Medical	9,021	12,572	9,223	8,878	7,771
Music	3,313	3,222	3,378	2,729	3,119
Nature	948	1,045	1,051	1,026	969
Performing arts	1,449	1,502	1,546	1,602	1,697
Pets	330	310	268	253	239
Philosophy	2,465	2,836	3,011	3,123	3,063
Photography	1,359	1,379	1,260	1,263	1,310
Poetry	2,321	2,248	2,859	2,629	2,177
Political science	5,925	6,239	6,480	6,632	6,727
Psychology	2,817	3,327	3,401	3,422	3,718
Reference	1,687	1,537	1,253	1,300	1,030
Religion	9,117	9,927	11,230	10,168	9,330
Science	8,266	12,575	9,217	9,173	6,877
Self-help	1,336	1,707	1,696	1,436	1,278
Social science	7,056	8,708	8,148	7,939	8,364
Sports and recreation	1,836	1,777	1,813	1,806	1,682
Study aids	999	626	628	1,908	816
Technology and engineering	5,060	7,971	5,935	7,017	5,288
Transportation	769	631	759	712	654
Travel	2,778	2,367	1,960	1,897	1,755
True crime	299	277	285	273	242
Young adult	5,163	5,618	4,209	5,140	4,338
Totals	190,533	210,772	204,402	205,978	191,576

Table 2 / Hardcover Average Per-Volume Prices, 2012–2015

BISAC Category	2012			2013			2014			2015		
	Vols.	$ Total	Prices	Vols.	$ Total	Prices	Vols.	$ Total	Prices	Vols.	$ Total	Prices
Antiques and collectibles	124	$8,625.88	$69.56	139	$9,835.83	$70.76	146	$9,787.90	$67.04	134	$12,820.49	$95.68
Architecture	762	61,463.81	80.66	926	82,744.31	89.36	799	71,495.57	89.48	895	89,025.09	99.47
Art	1,821	132,964.53	73.02	2,081	151,950.06	73.02	1,896	153,623.78	81.03	1,949	143,318.41	73.53
Bibles	199	7,454.48	37.46	189	7,162.74	37.90	137	4,618.52	33.71	178	6,361.42	35.74
Biography and autobiography	1,713	84,650.53	49.42	1,946	91,629.44	47.09	1,779	85,976.81	48.33	1,711	80,982.57	47.33
Body, mind, and spirit	132	4,926.32	37.32	240	7,910.46	32.96	158	7,369.69	46.64	150	4,404.89	29.37
Business and economics	4,126	576,674.56	139.77	4,506	696,067.00	154.48	4,370	637,061.42	145.78	4,659	684,419.92	146.90
Children	11,920	273,799.03	22.97	12,266	292,561.26	23.85	12,763	306,145.25	23.99	12,988	312,063.44	24.03
Comics and graphic novels	735	27,823.54	37.86	648	24,471.38	37.76	664	26,764.14	40.31	698	26,349.85	37.75
Computers	981	163,883.97	167.06	911	132,799.45	145.77	901	144,030.32	159.86	965	144,778.62	150.03
Cooking	1,135	32,966.80	29.05	1,214	36,161.73	29.79	1,244	35,987.89	28.93	1,225	34,549.83	28.20
Crafts and hobbies	210	6,536.84	31.13	201	5,890.82	29.31	204	5,867.39	28.76	172	4,950.11	28.78
Design	504	32,696.54	64.87	401	25,263.24	63.00	394	26,619.42	67.56	457	30,901.35	67.62
Drama	72	5,542.87	76.98	88	7,133.37	81.06	81	6,578.05	81.21	59	4,719.37	79.99
Education	1,616	214,220.22	132.56	1,794	220,807.27	123.08	1,930	236,406.94	122.49	2,155	259,523.69	120.43
Family and relationships	213	9,173.95	43.07	273	10,863.74	39.79	209	9,501.54	45.46	208	11,945.18	57.43
Fiction	4,421	133,663.96	30.23	5,146	155,859.00	30.29	4,625	138,968.43	30.05	4,345	129,659.68	29.84
Foreign language study	221	25,450.95	115.16	303	40,492.06	133.64	220	25,493.97	115.88	260	36,598.07	140.76
Games	122	4,392.79	36.01	114	4,717.26	41.38	95	3,756.34	39.54	111	4,469.05	40.26
Gardening	134	5,352.22	39.94	115	4,404.39	38.30	97	2,972.03	30.64	121	4,609.97	38.10
Health and fitness	321	23,555.04	73.38	382	24,840.64	65.03	353	20,632.91	58.45	359	24,469.10	68.16
History	4,950	427,995.44	86.46	5,385	487,856.44	90.60	5,489	519,594.73	94.66	5,784	540,589.99	93.46
House and home	88	3,935.94	44.73	108	3,971.65	36.77	91	3,062.99	33.66	109	3,880.42	35.60

Humor	245	4,842.66	19.77	246	4,876.22	19.82	288	6,838.36	23.74	292	7,216.81	24.72
Language arts and disciplines	1,147	151,273.33	131.89	1,328	195,738.83	147.39	1,302	192,447.26	147.81	1,543	221,538.42	143.58
Law	1,900	339,733.91	178.81	2,109	382,556.42	181.39	2,105	375,644.88	178.45	2,169	380,550.37	175.45
Literary collections	258	25,004.52	96.92	305	29,246.50	95.89	271	27,148.62	100.18	218	24,635.70	113.01
Literary criticism	2,027	250,008.05	123.34	2,210	276,713.60	125.21	2,284	289,859.58	126.91	2,257	273,588.20	121.22
Mathematics	963	145,702.22	151.30	961	139,720.81	145.39	963	136,189.64	141.42	979	145,804.91	148.93
Medical	3,546	639,621.95	180.38	3,527	672,625.04	190.71	3,488	711,937.72	204.11	4,116	746,936.40	181.47
Music	524	47,428.36	90.51	594	56,800.22	95.62	540	49,293.64	91.28	576	55,171.16	95.78
Nature	371	33,365.99	89.94	472	41,465.90	87.85	420	37,948.45	90.35	471	41,958.01	89.08
Performing arts	574	51,791.11	90.23	649	63,392.74	97.68	684	64,876.11	94.85	773	73,204.27	94.70
Pets	93	2,230.43	23.98	109	2,828.59	25.95	107	2,614.65	24.44	89	2,205.13	24.78
Philosophy	1,169	123,149.49	105.35	1,396	154,299.60	110.53	1,406	154,511.24	109.89	1,495	158,973.16	106.34
Photography	865	74,284.98	85.88	812	75,419.59	92.88	841	56,236.51	66.87	892	61,439.77	68.88
Poetry	287	11,933.43	41.58	422	14,567.61	34.52	352	12,192.55	34.64	282	12,234.42	43.38
Political science	2,654	299,398.54	112.81	2,807	325,881.22	116.10	3,036	354,242.40	116.68	3,145	379,431.66	120.65
Psychology	1,100	154,343.99	140.31	1,209	169,979.17	140.59	1,193	181,458.91	152.10	1,363	202,352.86	148.46
Reference	499	197,881.61	396.56	419	155,759.03	371.74	400	128,248.21	320.62	359	135,915.83	378.60
Religion	2,730	223,678.07	81.93	2,904	228,392.63	78.65	2,538	203,081.58	80.02	2,474	212,534.18	85.91
Science	3,331	652,311.72	195.83	3,486	772,346.52	221.56	3,536	705,705.43	199.58	4,143	772,647.68	186.49
Self-help	265	6,556.76	24.74	379	10,716.30	28.28	282	7,086.11	25.13	284	7,890.92	27.78
Social science	3,139	363,460.96	115.79	3,436	412,577.21	120.07	3,328	469,571.74	141.10	3,825	507,828.34	132.77
Sports and recreation	658	33,995.43	51.66	691	33,056.86	47.84	621	37,781.35	60.84	606	31,976.83	52.77
Study aids	14	1,548.35	110.60	14	1,629.34	116.38	19	1,762.30	92.75	14	1,419.40	101.39
Technology and engineering	2,653	465,522.95	175.47	2,583	465,501.51	180.22	2,567	487,613.19	189.95	3,439	575,927.46	167.47
Transportation	225	15,040.36	66.85	326	24,598.44	75.46	248	21,230.55	85.61	279	23,157.94	83.00
Travel	205	10,193.81	49.73	205	8,368.64	40.82	181	6,906.52	38.16	209	7,176.67	34.34
True crime	70	2,265.72	32.37	86	2,383.18	27.71	78	2,249.05	28.83	65	2,770.46	42.62
Young adult	2,256	83,170.95	36.87	1,975	62,425.67	31.61	2,169	73,589.21	33.93	2,044	65,872.45	32.23
Totals	70,288	$6,677,489.86	$95.00	75,036	$7,309,260.93	$97.41	73,892	$7,280,581.79	$98.53	78,093	$7,727,749.92	$98.96

Table 3 / Hardcover Average Per-Volume Prices, Less Than $81, 2012–2015

BISAC Category	2012			2013			2014			2015		
	Vols.	$ Total	Prices	Vols.	$ Total	Prices	Vols.	$ Total	Prices	Vols.	$ Total	Prices
Antiques and collectibles	95	$3,639.00	$38.31	112	$4,375.41	$39.07	112	$4,573.46	$40.83	89	$4,076.17	$45.80
Architecture	516	26,135.33	50.65	578	30,887.66	53.44	493	25,982.33	52.70	510	25,921.65	50.83
Art	1,413	66,651.03	47.17	1,550	73,837.42	47.64	1,397	66,750.34	47.78	1,448	69,110.32	47.73
Bibles	191	6,581.52	34.46	185	6,746.81	36.47	136	4,518.53	33.22	174	5,849.43	33.62
Biography and autobiography	1,536	47,993.56	31.25	1,794	56,737.95	31.63	1,625	50,630.07	31.16	1,557	48,553.47	31.18
Body, mind, and spirit	124	3,175.32	25.61	228	6,272.46	27.51	146	3,252.34	22.28	140	2,995.89	21.40
Business and economics	1,587	68,982.27	43.47	1,624	71,694.02	44.15	1,601	73,906.53	46.16	1,531	69,145.05	45.16
Children	11,652	223,824.32	19.21	11,965	234,239.70	19.58	12,452	249,944.50	20.07	12,642	253,259.29	20.03
Comics and graphic novels	698	22,543.70	32.30	606	19,741.65	32.58	615	19,290.33	31.37	654	20,655.03	31.58
Computers	180	11,008.45	61.16	189	11,487.51	60.78	205	12,824.02	62.56	224	14,242.25	63.58
Cooking	1,116	30,160.17	27.03	1,187	31,718.02	26.72	1,231	33,582.29	27.28	1,211	32,895.85	27.16
Crafts and hobbies	209	5,536.84	26.49	193	4,965.42	25.73	198	5,180.12	26.16	170	4,766.11	28.04
Design	411	19,224.47	46.77	327	15,469.19	47.31	312	15,209.12	48.75	354	16,440.17	46.44
Drama	41	1,710.41	41.72	43	2,093.46	48.69	41	1,858.67	45.33	28	1,529.20	54.61
Education	477	26,369.70	55.28	558	29,608.85	53.06	686	35,079.56	51.14	658	33,251.57	50.53
Family and relationships	183	4,152.36	22.69	240	6,014.54	25.06	166	3,972.21	23.93	153	3,336.45	21.81
Fiction	4,372	125,821.29	28.78	5,109	149,209.22	29.21	4,593	133,306.73	29.02	4,315	123,909.08	28.72
Foreign language study	101	5,930.85	58.72	126	7,058.40	56.02	94	5,454.75	58.03	91	5,508.49	60.53
Games	119	3,752.79	31.54	104	3,364.29	32.35	88	2,811.36	31.95	102	3,374.33	33.08
Gardening	127	4,232.27	33.32	107	3,215.89	30.06	96	2,792.03	29.08	117	4,194.97	35.85
Health and fitness	230	7,166.08	31.16	274	7,612.95	27.78	279	8,077.10	28.95	252	7,249.56	28.77
History	2,865	125,275.28	43.73	2,948	129,892.36	44.06	2,968	132,724.91	44.72	3,049	138,529.30	45.43
House and home	83	3,384.21	40.77	106	3,771.65	35.58	90	2,937.99	32.64	107	3,569.35	33.36

Humor	243	4,652.71	19.15	246	4,876.22	19.82	286	6,588.37	23.04	285	6,127.81	21.50
Language arts and disciplines	300	17,141.02	57.14	302	17,219.62	57.02	257	15,376.35	59.83	291	16,878.08	58.00
Law	319	18,678.81	58.55	344	20,088.16	58.40	290	16,935.64	58.40	282	15,711.62	55.71
Literary collections	141	5,669.72	40.21	141	5,698.67	40.42	152	5,695.43	37.47	123	4,854.97	39.47
Literary criticism	787	46,707.71	59.35	781	45,761.32	58.59	781	46,220.44	59.18	699	39,862.25	57.03
Mathematics	186	11,201.81	60.22	190	11,308.44	59.52	208	12,766.88	61.38	172	11,242.13	65.36
Medical	392	21,524.94	54.91	330	17,690.49	53.61	282	15,912.67	56.43	316	18,493.99	58.53
Music	313	14,173.73	45.28	291	12,970.94	44.57	307	13,963.85	45.48	263	11,417.28	43.41
Nature	230	8,416.78	36.59	275	9,185.68	33.40	238	8,563.18	35.98	230	8,484.19	36.89
Performing arts	319	15,524.46	48.67	282	13,979.00	49.57	301	15,167.17	50.39	289	14,218.65	49.20
Pets	93	2,230.43	23.98	109	2,828.59	25.95	106	2,509.65	23.68	87	1,946.13	22.37
Philosophy	476	26,754.50	56.21	523	29,341.82	56.10	501	28,350.42	56.59	515	27,775.12	53.93
Photography	756	36,270.44	47.98	705	33,661.99	47.75	730	34,846.78	47.74	759	36,540.40	48.14
Poetry	259	7,488.59	28.91	408	11,644.16	28.54	329	9,075.10	27.58	261	7,637.47	29.26
Political science	913	42,160.00	46.18	902	44,621.94	49.47	942	48,196.34	51.16	875	43,947.36	50.23
Psychology	366	18,870.64	51.56	332	16,197.03	48.79	327	15,931.90	48.72	352	17,992.57	51.12
Reference	181	6,063.91	33.50	172	5,427.63	31.56	159	4,729.06	29.74	144	4,126.77	28.66
Religion	1,713	56,736.05	33.12	1,871	63,128.53	33.74	1,579	57,535.48	36.44	1,399	49,752.95	35.56
Science	496	22,933.51	46.24	539	24,504.29	45.46	515	24,559.16	47.69	560	27,068.42	48.34
Self-help	262	6,259.77	23.89	369	9,382.30	25.43	278	6,523.11	23.46	272	6,301.71	23.17
Social science	1,100	60,821.33	55.29	1,204	66,309.79	55.07	1,031	57,581.77	55.85	1,074	60,048.79	55.91
Sports and recreation	572	17,875.67	31.25	606	19,133.04	31.57	514	16,365.97	31.84	510	16,032.13	31.44
Study aids	9	478.70	53.19	9	409.64	45.52	14	648.60	46.33	8	454.70	56.84
Technology and engineering	202	11,123.96	55.07	217	12,128.75	55.89	210	11,867.72	56.51	207	11,921.39	57.59
Transportation	180	6,882.24	38.23	251	10,255.76	40.86	170	7,134.70	41.97	207	8,617.19	41.63
Travel	181	5,460.97	30.17	187	5,813.74	31.09	169	5,281.70	31.25	201	6,085.77	30.28
True crime	68	1,949.77	28.67	85	2,302.18	27.08	78	2,249.05	28.83	59	1,870.46	31.70
Young adult	2,115	57,481.72	27.18	1,912	47,749.65	24.97	2,075	55,068.34	26.54	1,968	49,847.46	25.33
Totals	41,498	$1,394,785.11	$33.61	43,736	$1,473,634.20	$33.69	42,453	$1,440,304.12	$33.93	41,984	$1,417,620.74	$33.77

Table 4 / Mass Market Paperbacks Average Per-Volume Prices, 2012–2015

BISAC Category	2012			2013			2014			2015		
	Vols.	$ Total	Prices	Vols.	$ Total	Prices	Vols.	$ Total	Prices	Vols.	$ Total	Prices
Antiques and collectibles	5	$44.95	$8.99	5	$44.95	$8.99	4	$35.96	$8.99	n.a.	n.a.	n.a.
Architecture	n.a.	n.a.	n.a.	n.a.	n.a.	n.a.	n.a.	n.a.	n.a.	n.a.	n.a.	n.a.
Art	n.a.	n.a.	n.a.	n.a.	n.a.	n.a.	n.a.	n.a.	n.a.	n.a.	n.a.	n.a.
Bibles	n.a.	n.a.	n.a.	n.a.	n.a.	n.a.	n.a.	n.a.	n.a.	n.a.	n.a.	n.a.
Biography and autobiography	4	26.92	6.73	3	28.98	9.66	6	53.90	8.98	2	$16.98	$8.49
Body, mind and spirit	14	113.86	8.13	14	113.86	8.13	2	19.98	9.99	n.a.	n.a.	n.a.
Business and economics	1	7.99	7.99	n.a.	n.a.	n.a.	n.a.	n.a.	n.a.	1	8.99	8.99
Children	240	1,557.60	6.49	282	1,803.65	6.40	272	1,660.26	6.10	200	1,227.00	6.14
Comics and graphic novels	n.a.	n.a.	n.a.	n.a.	n.a.	n.a.	n.a.	n.a.	n.a.	n.a.	n.a.	n.a.
Computers	n.a.	n.a.	n.a.	n.a.	n.a.	n.a.	n.a.	n.a.	n.a.	n.a.	n.a.	n.a.
Cooking	n.a.	n.a.	n.a.	n.a.	n.a.	n.a.	n.a.	n.a.	n.a.	1	8.99	8.99
Crafts and hobbies	n.a.	n.a.	n.a.	n.a.	n.a.	n.a.	n.a.	n.a.	n.a.	n.a.	n.a.	n.a.
Design	n.a.	n.a.	n.a.	n.a.	n.a.	n.a.	n.a.	n.a.	n.a.	n.a.	n.a.	n.a.
Drama	2	9.90	4.95	n.a.	n.a.	n.a.	1	9.99	9.99	n.a.	n.a.	n.a.
Education	n.a.	n.a.	n.a.	n.a.	n.a.	n.a.	n.a.	n.a.	n.a.	n.a.	n.a.	n.a.
Family and relationships	n.a.	n.a.	n.a.	n.a.	n.a.	n.a.	1	8.99	8.99	1	8.99	8.99
Fiction	3,894	27,441.26	7.05	3,620	25,413.42	7.02	3,603	25,557.48	7.09	3,235	22,979.92	7.10
Foreign language study	n.a.	n.a.	n.a.	n.a.	n.a.	n.a.	1	6.99	6.99	n.a.	n.a.	n.a.
Games	n.a.	n.a.	n.a.	1	9.99	9.99	2	18.49	9.25	1	7.99	7.99
Gardening	n.a.	n.a.	n.a.	n.a.	n.a.	n.a.	n.a.	n.a.	n.a.	n.a.	n.a.	n.a.
Health and fitness	16	131.85	8.24	8	65.92	8.24	3	27.98	9.33	3	26.97	8.99
History	3	25.97	8.66	3	29.98	9.99	2	19.98	9.99	2	19.98	9.99
House and home	n.a.	n.a.	n.a.	n.a.	n.a.	n.a.	n.a.	n.a.	n.a.	n.a.	n.a.	n.a.

Humor	n.a.	n.a.	n.a.	2	15.99	8.00	n.a.	n.a.	n.a.	n.a.	n.a.	n.a.
Language arts and disciplines	n.a.	n.a.	n.a.	n.a.	n.a.	n.a.	1	7.99	7.99	n.a.	n.a.	n.a.
Law	n.a.	n.a.	n.a.	n.a.	n.a.	n.a.	1	4.95	4.95	n.a.	n.a.	n.a.
Literary collections	2	11.90	5.95	n.a.	n.a.	n.a.	n.a.	n.a.	n.a.	n.a.	n.a.	n.a.
Literary criticism	n.a.	n.a.	n.a.	n.a.	n.a.	n.a.	n.a.	n.a.	n.a.	n.a.	n.a.	n.a.
Mathematics	n.a.	n.a.	n.a.	n.a.	n.a.	n.a.	n.a.	n.a.	n.a.	n.a.	n.a.	n.a.
Medical	1	8.99	8.99	n.a.	n.a.	n.a.	1	7.99	7.99	n.a.	n.a.	n.a.
Music	n.a.	n.a.	n.a.	n.a.	n.a.	n.a.	n.a.	n.a.	n.a.	n.a.	n.a.	n.a.
Nature	1	7.99	7.99	1	10.99	10.99	n.a.	n.a.	n.a.	n.a.	n.a.	n.a.
Performing arts	1	9.99	9.99	1	7.99	7.99	1	10.99	10.99	1	9.99	9.99
Pets	n.a.	n.a.	n.a.	n.a.	n.a.	n.a.	n.a.	n.a.	n.a.	1	6.95	6.95
Philosophy	n.a.	n.a.	n.a.	n.a.	n.a.	n.a.	n.a.	n.a.	n.a.	n.a.	n.a.	n.a.
Photography	n.a.	n.a.	n.a.	3	19.85	6.62	n.a.	n.a.	n.a.	2	12.90	6.45
Poetry	2	14.90	7.45	3	19.48	6.49	1	9.99	9.99	3	23.93	7.98
Political science	n.a.	n.a.	n.a.	n.a.	n.a.	n.a.	n.a.	n.a.	n.a.	n.a.	n.a.	n.a.
Psychology	n.a.	n.a.	n.a.	n.a.	n.a.	n.a.	n.a.	n.a.	n.a.	1	7.99	7.99
Reference	3	24.93	8.31	n.a.	n.a.	n.a.	5	64.46	12.89	n.a.	n.a.	n.a.
Religion	2	14.98	7.49	n.a.	n.a.	n.a.	n.a.	n.a.	n.a.	n.a.	n.a.	n.a.
Science	n.a.	n.a.	n.a.	n.a.	n.a.	n.a.	n.a.	n.a.	n.a.	n.a.	n.a.	n.a.
Self-help	1	7.99	7.99	n.a.	n.a.	n.a.	n.a.	n.a.	n.a.	n.a.	n.a.	n.a.
Social science	1	9.99	9.99	n.a.	n.a.	n.a.	n.a.	n.a.	n.a.	n.a.	n.a.	n.a.
Sports and recreation	1	7.99	7.99	n.a.	n.a.	n.a.	n.a.	n.a.	n.a.	n.a.	n.a.	n.a.
Study aids	n.a.	n.a.	n.a.	n.a.	n.a.	n.a.	n.a.	n.a.	n.a.	n.a.	n.a.	n.a.
Technology and engineering	n.a.	n.a.	n.a.	n.a.	n.a.	n.a.	n.a.	n.a.	n.a.	1	7.99	7.99
Transportation	n.a.	n.a.	n.a.	1	5.99	5.99	n.a.	n.a.	n.a.	n.a.	n.a.	n.a.
Travel	n.a.	n.a.	n.a.	n.a.	n.a.	n.a.	n.a.	n.a.	n.a.	n.a.	n.a.	n.a.
True crime	38	315.62	8.31	26	220.74	8.49	20	173.80	8.69	13	107.87	8.30
Young adult	44	393.54	8.94	61	568.32	9.32	44	414.57	9.42	29	252.71	8.71
Totals	4,276	$30,189.11	$7.06	4,034	$28,380.10	$7.04	3,970	$28,105.75	$7.08	3,497	$24,736.14	$7.07

n.a. = not available

Table 5 / Trade Paperbacks Average Per-Volume Prices, 2012–2015

BISAC Category	2012			2013			2014			2015		
	Vols.	$ Total	Prices	Vols.	$ Total	Prices	Vols.	$ Total	Prices	Vols.	$ Total	Prices
Antiques and collectibles	160	$5,013.82	$31.34	139	$4,672.53	$33.62	139	$5,006.33	$36.02	118	$4,189.76	$35.51
Architecture	639	27,300.28	42.72	820	36,370.96	44.35	689	31,681.47	45.98	784	34,360.59	43.83
Art	1,718	65,165.45	37.93	1,942	94,634.29	48.73	1,679	66,455.05	39.58	1,800	66,111.54	36.73
Bibles	641	28,627.08	44.66	806	33,713.40	41.83	770	34,963.39	45.41	937	38,848.90	41.46
Biography and autobiography	2,648	53,221.08	20.10	3,176	63,288.72	19.93	2,920	59,600.10	20.41	2,604	53,004.46	20.36
Body, mind, and spirit	1,061	19,473.64	18.35	1,013	18,498.57	18.26	861	15,589.75	18.11	664	12,091.60	18.21
Business and economics	9,050	780,896.45	86.29	7,580	681,420.67	89.90	7,334	675,979.24	92.17	8,386	861,837.36	102.77
Children	10,137	140,160.48	13.83	10,461	125,925.45	12.04	11,493	149,042.21	12.97	11,260	174,132.25	15.46
Comics and graphic novels	2,206	36,152.82	16.39	1,847	30,718.11	16.63	2,077	36,463.18	17.56	1,998	35,190.46	17.61
Computers	4,289	402,287.48	93.80	3,814	342,365.27	89.77	3,506	293,638.64	83.75	2,784	214,245.74	76.96
Cooking	1,297	26,565.72	20.48	1,255	24,793.50	19.76	1,279	25,135.87	19.65	1,103	22,548.24	20.44
Crafts and hobbies	1,079	21,060.03	19.52	1,243	22,872.55	18.40	1,203	22,579.86	18.77	1,116	21,459.93	19.23
Design	386	16,011.01	41.48	331	12,981.36	39.22	308	12,974.68	42.13	254	11,426.02	44.98
Drama	504	9,877.77	19.60	615	12,460.59	20.26	584	12,118.54	20.75	531	11,884.39	22.38
Education	4,189	192,424.29	45.94	4,334	217,569.08	50.20	4,380	244,900.65	55.91	3,698	168,830.20	45.65
Family and relationships	763	14,635.11	19.18	770	15,480.74	20.10	756	17,307.38	22.89	650	13,126.19	20.19
Fiction	11,063	188,817.39	17.07	13,770	237,057.78	17.22	13,114	226,651.58	17.28	10,341	177,390.93	17.15
Foreign language study	1,224	52,211.37	42.66	1,108	63,542.06	57.35	1,370	61,346.00	44.78	822	40,409.24	49.16
Games	665	10,473.76	15.75	630	9,803.72	15.56	548	9,620.37	17.56	450	7,965.85	17.70
Gardening	236	5,568.52	23.60	200	4,569.29	22.85	163	3,576.37	21.94	157	3,920.20	24.97
Health and fitness	1,181	32,951.74	27.90	1,106	29,564.38	26.73	1,108	29,676.90	26.78	1,034	26,635.70	25.76
History	6,978	296,049.18	42.43	6,796	261,567.64	38.49	7,750	315,413.83	40.70	6,732	260,150.02	38.64
House and home	148	3,476.67	23.49	158	3,697.48	23.40	949	90,730.38	95.61	113	2,275.45	20.14

Humor	395	5,600.19	14.18	357	5,200.11	14.57	344	5,149.17	14.97	324	4,849.59	14.97
Language arts and disciplines	2,282	176,575.76	77.38	1,967	143,901.20	73.16	2,151	164,675.94	76.56	1,715	123,284.23	71.89
Law	3,492	267,877.35	76.71	3,322	259,091.99	77.99	3,690	295,619.73	80.11	3,618	305,619.57	84.47
Literary collections	492	17,272.72	35.11	498	17,486.91	35.11	673	14,412.07	21.41	318	10,651.19	33.49
Literary criticism	1,597	70,624.89	44.22	1,692	69,515.84	41.09	2,554	128,955.62	50.49	1,760	69,807.88	39.66
Mathematics	2,618	256,435.84	97.95	1,536	140,747.93	91.63	1,518	137,270.79	90.43	984	76,181.94	77.42
Medical	8,268	775,462.20	93.79	5,625	634,447.70	112.79	4,605	443,601.59	96.33	3,618	355,979.30	98.39
Music	2,683	69,462.84	25.89	2,782	70,511.07	25.35	2,188	63,168.82	28.87	2,517	64,560.52	25.65
Nature	651	24,378.54	37.45	575	18,773.91	32.65	593	18,815.35	31.73	498	15,339.09	30.80
Performing arts	922	35,636.18	38.65	892	32,184.86	36.08	924	33,923.10	36.71	908	32,806.26	36.13
Pets	217	3,947.06	18.19	158	2,950.43	18.67	146	2,726.10	18.67	149	2,650.95	17.79
Philosophy	1,481	72,676.07	49.07	1,586	77,919.52	49.13	1,776	85,079.41	47.91	1,549	64,677.66	41.75
Photography	514	17,254.98	33.57	445	15,421.04	34.65	420	15,012.44	35.74	418	17,278.65	41.34
Poetry	1,959	32,424.44	16.55	2,434	40,729.81	16.73	2,279	40,202.41	17.64	1,901	33,856.40	17.81
Political science	3,522	171,638.93	48.73	3,659	180,331.55	49.28	4,114	228,228.69	55.48	3,534	184,086.02	52.09
Psychology	2,039	143,593.12	70.42	1,977	138,997.64	70.31	2,121	123,365.31	58.16	2,255	114,800.86	50.91
Reference	1,022	109,796.48	107.43	824	84,308.77	102.32	891	88,689.36	99.54	670	110,097.14	164.32
Religion	7,158	164,496.45	22.98	8,275	187,160.47	22.62	7,585	179,954.12	23.72	6,786	164,764.87	24.28
Science	7,680	721,360.56	93.93	4,662	448,507.42	96.20	4,417	392,054.12	88.76	2,484	225,697.99	90.86
Self-help	1,440	24,946.68	17.32	1,308	23,213.62	17.75	1,153	21,682.71	18.81	981	16,737.98	17.06
Social science	5,442	296,247.46	54.44	4,623	241,344.93	52.21	4,673	254,906.87	54.55	4,422	214,045.31	48.40
Sports and recreation	1,118	26,237.08	23.47	1,119	26,982.96	24.11	1,185	28,869.47	24.36	1,073	26,220.70	24.44
Study aids	590	24,629.18	41.74	614	29,275.04	47.68	1,888	84,729.17	44.88	797	34,587.73	43.40
Technology and engineering	4,519	460,536.17	101.91	2,950	314,880.86	106.74	3,688	386,011.52	104.67	1,809	198,153.43	109.54
Transportation	405	13,963.19	34.48	432	17,210.84	39.84	465	19,689.21	42.34	374	14,808.26	39.59
Travel	2,160	43,811.42	20.28	1,752	36,177.72	20.65	1,716	35,350.68	20.60	1,551	31,943.25	20.60
True crime	169	3,175.80	18.79	173	3,446.61	19.92	175	3,326.61	19.01	164	3,078.28	18.77
Young adult	3,315	56,976.06	17.19	2,173	37,021.97	17.04	2,929	54,681.32	18.67	2,262	46,214.77	20.43
Totals	130,412	$6,515,458.76	$49.96	122,324	$5,645,310.86	$46.15	125,841	$5,790,603.47	$46.02	107,775	$4,824,814.84	$44.77

Table 6 / Audiobook Average Per-Volume Prices, 2012–2015

BISAC Category	2012 Vols.	2012 $ Total	2012 Prices	2013 Vols.	2013 $ Total	2013 Prices	2014 Vols.	2014 $ Total	2014 Prices	2015 Vols.	2015 $ Total	2015 Prices
Antiques and collectibles	n.a.	n.a.	n.a.	n.a.	n.a.	n.a.	n.a.	n.a.	n.a.	n.a.	n.a.	n.a.
Architecture	2	$64.90	$32.45	7	$299.77	$42.82	1	$59.95	$59.95	2	$29.94	$14.97
Art	12	448.82	37.40	4	149.80	37.45	9	353.91	39.32	9	284.89	31.65
Bibles	23	1,148.54	49.94	20	1,629.54	81.48	11	779.70	70.88	16	597.64	37.35
Biography and autobiography	1,018	47,926.38	47.08	1,215	50,171.75	41.29	982	40,855.38	41.60	1,231	45,120.53	36.65
Body, mind, and spirit	126	4,535.13	35.99	245	6,631.36	27.07	181	5,160.21	28.51	163	3,862.36	23.70
Business and economics	475	18,167.31	38.25	452	15,589.57	34.49	607	18,187.51	29.96	703	20,725.83	29.48
Children	1,283	41,118.66	32.05	1,743	71,387.45	40.96	1,032	36,755.87	35.62	2,335	93,347.09	39.98
Comics and graphic novels	4	149.92	37.48	2	29.98	14.99	n.a.	n.a.	n.a.	n.a.	n.a.	n.a.
Computers	4	170.92	42.73	2	104.94	52.47	18	742.73	41.26	8	242.90	30.36
Cooking	14	628.78	44.91	20	943.75	47.19	14	686.78	49.06	22	666.77	30.31
Crafts and hobbies	1	24.95	24.95	2	49.90	24.95	5	123.88	24.78	2	60.94	30.47
Design	3	171.90	57.30	2	74.94	37.47	n.a.	n.a.	n.a.	2	44.98	22.49
Drama	111	2,673.74	24.09	100	3,250.44	32.50	59	1,528.64	25.91	49	1,446.75	29.53
Education	37	1,292.12	34.92	33	1,296.50	39.29	32	1,178.72	36.84	25	908.77	36.35
Family and relationships	143	6,158.90	43.07	119	4,183.77	35.16	119	3,809.20	32.01	162	4,999.82	30.86
Fiction	11,408	477,403.65	41.85	11,561	445,335.72	38.52	11,447	445,467.43	38.92	12,979	414,030.64	31.90
Foreign language study	178	11,713.66	65.81	141	7,255.85	51.46	273	17,559.20	64.32	118	4,797.99	40.66
Games	5	224.88	44.98	n.a.	n.a.	n.a.	5	235.90	47.18	1	11.99	11.99
Gardening	5	159.93	31.99	n.a.	n.a.	n.a.	n.a.	n.a.	n.a.	1	14.99	14.99
Health and fitness	99	4,265.01	43.08	133	5,761.77	43.32	111	4,569.96	41.17	163	6,575.57	40.34
History	610	30,713.03	50.35	489	23,425.98	47.91	476	24,721.41	51.94	547	23,669.09	43.27
House and home	3	165.97	55.32	4	119.92	29.98	1	9.99	9.99	5	178.95	35.79

Humor	77	2,544.95	33.05	79	2,950.80	37.35	98	3,227.52	32.93	83	2,594.78	31.26
Language arts and disciplines	26	1,437.29	55.28	13	495.48	38.11	11	419.85	38.17	21	783.74	37.32
Law	18	918.69	51.04	16	1,038.88	64.93	12	748.88	62.41	10	475.94	47.59
Literary collections	35	1,395.31	39.87	18	667.57	37.09	41	2,218.06	54.10	56	2,262.87	40.41
Literary criticism	95	3,170.80	33.38	11	534.78	48.62	12	359.78	29.98	23	982.43	42.71
Mathematics	3	153.97	51.32	5	199.87	39.97	5	102.96	20.59	6	220.88	36.81
Medical	24	1,182.32	49.26	25	1,013.37	40.53	12	452.88	37.74	27	872.25	32.31
Music	51	2,338.88	45.86	33	1,352.91	41.00	25	1,281.28	51.25	15	516.30	34.42
Nature	13	670.79	51.60	27	1,094.38	40.53	23	1,072.54	46.63	34	1,073.43	31.57
Performing arts	16	550.68	34.42	58	2,403.87	41.45	65	2,575.33	39.62	65	2,441.24	37.56
Pets	20	858.69	42.93	30	1,178.29	39.28	13	481.64	37.05	17	668.67	39.33
Philosophy	42	1,669.98	39.76	38	1,125.56	29.62	25	800.54	32.02	17	493.75	29.04
Photography	n.a.	n.a.	n.a.	n.a.	n.a.	n.a.	n.a.	n.a.	n.a.	n.a.	n.a.	n.a.
Poetry	16	436.52	27.28	19	501.50	26.39	38	1,484.47	39.07	25	930.48	37.22
Political science	236	10,999.82	46.61	166	7,480.77	45.06	130	5,863.68	45.11	173	6,397.83	36.98
Psychology	85	3,353.42	39.45	74	3,268.54	44.17	96	3,126.47	32.57	102	3,634.78	35.64
Reference	11	389.81	35.44	5	248.87	49.77	8	207.91	25.99	4	61.96	15.49
Religion	577	19,067.79	33.05	677	19,698.58	29.10	698	20,059.46	28.74	941	24,646.58	26.19
Science	117	4,949.55	42.30	97	4,024.00	41.48	98	4,094.52	41.78	116	4,097.06	35.32
Self-help	386	14,247.32	36.91	212	6,589.63	31.08	231	7,028.94	30.43	285	8,593.79	30.15
Social science	116	5,045.79	43.50	111	4,229.66	38.11	103	3,652.24	35.46	120	3,727.33	31.06
Sports and recreation	37	1,630.38	44.06	48	1,916.81	39.93	52	2,003.15	38.52	64	2,195.16	34.30
Study aids	5	738.13	147.63	1	24.99	24.99	5	654.98	131.00	3	74.90	24.97
Technology and engineering	11	440.78	40.07	9	381.84	42.43	11	576.83	52.44	20	862.61	43.13
Transportation	7	323.86	46.27	10	486.78	48.68	5	261.95	52.39	9	323.80	35.98
Travel	49	1,758.00	35.88	37	1,327.79	35.89	9	429.84	47.76	26	685.59	26.37
True crime	80	3,623.44	45.29	137	5,499.55	40.14	94	3,214.65	34.20	105	3,050.53	29.05
Young adult	1,461	50,472.17	34.55	1,288	54,938.12	42.65	1,285	55,598.45	43.27	1,696	53,084.18	31.30
Totals	19,178	$783,696.23	$40.86	19,538	$762,365.89	$39.02	18,588	$724,785.17	$38.99	22,606	$747,371.29	$33.06

n.a. = not available

Table 7 / E-Book Average Per-Volume Prices, 2012–2015

BISAC Category	2012			2013			2014			2015		
	Vols.	$ Total	Prices	Vols.	$ Total	Prices	Vols.	$ Total	Prices	Vols.	$ Total	Prices
Antiques and collectibles	168	$3,800.79	$22.62	181	$3,655.88	$20.20	132	$2,251.26	$17.06	136	$1,250.16	$9.19
Architecture	830	39,720.21	47.86	926	59,043.35	63.76	1,083	156,573.26	144.57	501	30,444.42	60.77
Art	1,339	28,673.78	21.41	1,881	37,433.22	19.90	1,884	41,959.39	22.27	4,914	46,558.12	9.47
Bibles	165	2,206.87	13.37	516	4,419.77	8.57	247	2,263.10	9.16	191	1,659.92	8.69
Biography and autobiography	8,544	154,373.76	18.07	8,493	125,801.56	14.81	9,542	170,668.20	17.89	7,295	125,239.75	17.17
Body, mind, and spirit	2,744	35,389.78	12.90	1,997	21,040.54	10.54	1,815	19,086.88	10.52	1,361	15,456.01	11.36
Business and economics	12,688	522,358.69	41.17	12,835	632,939.18	49.31	10,599	517,119.53	48.79	21,266	455,374.56	21.41
Children	23,942	254,440.89	10.63	20,511	293,257.09	14.30	21,565	315,345.81	14.62	17,454	206,647.28	11.84
Comics and graphic novels	628	4,192.87	6.68	581	4,197.53	7.22	1,535	9,409.04	6.13	3,605	30,767.99	8.53
Computers	4,881	344,797.66	70.64	5,073	311,796.95	61.46	4,358	290,377.53	66.63	4,027	250,979.71	62.32
Cooking	2,680	30,965.36	11.55	3,554	44,226.31	12.44	2,870	34,481.13	12.01	3,023	36,195.53	11.97
Crafts and hobbies	1,270	13,268.39	10.45	1,437	14,003.52	9.74	960	11,462.67	11.94	1,202	11,091.35	9.23
Design	221	5,584.31	25.27	199	5,499.02	27.63	144	4,036.50	28.03	137	3,591.76	26.22
Drama	2,256	16,231.91	7.19	1,848	14,873.48	8.05	1,799	17,801.62	9.90	1,730	12,870.29	7.44
Education	3,878	184,802.91	47.65	5,305	265,959.51	50.13	4,642	180,118.87	38.80	4,178	116,587.90	27.91
Family and relationships	2,208	30,502.48	13.81	2,099	29,409.79	14.01	2,200	31,040.77	14.11	1,756	20,003.23	11.39
Fiction	108,916	1,054,636.72	9.68	100,029	674,571.51	6.74	104,416	670,233.30	6.42	90,988	685,892.94	7.54
Foreign language study	903	20,823.78	23.06	1,738	26,902.95	15.48	1,657	26,826.69	16.19	1,611	31,720.61	19.69
Games	492	4,142.80	8.42	529	4,811.65	9.10	682	5,591.37	8.20	652	4,760.04	7.30
Gardening	408	5,880.82	14.41	373	4,838.56	12.97	311	3,603.95	11.59	303	3,377.24	11.15
Health and fitness	3,179	42,891.46	13.49	3,765	46,743.20	12.42	3,170	37,128.71	11.71	2,991	39,049.02	13.06
History	9,697	314,778.53	32.46	11,010	467,959.52	42.50	12,548	429,850.67	34.26	9,738	355,572.19	36.51
House and home	309	3,982.29	12.89	442	4,344.72	9.83	310	2,996.65	9.67	302	3,241.56	10.73

Humor	1,297	16,071.41	12.39	1,125	9,936.70	8.83	1,080	10,117.32	9.37	893	10,683.30	11.96
Language arts and disciplines	2,009	90,968.66	45.28	2,900	193,052.28	66.57	2,274	175,067.42	76.99	1,738	152,865.46	87.95
Law	2,132	155,611.00	72.99	2,641	272,375.07	103.13	1,840	182,295.48	99.07	1,584	160,251.31	101.17
Literary collections	1,823	18,146.74	9.95	1,538	20,026.52	13.02	1,615	38,412.77	23.78	6,311	31,375.13	4.97
Literary criticism	2,444	90,185.27	36.90	2,730	214,535.08	78.58	2,354	178,963.40	76.03	2,423	156,557.12	64.61
Mathematics	1,973	147,047.70	74.53	1,572	135,922.36	86.46	1,425	134,546.94	94.42	1,136	96,017.24	84.52
Medical	5,638	541,053.54	95.97	9,492	700,007.81	73.75	3,737	388,814.98	104.04	2,625	270,950.82	103.22
Music	18,723	90,863.68	4.85	2,053	62,911.50	30.64	1,431	67,350.95	47.07	1,602	33,742.86	21.06
Nature	934	36,334.47	38.90	1,168	40,239.30	34.45	952	33,812.53	35.52	700	28,749.74	41.07
Performing arts	1,231	35,374.70	28.74	1,665	65,563.23	39.38	1,421	46,442.24	32.68	1,262	35,320.49	27.99
Pets	716	10,566.72	14.76	817	6,498.27	7.95	424	4,557.65	10.75	298	3,364.59	11.29
Philosophy	2,304	86,422.67	37.51	3,067	162,069.50	52.84	2,362	144,651.49	61.24	1,943	108,599.76	55.89
Photography	471	8,895.05	18.89	566	12,730.32	22.49	556	11,001.83	19.79	462	8,253.00	17.86
Poetry	2,398	17,226.54	7.18	3,272	22,040.23	6.74	3,813	26,903.93	7.06	3,575	22,141.95	6.19
Political science	4,959	203,959.25	41.13	5,274	259,462.37	49.20	3,913	218,284.16	55.78	3,589	185,214.10	51.61
Psychology	3,023	135,309.18	44.76	4,757	299,923.60	63.05	3,273	188,481.82	57.59	2,091	103,622.07	49.56
Reference	1,392	34,439.38	24.74	1,702	85,807.18	50.42	4,062	104,480.29	25.72	3,407	81,308.12	23.87
Religion	9,644	171,278.22	17.76	10,626	219,959.34	20.70	11,208	215,279.54	19.21	9,217	181,249.20	19.66
Science	5,935	605,906.19	102.09	4,823	514,561.79	106.69	4,710	558,419.82	118.56	3,680	355,621.70	96.64
Self-help	4,978	67,191.81	13.50	4,497	42,203.50	9.38	4,825	41,353.84	8.57	4,005	39,380.47	9.83
Social science	4,446	241,646.49	54.35	7,081	487,756.60	68.88	4,888	328,282.53	67.16	3,865	205,269.41	53.11
Sports and recreation	2,607	46,467.69	17.82	2,837	51,932.80	18.31	2,344	41,894.22	17.87	1,815	31,724.74	17.48
Study aids	13,402	307,735.80	22.96	6,165	115,936.64	18.81	4,721	87,747.44	18.59	813	10,298.17	12.67
Technology and engineering	4,044	477,385.35	118.05	4,106	476,087.09	115.95	3,859	562,712.67	145.82	2,914	358,605.72	123.06
Transportation	323	7,862.59	24.34	319	8,073.13	25.31	336	6,506.60	19.36	331	8,810.63	26.62
Travel	3,686	35,907.30	9.74	2,586	28,211.42	10.91	2,320	26,165.78	11.28	3,163	29,074.98	9.19
True crime	621	9,853.58	15.87	631	7,559.42	11.98	545	6,744.22	12.37	458	6,767.53	14.78
Young adult	5,980	102,305.51	17.11	6,485	88,563.26	13.66	6,613	89,272.68	13.50	5,424	72,530.73	13.37
Totals	301,479	$6,910,463.55	$22.92	281,817	$7,701,675.12	$27.33	271,370	$6,898,791.44	$25.42	250,685	$5,276,681.92	$21.05

Part 5
Reference Information

Bibliographies

The Librarian's Bookshelf

Karen Muller

Librarian, American Library Association

Gita Serpuja, MHI Candidate, University of Michigan School of Information

Alyssa Hanson, MSI Candidate, University of Michigan School of Information

Most of the books on this selective bibliography have been published since 2013; a few earlier titles are retained because of their continuing importance. Many are also available as e-books, although that has not been noted.

General

ALA Glossary of Library and Information Science, 4th ed. By Michael Levine-Clark and Toni M. Carter. ALA Editions, 2013.

American Library Directory, 2016–2017. Information Today, Inc., 2016. 2v. Print and online.

Annual Review of Information Science and Technology (ARIST). Ed. by Blaise Cronin. Information Today, Inc., 2010–

Encyclopedia of Library and Information Science. 3rd ed. Ed. by Miriam A. Drake. CRC, 2009. Print and online.

Exploring Digital Libraries: Foundations, Practice, Prospects. By Karen Calhoun. Neal-Schuman, 2014.

Foundations of Library and Information Science. 4th ed. By Richard E. Rubin. Neal-Schuman, 2016.

Historical Dictionary of Librarianship. By Mary Ellen Quinn. Rowman & Littlefield, 2014.

Information Services Today: An Introduction. By Sandra Hirsh. Rowman & Littlefield, 2015.

Introduction to the Library and Information Professions. 2nd ed. By Roger C. Greer, Robert J. Grover, and Susan G. Fowler. Libraries Unlimited, 2013.

Library and Book Trade Almanac, 2016. Ed. by Catherine Barr. Information Today, Inc., 2016.

Library and Information Science: A Guide to Key Literature and Sources. By Michael F. Bemis. ALA Editions, 2014.

Library and Information Science Source. EBSCO Publishing. Online database.

Library Programs and Services: The Fundamentals. 8th ed. By G. Edward Evans [and others]. Libraries Unlimited, 2015.

Library World Records. 2nd ed. By Godfrey Oswald. McFarland, 2009.

Academic Libraries

The Academic Library Administrator's Field Guide. By Bryce Eugene Nelson. ALA Editions, 2014.

Digital Humanities in the Library: Challenges and Opportunities for Subject Specialists. By Arianne Hartsell-Gundy, Laura Braunstein, and Liorah Golomb. Association of College and Research Libraries, 2015.

Embedded Librarianship: What Every Academic Librarian Should Know. Ed. by Alice L. Daugherty and Michael F. Russo. Libraries Unlimited, 2013.

Library Assessment in Higher Education. By Joseph R. Matthews. Libraries Unlimited, 2015.

Twenty-First Century Access Services: On the Front Line of Academic Librarianship. Ed. by Michael J. and Trevor A. Dawes. Association of College and Research Libraries, 2013.

Administration

Assessing Service Quality: Satisfying the Expectations of Library Customers. By Peter Hernon, Ellen Altman, and Robert E. Dugan. ALA Editions, 2015.

Balancing the Books: Accounting for Librarians. By Rachel A. Kirk. Libraries Unlimited, 2013.

Building Blocks for Planning Functional Library Space. 3rd ed. By the Library Leadership and Management Association. Scarecrow Press, 2011.

Building Science 101: A Primer for Librarians. By Lynn M. Piotrowicz and Scott Osgood. American Library Association, 2010.

Checklist of Library Building Design Consideration. 6th ed. By William W. Sannwald. ALA Editions, 2016.

The Complete Library Trustee Handbook. By Sally Gardner Reed and Jillian Kolonick. Neal-Schuman, 2010.

Digital Literacy and Digital Inclusion: Information Policy and the Public Library. By Kim M. Thompson et al. Rowman & Littlefield, 2014.

Exploring Digital Libraries: Foundations, Practice, Prospects. By Karen Calhoun. Neal-Schuman, 2014.

Five Steps of Outcome-Based Planning and Evaluation for Public Libraries. By Melissa Gross, Cindy Mediavilla, and Virginia A. Walter. ALA Editions, 2016.

How to Thrive as a Solo Librarian. Ed. by Carol Smallwood and Melissa J. Clapp. Scarecrow, 2012.

Letting Go of Legacy Services: Library Case Studies. By Mary Evangeliste and Katherine Furlong. ALA Editions, 2014.

Library and Information Center Management. 8th ed. By Barbara B. Moran, Robert D. Stueart, and Claudia J. Morner. Libraries Unlimited, 2013.

Library Consortia: Models for Collaboration and Sustainability. By Valerie Horton and Greg Pronevitz. ALA Editions, 2015.

Moving Materials: Physical Delivery in Libraries. Ed. by Valerie Horton and Bruce Smith. American Library Association, 2010.

Neal-Schuman Library Technology Companion: A Basic Guide for Library Staff. 5th ed. By John J. Burke. Neal-Schuman, 2016.

Running A Small Library: A How-to-Do-It Manual for Librarians. 2nd ed. By John A. Moorman. Neal-Schuman, 2015.

Strategic Planning for Results. By Sandra Nelson. American Library Association, 2008.

Useful, Usable, Desirable: Applying User Experience Design to Your Library. By Aaron Schmidt and Amanda Etches. American Library Association, 2014.

What Every Library Director Should Know. By Susan Carol Curzon. Rowman & Littlefield, 2014.

Advocacy and Public Awareness

Activism and the School Librarian: Tools for Advocacy and Survival. Ed. by Deborah D. Levitov. Libraries Unlimited, 2012.

ALA Book of Library Grant Money. 9th ed. Ed. by Nancy Kalikow Maxwell. American Library Association, 2014.

Beyond Book Sales: The Complete Guide to Raising Real Money for Your Library. Ed. by Susan Dowd for Library Strategies, a Consulting Group of the Friends of the Saint Paul Public Library. Neal-Schuman, 2014.

A Book Sale How-to Guide: More Money, Less Stress. By Pat Ditzler and JoAnn Dumas. American Library Association. 2012.

Crash Course in Dealing with Difficult Library Customers. By Shelley Mosley, Dennis C. Tucker, and Sandra Van Winkle. Libraries Unlimited, 2014.

Creative Library Marketing and Publicity: Best Practices. By Robert J. Lackie and M. Sandra Wood. Rowman & Littlefield, 2015.

Face2Face: Using Facebook, Twitter, and Other Social Media Tools to Create Great Customer Connections. By David Lee King. Information Today, 2012.

Grassroots Library Advocacy. By Lauren Comito, Aliqae Geraci, and Christian Zabriskie. American Library Association, 2012.

Listening to the Customer. By Peter Hernon and Joseph R. Matthews. Libraries Unlimited, 2011.

Marketing and Social Media: A Guide for Libraries, Archives, and Museums. By Christie Koontz and Lorri M. Mon. Rowman & Littlefield, 2014.

Marketing Your Library: Tips and Tools That Work. Ed. by Carol Smallwood, Vera Gubnitskaia, and Kerol Harrod. McFarland, 2012.

Say It With Data: A Concise Guide to Making Your Case and Getting Results. By Priscille Dando. ALA Editions, 2014.

School Libraries Matter. Ed. by Mirah J. Dow. Libraries Unlimited, 2013.

Start a Revolution: Stop Acting Like a Library. By Benn Bizzle and Maria Flora. ALA Editions, 2015.

Archives and Special Collections

Archives Alive: Expanding Engagement with Public Library Archives and Special Collections. By Diantha Dow Schull, ALA Editions, 2015.

Archives: Principles and Practices. By Laura A. Millar, Neal-Schuman, 2010.

Digitization and Digital Archiving: A Practical Guide for Librarians. By Elizabeth R. Leggett. Rowman & Littlefield, 2014.

Health Sciences Librarianship. Ed. by M. Sandra Wood. Rowman & Littlefield, 2014.

Rare Books and Special Collections. By Sidney E. Berger. Neal-Schuman, 2014.

Starting, Strengthening, and Managing Institutional Repositories: A How-to-Do-It Manual. By Jonathan A. Nabe. Neal-Schuman, 2010.

Cataloging, Bibliographic Control, and Technical Services

The Complete Guide to Acquisitions Management. 2nd ed. By Frances C. Wilkinson, Linda K. Lewis, and Rebecca L. Lubas. Libraries Unlimited, 2015.

Electronics Resources Management in the Academic Library: A Professional Guide. By Karin Wikoff. Libraries Unlimited, 2012.

Fundamentals of Technical Services. By John Sandstrom and Liz Miller. ALA Editions, 2015.

Integrated Library Systems: Planning, Selecting, and Implementing. By Desiree Webber and Andrew Peters. Libraries Unlimited, 2010.

Introduction to Cataloging and Classification. 11th ed. By Daniel N. Joudrey, Arlene G. Taylor, and David P. Miller. Libraries Unlimited, 2015.

Introduction to Indexing and Abstracting. 4th ed. By Donald Cleveland and Ana Cleveland. Libraries Unlimited, 2013.

Introduction to Technical Services. 8th ed. By C. Edward Evans, Sheila S. Intner, and Jean Weihs. Libraries Unlimited, 2011.

Library Automation: Core Concepts and Practical Systems Analysis. 3rd ed. By Dania Bilal. Libraries Unlimited, 2014.

Metadata. 2nd ed. By Marcia Lei Zeng and Jian Qin. ALA Editions, 2016.

RDA and Serials Cataloging. By Ed Jones. ALA Editions, 2013.

RDA Essentials. By Thomas Brenndorfer. ALA Editions, 2016.

RDA Made Simple: A Practical Guide to the New Cataloging Rules. By Amy Hart. Libraries Unlimited, 2014.

RDA: Resource Description and Access Print. Joint Steering Committee for Development of RDA (JSC). American Library Association, 2011–. Looseleaf.

RDA Toolkit, Joint Steering Committee for Development of RDA (JSC). American Library Association. Online resource.

Collection Development

The Collection Program in Schools: Concepts and Practice. 6th ed. By Marcia A. Mardis and Kay Bishop. Libraries Unlimited, 2016.

Developing and Managing Electronic Collections: The Essentials. By Peggy Johnson. ALA Editions, 2013.

Floating Collections: A Collection Development Model for Long-Term Success. By Wendy K. Bartlett. Libraries Unlimited, 2014.

Fundamentals of Collection Development and Management. 3rd ed. By Peggy Johnson. American Library Association, 2014.

Getting Started with Demand-Driven Acquisitions for E-Books. By Theresa S. Arndt. ALATechsource, 2015.

Rethinking Collection Development and Management. By Becky Albitz, Christine Avery, and Diane Zabel. Libraries Unlimited, 2014.

Rightsizing the Academic Library Collection. By Suzanne M. Ward. Association of College and Research Libraries, 2015.

The Weeding Handbook: A Shelf-by-Shelf Guide. By Rebecca Vnuk. ALA Editions, 2015.

Human Resources and Leadership

Being Indispensable: A School Librarian's Guide to Becoming an Invaluable Leader. By Ruth Toor and Hilda K. Weisburg. American Library Association, 2011.

Communicating Professionally: A How-to-Do-It Manual for Librarians. By Catherine Sheldrick Ross and Kirsti Nilsen. Neal-Schuman, 2013.

Fundamentals of Library Supervision. By Joan Giesecke and Beth McNeil. American Library Association, 2010.

Handbook of Academic Writing for Librarians. Rev. ed. By Christopher Vance Hollister. Association of College and Research Libraries, 2014.

Implementing an Inclusive Staffing Model for Today's Reference Services: A Practical Guide for Librarians. By Julia K. Nims, Paula Storm, and Robert Stevens. Rowman & Littlefield, 2014.

Mentoring A to Z. By Julie Todaro. ALA Editions, 2015.

Staff Development: A Practical Guide. 4th ed. Ed. by Andrea Wigbels Stewart, Carlette Washington-Hoagland, and Carol T. Zsulya. ALA Editions, 2013.

Success with Library Volunteers. By Leslie Edmonds Holt and Glen E. Holt. Libraries Unlimited, 2014.

Intellectual Freedom, Copyright, and Other Legal Issues

Banned Books Resource Guide. American Library Association/Office of Intellectual Freedom, 2014.

Book Banning in 21st Century America. By Emily Knox. Rowman & Littlefield, 2015.

Books Under Fire: A Hit List of Banned and Challenged Children's Books. By Pat Scales. ALA Editions, 2015.

Complete Copyright for K–12 Librarians and Educators. By Carrie Russell. American Library Association, 2012.

The Copyright Book: A Practical Guide. 6th ed. By William S. Strong. MIT Press, 2014.

Copyright Law for Librarians and Educators: Creative Strategies and Practical Solutions. 3rd ed. By Kenneth D. Crews. American Library Association, 2012.

Guide to Ethics in Acquisitions. By Wyoma VanDuinkerken, Wendi Arant Kaspar, and Jeanne Harrell. Association for Library Collections and Technical Services, 2014.

A History of ALA Policy on Intellectual Freedom: A Supplement to The Intellectual Freedom Manual, 9th ed. By Trina J. Magi and Martin Garnar. ALA Editions, 2015.

Intellectual Freedom for Teens: A Practical Guide for Young Adult and School Librarians. By Kristin Fletcher-Speak and Kelly Tyler. ALA Editions, 2014.

Intellectual Freedom Manual. 9th ed. By Trina J. Magi, Martin Garnar, and the Office for Intellectual Freedom. ALA Editions, 2015.

Intellectual Property for Nonprofit Organizations and Associations. By Jefferson C. Glassie, Eileen Morgan Johnson, and Dana O. Lynch. ASAE Association Management Press, 2012.

The Librarian's Legal Companion for Licensing Information Resources and Services. By Tomas A. Lipinski. Neal-Schuman, 2013.

Library Ethics. By Jean L. Preer. Libraries Unlimited, 2008.

Owning and Using Scholarship: An IP Handbook for Teachers and Researchers. By Kevin L. Smith. Association of College and Research Libraries, 2014.

Privacy and Confidentiality Issues: A Guide for Libraries and Their Lawyers. By Theresa Chmara. American Library Association, 2009.

Outreach, Programming, and Services

Assistive Technologies in the Library. By Barbara T. Mates; with contrib. by William R. Reed, IV. American Library Association, 2011.

Blueprint for a Job Center at Your Library. By Bernice Kao and Megan Pittsley-Fox. Libraries Unlimited, 2014.

Community Library Programs that Work: Building Youth and Family Literacy. By Beth Maddigan and Susan Bloos. Libraries Unlimited, 2014.

Crash Course in Gaming. By Suellen S. Adams. Libraries Unlimited, 2014.

El Día de los niños/El día de los libros: Building a Culture of Literacy in Your Community Through Día. By Jeanette Larson. American Library Association, 2011.

Dragons in the Stacks: A Teen Librarian's Guide to Tabletop Role-Playing. By Steven A. Torres-Roman and Cason E. Snow. Libraries Unlimited, 2015.

How to Launch an Author Awards Program at Your Library: Curating Self-Published Books, Reaching Out to the Community. By Julianne Stam and Elizabeth Clemmons. Libraries Unlimited, 2016.

Libraries and the Affordable Care Act: Helping the Community Understand Health-Care Options. By Francisca Goldsmith. ALA Editions, 2015.

Library Services for Adults in the 21st Century. By Elsie A. Rogers Halliday Okobi. Libraries Unlimited, 2014.

Library Services for Multicultural Patrons: Strategies to Encourage Library Use. Ed. by Carol Smallwood and Kim Becnel. Scarecrow, 2013.

Literacy: A Way Out for At-Risk Youth. By Jennifer Sweeney. Libraries Unlimited, 2012.

The Prison Library Primer: A Program for the Twenty-first Century. By Brenda Vogel. Scarecrow Press, 2009.

School Library Makerspaces: Grades 6–12. By Leslie Preddy. Libraries Unlimited, 2012.

Serving Grandfamilies in Libraries: A Handbook and Programming Guide. By Sarah Gough, Pat Feehan, and Denise R. Lyons. Scarecrow, 2014.

Small Business and the Public Library: Strategies for a Successful Partnership. By Luise Weiss, Sophia Serlis-McPhillips, and Elizabeth Malafi. American Library Association, 2011.

Streamlined Library Programming: How to Improve Services and Cut Costs. By Daisy Porter-Reynolds. Libraries Unlimited, 2014.

Technology and Literacy: 21st Century Library Programming for Children and Teens. By Jennifer Nelson and Keith Braafladt. American Library Association, 2012.

Preservation, Disaster Response, and Security

Disaster Response and Planning for Libraries. 3rd ed. By Miriam B. Kahn. American Library Association, 2012.

Emergency Preparedness and Disaster Recovery in School Libraries: Creating a Safe Haven. By Christie Kaaland and William M. Lokey. Libraries Unlimited, 2015.

Library Security: Better Communication, Safer Facilities. By Steve Albrecht. ALA Editions, 2015.

Personal Archiving: Preserving Our Digital Heritage. Ed. by Donald T. Hawkins. Information Today, 2013.

Practical Digital Preservation: A How-to Guide for Organizations of Any Size. By Adrian Brown. Neal-Schuman, 2013.

The Preservation Management Handbook: A 21st-Century Guide for Libraries, Archives, and Museums. Ed. by D. R. Harvey; Martha R. Mahard. Rowman & Littlefield, 2014.

Preserving Our Heritage: Perspectives from Antiquity to the Digital Age. By Michele Valerie Cloonan. Neal-Schuman, 2015.

Public Libraries

IFLA Public Library Service Guidelines. Ed. by Christie Koontz and Barbara Gubbin. De Gruyter Saur, 2010.

Libraries and the Reading Public in Twentieth-Century America. By Christine Pawley and Louise S. Robbins. University of Wisconsin Press, 2013.

Part of Our Lives: A People's History of the American Public Library. By Wayne A. Wiegand. Oxford University Press, 2015.

Public Libraries and Resilient Cities. Ed. by Michael Dudley. American Library Association, 2013.

Public Libraries in the 21st Century. By Ann E. Prentice. Libraries Unlimited, 2011.

The Public Library Policy Writer: A Guidebook with Model Policies on CD-ROM. By Jeanette C. Larson and Herman L. Totten. Neal-Schuman, 2008.

Small Public Library Management. By Jane Pearlmutter and Paul Nelson. American Library Association, 2012.

When Books Went to War: The Stories that Helped Us Win World War II. Molly Guptill Manning. Houghton Mifflin Harcourt, 2014.

Readers Advisory

Children's Literature in Action: A Librarian's Guide. 2nd ed. By Sylvia M. Vardell. Libraries Unlimited, 2014.

Coretta Scott King Award Books Discussion Guide: Pathways to Democracy. By Adelaide Poniatowski Phelps and Carole J. McCollough. ALA Editions, 2014.

The Coretta Scott King Awards, 1970–2014. ALA Editions, 2015.

Diversity in Youth Literature: Opening Doors Through Reading. By Jamie Campbell Naidoo and Sarah Park Dahlen. American Library Association, 2013.

The Mother of All Booklists: The 500 Most Recommended Nonfiction Reads for Ages 3 to 103. By William P. Martin. Rowman & Littlefield, 2015.

The Newbery and Caldecott Awards 2015: A Guide to the Medal and Honor Books. Association for Library Service to Children/ American Library Association, 2015.

Outstanding Books for the College Bound: Titles and Programs for a New Generation. Ed. by Angela Carstensen. American Library Association, 2011.

Pura Belpré Awards: Celebrating Latino Authors and Illustrators. By Rose Zertuche Trevino. ALA Editions, 2006.

Sex in the Library: A Guide to Sexual Content in Teen Literature. By Mary Jo Heller and Aarene Storms. VOYA Press, 2013.

The Slow Book Revolution: Creating a New Culture of Reading on College Campuses and Beyond. Ed. by Meagan Lacy. Libraries Unlimited, 2014.

Women's Fiction: A Guide to Popular Reading Interests . By Rebecca Vnuk and Nanette Donohue. Libraries Unlimited, 2013.

Reference and Information Literacy

Concise Guide to Information Literacy. By Scott Lanning. Libraries Unlimited, 2012.

Conducting the Reference Interview: A How-to-Do-It Manual for Librarians. 2nd ed. By Catherine Sheldrick Ross, Kristi Nilsen, and Marie L. Radford. Neal-Schuman, 2009.

How to Teach: A Practical Guide for Librarians. By Beverley E. Crane. Rowman & Littlefield, 2014.

Implementing Virtual Reference Services: A LITA Guide. Ed. by Beth C. Thomsett-Scott. ALA TechSource, 2013.

Interlibrary Loan Practices Handbook. 3rd ed. Ed. by Cherié L. Weible and Karen L. Janke. American Library Association, 2011.

Legal Reference for Librarians: How and Where to Find the Answers. By Paul D. Healey. ALA Editions, 2014.

Metaliteracy: Reinventing Information Literacy to Empower Learners. By Thomas P. Mackey and Trudi E. Jacobson. Neal-Schuman, 2014.

Modern Pathfinders: Creating Better Research Guides. By Jason Puckett. Association of College and Research Libraries, 2015.

The One-Shot Library Instruction Survival Guide. By Heidi E. Buchanan and Beth A. McDonough. ALA Editions, 2014.

Online Searching: A Guide to Finding Quality Information Efficiently and Effectively. By Karen Markey. Rowman & Littlefield, 2015.

Reference and Information Services: An Introduction. 4th ed. Ed. by Richard E. Bopp and Linda C. Smith. Libraries Unlimited, 2011.

Reference and Instructional Services for Information Literacy Skills in School Libraries. 3rd ed. By Scott Lanning. Libraries Unlimited, 2014.

Reference Sources and Services for Youth. By Meghan Harper. Neal-Shuman, 2011.

Web of Deceit: Misinformation and Manipulation in the Age of Social Media. Ed. by Anne P. Mintz. CyberAge Books, 2012.

Research and Statistics

Academic Library Trends and Statistics. Association of College and Research Libraries/American Library Association. Annual. Print and online.

The ALA–APA Salary Survey 2012: Librarian—Public and Academic. ALA–Allied Professional Association, American Library Association, 2012. Print and online.

ARL Annual Salary Survey. Association of Research Libraries. Annual. Print and online.

ARL Statistics. Association of Research Libraries. Annual. Print and online.

PLAmetrics: A PLDS Online Database. Public Library Association. Online database. http://www.plametrics.org/

Public Libraries in the United States Survey. Institute of Museum and Library Services. Annual. Online only. Free. https://www.imls.gov/research-evaluation/data-collection/public-libraries-united-states-survey

Research Methods in Information. 2nd ed. By Alison Jane Pickard and Susan Childs. Neal-Schuman, 2013.

School Libraries and Children's and Young Adult Services and Materials

Building a Core Print Collection for Preschoolers. By Alan R. Bailey. ALA Editions, 2014.

Diversity Programming for Digital Youth. By Jamie Campbell Naidoo. Libraries Unlimited, 2014.

Empowering Learners: Guidelines for School Library Programs. American Association of School Librarians, 2009.

Enhancing Teaching and Learning: A Leadership Guide for School Librarians. By Jean Donham. Neal-Schuman, 2013.

Evaluating Teen Services and Programs. By Sarah Flowers. Neal-Schuman, 2012.

The Handbook for Storytellers. By Judy Freeman and Caroline Feller Bauer. ALA Editions, 2015.

Independent School Libraries: Perspectives on Excellence. Ed. by Dorcas Hand. Libraries Unlimited, 2010.

Integrating Young Adult Literature Through the Common Core Standards. By Rachel L. Wadham and Jonathan W. Ostenson. Libraries Unlimited, 2013.

Managing Children's Services in Libraries. 4th ed. By Adele M. Fasick and Leslie Edmonds Holt. Libraries Unlimited, 2013.

The Power of Play: Designing Early Learning Spaces. By Dorothy Stoltz, Marisa Conner, and James Bradberry. ALA Editions, 2015.

The School Library Manager. 5th ed. By Blanche Woolls, Ann C. Weeks, and Sharon Coatney. Libraries Unlimited, 2014.

Standards for the 21st-Century Learner. American Association of School Librarians, 2007.

Standards for the 21st-Century Learner in Action. American Association of School Librarians, 2009.

Teen Services 101: A Practical Guide for Busy Library Staff. By Megan Fink. YALSA, 2015.

21st Century Learning in School Libraries: Putting the AASL Standards to Work. Ed. by Kristin Fontichiaro. Libraries Unlimited, 2009.

Young Adult Literature in Action: A Librarian's Guide. 2nd ed. By Rosemary Chance. Libraries Unlimited, 2014.

Trends

BiblioTech: Why Libraries Matter More Than Ever in the Age of Google. By John G. Palfrey. Basic Books, 2015.

Ecology, Economy, Equity: The Path to a Carbon-Neutral Library. By Mandy Henk. ALA Editions, 2014.

Global Mobile: Applications and Innovations for the Worldwide Mobile Ecosystem. Ed. by Peter A. Bruck and Madanmohan Rao. Information Today, 2013.

Greening Libraries. Ed. by Monika Antonelli and Mark McCullough. Library Juice Press, 2012.

Growing Young Minds: How Museums and Libraries Create Lifelong Learners. 2013. Institute of Museum and Library Services, 2013. http://purl.fdlp.gov/GPO/gpo38726.

The Library Beyond the Book. By Jeffrey T. Schnapp and Matthew Battles. Harvard University Press, 2014.

The Library in the Life of the User: Engaging with People Where They Live and Learn. By Lynn Silipigni Connaway and OCLC Research. OCLC Research, 2015. Also online.

Library 2020: Today's Leading Visionaries Describe Tomorrow's Library. By Joseph Janes. Scarecrow, 2013.

Reflecting on the Future of Academic and Public Libraries. Ed. by Peter Hernon and Joseph R Matthews. ALA Editions, 2013.

Reinventing the Library for Online Education. By Frederick J. Stielow. ALA, 2014.

UContent: The Information Professional's Guide to User-Generated Content. By Nicholas G. Tomaiuolo. Information Today, 2012.

Periodicals

This listing of key library periodical publications includes ISSNs for print and online formats; in general, newsletters are not included. Titles have been verified against the EBSCO database as active periodicals.

Against the Grain (1043-2094)

American Archivist (print, 0360-9081; online, 2165-6274)

American Libraries (0002-9769)

American Libraries Direct (online, 1559-369X)

Ariadne (1361-3200)

Archival Science (print, 1389-0166; online, 1573-7519)

Art Documentation (print, 0730-7187; online, 2161-9417)

Behavioral and Social Sciences Librarian (print , 0163-9269; online, 1544-4546)

Booklist (0006-7385); *Booklist Online* (2163-5544)

Bottom Line: Managing Library Finances (print + online, 0888-045X; online, 2054-1724)

Cataloging and Classification Quarterly (print, 0163-9374; online, 1544-4554)

Catholic Library World (0008-820X)

Children and Libraries: The Journal of the Association for Library Service to Children (print + online, 1542-9806)

CHOICE: Current Reviews for Academic Libraries (print, 0009-4978; online, 1523-8253)

Code4Lib Journal (1940-5758)

Collaborative Librarianship (online, 1943-7528)

Collection Building (print + online, 0160-4953; online 2054-5592)

Collection Management (print, 0146-2679; online, 1545-2549)

College & Research Libraries (online, 2150-6701)

Computers in Libraries (1041-7915)

D-Lib Magazine (1082-9873)

DttP: A Quarterly Journal of Government Information Practice & Perspective (0091-2085)

Education for Information (0167-8329)

Electronic Library (print + online, 0264-0473; online, 1758-616X)

Electronic Journal of Knowledge Management (1479-4411)

First Monday (1396-0466)

Government Information Quarterly (0740-624X)

Horn Book Magazine (0018-5078)

IFLA Journal (print, 0340-0352; online, 1745-2651)

In the Library with the Lead Pipe (online, 1944-6195)

Indexer (print, 0019-4131; online 1756-0632)

Information & Culture (print + online, 2164-8034; online, 2166-3033)

Information Outlook (print + online, 1091-0808; online, 1938-3819)

Information Research—An International Electronic Journal (1368-1613)

Information Standards Quarterly (print + online, 1041-0031; online, 2161-6205)

Information Technology and Libraries (online, 2163-5226)

Interlending & Document Supply (print + online, 0264-1615; online 1758-5848)

International Journal of Geographical Information Science (print 1365-8816; online 1362-3087)

International Journal of Law and Information Technology (0967-0769)

Internet @ Schools (print 1546-4636; online 2156-843X)

Internet Reference Services Quarterly (print, 1087-5301; online, 1540-4749)

Issues in Science and Technology Librarianship (online, 1092-1206)

Journal of Academic Librarianship (0099-1333)

Journal of Documentation (print + online, 0022-0418; online, 1758-7379)

Journal of Education for Library and Information Science (0748-5786)

Journal of Electronic Resources Librarianship (print, 1941-126X; online, 1941-1278)

Journal of Information Ethics (print, 1061-9321; online, 1941-2894)

Journal of Information Science (print, 0165-5515; online, 1741-6485)

Journal of Interlibrary Loan, Document Delivery and Information Supply (print + online, 1072-303X)

Journal of Librarianship & Information Science (print, 0961-0006; online, 1741-6477)

Journal of Library Administration (print, 0193-0826; online, 1540-3564)

Journal of Library Metadata (print, 1938-6389; online, 1937-5034)

Journal of Research on Libraries and Young Adults (2157-3980)

Journal of the American Society for Information Science and Technology (print, 2330-1635; online, (2330-1643)

Journal of Archival Organization (print, 1533-2748; online, 1533-2756)

Journal of the Medical Library Association (print, 1536-5050; online, 1558-9439)

Journal of Web Librarianship (print, 1932-2909; online, 1932-2917)

Knowledge Quest (1094-9046)

Law Library Journal (0023-9283)

Legal Reference Services Quarterly (print, 0270-319X; online, 1540-949X)

Library & Archival Security (print, 0196-0075; online, 1540-9511)

Library & Information Science Research (LIBRES) (0740-8188)

Library Collections Acquisitions & Technical Services (print, 1464-9055; online, 1873-1821)

Library Hi-Tech Journal (0737-8831)

Library Journal (0363-0277)

Library Leadership & Management (online, 1945-886X)

Library Management (print + online, 0143-5124; online, 1758-7921)

The Library Quarterly (print, 0024-2519; online, 1549-652X)

Library Resources & Technical Services, eLRTS (online, 2159-9610)

Library Technology Reports (print, 0024-2586; online, 1945-4538)

Library Trends (print, 0024-2594; online, 1559-0682)

Library Worklife: HR E-News for Today's Leaders (1550-3534)

Librarysparks (1544-9092)

New Library World (print, 0307-4803; online, 1758-6909)

New Review of Children's Literature and Librarianship (print, 1361-4541; online, 1740-7885)

News from the Library of Congress (1046-1663)

Newsletter on Intellectual Freedom (online, 1945-4546)

Notes (Music Library Association) (print, 0027-4380; online, 1534-150X)

Online Searcher (2324-9684)

portal: Libraries and the Academy (print, 1531-2542; online, 1530-7131)

Preservation Digital Technology & Culture (print, 2195-2957; online, 2195-2965)

Public Libraries (0163-5506; some content online at http://publiclibrariesonline.org)

Public Library Quarterly (print, 0161-6846; online, 1541-1540)

Publishing Research Quarterly (print, 1053-8801; online, 1936-4792)

RBM: A Journal of Rare Books, Manuscripts, and Cultural Heritage (print 1529-6407; online 2150-668X)

Reference & User Services Quarterly (online, 1094-9054)

Reference Librarian (print, 0276-3877; online, 1541-1117)

Reference Services Review (print + online, 0090-7324; online, 2054-1716)

Research Libraries Issues (1947-4911)

School Library Journal (0362-8930)

School Library Research (2165-1019)

The Scout Report (Online, 1092-3861)

Serials Librarian (print, 0361-526X; online, 1541-1095)

Serials Review (print, 0098-7913; online, 1879-095X)

State of America's Libraries Report (annual, online only)

Technical Services Quarterly (print, 0731-7131; online, 1555-3337)

Technicalities (0272-0884)

Theological Librarianship (1937-8904)

Voice of Youth Advocates (*VOYA*) (0160-4201)

Young Adult Library Services (1541-4302)

Blogs

(All sites checked March 3, 2016)

025.431: The Dewey Blog. Jonathan Furner, editor (http://ddc.typepad.com)

AASL Blog (http://www.aasl.ala.org/aaslblog)

ACRL Insider (http://acrl.ala.org/acrlinsider)

ACRLog (http://acrlog.org)

American Libraries: The Scoop (http://americanlibrariesmagazine.org/blogs)

ALSC Blog (http://www.alsc.ala.org/blog)

Annoyed Librarian (http://lj.libraryjournal.com/blogs/annoyedlibrarian)

AOTUS: Collector in Chief. By David Ferriero (http://blogs.archives.gov/aotus)

Archivesblogs: A syndicated collection of blogs by and for archivists (http://archivesblogs.com/category/eng)

ASCLA Blog (http://ascla.ala.org/blog)

Attempting Elegance. By Jennica Rogers (http://www.attemptingelegance.com)

Awful Library Books. By Holly Hibner and Mary Kelly (http://awfullibrarybooks.net)

Bibliographic Wilderness (http://bibwild.wordpress.com)

Blogging Censorship (http://ncac.org/blog)

Blue Skunk. By Doug Johnson (http://dougjohnson.squarespace.com)

The Booklist Reader (http://www.booklistreader.com)

The Daring Librarian (http://www.thedaringlibrarian.com/)

Deeplinks. From Electronic Frontier Foundation (https://www.eff.org/deeplinks)

Designing Better Libraries: Exploring the Application of Design, Innovation, and New Media to Create Better Libraries and User Experiences (http://dbl.lishost.org/blog)

The Digital Shift (http://www.thedigitalshift.com)

Digitization 101. By Jill Hurst-Wahl (http://hurstassociates.blogspot.com)

District Dispatch. By the ALA Washington Office (http://www.districtdispatch.org)

Early Word. By Nora Rawlinson (http://www.earlyword.com)

5 Minute Librarian (http://www.5minlib.com/)

A Fuse #8 Production. By Elizabeth Bird (http://blog.schoollibraryjournal.com/afuse-8production)

Go to Hellman. By Eric Hellman (http://go-to-hellman.blogspot.com)

Hack Library School (http://hacklibraryschool.com)

Hangingtogether.org (http://hangingtogether.org)

Hey Jude. By Judy O'Connell (http://heyjude.wordpress.com)

The Hub: Your Connection to Teen Reads. By the Young Adult Library Services Association (http://www.yalsa.ala.org/thehub)

INFOdocket. By Gary Price and Shirl Kennedy (http://infodocket.com)

Information Wants to Be Free. By Meredith Farkas (http://meredith.wolfwater.com/wordpress)

The Krafty Librarian (http://kraftylibrarian.com)

Law Librarians of Congress (http://blogs.loc.gov/law)

Leads from LLAMA (http://www.llama.ala.org/llamaleads)

Librarian.net. By Jessamyn West (http://www.librarian.net)

LibrarianInBlack. By Sarah Houghton-Jan (http://librarianinblack.net/librarianinblack)

Library as Incubator Project. By Laura Damon-Moore, Erinn Batykefer, and Christina Endres (http://www.libraryasincubatorproject.org)

Library History Buff Blog. By Larry T. Nix (http://libraryhistorybuff.blogspot.com)

Library Juice. By Rory Litwin (http://libraryjuicepress.com/blog)

Library of Congress Blog (http://blogs.loc.gov/loc)

Librarycity (http://librarycity.org)

LibUX (http://libux.co/)

LIS News. By Blake Carver (http://lisnews.org)

LITA Blog (http://litablog.org)

The 'M' Word—Marketing in Libraries. By Kathy Dempsey (http://themwordblog.blogspot.com)

NeverEndingSearch. By Joyce Valenza (http://blogs.slj.com/neverendingsearch)

NMRT Notes (http://www.nmrt.ala.org/notes)

No Shelf Required. By Sue Polanka (http://www.libraries.wright.edu/noshelfrequired)

Office for Intellectual Freedom Blog (http://www.oif.ala.org/oif)

Pattern Recognition. By Jason Griffey (http://www.jasongriffey.net/wp)

Planet Cataloging (http://planetcataloging.org)

Programming Librarian (http://www.programminglibrarian.org/blogs)

RA for All (http://raforall.blogspot.com)

RDA Toolkit Blog (http://www.rdatoolkit.org/blog)

Reader's Advisor Online (http://www.readersadvisoronline.com/blog)

RIPS Law Librarian (http://ripslawlibrarian.wordpress.com)

RUSA Blog (http://rusa.ala.org/blog)

SarahGlassmeyer(dot)com (http://sarahglassmeyer.com)

The Signal: Digital Preservation (http://blogs.loc.gov/digitalpreservation)

Tame the Web: Libraries and Technology. By Michael Stephens (http://tametheweb.com)

Teen Librarian Toolbox. By Karen Jensen, Stephanie Wilkes, Christie Ross Gibrich, and Heather Booth (http://www.teenlibrariantoolbox.com)

Techsoup for libraries (http://www.techsoupforlibraries.org/blog)

TechSource Blog. By Jason Griffey, Tom Peters, Kate Sheehan, Michael Stephens, Cindi Trainor, Michelle Boule, and Richard Wallis (http://www.alatechsource.org/blog)

TeleRead: News and views on e-books, libraries, publishing and related topics (http://www.teleread.com)

The Unquiet Librarian (http://theunquietlibrarian.wordpress.com)

Walt at Random. By Walt Crawford (http://walt.lishost.org)

YALSA Blog (http://yalsa.ala.org/blog)

Ready Reference

How to Obtain an ISBN

Beat Barblan

United States ISBN/SAN Agency

The International Standard Book Numbering (ISBN) system was introduced into the United Kingdom by J. Whitaker & Sons Ltd. in 1967 and into the United States in 1968 by R. R. Bowker. The Technical Committee on Documentation of the International Organization for Standardization (ISO TC 46) is responsible for the international standard.

The purpose of this standard is to "establish the specifications for the International Standard Book Number (ISBN) as a unique international identification system for each product form or edition of a monographic publication published or produced by a specific publisher." The standard specifies the construction of an ISBN, the rules for assignment and use of an ISBN, and all metadata associated with the allocation of an ISBN.

Types of monographic publications to which an ISBN may be assigned include printed books and pamphlets (in various product formats); electronic publications (either on the Internet or on physical carriers such as CD-ROMs or diskettes); educational/instructional films, videos, and transparencies; educational/instructional software; audiobooks on cassette or CD or DVD; braille publications; and microform publications.

Serial publications, printed music, and musical sound recordings are excluded from the ISBN standard as they are covered by other identification systems.

The ISBN is used by publishers, distributors, wholesalers, bookstores, and libraries, among others, in 217 countries and territories as an ordering and inventory system. It expedites the collection of data on new and forthcoming editions of monographic publications for print and electronic directories used by the book trade. Its use also facilitates rights management and the monitoring of sales data for the publishing industry.

The "new" ISBN consists of 13 digits. As of January 1, 2007, a revision to the ISBN standard was implemented in an effort to substantially increase the numbering capacity. The 10-digit ISBN identifier (ISBN-10) is now replaced by the ISBN 13-digit identifier (ISBN-13). All facets of book publishing are now expected to use the ISBN-13, and the ISBN agencies throughout the world are now issuing only ISBN-13s to publishers. Publishers with existing ISBN-10s need to convert their ISBNs to ISBN-13s by the addition of the EAN prefix 978 and recalculation of the new check digit:

ISBN-10: 0-8352-8235-X
ISBN-13: 978-0-8352-8235-2

When the inventory of the ISBN-10s has been exhausted, the ISBN agencies will start assigning ISBN-13s with the "979" prefix instead of the "978." There is no 10-digit equivalent for 979 ISBNs.

Construction of an ISBN

An ISBN currently consists of 13 digits separated into the following parts:

1 A prefix of "978" for an ISBN-10 converted to an ISBN-13
2 Group or country identifier, which identifies a national or geographic grouping of publishers
3 Publisher identifier, which identifies a particular publisher within a group
4 Title identifier, which identifies a particular title or edition of a title
5 Check digit, the single digit at the end of the ISBN that validates the ISBN-13

For more information regarding ISBN-13 conversion services provided by the U.S. ISBN Agency at R. R. Bowker, LLC, visit the ISBN Agency Web site at http://www.isbn.org, or contact the U.S. ISBN Agency at isbn-san@bowker.com.

Publishers requiring their ISBNs to be converted from the ISBN-10 to ISBN-13 format can use the U.S. ISBN Agency's free ISBN-13 online converter at http://isbn.org/converterpub.asp. Publishers can also view their ISBNs online by accessing their personal account at http://www.myidentifiers.com.

Displaying the ISBN on a Product or Publication

When an ISBN is written or printed, it should be preceded by the letters ISBN, and each part should be separated by a space or hyphen. In the United States, the hyphen is used for separation, as in the following example: ISBN 978-0-8352-8235-2. In this example, 978 is the prefix that precedes the ISBN-13, 0 is the group identifier, 8352 is the publisher identifier, 8235 is the title identifier, and 2 is the check digit. The group of English-speaking countries, which includes the United States, Australia, Canada, New Zealand, and the United Kingdom, uses the group identifiers 0 and 1.

The ISBN Organization

The administration of the ISBN system is carried out at three levels—through the International ISBN Agency in the United Kingdom, through the national agencies, and through the publishing houses themselves. The International ISBN Agency, which is responsible for assigning country prefixes and for coordinating the worldwide implementation of the system, has an advisory panel that represents the International Organization for Standardization (ISO), publishers, and libraries. The International ISBN Agency publishes the *Publishers International ISBN Directory,* which is a listing of all national agencies' publishers with their assigned ISBN publisher prefixes. R. R. Bowker, as the publisher of *Books In Print* with its extensive and varied database of publishers' addresses, was the obvious place to initiate the ISBN system and to provide the service to the U.S. publishing industry. To date, the U.S. ISBN Agency has entered more than 180,000 publishers into the system.

ISBN Assignment Procedure

Assignment of ISBNs is a shared endeavor between the U.S. ISBN Agency and the publisher. Publishers can apply online through the ISBN Agency's website www.myidentifiers.com. Once the order is processed, an e-mail confirmation will be sent with instructions for managing the account. The publisher then has the responsibility to assign an ISBN to each title, keep an accurate record of each number assigned, and register each title in the *Books In Print* database at www.myidentifiers.com. It is the responsibility of the ISBN Agency to validate assigned ISBNs and keep a record of all ISBN publisher prefixes in circulation.

ISBN implementation is very much market-driven. Major distributors, wholesalers, retailers, and so forth recognize the necessity of the ISBN system and request that publishers register with the ISBN Agency. Also, the ISBN is a mandatory bibliographic element in the International Standard Bibliographical Description (ISBD). The Library of Congress Cataloging in Publication (CIP) Division directs publishers to the agency to obtain their ISBN prefixes.

Location and Display of the ISBN

On books, pamphlets, and other printed material, the ISBN shall be printed on the verso of the title leaf or, if this is not possible, at the foot of the title leaf itself. It should also appear on the outside back cover or on the back of the jacket if the book has one (the lower right-hand corner is recommended). The ISBN shall also appear on any accompanying promotional materials following the provisions for location according to the format of the material.

On other monographic publications, the ISBN shall appear on the title or credit frames and any labels permanently affixed to the publication. If the publication is issued in a container that is an integral part of the publication, the ISBN shall be displayed on the label. If it is not possible to place the ISBN on the item or its label, then the number should be displayed on the bottom or the back of the container, box, sleeve, or frame. It should also appear on any accompanying material, including each component of a multi-type publication.

Printing of ISBN in Machine-Readable Coding

All books should carry ISBNs in the EAN-13 bar code machine-readable format. All ISBN EAN-13 bar codes start with the EAN prefix 978 for books. As of January 1, 2007, all EAN bar codes should have the ISBN-13 appearing immediately above the bar code in eye-readable format, preceded by the acronym "ISBN." The recommended location of the EAN-13 bar code for books is in the lower right-hand corner of the back cover (see Figure 1).

Figure 1 / Printing the ISBN in Bookland/EAN Symbology

Five-Digit Add-On Code

In the United States, a five-digit add-on code is used for additional information. In the publishing industry, this code is used for price information. The lead digit of the five-digit add-on has been designated a currency identifier, when the add-on is used for price. Number 5 is the code for the U.S. dollar, 6 denotes the Canadian dollar, 1 the British pound, 3 the Australian dollar, and 4 the New Zealand dollar. Publishers that do not want to indicate price in the add-on should print the code 90000 (see Figure 2).

Figure 2 / Printing the ISBN Bookland/EAN Number in Bar Code with the Five-Digit Add-On Code

978 = ISBN Bookland/EAN prefix   90000 means no information
5 = Code for U.S. $ in the add-on code
2499 = $24.99

Reporting the Title and the ISBN

After the publisher reports a title to the ISBN Agency, the number is validated and the title is listed in the many R. R. Bowker hard-copy and electronic publications, including *Books in Print; Forthcoming Books; Paperbound Books in Print; Books in Print Supplement; Books Out of Print; Books in Print Online; Books in Print Plus-CD ROM; Children's Books in Print; Subject Guide to Children's Books in Print; Books Out Loud: Bowker's Guide to AudioBooks; Bowker's Complete Video Directory; Software Encyclopedia; Software for Schools;* and other specialized publications.

For an ISBN application and information, visit the ISBN Agency website at www.myidentifiers.com, call the toll-free number 877-310-7333, fax 908-795-3515, or write to the United States ISBN Agency, 630 Central Ave., New Providence, NJ 07974.

The ISSN, and How to Obtain One

U.S. ISSN Center
Library of Congress

In the early 1970s the rapid increase in the production and dissemination of information and an intensified desire to exchange information about serials in computerized form among different systems and organizations made it increasingly clear that a means to identify serial publications at an international level was needed. The International Standard Serial Number (ISSN) was developed and became the internationally accepted code for identifying serial publications.

The ISSN is an international standard, ISO 3297: 2007, as well as a U.S. standard, ANSI/NISO Z39.9. The 2007 edition of ISO 3297 expands the scope of the ISSN to cover continuing resources (serials, as well as updating databases, looseleafs, and some websites).

The number itself has no significance other than as a brief, unique, and unambiguous identifier. The ISSN consists of eight digits in Arabic numerals 0 to 9, except for the last ("check") digit, which can be an X. The numbers appear as two groups of four digits separated by a hyphen and preceded by the letters ISSN—for example, ISSN 1234-5679.

The ISSN is not self-assigned by publishers. Administration of the ISSN is coordinated through the ISSN Network, an intergovernmental organization within the UNESCO/UNISIST program. The ISSN Network consists of national ISSN centers, coordinated by the ISSN International Centre, located in Paris. National ISSN Centers are responsible for registering serials published in their respective countries. Responsibility for the assignment of ISSN to titles from multinational publishers is allocated among the ISSN Centers in which the publisher has offices. A list of these publishers and the corresponding ISSN centers is located on the ISSN International Centre's website, http://www.issn.org.

The ISSN International Centre handles ISSN assignments for international organizations and for countries that do not have a national center. It also maintains and distributes the ISSN Register and makes it available in a variety of products, most commonly via the ISSN Portal, an online subscription database. The ISSN Register is also available via Z39.50 access, and as a data file. Selected ISSN data can also be obtained in customized files or database extracts that can be used, for example, to check the accuracy or completeness of a requestor's list of titles and ISSN. Another available ISSN service is OAI-PMH, a customizable "harvesting" protocol through which external applications can automatically and regularly gather new and updated metadata on a defined schedule. The ISSN Register contains bibliographic records corresponding to each ISSN assignment as reported by national ISSN centers. The database contains records for more than 1.7 million ISSNs.

The ISSN is used all over the world by serials publishers to identify their serials and to distinguish their titles from others that are the same or similar. It is used by subscription services and libraries to manage files for orders, claims, and back issues. It is used in automated check-in systems by libraries that wish to process receipts more quickly. Copyright centers use the ISSN as a means to collect and disseminate royalties. It is also used as an identification code by postal services and legal deposit services. The ISSN is included as a verification element in interlibrary lending activities and for union catalogs as a collocating device. In recent years, the ISSN has been incorporated into bar codes for optical recognition of serial publications and into the standards for the identification of issues and articles in serial publications. Other growing uses for the ISSN are in online systems where it can serve to connect catalog records or citations in abstracting and indexing databases with full-text journal content via OpenURL resolvers or reference linking services, and as an identifier and link in archives of electronic and print serials.

Because serials are generally known and cited by title, assignment of the ISSN is inseparably linked to the key title, a standardized form of the title derived from information in the serial issue. Only one ISSN can be assigned to a title in a particular medium. For titles issued in multiple media—e.g., print, online, CD-ROM—a separate ISSN is assigned to each medium version. If a major title change occurs or the medium changes, a new ISSN must be assigned. Centers responsible for assigning ISSNs also construct the key title and create an associated bibliographic record.

A significant new feature of the 2007 ISSN standard is the Linking ISSN (ISSN-L), a mechanism that enables collocation or linking among different media versions of a continuing resource. The Linking ISSN allows a unique designation (one of the existing ISSNs) to be applied to all media versions of a continuing resource while retaining the separate ISSN that pertains to each version. When an ISSN is functioning as a Linking ISSN, the eight digits of the base ISSN are prefixed with the designation "ISSN-L." The Linking ISSN facilitates search, retrieval, and delivery across all medium versions of a serial or other continuing resource for improved ISSN functionality in OpenURL linking, search engines, library catalogs, and knowledge bases. The 2007 standard also supports interoperability by specifying the use of ISSN and ISSN-L with other systems such as DOI, OpenURL, URN, and EAN bar codes. ISSN-L was implemented in the ISSN Register in 2008. To help ISSN users implement the ISSN-L in their databases, two free tables are available from the ISSN International Centre's home page: one lists each ISSN and its corresponding ISSN-L; the other lists each ISSN-L and its corresponding ISSNs.

In the United States, the U.S. ISSN Center at the Library of Congress is responsible for assigning and maintaining the ISSNs for all U.S. serial titles. Publishers wishing to have an ISSN assigned should download an application from the Center's website, and mail, e-mail, or fax the form to the U.S. ISSN Center. Assignment of the ISSN is free, and there is no charge for use of the ISSN.

To obtain an ISSN for a U.S. publication, or for more information about ISSN in the United States, libraries, publishers, and other ISSN users should visit the U.S. ISSN Center's website, http://www.loc.gov/issn, or contact the U.S. ISSN Center, U.S. Programs, Law, and Literature, Library of Congress, 101 Independence Ave. S.E., Washington, DC 20540-4284 (telephone 202-707-6452, fax 202-707-6333, e-mail issn@loc.gov).

For information about ISSN products and services, and for application procedures that non-U.S. parties should use to apply for an ISSN, visit the ISSN International Centre's website, http://www.issn.org, or contact the International Centre at 45 rue de Turbigo, 75003 Paris, France (telephone 33-1-44-88-22-20, fax 33-1-40-26-32-43, e-mail issnic@issn.org).

How to Obtain an SAN

Beat Barblan

United States ISBN/SAN Agency

SAN stands for Standard Address Number. The SAN system, an American National Standards Institute (ANSI) standard, assigns a unique identification number that is used to positively identify specific addresses of organizations in order to facilitate buying and selling transactions within the industry. It is recognized as the identification code for electronic communication within the industry.

For purposes of this standard, the book industry includes book publishers, book wholesalers, book distributors, book retailers, college bookstores, libraries, library binders, and serial vendors. Schools, school systems, technical institutes, and colleges and universities are not members of this industry, but are served by it and therefore included in the SAN system.

The purpose of the SAN is to ease communications among these organizations, of which there are several hundreds of thousands that engage in a large volume of separate transactions with one another. These transactions include purchases of books by book dealers, wholesalers, schools, colleges, and libraries from publishers and wholesalers; payments for all such purchases; and other communications between participants. The objective of this standard is to establish an identification code system by assigning each address within the industry a unique code to be used for positive identification for all book and serial buying and selling transactions.

Many organizations have similar names and multiple addresses, making identification of the correct contact point difficult and subject to error. In many cases, the physical movement of materials takes place between addresses that differ from the addresses to be used for the financial transactions. In such instances, there is ample opportunity for confusion and errors. Without identification by SAN, a complex record-keeping system would have to be instituted to avoid introducing errors. In addition, problems with the current numbering system—such as errors in billing, shipping, payments, and returns—are significantly reduced by using the SAN system. The SAN also eliminates one step in the order fulfillment process: the "look-up procedure" used to assign account numbers. Previously a store or library dealing with 50 different publishers was assigned a different account number by each of the suppliers. The SAN solved this problem. If a publisher prints its SAN on its stationery and ordering documents, vendors to whom it sends transactions do not have to look up the account number, but can proceed immediately to process orders by SAN.

Libraries are involved in many of the same transactions as book dealers, such as ordering and paying for books and charging and paying for various services to other libraries. Keeping records of transactions—whether these involve buying, selling, lending, or donations—entails operations suited to SAN use. SAN stationery speeds up order fulfillment and eliminate errors in shipping, billing, and crediting; this, in turn, means savings in both time and money.

History

Development of the Standard Address Number began in 1968 when Russell Reynolds, general manager of the National Association of College Stores (NACS), approached R. R. Bowker and suggested that a "Standard Account Number" system be implemented in the book industry. The first draft of a standard was prepared by an American National Standards Institute (ANSI) Committee Z39 subcommittee, which was co-chaired by Reynolds and Emery Koltay of Bowker. After Z39 members proposed changes, the current version of the standard was approved by NACS on December 17, 1979.

Format

The SAN consists of six digits plus a seventh *Modulus 11* check digit; a hyphen follows the third digit (XXX-XXXX) to facilitate transcription. The hyphen is to be used in print form, but need not be entered or retained in computer systems. Printed on documents, the Standard Address Number should be preceded by the identifier "SAN" to avoid confusion with other numerical codes (SAN XXXXXXX).

Check Digit Calculation

The check digit is based on *Modulus 11,* and can be derived as follows:

1. Write the digits of the basic number.   2 3 4 5 6 7
2. Write the constant weighting factors associated with each position by the basic number.   7 6 5 4 3 2
3. Multiply each digit by its associated weighting factor.   14 18 20 20 18 14
4. Add the products of the multiplications. $14 + 18 + 20 + 20 + 18 + 14 = 104$
5. Divide the sum by Modulus 11 to find the remainder. $104 \div 11 = 9$ plus a remainder of 5
6. Subtract the remainder from the Modulus 11 to generate the required check digit. If there is no remainder, generate a check digit of zero. If the check digit is 10, generate a check digit of X to represent 10, since the use of 10 would require an extra digit. $11 - 5 = 6$
7. Append the check digit to create the standard seven-digit Standard Address Number.   SAN 234-5676

SAN Assignment

R. R. Bowker accepted responsibility for being the central administrative agency for SAN, and in that capacity assigns SANs to identify uniquely the addresses of organizations. No SANs can be reassigned; in the event that an organization should cease to exist, for example, its SAN would cease to be in circulation entirely. If an organization using an SAN should move or change its name with no change in ownership, its SAN would remain the same, and only the name or address would be updated to reflect the change.

The SAN should be used in all transactions; it is recommended that the SAN be imprinted on stationery, letterheads, order and invoice forms, checks, and all other documents used in executing various book transactions. The SAN should always be printed on a separate line above the name and address of the organization, preferably in the upper left-hand corner of the stationery to avoid confusion with other numerical codes pertaining to the organization, such as telephone number, zip code, and the like.

SAN Functions

The SAN is strictly a Standard Address Number, becoming functional only in applications determined by the user; these may include activities such as purchasing, billing, shipping, receiving, paying, crediting, and refunding. It is the method used by Pubnet and PubEasy systems and is required in all electronic data interchange communications using the Book Industry Systems Advisory Committee (BISAC) EDI formats. Every department that has an independent function within an organization could have a SAN for its own identification.

For additional information or to make suggestions, write to ISBN/SAN Agency, R. R. Bowker, LLC, 630 Central Ave., New Providence, NJ 07974, call 877-310-7333, or fax 908-795-3515. The e-mail address is san@bowker.com. A SAN can be ordered online through the website www.myidentifiers.com, or an application can be requested by e-mail through san@bowker.com.

Distinguished Books

Notable Books of 2015

The Notable Books Council of the Reference and User Services Association, a division of the American Library Association, selected these titles for their significant contribution to the expansion of knowledge or for the pleasure they can provide to adult readers.

Fiction

Black River: A Novel by S.M. Hulse. Houghton Mifflin Harcourt.

The Book of Aron: A Novel by Jim Shepard. Alfred A. Knopf, a division of Random House.

Delicious Foods: A Novel by James Hannaham. Little, Brown and Company, Hachette Book Group.

Did You Ever Have a Family: A Novel by Bill Clegg. Scout Press, an imprint of Simon & Schuster.

Fortune Smiles: Stories by Adam Johnson. Random House, a division of Penguin Random House.

In the Country: Stories by Mia Alvar. Alfred A. Knopf, a division of Random House.

A Little Life: A Novel by Hanya Yanagihara. Doubleday, a division of Random House.

The Prophets of Eternal Fjord: A Novel by Kim Leine, translated by Martin Aitken. Liveright Publishing Corporation, a division of W.W. Norton.

The Sellout: A Novel by Paul Beatty. Farrar, Straus and Giroux.

The Sympathizer: A Novel by Viet Thanh Nguyen. Grove Press.

This Is the Life: A Novel by Alex Shearer. Washington Square Press, a division of Simon & Schuster.

The Tsar of Love and Techno: Stories by Anthony Marra. Hogarth, an imprint of Crown Publishing Group.

Nonfiction

The Interstellar Age: Inside the Forty-Year Voyager Mission by Jim Bell. Dutton, and imprint of Penguin Group.

Give Us the Ballot: The Modern Struggle for Voting Rights in America by Ali Berman. Farrar, Straus and Giroux.

The End of Plenty: The Race to Feed a Crowded World by Joel K. Bourne Jr. WW. Norton and Company.

Between the World and Me by Ta-Nehisi Coates. Spiegel & Grau, an imprint of Random House.

The Gay Revolution: The Story of the Struggle by Lillian Faderman. Simon & Schuster.

Romantic Outlaws: The Extraordinary Lives of Mary Wollstonecraft and Her Daughter, Mary Shelley by Charlotte Gordon. Random House, a division of Penguin Random House.

Dead Wake: The Last Crossing of the Lusitania by Erik Larson Crown Publishing Group, a division of Random House.

The Wright Brothers by David McCullough. Simon & Schuster.

The Soul of an Octopus: A Surprising Exploration into the Wonder of Consciousness by Sy Montgomery. Atria Books, Simon & Schuster.

M Train by Patti Smith. Alfred A. Knopf, a division of Random House.

Nagasaki: Life After Nuclear War by Susan Southard. Viking, an imprint of Penguin Random House.

Stalin's Daughter: The Extraordinary and Tumultuous Life of Svetlana Alliluyeva by Rosemary Sullivan. HarperCollins.

Poetry

Bastards of the Reagan Era by Reginald Dwayne Betts. Four Way Books.

Conflict Resolution for Holy Beings: Poems by Joy Harjo. W.W. Norton.

Best Fiction for Young Adults

Each year a committee of the Young Adult Library Services Association (YALSA), a division of the American Library Association, compiles a list of the best fiction appropriate for young adults ages 12 to 18. Selected on the basis of each book's proven or potential appeal and value to young adults, the titles span a variety of subjects as well as a broad range of reading levels. An asterisk denotes the title was selected as a top ten.

Ahdieh, Renée. *The Wrath and The Dawn*. Putnam. 2015. 416p. ISBN: 9780399171611.

*Albertalli, Becky. *Simon vs. the Homo Sapiens Agenda*. Harper/Balzer and Bray. 2015. 320p. ISBN: 9780062348678.

Almond, David. *A Song for Ella Grey*. Delacorte. 2015. 272p. ISBN: 9780553533590.

*Bardugo, Leigh. *Six of Crows*. Holt. 2015. 480p. ISBN: 9781627792127.

Black, Holly. *The Darkest Part of the Forest*. Little, Brown. 2015. 336p. ISBN: 9780316213073.

*Brooks, Kevin. *The Bunker Diary*. Lerner/Carolrhoda Lab. 2015. 264p. ISBN: 9781467754200.

Cameron, Sharon. *Rook*. Scholastic. 2015. 464p. ISBN: 9780545675994.

Carson, Rae. *Walk On Earth a Stranger*. Greenwillow. 2015. 448p. ISBN: 9780062242914.

*Crowder, Melanie. *Audacity*. Philomel. 2015. 400p. ISBN: 9780399168994.

Crowe, Chris. *Death Coming up the Hill*. HMH. 2014. 208p. ISBN: 9780544302159.

Demetrios, Heather. *I'll Meet You There*. Holt. 2015. 400p. ISBN: 9780805097955.

Dessen, Sarah. *Saint Anything*. Viking. 2015. 432p. ISBN: 9780451474704Donnelly, Jennifer. *These Shallow Graves*. Delacorte. 2015. 496p. ISBN: 9780385737654.

Fowley-Doyle, Moïra. *The Accident Season*. Penguin/Kathy Dawson. 2015. 304p. ISBN: 9780525429487.

Frank, E.R. *Dime*. Atheneum. 2015. 336p. ISBN: 9781481431606.

Gilbert, Kelly Loy. *Conviction*. Disney/Hyperion. 2015. 352p. ISBN: 9781423197386

Graudin, Ryan. *Wolf by Wolf*. Little, Brown. 2015. 400p. ISBN: 9780316405126.

The Great War: Stories Inspired by Objects from the First World War. Ill. by Jim Kay. Candlewick. 2015. 304p. ISBN: 9780763675547.

Hand, Cynthia. *The Last Time We Say Goodbye*. HarperTeen. 2015. 400p. ISBN: 9780062318473.

Hautman, Pete. *Eden West*. Candlewick. 2015. 320p. ISBN: 9780763674182.

Hellisen, Cat. *Beastkeeper*. Holt. 2015. 208p. ISBN: 9780805099805.

Heppermann, Christine. *Poisoned Apples: Poems for You, My Pretty*. Greenwillow. 2014. 128p. ISBN: 9780062289575.

Hunt, Leo. *13 Days of Midnight*. Candlewick. 2015. 336p. ISBN: 9780763678654.

Jensen, Cordelia. *Skyscraping*. Philomel. 2015. 352p. ISBN: 9780399167713.

Juby, Susan. *The Truth Commission*. Illustrated by Trevor Cooper. Viking. 2015. 320p. ISBN: 9780451468772.

Kaufman, Amie and Kristoff, Jay. *Illuminae: The Illuminae Files_01*. Knopf. 2015. 608p. ISBN: 9780553499117.

Battlestar Gallactica, part zombie story, and part 2001: A Space Odyssey.

Kern, Peggy. *Little Peach*. Harper/Balzer and Bray. 2015. 208p. ISBN: 978006266958

Konigsberg, Bill. *The Porcupine of Truth*. Scholastic/Arthur A. Levine. 2015. 336p. ISBN: 9780545648936.

Kornher-Stace, Nicole. *Archivist Wasp*. Big Mouth. 2015. 256p. ISBN: 9781618730978

Larbalestier, Justine. *Razorhurst*. Soho Teen. 2015. 320p. ISBN: 9781616955441.

Leavitt, Martine. *Calvin*. Farrar. 2015. 192p. ISBN: 9780374380731.

Lee, Stacey. *Under a Painted Sky*. Putnam. 2015. 384p. ISBN: 9780399168031.

Maas, Sarah J. *A Court of Thorns and Roses*. Bloomsbury. 2015. 432p. ISBN: 9781619634442.

Mackler, Carolyn. *Infinite in Between*. HarperTeen. 2015. 480p. ISBN: 9780061731075

McLemore, Anna-Marie. *The Weight of Feathers*. St. Martin's/Thomas Dunne. 2015. 320p. ISBN: 9781250058652.

Murphy, Julie. *Dumplin'*. Harper/Balzer and Bray. 2015. 384p. ISBN: 9780062327185

Ness, Patrick. *The Rest of Us Just Live Here*. HarperTeen. 2015. 336p. ISBN: 9780062403162.

Niven, Jennifer. *All the Bright Places*. Knopf. 2015. 400p. ISBN: 9780385755887.

Oakes, Stephanie. *The Sacred Lies of Minnow Bly*. Dial. 2015. 400p. ISBN: 9780803740709.

*Older, Daniel José. *Shadowshaper*. Scholastic/Arthur A. Levine Books. 2015. 304p. ISBN: 9780545591614.

Pérez, Ashley Hope. *Out of Darkness*. Lerner/Carolrhoda Lab. 2015. 408p. ISBN: 9781467742023.

Quintero, Sofia. *Show and Prove*. Knopf. 2015. 352p. ISBN: 9780375847073

Rabb, Margo. *Kissing in America*. HarperCollins. 2015. 400p. ISBN: 9780062322371.

Reid, Raziel. *When Everything Feels Like the Movies*. Perseus/Arsenal Pulp. 2015. 176p. ISBN: 9781551525747.

*Reynolds, Jason. *The Boy in the Black Suit*. Atheneum. 2015. 272p. ISBN: 9781442459502.

Ritter, William. *Beastly Bones: A Jackaby Novel*. Algonquin. 2015. 304p. ISBN: 9781616203542.

Rowell, Rainbow. *Carry On*. St. Martin's Griffin. 2015. 528p. ISBN: 9781250049551.

Rubin, Lance. *Denton Little's Deathdate*. Knopf. 2015. 352p. ISBN: 9780553496963.

*Ruby, Laura. *Bone Gap*. Harper/Balzer and Bray. 2015. 368p. ISBN: 9780062317605.

Schlitz, Laura. *The Hired Girl*. Candlewick. 400p. ISBN: 9780763678180.

*Shabazz, Ilyasah and Kekla Magoon. *X: A Novel*. Candlewick. 2015. 384p. ISBN: 9780763669676.

*Shusterman, Neal. *Challenger Deep*. HarperTeen. 2015. 320p. ISBN: 9780061134111.

*Silvera, Adam. *More Happy than Not*. Soho Teen. 2015. 304p. ISBN: 9781616955601.

Smith, Andrew. *The Alex Crow*. Dutton. 2015. 336p. ISBN: 9780525426530.

Spalding, Amy. *Kissing Ted Callahan (and Other Guys)*. Poppy. 2015. 320p. ISBN: 9780316371520.

Stead, Rebecca. *Goodbye Stranger*. Random/Wendy Lamb. 2015. 304p. ISBN: 9780385743174.

Suma, Nova Ren. *The Walls Around Us*. Algonquin. 2015. 336p. ISBN: 9781616203726.

Summers, Courtney. *All the Rage*. St. Martin's Griffin. 2015. 336p. ISBN: 9781250021915.

Tahir, Sabaa. *An Ember in the Ashes*. Razorbill. 2015. 464 p. ISBN: 978-1-595-14803-2.

Toten, Teresa. *The Unlikely Hero of Room 13B*. Delacorte. 2015. 304p. ISBN: 9780553507867.

Wagner, Laura Rose. *Hold Tight, Don't Let Go: A Novel of Haiti*. Abrams. 2015. 272p. ISBN: 9781419712043.

Wiviott, Meg. *Paper Hearts*. Simon & Schuster/Margaret K. McElderry Books. 2015. 352p. ISBN: 9781481439831.

Wynne-Jones, Tim. *The Emperor of Any Place*. Candlewick. 2015. 336p. ISBN: 9780763669737.

Yoon, Nicola. *Everything, Everything*. Delacorte. 2015. 320p. ISBN: 9780553496642.

Quick Picks for Reluctant Young Adult Readers

The Young Adult Library Services Association, a division of the American Library Association, annually chooses a list of outstanding titles that will stimulate the interest of reluctant teen readers. This list is intended to attract teens who, for whatever reason, choose not to read.

The list includes fiction and nonfiction titles published from late 2014 through 2015. An asterisk denotes the title was selected as a top ten.

Nonfiction

Benson, Richard. *F in Exams: Pop Quiz: All New Awesomely Wrong Test Answers.* 2015. Illus. Chronicle Books, $9.95. 9781452144030.

Chapman, Ryan. *Conversation Sparks: Trivia Worth Talking About.* Illus. 2015. Chronicle, $12.95. 9781452140025.

Clements, Frida. *Have a Little Pun: An Illustrated Play on Words.* Illus. 2015. Chronicle, $14.95. 9781452144160.

Ebrahim, Zak. *The Terrorist's Son: A Story of Choice.* 2014. Illus. TED/Simon & Schuster, $16.99. 9781476784809.

Gerry, Lisa M. *Puppy Love: True Stories of Doggy Devotion.* 2015. Illus. National Geographic Society Children's Books/ National Geographic Society, $12.99. 9781426318672.

Graham, Ali. *99 Problems: Superstars Have Bad Days Too.* 2015. Workman Publishing Company, $9.95. 9780761182153.

Heppermann, Christine. *Poisoned Apples: Poems for You, My Pretty.* 2014. Illus. Greenwillow/HarperCollins Children's, $17.99. 9780062289575.

Howell, Dan and Lester, Phil. *The Amazing Book Is Not on Fire: The World of Dan and Phil.* 2015. Illus. Random House Books for Young Readers, $18.99. 9781101939840.

Knapp, Andrew. *Find Momo Coast to Coast: My Dog Is Taking a Road Trip. Can You Find Him?* 2015. Illus. Quirk Books, $14.95. 9781594747625.

Light, Austin. *Movie Title Typos: Making Movies Better by Subtracting One Letter.* 2015. Illus. Chronicle Books, $14.95. 9781452149561.

*Maggs, Sam. The *Fangirl's Guide to the Galaxy: A Handbooks for Girl Geeks.* 2015. Illus. Quirk Books, $15.95. 9781594747892.

Miller, Shauna. *Penny Chic: How to Be Stylish on a Real Girl's Budget.* 2014. Little, Brown & Co/Hachette, $16.99.

Munroe, Randall. *What If?: Serious Scientific Answers to Absurd Hypothetical Questions.* 2014. Houghton Mifflin Harcourt, $20.00. 9780544272996.

National Geographic Society. *Weird But True Food: 300 Bite-Size Facts about Incredible Edibles.* 2015. National Geographic Society Children's Books, $7.99. 9781426318719.

Riordan, Rick. *Percy Jackson's Greek Heroes.* Illus. 2015. Disney Press, $24.99. 9781423183655.

Rissman, Rebecca. *Yoga for Your Mind & Body: A Teenage Practice for a Healthy, Balanced Life.* 2015. Switch Press/Capstone, $14.95. 9781630790134.

*Schatz, Kate. *Rad American Women A-Z: Rebels, Trailblazers, and Visionaries Who Shaped Our History . . . and Our Future!* 2015. Illus. City Lights Books, $14.95. 9780872866836.

Shecter, Vicky Alvear. *Hades Speaks!: A Guide to the Underworld by the Greek God of the Dead.* Illus. 2014. Boyds Mills Press/Highlights, $16.95. 9781620915981.

Shepherd, Jack. *67 Reasons Why Cats Are Better Than Dogs.* 2014. National Geographic Society, $12.99. 9781426213861.

Sobie, Brian. *MMA Now!: The Stars and Stories of Mixed Martial Arts.* 2014. Firefly Books, $19.95. 9781770852914.

Stones, Greg. *Ninjas Have Issues.* 2015. Chronicle Books, $9.95. 9781452144740.

Wicks, Maris. *Human Body Theater.* Illus. 2015. First: Second/Macmillan, $19.99. 9781626722774.

Fiction

Alender, Katie. *The Dead Girls of Hysteria Hall*. 2015. Point/Scholastic, $18.99. 9780545639996.

*Aveyard, Victoria. *Red Queen*. 2015. HarperTeen/HarperCollins, $17.99. 9780062310637.

Black, Holly. *The Darkest Part of the Forest*. 2015. Little, Brown Books for Young Readers/Hachette, $18.00. 9780316213073.

*Black, Holly and Clare, Cassandra. *The Iron Trial*. 2014. Illus. Scholastic Press, $17.99. 9780545522250.

Bow, Erin. *The Scorpion Rules*. 2015. Margaret E. McElderry/Simon & Schuster, $17.99. 9781481442718.

Charbonneau, Joelle. *Need*. 2015. Houghton Mifflin Harcourt, $17.99. 9780544416697.

Chmakova, Svetlana. *Awkward*. 2015. Yen Press/Hachette, $11.00. 9780316381307.

Cloonan, Becky. *Gotham Academy 1: Welcome to Gotham Academy*. 2015. Illus. DC Comics, $14.99. 9781401254728.

de la Cruz, Melissa. *The Isle of the Lost*. 2015. Hyperion/Disney, $17.99. 9781484720974.

Ducie, Joe. *The Rig*. 2015. Houghton Mifflin Harcourt, $16.99. 9780544503113.

Easton, T.S. *Boys Don't Knit (In Public)*. 2015. Feiwel & Friends/Macmillan, $16.99. 9781250053312.

Gonzalez, Christina Diaz. *Moving Target*. 2015. Scholastic Press/Scholastic, $17.99. 9780545773188.

Gratz, Alan. *Code of Honor*. 2015. Scholastic Press/Scholastic, $17.99. 9780545695190.

Gurevich, Margaret. *Making the Cut*. 2014. Illus. Stone Arch Books/Capstone Young Readers, $14.95. 9781623701123.

Harmon, Michael. *Stick*. 2015. Alfred A. Knopf Books for Young Readers/Random House, $17.99. 9780385754361.

Helms, Rhonda. *Promposal*. 2015. Simon Pulse/Simon and Schuster, $17.99. 9781481422321.

Hiaasen, Carl. *Skink No Surrender*. 2014. Alfred A. Knopf Books for Young Readers/Random House, $18.99. 9780375870514.

Howard, J.J. *Tracers*. 2015. G.P. Putnam's & Sons Books for Young Readers/Penguin, $17.99. 9780399173738.

Jamieson, Victoria. *Roller Girl*. 2015. Illus. Dial Books/Penguin, $20.99. 9780525429678.

Knowles, Jo. *Read Between the Lines*. 2015. Candlewick Press, $16.99. 9780763663872.

Latham, Jennifer. *Scarlett Undercover*. 2015. Little, Brown and Company/Hachette, $18.00. 9780316283939.

Laybourne, Emmy. *Sweet*. 2015. Feiwel & Friends/Macmillan, $17.99. 9781250055194.

*Lee, Fonda. *Zeroboxer*. 2015. Flux/Llewellyn Worldwide, $11.99. 9780738743387.

Matharu, Taran. *The Novice*. 2015. Feiwel & Friends/Macmillan, $18.99. 9781250067128.

*Murphy, Julie. *Dumplin'*. 2015. Balzer & Bray/HarperCollins, $17.99. 9780062327185.

*Myers, E.C. *The Silence of Six*. 2014. Adaptive Studios, $17.99. 9780996066624.

O'Connor, George. *Ares: Bringer of War*. 2015. Illus. First Second/Macmillan, $9.99. 9781626720138.

*Older, Daniel José. *Shadowshaper*. 2015. Arthur A. Levine/Scholastic, $17.99. 9780545591614.

Painchaud, Michelle. *Pretending to Be Erica*. 2015. Viking Books for Young Readers/Penguin, $17.99. 9780670014972.

Priest, Cherie. *I Am Princess X*. 2015. Arthur A. Levine/Scholastic, $18.99. 9780545620857.

Riordan, Rick. *The Sword of Summer*. 2015. Disney Press, $19.99. 9781423160915.

Saeed, Aisha. *Written in the Stars*. 2015. Nancy Paulsen Books/Penguin, $17.99. 9780399171703.

Smale, Holly. *Geek Girl*. 2015. HarperTeen/HarperCollins, $17.99. 9780062333575.

Smith, Greg. *Junior Braves of the Apocalypse: A Brave Is Brave*. 2015. Illus. Oni Press, $19.99. 9781620101445.

*Stevenson, Noelle. *Nimona*. 2015. Illus. HarperTeen/HarperCollins, $17.99. 9780062278234.

Stohl, Margaret. *Black Widow: Forever Red*. 2015. Marvel Press/Disney, $17.99. 9781484726433.

Stratton, Allan. *The Dogs*. Source Books Fire/Source Books, $16.99. 9781492609384.

Toten, Teresa. *The Unlikely Hero of Room 13 B*. 2015. Delacorte/Random House, $17.99. 9780553507867.

Traver, N. K. *Duplicity*. 2015. Thomas Dunne Books/Macmillan, $18.99. 9781250059147.

Tucholke, April G. *Slasher Girls and Monster Boys.* 2015. Dial/Penguin, $17.99. 9780803741737.

Tynion, James. *The Woods 1: The Arrow.* 2014. Illus. Boom! Entertainment/Boom! Studios, $9.99. 9781608864546.

Vega, Danielle. *Survive The Night.* 2015. Razorbill/Penguin, $17.99. 9781595147240.

Watters, Shannon, Grace Ellis, Noelle Stevenson & Brooke Allen. *Lumberjanes Vol. 1.* 2015. Illus. Boom! Studios, $14.99. 9781608866878.

Wilson, G. Willow. *Ms. Marvel 3: Crushed.* Marvel Enterprises, $15.99. 9780785192275.

*Yoon, Nicola. *Everything, Everything.* Illus. 2015. Delacorte Press/Random House, $18.99. 9780553496642.

Series

Jokulsson, Illugi. *James Rodriguez.* 2015. Abbeville Press, $13.95. 9780789212375.

Jokulsson, Illugi. *Stars of World Soccer.* 2015. Abbeville Press, $13.95. 9780789212399.

Jokulsson, Illugi. *U.S. Women's Team: Soccer Champions!.* 2015. Abbeville Press, $13.95. 9780789212153.

Matsui, Yusei. *Assassination Classroom V. 1.* 2014. Illus. Viz Media, $9.99. 9781421576077.

Matsui, Yusei. *Assassination Classroom V. 2.* 2015. Illus. Viz Media, $9.99. 9781421576084.

Matsui, Yusei. *Assassination Classroom V. 3.* 2014. Illus. Viz Media, $9.99. 9781421576091.

Matsui, Yusei. *Assassination Classroom V. 4.* 2015. Illus. Viz Media, $9.99. 9781421576107.

Matsui, Yusei. *Assassination Classroom V. 5.* 2015. Illus. Viz Media, $9.99. 9781421576114.

Matsui, Yusei. *Assassination Classroom V. 6.* 2015. Illus. Viz Media, $9.99. 9781421576121.

Amazing Audiobooks for Young Adults

Each year a committee of the Young Adult Library Services Association, a division of the American Library Association, compiles a list of the best audiobooks for young adults ages 12 to 18. The titles are selected for their teen appeal and recording quality, and because they enhance the audience's appreciation of any written work on which the recordings may be based. While the list as a whole addresses the interests and needs of young adults, individual titles need not appeal to this entire age range but rather to parts of it. An asterisk denotes the title was selected as a top ten.

Nonfiction

Unbroken (The Young Adult Adaptation): An Olympian's Journey from Airman to Castaway to Captive by Laura Hillenbrand, read by Edward Herrmann. Listening Library, 2014. 8 hours, 8 minutes; 7 discs. 9780553397116.

*What If? Serious Scientific Answers to Absurd Hypothetical Questions by Randall Munroe, read by Wil Wheaton. Blackstone Audio, 2014. 6 hours, 36 minutes; digital. 9781483030180.

Fiction

100 Sideways Miles by Andrew Smith, read by Kirby Heyborne. Tantor Audio, 2015. 7 hours. 6 discs. 9781494514099.

All American Boys by Jason Reynolds, Brendan Kiely, read by Keith Nobbs, Guy Lockard. Simon and Schuster, 2015. 6 hours, 35 minutes. Digital. 9781442398672.

All the Bright Places by Jennifer Niven, read by Kirby Heyborne and Ariadne Meyers. Listening Library, 2015. 11 hours, 4 minutes. 9 discs. 9780553552195.

Carry On, by Rainbow Rowell, read by Euan Morton. Macmillan Audio, 2015. 13 hours, 37 minutes. 11 discs. 9781427262028.

Crown of Three by J.D. Rinehart, read by Kirby Heyborne. Simon and Schuster, 2015. 11 hours, 30 minutes. 9 discs. 9781442385962.

*The Dead House by Dawn Kurtagich, read by Charlotte Parry and Christian Coulson. Hachette Audio, 2015. 10 hours, 30 minutes. Digital. 9781478959830.

Denton Little's Deathdate by Lance Rubin, read by Lance Rubin. Listening Library, 8 hours, 36 minutes. 8 discs. 9780553556018.

*Echo by Pam Munoz Ryan, read Mark Bramhall, David De Vries, Macleod Andrews, and Rebecca Soler. Scholastic, 2014. 10 hours, 22 minutes. 9 discs. 9780545788373.

An Ember in the Ashes by Sabaa Tahir, read by Fiona Hardingham and Steve West. Listening Library, 2015. 15 hours, 22 minutes. 12 discs. 9781101890752.

*Gabi, a Girl in Pieces by Isabel Quintero, read by Kyla Garcia. Listening Library, 2015. 7 hours, 59 minutes. 7 discs. 9781101917039.

Golden Son by Pierce Brown, read by Tim Gerard Reynolds. Recorded Books, 2015. 19 hours. 16 discs. 9781464042126.

The Graveyard Book by Neil Gaiman, read by Neil Gaiman, Derek Jacobi, Robert Madge, Clare Corbett, Miriam Margolyes, Andrew Scott, Julian Rhind-Tutt, Emilia Fox, Reece Shearsmith, Lenny Henry, and an ensemble cast. Harper Audio, 2014. 8 hours, 24 minutes. 7 discs. 9780062364463.

Guy in Real Life by Steve Brezenoff, read by MacLeod Andrews and Arielle DeLisle. Harper Audio, 2014. 9 hours, 33 minutes; 8 discs. 9781483004518.

*Half Wild by Sally Green, read by Carl Prekopp. Listening Library, 2015. 9 hours, 30 minutes; 8 discs. 9781101891094.

The Hollow Boy by Jonathan Stroud, read by Emily Bevan. Listening Library, 2015. 11 hours, 54 minutes. 10 discs. 9781101917398.

*Illuminae: The Illuminae Files_01 by Amie Kaufman and Jay Kristoff, read by Olivia Taylor Dudley, Lincoln Hoppe, Jonathan

McClain. Listening Library, 2015. 11 hours, 41 minutes; 10 discs. 9781101916643.

Journey to Star Wars: The Force Awakens Moving Target: A Princess Leia Adventure by Cecil Castellucci and Jason Fry, read by January LaVoy. Listening Library, 2015. 3 hours 53 minutes, digital. 9780147521828.

Lair of Dreams by Libba Bray, read by January LaVoy. Listening Library, 2015. 20 hours, 13 minutes; 16 discs. 9780449808795.

Library of Souls by Ransom Riggs, read by Kirby Heyborne. Blackstone Audio, 2015. 14 hours, 54 minutes; digital. 9781504634328.

The Rest of Us Just Live Here by Patrick Ness, read by James Fouhey. Harper Audio, 2015. 6 hours, 18 minutes, digital. 9780062421715.

Simon vs. the Homo Sapiens Agenda by Becky Albertalli, read by Michael Crouch. Harper Audio, 2015. 6 hours, 45 minutes; digital download. 9780062411501.

Slasher Girls and Monster Boys by April Genevieve Tucholke, read by Macleod Andrews, Emma Bering, Robbie Daymond, Nora Hunter, Jorjeana Marie, and Julia Whelan. Listening Library, 2015. 13 hours, 13 minutes; 11 discs. 9781101917466.

Trollhunters by Guillermo del Toro and Daniel Kraus, read by Kirby Heyborne. Recorded Books, 2015. 10 hours, 15 minutes; 9 discs. 9781490694320.

Waistcoats & Weaponry by Gail Carriger, read by Moira Quick. Hachette Audio, 2015. 9 hours; digital. 9780316279611.

The Witch Hunter by Virginia Boecker, read by Nicola Barber. Hachette Audio, 2015. 10 hours, digital. 9780062421715.

The Reading List

Established in 2007 by the Reference and User Services Association (RUSA), a division of the American Library Association, this list highlights outstanding genre fiction that merits special attention by general adult readers and the librarians who work with them.

RUSA's Reading List Council, which consists of 12 librarians who are experts in readers' advisory and collection development, selects books in eight categories: Adrenaline (suspense, thrillers, and action adventure), Fantasy, Historical Fiction, Horror, Mystery, Romance, Science Fiction, and Women's Fiction.

Adrenaline

Pretty Girls: A Novel by Karin Slaughter. William Morrow, a division of HarperCollins.

Fantasy

Uprooted by Naomi Novik. Del Rey, an imprint of Ballantine Books.

Historical Fiction

Crooked Heart: A Novel by Lissa Evans. Harper.

Horror

The Fifth House of the Heart: A Novel by Ben Tripp. Gallery Books, an imprint of Simon and Schuster.

Mystery

The Long and Faraway Gone by Lou Berney. William Morrow, an imprint of HarperCollins.

Romance

Taking the Heat by Victoria Dahl. HQN, Harlequin Books.

Science Fiction

Golden Son by Pierce Brown. Del Rey, an imprint of HarperCollins.

Women's Fiction

Re Jane by Patricia Park. Pamela Dorman Books, an imprint of Penguin Books.

The Listen List

Established in 2010 by the Reference and User Services Association (RUSA), the Listen List highlights outstanding audiobooks that merit special attention by general adult listeners and the librarians who work with them.

They are chosen by RUSA's Listen List Council, which annually selects a list of 12 titles that may include fiction, nonfiction, poetry, and plays. To be eligible, titles must be available for purchase and circulation by libraries. An annotated version of the list on the RUSA website includes more information on each choice.

All Involved by Ryan Gattis. Narrated by Anthony Rey Perez, Marisol Ramirez, Jim Cooper, Adam Lazarre-White, and James Chen. HarperAudio.

All the Old Knives by Olen Steinhauer. Narrated by Ari Fliakos and Juliana Francis Kelly. Macmillan Audio.

And Only to Deceive by Tasha Alexander. Narrated by Kate Reading. Recorded Books/Tantor Media.

Dead Wake: The Last Crossing of the Lusitania by Erik Larson. Narrated by Scott Brick. Books on Tape/Random House Audio.

Dracula by Bram Stoker. Narrated by David Horovitch, Jamie Parker, Joseph Kloska, Alison Pettitt, and cast. Naxos AudioBooks.

H is for Hawk by Helen MacDonald. Narrated by Helen MacDonald. Blackstone Audio.

The Invasion of the Tearling by Erika Johansen. Narrated by Davina Porter. HarperAudio.

The Jaguar's Children by John Vaillant. Narrated by Ozzie Rodriguez and David H. Lawrence XVII. Books on Tape/Random House Audio

The Knockoff: A Novel by Lucy Sykes and Jo Piazza. Narrated by Katherine Kellgren. Books on Tape/Random House Audio.

The Strangler Vine by M.J. Carter. Narrated by Alex Wyndham. Recorded Books/HighBridge Audio.

'Til the Well Runs Dry by Lauren Francis-Sharma. Narrated by Ron Butler and Bahni Turpin. Recorded Books/Tantor Media.

True Story: Murder, Memoir, Mea Culpa by Michael Finkel. Narrated by Rich Orlow. HarperAudio.

Alex Awards

The Alex Awards are given to ten books written for adults that have special appeal to young adults ages 12 through 18. The winning titles are selected by a committee of the Young Adult Library Services Association (YALSA), a division of the American Library Association, from among the previous year's publishing. The award is sponsored by the Margaret A. Edwards Trust.

All Involved by Ryan Gattis, published by Ecco, an imprint of HarperCollins Publishers (ISBN: 9780062378798).

Between the World and Me by Ta-Nehisi Coates, published by Spiegel & Grau, an imprint of Random House, a division of Penguin Random House LLC (ISBN: 9780812993547).

Bones & All by Camille DeAngelis, published by St. Martin's Press (ISBN: 9781250046505).

Futuristic Violence and Fancy Suits by David Wong, published by Thomas Dunne Books, an imprint of St. Martin's Press (ISBN: 9781250040190).

Girl at War by Sara Novic, published by Random House, an imprint and division of Penguin Random House LLC (ISBN: 9780812996340).

Half the World by Joe Abercrombie, published by Del Rey, an imprint of Random House, a division of Random House LLC, a Penguin Random House Company (ISBN: 9780804178426).

Humans of New York: Stories by Brandon Stanton, published by St. Martin's Press (ISBN: 9781250058904).

Sacred Heart by Liz Suburbia, published by Fantagraphics Books Inc. (ISBN: 9781606998410).

Undocumented: A Dominican Boy's Odyssey from a Homeless Shelter to the Ivy League by Dan-el Padilla Peralta, published by Penguin Press, an imprint of Penguin Random House LLC (ISBN: 9781594206528).

The Unraveling of Mercy Louis by Keija Parssinen, published by Harper, an imprint of HarperCollins Publishers (ISBN: 9780062319098) .

Notable Children's Videos

These DVD titles are selected by a committee of the Association for Library Service to Children, a division of the American Library Association. Recommendations are based on originality, creativity, and suitability for children.

Bugs in My Hair! 8 min., Weston Woods, 1-800-243-5020. Ages 4–8.

I'm Brave, 8 min., Weston Woods. Ages 4–8.

Peanut Butter and Jellyfish, 7 min., Weston Woods.

Same, Same But Different, 8 min., Weston Woods. Ages 4–7.

Scaredy Squirrel at Night, 11 min., Weston Woods. Ages 4–8.

That Is NOT a Good Idea! 7 min., Weston Woods & Mo Willems. Ages 4–8.

The Toxic Life Cycle of a Cigarette, 17 min., Human Relations Media, 1-800-431-2050. Grades 7–College.

Viva Frida, 11 min., Dreamscape, 1-877-983-7326. Ages 5–9.

Notable Recordings for Children

This list of notable CD recordings for children was selected by the Association for Library Service to Children, a division of the American Library Association. Recommended titles are chosen by children's librarians and educators on the basis of their originality, creativity, and suitability.

Appleblossom the Possum. Listening Library. 1-800-733-3000. Ages 6–10

The Boys in the Boat (Young Readers Adaptation): The True Story of an American Team's Epic Journey to Win Gold at the 1936 Olympics. Listening Library. Ages 12 and up

Bugs in My Hair. Weston Woods. 800-724-6527. Ages 3–8

Cartwheeling in Thunderstorms. Recorded Books. 877-732-2898. Ages 11–14

Echo. Scholastic Audio. 800-724-6527. Ages 10 and up

Goldilocks and the Three Dinosaurs. Weston Woods. Ages 3–8

Mo Willems narrates his own hilarious version of this familiar tale.

Hershel and the Hanukkah Goblins. Dreamscape. 877-983-7326. All Ages

The Hired Girl. Recorded Books. Ages 10–14

Infinity and Me. Live Oak Media. 800-788-1121. Ages 4–9

Ivan: The Remarkable True Story of the Shopping Mall Gorilla. Weston Woods. Ages 3–7

Jazz for Lil' Jumpers! Independent release. 781-254-8574. Ages 4–8

The Jumbies. Recorded Books. Ages 9–14

Jump Back, Paul: The Life and Poems of Paul Laurence Dunbar. Brilliance Audio. 800-648-2312. Ages 9–14

The Lightning Queen. Scholastic Audio. Ages 10–14

Most Dangerous: Daniel Ellsberg and the Secret History of the Vietnam War. Listening Library. Ages 12 and up

Ms. Rapscott's Girls. Listening Library. Ages 8–12

Nursery Rhyme Parade! Furious Rose Productions. www.lisaloeb.com. Ages 0–5

Nuts to You. Recorded Books. Ages 6–11

The Odds of Getting Even. Listening Library. Ages 9–12

Papa Is a Poet : A Story about Robert Frost. Weston Woods. Ages 5–10

Stella by Starlight. Simon & Schuster Audio. 212-698-7126. Ages 9–14

That Is NOT a Good Idea! Weston Woods. Ages 4–8

Trollhunters. Recorded Books. Ages 12–14

The War That Saved My Life. Listening Library. Ages 9–14

The Worst Class Trip Ever. Brilliance Audio. Ages 10–13

Notable Children's Books

A list of notable children's books is selected each year by the Notable Children's Books Committee of the Association for Library Service to Children, a division of the American Library Association. Recommended titles are selected by children's librarians and educators based on originality, creativity, and suitability for children. [See "Literary Prizes, 2015" later in Part 5 for Caldecott, Newbery, and other award winners—*Ed.*]

Younger Readers

An Ambush of Tigers: A Wild Gathering of Collective Nouns. By Betsy R. Rosenthal. Illus. by Jago. Lerner/Millbrook.

The Book Itch: Freedom, Truth, & Harlem's Greatest Bookstore. By Vaunda Micheaux Nelson. Illus. by R. Gregory Christie. Lerner/Carolrhoda.

Ballet Cat: The Totally Secret Secret. By Bob Shea. Illus. by the author. Disney/Hyperion.

Beep! Beep! Go to Sleep! By Todd Tarpley. Illus. by John Rocco. Little, Brown.

Boats for Papa. By Jessixa Bagley. Illus. by the author. Roaring Book/Neal Porter.

A Chicken Followed Me Home! Questions and Answers about a Familiar Fowl. By Robin Page. Illus. by the author. Simon & Schuster/Beach Lane.

Detective Gordon: The First Case. By Ulf Nilsson. Illus. by Gitte Spee. Tr. by Julia Marshall. Gecko.

Don't Throw It to Mo! By David A. Adler. Illus. by Sam Ricks. Penguin.

Drum Dream Girl: How One Girl's Courage Changed Music. By Margarita Engle. Illus. by Rafael López. HMH.

Emmanuel's Dream: The True Story of Emmanuel Ofosu Yeboah. By Laurie Ann Thompson. Illus. by Sean Qualls. Random/Schwartz & Wade.

Finding Winnie: The True Story of the World's Most Famous Bear. By Lindsay Mattick. Illus. by Sophie Blackall. Little, Brown.

Float. By Daniel Miyares. Illus. by the author. Simon & Schuster.

Flop to the Top! By Eleanor Davis and Drew Weing. Illus. by the authors. TOON.

Flutter & Hum / Aleteo y zumbido: Animal Poems / Poemas de animales. Ed. by Julie Paschkis. Illus. by the author. Holt.

Gingerbread for Liberty: How a German Baker Helped Win the American Revolution. By Mara Rockliff. Illus. by Vincent X. Kirsch. HMH.

Grandma Lives in a Perfume Village. By Fang Suzhen. Illus. by Sonja Danowski. Tr. by Huang Xiumin. NorthSouth.

The Grasshopper and the Ants. By Jerry Pinkney. Illus. by the author. Little, Brown.

Growing Up Pedro. By Matt Tavares. Illus. by the author. Candlewick.

Hippos Are Huge! By Jonathan London. Illus. by Matthew Trueman. Candlewick.

I Yam a Donkey! By Cece Bell. Illus. by the author. Clarion.

If You Plant a Seed. By Kadir Nelson. Illus. by the author. HarperCollins/Balzer + Bray.

Last Stop on Market Street. By Matt de la Peña. Illus. by Christian Robinson. Putnam.

Lenny & Lucy. By Philip C. Stead. Illus. by Erin E. Stead. Roaring Book/Neal Porter.

Leo: A Ghost Story. By Mac Barnett. Illus. by Christian Robinson. Chronicle.

Lillian's Right to Vote: A Celebration of the Voting Rights Act of 1965. By Jonah Winter. Illus. by Shane W. Evans. Random/Schwartz & Wade.

Mango, Abuela, and Me. By Meg Medina. Illus. by Angela Dominguez. Candlewick.

The Moon Is Going to Addy's House. By Ida Pearle. Illus. by the author. Penguin/Dial.

The Most Amazing Creature in the Sea. By Brenda Z. Guiberson. Illus. by Gennady Spirin. Holt.

Moving Blocks. By Yusuke Yonezu. Illus. by the author. Michael Neugebauer/Minedition.

Mr. Squirrel and the Moon. By Sebastian Meschenmoser. Illus. by the author. Tr. by David Henry Wilson. NorthSouth.

My Tata's Remedies = Los remedios de mi tata. By Roni Capin Rivera-Ashford. Illus. by Antonio Castro L. Cinco Puntos.

A Pig, a Fox, and a Box. By Jonathan Fenske. Illus. by the author. Penguin.

Piper Green and the Fairy Tree. By Ellen Potter. Illus. by Qin Leng. Knopf.

The Popcorn Astronauts: And Other Biteable Rhymes. By Deborah Ruddell. Illus. by Joan Rankin. Simon & Schuster/Margaret K. McElderry.

The Princess and the Pony. By Kate Beaton. Illus. by the author. Scholastic/Arthur A. Levine.

Raindrops Roll. By April Pulley Sayre. Illus. by the author. Simon & Schuster/Beach Lane.

Red. By Jan De Kinder. Illus. by the author. Tr. by Laura Watkinson. Eerdmans.

Roger Is Reading a Book. By Koen Van Biesen. Illus. by the author. Tr. by Laura Watkinson. Eerdmans.

Sidewalk Flowers. By JonArno Lawson. Illus. by Sydney Smith. Groundwood.

The Skunk. By Mac Barnett. Illus. by Patrick McDonnell. Roaring Brook.

Special Delivery. By Philip C. Stead. Illus. by Matthew Cordell. Roaring Brook/Neal Porter.

Supertruck. By Stephen Savage. Illus. by the author. Roaring Brook/Neal Porter.

Swan: The Life and Dance of Anna Pavlova. By Laurel Snyder. Illus. by Julie Morstad. Chronicle.

Tiptoe Tapirs. By Hanmin Kim. Illus. by the author. Tr. by Sera Lee. Holiday.

Trombone Shorty. By Troy Andrews. Illus. by Bryan Collier. Abrams.

Two Mice. By Sergio Ruzzier. Illus. by the author. Clarion.

Wait. By Antoinette Portis. Illus. by the author. Roaring Brook/Neal Porter.

Waiting. By Kevin Henkes. Illus. by the author. HarperCollins/Greenwillow.

Water Is Water: A Book about the Water Cycle. By Miranda Paul. Illus. by Jason Chin. Roaring Brook/Neal Porter.

Who Done It? By Olivier Tallec. Illus. by the author. Chronicle.

Wolfie the Bunny. By Ame Dyckman. Illus. by Zachariah OHora. Little, Brown.

The Wonderful Fluffy Little Squishy. By Beatrice Alemagna. Illus. by the author. Tr. by Claudia Zoe Bedrick. Enchanted Lion.

Woodpecker Wham! By April Pulley Sayre. Illus. by Steve Jenkins. Holt.

Written and Drawn by Henrietta. By Liniers. Illus. by the author. Tr. by the author. TOON.

Middle Readers

28 Days: Moments in Black History That Changed the World. By Charles R. Smith Jr. Illus. by Shane W. Evans. Roaring Brook/Neal Porter.

Adam and Thomas. By Aharon Appelfeld. Illus. by Philippe Dumas. Tr. by Jeffrey M. Green. Seven Stories/Triangle Square.

Adventures with Waffles. By Maria Parr. Illus. by Kate Forrester. Tr. by Guy Puzey. Candlewick.

Blackbird Fly. By Erin Entrada Kelly. HarperCollins/Greenwillow.

The Blackthorn Key. By Kevin Sands. Aladdin.

Echo. By Pam Muñoz Ryan. Scholastic.

Enormous Smallness: A Story of E. E. Cummings. By Matthew Burgess. Illus. by Kris Di Giacomo. Enchanted Lion.

Fish in a Tree. By Lynda Mullaly Hunt. Penguin/Nancy Paulsen.

Frederick's Journey: The Life of Frederick Douglass. By Doreen Rappaport. Illus. by London Ladd. Disney/Jump at the Sun.

Full Cicada Moon. By Marilyn Hilton. Penguin/Dial.

Funny Bones: Posada and His Day of the Dead Calaveras. By Duncan Tonatiuh. Illus. by the author. Abrams.

George. By Alex Gino. Scholastic.

Gone Crazy in Alabama. By Rita Williams-Garcia. HarperCollins/Amistad.

Hamster Princess: Harriet the Invincible. By Ursula Vernon. Illus. by the author. Penguin/Dial.

Lailah's Lunchbox: A Ramadan Story. By Reem Faruqi. Illus. by Lea Lyon. Tilbury.

Lost in the Sun. By Lisa Graff. Penguin/Philomel.

Mad about Monkeys. By Owen Davey. Illus. by the author. Flying Eye.

Mars Evacuees. By Sophia McDougall. HarperCollins.

The Marvels. By Brian Selznick. Illus. by the author. Scholastic.

Mesmerized: How Ben Franklin Solved a Mystery That Baffled All of France. By Mara

Rockliff. Illus. by Iacopo Bruno. Candlewick.

My Story, My Dance: Robert Battle's Journey to Alvin Ailey. By Lesa Cline-Ransome. Illus. by James E. Ransome. Simon & Schuster/Paula Wiseman.

My Two Blankets. By Irena Kobald. Illus. by Freya Blackwood. HMH.

Murder Is Bad Manners. By Robin Stevens. Simon & Schuster.

The Nest. By Kenneth Oppel. Illus. by Jon Klassen. Simon & Schuster.

Poet: The Remarkable Story of George Moses Horton. By Don Tate. Illus. by the author. Peachtree.

Red Butterfly. By A. L. Sonnichsen. Illus. by Amy June Bates. Simon & Schuster.

Roller Girl. By Victoria Jamieson. Illus. by the author. Penguin/Dial.

Sex Is a Funny Word: A Book about Bodies, Feelings, and YOU. By Cory Silverberg. Illus. by Fiona Smyth. Seven Stories/Triangle Square.

Stella by Starlight. By Sharon M. Draper. Atheneum.

Terrible Typhoid Mary: A True Story of the Deadliest Cook in America. By Susan Campbell Bartoletti. illus. HMH.

Tricky Vic: The Impossibly True Story of the Man Who Sold the Eiffel Tower. By Greg Pizzoli. Illus. by the author. Penguin/Viking.

Unusual Chickens for the Exceptional Poultry Farmer. By Kelly Jones. Illus. by Katie Kath. Knopf.

The War That Saved My Life. By Kimberly Brubaker Bradley. Penguin/Dial.

Older Readers

Baba Yaga's Assistant. By Marika McCoola. Illus. by Emily Carroll. Candlewick.

The Boys Who Challenged Hitler: Knud Pedersen and the Churchill Club. By Phillip Hoose. illus. Farrar.

Child Soldier: When Boys and Girls Are Used in War. By Jessica Dee Humphreys and Michel Chikwanine. Illus. by Claudia Dávila. Kids Can.

Cuckoo Song. By Frances Hardinge. Abrams/Amulet.

Drowned City: Hurricane Katrina and New Orleans. By Don Brown. Illus. by the author. HMH.

Enchanted Air: Two Cultures, Two Wings: A Memoir. By Margarita Engle. Atheneum.

First Flight around the World: The Adventures of the American Fliers Who Won the Race. By Tim Grove. illus. Abrams.

Goodbye Stranger. By Rebecca Stead. Random/Wendy Lamb.

The Hired Girl. By Laura Amy Schlitz. Candlewick.

The Lightning Queen. By Laura Resau. Scholastic.

Listen, Slowly. By Thanhhà Lai. HarperCollins.

Most Dangerous: Daniel Ellsberg and the Secret History of the Vietnam War. By Steve Sheinkin. illus. Roaring Brook.

My Seneca Village. By Marilyn Nelson. Namelos.

Orbiting Jupiter. By Gary D. Schmidt. Clarion.

Rhythm Ride: A Road Trip through the Motown Sound. By Andrea Davis Pinkney. illus. Roaring Brook.

The Seventh Most Important Thing. By Shelley Pearsall. Knopf.

The Smoking Mirror. By David Bowles. IFWG.

The Thing about Jellyfish. By Ali Benjamin. Little, Brown.

Turning 15 on the Road to Freedom: My Story of the 1965 Selma Voting Rights March. By Lynda Blackmon Lowery, as told to Elspeth Leacock and Susan Buckley. Illus. by P. J. Loughran. Penguin/Dial.

All Ages

Bird and Diz. By Gary Golio. Illus. by Ed Young. Candlewick.

Counting Lions. By Katie Cotton. Illus. by Stephen Walton. Candlewick.

Hiawatha and the Peacemaker. By Robbie Robertson. Illus. by David Shannon. Abrams.

Lost in NYC: A Subway Adventure. By Nadja Spiegelman. Illus. by Sergio García Sánchez. TOON Graphics.

My Pen. By Christopher Myers. Illus. by the author. Disney/Hyperion.

National Geographic Book of Nature Poetry: More Than 200 Poems with Photographs

That Float, Zoom, and Bloom! Ed. by J. Patrick Lewis. illus. National Geographic.

The Only Child. By Guojing. Illus. by the author. Random/Schwartz & Wade.

Pool. By JiHyeon Lee. Illus. by the author. Chronicle.

Sail Away. By Langston Hughes. Illus. by Ashley Bryan. Atheneum.

Voice of Freedom: Fannie Lou Hamer, Spirit of the Civil Rights Movement. By Carole Boston Weatherford. Illus. by Ekua Holmes. Candlewick.

The Year in Bestsellers: 2015

Daisy Maryles

Publishers Weekly

In 2015 an unusual event occurred in the world of bestsellers: a new category dominated the charts. For the first time, adult coloring books were the most successful players on the trade paperback lists. Four are among the longest-running bestsellers of the year, and 21 adult coloring books landed on the trade list in the course of 2015. The 21 coloring books spent a combined total of 175 weeks on the bestsellers lists; that accounts for 13.5 percent of the total positions on the trade paper bestseller lists for the year.

Adult coloring books are a long way from the subject matter of previous years' bestsellers—erotic romance was hot in 2012 thanks to the 50 Shades trilogy, the Duck Dynasty titles by members of the Robertson clan loudly quacked their way onto the charts in 2013, and movie tie-in sales in 2014 were big winners. The latter continued to do well in 2015. Three of the five longest-running mass market top sellers—*American Sniper*, *The Longest Ride*, and *The Martian*—were movie tie-ins, spending a total of 63 weeks on the charts. *American Sniper* and *The Martian* also made impressive showings on the 2015 trade paper longest-running chart. The movie tie-in editions of *Unbroken*, *Still Alice*, and *Wild* were also on that trade list, along with the regular editions of *Unbroken* and *The Martian*. That group added up to 238 weeks on the trade paper list. If any publisher can figure out how to do a movie tie-in adult coloring book, it would be a surefire winner.

Conglomerates Rock

The number of publishing conglomerates keeps shrinking, and that is a direct result of consolidation. While conglomerate clout on the bestseller charts continues to be powerful, the group keeps getting smaller. Three years ago, in 2013, we calculated the Bestsellers by Corporation chart for nine companies; in 2014 it was seven companies, and the latest chart only has five. It is also the first year that we combined the bestsellers from all the divisions and imprints of HarperCollins and Harlequin, and that had a significant boost on HC's paperback numbers. Adding the 2014 paperback totals for the two amounted to 126 titles and 549 weeks; the 2015 totals are 152 books and 543 weeks (the additional titles are due to the Harlequin acquisition).

In 2015 the Big Five owned 87.8 percent of all the hardcover bestseller positions available, and 80.1 percent in paperback. The group's leader, Penguin Random House, controlled 40.1 percent of the hardcover slots and 34.2 percent of paperbacks in 2015. It is unlikely that PRH will lose its first-place standing in the coming years. As separate publishers, Penguin and Random House were generally the top two players on these charts. As we point out each year, the bestsellers that make the weekly and annual charts represent less than 1 percent of total annual title output. And despite the conglomerates' dominance, there are 37 other hardcover publishers and 46 trade paperback houses that had titles on *PW's* weekly

Adapted from *Publishers Weekly*, January 8, 2016.

bestseller lists. However, most of the titles on the mass market lists belong to the Big Five. Only 41 of the 291 books that landed on the mass market list in 2015 were from publishers that were not part of the Big Five, and Kensington published 39 of those titles. The only two other publishers to crack the mass market list were Merriam-Webster with *The Merriam-Webster Official Scrabble Players Dictionary* and Sourcebooks with *I'll Stand by You* by Sharon Sala.

Tenure, Tenure, Tenure

The key to financial success is not just getting on the charts, but staying there. For example, Hachette had 61 hardcover bestsellers in 2015, much less than the 78 from HarperCollins—but Hachette's titles stayed on the lists for a combined total of 308 weeks, while HC had a total of 269. The result was a higher percentage of bestseller positions for Hachette. In another example, PRH had 150 paperback bestsellers in 2015, two books fewer than the HC total of 152, but PRH's titles racked up 889 weeks on the year's charts, compared to 543 for HC. That resulted in a 34.2 percent market share for PRH versus a 21 percent share for HC. An explanation of the significant difference is tenure. A total of 48 book titles in the HC group were on the weekly charts for only one or two weeks (mostly Harlequin romances). PRH had only 22 titles with one- or two-week runs. PRH also enjoyed nine of 21 titles that stayed on the charts for a double-digit number of weeks, and HC had only three.

Trade paperbacks tended to stay on the bestseller lists longer than mass market titles in 2015. Forty-one trade paperbacks stayed on the trade paperback lists for at least 10 weeks, and another 77 bestsellers had runs of five or more weeks, totaling 38 percent of the 240 on the list. There were still plenty of trade paperbacks that hit the lists for only a few weeks last year, with 93 books on the list for one week and another 34 for two weeks.

Multiple Hits

Veteran authors of fiction continue to be abundant on these annual charts, but there were some lucky debut writers. Debut holdovers from 2014 included Andy Weir's *The Martian* and Celeste Ng for *Everything I Never Told You*. Other debut novelists who arrived on the lists last year were David Duchovny with *Holy Cow* (FS&G), Stephanie Clifford with *Everybody Rise* (St. Martin's), and Garth Risk Hallberg with *City of Fire* (Knopf).

There were 20 authors that scored four or more mass market bestsellers during 2015. They included William W. Johnstone (18), Debbie Macomber (16), Nora Roberts/J.D. Robb (15), and James Patterson and his cowriters (11). Collectively books by those 20 writers occupied a total of 473 positions on the mass market charts, an impressive 36.4 percent of that list.

Eclectic is a good word to describe the assortment of nonfiction high rollers, including the leader of the pack, *The Life-Changing Magic of Tidying Up*, a book on decluttering and organizing—very important while New Year resolutions are still on the to-do list. Finance, health and fitness, and religion and spirituality continue to be strong nonfiction topics, as are books by Bill O'Reilly. Religion writers are again blessed on these charts, including Joel Osteen, Joyce Meyer, T.D. Jakes, Max Lucado, and Billy Graham. And with the 2016 elections looming and the presidential candidates causing a stir, there is no surprise to find many political books on the charts, including Ted Cruz's *A Time for Truth*, Ben Carson's *A More Perfect Union*, and Donald Trump's *Crippled America*.

Gold Goal Getters

It's hard to get to the top of the charts, and it's even harder to stay there. Only four of the 82 books that had double-digit runs on the 2015 weekly charts stayed at #1 for more than 10 weeks. In hardcover fiction, *The Girl on the Train* stayed at #1 for 14 weeks. In hardcover nonfiction, *The Life-Changing Magic of Tidying Up* was at the top of the charts for 12 weeks. And in trade paperback, the movie tie-in of *America Sniper* remained at #1 for 14 weeks, and *Grey* was there for 11 weeks. There were a total of 70 books with runs of one, two, or three weeks at #1. But even one week lets the author and publisher declare the book a chart topper.

Best Sellers of 2015 in Kindle eBooks

1. *The Girl on the Train: A Novel.* Paula Hawkins. (43,767).
2. *Grey: Fifty Shades of Grey as Told by* . . . . E. L. James. (12,960).
3. *All the Light We Cannot See: A Novel.* Anthony Doerr. (23,294).
4. *The Martian: A Novel.* Andy Weir. (27,677).
5. *The Nightingale.* Kristin Hannah. (23,911).
6. *Go Set a Watchman: A Novel.* Harper Lee. (10,592).
7. *Memory Man* (Amos Decker series). David Baldacci. (7,900).
8. *Big Little Lies.* Liane Moriarty. (11,620).
9. *American Sniper: The Autobiography of* . . . . Chris Kyle. (14,922).
10. *Rogue Lawyer.* John Grisham. (7,312).

Source: Amazon.

Nielsen BookScan Adult Fiction Top 20

1. *Go Set a Watchman.* Harper Lee (Harper). 1,599,189.
2. *Grey.* E. L. James (Vintage). 1,406,868.
3. *The Girl on the Train.* Paula Hawkins (Riverhead). 1,345,721.
4. *All the Light We Cannot See.* Anthony Doerr (Scribner). 1,013,616.
5. *The Martian* (trade paper). Andy Weir (Broadway). 673,041.
6. *Rogue Lawyer.* John Grisham (Doubleday). 576,362.
7. *To Kill a Mockingbird.* Harper Lee (Grand Central). 563,293.
8. *See Me.* Nicholas Sparks (Grand Central). 445,531.
9. *Gray Mountain.* John Grisham (Dell). 365,392.
10. *The Nightingale.* Kristin Hannah (St. Martin's). 331,384.

11. *The Bazaar of Bad Dreams.* Stephen King (Scribner). 322,298.
12. *The Girl in the Spider's Web.* David Lagercrantz (Knopf). 305,929.
13. *The Great Gatsby.* F. Scott Fitzgerald (Scribner). 296,641.
14. *The Alchemist.* Paulo Coelho (HarperOne). 285,264.
15. *Orphan Train.* Christina Baker Kline (Morrow). 280,379.
16. *Finders Keepers.* Stephen King (Scribner). 261,589.
17. *The Husband's Secret.* Liane Moriarty (Berkley). 253,512.
18. *Cross Justice.* James Patterson (Little, Brown). 250,996.
19. *Fahrenheit 451.* Ray Bradbury (Simon & Schuster). 247,900.
20. *The Martian* (mass market movie tie-in). Andy Weir (Broadway). 246,118.

Nielsen BookScan Adult Nonfiction Top 20

1. *The Life-Changing Magic of Tidying Up.* Marie Kondo (Ten Speed).1,143,422.
2. *Killing Reagan.* O'Reilly/Dugard (Holt). 851,980.
3. American Sniper (trade paperback movie tie-in). Chris Kyle (Morrow). 851,457.
4. *The Pioneer Woman Cooks: Dinnertime.* Ree Drummond (Morrow). 569,925.
5. *Jesus Calling.* Sarah Young (Thomas Nelson). 545,217.
6. *The Boys in the Boat.* Daniel James Brown (Penguin). 532,082.
7. *Strengths Finder 2.0.* Tom Rath (Gallup). 528,506.
8. *Lost Ocean.* Johanna Basford (Penguin). 492,684.
9. *The Wright Brothers.* David McCullough (Simon & Schuster). 443,801.
10. *American Sniper* (mass market movie tie-in). Chris Kyle (Harper). 354,536.
11. *The 5 Love Languages.* Gary Chapman (Northfield). 349,467.
12. *Guinness World Records.* Guinness World Records (Guinness World Records). 344,171.
13. *Unbroken.* Laura Hillenbrand (Random House). 341,446.
14. *Dead Wake.* Erik Larson (Crown). 333,989.
15. *Between the World and Me.* Ta-Nehisi Coates (Random/Spiegel & Grau). 319,352.
16. *Animal Kingdom.* Millie Marotta (Lark). 318,987.
17. *Being Mortal.* Atul Gawande (Metropolitan). 317,503.
18. *The 20/20 Diet.* Phil McGraw (Bird Street). 311,362.
19. *Creative Haven Creative Cats Coloring Book.* Marjorie Sarnat (Dover). 300,507.
20. *Mindset.* Carol Dweck (Ballantine). 297,407.

Nielsen BookScan Juvenile Top 20

1. *Old School* (Diary of a Wimpy Kid #10). Jeff Kinney (Abrams/Amulet). 1,483,855.

2. *Paper Towns*. John Green (Penguin/Speak). 919,478.
3. *Secret Garden*. Johanna Basford (Laurence King). 764,808.
4. *First 100 Words*. Roger Priddy (Priddy). 685,182.
5. *Enchanted Forest*. Johanna Basford (Laurence King). 674,705.
6. *The Long Haul* (Diary of a Wimpy Kid #9). Jeff Kinney (Abrams/Amulet). 554,250.
7. *Oh, the Places You'll Go!*. Dr. Seuss (Random House). 520,817.
8. *The Isle of the Lost* (Descendants). Melissa de la Cruz (Disney-Hyperion). 492,939.
9. *Laugh-Out-Loud Jokes for Kids*. Rob Elliott (Fleming H. Revell). 482,580.
10. *What Pet Should I Get?*. Dr. Seuss (Random House). 464,409.
11. *Green Eggs and Ham*. Dr. Seuss (Random House). 441,964.
12. *The Very Hungry Caterpillar*. Eric Carle (Philomel). 406,642.
13. *One Fish Two Fish Red Fish Blue Fish*. Dr. Seuss (Random House). 401,020.
14. *Goodnight Moon*. Brown/Hurd (HarperFestival). 398,319.
15. *Brown Bear, Brown Bear, What Do You See?*. Martin/Carle (Holt). 391,863.
16. *Love You Forever*. Robert N. Munsch (Firefly). 387,202.
17. *Wonder*. R.J. Palacio (Knopf). 384,871.
18. *Miss Peregrine's Home for Peculiar Children*. Ransom Riggs (Quirk). 368,816.
19. *The Day the Crayons Quit*. Daywalt/Jeffers (Philomel). 368,783.
20. *Looking for Alaska*. John Green (Penguin/Speak). 357,120.

Literary Prizes, 2015

Compiled by the staff of the *Library and Book Trade Almanac*

ABC-CLIO/Greenwood Award for Best Book in Library Literature ($5,000). To recognize works that improve library management principles and practice, understanding and application of new techniques, or further the education of librarians or other information specialists. *Sponsor:* ABC-CLIO. *Administered by:* American Library Association. *Winner:* Sidney E. Berger for *Rare Books and Special Collections* (ALA Neal-Schuman).

Academy of American Poets Fellowship ($25,000). For outstanding poetic achievement. *Offered by:* Academy of American Poets. *Winner:* Marie Howe.

Jane Addams Children's Book Awards. For children's books that effectively promote the cause of peace, social justice, world community, and equality. *Offered by:* Women's International League for Peace and Freedom and the Jane Addams Peace Association. *Winners:* (younger children), Duncan Tonatiuh, writer and illustrator, for *Separate Is Never Equal: Sylvia Mendez and Her Family's Fight for Desegregation* (Abrams); (older children) Teri Kanefield for *The Girl From the Tar Paper School: Barbara Rose Johns and the advent of the Civil Rights Movement* (Abrams).

Aesop Prize. For outstanding work in children's folklore, both fiction and nonfiction. *Offered by:* American Folklore Society. *Winners:* Rick Riordan for *Percy Jackson's Greek Heroes* (Disney-Hyperion) and Margi Preus for *West of the Moon* (Abrams).

Agatha Awards. For mystery writing in the method exemplified by author Agatha Christie. *Offered by:* Malice Domestic Ltd. *Winners:* (contemporary novel) Hank Phillippi Ryan for *Truth Be Told* (Forge); (first novel) Terrie Farley Moran for *Well Read, Then Dead* (Berkley Prime Crime); (historical) Rhys Bowen for *Queen of Hearts* (Berkley); (children's/YA) Penny Warner for *The Code Buster's Club, Case #4, The Mummy's Curse* (Egmont USA); (nonfiction) Hank Phillippi Ryan for *Writes of Passage: Adventures on the Writer's Journey* (Henery Press); (short story) Art Taylor for "The Odds Are Against Us" (EQMM).

American Academy of Arts and Letters Award of Merit ($25,000). Given annually, in rotation, for the short story, sculpture, novel, poetry, drama, and painting. *Offered by:* American Academy of Arts and Letters. *Winner:* Cormac McCarthy (novel).

American Academy of Arts and Letters Awards in Literature ($10,000). To honor writers of fiction and nonfiction, poets, dramatists, and translators of exceptional accomplishment. *Offered by:* American Academy of Arts and Letters. *Winners:* Annie Baker, Ann Goldstein, Glenn Greenwald, Lin-Manuel Miranda, Ibrahim Muhawi, Vijay Seshadri, Jeffrey Skinner, Naomi Wallace.

American Academy of Arts and Letters Rome Fellowships. For a one-year residency at the American Academy in Rome for young writers of promise. *Offered by:* American Academy of Arts and Letters. *Winners:* Will Boast, Lysley Tenorio.

American Book Awards. For literary achievement by people of various ethnic backgrounds. *Offered by:* Before Columbus Foundation. *Winners:* Hisham Aidi for *Rebel Music: Race, Empire, and the New Muslim Youth Culture* (Vintage); Arlene Biala for *her beckoning hands* (Word Poetry); Arthur Dong for *Forbidden City, USA: Chinese American Nightclubs, 1936–1970* (DeepFocus Productions); Roxanne Dunbar-Ortiz for *An Indigenous People's History of the United States* (Beacon Press); Peter J. Harris for *The Black Man of Happiness* (Black Man of Happiness Project); Marlon James for *A Brief History of Seven Killings* (Riverhead); Martin Kilson for *Transformation of the African American Intelligentsia, 1880–2012* (Harvard University Press); Naomi Klein for *This Changes Everything: Capitalism vs. The Climate* (Simon & Schuster); Laila Lalami for *The Moor's Account* (Pantheon); Manuel Luis Martinez for *Los Duros* (Floricanto Press); Craig Santos Perez for *from unincorporated territory [guma']* (Omnidawn); Carlos Santana, with

Ashley Kahn and Hal Miller for *The Universal Tone: Bringing My Story to Light* (Little, Brown); Ira Sukrungruang for *Southside Buddhist* (University of Tampa Press); Astra Taylor for *The People's Platform: Taking Back Power and Culture in the Digital Age* (Henry Holt); (lifetime achievement) Anne Waldman.

American Indian Youth Literature Awards. Offered biennially to recognize excellence in books by and about American Indians. *Offered by:* American Indian Library Association. *Winners:* (picture book) Richard Van Camp and Julie Flett, illustrator, for *Little You* (Orca); (middle school) Joseph Marshall III for *In the Footsteps of Crazy Horse* (Amulet); (young adult) Tim Tingle for *House of Purple Cedar* (Cinco Puntos).

American Poetry Review/Honickman First Book Prize in Poetry ($3,000 and publication of the book). To encourage excellence in poetry and to provide a wide readership for a deserving first book of poems. *Winner:* Alicia Jo Rabins for *Divinity School* (American Poetry Review).

Américas Book Award for Children's and Young Adult Literature. To recognize U.S. works of fiction, poetry, folklore, or selected nonfiction that authentically and engagingly portray Latin America, the Caribbean, or Latinos in the United States. *Sponsored by:* Consortium of Latin American Studies Programs (CLASP). *Winner:* Duncan Tonatiuh for *Separate is Never Equal: Sylvia Mendez & Her Family's Fight for Desegregation* (Abrams); Margarita Engle for *Silver People: Voices from the Panama Canal* (Houghton Mifflin Harcourt).

Rudolfo and Patricia Anaya Lecture on the Literature of the Southwest. To honor a Chicano or Chicana fiction writer. *Offered by:* National Hispanic Cultural Center, University of New Mexico. *Winner:* Anne Hillerman.

Hans Christian Andersen Literature Award (500,000 Danish kroner, about $73,000). To a writer whose work can be compared with that of Andersen. *Offered by:* Hans Christian Andersen Literary Committee. *Winner:* Haruki Murakami.

Anthony Awards. For superior mystery writing. *Offered by:* Boucheron World Mystery Convention. *Winners:* (novel) Laura Lippman for *After I'm Gone* (William Morrow); (first novel) Lori Rader-Day for *The Black Hour* (Seventh Street); (paperback original) Catriona McPherson for *The Day She Died* (Midnight Ink); (short story) Art Taylor for "The Odds Are Against Us" in *Ellery Queen Mystery Magazine* (Dell); (critical or nonfiction Work) Hank Phillippi Ryan, ed. for *Writes of Passage: Adventures on the Writer's Journey* (Henery); (anthology or collection) Laurie R. King & Leslie S. Klinger, eds. for *In the Company of Sherlock Holmes: Stories Inspired by the Holmes Canon* (Pegasus Crime).

Asian/Pacific American Awards for Literature. For books that promote Asian/Pacific American culture and heritage. *Sponsor:* Asian/Pacific American Librarians Association (APALA). *Winners:* (picture book) Chieri Uegaki and Qin Leng for *Hana Hashimoto, Sixth Violin* (Kids Can); (children's) Matt Faulkner for *Gaijin: American Prisoner of War* (Disney/Hyperion); (young adult) May-Lee Chai for *Tiger Girl* (GemmaMedia); (adult fiction) Celeste Ng for *Everything I Never Told You* (Penguin); (adult nonfiction) Robert Ji-Song Ku for *Dubious Gastronomy: The Cultural Politics of Eating Asian in the USA* (University of Hawaii Press).

Audio Publishers Association Awards (Audies). To recognize excellence in audiobooks. *Winners:* (audiobook of the year, original work) *Mandela: An Audio History* by Nelson Mandela, read by Desmond Tutu, Nelson Mandela, Joe Richman (HighBridge); (autobiography/memoir, narration by the author or authors) *Not My Father's Son: A Memoir* by Alan Cumming, read by the author (Blackstone); (distinguished achievement in production; children's, ages 8–12; multivoiced performance) *The Graveyard Book* by Neil Gaiman, read by Derek Jacobi, Robert Madge, Clare Corbett, Miriam Margolyes, Andrew Scott, Julian Rhind-Tutt, Emilia Fox, Reece Shearsmith, Lenny Henry, Neil Gaiman, and an Ensemble Cast (Harper); (solo narration, female) *Yellow Crocus* by Laila Ibrahim, read by Bahni Turpin (Brilliance); (solo narration, male) *The Hero's Guide to Being an Outlaw* by Christopher Healy, read by Bronson Pinchot (HarperCollins); (nonfiction) *Furious Cool: Richard Pryor and the World That Made Him* by David Henry, Joe Henry, read by the Dion

Graham (Tantor Media); (history/biography) *The Bully Pulpit: Theodore Roosevelt, William Howard Taft, and the Golden Age of Journalism* by Doris Kearns Goodwin, read by Edward Herrmann (Simon & Schuster); (inspirational/faith-based fiction) *The Auschwitz Escape* by Joel C. Rosenberg, read by Christopher Lane (Brilliance Audio); (inspirational/faith-based nonfiction) *Before Amen: The Power of a Simple Prayer* by Max Lucado, read by Read by Ben Holland (Thomas Nelson); (Judges Award, science & technology) *The Second Machine Age: Work, Progress, and Prosperity in a Time of Brilliant Technologies* by Erik Brynjolfsson, Andrew McAfee, read by Jeff Cummings (Brilliance); (literary fiction) *Euphoria* by Lily King, read by Simon Vance, Xe Sands (Blackstone); (business/educational) *A More Beautiful Question: The Power of Inquiry to Spark Breakthrough Ideas* by Warren Berger, read by Michael Quinlan (Brilliance Audio); (personal development) *What I Know For Sure* by Oprah Winfrey, read by the author (Macmillan); (fiction) *All the Light We Cannot See* by Anthony Doerr, read by Zach Appelman (Simon & Schuster); (classic) *The New York Stories* by John O'Hara, read by Becky Ann Baker, Dylan Baker, Bobby Cannavale, Jon Hamm, Richard Kind, Jan Maxwell, Gretchen Mol, Dallas Roberts, E. L. Doctorow (Penguin); (short stories/collections) *The Assassination of Margaret Thatcher: Stories* by Hilary Mantel, read by Jane Carr (Macmillan); (romance) *The Bridges of Madison County* by Robert James Waller, read by Kelli O'Hara, Steven Pasquale (Grand Central); (erotica) *Alpha* by Jasinda Wilder, read by Summer Roberts, Tyler Donne (Seth Clarke); (science fiction) *The Martian* by Andy Weir, read by R. C. Bray (Brilliance); (paranormal) *The Girl With All the Gifts* by M. R. Carey read by Finty Williams (Hachette); (fantasy) *Words of Radiance* by Brandon Sanderson, read by Michael Kramer, Kate Reading (Macmillan); (humor) *Yes Please* byAmy Poehler, read by Amy Poehler, Carol Burnett, Seth Meyers, Mike Schur, Eileen Poehler, William Poehler, Patrick Stewart, Kathleen Turner (Harper); (mystery) *The Silkworm* by Robert Galbraith, read by Robert Galbraith (Little, Brown); (thriller/suspense) *Those*

Who Wish Me Dead by Michael Koryta, read by Robert Petkoff (Hachette); (children's, ages 0–8) *H.O.R.S.E. A Game of Basketball and Imagination* by Christopher Myers, read by Dion Graham, Christopher Myers (Live Oak Media); (teens) *Egg and Spoon* by Gregory Maguire, read by Michael Page (Brilliance); (audio drama) *The Hound of the Baskervilles* by Sir Arthur Conan Doyle, read by Geoffrey Arend, Wilson Bethel, Seamus Dever, Sarah Drew, Henri Lubatti, James Marsters, Christopher Neame, Moira Quirk, Darren Richardson (Naxos).

Bad Sex in Fiction Award (United Kingdom). To "draw attention to the crude, badly written, often perfunctory use of redundant passages of sexual description in the modern novel, and to discourage it." *Sponsor:* Literary Review. *Winner:* Morrissey for *List of the Lost* (Penguin).

Baileys Women's Prize for Fiction (United Kingdom) (formerly the Orange Prize for Fiction) (£30,000). For the best novel written by a woman and published in the United Kingdom. *Winner:* Ali Smith for *How to Be Both* (Pantheon).

Bancroft Prizes ($10,000). For books of exceptional merit and distinction in American history, American diplomacy, and the international relations of the United States. *Offered by:* Columbia University. *Winners:* Sven Beckert for *Empire of Cotton: A Global History* (Knopf); Greg Grandin for *The Empire of Necessity* (Metropolitan/Henry Holt).

Barnes & Noble Discover Great New Writers Awards. To honor a first novel and a first work of nonfiction by American authors. *Offered by:* Barnes & Noble. *Winners:* (fiction) Evie Wyld for *All the Birds, Singing* (Pantheon); (nonfiction) Bryce Andrews for *Badluck Way: A Year on the Ragged Edge of the West* (Atria).

Mildred L. Batchelder Award. To the American publisher of a children's book originally published in a language other than English and subsequently published in English in the United States. *Offered by:* American Library Association, Association for Library Service to Children. *Winner:* Eerdmans for *Mikis and the Donkey* by Bibi Dumon Tak, illustrated by Philip Hopman, translated by Laura Watkinson.

BBC National Short Story Award (United Kingdom) (£15,000). *Winner:* Jonathan Buckley for "Briar Road."

Beacon of Freedom Award. For the best title introducing American history, from colonial times through the Civil War, to young readers. *Offered by:* Williamsburg (Virginia) Regional Library and the Colonial Williamsburg Foundation. *Winner:* Nathan Hale for *One Dead Spy* (Abrams). Final award was made in 2015.

Pura Belpré Awards. To a Latino/Latina writer and illustrator whose work portrays, affirms, and celebrates the Latino cultural experience in an outstanding work of literature for children and youth. *Offered by:* American Library Association, Association for Library Service to Children. *Winners:* (writer) Marjorie Agosín for *I Lived on Butterfly Hill* (Atheneum); (illustrator) Yuyi Morales, author and illustrator of *Viva Frida* (Roaring Brook).

Helen B. Bernstein Book Award for Excellence in Journalism ($15,000). To a journalist who has written at book length about an issue of contemporary concern. *Offered by:* New York Public Library. *Winner:* Anand Giridharadas for *The True American; Murder and Mercy in Texas* (W. W. Norton & Company).

Black Caucus of the American Library Association (BCALA) Literary Awards. *Winners:* (fiction) Lalita Tademy for *Citizens Creek: A Novel* (Atria); (nonfiction) Jeffrey B. Leak for *Visible Man: The Life of Henry Dumas* (University of Georgia Press); (first novelist award, to acknowledge outstanding achievement in writing and storytelling by a first-time fiction writer) Dwayne Alexander Smith for *Forty Acres: A Thriller* (Atria); (poetry) Kevin Young for *Books of Hours: Poems* (Knopf); (outstanding contribution to publishing citation) Ethelene Whitmire for *Regina Anderson Andrews, Harlem Renaissance Librarian* (University of Illinois Press).

Irma Simonton Black and James H. Black Award for Excellence in Children's Literature. To a book for young children in which the text and illustrations work together to create an outstanding whole. *Offered by:* Bank Street College of Education. *Winner:* Mac Barnett for *Sam and Dave Dig a Hole* (Candlewick).

James Tait Black Memorial Prize (United Kingdom) (£10,000). To recognize literary excellence in fiction and biography. *Offered by:* University of Edinburgh. *Winners:* (fiction) Zia Haider Rahman for *In the Light of What We Know* (Picador); (biography) Richard Benson for *The Valley: A Hundred Years in the Life of a Yorkshire Family* (Bloomsbury).

James Tait Black Prize for Drama (United Kingdom) (£10,000). *Offered by:* University of Edinburgh in partnership with the National Theatre of Scotland and in association with the Traverse Theatre. *Winner:* Gordon Dahlquist for *Tomorrow Come Today.*

Blue Peter Book of the Year (United Kingdom). To recognize excellence in children's books. Winners are chosen by a jury of viewers, ages 8–12, of the BBC television children's program "Blue Peter." *Winners:* (best story) Pamela Butchart for *The Spy Who Loved School Dinners* (Nosy Crow); (best book with facts) Andy Seed and Scott Garrett, illustrator, for *The Silly Book of Side-Splitting Stuff* (Bloomsbury).

Bookseller/Diagram Prize for Oddest Title of the Year. *Sponsor:* The *Bookseller* magazine. *Winner:* Margaret Meps Schulte for *Strangers Have the Best Candy* (Choose ART).

BookSense Book of the Year Awards. See Indies Choice Book Awards.

Boston Globe/Horn Book Awards. For excellence in children's literature. *Winners:* (fiction) Katherine Rundell for *Cartwheeling in Thunderstorms* (Simon & Schuster); (nonfiction) Candace Fleming for *The Family Romanov: Murder, Rebellion, and the Fall of Imperial Russia (Random House); (picture book) Marla Frazee for The Farmer and the Clown* (Simon & Schuster).

W. Y. Boyd Literary Award ($5,000). For a military novel that honors the service of American veterans during a time of war. *Offered by:* American Library Association. *Donor:* W. Y. Boyd II. *Winner:* Phil Klay for *Redeployment* (Penguin).

Branford Boase Award (United Kingdom). To the author and editor of an outstanding novel for young readers by a first-time writer. *Winners:* Rosie Rowell and editor Emily Thomas for *Leopold Blue* (Hot Key).

Bridport International Creative Writing Prizes (United Kingdom). For poetry and short stories. *Offered by:* Bridport Arts Centre. *Winners:* (poetry, £5,000) Kathy Miles for "An Elegy for Lace"; (short story, £5,000) Judith Edelman for "Ping at the Zoo"; (flash fiction, 250-word maximum, £1,000) Kit de Waal for "Crushing Big."

British Council Award for ELT writing (£2,000). To celebrate the best writing for English language teaching. *Winner:* Philip Kerr for *Translation And Own-Language Activities* (Cambridge University Press).

British Fantasy Awards. *Offered by:* British Fantasy Society. *Winners:* (novel) Francis Hardinge for *Cuckoo Song* (Abrams); (horror novel) Adam Nevill for *No One Gets Out Alive* (St. Martin's); (novella) Stephen Volk for *Newspaper Heart* in *The Spectral Book of Horror Stories*; (short story) Emma Newman for "A Woman's Place" in *Two Hundred and Twenty-One Baker Streets*; (anthology) Christie Yant, editor, for *Women Destroy Science Fiction* in *Lightspeed Magazine*; (collection) Adrian Cole for *Nick Nightmare Investigates* (Alchemy); (comic/graphic novel) Emily Carroll for *Through the Woods* (McElderry); (artist) Karla Ortiz; (nonfiction) S.T. Joshi , editor, for *Letters to Arkham: The Letters of Ramsey Campbell and August Derleth 1961 to 1971* (PS); (magazine/periodical) Laurel Sills and Lucy Smee, editors, for *Holdfast Magazine*; (film/television episode) for "Guardians of the Galaxy"; (newcomer) Sarah Lotz for *The Three* (Little, Brown); (British Fantasy Society Special Award, The Karl Edward Wagner Award) Juliet E. McKenna.

Sophie Brody Medal. For the U.S. author of the most distinguished contribution to Jewish literature for adults, published in the preceding year. *Donors:* Arthur Brody and the Brodart Foundation. *Offered by:* American Library Association, Reference and User Services Association. *Winner:* Boris Fishman for *A Replacement Life* (HarperCollins).

Witter Bynner Poetry Fellowships ($10,000). To encourage poets and poetry. *Sponsor* Witter Bynner Foundation for Poetry. *Winners:* Emily Fragos, Bobby C. Rogers.

Caine Prize for African Writing (£10,000). For a short story by an African writer, published in English. *Winner:* Namwali Serpell for "The Sack" in *Africa39* (Bloomsbury).

Randolph Caldecott Medal. For the artist of the most distinguished picture book. *Offered by:* American Library Association, Association for Library Service to Children. *Winner:* Dan Santat, writer and illustrator, for *The Adventures of Beekle: An Unimaginary Friend* (Little, Brown).

California Book Awards. To California residents to honor books of fiction, nonfiction, and poetry published in the previous year. *Offered by:* Commonwealth Club of California. *Winners:* (fiction) Rabih Alameddine for *An Unnecessary Woman* (Grove); (first fiction) Christina Nichol for *Waiting for the Electricity* (Overlook); (nonfiction) Miriam Pawel for *The Crusades of Cesar Chavez* (Bloomsbury); (poetry) Fred Moten for *The Feel Trio* (Letter Machine Editions); (juvenile) Jennifer L. Holm for *The Fourteenth Goldfish* (Random House); (young adult) Isabel Quintero for *Gabi, A Girl in Pieces* (Cinco Puntos); (contribution to publishing) Kim Bancroft for *The Heyday of Malcolm Margolin* (Heyday Books); (Californiana) Laura A. Ackley for *San Francisco's Jewel City: The Panama-Pacific International Exposition* (Heyday Books).

John W. Campbell Award. For the best new science fiction or fantasy writer whose first work of science fiction or fantasy was published in a professional publication in the previous two years. *Offered by:* Dell Magazines. *Winner:* Wesley Chu for *The Lives of Tao* (Angry Robot).

John W. Campbell Memorial Award. For science fiction writing. *Offered by:* Center for the Study of Science Fiction. *Winners:* Claire North for *The First Fifteen Lives of Harry August* (Redhook).

Canadian Library Association Book of the Year for Children. *Sponsor:* Library Services Centre. *Winner:* Jonathan Auxier for *The Night Gardener* (Penguin Canada).

Canadian Library Association Amelia Frances Howard-Gibbon Illustrator's Award. *Sponsor:* Library Services Centre. *Winner:* Marie-Louise Gay for *Any Questions?*, (Groundwood).

Canadian Library Association Young Adult Book Award. *Winners:* Mariko and Jillian Tamaki for *This One Summer* (Groundwood).

Andrew Carnegie Medal for Excellence in Fiction and Nonfiction. For adult books published during the previous year in the United States. *Sponsors:* Carnegie Corporation of New York, ALA/RUSA, and *Booklist.* *Winners:* (fiction) Anthony Doerr for *All The Light We Cannot See* (Scribner); (nonfiction) Bryan Stevenson for *Just Mercy: A Story of Justice and Redemption* (Spiegel & Grau).

Carnegie Medal (United Kingdom). See CILIP Carnegie Medal.

Center for Fiction Flaherty-Dunnan First Novel Prize. See Flaherty-Dunnan First Novel Prize.

Chicago Folklore Prize. For the year's best folklore book. *Offered by:* American Folklore Society. *Winner:* Jack Zipes for *Grimm Legacies: The Magic Spell of the Grimms' Folk and Fairy Tales* (Princeton University Press).

Chicago Tribune Nelson Algren Short Story Award ($5,000). For unpublished short fiction. *Offered by: Chicago Tribune. Winner:* Brenda Peynado for "The Great Escape."

Chicago Tribune Heartland Prize for Fiction ($7,500). *Offered by: Chicago Tribune. Winner:* Chang-Rae Lee for *On Such A Full Sea* (Riverhead).

Chicago Tribune Heartland Prize for Nonfiction ($7,500). *Offered by: Chicago Tribune. Winner:* Danielle Allen for *Our Declaration* (Liveright).

Chicago Tribune Literary Prize. For a lifetime of literary achievement by an author whose body of work has had great impact on American society. *Offered by: Chicago Tribune. Winner:* author Salman Rushdie.

Chicago Tribune Young Adult Literary Prize. To recognize a distinguished literary career. *Winner:* LeVar Burton.

Children's Africana Book Awards. To recognize and encourage excellence in children's books about Africa. *Offered by:* Africa Access, African Studies Association. *Winners:* Andrea Davis Pinkney and Shane W. Evans, illustrator, for *The Red Pencil* (Little, Brown).

Children's Book Council of Australia Book of the Year Awards. *Winners:* (older readers) Claire Zorn for *The Protected* (University of Queensland Press); (younger readers) Libby Gleeson for *The Cleo Stories: The Necklace and the Present* (Allen & Unwin); (early

childhood) Libby Gleeson and Freya Blackwood, illustrator, for *Go to Sleep, Jessie!* (Little Hare); (picture book) Freya Blackwood for *My Two Blankets* (Little Hare).

Young People's Poet Laureate ($25,000). For lifetime achievement in poetry for children. Honoree holds the title for two years. *Offered by:* The Poetry Foundation. *Winner:* Jacqueline Woodson.

Cholmondeley Awards for Poets (United Kingdom) (£1,500). For a poet's body of work and contribution to poetry. *Winners:* Patience Agbabi, Brian Catling, Christopher Middleton, Pascale Petit, J. H. Prynne.

CILIP Carnegie Medal (United Kingdom). For the outstanding children's book of the year. *Offered by:* CILIP: The Chartered Institute of Library and Information Professionals (formerly the Library Association). *Winner:* Tanya Landman for *Buffalo Soldier* (Walker).

CILIP Kate Greenaway Medal and Colin Mears Award (United Kingdom) (£5,000 plus £500 worth of books donated to a library of the winner's choice). For children's book illustration. *Offered by:* CILIP: The Chartered Institute of Library and Information Professionals. *Winner:* William Grill for *Shackleton's Journey* (Flying Eye).

Arthur C. Clarke Award. For the best science fiction novel published in the United Kingdom. *Offered by:* British Science Fiction Association. *Winner:* Emily St. John Mandel for *Station Eleven* (Picador).

David Cohen Prize for Literature (United Kingdom) (£40,000). Awarded biennially to a living British writer, novelist, poet, essayist, or dramatist in recognition of an entire body of work written in the English language. *Offered by:* David Cohen Family Charitable Trust. *Winner:* Tony Harrison.

Matt Cohen Award: In Celebration of a Writing Life (C$20,000). To a Canadian author whose life has been dedicated to writing as a primary pursuit, for a body of work. *Offered by:* Writers' Trust of Canada. *Sponsors:* Marla and David Lehberg. *Winner:* Richard Wagamese.

Commonwealth Book Prize (United Kingdom) (£10,000). To reward and encourage new Commonwealth fiction and ensure that works of merit reach a wider audience outside their country of origin. *Offered by:* Commonwealth Institute. *Winner:* The prize, formerly known as the Commonwealth Writers' Prize, was discontinued after the 2013 competition.

Commonwealth Short Story Prize (United Kingdom) (£5,000). To reward and encourage new short fiction by Commonwealth writers. *Offered by:* Commonwealth Institute. (Overall winner and regional winner, Canada and Europe) Jonathan Tel (United Kingdom) for "The Human Phonograph"; (regional winner, Africa) Lesley Nneka Arimah (Nigeria) for "Light"; (regional winner, Asia) Siddhartha Gigoo (India) for "The Umbrella Man"; (regional winner, Caribbean) Kevin Jared Hosein (Trinidad) for "The King of Settlement 4"; (regional winner, Pacific) Mary Rokonadravu (Fiji) for "Famished Eels."

Costa Book Awards (United Kingdom) (£5,000 plus an additional £25,000 for Book of the Year). For literature of merit that is readable on a wide scale. *Offered by:* Booksellers Association of Great Britain and Costa Coffee. *Winners:* (biography) Andrea Wulf for *The Invention of Nature* (John Murray); (novel) Kate Atkinson for *A God in Ruins* (Doubleday); (first novel) Andrew Michael Hurley for *The Loney* (John Murray); (poetry) Don Paterson for *40 Sonnets* (Faber and Faber); (children's and Book of the Year) Frances Hardinge for *The Lie Tree* (Macmillan).

Costa Short Story Award (United Kingdom) *Winners:* (first place, £3,500) Daniel Murphy for "Rogey"; (second place, £1,500) Erin Soros for "Fallen"; (third place, £500) Annalisa Crawford for "Watching the Storms Roll In."

Crab Orchard Review Literary Prizes ($2,000 and publication in *Crab Orchard Review*). *Winners:* (Jack Dyer Fiction Prize) Olivia Kate Cerrone for "A Member of the Tribe"; (John Guyon Literary Nonfiction Prize) Jocelyn Bartkevicius for "Mother Tongue"; (Richard Peterson Poetry Prize) T.J. McLemore for "The Bees, or Bringing Back Eurydice."

Crime Writers' Association (CWA) Dagger Awards (United Kingdom). *Winners:* (diamond dagger, for significant contribution to crime writing) Catherine Aird; (gold dagger, for best novel) Michael Robotham for *Life or Death* (Mulholland); (Ian Fleming steel dagger, for best thriller) Karin Slaughter for *Cop Town* (Dell); (John Creasey dagger, for best new crime writer) Smith Henderson for *Fourth Of July Creek* (Ecco); (international dagger, for a work translated into English) Pierre Lemaitre and Frank Wynne, translator, for *Camille* (Maclehose Press); (nonfiction dagger) Dan Davies for *In Plain Sight: The Life and Lies of Jimmy Savile* (Quercus); (CWA Dagger in the Library, for a body of work) Christopher Fowler; (debut dagger, for a previously unpublished crime writer) Greg Keen for *Last of the Soho Legends*; (short story) Richard Lange for "Apocrypha" in *Sweet Nothing Stories* (Mullholland Press); (CWA Endeavour historical dagger, for the best historical crime novel) S.G. MacLean for *The Seeker* (Quercus).

Benjamin H. Danks Award ($20,000). To a promising young writer, playwright, or composer, in alternate years. *Offered by:* American Academy of Arts and Letters. *Winner:* composer Alex Mincek.

Dartmouth Medal. For creating current reference works of outstanding quality and significance. *Donor:* Dartmouth College. *Offered by:* American Library Association, Reference and User Services Division. *Winner:* Princeton University Press *Princeton Dictionary of Buddhism.*

Derringer Awards. To recognize excellence in short crime and mystery fiction. *Sponsor:* Short Mystery Fiction Society. *Winners:* (flash story, up to 1,000 words) Joseph D'Agnese for "How Lil' Jimmie Beat the Big C" in *Shotgun Honey,* May 2014; (short story, 1,001–4,000 words) Cathi Stoler for "The Kaluki Kings of Queens" in *Murder New York Style: Family Matters,* August 2014; (long story, 4001–8,000 words) Hilary Davidson for "A Hopeless Case" in *All Due Respect #4,* September 2014; (novelette, 8,001–20,000 words) Doug Allyn for "The Snow Angel" in *Ellery Queen's Mystery Magazine,* January 2014; Edward D. Hoch Memorial Golden Derringer for Lifetime Achievement) James Powell.

Diagram Prize for Oddest Title of the Year. See Bookseller/Diagram Prize for Oddest Title of the Year.

Philip K. Dick Award. For a distinguished science fiction paperback published in the United States. *Sponsor:* Philadelphia Science Fiction Society and the Philip K. Dick Trust. *Winner:* Meg Elison for *The Book of the Unnamed Midwife* (Sybaritic).

Digital Book Awards. To recognize high-quality digital content available to readers as e-books and enhanced digital books. *Sponsor:* Digital Book World. *Winners:* (e-book, flowable: adult fiction) John Ashbery for *Chinese Whispers* (Open Road); (e-book, flowable: adult nonfiction) Sheila Heti, Heidi Julavits, and Leanne Shapton for *Women in Clothes* (Penguin); (e-book, flowable: children's) Laurie S. Sutton for *You Choose: Scooby-Doo! The Terror of the Bigfoot Beast* (Capstone); (e-book, fixed format/enhanced: adult fiction) Neil Gaiman for *The Truth Is a Cave in the Black Mountains* (Morrow); (e-book, fixed format/enhanced: adult nonfiction) Shauna Miller for *Penny Chic: How to Be Stylish on a Real Girl's Budget* (Little, Brown); (e-book, fixed format/enhanced: children's) Kyo Maclear, Danielle Mulhall, and Laura Brady for *Virginia Wolf* (Kids Can).

DSC Prize for South Asian Literature ($50,000). To recognize outstanding literature from or about the South Asian region and raise awareness of South Asian culture around the world. *Sponsor:* DSC Limited. *Winner:* Jhumpa Lahiri for *The Lowland* (Knopf).

Dundee International Book Prize (Scotland) (£10,000 and publication by Cargo). For an unpublished novel on any theme, in any genre. *Winner:* Martin Cathcart Froden for *Devil Take the Hindmost.*

Dundee Picture Book Award (Scotland) (£1,000). To recognize excellence in storytelling for children. The winner is chosen by the schoolchildren of Dundee. *Winners:* Sarah Warburton and Mark Sperring for *Max and the Won't Go To Bed Show* (HarperCollins).

Educational Writers' Award (United Kingdom) (£2,000). For noteworthy educational nonfiction for children. *Offered by:* Authors' Licensing and Collecting Society and Society of Authors. *Winners:* Rachel Williams and Lucy Letherland, illustrator, for *Atlas of Adventures* (Wide Eyed Editions).

Margaret A. Edwards Award ($2,000). To an author whose book or books have provided young adults with a window through which they can view their world and which will help them to grow and to understand themselves and their role in society. *Donor:* School Library Journal. *Winner:* Sharon M. Draper for *Tears of a Tiger, Forged by Fire, Darkness Before Dawn, Battle of Jericho, Copper Sun,* and *November Blues* (all Atheneum).

T. S. Eliot Prize for Poetry (United Kingdom) (£20,000). *Offered by:* Poetry Book Society. *Winner:* Sarah Howe for *Loop of Jade* (Random House UK).

Encore Award (United Kingdom) (£10,000). Awarded biennially for the best second novel of the previous two years. *Offered by* Society of Authors. *Sponsor:* Lucy Astor. *Winner:* Neel Mukherjee for *The Lives of Others* (Norton).

European Union Prize for Literature (€5,000). To recognize outstanding European writing. *Sponsors:* European Commission, European Booksellers Federation, European Writers' Council, Federation of European Publishers. *Winners:* (Austria) Carolina Schutti for *Once I Must Have Trodden Soft Grass*; (Croatia) Luka Bekavac for *Viljevo*; (France) Gaëlle Josse for *The Last Guardian of Ellis Island*; (Hungary) Edina Szvoren for *There Is None, Nor Let There Be*; (Ireland) Donal Ryan for *The Spinning Heart*; (Italy) Lorenzo Amurri for *Apnea*; (Lithuania) Undine Radzeviciute for *Fishes and Dragons*; (Norway) Ida Hegazi Høyer for *Forgive Me*; (Poland) Magdalena Parys for *Magician*; (Portugal) David Machado for *Average Happiness Index*; (Slovakia) Svetlana Zuchová for *Scenes from the Life of M.*; (Sweden) Sara Stridsberg for *The Gravity of Love.*

Fairfax Prize ($10,000). For a body of work that has "made significant contributions to American and international culture." *Sponsors:* Fairfax County (Virginia) Public Library Foundation and George Mason University. *Winner:* Tim O'Brien.

FIELD Poetry Prize ($1,000). For a book-length poetry collection. *Offered by:* FIELD: Contemporary Poetry and Poetics. *Winner:* Kenny Williams for *Blood Hyphen* (Oberlin).

FIL Literary Award in Romance Languages (formerly the Juan Rulfo International Latin American and Caribbean Prize (Mexico)

($150,000). For lifetime achievement in any literary genre. *Offered by:* Juan Rulfo International Latin American and Caribbean Prize Committee. *Winner:* Spanish author Enrique Vila-Matas.

Financial Times and McKinsey Business Book of the Year Award (£30,000). To recognize books that provide compelling and enjoyable insight into modern business issues. *Winner:* Martin Ford for *The Rise of the Robots: Technology and the Threat of a Jobless Future* (Basic).

Flaherty-Dunnan First Novel Prize ($10,000). *Offered by:* Center for Fiction, Mercantile Library of New York. *Winner:* Viet Thanh Nguyen for *The Sympathizer* (Grove Press).

Sid Fleischman Award for Humor. See Golden Kite Awards.

ForeWord Reviews Book of the Year Awards ($1,500). For independently published books. *Offered by: ForeWord Reviews* magazine. *Winners:* (editor's choice prize, fiction) Sarah Stark for *Out There* (Leaf Storm; (editor's choice prize, nonfiction) Rosie Price, Susan Kammeraad-Campbell, and Larry Price, photographer for *Edisto River: Black Water Crown Jewel* (Joggling Board Press).

E. M. Forster Award ($20,000). To a young writer from England, Ireland, Scotland, or Wales, for a stay in the United States. *Offered by:* American Academy of Arts and Letters. *Winner:* Adam Thirlwell.

Forward Prizes (United Kingdom). For poetry. *Offered by: The Forward. Winners:* (best collection, £10,000), Claudia Rankine for *Citizen: An American Lyric* (Penguin); (best first collection, £5,000) Mona Arshi for *Small Hands* (Liverpool University Press); (best single poem, £1,000) Claire Harman for "The Mighty Hudson."

H. E. Francis Short Story Competition ($1,000). For an unpublished short story no more than 5,000 words in length. *Sponsors:* Ruth Hindman Foundation and English Department, University of Alabama, Huntsville. *Winner:* Jeremy Kamps for "The Source of Everything."

Josette Frank Award. For a work of fiction in which children or young people deal in a positive and realistic way with difficulties in their world and grow emotionally and morally. *Offered by:* Bank Street College of Education and the Florence M. Miller Memorial Fund. *Winners:* (older readers) Jandy Nelson for *I'll Give You the Sun* (Penguin); (younger readers) Ann M. Martin for *Rain Reign* (Feiwel and Friends).

George Freedley Memorial Award. For the best English-language work about live theater published in the United States. *Offered by:* Theatre Library Association. *Winner:* Arnold Aronson for *Ming Cho Lee: A Life in Design* (Theatre Communications Group).

French-American Foundation Translation Prize ($10,000). For a translation or translations from French into English of works of fiction and nonfiction. *Offered by:* French-American Foundation. *Donor:* Florence Gould Foundation. *Winners:* (fiction) Donald Nicholson-Smith for his translation of *The Mad and The Bad* by Jean-Patrick Manchette (New York Review Books); (nonfiction) David Ball for his translation of *Diary of the Dark Years, 1940–1944* by Jean Guéhenno (Oxford University Press).

Frost Medal. To recognize achievement in poetry over a lifetime. *Offered by:* Poetry Society of America. *Winner:* Kamau Brathwaite.

Lewis Galantière Award. Awarded biennially for a literary translation into English from any language other than German. *Offered by:* American Translators Association. To be awarded next in 2016.

Galaxy National Book Awards. See Specsavers National Book Awards.

Theodor Seuss Geisel Award. For the best book for beginning readers. *Offered by:* American Library Association, Association for Library Service to Children. *Winner:* Anna Kang for *You Are (Not) Small,* illustrated by Christopher Weyant (Two Lions).

David Gemmell Legend Awards for Fantasy. For novels published for the first time in English during the year of nomination. *Winners:* (Legend Award for best fantasy novel) Brandon Sanderson for *Words of Radiance* (Gollancz); (Morningstar Award for best debut novel) Brian Stavely for *The Emperor's Blades* (Pan Macmillan/Tor UK); (Ravenheart Award for best cover art) Sam Green for *Words of Radiance* (Gollancz).

Giller Prize (Canada). See Scotiabank Giller Prize.

Gival Press Novel Award ($3,000 and publication by Gival Press). *Winner:* Robert Schirmer for *Barrow's Point.*

Giverny Award. For an outstanding children's science picture book. *Offered by:* 15 Degree Laboratory. *Winner:* Kate Messner and Christopher Silas Neal, illustrator, for *Up in the Garden and Down in the Dirt* (Chronicle).

Alexander Gode Medal. To an individual or institution for outstanding service to the translation and interpreting professions. *Offered by:* American Translators Association. *Winner:* Not awarded in 2015.

Golden Duck Awards for Excellence in Children's Science Fiction Literature. *Sponsored by:* Super-Con-Duck-Tivity. *Winners:* (picture book) Jeffrey Bennett for *Max Goes to the Space Station, A Science Adventure with Max the Dog* (Big Kid Science); (Eleanor Cameron Award for middle grades books) William Alexander for *Ambassador* (Margaret K. McElderry Books); (Hal Clement Award for young adult books) William Campbell Powell for *Expiration Day* (Tor Teen).

Golden Kite Awards. For children's books. *Offered by:* Society of Children's Book Writers and Illustrators. *Winners:* (picture book text) Kristy Dempsey for *A Dance Like Starlight: One Ballerina's Dream* (Philomel); (picture book illustration) Melissa Sweet for *The Right Word: Roget and His Thesaurus* (Eerdmans); (fiction) Deborah Wiles for *Revolution* (Scholastic); (nonfiction) Candice Fleming for *The Family Romanov; Murder, Rebellion and the Fall of Imperial Russia* (Schwartz & Wade); (Sid Fleischman Award for Humor) Michelle Knedsen for *Evil Librarian* (Candlewick).

Governor General's Literary Awards (Canada) (C$25,000, plus C$3,000 to the publisher). For works, in English and in French, of fiction, nonfiction, poetry, drama, and children's literature, and for translation. *Offered by:* Canada Council for the Arts. *Winners:* (fiction, English) Guy Vanderhaeghe for *Daddy Lenin and Other Stories* (Penguin Random House Canada); (fiction, French) Nicolas Dickner for *Six degrés de liberté* (Éditions Alto); (nonfiction, English) Mark L. Winston for *Bee Time: Lessons from the Hive* (Harvard University Press); (nonfiction, French) Jean-Philippe Warren for *Honoré Beaugrand : la plume et l'épée (1848-1906)* (Les Éditions du Boréal); (poetry, English)

Robyn Sarah for *My Shoes Are Killing Me* (Biblioasis); (poetry, French) Joël Pourbaix for *Le mal du pays est un art oublié* (Éditions du Noroît); (drama, English) David Yee for *carried away on the crest of a wave* (Playwrights Canada); (drama, French) Fabien Cloutier for *Pour réussir un poulet* (Les éditions de L'instant même and Dramaturges Éditeurs); (children's literature, text, English) Caroline Pignat for *The Gospel Truth* (Red Dee); (children's literature, text, French) Louis-Philippe Hébert for *Marie Réparatrice* (Les Éditions de La Grenouillère; (children's literature, illustration, English) Sydney Smith for *Sidewalk Flowers,* written by JonArno Lawson (Groundwood); (children's literature, illustration, French) Patrick Doyon for *Le voleur de sandwichs,* written by André Marois (Les Éditions de la Pastèque); (translation, French to English) Rhonda Mullins for *Twenty-One Cardinals* by Jocelyn Saucier (Coach House); (translation, English to French) Lori Saint-Martin and Paul Gagné for *Solomon Gursky* by Mordecai Richler (Éditions du Boréal).

Dolly Gray Children's Literature Awards. Presented biennially for fiction or biographical children's books with positive portrayals of individuals with developmental disabilities. *Offered by:* Council for Exceptional Children, Division on Autism and Developmental Disabilities. *Winners:* (intermediate book) Ann M. Martin for *Rain Reign* (MacMillan); (picture book) Shaila Abdullah and Aanyah Abdullah for *My Friend Suhana*(Loving Healing Press).

Kate Greenaway Medal and Colin Mears Award. See CILIP Kate Greenaway Medal.

Eric Gregory Awards (United Kingdom) (£4,000). For a published or unpublished collection by poets under the age of 30. *Winners:* Rowan Evans, Miriam Nash, Padraig Regan, Stewart Sanderson and Andrew Wynn Owen.

Griffin Poetry Prizes (Canada) (C$65,000). To a living Canadian poet or translator and a living poet or translator from any country, which may include Canada. *Offered by:* Griffin Trust. *Winners:* (international) Michael Longley for *The Stairwell* (Jonathan Cape); (Canadian) Jane Munro for *Blue Sonoma* (Brick).

Gryphon Award ($1,000). To recognize a noteworthy work of fiction or nonfiction for younger children. *Offered by:* The Center for Children's Books. *Winners:* English, Karen, and Laura Freeman, illustrator, for *Skateboard Party* (Clarion).

Guardian Children's Fiction Prize (United Kingdom) (£1,500). For an outstanding children's or young adult novel. *Offered by:* The *Guardian*. *Winner:* David Almond for *A Song for Ella Grey* (Hodder).

Guardian First Book Award (United Kingdom) (£10,000). To recognize a first book. *Offered by:* The *Guardian*. *Winner:* Andrew McMillan for his poetry collection *Physical* (Cape).

Dashiell Hammett Prize. For a work of literary excellence in the field of crime writing by a U.S. or Canadian writer. *Offered by:* North American Branch, International Association of Crime Writers. *Winner:* Stephen King for *Mr. Mercedes* (Scribner).

R. R. Hawkins Award. For the outstanding professional/scholarly work of the year. *Offered by:* Association of American Publishers. *Winner:* Thomas Piketty and Arthur Goldhammer, translator, for *Capital in the Twenty-First Century* (Belknap Press of Harvard University Press).

Anthony Hecht Poetry Prize ($3,000 and publication by Waywiser Press). For an unpublished first or second book-length poetry collection. *Winner:* Jaimee Hills for *How to Avoid Speaking.*

Drue Heinz Literature Prize ($15,000 and publication by University of Pittsburgh Press). For short fiction. *Winner:* Leslie Pietrzyk for *This Angel On My Chest* (University of Pittsburgh Press).

O. Henry Awards. See PEN/O. Henry Prize.

William Dean Howells Medal. In recognition of the most distinguished novel published in the preceding five years. *Offered by:* American Academy of Arts and Letters. *Winner:* William H. Gass for *Middle C* (Vintage).

Hugo Awards. For outstanding science fiction writing. *Offered by:* World Science Fiction Convention. *Winners:* (novel) Cixin Liu, Ken Liu translator for *The Three Body Problem* (Tor); (novella) no award; (novelette) Thomas Olde Heuvelt, Lia Belt translator for "The Day the World Turned Upside Down" (*Lightspeed*); (short story) no award;

(related work) no award; (graphic story) G. Willow Wilson, Adrian Alphona and Jake Wyatt, illustrators, for "Ms. Marvel Volume 1: No Normal" (Marvel Comics); (dramatic presentation, long form) James Gunn and Nicole Perlman, writers, and James Gunn, director, for *Guardians of the Galaxy,* (Marvel Studios, Moving Picture Company); (dramatic presentation, short form) Graeme Manson, writer, and John Fawcett, director, for *Orphan Black: "By Means Which Have Never Yet Been Tried"* (Temple Street Productions, Space/BBC America).

Hurston/Wright Legacy Awards. To writers of African American descent for a book of fiction, a book of nonfiction, and a book of poetry. *Offered by:* Hurston/Wright Foundation. *Winners:* (fiction) Laila Lalami for *The Moor's Account* (Vintage); (nonfiction) Elizabeth Nunez for *Not for Everyday Use* (Akashic); (poetry) Claudia Rankine for *Citizen: An American Lyric* (Graywolf).

IMPAC Dublin Literary Award (Ireland) (€100,000). For a book of high literary merit, written in English or translated into English; if translated, the author receives €75,000 and the translator €25,000. *Offered by:* IMPAC Corp. and the City of Dublin. *Winner:* Jim Crace for *Harvest* (Picador).

Independent Foreign Fiction Prize (United Kingdom) (£5,000 each for author and translator). For a work of fiction by a living author that has been translated into English from any other language and published in the United Kingdom. *Sponsor:* Arts Council England. *Winners:* Jenny Erpenbeck, author, and Susan Bernofsky, translator, for *The End of Days* (New Directions).

Indies Choice Book Awards (formerly Book-Sense Book of the Year Awards). Chosen by owners and staff of American Booksellers Association member bookstores. *Winners:* (adult fiction) Anthony Doerr for *All the Light We Cannot See* (Scribner); (adult nonfiction) Atul Gawande for *Being Mortal: Medicine and What Matters in the End* (Metropolitan); (adult debut) Andy Weir for *The Martian* (Crown); (young adult) Holly Black for *The Darkest Part of the Forest* (Little, Brown).

International Prize for Arabic Fiction ($50,000 and publication in English). To reward excellence in contemporary Arabic creative writing. *Sponsors:* Booker Prize Foundation, Emirates Foundation for Philanthropy. *Winner:* Shukri Mabkhout for *The Italian* (Dar Tanweer Tunis).

ILA Children's and Young Adults' Book Awards. For first or second books in any language published for children or young adults. *Offered by:* International Literacy Association. *Winners:* (primary fiction) Lois Brandt for *Maddi's Fridge* (Flashlight); (primary nonfiction) Katharine Hall for *Polar Bears and Penguins: A Compare and Contrast Book* (Abordale); (intermediate fiction) Jonathan Auxier for *The Night Gardener* (Amulet); (intermediate nonfiction) Cheryl Mullenbach for *The Industrial Revolution for Kids: The People and Technology That Changed the World* (Chicago Review); (young adult fiction) Tawni Waters for *Beauty of the Broken* (Simon Pulse).

Rona Jaffe Foundation Writers' Awards ($30,000). To identify and support women writers of exceptional talent in the early stages of their careers. *Offered by:* Rona Jaffe Foundation. *Winners:* Meehan Crist, Vanessa Hua, Ashley M. Jones, Britteney Black Rose Kapri, Amanda Rea, Natalie Haney Tilghman.

Jerusalem Prize (Israel). Awarded biennially to a writer whose works best express the theme of freedom of the individual in society. *Offered by:* Jerusalem International Book Fair. *Winner:* Ismail Kadare.

Jewish Book Council Awards. *Winners:* (Jewish Book of the Year) Bruce Hoffman for *Anonymous Soldiers: The Struggle For Israel, 1917–1947* (Knopf); (biography, autobiography, memoir) Joseph Polak, foreword by Elie Wiesel for *After the Holocaust the Bells Still Ring* (Urim); (contemporary Jewish life and practice) Shulem Deen for *All Who Go Do Not Return: A Memoir* (Graywolf); (education and Jewish identity) Ted Merwin for *Pastrami on Rye: An Overstuffed History of the Jewish Deli* (NYU Press); (fiction) Daniel Torday for *The Last Flight of Poxl West: A Novel* (St. Martin's); (history) Dennis Ross for *Doomed to Succeed: The U.S.-Israel Relationship from Truman to Obama* (Farrar, Straus and Giroux); (Holocaust) Anna Bikont and Alissa Valles, translator, for *The Crime and the Silence: Confronting the Massacre of Jews*

in Wartime Jedwabne (Farrar, Straus and Giroux); (illustrated children's book) Tanya Simon, Richard Simon, and Marc Siegel, illustrator, for *Oskar and the Eight Blessings* (Roaring Brook); (modern Jewish thought and experience) Rabbi Jonathan Sacks for *Not In God's Name: Confronting Religious Violence* (Schocken); (outstanding debut fiction) John Benditt for *The Boatmaker* (Tin House); (poetry) Edward Hirsch for *Gabriel: A Poem* (Knopf); (scholarship) Christine Hayes for *What's Divine About Divine Law? Early Perspectives* (Princeton University Press); (Sephardic culture) David A. Wacks for *Double Diaspora in Sephardic Literature: Jewish Cultural Production Before and After 1492* (Indiana University Press); (visual arts) Marc Michael Epstein, editor, for *Skies of Parchment, Seas of Ink: Jewish Illuminated Manuscripts* (Princeton University Press); (women's studies) Beverley Chalmers for *Birth, Sex and Abuse: Women's Voices Under Nazi Rule* (Grosvenor House); (writing based on archival material) Ethan B. Katz for *The Burdens of Brotherhood: Jews and Muslims from North Africa to France* (Harvard University Press); (young adult literature) Laura Amy Schlitz for *The Hired Girl* (Candlewick).

Samuel Johnson Prize for Nonfiction (United Kingdom) (£25,000). For an outstanding work of nonfiction. *Sponsor:* British Broadcasting Corporation. *Donor:* Anonymous. *Winner:* Steve Silberman for *Neurotribes: The Legacy of Autism and the Future of Neurodiversity* (Avery).

Sue Kaufman Prize for First Fiction ($5,000). For a first novel or collection of short stories. *Offered by:* American Academy of Arts and Letters. *Winner:* Michael Carroll for *Little Reef and Other Stories* (University of Wisconsin Press).

Ezra Jack Keats Awards. For children's picture books. *Offered by:* New York Public Library and the Ezra Jack Keats Foundation. *Winners:* (new writer award) Chieri Uegaki for *Hana Hashimoto, Sixth Violin,* illustrated by Qin Leng (Kids Can); (new illustrator award) Chris Haughton for *Shh! We Have a Plan* (Candlewick).

Kerlan Award. To recognize singular attainments in the creation of children's literature and in appreciation for generous donation of unique resources to the Kerlan Collection for the study of children's literature. *Offered by:* Kerlan Children's Literature Research Collections, University of Minnesota. *Winner:* Sharon Creech.

Coretta Scott King Book Awards ($1,000). To an African American author and illustrator of outstanding books for children and young adults. *Offered by:* American Library Association, Ethnic and Multicultural Exchange Round Table (EMIERT). *Winners:* (author) Jacqueline Woodson for *Brown Girl Dreaming* (Nancy Paulsen); (illustrator) Christopher Myers for *Firebird*, written by Misty Copeland (Penguin).

Coretta Scott King/John Steptoe Award for New Talent. To offer visibility to a writer or illustrator at the beginning of a career. *Sponsor:* Coretta Scott King Book Award Committee. *Winner:* Jason Reynolds *When I Was the Greatest*, (Atheneum).

Coretta Scott King/Virginia Hamilton Award for Lifetime Achievement. Given in even-numbered years to an African American author, illustrator, or author/illustrator for a body of books for children or young adults. In odd-numbered years, the award honors substantial contributions through active engagement with youth, using award-winning African American literature for children or young adults. *Winner:* librarian Deborah D. Taylor.

Kirkus Prize ($50,000). For outstanding fiction, nonfiction, and young readers literature. *Offered by Kirkus Reviews. Winners:* (fiction) Hanya Yanagihara for *A Little Life* (Doubleday); (nonfiction) Ta-Nehisi Coates for *Between The World and Me: Notes On The First 150 Years in America* (Spiegel & Grau); (young readers) Pam Muñoz Ryan for *Echo* (Scholastic).

Lambda Literary Awards. To honor outstanding lesbian, gay, bisexual, and transgender (LGBT) literature. *Offered by:* Lambda Literary Foundation. *Winners:* (transgender fiction) Casey Plett for *A Safe Girl To Love* (Topside); (gay general fiction) Tom Spanbauer for *I Loved You More* (Hawthorne); (lesbian general fiction) Alexis De Veaux for *Yabo* (RedBone); (LGBT debut fiction) Abdi Nazemian for *The Walk-In Closet* (Curtis Brown Unlimited); (transgender nonfiction) Thomas Page McBee for *Man Alive: A True*

Story of Violence, Forgiveness and Becoming a Man (City Lights); (bisexual fiction) Ana Castillo for *Give It to Me* (The Feminist Press); (bisexual nonfiction) Charles M. Blow for *Fire Shut Up In My Bones* (Houghton Mifflin Harcourt); (LGBT nonfiction) Martin Duberman for *Hold Tight Gently: Michael Callen, Essex Hemphill, and the Battlefield of AIDS* (The New Press); (gay poetry) Danez Smith for *[insert] boy* (YesYes); (lesbian poetry) Valerie Wetlaufer for *Mysterious Acts by My People* (Sibling Rivalry); (gay mystery) Katie Gilmartin for *Blackmail, My Love: A Murder Mystery* (Cleis); (lesbian mystery) Ellen Hart for *The Old Deep and Dark-A Jane Lawless Mystery* (Minotaur); (gay memoir/biography) Richard Blanco for *The Prince of Los Cocuyos* (HarperCollins/Ecco), John Lahr for *Tennessee Williams: Mad Pilgrimage of the Flesh* (Norton); (lesbian memoir/biography) Alethia Jones and Virginia Eubanks, with Barbara Smith for *Ain't Gonna Let Nobody Turn Me Around: Forty Years of Movement Building with Barbara Smith* (SUNY); (gay romance) Jeff Mann for *Salvation: A Novel of the Civil War* (Bear Bones); (lesbian romance) Robbi McCoy for *The Farmer's Daughter* (Bella); (gay erotica) Tiffany Reisz for *The King* (MIRA); (lesbian erotica) Diana Cage for *Lesbian Sex Bible* (Quiver); (LGBT anthology) Leila J. Rupp and Susan K. Freeman for *Understanding and Teaching US Lesbian, Gay, Bisexual, and Transgender History* (University of Wisconsin Press); (LGBT children's/young adult) Tim Federle for *Five, Six, Seven, Nate!* (Simon & Schuster); (LGBT drama) Robert O'Hara for *Bootycandy* (Samuel French); (LGBT graphic novel) Joyce Brabner for *Second Avenue Caper* (Farrar, Straus and Giroux); (LGBT science fiction/fantasy/horror) Chaz Brenchley for *Bitter Waters* (Lethe); (LGBT studies) Vincent Woodard, and Justin A. Joyce and Dwight McBride, editors, for *Delectable Negro: Human Consumption and Homoeroticism within US Slave Culture* (New York University Press).

Harold Morton Landon Translation Award ($1,000). For a book of verse translated into English. *Offered by:* Academy of American Poets. *Winner:* Roger Greenwald for *Guard-*

ing the Air: Selected Poems of Gunnar Harding (Black Widow Press).

David J. Langum, Sr. Prize in American Historical Fiction ($1,000). To honor a book of historical fiction published in the previous year. *Winner:* Kimberly Elkins for *What is Visible* (Twelve).

David J. Langum, Sr. Prize in American Legal History or Biography ($1,000). For a university press book that is accessible to the educated general public, rooted in sound scholarship, with themes that touch upon matters of general concern. *Winner:* Nathaniel Grow for *Baseball on Trial: The Origin of Baseball's Antitrust Exemption* (University of Illinois Press).

Latner Writers' Trust Poetry Prize (C$25,000). To a writer with an exceptional body of work in the field of poetry. *Winner:* Karen Solie.

James Laughlin Award ($5,000). To commend and support a second book of poetry. *Offered by:* Academy of American Poets. *Winner:* Kathryn Nuernberger for *The End of Pink* (BOA Editions).

Claudia Lewis Award. For the year's best poetry book or books for young readers. *Offered by:* Bank Street College of Education and the Florence M. Miller Memorial Fund. *Winner:* (older readers) Jacqueline Woodson for *Brown Girl Dreaming* (Penguin); (younger readers) Joyce Sidman and Rick Allen, illustrator for *Winter Bees* (Houghton Mifflin Harcourt).

Library of Congress Prize for American Fiction. To honor an American literary writer whose body of work is distinguished for its mastery of the art and for its originality of thought and imagination. *Offered by:* Library of Congress. *Winner:* Louise Erdrich.

Ruth Lilly and Dorothy Sargent Rosenberg Poetry Fellowships ($25,800). To emerging poets to support their continued study and writing of poetry. *Offered by:* the Poetry Foundation. *Winners:* Nate Marshall, Erika L. Sánchez, Danniel Schoonebeek, Safiya Sinclair, and Jamila Woods.

Ruth Lilly Poetry Prize ($100,000). To a U.S. poet in recognition of lifetime achievement. *Offered by:* the Poetry Foundation. *Winner:* Alice Notley.

Astrid Lindgren Memorial Award (Sweden) (5 million kroner, more than $575,000). In memory of children's author Astrid Lind-gren, to honor outstanding children's literature and efforts to promote it. *Offered by:* Government of Sweden and the Swedish Arts Council. *Winner:* The Project for the Study of Alternative Education in South Africa (PRAESA).

Locus Awards. For science fiction writing. *Offered by:* Locus Publications. *Winners:* (science fiction novel) Ann Leckie for *Ancillary Sword* (Orbit); (fantasy novel) Katherine Addison for *The Goblin Emperor* (Tor); (young adult book) Joe Abercrombie for *Half a King* (Del Rey); (first novel) Mary Rickert for *The Memory Garden* (Sourcebooks Landmark); (novella) Nancy Kress for *Yesterday's Kin* (Tachyon); (novelette) Joe Abercrombie for "Tough Times All Over" (Rogues); (short story) Elizabeth Bear for "Covenant" (Hieroglyph); (anthology) George R. R. Martin and Gardner Dozois, editors, for *Rogues* (Bantam); (collection) Jay Lake for *Last Plane to Heaven* (Tor); (nonfiction) Jo Walton for *What Makes This Book So Great* (Tor); (art book) John Fleskes, editor, for *Spectrum 21: The Best in Contemporary Fantastic Art* (Flesk).

London Book Festival Awards. To honor books worthy of further attention from the international publishing community. *Winners:* (science fiction and grand prize) Gary Grossman for *Old Earth* (Diversion); (general fiction) Everett DeMoirer for *Thirty-Three Cecils* (Blydyn Square); (general nonfiction) Kathy Gruver for *Journey of Healing* (Infinity); (children's) Ayn Cates Sullivan for *A Story of Becoming* (Infinite Light); (young adult) Mary A. Osborne for *Alchemy's Daughter* (Lake Street); (business) Bryony Thomas for *Watertight Marketing* (Panoma); (biography/autobiography/memoir) Freya Barrington for *Known to Social Services* (Faraxa); (how to) Onyx Jones for *The Unofficial Guide to Achieving Your Goals* (iUniverse); (wild card) Ann C. Pizzorusso for *Tweeting Da Vinci* (Da Vinci); (poetry) Eric Nelson for *Some Wonder* (Gival); (spiritual) James Stroud for *Mere Christian Apologetics* (Tate); (romance) Steven H. Manchester for *Gooseberry Island* (Story Plant); (photography/art) Charles Rawlings for *Living Mollusks* (The Peppertree Press); (cookbooks) Millie Snyder for *Lean and Luscious Meatless* (Headline); (history) Carl Schmitt for

Land and Sea: A World Historical Meditation (Telos).

Elizabeth Longford Prize for Historical Biography (United Kingdom) (£5,000). *Sponsors:* Flora Fraser and Peter Soros. *Winner:* Ben Macintyre for *A Spy Among Friends: Kim Philby and the Great Betrayal* (Bloomsbury).

Los Angeles Times Book Prizes. To honor literary excellence. *Offered by:* Los Angeles Times. *Winners:* (biography) Andrew Roberts for *Napoleon: A Life* (Viking); (current interest) Jeff Hobbs for *The Short and Tragic Life of Robert Peace: A Brilliant Young Man Who Left Newark for the Ivy League* (Scribner); (fiction) Siri Hustvedt for *The Blazing World* (Simon & Schuster); (Art Seidenbaum Award for First Fiction) Valeria Luiselli for *Faces in the Crowd* (Coffee House Press); (graphic novel/comics) Jaime Hernandez for *The Love Bunglers* (Fantagraphics); (history) Adam Tooze for *The Deluge: The Great War, America and the Remaking of the Global Order, 1916–1931* (Viking); (mystery/thriller) Tom Bouman for *Dry Bones in the Valley* (W.W. Norton & Company); (poetry) Claudia Rankine for *Citizen: An American Lyric* (Graywolf Press); (science and technology) Elizabeth Kolbert for *The Sixth Extinction: An Unnatural History* (Henry Holt and Co.); (young adult literature) Candace Fleming for *The Family Romanov: Murder, Rebellion, and the Fall of Imperial Russia* (Schwartz & Wade / Random House Children's); (Robert Kirsch Award for lifetime achievement) Author T.C. Boyle; (innovator's award) LeVar Burton.

Amy Lowell Poetry Traveling Scholarship. For one or two U.S. poets to spend one year outside North America in a country the recipients feel will most advance their work. *Offered by:* Amy Lowell Poetry Traveling Scholarship. *Winner:* Meg Day.

J. Anthony Lukas Awards. For nonfiction writing that demonstrates literary grace, serious research, and concern for an important aspect of American social or political life. *Offered by:* Columbia University Graduate School of Journalism and the Nieman Foundation for Journalism at Harvard. *Winners:* (Lukas Book Prize, $10,000) Jenny Nordberg for *The Underground Girls of Ka-*

bul (Crown); (Mark Lynton History Prize, $10,000) Harold Holzer for *Lincoln and the Power of the Press: The War for Public Opinion* (Simon & Schuster); (Work-in-Progress Award, $30,000) Dan Egan for *Liquid Desert: Life and Death of the Great Lakes* (Norton).

Macavity Awards. For excellence in mystery writing. *Offered by:* Mystery Readers International. *Winners:* (mystery novel) Alex Marwood for *The Killer Next Door* (Penguin); (first mystery) Julia Dahl for *Invisible City* (Minotaur); (short story) Craig Faustus Buck for "Honeymoon Sweet" in *Murder at the Beach: The Bouchercon Anthology 2014,* edited by Dana Cameron (Down & Out); (nonfiction) Hank Phillippi Ryan, editor, for *Writes of Passage: Adventures on the Writer's Journey* (Henery); (Sue Feder Historical Mystery Award) Catriona McPherson for *A Deadly Measure of Brimstone* (Minotaur).

McKitterick Prize (United Kingdom) (£4,000). To an author over the age of 40 for a first novel, published or unpublished. *Winner:* Robert Allison for *The Letter Bearer* (Granta.

Man Booker International Prize (United Kingdom) (£60,000). Awarded biennially to a living author for a significant contribution to world literature. *Offered by:* Man Group. *Winner:* László Krasznahorkai.

Man Booker Prize for Fiction (United Kingdom) (£50,000). For the best novel written in English by a Commonwealth author. *Offered by:* Booktrust and the Man Group. *Winner:* Marlon James for *A Brief History of Seven Killings* (Oneworld).

Lenore Marshall Poetry Prize ($25,000). For an outstanding book of poems published in the United States. *Offered by:* Academy of American Poets. *Winner:* Kevin Young for *Book of Hours* (Knopf).

Mason Award ($10,000). To honor an author whose body of work has made extraordinary contributions to bringing literature to a wide reading public. *Sponsors:* George Mason University and Fall for the Book. *Winner:* Diana Gabaldon.

Somerset Maugham Awards (United Kingdom) (£2,500). For works in any genre except drama by a writer under the age of 35, to enable young writers to enrich their work by gaining experience of foreign countries. *Winners:* Jonathan Beckman for *How To Ruin A Queen: Marie Antoinette, the Stolen Diamonds and the Scandal That Shook The French Throne* (John Murray), Liz Berry for *Black Country* (Chatto & Windus); Ben Brooks for *Lolito* (Canongate); Zoe Pilger for *Eat My Heart Out* (Serpent's Tail).

Addison M. Metcalf Award in Literature ($2,000). Awarded biennially in alternation with the Addison M. Metcalf Award in Art, to a young writer of great promise. *Offered by:* American Academy of Arts and Letters. *Winner:* Amy Rowland.

Vicky Metcalf Award for Literature for Young People (Canada) (C$20,000). To a Canadian writer of children's literature for a body of work. *Offered by:* Metcalf Foundation. *Winner:* Jan Thornhill.

Midwest Booksellers Choice Awards. *Offered by:* Midwest Booksellers Association. *Winners:* (fiction) Julie Schumacher for *Dear Committee Members* (Wheeler); (nonfiction) Pamela Smith Hill, editor, for *Pioneer Girl* (South Dakota Historical Society); (poetry) Ted Kooser for *Splitting an Order* (Copper Canyon); (young adult) Michael Perry for *The Scavengers* (HarperCollins); (picture book) Joyce Sidman for *Winter Bees* (Houghton Mifflin Harcourt).

William C. Morris YA Debut Award. To honor a debut book published by a first-time author writing for teens and celebrating impressive new voices in young adult literature. *Offered by:* American Library Association, Young Adult Library Services Association. *Donor:* William C. Morris Endowment. *Winner:* Isabel Quintero for *Gabi, a Girl in Pieces* (Cinco Puntos).

Mythopoeic Fantasy Awards. To recognize fantasy or mythic literature for children and adults that best exemplifies the spirit of the Inklings, a group of fantasy writers that includes J. R. R. Tolkien, C. S. Lewis, and Charles Williams. *Offered by:* Mythopoeic Society. *Winners:* (adult literature) Sarah Avery for *Tales from Rugosa Coven* (Dark Quest); (children's literature) Natalie Lloyd for *A Snicker of Magic* (Scholastic); (Mythopoeic Scholarship Award in Inklings Studies) Robert Boenig for *C.S. Lewis and the Middle Ages* (Kent State University Press); (Mythopoeic Scholarship Award in Myth

and Fantasy Studies) Brian Attebery for *Stories About Stories: Fantasy and the Remaking of Myth* (Oxford University Press).

National Book Awards. To celebrate the best in American literature. *Offered by:* National Book Foundation. *Winners:* (fiction) Phil Klay for *Redeployment* (Penguin); (nonfiction) Evan Osnos for *Age of Ambition: Chasing Fortune, Truth, and Faith in the New China* (Farrar, Straus & Giroux); (poetry) Louise Glück for *Faithful and Virtuous Night* Farrar, Straus & Giroux); (young people's literature) Jacqueline Woodson for *Brown Girl Dreaming* (Penguin).

National Book Awards (United Kingdom). See Specsavers National Book Awards.

National Book Critics Circle Awards. For literary excellence. *Offered by:* National Book Critics Circle. *Winners:* (fiction) Marilynne Robinson for *Lila* (Farrar, Straus & Giroux); (nonfiction) David Brion Davis for *The Problem of Slavery in the Age of Emancipation* (Knopf); (biography) John Lahr for *Tennessee Williams: Mad Pilgrimage of the Flesh* (Norton); (autobiography) Roz Chast for *Can't We Talk About Something More Pleasant?* (Bloomsbury); (poetry) Claudia Rankine for *Citizen: An American Lyric* (Graywolf); (criticism) Nona Willis Aronowitz for *The Essential Ellen Willis* (University of Minnesota Press); (Nona Balakian Citation for Excellence in Reviewing) Alexandra Schwartz; (Ivan Sandrof Lifetime Achievement Award) Toni Morrison.

National Book Foundation Literarian Award for Outstanding Service to the American Literary Community. *Offered by:* National Book Foundation. *Winner:* James Patterson, novelist and literary activist.

National Book Foundation Medal for Distinguished Contribution to American Letters ($10,000). To a person who has enriched the nation's literary heritage over a life of service or corpus of work. *Offered by:* National Book Foundation. *Winner:* Don DeLillo.

National Translation Awards ($5,000). To honor translators whose work has made a valuable contribution to literary translation into English. *Offered by:* American Literary Translators Association. *Winners:* (prose) William M. Hutchins, translator from Arabic, for *The New Waw: Saharan Oasis* by Ibrahim al-Koni (Center for Middle Eastern

Studies at the University of Texas at Austin); (poetry) Pierre Joris, translator from German, for *Breathturn into Timestead* by Paul Celan (Farrar, Straus & Giroux); (Lucien Stryk Asian Translation Prize) Eleanor Goodman for *Something Crosses My Mind* by Wang Xiaoni (Zephyr).

Nebula Awards. For science fiction writing. *Offered by:* Science Fiction and Fantasy Writers of America (SFWA). *Winners:* (novel) Jeff VanderMeer for *Annihilation* (HarperCollins Canada); (novella) Nancy Kress for *Yesterday's Kin* (Tachyon); (novelette) Alaya Dawn Johnson for "A Guide to the Fruits of Hawai'i" in *F&SF,* July–August 2014; (short story) Ursula Vernon for "Jackalope Wives" in *Apex,* January 2014; (Ray Bradbury Award for Outstanding Dramatic Presentation) James Gunn and Nicole Perlman for *Guardians of the Galaxy* (Walt Disney Studios); (Andre Norton Award for Young Adult Science Fiction and Fantasy) Alaya Dawn Johnson for *Love Is the Drug* (Levine); (Damon Knight Grand Master Award) Larry Niven.

John Newbery Medal. For the most distinguished contribution to literature for children. *Offered by:* American Library Association, Association for Library Service to Children. *Winner:* Kwame Alexander for *The Crossover* (HMH Books for Young Readers).

Nimrod Literary Awards ($2,000 plus publication). *Offered by:* Nimrod International *Journal of Prose and Poetry. Winners:* (Pablo Neruda Prize in Poetry) Heather Altfeld for "Two Pockets" and other poems; (Katherine Anne Porter Prize in Fiction) J. Duncan Wiley for "Inclusions."

Nobel Prize in Literature (Sweden). For the total literary output of a distinguished career. *Offered by:* Swedish Academy. *Winner:* Svetlana Alexievich.

Eli M. Oboler Memorial Award. Given biennially to an author of a published work in English or in English translation dealing with issues, events, questions, or controversies in the area of intellectual freedom. *Offered by:* Intellectual Freedom Round Table, American Library Association. *Winners:* Mark Alfino and Laura Koltutsky, editors, for *The Library Juice Press Handbook of Intellectual Freedom* (Library Juice).

Flannery O'Connor Awards for Short Fiction. For collections of short fiction. *Offered by:* University of Georgia Press. *Winners:* Lisa Graley for *The Current That Carries*, Anne Raeff for *The Jungle All Around Us* (both UGA Press).

Frank O'Connor Short Story Award (£25,000). An international award for a collection of short stories. *Offered by:* Munster Literature Centre, Cork, Ireland. *Sponsor:* Cork City Council. *Winner:* Carys Davies for *The Redemption of Galen Pike* (Salt).

Oddest Book Title of the Year Award. See Bookseller/Diagram Prize for Oddest Title of the Year.

Scott O'Dell Award for Historical Fiction ($5,000). *Offered by: Bulletin of the Center for Children's Books,* University of Chicago. *Winner:* Kirby Larson for *Dash* (Scholastic).

Odyssey Award. To the producer of the best audiobook for children and/or young adults available in English in the United States. *Sponsors:* American Library Association, ALSC/Booklist/YALSA. *Winner:* Live Oak Media for *H. O. R. S. E. A Game of Basketball and Imagination* by Christopher Myers, narrated by Dion Graham and Christopher Myers.

Seán Ó Faoláin Short Story Competition (€2,000 and publication in the literary journal *Southword. Offered by:* Munster Literature Centre, Cork, Ireland. *Winner:* Evelyn Walsh for "'White Rabbit."

Dayne Ogilvie Prize (Canada) (C$4,000). To an emerging Canadian writer from the LGBT community who demonstrates promise through a body of quality work. *Offered by:* Writers' Trust of Canada. *Sponsor:* Robin Pacific. *Winner:* Alex Leslie.

Orbis Pictus Award for Outstanding Nonfiction for Children. *Offered by:* National Council of Teachers of English. *Winners:* Candace Fleming for *The Family Romanov: Murder, Rebellion and the Fall of Imperial Russia* (Schwartz & Wade).

Orion Book Awards ($3,000). To recognize books that deepen connection to the natural world, present new ideas about mankind's relationship with nature, and achieve excellence in writing. *Sponsors: Orion Magazine* and the Geraldine R. Dodge Foundation. *Winners:* (fiction) Laline Paull for *The Bees*

(Ecco Press); (nonfiction) George Monbiot for *Feral: Rewilding the Land, the Sea, and Human Life* (University of Chicago Press).

Oxford-Weidenfeld Translation Prize. *Winner:* Susan Bernofsky for her translation of Jenny Erpenbeck's *The End of Days* (Portobello).

PEN Award for Poetry in Translation ($3,000). For a book-length translation of poetry from any language into English, published in the United States. *Offered by:* PEN American Center. *Winner:* Eliza Griswold for her translation from the Pashto of *I Am the Beggar of the World: Landays from Contemporary Afghanistan* (Farrar, Straus and Giroux).

PEN/Saul Bellow Award for Achievement in American Fiction ($25,000). Awarded biennially to a distinguished living American author of fiction. *Offered by:* PEN American Center. *Winner:* To be awarded next in 2016.

PEN/Bellwether Prize for Socially Engaged Fiction ($25,000). Awarded biennially to the author of a previously unpublished novel that addresses issues of social justice and the impact of culture and politics on human relationships. *Founder:* Barbara Kingsolver. *Winner:* To be awarded next in 2016.

PEN Beyond Margins Awards. See PEN Open Book Awards.

PEN/Robert W. Bingham Prize ($25,000). To a writer whose first novel or short story collection represents distinguished literary achievement and suggests great promise. *Offered by:* PEN American Center. *Winner:* Jack Livings for *The Dog* (Farrar, Straus and Giroux).

PEN/Diamonstein-Spielvogel Award for the Art of the Essay ($10,000). For a book of essays by a single author that best exemplifies the dignity and esteem of the essay form. *Winner:* Ian Buruma for *Theater of Cruelty: Art, Film, and the Shadow of War* (New York Review Books).

PEN/ESPN Award for Literary Sports Writing ($5,000). To a living writer or writers for exceptional contributions to the field of literary sports writing. *Winner:* John Branch for *Boy on Ice: The Life and Death of Derek Boogaard* (W. W. Norton & Company).

PEN/ESPN Lifetime Achievement Award for Literary Sports Writing ($5,000). For a writer whose body of work represents an exceptional contribution to the field. *Winner:* Bob Ryan.

PEN/Faulkner Award for Fiction ($15,000). To honor the year's best work of fiction published by an American. *Winner:* Atticus Lish for *Preparation for the Next Life* (Tyrant Books).

PEN/John Kenneth Galbraith Award for Nonfiction ($10,000). Given biennially for a distinguished book of general nonfiction. *Offered by:* PEN American Center. *Winner:* Sheri Fink for *Five Days at Memorial: Life and Death in a Storm-Ravaged Hospital* (Crown).

PEN/Heim Translation Fund Grants ($2,000–$4,000). To support the translation of book-length works of fiction, creative nonfiction, poetry, or drama that have not previously appeared in English or have appeared only in an egregiously flawed translation. *Winners:* Allison Charette, Jennifer Croft, Stephan Delbos, Amanda DeMarco, Adriana Jacobs, Roy Kesey, Lee Klein, Dong Li, Meg Matich, Jacob Moe, Rajiv Mahabir, Takami Nieda, Zoë Perry, Will Schutt, Sophie Seita and Simon Wickham-Smith.

PEN/Ernest Hemingway Foundation Award. For a distinguished work of first fiction by an American. *Offered by:* PEN New England. *Winner:* Arna Bontemps Hemenway for *Elegy on Kinderklavier* (Sarabande).

PEN/O. Henry Prize. For short stories of exceptional merit, in English, published in U.S. and Canadian magazines. *Winners:* Percival Everett for "Finding Billy White Feather" in the *Virginia Quarterly Review*; Lydia Davis for "The Seals" in *The Paris Review*; Lionel Shriver for "Kilifi Creek" in the *New Yorker*; Manuel Muñoz for "The Happiest Girl in the Whole USA" in *Glimmer Train*; Russell Banks for "A Permanent Member of the Family" in *Conjunctions*; Dina Nayeri for "A Ride Out of Phrao" in *Alaska Quarterly Review*; Emily Ruskovich for "Owl" in *One Story*; Becky Hagenston for "The Upside-Down World" in *Subtropics*; Lynn Freed for "The Way Things Are Going" in *Harper's*; Brenda Peynado for "The History of Happiness" in the *Cimarron Review*; Naira Kuzmich for "The Kingsley Drive Chorus" in *Salamander* Emma Törzs for "Word of Mouth" in *The Threepenny Review*; Christopher Merkner for "Cabins" in

Subtropics; Molly Antopol for "My Grandmother Tells Me This Story" in *Ecotone*; Lynne Sharon Schwartz for "The Golden Rule" in *Fifth Wednesday Journal*; Joan Silber for "About My Aunt" in *Tin House*; Thomas Pierce for "Ba Baboon" in the *New Yorker*; Elizabeth Strout for "Snow Blind" in *Virginia Quarterly Review*; Vauhini Vara for "I, Buffalo" in *Tin House*; Elizabeth McCracken for "Birdsong from the Radio" in *Zoetrope: All-Story.*

PEN/Nora Magid Award ($2,500). Awarded biennially to honor a magazine editor who has contributed significantly to the excellence of the publication he or she edits. *Winners:* Rob Spillman for *Tin House.*

PEN/Malamud Award. To recognize a body of work that demonstrates excellence in the art of short fiction. *Winner:* Deborah Eisenberg.

PEN/Ralph Manheim Medal for Translation. Given triennially to a translator whose career has demonstrated a commitment to excellence. *Winner:* Burton Watson.

PEN/Phyllis Naylor Working Writer Fellowship ($5,000). To a published author of children's or young adults' fiction to aid in completing a book-length work in progress. *Offered by:* PEN American Center. *Winner:* Stephanie Kuehn for *The Pragmatist* (Forthcoming from Dutton/ Penguin Books).

PEN New England Awards. For works of fiction, nonfiction, and poetry by New England writers or with New England topics or settings. *Winners:* (nonfiction) Kevin Birmingham for *The Most Dangerous Book: The Battle for James Joyce's Ulysses* (Penguin); (fiction) Carolyn Chute for *Treat Us Like Dogs and We Will Become Wolves* (Grove), (poetry) Wesley McNair for *The Lost Child* (David R Godine).

PEN New England Susan P. Bloom Children's Book Discovery Award. For noteworthy unpublished children's or young adult literature. *Winners:* Alice Caldwell for "Sly as a Sheep"; Sheryl DePaolo for "Child Star"; Kristy Acevedo for "Consider."

PEN New England Henry David Thoreau Prize for Literary Excellence in Nature Writing. *Winner:* Diane Ackerman.

PEN Open Book Award (formerly PEN Beyond Margins Award) ($5,000). For book-length writings by authors of color, published in the United States during the current calendar year. *Offered by:* PEN American Center. *Winner:* Claudia Rankine for *Citizen: An American Lyric* (Graywolf).

PEN/Joyce Osterweil Award for Poetry ($5,000). A biennial award given in odd-numbered years to recognize a new and emerging American poet. *Offered by:* PEN American Center. *Winner:* Saeed Jones for *Prelude to Bruise* (Coffee House Press).

PEN/Laura Pels Foundation Awards for Drama. To recognize a master American dramatist, an American playwright in mid-career, and an emerging American playwright. *Offered by:* PEN American Center. *Winners:* (master dramatist, $7,500) Tina Howe; (mid-career, $7,500) Anne Washburn; (emerging playwright, $2,500) Jennifer Blackmer.

PEN Translation Prize ($3,000). To promote the publication and reception of translated world literature in English. *Winner:* Denise Newman for her translation from Danish of *Baboon* by Naja Marie Aidt (Two Lines).

PEN/Voelcker Award for Poetry. Given in even-numbered years to an American poet at the height of his or her powers. *Offered by:* PEN American Center. *Winner:* To be awarded next in 2016.

PEN/Jacqueline Bograd Weld Award for Biography ($5,000). To the author of a distinguished biography published in the United States during the previous calendar year. *Offered by:* PEN American Center. *Winner:* Anna Whitelock for *The Queen's Bed: An Intimate History of Elizabeth's Court* (Farrar, Straus & Giroux).

PEN/E. O. Wilson Literary Science Writing Award ($10,000). For a book of literary nonfiction on the subject of the physical and biological sciences. *Winner:* Joshua Horwitz for *War of the Whales: A True Stor* (Simon & Schuster).

Maxwell E. Perkins Award. To honor an editor, publisher, or agent who has discovered, nurtured, and championed writers of fiction in the United States. *Offered by:* Center for Fiction, Mercantile Library of New York. *Winner:* Daniel Halpern, Publisher and President of Ecco, an imprint of HarperCollins Publishers.

Phoenix Awards. To the authors of English-language children's books that failed to win a major award at the time of publication 20 years earlier. *Winner:* Kyoko Mori for *One*

Bird (Henry Holt, 1995); (picture book) Sara Fanelli for *My Map Book* (HarperCollins, 1995).

Edgar Allan Poe Awards. For outstanding mystery, suspense, and crime writing. *Offered by:* Mystery Writers of America. *Winners:* (novel) Stephen King for *Mr. Mercedes* (Simon & Schuster); (first novel) Tom Bouman for *Dry Bones in the Valley* (W.W. Norton); (paperback original) Chris Abani for *The Secret History of Las Vegas* (Penguin); (fact crime) William J. Mann for *Tinseltown: Murder, Morphine, and Madness at the Dawn of Hollywood* (HarperCollins); (critical/biographical) J.W. Ocker for *Poe-Land: The Hallowed Haunts of Edgar Allan Poe* (W.W. Norton); (short story) Gillian Flynn for "What Do You Do?" (Penguin); (juvenile) Kate Milford for *Greenglass House* (Clarion); (young adult) James Klise for *The Art of Secrets* (Algonquin); (television episode) Sally Wainwright for "Episode 1" – Happy Valley (Netflix); (Robert L. Fish Memorial Award) Zoë Z. Dean for "Getaway Girl" in *Ellery Queen Mystery Magazine* (Dell); (grand master) Lois Duncan, James Ellroy; (Raven Awards) Ruth and Jon Jordan for *Crimespree Magazine*Kathryn Kennison, *Magna Cum Murder*; (Ellery Queen Award) Charles Ardai, Editor and Founder, *Hard Case Crime*; (Simon & Schuster Mary Higgins Clark Award) Jane Casey for *The Stranger You Know* (Minotaur).

Poets Out Loud Prize ($1,000 and publication by Fordham University Press). For a book-length poetry collection. *Sponsor:* Fordham University. *Winners:* Gregory Mahrer for "A Provisional Map of the Lost Continent"; (editor's prize) Nancy K. Pearson for "The Whole By Contemplation of a Single Bone."

Katherine Anne Porter Award ($20,000). Awarded biennially to a prose writer of demonstrated achievement. *Offered by:* American Academy of Arts and Letters. *Winner:* Matt Cashion for *Last Words of the Holy Ghost* (University of North Texas Press).

Michael L. Printz Award. For excellence in literature for young adults. *Offered by:* American Library Association, Young Adult Library Services Association. *Winner:* Jandy Nelson for *I'll Give You the Sun* (Dial).

V. S. Pritchett Memorial Prize (United Kingdom) (£1,000). For a previously unpublished short story. *Offered by:* Royal Society of Literature. *Winner:* Jonathan Tel for "The Seduction of a Provincial Accountant."

Pritzker Military Library Literature Award ($100,000). To recognize a living author for a body of work that has profoundly enriched the public understanding of American military history. *Sponsor:* Tawani Foundation. *Winner:* David Hackett Fischer.

Prix Aurora Awards (Canada). For science fiction. *Winners:* (novel) Julie E. Czerneda for *A Play of Shadow* (DAW); (young adult novel) Karl Schroeder for *Lockstep* (Tor) and Charles de Lint for *Out of This World* (Razorbill Canada); (short fiction) Eric Choi for "Crimson Sky" in *Analog*; (poem/song) Tony Pi for "A Hex, With Bees" in *Wrestling With Gods: Tesseracts Eighteen* (Edge); (graphic novel) Kari Maaren for the webcomic *It Never Rains*; (related work) *On Spec* (Copper Pig Writers' Society).

Prix Goncourt (France). For "the best imaginary prose work of the year." *Offered by:* Société des Gens des Lettres. *Winner:* Mathias Énard for *La Boussole* (The Compass) (French and European Publications).

Pulitzer Prizes in Letters ($10,000). To honor distinguished work dealing preferably with American themes. *Offered by:* Columbia University Graduate School of Journalism. *Winners:* (fiction) Anthony Doerr for *All the Light We Cannot See* (Scribner); (drama) Stephen Adly Guirgisfor *Between Riverside and Crazy*; (history) Elizabeth A. Fenn for *Encounters at the Heart of the World: A History of the Mandan People* (Hill and Wang); (biography/autobiography) David I. Kertzer for *The Pope and Mussolini: The Secret History of Pius XI and the Rise of Fascism in Europe* (Random House); (poetry) Gregory Pardlo for *Digest* (Four Way Books); (general nonfiction) Elizabeth Kolbert for *The Sixth Extinction: An Unnatural History* (Henry Holt and Co.).

Raiziss/De Palchi Translation Award ($5,000 prize and a $25,000 fellowship, awarded in alternate years). For a translation into English of a significant work of modern Italian poetry by a living translator. *Offered by:* Academy of American Poets. *Winner:* Todd Portnowitz for his translation of *Go Tell It to the Emperor: Selected Poems* by Pierluigi Cappello.

RBC Bronwen Wallace Award for Emerging Writers (C$5,000) (Canada). For a writer under the age of 35 who has not yet been published in book form. *Sponsor: RBC Foundation. Winner:* Alessandra Naccarato for the short story "Re-Origin of Species."

Arthur Rense Poetry Prize ($20,000). Awarded triennially to an exceptional poet. *Offered by:* American Academy of Arts and Letters. *Winner:* To be awarded next in 2017.

Harold U. Ribalow Prize. For Jewish fiction published in English. *Sponsor: Hadassah* magazine. *Winner:* Molly Antopol for *The UnAmericans* (W. W. Norton).

Rita Awards. *Offered by:* Romance Writers of America. *Winners:* (first book) Clara Kensie for *Run to You* (Harlequin); (short contemporary romance) Caro Carson for *A Texas Rescue Christmas* (Harlequin); (mid-length contemporary romance) Jill Shalvis for *One in a Million* (Grand Central); (long contemporary romance) Jane Graves for *Baby, It's You* (Grand Central); (erotic) Tiffany Reisz for *The Saint* (Harlequin); (long historical) Meredith Duran for *Fool Me Twice* (Simon & Schuster); (short historical) Tessa Dare for *Romancing the Duke* (HarperCollins); (inspirational) Irene Hannon for *Deceived* (Baker); (paranormal) Kristen Callihan for *Evernight* (Grand Central); (novella) Anna Richland for *His Road Home* (Harlequin); (suspense) J. D. Robb for *Concealed in Death* (Penguin); (young adult) Juliana Stone for *Boys Like You* (Sourcebooks).

Rita Golden Heart Awards. For worthy unpublished romance manuscripts. *Offered by:* Romance Writers of America. *Winners:* (contemporary) Kimberly Buckner for "Call Me Mrs. Whitlock"; (short contemporary) Alexa Rowan for "Winning Her Over"; (historical) Sara Leyton for "The Reunion"; (paranormal) Jeanne Oates Estridge for "Demons Don't"; (erotic) Michele Arris for "A Deal for Love"; (suspense) Tracy Poole for "A Shot Worth Taking"; (young adult) Stephanie Winkelhake for "When I Wake."

Rodda Book Award. To recognize a book that exhibits excellence in writing and has contributed significantly to congregational libraries through promotion of spiritual growth. The award is given to books for adults, young adults, and children on a rotational basis. *Offered by:* Church and Synagogue Library Association. *Winner:* (adult) Rabbi David Zaslow for *Jesus: First-Century Rabbi* (Paraclete).

Rogers Writers' Trust Fiction Prize (Canada) (C$25,000). To a Canadian author of a novel or short story collection. *Offered by:* Rogers Communications. *Winner:* André Alexis for *Fifteen Dogs* (Coach House).

Sami Rohr Prize for Jewish Literature ($100,000). For emerging writers of Jewish literature. *Offered by:* Family of Sami Rohr. *Winner:* Ayelet Tsabari for *The Best Place on Earth: Stories* (HarperCollins Canada).

Rosenthal Foundation Award ($10,000). To a young novelist of considerable literary talent. *Offered by:* American Academy of Arts and Letters. *Winner:* Tiphanie Yanique for *Land of Love and Drowning* (Riverhead).

Royal Society of Literature Benson Medal (United Kingdom). To recognize meritorious works in poetry, fiction, history and belles letters, honoring an entire career. The recipient may be someone who is not a writer but has done conspicuous service to literature. *Winner:* Nancy Sladek.

Royal Society of Literature Jerwood Awards for Nonfiction (United Kingdom). For authors engaged on their first major commissioned works of nonfiction. *Offered by:* Royal Society of Literature. *Winners:* (£10,000) Thomas Morris for "The Matter of the Heart"; (£5,000) Catherine Nixey for "The Darkening Age"; Duncan White for "Cold Warriors: Waging Literary War Across the Iron Curtain."

Royal Society of Literature Ondaatje Prize (United Kingdom) (£10,000). For a distinguished work of fiction, nonfiction, or poetry evoking the spirit of a place. *Offered by:* Royal Society of Literature. *Winner:* Justin Marozzi for *Baghdad: City of Peace, City of Blood* (Allen Lane).

Juan Rulfo International Latin American and Caribbean Prize. See FIL Literary Award in Romance Languages.

Saltire Society Scotland Literary Awards. To recognize noteworthy work by writers of Scottish descent or living in Scotland, or by anyone who deals with the work or life of a Scot or with a Scottish problem, event, or situation. *Offered by:* Saltire Society. *Sponsors:* Creative Scotland, the National Library of Scotland, the Scottish Poetry

Library, the Scottish Historical Review Trust, Tamdhu Speyside Single Malt Scotch Whisky. *Winners (book of the year £5,000, individual categories £2,000):* (fiction book of the year) Michel Faber for *The Book of Strange New Things* (Canongate); (research book of the year) Tanja Bueltmann for *Clubbing Together: Ethnicity, Civility and Formal Sociability in the Scottish Diaspora to 1930* (Liverpool University Press); (poetry book of the year) Ryan Van Winkle for *The Good Dark* (Penned in the Margins); (first book) Helen McClory for *On the Edges of Vision* (Queen's Ferry Press); (history book) Patricia R. Andrew for *A Chasm In Time — Scottish War Art And Artists in the Twentieth Century* (Birlinn).

Carl Sandburg Literary Awards. To honor a significant body of work that has enhanced public awareness of the written word. *Sponsor:* Chicago Public Library Foundation. *Winners:* Stephen Sondheim, composer and lyricist; (21st Century Award, for significant recent achievement by a Chicago-area writer) Eric Charles May, author of *Bedrock Faith.*

Schneider Family Book Awards ($5,000). To honor authors and illustrators for books that embody artistic expressions of the disability experience of children and adolescents. *Offered by:* American Library Association. *Donor:* Katherine Schneider. *Winners:* (ages 0–10) Alan Rabinowitz and Catia Chien, illustrator, for *A Boy and a Jaguar* (Houghton Mifflin Harcourt); (ages 11–13) Ann M. Martin for *Rain Reign* (Feiwel and Friends); (ages 13–18) Gail Giles for *Girls Like Us* (Candlewick).

Scotiabank Giller Prize (Canada) (C$100,000 first place, C$10,000 to each of the finalists). For the best Canadian novel or short story collection written in English. *Offered by:* Giller Prize Foundation and Scotiabank. *Winners:* Kathy Stinson and Dusan Petricic, illustrator, for *The Man with the Violin* (Annick); (finalists) André Alexis for *Fifteen Dogs* (Coach House Books); Samuel Archibald and Donald Winkler, translator, for *Arvida* (Biblioasis); Rachel Cusk for *Outline* (HarperCollins); Heather O'Neill for *Daydreams of Angels* (HarperCollins);

Anakana Schofield for *Martin John* (Biblioasis).

Shamus Awards. To honor mysteries featuring independent private investigators. *Offered by:* Private Eye Writers of America. *Winners:* (hardcover novel) David Rosenfelt for *Hounded* (Minotaur); (first novel) Julia Dahl for *Invisible City* (Minotaur); (original paperback) Vincent Zandri for *Moonlight Weeps* (Down & Out); (short story) Gon Ben Ari for "Clear Recent History" in *Tel Aviv Noir*; (indie novel) Trace Conger for *The Shadow Broker* (CreateSpace Independent Publishing); (Shamus Award for Lifetime Achievement) Parnell Hall.

Shelley Memorial Award ($6,000 to $9,000). To a poet or poets living in the United States, chosen on the basis of genius and need. *Offered by:* Poetry Society of America. *Winner:* D. A. Powell.

Robert F. Sibert Medal. For the most distinguished informational book for children. *Offered by:* American Library Association, Association for Library Service to Children. *Winner:* Jen Bryant for *The Right Word: Roget and His Thesaurus* (Eerdmans).

Society of Authors Traveling Scholarships (United Kingdom) (£1,750). *Winners:* Tahmima Anam, James Hall, Philip Terry, and Rupert Thomson.

Specsavers National Book Awards (United Kingdom) (formerly the Galaxy National Book Awards, earlier the British Book Awards). *Winners:* no awards event in 2015.

Spur Awards. *Offered by:* Western Writers of America. *Winners:* (contemporary novel) CB McKenzie for *Bad Country* (Minotaur); (historical novel and first novel) James D. Crownover for *Wild Ran the Rivers* (Five Star); (traditional novel) Patrick Dearen for *The Big Drift* (TCU Press); (historical nonfiction) Jerome A. Greene for *American Carnage: Wounded Knee, 1890* (University of Oklahoma Press); (contemporary nonfiction) Angela Day for *Red Light to Starboard: Recalling the Exxon Valdez Disaster* (Washington State University Press); (nonfiction biography) Philip Burnham for *Song of Dewey Beard: Last Survivor of the Little Bighorn* (Bison Book/University Nebraska Press); (juvenile fiction) Rod Miller for *Rawhide Robinson Rides The Range: True Adventures of Bravery And Daring in the Wild West* (Five Star); (juvenile nonfiction) Nancy Oswald for *Edward Wynkoop: Soldier and Indian Agent* (Filter Press); (storyteller) Donald F. Montileaux for *Tasunka: A Lakota Horse Legend* (South Dakota State Historical Society Press); (short fiction) Andrew Geyer for "Fingers" (Steven F. Austin University Press); (short nonfiction) Richard W. Etulain for "Calamity Jane: A Life and Legends" (*Montana, The Magazine of Western History*); (poem) Alan Birkelbach for "A Little Longer Than the Moment" (Cowboy Poetry Press); (song) Doug Figgs and Todd Carter for "Charlie and Evangeline" (Figgs/Carter); (documentary script) Kami Horton for "IState of Jefferson" (Oregon Public Broadcasting).

Wallace Stevens Award ($100,000). To recognize outstanding and proven mastery in the art of poetry. *Offered by:* Academy of American Poets. *Winner:* Joy Harjo.

Bram Stoker Awards. For superior horror writing. *Offered by:* Horror Writers Association. *Winners:* (novel) Steve Rasnic Tem for *Blood Kin* (Solaris); (first novel) Maria Alexander for *Mr. Wicker* (Raw Dog Screaming Press); (young adult novel) John Dixon for *Phoenix Island* (Simon & Schuster); (graphic novel) Jonathan Maberry for *Bad Blood* (Dark Horse); (long fiction) Joe R. Lansdale "Fishing for Dinosaurs" in *Limbus, Inc., Book II* (JournalStone); (short fiction tie) Usman T. Malik for "The Vaporization Enthalpy of a Peculiar Pakistani Family" in *Qualia Nous* (Written Backwards), Rena Mason for "Ruminations" in *Qualia Nous* (Written Backwards); (screenplay) Jennifer Kent for "The Babadook" (Causeway Films); (lifetime achievement) Jack Ketchum, Tanith Lee.

Stonewall Book Awards. *Offered by:* Gay, Lesbian, Bisexual, and Transgender Round Table, American Library Association. *Winners:* (Barbara Gittings Literature Award) Saeed Jones for *Prelude to Bruise* (Coffee House); (Israel Fishman Nonfiction Award) Scott Siraj al-Haqq Kugle for *Living Out Islam: Voices of Gay, Lesbian, and Transgender Muslims* (New York University Press); (Mike Morgan and Larry Romans Children's and Young Adult Literature Award) Gayle E. Pitman, Ph.D. for *This Day in June* (Magination).

Story Prize ($20,000). For a collection of short fiction. *Offered by:* Story magazine. *Winner:* Elizabeth McCracken for *Thunderstruck*(Dial).

Flora Stieglitz Straus Award. For nonfiction books that serve as an inspiration to young readers. *Offered by:* Bank Street College of Education and the Florence M. Miller Memorial Fund. *Winner:* Susan Kuklin for *Beyond Magenta: Transgender Teens Speak Out* (Candlewick).

Theodore Sturgeon Memorial Award. For the year's best short science fiction. *Offered by:* Center for the Study of Science Fiction. *Winner:* Cory Doctorow for "The Man Who Sold the Moon" in *Hieroglyph: Stories and Visions for a Better Future* (Morrow).

Sunburst Awards for Canadian Literature of the Fantastic (C$1,000). *Winners:* (adult) Thomas King for *The Back of the Turtle* (HarperCollins); (young adult) Cecil Castellucci for *Tin Star* (Roaring Brook).

Sunday Times EFG Short Story Award (United Kingdom) (£30,000). To an author from any country for an English-language story of 6,000 words or less *Winner:* Yiyun Li for "A Sheltered Woman."

Tanizaki Junichiro Prize (Japan) (1 million yen, approximately $8,450). For a full-length work of fiction or drama by a professional writer. *Offered by:* Chuokoron-Shinsha, Inc. *Winner:* Kaori Ekuni for *Geckos, Frogs, and Butterflies* (Asahi Shimbun).

Charles Taylor Prize for Literary Nonfiction (Canada) (C$25,000). To honor a book of creative nonfiction widely available in Canada and written by a Canadian citizen or landed immigrant. *Offered by:* Charles Taylor Foundation. *Winner:* Plum Johnson for *They Left Us Everything* (Penguin Canada).

Sydney Taylor Children's Book Awards. For a distinguished contribution to Jewish children's literature. *Offered by:* Association of Jewish Libraries. *Winners:* (younger readers) Jim Aylesworth and Barbara McClintock, illustrator, for *My Grandfather's Coat.* (Scholastic); (older readers) Loïc Dauvillier for *Hidden: A Child's Story of the Holocaust* (First Second); (teen readers) Donna Jo Napoli for *Storm* (Simon & Schuster).

Sydney Taylor Manuscript Competition ($1,000). For the best fiction manuscript appropriate for readers ages 8–13, both Jewish and non-Jewish, revealing positive aspects of Jewish life, and written by an unpublished author. *Winner:* Meira Drazin for *Honey and Me.*

Theatre Library Association Award. See Richard Wall Memorial Award.

Dylan Thomas Prize (United Kingdom) (£30,000). For a published or produced literary work in the English language, written by an author under 30. *Offered by:* University of Wales. *Winner:* not awarded in 2015.

Thriller Awards. *Offered by:* International Thriller Writers. *Winners:* (hardcover novel) Megan Abbott for *The Fever* (Little, Brown); (paperback original) Vincent Zandri for *Moonlight Weeps* (Down & Out); (first novel) Laura McHugh for *The Weight of Blood* (Spiegel & Grau); (e-book original) C.J. Lyons for *Hard Fall* (Legacy); (young adult) Elle Cosimano for *Nearly Gone* (Kathy Dawson Books); (short story) Tim L. Williams for "The Last Wrestling Bear In West Kentucky" in *Ellery Queen Mystery Magazine.*

Thurber Prize for American Humor ($5,000). For a humorous book of fiction or nonfiction. *Offered by:* Thurber House. *Winner:* Julie Schumacher for *Dear Committee Members* (Wheeler).

Tom-Gallon Trust Award (United Kingdom) (£1,000). For a short story. *Offered by:* Society of Authors. *Sponsor:* Authors' Licensing and Collecting Society. *Winner:* Maria C. McCarthy for "More Katharine Than Audrey."

Betty Trask Prize and Awards (United Kingdom). To Commonwealth writers under the age of 35 for "romantic or traditional" first novels. *Offered by:* Society of Authors. *Winners:* (Betty Trask Prize, £10,000) Ben Fergusson for *The Spring of Kasper Meier* (Little, Brown); (Betty Trask Awards, £5,000) Emma Healey for *Elizabeth Is Missing* (Viking), Zoe Pilger for *Eat My Heart Out* (Serpent's Tail), Simon Wroe for *Chop Chop* (Viking).

Kate Tufts Discovery Award ($10,000). For a first or very early book of poetry by an emerging poet. *Offered by:* Claremont Graduate University. *Winner:* Brandon Som for *The Tribute Horse* (Nightboat).

Kingsley Tufts Poetry Award ($100,000). For a book of poetry by a mid-career poet. *Offered by:* Claremont Graduate School. *Winner:* Angie Estes for *Enchantée* (Oberlin College Press).

21st Century Award. To honor recent achievement in writing by an author with ties to Chicago. See Carl Sandburg Literary Awards.

UKLA Children's Book Awards (United Kingdom). *Sponsor:* United Kingdom Literacy Association. *Winners:* (ages 3–6) Drew Daywalt, and Oliver Jeffers, illustrator, for *The Day the Crayons Quit* (HarperCollins); (ages 7–11) Philip Reeve and Sarah McIntyre for *Oliver and the Seawigs* (Oxford University Press); (ages 12–16) David Levithan for *Every Day* (Egmont).

Ungar German Translation Award ($1,000). Awarded biennially for a distinguished literary translation from German into English that has been published in the United States. *Offered by:* American Translators Association. *Winner:* Susan Bernofsky for her translation of Jenny Erpenbeck's *The End of Days.*

John Updike Award ($20,000). Given biennially to a writer in mid-career who has demonstrated consistent excellence. *Offered by:* American Academy of Arts and Letters. *Winner:* Zachary Lazar.

VCU/Cabell First Novelist Award ($5,000). For a first novel published in the previous year. *Offered by:* Virginia Commonwealth University. *Winner:* Boris Fishman for *A Replacement Life* (HarperCollins).

Harold D. Vursell Memorial Award ($20,000). To a writer whose work merits recognition for the quality of its prose style. *Offered by:* American Academy of Arts and Letters. *Winner:* John Lahr.

Amelia Elizabeth Walden Award ($5,000). To honor a book relevant to adolescents that has enjoyed a wide teenage audience. *Sponsor:* Assembly on Literature for Adolescents, National Council of Teachers of English. *Winner:* A.S. King for *Glory O'Brien's History of the Future* (Little, Brown).

Richard Wall Memorial Award (formerly the Theatre Library Association Award). To honor an English-language book of exceptional scholarship in the field of recorded performance, including motion pictures, television, and radio. *Offered by:* Theatre

Library Association. *Winner:* Mark Harris for *Five Came Back* (Penguin).

George Washington Book Prize ($50,000). To recognize an important new book about America's founding era. *Offered by:* Washington College and the Gilder Lehrman Institute of American History. *Winner:* Nick Bunker for *An Empire on the Edge: How Britain Came to Fight America* (Knopf).

Carole Weinstein Poetry Prize ($10,000). To poets with strong connections to the Commonwealth of Virginia who have made a "significant recent contribution to the art of poetry." *Winner:* Joshua Poteat.

Hilary Weston Writers' Trust Prize for Nonfiction (C$60,000) (Canada). *Winner:* Rosemary Sullivan for *Stalin's Daughter: The Extraordinary and Tumultuous Life of Svetlana Alliluyeva* (HarperCollins Canada).

Hilary Weston Writers' Trust Prize for Student Nonfiction (C$2,500 plus C$1,000 for the winner's school, and publication on Macleans.ca and Writerstrust.com) (Canada). For students in grades 9–12. *Winner:* Rosemary Sullivan for *Stalin's Daughter: The Extraordinary and Tumultuous Life of Svetlana Alliluyeva* (HarperCollins Canada).

Whitbread Book Awards. See Costa Book Awards.

E. B. White Award ($10,000). For achievement in children's literature. *Offered by:* American Academy of Arts and Letters. *Winner:* Christopher Paul Curtis.

E. B. White Read-Aloud Awards. For children's books with particular appeal as read-aloud books. *Offered by:* American Booksellers Association/Association of Booksellers for Children. *Winners:* (picture book) Mac Barnett and Jon Klassen, illustrator, for *Sam and Dave Dig a Hole* (Candlewick); (middle readers) Jacqueline Woodson for *Brown Girl Dreaming* (Nancy Paulsen).

Whiting Writers' Awards ($50,000). For emerging writers of exceptional talent and promise. *Offered by:* Mrs. Giles Whiting Foundation. *Winners:* (poetry) Anthony Carelli, Jenny Johnson, Aracelis Girmay, Roger Reeves; (fiction) Leopoldine Core, Dan Josefson, Azareen Van der Vliet Oloomi; (nonfiction) Elena Passarello; (drama) Lucas Hnath, Anne Washburn.

Walt Whitman Award ($5,000). To a U.S. poet who has not published a book of poems in a standard edition. *Offered by:* Academy of American Poets. *Winner:* Sjohnna McCray for "Rapture."

Richard Wilbur Award ($1,000 and publication by University of Evansville Press). For a book-length poetry collection. *Winner:* Midge Goldberg for "Snowman's Code."

Laura Ingalls Wilder Award. Awarded biennially to an author or illustrator whose books have made a substantial and lasting contribution to children's literature. *Offered by:* American Library Association, Association for Library Service to Children. *Winner:* Donald Crews.

Robert H. Winner Memorial Award ($2,500). To a mid-career poet over 40 who has published no more than one book of poetry. *Offered by:* Poetry Society of America. *Winner:* Karen Skolfield.

George Wittenborn Memorial Book Awards. To North American art publications that represent the highest standards of content, documentation, layout, and format. *Offered by:* Art Libraries Society of North America (ARLIS/NA). *Winner:* Arthur K. Wheelock, Jr. for *Dutch Paintings of the Seventeenth Century* (A National Gallery of Art Online Edition).

Thomas Wolfe Prize and Lecture. To honor writers with distinguished bodies of work. *Offered by:* Thomas Wolfe Society and University of North Carolina at Chapel Hill. *Winner:* Clyde Edgerton.

Thomas Wolfe Fiction Prize ($1,000). For a short story that honors Thomas Wolfe. *Offered by:* North Carolina Writers Network. *Winner:* Mesha Maren for "Chokedamp".

Helen and Kurt Wolff Translator's Prize ($10,000). For an outstanding translation from German into English, published in the United States. *Offered by:* Goethe Institut Inter Nationes, New York. *Winner:* Catherine Schelbert for her translation of Hugo Ball's *Flametti: oder vom Dandysmus der Armen (Flametti, or The Dandyism of the Poor))* (Wakefield).

World Fantasy Convention Awards. For outstanding fantasy writing. *Offered by:* World Fantasy Convention. *Winners:* (novel) David Mitchell for *The Bone Clocks* (Random House); (novella) Daryl Gregory for *We Are All Completely Fine* (Tachyon); (short story) Scott Nicolay for "Do You Like to Look at

Monsters?" in *Fedogan & Bremer, chapbook*; (anthology) Kelly Link and Gavin J. Grant, editors, for *Monstrous Affections: An Anthology of Beastly Tales* (Candlewick); (collection) Helen Marshall for *Gifts for the One Who Comes After* (ChiZine), and Angela Slatter for *The Bitterwood Bible and Other Recountings* (Tartarus).

Writers' Trust Engel/Findley Award (C$25,000). To a Canadian writer predominantly of fiction, for a body of work. *Winner:* Annabel Lyon.

Writers' Trust Poetry Prize. See Latner Writers' Trust Poetry Prize.

Writers' Trust Shaughnessy Cohen Prize for Political Writing (Canada) (C$25,000). For a nonfiction book that captures a subject of political interest. *Sponsor:* CTV. *Winner:* Joseph Heath for *Enlightenment 2.0: Restoring Sanity to Our Politics, Our Economy, and Our Lives* (HarperCollins).

Writers' Trust/McClelland & Stewart Journey Prize (Canada) (C$10,000). To a new, developing Canadian author for a short story or an excerpt from a novel in progress. *Offered by:* McClelland & Stewart. *Winner:* Deirdre Dore for "The Wise Baby" in *Geist.*

Writers' Trust Hilary Weston Prize for Nonfiction (Canada). See Hilary Weston Writers' Trust of Canada Prize for Nonfiction.

YALSA Award for Excellence in Nonfiction. For a work of nonfiction published for young adults (ages 12–18). *Offered by:* American Library Association, Young Adult Library Services Association. *Winner:* Maya Van Wagenen for *Popular: Vintage Wisdom for a Modern Geek* (Dutton).

Young Lions Fiction Award ($10,000). For a novel or collection of short stories by an American under the age of 35. *Offered by:* Young Lions of the New York Public Library. *Winner:* Molly Antopol for *The UnAmericans* (W. W. Norton).

Morton Dauwen Zabel Award ($10,000). Awarded biennially, in rotation, to a progressive and experimental poet, writer of fiction, or critic. *Offered by:* American Academy of Arts and Letters. *Winner:* To be awarded next in 2016.

Zoetrope Short Fiction Prizes. *Offered by: Zoetrope: All-Story. Winners:* (first, $1,000) David Goguen for "A Soft Projection for Q4"; (second, $500) Bill Gaston for "Carla's Dead Wife"; (third, $250) Katherine Davis for "The Missing."

Charlotte Zolotow Award. For outstanding writing in a picture book published in the United States in the previous year. *Offered by:* Cooperative Children's Book Center, University of Wisconsin–Madison. *Winners:* Jenny Offill for *Sparky!,* illustrated by Chris Appelhans (Schwartz & Wade).

Part 6
Directory of Organizations

Directory of Library and Related Organizations

Networks, Consortia, and Other Cooperative Library Organizations

This list is taken from the current edition of *American Library Directory* (Information Today, Inc.), which includes additional information on member libraries and primary functions of each organization.

United States

Alabama

Alabama Health Libraries Assn., Inc. (AL-HeLa), Lister Hill Lib., Univ. of Alabama, Birmingham 35294-0013. SAN 372-8218. Tel. 205-975-8313, fax 205-934-2230. *Pres.* Justin Robertson.

Library Management Network, Inc. (LMN), 2132 6th Ave S.E., Suite 106, Decatur 35601. SAN 322-3906. Tel. 256-308-2529, fax 256-308-2533. *Systems Coord.* Charlotte Moncrief.

Marine Environmental Sciences Consortium, Dauphin Island Sea Laboratory, Dauphin Island 36528. SAN 322-0001. Tel. 251-861-2141, fax 251-861-4646, e-mail disl@disl.org. *Coord.* John Dindo.

Network of Alabama Academic Libraries, c/o Alabama Commission on Higher Education, Montgomery 36104. SAN 322-4570. Tel. 334-242-2211, fax 334-242-0270. *Dir.* Ron P. Leonard.

Alaska

Alaska Library Network (ALN), 344 W. Third Ave., No. 125, Anchorage 99501-2338. SAN 371-0688. Tel. 907-269-6567, e-mail info@aklib.net. *Exec. Dir.* Tracy Swaim.

Arkansas

Northeast Arkansas Hospital Library Consortium, 223 E. Jackson, Jonesboro 72401. SAN 329-529X. Tel. 870-972-1290, fax 870-931-0839. *Dir.* Karen Crosser.

California

49-99 Cooperative Library System, c/o Southern California Lib. Cooperative, Monrovia 91016. SAN 301-6218. Tel. 626-359-6111, fax 626-359-0001. *Dir.* Diane R. Satchwell.

Bay Area Library and Information Network (BayNet), 1462 Cedar St., Berkeley 94702. SAN 371-0610. Tel. 415-355-2826, e-mail infobay@baynetlibs.org. *Pres.* Debbie Abilock.

Califa, 32 W. 25 Ave., Suite 201, San Mateo 94403. Tel. 650-572-2746, fax 650-349-5089, e-mail califa@califa.org. *Exec. Dir.* Linda Crowe.

Claremont University Consortium (CUC), 150 E. 8 St., Claremont 91711. Tel. 909-621-8000; 909-621-8150, fax 909-621-8681. *CEO* Stig Lanesskog.

Consumer Health Information Program and Services (CHIPS), 12350 Imperial Hwy., Norwalk 90650. SAN 372-8110. Tel. 562-868-4003, fax 562-868-4065, e-mail reference services@gw.colapl.org. *Libn.* James Balducki.

Consortium for Open Learning, 333 Sunrise Ave., No. 229, Roseville 95661-3480. SAN 329-4412. Tel. 916-788-0660, fax 916-788-0696. *Operations Mgr.* Sandra Scott-Smith.

Gold Coast Library Network, 3437 Empresa Drive, Suite C, San Luis Obispo 93401-7355. Tel. 805-543-6082, fax 805-543-9487. *Admin. Dir.* Maureen Theobald.

National Network of Libraries of Medicine–Pacific Southwest Region (NN/LM-PSR), Louise M. Darling Biomedical Lib., Los Angeles 90095-1798. SAN 372-8234. Tel. 310-825-1200, fax 310-825-5389, e-mail psr-nnlm@library.ucla.edu. *Dir.* Judy Consales.

Nevada Medical Library Group (NMLG), Barton Memorial Hospital Lib., South Lake Tahoe 96150. SAN 370-0445. Tel. 530-543-5844, fax 530-541-4697. *Senior Exec. Coord.* Laurie Anton.

Northern and Central California Psychology Libraries (NCCPL), 2040 Gough St., San Francisco 94109. SAN 371-9006. Tel. 415-771-8055. *Pres.* Scott Hines.

Northern California Assn. of Law Libraries (NOCALL), 268 Bush St., No. 4006, San Francisco 94104. SAN 323-5777. E-mail admin@nocall.org. *Pres.* Ellen Platt.

Peninsula Libraries Automated Network (PLAN), 2471 Flores St., San Mateo 94403-4000. SAN 371-5035. Tel. 650-349-5538, fax 650-349-5089. *Dir., Information Technology.* Monica Schultz.

San Bernardino, Inyo, Riverside Counties United Library Services (SIRCULS), 555 W. 6th St., San Bernardino 92410. Tel. 909-381-8257, fax 909-888-3171, e-mail ils@inlandlib.org. *Exec. Dir.* Vera Skop.

San Francisco Biomedical Library Network (SFBLN), San Francisco General Hospital UCSF/Barnett-Briggs Medical Lib., San Francisco 94110. SAN 371-2125. Tel. 415-206-6639, e-mail fishbon@ucsfmedctr.org. *Lib. Dir.* Stephen Kiyoi.

Santa Clarita Interlibrary Network (SCIL-NET), Powell Lib., Santa Clarita 91321. SAN 371-8964. Tel. 661-362-2271, fax 661-362-2719. *Libn.* John Stone.

Serra Cooperative Library System, c/o San Diego Public Lib., San Diego 92101. SAN

301-3510. Tel. 619-236-5800. *Exec. Dir.* Diane R. Satchwell.

Southern California Library Cooperative (SCLC), 248 E. Foothill Blvd., Suite 101, Monrovia 91016-5522. SAN 371-3865. Tel. 626-359-6111, fax 626-359-0001, e-mail sclchq@socallibraries.org. *Dir.* Diane R. Satchwell.

Colorado

Automation System Colorado Consortium (ASCC), c/o Delta Public Lib., Delta 81416. Tel. 970-874-9630, fax 970-874-8605. *Regional Mgr.* Lea Hart.

Colorado Alliance of Research Libraries, 3801 E. Florida Ave., Suite 515, Denver 80210. SAN 322-3760. Tel. 303-759-3399, fax 303-759-3363. *Exec. Dir.* George Machovec.

Colorado Assn. of Law Libraries, P.O. Box 13363, Denver 80201. SAN 322-4325. Tel. 303-492-7535, fax 303-492-2707. *Pres.* Mark Popielarski.

Colorado Council of Medical Librarians (CCML), P.O. Box 101058, Denver 80210-1058. SAN 370-0755. Tel. 303-724-2124, fax 303-724-2154. *Pres.* Peggy Cruse.

Colorado Library Consortium (CLiC), 7400 E. Arapahoe Rd., Suite 75, Centennial 80112. SAN 371-3970. Tel. 303-422-1150, fax 303-431-9752. *Exec. Dir.* Jim Duncan.

Western Council of State Libraries, Inc., Colorado State Libraries, Denver 80203-1799. Tel. 303-866-6733, fax 303-866-6940. *Pres.* Eugene Hainer.

Connecticut

Bibliomation, 24 Wooster Ave., Waterbury 06708. Tel. 203-577-4070. *Exec. Dir.* Carl DeMilia.

Connecticut Library Consortium, 234 Court St., Middletown 06457-3304. SAN 322-0389. Tel. 860-344-8777, fax 860-344-9199, e-mail clc@ctlibrarians.org. *Exec. Dir.* Jennifer Keohane.

Council of State Library Agencies in the Northeast (COSLINE), Connecticut State Lib., Hartford 06106. SAN 322-0451. Tel. 860-757-6510, fax 860-757-6503.

CTW Library Consortium, Olin Memorial Lib., Middletown 06459-6065. SAN 329-4587.

Tel. 860-685-3887, fax 860-685-2661. *Libn. for Collaborative Projects* Lorri Huddy.

Hartford Consortium for Higher Education: 31 Pratt St., 4th fl., Hartford 06103. SAN 322-0443. Tel. 860-702-3801, fax 860-241-1130. *Exec. Dir.* Martin Estey.

Libraries Online, Inc. (LION), 100 Riverview Center, Suite 252, Middletown 06457. SAN 322-3922. Tel. 860-347-1704, fax 860-346-3707. *Exec. Dir.* Alan Hagyard.

Library Connection, Inc., 599 Matianuck Ave., Windsor 06095-3567. Tel. 860-298-5322, fax 860-298-5328. *Exec. Dir.* George Christian.

Delaware

Central Delaware Library Consortium, Dover Public Lib., Dover 19901. SAN 329-3696. Tel. 302-736-7030, fax 302-736-5087. *Dir.* Margery Kirby Cyr.

District of Columbia

Council for Christian Colleges and Universities, 321 8th St. N.E., Washington 20002. SAN 322-0524. Tel. 202-546-8713, fax 202-546-8913, e-mail council@cccu.org. *Pres.* Charles "Chip" W. Pollard.

District of Columbia Area Health Science Libraries (DCAHSL), P.O. Box 96920, Washington 20090. SAN 323-9918. Tel. 202-863-2518, fax 202-484-1595, e-mail mtaliaferro@aamc.org. *Pres.* Wanda Whitney.

FEDLINK/Federal Library and Information Network, c/o Federal Lib. and Info. Center Committee, Washington 20540-4935. SAN 322-0761. Tel. 202-707-4800, fax 202-707-4818, e-mail flicc@loc.gov. *Mgr.* Joan Fitts.

Interlibrary Users Assn. (IUA), c/o Urban Institute Lib., Washington 20037. SAN 322-1628. Tel. 202-261-5534, fax 202-223-3043. *Pres.* Nancy L. Minter.

Washington Theological Consortium, 487 Michigan Ave. N.E., Washington 20017-1585. SAN 322-0842. Tel. 202-832-2675, fax 202-526-0818, e-mail wtc@washtheocon.org. *Exec. Dir.* Larry Golemon.

Florida

Florida Library Information Network, R. A. Gray Bldg., Tallahassee 32399-0250. SAN 322-0869. Tel. 850-245-6600, fax 850-245-6744, e-mail library@dos.myflorida.com. *Bureau Chief* Cathy Moloney.

Northeast Florida Library Information Network (NEFLIN), 2233 Park Ave., Suite 402, Orange Park 32073. Tel. 904-278-5620, fax 904-278-5625, e-mail office@neflin.org. *Exec. Dir.* Brad Ward.

Panhandle Library Access Network (PLAN), Five Miracle Strip Loop, Suite 8, Panama City Beach 32407-3850. SAN 370-047X. Tel. 850-233-9051, fax 850-235-2286. *Pres.* Lori Driscoll.

SEFLIN/Southeast Florida Library Information Network, Inc, Wimberly Lib., Office 452, Boca Raton 33431. SAN 370-0666. Tel. 561-208-0984, fax 561-208-0995. *Exec. Dir.* Jennifer Pratt.

Southwest Florida Library Network (SWFLN), 13120 Westlinks Terrace, Unit 3, Fort Myers 33913. Tel. 239-313-6338, fax 239-313-6329, e-mail swfln@fgcu.edu. *Exec. Dir.* Luly Castro.

Tampa Bay Library Consortium, Inc., 1202 Tech Blvd., Suite 202, Tampa 33619. SAN 322-371X. Tel. 813-740-3963; 813-622-8252, fax 813-628-4425. *Exec. Dir.* Charlie Parker.

Tampa Bay Medical Library Network: Medical Lib., Department 7660, Saint Petersburg 33701. SAN 322-0885. Tel. 727-767-8557. *Chair* Joshua Brown.

Georgia

Association of Southeastern Research Libraries (ASERL), Georgia State University, Atlanta 30303-3202. SAN 322-1555. Tel. 404-413-2896. *Exec. Dir.* John Burger.

Atlanta Health Science Libraries Consortium, Fran Golding Medical Lib. at Scottish Rite, Atlanta 30342-1600. Tel. 404-785-2157, fax 404-785-2155. *Pres.* Kate Daniels.

Atlanta Regional Council for Higher Education (ARCHE), 133 Peachtree St., Suite 4925, Atlanta 30303. SAN 322-0990. Tel. 404-651-2668, fax 404-880-9816, e-mail arche@atlantahighered.org. *Pres.* Elizabeth Kiss.

Georgia Online Database (GOLD), c/o Georgia Public Lib. Service, Atlanta 30345-4304. SAN 322-094X. Tel. 404-235-7200, fax 404-235-7201. *Project Mgr.* Elaine Hardy.

LYRASIS, 1438 W. Peachtree St. N.W., Suite 200, Atlanta 30309-2955. SAN 322-0974. Tel. 404-892-0943, fax 404-892-7879. *CEO* Robert Miller.

Metro Atlanta Library Assn. (MALA), P.O. Box 14948, Atlanta 30324. SAN 378-2549. https://www.facebook.com/MAtlantaLA/info/?tab=overview.

Hawaii

Hawaii Library Consortium (HLC), http://web.hawaii.edu/hlc. Tel. 808-875-2408. *Pres.* Nori Leong.

Hawaii-Pacific Chapter, Medical Library Assn. (HPC-MLA), Health Sciences Lib., Honolulu 96813. SAN 371-3946. Tel. 808-692-0810, fax 808-692-1244. *Chair* Walter Benavitz.

Idaho

Canyon Owyhee Library Group (COLG), 203 E. Owyhee Ave., Homedale 83628. Tel. 208-337-4613, fax 208-337-4933. *Pres.* Pam Herman.

Cooperative Information Network (CIN), 8385 N. Government Way, Hayden 83835-9280. SAN 323-7656. Tel. 208-772-5612, fax 208-772-2498.

LYNX Consortium, c/o Boise Public Lib., Boise 83702-7195. SAN 375-0086. Tel. 208-384-4238, fax 208-384-4025. *Dir.* Kevin Booe.

Illinois

Areawide Hospital Library Consortium of Southwestern Illinois (AHLC), c/o St. Elizabeth Hospital Health Sciences Lib., Belleville 62222. SAN 322-1016. Tel. 618-234-2120 ext. 2011, fax 618-222-4614.

Assn. of Chicago Theological Schools (ACTS), Univ. of St. Mary of the Lake, Mundelein 60060-1174. SAN 370-0658. Tel. 847-566-6401. *Chair* Thomas Baima.

Center for Research Libraries, 6050 S. Kenwood, Chicago 60637-2804. SAN 322-1032. Tel. 773-955-4545, fax 773-955-4339. *Pres.* Bernard F. Reilly.

Chicago and South Consortium, Jackson Park Hospital and Medical Center, Chicago 60649-3993. SAN 322-1067. Tel. 773-947-7653. *Coord.* Andrew Paradise.

Chicago Area Museum Libraries (CAML), c/o Lib., Field Museum, Chicago 60605-2496. SAN 371-392X. Tel. 312-665-7970, fax 312-665-7893. *Museum Libn.* Christine Giannoni.

Committee on Institutional Cooperation, 1819 S. Neil St., Suite D, Champaign 61820-7271. Tel. 217-333-8475, fax 217-244-7127, e-mail cic@staff.cic.net. *Dir.* Barbara Mcfadden Allen.

Consortium of Academic and Research Libraries in Illinois (CARLI), 100 Trade Center Drive, Suite 303, Champaign 61820. SAN 322-3736. Tel. 217-244-7593, fax 217-244-7596, e-mail support@carli.illinois.edu. *Exec. Dir.* Susan Singleton.

Council of Directors of State University Libraries in Illinois (CODSULI), Southern Illinois Univ. School of Medicine Lib., Springfield 62702-4910. SAN 322-1083. Tel. 217-545-0994, fax 217-545-0988.

East Central Illinois Consortium, Booth Lib., Eastern Illinois Univ., Charleston 61920. SAN 322-1040. Tel. 217-581-7549, fax 217-581-7534. *Mgr.* Stacey Knight-Davis.

Fox Valley Health Science Library Consortium, c/o Delnor-Community Hospital, Geneva 60134. SAN 329-3831. Tel. 630-208-4299.

Heart of Illinois Library Consortium, 511 N.E. Greenleaf, Peoria 61603. SAN 322-1113. *Chair* Leslie Menz.

Illinois Library and Information Network (IL-LINET), c/o Illinois State Lib., Springfield 62701-1796. SAN 322-1148. Tel. 217-782-2994, fax 217-785-4326. *Dir.* Anne Craig.

LIBRAS, Inc., North Park Univ., Chicago 60625-4895. SAN 322-1172. Tel. 773-244-5584, fax 773-244-4891. *Pres.* Rebecca Miller.

Metropolitan Consortium of Chicago, Chicago School of Professional Psychology, Chicago 60610. SAN 322-1180. Tel. 312-329-6630, fax 312-644-6075. *Coord.* Margaret White.

National Network of Libraries of Medicine–Greater Midwest Region (NN/LM-GMR), c/o Lib. of Health Sciences, Univ. of Illinois at Chicago, Chicago 60612-4330. SAN 322-1202. Tel. 312-996-2464, fax 312-996-2226. *Dir.* Kathryn Carpenter.

Network of Illinois Learning Resources in Community Colleges (NILRC), P.O. Box 120, Blanchardville 53516-0120. Tel. 608-

523-4094, fax 608-523-4072. *Business Mgr.* Lisa Sikora.

System Wide Automated Network (SWAN), c/o Metropolitan Lib. System, Burr Ridge 60527-5783. Tel. 630-734-5000, fax 630-734-5050. *Dir.* Aaron Skog.

Indiana

Central Indiana Health Science Libraries Consortium, Indiana Univ. School of Medicine Lib., Indianapolis 46202. SAN 322-1245. Tel. 317-274-8358, fax 317-274-4056. *Officer* Elaine Skopelja.

Consortium of College and University Media Centers (CCUMC), Indiana Univ., Bloomington 47405-1223. SAN 322-1091. Tel. 812-855-6049, fax 812-855-2103, e-mail ccumc@ccumc.org. *Exec. Dir.* Aileen Scales.

Evansville Area Library Consortium, 3700 Washington Ave., Evansville 47750. SAN 322-1261. Tel. 812-485-4151, fax 812-485-7564. *Coord.* Jane Saltzman.

Evergreen Indiana Consortium, Indiana State Lib., Indianapolis 46202. Tel. 317-234-6624, fax 317-232-0002. *Coord.* Anna Goben.

Iowa

Consortium of User Libraries (CUL), Lib. for the Blind and Physically Handicapped, Des Moines 50309-2364. SAN 305-344X. Tel. 515-281-1333, fax 515-281-1378; 515-281-1263. *Dir.* Randall E. Landgrebe.

Dubuque (Iowa) Area Library Information Consortium, c/o Burton Payne Lib., N.E. Iowa Community College, Peosta 52068. Tel. 563-556-5110 ext. 269, fax 563-557-0340. *Coord.* Deb Seiffert.

Iowa Private Academic Library Consortium (IPAL), http://www.ipalgroup.org. SAN 329-5311. Tel. 712-749-2127, 712-749-2203, fax 712-749-2059, e-mail library@bvu.edu. *Chair* Paul Waelchli.

Polk County Biomedical Consortium, c/o Broadlawns Medical Center Lib., Des Moines 50314. SAN 322-1431. Tel. 515-282-2394, fax 515-282-5634. *Treas.* Elaine Hughes.

Quad City Area Biomedical Consortium, Great River Medical Center Lib., West Burlington 52655. SAN 322-435X. Tel. 319-768-4075, fax 319-768-4080. *Coord.* Sarah Goff.

Sioux City Library Cooperative (SCLC), c/o Sioux City Public Lib., Sioux City 51101-1203. SAN 329-4722. Tel. 712-255-2933 ext. 255, fax 712-279-6432. *Chair* Betsy Thompson.

State of Iowa Libraries Online (SILO), State Lib. of Iowa, Des Moines 50319. SAN 322-1415. Tel. 515-281-4105, fax 515-281-6191. *State Libn.* Michael Scott.

Kansas

Associated Colleges of Central Kansas (ACCK), 210 S. Main St., McPherson 67460. SAN 322-1474. Tel. 620-241-5150, fax 620-241-5153. *Dir.* Cindy Sutton.

Dodge City Library Consortium, c/o Comanche Intermediate Center, Dodge City 67801. SAN 322-4368. Tel. 620-227-1609, fax 620-227-4862.

State Library of Kansas/Statewide Resource Sharing Div., 300 S.W. 10 Ave., Room 343 N., Topeka 66612-1593. SAN 329-5621. Tel. 785-296-3875, fax 785-368-7291. *Dir.* Jeff Hixon.

Kentucky

Assn. of Independent Kentucky Colleges and Universities (AIKCU), 484 Chenault Rd., Frankfort 40601. SAN 322-1490. Tel. 502-695-5007, fax 502-695-5057. *Pres.* Gary S. Cox.

Eastern Kentucky Health Science Information Network (EKHSIN), c/o Camden-Carroll Lib., Morehead 40351. SAN 370-0631. Tel. 606-783-6860, fax 606-784-2178. *Lib. Dir.* Tammy Jenkins.

Kentuckiana Metroversity, Inc., 200 W. Broadway, Suite 800, Louisville 40202. SAN 322-1504. Tel. 502-897-3374, fax 502-895-1647.

Kentucky Medical Library Assn., VA Medical Center, Lib. Serices 142D, Louisville 40206-1499. SAN 370-0623. Tel. 502-287-6240, fax 502-287-6134. *Head Libn.* Gene M. Haynes.

Theological Education Assn. of Mid America (TEAM-A), Southern Baptist Theological Seminary, Louisville 40280. SAN 377-5038. Tel. 502-897-4807, fax 502-897-4600. *Dir., Info. Resources* Ken Boyd.

Louisiana

Central Louisiana Medical Center Library Consortium (CLMLC), 2495 Shreveport Hwy., 142D, Alexandria 71306. Tel. 318-619-9102, fax 318-619-9144, e-mail clmlc 8784@yahoo.com. *Coord.* Miriam J. Brown.

Health Sciences Library Assn. of Louisiana (HSLAL), 1501 Kings Hwy., Shreveport 71103. SAN 375-0035. Tel. 318-675-5679. *Pres.* Deidra Woodson.

Loan SHARK, State Lib. of Louisiana, Baton Rouge 70802. SAN 371-6880. Tel. 225-342-4920, 342-4918, fax 225-219-4725. *Head, Access Services* Kytara A. Gaudin.

LOUIS/Louisiana Library Network, Info. Technology Services, Baton Rouge 70803. *Exec. Dir.* Sara Zimmerman.

New Orleans Educational Telecommunications Consortium, 6400 Press Dr., New Orleans 70126. SAN 329-5214. Tel. 504-524-0350, e-mail noetc@noetc.org.

Southeastern Chapter of the American Assn. of Law Libraries (SEAALL), c/o Supreme Court of Louisiana, New Orleans 70130-2104. Tel. 504-310-2405, fax 504-310-2419. *Pres.* Michelle Cosby.

Maine

Health Science Library Information Consortium (HSLIC), 211 Marginal Way, No 245, Portland 04101. SAN 322-1601. Tel. 207-795-2561, fax 207-795-2569. *Chair* Kathy Brunjes.

Maryland

Maryland Interlibrary Loan Organization (MILO), c/o Enoch Pratt Free Lib., Baltimore 21201-4484. SAN 343-8600. Tel. 410-396-5498, fax 410-396-5837, e-mail milo@prattlibrary.org. *Mgr.* Emma E. Beaven.

National Network of Libraries of Medicine (NN/LM), National Lib. of Medicine, Bethesda 20894. SAN 373-0905. Tel. 301-496-4777, fax 301-480-1467. *Dir.* Angela Ruffin.

National Network of Libraries of Medicine–Southeastern Atlantic Region (NN/LM-SEA), Univ. of Maryland Health Sciences and Human Services Lib., Baltimore 21201-1512. SAN 322-1644. Tel. 410-706-2855, fax 410-706-0099, e-mail hshsl-nlmsea@hshsl.umaryland.edu. *Dir.* Diana Babski.

U.S. National Library of Medicine (NLM), 8600 Rockville Pike, Bethesda 20894. SAN 322-1652. Tel. 301-594-5983, fax 301-402-1384, e-mail custserv@nlm.nih.gov. *Coord.* Martha Fishel.

Washington Research Library Consortium (WRLC), 901 Commerce Drive, Upper Marlboro 20774. SAN 373-0883. Tel. 301-390-2000, fax 301-390-2020. *Exec. Dir.* Mark Jacobs.

Massachusetts

Boston Biomedical Library Consortium (BBLC), c/o Dana Farber Cancer Trust, Boston 02115. SAN 322-1725. *Pres.* Christine Fleuried.

Boston Library Consortium, Inc., 10 Milk St., Suite 354, Boston 02108. SAN 322-1733. Tel. 617-262-0380, fax 617-262-0163, e-mail admin@blc.org. *Exec. Dir.* Susan Stearns.

Cape Libraries Automated Materials Sharing Network (CLAMS), 270 Communication Way, Unit 4E, Hyannis 02601. SAN 370-579X. Tel. 508-790-4399, fax 508-771-4533. *Exec. Dir.* Gayle Simundza.

Central and Western Massachusetts Automated Resource Sharing (C/W MARS), 67 Millbrook St., Suite 201, Worcester 01606. SAN 322-3973. Tel. 508-755-3323 ext. 30, fax 508-755-3721. *Exec. Dir.* Timothy Spindler.

Cooperating Libraries of Greater Springfield (CLGS), Springfield Technical Community College, Springfield 01102. SAN 322-1768. Tel. 413-755-4565, fax 413-755-6315, e-mail lcoakley@stcc.edu. *Coord.* Lynn Coakley.

Fenway Libraries Online, Inc. (FLO), c/o Wentworth Institute of Technology, Boston 02115. SAN 373-9112. Tel. 617-442-2384, fax 617-442-1519. *Exec. Dir.* Kevin Kidd.

Massachusetts Health Sciences Libraries Network (MAHSLIN), Lamar Soutter Lib., Univ. of Massachusetts Medical School, Worcester 01655. SAN 372-8293. http://nahsl.libguides.com/mahslin/home. *Pres.* Donna Beales.

Merrimack Valley Library Consortium, 4 High St., North Andover 01845. SAN 322-4384. Tel. 978-557-1050, fax 978-557-8101, e-mail netmail@mvlc.org. *Exec. Dir.* Eric C. Graham.

Minuteman Library Network, 10 Strathmore Rd., Natick 01760-2419. SAN 322-4252. Tel. 508-655-8008, fax 508-655-1507. *Exec. Dir.* Susan McAlister.

National Network of Libraries of Medicine–New England Region (NN/LM-NER), Univ. of Massachusetts Medical School, Worcester 01655. SAN 372-5448. Tel. 508-856-5979, fax 508-856-5977. *Dir.* Elaine Martin.

North of Boston Library Exchange, Inc. (NOBLE), 26 Cherry Hill Drive, Danvers 01923. SAN 322-4023. Tel. 978-777-8844, fax 978-750-8472. *Exec. Dir.* Ronald A. Gagnon.

Northeast Consortium of Colleges and Universities in Massachusetts (NECCUM), Merrimack College, North Andover 01845. SAN 371-0602. Tel. 978-556-3400, fax 978-556-3738. *Pres.* Richard Santagati.

Northeastern Consortium for Health Information (NECHI), Lowell General Hospital Health Science Lib., Lowell 01854. SAN 322-1857. Tel. 978-937-6247, fax 978-937-6855. *Libn.* Donna Beales.

SAILS Library Network, 10 Riverside Dr., Suite 102, Lakeville 02347. SAN 378-0058. Tel. 508-946-8600, fax 508-946-8605, e-mail support@sailsinc.org. *Pres.* Melissa Campbell.

Western Massachusetts Health Information Consortium, Baystate Medical Center Health Sciences Lib., Springfield 01199. SAN 329-4579. Tel. 413-794-1865, fax 413-794-1974. *Pres.* Susan La Forter.

Michigan

Detroit Area Consortium of Catholic Colleges, c/o Wayne State University, Detroit 48202. SAN 329-482X. Tel. 313-883-8500, fax 313-883-8594. *Dir.* Chris Spilker.

Detroit Area Library Network (DALNET), 6th Floor SEL, 5048 Gullen Mall, Detroit 48202. Tel. 313-577-6789, fax 313-577-1231, info@dalnet.org. *Exec. Dir.* Steven K. Bowers.

Lakeland Library Cooperative, 4138 Three Mile Rd. N.W., Grand Rapids 49534-1134. SAN 308-132X. Tel. 616-559-5253, fax 616-559-4329. *Dir.* Sandra Wilson.

The Library Network (TLN), 41365 Vincenti Ct., Novi 48375. SAN 370-596X. Tel. 248-536-3100, fax 248-536-3099. *Dir.* James Pletz.

Michigan Health Sciences Libraries Assn. (MHSLA), 1407 Rensen St., Suite 4, Lansing 48910. SAN 323-987X. Tel. 517-394-2774, fax 517-394-2675. *Pres.* Jennifer Bowen.

Mideastern Michigan Library Cooperative, 503 S. Saginaw St., Suite 839, Flint 48502. SAN 346-5187. Tel. 810-232-7119, fax 810-232-6639. *Dir.* Denise Hooks.

Mid-Michigan Library League, 210 1/2 N Mitchell, Cadillac 49601-1835. SAN 307-9325. Tel. 231-775-3037, fax 231-775-1749. *Dir.* Sheryl L. Mase.

PALnet, 1040 W Bristol Rd., Flint 48507. Tel. 810-766-4070. *Dir.* Vince Molosky.

Southeastern Michigan League of Libraries (SEMLOL), Lawrence Technological Univ., Southfield 48075. SAN 322-4481. Tel. 248-204-3000, fax 248-204-3005. *Treas.* Gary Cocozzoli.

Southwest Michigan Library Cooperative, Willard Public Library, Battle Creek, 49017. SAN 308-2156. Tel. 269-968-8166, e-mail rhulsey@willard.lib.mi.us. *Dir.* John Mohney.

Suburban Library Cooperative (SLC), 44750 Delco Blvd., Sterling Heights 48313. SAN 373-9082. Tel. 586-685-5750, fax 586-685-3010. *Dir.* Tammy Turgeon.

Upper Peninsula of Michigan Health Science Library Consortium, c/o Marquette Health System Hospital, Marquette 49855. SAN 329-4803. Tel. 906-225-3429, fax 906-225-3524. *Lib. Mgr.* Janis Lubenow.

Upper Peninsula Region of Library Cooperation, Inc., 1615 Presque Isle Ave., Marquette 49855. SAN 329-5540. Tel. 906-228-7697, fax 906-228-5627. *Treas.* Suzanne Dees.

Valley Library Consortium, 3210 Davenport Ave., Saginaw 48602-3495. Tel. 989-497-0925, fax 989-497-0918. *Exec. Dir.* Randall Martin.

Minnesota

Capital Area Library Consortium (CALCO), c/o Minnesota Dept. of Transportation, Lib. MS155, Saint Paul 55155. SAN 374-6127. Tel. 651-296-5272, fax 651-297-2354. *Libn.* Shirley Sherkow.

Central Minnesota Libraries Exchange (CMLE), Miller Center, Room 130-D, Saint Cloud 56301-4498. SAN 322-3779. Tel. 320-308-2950, fax 320-654-5131, e-mail cmle@stcloudstate.edu. *Dir.* Patricia A. Post.

Cooperating Libraries in Consortium (CLIC), 1619 Dayton Ave., Suite 204, Saint Paul 55104. SAN 322-1970. Tel. 651-644-3878, fax 651-644-6258. *Exec. Dir.* Ruth Dukelow.

Metronet, 1619 Dayton Ave., Suite 314, Saint Paul 55104. SAN 322-1989. Tel. 651-646-0475, fax 651-649-3169, e-mail information @metrolibraries.net. *Exec. Dir.* Ann Walker Smalley.

Metropolitan Library Service Agency (MEL-SA), 1619 Dayton Ave., No. 314, Saint Paul 55104-6206. SAN 371-5124. Tel. 651-645-5731, fax 651-649-3169, e-mail melsa@melsa.org. *Exec. Dir.* Ken Behringer.

MINITEX Library Information Network, 15 Andersen Lib., Univ. of Minnesota–Twin Cities, Minneapolis 55455-0439. SAN 322-1997. Tel. 612-624-4002, fax 612-624-4508. *Dir.* Valerie Horton.

Minnesota Library Information Network (MnLINK), Univ. of Minnesota–Twin Cities, Minneapolis 55455-0439. Tel. 612-624-8096, fax 612-624-4508. *Info. Specialist* Nick Banitt.

Minnesota Theological Library Assn. (MTLA), Luther Seminary Lib., Saint Paul 55108. SAN 322-1962. Tel. 651-641-3447. *Chair* Sue Ebbers.

Northern Lights Library Network, 104 7th Ave. S., Moorhead 56563. SAN 322-2004. Tel. 218-847-2825, fax 218-847-1461, e-mail nloffice@nlln.org. *Exec. Dir.* Kathy B. Enger.

Southeastern Libraries Cooperating (SELCO), 2600 19th St. N.W., Rochester 55901-0767. SAN 308-7417. Tel. 507-288-5513, fax 507-288-8697. *Exec. Dir.* Ann Hutton.

Southwest Area Multicounty Multitype Interlibrary Exchange (SAMMIE), Southwest Minnesota State University Library, Marshall 56258. SAN 322-2039. Tel. 507-532-9013, fax 507-532-2039, e-mail info@sammie.org. *Exec. Dir.* Shelly Grace.

Twin Cities Biomedical Consortium (TCBC), c/o Fairview Univ. Medical Center, Minneapolis 55455. SAN 322-2055. Tel. 612-273-6595, fax 612-273-2675. *Mgr.* Colleen Olsen.

Mississippi

Central Mississippi Library Council (CMLC), c/o Millsaps College Lib., Jackson 39210. SAN 372-8250. Tel. 601-974-1070, fax 601-974-1082. *Chair* Stephen Parks.

Mississippi Electronic Libraries Online (MELO), Mississippi State Board for Community and Junior Colleges, Jackson 39211. Tel. 601-432-6518, fax 601-432-6363, e-mail melo@colin.edu. *Dir.* Audra Kimball.

Missouri

Greater Western Library Alliance (GWLA), 5109 Cherry St., Kansas City 64110. Tel. 816-926-8765, fax 816-926-8790. *Exec. Dir.* Joni Blake.

Health Sciences Library Network of Kansas City (HSLNKC), Univ. of Missouri–Kansas City Health Sciences Lib., Kansas City 64108-2792. SAN 322-2098. Tel. 816-235-1880, fax 816-235-6570. *Pres.* Kitty Serling.

Kansas City Library Service Program (KC-LSP), 14 W. 10 St., Kansas City 64105.Tel. 816-701-3520, fax 816-701-3401, e-mail kclcsupport@kclibrary.org. *Library Systems and Service Program Mgr.* Melissa Carle.

Mid-America Law Library Consortium (MALLCO), 100 North Tucker Blvd., St. Louis 63101. Tel. 314-977-3449, fax 314-977-3966, e-mail cdugas@slu.edu. *Exec. Dir.* Corie Dugas.

Mid-America Library Alliance/Kansas City Metropolitan Library and Information Network, 15624 E. 24 Hwy., Independence 64050. SAN 322-2101. Tel. 816-521-7257, fax 816-461-0966. *Exec. Dir.* Susan Burton.

Saint Louis Regional Library Network, 1190 Meramec Station Rd., Ballwin 63021. SAN 322-2209. Tel. 800-843-8482. *Pres.* Heidi Vix.

Nebraska

ICON Library Consortium, McGoogan Lib. of Medicine, Univ. of Nebraska, Omaha 68198-6705. Tel. 402-559-7099, fax 402-559-5498.

Nevada

Desert States Law Library Consortium, Wiener-Rogers Law Lib., William S. Boyd School of Law, Las Vegas 89154-1080. Tel. 702-895-2400, fax 702-895-2416. *Collection Development Libn.* Matthew Wright.

Information Nevada, Interlibrary Loan Dept., Nevada State Lib. and Archives, Carson City 89701-4285. SAN 322-2276. Tel. 775-684-3328, fax 775-684-3330. *Asst. Admin., Lib. and Development Services* Karen Starr.

New Hampshire

GMILCS, Inc., 31 Mount Saint Mary's Way, Hooksett 03106. Tel. 603-485-4286, fax 603-485-4246, e-mail helpdesk@gmilcs. org. *Systems Libn.* Kevin French.

Health Sciences Libraries of New Hampshire and Vermont, Breene Memorial Lib., New Hampshire Hospital, Concord 03246. SAN 371-6864. Tel. 603-527-2837, fax 603-527-7197. *Admin. Coord.* Anne Conner.

Librarians of the Upper Valley Coop. (LUV Coop), c/o Hanover Town Lib., Etna 03750. SAN 371-6856. Tel. 603-643-3116. *Coord.* Barbara Prince.

Merri-Hill-Rock Library Cooperative, c/o Kimball Lib., Atkinson 03811-2299. SAN 329-5338. Tel. 603-362-5234, fax 603-362-4791. *Dir.* Jon Godfrey.

New Hampshire College and University Council, 3 Barrell Court, Suite 100, Concord 03301-8543. SAN 322-2322. Tel. 603-225-4199, fax 603-225-8108. *Pres.* Thomas R. Horgan.

Nubanusit Library Cooperative, c/o Peterborough Town Lib., Peterborough 03458. SAN 322-4600. Tel. 603-924-8040, fax 603-924-8041.

New Jersey

Basic Health Sciences Library Network (BHSL), Overlook Hospital Health Science Lib., Summit 07902. SAN 371-4888. Tel. 908-522-2886, fax 908-522-2274. *Coord.* Pat Regenberg.

Bergen Passaic Health Sciences Library Consortium, c/o Health Sciences Lib., Englewood Hospital and Medical Center, Englewood 07631. SAN 371-0904. Tel. 201-894-3069, fax 201-894-9049. *Coord.* Lia Sabbagh.

Burlington Libraries Information Consortium (BLINC), 5 Pioneer Blvd., Westampton 08060. Tel. 609-267-9660, fax 609-267-4091, e-mail hq@bcls.lib.nj.us. *Dir.* Ranjna Das.

Libraries of Middlesex Automation Consortium (LMxAC), 1030 Saint Georges Ave., Suite 203, Avenel 07001. SAN 329-448X. Tel. 732-750-2525, fax 732-750-9392. *Exec. Dir.* Eileen Palmer.

LibraryLinkNJ, New Jersey Library Cooperative, 44 Stelton Rd., Suite 330, Piscataway 08854. SAN 371-5116. Tel. 732-752-7720, fax 732-752-7785. *Exec. Dir.* Kathy Schalk-Greene.

Morris Automated Information Network (MAIN), c/o Morris County Lib., 30 East Hanover Ave., Whippany 07981. SAN 322-4058. Tel. 973-631-5353, fax 973-631-5366. *Exec. Dir.* Phillip Berg.

Morris-Union Federation, 214 Main St., Chatham 07928. SAN 310-2629. Tel. 973-635-0603, fax 973-635-7827.

New Jersey Health Sciences Library Network (NJHSN), Overlook Hospital Lib., Summit 07902. SAN 371-4829. Tel. 908-522-2886, fax 908-522-2274. *Lib. Mgr.* Patricia Regenberg.

New Jersey Library Network, Lib. Development Bureau, Trenton 08608. SAN 372-8161. Tel. 609-278-2640 ext. 152, fax 609-278-2650. *Assoc. State Libn. for Lib. Development* Kathleen Moeller-Peiffer.

Virtual Academic Library Environment (VALE), William Paterson Univ. Lib., Wayne 07470-2103. Tel. 973-720-3179, fax 973-720-3171. *Coord.* Judy Avrin.

New Mexico

Estacado Library Information Network (ELIN), 509 N. Shipp, Hobbs 88240. Tel. 505-397-9328, fax 505-397-1508.

New Mexico Consortium of Academic Libraries, Dean's Office, Albuquerque 87131-0001. SAN 371-6872. *Pres.* Barbara Lovato.

New Mexico Consortium of Biomedical and Hospital Libraries, c/o St. Vincent Hospital, Santa Fe 87505. SAN 322-449X. Tel. 505-820-5218, fax 505-989-6478. *Chair* Albert Robinson.

New York

Academic Libraries of Brooklyn, Long Island Univ. Lib. LLC 517, Brooklyn 11201. SAN 322-2411. Tel. 718-488-1081, fax 718-780-4057. *Dir.* Ingrid Wang.

Associated Colleges of the Saint Lawrence Valley, SUNY Potsdam, Potsdam 13676-2299. SAN 322-242X. Tel. 315-267-3331, fax 315-267-2389. *Exec. Dir.* Anneke J. Larrance.

Brooklyn-Queens-Staten Island-Manhattan-Bronx Health Sciences Librarians (BQSIMB), 150 55th St., Brooklyn 11220. Tel. 718-630-7200, fax 718-630-8918. *Pres.* Sheryl Ramer Gesoff.

Capital District Library Council (CDLC), 28 Essex St., Albany 12206. SAN 322-2446. Tel. 518-438-2500, fax 518-438-2872. *Exec. Dir.* Kathleen Gundrum.

Central New York Library Resources Council (CLRC), 6493 Ridings Rd., Syracuse 13206-1195. SAN 322-2454. Tel. 315-446-5446, fax 315-446-5590. *Exec. Dir.* Debby Emerson.

ConnectNY, Rochester Institute of Technology, Rochester 14623. Tel. 585-475-2050. *Exec. Dir.* Pamela Jones.

Library Assn. of Rockland County (LARC), P.O. Box 917, New City 10956-0917. Tel. 845-359-3877. *Pres.* Carol Connell Cannon.

Library Consortium of Health Institutions in Buffalo (LCHIB), Abbott Hall, SUNY at Buffalo, Buffalo 14214. SAN 329-367X. Tel. 716-829-3900 ext. 143, fax 716-829-2211, e-mail hubnet@buffalo.edu; ulb-lchib@buffalo.edu. *Exec. Dir.* Martin E. Mutka.

Long Island Library Resources Council (LILRC), 627 N. Sunrise Service Rd., Bellport 11713. SAN 322-2489. Tel. 631-675-1570. *Dir.* Herbert Biblo.

Medical and Scientific Libraries of Long Island (MEDLI), c/o Palmer School of Lib. and Info. Science, Brookville 11548. SAN 322-4309. Tel. 516-299-2866, fax 516-299-4168. *Chair* Mary Westermann-Cicio.

Metropolitan New York Library Council (METRO), 57 E. 11 St., 4th flr., New York 10003-4605. SAN 322-2500. Tel. 212-228-2320, fax 212-228-2598. *Exec. Dir.* Nate Hill.

New England Law Library Consortium (NELLCO), 80 New Scotland Ave., Albany 12208. SAN 322-4244. Tel. 518-694-3025, fax 518-694-3027. *Exec. Dir.* Tracy L. Thompson.

New York State Higher Education Initiative (NYSHEI), 22 Corporate Woods Blvd., Albany 12211-2350. Fax 518-432-4346, e-mail nyshei@nyshei.org. *Exec. Dir.* Stanley S. Hansen.

Northeast Foreign Law Libraries Cooperative Group, Columbia Univ. Lib., New York 10027. SAN 375-0000. Tel. 212-854-1411, fax 212-854-3295. *Coord.* Silke Sahl.

Northern New York Library Network, 6721 U.S. Hwy. 11, Potsdam 13676. SAN 322-2527. Tel. 315-265-1119, fax 315-265-1881, e-mail info@nnyln.org. *Exec. Dir.* John J. Hammond.

Rochester Regional Library Council, 390 Packetts Landing, Fairport 14450. SAN 322-2535. Tel. 585-223-7570, fax 585-223-7712, e-mail rrlc@rrlc.org. *Exec. Dir.* Kathleen M. Miller.

South Central Regional Library Council, Clinton Hall, Ithaca 14850. SAN 322-2543. Tel. 607-273-9106, fax 607-272-0740, e-mail scrlc@scrlc.org. *Exec. Dir.* Mary-Carol Lindbloom.

Southeastern New York Library Resources Council (SENYLRC), 21 S. Elting Corners Rd., Highland 12528-2805. SAN 322-2551. Tel. 845-883-9065, fax 845-883-9483. *Exec. Dir.* Tessa Killian.

SUNYConnect, Office of Lib. and Info. Services, Albany 12246. Tel. 518-443-5577, fax 518-443-5358. *Asst. Provost for Lib. and Info. Services* Carey Hatch.

United Nations System Electronic Information Acquisitions Consortium (UNSEIAC), c/o United Nations Lib., New York 10017. SAN 377-855X. Tel. 212-963-2026, fax 212-963-2608, e-mail unseiac@un.org. *Coord.* Kikuko Maeyama.

Western New York Library Resources Council, 4950 Genesee St., Buffalo 14225. SAN 322-2578. Tel. 716-633-0705, fax 716-633-1736. *Exec. Dir.* Sheryl Knab.

North Carolina

AHEC Digital Library, http://library.ncahec.net. *Dir.* Diana McDuffee.

Cape Fear Health Sciences Information Consortium, 1601 Owen Drive, Fayetteville

28301. SAN 322-3930. Tel. 910-671-5046, fax 910-671-5337. *Dir.* Katherine Mcginniss.

North Carolina Community College System, 200 W. Jones St., Raleigh 27603-1379. SAN 322-2594. Tel. 919-807-7100, fax 919-807-7175; 919-807-7164. *Assoc. V.P. for Learning Technology Systems* Bill Randall.

Triangle Research Libraries Network, Wilson Lib., Chapel Hill 27514-8890. SAN 329-5362. Tel. 919-962-8022, fax 919-962-4452. *Interim Dir.* Lisa Croucher.

Western North Carolina Library Network (WNCLN), c/o Ramsey Lib., 1 University Heights, Asheville 28804. Tel. 828-668-2368. *Network Libn.* Ben Shirley.

North Dakota

Central Dakota Library Network, Morton Mandan Public Lib., Mandan 58554-3149. SAN 373-1391. Tel. 701-667-5365, e-mail mortonmandanlibrary@cdln.info. *Dir.* Kelly Steckler.

Tri-College University Libraries Consortium, NDSU Downtown Campus, Fargo 58102. SAN 322-2047. Tel. 701-231-8170, fax 701-231-7205. *In Charge* Sonia Hohnadel.

Ohio

Assn. of Christian Librarians (ACL), P.O. Box 4, Cedarville 45314. Tel. 937-766-2255, fax 937-766-5499, e-mail info@acl.org. *Pres.* Frank Quinn.

Central Ohio Hospital Library Consortium, 127 S. Davis Ave., Columbus 43222. SAN 371-084X. Tel. 614-234-5214, fax 614-234-1257, e-mail library@mchs.com. *Dir.* Stevo Roksandic.

Christian Library Consortium (CLC), c/o ACL, Cedarville 45314. Tel. 937-766-2255, fax 937-766-5499, e-mail info@acl.org. *Coord.* Beth Purtee.

Columbus Area Library and Information Council of Ohio (CALICO), c/o Westerville Public Lib., Westerville 43081. SAN 371-683X. Tel. 614-882-7277, fax 614-882-5369.

Consortium of Popular Culture Collections in the Midwest (CPCCM), c/o Popular Culture Lib., Bowling Green 43403-0600. SAN 370-5811. Tel. 419-372-2450, fax 419-372-7996. *Head Libn.* Nancy Down.

Five Colleges of Ohio, 102 Allen House, Gambier 43022. Tel. 740-427-5377, fax 740-427-5390, e-mail ohiofive@gmail.com. *Exec. Dir.* Susan Palmer.

Northeast Ohio Regional Library System (NEO-RLS), 1580 Georgetown Rd., Hudson 44236. SAN 322-2713. Tel. 330-655-0531, fax 330-655-0568. *Exec. Dir.* Catherine Hakala-Ausperk.

Northwest Regional Library System (NORWELD), 181½ S. Main St., Bowling Green 43402. SAN 322-273X. Tel. 419-352-2903, fax 419-353-8310. *Exec. Dir.* Arline V. Radden.

OCLC Online Computer Library Center, Inc., 6565 Kilgour Place, Dublin 43017-3395. SAN 322-2748. Tel. 614-764-6000, fax 614-718-1017, e-mail oclc@oclc.org. *Pres./CEO* Skip Pritchard.

Ohio Health Sciences Library Assn. (OHSLA), Medical Lib., South Pointe Hospital, Warrensville Heights 44122. Tel. 216-491-7454, fax 216-491-7650. *Pres.* Debra Orr.

Ohio Library and Information Network (OhioLINK), 35 E. Chestnut St., 8th fl., Columbus 43215-2541. SAN 374-8014. Tel. 614-485-6722, fax 614-228-1807, email info@ohiolink.edu. *Exec. Dir.* Gwen Evans.

Ohio Network of American History Research Centers, Ohio Historical Society Archives-Lib., Columbus 43211-2497. SAN 323-9624. Tel. 614-297-2510, fax 614-297-2546, e-mail reference@ohiohistory.org.

Ohio Public Library Information Network (OPLIN), 2323 W. 5 Ave., Suite 130, Columbus 43204. Tel. 614-728-5252, fax 614-728-5256, e-mail support@oplin.org. *Exec. Dir.* Stephen Hedges.

OHIONET, 1500 W. Lane Ave., Columbus 43221-3975. SAN 322-2764. Tel. 614-486-2966, fax 614-486-1527. *Exec. Officer* Michael P. Butler.

SEO (Serving Every Ohioan) Library Center, 40780 Marietta Rd., Caldwell 43724. SAN 356-4606. *Dir.* Dianna Clark.

Southeast Regional Library System (SERLS), 252 W. 13 St., Wellston 45692. SAN 322-2756. Tel. 740-384-2103, fax 740-384-2106, e-mail dirserls@oplin.org. *Dir.* Jay Burton.

SWON Libraries Consortium, 10250 Alliance Rd., Suite 225, Blue Ash 45242. SAN 322-2675. Tel. 513-751-4422, fax 513-751-

0463, e-mail info@swonlibraries.org. *Exec. Dir.* Melanie A. Blau-McDonald.

Southwestern Ohio Council for Higher Education (SOCHE), Miami Valley Research Park, Dayton 45420-4015. SAN 322-2659. Tel. 937-258-8890, fax 937-258-8899, e-mail soche@soche.org.

State Assisted Academic Library Council of Kentucky (SAALCK), 12031 Southwick Lane, Cincinnati 45241. SAN 371-2222. Tel. 800-771-1972, e-mail saalck@saalck. org. *Exec. Dir.* Anne Abate.

Theological Consortium of Greater Columbus (TCGC), Trinity Lutheran Seminary, Columbus 43209-2334. Tel. 614-384-4646, fax 614-238-0263. *Lib. Systems Mgr.* Ray Olson.

Oklahoma

Oklahoma Health Sciences Library Assn. (OHSLA), HSC Bird Health Science Lib., Univ. of Oklahoma, Oklahoma City 73190. SAN 375-0051. Tel. 405-271-2285 ext. 48755, fax 405-271-3297.

Oregon

Chemeketa Cooperative Regional Library Service, c/o Chemeketa Community College, Salem 97305-1453. SAN 322-2837. Tel. 503-399-5105, fax 503-399-7316, e-mail contact@cclrs.org. *Dir.* John Goodyear.

Library Information Network of Clackamas County (LINCC), 1810 Red Soils Court, #110, Oregon City 97045. SAN 322-2845. Tel. 503-723-4888, fax 503-794-8238. *Lib. System Analyst* George Yobst.

Orbis Cascade Alliance, 2288 Oakmont Way, Eugene 97401. SAN 377-8096. Tel. 541-246-2470. *Exec. Dir.* John Helmer.

Oregon Health Sciences Libraries Assn. (OHSLA), Oregon Health and Science Univ. Lib., Portland 97239-3098. SAN 371-2176. Tel. 503-494-3462, fax 503-494-3322, e-mail library@ohsu.edu.

Southern Oregon Library Federation, c/o Klamath County Lib., Klamath Falls 97601. SAN 322-2861. Tel. 541-882-8894, fax 541-882-6166. *Dir.* Christy Davis.

Washington County Cooperative Library Services, 111 N.E. Lincoln St., MS No. 58, Hillsboro 97124-3036. SAN 322-287X. Tel.

503-846-3222, fax 503-846-3220. *Mgr.* Eva Calcagno.

Pennsylvania

Associated College Libraries of Central Pennsylvania, c/o 648 State St., Lancaster 17603. E-mail webmaster@aclcp.org. *Chair* Robin Wagner.

Berks County Library Assn. (BCLA), Reading Public Lib., Reading 19602. SAN 371-0866. Tel. 610-478-9035; 610-655-6350. *Pres.* Jennifer Balas.

Central Pennsylvania Consortium (CPC), Dickinson College, Carlisle 17013. SAN 322-2896. Tel. 717-245-1984, fax 717-245-1807, e-mail cpc@dickinson.edu. *Pres.* Katherine Haley Will.

Central Pennsylvania Health Sciences Library Assn. (CPHSLA), Office for Research Protections, Pennsylvania State Univ., University Park 16802. SAN 375-5290. Fax 814-865-1775. *Pres.* Helen Houpt.

Cooperating Hospital Libraries of the Lehigh Valley Area, Estes Lib., Saint Luke's Hospital, Bethlehem 18015. SAN 371-0858. Tel. 610-954-3407, fax 610-954-4651.

Delaware Valley Information Consortium (DEVIC), St. Mary Medical Center Medical Lib., Langhorne 19047. Tel. 215-710-2012, fax 215-710-4638.

Eastern Mennonite Associated Libraries and Archives (EMALA), 2215 Millstream Rd., Lancaster 17602. SAN 372-8226. Tel. 717-393-9745, fax 717-393-8751. *Chair* John Weber.

Greater Philadelphia Law Library Assn. (GPLLA), PO Box 335, Philadelphia 19105. SAN 373-1375. *Pres.* Lori Strickler Corso.

HSLC/Access PA (Health Science Libraries Consortium), 3600 Market St., Suite 550, Philadelphia 19104-2646. SAN 323-9780. Tel. 215-222-1532, fax 215-222-0416, e-mail support@hslc.org. *Exec. Dir.* Maryam Phillips.

Interlibrary Delivery Service of Pennsylvania (IDS), c/o Bucks County IU, No. 22, Doylestown 18901. SAN 322-2942. Tel. 215-348-2940 ext. 1620, fax 215-348-8315, e-mail ids@bucksiu.org. *Admin. Dir.* Pamela Newman Dinan.

Keystone Library Network, Dixon Univ. Center, Harrisburg 17110-1201. Tel. 717-720-

4088, fax 717-720-4453. *Coord.* Mary Lou Sowden.

Laurel Highlands Health Science Library Consortium, 361 Sunrise Rd., Dayton 16222. SAN 322-2950. Tel. 814-341-0242, fax 814-266-8230. *Dir.* Rhonda Yeager.

Lehigh Valley Assn. of Independent Colleges, 130 W. Greenwich St., Bethlehem 18018. SAN 322-2969. Tel. 610-625-7888, fax 610-625-7891. *Exec. Dir.* Diane Dimitroff.

Montgomery County Library and Information Network Consortium (MCLINC), 301 Lafayette St., 2nd flr., Conshohocken 19428. Tel. 610-238-0580, fax 610-238-0581, e-mail webmaster@mclinc.org. *Pres.* Cherilyn Fiory.

National Network of Libraries of Medicine–Middle Atlantic Region (NN/LM-MAR), Univ. of Pittsburgh, Pittsburgh 15261. E-mail nnlmmar@pitt.edu. *Exec. Dir.* Renae Barger.

Northeastern Pennsylvania Library Network, c/o Marywood Univ. Lib., Scranton 18509-1598. SAN 322-2993. Tel. 570-348-6260, fax 570-961-4769. *Exec. Dir.* Catherine H. Schappert.

Northwest Interlibrary Cooperative of Pennsylvania (NICOP), Mercyhurst College Lib., Erie 16546. SAN 370-5862. Tel. 814-824-2190, fax 814-824-2219. *Archivist* Earleen Glaser.

Pennsylvania Library Assn., 220 Cumberland Pkwy, Suite 10, Mechanicsburg 17055. Tel. 717-766-7663, fax 717-766-5440. *Exec. Dir.* Glenn R. Miller.

Philadelphia Area Consortium of Special Collections Libraries (PACSCL), P.O. Box 22642, Philadelphia 19110-2642. Tel. 215-985-1445, fax 215-985-1446, email lblanchard@pacscl.org. *Exec. Dir.* Laura Blanchard.

Southeastern Pennsylvania Theological Library Assn. (SEPTLA), c/o Biblical Seminary, Hatfield 19440. SAN 371-0793. Tel. 215-368-5000 ext. 234. *Pres.* Jenifer Gundry.

State System of Higher Education Library Cooperative (SSHELCO), c/o Bailey Lib., Slippery Rock 16057. Tel. 724-738-2630, fax 724-738-2661. *Dir.* Philip Tramdack.

Susquehanna Library Cooperative (SLC), Stevenson Lib., Lock Haven Univ., Lock Haven 17745. SAN 322-3051. Tel. 570-484-2310,

fax 570-484-2506. *Interim Dir. of Lib. and Info. Services* Joby Topper.

Tri-State College Library Cooperative (TCLC), c/o Rosemont College Lib., Rosemont 19010-1699. SAN 322-3078. Tel. 610-525-0796, fax 610-525-1939, e-mail office@tclclibs.org. *Coord.* Ellen Gasiewski.

Rhode Island

Library of Rhode Island Network (LORI), c/o Office of Lib. and Info. Services, Providence 02908-5870. SAN 371-6821. Tel. 401-574-9300, fax 401-574-9320. *Chair of Lib. Services* Karen Mellor.

Ocean State Libraries (OSL), 300 Centerville Rd., Suite 103S, Warwick 02886-0226. SAN 329-4560. Tel. 401-738-2200, fax 401-736-8949, e-mail support@oslri.net. *Exec. Dir.* Joan Gillespie.

South Carolina

Charleston Academic Libraries Consortium (CALC), P.O. Box 118067, Charleston 29423-8067. SAN 371-0769. Tel. 843-574-6088, fax 843-574-6484. *Chair* Drucie Gullion.

Partnership Among South Carolina Academic Libraries (PASCAL), 1122 Lady St., Suite 300, Columbia 29201. Tel. 803-734-0900, fax 803-734-0901. *Exec. Dir.* Rick Moul.

South Carolina AHEC, c/o Medical Univ. of South Carolina, Charleston 29425. SAN 329-3998. Tel. 843-792-4431, fax 843-792-4430. *Exec. Dir.* David Garr.

South Carolina Library Network, 1430 and 1500 Senate St., Columbia 29201. SAN 322-4198. Tel. 803-734-8666, fax 803-734-8676. *Dir., Lib. Development* Kathy Sheppard.

South Dakota

South Dakota Library Network (SDLN), 1200 University, Unit 9672, Spearfish 57799-9672. SAN 371-2117. Tel. 605-642-6835, fax 605-642-6472. *Dir.* Warren Wilson.

Tennessee

Consortium of Southern Biomedical Libraries (CONBLS), Meharry Medical College, Nashville 37208. SAN 370-7717. Tel. 615-

327-6728, fax 615-327-6448. *Chair* Brenda Seago.

Knoxville Area Health Sciences Library Consortium (KAHSLC), Univ. of Tennessee Preston Medical Lib., Knoxville 37920. SAN 371-0556. Tel. 865-305-9525, fax 865-305-9527. *Pres.* Cynthia Vaughn.

Tennessee Health Science Library Assn. (THeSLA), Holston Valley Medical Center Health Sciences Lib., Kingsport 37660. SAN 371-0726. Tel. 423-224-6870, fax 423-224-6014. *Pres.* Sandy Oelschlegel.

Tri-Cities Area Health Sciences Libraries Consortium (TCAHSLC), James H. Quillen College of Medicine, East Tennessee State Univ., Johnson City 37614. SAN 329-4099. Tel. 423-439-6252, fax 423-439-7025. *Dir.* Biddanda Ponnappa.

Texas

Abilene Library Consortium, 3305 N. 3 St., Suite 301, Abilene 79603. SAN 322-4694. Tel. 325-672-7081, fax 325-672-7082. *Coord.* Edward J. Smith.

Amigos Library Services, Inc., 14400 Midway Rd., Dallas 75244-3509. SAN 322-3191. Tel. 972-851-8000, fax 972-991-6061, e-mail amigos@amigos.org. *Pres./CEO* Bonnie Juergens.

Council of Research and Academic Libraries (CORAL), P.O. Box 290236, San Antonio 78280-1636. SAN 322-3213. Tel. 210-458-4885. *Coord.* Rosemary Vasquez.

Del Norte Biosciences Library Consortium, El Paso Community College, El Paso 79998. SAN 322-3302. Tel. 915-831-4149, fax 915-831-4639. *Coord.* Becky Perales.

Harrington Library Consortium, 413 E. 4 Ave., Amarillo 79101. SAN 329-546X. Tel. 806-378-6037, fax 806-378-6038. *Dir.* Amanda Barrera.

Health Libraries Information Network (Health LINE), 3500 Camp Bowie Blvd. LIB-222, Fort Worth 76107-2699. SAN 322-3299. E-mail dfwhealthline@gmail.com. *Chair* Mary Ann Huslig.

Houston Area Library Automated Network (HALAN), Houston Public Lib., Houston 77002. Tel. 832-393-1411, fax 832-393-1427, e-mail website@hpl.lib.tx.us. *Chief* Judith Hiott.

Houston Area Research Library Consortium (HARLiC), c/o Univ. of Houston Libs., Houston 77204-2000. SAN 322-3329. Tel. 713-743-9807, fax 713-743-9811. *Pres.* Dana Rooks.

National Network of Libraries of Medicine–South Central Region (NN/LM-SCR), c/o HAM-TMC Library, Houston 77030-2809. SAN 322-3353. Tel. 713-799-7880, fax 713-790-7030, e-mail nnlm-scr@exch.library.tmc.edu. *Dir.* L. Maximillian Buja.

South Central Academic Medical Libraries Consortium (SCAMeL), c/o Lewis Lib.-UNTHSC, Fort Worth 76107. SAN 372-8269. Tel. 817-735-2380, fax 817-735-5158. *Dir.* Daniel Burgard.

Texas Council of Academic Libraries (TCAL), VC/UHV Lib., Victoria 77901. SAN 322-337X. Tel. 361-570-4150, fax 361-570-4155. *Chair* Karen Baen.

Texas Navigator Group, P.O. Box 12927, Austin 78711. SAN 322-3396. Tel. 512-463-5406, fax 512-936-2306. *Coord.* Sue Bennett.

Texas State Library and Archives Commission (TexSHARE), P.O. Box 12927, Austin 78711. Tel. 512-463-5455, fax 512-936-2306, e-mail texshare@tsl.state.tx.us. *Dir. and State Libn.* Edward Seidenberg.

Utah

National Network of Libraries of Medicine–MidContinental Region (NN/LM-MCR), Spencer S. Eccles Health Sciences Lib., Univ. of Utah, Salt Lake City 84112-5890. SAN 322-225X. Tel. 801-587-3412, fax 801-581-3632. *Dir.* Jean Shipman.

Utah Academic Library Consortium (UALC), Univ. of Utah, Salt Lake City 84112-0860. SAN 322-3418. Tel. 801-581-7701, 801-581-3852, fax 801-585-7185, e-mail UALC mail@library.utah.edu. *Fiscal Agent* Parker M. Dougherty.

Utah Health Sciences Library Consortium, c/o Spencer S. Eccles Health Sciences Lib., Univ. of Utah, Salt Lake City 84112-5890. SAN 376-2246. Tel. 801-585-5743, fax 801-581-3632. *Chair* Emily Eresuma.

Vermont

North Atlantic Health Sciences Libraries, Inc. (NAHSL), Dana Medical Lib., Univ. of Vermont Medical School, Burlington 05405. SAN 371-0599. Tel. 508-656-3483, fax 508-656-0762. *Chair* Donna Belcinski.

Vermont Resource Sharing Network, c/o Vermont Dept. of Libs., Montpelier 05609-0601. SAN 322-3426. Tel. 802-828-3261, fax 802-828-1481. *Ref. Libn.* Gerrie Denison.

Virgin Islands

Virgin Islands Library and Information Network (VILINET), c/o Div. of Libs., Archives, and Museums, Saint Thomas 00802. SAN 322-3639. Tel. 340-773-5715, fax 340-773-3257, e-mail info@vilinet.net. *Territorial Dir. of Libs., Archives, and Museums* Ingrid Bough.

Virginia

American Indian Higher Education Consortium (AIHEC), 121 Oronoco St., Alexandria 22314. SAN 329-4056. Tel. 703-838-0400, fax 703-838-0388, e-mail info@aihec.org.

Lynchburg Area Library Cooperative, c/o Sweet Briar College Lib., Sweet Briar 24595. SAN 322-3450. Tel. 434-381-6315, fax 434-381-6173.

Lynchburg Information Online Network (LION), 2315 Memorial Ave., Lynchburg 24503. SAN 374-6097. Tel. 434-381-6311, fax 434-381-6173. *Dir.* John G. Jaffee.

NASA Libraries Information System–NASA Galaxie, NASA Langley Research Center, MS 185-Technical Lib., Hampton 23681-2199. SAN 322-0788. Tel. 757-864-2356, fax 757-864-2375. *Coord.* Phyllis Kay Costulis.

Richmond Academic Library Consortium (RALC), James Branch Cabell Lib., Virginia Commonwealth Univ., Richmond 23284. SAN 322-3469. Tel. 804-828-1110, fax 804-828-1105. *Univ. Libn.* Kevin Butterfield.

Southside Virginia Library Network (SVLN), Longwood Univ., Farmville 23909-1897. SAN 372-8242. Tel. 434-395-2431; 434-395-2433, fax 434-395-2453. *Dean of Lib.* Suzy Szasz Palmer.

United States Army Training and Doctrine Command (TRADOC)/Lib. Program Office, U.S. Army Hq TRADOC, Fort Monroe 23651. SAN 322-418X. Tel. 757-788-2155, fax 757-788-5544. *Dir.* Amy Loughran.

Virginia Independent College and University Library Assn., c/o Mary Helen Cochran Lib., Sweet Briar 24595. SAN 374-6089. Tel. 434-381-6139, fax 434-381-6173. *Dir.* John Jaffee.

Virginia Tidewater Consortium for Higher Education (VTC), 4900 Powhatan Ave., Norfolk 23529. SAN 329-5486. Tel. 757-683-3183, fax 757-683-4515, e-mail lgdotolo@aol.com. *Pres.* Lawrence G. Dotolo.

Virtual Library of Virginia (VIVA), George Mason Univ., Fairfax 22030. Tel. 703-993-4652, fax 703-993-4662. *Dir.* Anne Osterman.

Washington

Cooperating Libraries in Olympia (CLIO), Evergreen State College Library, L2300, Olympia 98505. SAN 329-4528. Tel. 360-867-6260, fax 360-867-6790. *Dean, Lib. Services* Greg Mullins.

Inland NorthWest Health Sciences Libraries (INWHSL), P.O. Box 10283, Spokane 99209-0283. SAN 370-5099. Tel. 509-368-6973, fax 509-358-7928. *Dir. of Lib. Services* Anne Mackereth.

National Network of Libraries of Medicine–Pacific Northwest Region (NN/LM-PNR), T-344 Health Sciences Bldg., Univ. of Washington, Seattle 98195. SAN 322-3485. Tel. 206-543-8262, fax 206-543-2469, e-mail nnlm@u.washington.edu. *Assoc. Dir.* Catherine Burroughs.

Palouse Area Library Information Services (PALIS), c/o Neill Public Lib., Pullman 99163. SAN 375-0132. Tel. 509-334-3595, fax 509-334-6051. *Dir.* Andriette Pieron.

Washington Idaho Network (WIN), Foley Center Lib., Gonzaga Univ., Spokane 99258. Tel. 509-323-6545, fax 509-324-5904, e-mail winsupport@gonzaga.edu. *Pres.* Kathleen Allen.

Wisconsin

Fox River Valley Area Library Consortium (FRVALC), c/o Polk Lib., Univ. of Wisconsin–Oshkosh, Oshkosh 54901. SAN 322-3531. Tel. 920-424-3348, 920-424-4333, fax 920-424-2175.

Fox Valley Library Council, c/o OWLS, Appleton 54911. SAN 323-9640. Tel. 920-832-6190, fax 920-832-6422. *Pres.* Paula Wright.

North East Wisconsin Intertype Libraries, Inc. (NEWIL), 515 Pine St., Green Bay 54301. SAN 322-3574. Tel. 920-448-4413, fax 920-448-4420. *Coord.* Jamie Matczak.

Northwestern Wisconsin Health Science Library Consortium, c/o Gundersen Lutheran Medical Center, Lacrosse 54601. Tel. 608-775-5410, fax 608-775-6343. *Treas.* Eileen Severson.

South Central Wisconsin Health Science Library Consortium, c/o Fort Healthcare Medical Lib., Fort Atkinson 53538. SAN 322-4686. Tel. 920-568-5194, fax 920-568-5195. *Coord.* Carrie Garity.

Southeastern Wisconsin Health Science Library Consortium, Veterans Admin. Center Medical Lib., Milwaukee 53295. SAN 322-3582. Tel. 414-384-2000 ext. 42342, fax 414-382-5334. *Coord.* Kathy Strube.

Southeastern Wisconsin Information Technology Exchange, Inc. (SWITCH), 6801 North Yates Rd., Milwaukee 53217. Tel. 414-382-6710. *Coord.* Jennifer Schmidt.

University of Wisconsin System School Library Education Consortium (UWSSLEC), Graduate and Continuing Educ., Univ. of Wisconsin–Whitewater, Whitewater 53190. Tel. 262-472-1463, fax 262-472-5210, e-mail lenchoc@uww.edu. *Dir.* Eileen Schroeder.

Wisconsin Library Services (WILS), 1360 Regent St., No. 121, Madison 53715-1255. Tel. 608-216-8399, e-mail information@wils.org. *Dir.* Stef Morrill.

Wisconsin Public Library Consortium (WPLC), c/o WILS, 1360 Regent St., No. 121, Madison 53715-1255. Tel. 608-216-8399, e-mail information@wils.org.

Wisconsin Valley Library Service (WVLS), 300 N. 1 St., Wausau 54403. SAN 371-3911. Tel. 715-261-7250, fax 715-261-7259. *Dir.* Marla Rae Sepnafski.

WISPALS Library Consortium, c/o Gateway Technical College, Kenosha 53144-1690. Tel. 262-564-2602, fax 262-564-2787. *Chair* Scott Vrieze.

Wyoming

WYLD Network, c/o Wyoming State Lib., Cheyenne 82002-0060. SAN 371-0661. Tel. 307-777-6339, fax 307-777-6289, e-mail wyldstaff@will.state.wy.us. *Pres.* Marci Mock.

Canada

Alberta

The Alberta Library (TAL), 6-14, 7 Sir Winston Churchill Sq., Edmonton T5J 2V5. Tel. 780-414-0805, fax 780-414-0806, e-mail admin@thealbertalibrary.ab.ca. *CEO* Grant Chaney.

Council of Prairie and Pacific University Libraries (COPPUL), LCR Admin. Suite, 6th fl. TFDL, Calgary T2N 1N4. Tel. 403-220-8133, fax 403-282-1218. *Exec. Dir.* Andrew Waller.

NEOS Library Consortium, Cameron Lib., 5th flr., Edmonton T6G 2J8. Tel. 780-492-0075, fax 780-492-8302. *Mgr.* Anne Carr-Wiggin.

British Columbia

British Columbia Academic Health Council (BCAHC), 1847 W. Broadway, Vancouver V6J 1Y6. Tel. 604-739-3910 ext. 228, fax 604-739-3931, e-mail info@bcahc.ca. *CEO* Laureen Styles.

British Columbia College and Institute Library Services, Langara College Lib., Vancouver V5Y 2Z6. SAN 329-6970. Tel. 604-323-5639, fax 604-323-5544, e-mail cils@langara.bc.ca. *Dir.* Mary Anne Epp.

British Columbia Electronic Library Network (BCELN), WAC Bennett Lib., 7th flr., Simon Fraser Univ., Burnaby V5A 1S6. Tel. 778-782-7003, fax 778-782-3023, e-mail office@eln.bc.ca. *Exec. Dir.* Anita Cocchia.

Council of Prairie and Pacific University Libraries (COPPUL), LCR Administrative Suite, 6th Floor TFDL, University of Calgary, Calgary T2N 1N4. *Exec. Dir.* Andrew Waller.

Electronic Health Library of British Columbia (e-HLbc), c/o Bennett Lib., Burnaby V5A 1S6. Tel. 778-782-5440, fax 778-782-3023, e-mail info@ehlbc.ca. *Coord.* Leigh Anne Palmer.

Public Library InterLINK, 5489 Byrne Rd., No 158, Burnaby V5J 3J1. SAN 318-8272. Tel. 604-517-8441, fax 604-517-8410, e-mail info@interlinklibraries.ca. *Operations Mgr.* Rita Avigdor.

Manitoba

Manitoba Library Consortium, Inc. (MLCI), c/o Lib. Admin., Univ. of Winnipeg, Winnipeg R3B 2E9. SAN 372-820X. Tel. 204-786-9801, fax 204-783-8910. *Chair* Louise Ayotte-Zaretski.

Nova Scotia

Maritimes Health Libraries Assn. (MHLA-AB-SM), W. K. Kellogg Health Sciences Lib., Halifax B3H 1X5. SAN 370-0836. Tel. 902-494-2483, fax 902-494-3750. *Libn.* Shelley McKibbon.

NOVANET, 84 Chain Lake Drive, Suite 402, Halifax B3S 1A2. SAN 372-4050. Tel. 902-453-2461, fax 902-453-2369, e-mail office@novanet.ns.ca. *Mgr.* Bill Slauenwhite.

Ontario

Canadian Assn. of Research Libraries (Association des Bibliothèques de Recherche du Canada), 203-309 Cooper St., Ottawa K2P 0G5. SAN 323-9721. Tel. 613-482-9344, fax 613-562-5297, e-mail info@carl-abrc.ca. *Exec. Dir.* Susan Haigh.

Canadian Health Libraries Assn. (CHLA-AB-SC), 468 Queen St. E., LL-02, Toronto M5A 1T7. SAN 370-0720. Tel. 416-646-1600, fax 416-646-9460, e-mail info@chla-absc.ca. *Pres.* Jeanna Hough.

Canadian Research Knowledge Network (CRKN), 301-11 Holland Ave., Ottawa K1Y 4S1. Tel. 613-907-7040, fax 866-903-9094. *Exec. Dir.* Clare Appavoo.

Hamilton and District Health Library Network, c/o St Josephs Healthcare Hamilton, Sherman Lib., Room T2305, Hamilton L8N 4A6. SAN 370-5846. Tel. 905-522-1155 ext. 3410, fax 905-540-6504. *Coord.* Jean Maragno.

Health Science Information Consortium of Toronto, c/o Gerstein Science Info. Center, Univ. of Toronto, Toronto M5S 1A5. SAN 370-5080. Tel. 416-978-6359, fax 416-971-2637. *Exec. Dir.* Miriam Ticoll.

Ontario Council of University Libraries (OCUL), 130 Saint George St., Toronto M5S 1A5. Tel. 416-946-0578, fax 416-978-6755. *Exec. Dir.* John Barnett.

Ontario Library Consortium (OLC), c/o Georgina Public Lib., Keswick L4P 3P7. *Pres.* Gay Kozak Selby.

Parry Sound and Area Access Network, c/o Parry Sound Public Lib., Parry Sound P2A 1E3. Tel. 705-746-9601, fax 705-746-9601, e-mail pspl@vianet.ca. *Chair* Laurine Tremaine.

Perth County Information Network (PCIN), c/o Stratford Public Lib., Stratford N5A 1A2. Tel. 519-271-0220, fax 519-271-3843, e-mail webmaster@pcin.on.ca. *CEO* Sam Coglin.

Shared Library Services (SLS), Woodstock General Hospital, Woodstock N4V 0A4. SAN 323-9500. Tel. 519-421-4233, ext. 2735, fax 519-421-4236. *Libn.* Linda Wilcox.

Southwestern Ontario Health Libraries and Information Network (SOHLIN), London Health Sciences Centre, London N6A 5W9. Tel. 519-685-8500, ext. 56038. *Pres.* Jill McTavish.

Toronto Health Libraries Assn. (THLA), 3409 Yonge St., Toronto M4N 2L0. SAN 323-9853. Tel. 416-485-0377, fax 416-485-6877, e-mail medinfoserv@rogers.com. *Pres.* Graziela Alexandria.

Quebec

Assn. des Bibliothèques de la Santé Affiliées a l'Université de Montréal (ABSAUM), c/o Health Lib., Univ. of Montreal, Montreal H3C 3J7. SAN 370-5838. Tel. 514-343-6826, fax 514-343-2350. *Dir.* Monique St-Jean.

Canadian Heritage Information Network (CHIN), 15 Eddy St., 4th flr., Gatineau K1A 0M5. SAN 329-3076. Tel. 819-994-1200, fax 819-994-9555, e-mail service@chin.gc.ca. *Acting Exec. Dir.* Charlie Costain.

Réseau BIBLIO de l'Ouatouais, 2295 Saint-Louis St., Gatineau, Quebec J8T 5L8. SAN 319-6526. Tel. 819-561-6008. *Exec. Gen.* Sylvie Thibault.

National Library and Information-Industry Associations, United States and Canada

AIIM—The Association for Information and Image Management

President and CEO, John F. Mancini
1100 Wayne Ave., Suite 1100, Silver Spring, MD 20910
800-477-2446, 301-587-8202, e-mail aiim@aiim.org
World Wide Web http://www.aiim.org
European Office: 8 Canalside, Lowesmoor Wharf, Worcester WR1 2RR, England
Tel. 44-1905-727600, fax 44-1905-727609, e-mail info@aiim.org.uk

Object

AIIM is an international authority on enterprise content management, the tools and technologies that capture, manage, store, preserve, and deliver content in support of business processes. Founded in 1943.

Officers

Chair Paul Engel, VeBridge; *V. Chair* Anthony Peleska, Minnesota Housing Finance Agency; *Treas.* Daniel Antion, American Nuclear Insurers; *Past Chair* Timothy Elmore, Federal Credit Union.

Publication

Connect (weekly, memb., online).

American Association of Law Libraries

Executive Director, Kate Hagan
105 W. Adams St., Suite 3300, Chicago, IL 60603
312-939-4764, fax 312-431-1097, e-mail khagan@aall.org
World Wide Web http://www.aallnet.org

Object

The American Association of Law Libraries (AALL) is established for educational and scientific purposes. It shall be conducted as a nonprofit corporation to promote and enhance the value of law libraries to the public, the legal community, and the world; to foster the profession of law librarianship; to provide leadership in the field of legal information; and to foster a spirit of cooperation among the members of the profession. Established 1906.

Membership

Memb. 5,000+. Persons officially connected with a law library or with a law section of a state or general library, separately maintained. Associate membership available for others. Dues (Indiv.) $222; (Associate) $222; (Retired) $56; (Student) $56. Year. July–June.

Officers (2015–2016)

Pres. Keith Ann Stiverson kstivers@kentlaw.iit.edu; *V.P.* Ronald E. Wheeler Jr.. E-mail rewheeler@suffolk.edu; *Secy.* Katherine K. Coolidge. E-mail kcoolidge@bulkley.com; *Treas.* Gail Warren. E-mail gail.warren.56@comcast.net; *Past Pres.* Holly M. Riccio. E-mail hriccio@omm.

Executive Board Members

John W. Adkins. E-mail jadkins@sdlawlibrary.org; Femi Cadmus. E-mail femi.cadmus@cornell.edu; Kenneth J. Hirsh. E-mail hirshkh@ucmail.uc.edu; Donna Nixon. E-mail dnixon@email.unc.edu Emily R. Florio. E-mail florio@fr.com; Mary E. Matuszak.

American Indian Library Association

President, Paulita Aguilar
World Wide Web http://www.ailanet.org

Object

To improve library and information services for American Indians. Founded in 1979; affiliated with American Library Association in 1985.

Membership

Any person, library, or other organization interested in working to improve library and information services for American Indians may become a member. Dues (Inst.) $40; (Indiv.) $20; (Student) $10.

Officers (July 2014–June 2015)

Pres. Paulita Aguilar. Email paulita@umn.edu; *V.P./Pres.-Elect* Omar Poler (Mole Lake Soka-ogon Chippewa Community). Email poler@wisc.edu; *Secy.* Angela Thornton (Cherokee Nation). E-mail athornton@hdpl.org; *Treas.* Carlene Engstrom (Salish/Kootenai). E-mail carleneengstrom@yahoo.com; *Past Pres.* Zora Sampson (Choctaw). Email sampson@uwplatt.edu; *Exec. Dir.* Keith Michael Fiels. Email kfiels@ala.org; *Membs. at Large* Antonio Arce (2014–2016); Aaron LaFromboise (Blackfeet) (2015–2017); Patricia Cutright (Lakota) (2015–2017).

Publication

AILA Newsletter (irregular). *Ed.* Danielle Geller (Navajo).

American Library Association

Executive Director, Keith Michael Fiels
50 E. Huron St., Chicago, IL 60611
800-545-2433, 312-280-1392, fax 312-440-9374
World Wide Web http://www.ala.org

Object

The mission of the American Library Association (ALA) is to provide leadership for the development, promotion, and improvement of library and information services and the profession of librarianship in order to enhance learning and ensure access to information for all. Founded 1876.

Memb. (Indiv.) 52,841; (Inst.) 2,415; (Corporate) 183; (Total) 55,439 (as of November 2014). Any person, library, or other organization interested in library service and librarians. Dues (Indiv.) 1st year, $67; 2nd year, $102; 3rd year and later, $135; (Trustee and Assoc. Memb.) $61; (Lib. Support Staff) $48; (Student) $35; (Foreign Indiv.) $81; (Non-salaried/Unemployed/Retired) $48; (Inst.) $175 and up, depending on operating expenses of institution.

Officers (2015–2016)

Pres. Sari Feldman, Cuyahoga County Lib. sfeldman@cuyahogalibrary.org; *Pres.-Elect* Dr. Julia B. Todaro, Austin Community College jtodaro@austincc.edu; *Past Pres.* Courtney Young, Penn State University cly11@psu.edu; *Treas.* Mario M. Gonzalez, Passaic (New Jersey) Public Lib. E-mail mgonzalez@passaicpubliclibrary.org.

Executive Board

Robert E. Banks (2016); Loida A. Garcia-Febo (2018); Peter Hepburn (2017); Julius C. Jefferson Jr. (2018); Sara Kelly Johns (2016); Mike L. Marlin (2018); James Neal (2016); Gina Persichini (2017).

Endowment Trustees

Rodney M. Hersberger, Robert Randolph Newlan, Sioban A. Reardon, Brian E.C. Schottlaender, Teri R. Switzer, Patricia A. Wand; Staff Liaisons: Keith D. Brown, Latasha Bryant, Keith Michael Fiels, Mark Leon

Divisions

See the separate entries that follow: American Assn. of School Libns.; Assn. for Lib. Collections and Technical Services; Assn. for Lib. Service to Children; Assn. of College and Research Libs.; Assn. of Specialized and Cooperative Lib. Agencies; Lib. Leadership and Management Assn.; Lib. and Info. Technology Assn.; Public Lib. Assn.; Reference and User Services Assn.; United for Libraries; Young Adult Lib. Services Assn.

Publications

ALA Handbook of Organization (online).
American Libraries (6 a year with occasional digital supplements; memb.; organizations $70; foreign $80; single copy $11.50).
Booklist (22 a year with 4 *Book Links* print issues and access to *Booklist Online*; U.S. and Canada $147.50; foreign $170; single copy $9).

Round Table Chairs

(ALA staff liaison in parentheses)
Ethnic and Multicultural Information Exchange. Leslie Campbell Hime (Gwendolyn Prellwitz).

Exhibits. Kelly Coyle- Crivelli (Paul Graller).

Federal and Armed Forces Libraries. Amanda J. Wilson (Rosalind Reynolds).

Games and Gaming. Christopher Harris (Tina Coleman).

Gay, Lesbian, Bisexual, and Transgender. Peter D. Coyle (John Amudson).

Government Documents. Steven Woods (Rosalind Reynolds).

Intellectual Freedom. Pamela R. Klipsch (Shumeca Pickett).

International Relations. John Hickok (Delin R. Guerra).

Learning. Caitlin Moen (Kimberly L. Redd).

Library History. Eric C. Novotny (Norman Rose).

Library Instruction. Andrew Revelle (Lorelle Swader).

Library Research. Karen W. Gavigan (Norman Rose).

Library Support Staff Interests. Nina Manning (Lorelle Swader).

Map and Geospatial Information. Elizabeth Cox (Danielle M. Alderson).

New Members. .Kirby McCurtis (Kimberly L. Redd).

Retired Members. Vivian R. Wynn (Danielle M. Alderson).

Social Responsibilities. Nikki Winslow (John Admunson).

Staff Organizations. Leon S. Bay (Kimberly L. Redd).

Sustainability. Madeleine Charney (John Admunson).

Video. Brian Wesley Boling (Danielle M. Alderson).

Committee Chairs

(ALA staff liaison in parentheses)

Accreditation (Standing). Joan S. Howland (Laura Dare).

American Libraries Advisory (Standing). Luren E. Dickinson (Laurie Borman).

Appointments (Standing). Julie B. Todaro (Kerri Price).

Awards (Standing). Susan G. Hess (Cheryl Malden).

Budget Analysis and Review (Standing). Ann M. Martin (Keith D. Brown).

Chapter Relations (Standing). Ben Allen Hunter (Michael Dowling).

Committee on Committees (Elected Council Committee). Julie B. Todaro (Lois Ann Gregory-Wood).

Conference Committee (Standing). Clara Nalli Bohrer (Amy McGuigan).

Conference Program Coordinating Team. .

Constitution and Bylaws (Standing). James R. Rettig (JoAnne M. Kempf).

Council Orientation (Standing). Joseph M. Eagan (Lois Ann Gregory-Wood).

Diversity (Standing). April Grey (Gwendolyn Prellwitz).

Education (Standing). Michael Gutierrez (Kimberly L. Redd).

Election (Standing). Sarah Ann Long (Lois Ann Gregory-Wood).

Human Resource Development and Recruitment (Standing). Neely Tang (Lorelle R. Swader).

Information Technology Policy Advisory (Standing). Daniel R. Lee (Alan Inouye).

Intellectual Freedom (Standing). Pamela R. Klipsch (Barbara Jones).

International Relations (Standing). Clem Guthro (Michael Dowling)

Legislation (Standing). Ann Dutton Ewbank (Emily Sheketoff).

Library Advocacy (Standing). Gina J. Millsap (Marci Merola)

Literacy (Standing). Jessica Shira Sender (Kristin Lahurd).

Literacy and Outreach Services Advisory (Standing). Mimi Lee (Gwendolyn Prellwitz).

Membership (Standing). Laurel M. Bliss (Cathleen Bourdon).

Membership Meetings. Derek Mosley (Lois Ann Gregory-Wood)

Nominating.

Organization (Standing). Susan Considine (Kerri Price).

Policy Monitoring (Standing). Vicky L. Crone (Lois Ann Gregory-Wood).

Professional Ethics (Standing). Mary Jane Santos (Kristin Pekoll).

Public and Cultural Programs Advisory (Standing). Timothy P. Grimes (Sarah Ostman).

Public Awareness (Standing). Nancy R. Dowd (Cathleen Bourdon).

Publishing (Standing). Sandra Hirsh (Donald E. Chatham).

Research and Statistics (Standing). Linda Hofschire (Kathy Rosa).

Resolutions. Larry Romans (Lois Ann Gregory-Wood).

Rural, Native, and Tribal Libraries of All Kinds. Megan Kathleen Beard (Gwendolyn Prellwitz).

Scholarships and Study Grants. Tim Jiping Zou (Kimberly L. Redd).

Status of Women in Librarianship (Standing). Susan Antoinette Alteri (Lorelle R. Swader).

Training, Orientation, and Leadership Development. Kim Copenhaver (Lorelle R. Swader).

Website Advisory. Ron Block (Sherri L. Vanyek)

American Library Association
American Association of School Librarians

Executive Director, Sylvia Knight Norton
50 E. Huron St., Chicago, IL 60611
312-280-4382, 800-545-2433 ext. 4382, fax 312-280-5276, e-mail aasl@ala.org
World Wide Web http://www.aasl.org

Object

The American Association of School Librarians empowers leaders to transform teaching and learning. AASL works to ensure that all members of the field collaborate to provide leadership in the total education program; participate as active partners in the teaching/learning process; connect learners with ideas and information; and prepare students for lifelong learning, informed decision making, a love of reading, and the use of information technologies.

Established in 1951 as a separate division of the American Library Association.

Membership

Memb. 7,000+. Open to all libraries, school librarians, interested individuals, and business firms, with requisite membership in ALA.

Officers (2015–2016)

Pres. Leslie Predi; *Pres.-Elect* Audrey Church; *Treas.* Robbie Nickel; *Past Pres.* Terri Grief

Board of Directors

Melissa Jacobs, Steven Yates, Diane Chen, Pamela Harland, Eileen Kern, Linda Weatherspoon, Pamela Renfrow, Lisa Hathcock, Kathryn Roots Lewis, Katie Williams, Craig Seasholes, Ken Stewart, Jody Howard, Robert Hilliker, Devona J. Pendergrass, Sylvia Knight Norton (ex officio).

Publications

AASL Hotlinks (mo.; electronic, memb.).

Knowledge Quest (5 a year; $50, $60 outside U.S.). *Ed.* Meg Featheringham. E-mail mfeatheringham@ala.org.

School Library Research (electronic, free, at http://www.ala.org/aasl/slr). *Eds.* Ruth Small. E-mail drruth@syr.edu; Mega Subramaniam. E-mail manis2@gmail.com.

Section Leadership

AASL/ESLS Executive Committee. Karla Collins, Karen Gavigan, Jody Howard, Rebecca Morris, Deborah Parrott.

AASL/ISS Executive Committee. Robert Hilliker, Sarah Jane Levin, Yapha Mason.
AASL/SPVS Executive Committee. Lori Donovan, Mary Keeling, Margaret Montgomery, Suzanna Panter, Devona J. Pendergrass.

Committee Chairs

AASL/ACRL Interdivisional Committee on Information Literacy. Floyd Pentlin.
AASL/ALSC/YALSA Joint Committee on School/Public Library Cooperation. Jenna Nemec-Loise (ALSC).
Advocacy. Dorcus Hand.
Affiliate Assembly. Lori Donovan.
Alliance for Association Excellence. Robbie Nickel.
American University Press Book Selection. Annemarie Roscello.
Annual Conference. Lee Gordon.
Awards. Carlyn Gray.
Banned Websites Awareness Day. Michelle Luhtala.
Best Apps for Teaching and Learning. Catharine Potter.
Best Websites for Teaching and Learning. Lucy Santos Green.
Beyond Words Grant Jury. Jennifer Jamison.
Blog Group. .
Bylaws and Organization. Lynn Gordon.
CAEP Coordinating Committee. Mona Kerby.
Fall Forum (National Institute) 2015. .
Leadership Development Committee. Terri Grief.
National Conference. Debra Kay Logan, Katherine E. Lowe.
Research/Statistics. Sue Kimmel.
School Library Month Committee. Suzanne Dix.
Standards and Guidelines Implementation. Katherine Lehman.

Editorial Board Chairs

Essential Links Editorial Board. Floyd Pentlin.
Knowledge Quest Editorial Board. Ann Dutton Ewbank.

School Library Research Editorial Board. Ruth Small, Mega Subramaniam.

Task Force Chairs

Committee Review.
Community of Scholars. Jeffrey DiScala.
External Relations. Debra Kachel.
Presidential Initiative. Carl Harvey.
65th Celebration. Carl A. Harvey.
STEM.
Underserved Student Populations.

Awards Committee Chairs

ABC-CLIO Leadership Grant. Michelle Bayuk.
Collaborative School Library Award. Floyd Pentlin.
Distinguished School Administrator Award. Pamela Renfrow.
Distinguished Service Award. Terrence Young.
Frances Henne Award. Krista Britton.
Information Technology Pathfinder Award. Carolyn J. Starkey.
Innovative Reading Grant. Kelly Hincks.
Intellectual Freedom Award. Carolyn Starkey.
National School Library Program of the Year Award. Barbara Stripling.
Roald Dahl's Miss Honey Social Justice Award. Terrence Young.
Ruth Toor Grant for Strong Public School Libs.: Karen Meier

Advisory Group Staff Liaisons

Professional Development. Jennifer Habley.
Publications. Stephanie Book.

American Library Association
Association for Library Collections and Technical Services

Executive Director, Keri Cascio
50 E. Huron St., Chicago, IL 60611
800-545-2433 ext. 5030, fax 312-280-5033, e-mail kcascio@ala.org
World Wide Web http://www.ala.org/alcts

Object

The Association for Library Collections and Technical Services (ALCTS) envisions an environment in which traditional library roles are evolving. New technologies are making information more fluid and raising expectations. The public needs quality information anytime, anyplace. ALCTS provides frameworks to meet these information needs.

ALCTS provides leadership to the library and information communities in developing principles, standards, and best practices for creating, collecting, organizing, delivering, and preserving information resources in all forms. It provides this leadership through its members by fostering educational, research, and professional service opportunities. ALCTS is committed to quality information, universal access, collaboration, and lifelong learning.

Standards—Develop, evaluate, revise, and promote standards for creating, collecting, organizing, delivering, and preserving information resources in all forms.

Best practices—Research, develop, evaluate, and implement best practices for creating, collecting, organizing, delivering, and preserving information resources in all forms.

Education—Assess the need for, sponsor, develop, administer, and promote educational programs and resources for lifelong learning.

Professional development—Provide opportunities for professional development through research, scholarship, publication, and professional service.

Interaction and information exchange—Create opportunities to interact and exchange information with others in the library and information communities.

Association operations—Ensure efficient use of association resources and effective delivery of member services.

Established in 1957; renamed in 1988.

Membership

Memb. 3,800. Any member of the American Library Association may elect membership in this division according to the provisions of the bylaws.

Officers (2015–2016)

Pres. Norm Madeiros, Haverford College, 370 Lancaster Ave., Haverford, PA 19041. Tel. 610.896.1173, email nmedeiro@haverford.ed; *Pres.-Elect* Vicki L. Sipe, Albin O. Kuhn Lib. & Gallery, University of Maryland, Baltimore County, 1000 HillTop Cir., Baltimore, MD 21250. Tel. 410.455.6751 sipe@umbc.edu; *Past Pres.* Mary Page, University of Central Florida, P.O. Box 162666, Orlando, FL 32816. Tel. 407.823.2564. Fax 407.823.2529. email mary.page@ucf.edu.

Address correspondence to the executive director.

Board of Directors

Erin E. Boyd, Maria Davidson-DePalma Collins, Karla L. Strieb, James J. Dooley, Michele Seikel, Shannon Tennant, Santi Allen Thompson, Bobby Bothman, Jeanne Harrell, Erin Leach, Annie Peterson, Andrea Wirth, Rebecca L. Mugridge, Hannah Buckland, Keri Cascio, Julia Reese.

Publications

ALCTS News (q.; free; posted at http://www.ala.org/alcts). *Ed.* Rebecca Mugridge, Univ. Libs., Univ. at Albany, SUNY, UAB 121, Albany, NY 12222. Tel. 518-437-5062, e-mail rmugridge@albany.edu.

Library Resources and Technical Services (*LRTS*) (q.; nonmemb. $100; international $100). Electronic only. *Ed.* Mary Beth Weber, Technical and Automated Services Dept., Rutgers Univ. Libs., 47 Davidson Rd., Piscataway, NJ 08854. Tel. 732-445-0500, fax 732-445-5888, e-mail mbfecko@rci.rutgers.edu.

Section Chairs

Acquisitions. Lisa Spagnolo.
Cataloging and Metadata Management. Melinda Reagor Flannery.
Collection Management. Michael Levine-Clark.
Continuing Resources. Jennifer Young.
Preservation and Reformatting. Kara McClurken.

Committee Chairs

Affiliate Relations. Elaine Franco.
ALCTS Outstanding Publications Award Jury. Rene Erlandson.
Hugh C. Atkinson Memorial Award (ALCTS/ACRL/LLAMA/LITA). Nancy Gibbs.
Ross Atkinson Lifetime Achievement Award Jury. Emily McElroy.
Budget and Finance. Vicki Sipe.
Continuing Education. Maria Pinkas.
Fund Raising. Lenore England.
International Relations. Qiang Jin.
Leadership Development. Donia Conn.
LRTS Editorial Board. Mary Beth Weber.
Membership. Susan Wynne.
Nominating. Carolynne Myall.
Organization and Bylaws. Lucas Mak.

Outstanding Collaboration Citation Jury. Ginger Williams.
Esther J. Piercy Award Jury. Harriet Lightman.
Planning. Meg Mering.
Program. Susan Davis, Reeta Sinha.
Publications. Mary Miller.
Edward Swanson Memorial Best of *LRTS* Award Jury. Arthur Miller.

Interest Group Chairs

Authority Control (ALCTS/LITA). Nathan Putnam.
Creative Ideas in Technical Services. Erin Leach.
Electronic Resources. Jeanne Castro.
Functional Requirements for Bibliographic Records (FRBR). Scott Piepenburg.
Linked Library Data (ALCTS/LITA). Violeta Ilik, Sarah Quimby.
MARC Formats (ALCTS/LITA). Carolyn Hansen, Victoria Mueller.
New Members. Elyssa Gould, Deana Groves.
Newspapers. Brian Geiger.
Public Libraries Technical Services. Carolyn Saccucci.
Role of the Professional in Academic Research Technical Service Departments. Christine Dulaney, Harriet Wintermute.
Scholarly Communications. Doug Way.
Technical Services Directors of Large Research Libraries. Jennifer Marill.
Technical Services Managers in Academic Libraries. Amy Lana.
Technical Services Workflow Efficiency. Margaret Glerum, Michael Winecoff.

American Library Association
Association for Library Service to Children

Executive Director, Aimee Strittmatter
50 E. Huron St., Chicago, IL 60611
312-280-2163, 800-545-2433 ext. 2163, fax 312-280-5271, e-mail alsc@ala.org
World Wide Web http://www.ala.org/alsc

Object

The core purpose of the Association for Library Service to Children (ALSC) is to create a better future for children through libraries. Its primary goal is to lead the way in forging excellent library services for all children. ALSC offers creative programming, information about best practices, continuing education, an awards and media evaluation program, and professional connections. Founded in 1901.

Membership

Memb. 4,000. Open to anyone interested in library services to children. For information on dues, see ALA entry.

Address correspondence to the executive director.

Officers

Pres. Andrew Medlar; *V.P./Pres.-Elect* Betsy Orsburn; *Past Pres.* Ellen Riordan; *Fiscal Officer* Diane Foote; *Div. Councilor* Lisa Von Drasek.

Directors

Rita Auerbach, Gretchen Caserotti, Doris Gebel, Jamie Campbell Naidoo, Julie Roach, Michael Santangelo, Megan Schliesman, Kay Weisman.

Publications

ALSC Matters! (q., electronic; memb. Not available by subscription.)
Children and Libraries: The Journal of the Association for Library Service to Children (q.; print and online; memb; nonmemb. $50; foreign $60).
Everyday Advocacy Matters (q., electronic; memb. Not available by subscription.)

Committee Chairs

AASL/ALSC/YALSA Interdivisional Committee on School/Public Library Cooperation. Jenna Nemec-Loise.
Advocacy and Legislation. Robyn M. Lupa.
ALSC/Booklist/YALSA Odyssey Award Selection 2015. Dawn Rutherford.
ALSC/Booklist/YALSA Odyssey Award Selection 2016. Jennifer Duffy.
Arbuthnot Honor Lecture 2015. Sue McCleaf Nespeca.
Arbuthnot Honor Lecture 2016. Julie Corsaro.
Arbuthnot Honor Lecture 2017. Ellen Ruffin.
Mildred L. Batchelder Award 2015. Diane Janoff.
Mildred L. Batchelder Award 2016. Elizabeth Stalford.
Pura Belpré Award 2015. Tim Wadham.
Pura Belpré Award 2016. Ana-Elba Pavon.
Budget. Paula Holmes.
Randolph Caldecott Award 2015. Junko Yokota.
Randolph Caldecott Award 2016. Rachel Payne.
Andrew Carnegie Medal/Notable Children's Videos 2015. Caitlin Dixon Jacobson.
Andrew Carnegie Medal/Notable Children's Videos 2016. Lizabeth Deskins.
Children and Libraries Advisory Committee. Judi Moreillon.
Children and Technology. Amy Graves.
Distinguished Service Award 2015. Julie Cummins.
Distinguished Service Award 2016. Julie A. Corsaro.
Early Childhood Programs and Services. Matthew McLain.

Education. Nina Lindsay.

Every Child Ready to Read Oversight. Dorothy M. Stoltz.

Theodor Seuss Geisel Award 2015. Kevin Delecki.

Theodor Seuss Geisel Award 2016. Robin Lynn Smith.

Grant Administration Committee. Susan A. M. Poulter.

Great Websites. Lara Crews, Lisa Taylor.

Intellectual Freedom. Heather Acerro.

Interdivisional Committee on School/Public Library Partnerships. Jenna Nemec-Loise.

Liaison with National Organizations. Lori Coffey Hancock, Beth Munk.

Library Service to Special Population Children and Their Caregivers. Africa S. Hands.

Local Arrangements (San Francisco). Christy Estrovitz.

Managing Children's Services. Thomas J. Barthelmess.

Membership. Amanda Jean Roberson.

John Newbery Award 2015. Randall Enos.

John Newbery Award 2016. Ernie Cox.

Nominating 2015. Mary Fellows.

Nominating 2016. Jan S. Watkins.

Notable Children's Books. Maralita L. Freeny.

Notable Children's Recordings. Barbara Scotto.

Odyssey Award 2015. Dawn M. Rutherford.

Odyssey Award 2016. Cindy Lombardo.

Oral History. Deborah Sharon Cooper.

Organization and Bylaws. Samuel Eddington, Vicky Smith.

Program Coordinating. Patricia Ann Carleton.

Public Awareness. Amy E. Koester.

Quicklists Consulting. Krista K. Britton, Mary R. Voors.

Charlemae Rollins President's Program. Christine D. Caputo, Carol K. Phillips.

Scholarships. Miriam Budin.

School Age Programs and Service. Amber Lea Creger.

Robert F. Sibert Award 2015. Deborah Taylor.

Robert F. Sibert Award 2016. Elizabeth Overmeyer.

Special Collections and Bechtel Fellowship. Mary Beth Dunhouse.

Laura Ingalls Wilder Award 2015. Karen Nelson Hoyle.

Laura Ingalls Wilder Award 2016. Chrystal Carr-Jeter.

American Library Association
Association of College and Research Libraries

Executive Director, Mary Ellen K. Davis
50 E. Huron St., Chicago, IL 60611-2795
312-280-2523, 800-545-2433 ext. 2523, fax 312-280-2520, e-mail acrl@ala.org
World Wide Web http://www.ala.org/acrl

Object

The Association of College and Research Libraries (ACRL) leads academic and research librarians and libraries in advancing learning and transforming scholarship. Founded 1940.

Membership

Memb. 11,172. For information on dues, see ALA entry.

Officers

Pres. Ann Campion Riley, 104 Ellis Lib. University of Missouri, Columbia, MO 65201 Tel. 573.882.1685 Email kaw@umn.edu; *Pres.-Elect* Irene M. Herold, University of Hawai'i at Manoa Lib., 2550 McCarthy Mall, Honolulu, HI 96822 Tel. 808.956.7205 Email heroldi@hawaii.edu; *Past Pres.* Karen A. Williams, University of Arizona, Tucson, AZ 85718 Tel. 520-621-9733 Email karenwilliams.email.arizona.edu; *Budget and Finance Chair* Cynthia K.

Steinhoff, Anne Arundel Community College, 101 College Pkwy., Arnold, MD 21012-1895. Tel. 410-777-2483, fax 410-777-4483, e-mail ck steinhoff@aacc.edu; *ACRL Councilor* Douglas K. Lehman, Wittenberg Univ., P.O. Box 7207, Springfield, OH 45501-7207. Tel. 937-327-7016, fax 937-327-6139, e-mail dlehman@ wittenberg.edu.

Board of Directors

Officers; John P. Culshaw, Julie Ann Garrison, Julia M. Gelfand, Irene M. H. Herold, Marilyn Nabua Ochoa, Loretta R. Parham, Kim Leeder Reed, Susan Barnes Whyte.

Publications

Choice (12 a year; $429; Canada and Mexico $465; other international $549). *Ed.* Mark Cummings.

Choice Reviews-on-Cards (available only to subscribers of *Choice* and/or *Choice Reviews Online*) $529; Canada and Mexico $565; other international $659).

Choice Reviews Online 2.0 (academic libraries FTE 10,000+, $625; academic libraries FTE 2,500–9,999, $589; academic libraries FTE fewer than 2,500, $555; school libraries K–12, $375; foreign academic libraries [includes Mexico and Canada] $619; public libraries, $530; government libraries, $600; other libraries, $600; publishers/dealers, $600).

College & Research Libraries (*C&RL*) (6 a year; open access online-only). *Ed.* Scott Walter.

College & Research Libraries News (*C&RL News*) (11 a year; memb.; nonmemb. $54; Canada and other PUAS countries $59; other international $64). *Ed.* David Free.

Publications in Librarianship (formerly ACRL Monograph Series) (occasional). *Ed.* To be announced.

RBM: A Journal of Rare Books, Manuscripts, and Cultural Heritage (s. ann.; $48; Canada

and other PUAS countries $54; other international $64). *Ed.* Jennifer K. Sheehan.

Committee and Task Force Chairs

AASL/ACRL Information Literacy (interdivisional). Jennifer Leigh Fabbi, Mary O. Keeling.

Academic/Research Librarian of the Year Award. Tyrone Heath Cannon.

ACRL Academic Library Trends and Statistics Survey. Robert E. Dugan.

ACRL 2015 Colleagues Committee. Julia M. Gelfand, Karin A. Trainer.

ACRL 2015 Contributed Papers. Beth McNeil, Janice D. Welburn.

ACRL 2015 Coordinating Committee (Portland). Lori Goetsch.

ACRL 2015 Innovations. Heidi Steiner Burkhardt, Beth Filar-Williams.

ACRL 2015 Invited Papers. Adele L. Barsh, Lisa Janicke Hinchliffe.

ACRL 2015 Keynote Speakers. Elizabeth A. Dupuis, Maggie Farrell.

ACRL 2015 Local Arrangements. Rachel Bridgewater, Dena Holiman Hutto.

ACRL 2015 Panel Sessions. Elizabeth Blakesley, Scott Walter.

ACRL 2015 Poster Sessions. Kim Leeder Reed, Tanner Wray III.

ACRL 2015 Preconference. Penny M. Beile, Jennifer Leigh Fabbi.

ACRL 2015 Roundtable Discussions. John P. Culshaw, Rita Cecilia Knight.

ACRL 2015 Scholarships. Latrice Booker, Adriana Gonzalez.

ACRL 2015 TechConnect Presentations. Heidi Gauder, John Leonard.

ACRL 2015 Virtual Conference. Ameet Doshi, Melanie Hawks.

ACRL 2015 Workshop Programs. Elizabeth L. Bagley, Madeleine Charney.

ACRL/LLAMA Interdivisional Committee on Building Resources. Frank R. Allen, Felice E. Maciejewski.

Appointments. John M. Budd.

Hugh C. Atkinson Memorial Award. Nancy Jean Gibbs.

Budget and Finance. Cynthia K. Steinhoff.

Choice Editorial Board. Peggy Seiden.

College & Research Libraries Editorial Board. Scott Walter.

College & Research Libraries News Editorial Board. Cassandra Kvenild.

Diversity. Martha Alvarado Parker.

Excellence in Academic Libraries Award. Steven J. Bell.

Government Relations. Jonathan Miller.

Immersion Program. Elin Anne O'Hara-Gonya.

Information Literacy Standards. Jeanne R. Davidson.

Dr. E. J. Josey Spectrum Scholar Mentor Program. Harriett E. Green.

Leadership Recruitment and Nomination. Gillian S. Gremmels.

Liaison Assembly. Elizabeth G. McClenney.

Liaison Coordinating. Lori J. Phillips.

Liaison Grants. Andrea M. Falcone.

Liaisons Training and Development. Elizabeth G. McClenney.

Membership. Kathy M. Irwin.

New Publications Advisory. Barbara Irene Dewey.

President's Program Planning Committee, 2015. Deborah B. Dancik.

Professional Development. Paul A. Sharpe.

Publications Coordinating. Priscilla J. Finley.

Publications in Librarianship Editorial Board. To be announced.

RBM Editorial Board. Jennifer Karr Sheehan.

Research Planning and Review. Jeanne R. Davidson.

Resources for College Libraries Editorial Board. E. Chisato Uyeki.

Section Membership. Katie E. Gibson, Dalena Estelle Hunter.

Standards. Susanna D. Boylston.

Student Learning and Information Literacy. Carrie Donovan.

Value of Academic Libraries. Lynn Silipigni Connaway.

Discussion Group Chairs

Assessment. Charla M. Gilbert, Nancy B. Turner.

Balancing Baby and Book. Laura Bonella.

Continuing Education/Professional Development. Rich Paustenbaugh.

Copyright. Tomas A. Lipinski.

First Year Experience. Danielle L. Rowland.

Heads of Public Services. Patricia Flanagan.

Information Commons. Carolyn L. Cunningham, Michael Whitchurch.

International Perspectives on Academic and Research Libraries. Evviva Weinraub Lajoie.

Leadership. Rudy Leon.

Library and Information Science Collections. Cynthia H. Krolikowski, Daniel G. Tracy.

Library Support for Massive Open Online Courses (MOOCs). Kyle Kenneth Courtney, Michele Ostrow.

Media Resources. Monique L. Threatt.

MLA International Bibliography. Sarah G. Wenzel.

New Members. Tyler Dzuba, Elizabeth Psyck.

Personnel Administrators and Staff Development Officers. Leo G. Agnew, Tiffany Allen.

Philosophical, Religious, and Theological Studies. Wayne Bivens-Tatum.

Popular Cultures. Jenny E. Robb.

Scholarly Communications. Devin Savage.

Student Retention. Jaime Corris Hammond, Nicole Pagowsky.

Undergraduate Libraries. Doug Worsham.

Interest Group Conveners

Academic Library Services to International Students. Arianne Hartsell-Gundy, Qing Meade.

Digital Badges. Cinthya Ippoliti, Emily L. Rimland.

Digital Curation. Megan Toups.

Digital Humanities. Zach Coble.

Health Sciences. Julie Planchon Wolf.

Image Resources. Kasia Leousis.

Librarianship in For-Profit Educational Institutions. Julie Evener.

Library and Information Science (LIS) Education. Michael A. Crumpton.

Library Marketing and Outreach Interest Group. Virginia A. Alexander, Adam Haigh.

Numeric and Geospatial Data Services in Academic Libraries. Jeremy Darrington.

Residency. Tarida Anantachai.

Technical Services. Gwen Gregory.

Universal Accessibility. John Siegel.

Virtual Worlds. JJ Jacobson.

Section Chairs

African American Studies Librarians. Malaika Grant.
Anthropology and Sociology. Erin F. Gratz.
Arts. Ngoc-Yen Tran.
Asian, African, and Middle Eastern. Jingfeng Xia.
College Libraries. Erin T. Smith.
Community and Junior College Libraries. Theresa C. Stanley.

Distance Learning. Alice Daugherty.
Education and Behavioral Sciences. Dana Scott Peterman.
Instruction. Mark Szarko.
Law and Political Science. Jeremy Darrington.
Literatures in English. Laura Lynne Taddeo.
Rare Books and Manuscripts. R. Arvid Nelsen.
Science and Technology. Marianne Stowell Bracke.
Slavic and East European. Kirill Tolpygo.
University Libraries. Marilyn Myers.
Western European Studies. Sarah Sussman.
Women and Gender Studies. Diane M. Fulkerson.

American Library Association
Association of Specialized and Cooperative Library Agencies

Executive Director, Susan Hornung
50 E. Huron St., Chicago, IL 60611-2795
312-280-4395, 800-545-2433 ext. 4395, fax 312-280-5273, e-mail shornung@ala.org
World Wide Web http://www.ala.org/ascla

Object

The Association for Specialized and Cooperative Library Agencies (ASCLA) enhances the effectiveness of library service by advocating for and providing high-quality networking, enrichment, and educational opportunities for its diverse members, who represent state library agencies, libraries serving special populations, library cooperatives, and library consultants. ASCLA's members are

- Librarians, library agencies, and staff serving populations with special needs, such as those with sensory, physical, health, or behavioral conditions or those who are incarcerated or detained
- Librarians and staff of state library agencies, and state library consultants—organizations created or authorized by state governments to promote library services
- Library networks and cooperatives, organizations of one or more types of libraries—academic, public, special, or school—that collaborate to maximize the funds available for provision of library services to all citizens; they may serve a

community, a metropolitan area, a region, or a statewide or multistate area

- Consultants, independent or contract librarians, as well as those who work outside traditional library settings

Member activity is centered around interest groups.

Membership

Memb. 800+. For information on dues, see ALA entry.

Officers and Directors (2015–2016)

Pres. Rhonda K. Puntney Gould; *Pres.-Elect* Michael A. Golrick; *Past Pres.* Kathleen Ann Moeller-Pfeiffer; *Div. Councilor* Lizbeth Bishoff; *Secy.* Tracy Byerly; *Dirs.-at-Large* Jana R. Fine, Raye L. Oldham; *Dir., Cooperatives and Networks* Gregory Pronevitz; *Dirs., Special Populations* Christopher John Corrigan, Lily J. Sacharow; *Dir., Lib. Consultants/Independent*

Libns. Allan Martin Kleiman; *Dir., State Lib. Agencies* Shannon O'Grady.

Interest Group Leaders

Alzheimer's and Related Dementias. Mary Beth Riedner.

Bridging Deaf Cultures @ your library. Alec McFarlane.

Collaborative Digitization. Sandra McIntyre.

Consortial eBooks. Dee Brennan, Veronda Pitchford.

Consortium Management Discussion. Sheryl Knab.

Future of Libraries. Peggy Cadigan.

Interlibrary Cooperation. To be announced.

Library Consultants. Carson Block.

Library Services for Youth in Custody. Camden Eadoin Tadhg.

Library Services to People with Visual or Physical Disabilities that Prevent Them from Reading Standard Print. Carli Spina.

Library Services to the Incarcerated and Detained. Elizabeth Marshak.

LSTA Coordinators. Katie McDonough.

Physical Delivery. James E. Pletz.

State Library Agencies—Library Development. Carol Desch.

Tribal Librarians. Lillian Chavez.

Universal Access. Marti Goddard.

Youth Services Consultants. Sharon Rawlins.

For more information on ASCLA interest groups, see http://www.ala.org/ascla/ascla ourassoc/asclainterest/list.

Publication

Interface (q.; online). *Ed.* Anne Abate. E-mail anne@librarydiscountnetwork.com.

Committees

Accessibility Assembly; Awards; Board of Directors; Conference Programming; Executive; Finance and Planning; Guidelines for Library and Information Services for the American Deaf Community; Interest Group Coordinating; Membership; Nominating; Online Learning; President's Program Planning; Publications; Web Presence.

For more information on ASCLA committees, see http://www.ala.org/ascla/asclaour assoc/asclarosters/rosters.

American Library Association
Library and Information Technology Association

Executive Director, Mary C. Taylor
50 E. Huron St., Chicago, IL 60611
312-280-4267, 800-545-2433, e-mail mtaylor@ala.org
World Wide Web http://www.lita.org

Object

As a center of expertise about information technology, the Library and Information Technology Association (LITA) leads in exploring and enabling new technologies to empower libraries. LITA members use the promise of technology to deliver dynamic library collections and services.

LITA educates, serves, and reaches out to its members, other ALA members and divisions, and the entire library and information community through its publications, programs, and other activities designed to promote, develop, and aid in the implementation of library and information technology.

Membership

Memb. 2,900. For information on dues, see ALA entry.

Officers (2015–2016)

Pres. Thomas P. Dowling; *V.P.* Aimee Fifarek; *Past Pres.* Rachel Vacek.

Directors

Aimee Fifarek, Cody Hanson, S. G. Ranti Junus, Bohyun Kim, Jennifer Reiswig, Jennifer Emanuel Taylor, Andromeda Yelton, *Div. Councilor* Aaron Dobbs.

Publication

Information Technology and Libraries (ITAL) (open source at http://ejournals.bc.edu/ojs/index.php/ital/issue/current). *Ed.* Robert Gerrity. For information or to send manuscripts, contact the editor.

American Library Association
Library Leadership and Management Association

Executive Director, Kerry Ward
50 E. Huron St., Chicago, IL 60611
312-280-5032, 800-545-2433 ext. 5032, fax 312-280-5033
e-mail kward@ala.org
World Wide Web http://www.ala.org/llama

Object

The Library Leadership and Management Association (LLAMA) Strategic Plan sets out the following:

Mission: The Library Leadership and Management Association advances outstanding leadership and management practices in library and information services by encouraging and nurturing individual excellence in current and aspiring library leaders.

Vision: As the foremost organization developing present and future leaders in library and information services, LLAMA provides a welcoming community where aspiring and experienced library leaders and library supporters from all types of libraries can seek and share knowledge and skills in leadership, administration, and management in a manner that creates meaningful transformation in libraries around the world.

Core Values: LLAMA believes advancing leadership and management excellence is achieved by fostering the following values—exemplary and innovative service to and for our members, and leadership development and continuous learning opportunities for our members.

Established in 1957.

Membership

Memb. 3,900+. For information on dues, see ALA entry.

Officers (2015–2016)

Pres. Jeff Steely, Baylor Univ., Tel. 254-710-2464. E-mail Jeffrey_Steely@baylor.edu; *Pres.-Elect* John Spears, Salt Lake City Public Lib., Tel. 801-524-8205. Email jspears@slcpl.org; *Treas.* James Rettig; *Past Pres.* Diane Bruxvoort.

Address correspondence to the executive director.

Publication

Library Leadership and Management (LL&M) (open access at http://journals.tdl.org/llm/index.php/llm). *Ed.* Bradford Lee Eden. E-mail brad.eden@valpo.edu.

Section Chairs

Buildings and Equipment. Melissa B. Bennett.
Fund Raising and Financial Development. James Michael Thompson.
Human Resources Marcy L. Simons.

Library Organization and Management. Leo S. Lo.

Measurement, Assessment, and Evaluation. Lisa R. Horowitz.

New Professionals. Tyler Dzuba.

Public Relations and Marketing. Kimberly Terry.

Systems and Services. Paul A. Sharpe.

American Library Association
Public Library Association

Executive Director, Barbara A. Macikas
50 E. Huron St., Chicago, IL 60611
312-280-5752, 800-545-2433 ext. 5752, fax 312-280-5029, e-mail pla@ala.org
World Wide Web http://www.pla.org

The Public Library Association (PLA) has specific responsibility for

1. Conducting and sponsoring research about how the public library can respond to changing social needs and technical developments
2. Developing and disseminating materials useful to public libraries in interpreting public library services and needs
3. Conducting continuing education for public librarians by programming at national and regional conferences, by publications such as the newsletter, and by other delivery means
4. Establishing, evaluating, and promoting goals, guidelines, and standards for public libraries
5. Maintaining liaison with relevant national agencies and organizations engaged in public administration and human services, such as the National Association of Counties, the Municipal League, and the Commission on Postsecondary Education
6. Maintaining liaison with other divisions and units of ALA and other library organizations, such as the Association for Library and Information Science Education and the Urban Libraries Council
7. Defining the role of the public library in service to a wide range of user and potential user groups
8. Promoting and interpreting the public library to a changing society through legislative programs and other appropriate means
9. Identifying legislation to improve and to equalize support of public libraries

PLA enhances the development and effectiveness of public librarians and public library services. This mission positions PLA to

- Focus its efforts on serving the needs of its members
- Address issues that affect public libraries
- Commit to quality public library services that benefit the general public

The goals of PLA are

- Advocacy and Awareness: PLA is an essential partner in public library advocacy.
- Leadership and Transformation: PLA is the leading source for learning opportunities to advance transformation of public libraries.
- Literate Nation: PLA will be a leader and valued partner of public libraries' initiatives to create a literate nation.
- Organizational Excellence: PLA is positioned to sustain and grow its resources to advance the work of the association.

Membership

Memb. 8,000+. Open to all ALA members interested in the improvement and expansion of public library services to all ages in various types of communities.

Officers (2015–2016)

Pres. Vailey Oehlke, Multonomah County (Oregon) Lib. E-mail vaileyo@multcolib. org; *Pres.-Elect* Felton Thomas, Jr, Cleveland Public Lib., 325 Superior Ave., Cleveland, OH 44114. Tel. 216-623-2827. Email felton. Thomas@cpl.org; *Past Pres.* Larry Neal, Clinton-Macomb (Michigan) Public Lib. E-mail lneal@cmpl.org.

Publication

Public Libraries (bi-mo.; memb.; nonmemb. $65; foreign $75; single copy $10). *Ed.* Kathleen Hughes, PLA, 50 E. Huron St., Chicago, IL 60611. E-mail khughes@ala. org.

Committee Chairs

Baker & Taylor Entertainment Audio Music/ Video Product Award. Nick Taylor.

Budget and Finance. Clara Nalli Bohrer.

Gordon M. Conable Award Jury. Susan Wray.

Continuing Education Advisory Group. James D. Cooper.

DEMCO New Leaders Travel Grant Jury. Marla J. Ehlers.

EBSCO Excellence in Small and/or Rural Public Library Service Award. Luren E. Dickinson.

Intellectual Freedom. Robert Hubsher.

Leadership Development. Karen Danczak-Lyons.

Legislation and Advocacy. Jan W. Sanders.

Allie Beth Martin Award Jury. Kristen Rae Allen-Vogel.

Membership Advisory Group. Richard Kong.

Nominating 2015. Eva D. Poole.

Performance Measurement Task Force. Denise Marie Davis.

Charlie Robinson Award Jury. Skip Auld.

PLA 2016 Local Arrangements. Diane Lapierre.

PLA 2016 National Conference. Marcellus Turner.

PLA 2016 National Conference Program Subcommittee. Pamela Sandlian Smith.

PLA/ALSC Every Child Ready to Read Oversight Committee. Dorothy M. Stoltz.

PLA Annual Conference Program Subcommittee. Trisha A. Burns.

PLDS Statistical Report Advisory. Kristin Whitehair.

Polaris Innovation in Technology John Iliff Award. Tricia Bengel.

Public Libraries Advisory. Monique Le Conge Ziesenhenne.

Romance Writers of America Library Grant Jury. Kara A. Kohn.

Technology. Brian Auger.

Upstart Library Innovation Award Jury. Monica Harris.

American Library Association
Reference and User Services Association

Executive Director, Susan Hornung
50 E. Huron St., Chicago, IL 60611
800-545-2433 ext. 4395, 312-280-4395, fax 312-280-5273, e-mail shornung@ala.org
World Wide Web http://www.ala.org/rusa

Object

The Reference and User Services Association (RUSA) is responsible for stimulating and supporting excellence in the delivery of general library services and materials, and the provision of reference and information services, collection development, readers' advisory, and resource sharing for all ages, in every type of library.

The specific responsibilities of RUSA are:

1. Conduct of activities and projects within the association's areas of responsibility

2. Encouragement of the development of librarians engaged in these activities, and stimulation of participation by members of appropriate type-of-library divisions

3. Synthesis of the activities of all units within the American Library Association that have a bearing on the type of activities represented by the association

4. Representation and interpretation of the association's activities in contacts outside the profession

5. Planning and development of programs of study and research in these areas for the total profession

6. Continuous study and review of the association's activities

Membership

Memb. 3,800+

Officers

Pres. Joseph Thompson; *Pres.-Elect* Liane Taylor; *Secy.* Erin Rushton; *Past Pres.* M. Kathleen Kern; *Div. Councilor* Jennifer C. Boettcher.

Publications

Reference & User Services Quarterly (online only at http://rusa.metapress.com) (memb.). *Ed.* Barry Trott, Williamsburg Regional Lib., 7770 Croaker Rd., Williamsburg, VA 23188-7064. E-mail btrott@wrl.org.
RUSA Update, (q., online newsletter, at http://www.rusa.ala.org/rusaupdate).

Sections

Business Reference and Services (BRASS); Collection Development and Evaluation (CODES); History (HS); MARS: Emerging Technologies in Reference (MARS); Reference Services (RSS); Sharing and Transforming Access to Resources (STARS).

Committees

Access to Information; AFL-CIO/ALA Library Service to Labor Groups; Andrew Carnegie Medals for Excellence in Fiction and Nonfiction; Awards Coordinating; Board of Directors; Budget and Finance; Conference Program Coordinating; Executive; Free School (subcommittee); Gale Cengage Award for Excellence in Reference and Adult Services; Isadore Gilbert Mudge Award; Just Ask Council (ad hoc); Learning Opportunities Task Force (ad hoc); John Sessions Memorial Award; Margaret E. Monroe Library Adult Services Award; Membership; Nominating; Organization and Planning; President's Program Planning; Professional Development; Publications and Communications; *Reference & User Services Quarterly* Editorial Advisory; Reference Service Press Awards; Resource Development Committee (ad hoc); Review Professional Competencies for Reference and User Services Librarians; Review Task Force (ad hoc);

Standards and Guidelines; Strategic Plan Co-ordinating Task Force (ad hoc); Task Force on Legislative Issues (ad-hoc); Trends Task Force.

For section committees, and committee chairpersons, see http://www.ala.org/rusa/contact/rosters#rss.

American Library Association
United for Libraries: Association of Library Trustees, Advocates, Friends, and Foundations

Executive Director, Sally Gardner Reed
109 S. 13 St., Suite 117B, Philadelphia, PA 19107
312-280-2161, fax 215-545-3821, e-mail sreed@ala.org
World Wide Web http://www.ala.org/united

Object

United for Libraries was founded in 1890 as the American Library Trustee Association (ALTA). It was the only division of the American Library Association (ALA) dedicated to promoting and ensuring outstanding library service through educational programs that develop excellence in trusteeship and promote citizen involvement in the support of libraries. ALTA became an ALA division in 1961. In 2008 the members of ALTA voted to expand the division to more aggressively address the needs of friends of libraries and library foundations, and through a merger with Friends of Libraries USA (FOLUSA) became the Association of Library Trustees, Advocates, Friends and Foundations (ALTAFF). In 2012 members voted to add "United for Libraries" to its title.

Memb. 5,200. Open to all interested persons and organizations. For dues and membership year, see ALA entry.

Officers

Pres. Rod Wagner; *Pres-Elect* Christine Lind Hage; *Councilor* Susan Schmidt; *Past Pres.* Gail Guidry Griffin.

Publications

Citizens-Save-Libraries: A Power Guide for Successful Advocacy.
The Complete Trustee Handbook.
Even More Great Ideas for Libraries and Friends.
101+ Great Ideas for Libraries and Friends.
The Voice for America's Libraries (q.; memb.).

Committee Chairs

Annual Conference Program. Robin Hoklotubbe.
Library Issues. Jeff Smith.
Newsletter and Website Advisory. Cindy Friedemann.
Nominating. Susan Schmidt.
PLA Conference Program. Deloris Lynch.
United for Libraries Leaders Orientation. Peggy Danhof.

American Library Association
Young Adult Library Services Association

Executive Director, Beth Yoke
50 E. Huron St., Chicago, IL 60611
312-280-4390, 800-545-2433 ext. 4390, fax 312-280-5276, e-mail yalsa@ala.org
World Wide Web http://www.ala.org/yalsa
YALSA blog http://yalsa.ala.org/blog, The Hub (http://yalsa.ala.org/thehub),
Wiki (http://wikis.ala.org/yalsa), Twitter (http://twitter.com/yalsa)
Facebook (http://www.facebook.com/YALSA)

Object

In every library in the nation, high-quality library service to young adults is provided by a staff that understands and respects the unique informational, educational, and recreational needs of teenagers. Equal access to information, services, and materials is recognized as a right, not a privilege. Young adults are actively involved in the library decision making process. The library staff collaborates and cooperates with other youth-serving agencies to provide a holistic, community-wide network of activities and services that support healthy youth development. To ensure that this vision becomes a reality, the Young Adult Library Services Association (YALSA)

1. Advocates extensive and developmentally appropriate library and information services for young adults ages 12 to 18

2. Promotes reading and supports the literacy movement

3. Advocates the use of information and digital technologies to provide effective library service

4. Supports equality of access to the full range of library materials and services, including existing and emerging information and digital technologies, for young adults

5. Provides education and professional development to enable its members to serve as effective advocates for young people

6. Fosters collaboration and partnerships among its individual members with the library community and other groups involved in providing library and information services to young adults

7. Influences public policy by demonstrating the importance of providing library and information services that meet the unique needs and interests of young adults

8. Encourages research and is in the vanguard of new thinking concerning the provision of library and information services for youth

Membership

Memb. 5,100. Open to anyone interested in library services for and with young adults. For information on dues, see ALA entry.

Officers

Pres. Christopher Shoemaker. E-mail cinf-0master@gmail.com; *Pres.-Elect* Candice Mack. E-mail cmack@lapl.org; *Div. Councilor* Vicki Emery. E-mail vemery@fcps.edu; *Fiscal Officer* Linda W. Braun. E-mail lbraun2000@gmail.com; *Secy.* Carrie Kausch. E-mail ckaush@gmail.com; *Past Pres.* Shannon Peterson. E-mail shannon.peterson@gmail.com.

Directors

Maureen Hartman, Joy Kim, Gretchen Kolderup, Jennifer Korn, Carla Land, Nicola McDonald, Rachel McDonald, Krista McKenzie, Jack Martin, Sarah Sogigian, Sarah Townsend.

Publications

Journal of Research on Libraries and Young Adults (q.) (online, open source, peer-reviewed). *Ed.* Denise Agosto.

Young Adult Library Services (q.) (memb.; nonmemb. $70; foreign $80). *Ed.* Linda W. Braun.

YALSA E-News (weekly, memb.). *Ed.* Anna Lam.

American Merchant Marine Library Association (AMMLA)

Executive Director, Roger T. Korner
104 Broadway, Jersey City, NJ 07306
201-369-1100, fax 201-369-1105, e-mail ussammla@ix.netcom.com
World Wide Web http://unitedseamensservice.org

Object

Known as "the public library of the high seas," AMMLA provides ship and shore library service for American-flag merchant vessels and for the Military Sealift Command, the U.S. Coast Guard, and other waterborne operations of the U.S. government. Established in 1921.

In 2012 it distributed more than 23,000 books and magazines to American Merchant Marine, the U.S. Navy and Coast Guard, and seafarers of allied nations. A total of 240 libraries were mailed to U.S. merchant vessels transporting supplies to U.S. forces.

Executive Committee

Pres. Edward R. Morgan; *Chair* F. Anthony Naccarato; *Secy.* Donald E. Kadlac; *Treas.* William D. Potts; *Gen. Counsel* John L. DeGurse, Jr.; *V.P.s* Thomas J. Bethel, Capt. Timothy A. Brown, James Capo, David Cockroft, Capt. Remo Di Fiore, Yoji Fujisawa, John Halas, Richard P. Hughes, Michael B. Jewell, Rene Lioeanjie, George E. Murphy, Conrado F. Oca, Michael Sacco, Richard L. Trumka.

American Theological Library Association

Executive Director, Brenda Bailey-Hainer
300 S. Wacker Drive, Suite 2100, Chicago, IL 60606-6701
888-665-2852, 312-454-5100, fax 312-454-5505, e-mail atla@atla.com
World Wide Web http://www.atla.com

Mission

The mission of the American Theological Library Association (ATLA) is to foster the study of theology and religion by enhancing the development of theological and religious libraries and librarianship.

Membership

(Inst.) 249; (International Inst.) 19; (Indiv.) 401; (Student) 99; (Lifetime) 92; (Affiliates) 69.

Officers

Pres. Beth Bidlack, Burke Lib. at Union Theological Seminary, New York. E-mail beth.bidlack@columbia.edu; *V.P.* Kelly Campbell, John Bulow Campbell Lib., Columbia Theological Seminary, Decatur, Ga.; *Secy.* Stephen Z. Perisho, Seattle Pacific Univ. Lib., Seattle; *Past Pres.* Andrew Keck, Luther Seminary, 2481 Como Ave., St. Paul, MN 55108.

Directors

H. D. "Sandy" Ayer, Jennifer Bartholomew, Carrie M. Hackney, Andrew Keck, Amy E. Limpitlaw, Timothy D. Lincoln, Melody Layton McMahon, Matthew Ostercamp, Eileen K. Saner.

Publications

ATLA Indexes in MARC Format (q.).

ATLA Religion Database, 1949– (q., on EBSCO, Ovid).
ATLASerials, 1949– (q., full-text, on EBSCO, Ovid).
ATLA Catholic Periodical and Literature Index (q., on EBSCO).
Old Testament Abstracts (ann., on EBSCO).
New Testament Abstracts (ann., on EBSCO).
Proceedings (ann.; memb.; nonmemb. $60). *Ed.* Tawny Burgess.
Research in Ministry: An Index to Doctor of Ministry Project Reports (ann.) online. *Ed.* Justin Travis.

Archivists and Librarians in the History of the Health Sciences

President, Stephen E. Novak
E-mail sen13@columbia.edu
World Wide Web http://www.alhhs.org

Object

The association was established exclusively for educational purposes, to serve the professional interests of librarians, archivists, and other specialists actively engaged in the librarianship of the history of the health sciences by promoting the exchange of information and by improving the standards of service.

Membership

Memb. Approximately 150.

Officers

Pres. Stephen E. Novak. E-mail sen13@columbia.edu; *Secy.* Phoebe Evans Letocha. E-mail pletocha@jhmi.edu; *Treas.* Barbara J. Niss. E-mail barbara.niss@mssm.edu; *Past Pres.* Christopher Lyons. E-mail christopher.lyons@mcgill.ca; *Membs.-at-Large* Elisabeth Brander, Deborah Coltham, Bob Vietrogoski, Renee Ziemer.

Publication

Watermark (q.; memb.). *Ed.* Martha Stone, Massachusetts General Hospital. E-mail mstone@partners.org

ARMA International

President, Fred Pulzello
ARMA International, 11880 College Blvd., Suite 450, Overland Park, KS 66210
800-422-2762, 913-341-3808, fax 913-341-3742
World Wide Web http://www.arma.org

Object

To advance the practice of records and information management as a discipline and a profession; to organize and promote programs of research, education, training, and networking within that profession; to support the enhancement of professionalism of the membership; and to promote cooperative endeavors with related professional groups.

Membership

Approximately 26,000 in more than 30 countries. Annual dues $175; Chapter dues vary.

Officers

Pres. Fred Pulzello; *Past-Pres.* Julie J. Colgan; *Pres.-Elect* Peter Kurilecz; *Treas.* Brenda Prowse.

Directors

Patricia Burns, Robert E. Calabrese, Tod Chernikoff, Melissa G. Dederer, Tera Ladner, Peggy Neal, Alison North, Denise Pickett, Marc Simpson, Richard Vestuto.

Publication

Information Management (*IM*) (bi-mo.).

Art Libraries Society of North America

President, Carole Ann Fabian
Executive Director, Robert J. Kopchinski
414-908-4954 ext. 136, e-mail r.kopchinski@arlisna.org
World Wide Web https://www.arlisna.org

Object

The object of the Art Libraries Society of North America (ARLIS/NA) is to foster excellence in art librarianship and visual resources curatorship for the advancement of the visual arts. Established 1972.

Membership

Memb. 1,000+. Dues (Inst./Business Affiliate) $145; (Introductory) $90 (one-year limit); (Indiv.) $120; (Student) $50 (three-year limit); (Retired/Unemployed) $60. Year. Jan. 1–Dec. 31. Membership is open to all those interested in visual librarianship, whether they be professional librarians, students, library assistants, art book publishers, art book dealers, art historians, archivists, architects, slide and photograph curators, or retired associates in these fields.

Officers

Pres. Carole Ann Fabian, Avery Architectural and Fine Arts Lib., Columbia Univ., 1172 Amsterdam Ave., MC0301, New York, NY 10027. Tel. 212-854-3068, e-mail caf2141@columbia.edu; *V.P./Pres.-Elect* Kristen Regina, Hillwood Estate, Museum and Gardens, Washington, D.C. Tel. 202-243-3934, e-mail kregina@

hillwoodmuseum.org; *Secy.* Eric Wolf, the Menil Collection, 1511 Branard St., Houston, TX 77006. Tel. 713-525-9426, e-mail ewolf@menil.org; *Treas.* Mark Pompelia, Rhode Island School of Design, Providence. Tel. 401-709-5935, e-mail mpompeli@risd.edu; *Past Pres.* Gregory P. J. Most, National Gallery of Art, Washington, DC 20565. Tel. 202-842-6100, e-mail g-most@nga.gov.

Address correspondence to Robert J. Kopchinski, Technical Enterprises, Inc., 7044 S. 13 St., Oak Creek, WI 53154.

Publications

ARLIS/NA Update (bi-mo.; memb.).
Art Documentation (2 a year; memb., subscription).
Handbook and List of Members (ann.; memb.).
Occasional papers (price varies).
Miscellaneous others (request current list from headquarters).

Asian/Pacific American Librarians Association

Executive Director, Buenaventura "Ven" Basco
P.O. Box 677593, Orlando, FL 32867-7593
E-mail buenaventura.basco@ucf.edu
World Wide Web http://www.apalaweb.org

Object

To provide a forum for discussing problems and concerns of Asian/Pacific American librarians; to provide a forum for the exchange of ideas by Asian/Pacific American librarians and other librarians; to support and encourage library services to Asian/Pacific American communities; to recruit and support Asian/Pacific American librarians in the library/information science professions; to seek funding for scholarships in library/information science programs for Asian/Pacific Americans; and to provide a vehicle whereby Asian/Pacific American librarians can cooperate with other associations and organizations having similar or allied interests. Founded in 1980; incorporated 1981; affiliated with American Library Association 1982.

Membership

Approximately 300. Open to all librarians and information specialists of Asian/Pacific descent working in U.S. libraries and information centers and other related organizations, and to others who support the goals and purposes of the association. Asian/Pacific Americans are defined as people residing in North America who self-identify as Asian/Pacific American.

Officers

Pres. Eileen K. Bosch, Bowling Green State Univ. E-mail ebosch@bgsu.edu; *V.P./Pres.-Elect* Janet H. Clarke, Stony Brook Univ. Libs. E-mail janet.clarke@stonybrook.edu; *Secy.* Sarah Jeong, Wake Forest Univ. E-mail jeongsh@wfu.edu; *Treas.* Dora Ho, Los Angeles Public Lib. E-mail dorah2005@gmail.com; *Past Pres.* Eugenia Beh, Massachusetts Institute of Technology. E-mail eugenia_beh@yahoo.com; *Board Membs.-at-Large* Anna Coats, Melissa Cardenas-Dow, Paolo Gujilde, Annie Pho.

Publication

APALA Newsletter (q.).

Committee Chairs

Constitution and Bylaws. Paul Lai.
Family Literacy Focus. Lessa Pelayo-Lozada.
Finance and Fund Raising. Sandy Wee.
Literature Awards. Ven Basco, Dora Ho.
Membership. Maria Pontillas.
Newsletter and Publications. Melissa Cardenas-Dow, Gary A. Colmenar.
Nominating. Eugenia Beh.

Program Planning, 2015. Janet Clarke, Peter Spyers-Duran.
Publicity. Holly Okuhara, Ngoc-Yen Tran.
Scholarships and Awards. Tassanee Chitcharoen, Valeria Molteni.
Web. Alvin Dantes.

Association for Information Science and Technology

Executive Director, Richard B. Hill
8555 16th St., Suite 850, Silver Spring, MD 20910
301-495-0900, fax 301-495-0810, e-mail asis@asis.org
World Wide Web http://www.asist.org

Object

The Association for Information Science and Technology (ASIS&T, formerly the American Society for Information Science and Technology) provides a forum for the discussion, publication, and critical analysis of work dealing with the design, management, and use of information, information systems, and information technology.

Membership

Regular Memb. (Indiv.) 1,100; (Student) 500; (Early/Transitional Professional) 140; (Developing Nation) 30; (Inst.) 120. Dues (Indiv.) $140; Early/Transitional Professional $65; Developing Nation (varies by category); (Student) $40; (Inst.) $650 and $800.

Officers

Pres. Sandra G. Hirsh, San José State Univ.; *Pres.-Elect* Nadia Caidi, Univ. of Toronto; *Treas.* Vicki Gregory, Univ. of South Florida; *Past Pres.* Harry Bruce, University of Washington.

Address correspondence to the executive director.

Directors

June Abbas, Jamshid Beheshti, Lynn Silipigni Connaway, Sanda Erdelez, Lauren D. Harrison, Fidelia Ibekwe-SanJuan.

Publications

Periodicals

Journal of the Association for Information Science and Technology. Available with ASIS&T membership or from Wiley Blackwell.
Bulletin of the Association for Information Science and Technology (online only).
Proceedings of the ASIS&T Annual Meeting. Available from ASIS&T.

Books and Monographs

ASIST Thesaurus of Information Science, Technology, and Librarianship, 3rd ed.
Computerization Movements and Technology Diffusion: From Mainframes to Ubiquitous Computing.
Covert and Overt.
Digital Inclusion.
Editorial Peer Review: Its Strengths and Weaknesses.
Electronic Publishing: Applications and Implications.
Evaluating Networked Information Services: Techniques, Policy and Issues.
From Print to Electronic: The Transformation of Scientific Communication.
Historical Information Science.
Historical Studies in Information Science.
The History and Heritage of Scientific and Technological Information Systems.
Information and Emotion: The Emergent Affective Paradigm in Information Behavior Research and Theory.
Information Management for the Intelligent Organization, 3rd ed.
Information Need: A Theory Connecting Information Search to Knowledge Formation.

Information Representation and Retrieval in the Digital Age, 2nd ed.

Intelligent Technologies in Library and Information Service Applications.

International Perspectives on the History of Information Science and Technology.

Introduction to Information Science and Technology.

Introductory Concepts in Information Science, 2nd ed.

Knowledge Management: The Bibliography.

Knowledge Management for the Information Professional.

Knowledge Management in Practice: Connections and Context.

Knowledge Management Lessons Learned: What Works and What Doesn't.

The New Digital Scholar.

The Next Digital Scholar.

Powering Search: The Role of Thesauri in New Information Environments.

Scholarly Metrics Under the Microscope.

Statistical Methods for the Information Professional.

Theories of Information Behavior.

The Web of Knowledge: A Festschrift in Honor of Eugene Garfield.

The above books and monographs are available from Information Today, Inc., 143 Old Marlton Pike, Medford, NJ 08055. Many are available as e-books.

Association for Library and Information Science Education

Executive Director, Andrew Estep
ALISE Headquarters, 2150 N. 107 St., Suite 205, Seattle WA 98133
Tel. 206-209-5267, fax 206-367-8777, e-mail office@alise.org
World Wide Web http://www.alise.org

The Association for Library and Information Science Education (ALISE) is an independent nonprofit professional association whose mission is to promote excellence in research, teaching, and service for library and information science education through leadership, collaboration, advocacy, and dissemination of research. Its enduring purpose is to promote research that informs the scholarship of teaching and learning for library and information science, enabling members to integrate research into teaching and learning. The association provides a forum in which to share ideas, discuss issues, address challenges, and shape the future of education for library and information science. Founded in 1915 as the Association of American Library Schools, it has had its present name since 1983.

Membership

700+ in four categories: Personal, Institutional, International Affiliate Institutional, and Associate Institutional. Personal membership is open to anyone with an interest in the association's objectives.

Officers

Pres. Samantha K. Hastings, Univ. of South Carolina. E-mail hastings@sc.edu; *V.P./Pres.-Elect* Louise Spiteri, Dalhousie Univ. E-mail louise.spiteri@dal.ca; *Secy.-Treas.* Denice Adkins, Univ. of Missouri. E-mail adkinsde@missouri.edu; *Dirs.* Laurie Bonnici, Univ. of Alabama; Carol L. Tilley, Univ. of Illinois at Urbana-Champaign; *Past Pres.* Clara Chu, Univ. of North Carolina–Greensboro. E-mail cmchu@uncg.edu.

Publication

Journal of Education for Library and Information Science (JELIS) (q.). *Ed.* Peta Wellstead, Open Polytechnic of New Zealand/Kuratini Tuwhera. E-mail jeliseditor@alise.org.

Association for Rural and Small Libraries

201 E. Main St., Suite 1405, Lexington, KY 40507
Tel. 859-514-9178, e-mail szach@amrms.com
World Wide Web http://www.arsl.info

Object

The Association for Rural and Small Libraries (ARSL) was established in 1978, in the Department of Library Science at Clarion University of Pennsylvania, as the Center for Study of Rural Librarianship.

ARSL is a network of people throughout the United States dedicated to the positive growth and development of libraries. ARSL believes in the value of rural and small libraries, and strives to create resources and services that address national, state, and local priorities for libraries situated in rural communities.

Its objectives are

- To organize a network of members concerned about the growth and development of useful library services in rural and small libraries
- To provide opportunities for the continuing education of members
- To provide mechanisms for members to exchange ideas and to meet on a regular basis
- To cultivate the practice of librarianship and to foster a spirit of coopera-

tion among members of the profession, enabling them to act together for mutual goals

- To serve as a source of current information about trends, issues, and strategies
- To partner with other library and nonlibrary groups and organizations serving rural and small library communities
- To collect and disseminate information and resources that are critical to this network
- To advocate for rural and small libraries at the local, state, and national levels

Officers

Pres. Donna Brice, Eastern Lancaster County Lib., 11 Chestnut, New Holland, PA 17557. Tel. 717-354-0525, e-mail dbrice@elanco library.org; *V.P./Pres.-Elect* Lisa Lewis, Tel. 520-226-6063, e-mail minefee2001@yahoo. com; *Past Pres.* Tena Hanson, Estherville Public Lib., 613 Central Ave., Estherville, IA 51334. Tel. 712-362-7731, e-mail thanson librarian@gmail.com.

Association of Academic Health Sciences Libraries

Executive Director, Louise S. Miller
2150 N. 107 St., Suite 205, Seattle, WA 98133
206-367-8704, fax 206-367-8777, e-mail aahsl@sbims.com
World Wide Web http://www.aahsl.org

Object

The Association of Academic Health Sciences Libraries (AAHSL) comprises the libraries serving the accredited U.S. and Canadian medical schools belonging to or affiliated with the Association of American Medical Colleges. Its goals are to promote excellence in academic health science libraries and to ensure that the next generation of health practitioners is trained in information-seeking skills that enhance the quality of health care delivery, education, and research. Founded in 1977.

Membership

Memb. 150+. Full membership is available to nonprofit educational institutions operating a school of health sciences that has full or provisional accreditation by the Association of American Medical Colleges. Full members are represented by the chief administrative officer of the member institution's health sciences library. Associate membership (and nonvoting representation) is available to organizations having an interest in the purposes and activities of the association. For dues information, contact the association.

Officers

Pres. (2015–2016) Paul Schoening, Bernard Becker Medical Lib., Washington Univ. School of Medicine. Tel. 314-362-3119, e-mail pas@wusm.wustl.edu; *Pres.-Elect (2015–2016)* Ruth Riley, School of Medicine Lib., Univ. of South Carolina. Tel. 803-216-3220, e-mail ruth.riley@uscmed.sc.edu; *Past Pres.* A. James Bothmer, Health Sciences Lib./Learning Resources Center, Creighton Univ. Tel. 402-280-5120, e-mail jbothmer@creighton.edu; *Secy./Treas. (2013–2016)* Kathryn Carpenter, Lib. of the Health Sciences, Univ. of Illinois at Chicago. Tel. 312-996-8966, e-mail khc@uic.edu.

Directors

Barbara Epstein (2012–2015), Health Sciences Lib. System, Univ. of Pittsburgh. Tel. 412-648-8866, e-mail bepstein@pitt.edu; Neville Prendergast (2013–2016), Rudolph Matas Lib. of the Health Sciences, Tulane Univ. Medical Center. Tel. 614-292-4852, e-mail nprender@tulane.edu; Pamela Bradigan (2014–2017), Health Sciences Lib., Ohio State Univ. Tel. 212-263-6990, e-mail pamela.bradigan@osumc.edu.

Association of Christian Librarians

Executive Director, Janelle Mazelin
P.O. Box 4, Cedarville, Ohio 45314
Tel. 937-766-2255, fax 937-766-5499, e-mail info@acl.org

Object

The mission of the Association of Christian Librarians (ACL) is to strengthen libraries through professional development of evangelical librarians, scholarship, and spiritual encouragement for service in higher education. ACL is a growing community that integrates faith, ministry, and academic librarianship through development of members, services, and scholarship.

Founded 1957.

Membership

500+ at about 150 institutions. Membership is open to those who profess the Christian faith as outlined by the association's statement of faith, and are employed at an institution of higher education. Associate memberships are available for non-librarians who both agree with ACL's statement of faith and are interested in libraries or librarianship.

Officers

Pres. (2012–2016) Frank Quinn, Point Loma Nazarene Univ.; *V.P. (2011–2015)* Rodney Birch, George Fox Univ.; *Secy. (2014–2017)* Denise Nelson, Point Loma Nazarene Univ., *Treas. (2008–-2016)* Sheila O. Carlblom; *Dirs.-at-Large* Jennifer Ewing, Nate Farley, Alison Jones, Linda Poston, Paul Roberts, Bob Triplett.

Association of Independent Information Professionals

8550 United Plaza Blvd., Suite 1001, Baton Rouge, LA 70809
225-408-4400, fax 225-408-4422, e-mail office@aiip.org
World Wide Web http://www.aiip.org

Object

Members of the Association of Independent Information Professionals (AIIP) are owners of firms providing such information-related services as online and manual research, document delivery, database design, library support, consulting, writing, and publishing.

The objectives of the association are

- To advance the knowledge and understanding of the information profession
- To promote and maintain high professional and ethical standards among its members
- To encourage independent information professionals to assemble to discuss common issues
- To promote the interchange of information among independent information professionals and various organizations
- To keep the public informed of the profession and of the responsibilities of the information professional

Membership

Memb. 50+.

Officers

Pres. Connie Clem, Clem Information Strategies. E-mail president@aiip.org; *Pres.-Elect* June Boyle, CeRCo Research and Consulting;

Secy. Joann M. Wleklinski, Wleklinski Information Services; *Treas.* Marilyn Harmacek, MHC Info Solutions; *Past Pres.* Jocelyn Sheppard, Red House Consulting.

Publications

AIIP Connections (q.).
Membership Directory (ann.).
Professional papers series.

Association of Jewish Libraries

P.O. Box 1118, Teaneck, NJ 07666
201-371-3255
World Wide Web http://www.jewishlibraries.org

Object

The Association of Jewish Libraries (AJL) is an international professional organization that fosters access to information and research in all forms of media relating to all things Jewish. The association promotes Jewish literacy and scholarship and provides a community for peer support and professional development.

AJL membership is open to individuals and libraries, library workers, and library supporters. There are two divisions within AJL: RAS (Research Libraries, Archives, and Special Collections) and SSC (Schools, Synagogues, and Centers). The diverse membership includes libraries in synagogues, JCCs, day schools, yeshivot, universities, Holocaust museums, and the Library of Congress. Membership is drawn from North America and places beyond, including China, the Czech Republic, the Netherlands, Israel, Italy, South Africa, Switzerland, and the United Kingdom.

Goals

The association's goals are to

- Maintain high professional standards for Judaica librarians and recruit qualified individuals into the profession
- Facilitate communication and exchange of information on a global scale
- Encourage quality publication in the field in all formats and media, print, digital, and so forth, and to stimulate publication of high-quality children's literature
- Facilitate and encourage establishment of Judaica library collections

- Enhance information access for all through application of advanced technologies
- Publicize the organization and its activities in all relevant venues: stimulate awareness of Judaica library services among the public at large; promote recognition of Judaica librarianship within the wider library profession; and encourage recognition of Judaica library services by other organizations and related professions
- Ensure continuity of the association through sound management, financial security, effective governance and a dedicated and active membership

AJL conducts an annual convention in the United States or Canada in late June.

Membership

Memb. 600. Year: Oct.–Sept. For dues information, contact Sheryl Stahl at sstahl@huc.edu.

Officers

Pres. Yaffa Weisman; *V.P./Pres.-Elect* Amalia Warshenbrot; *V.P. Membership* Sheryl Stahl; *Secy.* Marga Hirsch; *Treas.* Deborah Stern; *Past Pres.* Heidi Estrin; *V.P. Development* James P. Rosenbloom; *RAS Pres.* Sharon Benamou; *SSC Pres.* Aimee Lurie.

Address correspondence to info@jewish libraries.org.

Publications

AJL Conference Proceedings.

AJL News (q., digital).
AJL Reviews (q., digital).
Judaica Librarianship (annual, digital).

Association of Research Libraries

Executive Director, Elliott Shore
21 Dupont Circle N.W., Suite 800, Washington, D.C. 20036
202-296-2296, fax 202-872-0884, e-mail arlhq@arl.org
World Wide Web http://www.arl.org

Object

The Association of Research Libraries (ARL) is a nonprofit organization of 125 research libraries in the United States and Canada. ARL's mission is to influence the changing environment of scholarly communication and the public policies that affect research libraries and the diverse communities they serve. ARL pursues this mission by advancing the goals of its member research libraries, providing leadership in public and information policy to the scholarly and higher education communities, fostering the exchange of ideas and expertise, facilitating the emergence of new roles for research libraries, and shaping a future environment that leverages its interests with those of allied organizations.

Membership

Memb. 125. Membership is institutional. Dues: $26,744 for 2015.

Officers

Pres. Deborah Jakubs, Duke Univ.; *V.P./Pres.-Elect* Larry Alford, Univ. of Toronto; *Past Pres.* Carol Pitts Diedrichs, Ohio State Univ.

Board of Directors

Larry Alford, Univ. of Toronto; David H. Carlson (ex officio), Texas A&M Univ.; Mary Case, Univ. of Illinois at Chicago; Carol Pitts Diedrichs, Ohio State Univ.; Susan Gibbons, Yale Univ.; Thomas Hickerson, Univ. of Calgary; Jeffrey L. Horrell (ex officio), Dartmouth College; Deborah Jakubs, Duke Univ.; Richard E. Luce, Univ. of Oklahoma; Bonnie MacEwan, Auburn Univ.; Mary Ann Mavrinac, Univ. of Rochester; Brian E. C. Schottlaender (ex officio), Univ. of California, San Diego; Elliott Shore (ex officio), ARL; Ann Thornton, New York Public Lib.; John Wilkin, Univ. of Illinois at Urbana-Champaign.

Publications

Research Library Issues: A Report from ARL, CNI, and SPARC (4 per year).
ARL Academic Health Sciences Library Statistics (ann.).
ARL Academic Law Library Statistics (ann.).
ARL Annual Salary Survey (ann.).
ARL Statistics (ann.).
SPEC Kit series (4 a year).

Committee and Working Group Chairs

Accessibility and Universal Design Working Group. Ed Van Gemert, Univ. of Wisconsin–Madison.
Advancing Scholarly Communication. Brian E. C. Schottlaender, Univ. of California, San Diego.
ARL Licensing Working Group. Jay Starratt, Washington State Univ.
Diversity and Leadership. Joyce Backus, National Lib. of Medicine.
E-Research Working Group. Harriette Hemmasi, Brown Univ.
Fair Use and Related Exemptions Working Group. Betsy Wilson, Univ. of Washington.

Influencing Public Policies. David Carlson, Texas A&M Univ.

Membership. Sarah Thomas, Harvard Univ.

Regional Federal Depository Libraries Working Group. Judith C. Russell, Univ. of Florida.

Statistics and Assessment. Robert E. Fox, Jr., Univ. of Louisville.

Strategic Thinking and Design Transition Team. Brian E. C. Schottlaender, Univ. of California, San Diego.

Transforming Research Libraries. Jeffrey Horrell, Dartmouth College.

Transforming Special Collections in the Digital Age Working Group, Thomas Hickerson, Univ. of Calgary.

ARL Membership

Non-university Libraries

Boston Public Lib.; Center for Research Libs.; Lib. of Congress; National Agricultural Lib.; National Archives and Records Administration; National Lib. of Medicine; National Research Council Canada, Knowledge Management; New York Public Lib.; New York State Lib.; Smithsonian Institution Libs.

University Libraries

Alabama; Albany (SUNY); Alberta; Arizona; Arizona State; Auburn; Boston College; Bos-
ton Univ.; Brigham Young; British Columbia; Brown; Buffalo (SUNY); Calgary; California, Berkeley; California, Davis; California, Irvine; California, Los Angeles; California, Riverside; California, San Diego; California, Santa Barbara; Case Western Reserve; Chicago; Cincinnati; Colorado; Colorado State; Columbia; Connecticut; Cornell; Dartmouth; Delaware; Duke; Emory; Florida; Florida State; George Washington; Georgetown; Georgia; Georgia Inst. of Technology; Guelph; Harvard; Hawaii; Houston; Howard; Illinois, Chicago; Illinois, Urbana-Champaign; Indiana; Iowa; Iowa State; Johns Hopkins; Kansas; Kent State; Kentucky; Laval; Louisiana State; Louisville; McGill; McMaster; Manitoba; Maryland; Massachusetts; Massachusetts Inst. of Technology; Miami (Florida); Michigan; Michigan State; Minnesota; Missouri; Montreal; Nebraska, Lincoln; New Mexico; New York; North Carolina; North Carolina State; Northwestern; Notre Dame; Ohio; Ohio State; Oklahoma; Oklahoma State; Oregon; Ottawa; Pennsylvania; Pennsylvania State; Pittsburgh; Princeton; Purdue; Queen's (Kingston, Ontario); Rice; Rochester; Rutgers; Saskatchewan; South Carolina; Southern California; Southern Illinois; Stony Brook (SUNY); Syracuse; Temple; Tennessee; Texas; Texas A&M; Texas Tech; Toronto; Tulane; Utah; Vanderbilt; Virginia; Virginia Tech; Washington; Washington (Saint Louis); Washington State; Waterloo; Wayne State; Western Ontario; Wisconsin; Yale; York.

Association of Vision Science Librarians

Co-Chairs, D. J. Matthews, Kristin Motte
World Wide Web http://www.avsl.org

Object

To foster collective and individual acquisition and dissemination of vision science information, to improve services for all persons seeking such information, and to develop standards for libraries to which members are attached. Founded in 1968.

Officers

Co-Chairs D. J. Matthews, Marshall B. Ketchum Univ. E-mail djmatthews@ketchum.edu; Kristin Motte, New England College of Optometry. E-mail mottek@neco.edu; *Treas.* Elaine Wells, Harold Kohn Vision Science Lib., SUNY College of Optometry; *Member-ship Chair* Christine Weber, Illinois College of Optometry.

Publications

Guidelines for Vision Science Librarians.
Opening Day Book, Journal and AV Collection List–Visual Science.
Standards for Vision Science Libraries.
Union List of Vision-Related Serials (irreg.).

Meetings

Annual meeting held in the fall, mid-year mini-meeting with the Medical Library Association.

Beta Phi Mu
(International Library and Information Studies Honor Society)

Executive Director, Alison M. Lewis
Drexel University, College of Computing and Informatics
Philadelphia, PA 19104
215-895-5959, fax 215-895-2494, e-mail alewis@drexel.edu or betaphimu@drexel.edu
World Wide Web http://www.beta-phi-mu.org

Object

To recognize distinguished achievement in and scholarly contributions to librarianship, information studies, or library education, and to sponsor and support appropriate professional and scholarly projects relating to these fields. Founded at the University of Illinois in 1948.

Membership

Memb. 36,000. Eligibility for membership in Beta Phi Mu is by invitation of the faculty from institutions where the American Library Association, or other recognized accrediting agency approved by the Beta Phi Mu Executive Board, has accredited or recognized a professional degree program. Candidates must be graduates of a library and information science program and fulfill the following requirements: complete the course requirements leading to a master's degree with a scholastic average of 3.75 where A equals 4 points, or complete a planned program of advanced study beyond the master's degree which require full-time study for one or more academic years with a scholastic average of 3.75 where A equals 4.0. Each chapter or approved institution is allowed to invite no more than 25 percent of the annual graduating class, and the faculty of participating library schools must attest to their initiates' professional promise.

Officers

Pres. Eileen Abels, Graduate School of Lib. and Info. Science, Simmons College, Boston; *V.P.* Charles McElroy, Florida State Univ. Lib.

Directors

Susan W. Alman, Lynn Silipigni Connaway, Marie Radford, Vinette Thomas, Elaine Yontz.

Publications

Beta Phi Mu Scholar Series. Available from Rowman & Littlefield, Publishers, 4501 Forbes Blvd., Suite 200, Lanham, MD 20706. *Ed.* Lorraine J. Haricombe; *Assoc. Ed.* Keith Russell.
Newsletter. *The Pipeline* (biennial; electronic only). *Ed.* Isabel Gray.

Chapters

Alpha. Univ. of Illinois at Urbana-Champaign, Grad. School of Lib. and Info. Science; *Gamma.* Florida State Univ., College of Communication and Info.; *Epsilon.* Univ. of North Carolina at Chapel Hill, School of Info. and Lib. Science; *Theta.* Pratt Inst., Grad. School of Lib. and Info. Science; *Iota.* Catholic Univ. of America, School of Lib. and Info. Science; Univ. of Maryland, College of Info. Studies; *Lambda.* Univ. of Oklahoma, School of Lib. and Info. Studies; *Xi.* Univ. of Hawaii at Manoa, School of Lib. and Info. Studies; *Omicron.* Rutgers Univ., Grad. School of Communication, Info., and Lib. Studies; *Pi.* Univ. of Pittsburgh, School of Info. Sciences; *Rho.* Kent State Univ., School of Lib. and Info. Science; *Sigma.* Drexel Univ., College of Computing and Informatics; *Phi.* Univ. of Denver, Grad. School of Lib. and Info. Science; *Psi.* Univ. of Missouri at Columbia, School of Lib. and Info. Science; *Omega.* San Jose State Univ., School of Lib. and Info. Science; *Beta Beta.* Simmons College, Grad. School of Lib. and Info. Science; *Beta Delta.* State Univ. of New York at Buffalo, Dept. of Lib. and Info. Studies; *Beta Epsilon.* Emporia State Univ., School of Lib. and Info. Management; *Beta Zeta.* Louisiana State Univ., School of Lib. and Info. Science; *Beta Eta.* Univ. of Texas at Austin, Grad. School of Lib. and Info. Science; *Beta Iota.* Univ. of Rhode Island, Grad. School of Lib. and Info. Studies; *Beta Kappa.* Univ. of Alabama, School of Lib. and Info. Studies; *Beta Lambda.* Texas Woman's Univ., School of Lib. and Info. Sciences; *Beta Mu.* Long Island Univ., Palmer School of Lib. and Info. Science; *Beta Xi.* North Carolina Central Univ., School of Lib. and Info. Sciences; *Beta Omicron.* Univ. of Tennessee at Knoxville, School of Info. Sciences; *Beta Pi.* Univ. of Arizona, School of Info. Resources and Lib. Science; *Beta Rho.* Univ. of Wisconsin at Milwaukee, School of Info.; *Beta Sigma.* Clarion Univ. of Pennsylvania, Dept. of Lib. Science; *Beta Phi.* Univ. of South Florida, School of Lib. and Info. Science; *Beta Psi.* Univ. of Southern Mississippi, School of Lib. and Info. Science; *Beta Omega.* Univ. of South Carolina, College of Lib. and Info. Science; *Beta Beta Epsilon.* Univ. of Wisconsin at Madison, School of Lib. and Info. Studies; *Beta Beta Theta.* Univ. of Iowa, School of Lib. and Info. Science; *Beta Beta Kappa.* Univ. of Puerto Rico, Grad. School of Info. Sciences and Technologies; *Pi Lambda Sigma.* Syracuse Univ., School of Info. Studies; *Beta Beta Mu.* Valdosta State Univ., School of Lib. and Info. Science; *Beta Beta Nu.* Univ. of North Texas, College of Info.; *Beta Beta Xi.* St. Catherine Univ., Master of Lib. and Info. Science program.

Bibliographical Society of America

Executive Secretary, Michèle E. Randall
P.O. Box 1537, Lenox Hill Sta., New York, NY 10021
212-452-2710 (tel./fax), e-mail bsa@bibsocamer.org
World Wide Web http://www.bibsocamer.org

Object

To promote bibliographical research and to issue bibliographical publications. Organized in 1904.

Membership

Memb. Dues (Indiv.) $65; (Sustaining) $250; (Contributing) $100; (Student) $20; (Inst.) $100; (Lifetime) $1,250. Year. Jan.–Dec.

Officers

Pres. Martin Antonetti, Smith College. E-mail mantonet@smith.edu; *V.P.* John Crichton, Brick Row Book Shop, San Francisco. E-mail jcrichton@brickrow.com; *Secy.* Barbara Heritage, Rare Book School. E-mail beh7v@virginia.edu; *Treas.* G. Scott Clemons, Brown Brothers Harriman. E-mail scott.clemons@bbh.com.

Council

(2015) Christina Geiger, Michael Suarez, David J. Supino, Michael Thompson; (2016) John A. Buchtel, Gerald Cloud, David Alan Richards, Marcia Reed; (2017) William T. LaMoy, Nina Musinsky, George Ong, Heather Wolfe.

Publication

Papers of the Bibliographical Society of America (q.; memb.).

Bibliographical Society of Canada
(La Société Bibliographique du Canada)

President, Linda Quirk
World Wide Web http://www.bsc-sbc.ca/index.html
360 Bloor St. W., P.O. Box 19035, Toronto, ON M5S 3C9

Object

The Bibliographical Society of Canada is a bilingual (English/French) organization that has as its goal the scholarly study of the history, description, and transmission of texts in all media and formats, with a primary emphasis on Canada, and the fulfillment of this goal through the following objectives:

- To promote the study and practice of bibliography: enumerative, historical, descriptive, analytical, and textual
- To further the study, research, and publication of book history and print culture
- To publish bibliographies and studies of book history and print culture
- To encourage the publication of bibliographies, critical editions, and studies of book history and print culture
- To promote the appropriate preservation and conservation of manuscript, archival, and published materials in various formats
- To encourage the utilization and analysis of relevant manuscript and archival sources as a foundation of bibliographical scholarship and book history

- To promote the interdisciplinary nature of bibliography, and to foster relationships with other relevant organizations nationally and internationally
- To conduct the society without purpose of financial gain for its members, and to ensure that any profits or other accretions to the society shall be used in promoting its goal and objectives

Membership

The society welcomes as members all those who share its aims and wish to support and participate in bibliographical research and publication.

Officers

Pres. Linda Quirk. E-mail president@bsc-sbc. ca; *1st V.P.* Nancy Earle; *2nd V.P.* Ruth Panofsky; *Secy.* Greta Golick. E-mail secretary@ bsc-sbc.ca; *Assoc. Secy.* Roger Meloche; *Treas.* Tom Vincent; *Past Pres.* Janet Friskney.

Publications

Papers of the Bibliographical Society of Canada/Cahiers de la Société Bibliographique du Canada (s. ann).
The Bulletin/Le Bulletin (s. ann).

For a full list of the society's publications, see http://www.library.utoronto.ca/bsc/publicationseng.html.

Black Caucus of the American Library Association

President, Kelvin A. Watson
P.O. Box 1738, Hampton, VA 23669
World Wide Web http://www.bcala.org

Mission

The Black Caucus of the American Library Association (BCALA) serves as an advocate for the development, promotion, and improvement of library services and resources for the nation's African American community and provides leadership for the recruitment and professional development of African American librarians. Founded in 1970.

Membership

Membership is open to any person, institution, or business interested in promoting the development of library and information services for African Americans and other people of African descent and willing to maintain good financial standing with the organization. The membership is currently composed of librarians and other information professionals, library support staff, libraries, publishers, authors, vendors, and other library-related organizations in the United States and abroad. Dues (Lifetime)

$500; (Corporate) $200; (Institutional) $60; (Regular) $45; (Library Support Staff) $20; (Student) $10; (Retired) $0.

Officers

Pres. Kelvin A. Watson. E-mail kantoniow@ yahoo.com; *V.P./Pres.-Elect* Denyvetta Davis; *Secy.* kYmberly Keeton; *Past Pres.* Jerome Offord, Jr.

Executive Board

Richard Ashby, Bettye Black, Wanda K. Brown, Elizabeth Jean Brumfield, Rudolf Clay, Eboni Curry, Tiffany A. Duck, Michele Fenton, Emily Guss, Andrew P. Jackson, Karen Lemons, Carol Nurse, Kirby McCurtis, Monya Tomlinson.

Publication

BCALA Newsletter (bi-mo; memb.).

Canadian Association for Information Science
(L'Association Canadienne des Sciences de l'Information)

President, Diane Rasmussen Pennington
World Wide Web http://www.cais-acsi.ca

Object

To promote the advancement of information science in Canada and encourage and facilitate the exchange of information relating to the use, access, retrieval, organization, management, and dissemination of information.

Officers

Pres. Diane Rasmussen Pennington, Ashford Univ. E-mail diane.m.rasmussen@gmail.com; *Secy.* Deborah Hicks, Univ. of Alberta. E-mail deborah.hicks@ualberta.ca; *Treas.* Anatoliy Gruzd, Dalhousie Univ. E-mail gruzd@dal.ca.

Membership

Institutions and individuals interested in information science and involved in the gathering, organization, and dissemination of information (such as information scientists, archivists, librarians, computer scientists, documentalists, economists, educators, journalists, and psychologists) and who support CAIS's objectives can become association members.

Publication

Canadian Journal of Information and Library Science. Ed. Clément Arsenault, Univ. de Montréal. E-mail clement.arsenault@umontreal.ca.

Canadian Association of Research Libraries
(Association des Bibliothèques de Recherche du Canada)

Executive Director, Susan Haigh
309 Cooper St., Suite 203, Ottawa, ON K2P 0G5
613-482-9344 ext. 101, e-mail info@carl-abrc.ca
World Wide Web http://www.carl-abrc.ca

Membership

The Canadian Association of Research Libraries (CARL), established in 1976, is the leadership organization for the Canadian research library community. The association's members are the 29 major academic research libraries across Canada together with Library and Archives Canada and the Canada Institute for Scientific and Technical Information (CISTI). Membership is institutional, open primarily to libraries of Canadian universities that have doctoral graduates in both the arts and the sciences. CARL is an associate member of the Association of Universities and Colleges of Canada (AUCC) and is incorporated as a not-for-profit organization under the Canada Corporations Act.

Mission

The association provides leadership on behalf of Canada's research libraries and enhances their capacity to advance research and higher education. It promotes effective and sustainable scholarly communication, and public policy that enables broad access to scholarly information.

Officers

Pres. Gerald Beasley, Univ. of Alberta; *V.P./
Pres.-Elect* Martha Whitehead, Queen's Univ.;
Secy. Lynda Gadoury, Université du Québec à
Montréal; *Treas.* Donna Bourne-Tyson, Dal-
housie Univ.; *Past Pres.* Thomas Hickerson,
Univ. of Calgary. E-mail tom.hickerson@
ucalgary.ca; *Dirs.* Jonathan Bengtson, Univ. of
Victoria; Vivian Lewis, McMaster Univ.; *Exec.
Dir.* Susan Haigh. E-mail susan.haigh@carl-
abrc.ca.

Member Institutions

Univ. of Alberta, Univ. of British Columbia,
Brock Univ., Univ. of Calgary, Carleton Univ.,
CISTI (Canada Institute for Scientific and
Technical Information), Concordia Univ., Dal-
housie Univ., Univ. of Guelph, Université La-
val, Lib. and Archives Canada, McGill Univ.,
McMaster Univ., Univ. of Manitoba, Memorial
Univ. of Newfoundland, Université de Montré-
al, Univ. of New Brunswick, Univ. of Ottawa,
Université du Québec à Montréal, Queen's
Univ., Univ. of Regina, Ryerson Univ., Univ.
of Saskatchewan, Université de Sherbrooke,
Simon Fraser Univ., Univ. of Toronto, Univ. of
Victoria, Univ. of Waterloo, Univ. of Western
Ontario, Univ. of Windsor, York Univ.

Canadian Library Association
(Association Canadienne des Bibliothèques)

Executive Director, Valoree McKay
1150 Morrison Drive, Suite 400, Ottawa, ON K1Y 0K4
613-232-9625 ext. 306, fax 613-563-9895, e-mail vmckay@cla.ca
World Wide Web http://www.cla.ca

Object

The Canadian Library Association (CLA) is
the national voice for Canada's library communities. CLA champions library values and
the value of libraries, influences public policy
affecting libraries, inspires and supports learning, and collaborates to strengthen the library
community. The association represents Canadian librarianship to the federal government
and media, carries on international liaison
with other library associations and cultural
agencies, offers professional development programs, and supports such core library values
as intellectual freedom and access to information, particularly for disadvantaged populations. Founded in 1946, CLA is a not-for-profit
voluntary organization governed by an elected
executive council.

Membership

Memb. (as of December 2014) (Indiv.) 957;
(Inst.) 249; (Corporate) 50; (Associate) 27.

Open to individuals, institutions, library
boards, and groups interested in librarianship
and in library and information services.

Officers

Pres. Sandra Singh, Vancouver Public Lib., 350
W. Georgia St., Vancouver, BC V6B 6B1. Tel.
604-331-4007, e-mail sandra.singh@vpl.ca;
V.P./Pres.-Elect Rosemary Bonanno, Vancouver Island Regional Lib. E-mail rbonanno@
virl.bc.ca; *Treas.* Michael Ridley, Univ. of
Guelph. E-mail mridley@uoguelph.ca; *Past
Pres.* Marie DeYoung, Saint Mary's Univ. E-
mail marie.deyoung@smu.ca.

Publications

*Feliciter: Linking Canada's Information Pro-
fessionals* (6 a year; electronic).
CLA Digest (bi-w.; electronic newsletter).

Catholic Library Association

President, Sara B. Baron
8550 United Plaza Blvd., Suite 1001, Baton Rouge, LA 70809
Tel. 225-408-4417, e-mail cla@cathla.org
World Wide Web http://www.cathla.org

Object

The promotion and encouragement of Catholic literature and library work through cooperation, publications, education, and information. Founded in 1921.

Membership

Memb. 1,000. Dues $55–$500. Year. July–June.

Officers

Pres. Sara B. Baron, Regent Univ. Lib., Virginia Beach. E-mail sbaron@regent.edu; *V.P./Pres.-Elect* Mary Kelleher, Univ. of St.

Thomas, Houston. E-mail kellehm@stthom.edu; *Past Pres.* Malachy R. McCarthy, Claretian Missionaries Archives, Chicago. E-mail mmccarthy@cathla.org.

Address correspondence to the executive director.

Executive Board

Officers; Susan B. Finney; Cait C. Kokolus; Pat Lawton; Ann O'Hara.

Publication

Catholic Library World (q.; memb.; nonmemb. $125). *General Ed.* Sigrid Kelsey.

Chief Officers of State Library Agencies

Executive Director, Timothy Cherubini
201 E. Main St., Suite 1405, Lexington, KY 40507
859-514-9826, fax 859-514-9166, e-mail tcherubini@cosla.org
World Wide Web http://www.cosla.org

Object

Chief Officers of State Library Agencies (COSLA) is an independent organization of the chief officers of state and territorial agencies designated as the state library administrative agency and responsible for statewide library development. Its purpose is to identify and address issues of common concern and national interest; to further state library agency relationships with federal government and national organizations; and to initiate cooperative action for the improvement of library services to the people of the United States.

COSLA's membership consists solely of these top library officers, variously designated

as state librarian, director, commissioner, or executive secretary. The organization provides a continuing mechanism for dealing with the problems and challenges faced by these officers. Its work is carried on through its members, a board of directors, and committees.

Board of Directors (2014–2016)

Pres. Kendall Wiggin, State Libn., Connecticut State Lib., 231 Capitol Ave., Hartford, CT 06106. Tel. 860-757-6510, e-mail kendall.wiggin@ct.gov; *V.P./Pres.-Elect* Sandra Treadway, Libn. of Virginia, Lib. of Virginia, 800 E. Broad St., Richmond, VA 23219. Tel. 804-692-

3535, e-mail sandra.treadway@lva.virginia. gov; *Treas.* Stacey Aldrich, Deputy Secy. for Libs., Office of Commonwealth Libs., Pennsylvania Dept. of Educ., 607 South Drive, Forum Bldg., Room 200, Harrisburg, PA 17120-0600. Tel. 717-787-2646, e-mail saldrich@pa.gov; *Secy.* Kurt Kiefer, State Libn., Div. for Libraries, Technology, and Community Learning, Wisconsin Dept. of Public Instruction, P.O. Box 7841, Madison, WI 53707. Tel. 608-266-2205, e-mail kurt.kiefer@dpi.wi.gov;

Past Pres. Ann Joslin, State Libn., Idaho Commission for Libs., 325 W. State St., Boise, ID 83702. Tel. 208-334-2150, e-mail ann.joslin@libraries.idaho.gov; *Dirs.* Cal Shepard, State Libn., North Carolina State Lib., 4640 Mail Service Center, Raleigh, NC 27699-4640. Tel. 919-807-7410, e-mail cal.shepard@ncdcr.gov; Charles Sherrill, State Libn. and Archivist, Tennessee State Lib. and Archives, 403 Seventh Ave. North, Nashville, TN 37243. Tel. 615-741-7996, e-mail chuck.sherrill@tn.gov.

Chinese American Librarians Association

Executive Director, Li Fu
E-mail ailifaha@gmail.com
World Wide Web http://cala-web.org

Object

To enhance communications among Chinese American librarians as well as between Chinese American librarians and other librarians; to serve as a forum for discussion of mutual problems and professional concerns among Chinese American librarians; to promote Sino-American librarianship and library services; and to provide a vehicle whereby Chinese American librarians can cooperate with other associations and organizations having similar or allied interests.

Membership

Memb. About 600. Membership is open to anyone interested in the association's goals and activities. Dues (Regular) $30; (International/Student/Non-salaried) $15; (Inst.) $100; (Affiliated) $100; (Life) $300.

Officers

Pres. Carol Kachuen Gee. E-mail kachuen. gee@lehman.cuny.edu; *V.P./Pres.-Elect* Lian Ruan. E-mail lruan@illinois.edu; *Incoming V.P./Pres.-Elect; Treas.* Hong Miao. E-mail miao hong818@gmail.com; *Past Pres.* Lisa Zhao. E-mail zhzhls200@gmail.com.

Publications

CALA Newsletter (2 a year; memb.; online). *Eds.* Priscilla Yu. E-mail pcyu@illinois.edu; Sai Deng. E-mail saideng@gmail.com.
Journal of Library and Information Science (*JLIS*) (2 a year). *Editorial Board Chair* (2012–2015) Chengzhi Wang, Columbia Univ. Libs. E-mail cw2165@columbia.edu.
Membership Directory (memb.).
Occasional Paper Series (OPS) (online). *Ed.* (2012–2015) Yunshan Ye. E-mail yye@jhu. edu.

Church and Synagogue Library Association

10157 S.W. Barbur Blvd., No.102C, Portland, OR 97219
503-244-6919, 800-542-2752, fax 503-977-3734, e-mail csla@worldaccessnet.com
World Wide Web http://www.cslainfo.org

Object

The Church and Synagogue Library Association (CSLA) provides educational guidance in the establishment and maintenance of congregational libraries.

Its purpose is to act as a unifying core for congregational libraries; to provide the opportunity for a mutual sharing of practices and problems; to inspire and encourage a sense of purpose and mission among congregational librarians; to study and guide the development of congregational librarianship toward recognition as a formal branch of the library profession. Founded in 1967.

Membership

Memb. 1,000. Dues (Inst.) $200; (Affiliated) $100; (Church or Synagogue) $70 ($75 foreign); (Indiv.) $50 ($55 foreign).

Officers

Pres. Cheryl Cutchin; *1st V.P./Pres.-Elect* to be announced; *2nd V.P.* Maria Isabel Garcia; *Treas.* Alice Campbell; *Past Pres.* Evelyn Pockrass; *Ed., Congregational Libraries Today* Sue Poss; *Admin.* Judith Janzen.

Executive Board

Officers; committee chairs.

Publications

Bibliographies (4; price varies).
Congregational Libraries Today (q.; memb.; nonmemb. $50; Canada $60).
CSLA Guides (price varies).

Coalition for Networked Information

Executive Director, Clifford A. Lynch
21 Dupont Circle, Suite 800, Washington, DC 20036
202-296-5098, fax 202-872-0884, e-mail http://www.cni.org/contact
World Wide Web http://www.cni.org
Twitter http://twitter.com/cni_org
YouTube https://www.youtube.com/cnivideo
Vimeo http://vimeo.com/cni

Mission

The Coalition for Networked Information (CNI) promotes the transformative promise of networked information technology for the advancement of scholarly communication and the enrichment of intellectual productivity.

Membership

Memb. 232. Membership is institutional. Dues $7,500. Year. July–June.

Steering Committee

John P. Barden, Univ. of Rochester; Daniel Cohen, Digital Public Lib. of America; Joseph D. Combs, Vanderbilt Univ.; Rebecca A. Graham, Univ. of Guelph; Geneva L. Henry, George Washington Univ.; Thomas C. Leonard, Univ. of California, Berkeley; Clifford A. Lynch (ex officio), Coalition for Networked Information; Diana G. Oblinger (ex officio) EDUCAUSE; Elliott Shore (ex officio), Assn. of Research Libs.; John Unsworth, Brandeis Univ.; Donald J. Waters, Andrew W. Mellon Foundation.

Publication

CNI-Announce (subscribe by e-mail to cni-announce-subscribe@cni.org).
Periodic reports (http://www.cni.org/resources/publications/other-publications-by-cni-staff).

Council on Library and Information Resources

1707 L St. N.W., Suite 650, Washington, DC 20036
202-939-4750, fax 202-600-9628
World Wide Web http://www.clir.org

Object

In 1997 the Council on Library Resources (CLR) and the Commission on Preservation and Access (CPA) merged and became the Council on Library and Information Resources (CLIR). CLIR is an independent, nonprofit organization that forges strategies to enhance research, teaching, and learning environments in collaboration with libraries, cultural institutions, and communities of higher learning.

CLIR promotes forward-looking collaborative solutions that transcend disciplinary, institutional, professional, and geographic boundaries in support of the public good. CLIR identifies and defines the key emerging issues relating to the welfare of libraries and the constituencies they serve, convenes the leaders who can influence change, and promotes collaboration among the institutions and organizations that can achieve change. The council's interests embrace the entire range of information resources and services from traditional library and archival materials to emerging digital formats. It assumes a particular interest in helping institutions cope with the accelerating pace of change associated with the transition into the digital environment.

While maintaining appropriate collaboration and liaison with other institutions and organizations, CLIR operates independently of any particular institutional or vested interests. Through the composition of its board, it brings the broadest possible perspective to bear upon defining and establishing the priority of the issues with which it is concerned.

Board

CLIR's Board of Directors currently has 23 members.

Officers

Chair David Gift, Internet2; *Pres.* Charles Henry. E-mail chenry@clir.org; *V. Chair* Leslie Weir, Univ. of Ottawa; *Treas.* Kathleen Fitzpatrick, Modern Language Assn.

Address correspondence to headquarters.

Publications

Annual Report.
CLIR Issues (bi-mo.).
Technical reports.

Federal Library and Information Network

Interim Executive Director, Kathryn Mendenhall
Library of Congress, Washington, DC 20540-4935
202-707-4800, World Wide Web http://www.loc.gov/flicc

Object

The Federal Library and Information Network (FEDLINK) is an organization of federal agencies working together to achieve optimum use of the resources and facilities of federal libraries and information centers by promoting common services, coordinating and sharing available resources, and providing continuing professional education for federal library and information staff. FEDLINK serves as a forum for discussion of the policies, programs, procedures, and technologies that affect federal libraries and the information services they provide to their agencies, to Congress, the federal courts, and the public.

Membership

The FEDLINK voting membership is composed of representatives of the following U.S. federal departments and agencies: Each of the national libraries (the Library of Congress, National Agricultural Library, National Library of Education, National Library of Medicine, and the National Transportation Library); each cabinet-level executive department, as defined in 5 U.S.C. § 101; additional departments and agencies (the Defense Technical Information Center; departments of the Air Force, Army, and Navy; Executive Office of the President, Government Accountability Office, General Services Administration, Government Printing Office, Institute of Museum and Library Services, National Aeronautics and Space Administration, National Archives and Records Administration, National Technical Information Service [Department of Commerce], Office of Management and Budget, Office of Personnel Management, Office of Scientific and Technical Information [Department of Energy], Office of the Director of National Intelligence, and the Smithsonian Institution); the U.S. Supreme Court and the Administrative Office of the U.S. Courts; the District of Columbia; and other federal independent agencies and government corporations.

Officers

Co-Chairs Kathryn Mendenhall and Mark Sweeney, Library of Congress.

Address correspondence to the interim executive director.

Medical Library Association

Executive Director, Carla Funk
65 E. Wacker Place, Suite 1900, Chicago, IL 60601-7298
312-419-9094, fax 312-419-8950, e-mail info@mlahq.org
World Wide Web http://www.mlanet.org

Object

The Medical Library Association (MLA) is a nonprofit professional education organization with nearly 4,000 health sciences information professional members and partners worldwide. MLA provides lifelong educational opportunities, supports a knowledge base of health information research, and works with a global network of partners to promote the importance of high-quality information for improved health to the health care community and the public.

Membership

Memb. (Inst.) 400+; (Indiv.) 3,200+, in more than 50 countries. Institutional members are medical and allied scientific libraries. Individual members are people who are (or were at the time membership was established) engaged in professional library or bibliographic work in medical and allied scientific libraries or people who are interested in medical or allied scientific libraries. Members can be affiliated with one or more of MLA's more than 20 special-interest sections and its regional chapters.

Officers

Pres. Linda Walton. E-mail linda-walton@ uiowa.edu; *Pres.-Elect* Michelle Kraft. E-mail kraftm@ccf.org; *Secy.* Sandra Franklin; *Treas.* Chris Shaffer; *Past Pres.* Dixie Jones.

Directors

Kris Alpi (2016), Melissa De Santis (2017), Angela Dixon (2016), Julia Esparza (2015), Sandra Franklin (2016), Heidi Heilemann (2017), Teresa L. Knott (2017), Jodi L. Philbrick (2016), Chris Shaffer (2015).

Publications

Journal of the Medical Library Association (q.; $190).
MLA News (10 a year; $120).

Music Library Association

8551 Research Way, Suite 180, Middleton, WI 53562
608-836-5825, fax 608-831-8200, e-mail mla@areditions.com
World Wide Web http://www.musiclibraryassoc.org

Object

The Music Library Association provides a professional forum for librarians, archivists, and others who support and preserve the world's musical heritage. To achieve this mission, it

- Provides leadership for the collection and preservation of music and information about music in libraries and archives
- Develops and delivers programs that promote continuing education and professional development in music librarianship
- Ensures and enhances intellectual access to music for all by contributing to the development and revision of national and international codes, formats, and other standards for the bibliographic control of music
- Ensures and enhances access to music for all by facilitating best practices for housing, preserving, and providing access to music
- Promotes legislation that strengthens music library services and universal access to music
- Fosters information literacy and lifelong learning by promoting music reference services, library instruction programs, and publications
- Collaborates with other groups in the music and technology industries, government, and librarianship, to promote its mission and values

Membership

Memb. 1,200+. Dues (Inst.) $135; (Indiv.) $100; (Retired or Assoc.) $70; (Paraprofessional) $55; (Student) $45. (Foreign, add $10.) Year. July–June.

Officers

Pres. Michael Colby. E-mail mdcolby@ucdavis. edu; *V.P./Pres.-Elect* Michael Rogan. E-mail michael.rogan@tufts.edu; *Recording Secy.* Lisa Shiota. E-mail lshi@loc.gov; *Admin. Officer* Paul Cary. E-mail pcary@bw.edu; *Past Pres.* Jerry L. McBride. E-mail jerry.mcbride@ stanford.edu.

Members-at-Large

(2013–2015) Stephanie Bonjack, Michael J. Duffy IV, Rick McRae; (2014–2016) Damian Iseminger, Tracey Rudnick, John Shepard.

Publications

MLA Index and Bibliography Series (irreg.; price varies).
MLA Newsletter (q.; memb.).
MLA Technical Reports (irreg.; price varies).
Music Cataloging Bulletin (mo.; online subscription only, $35).
Notes (q.; indiv. $85; inst. $100).

National Association of Government Archives and Records Administrators

1450 Western Ave., Suite 101, Albany, NY 12203
518-694-8472, World Wide Web http://www.nagara.org

Object

Founded in 1984, the National Association of Government Archives and Records Administrators (NAGARA) is a nationwide association of local, state, and federal archivists and records administrators, and others interested in improved care and management of government records. NAGARA promotes public awareness of government records and archives management programs, encourages interchange of information among government archives and records management agencies, develops and implements professional standards of government records and archival administration, and encourages study and research into records management problems and issues.

Membership

Most NAGARA members are federal, state, and local archival and records management agencies.

Officers

Pres. Tanya Marshall, Vermont State Archives and Records Admin., 1078 U.S. Route 2, Middlesex, Montpelier 05633-7701. Tel. 802-828-0405, fax 802-828-3710, e-mail tanya.marshall @sec.state.vt.us; *Pres.-Elect* Pari Swift, Ohio Attorney General`s Office, 30 E. Broad St., Co-

lumbus 43215-3428. Tel. 614-466-1356, e-mail pari.swift@ohioattorneygeneral.gov; *V.P.* Cathi Carmack, Tennessee State Lib. and Archives, 403 7th Ave. North, Nashville 37243. Tel. 615-253-3468, fax 615-532-5315 e-mail Cathi. Carmack@tn.gov; *Secy.* Jannette Goodall, City of Austin, 301 W. 2 St., P.O. Box 1088, Austin 78767. Tel. 512-974-9045, e-mail jannette. goodall@austintexas.gov; *Treas.* Galen Wilson, National Archives and Records Admin., 3150 Springboro Rd., Dayton, OH 45439-1883. Tel. 937-425-0613, e-mail galen.wilson@nara.gov; *Past Pres.* Daphne DeLeon, Nevada State Lib. and Archives, 100 N. Stewart St., Carson City, NV 89701-4285. Tel. 775-684-3315, fax 775-684-3311, e-mail ddeleon@nevadaculture.org.

Directors

Debbie Bahn, Patricia Franks, Anne Mills, Arian Ravanbakhsh, Shawn Rounds, Michael Sherman, Amelia Winstead.

Publications

Clearinghouse (q.; memb.).

Crossroads (q.; memb.).

Government Records Issues (series).

Preservation Needs in State Archives.

Program Reporting Guidelines for Government Records Programs.

National Federation of Advanced Information Services

Executive Director, Marcie Granahan
801 Compass Way, Suite 201, Annapolis, MD 21401
443-221-2980, fax 443-221-2981, e-mail nfais@nfais.org
World Wide Web http://www.nfais.org

Object

The National Federation of Advanced Information Services (NFAIS) is an international nonprofit membership organization composed of leading information providers. Its membership includes government agencies, nonprofit scholarly societies, private sector businesses, and libraries. NFAIS is committed to promoting the value of credible, high-quality content. It serves all groups that create, aggregate, organize, or facilitate access to such information. In order to improve members' capabilities and to contribute to their ongoing success, NFAIS provides opportunities for education, advocacy, and a forum in which to address common interests. Founded in 1958.

Membership

Memb. 60. Full members are organizations whose main focus is any of the following activities: information creation, organization, aggregation, dissemination, access, or retrieval. Organizations are eligible for associate member status if they do not meet the qualifications for full membership.

Officers

Pres. Chris McCue, CAS; *Pres.-Elect* Mary Sauer-Games, OCLC; *Secy.* Lynn Willis, American Psychological Assn.; *Treas.* Christopher Burghardt, Thomson Reuters; *Past Pres.* Suzanne BeDell, Elsevier.

Directors

Brenda Bailey-Hainer, American Theological Lib. Assn.; Nancy Blair-DeLeon; Chris Cole, National Agricultural Lib.; Don Hagen, National Technical Info. Service; Cynthia Murphy, Thomson Reuters IP Solutions; Deborah Ozga, National Lib. of Medicine; Judith Russell, Univ. of Florida; Judy Salk, Elsevier; Peter Simon, NewsBank.

Staff

Exec. Dir. Marcie Granahan. E-mail mgranahan @nfais.org; *Dir., Professional Development* Jill O'Neill. E-mail jilloneill@nfais.org.

Publications

For a detailed list of NFAIS publications, go to http://www.nfais.org/publications.

National Information Standards Organization (NISO)

Executive Director, Todd Carpenter
3600 Clipper Mill Rd., Suite 302, Baltimore, MD 21211
301-654-2512, fax 410-685-5278, e-mail nisohq@niso.org
World Wide Web http://www.niso.org

Object

The National Information Standards Organization (NISO) fosters the development and maintenance of standards that facilitate the creation, persistent management, and effective interchange of information so that it can be trusted for use in research and learning. To fulfill this mission, NISO engages libraries, publishers, information aggregators, and other organizations that support learning, research, and scholarship through the creation, organization, management, and curation of knowledge. NISO works with intersecting communities of interest and across the entire lifecycle of an information standard. NISO standards apply both traditional and new technologies to the full range of information-related needs, including discovery, retrieval, repurposing, storage, metadata, business information, and preservation.

NISO also develops and publishes recommended practices, technical reports, white papers, and information publications. NISO holds regular educational programs on standards, technologies, and related topics where standards-based solutions can help solve problems. These programs include webinars, online virtual conferences, in-person forums, and teleconferences.

Experts from the information industry, libraries, systems vendors, and publishing participate in the development of NISO standards and recommended practices. The standards are approved by the consensus body of NISO's voting membership, representing libraries, publishers, vendors, government, associations, and private businesses and organizations. NISO is supported by its membership and grants.

NISO is a not-for-profit association accredited by the American National Standards Institute (ANSI) and serves as the U.S. Technical Advisory Group Administrator to ISO/TC 46 Information and Documentation as well as the secretariat for ISO/TC 46/SC 9, Identification and Description.

Membership

Voting Members: 80+. Open to any organization, association, government agency, or company willing to participate in and having substantial concern for the development of NISO standards. Library Standards Alliance Members: 60+. Open to any academic, public, special, or government-supported library interested in supporting the mission of NISO.

Officers

Chair Gerry Grenier, IEEE; *V. Chair/Chair-Elect* Mike Teets, OCLC; *Treas.* Janice Fleming, American Psychological Assn.; *Past Chair* Heather Reid, Copyright Clearance Center.

Directors

Marian Hollingsworth, Thomson Reuters; Evan Owens, Cenveo Publisher Services; Oliver Pesch, EBSCO; Barbara Preece, Loyola/Notre Dame Lib.; Chris Shillum, Elsevier; B. Tommie Usdin, Mulberry Technologies; Tyler Walters, Virginia Tech Univ. Libs.; Keith Webster, Carnegie Mellon Univ.; Jabin White, ITHAKA.

Publications

Information Standards Quarterly (print: $130/year domestic, $165/year international, back issues $36; electronic version available in open access from the NISO website).
NISO Newsline (free e-newsletter released on the first Wednesday of each month; dis-

tributed by e-mail and posted on the NISO website).

Working Group Connection (free quarterly e-newsletter supplement to *Newsline* that provides updates on the activities of NISO's working groups; distributed by e-mail and posted on the NISO website).

For other NISO publications, see the article "National Information Standards Organization

(NISO) Standards" later in Part 6 of this volume.

NISO's published standards, recommended practices, and technical reports are available free of charge as downloadable PDF files from the NISO website (http://www.niso.org). Hardcopy documents are available for sale from the website.

Patent and Trademark Resource Center Association

World Wide Web http://www.ptrca.org

Object

The Patent and Trademark Resource Center Association (PTRCA) provides a support structure for the more than 80 patent and trademark resource centers (PTRCs) affiliated with the U.S. Patent and Trademark Office (USPTO). The association's mission is to discover the interests, needs, opinions, and goals of the PTRCs and to advise USPTO in these matters for the benefit of PTRCs and their users, and to assist USPTO in planning and implementing appropriate services. Founded in 1983 as the Patent Depository Library Advisory Council; name changed to Patent and Trademark Depository Library Association in 1988; became an American Library Association affiliate in 1996. In 2011 the association was renamed the Patent and Trademark Resource Center Association.

Membership

Open to any person employed in a patent and trademark resource center library whose responsibilities include the patent and trademark collection. Affiliate membership is also available. Dues $65 in 2015.

Officers

Pres. Spruce Fraser. E-mail sfraser@slpl.org; *V.P./Pres.-Elect* Karen Kitchens. E-mail karen.kitchens@wyo.gov; *Secy.* Suzanne Reinman. E-mail suzanne.reinman@okstate.edu; *Treas.* Jim Miller. E-mail jmiller2@umd.edu; *Past Pres.* Ran Raider. E-mail ran.raider@wright.edu.

Divisional Representatives

(Academic) Connie Wu (2013–2015). E-mail conniewu@rutgers.edu; Lisha Li (2014–2016). E-mail lisha.li@library.gatech.edu; (Public) Mary Kordyban (2013–2015). E-mail mkordyban@detroitpubliclibrary.org; Irene Yelovich (2014–2016). E-mail yelovichi@carnegielibrary.org.

Publication

PTRCA Journal. Electronic at http://ptrca.org/newsletters. *Ed.* Suzanne Reinman. E-mail suzanne.reinman@okstate.edu.

Polish American Librarians Association

President, Ronald V. Stoch
P.O. Box 7232, Prospect Heights, IL 60070-7232
World Wide Web http://www.palalib.org

Object

The mission of the Polish American Librarians Association (PALA) is to positively affect services provided to library patrons of Polish descent and individuals interested in Polish culture.

The organization's vision is

- To enhance professional knowledge by developing forums for discussion and networks of communication among library staff working with Polish collections and patrons of Polish origin
- To promote understanding and respect among all cultures by expanding the means to access reliable, current information about Polish and Polish American culture
- To promote Polish American librarianship
- To provide opportunities for cooperation with other library associations

Founded in 2009.

Membership

Membership is open to librarians, students of library schools, library support staff, and others who support the vision of PALA. Dues (Regular) $25; (Support Staff, Student, Retired, Unemployed) $15.

Officers

Pres. Ronald V. Stoch, 1827 N. 74 Ct., Elmwood Park, IL 60707. Tel. 708-453-9274, e-mail yukon981973@att.net; *V.P./Pres.-Elect* Joanna Klos, Wood Dale Public Lib. Dist., 520 N. Wood Dale Rd., Wood Dale, IL 60191. Tel. 630-766-6762, fax 630-766-5715, e-mail jklos@wooddalelibrary.org; *Secy.* Pamela Cipkowski, Creek Public Lib. Dist., 1405 S. Park Ave., Streamwood, IL 60107. Tel. 630-483-4946, e-mail secretary@palalib.org; *Treas.* Malgorzata Bylinska, Arlington Heights Memorial Lib., 500 N. Dunton Ave., Arlington Heights, IL 60004. Tel. 847-870-4401; *Past Pres.* Elizabeth Marszalik, Oak Park Public Lib., 834 Lake St., Oak Park, IL 60301. Tel. 708-697-6917, e-mail emarszalik@oppl.org; *Dirs.-at-Large* Diane Bartkowiak, Wanda Jacak, Grazyna Krzycka-Langguth, Felice E. Maciejewski, Renata Schneider; *Exec. Dir.* Leonard Kniffel, 2743 N. Greenview Ave., Chicago, IL 60614. Tel. 773-935-3635, e-mail lkniffe@sbcglobal.net.

REFORMA (National Association to Promote Library and Information Services to Latinos and the Spanish-Speaking)

President, Silvia Cisneros
P.O. Box 832, Anaheim, CA 92815
Tel. 209-379-5637, e-mail info@reforma.org
World Wide Web http://www.reforma.org

Object

Promoting library services to the Spanish-speaking for nearly 40 years, REFORMA, an affiliate of the American Library Association, works in a number of areas to advance the development of library collections that include Spanish-language and Latino-oriented materials; the recruitment of more bilingual and bicultural professionals and support staff; the development of library services and programs that meet the needs of the Latino community; the establishment of a national network among individuals who share its goals; the education of the U.S. Latino population in regard to the availability and types of library services; and lobbying efforts to preserve existing library resource centers serving the interest of Latinos.

Membership

Memb. 800+. Membership is open to any person who is supportive of the goals and objectives of REFORMA.

Officers

Pres. Silvia Cisneros, Santa Ana Public Lib., 26 Civic Center Plaza, Santa Ana, CA 92701. Tel. 714-647-5244, e-mail president@reforma. org; *V.P./Pres.-Elect* Beatriz Guevara, Charlotte Mecklenburg Lib./Independence Regional Lib., 6000 Conference Drive, Charlotte, NC 28212. Tel. 704-416-4833, e-mail vice-president@ reforma.org; *Secy./Recorder* Louis Munoz, Brooklyn Public Lib. Tel. 718-230-2417, e-mail secretary@reforma.org; *Treas.* Sarah Dahlen, California State Univ., Monterey Bay. Tel. 831-582-4432, e-mail treasurer@reforma. org; *Memb.-at-Large* Cristina Ramirez, Richmond (Virginia) Public Lib. Tel. 804-646-8488, e-mail cristina.ramirez@richmondgov. com; *Past Pres.* Isabel Espinal, W. E. B. Du Bois Lib., Univ. of Massachusetts. Tel. 413-545-6817, e-mail past-president@reforma.org.

Committees

Pura Belpré Award. Ana E. Pavon.
Children's and Young Adult Services. Lucía González, Celia Perez.
Education. Lori S. Mestre.
Finance. Isabel Espinal.
Information Technology. Juan Carlos Rodríguez.
International Relations. Ady Huertas.
Legislative. Angélica Fortín, Millie González.
Librarian of the Year Award. Roxana Benavides.
Membership. Juan Carlos Rodriguez, Jose Miguel Ruiz.
Nominations. Maria Kramer.
Organizational Development. Martha A. Parker.
Program. Beatriz Guevara.
National Conferences. Jacqueline Ayala, Loanis Menéndez-Cuesta
Public Relations. David Lopez.
Recruitment and Mentoring. Minerva Alaniz.
Scholarship. Mary A. Donley.
Translations. Nicanor Diaz.

Publication

REFORMA (online newsletter).

Meetings

General membership and board meetings take place at the American Library Association Midwinter Meeting and Annual Conference.

Society for Scholarly Publishing

Executive Director, Ann Mehan Crosse
10200 W. 44 Ave., Suite 304, Wheat Ridge, CO 80033
303-422-3914, fax 720-881-6101, e-mail info@sspnet.org or amcrosse@kellencompany.com
World Wide Web http://www.sspnet.org

Object

To draw together individuals involved in the process of scholarly publishing. This process requires successful interaction of the many functions performed within the scholarly community. The Society for Scholarly Publishing (SSP) provides the leadership for such interaction by creating opportunities for the exchange of information and opinions among scholars, editors, publishers, librarians, printers, booksellers, and all others engaged in scholarly publishing.

Membership

Memb. 1,180+. Open to all with an interest in the scholarly publishing process and dissemination of information. Dues (New Member) $160; (Indiv. Renewal) $175; (Libn.) $85; (Early Career) $80; (Student) $40; (Supporting Organization) $1,750; (Sustaining Organization) $4,100. Year. Jan.–Dec.

Executive Committee

Pres. Howard Ratner, *CHOR, Inc.* E-mail hratner @chorusaccess.org; *Pres.-Elect* Ann Michael, DeltaThink. E-mail ann.michael@deltathink. com; *Past Pres.* Kent Anderson, AAAS/Science. Email kanderso@aaas.org; *Secy./Treas.* Byron Laws, vPrompt eServices. Email byron @vprompt.com.

Directors

Jocelyn Dawson, Emilie Delquie, Marian Hollingsworth, Michelle Norell, Jennifer Pesanelli, Jean Shipman, David Smith, Heather Staines, Greg Suprock.

Meetings

An annual meeting is held in late May/early June. SSP also conducts a Librarian Focus Group (February), the Spring Seminar Series (May/early June), and the Fall Seminar Series (September).

Society of American Archivists

Executive Director, Nancy P. Beaumont
17 N. State St., Suite 1425, Chicago, IL 60602
866-722-7858, 312-606-0722, fax 312-606-0728, e-mail nbeaumont@archivists.org
World Wide Web http://www.archivists.org

Object

Founded in 1936, the Society of American Archivists (SAA) is North America's oldest and largest national archival professional association. Representing more than 6,000 individual and institutional members, SAA promotes the value and diversity of archives and archivists and is the preeminent source of professional resources and the principal communication hub for American archivists.

Membership

Memb. 6,200+. Dues (Indiv.) $50 to $250, graduated according to salary; (Assoc. domestic) $100; (Student or Bridge) $50; (Inst.) $300; (Sustaining Inst.) $550.

Officers

Pres. Kathleen Roe, Troy Archival Consulting. Tel. 518-961-1550, e-mail kathleen.d.roe@gmail.com; *V.P.* Dennis Meissner, Minnesota Historical Society; *Treas.* Mark Duffy, Archives of the Episcopal Church.

Staff

Exec. Dir. Nancy Beaumont. E-mail nbeaumont@archivists.org; *Admin., Web and Information Systems* Matt Black. E-mail mblack@archivists.org; *Dir., Publishing* Teresa Brinati. E-mail tbrinati@archivists.org; *Educ. Program Coord.* Mia Capodilupo. E-mail mcapodilupo@archivists.org; *Dir., Educ.* Solveig De Sutter. E-mail sdesutter@archivists.org; *Dir., Finance and Admin.* Peter Carlson. E-mail pcarlson@archivists.org; *Mgr., Service Center* Carlos Salgado. E-mail csalgado@archivists.org; *Program Coord.* René Craig. E-mail rcraig@archivists.org; *Editorial and Production Coord.* Anne Hartman. E-mail ahartman@archivists.org; *Educ. Program Coord.* Ania Jaroszek. E-mail ajaroszek@archivists.org; *Service Center Reps.* Lee Gonzalez. E-mail lgonzalez@archivists.org; Jeanette Spears. E-mail jspears@archivists.org.

Publications

American Archivist (2 a year) individual print or online edition, $169; print and online, $199; institutional, $209 print or online, $259 print and online). *Ed.* Gregory Hunter; *Reviews Ed.* Amy Cooper Cary.
Archival Outlook (bi-mo.; memb.). *Eds.* Teresa Brinati, Anne Hartman.

Software and Information Industry Association

1090 Vermont Ave. N.W., Washington, DC 20005-4095
202-289-7442, fax 202-289-7097
World Wide Web http://www.siia.net

The Software and Information Industry Association (SIIA) was formed January 1, 1999, through the merger of the Software Publishers Association (SPA) and the Information Industry Association (IIA).

Membership

Memb. 800+ companies. Open to companies that develop software and digital information content. For details on membership and dues, see the SIIA website, http://www.siia.net.

Staff

Pres. Kenneth Wasch. E-mail kwasch@siia. net; *CFO* Tom Meldrum; *Gen. Counsel and Senior V.P.* Keith Kupferschmid; *Senior V.P.* Tom Davin; *V.P.s* Jennifer Baranowski, Karen Billings, Eileen Bramlet, Rhianna Collier, Eric Fredell, Luis Hernandez, Mark MacCarthy, Michael Marchesano; *Senior Dirs.* Matthew Kinsman, David LeDuc, Mark Schneiderman, Katrina Styles-Hunt.

Board of Directors

Ann Amstutz-Hayes, Scholastic; Richard Atkinson, Adobe Systems; Simon Beale; Mark Bohannon, Red Hat; Cynthia Braddon (chair), McGraw Hill Financial; Antoinette Bush, Dow Jones; Denise Elliott, Kiplinger Washington Editors; Kate Friedrich, Thomson Reuters; Randall Hopkins, NASDAQ OMX; Stephen Laster, McGraw Hill Education; Bernard McKay, Intuit; Jason Mahler, Oracle; Douglas Manoni, SourceMedia; Steve Manzo, Reed Elsevier; Peter Marney, Wiley; Chuck Melley, Pearson; Timothy Sheehy, IBM; Johanna Shelton, Google; Neal Vitale, 1105 Media; Ken Wasch, SIIA.

SPARC

Executive Director, Heather Joseph
21 Dupont Circle, Suite 800, Washington, DC 20036
202-296-2296, fax 202-872-0884, e-mail sparc@arl.org
World Wide Web http://www.sparc.arl.org

SPARC, the Scholarly Publishing and Academic Resources Coalition, is a global organization that promotes expanded sharing of scholarship in the networked digital environment. It is committed to faster and wider sharing of outputs of the research process to increase the impact of research, fuel the advancement of knowledge, and increase the return on research investments.

Developed by the Association of Research Libraries, SPARC has become a catalyst for change. Its pragmatic focus is to stimulate the emergence of new scholarly communication models that expand the dissemination of scholarly research and reduce financial pressures on libraries. Action by SPARC in collaboration with stakeholders—including authors, publishers, and libraries—builds on the unprecedented opportunities created by the networked digital environment to advance the conduct of scholarship.

SPARC's role in stimulating change focuses on

- Educating stakeholders about the problems facing scholarly communication and the opportunities for them to play a role in achieving positive change

- Advocating policy changes that advance scholarly communication and explicitly recognize that dissemination of scholarship is an essential, inseparable component of the research process
- Incubating demonstrations of new publishing and sustainability models that benefit scholarship and academe

SPARC is a visible advocate for changes in scholarly communication that benefit more than the academic community alone. Founded in 1997, it has expanded to represent more than 800 academic and research libraries in North America, the United Kingdom, Europe, and Japan.

Membership

SPARC membership is open to international academic and research institutions, organizations, and consortia that share an interest in creating a more open and diverse marketplace for scholarly communication. Dues are scaled by membership type and budget. For more information, visit SPARC's website at http://www.sparc.arl.org/membership, SPARC Europe at http://www.sparceurope.org, or SPARC Japan at http://www.nii.ac.jp/sparc.

Publications

HowOpenIsIt? Open Access Spectrum (2014 revision) by Greg Tananbaum.

North American Campus-Based Open Access Funds: A Five-Year Progress Report (2014) by Greg Tananbaum.

Article-Level Metrics: A SPARC Primer (2013) by Greg Tananbaum.

The Collective Provision of Open Access Resources (2013) by Raym Crow in collaboration with Knowledge Exchange.

Implementing an Open Data Policy (2013) by Greg Tananbaum.

You've Signed the Boycott, Now What? A SPARC Guide for Campus Action (2012) (http://www.arl.org/sparc/bm~doc/sparc_boycott_next_steps.pdf).

Open-Access Journal Publishing Resource Index (2011) by Raym Crow.

Library Publishing Services: Strategies for Success (2011) by Raym Crow, October Ivins, Allyson Mower, Daureen Nesdill, Mark Newton, Julie Speer, and Charles Watkinson.

Library Publishing Services: Strategies for Success Report, Version 1.0 (2011) by Raym Crow, October Ivins, Allyson Mower, Daureen Nesdill, Mark Newton, Julie Speer, and Charles Watkinson.

Campus-Based Open-Access Publishing Funds: A Practical Guide to Design and Implementation (2010) by Greg Tananbaum.

Campus-Based Publishing Partnerships: A Guide to Critical Issues (2009) by Raym Crow.

Income Models for Open Access: An Overview of Current Practice (2009) by Raym Crow.

The Right to Research: The Student Guide to Opening Access to Scholarship (2008), part of a campaign to engage students on the issue of research access.

Greater Reach for Research: Expanding Readership Through Digital Repositories (2008), the initiative to educate faculty on the benefits of open repositories and emerging research access policies.

Author Rights (2006), an educational initiative and introduction to the SPARC Author Addendum, a legal form that enables authors of journal articles to modify publishers' copyright transfer agreements and allow authors to keep key rights to their articles.

"Open Access News Blog," daily updates on the worldwide movement for open access to science and scholarship, written by Peter Suber and cosponsored by SPARC.

SPARC Open Access Newsletter, a monthly roundup of developments relating to open access publishing, written by Peter Suber.

SPARC e-news, SPARC's monthly newsletter featuring SPARC activities, an industry roundup, upcoming workshops and events, and articles relating to developments in scholarly communication.

Publishing Cooperatives: An Alternative for Society Publishers (2006) by Raym Crow.

Sponsorships for Nonprofit Scholarly and Scientific Journals: A Guide to Defining and Negotiating Successful Sponsorships (2005) by Raym Crow.

A more-complete list of SPARC publications, including brochures, articles, and guides, is available at http://www.sparc.arl.org/resources.

Special Libraries Association (SLA)

Interim Executive Director, Cindy Shamel
Interim Strategic Director Ulla de Stricker
331 S. Patrick St., Alexandria, VA 22314
703-647-4900, fax 703-647-4901, e-mail resources@sla.org
World Wide Web http://www.sla.org

Mission

The Special Libraries Association promotes and strengthens its members through learning, advocacy, and networking initiatives.

Strategic Vision

SLA is a global association of information and knowledge professionals who are employed in every sector of the economy. Its members thrive where data, information, and knowledge intersect, and its strategic partners support SLA because they believe in the association's mission and the future of its members. SLA's goal is to support information professionals as they contribute, in their varied and evolving roles, to the opportunities and achievements of organizations, communities, and society.

Membership

Memb. 9,000+ in 75 countries. Dues (Organizational) $750; (Indiv.) $114–$200; (Student/ Retired/Salary less than $18,000 income per year) $40.

Officers

Pres. Jill Strand. E-mail jillstrand@gmail. com; *Pres.-Elect* Tom Rink. E-mail rink@ nsuok.edu; *Treas.* John DiGilio. E-mail jdigilio @reedsmith.com; *Chapter Cabinet Chair* James King. E-mail james.king@nih.gov; *Chapter Cabinet Chair-Elect* Kim Silk. E-mail kimberly.silk@rotman.utoronto.ca; *Div. Cabinet Chair* Juliane Schneider. E-mail juliane _schneider@hms.harvard.edu; *Div. Cabinet Chair-Elect* Ruth Kneale. E-mail rkneale@ nso.edu; *Past Pres.* Kate Arnold. E-mail kate arnold64@yahoo.co.uk.

Directors

Officers; Kevin Adams, Catherine Lavalee-Welch; Moy McIntosh, Bethan Ruddock.

Publication

Information Outlook (memb., nonmemb. $125/ yr.)

Theatre Library Association

c/o New York Public Library for the Performing Arts
40 Lincoln Center Plaza, New York, NY 10023
E-mail theatrelibraryassociation@gmail.com
World Wide Web http://www.tla-online.org

Object

To further the interests of collecting, preserving, and using theater, cinema, and performing arts materials in libraries, museums, and private collections. Founded in 1937.

Membership

Memb. 300. Dues (Indiv.) $25–$50, (Inst.) $75–$95. Year. Jan.–Dec.

Officers

Pres. Nancy Friedland, Columbia Univ.; *V.P.* Angela Weaver, Univ. of Washington; *Exec. Secy.* Laurie Murphy, New York Univ.; *Treas.* Colleen Reilly, Slippery Rock Univ.

Executive Board

Noreen Barnes, Diana Bertolini, Jody Blake, John Calhoun, Leahkim Gannett, Tanisha Jones, Beth Kattelman, Diana King, Doug Reside, Kenneth Schlesinger, Morgen Stevens-Garmon, Joseph Tally, Annemarie van Roessel; *Honorary* Louis A. Rachow; *Legal Counsel* Georgia Harper.

Publications

Broadside (3 a year; memb.). *Ed.* Angela Weaver.
Performing Arts Resources (occasional; memb.).
Membership Directory (annual; memb.). *Ed.* Laurie Murphy.

Committee Chairs

Book Awards. Linda Miles, Tiffany Nixon.
Conference Planning. Angela Weaver.
Membership. Beth Kattelman.
Nominating. Kenneth Schlesinger.
Professional Awards. Francesca Marini.
Publications. Leahkim Gannett.
Strategic Planning. Angela Weaver.
Website Editorial. David Nochimson, Angela Weaver.

Urban Libraries Council

CEO and President, Susan B. Benton
125 S. Wacker Drive, Suite 1050, Chicago, IL 60606
312-676-0999, fax 312-676-0950, e-mail info@urbanlibraries.org
World Wide Web http://www.urbanlibraries.org

Object

Since 1971 the Urban Libraries Council (ULC) has worked to strengthen public libraries as an essential part of urban life. A member organization of North America's leading public library systems, ULC serves as a forum for research widely recognized and used by public and private sector leaders. Its members are thought leaders dedicated to leadership, innovation, and the continuous transformation of libraries to meet community needs.

ULC's work focuses on helping public libraries to identify and utilize skills and strategies that match the challenges of the 21st century.

Membership

Membership is open to public libraries and to corporate partners specializing in library-related materials and services. The organization also offers associate memberships.

Officers

Chair Karen "Kari" Glover; *V. Chair/Chair-Elect* Matthew K. Poland; *Secy./Treas.* Jan Harder; *Past Chair* Melanie Huggins; *Member-at-Large* Michael Sherrod.

Officers serve one-year terms, members of the executive board two-year terms. New officers are elected and take office at the summer annual meeting of the council.

Executive Board

Ruth Anna, Jill Bourne, Rhea Brown Lawson, Irvin Mayfield, William H. Meadows, Vailey Oehlke, Mary Blankenship Pointer, Gloria Rubio-Cortés, Gary A. Wasdin, Ed Williams, Rashad Young.

State, Provincial, and Regional Library Associations

The associations in this section are organized under three headings: United States, Canada, and Regional. Both the United States and Canada are represented under Regional associations.

United States

Alabama

Memb. 1,200. Publication. *The Alabama Librarian* (q.).

Pres. Wendy Stephens, 204 California St., Huntsville 35801. Tel. 256-520-1878, e-mail wendysteadmanstephens@gmail.com; *Pres.-Elect* Paula Laurita, Athens-Limestone Public Lib., 405 E. South St., Athens 35611. Tel. 256-232-1233, e-mail drago.biblioteche@gmail.com; *Secy.* James Gilbreath, Brown Mackie College Lib., 105 Vulcan Rd., Suite 400, Birmingham 35209. Tel. 205-909-1554, e-mail jgilbreath@brownmackie.edu; *Treas.* John Gantt, Auburn Univ. at Montgomery, P.O. Box 244023, Montgomery 36124-4023. Tel. 334-244-3781, e-mail jgantt2@aum.edu; *Past Pres.* Jeff Simpson, Lib./Wallace Hall, 501 University Ave., Troy 36082. Tel. 334-670-3257, e-mail jsimpson25000@outlook.com; *Assn. Admin.* Angela Moore.

Address correspondence to the association, 6030 Monticello Drive, Montgomery 36117. Tel. 334-414-0113, e-mail allibraryassoc@gmail.com.

World Wide Web http://allanet.org.

Alaska

Memb. 450+. Publication. *Newspoke* (q.) (online at http://akla.org/newspoke).

Pres. Karen Jensen. E-mail kljensen@alaska.edu; *Pres.-Elect* Patty Brown. E-mail director@haineslibrary.org; *Secy.* Maeghan Kearney. E-mail maeghan.kearney@alaska.gov; *Interim Treas.* Robert Barr. E-mail robert_barr@juneau.lib.ak.us; *Conference Coords.* MJ Grande. E-mail mjgrande@juneau.lib.ak.us; Linda Wynne. E-mail lindaleewynne@gmail.com; *Past Pres.* Stacey Glaser. E-mail sglaser@alaska.edu; *Exec. Officer* Patty Linville. E-mail eo@akla.org.

Address correspondence to the secretary, Alaska Lib. Assn., P.O. Box 81084, Fairbanks 99708. E-mail akla@akla.org.

World Wide Web http://www.akla.org.

Arizona

Memb. 1,000. Term of Office. Nov.–Nov. Publication. *AzLA Newsletter* (mo.).

Pres. Dan Stanton, Arizona State Univ. Libs. Tel. 480-965-1798, e-mail danton@asu.edu or president@azla.org; *Pres.-Elect* Amber Mathewson, Pima County Public Lib. Tel. 520-594-5650, e-mail amber.mathewson@pima.gov; *Secy.* Joyce Martin, Labriola National American Indian Data Center, ASU Libs. Tel. 480-965-0298, e-mail joyce.martin@asu.edu; *Treas.* Denise Keller, Pinal County Lib. Dist., Florence 85132. Tel. 520-866-6457, e-mail denise.keller@pinalcountyaz.gov; *Past Pres.* Ann Boles, Wickenburg Public Lib. Tel. 928-533-2276, e-mail ann.boles@gmail.com; *Exec. Secy.* Debbie J. Hanson, Arizona Lib. Assn., 950 E. Baseline Rd., No. 104-1025, Tempe 85283. Tel. 480-609-3999, fax 480-609-3939, e-mail admin@azla.org.

Address correspondence to the executive secretary.

World Wide Web http://www.azla.org.

Arkansas

Memb. 600. Publication. *Arkansas Libraries* (bi-mo.).

Pres. Devona Pendergrass, Mountain Home H.S. Tel. 870-425-2541, e-mail dpendergrass@mtnhome.k12.ar.us; *V.P./Pres.-Elect* Jud Copeland, Univ. of Central Arkansas, Conway. Tel. 501-499-5414, e-mail jcopeland@uca.edu; *Secy./Treas.* Jamie Melson, Central Arkansas Lib. System, Little Rock. Tel. 501-918-3074, e-mail jamiem@cals.lib.ar.us; *Past Pres.* Trish Miller, Remington College, Little Rock. Tel. 501-312-0007, e-mail trish.miller@remington college.edu; *Exec. Admin.* Lynda Hampel, Arkansas Lib. Assn., P.O. Box 958, Benton 72018-0958. Tel. 501-860-7585, fax 501-778-4014, e-mail arlib2@sbcglobal.net.

Address correspondence to the executive administrator.

World Wide Web http://www.arlib.org.

California

Memb. 2,500. Publication. *CLA Insider* (online).

Pres. Robert Karatsu, Rancho Cucamonga Public Lib. E-mail robert.karatsu@cityofrc.us; *V.P./Pres.-Elect* Misty Jones, San Diego Public Lib. System. E-mai lmnjones@sandiego.gov; *Secy.* Hillary Theyer, Torrance Public Lib. E-mail librarylady16@yahoo.com; *Treas.* Beth Wrenn-Estes, San José State Univ. E-mail bwestes@mac.com; *Past Pres.* Deborah Doyle, CALTAC. E-mail zorrah@gmail.com; *Interim Exec. Dir.* Natalie Cole. Tel. 650-376-0886, e-mail execdir@cla-net.org or ncole@cla-net.org

Address correspondence to the executive director, California Lib. Assn., 2471 Flores St., San Mateo 94403. Tel. 650-376-0886, fax 650-539-2341.

World Wide Web http://www.cla-net.org.

Colorado

Pres. Kari May, Elbert County Lib. Dist. E-mail director@elbertcountylibrary.org; *V.P./ Pres.-Elect* Joanna Primus, Community College of Aurora. E-mail joanna.primus@ccaurora.edu; *Secy.* Dinah Kress, Prairie Hills Elementary School. E-mail dinah.kress@asd20.org; *Treas.* Mike Varnet, Pikes Peak Lib. Dist. E-mail mvarnet@ppld.org; *Past Pres.* Stephen Sweeney. E-mail stephen.sweeney@archden.org; *Business Mgr.* Jesse Haynes; *Business Admin.* Amanda Rewerts.

Address correspondence to the president, Colorado Assn. of Libs., 12011 Tejon St., Suite 700, Westminster 80234. Tel. 303-463-6400, fax 303-458-0002.

World Wide Web http://www.cal-webs.org.

Connecticut

Memb. 1,000+. Term of Office. July–June. Publication. *CLA Today* (online). E-mail editor@ctlibrarians.org.

Pres. Dawn La Valle, Connecticut State Lib., 231 Capitol Ave., Hartford 06106. Tel. 860-757-6665, e-mail dawn.lavalle@ct.gov; *V.P./Pres.-Elect* Beth A Crowley, Scranton Memorial Lib., 801 Boston Post Rd., Madison 06443. Tel. 203 245-7365, e-mail crowleyb@madisonct.org; *Recording Secy.* Michele Martin, Greenwich Lib., 101 W. Putnam Ave., Greenwich 06830. Tel. 203-625-6533, e-mail mmartin@greenwichlibrary.org; *Treas.* Nicole Greco, Milford Public Lib., 57 New Haven Ave., Milford 06460. Tel. 203-783-3307, e-mail ngreco@ci.milford.ct.us; *Past Pres.* Richard Conroy, Essex Lib. Assn., 33 West Ave., Essex 06426. Tel. 860-767-1560, e-mail rconroy@essexlib.org.

Address correspondence to Connecticut Lib. Assn., 234 Court St., Middletown 06457. Tel. 860-346-2444, fax 860-344-9199, e-mail cla@ctlibrarians.org.

World Wide Web http://www.ctlibrary association.org.

Delaware

Memb. 200+. Publication. *DLA Bulletin* (online only).

Pres. Beth Borene, Bear Public Lib., 101 Governors Place, Bear 19701. Tel. 302-838-3300, e-mail eborene@nccde.org; *V.P.* Laurel Ferris, John Eugene Derrickson Memorial Lib., Delaware Technical Community College, 333 N. Shipley St., Wilmington 19801. Tel. 302-573-5431, e-mail lferris@dtcc.edu; *Secy.* Janice Haney, Appoquinimink H.S., 1080 Bunker Hill Rd., Middletown 19709. E-mail janice.haney@appo.k12.de.us; *Treas.* Ed Goyda, Lewes Public Lib., 111 Adams Ave., Lewes 19958. E-mail ed.goyda@lib.de.us; *Past Pres.* Christine Payne, Appoquinimink H.S., 1080 Bunker Hill Rd., Middletown 19709. Tel. 302-449-3840, e-mail christine.payne@appo.k12.de.us; *Exec. Dir.* Cathay Keough, Delaware Div. of Libs., 121 Martin Luther King, Jr. Blvd. N., Dover 19901. Tel. 302-983-1430, e-mail cathay.keough@lib.de.us.

World Wide Web http://www2.lib.udel.edu/dla.

District of Columbia

Memb. 300+. Term of Office. July–June. Publication. *Capital Librarian* (s. ann.).

Pres. Christina Bailey. E-mail dclapresident @gmail.com; *V.P./Pres.-Elect* Julius C. Jefferson, Jr. E-mail dclavicepresident@gmail.com; *Secy.* Victor Benitez. E-mail dclasecretary@ gmail.com; *Treas.* TaChalla Ferris. E-mail dclatreasurer@gmail.com; *Past Pres.* Amanda J. Wilson.

Address correspondence to the association, Box 14177, Benjamin Franklin Sta., Washington 20044.

World Wide Web http://www.dcla.org.

Florida

Memb. (Indiv.) 1,000+. Publication. *Florida Libraries* (s. ann.).

Pres. (2013–2016) Linda McCarthy, Florida Virtual Campus. Tel. 850-922-6044, e-mail lmccarthy@flvc.org; *V.P./Pres.-Elect (2014– 2017)* Gene Coppola, Palm Harbor Lib. Tel. 727-784-3332 ext. 3001, e-mail gene@phlib. org; *Secy. (2013–2015)* Anne Haywood, Bruton Memorial Lib. Tel. 813-757-9215, e-mail ahaywood@plantcitygov.com; *Treas. (2014– 2016)* Sarah Hammill, Florida International Univ. Tel. 305-348-3009, e-mail hammills@ fiu.edu; *Past Pres.* Gladys Roberts, Polk County Lib. Cooperative. Tel. 863-519-7958, e-mail gladys.roberts@mypclc.info; *Exec. Dir.* Martina Brawer, Florida Lib. Assn., 541 E. Tennessee St., Suite 103, Tallahassee 32308. Tel. 850-270-9205, fax 850-270-9405, e-mail martina. brawer@comcast.net.

Address correspondence to the executive director.

World Wide Web http://www.flalib.org.

Georgia

Memb. 800+. Publication. *Georgia Library Quarterly. Ed.* Virginia Feher, Univ. of North Georgia. Tel. 706-310-6305, e-mail virginia. feher@ung.edu.

Pres. Lace Keaton, Newton County Lib. System; *1st V.P./Pres.-Elect* Cathy Jeffrey, Clayton State Univ. Tel. 678-466-4336, e-mail cathy jeffrey@clayton.edu; *2nd V.P./Membership Chair* Karen Manning, Georgia Tech Lib. and Info. Center. Tel. 404-385-8353, e-mail km17@ mail.gatech.edu; *Secy.* Ariel Turner, Horace W. Sturgis Lib., Kennesaw State Univ. Tel. 470-578-6273, e-mail aturne93@kennesaw. edu; *Treas.* Ashley Dupuy, Kennesaw State

Univ.; *Past Pres.* Susan Morris, Univ. of Georgia. Tel. 706-542-0642, e-mail smorris@uga. edu.

Address correspondence to the president, Georgia Lib. Assn., P.O. Box 793, Rex 30273-0793.

World Wide Web http://gla.georgialibraries. org.

Hawaii

Memb. 250. Publication. HLA Blog, "Hawaii Library Association" (http://hawaiilibraryasso-ciation.blogspot.com).

Pres. Tim Arnold, Meader Lib., Hawaii Pacific Univ. Tel. 808-544-9330, e-mail tarnold@ hpu.edu; *V.P./Pres.-Elect* Kimball Boone, Brigham Young Univ.–Hawaii; *Secy.* Susan Hammer, Mid-Pacific Institute; *Treas.* Jude Y. Yang, University of Hawaii at Manoa; *Past Pres.* Christina Abelardo, Sgt. Yano Lib., Schofield Barracks. E-mail christinathelibrarian@ gmail.com.

Address correspondence to the association at P.O. Box 4441, Honolulu 96812-4441 or by e-mail at hawaii.library.association@gmail. com.

World Wide Web http://hla.chaminade.edu.

Idaho

Memb. 420. Term of Office. Oct.–Oct.

Pres. Becky Proctor, West Junior H.S., 8371 W. Salt Creek Court, Boise 83709. Tel. 208-854-6456, e-mail becky.proctor@boiseschools. org; *V.P./ Pres.-Elect* Kristi Haman, Ada Community Lib., Boise 83709. Tel. 208-362-0181 ext.124, e-mail khaman@adalib.org; *Secy.* Kathleen McVey, Meridian Lib. Dist.,1326 W. Cherry Lane, Meridian 83642. Tel. 208-888-4451, e-mail kathleen@mld.org; *Treas.* Danielle Persinger, College of Western Idaho, P.O. Box 3010, Nampa 83653. Tel. 208-562-2154, e-mail daniellepersinger@cwidaho.cc; *Past Pres.* Rami Attebury, Univ. of Idaho Lib., P.O. Box 442350, Moscow 88344-2350. Tel. 208-885-2503, e-mail rattebur@uidaho.edu.

Address correspondence to the association, P.O. Box 8533, Moscow 83844.

World Wide Web http://www.idaholibraries. org.

Illinois

Memb. 3,500. Publication. *ILA Reporter* (bi-mo.).

Pres. Jeannie Dilger, La Grange Public Lib., 10 W. Cossitt Ave., La Grange 60525. Tel. 708-215-3273, fax 708-352-1620, e-mail dilgerj@lagrangelibrary.org; *V.P./Pres.-Elect* Betsy Adamowski, Wheaton Public Lib., 225 N. Cross St. Wheaton 60187-5376. Tel. 630-668-1374, fax 630-668-1465, e-mail betsy@wheatonlibrary.org; *Treas.* Leora Siegel, Lenhardt Lib., Chicago Botanic Garden, 1000 Lake Cook Rd., Glencoe 60022. Tel. 847-835-8202, fax 847-835-6885, e-mail lsiegel@chicagobotanic.org; *Past Pres.* Su Erickson, Robert Morris Univ., 905 Meridan Lake Drive, Aurora 60504. Tel. 630-375-8209, fax 630-375-8193, e-mail serickson@robertmorris.edu; *Exec. Dir.* Robert P. Doyle, Illinois Lib. Assn., 33 W. Grand Ave., Suite 401, Chicago 60654-6799. Tel. 312-644-1896, fax 312-644-1899, e-mail doyle@ila.org.

Address correspondence to the executive director.

World Wide Web http://www.ila.org.

Indiana

Indiana Lib. Federation. Memb. 2,000+. Publications. *Indiana Libraries* (s. ann.). *Ed.* Kristi Palmer, IUPUI Univ. Lib., 755 W. Michigan, Indianapolis 46202. Tel. 317-274-8230, e-mail klpalmer@iupui.edu; *Focus on Indiana Libraries* (11 a year, memb.). *Ed.* Diane J. Bever, Kokomo Lib., Indiana Univ., 2300 S. Washington St., P.O. Box 9003, Kokomo 46904-9003. Tel. 765-455-9345, fax 765-455-9276, e-mail dbever@iuk.edu.

Pres. Beverly Gard, Hancock County Public Lib., Greenfield. Tel. 317-462-5141, e-mail bevjgard@gmail.com; *Pres.-Elect* Robyn Young, Avon Community School Corp., 7575 E. CR 150 S., Avon 46123. Tel. 317-544-5031, e-mail rryoung@avon-schools.org; *Secy.* Kathy Burnette, Discovery Middle School, Granger. Tel. 574-674-6010, e-mail teach46530@gmail.com; *Treas.* Amy Harshbarger, Logan Lib., Rose-Hulman Institute of Technology, Terre Haute. E-mail harshbarg@rose-hulman.edu; *Past Pres.* Marcia Learned Au, Evansville Vanderburgh Public Lib., Evansville. E-mail mau@evpl.org; *Exec. Dir.* Susan Akers. Tel. 317-257-2040 ext. 101, e-mail sakers@ilfonline.org.

Address correspondence to Indiana Lib. Federation, 941 E. 86 St., Suite 260, Indianapolis 46240. Tel. 317-257-2040, fax 317-257-1389.

World Wide Web http://www.ilfonline.org.

Iowa

Memb. 1,500. Publication. *Catalyst* (bi-mo.).

Pres. Sarah Willeford; *V.P./Pres.-Elect* Duncan Stewart; *Secy.* Marilyn Murphy; *Treas.* Nancy Trask; *Past Pres.* Mary Heinzman.

Address correspondence to the association, 6919 Vista Drive, West Des Moines 50266. Tel. 515-282-8192.

World Wide Web http://www.iowalibraryassociation.org.

Kansas

Kansas Lib. Assn. Memb. 1,500. Term of Office. July–June. Publication. *KLA Connects* (q.).

Pres. Terri Summey, Emporia State Univ. Libs. and Archives, Campus Box 4051, Emporia 66801. Tel. 620-341-5058, e-mail tsummey@emporia.edu; *V.P.* Kelly Fann, Lawrence Public Lib., 707 Vermont St., Lawrence 66044. Tel. 785-843-3833, e-mail kfann@lawrence.lib.ks.us; *2nd V.P.* Kim Gile, Johnson County Lib., 9875 W. 87 St., Overland Park 66212. Tel. 913-826-4600 ext. 64479, e-mail gilek@jocolibrary.org; *Secy.* Julie Hildebrand, Independence Public Lib., 220 E. Maple St., Independence 67301. Tel. 620-331-3030, e-mail julie.hildebrand@iplks.org; *Treas.* Gary Landeck, Atchison Public Lib., 401 Kansas Ave., Atchison 66002. Tel. 913-367-1902 ext. 208, e-mail glandeck@atchisonlibrary.org; *Past Pres.* Cathy Reeves, Dodge City Public Lib., 1001 N. 2 Ave., Dodge City 67801. Tel. 620-225-0248, e-mail cathyr@dcpl.info; *Exec. Secy.* Cary Pressley.

Address correspondence to the president, Kansas Lib. Assn., 1020 S.W. Washburn, Topeka 66604. Tel. 785-580-4518, fax 785-580-4595, e-mail kansaslibraryassociation@yahoo.com.

World Wide Web http://www.kslibassoc.org.

Kentucky

Memb. 1,600. Publication. *Kentucky Libraries* (q.).

Pres. Laura Whayne, Kentucky Transportation Center, 176 Raymond Bldg., Lexington 40506. Tel. 859-257-2155, e-mail laura. whayne@uky.edu; *Pres.-Elect* Julie Howe, Somerset Community College, Laurel North Campus, Bldg. 2, Room 125, 100 University Drive, Somerset 40741. Tel. 606-878-4724, e-mail julie.howe@kctcs.edu; *Secy.* Dave Schroeder, Kenton County Public Lib., Admin. Center, 2171 Chamber Center Drive, Ft. Mitchell 41017. Tel. 859-578-3600, e-mail dave. schroeder@kentonlibrary.org; *Past Pres.* Brenda Metzger, McCracken County H.S., 6530 New Hwy. 60 W., Paducah 42001. Tel. 270-538-4356, e-mail brenda.metzger@mccracken. kyschools.us; *Exec. Dir.* Tom Underwood, 1501 Twilight Trail, Frankfort 40601. Tel. 502-223-5322, fax 502-223-4937, e-mail info@ kylibasn.org.

Address correspondence to the executive director.

World Wide Web http://www.klaonline.org

Louisiana

Memb. 1,000+. Term of Office. July–June. Publication. *Louisiana Libraries* (q.). *Ed.* Celise Reech-Harper. Tel. 337-463-6217 ext. 22, e-mail celise@beau.org.

Pres. Robert Bremer. Tel. 985-448-4657, e-mail robert.bremer@nicholls.edu; *1st V.P./ Pres.-Elect* Paula Clemmons. Tel. 337-433-5246, e-mail pclemmons@episcopaldayschool. org; *2nd V.P.* Kathlyn Bowersox. Tel. 225-771-2666, e-mail kathlyn_bowersox@subr. edu; *Secy.* Holly Priestley. Tel. 318-327-1490, e-mail hpriestley@oplib.org; *Past Pres.* Vivian McCain. Tel. 318-251-5030, e-mail vmccain@ mylpl.org.

Address correspondence to Louisiana Lib. Assn., 8550 United Plaza Blvd., Suite 1001, Baton Rouge 70809. Tel. 225-922-4642, 877-550-7890, fax 225-408-4422, e-mail office@ llaonline.org.

World Wide Web http://www.llaonline.org.

Maine

Maine Lib. Assn. Memb. 950. Publication. *MLA-to-Z* (q., online).

Pres. Nissa Flanagan, Merrill Memorial Lib., 215 Main St., Yarmouth 04096. Tel. 207-846-4763, e-mail nflanagan@maine.rr.com;

V.P./Pres.-Elect Bryce Cundick, Mantor Lib., Univ. of Maine at Farmington, 116 South St., Farmington 04938-1998. Tel. 207-240-7565, e-mail bryce.cundick@maine.edu; *Secy.* Lisa Shaw. E-mail librarydirector@cariboumaine. org; *Treas.* Michael Dignan, Paris Public Lib., 37 Market Sq., Paris 04291-1509. Tel. 207-743-6994, e-mail mdignan@paris.lib. me.us; *Past Pres.* Andi Jackson-Darling, Falmouth Memorial Lib., 5 Lunt Rd., Falmouth 04105. Tel. 207-781-2351, e-mail ajdarling@ falmouth.lib.me.us; *Business Mgr.* Edna Comstock. E-mail mla1@gwi.net.

Address correspondence to the association, P.O. Box 634, Augusta 04332-0634. Tel. 207-441-1410.

World Wide Web http://mainelibraries.org.

Maryland

Maryland Lib. Assn. Memb. 1,000+. Term of Office. July–July. Publication. *The Crab* (q., online). *Ed.* Annette Haldeman. E-mail annette. haldeman@mlis.state.md.us.

Pres. John Venditta; *1st V.P./Pres.-Elect* Mary Hastler; *Secy.* Katy Sullivan; *Treas.* Daria Parry; *Past Pres.* Carrie Willson-Plymire; *Exec. Dir.* Margaret Carty. E-mail mcarty@carr.org.

Address correspondence to the association, 1401 Hollins St., Baltimore 21223. Tel. 410-947-5090, fax 410-947-5089, e-mail mla@ mdlib.org.

World Wide Web http://www.mdlib.org.

Massachusetts

Massachusetts Lib. Assn. Memb. (Indiv.) 1,000; (Inst.) 100. Publication. *Bay State Libraries* (q.).

Pres. Maureen Ambrosino, Westborough Public Lib., 55 W. Main St., Westborough 01581. Tel. 508-871-5280, e-mail mambrosino@town.westborough.ma.us; *V.P.* Eric Poulin, Nahman-Watson Lib., Greenfield Community College, 1 College Drive, Greenfield 01301. Tel. 413-775-1834, e-mail pouline@ gcc.mass.edu; *Secy.* Debby Conrad, SAILS Lib. Network, 10 Riverside Drive, Suite 102, Lakeville 02347. Tel. 508-946-8600, e-mail dconrad@sailsinc.org; *Treas.* Ryan Livergood, Robbins Lib., 700 Massachusetts Ave., Arlington 02476. Tel. 781-316-3200, e-mail rlivergood@minlib.net; *Past Pres.* Elizabeth

Marcus, Brockton Public Lib., 304 Main St., Brockton 02301. Tel. 508-580-7890 ext. 101, e-mail emarcus@cobma.us; *Exec. Mgr.* Sarah Hagan, Massachusetts Lib. Assn., P.O. Box 240813, Boston 01730. Tel. 781-698-7764, e-mail manager@masslib.org.

Address correspondence to the executive manager.

World Wide Web http://www.masslib.org.

Michigan

Memb. 1,200+. Publication. *MLA Weekly* (e-newsletter).

Pres. Asante Cain, Grand Rapids Public Lib.; *Pres.-Elect* Leslie Warren, Olson Lib., Northern Michigan Univ.; *Treas.* Richard Schneider, Muskegon Dist. Lib.; *Past Pres.* Cathy Wolford, DALNET.

Address correspondence to Gail Madziar, Exec. Dir., Michigan Lib. Assn., 3410 Belle Chase Way, Suite 100, Lansing 48911. Tel. 517-394-2774 ext. 224, e-mail madziarg@mlcnet.org.

World Wide Web http://www.mla.lib.mi.us.

Minnesota

Memb. 1,100. Term of Office. (*Pres., Pres.-Elect*) Jan.–Dec.

Pres. Maggie Snow, Anoka County Lib. E-mail maggie.snow@co.anoka.mn.us; *Pres.-Elect* Margaret Stone, Washington County Lib. E-mail margaret.stone@co.washington.mn.us; *Secy.* Laura Morlcok, St. Catherine Univ. MLIS Program. E-mail llmorlock@stkate.edu; *Treas.* Jennifer Hootman, MINITEX. E-mail hootm001@umn.edu; *Past Pres.* Michele Mc-Graw, Hennepin County Lib. E-mail mmcgraw@hclib.org.

Address correspondence to the association, 400 S. 4 St., Suite 401-223, Minneapolis 55415. Tel. 877-867-0982, 612-294-6549, e-mail mla@management-hq.com.

World Wide Web http://www.mnlibrary association.org.

Mississippi

Memb. 625. Term of Office. Jan.–Dec. Publication. *Mississippi Libraries* (q.).

Pres. Patsy C. Brewer, Waynesboro-Wayne County Lib. Tel. 601-735-2268, e-mail wlib@ wwcls.lib.ms.us; *V.P.* Molly McManus, U.S. Army Engineer Research and Development Center, Vicksburg. Tel. 601-634-4122, e-mail molly.s.mcmanus@usace.army.mil; *Secy.* Selina Swink, Lake Public Lib. Tel. 601-775-3560, e-mail sswink@cmrls.lib.ms.us; *Treas.* Blair Booker, Holmes Community College. Tel. 601-605-3303, e-mail bbooker@holmescc. edu; *Past Pres.* Amanda Clay Powers, MSU-Mitchell Memorial Lib. Tel. 662-325-7677, e-mail apowers@library.msstate.edu; *MLA Admin.* Barbara J. Price, P.O. Box 13687, Jackson 39236-3687. Tel. 601-981-4586, e-mail info@misslib.org.

Address correspondence to the administrator.

World Wide Web http://www.misslib.org.

Missouri

Memb. 800+. Term of Office. Jan.–Dec. Publication. *MO INFO* (bi-mo.).

Pres. Christina Prucha, Logan Univ. E-mail christina.prucha@logan.edu; *Pres.-Elect* Sharla Lair, MOBIUS Consortium, Columbia; *Past Pres.* Gerald S. Brooks, St. Louis Public Lib. E-mail gbrooks@slpl.org.

Address correspondence to the president.

World Wide Web http://www.molib.org.

Montana

Memb. 600. Term of Office. July–June. Publication. *Focus* (bi-mo.).

Pres. Sheila Bonnand, Renne Lib., MSU, P.O. Box 173320, Bozeman 59717. Tel. 406-994-4130, e-mail sbonnand@montana.edu; *V.P./Pres.-Elect* Dawn Kingstad, Glendive Public Lib., P.O. Box 576, Glendive 59330. Tel. 406-989-1561, e-mail booksrus@midrivers. com; *Secy./Treas.* Lisa Mecklenberg Jackson, State Law Lib. of Montana, 215 N. Sanders, P.O. Box 203004, Helena 59620. Tel. 406-444-3660, e-mail lisameckjack@gmail.com; *Past Pres.* Beth Boyson, Bozeman Public Lib., 626 Main St., Bozeman 59715. Tel. 406-582-2402, fax 406-582-2424, e-mail bboyson@bozeman. net; *Admin. Dir.* Debbi Kramer, P.O. Box 1352, Three Forks 59752. Tel. 406-579-3121, fax 406-285-3091, e-mail debkmla@hotmail.com.

Address correspondence to the administrative director.

World Wide Web http://www.mtlib.org.

Nebraska

Term of Office. Jan.–Dec.

Pres. Gayle Roberts, Blair Public Lib. E-mail groberts@ci.blair.ne.us; *V.P./Pres.-Elect* Julee Hector, Lincoln City Libs. E-mail j.hector@lincolnlibraries.org; *Secy.* Terry Wingate, Omaha Public Libs. E-mail twingate @omahalibrary.org; *Treas.* Megan Klein-Hewitt, Omaha Public Libs. E-mail nlatreasurer @gmail.com; *Past Pres.* Robin Clark, Sump Memorial Lib. E-mail robin.r.clark@gmail. com; *Exec. Dir.* Michael Straatmann.

Address correspondence to the executive director, P.O. Box 21756, Lincoln 68542-1756. Tel. 402-216-0727, e-mail nlaexecutivedirector @gmail.com.

World Wide Web http://nebraskalibraries. site-ym.com.

Nevada

Memb. 450. Term of Office. Jan.–Dec. Publication. *Nevada Libraries* (q.).

Pres. Carol Lloyd, Churchill County Lib. E-mail celloyd@clan.lib.nv.us; *Pres.-Elect* Scott Clonan, Las Vegas-Clark County Lib. Dist. E-mail clonans@lvccld.org; *Treas.* Tammy Westergard, Carson City Lib. E-mail twestergard @carson.org; *Past Pres.* Ann-Marie White, Las Vegas-Clark County Lib. System. E-mail whitea@lvccld.org; *Exec. Secy.* Kristy Isla. E-mail ardainia@yahoo.com.

Address correspondence to the executive secretary.

World Wide Web http://www.nevada libraries.org.

New Hampshire

Memb. 700. Publication. *NHLA News* (q.).

Pres. Amy Lapointe, Amherst Town Lib., 14 Main St., Amherst 03031. Tel. 603-673-2288, e-mail alapointe@amherstlibrary.org; *V.P./Pres.-Elect* Jenn Hosking, Nashua Public Lib., 2 Court St., Nashua 03060. Tel. 603-589-4621, e-mail jenn.hosking@nashualibrary. org; *Secy.* Mary White, Howe Lib., 13 South St., Hanover 03755. Tel. 603-640-3267, e-mail mary.h.white@thehowe.org; *Treas.* Cara Barlow, Derry Public Lib., 64 E. Broadway, Derry 03038. Tel. 603-432-6128, e-mail carab@ derrypl.org; *Past Pres.* Linda Taggart, Nashua Public Lib., 2 Court St., Nashua 03060. Tel.

603-589-4600, e-mail linda.taggart@nashua library.org.

Address correspondence to the association, c/o New Hampshire State Lib., Attn: Michael York, State Libn., 20 Park St., Concord 03301-6314.

World Wide Web http://nhlibrarians.org.

New Jersey

Memb. 1,800. Term of Office. July–June. Publication. *New Jersey Libraries NEWSletter* (q.).

Pres. Terrie McColl, New Milford Public Lib., 200 Dahlia Ave., New Milford 07646. Tel. 201-262-1221, e-mail mccoll@bccls.org; *V.P.* James Keehbler, Piscataway Public Lib., 500 Hoes Lane, Piscataway 08854. Tel. 732-463-1633, fax 908-463-1007, e-mail jkeehbler@ piscatawaylibrary.org; *2nd V.P.* Keith McCoy, Somerset County Lib. System, Bridgewater Lib., 1 Vogt Drive, Bridgewater 08807. Tel. 908-526-4016 ext.128, e-mail kmccoy@sclibnj. org; *Secy.* Leslie Kahn, Newark Public Lib., 5 Washington St., Newark 07102. Tel. 973-733-7820, fax 973-733-5648, e-mail lkahn@npl. org; *Treas.* Chris Carbone, South Brunswick Public Lib., 110 Kingston Lane, Monmouth Junction 08852. Tel. 732-329-4000 ext. 7287, fax 732-329-0573, e-mail ccarbone@sbpl.info; *Past Pres.* Eileen Palmer, Libs. of Middlesex Automation Consortium, 1030 St. Georges Ave., Suite 203, Avenel 00701. Tel. 732-750-2525, e-mail empalmer@lmxac.org; *Exec. Dir.* Patricia Tumulty, NJLA, P.O. Box 1534, Trenton 08607. Tel. 609-394-8032, fax 609-394-8164, e-mail ptumulty@njla.org.

Address correspondence to the executive director.

World Wide Web http://www.njla.org.

New Mexico

Memb. 550. Term of Office. Apr.–Apr. Publication. *NMLA Bulletin* (online, 6 a year).

Pres. Janice Kowemy. E-mail lagunapueblo-nsn.gov; *V.P./Pres.-Elect* Sharon Jenkins. E-mail djenkins@nmsu.edu; *Secy.* Melanie Chavez. E-mail melchavez10@gmail.com; *Treas.* Paulita Aguilar. E-mail paulita@unm. edu; *Past Pres.* Mary Ellen Pellington. E-mail mepellington@ci.gallup.nm.us.

Address correspondence to the association, Box 26074, Albuquerque 87125. Tel. 505-400-7309, e-mail contact@nmla.org.

World Wide Web http://nmla.org.

New York

Memb. 4,000. Term of Office. Nov.–Nov. Publication. *NYLA e-Bulletin* (q.).

Pres. Geoffrey S. Kirkpatrick. Tel. 518-439-9314, e-mail geoff@bethpl.org; *Pres.-Elect* Debby Emerson. Tel. 315-446-5446, e-mail demerson@clrc.org; *Treas.* Timothy G. Burke. Tel. 518-437-9882, e-mail tim.burke@uhls.lib.ny.us; *Past Pres.* Sara Kelly Johns. Tel. 518-891-2339, e-mail skjohns@gmail.com.

Address correspondence to Jeremy Johannesen, executive director, New York Lib. Assn., 6021 State Farm Rd., Guilderland 12084. Tel. 800-252-6952 ext. 101 or 518-432-6952, fax 518-427-1697, e-mail director@nyla.org.

World Wide Web http://www.nyla.org.

North Carolina

Memb. 1,100. Term of Office. Oct.–Oct. Publications. *North Carolina Library Association E-news* (online, bi-mo.). *Ed.* Marilyn Schuster, Local Documents/Special Collections, Univ. of North Carolina–Charlotte. E-mail mbschust@email.uncc.edu; *North Carolina Libraries* (online, 2 a year). *Ed.* Ralph Scott, Joyner Lib., East Carolina Univ., Greenville 27858. Tel. 252-328-0265, e-mail scottr@ecu.edu.

Pres. Dale Cousins, Wake County Public Libs., 404 Perry St., Raleigh 27605. Tel. 919-856-6726, e-mail dale.cousins@wakegov.com; *V.P./Pres.-Elect* Rodney Lippard, Rowan-Cabarrus Community College, P.O. Box 1595, Salisbury 28145. Tel. 704-216-3686, e-mail rodney.lippard@rccc.edu; *Secy.* To be announced; *Treas.* M. J. Wilkerson, Alamance County Public Libs., 342 S. Spring St., Burlington 27215. Tel. 336-513-4753, e-mail mgoodrum@alamancelibraries.org; *Past Pres.* Wanda Brown, Z. Smith Reynolds Lib., Wake Forest Univ., Box 7777 Reynolda Sta., Winston-Salem 27109. Tel. 336-758-5094, e-mail brownw@wfu.edu; *Admin. Asst.* Kim Parrott, North Carolina Lib. Assn., 1841 Capital Blvd., Raleigh 27604. Tel. 919-839-6252, fax 919-839-6253, e-mail nclaonline@gmail.com.

Address correspondence to the administrative assistant.

World Wide Web http://www.nclaonline.org.

North Dakota

Memb. (Indiv.) 300+. Term of Office. Sept.–Sept. Publication. *The Good Stuff* (q.). *Ed.* Marlene Anderson, Bismarck State College Lib., Box 5587, Bismarck 58506-5587. Tel. 701-224-5578, fax 701-224-5551, e-mail marlene.anderson@bismarckstate.edu.

Pres. Greta Guck, Leach Public Lib., 417 Second Ave. N, Wahpeton 58075-4416. Tel. 701-642-5732, e-mail greta.leachplib@midconetwork.com; *Pres.-Elect* Stephen Banister, Minot State Univ. Tel. 701-858-3855, fax 701-858-3581, e-mail stephen.banister@minotstateu.edu; *Secy.* Mary Lorenz, Grand Forks Public Lib. Tel. 701-772-8116, fax 701-772-1379, e-mail mary.lorenz@gflibrary.com; *Treas.* Michael Safratowich, UND Lib. of the Health Sciences. Tel. 701-777-2602, fax 701-777-4790, e-mail michael.safratowich@med.und.edu; *Past Pres.* Victor Lieberman, Chester Fritz Lib., Univ. of North Dakota. Tel. 701-777-4639, fax 701-777-3319, e-mail victor.lieberman@library.und.edu.

Address correspondence to the president.

World Wide Web http://www.ndla.info.

Ohio

Memb. 2,700+. Term of Office. Jan.–Dec. Publication. *Access* (memb., weekly, online).

Pres. Jeff Winkle, Findlay Hancock County Public Lib. Tel. 419-422-1712, e-mail winkleje@findlaylibrary.org; *V.P./Pres.-Elect* Alan Radnor, Bexley Public Lib. Tel. 614-464-6326; *Secy./Treas.* Deborah Dubois, Mansfield-Richland County Public Lib. Tel. 419-522-3001, e-mail ddubois@mrcpl.org; *Past Pres.* Meg Delaney, Toledo-Lucas County Public Lib. Tel. 419-259-5333, e-mail meg.delaney@toledolibrary.org; *Exec. Dir.* Douglas S. Evans. E-mail devans@olc.org.

Address correspondence to the executive director, OLC, 1105 Schrock Rd., Suite 440, Columbus 43229-1174. Tel. 614-410-8092, fax 614-410-8098, e-mail olc@olc.org.

World Wide Web http://www.olc.org.

Oklahoma

Memb. (Indiv.) 1,000; (Inst.) 60. Term of Office. July–June. Publication. *Oklahoma Librarian* (bi-mo.).

Pres. Shari Clifton; *V.P./Pres.-Elect* Calypso Gilstrap; *Secy.* Chris Kennedy; *Treas.* Tim Miller; *Past Pres.* Lynda Reynolds; *Exec. Dir.* Kay Boies, 300 Hardy Drive, P.O. Box 6550, Edmond 73083. Tel. 405-525-5100, fax 405-525-5103, e-mail exec_director@oklibs.org.

Address correspondence to the executive director.

World Wide Web http://www.oklibs.org.

Oregon

Memb. (Indiv.) 1,000+. Publications. *OLA Hotline* (bi-w.), *OLA Quarterly.*

Pres. Candice Watkins, Clatsop Community College Lib. E-mail cwatkins@clatsopcc.edu; *V.P./Pres.-Elect* Jane Corry, Multnomah County Lib. E-mail janec@multcolib.org; *Secy.* Stephanie Debner, Mt. Hood Community College Lib. E-mail stephanie.debner@mhcc.edu; *Treas.* Valery King, Oregon State Univ. Lib. E-mail valery.king@oregonstate.edu; *Past Pres.* Penny Hummel, Canby Public Lib. E-mail phummel.ola@gmail.com; *Assn. Mgr.* Shirley Roberts. E-mail sroberts.ola@gmail.com.

Address correspondence to Oregon Lib. Assn., P.O. Box 3067, La Grande 97850. Tel. 541-962-5824, e-mail olaweb@olaweb.org.

World Wide Web http://www.olaweb.org.

Pennsylvania

Memb. 1,900+. Term of Office. Jan.–Dec. Publication. *PaLA Bulletin* (10 a year).

Pres. Janis Stubbs, Delaware County Lib. System. Tel. 610-891-8622, e-mail jstubbs@delcolibraries.org; *1st V.P.* David Schappert, Marywood Univ. Tel. 570-961-4764, e-mail dschappert@gmail.com; *2nd V.P./Conference Chair* Chris Snyder, Bucks County Free Lib. Tel. 215-348-9083, e-mail snyderc@buckslib.org; *3rd V.P.* Carolyn Blatchley, Cumberland County Lib. Tel. 717-240-5379, e-mail cblatchley@ccpa.net; *Treas.* Marguerite Dube, Chester County Lib. Tel. 610-280-2645, e-mail mdube@ccls.org; *Past Pres.* Paula Gilbert, Martin Lib. Tel. 717-846-5300, e-mail pgilbert@yorklibraries.org; *Exec. Dir.* Glenn R. Miller, Pennsylvania Lib. Assn., 220 Cumberland Pkwy., Suite 10, Mechanicsburg 17055. Tel. 717-766-7663, fax 717-766-5440, e-mail glenn@palibraries.org.

Address correspondence to the executive director.

World Wide Web http://www.palibraries.org.

Rhode Island

Memb. (Indiv.) 350+; (Inst.) 50+. Term of Office. June–June. Publication. *RILA Bulletin.* *Eds.* Brandi Kenyon, Andria Tieman. E-mail rilabulletin@gmail.com.

Pres. Jenifer Bond, Douglas and Judith Krupp Lib., Bryant Univ., Smithfield 02917. Tel. 401-232-6299, e-mail jbond2@bryant.edu; *V.P./Pres.-Elect* Aaron Coutu, Cumberland Lib. Tel. 401-333-2552 ext. 5, e-mail acoutu@cumberlandlibrary.org; *Secy.* Emily Grace LeMay. E-mail secretary@rilibraryassoc.org; *Treas.* Patricia Lombardi. Tel. 401-232-6296, e-mail treasurer@rilibraryassoc.org; *Past Pres.* Eileen Dyer, Cranston Public Lib., 140 Sockanossett Cross Rd., Cranston 02920. Tel. 401-943-9080 ext. 119, e-mail eadyer@gmail.com.

Address correspondence to Rhode Island Library Assn., P.O. Box 6765, Providence 02940.

World Wide Web http://www.rilibraries.org.

South Carolina

Memb. 350+. Term of Office. Jan.–Dec. Publication. *News and Views.*

Pres. Crystal Johnson, Richland Lib., 2916 Broad River Rd., Columbia 29210. Tel. 803-772-6675, e-mail cjohnson@richlandlibrary.com; *1st V.P./Conference Chair* John Kennerly, Erskine College, P.O. Box 188, 1 Depot St., Due West 29639. Tel. 864-379-8788, e-mail kennerly@erskine.edu; *2nd V.P.* Amber Conger, Richland Lib., 1431 Assembly St., Columbia 29212. Tel. 803-929-3401, e-mail aconger@richlandlibrary.com; *Secy.* Virginia Alexander, USC Upstate, 800 University Way, Spartanburg 29303. Tel. 864-503-5735, e-mail alexanva@uscupstate.edu; *Treas.* Sarah Hood, J. Drake Edens Lib., Columbia College, 1301 Columbia College Drive, Columbia 29203. Tel. 803-786-3570, e-mail shood@columbiasc.edu; *Past Pres.* Edward Rock, Clemson Univ. Libs., Box 343001, Clemson 29643. Tel. 864-656-1879, e-mail erock@clemson.edu; *Exec.*

Secy. Donald Wood, SCLA, P.O. Box 1763, Columbia 29202. Tel. 803-252-1087, fax 803-252-0589. E-mail scla@capconsc.com. Address correspondence to the executive secretary.

World Wide Web http://www.scla.org.

South Dakota

Memb. (Indiv.) 450+; (Inst.) 60+. Publication. *Book Marks* (q.). *Ed.* Melissa Weber, Canistota School Lib., Canistota 57012. E-mail book markssd@gmail.com.

Pres. Amber Wilde, Grace Balloch Memorial Lib., Spearfish. E-mail amber.wilde@cityofspearfish.com; *V.P./Pres.-Elect* Kathy Jacobs-Wibbels, Yankton Community Lib. E-mail kwibbles@cityofyankton.org; *Recording Secy.* Nita Gill, Brookings Public Lib. E-mail ngill@cityofbrookings.org; *Past Pres.* Scott Ahola, Black Hills State Univ., Spearfish. E-mail scott.ahola@bhsu.edu; *Exec. Secy./Treas.* Laura G. Olson, Canton Public Lib. E-mail sdlaest@gmail.com.

Address correspondence to the executive secretary, SDLA, 28363 472nd Ave., Worthing 57077-5722. Tel. 605-372-0235, e-mail sdlaest@gmail.com.

World Wide Web http://www.sdlibrary association.org.

Tennessee

Memb. 600+. Term of Office. July–June. Publications. *Tennessee Libraries* (q.). *Ed.* Amy York. E-mail ayork@mtsu.edu; *TLA Newsletter* (q.). *Ed.* Anthony Prince. E-mail aprince1@tnstate.edu. Both online at http://www.tnla.org.

Pres. Susan Jennings. E-mail suzyjenn620@gmail.com; *V.P./Pres.-Elect* Pam Dennis. E-mail pdennis@memphis.edu; *Recording Secy.* Heather Lanier. E-mail lanierh@brentwood-tn.org; *Past Pres.* Ruth Kinnersley. E-mail rkinnersley@trevecca.edu; *Exec. Dir.* Annelle R. Huggins, Tennessee Lib. Assn., Box 241074, Memphis 38124. Tel. 901-485-6952, e-mail arhuggins1@comcast.net.

Address correspondence to the executive director.

World Wide Web http://tnla.org.

Texas

Memb. 6,500+. Term of Office. Apr.–Apr. Publications. *Texas Library Journal* (q.), *TLACast* (9 a year).

Pres. Sharon Amastae; *Pres.-Elect* Susan Mann; *Treas.* Gretchen Pruett; *Past Pres.* Yvonne Chandler; *Exec. Dir.* Patricia H. Smith, TXLA, 3355 Bee Cave Rd., Suite 401, Austin 78746-6763. Tel. 512-328-1518, fax 512-328-8852, e-mail pats@txla.org or tla@txla.org.

Address correspondence to the executive director.

World Wide Web http://www.txla.org.

Utah

Memb. 650. Publication. *Utah Libraries News* (q.) (online at http://www.ula.org/newsletter).

Pres. Pamela Martin, Merrill Cazier Lib., Utah State Univ., 3000 Old Main Hill, Logan 84322. Tel. 435-797-2685, fax 435-797-2677, e-mail pamela.martin@usu.edu; *V.P./Pres.-Elect* Dustin Fife, San Juan County Lib., 25 W. 300 South, Blanding 84511. Tel. 435-678-2335, e-mail d.t.fife@sanjuancounty.org; *Recording Secy.* Andrea Payant, USU Merrill-Cazier Lib. E-mail andrea.payant@usu.edu; *Treas.* Javaid Lal. E-mail jlal@ula.org; *Past Pres.* Patricia Hull, Magna Branch, Salt Lake County Lib. System, 8339 W. 3500 South, Magna 84044. Tel. 801-944-7626, e-mail phull@slcolibrary.org; *Exec. Dir.* Barbara Hopkins, Canyons School Dist. Tel. 801-810-7149, e-mail barbaraw.hopkins@gmail.com.

Address correspondence to the executive director, Utah Lib. Assn., P.O. Box 708155, Sandy 84070-8155.

World Wide Web http://www.ula.org.

Vermont

Memb. 400. Publication. *VLA News* (q.).

Pres. Toni Josey. E-mail vermontlibraries president@gmail.com; *V.P./Pres.-Elect* Virgil Fuller, Chelsea Public Lib., 296 Vermont Route 1110, Chelsea 05038. Tel. 802-685-2188, e-mail vermontlibrariesvicepresident@gmail.com; *Secy.* Sarah Costa, Aldrich Public Lib., 6 Washington St., Barre 05641. Tel. 802-839-5045, e-mail sbjackman@gmail.com; *Treas.* James Allen, Bailey/Howe Lib., Univ. of Vermont, 538 Main St., Burlington 05405. Tel. 802-656-3254, e-mail jpallen@uvm.edu; *Past*

Pres. Amber Billey, Bailey/Howe Lib., Univ. of Vermont, 538 Main St., Burlington 05405-0036. Tel. 802-656-8568, e-mail amber.billey @uvm.edu.

Address correspondence to VLA, Box 803, Burlington 05402.

World Wide Web http://www.vermont libraries.org.

Virginia

Memb. 950+. Term of Office. Oct.–Oct. Publication. *Virginia Libraries* (q.).

Pres. Suzy Szasz Palmer, Greenwood Lib., Longwood Univ., 201 High St., Farmville 23909. Tel. 434-395-2083, e-mail palmerss@ longwood.edu; *Pres.-Elect* Martha Hutzel, England Run Branch, Central Rappahannock Regional Lib., 806 Lyons Blvd., Fredericksburg 22406. Tel. 540-899-1703, e-mail mhutzel @crrl.org; *2nd V.P.* Shari Henry, Westover Branch, Arlington Public Lib., 1644 N. McKinley Rd., Arlington 22205. Tel. 703-228-5261, e-mail shenry@arlingtonva.us; *Secy.* Cindy S. Church, Lib. of Virginia, 800 E. Broad St., Richmond 23219-8000. Tel. 804-692-3773, e-mail cindy.church@lva.virginia.gov; *Treas.* Nathan Flinchum, Roanoke Public Libs., 706 S. Jefferson St. S.W., Roanoke 24016. Tel. 540-853-2073, e-mail nathan.flinchum@roanokeva.gov; *Past Pres.* Kevin Smith, Yorktown Public Lib., 100 Long Green Blvd., Yorktown 23693. Tel. 757-890-5134, e-mail smithk@yorkcounty. gov; *Exec. Dir.* Lisa Varga, P.O. Box 56312, Virginia Beach 23456. Tel. 757-689-0594, fax 757-447-3478, e-mail vla.lisav@cox.net.

Address correspondence to the executive director.

World Wide Web http://www.vla.org.

Washington

Memb. (Indiv.) 742, (Inst.) 47. Publications. *Alki: The Washington Library Association Journal* (3 a year). *Ed.* Joyce Hansen, Seattle Public Lib., 1000 Fourth Ave., Seattle 98104. Tel. 206-713-9497, e-mail alkieditor@alki.org; *Connect* (e-newsletter, mo.).

Pres. Nancy Ledeboer, Spokane County Lib. Dist. Tel. 509-893-8200, e-mail nledeboer@ scld.org; *V.P./Pres.-Elect* Darcy Brixey, Bellevue Regional Lib. Tel. 425-450-1765. E-mail dbrixey@kcls.org; *Secy./Treas.* Phil Heikkinen,

Orcas Island Public Lib. Tel. 360-376-2308, e-mail pheikkinen@orcaslibrary.org; *Past Pres.* Jennifer Wiseman, King County Lib. System. Tel. 425-369-3221, e-mail jlwiseman@kcls. org; *Exec. Dir.* Dana Murphy-Love, WLA, 23607 Hwy. 99, Suite 2-C, Edmonds 98026. Tel. 425-967-0739, e-mail dana@wla.org.

Address correspondence to the executive director.

World Wide Web http://www.wla.org.

West Virginia

Memb. 650+. Publication. *West Virginia Libraries* (6 a year). *Ed.* Pamela K. Coyle, Martinsburg-Berkeley County Public Lib., 101 W. King St., Martinsburg 25401. Tel. 304-267-8933, fax 304-267-9720, e-mail pam.coyle@ martin.lib.wv.us.

Pres. Amy Lilly, Raleigh County Public Lib., 221 N. Kanawha St., Beckley 25801. Tel. 304-255-0511 ext. 100, e-mail amy.lilly@ raleigh.lib.wv.us; *1st V.P./Pres.-Elect* Emilee Seese, Ritchie County Public Lib., P.O. Box 122, Ellenboro 26346. Tel. 304-643-5122, fax 304-643-4019, e-mail seesee@mail.mln. lib.wv.us; *2nd V.P.* Ivonne Martinez, Mountaintop Public Lib., P.O. Box 217, 384 Quail Ridge Rd., Thomas 26292. Tel. 304-463-4582, fax 304-463-5789, e-mail ivonne.martinez@ mail.nln.lib.wv.us; *Secy.* Jessica Tapia, WVU Libs., P.O. Box 6069, 1549 University Ave., Morgantown 26506. Tel. 304-293-0312, e-mail jessica.tapia@mail.wvu.edu; *Treas.* Brian E. Raitz, Parkersburg and Wood County Public Lib., 3100 Emerson Ave., Parkersburg 26104-2414. Tel. 304-420-4587 ext. 11, fax 304-420-4589, e-mail raitzb@mail.mln.lib.wv.us; *Past Pres.* Beth Royall, Evansdale Lib., West Virginia Univ. Libs., P.O. Box 6105, Morgantown 26506-6105. Tel. 304-293-9755, fax 304-293-7330, e-mail beth.royall@mail.wvu.edu.

Address correspondence to the president.

World Wide Web http://www.wvla.org.

Wisconsin

Memb. 1,900. Term of Office. Jan.–Dec. Publication. *WLA Newsletter* (q.).

Pres. John Politz, McIntyre Lib., UW–Eau Claire. Tel. 715-836-4827, e-mail pollitjh@ uwec.edu; *Pres.-Elect* Pamela Westby, Middleton Public Lib., Middleton. Tel. 608-827-7425, e-mail pamela@midlibrary.org; *Treas.* Jen Gerber, Oscar Grady Public Lib., Saukville. Tel. 262-284-6022, e-mail jgerber@esls.lib. wi.us; *Past Pres.* Krista L. Ross, Southwest Wisconsin Lib. System, Fennimore. Tel. 608-822-3393, e-mail kross@swls.org; *Exec. Dir.* Plumer Lovelace. E-mail lovelace@wisconsin libraries.org.

Address correspondence to the association, 4610 S. Biltmore Lane, No. 100, Madison 53718-2153. Tel. 608-245-3640, fax 608-245-3646, e-mail wla@wisconsinlibraries.org.

World Wide Web http://wla.wisconsin libraries.org.

Wyoming

Memb. 450+. Term of Office. Oct.–Oct.

Pres. Rebecca Lehman, Campbell County Public Lib. Tel. 307-682-3223, e-mail president @wyla.org; *V.P.* Sid Stanfill. E-mail vicepresident @wyla.org; *Past Pres.* Richard Landreth, Westwood H.S./4J Elementary Libs. E-mail landreth@ccsd.k12.wy.us; *Exec. Secy.* Laura Grott, P.O. Box 1387, Cheyenne 82003-1387. Tel. 307-632-7622, fax 307-638-3469, e-mail executivesecretary@wyla.org.

Address correspondence to the executive secretary.

World Wide Web http://www.wyla.org.

Canada

Alberta

Memb. 500. Term of Office. May–Apr. Publication. *Letter of the LAA* (q.).

Pres. Karen Hildebrandt, Concordia Univ. College of Alberta. E-mail president@laa. ca; *1st V.P.* Jason Openo, Medicine Hat College. E-mail 1stvicepresident@laa.ca; *2nd V.P.* Norene James, Grant MacEwan Univ. E-mail 2ndvicepresident@laa.ca; *Treas.* Jackie Flowers, Calgary Public Lib. E-mail treasurer@ laa.ca; *Past Pres.* Lisa Hardy, Calgary Public Lib. E-mail pastpresident@laa.ca; *Exec. Dir.* Christine Sheppard, 80 Baker Crescent N.W., Calgary T2L 1R4. Tel. 403-284-5818, fax 403-282-6646, e-mail info@laa.ca.

Address correspondence to the executive director.

World Wide Web http://www.laa.ca.

British Columbia

Memb. 750+. Term of Office. April–April. Publication. *BCLA Browser* (q.; online at http://bclabrowser.ca). *Ed.* Leanna Jantzi. E-mail browser@bcla.bc.ca.

Pres. Heather Buzzell, Penticton Public Lib.; *Past Pres.* Gwen Bird, Council of Prairie and Pacific Univ. Libs.; *Exec. Dir.* Annette De-Faveri. E-mail execdir@bcla.bc.ca.

Address correspondence to the association, 900 Howe St., Suite 150, Vancouver V6Z 2M4. Tel. 604-683-5354, e-mail exdir@bcla.bc.ca.

World Wide Web http://www.bcla.bc.ca.

Manitoba

Memb. 500+. Term of Office. May–May. Publications. *Newsline* (mo.); *Manitoba Libraries* (mo., online, open access journal).

Pres. Camille Callison, Elizabeth Dafoe Lib., Univ. of Manitoba, Winnipeg. Tel. 204-480-1054, e-mail president@mla.mb.ca; *V.P.* Alix-Rae Stefanko. E-mail awards@mla. mb.ca; *Secy.* Evelyn Bruneau, Elizabeth Dafoe Lib., Univ. of Manitoba, Winnipeg. Tel. 204-474-6780, e-mail evelyn_bruneau@umanitoba. ca; *Treas.* Laura Hochheim, Neil John Maclean Health Sciences Lib., Univ. of Manitoba, Winnipeg. Tel. 204-480-1346, e-mail laura.hochheim @umanitoba.ca; *Past Pres.* Dawn Bassett, Canadian Grain Commission. E-mail dbassett69 @gmail.com.

Address correspondence to the association, 606-100 Arthur St., Winnipeg R3B 1H3. Tel. 204-943-4567, e-mail manitobalibrary@gmail. com.

World Wide Web http://www.mla.mb.ca.

Ontario

Memb. 5,000+. Publications. *Access* (q.); *Teaching Librarian* (3 a year).

Pres. Jane Hilton, Whitby Public Lib. E-mail janehilton.ca@gmail.com; *V.P./Pres.-Elect* Todd Kyle, Newmarket Public Lib. E-mail tkyle@newmarketpl.ca; *Treas.* Lesa Balch, Kitchener Public Lib. E-mail lesa.balch@kpl. org; *Past Pres.* Anita Brooks Kirkland. E-mail anitabk@bythebrooks.ca; *Exec. Dir.* Shelagh Paterson. E-mail spaterson@accessola.com.

Address correspondence to the association, 2 Toronto St., Toronto M5C 2B6. Tel. 416-363-

3388 or 866-873-9867, fax 416-941-9581 or 800-387-1181, e-mail info@accessola.com.

World Wide Web http://www.accessola. com.

Quebec

Memb. (Indiv.) 100+. Term of Office. May–April. Publication. *ABQLA Bulletin* (3 a year). *Pres.* Shannon Babcock. E-mail shannon. babcock@mels.gouv.qc.ca; *V.P.* Sonia Smith. E-mail sonia.smith@mcgill.ca; *Treas.* Anne Wade. E-mail wada@education.concordia.ca; *Past Pres.* Robin Canuel. E-mail robin.canuel @mcgill.ca; *Exec. Secy.* Margaret Goldik, P.O. Box 26717, CPS Beaconsfield, Beaconsfield H9W 6G7. Tel./fax 514-697-0146, e-mail abqla@abqla.qc.ca.

Address correspondence to the executive secretary.

World Wide Web http://www.abqla.qc.ca.

Saskatchewan

Memb. 200+. Publication. *Forum* (q.). *Pres.* Gwen Schmidt, Saskatoon Public Lib. 311 23rd St., Saskatoon S7K 0J6. Tel. 306-975-7606, e-mail gwen.m.schmidt@gmail.com; *V.P., Membership and Publications* Michael Shires, Dr. John Archer Lib., Univ. of Regina. Tel. 306-585-4493, e-mail michael.shires@ uregina.ca; *V.P., Advocacy and Development* Gillian Nowlan, Dr. John Archer Lib., Univ. of Regina. Tel. 306-337-2434, e-mail gillian. nowlan@uregina.ca; *Treas.* Deborah McConkey, Horizon College and Seminary Lib., 1303 Jackson Ave., Saskatoon S7H 2M9. Tel. 306-374-6655, e-mail library@horizon.edu; *Exec. Dir.* Judy Nicholson, SLA Office, No. 15, 2010 7th Ave., Regina S4R 1C2. Tel. 306-780-9413, fax 306-780-9447, e-mail slaexdir@sasktel. net.

Address correspondence to the executive director.

World Wide Web http://www.saskla.ca.

Regional

Atlantic Provinces: N.B., N.L., N.S., P.E.I.

Memb. (Indiv.) 320+; (Inst.) Publication. *APLA Bulletin* (4 a year).

Pres. Crystal Rose, Ferriss Hodgett Lib., Grenfell Campus, Memorial Univ. of Newfoundland, 20 University Drive, Corner Brook A2H 5G4. Tel. 709-637-6236 or 709-637-2183, e-mail crose@grenfell.mun.ca; *V.P./Pres.-Elect* Lynn Somers, Nova Scotia Provincial Library, Dept. of Communities, Culture, and Heritage, 1741 Brunswick St., Halifax NS B3J 3X8. Tel. 902 424-4852, fax 902-424-0633; *V.P., Membership* Suzanne van den Hoogen, Angus L. Macdonald Lib., St. Francis Xavier Univ., P.O. Box 5000, Antigonish, NS B2G 2W5. Tel. 902-867-4535, e-mail svandenh@stfx.ca; *V.P. Nova Scotia* Stan Orlov, Mount Saint Vincent Univ., 166 Bedford Hwy., Halifax, NS B3M 2J6. Tel. 902-457-6212, fax 902-457-6445, e-mail stan.orlov@msvu.ca; *V.P. New Brunswick* Leah Brisco, New Brunswick Public Lib. Service, 250 King St., P.O. Box 6000, Fredericton, NB E3B 5H1. Tel. 506-453-3442, e-mail leah. brisco@gnb.ca; *V.P. Newfoundland and Labrador* Krista Godfrey, Queen Elizabeth II Lib., Memorial Univ. of Newfoundland, St. John's, NL A1B 3Y1. Tel. 709-864-3753, e-mail kgodfrey@mun.ca; *V.P. Prince Edward Island* Patricia Doucette, Holland College, 140 Weymouth St., Charlottetown, PE C1A 4Z1. Tel. 902-566-9558, e-mail pmdoucette@hollandcollege.com; *Secy.* Anne Bowden, Dr. C. R. Barrett Lib., Marine Institute, Memorial Univ. of Newfoundland, P.O. Box 4920, St. John's, NL A1C 5R3. Tel. 709-778-0445, e-mail anne. bowden@mi.mun.ca; *Treas.* Gail Fraser, W. K. Kellogg Health Sciences Lib., Dalhousie Univ., P.O. Box 15000, Halifax, NS B3H 4R2. E-mail gail.fraser@dal.ca; *Past Pres.* Louise White, Marine Institute, Memorial Univ. of Newfoundland, P.O. Box 4920, St. John's, NL A1C 5R3. Tel. 709-757-0719, e-mail louise.white@ mi.mun.ca.

Address correspondence to Atlantic Provinces Lib. Assn., c/o SIM, Kenneth C. Rowe Mgt. Bldg., Dalhousie Univ., Suite 4010, 6100 University Ave., Halifax, NS B3H 4R2.

World Wide Web http://www.apla.ca.

Mountain Plains: Ariz., Colo., Kan., Mont., Neb., Nev., N.Dak., N.Mex., Okla., S.Dak., Utah, Wyo.

Memb. 700. Term of Office. Oct.–Oct. Publications. *MPLA Newsletter* (bi-mo., online only). *Ed.* Abby Moore, I. D. Weeks Lib., Univ. of

South Dakota, 414 E. Clark St., Vermillion 57069. Tel. 605-677-6094, e-mail editor@ mpla.us.

Pres. Annie Epperson, Michener Lib., Univ. of Northern Colorado, Campus Box 48, Greeley 80639-0091. Tel. 970-351-1535, fax 970-351-2963, president@mpla.us; *V.P./Pres.-Elect* Eric Stroshane, North Dakota State Lib. E-mail vicepresident@mpla.us; *Recording Secy.* Valerie Nye, Inst. of American Indian Arts, Santa Fe. E-mail secretary@mpla.us; *Past Pres.* Wendy Wendt, Grand Forks Public Lib. Tel. 701-772-8116, fax 701-771-1379, e-mail past president@mpla.us; *Exec. Secy.* Judy Zelenski, 14293 W. Center Drive, Lakewood, CO 80228. Tel. 303-985-7795, e-mail execsecretary@ mpla.us.

Address correspondence to the executive secretary.

World Wide Web http://www.mpla.us.

New England: Conn., Maine, Mass., N.H., R.I., Vt.

Memb. (Indiv.) 650+. Term of Office. Nov.–Oct. Publication. *NELA News* (online, mo.).

Pres. Stephen Spohn, Massachusetts Lib. System, Marlborough. E-mail president@ nelib.org; *V.P./Pres.-Elect* Deb Hoadley, Massachusetts Lib. System, Marlborough. Tel. 508-357-2121, e-mail vice-president@nelib.org; *Secy.* Betsy Solon. E-mail secretary@nelib. org; *Treas.* Denise Van Zanten, Manchester City Lib., Manchester, N.H. E-mail treasurer@ nelib.org; *Senior Dir.* Amy Howlett, Vermont Dept. of Libs., Chester. E-mail director-sr@ nelib.org; *Junior Dir.* Meaghan Thompson, Turner Free Lib., Randolph, Mass. E-mail director-jr@nelib.org; *Admin.* Robert Scheier, New England Lib. Assn., 55 N. Main St., Unit 49, Belchertown, MA 01007. Tel. 413-813-5254, e-mail library-association-administrator@nelib.org.

World Wide Web http://www.nelib.org.

Pacific Northwest: Alaska, Idaho, Mont., Ore., Wash., Alberta, B.C.

Memb. 170+. Term of Office. Aug.–Aug. Publication. *PNLA Quarterly. Ed.* Mary Bolin, 322B Love Lib., Univ. of Nebraska, P.O. Box 881140, Lincoln, NE 68588-4100. Tel. 402-472-4281, e-mail mbolin2@unlnotes.unl.edu.

Pres. Honore Bray, Missoula Public Lib., Missoula, Mont. Tel. 406-721-2665, e-mail hbray@missoula.lib.mt.us; *1st V.P./Pres.-Elect* Gwendolyn Haley, Spokane County (Washington) Lib. Dist.; *2nd V.P.* Jay Peters, Coquitlam Public Lib., 575 Poirier St., Coquitlam, BC V3J 6A. Tel. 604-937-4148 ext. 4248, e-mail jpeters@library.coquitlam.bc.ca; *Secy.* Candice Stenstrom, Public Lib. InterLINK, 5489 Byrne Rd., Burnaby, BC V5J 3J1. Tel. 604-437-8441, fax 604-437-8410, e-mail candice.stenstrom@ interlink; *Treas.* Katie Cargill, Eastern Washington Univ. Libs., 816 F St., Cheney, WA 99004. Tel. 509-999-6714, e-mail kcargill@ ewu.edu; *Past Pres.* Kelsey Keyes, Albertsons Lib., Boise State Univ., Boise, ID. Tel. 208-426-1139, e-mail kelseykeyes@boisestate.edu.

Address correspondence to the president, Pacific Northwest Lib. Assn.

World Wide Web http://www.pnla.org.

Southeastern: Ala., Ark., Fla., Ga., Ky., La., Miss., N.C., S.C., Tenn., Va., W.Va.

Memb. 500. Publication. *The Southeastern Librarian (SELn)* (q.). *Ed.* Perry Bratcher, 503A Steely Lib., Northern Kentucky Univ., Highland Heights, KY 41099. Tel. 859-572-6309, fax 859-572-6181, e-mail bratcher@nku.edu.

Pres. Camille McCutcheon. E-mail cmccutcheon@uscupstate.edu; *V.P.* Linda Suttle Harris. *Secy.* Sue Alexander; *Treas.* Beverly James; *Past Pres.* Gordon N. Baker, Clayton State Univ. Lib. E-mail gordonbaker@clayton. edu.

Address correspondence to Southeastern Lib. Assn., Admin. Services, P.O. Box 950, Rex, GA 30273-0950. Tel. 770-961-3520, fax 770-961-3712.

World Wide Web http://selaonline.org.

State and Provincial Library Agencies

The state library administrative agency in each of the U.S. states will have the latest information on its state plan for the use of federal funds under the Library Services and Technology Act (LSTA). The directors and addresses of these state agencies are listed below.

Alabama

Nancy C. Pack, Dir., Alabama Public Lib. Service, 6030 Monticello Drive, Montgomery 36130-6000. Tel. 334-213-3901, fax 334-213-3993, e-mail npack@apls.state.al.us. World Wide Web http://statelibrary.alabama.gov.

Alaska

Linda S. Thibodeau, State Libn. and Dir., Alaska Dept. of Educ., Div. of Libs., Archives, and Museums, P.O. Box 110571, Juneau 99811. Tel. 907-465-2911, fax 907-465-2151, e-mail linda.thibodeau@alaska.gov. World Wide Web http://library.state.ak.us.

Arizona

Joan Clark, State Libn., Arizona State Lib., Archives, and Public Records, 1700 W. Washington, Phoenix 85007. Tel. 602-926-4035, fax 602-256-7983, e-mail jclark@azlibrary.gov. World Wide Web http://www.lib.az.us.

Arkansas

Carolyn Ashcraft, State Libn., Arkansas State Lib., 900 W. Capitol, Suite 100, Little Rock 72201-3108. Tel. 501-682-1526, fax 501-682-1899, e-mail carolyn@library.arkansas.gov. World Wide Web http://www.library.arkansas.gov.

California

Greg Lucas, State Libn., California State Lib., P.O. Box 942837, Sacramento 94237-0001. Tel. 916-323-9750, fax 916-323-9768, e-mail greg.lucas@library.ca.gov. World Wide Web http://www.library.ca.gov.

Colorado

Eugene Hainer, Dir. and State Libn., Colorado State Lib., Rm. 309, 201 E. Colfax Ave., Denver 80203-1799. Tel. 303-866-6733, fax 303-866-6940, e-mail hainer_g@cde.state.co.us. World Wide Web http://www.cde.state.co.us/cdelib.

Connecticut

Kendall F. Wiggin, State Libn., Connecticut State Lib., 231 Capitol Ave., Hartford 06106. Tel. 860-757-6510, fax 860-757-6503, e-mail kendall.wiggin@ct.gov. World Wide Web http://www.cslib.org.

Delaware

Annie Norman, State Libn. and Dir., Delaware Div. of Libs., 121 Martin Luther King Jr. Blvd. N., Dover 19901. Tel. 302-257-3001, fax 302-739-8436, e-mail annie.norman@state.de.us. World Wide Web http://www.state.lib.de.us.

District of Columbia

Richard Reyes-Gavilan, Exec. Dir., District of Columbia Public Lib., 901 G St. N.W., Suite 400, Washington 20001-4599. Tel. 202-727-1101, fax 202-727-1129, e-mail rrg@dc.gov. World Wide Web http://www.dclibrary.org.

Florida

Judith A. Ring, State Libn., Div. of Lib. and Info. Services, R. A. Gray Bldg., 500 S. Bronough St., Tallahassee 32399-0250. Tel. 850-245-6604, fax 850-488-2746, e-mail jring@dos.state.fl.us. World Wide Web http://dlis.dos.state.fl.us/library.

Georgia

Julie Walker, State Libn., Georgia Public Lib. Services, 1800 Century Place, Suite 150, Atlanta 30345-4304. Tel. 404-235-7140, fax 404-235-7201, e-mail jwalker@georgialibraries.org. World Wide Web http://www.georgialibraries.org.

Hawaii

Richard Burns, State Libn., Hawaii State Public Lib. System, 44 Merchant St., Honolulu 96813. Tel. 808-586-3704, fax 808-586-3715, e-mail stlib@librarieshawaii.org. World Wide Web http://www.librarieshawaii.org.

Idaho

Ann Joslin, State Libn., Idaho Commission for Libs., 325 W. State St., Boise 83702-6072. Tel. 208-334-2150, fax 208-334-4016, e-mail ann.joslin@libraries.idaho.gov. World Wide Web http://libraries.idaho.gov.

Illinois

Anne Craig, Dir., Illinois State Lib., 300 S. 2 St., Springfield 62701-1703. Tel. 217-782-2994, fax 217-785-4326, e-mail acraig@ilsos.net. World Wide Web http://www.cyberdrive illinois.com/departments/library/home.html.

Indiana

Jacob Speer, Dir. and State Libn., Indiana State Lib., 315 W. Ohio St., Indianapolis 46202. Tel. 317-232-3693, fax 317-232-3728, e-mail jspeer1@library.in.gov. World Wide Web http://www.in.gov/library.

Iowa

Barbara Corson, Interim State Libn., State Lib. of Iowa, 1112 E. Grand Ave., Des Moines 50319. Tel. 515-281-4105, fax 515-281-6191, e-mail barb.corson@lib.state.ia.us. World Wide Web http://www.statelibraryofiowa.org.

Kansas

Jo Budler, State Libn., State Lib. of Kansas, Rm. 312-N, 300 S.W. 10 Ave., Topeka 66612-1593. Tel. 785-296-5466, fax 785-296-6650, e-mail jo.budler@library.ks.gov. World Wide Web http://www.kslib.info.

Kentucky

Wayne Onkst, State Libn. and Commissioner, Kentucky Dept. for Libs. and Archives, P.O. Box 537, 300 Coffee Tree Rd., Frankfort 40602-0537. Tel. 502-564-8300 ext. 312, fax 502-564-5773, e-mail wayne.onkst@ky.gov. World Wide Web http://www.kdla.ky.gov.

Louisiana

Rebecca Hamilton, State Libn., State Lib. of Louisiana, P.O. Box 131, 701 N. 4 St., Baton Rouge 70821-0131. Tel. 225-342-4923, fax 225-219-4804, e-mail rhamilton@crt.state.la.us. World Wide Web http://www.state.lib.la.us.

Maine

James Ritter, State Libn., Maine State Lib., 64 State House Sta., Augusta 04333-0064. Tel. 207-287-5620, fax 207-287-5624, e-mail linda.lord@maine.gov. World Wide Web http://www.state.me.us/msl.

Maryland

Irene Padilla, Asst. State Superintendent for Libs., State Dept. of Educ., Div. of Lib. Development and Services, 200 W. Baltimore St., Baltimore 21201. Tel. 410-767-0435, fax 410-333-2507, e-mail ipadilla@msde.state.md.us. World Wide Web http://www.marylandpublic schools.org/MSDE/divisions/library.

Massachusetts

Dianne Carty, Dir., Massachusetts Board of Lib. Commissioners, 98 N. Washington St., Suite 401, Boston 02114-1933. Tel. 617-725-1860 ext. 222, fax 617-725-0140, e-mail dianne.carty@state.ma.us. World Wide Web http://mblc.state.ma.us.

Michigan

Randy Riley, State Libn., Lib. of Michigan, 702 W. Kalamazoo St., P.O. Box 30007, Lansing 48909-7507. Tel. 517-373-5860, fax 517-373-5700, e-mail rileyr@michigan.gov. World Wide Web http://www.michigan.gov/libraryofmichigan.

Minnesota

Jennifer R. Nelson, Dir. of State Lib Services, Minnesota State Lib. Agency, Div. of State Lib. Services, Dept. of Educ., 1500 Hwy. 36 W., Roseville 55113-4266. Tel. 651-582-8791, fax

651-582-8752, e-mail jennifer.r.nelson@state.mn.us. World Wide Web http://education.state.mn.us/MDE/stusuc/lib.statelibserv/index.html.

Mississippi

Susan Cassagne, Exec. Dir., Mississippi Lib. Commission, 3881 Eastwood Drive, Jackson 39211. Tel. 601-432-4039, fax 601-432-4480, e-mail susan@mlc.lib.ms.us. World Wide Web http://www.mlc.lib.ms.us.

Missouri

Barbara A. Reading, State Libn., Missouri State Lib., P.O. Box 387, 600 W. Main, Jefferson City 65102-0387. Tel. 573-526-4783, fax 573-751-3612, e-mail barbara.reading@sos.mo.gov. World Wide Web http://www.sos.mo.gov/library.

Montana

Jennie Stapp, State Libn., Montana State Lib., 1515 E. 6 Ave., P.O. Box 201800, Helena 59620-1800. Tel. 406-444-3116, fax 406-444-0266, e-mail jstapp2@mt.gov. World Wide Web http://msl.mt.gov.

Nebraska

Rodney G. Wagner, Dir., Nebraska Lib. Commission, Suite 120, The Atrium, 1200 N St., Lincoln 68508-2023. Tel. 402-471-4001, fax 402-471-2083, e-mail rod.wagner@nebraska.gov. World Wide Web http://www.nlc.nebraska.gov.

Nevada

Daphne DeLeon, State Lib. and Archives Admin., Nevada State Lib. and Archives, 100 N. Stewart St., Carson City 89710-4285. Tel. 775-684-3315, fax 775-684-3311, e-mail ddeleon@admin.nv.gov. World Wide Web http://nsla.nv.gov.

New Hampshire

Michael York, State Libn., New Hampshire State Lib., 20 Park St., Concord 03301-6314. Tel. 603-271-2397, fax 603-271-6826, e-mail michael.york@dcr.nh.gov. World Wide Web http://www.state.nh.us/nhsl.

New Jersey

Mary Chute, State Libn., New Jersey State Lib., P.O. Box 520, Trenton 08625-0520. Tel. 609-278-2640 ext. 101, fax 609-278-2652, e-mail mchute@njstatelib.org. World Wide Web http://www.njstatelib.org.

New Mexico

Michael Delello, Interim State Libn., New Mexico State Lib., 1209 Camino Carlos Rey, Santa Fe 87507. Tel. 505-827-6354, fax 505-476-9761, e-mail michael.delello@state.nm.us. World Wide Web http://www.nmstatelibrary.org.

New York

Bernard A. Margolis, State Libn. and Assistant Commissioner for Libs., New York State Lib., Room 10C34, 222 Madison Ave., Albany 12230. Tel. 518-486-4865, fax 518-486-6880, e-mail bmargolis@mail.nysed.gov. World Wide Web http://www.nysl.nysed.gov.

North Carolina

Caroline "Cal" Shepard, State Libn., State Lib. of North Carolina, Admin. Section, 4640 Mail Service Center, 109 E. Jones St., Raleigh 27699-4640. Tel. 919-807-7410, fax 919-733-8748, e-mail cal.shepard@ncdcr.gov. World Wide Web http://statelibrary.ncdcr.gov.

North Dakota

Mary J. Soucie, State Libn., North Dakota State Lib., 604 E. Boulevard Ave., Dept. 250, Bismarck 58505-0800. Tel. 701-328-2492, fax 701-328-2040, e-mail msoucie@nd.gov. World Wide Web http://ndsl.lib.state.nd.us.

Ohio

Beverly Cain, State Libn., State Lib. of Ohio, Suite 100, 274 E. 1 Ave., Columbus 43201. Tel. 614-644-6843, fax 614-466-3584, e-mail bcain@library.ohio.gov. World Wide Web http://www.library.ohio.gov.

Oklahoma

Susan C. McVey, Dir., Oklahoma Dept. of Libs., 200 N.E. 18 St., Oklahoma City 73105-

3298. Tel. 405-522-3173, fax 405-522-1077, e-mail smcvey@oltn.odl.state.ok.us. World Wide Web http://www.odl.state.ok.us.

Oregon

MaryKay Dahlgreen, State Libn., Oregon State Lib., 250 Winter St. N.E., Salem 97301. Tel. 503-378-4367, fax 503-585-8059, e-mail marykay.dahlgreen@state.or.us. World Wide Web http://oregon.gov/OSL.

Pennsylvania

Stacey Aldrich, Deputy Secy. of Educ. and Commissioner for Libs., Pennsylvania Office of Commonwealth Libs., 607 South Drive, Harrisburg 17120-0600. Tel. 717-783-2466, fax 717-772-3265, e-mail saldrich@pa.gov. World Wide Web http://www.portal.state.pa.us/portal/server.pt/community/bureau_of_state_library/8811.

Rhode Island

Karen Mellor, Acting Chief Lib. Officer, Rhode Island Office of Lib. and Info. Services, 1 Capitol Hill, second flr., Providence 02908-5803. Tel. 401-574-9304, fax 401-574-9320, e-mail karen.mellor@olis.ri.gov. World Wide Web http://www.olis.ri.gov.

South Carolina

Leesa Benggio, Acting Dir., South Carolina State Lib., 1430 Senate St., P.O. Box 11469, Columbia 29211. Tel. 803-734-8668, fax 803-734-8676, e-mail lbenggio@statelibrary.sc.gov. World Wide Web http://www.statelibrary.sc.gov.

South Dakota

Daria Bossman, State Libn., South Dakota State Lib., 800 Governors Drive, Pierre 57501-2294. Tel. 605-773-3167, fax 605-773-6962, e-mail daria.bossman@state.sd.us. World Wide Web http://library.sd.gov.

Tennessee

Chuck Sherrill, State Libn. and Archivist, Tennessee State Lib. and Archives, 403 Seventh Ave. N., Nashville 37243-0312. Tel. 615-741-7996, fax 615-532-9293, e-mail chuck.sherrill@tn.gov. World Wide Web http://www.tennessee.gov/tsla.

Texas

Mark Smith, Dir. and Libn., Texas State Lib. and Archives Commission, 1201 Brazos St., P.O. Box 12927, Austin 78711-2927. Tel. 512-463-6856, fax 512-463-5436, e-mail msmith@tsl.state.tx.us. World Wide Web http://www.tsl.state.tx.us.

Utah

Donna Jones Morris, Dir. and State Libn., Utah State Lib. Div., Suite A, 250 N. 1950 W., Salt Lake City 84116-7901. Tel. 801-715-6770, fax 801-715-6767, e-mail dmorris@utah.gov. World Wide Web http://library.utah.gov.

Vermont

Martha Reid, State Libn., Vermont Dept. of Libs., 109 State St., Montpelier 05609. Tel. 802-828-3265, fax 802-828-2199, e-mail martha.reid@mail.dol.state.vt.us. World Wide Web http://dol.state.vt.us.

Virginia

Sandra G. Treadway, Libn. of Virginia, Lib. of Virginia, 800 E. Broad St., Richmond 23219-8000. Tel. 804-692-3535, fax 804-692-3594, e-mail sandra.treadway@lva.virginia.gov. World Wide Web http://www.lva.virginia.gov.

Washington

Rand Simmons, State Libn., Washington State Lib., Office of the Secy. of State, 6880 Capitol Blvd., P.O. Box 42460, Olympia 98504. Tel. 360-570-5585, fax 360-586-7575, e-mail rand.simmons@sos.wa.gov. World Wide Web http://www.sos.wa.gov/library.

West Virginia

Karen Goff, Dir./State Libn., West Virginia Lib. Commission, Cultural Center, 1900 Kanawha Blvd. E., Charleston 25305. Tel. 304-558-2041, fax 304-558-2044, e-mail karen.e.goff@wv.gov. World Wide Web http://www.librarycommission.wv.gov.

Wisconsin

Kurt Kiefer, Asst. State Superintendent, Wisconsin Dept. of Public Instruction, Div. for Libs. and Technology, P.O. Box 7841, Madison 53707-7841. Tel. 608-266-2205, fax 608-266-9207, e-mail kurt.kiefer@dpi.wi.gov. World Wide Web http://dlt.dpi.wi.gov.

Wyoming

Lesley Boughton, State Libn., Wyoming State Lib., 2800 Central Ave., Cheyenne 82002. Tel. 307-777-5911, fax 307-777-6289, e-mail lbough@wyo.gov. World Wide Web http://www-wsl.state.wy.us.

American Samoa

Justin H. Maga, Acting Territorial Libn., Feleti Barstow Public Lib., P.O. Box 997687, Pago Pago, AS 96799. Tel. 684-633-5816, fax 684-633-5823, e-mail justinmaga@gmail.com. World Wide Web http://fbpl.org.

Federated States of Micronesia

Augustine Kohler, Acting Dir., National Archives, Culture, and Historic Preservation, P.O. Box PS 175, Palikir, Pohnpei, FM 96941. Tel. 691-320-2343, fax 691-320-5634, e-mail hpo@mail.fm. World Wide Web http://www.fsmgov.org.

Guam

Sandra Stanley, Admin. Officer, Guam Public Lib. System, 254 Martyr St., Hagatna 96910-5141. Tel. 671-475-4765, fax 671-477-9777, e-mail sandra.stanley@gpls.guam.gov. World Wide Web http://gpls.guam.gov.

Northern Mariana Islands

John Oliver Gonzales, Exec. Dir., CNMI Joeten-Kiyu Public Lib., P.O. Box 501092, Saipan, MP 96950-1092. Tel. 670-235-7324, fax 670-235-7550, e-mail joetenkiyupublic library@gmail.com. World Wide Web http://www.cnmilibrary.com.

Palau

Sinton Soalablai, Chief of School Mgt., Palau Ministry of Educ., P.O. Box 189, Koror, PW 96940. Tel. 680-488-2952, fax 680-488-8465, e-mail ssoalablai@palaumoe.net. World Wide Web http://palaugov.net.

Puerto Rico

Miguel A. Hernández, Dir., Lib. and Info. Services Program, Puerto Rico Dept. of Educ., P.O. Box 190759, San Juan 00919-0759. Tel. 787-773-3564, fax 787-753-6945, e-mail hernandez _mi@de.gobierno.pr. World Wide Web http://www.de.gobierno.pr/tags/bibliotecas.

Republic of the Marshall Islands

Amenta Matthew, Exec. Dir., Alele Museum, Lib., National Archives, P.O. Box 629, Majuro, MH 96960. Tel. 692-455-5707, fax 692-625-3226, e-mail alelemuseum@gmail.com. World Wide Web http://alelemuseum.tripod.com/index.html.

U.S. Virgin Islands

Ingrid Bough, Territorial Dir., Div. of Libs., Archives, and Museums, Dept. of Planning and Natural Resources, 1122 King St., Christiansted, St. Croix, VI 00820. Tel. 340-773-5715, fax 340-773-5327, e-mail ingrid.bough@dpnr.vi.gov. World Wide Web http://www.virgin islandspace.org/division%20of%20libraries/dlamhome.htm.

Canada

Alberta

Diana Davidson, Dir., Public Lib. Services Branch, Alberta Municipal Affairs, 803 Standard Life Centre, 10405 Jasper Ave., Edmonton T5J 4R7. Tel. 780-415-0284, fax 780-415-8594, e-mail diana.davidson@gov.ab.ca or libraries@gov.ab.ca. World Wide Web http://www.municipalaffairs.alberta.ca/alberta_libraries.cfm.

British Columbia

Beverley Shaw, Dir., Public Lib. Services Branch, Ministry of Educ., P.O. Box 9161, Stn. Prov. Govt., Victoria V8W 9H3. Tel. 250-415-1662, fax 250 953-4985, e-mail bev.shaw@gov.bc.ca. World Wide Web http://www.bced.gov.bc.ca/pls.

Manitoba

Dir., Public Lib. Services, Manitoba Dept. of Tourism, Culture, Heritage, Sport and Consumer Protection, 300-1011 Rosser Ave., Brandon R7A OL5. Tel. 204-726-6590, fax 204-726-6868, e-mail pls@gov.mb.ca. World Wide Web http://www.gov.mb.ca/chc/pls/index.html.

New Brunswick

Sylvie Nadeau, Exec. Dir., New Brunswick Public Lib. Service, Place 2000, 250 King St., P.O. Box 6000, Fredericton E3B 5H1. Tel. 506-453-2354, fax 506-444-4064, e-mail sylvie.nadeau@gnb.ca. World Wide Web http://www.gnb.ca/0003/index-e.asp.

Newfoundland and Labrador

Shawn Tetford, Exec. Dir., Provincial Info. and Lib. Resources Board, 48 St. George's Ave., Stephenville A2N 1K9. Tel. 709-643-0902, fax 709-643-0925, e-mail stetford@nlpl.ca. World Wide Web http://www.nlpl.ca.

Northwest Territories

Alison Hopkins, Territorial Libn., NWT Lib. Services, 75 Woodland Drive, Hay River X0E 1G1. Tel. 867-874-6531, fax 867-874-3321, e-mail alison_hopkins@gov.nt.ca. World Wide Web http://www.nwtpls.gov.nt.ca.

Nova Scotia

Jennifer Evans, Dir., Provincial Libn., Nova Scotia Provincial Lib., 3770 Kempt Rd., Halifax B3K 4X8. Tel. 902-424-2457, fax 902-424-0633, World Wide Web http://www.library.ns.ca.

Nunavut

Ron Knowling, Mgr., Nunavut Public Lib. Services, Box 270, Baker Lake X0C 0A0. Tel. 867-793-3353, fax 867-793-3360, e-mail rknowling@gov.nu.ca. World Wide Web http://www.publiclibraries.nu.ca.

Ontario

Rod Sawyer, Ontario Government Ministry of Tourism, Culture, and Sport, Hearst Block, 900 Bay St., Toronto M7A 2E1. Tel. 416-326-9326. World Wide Web http://www.mtc.gov.on.ca/en/libraries/contact.shtml.

Ontario Lib. Service–North, 334 Regent St., Sudbury P3C 4E2. Tel. 705-675-6467. World Wide Web http://www.olsn.ca. Joyce Cunningham, Chair.

Southern Ontario Lib. Service, No. 1504, 1 Yonge St., Toronto M5E 1E5. Tel. 416-961-1669, fax 416-961-5122. World Wide Web http://www.sols.org. Barbara Franchetto, CEO. E-mail bfranchetto@sols.org.

Prince Edward Island

Public Lib. Service of Prince Edward Island, P.O. Box 7500, Morell C0A 1S0. Tel. 902-961-7320, fax 902-961-7322, e-mail plshq@gov.pe.ca. World Wide Web http://www.library.pe.ca.

Quebec

Christiane Barbe, Chair and CEO, Bibliothèque et Archives Nationales du Québec (BAnQ), 2275 rue Holt, Montreal H2G 3H1. Tel. 800-363-9028 or 514-873-1100, fax 514-873-9312, info@banq.qc.ca. World Wide Web http://www.banq.qc.ca/portal/dt/accueil.jsp.

Saskatchewan

Brett Waytuck, Provincial Libn., Provincial Lib. and Literacy Office, Ministry of Educ., 409A Park St., Regina S4N 5B2. Tel. 306-787-2972, fax 306-787-2029, e-mail brett.waytuck@gov.sk.ca. World Wide Web http://www.education.gov.sk.ca/provincial-library/public-library-system.

Yukon Territory

Julie Ourom, Dir., Public Libs., Community Development Div., Dept. of Community Services, Government of Yukon, P.O. Box 2703, Whitehorse Y1A 2C6. Tel. 867-667-5447, fax 867-393-6333, e-mail julie.ourom@gov.yk.ca. World Wide Web http://www.ypl.gov.yk.ca.

State School Library Media Associations

Alabama

Children's and School Libns. Div., Alabama Lib. Assn. Memb. 600+. Publication. *The Alabama Librarian* (q.).

Chair Susan Cordell, Sta. 33, Univ. of West Alabama, Livingston 35470. Tel. 205-652-5421, fax 205-652-3706, e-mail scordell@uwa.edu; *V. Chair/Chair-Elect* Cendy Cooper, Tarrant Middle/H.S., 91 Black Creek Rd., Tarrant 35217. Tel. 205-849-0172, e-mail cooperc@tarrant.k12.al.us; *Past Chair* Carolyn Starkey, Buckhorn H.S., 25 Warren Rd., Albertville 35950. Tel. 256-302-1009, e-mail admin@jojo-starkey.com.

Address correspondence to the association administrator, Alabama Lib. Assn., 6030 Monticello Drive, Montgomery 36117. Tel. 334-414-0113, e-mail allibraryassoc@gmail.com.

World Wide Web http://allanet.org.

Alaska

Alaska Assn. of School Libns. Memb. 100+. Publication. *The Puffin* (3 a year), online at http://akasl.org/puffin-newsletter. *Ed.* Alta Collins, Northern Lights ABC School, Anchorage. E-mail collins_alta@asdk12.org.

Pres. Deborah Rinio, North Pole Middle School, Fairbanks. E-mail akasl.president@gmail.com; *Pres.-Elect* Dona Helmer, College Gate Elementary, Anchorage. E-mail helmer_dona@asdk12.org; *Secy.* Amelia Mitchell, Ryan Middle School, Northstar, Fairbanks; *Treas.* Laura Guest, Turnagain Elementary, Anchorage. E-mail guest_laura@asdk12.us; *Past Pres.* Wendy Stout, Larson Elementary, Wasilla. E-mail wendy.stout@matsuk12.us.

World Wide Web http://www.akasl.org.

Arizona

Teacher-Libn. Div., Arizona Lib. Assn. Memb. 1,000. Term of Office. Jan.–Dec. Publication. *AZLA Newsletter.*

Chair Shirley Berow, Desert Harbor Elementary, 15585 N. 91 Ave., Peoria 85382. Tel. 623-486-6216, e-mail sberow@cox.net.

Address correspondence to the chairperson.

World Wide Web http://www.azla.affiniscape.com.

Arkansas

Arkansas Assn. of School Libns., div. of Arkansas Lib. Assn.

Chair Wendy Rickman, Univ. of Central Arkansas, Conway 72035. Tel. 501-450-5431, e-mail arasl@uca.edu; *Past Chair* Erin Shaw, Greenbrier Middle School, 13 School Drive, Greenbrier 72058. Tel. 501-679-2113, e-mail shawe@greenbrierschools.org.

Address correspondence to the president.

World Wide Web http://www.arlib.org/organization/aasl/index.php.

California

California School Lib. Assn. Memb. 1,200+. Publications. *CSLA Journal* (2 a year). *Ed.* Jeanne Nelson. E-mail nelson.jeanne914@gmail.com; *CSLA Newsletter* (10 a year, memb., via e-mail).

(State Board) *Pres.* Liz Dodds, Bullard H.S., 5445 N. Palm Ave., Fresno 93704. Tel. 559-451-4405, e-mail liz.dodds@gmail.com; *Pres.-Elect* Beth Olshewsky, 1290 Ridder Park Drive, MC232, San José 95131-2304. Tel. 408-453-6670, fax 408-453-6815, e-mail beth_olshewsky@sccoe.org; *Secy:* Nina Jackson; *Treas.* Kathie Maier; *Past Pres.* Janice Gilmore-See; (Northern Region) *Pres.* Jessica Lee; *Pres.-Elect* Lisa Bishop; (Southern Region) *Pres.* Sondra Keckley; *Pres.-Elect* Sharlene Paxton.

Address correspondence to the association at 6444 E. Spring St., No. 237, Long Beach 90815-1553. Tel./fax 888-655-8480, e-mail info@csla.net.

World Wide Web http://www.csla.net.

Colorado

Colorado Assn. of School Libns. Memb. 250+.

Pres. Megan McQuinn, Farrell B. Howell ECE-8, Denver. E-mail megan_mcquinn@dpsk12.org.

World Wide Web http://www.cal-webs. org/?page=CASL.

Connecticut

Connecticut Assn. of School Libns. (formerly Connecticut Educ. Media Assn.). Memb. 500+. Term of Office. July–June.

Pres. Mary Ellen Minichiello. E-mail meminichiello@milforded.org; *V.P.* Shelley Stedman. E-mail slstedman@hotmail.com; *Recording Secy.* Christopher Barlow. E-mail christophbarlow@sbcglobal.net; *Treas.* Jody Pillar. E-mail pillarj@gilbertschool.org; *Past Pres.* Sara Kelley-Mudie. E-mail librarian. skm@gmail.com; *Admin. Secy.* Anne Weimann, 25 Elmwood Ave., Trumbull 06611. Tel. 203-372-2260, e-mail aweimann@snet.net.

Address correspondence to the administrative secretary.

World Wide Web http://www.ctcasl.com.

Delaware

Delaware School Lib. Assn., div. of Delaware Lib. Assn. Memb. 100+. Publications. *DSLA Newsletter* (online; irreg.); column in *DLA Bulletin* (3 a year).

Pres. Jen Delgado, Henry B. duPont Middle School, 735 Meeting House Rd., Hockessin 19707. Tel. 302-239-3420, e-mail jennifer. delgado@redclay.k12.de.us; *V.P./Pres.-Elect* Bonnie Gaus, May B. Leasure School, 1015 Church Rd., Newark 19702. Tel. 302-454-2103 ext. 408, fax 302-454-2109, e-mail gausb@ christina.k12.de.us; *Secy.* Tamara Carr. E-mail tcarr@caravel.org; *Past Pres.* Janice Haney, Appoquinimink H.S., 1080 Bunker Hill Rd., Middletown 19709. E-mail janice.haney@ appo.k12.de.us.

Address correspondence to the president.

World Wide Web http://www2.lib.udel.edu/ dla/divisions/dsla13.htm.

District of Columbia

District of Columbia Assn. of School Libns. Memb. 8. Publication. *Newsletter* (4 a year).

Pres. André Maria Taylor. E-mail diva librarian2@aol.com.

Address correspondence to André Maria Taylor, 330 10th St. N.E., Washington, DC 20002. Tel. 301-502-4203.

Florida

Florida Assn. for Media in Educ. Memb. 1,400+. Term of Office. Nov.–Oct. Publication. *Florida Media Quarterly. Ed.* Maggie Josephson.

Pres. Michelle Jarret. E-mail jarrettm@ osceola.k12.fl.us; *Pres.-Elect* Lucretia Miller. E-mail millerL7@duvalschools.org; *Secy.* Andrea Parisi; *Treas.* Lorri Cosgrove. E-mail cosgrol@stjohns.k12.fl.us; *Past Pres.* Henry Haake. E-mail henry.haake@polk-fl.net.

Address correspondence to FAME, P.O. Box 4778, Haines City 33845-4778. Tel. 813-380-5673, e-mail floridamediaed@gmail.com.

World Wide Web http://www.floridamedia. org.

Georgia

Georgia Assn. of School Libns.

Chair Lucy Green, Georgia Southern Univ. E-mail lgreen@georgiasouthern.edu; *Chair-Elect* Stephanie Jones, Georgia Southern Univ., P.O. Box 8131, Statesboro 30460-8131. Tel. 912-478-5250, e-mail sjones@georgiasouthern.edu.

Address correspondence to School Lib. Media Div., Georgia Lib. Assn., P.O. Box 793, Rex, GA 30273.

World Wide Web http://gla.georgialibraries. org/div_media.htm.

Georgia Lib. Media Assn. Memb. 700+.

Pres. Beth Miller; *Pres.-Elect* Debbie Sandford; *Secy.* Janelle McClure; *Treas.* Lora Taft; *Past Pres.* Andy Spinks; *Exec. Dir.* Lasa Joiner.

Address correspondence to GLMA Executive Office, 2711 Irvin Way, Suite 111, Decatur 30030. Tel. 404-299-7700, fax 404-299-7029, e-mail glma@jlh-consulting.com.

World Wide Web http://www.glma-inc.org.

Hawaii

Hawaii Assn. of School Libns. Memb. 145. Term of Office. June–May. Publication. *HASL Newsletter* (3 a year).

Pres. Sherry Rose; *V.P., Programming* Nalani Naluai; *V.P., Membership* Diane Mokuau; *Corresponding Secy.* Terry Heckman; *Recording Secy.* Deb Peterson; *Treas.* Danielle Fujii.

Address correspondence to the association, P.O. Box 235284, Honolulu 96823.

World Wide Web https://sites.google.com/site/haslsite.

Idaho

Educ. Media Div., Idaho Lib. Assn. Memb. 40+.

Chair Sara Murphy, Meridian Middle School, West Ada School Dist. E-mail murphy.sara@meridianschools.org; *Chair-Elect* Jessica Bowman, Sandpoint Middle School, Lake Pend Oreille School Dist. E-mail bowm9663@gmail.com; *Past Chair* Debbie Jenson, Fairmont Junior H.S., Boise School Dist. Tel. 208-854-4796, e-mail deborah.jenson@boiseschools.org.

Address correspondence to the chairperson.

World Wide Web http://www.idaholibraries.org/about-us/officersdivisionscommittees/educational-media-division.

Illinois

Illinois School Lib. Media Assn. Memb. 1,000. Term of Office. July–June. Publications. *ISLMA News* (4 a year); *Linking for Learning: The Illinois School Library Media Program Guidelines* (3rd ed., 2010); *Powerful Libraries Make Powerful Learners: The Illinois Study.*

Pres. Stephanie Stieglitz, Lane School, Hinsdale. E-mail sstieglitz@d181.org; *Pres.-Elect* Angie Green, Illini Bluffs SD No. 327, Glasford. E-mail angela.green0905@gmail.com; *Secy.* Christy Semande, Canton USD 66, Canton. E-mail csemande@yahoo.com; *Treas.* Lauren Ochs, Warrensburg-Latham H.S., Warrensburg. E-mail ochsl@wl.k12.il.us; *Past Pres.* Debra Turner, Metea Valley H.S., 1801 N. Eola Rd., Aurora, IL 60502. Tel. 630-375-8851. E-mail debbie_turner@ipsd.org; *Exec. Secy./Membership* Becky Robinson, ISLMA, P.O. Box 1326, Galesburg 61402-1326. Tel. 309-341-1099, e-mail ISLMAexsec@gmail.com.

World Wide Web http://www.islma.org.

Indiana

Assn. of Indiana School Library Educators (AISLE). Publications. *Focus on Indiana Libraries* (mo.); *Indiana Libraries* (q.).

Pres. Gigi Shook, Center Grove H.S., 2717 S. Morgantown Rd., Greenwood 46143. Tel. 317-881-0581, e-mail shookg@centergrove. k12.in.us; *V.P.* Michelle Houser, 1000 E. North Adams Drive, Decatur 46733. Tel. 260-724-7121 ext. 2143, e-mail houserm@nadams.k12.in.us; *Secy.* Liz Green, Mitchell Elementary, 2809 W. Purdue Ave., Muncie 47304. Tel. 765-747-5413, e-mail lgreen@muncie.k12.in.us; *Treas.* Debbie Acord, Wells County Public Lib., 200 W. Washington St., Bluffton 46714. Tel. 260-824-1612, e-mail debbie.acord@gmail.com; *Past Pres.* Susie Highley, Creston Middle School, 10925 E. Prospect, Indianapolis 46239. Tel. 812-532-6806, fax 812-532-6891, e-mail shighley@warren.k12.in.us.

Address correspondence to the association, c/o Indiana Lib. Federation, 941 E. 86 St., Suite 260, Indianapolis 46240. Tel. 317-257-2040, fax 317-257-1389, e-mail ilf@indy.net.

World Wide Web http://www.ilfonline.org/?AISLE.

Iowa

Iowa Assn. of School Libns., div. of the Iowa Lib. Assn. Memb. 180+. Term of Office. Jan.–Jan. Publication. *IASL Journal* (online, 4 a year).

Chair Dixie Forcht. E-mail dixieforcht@gmail.com; *V. Chair* Kathrine Rogers. E-mail kathrine.rogers@mcsdonline.org; *Secy./Treas.* Sue Inhelder. E-mail sinhelder@marshalltown.k12.ia.us; *Past Chair* Christine Sturgeon. E-mail csturgeon@mnwcougars.com.

Address correspondence to the chairperson.

World Wide Web http://www.iasl-ia.org.

Kansas

Kansas Assn. of School Libns. Memb. 600. Publication. *KASL News* (online, q.).

Pres. Nancy McFarlin. E-mail kaslpresident@gmail.com; *Pres.-Elect* Marla Wigton. E-mail kaslpresidentelect@gmail.com; *Secy.* Sharon Parks. E-mail kaslsecretary@gmail.com; *Treas.* Brenda Lemon. E-mail kasltreasurer@gmail.com; *Past Pres.* Carmaine Ternes; E-mail kaslpastpresident@gmail.com; *Exec. Secy.* Barb Bahm. E-mail kaslexecsecretary@gmail.com.

Address correspondence to the executive secretary.

World Wide Web http://kasl.typepad.com/kasl.

Kentucky

Kentucky Assn. of School Libns. (KASL), section of Kentucky Lib. Assn. Memb. 600+. Publication. *KASL Newsletter* (q.).

Pres. Lisa Hughes, Lone Oak Intermediate School, 300 Cumberland Ave., Paducah 42001. Tel. 270-538-4160, e-mail lisa.hughes@mccracken.kyschools.us; *Pres.-Elect* James Allen. E-mail james.allen@oldham.kyschools.us; *Secy.* Renee Hale. E-mail renee.hale@warren.kyschools.us; *Treas.* Fred Tilsley. E-mail ftilsley@windstream.net; *Past Pres.* Janet Wells, Rockcastle County H.S. Tel. 606-256-4816, e-mail janet.wells@rockcastle.kyschools.us.

Address correspondence to the president.

World Wide Web http://www.kysma.org.

Louisiana

Louisiana Assn. of School Libns., section of Louisiana Lib. Assn. Memb. 230. Term of Office. July–June.

Pres. Kristy Sturm. Tel. 337-521-7411 ext. 18919, e-mail kasturm@lpssonline.com; *1st V.P./Pres.-Elect* Jade Calais. Tel. 337-521-7950, fax 337-521-7951, e-mail rjrcampbell@lpssonline.com; *2nd V.P.* Desiree Alexander. E-mail educatoralexander@gmail.com; *Secy.* Janet Gary. Tel. 337-364-3927, fax 337-365-9681, e-mail jgary@iberia.k12.la.us; *Past Pres.* Amanda Graves. Tel. 225-383-0397 ext.118, e-mail agraves@catholichigh.org.

Address correspondence to the association, c/o Louisiana Lib. Assn., 8550 United Plaza Blvd., Suite 1001, Baton Rouge 70809. Tel. 225-922-4642, fax 225-408-4422, e-mail office@llaonline.org.

World Wide Web http://llaonline.org/sig/lasl.php.

Maine

Maine Assn. of School Libs. Memb. 200+.

Pres. Joyce Lucas, Winslow H.S. E-mail jolukeme@gmail.com; *Pres.-Elect* Tina Taggart, Foxcroft Academy. E-mail tina.taggart@staff.foxcroftacademy.org; *Secy.* Janet Patterson. E-mail janet.patterson.mls@gmail.com; *Treas.* Dorothy Hall-Riddle. E-mail dorothy hallriddle@gmail.com; *Past Pres.* Eileen Broderick. E-mail ebroderick@rus10.org; *Business Mgr.* Edna Comstock, MASL, P.O. Box 634,

Augusta 04332-0634. Tel. 207-441-1410, e-mail masl@gwi.net.

Address correspondence to the president.

World Wide Web http://www.maslibraries.org.

Maryland

Maryland Assn. of School Libns. (formerly Maryland Educ. Media Organization).

Pres. Mary Jo Richmond, Frederick County Public Schools. E-mail president@maslmd.org; *Secy.* Linda S. Langr, High Point H.S., Prince George's County Public Schools. E-mail secretary@maslmd.org; *Treas.* Lynda Baker, Frederick County Public Schools. E-mail treasurer@maslmd.org; *Past Pres.* Michele Forney, Prince George's County Public Schools. E-mail michele.forney@gmail.com.

Address correspondence to the association, Box 21127, Baltimore 21228.

World Wide Web http://maslmd.org.

Massachusetts

Massachusetts School Lib. Assn. Memb. 800. Publication. *MSLA Forum* (3 a year).

Pres. Judi Paradis, Plympton Elementary, Waltham. Tel. 781-314-5767, e-mail jparadis@maschoolibraries.org; *Pres.-Elect* Anita Cellucci, Westborough H.S. Tel. 508-836-7720 ext. 5180; *Secy.* Carrie Tucker, E. Bridgewater H.S. Tel. 508-378-5841; *Treas.* Linda Friel. E-mail lafriel@maschoolibraries.org; *Past Pres.* Valerie Diggs, Chelmsford H.S. Tel. 978-251-5111; *Exec. Dir.* Kathy Lowe, Massachusetts School Lib. Assn., P.O. Box 658, Lunenburg 01462. Tel. 978-582-6967, e-mail klowe@maschoolibraries.org.

Address correspondence to the executive director.

World Wide Web http://www.maschoolibraries.org.

Michigan

Michigan Assn. for Media in Educ. Memb. 1,200. Publications. *Media Spectrum* (2 a year); *MAME Newsletter* (6 a year).

Pres. Kathy Lester, East Middle School, 1042 S. Mill St., Plymouth 48170. Tel. 734-416-4951, e-mail kathyl@mimame.org; *Pres.-Elect* Gwenn Marchesano, Pioneer Middle School, 46081 Ann Arbor Rd., Plymouth

48170. Tel. 734-416-7561, e-mail gmarchesano @mimame.org; *Secy.* Jeanna Walker, Portage Public Schools, 1000 Idaho St., Portage 49024. Tel. 269-323-5489, e-mail jwalker@portageps. org; *Past Pres.* Tom Stream, 15681 High Ridge Drive, Grand Haven 49417. Tel. 616-842-3335, e-mail tom.stream@mimame.org.

Address correspondence to MAME, 1407 Rensen, Suite 3, Lansing 48910. Tel. 517-394-2808, fax 517-394-2096, e-mail mame@ mimame.org.

World Wide Web http://www.mimame.org.

Minnesota

Info. and Technology Educators of Minnesota (ITEM) (formerly Minnesota Educ. Media Organization). Memb. 400+. Term of Office. July–June.

Pres. Mary Mehsikomer, TIES, 1667 Snelling Ave. N., St. Paul 55108. Tel. 651-999-6510, e-mail mary.mehsikomer@ties.k12. mn.us; *Co-Pres.-Elect* Andi Bodeau, Bloomington Public Schools. E-mail bodeaua@gmail. com; Jen Legatt, Hopkins Public Schools. E-mail jen.m.legatt@gmail.com; *Secy.* Rosalyn Obando, Richfield Middle School, 7461 Oliver Ave. S., Richfield 55423. Tel. 612-798-6400, e-mail rjobando@gmail.com; *Treas.* Robin Weber, Isanti 55040. Tel. 763-464-1503, e-mail weber@usinternet.com; *Past Co-Pres.* Karen Qualey, Hubert Olson Middle School, 4551 W. 102 St., Bloomington 55437. E-mail karenjoy113@gmail.com; Donna Ohlgren, Oak View Elementary, 6710 E. Fish Lake Rd., Maple Grove 55369. E-mail ohlgrend@gmail. com; *Admin. Asst.* Deanna Sylte, P.O. Box 130555, Roseville 55113. Tel. 651-771-8672, e-mail admin@memoweb.org.

World Wide Web http://mnitem.org.

Mississippi

School Lib. Section, Mississippi Lib. Assn. Memb. 1,300.

Chair Holly Gray, Tupelo High Schools. Tel. 662-841-8979, e-mail ehgray@gmail.com. *Exec. Secy.* Barbara J. Price.

Address correspondence to School Section, Mississippi Lib. Assn., P.O. Box 13687, Jackson 39236-3687. Tel. 601-981-4586, e-mail info@misslib.org.

World Wide Web http://www.misslib.org.

Missouri

Missouri Assn. of School Libns. Memb. 1,000. Term of Office. July–June. Publication. *Connections* (q.).

Pres. Lysha Thompson, Miller County R-3 Schools. E-mail lthompson@tuscumbialions. k12.mo.us; *1st V.P./Pres.-Elect* Margaret Sullivan, Rockwood Summit H.S., Marquette H.S., Rockwood School Dist. E-mail sullivan margaret@rockwood.k12.mo.us; *2nd V.P.* Amy Taylor, Lee's Summit West H.S. E-mail amy. taylor@leesummit.k12.mo.us; *Secy.* Rene Burress, Univ. of Central Missouri. E-mail burress@ucmo.edu; *Treas.* Kris Baughman, Eastwood Hills Elementary, Raytown C-2 School Dist. E-mail kris.baughman@raytown schools.org; *Past Pres.* Ellen Wickham, Raytown South H.S. E-mail wickhame@raytown schools.org.

Address correspondence to the association, P.O. Box 684, Jefferson City 65102. Tel. 573-635-6044, e-mail info@maslonline.org.

World Wide Web http://www.maslonline. org.

Montana

School Lib. Div., Montana Lib. Assn. Memb. 200+. Publication. *FOCUS* (published by Montana Lib. Assn.) (q.).

Chair Dana Carmichael, Whitefish Middle School, 221 Peregrine Lane, Whitefish 59937. Tel. 406-862-8650, e-mail carmichaeld@wfps. k12.mt.us; *V. Chair* Niki Keuch, Chief Joseph Middle School, 4255 Kimberwicke, Bozeman 59718. Tel. 406-522-6307, e-mail nkeuch@ gmail.com; *Past Chair* Lisa Lykins, Glacier H.S., 851 N. Main St., Kalispell 59901. Tel. 406-261-2338, e-mail lykinsl@sd5.k12.mt.us; *Exec. Dir., Montana Lib. Assn.* Debbi Kramer, P.O. Box 1352, Three Forks 59752. Tel. 406-579-3121, e-mail debkmla@hotmail.com.

World Wide Web http://www.mtlib.org.

Nebraska

Nebraska School Libns. Assn. Memb. 300+. Term of Office. July–June. Publication. *NSLA News* (q.).

Pres. Beth Kabes. E-mail bkabes@esu7. org; *Pres.-Elect* Laura Pietsch. E-mail laura. pietsch@ops.org; *Secy.* Stephanie Dannehl. E-mail sdannehl@esu11.org; *Treas.* Angie

Richeson. E-mail aricheso@esu10.org; *Past Pres.* Sherry Crow. E-mail crowsr@unk.edu; *Exec. Secy.* Kim Gangwish. E-mail contact nsla@gmail.com.

Address correspondence to the executive secretary, Bellevue West H.S., 1501 Thurston Ave., Bellevue 68123.

World Wide Web http://www.neschoollibrarians.org.

Nevada

Nevada School and Children Libns. Section, Nevada Lib. Assn. Memb. 120.

Chair Shar Murphy, Honors Academy of Literature. E-mail ms.shar@academyoflit.org; *Past Chair* Carla Land, Las Vegas-Clark County Lib. Dist. E-mail landc@lvccld.org; *Exec. Secy.* Kristy Isla. E-mail ardainia@yahoo.com.

Address correspondence to the executive secretary.

World Wide Web http://www.nevadalibraries.org/handbook/nscls.html.

New Hampshire

New Hampshire School Lib. Media Assn. Memb. 250+. Term of Office. July–June. Publication. *Online News* (winter, spring; online and print).

Pres. Carol Sweny, Henniker Community School. E-mail cdsweny@comcast.net; *V.P.* Donna Zecha, Hopkinton Middle/H.S. Lib., Contoocook. E-mail hophslibrary@hopkintonschools.org; *Recording Secy.* Caitlin Ahearn. E-mail cahearn@londonderry.org; *Treas.* Helen Burnham, Lincoln Street School, Exeter. E-mail hburnham@sau16.org; *Past Pres.* Pam Harland, Sanborn Regional H.S., Kingston. E-mail pharland@sau17.org.

Address correspondence to the president, NHSLMA, Box 418, Concord 03302-0418.

World Wide Web World Wide Web http://nhslma.org.

New Jersey

New Jersey Assn. of School Libns. (NJASL). Memb. 1,000+. Term of Office. Aug.–July.

Pres. Arlen Kimmelman, Clearview Regional H.S., Mullica Hill. E-mail president@njasl.org; *Pres.-Elect* Janet Clark, Cleveland Street School, Orange. E-mail presidentelect@njasl.org; *V.P.* Bruce DuBoff, Pennsauken

Intermediate School and Howard M. Phifer Middle School, Pennsauken. E-mail vicepresident@njasl.org; *Recording Secy.* Michelle McGreivey. E-mail recordingsecretary@njasl.org; *Treas.* Jean Stock. E-mail treasurer@njasl.org; *Past Pres.* Pam Gunter. E-mail immediatepastpresident@njasl.org.

Address correspondence to Elizabeth McArthur, Mgr., NJASL, P.O. Box 460, Collingswood 08108. E-mail associationmanager@njasl.org.

World Wide Web http://www.njasl.org.

New York

Section of School Libns., New York Lib. Assn., 6021 State Farm Rd., Guilderland, NY 12084. Tel. 518-432-6952, fax 518-427-1697, e-mail info@nyla.org†. Memb. 800+. Term of Office. Nov.–Oct. Publications. *SLMSGram* (q.); participates in *NYLA Bulletin* (mo. except July and Aug.).

Pres. Jill Leinung. E-mail mfleinung@gmail.com; *Pres.-Elect* Susan Polos; *Past Pres.* Karen Sperrazza. E-mail krnsprzz@gmail.com.

World Wide Web http://nylassl.weebly.com.

North Carolina

North Carolina School Lib. Media Assn. Memb. 1,000+. Term of Office. Nov.–Oct.

Pres. Joanna Gerakios, Pitt County Schools. Tel. 252-830-3516, fax 252-830-0206, e-mail gerakij@pitt.k12.nc.us; *Pres.-Elect* Walter Carmichael, Kimmel Farm Elementary, Winston Salem 27127. Tel. 336-703-6760, fax 336-784-4427, e-mail ncslmawalter@gmail.com; *Secy.* Jennifer Umbarger, Rogers-Herr Middle School, Durham Public Schools, Durham 27707. Tel. 919-560-3970 ext. 70235, e-mail jennifer.umbarger@dpsnc.net; *Treas.* Laura Bowers, Westwood Elementary, West Jefferson 28694. Tel. 336-877-2921, e-mail laura.bowers@ashe.k12.nc.us; *Past Pres.* Joann Absi, New Hanover County Schools, Wilmington 28412. Tel. 910-790-2360, fax 910-790-2356, e-mail joann.absi@nhcs.net.

Address correspondence to the president.

World Wide Web http://www.ncslma.org.

North Dakota

School Lib. and Youth Services Section, North Dakota Lib. Assn. Memb. 100. Publication. *The Good Stuff* (q.).

Chair Amber Emery, Fargo Public Lib. Tel. 701-241-1495,fax701-241-8581,e-mailaemery @cityoffargo.com.

World Wide Web http://ndlaonline.org.

Ohio

Ohio Educ. Lib. Media Assn. Memb. 1,000. Publications. *OELMA News* (3 a year); *Ohio Media Spectrum* (q.).

Pres. Angela Wojtecki, Nordonia Hills H.S., 8006 S. Bedford Drive, Macedonia 44056. Tel. 330-908-6030, e-mail oelma.awojtecki@ gmail.com; *V.P.* Liz Deskins, Hilliard Bradley H.S. 4629 Shaler Drive, Columbus 43228. Tel. 614-870-1641; *Secy.* Karen Gedeon, Cuyahoga Falls Middle School, 1057 Thornton Court, Macedonia 44056. Tel. 330-467-2017, e-mail kgedeon2@gmail.com; *Treas.* Lisa Barnes Prince, Stanton Middle School, 1175 Hudson Rd., Kent 44240. E-mail lbarnesprince@att. net; *Past Pres.* Susan Yutze. E-mail oelmasdy@ gmail.com; *Dir. of Services* Kate Brunswick, 17 S. High St., Suite 200, Columbus 43215. Tel. 614-221-1900, fax 614-221-1989, e-mail kate@assnoffices.com.

Address correspondence to the director of services.

World Wide Web http://www.oelma.org.

Oklahoma

Oklahoma School Libns. Div., Oklahoma Lib. Assn. Memb. 200+. Publication. *Oklahoma Librarian.*

Chair Kristi Merchant. E-mail oksl@oklibs. org; *Past Chair* Earon Cunningham.

Address correspondence to the chairperson, School Libs. Div., Oklahoma Lib. Assn., P.O. Box 6550, Edmond, OK 73083. Tel. 405-348-0506.

World Wide Web http://www.oklibs.org/ ?page=OKSL.

Oregon

Oregon Assn. of School Libs. Memb. 600. Publication. *Interchange* (3 a year).

Pres. Stephanie Thomas. E-mail president@ oasl.olaweb.org; *Pres.-Elect* Robin Rolfe. E-mail presidentelect@oasl.olaweb.org; *Secy.* Jenny Takeda. E-mail secretary@oasl.olaweb. org; *Treas.* Stuart Levy. E-mail treasurer@oasl. olaweb.org; *Past Pres.* Nancy Sullivan. E-mail pastpresident@oasl.olaweb.org.

Address correspondence to the association, P.O. Box 3067, La Grande 97850.

World Wide Web http://ola.memberclicks. net/oasl-home.

Pennsylvania

Pennsylvania School Libns. Assn. Memb. 800+.

Pres. Michael Nailor. E-mail mnailor@psla. org; *V.P./Pres.-Elect* Allison Burrell. E-mail aburrell@psla.org; *Secy.* Lindsey Long. E-mail pslaboard@psla.org; *Treas.* Natalie Hawley. E-mail pslaboard@psla.org; *Past Pres.* Eileen Kern. E-mail ekern@psla.org.

Address correspondence to the president.

World Wide Web http://www.psla.org.

Rhode Island

School Libns. of Rhode Island (formerly Rhode Island Educ. Media Assn.). Memb. 350+.

Pres. Jane Perry. *V.P.* Sarah Hunicke; *Secy.* Lisa Casey; *Treas.* Jen Simoneau; *Past Pres.* Darshell Silva.

World Wide Web http://www.slri.info.

South Carolina

South Carolina Assn. of School Libns. Memb. 900. Term of Office. July–June.

Pres. Diana Carr. E-mail dcarr@richland one.org; *V.P./Pres.-Elect* Jennifer Tazerouti; *Secy.* Andi Fansher. E-mail andifansher@ gmail.com; *Treas.* Gloria Coleman; *Past Pres.* Anne Lemieux. E-mail lemieux.anne@gmail. com; *Exec. Secy.* Diane Ervin. E-mail ervin scasl@gmail.com.

Address correspondence to the association, P.O. Box 2442, Columbia 29202. Tel./fax 803-492-3025.

World Wide Web http://www.scasl.net.

South Dakota

South Dakota School Lib. Media Section, South Dakota Lib. Assn., 28363 472nd Ave.,

Worthing 57077. Tel. 605-372-0235. Memb. 140+. Term of Office. Oct.–Sept.

Chair Sharlene Lien, Discovery Elementary, Sioux Falls. E-mail sharlene.lien@k12.sd.us.

Tennessee

Tennessee Assn. of School Libns. Memb. 450. Term of Office. Jan.–Dec. Publication. *TASL Talks.*

Pres. Lora Ann Black, Stewart County H.S. E-mail loraannblack.tasl@gmail.com; *V.P./ Pres.-Elect* Mindy Nichols, Crockett County H.S. E-mail mindy.nichols.tasl@gmail.com; *Secy.* Shannon Minner, Reeves Rogers Elementary. E-mail shannon.minner.tasl@gmail.com; *Treas.* Nancy Dickinson, Hillsboro Elementary. E-mail tasltennessee@gmail.com; *Past Pres.* Mona Batchelor, McKenzie H.S. E-mail mona.batchelor.tasl@gmail.com.

Address correspondence to the president.

World Wide Web http://www.tasltn.org.

Texas

Texas Assn. of School Libns., div. of Texas Lib. Assn. Memb. 4,000+. Term of Office. Apr.–Mar.

Chair Julie Briggs. E-mail julie.briggs@risd.org; *Chair-Elect* Renee Dyer. E-mail rdyer@wisd.us; *Secy.* Jill Bellomy. E-mail jill bellomy@gmail.com; *Past Chair* Karen Kessel. E-mail karen_kessel@yahoo.com.

Address correspondence to Texas Lib. Assn., 3355 Bee Cave Rd., Suite 401, Austin 78746. Tel. 512-328-1518, fax 512-328-8852, e-mail tla@txla.org.

World Wide Web http://www.txla.org/groups/tasl.

Utah

Utah Educ. Lib. Media Assn. Memb. 500+. Publication. *UELMA Newsletter* (q.).

Pres. Jessica Moody, Olympus Junior H.S., 2217 E. 4800 S., Holladay 84117-5309. Tel. 385-646-5224, e-mail jmoody@graniteschools. org; *Pres.-Elect* Michelle Miles, Riverton H.S., 12476 S. 2700 W., Riverton 84065. Tel. 801-256-5800, e-mail michelle.miles@jordan district.org; *Secy.* Nikki Ann Gregerson, Granite School Dist., 2500 S. State St., Salt Lake City. Tel. 801-824-8478, e-mail ngregerson

@graniteschools.org; *Past Pres.* Amanda Porter, Rocky Mountain Middle School, 800 W. School House Way, Heber City 84032. Tel. 435-654-9350 ext. 2610, e-mail amanda.porter @wasatch.edu; *Exec. Dir.* Brian Rollins. Tel. 801-232-6531, e-mail brollins04@comcast. net.

Address correspondence to the executive director.

World Wide Web http://www.uelma.org.

Vermont

Vermont School Lib. Assn. (formerly Vermont Educ. Media Assn.). Memb. 220+. Term of Office. May–May. Publication. *VSLA Newsletter Online* (q.).

Pres. Linda McSweeney, Stowe Middle/ H.S., 413 Barrows Rd., Stowe 05672. Tel. 802-253-7229, e-mail linda.mcsweeney@lssuvt. org; *Pres.-Elect* Kathy Lawrence. E-mail klawrence@ccsuvt.org; *Secy.* Kate Davie, Blue Mountain Union School, 2420 Rte. 302, Wells River 05081. Tel. 802-757-2711 ext.1142, e-mail kate.davie@bmuschool.org; *Treas.* Susan Monmaney, Montpelier H.S., 5 High School Drive, Montpelier 05602. Tel. 802-225-8020, e-mail susanm@mpsvt.org; *Past Pres.* Denise Wentz, Allen Brook School, 497 Talcott Rd., Williston 05495. Tel. 802-879-5848, e-mail dwentz@cssu.org.

Address correspondence to the president.

World Wide Web https://sites.google.com/site/vermontschoollibraries/home.

Virginia

Virginia Assn. of School Libns. (VAASL) (formerly Virginia Educ. Media Assn. [VEMA]). Memb. 1,200. Term of Office. Nov.–Nov. Publication. *VAASL Voice* (q.).

Pres. Eileen Godwin. E-mail president@vaasl.org; *Pres.-Elect* Carolyn Vibbert. E-mail presidentelect@vaasl.org; *Secy.* Schenell Agee. E-mail secretary@vaasl.org; *Treas.* Judy Deichman. E-mail treasurer@vaasl.org; *Past Pres.* Lori Donovan. E-mail pastpresident@vaasl.org; *Exec. Dir.* Margaret Baker. Tel. 540-416-6109, e-mail executive@vaasl.org.

Address correspondence to the association, P.O. Box 2015, Staunton 24402-2015. Tel. 540-416-6109.

World Wide Web http://vaasl.org.

Washington

Washington Lib. Media Assn. Memb. 700+. Term of Office. Oct.–Oct. Publication. *Medium* (3 a year). *Ed.* Jodeana Kruse. E-mail medium @wlma.org.

Pres. Sharyn Merrigan. E-mail president@ wlma.org; *Pres.-Elect* Craig Seasholes. E-mail pres-elect@wlma.org; *V.P.* Carrie Willenbring. E-mail vicepresident@wlma.org; *Secy.* Kimberly Rose. E-mail secretary@wlma.org; *Treas.* Merrilyn Tucker. E-mail treasurer@wlma. org; *Past Pres.* Anne Bingham. E-mail past president@wlma.org.

Address correspondence to the association. E-mail wlma@wlma.org.

World Wide Web http://www.wlma.org.

West Virginia

School Lib. Div., West Virginia Lib. Assn. Memb. 50. Term of Office. Nov.–Nov. Publication. *WVLA School Library News* (5 a year).

Chair Lynda Suzie Martin, Brookhaven Elementary, 147 Estate Drive, Morgantown 26508. Tel. 304-282-0147, e-mail library nbct@gmail.com; *Past Chair* Cathy Davis, East Fairmont Junior H.S., 1 Orion Lane, Fairmont 26554. Tel. 304-367-2123, e-mail davisc57@ hotmail.com.

Address correspondence to the chairperson. World Wide Web http://www.wvla.org.

Wisconsin

Wisconsin Educ. Media and Technology Assn. Memb. 1,100+. Publication. *WEMTA Dispatch* (q.).

Pres. Donna Smith. E-mail president@ wemta.org; *Pres.-Elect* Kim Bannigan. E-mail pres-elect@wemta.org; *Secy.* Eileen Schroeder. E-mail secretary@wemta.org; *Treas.* Renee Disch. E-mail treasurer@wemta.org; *Past Pres.* Joel VerDuin. E-mail joelverduin@ yahoo.com.

Address correspondence to WEMTA, P.O. Box 44578, Madison 53744-4578. Tel. 608-848-1232, fax 608-848-9266, e-mail wemta@ wiscow.com.

World Wide Web http://www.wemta.org.

Wyoming

Teacher-Libn. Interest Group, Wyoming Lib. Assn. Memb. 100+.

Group Leader Laura Miller. E-mail lamiller @ccsd.k12.wy.us.

Address correspondence to the group leader. World Wide Web https://sites.google.com/ site/wlateacherlibrarians.

International Library Associations

International Association of Agricultural Information Specialists

Federico Sancho Guevara, President
IAALD, P.O. Box 63, Lexington, KY 40588-0063
Fax 859-257-8379, e-mail info@iaald.org
World Wide Web http://www.iaald.org

Object

The International Association of Agricultural Information Specialists (IAALD) facilitates professional development of and communication among members of the agricultural information community worldwide. Its goal is to enhance access to and use of agriculture-related information resources. To further this mission, IAALD will promote the agricultural information profession, support professional development activities, foster collaboration, and provide a platform for information exchange. Founded 1955.

Membership

Memb. 400+ in more than 75 countries. Dues (Inst.) US$130; (Indiv.) US$60.

Officers

Pres. Federico Sancho Guevara (Costa Rica); *V.P./Pres.-Elect* Peter Walton (Australia); *Secy.-Treas.* Toni Greider (USA); *Past Pres.* Edith Hesse (Austria).

Board Members

Krishan Bheenick (Mauritius), Jerry Miner (Canada), Jaron Porciello (USA), Margaret Sraku-Lartey (Ghana).

Publication

Agricultural Information Worldwide (q.) (memb.).

International Association of Law Libraries

Jeroen Vervliet, President
Peace Palace Library, The Hague, Netherlands
Tel. 31-70-302-4242, e-mail j.vervliet@ppl.nl
World Wide Web http://www.iall.org

Object

The International Association of Law Libraries (IALL) is a worldwide organization of librarians, libraries, and other persons or institutions concerned with the acquisition and use of legal information emanating from sources other than their jurisdictions and from multinational and international organizations.

IALL's purpose is to facilitate the work of librarians who acquire, process, organize, and provide access to foreign legal materials. IALL has no local chapters but maintains liaison with national law library associations in many countries and regions of the world.

Membership

More than 800 members in more than 50 countries on five continents.

Officers

Pres. Jeroen Vervliet, Peace Palace Lib., Carnegieplein 2, 2517 KJ The Hague, Netherlands. Tel. 31-70-302-4242, e-mail j.vervliet@ppl.nl; *1st V.P.* Ruth Bird, Bodleian Law Lib., Univ. of Oxford, St. Cross Bldg., Manor Rd., Oxford OX1 3UR, England. Tel. 44-1865-271451, fax 44-1865-271475, e-mail ruth.bird@bodleian.ox.ac.uk; *2nd V.P.* Bård Tuseth, Dept. of Public and International Law Lib., Domus Bibliotheca, Karl Johansgt. 47, 0162 Oslo, Norway. Tel. 47-2285-9494, fax 47-2285-9493, e-mail b.s.tuseth@ub.uio.no; *Secy.* Barbara Garavaglia, Univ. of Michigan Law Lib., Ann Arbor, MI 48109-1210. Tel. 734-764-9338, fax 734-764-5863, e-mail bvaccaro@umich.edu; *Treas.* Xinh Luu, Univ. of Virginia Law Lib., 580 Massie Rd., Charlottesville, VA 22903. E-mail xtl5d@virginia.edu; *Past Pres.* Petal Kinder, High Court of Australia, Parkes Place, Parkes, Canberra, ACT 2600. Tel. 61-2-6270-6922, fax 61-2-6273-2110, e-mail pkinder@hcourt.gov.au.

Board Members

Kristina Alayan, Duke Univ. School of Law; Daniel Boyer, Nahum Gelber Law Lib., McGill Univ.; Kurt Carroll, Lib. of Congress; Lily Echiverri, Univ. of the Philippines; Mark D. Engsberg (ex officio), MacMillan Law Lib., Emory Univ. School of Law, Atlanta; David Gee, Inst. of Advanced Legal Studies, Univ. of London; Marci Hoffman (ex officio), Univ. of California, Berkeley, School of Law Lib.; Kerem Kahvecioglu, Istanbul Bilgi Univ., Istanbul; Ivo Vogel, Sondersammelgebiet und Virtuellen Fachbibliothek Recht, Berlin.

Publication

International Journal of Legal Information (*IJLI*) (3 a year; memb.).

International Association of Music Libraries, Archives, and Documentation Centres

Pia Shekhter, Secretary-General
Gothenburg University Library, P.O. Box 210, SE 405 30 Gothenburg, Sweden
Tel. 46-31-786-4057, cell 46-703-226-092, fax 46-31-786-40-59, e-mail secretary@iaml.info.
World Wide Web http://www.iaml.info.

Object

The object of the International Association of Music Libraries, Archives, and Documentation Centres (IAML) is to promote the activities of music libraries, archives, and documentation centers and to strengthen the cooperation among them; to promote the availability of all publications and documents relating to music and further their bibliographical control; to encourage the development of standards in all areas that concern the association; and to support the protection and preservation of musical documents of the past and the present.

Membership

Memb. 1,700.

Board Members

Pres. Barbara Dobbs Mackenzie, *Répertoire International de Littérature Musicale* (*RILM*), New York. E-mail president@iaml.info; *Secy.-Gen.* Pia Shekhter, Gothenburg Univ. Lib., Box 210, SE 405 30 Gothenburg. Tel. 46-31-786-40-57; *Treas.* Thomas Kalk, Stadtbüchereien Düsseldorf. E-mail treasurer@iaml.info; *V.P.s* Stanisław Hrabia, Uniwersytet Jagiellonski,

Kraków; Antony Gordon, British Lib., London; Johan Eeckeloo, Koninklijk Conservatorieum, Brussels; Joseph Hafner, McGill Univ., Montreal; *Past Pres.* Roger Flury, National Lib. of New Zealand (retired), P.O. Box 1467, Wellington.

Publication

Fontes Artis Musicae (4 a year; memb.). *Ed.* Maureen Buja, Hong Kong Gold Coast Block 22, Flat 1-A, 1 Castle Peak Rd., Tuen Mun, NT, Hong Kong. Tel. 852-2146-8047, e-mail fontes@iaml.info.

Professional Branches

Archives and Music Documentation Centres. *Chair* Marie Cornaz, Bibliothèque Royale de Belgique, Brussels. E-mail archives@iaml.info.

Broadcasting and Orchestra Libraries. *Chair* Nienke de Boer, Holland Symfonia, Haarlem. E-mail broadcasting@iaml.info.

Libraries in Music Teaching Institutions. *Chair* Johan Eeckeloo, Koninklijk Conservatorium, Brussels. E-mail teaching@iaml.info.

Public Libraries. *Chair* Carolyn Dow, Polley Music Lib., Lincoln City Libs., Lincoln, Nebraska. E-mail publiclibraries@iaml.info.

Research Libraries. *Chair* Thomas Leibnitz. Musiksammlung der Österreichischen Nationalbibliothek, Vienna. E-mail research libraries@iaml.info.

Subject Commissions

Audio-Visual Materials. *Chair* Andrew Justice. University of North Texas, Denton. E-mail av@iaml.info.

Bibliography. *Chair* Rupert Ridgewell, British Lib., London. E-mail bibliography@iaml.info.

Cataloguing. *Chair* Joseph Hafner. McGill Univ., Montreal. E-mail cataloguing@iaml.info.

Service and Training. *Chair* Jane Gottlieb. Juilliard School, New York. E-mail service@iaml.info.

Sub-commission on Unimarc. *Chair* Isabelle Gauchet Doris. Centre de Documentation de la Musique Contemporaine, Paris. E-mail unimarc@iaml.info.

International Association of School Librarianship

Kathleen Combs, Executive Director
65 E. Wacker Place, Suite 1900, Chicago, IL 60601
e-mail iasl@mlahq.org
World Wide Web http://iasl-online.mlanet.org

Mission and Objectives

The mission of the International Association of School Librarianship (IASL) is to provide an international forum for those interested in promoting effective school library programs as viable instruments in the education process. IASL also provides guidance and advice for the development of school library programs and the school library profession. IASL works in cooperation with other professional associations and agencies.

Membership is worldwide and includes school librarians, teachers, librarians, library advisers, consultants, education administrators, and others who are responsible for library and information services in schools. The membership also includes professors and instructors in universities and colleges where there are programs for school librarians, and students who are undertaking such programs.

The objectives of IASL are to advocate the development of school libraries throughout all countries; to encourage the integration of school library programs into the instruction and curriculum of the school; to promote the professional preparation and continuing education of school library personnel; to foster a sense of community among school librarians in all parts of the world; to foster and extend relationships between school librarians and other professionals in connection with children and youth; to foster research in the field of school librarianship and the integration of its findings with pertinent knowledge from related fields; to promote the publication and dissemination of information about successful advocacy and program initiatives in school librarianship; to share information about programs and materials for children and youth throughout the international community; and to initiate and coordinate activities, conferences, and other projects in the field of school librarianship and information services.

Founded 1971.

Membership

Approximately 600.

Officers and Executive Board

Pres. Diljit Singh, Malaysia; *V.P.s.* Mihaela Banek Zorica, Association Operations, Croatia; Kay Hones, Association Relations, USA; Elizabeth Greef, Advocacy and Promotion, Australia; *Treas.* Katy Manck, USA; *Dirs.* Geraldine Howell, Oceania; Busi Dlamini, Africa–Sub Sahara; Lourdes T. David, East Asia; Luisa Marquardt, Europe; Dianne Oberg, Canada; Madhu Bhargava, International Schools; Nancy Everhart, USA; Ayse Yuksel-Durukan, North Africa/Middle East; Hanna Chaterina George, Asia; Paulette Stewart, Latin America/Caribbean.

Publications

Proceedings of annual conferences (available on the EBSCO, Proquest, and Gale Cengage databases).

School Libraries Worldwide (http://www.iasl-online.org/publications/slw/index.html), the association's refereed research and professional journal (2 a year).

IASL Newsletter (http://www.iasl-online.org/publications/newsletter.html) (4 a year).

International Association of Scientific and Technological University Libraries (IATUL)

President, Reiner Kallenborn
World Wide Web http://www.iatul.org

Object

The main object of the International Association of Scientific and Technological University Libraries (IATUL) is to provide a forum where library directors and senior managers can meet to exchange views on matters of current significance and to provide an opportunity for them to develop a collaborative approach to solving problems. IATUL also welcomes into membership organizations that supply services to university libraries, if they wish to be identified with the association's activities.

Membership

250+ in 60 countries.

Officers

Pres. Reiner Kallenborn, Technische Universität München, Munich, Germany; *V.P.* Gwendolyn Ebbett, Univ. of Windsor, Ontario, Canada; *Secy.* Elisha R. T. Chiware, Cape Peninsula Univ. of Technology, South Africa; *Treas.* Irma Pasanen, Aalto Univ. Lib., Helsinki, Finland.

Publication

IATUL Conference Proceedings (on IATUL
website, http://www.iatul.org) (ann.).

International Council on Archives

David A. Leitch, Secretary-General
60 rue des Francs-Bourgeois, 75003 Paris, France
Tel. 33-1-40-27-63-06, fax 33-1-42-72-20-65, e-mail ica@ica.org
World Wide Web http://www.ica.org

Object

The mission of the International Council on
Archives (ICA) is to establish, maintain, and
strengthen relations among archivists of all
lands, and among all professional and other
agencies or institutions concerned with the
custody, organization, or administration of
archives, public or private, wherever located.
Established 1948.

Membership

Memb. Approximately 1,400 (representing
nearly 200 countries and territories).

Officers

Pres. David Fricker, Australia; *V.P.s* Andreas
Kellerhals, Switzerland; Henri Zuber, France.

Executive Board

Haman bin Mohammed al-Dhawyani, Oman;
Atakitty Assefa Asgedom, Ethiopia; Esther
Cruces Blanco, Spain; Paola Caroli, Italy; Eric
Sze Choong, Singapore; Bryan Corbett, Cana-
da; Margaret Crockett, United Kingdom; Jaime
Antunes da Silva, Brazil; Deborah Jenkins,
United Kingdom; Antoine Lumenganeso Ki-
obe, Congo; Alphonse Labitan, Benin; Hervé
Lemoine, France; Emilie Gagnet Leumas,
United States; William J. Maher, United States;
Milovan Misic, Switzerland; Francis Mwangi,
Kenya; Donghoon Park, South Korea; Günther
Schefbeck, Austria; Amela Silipa, Western Sa-
moa; Kenth Sjöblom, Finland; David Sutton,
United Kingdom; Rita Tjien-Fooh, Suriname;
Sarah Tyacke, United Kingdom; F. J. W. Van
Kan, Netherlands; Karel Velle, Belgium; Ama-
tuni Virabyan, Armenia; Geir Magnus Walder-
haug, Norway; Saroja Wettasinghe, Sri Lanka.

Publications

Comma (memb.) (2 a year, memb.).
Flash (2 a year; memb.).
Guide to the Sources of the History of Nations
(Latin American Series, 11 vols. pub.; Africa South of the Sahara Series, 20 vols. pub.;
North Africa, Asia, and Oceania Series, 15
vols. pub.).
Guide to the Sources of Asian History (English-language series [India, Indonesia, Korea, Nepal, Pakistan, Singapore], 14 vols.
pub.; national language series [Indonesia,
Korea, Malaysia, Nepal, Thailand], 6 vols.
pub.; other guides, 3 vols. pub.).

International Federation of Film Archives
(Fédération Internationale des Archives du Film)

Secretariat, 42 rue Blanche, B-1060 Brussels, Belgium
Tel. 32-2-538-30-65, fax 32-2-534-47-74, e-mail info@fiafnet.org
World Wide Web http://www.fiafnet.org

Object

Founded in 1938, the International Federation of Film Archives (FIAF) brings together not-for-profit institutions dedicated to rescuing films and any other moving-image elements considered both as cultural heritage and as historical documents.

FIAF is a collaborative association of the world's leading film archives whose purpose has always been to ensure the proper preservation and showing of motion pictures. More than 150 archives in more than 75 countries collect, restore, and exhibit films and cinema documentation spanning the entire history of film.

FIAF seeks to promote film culture and facilitate historical research, to help create new archives around the world, to foster training and expertise in film preservation, to encourage the collection and preservation of documents and other cinema-related materials, to develop cooperation between archives, and to ensure the international availability of films and cinema documents.

Officers

Pres. Eric Le Roy; *Secy.-Gen.* Michael Loebensten; *Treas.* Jon Wengström.

Address correspondence to Christophe Dupin, Senior Administrator, c/o FIAF Secretariat. E-mail c.dupin@fiafnet.org.

Publications

Journal of Film Preservation.
International Index to Film Periodicals.
FIAF International Filmarchive database (OVID).
FIAF International Index to Film Periodicals (ProQuest).

For additional FIAF publications, see http://www.fiafnet.org.

International Federation of Library Associations and Institutions

Jennefer Nicholson, Secretary-General
P.O. Box 95312, 2509 CH The Hague, Netherlands
Tel. 31-70-314-0884, fax 31-70-383-4827
E-mail ifla@ifla.org, World Wide Web http://www.ifla.org

Object

The object of the International Federation of Library Associations and Institutions (IFLA) is to promote international understanding, cooperation, discussion, research, and development in all fields of library activity, including bibliography, information services, and the education of library personnel, and to provide a body through which librarianship can be represented in matters of international interest. IFLA is the leading international body representing the interests of library and information services and their users. It is the global voice of the library and information profession. Founded 1927.

Officers and Governing Board

Pres. Sinikka Sipilä, Finnish Lib. Assn.; *Pres.-Elect* Donna Scheeder, Lib. of Congress; *Treas.* Frédéric Blin, Bibliothèque Nationale et Universitaire de Strasbourg.

Governing Board

Kent Skov Andreasen (Denmark), Ingrid Bon (Netherlands), Genevieve Clavel-Merrin (Switzerland), Loida Garcia-Febo (United States), Ngian Lek Choh (Singapore), Barbara Lison (Germany), Inga Lundén (Sweden), Ellen Ndeshi Namhila (Namibia), and Glòria Pérez-Salmerón (Spain), plus the chairs of the IFLA Professional Committee and divisions.

Publications

IFLA Annual Report.
IFLA Journal (4 a year).
IFLA Professional Reports.
IFLA Publications Series.
IFLA Series on Bibliographic Control.
International Preservation News.

American Membership

Associations

American Lib. Assn., Assn. for Lib. and Info. Science Educ., Assn. of Research Libs., Chief Officers of State Lib. Agencies, Medical Lib. Assn., Special Libs. Assn., Urban Libs. Council, Chinese American Libns. Assn., Polish American Lib. Assn.

Institutional Members

More than 100 libraries and related institutions are institutional members or consultative bodies and sponsors of IFLA in the United States (out of a total of more than 1,000 globally), and more than 100 are individual affiliates (out of a total of more than 300 affiliates globally).

International Organization for Standardization

Rob Steele, Secretary-General
ISO Central Secretariat, Chemin de Blandonnet 8, CP 401
1214 Vernier, Geneva, Switzerland
Tel. 41-22-749-01-11, fax 41-22-733-34-30, e-mail central@iso.org
World Wide Web http://www.iso.org

Object

The International Organization for Standardization (ISO) is a worldwide federation of national standards bodies, founded in 1947, at present comprising 163 members, one in each country. The object of ISO is to promote the development of standardization and related activities in the world with a view to facilitating international exchange of goods and services, and to developing cooperation in the spheres of intellectual, scientific, technological, and economic activity. The scope of ISO covers international standardization in all fields except electrical and electronic engineering standardization, which is the responsibility of the International Electrotechnical Commission (IEC). The results of ISO technical work are published as international standards.

Officers

Pres. Zhang Xiaogang, China; *V.P. (Policy)* John Walter, Canada; *V.P. (Technical Management)* Elisabeth Stampfl-Blaha, Austria; *V.P. (Finance)* Olivier Peyrat, France; *Treas.* Miguel Payró, Argentina/United Kingdom.

Technical Work

The technical work of ISO is carried out by more than 200 technical committees. These include:
ISO/TC 46—Information and documentation (Secretariat, Association Française de Normalization, 11 ave. Francis de Pressensé, 93571 La Plaine Saint-Denis, Cedex, France). Scope: Standardization of practices relating to librar-

ies, documentation and information centers, indexing and abstracting services, archives, information science, and publishing.

ISO/TC 37—Terminology and language and content resources (Secretariat, INFOTERM, Aichholzgasse 6/12, 1120 Vienna, Austria, on behalf of Österreichisches Normungsinstitut). Scope: Standardization of principles, methods, and applications relating to terminology and other language and content resources in the contexts of multilingual communication and cultural diversity.

ISO/IEC JTC 1—Information technology (Secretariat, American National Standards Institute, 25 W. 43 St., 4th fl., New York, NY 10036). Scope: Standardization in the field of information technology.

Publications

ISO Annual Report.
ISOfocus (6 a year).
ISO International Standards.
ISO Online information service on World Wide Web (http://www.iso.org).

Foreign Library Associations

The following is a list of regional and national library associations around the world. A more complete list can be found in *International Literary Market Place* (Information Today, Inc.).

Regional

Africa

Standing Conference of Eastern, Central, and Southern African Lib. and Info. Assns. (SCECSAL), c/o Swaziland Lib. Assn., P.O. Box 2309, Mbabane H100, Swaziland. Tel. 268-404-2633, fax 268-404-3863, e-mail fmkhonta@uniswacc.uniswa.sz, World Wide Web http://www.swala.sz.

The Americas

Assn. of Caribbean Univ., Research, and Institutional Libs. (ACURIL), P.O. Box 21609, San Juan, Puerto Rico 00931-1906. Tel. 787-763-6199, e-mail executivesecretariat@acuril.org. *Pres.* Dorcas R. Bowler; *Exec. Secy.* Luisa Vigo-Cepeda.

Seminar on the Acquisition of Latin American Lib. Materials (SALALM), c/o *Exec. Secy.* Hortensia Calvo, SALALM Secretariat, Latin American Lib., 422 Howard Tilton Memorial Lib., Tulane Univ., 7001 Freret St., New Orleans, LA 70118-5549. Tel. 504-247-1366, fax 504-247-1367, e-mail salalm@tulane.edu, World Wide Web http://www.salalm.org. *Pres.* Luis Gonzales. E-mail luisgonz@indiana.edu.

Asia

Congress of Southeast Asian Libns. (CONSAL), c/o Jl Salemba Raya 28A, Jakarta 10430, Indonesia. Tel. 21-310-3554, World Wide Web http://www.consal.org. *Secy.-Gen.* Aristianto Hakim.

The Commonwealth

Commonwealth Lib. Assn. (COMLA), P.O. Box 144, Mona, Kingston 7, Jamaica. Tel. 876-978-2274, fax 876-927-1926, e-mail comla72@yahoo.com. *Interim Pres.* Elizabeth Watson.

National and State Libs. Australasia, c/o State Lib. of Victoria, 328 Swanston St., Melbourne, Vic. 3000, Australia. Tel. 3-8664-7512, fax 3-9639-4737, e-mail nsla@slv.vic.gov.au, World Wide Web http://www.nsla.org.au. *Chair* Alan Smith.

U.K. Library and Archives Group on Africa (SCOLMA, formerly the Standing Conference on Lib. Materials on Africa), c/o Marion Wallace, Social Science Collections and Research, British Lib., St. Pancras, 96 Euston Rd., London NW1 2DB, England. Tel. 20-7412-7829, World Wide Web http://scolma.org.

Europe

Ligue des Bibliothèques Européennes de Recherche (LIBER) (Assn. of European Research Libs.), Postbus 90407, 2509 LK The Hague, Netherlands. Tel. 070-314-07-67, fax 070-314-01-97, e-mail liber@kb.nl, World Wide Web http://www.libereurope.eu. *Pres.* Kristiina Hormia-Poutanen. E-mail kristiina.hormia@helsinki.fi; *V.P.* Jeannette Frey. E-mail jeannette.frey@bcu.unil.ch; *Secy.-Gen.* Ann Matheson. E-mail a.matheson@tinyworld.co.uk.

National

Argentina

Asociación de Bibliotecarios Graduados de la República Argentina (ABGRA) (Assn. of Graduate Libns. of Argentina), Parana 918, 2do Piso, C1017AAT Buenos Aires. Tel. 11-4811-0043, fax 11-4816-3422, e-mail info@abgra.org.ar, World Wide Web http://www.abgra.org.ar. *Pres.* Antonio Bellofatto; *V.P.* Tatiana María Carsen; *Secy.-Gen.* Mirta Estela Villalba.

Australia

Australian Lib. and Info. Assn., Box 6335, Kingston, ACT 2604. Tel. 2-6215-8222, fax 2-6282-2249, e-mail enquiry@alia.org.au, World Wide Web http://www.alia.org.au. *Pres.* Damian Lodge; *CEO* Sue McKerracher. E-mail sue.mckerracher@alia.org.au.

Australian Society of Archivists, P.O. Box A623, Sydney South, NSW 1235. Tel. 618-8411-5550, e-mail office@archivists.org.au, World Wide Web http://www.archivists.org. au. *Pres.* Kylie Percival; *V.P.* Adelaide Parr.

Austria

Österreichische Gesellschaft für Dokumentation und Information (Austrian Society for Documentation and Info.), c/o OGDI, Wollzeile 1-3, P.O. Box 43, 1022 Vienna. E-mail office@oegdi.at, World Wide Web http://www.oegdi.at. *Secy.-Gen.* Hermann Huemer. E-mail hermann.huemer@oegdi.at.

Vereinigung Österreichischer Bibliothekarinnen und Bibliothekare (VOEB) (Assn. of Austrian Libns.), Vorarlberg State Lib., Fluherstr. 4, 6900 Bregenz. E-mail voeb@ub.tuwein.ac.at, World Wide Web http://www.univie.ac.at/voeb/php. *Pres.* Werner Schlacher, Universitätsbibliothek Graz, Universitätsplatz 3, 8010 Graz. E-mail werner.schlacher@uni-graz.at.

Bangladesh

Bangladesh Assn. of Libns., Info. Scientists and Documentalists (BALID), 67/B, Rd. 9/A, Dhanmondi, Dhaka 1209. *Chair* Mirza Mohd Rezaul Islam. E-mail balidbd@gmail.com.

Barbados

Lib. Assn. of Barbados, P.O. Box 827E, Bridgetown, Barbados. E-mail milton@uwichill.edu.bb. *Pres.* Junior Browne.

Belgium

Archief- en Bibliotheekwezen in België (Belgian Assn. of Archivists and Libns.), Keizerslaan 4, 1000 Brussels. Tel. 2-519-53-93, fax 2-519-56-10.

Association Belge de Documentation/Belgische Vereniging voor Documentatie (Belgian Assn. for Documentation), Chaussée de Wavre 1683, B-1160 Brussels. Tel. 2-675-58-62, fax 2-672-74-46, e-mail abdbvd@abd-bvd.be, World Wide Web http://www.abd-bvd.be. *Pres.* Guy Delsaut. E-mail guy.delsaut@skynet.be; *Secy.-Gen.* Marc Van Den Bergh. E-mail mvdbergh@serv.be.

Association Professionnelle des Bibliothécaires et Documentalistes (Assn. of Libns. and Documentation Specialists), Chaussée de Charleroi 85, 5000 Namur, Belgique. Tel. 71-52-31-93, fax 71-52-23-07, World Wide Web http://www.apbd.be. *Pres.* Françoise Dury.

Vlaamse Vereniging voor Bibliotheek-, Archief-, en Documentatiewezen (Flemish Assn. of Libns., Archivists, and Documentalists), Statiestraat 179, B-2600 Berchem, Antwerp. Tel. 3-281-44-57, e-mail vvbad@vvbad.be, World Wide Web http://www.vvbad.be. *Coord.* Bruno Vermeeren.

Belize

Belize National Lib. Service and Info. System (BNLSIS), P.O. Box 287, Belize City. Tel. 223-4248, fax 223-4246, e-mail nls@btl.net, World Wide Web http://www.nlsbze.bz. *Chief Libn.* Joy Ysaguirre.

Bolivia

Centro Nacional de Documentación Cientifica y Tecnológica (National Scientific and Technological Documentation Center), Av. Mariscal Santa Cruz 1175, Esquina c Ayacucho, La Paz. Tel. 02-359-583, fax 02-359-586, e-mail iiicndct@huayna.umsa.edu.bo, World Wide Web http://www.bolivian.com/industrial/cndct.

Bosnia and Herzegovina

Drustvo Bibliotekara Bosne i Hercegovine (Libns. Society of Bosnia and Herzegovina), Zmaja od Bosne 8B, 71000 Sarajevo. Tel. 33-275-5325, fax 33-212-435, e-mail nubbih@nub.ba, World Wide Web http://www.nub.ba. *Pres.* Nevenka Hajdarovic. E-mail nevenka@nub.ba.

Botswana

Botswana Lib. Assn., Box 1310, Gaborone. Tel. 371-750, fax 371-748, World Wide Web http://www.bla.org.bw. *Pres.* Kgomotso Radijeing. E-mail president@bla.org.bw.

Brazil

Associação dos Arquivistas Brasileiros (Assn. of Brazilian Archivists), Av. Presidente Vargas 1733, Sala 903, 20210-030 Rio de Janiero RJ. Tel. 21-2507-2239, fax 21-3852-2541, e-mail aab@aab.org.br, World Wide Web http://www.aab.org.br. *Pres.* Margareth da Silva.

Brunei Darussalam

Persatuan Perpustakaan Negara Brunei Darussalam (National Lib. Assn. of Brunei), c/o Class 64 Lib., SOASC, Jalan Tengah, Bandar Seri Begawan BS8411. Fax 2-222-330, e-mail pobox.bla@gmail.com, World Wide Web http://bruneilibraryassociation.word press.com. *Hon. Secy.* Hjh Rosnani. E-mail rosnaniy@hotmail.com.

Cameroon

Assn. des Bibliothécaires, Archivistes, Documentalistes et Muséographes du Cameroun (Assn. of Libns., Archivists, Documentalists, and Museum Curators of Cameroon), BP 14077, Yaoundé. World Wide Web http://www.abadcam.sitew.com. *Pres.* Jérôme Ndjock.

Chile

Colegio de Bibliotecarios de Chile (Chilean Lib. Assn.), Avda. Diagonal Paraguay 383, Torre 11, Oficina 122, 6510017 Santiago. Tel. 2-222-5652, e-mail cbc@bibliotecarios.cl, World Wide Web http://www.bibliotecarios. cl. *Pres.* Gabriela Pradenas Bobadilla; *Secy.-Gen.* Victor Candia Arancibia.

China

Lib. Society of China, 33 Zhongguancun S, Beijing 100081. Tel. 10-8854-5283, fax 10-6841-7815, e-mail ztxhmsc@nlc.gov. cn, World Wide Web http://www.nlc.gov.cn. *Dir.* Zhou Heping.

Colombia

Asociación Colombiana de Bibliotecólogos y Documentalistas (Colombian Assn. of Libns. and Documentalists), Calle 21, No. 6-58, Oficina 404, Bogotá D.C. Tel. 1-282-3620, fax 1-282-5487, e-mail secretaria@ ascolbi.org, World Wide Web http://www. ascolbi.org. *Pres.* Marisol Goyeneche Reina.

Congo (Republic of)

Assn. des Bibliothécaires, Archivistes, Documentalistes et Muséologues du Congo (ABADOM) (Assn. of Librarians, Archivists, Documentalists, and Museologists of Congo), BP 3148, Kinshasa-Gombe. *Pres.* Desire Didier Tengeneza. E-mail didier teng@yahoo.fr.

Côte d'Ivoire

Direction des Archives Nationales et de la Documentation, BP V 126, Abidjan. Tel. 20-21-75-78. *Dir.* Venance Bahi Gouro.

Croatia

Hrvatsko Knjiznicarsko Drustvo (Croatian Lib. Assn.), c/o National and Univ. Lib., Hrvatske bratske zajednice 4, 10 000 Zagreb. Tel./fax 1-615-93-20, e-mail hkd@nsk.hr, World Wide Web http://www.hkdrustvo.hr. *Pres.* Marijana Misetic. E-mail mmisetic@ffzg.hr.

Cuba

Asociación Cubana de Bibliotecarios (ASCUBI) (Lib. Assn. of Cuba), P.O. Box 6670, Havana. Tel. 7-555-442, fax 7-816-224, e-mail ascubi@bnjm.cu, World Wide Web http://www.bnjm.cu/ascubi. *Chair* Margarita Bellas Vilariño. E-mail ascubi@bnjm.cu.

Cyprus

Kypriakos Synthesmos Vivliothicarion (Lib. Assn. of Cyprus), c/o Pedagogical Academy, P.O. Box 1039, Nicosia.

Czech Republic

Svaz Knihovniku a Informacnich Pracovniku Ceske Republiky (SKIP) (Assn. of Lib. and Info. Professionals of the Czech Republic),

National Lib., Klementinum 190, 110 00 Prague 1. Tel. 221-663-379, fax 221-663-175, e-mail skip@nkp.cz, World Wide Web http://skipcr.cz. *Pres.* Roman Giebisch. E-mail roman.giebisch@nkp.cz.

Denmark

Arkivforeningen (Archives Society), c/o Rigsarkivet, Rigsdagsgarden 9, 1218 Copenhagen. Tel. 3392-3310, fax 3315-3239, World Wide Web http://www.arkivarforeningen. no. *Chair* Lars Schreiber Pedersen. E-mail lape02@frederiksberg.dk.

Danmarks Biblioteksforening (Danish Lib. Assn.), Vartov, Farvergade 27D, 1463 Copenhagen K. Tel. 3325-0935, fax 3325-7900, e-mail db@db.dk, World Wide Web http://www.db.dk. *Pres.* Steen Bording Andersen. E-mail sba@byr.aarhus.dk.

Danmarks Forskningsbiblioteksforening (Danish Research Lib. Assn.), c/o Statsbiblioteket, Tangen 2, 8200 Arhus N. Tel. 89-46-22-07, e-mail df@statsbiblioteket.dk, World Wide Web http://www.dfdf.dk. *Pres.* Michael Cotta-Schønberg. E-mail mcs@kb.dk; *Secy.* Hanne Dahl.

Dansk Musikbiblioteks Forening (Assn. of Danish Music Libs.), c/o Koge Lib., Kirkestr. 18, 4600 Koge. E-mail sekretariat @dmbf.nu, World Wide Web http://www. dmbf.nu. *Pres.* Emilie Wieth-Knudsen. E-mail emwk@ltk.dk.

Kommunernes Skolebiblioteksforening (Assn. of Danish School Libs.), Farvergade 27 D, 2 sal, 1463 Copenhagen K. Tel. 33-11-13-91, e-mail ksbf@ksbf.dk, World Wide Web http://www.ksbf.dk. *Dir.* Gitte Frausing. E-mail gf@ksbf.dk.

Ecuador

Asociación Ecuatoriana de Bibliotecarios (Ecuadoran Lib. Assn.), c/o Casa de la Cultura Ecuatoriana, Casillas 87, Quito. E-mail asoecubiblio@gmail.com. *Pres.* Eduardo Puente. E-mail epuente@flacso.edu.ec.

El Salvador

Asociación de Bibliotecarios de El Salvador (ABES) (Assn. of Salvadorian Libns.), Jardines de la Hacienda Block D pje, 19 No. 158, Ciudad Merliot, Antiguo Cuscatlan,

La Libertad. Tel. 503-2534-8924, fax 523-2228-2956, e-mail abeselsalvador@gmail. com. *Co-Chairs* Ernesto Jonathan Menjivar, Ana Yensi Vides.

Finland

Suomen Kirjastoseura (Finnish Lib. Assn.), Runeberginkatu 15 A 23, 00100 Helsinki. Tel. 44-522-2941, e-mail info@fla.fi, World Wide Web http://www.fla.fi. *Exec. Dir.* Sinikka Sipilä.

France

Association des Archivistes Français (Assn. of French Archivists), 8 rue Jean-Marie Jego, 75013 Paris. Tel. 1-46-06-39-44, fax 1-46-06-39-52, e-mail secretariat@ archivistes.org, World Wide Web http:// www.archivistes.org. *Pres.* Katell Auguié; *Secy.* Marie-Edith Enderlé-Naud.

Association des Bibliothécaires Français (Assn. of French Libns.), 31 rue de Chabrol, F-75010 Paris. Tel. 1-55-33-10-30, fax 1-55-30-10-31, e-mail info@abf.asso.fr, World Wide Web http://www.abf.asso.fr. *Pres.* Anne Verneuil; *Gen. Secy.* Sophie Rat.

Association. des Professionnels de l'Information et de la Documentation (Assn. of Info. and Documentation Professionals), 25 rue Claude Tillier, F-75012 Paris. Tel. 1-43-72-25-25, fax 1-43-72-30-41, e-mail adbs@ adbs.fr, World Wide Web http://www.adbs. fr. *Co-Pres.* Anne-Marie Libmann, Véronique Mesguich; *CEO* Karine Cuney.

Germany

Arbeitsgemeinschaft der Spezialbibliotheken (Assn. of Special Libs.), c/o Herder-Institute eV, Bibliothek, Gisonenweg 5-7, 35037 Marburg. Tel. 6421-184-151, fax 6421-184-139, e-mail geschaeftsstelle@aspb.de, World Wide Web http://aspb.de. *Chair* Henning Frankenberger. E-mail frankenberger@ mpisoc.mpg.de.

Berufsverband Information Bibliothek (Assn. of Info. and Lib. Professionals), Gartenstr. 18, 72764 Reutlingen. Tel. 7121-3491-0, fax 7121-3004-33, e-mail mail@bib-info. de, World Wide Web http://www.bib-info. de. *Deputy Chairs* Tom Becker. E-mail tom. becker@fh-koeln.de; Petra Kille. E-mail kille@ub.uni-kl.de; *Acting Managing Dir.* Bernd Raja. E-mail schleh@bib-info.de.

Deutsche Gesellschaft für Informationswissenschaft und Informationspraxis eV (German Society for Information Science and Practice eV), Windmühlstr. 3, 603294 Frankfurt-am-Main. Tel. 69-43-03-13, fax 69-490-90-96, e-mail mail@dgi-info.de, World Wide Web http://www.dgi-info.de. *Pres.* Reinhard Karger, German Research Center for Artificial Intelligence.

Deutscher Bibliotheksverband eV (German Lib. Assn.), Fritschestr. 27–28, 10585 Berlin. Tel. 30-644-98-99-10, fax 30-644-98-99-29, e-mail dbv@bibliotheksverband.de, World Wide Web http://www.bibliotheksverband. de. *Pres.* Gudrun Heute-Bluhm.

VdA—Verband Deutscher Archivarinnen und Archivare (Assn. of German Archivists), Woerthstr. 3, 36037 Fulda. Tel. 661-29-109-72, fax 661-29-109-74, e-mail info@vda.archiv. net, World Wide Web http://www.vda.archiv. net. *Chair* Irmgard Christa Becker.

Verein Deutscher Bibliothekare eV (Society of German Libns.), Universitaetsbibliothek München, Geschwister-Scholl-Platz 1, 80539 Munich. Tel. 89-2180-2420, e-mail geschaeftsstelle@vdb-online.org, World Wide Web http://www.vdb-online.org. *Chair* Klaus-Rainer Brintzinger, Munich Univ. Lib., Geschwister-Scholl-Platz 1, 80539 Munich. E-mail vorsitzender@vdb-online.org.

Ghana

Ghana Lib. Assn., Box GP 4105, Accra. Tel. 244-17-4930, e-mail ghanalibassoc@gmail. com, World Wide Web http://gla-net.org. *Pres.* Perpetua S. Dadzie; *V.P.* Samuel B. Aggrey.

Greece

Enosis Hellinon Bibliothekarion (Assn. of Greek Libns.), Skoufa 52, P.O. Box 10672, Athens. Tel./fax 210-330-2128, e-mail info@eebep.gr, World Wide Web http://www.eebep.gr. *Pres.* George Glossa. E-mail glossiotis@gmail.com; *Gen. Secy.* Rena Choremi-Thomopoulou. E-mail rhoremi@hotmail.com.

Guyana

Guyana Lib. Assn., c/o National Lib., P.O. Box 10240, Georgetown.

Hong Kong

Hong Kong Lib. Assn., GPO Box 10095, Hong Kong, China. E-mail hkla@hkla.org, World Wide Web http://www.hkla.org. *Pres.* Bryant McEntyre. E-mail mbmcentire@yahoo. com.

Hungary

Magyar Könyvtárosok Egyesülete (Assn. of Hungarian Libns.), H-1054, Hold u 6, Budapest. Tel./fax 1-311-8634, e-mail mke@oszk.hu, World Wide Web http://www.mke. oszk.hu. *Pres.* Klara Bakos; *Secy. Gen.* Miklós Fehér.

Iceland

Upplysing—Felag bokasafns-og upplysingafraeoa (Information—The Icelandic Lib. and Info. Science Assn.), Lyngas 18, 210 Gardabaer. Tel. 354-864-6220, e-mail upplysing@upplysing.is, World Wide Web http://www.upplysing.is.

India

Indian Assn. of Special Libs. and Info. Centres, P-291, CIT Scheme 6M, Kankurgachi, Kolkata 700-054. Tel. 33-2362-9651, e-mail iaslic@vsnl.net, World Wide Web http://www.iaslic1955.org.in. *Pres.* Barun Mukherjee. *Gen. Secy.* Pijushkanti Panigrahi. E-mail panigrahipk@yahoo.com.

Indian Lib. Assn., A/40-41, Flat 201, Ansal Bldg., Mukerjee Nagar, New Delhi 110009. Tel./fax 11-2765-1743, e-mail dvs-srcc@rediffmail.com, World Wide Web http://www.ilaindia.net. *Pres.* Ashu Shokeen. E-mail shokeen_ashu@rediffmail.com; *Gen. Secy.* Pardeep Rai. E-mail raipardeep@gmail.com.

Indonesia

Ikatan Pustakawan Indonesia (Indonesian Lib. Assn.), 11 Jalan Medan Merdeka Selatan, Jakarta 10110. Tel./fax 21-385-5729, e-mail pi2012_2015@yahoo.com, World Wide Web http://ipi.pnri.go.id.

Ireland

Cumann Leabharlann na hEireann (Lib. Assn. of Ireland), c/o 138–144 Pearce St., Dublin 2. E-mail president@libraryassociation.ie, World Wide Web http://www.libraryassociation. ie. *Pres.* Jane Cantwell. E-mail president@libraryassociation.ie.

Israel

Israeli Center for Libs., 22 Baruch Hirsch St., P.O. Box 801, 51108 Bnei Brak. Tel. 03-6180151, fax 03-5798048, e-mail meida@gmail.com or icl@icl.org.il; World Wide Web http://www.icl.org.il.

Italy

Associazione Italiana Biblioteche (Italian Lib. Assn.), Biblioteca Nazionale Centrale, Viale Castro Pretorio 105, 00185 Rome RM. Tel. 6-446-3532, fax 6-444-1139, e-mail aib@legalmail.it, World Wide Web http://www.aib.it. *CEO* Enrica Manenti. E-mail manenti@aib.it.

Jamaica

Lib. and Info. Assn. of Jamaica, P.O. Box 125, Kingston 5. Tel./fax 876-927-1614, e-mail liajapresident@yahoo.com, World Wide Web http://www.liaja.org.jm. *Pres.* Viviene Kerr-Williams. E-mail vskwilliams@gmail.com.

Japan

Info. Science and Technology Assn., Sasaki Bldg., 2-5-7 Koisikawa, Bunkyo-ku, Tokyo 112-0002. Tel. 3-3813-3791, fax 3-3813-3793, e-mail infosta@infosta.or.jp, World Wide Web http://www.infosta.or.jp.
Nihon Toshokan Kyokai (Japan Lib. Assn.), 1-11-14 Shinkawa, Chuo-ku, Tokyo 104 0033. Tel. 3-3523-0811, fax 3-3523-0841, e-mail info@jla.or.jp, World Wide Web http://www.jla.or.jp. *Pres.* Shiomi Noboru.
Senmon Toshokan Kyogikai (Japan Special Libs. Assn.), c/o Japan Lib. Assn., Bldg. F6, 1-11-14 Shinkawa Chuo-ku, Tokyo 104-

0033. Tel. 3-3537-8335, fax 3-3537-8336, e-mail jsla@jsla.or.jp, World Wide Web http://www.jsla.or.jp.

Jordan

Jordan Lib. and Info. Assn., P.O. Box 6289, Amman 11118. Tel./fax 6-462-9412, e-mail jorla_1963@yahoo.com, World Wide Web http://www.jorla.org. *Pres.* Omar Mohammad Jaradat.

Kenya

Kenya Assn. of Lib. and Info. Professionals (formerly Kenya Lib. Assn.), Buruburu, P.O. Box 49468, 00100 Nairobi. Tel. 20-733-732-799, e-mail gitachur@yahoo.com, World Wide Web http://www.kenyalibrary association.or.ke. *Chair* Rosemary Gitachu.

Korea (Democratic People's Republic of)

Lib. Assn. of the Democratic People's Republic of Korea, c/o Grand People's Study House, P.O. Box 200, Pyongyang. E-mail korea@korea-dpr.com.

Korea (Republic of)

Korean Lib. Assn., San 60-1, Banpo-dong, Seocho-gu, Seoul 137-702. Tel. 2-535-4868, fax 2-535-5616, e-mail license@kla.kr, World Wide Web http://www.kla.kr.

Laos

Association des Bibliothécaires Laotiens (Lao Lib. Assn.), c/o Direction de la Bibliothèque Nationale, Ministry of Educ., BP 704, Vientiane. Tel. 21-21-2452, fax 21-21-2408, e-mail bailane@laotel.com.

Latvia

Latvian Libns. Assn., Terbatas iela 75, Riga LV-1001. Tel./fax 6731-2791, e-mail lbb@lbi.lnb.lv, World Wide Web http://www.lnb.lv.

Lebanon

Lebanese Lib. Assn., P.O. Box 13-5053, Beirut 1102 2801. Tel. 1-786-456, e-mail kjaroudy@lau.edu.lb, World Wide Web http://www.llaweb.org. *Pres.* Randa Chidiac. E-mail randachidiac@usek.edu.lb.

Lesotho

Lesotho Lib. Assn., Private Bag A26, Maseru 100. Tel. 213-420, fax 340-000, e-mail s.mohai@nul.ls. *Contact* Makemang Ntsasa.

Lithuania

Lietuvos Bibliotekininku Draugija (Lithuanian Libns. Assn.), S Dariaus ir S Gireno g 12, LT-59212 Birstonas. Tel./fax 8-319-65760, e-mail lbd.sekretore@gmail.com, World Wide Web http://www.lbd.lt. *Pres.* Irma Kleiziene. E-mail bmb@is.lt.

Luxembourg

Association Luxembourgeoise des Bibliothécaires, Archivistes, et Documentalistes (ALBAD) (Luxembourg Assn. of Libns., Archivists, and Documentalists), c/o National Lib. of Luxembourg, BP 295, L-2012 Luxembourg. Tel. 352-22-97-55-1, fax 352-47-56-72, World Wide Web http://www.albad.lu. *Pres.* Jean-Marie Reding; *Secy. Gen.* Bernard Linster. E-mail bernard.linster@hotmail.com.

Malawi

Malawi Lib. Assn., c/o Univ. Libn., P.O. Box 429, Zomba. Tel. 524-265, fax 525-255, World Wide Web http://www.mala.mw. *Pres.* Fiskani Ngwire; *Secy. Gen.* Robin Mwanga.

Malaysia

Persatuan Pustakawan Malaysia (Libns. Assn. of Malaysia), P.O. Box 12545, 50782 Kuala Lumpur. Tel./fax 3-2694-7390, e-mail ppm55@po.jaring.my, World Wide Web http://ppm55.org.

Mali

Association Malienne des Bibliothécaires, Archivistes et Documentalistes (Mali Assn. of Libns., Archivists, and Documentalists) (AMBAD), BP E4473, Bamako. Tel. 20-

29-94-23, fax 20-29-93-76, e-mail dnbd@afribone.net.ml.

Malta

Malta Lib. and Info. Assn. (MaLIA), c/o Univ. of Malta Lib., Msida MSD 2080. E-mail info@malia-malta.org, World Wide Web http://www.malia-malta.org. *Chair* Mark Camilleri.

Mauritania

Association Mauritanienne des Bibliothécaires, Archivistes, et Documentalistes (Mauritanian Assn. of Libns., Archivists, and Documentalists), c/o Bibliothèque Nationale, BP 20, Nouakchott. Tel. 525-18-62, fax 525-18-68, e-mail bibliothequenationale@yahoo.fr.

Mauritius

Mauritius Lib. Assn., Ministry of Educ. Public Lib., Moka Rd., Rose Hill. Tel. 403-0200, fax 454-9553. *Pres.* Abdool Fareed Soogali.

Mexico

Asociación Mexicana de Bibliotecarios (Mexican Assn. of Libns.), Angel Urraza 817-A, Colonia Del Valle, Benito Juárez, Mexico DF, CP 03100. Tel. 55-55-75-33-96, e-mail correo@ambac.org.mx, World Wide Web http://www.ambac.org.mx. *Pres.* María Asunción Mendoza Becerra; *V.P.* Armendáriz Saúl Sánchez.

Myanmar

Myanmar Lib. Assn., c/o National Lib. of Myanmar, 85 Thirimingalar Yeiktha Lane, Kabar Aye Pagoda Rd., Yankin Township, Yangon. Tel. 1-662-470, e-mail myanmarlibraryassociation.mla@gmail.com, World Wide Web https://www.facebook.com/pages/Myanmar-Library-Association/759155320812626.

Nepal

Nepal Lib. Assn., GPO 2773, Kathmandu. Tel. 977-1-441-1318, e-mail info@nla.org.np, World Wide Web http://www.nla.org.np. *Pres.* Prakash Kumar Thapa. E-mail kyammuntar@yahoo.com.

The Netherlands

KNVI—Koninklijke Nederlandse Vereniging van Informatieprofessionals (Royal Dutch Association of Information Professionals) (formerly Nederlandse Vereniging voor Beroepsbeoefenaren in de Bibliotheek-Informatie-en Kennissector or Netherlands Assn. of Libns., Documentalists, and Info. Specialists), Mariaplaats 3, 3511 LH Utrecht. Tel. 30-233-0050, e-mail info@knvi.net, World Wide Web http://http://knvi.net. *Chair* Michel Wesseling. E-mail m.g.wesseling@gmail.com.

New Zealand

New Zealand Lib. Assn. (LIANZA), P.O. Box 12212, Thorndon, Wellington 6144. Tel. 4-801-5542, fax 4-801-5543, e-mail officeadmin@lianza.org.nz, World Wide Web http://www.lianza.org.nz. *Pres.* Corin Haines. E-mail librarianboy@gmail.com; *Pres.-Elect* Kris Wehipeihana. E-mail kris.wehipeihana@toiwhakaari.ac.nz; *Exec. Dir.* Joanna Matthew. E-mail joanna@lianza.org.nz.

Nicaragua

Asociación Nicaraguense de Bibliotecarios y Profesionales Afines (ANIBIPA) (Nicaraguan Assn. of Libns.), Bello Horizonte, Tope Sur de la Rotonda 1/2 cuadra abajo, J-11-57, Managua. Tel. 277-4159, e-mail anibipa@hotmail.com. *Pres.* Yadira Roque. E-mail r-yadira@hotmail.com.

Nigeria

National Lib. of Nigeria, Sanusi Dantata House, Central Business District, PMB 1, Abuja GPO 900001. Tel. 805-536-5245, fax 9-234-6773, e-mail info@nla-ng.org, World Wide Web http://www.nla-ng.org. *Pres.* Alhaji Rilwanu Abdulsala.

Norway

Arkivarforeningen (Assn. of Archivists), Fredrik Glads gate 1, 0482 Oslo. Tel. 913-16-895, e-mail imb@steria.no, World Wide Webhttp://www.arkivarforeningen.no.*Chair* Inge Manfred Bjorlin. E-mail inge.bjorlin@gmail.com.

Norsk Bibliotekforening (Norwegian Lib. Assn.), Postboks 6540, 0606 Etterstad, Oslo. Tel. 23-24-34-30, fax 22-67-23-68, e-mail nbf@norskbibliotekforening.no, World Wide Web http://www.norskbibliotekforening.no. *Gen. Secy.* Hege Newth Nouri. E-mail hege.newth.nouri@norskbibliotekforening.no.

Pakistan

Library Promotion Bureau, Karachi Univ. Campus, P.O. Box 8421, Karachi 75270. Tel./fax 21-3587-6301. *Pres.* Ghaniul Akram Sabzwari, 4213 Heritage Way Drive, Fort Worth, TX 76137. E-mail gsabzwari@hotmail.com, World Wide Web http://www.lpb-pak.com,.

Panama

Asociación Panameña de Bibliotecarios (Lib. Assn. of Panama), c/o Biblioteca Interamericana Simón Bolivar, Estafeta Universitaria, Panama City. E-mail biblis2@arcon.up.ac.pa, World Wide Web https://www.facebook.com/asociacionpanamenabibliotecarios/info.

Paraguay

Asociación de Bibliotecarios Graduados del Paraguay (Assn. of Paraguayan Graduate Libns.), Facultad Politecnica, Universidad Nacional de Asunción, 2160 San Lorenzo. Tel. 21-585-588, e-mail abigrap@pol.una.py, World Wide Web http://www.pol.una.py/abigrap. *Chair* Emilce Sena Correa. E-mail esena@pol.una.py.

Peru

Asociación de Archiveros del Perú (Peruvian Assn. of Archivists), Av. Manco Capac No. 1180, Dpto 201, La Victoria, Lima. Tel. 1-472-8729, fax 1-472-7408, e-mail contactos@adapperu.com. *Pres.* Juan Manuel Serrano Valencia.

Philippines

Assn. of Special Libs. of the Philippines, c/o Goethe-Institut Philippinen, G/4-5/F Adamson Centre, 121 Leviste St., Salcedo Village,

1227 Makati City. Tel. 2-840-5723, e-mail aslpboard@yahoo.com.ph, World Wide Web http://aslpwiki.wikispaces.com. *Pres.* Brinerdine G. Alejandrino. Philippine Libns. Assn., Room 301, National Lib. Bldg., T. M. Kalaw St., 1000 Ermita, Manila. Tel. 525-9401. World Wide Web http://plai.org.ph. *Pres.* Elizabeth R. Peralejo.

Poland

Stowarzyszenie Bibliotekarzy Polskich (Polish Libns. Assn.), al Niepodleglosci 213, 02-086 Warsaw. Tel. 22-825-83-74, fax 22-825-53-49, e-mail biuro@sbp.pl, World Wide Web http://www.sbp.pl. *Chair* Elizabeth Stefanczyk. E-mail e.stefanczyk@bn.org.pl; *Secy. Gen.* Marzena Przybysz.

Portugal

Associação Portuguesa de Bibliotecários, Arquivistas e Documentalistas (Portuguese Assn. of Libns., Archivists, and Documentalists), Rua Morais Soares, 43C, 1 Dto e Frte, 1900-341 Lisbon. Tel. 21-816-19-80, fax 21-815-45-08, e-mail apbad@apbad.pt, World Wide Web http://www.apbad.pt.

Puerto Rico

Sociedad de Bibliotecarios de Puerto Rico (Society of Libns. of Puerto Rico), Apdo 22898, San Juan 00931-2898. Tel./fax 787-764-0000, World Wide Web http://www. sociedadbibliotecarios.org. *Pres.* Juan Vargas. E-mail juan.vargas3@upr.edu.

Russia

Rossiiskaya Bibliotechnaya Assotsiatsiya (Russian Lib. Assn.), 18 Sadovaya St., St. Petersburg 191069. Tel./fax 812-110-5861, e-mail rba@nlr.ru, World Wide Web http://www.rba.ru. *Exec. Secy.* Elena Tikhonova.

Senegal

Association Sénégalaise des Bibliothécaires, Archivistes et Documentalistes (Senegalese Assn. of Libns., Archivists, and Documentalists), BP 2006, Dakar RP, Université Cheikh Anta Diop, Dakar. Tel. 77-651-00-

33, fax 33-824-23-79, e-mail asbad200@ hotmail.com, World Wide Web http://www. asbad.org. *Pres.* Lawrence Gomis Baaya; *Secy. Gen.* Alassane Ndiath.

Serbia and Montenegro

Jugoslovenski Bibliografsko Informacijski Institut, Terazije 26, 11000 Belgrade. Tel. 11-2687-836, fax 11-2687-760.

Sierra Leone

Sierra Leone Assn. of Archivists, Libns., and Info. Scientists, c/o Sierra Leone Lib. Board, Rokel St., P.O. Box 326, Freetown. Tel. 022-220-758.

Singapore

Lib. Assn. of Singapore, National Lib. Board, 100 Victoria St., No. 14-01, Singapore 188064. Tel. 6332-3255, fax 6332-3248, e-mail lassec@las.org.sg, World Wide Web http://www.las.org.sg. *Pres.* Lee Cheng Ean. E-mail president@las.org.sg.

Slovenia

Zveza Bibliotekarskih Druötev Slovenije (Union of Assns. of Slovene Libns.), Turjaöka 1, 1000 Ljubljana. Tel. 1-2001-176, fax 1-4257-293, e-mail info@zbds-zveza.si, World Wide Web http://www.zbds-zveza.si. *Pres.* Sabina Fras Popovic. E-mail sabina. fras-popovic@mb.sik.si.

South Africa

Lib. and Info. Assn. of South Africa, P.O. Box 1598, Pretoria 0001. Tel. 12-328-2010, fax 12-323-4912, e-mail liasa@liasa.org. za, World Wide Web http://www.liasa.org. za. *Pres.* Ujala Satgoor. E-mail president@ liasa.org.za.

Spain

Federación Española de Archiveros, Bibliotecarios, Museólogos y Documentalistas (ANABAD) (Spanish Federation of Assns. of Archivists, Libns., Archaeologists, Museum Curators, and Documentalists), de las Huertas, 37, 28014 Madrid. Tel. 91-575-1727, fax 91-578-1615, e-mail anabad@

anabad.org, World Wide Web http://www. anabad.org. *Pres.* Miguel Ángel Gacho Santamaría.

Sri Lanka

Sri Lanka Lib. Assn., Sri Lanka Professional Centre 275/75, Stanley Wijesundara Mawatha, Colombo 7. Tel./fax 11-258-9103, e-mail slla@slltnet.lk, World Wide Web http://www.slla.org.lk. *Pres.* Shivanthi Weerasinghe; *Gen. Secy.* Lilamani Amerasekera.

Swaziland

Swaziland Lib. Assn. (SWALA), P.O. Box 2309, Mbabane H100. Tel. 404-2633, fax 404-3863.

Sweden

Svensk Biblioteksförening Kansli (Swedish Lib. Assn.), World Trade Center, D5, Box 70380, 107 24 Stockholm. Tel. 8-545-132-30, fax 8-545-132-31, e-mail info@biblioteksforeningen.org, World Wide Web http://www.biblioteksforeningen.org. *Chair* Calle Nathanson; *Secy. Gen.* Niclas Lindberg. E-mail nl@biblioteksforeningen.org.

Svensk Förening för Informationsspecialister (Swedish Assn. for Info. Specialists), Box 2001, 135 02 Tyresö. E-mail kansliet@sfis.nu, World Wide Web http://www.sfis.nu/om. *Chair* Ann-Christin Karlén Gramming. E-mail ann-christin.karlen@vinge.se.

Svenska Arkivsamfundet (Swedish Archival Society), Association Hall, Virkesvägen 26, 120 30 Stockholm. E-mail info@arkivsamfundet.se, World Wide Web http://www.arkivsamfundet.se.

Switzerland

Bibliothek Information Schweiz/Bibliothèque Information Suisse/Biblioteca Informazione Swizzera/Library Information Switzerland (BIS), Bleichemattstrasse 42, 5000 Aarau. Tel. 41-62-823-19-38, fax 41-62-823-19-39, e-mail info@bis.ch. *Managing Dir.* Hans Ulrich Locher. E-mail halo.locher@bis.info.

Verein Schweizer Archivarinnen und Archivare (Assn. of Swiss Archivists), Schweizerisches Bundesarchiv, Büro Pontri GmbH, Solohurnstr. 13, Postfach CH-3322, Urtenen Schönbühl. Tel. 41-31-312-26-66, fax 41-31-312-26-68, e-mail info@vsa-aas.ch, World Wide Web http://www.vsa-aas.org. *Pres.* Claudia Engler.

Taiwan

Lib. Assn. of the Republic of China (LAROC), 20 Zhongshan South Rd., Taipei 10001. Tel. 2-2361-9132, fax 2-2370-0899, e-mail lac@msg.ncl.edu.tw, World Wide Web http://www.lac.org.tw.

Tanzania

Tanzania Lib. Assn., P.O. Box 33433, Dar es Salaam. Tel./fax 255-744-296-134, e-mail tla_tanzania@yahoo.com, World Wide Web http://www.tla.or.tz.

Thailand

Thai Lib. Assn., 1346 Akarnsongkhro 5 Rd., Klongchan, Bangkapi, Bangkok 10240. Tel. 02-734-9022, fax 02-734-9021, e-mail tla2497@yahoo.com, World Wide Web http://tla.or.th.

Trinidad and Tobago

Lib. Assn. of Trinidad and Tobago, P.O. Box 1275, Port of Spain. Tel. 868-687-0194, e-mail info@latt.org.tt, World Wide Web http://www.latt.org.tt. *Pres.* Selwyn Rodulfo.

Tunisia

Association Tunisienne des Documentalistes, Bibliothécaires et Archivistes (Tunisian Assn. of Documentalists, Libns., and Archivists), BP 380, 1000 Tunis RP. Tel. 895-450.

Turkey

Türk Kütüphaneciler Dernegi (Turkish Libns. Assn.), Necatibey Cad Elgun Sok 8/8, 06440 Kizilay, Ankara. Tel. 312-230-13-25, fax 312-232-04-53, e-mail tkd.dernek@gmail.com, World Wide Web http://www.kutuphaneci.org.tr. *Pres.* Ali Fuat Kartal.

Uganda

Uganda Lib. and Info. Assn., P.O. Box 8147, Kampala. Tel. 772-488-937, e-mail info@ulia.or.ug. *Pres.* Constant Okello-Obura; *Gen. Secy.* Simon Engitu.

Ukraine

Ukrainian Lib. Assn., Vasylkovska 12, Office 5, Code 5, 01004, Kyiv. Tel. 380-44-239-74-87, fax 380-44-35-45-47, e-mail u_b_a@ukr.net, World Wide Web http://www.uba.org.ua.

United Kingdom

Archives and Records Assn., UK and Ireland (formerly the Society of Archivists), Priaryfield House, 20 Canon St., Taunton TA1 1SW, England. Tel. 1823-327-077, fax 1823-271-719, e-mail societyofarchivists@archives.org.uk, World Wide Web http://www.archives.org.uk. *Chief Exec.* John Chambers; *Chair* David Mander.

ASLIB, the Assn. for Info. Management, Howard House, Wagon Lane, Bingley BD16 1WA, England. Tel. 01274-777-700, fax 01274-785-201, e-mail support@aslib.com, World Wide Web http://www.aslib.com.

Bibliographical Society, Institute of English Studies, Senate House, Malet St., London WC1E 7HU, England. E-mail admin@bibsoc.org.uk, World Wide Web http://www.bibsoc.org.uk. *Pres.* Henry Woudhuysen. E-mail president@bibsoc.org.uk.

Chartered Institute of Lib. and Info. Professionals (CILIP) (formerly the Lib. Assn.), 7 Ridgmount St., London WC1E 7AE, England. Tel. 20-7255-0500, fax 20-7255-0501, e-mail info@cilip.org.uk, World Wide Web http://www.cilip.org.uk. *Pres.* Jan Parry. E-mail jan.parry@cilip.org.uk; *Chief Exec.* Annie Mauger. E-mail annie.mauger@cilip.org.uk.

School Lib. Assn., 1 Pine Court, Kembrey Park, Swindon SN2 8AD, England. Tel. 1793-530-166, fax 1793-481-182, e-mail info@sla.org.uk, World Wide Web http://www.sla.org.uk. *Pres.* Kevin Crossley-Holland; *Chair* Karen Horsfield; *Dir.* Tricia Adams.

Scottish Lib. and Info. Council, 151 W. George St., Glasgow G2 2JJ, Scotland. Tel. 141-228-4790, e-mail info@scottishlibraries.org, World Wide Web http://www.scottishlibraries.org. *CEO* Amina Shah. E-mail a.shah@scottishlibraries.org.

Society of College, National, and Univ. Libs (SCONUL) (formerly Standing Conference of National and Univ. Libs.), 94 Euston St., London NW1 2HA, England. Tel. 20-7387-0317, fax 20-7383-3197, e-mail info@sconul.ac.uk, World Wide Web http://www.sconul.ac.uk. *Chair* Liz Jolly; *Exec. Dir.* Ann Rossiter.

Uruguay

Agrupación Bibliotecológica del Uruguay (Uruguayan Lib. and Archive Science Assn.) and Asociación de Bibliotecólogos del Uruguay (Uruguayan Libns. Assn.), Eduardo V. Haedo 2255, CP 11200, Montevideo. Tel. 2409-9989, e-mail abu@adinet.com.uy. *Pres.* Alicia Ocaso.

Vietnam

Hôi Thu-Vien Viet Nam (Vietnam Lib. Assn.), National Lib. of Vietnam, 31 Trang Thi, Hoan Kiem, 10000 Hanoi. Tel. 4-3825-5397, fax 4-3825-3357, e-mail info@nlv.gov.vn, World Wide Web http://www.nlv.gov.vn.

Zambia

Zambia Lib. Assn., P.O. Box 38636, 10101 Lusaka. *Chair* Benson Njobvu. E-mail benson njobvu@hotmail.com.

Zimbabwe

Zimbabwe Lib. Assn., Harare City Lib., Civic Centre, Rotten Row, P.O. Box 1987, Harare. Tel. 263-773-060-307, e-mail info@zimla.co.za, World Wide Web http://zimbabwe reads.org/zimla. *Chair* T. G. Bohwa.

Directory of Book Trade and Related Organizations

Book Trade Associations, United States and Canada

For more extensive information on the associations listed in this section, see the annual edition of *Literary Market Place* (Information Today, Inc.).

AIGA—The Professional Assn. for Design (formerly American Institute of Graphic Arts), 164 Fifth Ave., New York, NY 10010. Tel. 212-807-1990, fax 212-807-1799, e-mail aiga@aiga.org, World Wide Web http://www.aiga.org. *Pres.* Sean Adams, Adams-Morioka, Inc. E-mail sean_a@adamsmorioka.com; *Secy.-Treas.* Darralyn Rieth. E-mail darralynrieth@gmail.com; *Exec. Dir.* Richard Grefé. E-mail grefe@aiga.org.

American Book Producers Assn. (ABPA), 151 W. 19 St., third fl., New York, NY 10011. Tel. 212-675-1363, fax 212-675-1364, e-mail office@ABPAonline.org, World Wide Web http://www.abpaonline.org. *Pres.* Richard Rothschild; *V.P.* Nancy Hall; *Treas.* Valerie Tomaselli; *Admin.* Kirsten Hall.

American Booksellers Assn., 200 White Plains Rd., Tarrytown, NY 10591. Tel. 800-637-0037, 914-591-2665, fax 914-591-2720, World Wide Web http://www.bookweb.org. *Pres.* Steve Bercu, BookPeople, Austin. Tel. 512-472-5050, e-mail steve@bookpeople.com; *V.P./Secy.* Betsy Burton, The King's English Bookshop, Salt Lake City. Tel. 801-484-9100, e-mail btke@comcast.net; *CEO* Oren Teicher. E-mail oren@bookweb.org.

American Literary Translators Assn. (ALTA), Univ. of Texas at Dallas, 800 W. Campbell Rd., Mail Sta. JO51, Richardson, TX 75080. Tel. 972-883-2092, fax 972-883-6303, World Wide Web http://www.utdallas.edu/alta. *Managing Dir.* Erica Mena. E-mail erica@literarytranslators.org.

American Printing History Assn., Box 4519, Grand Central Sta., New York, NY 10163-4519. World Wide Web http://www.printinghistory.org. *Pres.* Robert McCamant; *Exec. Secy.* Lyndsi Barnes. E-mail secretary@printinghistory.org.

American Society for Indexing, 1628 E. Southern Ave., No. 9-223, Tempe, AZ 85282. Tel. 480-245-6750, e-mail info@asindexing.org, World Wide Web http://www.asindexing.org. *Pres.* Charlee Trantino. E-mail president@asindexing.org; *V.P./Pres.-Elect* Fred Leise. E-mail presidentelect@asindexing.org; *Exec. Dir.* Gwen Henson. E-mail gwen@asindexing.org.

American Society of Journalists and Authors, 1501 Broadway, Suite 403, New York, NY 10036. Tel. 212-997-0947, fax 212-937-2315, e-mail asjaoffice@asja.org, World Wide Web http://www.asja.org. *Pres.* Randy Dotinga. E-mail president@asja.org; *V.P.* Sherry Beck Paprocki. E-mail vicepresident@asja.org; *Exec. Dir.* Alexandra Cantor Owens.

American Society of Media Photographers, 150 N. 2 St., Philadelphia, PA 19106. Tel. 215-451-2767, fax 215-451-0880, e-mail mopsik@asmp.org, World Wide Web http://www.asmp.org. *Pres.* Gail Mooney. E-mail mooney@asmp.org; *V. Chair* Jenna Close; *Exec. Dir.* Eugene Mopsik.

American Society of Picture Professionals, 201 E. 25 St., No. 11C, New York, NY 10010. Tel. 516-500-3686, e-mail director@aspp.com, World Wide Web http://www.aspp.

com. *Pres.* Cecilia de Querol. E-mail president@aspp.com; *Exec. Dir.* Sam Merrell. E-mail director@aspp.com.

American Translators Assn., 225 Reinekers Lane, Suite 590, Alexandria, VA 22314. Tel. 703-683-6100, fax 703-683-6122, e-mail ata@atanet.org, World Wide Web http://www.atanet.org. *Pres.* Caitilin Walsh; *Pres.-Elect* David C. Rumsey; *Secy.* Boris Silversteyn; *Treas.* Ted R. Wozniak; *Exec. Dir.* Walter W. Bacak, Jr. E-mail walter@atanet. org.

Antiquarian Booksellers Assn. of America, 20 W. 44 St., No. 507, New York, NY 10036-6604. Tel. 212-944-8291, fax 212-944-8293, e-mail inquiries@abaa.org, World Wide Web http://www.abaa.org. *Pres.* Thomas Goldwasser; *V.P./Secy.* Mary Gilliam; *Treas.* Charles Kutcher; *Exec. Dir.* Susan Benne. E-mail sbenne@abaa.org.

Assn. Media and Publishing, 12100 Sunset Hills Road, Suite 130, Reston, VA 20190. Tel. 703-234-4063, fax 703-435-4390, e-mail info@associationmediaandpublishing.org, World Wide Web http://www.association mediaandpublishing.org. *Pres.* Kim Howard; *V.P.* Erin Pressley; *Exec. Dir.* Elissa Myers. Tel. 703-234-4107, e-mail elissa@association mediaandpublishing.org.

Assn. of American Publishers, 71 Fifth Ave., New York, NY 10003. Tel. 212-255-0200, fax 212-255-7007. Washington Office 455 Massachusetts Ave. N.W., Suite 700, Washington, DC 20001. Tel. 202-347-3375, fax 202-347-3690, World Wide Web http://www.publishers.org. *Pres./CEO* Tom Allen. E-mail tallen@publishers.org; *General Counsel and V.P., Government Affairs* Allan R. Adler. E-mail adler@publishers.org; *Exec. Dir., Higher Educ.* David Anderson. E-mail danderson@publishers.org; *Exec. Dir., Pre-K–12 Learning Group* Jay Diskey. E-mail jdiskey@publishers.org; *Senior Dir., Pre-K–12 Learning Group* Susan Fletcher. E-mail sfletcher@publishers.org; *V.P.* Tina Jordan. E-mail tjordan@publishers.org; *Dir., Membership Marketing* Gail Kump. E-mail gkump@publishers.org; *Exec. Dir., Digital, Environmental and Accessibility Affairs* Ed McCoyd. E-mail emccoyd@ publishers.org; *Strategic Partnerships Exec.* Jo-Ann McDevitt. E-mail jmcdevitt@ publishers.org; *Dir., Free Expression Advocacy* Judith Platt. E-mail jplatt@publishers. org; *Exec. Dir., International Copyright Enforcement and Trade Policy* M. Lui Simpson. E-mail lsimpson@publishers.org; *V.P. and Exec. Dir., Professional and Scholarly Publishing* John Tagler. E-mail jtagler@ publishers.org.

Assn. of American University Presses, 28 W. 36 St., Suite 602, New York, NY 10018. Tel. 212-989-1010, fax 212-989-0275, e-mail info@aaupnet.org, World Wide Web http://aaupnet.org. *Pres.* Barbara Kline Pope, National Academies Press; *Pres.-Elect* Meredith Babb, Univ. Press of Florida; *Past Pres.* Philip Cercone, McGill-Queen's Univ. Press; *Exec. Dir.* Peter Berkery. Tel. 212-989-1010 ext. 29, e-mail pberkery@ aaupnet.org.

Assn. of Canadian Publishers, 174 Spadina Ave., Suite 306, Toronto, ON M5T 2C2. Tel. 416-487-6116, fax 416-487-8815, World Wide Web http://www.publishers.ca. *Pres.* Erin Creasy, ECW Press, 2120 Queen St. E., Suite 200 Toronto, ON M4E 1E2. Tel. 416-694-3348, fax 416-698-9906, e-mail erin@ecwpress.com; *V.P./Treas.* Matt Williams, House of Anansi/Groundwood, 110 Spadina Ave., Suite 801, Toronto, ON M5V 2M5. Tel. 416-363-4343, fax 416-363-1017, e-mail matt@anansi.ca; *Exec. Dir.* Carolyn Wood. Tel. 416-487-6116 ext. 222, e-mail carolyn_wood@canbook.org.

Assn. of Educational Publishers (AEP). Merged in 2013 with the School Division of the Assn. of American Publishers (AAP).

Audio Publishers Assn., 100 N. 20 St., Suite 400, Philadelphia, PA 19103. Tel. 215-564-2729, e-mail info@audiopub.org; World Wide Web http://www.audiopub.org. *Pres.* Michele Cobb; *V.P.* Linda Lee; *V.P., Member Communications* Robin Whitten; *Secy.* Janet Benson; *Treas.* Sean McManus; *Exec. Dir.* Denise Daniels.

Authors Guild, 31 E. 32 St., seventh fl., New York, NY 10016. Tel. 212-563-5904, fax 212-564-5363, e-mail staff@authorsguild. org, World Wide Web http://www.authors guild.org. *Pres.* Roxana Robinson; *V.P.s* Judy Blume, Richard Russo, James Shapiro; *Secy.* Pat Cummings; *Treas.* Peter Petre.

Book Industry Study Group, 145 W. 45 St., Suite 601, New York, NY 10017. Tel. 646-336-7141, fax 646-336-6214, e-mail info@

bisg.org, World Wide Web http://www.bisg. org. *Chair* Tara Catogge, Quarto Publishing; *V. Chair* Andrew Savikas, Safari Books Online; *Secy.* Fran Toolan, Firebrand Technologies; *Treas.* Maureen McMahon, Kaplan Publishing; *Exec. Dir.* Len Vlahos. E-mail len@bisg.org.

Book Manufacturers' Institute, 2 Armand Beach Drive, Suite 1B, Palm Coast, FL 32137. Tel. 386-986-4552, fax 386-986-4553, e-mail info@bmibook.com, World Wide Web http://www.bmibook.org. *Pres.* Jac B. Garner, Webcrafters; *Exec. V.P./Secy.* Daniel N. Bach; *V.P./Pres.-Elect* Kent H. Larson, Bridgeport National Bindery; *Treas.* Paul Genovese, Lake Book Manufacturing. Address correspondence to the executive vice president.

Bookbuilders of Boston, 115 Webster Woods Lane, North Andover, MA 01845. Tel. 781-378-1361, fax 419-821-2171, e-mail office @bbboston.org, World Wide Web http://www.bbboston.org. *Pres.* Jamie Carter. E-mail jcarter@copyright.com; *1st V.P.* Christopher Hartman. E-mail hartman.cg@gmail.com; *2nd V.P.* Tom Delano. E-mail tom.delano@gmail.com; *Treas.* James Taylor. E-mail jtaylor@vistahigherlearning.com; *Clerk* Laura Wind. E-mail lwind@bedford stmartins.com.

Bookbuilders West. See Publishing Professionals Network.

Canadian Booksellers Assn. Now part of Retail Council of Canada. Toronto office: 1255 Bay St., Suite 902, Toronto, ON M5R 2A9.

Canadian International Standard Numbers (ISN) Agency, c/o Published Heritage, Lib. and Archives Canada, 395 Wellington St., Ottawa, ON K1A 0N4. Tel. 866-578-7777 (toll-free) or 613-996-5115, World Wide Web http://www.collectionscanada.ca/isn/index-e.html.

Canadian Printing Industries Assn., P.O. Box 58033, Orleans Garden, 1619 Orleans Blvd., Ottawa, ON K1C 7E2. Tel. 613-236-7208, toll free (Canada and USA) 800-267-7280, fax 613-232-1334, World Wide Web http://www.cpia-aci.ca. *Chair* Sandy Stephens, Informco; *Exec. Dir.* Brian Ellis. E-mail brian ellis@cpia-aci.ca.

CBA: The Assn. for Christian Retail (formerly Christian Booksellers Association), 9240 Explorer Drive, Suite 200, Colorado Springs, CO 80920. Tel. 719-265-9895, fax 719-272-3510, e-mail info@cbaonline.org, World Wide Web http://www.cbaonline. org. *Chair* Sue Smith, Baker Book House; *V. Chair* Robin Hogan, Christian Cultural Center Bookstore.

Chicago Book Clinic. See Midwest Publishing Assn.

Children's Book Council, 54 W. 39 St., 14th fl., New York, NY 10018. Tel. 212-966-1990, fax 212-966-2073, e-mail cbc.info@cbc books.org, World Wide Web http://www.cbc books.org. *Chair* Betsy Groban, Houghton Mifflin Harcourt; *V. Chair* Jon Anderson, Simon & Schuster; *Exec. Dir.* Robin Adelson. E-mail robin.adelson@cbcbooks.org.

Christian Booksellers Association. See CBA: The Assn. for Christian Retail.

Copyright Society of the USA, 1 E. 53 St., eighth fl., New York, NY 10022. World Wide Web http://www.csusa.org. *Pres.* Eric J. Schwartz; *V.P.* Nancy E. Wolff; *Secy.* Judith Finell; *Treas.* Michael Donaldson; *Dir. Operations* Kaitland Kubat.

Council of Literary Magazines and Presses, 154 Christopher St., Suite 3C, New York, NY 10014. Tel. 212-741-9110, fax 212-741-9112, e-mail info@clmp.org, World Wide Web http://www.clmp.org. *Co-chairs* Nicole Dewey, Gerald Howard; *Exec. Dir.* Jeffrey Lependorf. E-mail jlependorf@clmp.org.

Educational Book and Media Assn. (formerly Educational Paperback Assn.), P.O. Box 3363, Warrenton, VA 20188. Tel. 540-318-7770, e-mail info@edupaperback.org, World Wide Web http://www.edupaperback. org. *Pres.* Jennifer Allen; *V.P.* Jill Faherty; *Treas.* Joyce Skokut; *Past Pres.* Dan Walsh.

Evangelical Christian Publishers Assn., 9633 S. 48 St., Suite 140, Phoenix, AZ 85044. Tel. 480-966-3998, fax 480-966-1944, e-mail info@ecpa.org, World Wide Web http://www.ecpa.org. *Pres. and CEO* Mark W. Kuyper.

Graphic Artists Guild, 32 Broadway, Suite 1114, New York, NY 10004. Tel. 212-791-3400, fax 212-792-0333, e-mail admin@ gag.org, World Wide Web http://www. graphicartistsguild.org. *Pres.* Haydn S. Adams. E-mail president@gag.org; *V.P.* Lara Kisielewska; *Exec. Dir.* Patricia McKiernan. E-mail admin@gag.org.

Great Lakes Independent Booksellers Assn., c/o Exec. Dir. Deb Leonard, 2113 Roosevelt, Ypsilanti, MI 48197. Tel. 888-736-3096, fax 734-879-11291, e-mail deb@gliba.org, World Wide Web http://www.gliba.org. *Pres.* Tom Lowry, Lowry's Books, 22 N. Main St., Three Rivers, MI 49093. Tel. 269-273-7323, e-mail hiphop@net-link.net.

Guild of Book Workers, 521 Fifth Ave., New York, NY 10175. Tel. 212-292-4444, e-mail secretary@guildofbookworkers.org, World Wide Web http://www.guildofbook workers.org. *Pres.* Mark Andersson. E-mail president@guildofbookworkers.org; *V.P.* Bexx Caswell. E-mail vicepresident@ guildofbookworkers.org.

Horror Writers Assn., P.O. Box 56687, Sherman Oaks, CA 91413. E-mail hwa@horror. org, World Wide Web http://www.horror. org. *Pres.* Rocky Wood. E-mail president@ horror.org; *V.P.* Lisa Morton. E-mail vp@ horror.org; *Secy.* Joe McKinney. E-mail secretary@horror.org; *Treas.* Leslie Klinger. E-mail treasurer@horror.org.

IAPHC—The Graphic Professionals Resource Network (formerly the International Assn. of Printing House Craftsmen), P.O. Box 2549, Maple Grove, MN 55311-7549. Tel. 800-466-4274 (toll-free) or 763-560-1620, fax 763-560-1350, e-mail headquarters@ iaphc.org, World Wide Web http://www. iaphc.org. *Pres./CEO* Kevin P. Keane. E-mail kkeane1069@aol.com.

Independent Book Publishers Assn. (formerly PMA), 1020 Manhattan Beach Blvd., Suite 204, Manhattan Beach, CA 90266. Tel. 310-546-1818, fax 310-546-3939, e-mail info@ ibpa-online.org, World Wide Web http:// www.ibpa-online.org. *Chair* Deltina Hay, Dalton Publishing, 9101 La Cresada Drive, No. 1934, Austin, TX 78749. Tel. 512-567-4955; *Exec. Dir.* Angela Bole. Tel. 310-546-1818, e-mail angela@ibpa-online.org; *COO/Secy.* Terry Nathan. E-mail terry@ ibpa-online.org.

International Standard Book Numbering U.S. Agency, 630 Central Ave., New Providence, NJ 07974. Tel. 888-269-5372, fax 908-219-0188, e-mail isbn-san@bowker.com, World Wide Web http://www.isbn.org. *Dir., Identifier Services* Beat Barblan.

Jewish Book Council, 520 Eighth Ave., fourth fl., New York, NY 10018. Tel. 212-201-2920, fax 212-532-4952, e-mail jbc@jewish books.org, World Wide Web http://www. jewishbookcouncil.org. *Pres.* Lawrence J. Krule; *V.P.* Judith Lieberman; *Secy.* Mimi S. Frank.

Library Binding Institute/Hardcover Binders International, 4400 PGA Blvd., Suite 600, Palm Beach Gardens, FL 33410. Tel. 561-745-6821, fax 561-775-0089, e-mail info@ lbibinders.org, World Wide Web http://www. lbibinders.org. *Pres.* Duncan Campbell, Campbell-Logan Bindery. E-mail duncan@ campbell-logan.com; *Exec. Dir.* Debra Nolan. E-mail dnolan@lbibinders.org.

Midwest Independent Publishers Assn. (MIPA), P.O. Box 18536, St. Paul, MN 55118-0536. Tel. 651-917-0021 or 651-917-0021, World Wide Web http://www.mipa. org. *Pres.* Sherry Roberts, Roberts Group. Tel. 952-322-4005, e-mail sherry@editorial service.com; *Secy.* Judith Palmateer, Amber Skye Publishing. Tel. 651-452-0463, e-mail jpalmateer0463@comcast.net; *Treas.* Dorie McClelland, Spring Book Design. Tel. 651-457-0258, e-mail dorie@springbookdesign. com.

Midwest Publishing Assn., 275 N. York St., Suite 401, Elmhurst, IL 60126. Tel. 630-833-4220, e-mail info@midwestpublish. org, World Wide Web http://www.midwest publish.org. *Pres.* Del Bishop, The Bishop Group, 3 Burning Oak Trail, Barrington Hills, IL 60019. Tel. 847-462-1877, e-mail bishopgroup@comcast.net.

Miniature Book Society. *Pres.* Stephen Byrne. E-mail sb@finalscore.demon.co.uk; *V.P.* Jim Brogan; *Secy.* Gail Faulkner; *Treas.* Karen Nyman. World Wide Web http://www.mbs. org.

Minnesota Book Publishers' Roundtable. E-mail information@publishersroundtable.org, World Wide Web http://www.publishers roundtable.org. *Pres.* Katie Nickerson, Univ. of Minnesota Press, 111 Third Ave. S., Suite 290, Minneapolis, MN 55401. E-mail nickerso @umn.edu; *V.P.* Kate Kjorlien, Hazelden Publishing, 15251 Pleasant Valley Rd., Center City, MN 55012. E-mail kkjorlien@ hazelden.org.

Mountains and Plains Independent Booksellers Assn., 3278 Big Spruce Way, Park City, UT 84098. Tel. 435-649-6079, fax 435-649-6105, e-mail laura@mountainsplains.org,

World Wide Web http://www.mountains plains.org. *Pres.* Andrea Avantaggio, Maria's Bookshop, 960 Main Ave., Durango, CO 81301. Tel. 970-247-1438, fax 970-247-5916, e-mail andrea@mariasbookshop.com; *Exec. Dir.* Laura Ayrey.

MPA—The Assn. of Magazine Media (formerly Magazine Publishers of America), 757 Third Ave., 11th fl., New York, NY 10017. Tel. 212-872-3700, e-mail mpa@magazine. org, World Wide Web http://www.magazine. org. *Pres. and CEO* Mary Berner. Tel. 212-872-3710, e-mail president@magazine.org.

NAPL (formerly National Assn. for Printing Leadership), 1 Meadowlands Plaza, Suite 1511, East Rutherford, NJ 07073. Tel. 800-642-6275, 201-634-9600, fax 201-634-0324, e-mail info@napl.org, World Wide Web http://www.napl.org. *Pres./CEO* Joseph P. Truncale. E-mail jtruncale@napl. org.

National Assn. of College Stores, 500 E. Lorain St., Oberlin, OH 44074-1294. Tel. 800-622-7498, 440-775-7777, fax 440-775-4769, e-mail info@nacs.org, World Wide Web http:// www.nacs.org. *Pres.* Todd Summer; *Pres.-Elect* Anthony Martin; *CEO* Brian Cartier. E-mail bcartier@nacs.org.

National Book Foundation, 90 Broad St., Suite 604, New York, NY 10004. Tel. 212-685-0261, fax 212-213-6570, e-mail national book@nationalbook.org, World Wide Web http://www.nationalbook.org. *Pres./CEO* David Steinberger, Perseus Books Group; *V.P.* Morgan Entrekin, Grove/Atlantic; *Exec. Dir.* Harold Augenbraum. E-mail haugenbraum @nationalbook.org.

National Coalition Against Censorship (NCAC), 19 Fulton St., Suite 407, New York, NY 10038. Tel. 212-807-6222, fax 212-807-6245, e-mail ncac@ncac.org, World Wide Web http://www.ncac.org. *Exec. Dir.* Joan E. Bertin; *Dirs.* Jon Anderson, Michael Bamberger, Joan E. Bertin, Judy Blume, Susan Clare, Martha Gershun, Robie Harris, Phil Harvey, Michael Jacobs, Eric M. Freedman, Chris Peterson, Larry Siems, Emily Whitfield.

New Atlantic Independent Booksellers Assn. (NAIBA), 2667 Hyacinth St., Westbury, NY 11590. Tel. 516-333-0681, fax 516-333-0689, e-mail info@naiba.com, World Wide Web http://www.newatlanticbooks.

com. *Pres.* Mark LaFramboise, Politics and Prose; *V.P.* Todd Dickinson, Aaron's Books; *Exec. Dir.* Eileen Dengler.

New England Independent Booksellers Assn. (NEIBA), 1955 Massachusetts Ave., Cambridge, MA 02140-1405, e-mail steve@ neba.org, World Wide Web http://www.new englandbooks.org. *Pres.* Suzanna Hermans, Oblong Books & Music, Rhinebeck, NY; *V.P.* Susan Mercier, Edgartown Books, Edgartown, MA; *Exec. Dir.* Steve Fischer.

New York Center for Independent Publishing (formerly the Small Press Center), c/o General Society of Mechanics and Tradesmen Lib., 20 W. 44 St., New York, NY 10036. Tel. 212-764-7021, e-mail info@nycip.org, World Wide Web http://nycip.wordpress. com.

Northern California Independent Booksellers Assn., The Presidio, 1007 General Kennedy Ave., P.O. Box 29169, San Francisco, CA 94129. Tel. 415-561-7686, fax 415-561-7685, e-mail office@nciba.com, World Wide Web http://www.nciba.com. *Pres.* Calvin Crosby; *V.P.* John Russel; *Exec. Dir.* Hut Landon.

PEN American Center, Div. of International PEN, 588 Broadway, Suite 303, New York, NY 10012. Tel. 212-334-1660, fax 212-334-2181, e-mail pen@pen.org, World Wide Web http://www.pen.org. *Pres.* Peter Godwin; *Exec. V.P.* John Troubh; *V.P.s* Jeri Laber, Joanne Leedom-Ackerman, Annette Tapert; *Secy.* Theresa Rebeck; *Treas.* John Oakes; *Exec. Dir.* Susanne Nossel. E-mail snossel@pen.org.

Periodical and Book Assn. of America, 481 Eighth Ave., Suite 526, New York, NY 10001. Tel. 212-563-6502, fax 212-563-4098, World Wide Web http://www.pbaa. net. *Pres.* Jay Annis. E-mail jannis@taunton. com; *Chair* William Michalopoulos. E-mail wmichalopoulos@hearst.com; *Exec. Dir.* Lisa W. Scott. E-mail lisawscott@hotmail. com; *Assoc. Dir.* Jose Cancio. E-mail jcancio @pbaa.net.

Publishers Marketing Assn. (PMA). See Independent Book Publishers Assn.

Publishing Professionals Network (formerly Bookbuilders West), 9328 Elk Grove Blvd., Suite 105, Elk Grove, CA 95624. Tel. 415-670-9564, e-mail operations@bookbuilders. org, World Wide Web http://pubpronetwork.

org. *Pres.* David Zielonka; *V.P.* Tona Pearce Myers.

Romance Writers of America, 14615 Benfer Rd., Houston, TX 77069. Tel. 832-717-5200, fax 832-717-5201, e-mail info@rwa.org, World Wide Web http://www.rwa.org. *Pres.* Cindy Kirk. E-mail cindykirk@aol.com; *Pres.-Elect* Diane Kelly. E-mail diane@dianekelly.com; *Exec. Dir.* Allison Kelley. E-mail allison.kelley@rwa.org.

Science Fiction and Fantasy Writers of America, P.O. Box 3238, Enfield, CT 06083-3238. World Wide Web http://www.sfwa.org. *Pres.* Steven Gould. E-mail president@sfwa.org; *V.P.* Cat Rambo. E-mail vp@sfwa.org; *Secy.* Susan Forest. E-mail secretary@sfwa.org; *CFO* Bud Sparhawk. E-mail treasurer@sfwa.org; *Operations Mgr.* Kate Baker. E-mail office@sfwa.org.

Society of Children's Book Writers and Illustrators (SCBWI), 8271 Beverly Blvd., Los Angeles, CA 90048. Tel. 323-782-1010, fax 323-782-1892, e-mail scbwi@scbwi.org, World Wide Web http://www.scbwi.org. *Pres.* Stephen Mooser. E-mail stephen mooser@scbwi.org; *Exec. Dir.* Lin Oliver.

Society of Illustrators (SI), 128 E. 63 St., New York, NY 10065. Tel. 212-838-2560, fax 212-838-2561, e-mail info@society illustrators.org, World Wide Web http://www.societyillustrators.org. *Pres.* Tim O'Brien; *Exec. V.P.* Victor Juhasz; *V.P.* Kar-en Green; *Secy.* Leslie Cober-Gentry; *Exec. Dir.* Anelle Miller. E-mail anelle@society illustrators.org.

Southern Independent Booksellers Alliance (SIBA), 3806 Yale Ave., Columbia, SC 29205. Tel. 803-994-9530, fax 309-410-0211, e-mail info@sibaweb.com, World Wide Web http://www.sibaweb.com. *Exec. Dir.* Wanda Jewell. E-mail wanda@sibaweb.com.

Western Writers of America, c/o Candy Moulton, 271 CR 219, Encampment, WY 82325 Tel. 307-329-8942, e-mail wwa.moulton@gmail.com, World Wide Web http://www.westernwriters.org. *Pres.* Sherry Monahan; *V.P.* Kirk Ellis; *Past Pres.* Dusty Richards; *Exec. Dir./Secy.-Treas.* Candy Moulton.

Women's National Book Assn., P.O. Box 237, FDR Sta., New York, NY 10150. Tel./fax 212-208-4629, e-mail info@wnba-books.org, World Wide Web http://www.wnba-books.org. *Pres.* Carin Siegfried, 7308 Quail Meadow Lane, Charlotte, NC 28210. Tel. 704-608-6559, e-mail carinsiegfried@earthlink.net; *V.P./Pres.-Elect* Jane Kinney-Denning, 1629 NYS Rt. 94, New Windsor, NY 12533. Tel. 845-496-1593, e-mail jdenning@pace.edu; *Secy.* Shannon Janeczek; *Treas.* Gloria Toler; *Past Pres.* Valerie Tomaselli.

International and Foreign Book Trade Associations

For Canadian book trade associations, see the preceding section, "Book Trade Associations, United States and Canada." For a more extensive list of book trade organizations outside the United States and Canada, with more detailed information, consult *International Literary Market Place* (Information Today, Inc.), which also provides extensive lists of major bookstores and publishers in each country.

International

African Publishers' Network, c/o Ghana Book Publishers Assn. (GBPA), P.O. Box LT 471, Lartebiokorshie, Accra, Ghana. Tel. 233-21-912765, e-mail ghanabookpubs@yahoo.com.

Afro-Asian Book Council, 4835/24 Ansari Rd., New Delhi 110002, India. Tel. 11-2325-8865, fax 11-2326-7437, e-mail afro@aab-council.org, World Wide Web http://www.aabcouncil.org. *Secy.-Gen.* Sukumar Das. E-mail sukumar4das21@gmail.com; *Dir.* Saumya Gupta. E-mail sgupta@aabcouncil.org.

Centro Régional para el Fomento del Libro en América Latina y el Caribe (CERLALC) (Regional Center for Book Promotion in Latin America and the Caribbean), Calle 70, No. 9-52, Bogotá, Colombia. Tel. 1-540-2071, fax 1-541-6398, e-mail libro@cerlalc.com, World Wide Web http://www.cerlalc.org. *Dir.* Fernando Zapata López.

Federation of European Publishers, rue Montoyer 31, Boîte 8, 1000 Brussels, Belgium. Tel. 2-770-11-10, fax 2-771-20-71, e-mail info@fep-fee.eu, World Wide Web http://www.fep-fee.eu. *Pres.* Pierre Dutilleul; *Dir.-Gen.* Anne Bergman-Tahon.

International Board on Books for Young People (IBBY), Nonnenweg 12, 4003 Basel, Switzerland. Tel. 61-272-29-17, fax 61-272-27-57, e-mail ibby@ibby.org, World Wide Web http://www.ibby.org. *Exec. Dir.* Elizabeth Page.

International League of Antiquarian Booksellers (ILAB), c/o Rue Toepffer 5, Case postale 499, 1211 Geneva 12, Switzerland. E-mail secretary@ilab.org, World Wide Web http://www.ilab.org. *Pres.* Norbert Donhofer; *Gen. Secy.* Ulrich Hobbeling.

International Publishers Assn. (Union Internationale des Editeurs), 23 ave. de France, CH-1202 Geneva, Switzerland. Tel. 22-704-1820, e-mail secretariat@internationalpublishers.org, World Wide Web http://www.internationalpublishers.org. *Pres.* Youngsuk Chi; *Secy.-Gen.* Jens Bammel.

STM: The International Assn. of Scientific, Technical, and Medical Publishers, 267 Banbury Rd., Oxford OX2 7HT, England. Tel. 44-1865-339-321, fax 44-1865-339-325, e-mail info@stm-assoc.org, World Wide Web http://www.stm-assoc.org. *CEO* Michael Mabe.

National

Argentina

Cámara Argentina del Libro (Argentine Book Assn.), Av. Belgrano 1580, 4 piso, C1093AAQ Buenos Aires. Tel. 11-4381-8383, fax 11-4381-9253, e-mail cal@editores.org.ar, World Wide Web http://www.editores.org.ar. *Pres.* Isaac Rubizal.

Fundación El Libro (Book Foundation), Yrigoyen 1628, 5 piso, C1089AAF Buenos Aires. Tel. 11-4370-0600, fax 11-4370-0607, e-mail fundacion@el-libro.com.ar, World Wide Web http://www.el-libro.org.ar. *Admin. Mgr.* Daniel Monzo; *Chair* Martin Gremmelspacher.

Australia

Australian and New Zealand Assn. of Antiquarian Booksellers (ANZAAB), Apartment 1, 122 Raglan St., Mosman, NSW 2088. E-mail admin@anzaab.com, World Wide Web http://www.anzaab.com. *Pres.* Jörn Harbeck; *Secy.* Rachel Robarts.

Australian Booksellers Assn., 828 High St., Unit 9, Kew East, Vic. 3102. Tel. 3-9859-7322, fax 3-9859-7344, e-mail mail@aba.org.au, World Wide Web http://www.aba.

org.au. *Pres.* Patricia Genat; *CEO* Joel Becker.

Australian Publishers Assn., 60/89 Jones St., Ultimo, NSW 2007. Tel. 2-9281-9788, e-mail apa@publishers.asn.au, World Wide Web http://www.publishers.asn.au. *Pres.* Louise Adler; *CEO* Maree McCaskill. E-mail maree.mccaskill@publishers.asn.au.

Austria

Hauptverband des Österreichischen Buchhandels (Austrian Publishers and Booksellers Assn.), Grünangergasse 4, A-1010 Vienna. Tel. 1-512-15-35-26, fax 1-512-84-82, e-mail sekretariat@hvb.at, World Wide Web http://www.buecher.at. *Mgr.* Inge Kralupper. E-mail kralupper@hvb.at.

Verband der Antiquare Österreichs (Austrian Antiquarian Booksellers Assn.), Grünangergasse 4, A-1010 Vienna. Tel. 1-512-1535-14, e-mail sekretariat@hvb.at, World Wide Web http://www.antiquare.at.

Belarus

National Book Chamber of Belarus, 31a V Khoruzhei Str., Rm. 707, 220002 Minsk. Tel. 17-289-33-96, fax 17-334-78-47, World Wide Web http://natbook.org.by. *Dir.* Elena V. Ivanova. E-mail elvit@natbook.org.by.

Belgium

Boek.be (formerly Vlaamse Boekverkopersbond, Flemish Booksellers Assn.), Te Buelaerlei 37, 2140 Borgerhout. Tel. 03-230-89-23, fax 3-281-22-40, World Wide Web http://www.boek.be. *CEO* Geert Joris; *Communication Mgr.* Patricia De Laet. E-mail patricia.delaet@boek.be.

Vlaamse Uitgevers Vereniging (Flemish Publishers Assn.). See Boek.be.

Bolivia

Cámara Boliviana del Libro (Bolivian Book Chamber), Calle Capitan Ravelo No. 2116, 682 La Paz. Tel. 2-211-3264, e-mail cabolib@entelnet.bo, World Wide Web http://www.cabolib.org.bo. *Gen. Mgr.* Ana Patricia Navarro.

Brazil

Cámara Brasileira do Livro (Brazilian Book Assn.), Rua Cristiano Viana 91, Jardim Paulista, 05411-000 Sao Paulo-SP. Tel./fax 11-3069-1300, e-mail cbl@cbl.org.br, World Wide Web http://www.cbl.org.br. *Pres.* Karine Goncalves Pansa.

Sindicato Nacional dos Editores de Livros (Brazilian Publishers Assn.), Rue da Ajuda 35-18 andar, 20040-000 Rio de Janeiro-RJ. Tel. 21-2533-0399, fax 21-2533-0422, e-mail snel@snel.org.br, World Wide Web http://www.snel.org.br. *Pres.* Sonia Machado Jardim.

Chile

Cámara Chilena del Libro AG (Chilean Assn. of Publishers, Distributors, and Booksellers), Av. Libertador Bernardo O'Higgins 1370, Oficina 501, Santiago. Tel. 2-672-0348, fax 2-687-4271, e-mail prolibro@tie.cl, World Wide Web http://www.camlibro.cl. *Pres.* Arturo Infante.

Colombia

Cámara Colombiana del Libro (Colombian Book Assn.), Calle 35, No. 5A 05, Bogotá. Tel. 57-1-323-01-11, fax 57-1-285-10-82, e-mail camlibro@camlibro.com.co, World Wide Web http://www.camlibro.com.co. *Exec. Chair* Enrique González Villa; *Secy.-Gen.* José Manuel Ramirez Sarmiento.

Czech Republic

Svaz ceských knihkupcu a nakladatelu (Czech Publishers and Booksellers Assn.), P.O. Box 177, 110 01 Prague. Tel. 224-219-944, fax 224-219-942, e-mail sckn@sckn.cz, World Wide Web http://www.sckn.cz. *Chair* Martin Vopěnka.

Denmark

Danske Boghandlerforening (Danish Booksellers Assn.), Slotsholmsgade 1 B, 1216 Copenhagen K. Tel. 3254-2255, fax 3254-0041, e-mail ddb@bogpost.dk, World Wide Web http://www.boghandlerforeningen.dk. *Chair* Mogens Eliasson.

Danske Forlæggerforening (Danish Publishers Assn.), Børsen DK-1217 Copenhagen K. Tel. 45-33-15-66-88, e-mail danishpublishers@danishpublishers.dk, World Wide Web http://www.danskeforlag.dk.

Ecuador

Cámara Ecuatoriana del Libro, Avda. Eloy Alfaro, N29-61 e Inglaterra, Edf. Eloy Alfaro, 9 no. piso, Quito. Tel. 2-5533-11, fax 2-222-150, e-mail celnp@uio.satnet.net, World Wide Web http://celibro.org.ec. *Pres.* Fabian Luzuriaga.

Egypt

General Egyptian Book Organization (GEBO), P.O. Box 235, Cairo 11511. Tel. 2-257-7531, fax 2-257-54213, e-mail info@gebo.gov.eg, World Wide Web http://www.gebo.gov.eg. *Chair* Nasser Al-Ansary.

Estonia

Estonian Publishers Assn., Roosikrantsi 6-207,10119 Tallinn. Tel. 372-644-9866, fax 372-617-7550, e-mail kirjastusteliit@eki.ee, World Wide Web http://www.estbook.com. *Managing Dir.* Kaidi Urmet.

Finland

Kirjakauppaliitto Ry (Booksellers Assn. of Finland), Urho Kekkosen Katu 8 C 34b, 00100 Helsinki. Tel. 9-6899 112, e-mail toimisto@kirjakauppaliitto.fi, World Wide Web http://www.kirjakauppaliitto.fi. *CEO* Katriina Jaakkola.

Suomen Kustannusyhdistys (Finnish Book Publishers Assn.), P.O. Box 177, Lönnrotinkatu 11 A, FIN-00121, Helsinki. Tel. 358-9-228-77-250, fax 358-9-612-1226, World Wide Web http://www.kustantajat.fi/en. *Chair* Pasi Vainio; *Dir.* Sakari Laiho.

France

Bureau International de l'Edition Française (BIEF) (International Bureau of French Publishing), 115 blvd. Saint-Germain, F-75006 Paris. Tel. 01-44-41-13-13, fax 01-46-34-63-83, e-mail info@bief.org, World Wide Web http://www.bief.org. *Pres.* Vera

Michalski-Hoffmann; *CEO.* Jean-Guy Boin. *New York Branch* French Publishers Agency, 853 Broadway, Suite 1509, New York, NY 10003-4703. Tel./fax 212-254-4540, World Wide Web http://frenchpubagency.com.

Cercle de la Librairie (Circle of Professionals of the Book Trade), 35 rue Grégoire-de-Tours, F-75006 Paris. Tel. 01-44-41-28-00, fax 01-44-41-28-65, e-mail commercial@electre.com, World Wide Web http://www.electre.com.

Syndicat de la Librairie Française, Hotel Massa, 38 rue du Faubourg Saint-Jacques, F-75014 Paris. Tel. 01-53-62-23-10, fax 01-53-62-10-45, e-mail contact@union-librarie.fr, World Wide Web http://www.syndicat-librairie.fr. *Mgr.* Guillaume Husson.

Syndicat National de la Librairie Ancienne et Moderne (SLAM) (National Assn. of Antiquarian and Modern Booksellers), 4 rue Gît-le-Coeur, F-75006 Paris. Tel. 01-43-29-46-38, fax 01-43-25-41-63, e-mail slam-livre@wanadoo.fr, World Wide Web http://www.slam-livre.fr. *Pres.* Frederic Castaing.

Syndicat National de l'Edition (SNE) (National Union of Publishers), 115 blvd. Saint-Germain, F-75006 Paris. Tel. 01-44-41-40-50, fax 01-44-41-40-77, World Wide Web http://www.sne.fr. *Pres.* Vincent Mountain.

Germany

Börsenverein des Deutschen Buchhandels e.V. (Stock Exchange of German Booksellers), Braubachstr. 16, 60311 Frankfurt-am-Main. Tel. 49-69-1306-0, fax 49-69-1306-201, e-mail info@boev.de, World Wide Web http://www.boersenverein.de. *CEO* Alexander Skipis.

Verband Deutscher Antiquare e.V. (German Antiquarian Booksellers Assn.), Geschäftsstelle, Seeblick 1, 56459 Elbingen. Tel. 6435-90-91-47, fax 6435-90-91-48, e-mail buch@antiquare.de, World Wide Web http://www.antiquare.de. *Chair* Christian Hesse.

Greece

Hellenic Federation of Publishers and Booksellers, 73 Themistocleous St., 106 83 Athens. Tel. 2103-300-924, fax 2133-301-617, e-mail secretary@poev.gr, World Wide Web http://www.poev.gr. *Pres.* Annie Ragia; *Secy.-Gen.* Nicholas Stathatos.

Hungary

Magyar Könyvkiadók és Könyvterjesztök Egyesülése (Assn. of Hungarian Publishers and Booksellers), Postfach 130, 1367 Budapest. Tel. 1-343-2540, fax 1-343-2541, e-mail mkke@mkke.hu, World Wide Web http://www.mkke.hu. *Managing Dir.* Péter László Zentai.

Iceland

Félag Islenskra Bókaútgefenda (Icelandic Publishers Assn.), Baronsstig 5, 101 Reykjavik. Tel. 511-8020, fax 511-5020, e-mail fibut@fibut.is, World Wide Web http://www. bokautgafa.is. *Chair* Egill Örn Jóhannsson.

India

Federation of Indian Publishers, Federation House, 18/1C Institutional Area, Aruna Asaf Ali Marg, New Delhi 110067. Tel. 11-2696-4847, fax 11-2686-4054, e-mail fip1@sify. com, World Wide Web http://www.fipindia. org. *Exec. Dir.* P. K. Arora.

Indonesia

Ikatan Penerbit Indonesia (Assn. of Indonesian Book Publishers), Jl. Kalipasir 32, Cikini Jakarta Pusat 10330. Tel. 21-3190-2532, fax 21-3192-6124, e-mail sekretariat@ikapi. org, World Wide Web http://www.ikapi.org.

Ireland

Publishing Ireland/Foilsiu Eireann (formerly CLÉ: The Irish Book Publishers' Assn.), 25 Denzille Lane, Dublin 2. Tel. 639-4868, e-mail info@publishingireland.com, World Wide Web http://www.publishingireland. com. *Pres.* Michael McLouglin. E-mail president@publishingireland.com.

Israel

Book Publishers' Assn. of Israel, 29 Carlebach St., 67132 Tel Aviv. Tel. 3-561-4121, fax 3-561-1996, e-mail info@tbpai.co.il, World Wide Web http://www.tbpai.co.il. *Chair* Rachel Edelman.

Italy

Associazione Italiana Editori (Italian Publishers Assn.), Corso di Porta Romana 108, 20122 Milan. Tel. 2-89-28-0800, fax 2-89-28-0860, e-mail aie@aie.it, World Wide Web http://www.aie.it. *Dir.* Alfieri Lorenzon.

Associazione Librai Antiquari d'Italia (Antiquarian Booksellers Assn. of Italy), Via dei Bononcini 24, 41121 Modena. Tel. 347 646-9147, fax 06 9293-3756, e-mail alai@alai. it, World Wide Web http://www.alai.it. *Pres.* Fabrizio Govi.

Japan

Antiquarian Booksellers Assn. of Japan, 27 Sakamachi, Shinjuku-ku, Tokyo 160-0002. Tel. 3-3357-1417, fax 3-3356-8730, e-mail abaj@abaj.gr.jp, World Wide Web http:// www.abaj.gr.jp. *Pres.* Masaji Yagi.

Japan Assn. of International Publications (formerly Japan Book Importers Assn.), c/o UPS, 1-32-5 Higashi-shinagawa, Shinagawa-ku, Toyko 140-0002. Tel. 3-5479-7269, fax 3-5479-7307, e-mail office@jaip.jp, World Wide Web http://www.jaip.jp. *Exec. Dir.* Takashi Yamakawa.

Japan Book Publishers Assn., 6 Fukuro-machi, Shinjuku-ku, Tokyo 162-0828. Tel. 3-3268-1302, fax 3-3268-1196, e-mail research@ jbpa.or.jp, World Wide Web http://www. jbpa.or.jp. *Pres.* Masahiro Oga.

Kenya

Kenya Publishers Assn., P.O. Box 42767, Nairobi 00100. Tel. 20-375-2344, e-mail info@kenyapublishers.org, World Wide Web http://www.kenyapublishers.org. *Chair* Lawrence Njagi.

Korea (Republic of)

Korean Publishers Assn., 105-2 Sagan-dong, Jongro-gu, Seoul 110-190. Tel. 735-2701-4, fax 2-738-5414, e-mail webmaster@kpa21. or.kr, World Wide Web http://eng.kpa21. or.kr. *Pres.* Sok-Ghee Baek.

Latvia

Latvian Publishers' Assn., Baznicas iela 37-3, LV-1010 Riga. Tel./fax 67-217-730, e-mail lga@gramatizdeveji.lv, World Wide Web http://www.gramatizdeveji.lv. *Pres.* Renāte Punka.

Lithuania

Lithuanian Publishers Assn., The Capitol, 5-317, LT-01108 Vilnius. Tel./fax 5-261-77-40, e-mail info@lla.lt, World Wide Web http://www.lla.lt. *Pres.* Remigijus Jokubauskas; *Exec. Dir.* Aida Dobkevičiūtė.

Malaysia

Malaysian Book Publishers' Assn., No. 7-6, Block E2, Jl PJU 1/42A, Dataran Prima, 47301 Petaling Jaya, Selangor. Tel. 3-7880-5840, fax 3-7880-5841, e-mail info@mabopa.com.my, World Wide Web http://www.mabopa.com.my. *Pres.* Husammuddin Haji Yaacub.

Mexico

Cámara Nacional de la Industria Editorial Mexicana (Mexican Publishers' Assn.), Holanda No. 13, Col. San Diego Churubusco, Deleg. Coyoacan, 04120 Mexico DF. Tel. 155-56-88-20-11, fax 155-56-04-31-47, e-mail contacto@caniem.com, World Wide Web http://www.caniem.com. *Pres.* José Ignacio Echeverría.

The Netherlands

KVB—Koninklijke Vereeniging van het Boekenvak (Royal Society for the Book Trade), P.O. Box 12040, AA Amsterdam-Zuidoost. Tel. 20-624-02-12, fax 20-620-88-71, e-mail info@kvb.nl, World Wide Web http://www.kvb.nl. *Dir.* Marty Langeler.

Nederlands Uitgeversverbond (Royal Dutch Publishers Assn.), Postbus 12040, 1100 AA Amsterdam. Tel. 20-430-9150, fax 20-430-9199, e-mail info@nuv.nl, World Wide Web http://www.nuv.nl. *Pres.* Loek Hermans.

Nederlandsche Vereeniging van Antiquaren (Netherlands Assn. of Antiquarian Booksellers), Singel 319, 1012 WJ Amsterdam. Tel. 70-364-98-40, fax 70-364-33-40, e-mail info@nvva.nl, World Wide Web http://www.nvva.nl. *Pres.* Frank Rutten.

Nederlandse Boekverkopersbond (Dutch Booksellers Assn.), Postbus 32, 3720 AA Bilthoven. Tel. 30-228-79 56, fax 30-228-45-66, e-mail info@boekbond.nl, World Wide Web http://www.boekbond.nl. *Pres.* Dick Anbeek.

New Zealand

Booksellers New Zealand, Featherstone St., P.O. Box 25033, Wellington 6011. Tel. 4-472-1908, fax 4-472-1912, e-mail info@booksellers.co.nz, World Wide Web http://www.booksellers.co.nz. *Chair* Mary Sangster; *CEO* Lincoln Gould.

Nigeria

Nigerian Publishers Assn., GPO Box 2541, Dugbe, Ibadan. Tel. 2-751-5352, e-mail info@nigerianpublishers.org, World Wide Web http://www.nigerianpublishers.org. *Pres.* N. O. Okereke.

Norway

Norske Bokhandlerforening (Norwegian Booksellers Assn.), Øvre Vollgate 15, 0158 Oslo. Tel. 22-40-45-40, fax 22-41-12-89, e-mail post@bokogsamfunn.no, World Wide Web http://www.bokogsamfunn.no. *Editor* Dag H. Nestegard.

Norske Forleggerforening (Norwegian Publishers Assn.), Øvre Vollgate 15, 0158 Oslo. Tel. 22-00-75-80, fax 22-33-38-30, e-mail dnf@forleggerforeningen.no, World Wide Web http://www.forleggerforeningen.no. *Chair* Tom Harald Jenssen; *CEO* Kristenn Einarsson.

Peru

Cámara Peruana del Libro (Peruvian Publishers Assn.), Av. Cuba 427, Jesús María, Apdo. 10253, Lima 11. Tel. 1-472-9516, fax 1-265-0735, e-mail cp-libro@cpl.org.pe, World Wide Web http://www.cpl.org.pe. *Pres.* Coronado Germán Vallenas.

Philippines

Philippine Educational Publishers Assn., c/o St. Mary's Publishing Corporation, 1308 P. Guevarra St., Sta. Cruz, Manila. Tel. 2-734-7790, fax 2-735-0955.

Poland

Polish Society of Book Editors, Holy Cross 30, lok 156, 00-116 Warsaw. Tel. 22-407-77-30, e-mail ptwk@ptwk.pl, World Wide Web http://www.wydawca.com.pl. *Dir.* Maria Kuisz.

Władze Stowarzyszenia Księgarzy Polskich (Assn. of Polish Booksellers), ul. Mazowiecka 6.8 def. 414, 00-048 Warsaw. Tel./fax 0-22-827-93-81, e-mail skp@ksiegarze.org.pl, World Wide Web http://www.ksiegarze.org.pl. *Chair* Waldemar Janaszkiewicz.

Portugal

Associação Portuguesa de Editores e Livreiros (Portuguese Assn. of Publishers and Booksellers), Av. dos Estados Unidas da America 97, 6 Esq., 1700-167 Lisbon. Tel. 21-843-51-80, e-mail geral@apel.pt, World Wide Web http://www.apel.pt. *Pres.* João Alvim.

Russia

Assn. of Book Publishers of Russia, ul. B. Nikitskaya 44, 121069 Moscow. Tel. 495-202-1174, fax 495-202-3989, e-mail askibook@gmail.com, World Wide Web http://www.aski.ru. *Pres.* Konstantin V. Checkenev.

Rossiiskaya Knizhnaya Palata (Russian Book Chamber), Kremlin Embankment, 1.09, Bldg. 8, 19019 Moscow. Tel. 495-688-96-89, fax 495-688-99-91, e-mail info@bookchamber.ru, World Wide Web http://www.bookchamber.ru. *Dir. Gen.* Elena Nogina.

Serbia and Montenegro

Assn. of Yugoslav Publishers and Booksellers, Kneza Milosa 25/I, 11000 Belgrade. Tel. 11-642-533, fax 11-646-339.

Singapore

Singapore Book Publishers Assn., 86 Marine Parade Central No. 03-213, Singapore 440086. Tel. 6344-7801, fax 6344-0897, e-mail info@singaporebookpublishers.sg, World Wide Web http://www.singaporebookpublishers.sg. *Pres.* Triena Noeline Ong.

Slovenia

Zdruzenie Zaloznikov in Knjigotrzcev Slovenije Gospodarska Zbornica Slovenije (Assn. of Publishers and Booksellers of Slovenia), Dimieva ulica 13, SI 1000 Ljubljana. Tel. 1-5898-000, fax 1-5898-100, e-mail info@gzs.si, World Wide Web http://www.gzs.si/slo.

South Africa

Publishers Assn. of South Africa (PASA), P.O. Box 18223, Wynberg 7824. Tel. 21-762-9083, fax 21-762-2763, e-mail pasa@publishsa.co.za, World Wide Web http://www.publishsa.co.za. *Chair* Mandla Balisa; *Exec. Dir.* Brian Wafawarowa.

South African Booksellers Assn. (formerly Associated Booksellers of Southern Africa), P.O. Box 870, Bellville 7535. Tel. 21-945-1572, fax 21-945-2169, e-mail saba@sabooksellers.com, World Wide Web http://sabooksellers.com. *Chair and Pres.* Sydwell Molosi.

Spain

Federación de Gremios de Editores de España (Federation of Spanish Publishers Assns.), Cea Bermúdez 44-2, 28003 Madrid. Tel. 91-534-51-95, fax 91-535-26-25, e-mail fgee@fge.es, World Wide Web http://www.federacioneditores.org. *Pres.* Xavier Mallafré; *Exec. Dir.* Antonio María Ávila.

Sri Lanka

Sri Lanka Book Publishers Assn., 53 Maligakanda Rd., Colombo 10. Tel./fax 0094-112-696-821, fax, e-mail bookpub@sltnet.lk, World Wide Web http://www.bookpublishers.lk. *Pres.* Vijitha Yapa.

Sudan

Sudanese Publishers' Assn., c/o Institute of African and Asian Studies, Khartoum Univ., P.O. Box 321, Khartoum 11115. Tel. 11-77-0022. *Dir.* Al-Amin Abu Manga Mohamed.

Sweden

Svenska Förläggareföreningen (Swedish Publishers Assn.), Queen St. 97, S-11360 Stockholm. Tel. 8-736-19-40, e-mail info@forlaggare.se, World Wide Web http://www.forlaggare.se. *Pres. and Dir.* Kristina Ahlinder.

Switzerland

Swiss Booksellers and Publishers Association (SBVV), Alder Strasse 40, P.O. Box 8034, Zurich. Tel. 44-421-36-00, fax 44-421-36-18, e-mail info@sbvv.ch, World Wide Web https://www.sbvv.ch. *CEO* Dani Landolf.

Thailand

Publishers and Booksellers Assn. of Thailand, 83/159 Moo Chinnakhet 2, Ngam Wong Wan Rd., Tungsonghong Lak Si, Bangkok 10210. Tel. 2-954-9560-4, fax 2-954-9566, e-mail info@pubat.or.th, World Wide Web http://www.pubat.or.th. *Pres.* Charun Homtientong.

Uganda

Uganda Publishers Assn., P.O. Box 7732, Kampala. Tel. 414-286-093, fax 414-286-397. *Chair* David Kibuuka; *Gen. Secy.* Martin Okia.

United Kingdom

Antiquarian Booksellers Assn., Sackville House, 40 Piccadilly, London W1J 0DR, England. Tel. 20-7439-3118, fax 20-7439-3119, e-mail admin@aba.org.uk, World Wide Web http://www.aba.org.uk. *Admin.* Clare Pedder; *Secy.* Tony Russ.

Assn. of Learned and Professional Society Publishers, 1-3 Ship St., Shoreham-by-Sea, West Sussex BN43 5DH, England. Tel. 1275-858-837, World Wide Web http://www.alpsp.org. *Chief Exec.* Audrey McCulloch.

Booktrust, Book House, 45 East Hill, Wandsworth, London SW18 2QZ, England. Tel. 20-8516-2977, fax 20-8516-2978, e-mail query@booktrust.org.uk, World Wide Web http://www.booktrust.org.uk. *Pres.* Michael Morpurgo; *Chair* Karen Brown.

Publishers Assn., 29B Montague St., London WC1B 5BW, England. Tel. 20-7691-9191, fax 20-7691-9199, e-mail mail@publishers.org.uk, World Wide Web http://www.publishers.org.uk. *Pres.* Dominic Knight; *Chief Exec.* Richard Mollet.

Scottish Book Trust, Sandeman House, Trunk's Close, 55 High St., Edinburgh EH1 1SR, Scotland. Tel. 131-524-0160, e-mail info@scottishbooktrust.com, World Wide Web http://www.scottishbooktrust.com. *CEO* Marc Lambert.

Welsh Books Council (Cyngor Llyfrau Cymru), Castell Brychan, Aberystwyth, Ceredigion SY23 2JB, Wales. Tel. 1970-624-151, fax 1970-625-385, e-mail info@wbc.org.uk, World Wide Web http://www.cllc.org.uk. *Chief Exec.* Elwyn Jones.

Uruguay

Cámara Uruguaya del Libro (Uruguayan Publishers Assn.), Colon 1476, Apdo. 102, 11000 Montevideo. Tel. 2-916-93-74, fax 2-916-76-28, e-mail gerencia@camaradellibro.com.uy, World Wide Web http://www.camaradellibro.com.uy. *Pres.* Alicia Guglielmo.

Venezuela

Cámara Venezolana del Libro (Venezuelan Publishers Assn.), Av. Andrés Bello, Centro Andrés Bello, Torre Oeste 11, piso 11, of. 112-0, Caracas 1050. Tel. 212-793-1347, fax 212-793-1368, e-mail cavelibrocgeneral@gmail.com, World Wide Web http://www.cavelibro.org. *Pres.* Ivan Dieguez Vazquez; *Exec. Dir.* Dalila Da Silva.

Zambia

Booksellers Assn. of Zambia, P.O. Box 51109, 10101 Lusaka. E-mail bpaz@zamtel.zm.

Zimbabwe

Zimbabwe Book Publishers Assn., P.O. Box 3041, Harare. Tel. 4-773-236, fax 4-754-256.

National Information Standards Organization (NISO)

Content and Collection Management

ANSI/NISO Z39.2-1994 (R2009)	Information Interchange Format ISBN 978-1-937522-23-0
ANSI/NISO Z39.14-1997 (R2015)	Guidelines for Abstracts ISBN 978-1-937522-44-5
ANSI/NISO Z39.18-2005 (R2010)	Scientific and Technical Reports— Preparation, Presentation, and Preservation ISBN 978-1-937522-21-6
ANSI/NISO Z39.19-2005 (R2010)	Guidelines for the Construction, Format, and Management of Monolingual Controlled Vocabularies ISBN 978-1-937522-22-3
ANSI/NISO Z39.23-1997 (S2015)	Standard Technical Report Number Format and Creation ISBN 978-1-937522-45-2
ANSI/NISO Z39.29-2005 (R2010)	Bibliographic References ISBN 978-1-937522-26-1
ANSI/NISO Z39.32-1996 (R2012)	Information on Microfiche Headers ISBN 978-1-937522-29-2
ANSI/NISO Z39.41-1997 (S2015)	Placement Guidelines for Information on Spines ISBN 978-1-937522-46-9
ANSI/NISO Z39.43-1993 (R2011)	Standard Address Number (SAN) for the Publishing Industry ISBN 978-1-937522-28-5
ANSI/NISO Z39.48-1992 (R2009)	Permanence of Paper for Publications and Documents in Libraries and Archives ISBN 978-1-937522-30-8
ANSI/NISO Z39.71-2006 (R2011)	Holdings Statements for Bibliographic Items ISBN 978-1-937522-31-5
ANSI/NISO Z39.73-1994 (R2012)	Single-Tier Steel Bracket Library Shelving ISBN 978-1-937522-32-2
ANSI/NISO Z39.74-1996 (R2012)	Guides to Accompany Microform Sets ISBN 978-1-937522-40-7

ANSI/NISO Z39.78-2000 (R2010)   Library Binding
ISBN 978-1-937522-33-9

ANSI/NISO Z39.84-2005 (R2010)   Syntax for the Digital Object Identifier
ISBN 978-1-937522-34-6

ANSI/NISO Z39.85-2012   The Dublin Core Metadata Element Set
ISBN 978-1-937522-14-8

ANSI/NISO Z39.86-2005 (R2012)   Specifications for the Digital Talking Book
ISBN 978-1-937522-35-3

ANSI/NISO Z39.96-2012   JATS: Journal Article Tag Suite
ISBN 978-1-937522-10-0

ANSI/NISO Z39.98-2012   Authoring and Interchange Framework for
Adaptive XML Publishing Specification
ISBN 978-1-937522-07-0

ANSI/NISO/ISO 12083-1995
(R2009)   Electronic Manuscript Preparation and
Markup
ISBN 978-1-880124-20-8

Standards for Discovery to Delivery

ANSI/NISO Z39.19-2005 (R2010)   Guidelines for the Construction, Format,
and Management of Monolingual
Controlled Vocabularies
ISBN 978-1-937522-22-3

ANSI/NISO Z39.50-2003 (S2014)   Information Retrieval (Z39.50) Application
Service Definition and Protocol
Specification
ISBN 978-1-937522-42-1

ANSI/NISO Z39.83-1-2012   NISO Circulation Interchange Part 1:
Protocol (NCIP) version 2.02
ISBN 978-1-937522-03-2

ANSI/NISO Z39.83-2-2012   NISO Circulation Interchange Protocol
(NCIP) Part 2: Implementation Profile 1,
version 2.02
ISBN 978-1-937522-04-9

ANSI/NISO Z39.85-2012   The Dublin Core Metadata Element Set
ISBN 978-1-937522-14-8

ANSI/NISO Z39.87-2006 (R2011)   Data Dictionary—Technical Metadata for
Digital Still Images
ISBN 978-1-937522-37-7

ANSI/NISO Z39.88-2004 (R2010)   The OpenURL Framework for Context-
Sensitive Services
ISBN 978-1-937522-38-4

ANSI/NISO Z39.89-2003 (S2014)   The U.S. National Z39.50 Profile for
Library Applications
ISBN 978-1-937522-43-8

ANSI/NISO Z39.99-2014   ResourceSync Framework Specification
ISBN 978-1-937522-19-3

Business Information

ANSI/NISO Z39.7-2013   Information Services and Use: Metrics and
Statistics for Libraries and Information
Providers—Data Dictionary
ISBN 978-1-937522-15-5

ANSI/NISO Z39.93-2014   The Standardized Usage Statistics
Harvesting Initiative (SUSHI) Protocol
ISBN 978-1-937522-47-6

Preservation and Storage

ANSI/NISO Z39.32-1996 (R2012)   Information on Microfiche Headers
ISBN 978-1-937522-29-2

ANSI/NISO Z39.48-1992 (R2009)   Permanence of Paper for Publications and
Documents in Libraries and Archives
ISBN 978-1-937522-30-8

ANSI/NISO Z39.73-1994 (R2012)   Single-Tier Steel Bracket Library Shelving
ISBN 978-1-937522-32-2

ANSI/NISO Z39.78-2000 (R2010)   Library Binding
ISBN 978-1-937522-33-9

In Development/NISO Initiatives

NISO develops new standards, reports, and best practices on a continuing basis
to support its ongoing standards development program. NISO working groups are
currently developing or exploring the following:

- Alternative Metrics Recommended Practices
- Bibliographic Vocabulary Use and Reuse; Vocabulary Documentation; and
  Vocabulary Preservation
- Journal Article Versions (JAV) Addendum (NISO RP-8-201x)
- Protocol for Exchanging Serial Content (NISO RP-23-201x)
- Standard Interchange Protocol (SIP) (NISO Z39.100-201x)
- Permanence of Paper for Publications and Documents in Libraries and Ar-
  chives (revision to Z39.48)
- SUSHI Lite (NISO TR-06-201x)

NISO Recommended Practices

A Framework of Guidance for Building Good Digital Collections, 3rd ed., 2007
ISBN 978-1-880124-74-1

NISO RP-2005-01   Ranking of Authentication and Access Methods Available to the Metasearch Environment
ISBN 978-1-880124-89-5

NISO RP-2005-02   Search and Retrieval Results Set Metadata
ISBN 978-1-880124-88-8

NISO RP-2005-03   Search and Retrieval Citation Level Data Elements
ISBN 978-1-880124-87-1

NISO RP-2006-01   Best Practices for Designing Web Services in the Library Context
ISBN 978-1-880124-86-4

NISO RP-2006-02   NISO Metasearch XML Gateway Implementers Guide
ISBN 978-1-880124-85-7

NISO RP-6-2012   RFID in U.S. Libraries
ISBN 978-1-937522-02-5

NISO RP-7-2012   SERU: A Shared Electronic Resource Understanding
ISBN 978-1-937522-08-7

NISO RP-8-2008   Journal Article Versions (JAV)
ISBN 978-1-880124-79-6

NISO RP-9-2014   KBART: Knowledge Bases and Related Tools
ISBN 978-1-937522-41-4

NISO RP-10-2010   Cost of Resource Exchange (CORE) Protocol
ISBN 978-1-880124-84-0

NISO RP-11-2011   ESPReSSO: Establishing Suggested Practices Regarding Single Sign-On
ISBN 978-1-880124-98-7

NISO RP-12-2012   Physical Delivery of Library Resources
ISBN 978-1-937522-01-8

NISO RP-14-2014   NISO SUSHI Protocol: COUNTER-SUSHI Implementation Profile
ISBN 978-1-937522-45-2

NISO RP-15-2013   Recommended Practices for Online Supplemental Journal Article Materials
ISBN 978-1-937522-12-4

NISO RP-16-2013   PIE-J: The Presentation and Identification of E-Journals
ISBN 978-1-937522-05-6

NISO RP-17-2013   Institutional Identification: Identifying Organizations in the Information Supply Chain
ISBN 978-1-937522-11-7

NISO RP-20-2014   Open Discovery Initiative: Promoting Transparency in Discovery
ISBN 978-1-937522-42-1

NISO RP-21-2013   Improving OpenURLs Through Analytics (IOTA):
                      Recommendations for Link Resolver Providers
                      ISBN 978-1-937522-18-6

NISO RP-22-2015   Access License and Indicators
                      ISBN 978-1-937522-49-0

NISO RP-24-2015   Transfer Code of Practice, version 3.0
                      ISBN 978-1-937522-40-7

NISO Technical Reports

NISO TR01-1995   Environmental Guidelines for the Storage of Paper Records
                      by William K. Wilson
                      ISBN 978-1-800124-21-5

NISO TR02-1997   Guidelines for Indexes and Related Information Retrieval
                      Devices
                      by James D. Anderson
                      ISBN 978-1-880124-36-9

NISO TR03-1999   Guidelines for Alphabetical Arrangement of Letters and
                      Sorting of Numerals and Other Symbols
                      by Hans H. Wellisch
                      ISBN 978-1-880124-41-3

NISO TR04-2006   Networked Reference Services: Question/Answer
                      Transaction Protocol
                      ISBN 978-1-880124-71-0

NISO TR-05-2013   IOTA Working Group Summary of Activities and
                      Outcomes
                      ISBN 978-1-937522-17-9

Other NISO Publications

The Case for New Economic Models to Support Standardization
    by Clifford Lynch
    ISBN 978-1-880124-90-1

The Exchange of Serials Subscription Information
    by Ed Jones
    ISBN 978-1-880124-91-8

The Future of Library Resource Discovery
    by Marshall Breeding
    ISBN 978-1-937522-41-4

Information Standards Quarterly (ISQ) [NISO quarterly open access magazine]
    ISSN 1041-0031

Internet, Interoperability and Standards—Filling the Gaps
    by Janifer Gatenby
    ISBN 978-1-880124-92-5

Issues in Crosswalking Content Metadata Standards
by Margaret St. Pierre and William P. LaPlant
ISBN 978-1-880124-93-2

Making Good on the Promise of ERM: A Standards and Best Practices
Discussion Paper
by the ERM Data Standards and Best Practices Review Steering Committee
ISBN 978-1-9357522-00-1

Metadata Demystified: A Guide for Publishers
by Amy Brand, Frank Daly, and Barbara Meyers
ISBN 978-1-880124-59-8

The Myth of Free Standards: Giving Away the Farm
by Andrew N. Bank
ISBN 978-1-880124-94-9

NISO Newsline [free monthly e-newsletter]
ISSN 1559-2774

NISO Working Group Connection (free quarterly supplement to Newsline)
Patents and Open Standards
by Priscilla Caplan
ISBN 978-1-880124-95-6

The RFP Writer's Guide to Standards for Library Systems
by Cynthia Hodgson
ISBN 978-1-880124-57-4

Streamlining Book Metadata Workflow
by Judy Luther
ISBN 978-1-880124-82-6

Understanding Metadata
ISBN 978-1-880124-62-8

Up and Running: Implementing Z39.50: Proceedings of a Symposium
Sponsored by the State Library of Iowa
edited by Sara L. Randall
ISBN 978-1-880124-33-8

Z39.50: A Primer on the Protocol
ISBN 978-1-880124-35-2

Z39.50 Implementation Experiences
ISBN 978-1-880124-51-2

NISO standards are available online at http://www.niso.org/standards. Recommended Practices, Technical Reports, White Papers, and other publications are available on the NISO website at http://www.niso.org/publications.

For more information, contact NISO, 3600 Clipper Mill Rd., Suite 302, Baltimore, MD 21211. Tel. 301-654-2512, fax 410-685-5278, e-mail nisohq@niso.org, World Wide Web http://www.niso.org.

Calendar, 2016–2024

The list below contains information on association meetings or promotional events that are, for the most part, national or international in scope. State and regional library association meetings are also included. To confirm the starting or ending date of a meeting, which may change after the *Library and Book Trade Almanac* has gone to press, contact the association directly. Addresses of library and book trade associations are listed in Part 6 of this volume. For information on additional book trade and promotional events, see *Literary Market Place* and *International Literary Market Place,* published by Information Today, Inc., and other library and book trade publications such as *Library Journal, School Library Journal,* and *Publishers Weekly.* The American Library Association (ALA) keeps an online calendar at http://www.ala.org/conferencesevents/planning-calendar. An Information Today events calendar can be found at http://www.infotoday.com/calendar.shtml.

2016

June

1–3	Canadian Assn. for Information Science (CAIS)	Calgary, AB
1–3	Canadian Library Assn. National Forum	Ottawa, ON
5–9	Assn. of Caribbean University, Research and Institutional Libraries (ACURIL)	Petion-Ville, Haiti
6–8	Specialized Information Publishers Assn.	Washington, DC
8–10	Assn. of Canadian Publishers Annual Meeting	Winnipeg, MB
12–14	Special Libraries Assn.	Philadelphia, PA
13–16	Assn. of Christian Librarians	Newberg, OR
15–19	Seoul International Book Fair	Seoul, South Korea
16–18	Assn. of American University Presses	Philadelphia, PA
23–28	American Library Assn. Annual Conference	Orlando, FL
23–28	American Assn. of School Librarians @ ALA	Orlando, FL
29–July 1	Assn. of European Research Libraries (LIBER)	Helsinki, Finland

July 2016

3–8	International Assn. of Music Libraries Annual Conference	Rome, Italy
9–11	International Literacy Assn.	Boston, MA
13–15	IEEE Technically Sponsored SAI Computing Conference (formerly Science and Information Conference)	London, UK
13–16	National Assn. of Government Archives and Records Administrators (NAGARA)	Lansing, MI
16–19	American Assn. of Law Libraries (AALL)	Chicago, IL
19–22	Assn. of Jewish Libraries	Charleston, SC
20–26	Hong Kong Book Fair	Hong Kong
27–29	Church and Synagogue Library Assn.	Kent, OH
31–Aug. 6	Society of American Archivists	Atlanta, GA

August

3–5	Pacific Northwest Library Assn.	Calgary, AB
13–19	81st IFLA General Conference and Assembly	Columbus, OH
14–30	Edinburgh International Book Fair	Edinburgh, UK
22–26	International Assn. of School Librarianship (IASL)	Tokyo, Japan
24–28	Beijing International Book Fair	Beijing, China
29–31	International Symposium on Information Management	Cusco, Peru

September

13–14	Web Search University 2016	Arlington, VA
15–18	North Carolina Library Assn.	Black Mountain, NC
21–23	North Dakota Library Assn.	Dickinson, ND
21–23	Wyoming Library Assn.	Jackson Hole, WY
21–24	Kentucky Library Assn.	Louisville, KY
23–25	Tokyo International Book Fair	Tokyo, Japan
28–30	Ohio Library Council	Sandusky, OH
28–30	South Dakota Library Assn.	Watertown, SD
29–30	Minnesota Library Assn.	Duluth, MN
29–Oct. 2	Goteborg Book Fair	Gothenburg, Sweden

October

5–7	Georgia Library Assn./Georgia Council of Media Organizations	Athens, GA
5–7	Idaho Library Assn.	Idaho Falls, ID

5–7	Missouri Library Assn.	Springfield, MO
5–7	West Virginia Library Assn.	Glade Springs Resort, WV
11–12	International Conference of Indigenous Archives, Libraries, and Museums	Phoenix, AZ
12–14	Iowa Library Assn.	Dubuque, IA
14–18	Association for Information Science and Technology (ASIS&T)	Copenhagen, Denmark
16–18	New England Library Assn.	Danvers, MA
16–19	Pennsylvania Library Assn.	Pocono Manor, PA
17–19	Nevada Library Assn.	Las Vegas, NV
18–20	Nebraska Library Assn.	Omaha, NE
19–21	Kansas Library Assn.	Wichita, KS
19–23	Frankfurt Book Fair	Frankfurt, Germany
17–19	Internet Librarian 2016	Monterey, CA
18–19	Internet Librarian International 2016	London, UK
18–20	Illinois Library Assn.	Rosemont, IL
18–21	Mississippi Library Assn.	Vicksburg, MS
20–22	Colorado Assn. of Libraries./Mountain Plains Library Assn.	Loveland, CO
24–28	International Conference on Information and Knowledge Management (CIKM)	Indianapolis, IN
25–28	Wisconsin Library Assn.	Milwaukee, WI
25–Nov. 1	Belgrade International Book Fair	Belgrade, Serbia
26–28	Michigan Library Assn.	Lansing, MI
26–28	Virginia Library Assn.	Hot Springs, VA
27–30	Helsinki Book Fair	Helsinki, Finland

November

1–2	Streaming Media West	Huntington Beach, CA
2–4	Arizona Library Assn.	Tucson AZ
2–4	New Mexico Library Assn.	Albuquerque, NM
2–5	New York Library Assn.	Saratoga Springs, NY
3–4	New Hampshire Library Assn.	Hooksett, NH
3–5	California Library Assn.	Sacramento, CA
8–10	Indiana Library Federation	Indianapolis, IN
8–11	Istanbul International Book Fair	Istanbul, Turkey
9–11	South Carolina Library Assn.	Columbia, SC
12–15	Buch Wien International Book Fair	Graz, Austria
11–12	Hawaii Library Assn.	Hilo, HI
13–15	Arkansas Library Assn.	Little Rock

November 2016 *(cont.)*

15–17	KMWorld 2016	Washington, DC
16–21	Salon du Livre de Montréal	Montreal, QC
21–22	Bibliographical Society of Australia and New Zealand	Hamilton, New Zealand
28–30	Guadalajara International Book Fair	Guadalajara, Mexico
30–Dec. 4	Moscow International Book Fair	Moscow, Russia

December

11–14	International Conference on Information Systems (ICIS)	Dublin, Ireland

2017

January

4–7	Hawaii International Conference on System Sciences	Waikoloa Village, HI
20–24	American Library Assn. Midwinter Meeting	Atlanta, GA

March

22–25	Assn. of College and Research Libraries (ACRL)	Baltimore, MD
28–30	Computers in Libraries 2017	Arlington, VA

April

5–7	Tennessee Library Assn.	Knoxville, TN
19–22	Texas Library Assn.	San Antonio, TX

May

10–12	Maryland Library Assn./Delaware Library Assn.	Ocean City, MD
16–17	Streaming Media East	New York, NY
31–June 2	Book Expo America (BEA)	New York, NY

June

22–27	American Library Assn. Annual Conference	Chicago, IL
22–27	American Assn. of School Librarians @ ALA	Chicago, IL

July

15–18	American Assn. of Law Libraries (AALL)	Austin, TX

September

| 20–23 | Kentucky Library Assn. | Louisville, KY |
| 27–29 | South Dakota Library Assn. | Cedar Shore, SD |

October

4–6	Missouri Library Assn.	St. Louis, MO
4–6	North Dakota Library Assn.	Grand Forks, ND
10–12	Illinois Library Assn.	Tinley Park, IL
10–13	Nebraska Library Assn./Nebraska School Library Assn.	Kearney, NE
15–18	Pennsylvania Library Assn.	Pittsburgh, PA
16–20	North Carolina Library Assn.	Winston-Salem, NC
25–28	Wisconsin Library Assn.	Wisconsin Dells, WI

November

1–3	New Mexico Library Assn.	Albuquerque, NM
2–3	Streaming Media West	Huntington Beach, CA
7–9	KM World 2017	Washington, DC
15–20	Salon du Livre de Montréal	Montreal, QC

2018

January

| 3–6 | Hawaii International Conference on System Sciences | Waikoloa Village, HI |
| 19–23 | American Library Assn. Midwinter Meeting | Los Angeles, CA |

March

| 20–24 | Public Libraries Assn. | Philadelphia, PA |

April

4–6	Tennessee Library Assn.	Memphis, TN
10–13	Texas Library Assn.	Dallas, TX
17–19	Computers in Libraries 2018	Arlington, VA

June

| 21–26 | American Library Assn. Annual Conference | New Orleans, LA |
| 21–26 | American Assn. of School Librarians @ ALA | New Orleans, LA |

July 2018

14–17	American Assn. of Law Libraries (AALL)	Baltimore, MD

October

14–17	Pennsylvania Library Assn.	Harrisburg, PA

November

14–19	Salon du Livre de Montréal	Montreal, QC

2019

January

7–10	Hawaii International Conference on System Sciences	Maui, HI
25–29	American Library Assn. Midwinter Meeting	Seattle, WA

April

2–5	Texas Library Assn.	Austin, TX

June

27–July 2	American Library Assn. Annual Conference	New York, NY
27–July 2	American Assn. of School Librarians @ ALA	New York, NY

July

13–16	American Assn. of Law Libraries (AALL)	Washington, DC

October

8–11	Wisconsin Library Assn.	Wisconsin Dells, WI

2020

January

6–9	Hawaii International Conference on System Sciences	Maui, HI
17–21	American Library Assn. Midwinter Meeting	Philadelphia, PA

March

25–28	Texas Library Assn.	Houston, TX

June

25–30	American Library Assn. Annual Conference	Chicago, IL
25–30	American Assn. of School Librarians @ ALA	Chicago, IL

2021

January

22–26	American Library Assn. Midwinter Meeting	Indianapolis, IN

June

24–29	American Library Assn. Annual Conference	San Francisco, CA
24–29	American Assn. of School Librarians @ ALA	San Francisco, CA

2022

January

21–25	American Library Assn. Midwinter Meeting	San Antonio, TX

June

23–28	American Library Assn. Annual Conference	Washington, DC
23–28	American Assn. of School Librarians @ ALA	Washington, DC

2023

January

27–31	American Library Assn. Midwinter Meeting	New Orleans, LA

June

22–27	American Library Assn. Annual Conference	Chicago, IL
22–27	American Assn. of School Librarians @ ALA	Chicago, IL

2024

February

9–13	American Library Assn. Midwinter Meeting	Denver, CO

June

27–July 2	American Library Assn. Annual Conference	San Diego, CA
27–July 2	American Assn. of School Librarians @ ALA	San Diego, CA

Acronyms

A

AALL. American Association of Law Libraries

AASL. American Association of School Librarians

ABA. American Booksellers Association

ABOS. Association of Bookmobile and Outreach Services

AC. Access Copyright

ACRL. Association of College and Research Libraries

AIIP. Association of Independent Information Professionals

AILA. American Indian Library Association

AJL. Association of Jewish Libraries

ALA. American Library Association

ALCTS. Association for Library Collections and Technical Services

ALIC. Archives Library Information Center

ALISE. Association for Library and Information Science Education

ALS. Academic Libraries Survey

ALSC. Association for Library Service to Children

ALTAFF. Association of Library Trustees, Advocates, Friends, and Foundations

AMMLA. American Merchant Marine Library Association

APALA. Asian/Pacific American Librarians Association

ARL. Association of Research Libraries

ARLIS/NA. Art Libraries Society of North America

ARSL. Association for Rural and Small Libraries

ASCLA. Association of Specialized and Cooperative Library Agencies

ASIS&T. American Association for Information Science and Technology

ATLA. American Theological Library Association

ATN. Access Text Network

B

BARD. Braille and Audio Reading Download

BCALA. Black Caucus of the American Library Association

BEA. BookExpo America

BLC. Brody Learning Commons

BSA. Bibliographical Society of America

C

CACUL. Canadian Association of College and University Libraries

CAIS. Canadian Association for Information Science

CALA. Chinese-American Librarians Association

CAPL. Canadian Association of Public Libraries

CARL. Canadian Association of Research Libraries

CASLIS. Canadian Association of Special Libraries and Information Services

CGP. Catalog of U.S. Government Publications

CLA. Canadian Library Association

CLIR. Council on Library and Information Resources

CLTA. Canadian Library Trustees Association

CNI. Coalition for Networked Information

COSLA. Chief Officers of State Library Agencies

CSLA. Church and Synagogue Library Association

CWA. Crime Writers' Association

D

DLF. Digital Library Federation
DPLA. Digital Public Library of America
DRM. Digital rights management
DTIC. Defense Technical Information
Center

E

EAR. Export Administration Regulations
EDB. Energy Science and Technology
Database
EMIERT. Ethnic and Multicultural
Information and Exchange Round
Table
ESEA. Elementary and Secondary Education
Act

F

FAA. Foreign Intelligence Surveillance Act
FAFLRT. Federal and Armed Forces
Librarians Round Table
FAIFE. Freedom of Access to Information
and Freedom of Expression
FBI. Federal Bureau of Investigation
FDLP. Federal Depository Library Program
FDsys. Federal Digital System
FEDRIP. Federal Research in Progress
Database
FIAF. International Federation of Film
Archives
FRPAA. Federal Research Public Access Act

G

GLBTRT. Gay, Lesbian, Bisexual, and
Transgendered Round Table
GLIN. Global Legal Information Network
GODORT. Government Documents Round
Table
GPO. Government Printing Office
GSU. Georgia State University

I

IAALD. International Association of
Agricultural Information Specialists
IACs. Information Analysis Centers
IALL. International Association of Law
Libraries
IAML. International Association of
Music Libraries, Archives and
Documentation Centres
IASL. International Association of School
Librarians
ICA. International Council on Archives
ICBS. International Committee of the Blue
Shield
IDPF. International Digital Publishing
Forum
IFLA. International Federation of Library
Associations and Institutions
ILS. Integrated Library System
IMLS. Institute of Museum and Library
Services
ISBN. International Standard Book Number
ISO. International Organization for
Standardization
ISOO. Information Security Oversight
Office
ISSN. International Standard Serial Number

L

LAC. Library and Archives Canada
LC. Library of Congress
LCA. Library Copyright Alliance
LCI. Leading Change Institute
LEED. Leadership in Energy and
Environmental Design
LHHS. Labor, Health, and Human Services
Appropriations Bill
LHRT. Library History Round Table
LIS. Library/information science
LITA. Library and Information Technology
Association
LJ. Library Journal
LLAMA. Library Leadership and
Management Association
LRRT. Library Research Round Table
LSCM. Library Services and Content
Management
LSTA. Library Services and Technology Act

M

MLA. Medical Library Association; Music
   Library Association
MOOCs. massively open online courses

N

NAGARA. National Association of
   Government Archives and Records
   Administrators
NAL. National Agricultural Library
NARA. National Archives and Records
   Administration
NCBI. National Center for Biotechnology
   Information
NCES. National Center for Education
   Statistics
NDC. National Declassification Center
NDIIPP. National Digital Information
   Infrastructure and Preservation
   Program
NEH. National Endowment for the
   Humanities
NFAIS. National Federation of Advanced
   Information Services
NIH. National Institutes of Health
NISO. National Information Standards
   Organization
NLE. National Library of Education
NLM. National Library of Medicine
NMRT. New Members Round Table
NTIS. National Technical Information
   Service
NTRL. National Technical Reports Library

O

ORI. Owners' Rights Initiative
OWF. Operation Warfighter

P

PLA. Public Library Association
PTDLA. Patent and Trademark Depository
   Library Association
PW. Publishers Weekly

R

RDA. Resource Description and Access
RUSA. Reference and User Services
   Association

S

SAA. Society of American Archivists
SAN. Standard Address Number
SIIA. Software and Information Industry
   Association
SLA. Special Libraries Association
SPARC. Scholarly Publishing & Academic
   Resources Coalition
SRRT. Social Responsibilities Round Table
SRS. Selected Research Service
SSP. Society for Scholarly Publishing
STEM. science, technology, engineering,
   and mathematics
StLA. state libraries and library agencies

T

TLA. Theatre Library Association

U

ULC. Urban Libraries Council
USCIS. United States Citizenship and
   Immigration Service

W

WDL. World Digital Library
WIPO. World Intellectual Property
   Organization
WISE. Web-based Information Science
   Education Consortium
WNC. World News Connection
WRP. Workforce Recruitment Program

Y

YALSA. Young Adult Library Services
   Association

Index of Organizations

Please note that many cross-references refer to entries in the Subject Index.

A

Academic Libraries Survey (ALS). See under National Center for Education Statistics

AGRICOLA (Agricultural OnLine Access), 81, 93

AIIM (The Association for Information and Image Management), 492

Alabama Humanities Council, 213

Alaska Humanities Council, 213

American Association of Law Libraries (AALL), 249, 492–93
awards, 278–79
scholarships, 274, 278–79

American Association of School Librarians (AASL), 13, 141, 249, 496–97
awards/scholarships, 281–82

American Booksellers Association (ABA), 150–58
advocacy, 157–58
association and governance, 152–53
book awards, 153–54
conferences, 155–57
membership growth, 150
personnel, 155

American Booksellers Foundation for Free Expression (ABFFE), 158

American Folklife Center, 64–65

American Indian Library Association (AILA), 493

American Library Association (ALA), 135–36, 494–512
academic libraries, 141–42
ALA Editions/ALA Neal-Schuman, 147
ALA Graphics, 148
ALA TechSource, 147–48
awards, 279–91
Building STEAM with Día Toolkit, 143
Center for the Future of Libraries, 140

conferences and workshops, 143–46, 149
divisions, 135
Ethnic and Multicultural Information and Exchange Round Table (EMIERT) awards, 286
Exhibits Round Table (ERT) awards, 286
Federal and Armed Forces Librarians Round Table (FAFLRT) awards, 286
focus on school libraries and librarians, 141
Gay, Lesbian, Bisexual, and Transgendered Round Table (GLBTRT), 286
Government Documents Round Table (GODORT) awards, 286–87
grants and contributions, 146–47
Beyond Words disaster relief grants, 143
Curiosity Create grants, 146
public programming, 146–47
research on student achievement, 146
highlights, 137–42
intellectual freedom, 142
Intellectual Freedom Round Table (IFRT), 287
International Relations Committee, scholarships from, 274–75
JobLIST, 247
leadership and strategic planning, 136–37
Libraries Transforming Communities (LTC), 143
Library History Round Table (LHRT) awards, 287
Library Research Round Table (LRRT) awards, 288
library services for children, 140
Map and Geospatial Information Round Table (MAGIRT) award, 288
membership, 135, 142
national celebrations and observances, 139–40

I

Subject Index

Please note that many cross-references refer to entries in the Index of Organizations.

A

ABACUS project, 156, 157
academic books
  e-books, 351, 356–57t, 360–61, 363
  prices and price indexes
    British books, 380–81t, 382–84
    North American, 351, 354–55t
    U.S. college books, 363, 364–65t
  See also textbooks
academic libraries
  acquisition expenditures, 320–21t
  advocacy and public awareness
    bibliography for librarians, 404–5
  bibliography (for librarians) on, 403–4
  Canadian, 309t
  CLIR fellowship, 179–81
  NCES survey, 120
  number of, 307–9t
  placement sources, online, 249–50
  salary levels in, 260, 262
  SPARC campus education, 173
academic library buildings
  new, 336–37t
  renovations/additions, 336–37t
Access to Information Act (ATI/ATIA),
    35–36, 43–44
Access to Information and Protection of
    Privacy Act of 2015 (ATIPPA/ATIPP
    Act), 45–46, 48–49
acquisitions
  expenditures, 317–25
    academic libraries, 320–21t
    government libraries, 324–25t
    public libraries, 318–19t
    special libraries, 322–23t
  Library of Congress, 56–57, 60

Alabama
  library associations, 550
  networks and cooperative library
    organizations, 475
  school library media associations, 570
  state library agencies, 564
Alaska
  library associations, 550
  networks and cooperative library
    organizations, 475
  school library media associations, 570
  state library agencies, 564
Alberta, Canada, 568
  freedom of Information and privacy
    legislation in, 43–44
Alex Awards, 435
American Libraries magazine, 149
American Samoa, 568
apps for teaching and learning, 13
archives
  acquisition expenditures
    academic libraries, 320–21t
    government libraries, 324–25t
    public libraries, 318–19t
    special libraries, 322–23t
  bibliography (for librarians) on, 405
  salary levels in, 260, 262
  Web archiving, 66
Arizona
  library associations, 550
  school library media associations, 570
  state library agencies, 564
Arkansas
  library associations, 550–51
  networks and cooperative library
    organizations, 475
  school library media associations, 570
armed forces, number of libraries in, 307–9t